UK VISITOR
ATTRACTIONS
DIRECTORY

UK VISITOR ATTRACTIONS DIRECTORY

Oxford Centre for Tourism and Leisure Studies (OCTALS),
Oxford Brookes University

CASSELL

Cassell
Villiers House
41/47 Strand
London WC2N 5JE

First published 1994

British Library Cataloguing-in-Publication Data
A catalogue entry for this book is available from the British Library.

ISBN 0-304-32694-1

Typeset by Colset Ptd Ltd, Singapore
Printed and bound in Great Britain by Short Run Press Ltd, Exeter

CONTENTS

PREFACE

UK Visitor Attractions Directory records and presents information about UK visitor attractions, a previously under-researched sector of the tourist industry. It incorporates information on the type and category of attractions; their ownership, size, and location; the activities undertaken; and lists the range of facilities provided for visitors at each attraction. The directory will therefore be of interest and use to:

- participants in the industry who wish to analyse their competitive environment;
- students and researchers investigating the sector;
- policy makers and/or financiers examining resource use and allocation;
- suppliers who seek additional market outlets.

The current edition is based on replies to a structured sample of the sector. It is envisaged that the *Directory* will be produced on a biennial basis and the contents expanded and refined from the insights already obtained. Attractions currently listed will be invited to amend and update their entries, and additional attractions will be invited to participate in order to widen the database. There is no charge for entry and interested parties should contact the OCTALS Manager or H. Anthea Rogers, OCTALS, Oxford Brookes University, Oxford, tel. 0865 484824/484825.

Specific information in the form of tables or mailing lists may be abstracted from the information held on the database. A sample table (retailing) of the type of analysis that can be abstracted is recorded in Appendix A. If you are interested in acquiring particular data please contact the OCTALS Manager or H. Anthea Rogers, as above.

ACKNOWLEDGEMENTS

This *Directory* has been a collaborative venture involving
numerous staff. Grateful appreciation is expressed to the following
individuals who assisted.

Judith Thomas, who was involved in the inception and initial
development of the concept; Rob Stevens, who helped to devise
the mailing list and questionnaire; Chris Murphy, who organised
the computer database, its technical operation and the analysis of
the information collected; Angela Mayer and Nina Downie, who
entered all the data; Coral Dutson for her secretarial support;
Geoff Cole, who helped with library searches and background
information for desk research that underpinned the project;
H. Anthea Rogers, who researched and wrote the overview and
analysis; and Steve Cook from Cassell, who encouraged and
supported the whole exercise.

Their efficiency, competence and patience ensured that my role
in managing the project was made much easier.

Also, a particular thank-you to owners and managers in the
sector who responded to our requests for information.

Leigh Guyatt
Oxford Brookes University

INTRODUCTION: GENERAL REVIEW OF VISITOR ATTRACTIONS IN THE UK

This *Directory* focuses on the attractions sector of the UK tourist industry: a sector that has seen rapid growth over the last two decades and, though affected to some degree by the current recession, still has a high activity level in comparison to other industries.

DEFINITION OF THE TOURIST INDUSTRY

The industry is difficult to define from the supply side since it is fragmented and diverse. Approaching it as a phenomenon or activity makes the task easier. For this reason the definition in most general use in the UK is that of the Tourism Society:

> Tourism denotes the temporary short term movement of people to destinations outside the places where they normally live and work and their activities during their stay at these destinations . . . this definition includes domestic and international tourism comprising day visits as well as staying visits, for the following main purposes: holidays, leisure and recreation; business and conferences.

This is a good workable definition for the *Directory* since it spans tourism and leisure activities, includes staying visits (sometimes referred to as trips), and also day visits from home for leisure and recreational purposes. It means that anyone who travels further than to the place where they normally live and work inadvertently becomes a participant in this pervasive industry.

Tourism has been one of the few growth industries in the UK over the last two decades. Throughout the 1980s it accounted for just under 5% of world-wide tourist arrivals. In 1991 16.6 million foreign visitors are estimated to have spent £7,168 million within the UK. In 1991, domestic tourism accounted for 94.4 million trips and an additional £10,470 million of expenditure. In addition, day leisure visits were estimated by the Department of Employment in 1989 to generate another 1,684 million visits, although only around 10% may have been solely for the purpose of visiting an attraction. The tourism industry is therefore big business, accounting for 3% of national output and, directly or indirectly, employing 1.5 million people. It is however difficult to analyse statistically since the component sectors overlap: a tourism 'product' is enjoyed usually in conjunction with other complementary services such as accommodation, transport and/or food and drink. In addition, many of the facilities are used by a variety of participants with diverse motivations.

The following categorisation is normally used when analysing the industry:

- Attractions
- Facilities
- Infrastructure
- Transport
- Hospitality

Tourist attractions are the central hub of the industry, and provide a key role in the motivation for travel both for domestic and foreign tourists. They are provided by a diverse group of organisations, both in terms of ownership and size, and offer a variety of experiences to the visitor that includes sheer hedonistic pleasure, entertainment and education.

DEFINITION OF TOURIST ATTRACTIONS

After much debate the national tourist boards for England, Scotland and Wales have agreed on the following definition:

> A permanently established excursion destination, a primary purpose of which is to allow public access for entertainment, interest or education; rather than being a primary retail outlet or a venue for sporting, theatrical, or film performances. It must be open to the public, without prior booking, for published periods each year, and should be capable of attracting day visitors or tourists, as well as local residents.

These criteria form the basis for inclusion in the *Directory*. Included are theme parks, historic houses, castles, monuments, heritage centres, gardens, museums, galleries, zoos, cathedrals, collieries, water-mills, model villages, steamboats, rare breed farm parks, sea-life centres, industrial tourism centres, and much more. The diversity is apparent and this makes taxonomy difficult, since many can be recorded in more than one category when they offer overlapping experiences. Shopping centres or sporting complexes have been excluded together with natural attractions such as beauty spots or temporary events such as flower festivals.

PROFILE OF THE SECTOR

The sector has grown substantially in the last two decades. Only 25% of current attractions were open prior to 1960. A third of the attractions now available to the public have opened since 1979 and 58 new attractions opened in 1991. Investment has been considerable, as the sector is capital intensive. The White Cliffs of Dover attraction involved £13.75 million, and newly-revealed plans for redevelopment at Stonehenge will require an anticipated £10 million. Much of the funding has come from private sector sources, but local authority and central government funding supported and acted as catalysts for substantial investment until the late 1980s. However, in 1989 grant aid for tourist development in England was withdrawn, although it continues for Wales and Scotland via their development boards and respective offices.

Tourist development action programmes are still being used to initiate joint public and private sector development initiatives and many local authorities have encouraged strategic development initiatives, particularly in areas of high unemployment. European Funding is also available to developments that meet EEC specific criteria for support. In 1991 an estimated £134 million was spent on capital improvements, reflecting not merely depreciation but pro-active strategies that included the updating of facilities to keep pace with technological innovation and changing visitor tastes.

Visits to attractions are highly seasonal, being concentrated primarily in the summer months. In addition, there is a focus on weekend visits by day excursionists. The Survey of Leisure Day Visits estimated that almost 35% of all visits made to tourist attractions by UK residents take place on Sundays, the majority in family groups, and that 66% of these use their own car as a means of transport. Children are estimated to account for 30% of all visitors and this would reinforce the peaking of demand in certain periods.

Ownership patterns within any industry are important, since there are well-documented links between ownership, mission, behaviour and performance. Details regarding ownership have been very limited. Tourist board estimates suggest that of their registered attractions the government owns approximately 12%, local authorities 29%, while the remaining 59% are classed as 'private'. The latter category does not really reflect the complex ownership pattern that actually exists in the sector and, as we shall examine later, hides a diversity of missions, objectives and strategy that enriches the sector even if it does make the work of analysts more difficult.

The range of amenities offered by each attraction reflects the specific nature of the experience they offer to visitors. Some basic requirements are necessary to meet visitors' expectations and health and safety regulations: initial access requires signposting and the ubiquitous car-parking facilities; public lavatories, refreshment facilities and basic interpretation is the norm. Further amenities may be provided: commercial considerations have resulted in most attractions providing shopping opportunities, and increasingly these are seen as desirable from the visitor's perspective. Guides and/or guidebooks are the norm in most attractions, facilities for the disabled, seating for the enjoyment of all, shelter from adverse weather, facilities for children, and numerous other quality enhancers are offered by attractions which are aware of the increasing expectations of their visitors.

All these facilities require effective site and operations management to ensure that the whole attraction runs smoothly to plan. The more progressive attractions offer additional facilities such as very sophisticated interpretation with advanced technology being harnessed to enhance visitors' experiences. The amenities and concepts combine to offer a total 'package' to the visitor, but though physical attributes are important the psychological needs of the visitor must also be met. Whether this involves cosseting and personal attention, freedom to explore at their own pace, the adrenalin-raising thrill of white-knuckle rides or the peace and serenity of a beautiful garden, an overriding need is for the visitor to feel welcome, comfortable and secure. The role of staff in this context is vital. Visitors come with preconceptions that have been built up in a variety of ways: these expectations must be met fully if satisfaction is to be guaranteed. In fact they should be exceeded if a reputation for excellence, value for money or other desirable qualitative images are central to the mission of the attraction.

DIMENSIONS OF THE ATTRACTIONS SECTOR

Annual surveys are made by tourist boards to obtain information on visits, usage and capacity of all attractions 'where it is feasible to charge admission for the sole purpose of sightseeing'. It is estimated that 5,188 attractions exist in the UK: 4,019 in England, 795 in Scotland, 236 in Wales and 138 in Northern Ireland. *Sightseeing*, a syndicate tourist board publication, counted 345 million visits in 1991: 76 million to historic properties, 58 million to museums, 23 million to wildlife attractions, 19 million to art galleries, 15 million to gardens and 154 million to a variety of other attractions. Since these figures refer only to the attractions that charge, an estimated 64%, they must significantly underestimate the amount of activity in the sector as a whole. The 1991 Visitor Attraction Survey undertaken by the BTA revealed the following numbers for the top five attractions charging for admission:

   i)   Madame Tussauds 2,248,956;
   ii) Alton Towers 1,968,000;
   iii) Tower of London 1,923,520;
   iv) Natural History Museum 1,571,681;
   v)   St Paul's Cathedral 1,500,000.

Top of the list for Historic properties was the Tower of London, with 1.9 million visitors; the top garden was Tropical World at Leeds, with 1.1 million, closely followed by Hampton Court with 1 million; in museums and galleries the British Museum had over 5 million visitors; for the wildlife category London Zoo had 1.1 million and Windsor Safari Park 899,076; Blackpool Pleasure Beach topped all attendances with 6.5 million, followed by the Palace Pier at Brighton with 3.5 million; and the most visited country park was Strathclyde Country Park with 4.2 million visitors.

FEATURES OF OPERATIONS AND MANAGEMENT

It has already been established that successful attractions meet and hopefully exceed visitor expectations. Managing the intangible service provided by attractions in this context requires skill and flair. Managing an attraction poses a challenge that is very different from that encountered in manufacturing.

- The product is intangible and elusive: it is not carried home in a carrier bag! To the visitor the experience is unique, sometimes never to be repeated, while to the supplier and staff it is routine, maybe even at times regrettably tedious. This poses a real challenge for the selection, training and management of staff as well as for the marketeer, who has to monitor the way expectations are aroused and the product delivered.

- The product is delivered in real time with the resulting peaks and troughs of seasonal, weekly and daily fluctuations in demand. This highlights operational issues of capacity planning, scheduling of activities and staffing, etc. that have to be carefully planned and executed.

- The attraction's actual location or site is the factory floor, where the service is delivered in full sight of the customer. This involves the visitor in the production process and means that the environs have to be meticulously planned for aesthetic, ergonomic and safety reasons. Interpretation is also crucial in this context, as well as the provision of adequate facilities. The need for facilities for disadvantaged or special needs groups is also at last being recognised.

- Environmental issues are of great concern to society and will play an increasing role in attraction management. All attractions have impacts on the environment in which they are located: costs and benefits result from their operation. This applies to rural attractions located in the countryside as well as to heritage-based attractions in built up environments. Net effects are difficult to quantify as the interests of affected parties may conflict. In this context the codes of practice drawn up by tourist boards are a welcome development, and offer hope for an improved recognition of the problems and how they may be mitigated.

We have so far focused on the internal factors that affect the management of attractions, but external forces are also influential. The economic, social, political and technological environments set the contexts in which attractions operate and so impinge on strategy and determine performance. Though at times they may constrain activity, opportunities are also offered. The current long and continuing recession in the UK has reduced activity and depressed income and employment levels for the economy as a whole. Sample surveys taken by tourist boards indicate that from 1988 to 1991 visits to attractions showed an overall rise of 8%, although between 1990 and 1991 there was a 1% fall. This 1% average drop hides significant fluctuations within individual categories: historic properties down 4%; wildlife parks and zoos down 6%; gardens up 4%; country parks up 3% and farms up 6%. In addition, the blanket averages overlook the fact that many new attractions opened over the period and some were very successful, e.g. Tullie house in Carlisle attracted 300,000 visitors. Some attractions, aware of the potential negative effects of the recession, altered their marketing strategy to keep up visitor numbers, though in some instances this may have had an adverse effect on overall performance. In a gloomy world of uncertainty, attractions able to offer an opportunity for escapism or real pleasure still have potential to draw visitors. Attractions dependent on international visitors were in the main adversely affected by the after-effects of the Gulf War, but even here the vulnerability was not uniform: Blenheim Palace experienced a 1.6% drop, while Windsor State Apartments had a 26% decline.

Socially, leisure is increasingly seen as a merit that is central to people's lives. For leisure outside the home there is a move towards active and participative activities, a trend exploited effectively by many attractions. The search for educational experiences explains some of the observable trends in the sector. Industrial tourism is a growing sector, with 294 registered centres that range from porcelain, chocolate, or alcoholic production centres with lucrative retailing outlets to nuclear disposal plants or pump storage power generating stations with intangible products. Farm tourism, especially working farms, has caught the imagination of the public, particularly families and schoolchildren. This is a fast-growing section offering education and entertainment locally through access to animals and the countryside and a glimpse of different life-styles.

Demographic changes for the 1990s indicate that the 45–59 age group, with its high disposable income and free time, will comprise 25% of the population by the year 2000. In addition, a growth in families with young children is anticipated. These changes will influence visitor numbers.

We have already seen that green issues and concern for the environment have entered this sector. Impact analysis is increasingly required for new developments. In a rural context this is perhaps to be expected, but it also applies to the heritage sector, where conservation and preservation are hotly contested issues of great concern to the public at large.

Technological innovation has been harnessed by the sector in a variety of ways, such as interpretation, automatic ticketing and booking systems, animatronics, etc., but more opportunities exist as virtual reality and other simulations are increasingly adapted to leisure and entertainment usage.

Throughout the 1980s the government encouraged tourism by underpinning marketing at international level and supporting investment programmes or initiatives that offered employment prospects. At the beginning of the 1990s this support can no longer be guaranteed, and changed funding arrangements between national and regional boards, at least in England, suggest that less support will be forthcoming. Wales and Scotland however seem to have mechanisms through their respective offices which should allow continuity of their existing policies.

Overall, there is quiet optimism in the sector that, with imagination and effective management, the vigour of the sector can be maintained through the 1990s.

THE DIRECTORY

The survey has increased the knowledge base for the sector, and individual entries list all the specific information that has been collected. The database on which these were recorded can be manipulated so that individual components, interrelationships features and attributes can be abstracted for detailed analysis and appraisal.

THE COVERAGE OF THE SURVEY

Data was collected by a postal questionnaire that was designed to elicit in-depth information about the tourist attractions operating in the UK. A pilot study was undertaken in early 1992 to check the robustness of the questionnaire and likely response rate. The results were encouraging and, after some adjustments, a full survey was conducted during 1992. The structured sample was based on desk research that reviewed published information (albeit piecemeal) regarding the structure and participants in the sector. Tourist board registrations were the primary source for mailing lists. An initial sample (3,000) based on type of attraction, regional distribution, size and ownership was selected. Replies were received from 33% of those approached. As an initial first-time response rate this was deemed satisfactory. Additional questionnaires were mailed and previous recipients followed up in order to maintain the desired structured response, but time constraints did not allow the sample to be increased substantially. It is hoped that as the project develops a wider response rate will be achieved to increase the accuracy of the analysis that can be drawn from the respondents.

An alphabetical list of all respondents (1,200) is listed in Appendix B. Some background information is presented before the analysis.

The distribution of the respondents according to category, region, size and ownership is given in Figures 1, 2, 3 and 4 respectively. Information on the sector for these particular variables is too sparse to conclude with absolute certainty how representative the sample is. From previously published information there is no reason to suspect that there are major distortions.

Type and ownership (Figures 1 and 4) were categories that caused some problems for the current analysis, but have provided insights for future research that will be invaluable in mapping out the distribution of organisations within these categories.

The 'type' category was extended deliberately, from the rather restricted categories traditionally used in the sector to encompass the increasingly diverse portfolio of type that is developing. Even so, the twelve categories used failed to reduce 'the other' miscellaneous remainder below 16%. Each respondent determined their own classification category. Many attractions felt that they overlapped the designated categories sufficiently to warrant classification in more than one. This was permitted and the bases adjusted for multiple classification when percentages were calculated for type. In future editions this categorisation will be re-examined.

Ownership patterns in the sector are more heterogeneous than any other industrial sector known to the author. The original intention of offering a fivefold classification proved inadequate to meet this diversity. Respondents classified themselves as trust/charity status (21%), limited company (13%), PLC (2%), local authority (24%), other (40%). The largest entries under 'other' categories, re-analysed and expressed as a percentage of the

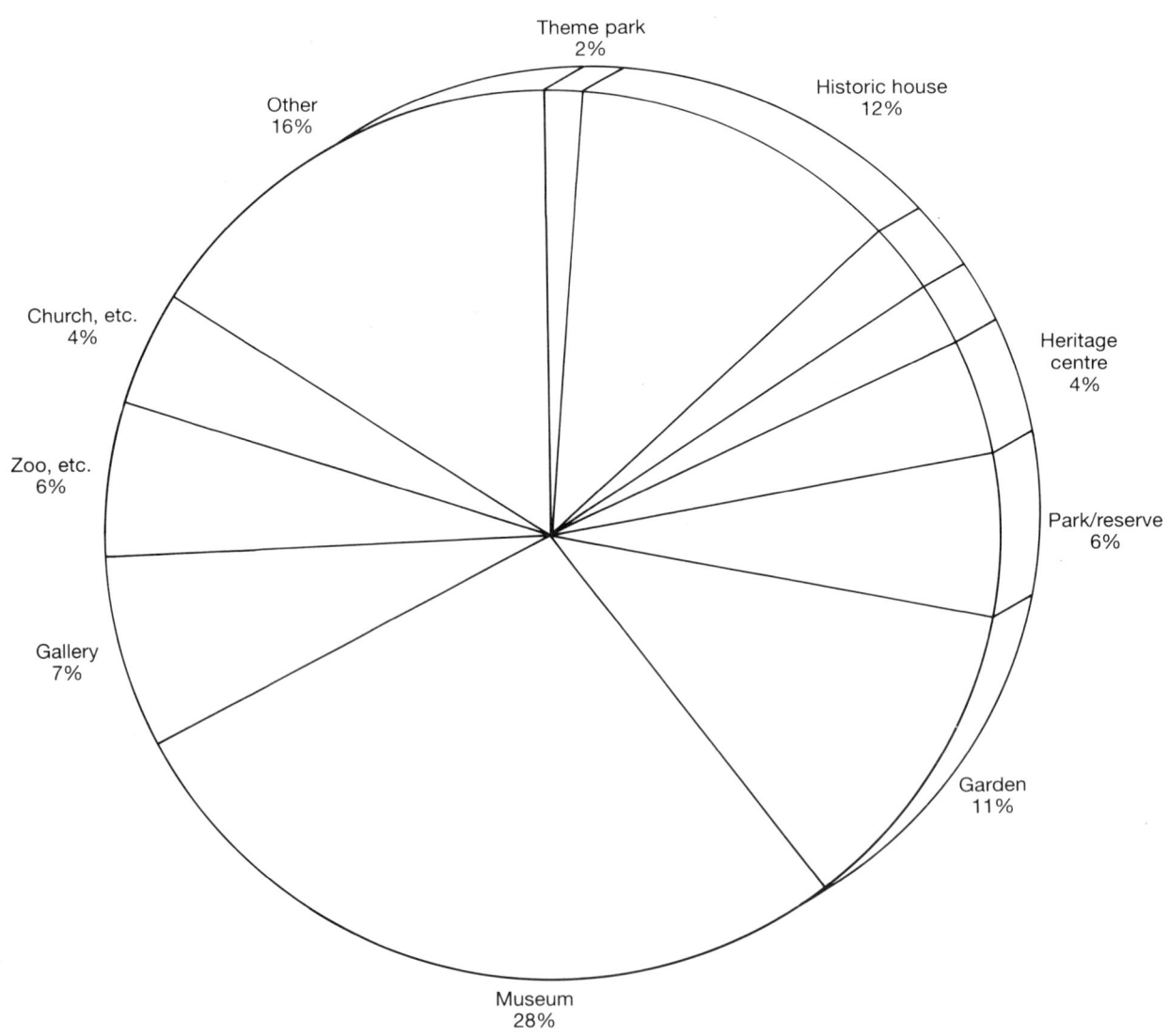

Figure 1

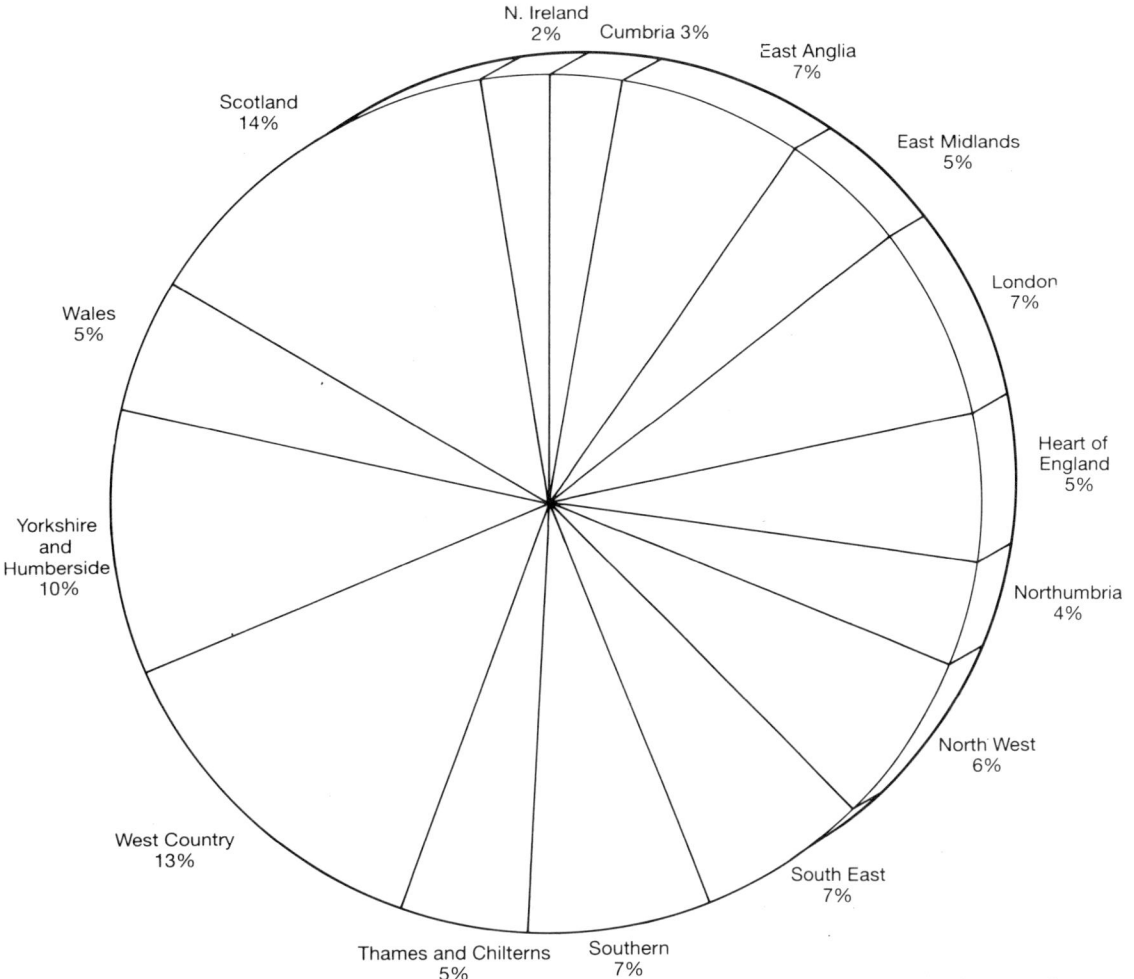

Figure 2

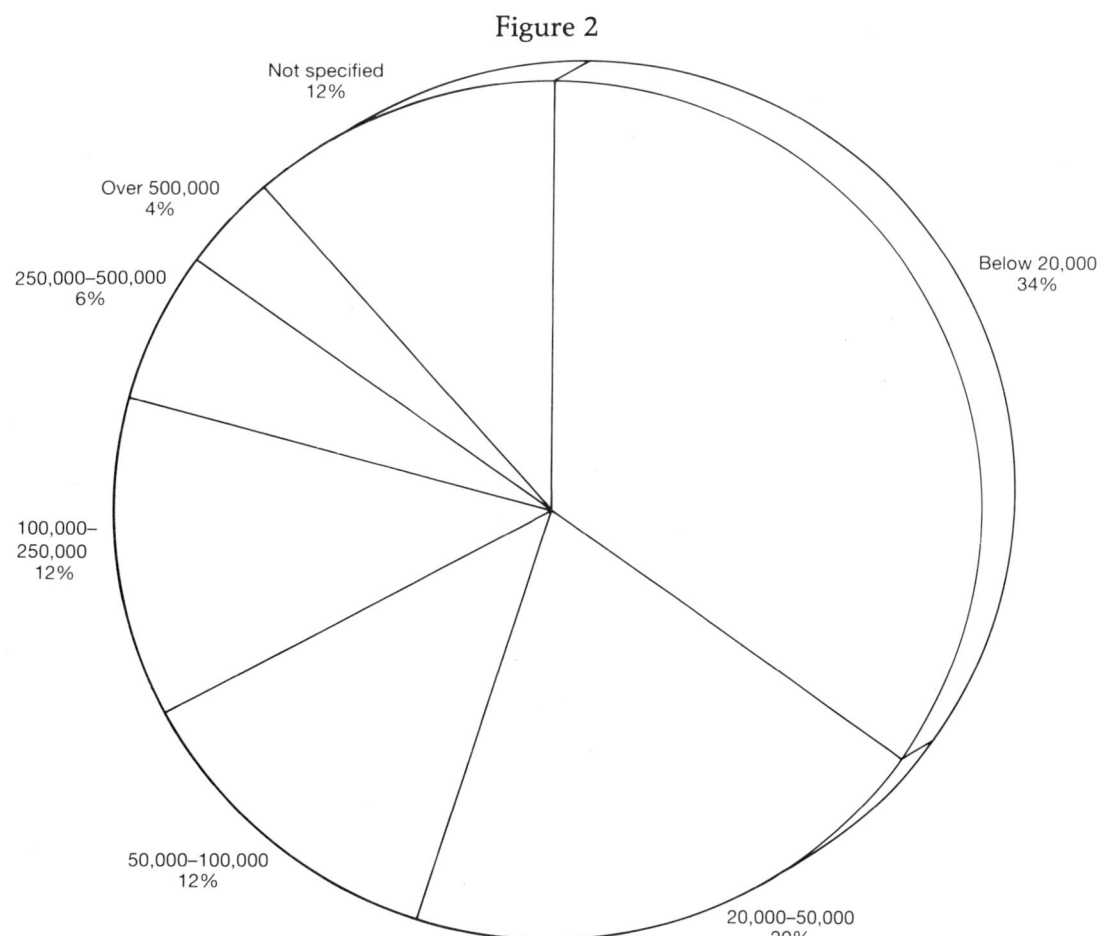

Figure 3

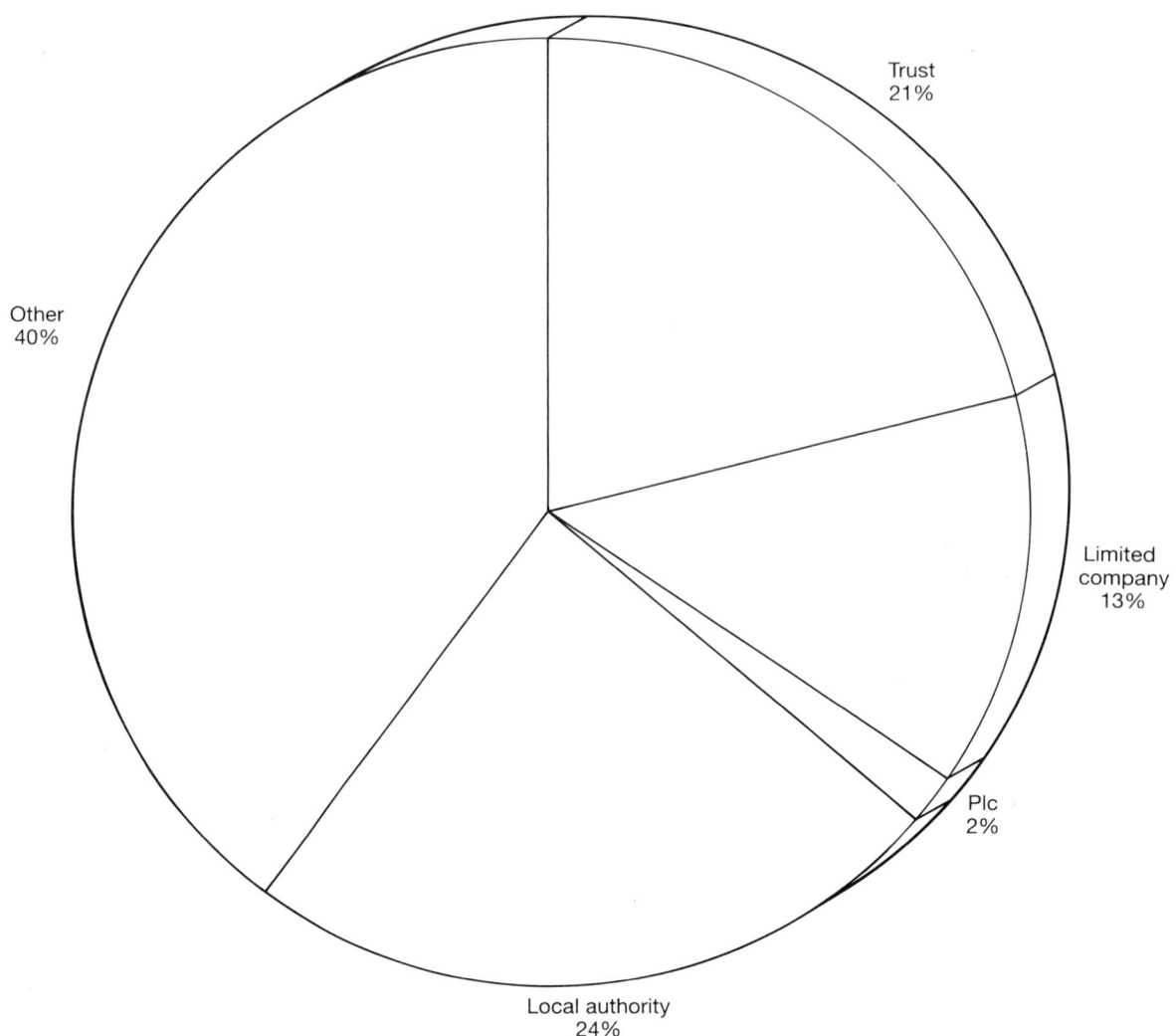

Figure 4

total sample, were: private ownership (12%), Ecclesiastical (6%), government (4%), dual ownerships (3%). Again, this is an area which will be made more specific in the next edition but further analysis of the data is already being undertaken.

ANALYSIS OF DATA

More detailed analysis and cross-tabulations of the entries by categories are shown in Tables 1 to 4. Readers are reminded that these are sample-based, but there are interesting insights. The tables should be read horizontally from the classification on the left-hand side. The percentages will then total 100%. For example, using Table 1 to illustrate: 50% of all the theme parks responding were owned by limited companies, but only 10.5% of museums had limited company status. Using category as a base for calculating percentages, we can also see that 23.5% of theme parks have over 500,000 visitors, while only 2.5% of museums are in this category.

Museums, historic houses and heritage centres are predominantly small, with 41.4%, 41.3% and 38.9% respectively falling in the below 20,000 group.

Table 2 analyses the sample according to the regional tourist boards as they were when the survey was conducted. On this basis the predominant size of tourism attractions in Scotland is small; Northumbria also has a high proportion of small tourist attractions as well as a high percentage of local authority ownership. Analysis along these lines can be undertaken from Tables 3 and 4.

All attractions were asked to provide a mission statement. These were to be reviewed in light of ownership, type and size. Regrettably, the pilot gave no indication of the rather curious interpretations of 'mission' that respondents were to come up with. The majority described the activities that went on in their attraction rather than the motivating purpose; others failed to complete the statement. It is sometimes suggested that mission statements are public relations exercises and do not reflect true motivation. Allowing for this distortion, the respondents provide some fascinating insights into the web of complex aims and objectives that prevail in the sector.

One would expect commercial organisations to include 'profitability' as one of their aims, but in almost all the usable replies this was tempered by additional qualitative statements that involved other stakeholders such as:

- to make profits for shareholders;
- to benefit staff by running a successful business which provides exceptional service to its customers;
- to make a satisfactory profit and to provide an enjoyable experience for young and old.

One commercial organisation expressed the following wish:

- to be pioneering, enterprising and innovative as well as professional in all that we do.

Local authorities have a wide range of stakeholders to satisfy and this is reflected in a typical mission for a local authority country park:

- to achieve 300,000 visitors per annum;
- to change perceptions of the area and establish it as a tourist area;
- to increase awareness and access to the countryside for the benefit of all.

One local authority museum stated:

- the museum is responsible for the acquisition, preservation, interpretation, communication and exhibition of the material culture, history and natural environment of . . . and its environs for the benefit of the local community and visitors to the area.

Trust status produced some of the most noble missions, for example:

Table 1

UK tourist attraction database: percentage analysis of entries by category

| | Ownership | | | | | No. of visitors (1992) | | | | | | |
	trust	limited company	plc	local authority	other	under 20,000	20,000-50,000	50,000-100,000	100,000-250,000	250,000-500,000	over 500,000	not known
theme park	2.94	50.00	5.88	8.82	32.35	8.82	20.59	8.82	14.71	17.65	23.53	5.88
historic house	35.04	7.09	0.39	23.62	33.86	41.34	22.44	12.99	6.69	4.33	2.36	9.84
castle	20.75	11.32	1.89	16.98	49.06	28.30	16.98	22.64	16.98	1.89	5.66	7.55
monument	23.40	2.13	0.00	21.28	53.19	29.79	21.28	14.89	6.38	10.64	8.51	8.51
heritage centre	23.33	16.67	2.22	25.56	32.22	38.89	17.78	10.00	12.22	7.78	2.22	11.11
park/reserve	20.00	8.80	0.80	36.80	33.60	17.60	16.80	15.20	20.00	12.00	7.20	11.20
garden	31.12	8.30	0.41	18.26	41.91	39.00	20.75	15.35	9.13	3.32	3.32	9.13
museum	26.29	10.48	1.66	31.11	30.45	41.43	21.96	11.15	9.65	3.66	2.50	9.65
gallery	19.73	5.44	1.36	46.26	27.21	28.57	25.17	12.24	13.61	4.76	4.76	10.88
zoo, etc.	20.17	23.53	3.36	9.24	43.70	16.81	20.17	14.29	17.65	10.08	9.24	11.76
church, etc.	10.00	3.33	0.00	1.11	85.56	32.22	8.89	12.22	10.00	13.33	7.78	15.56
other	14.54	22.85	3.86	19.29	39.47	27.89	21.96	12.17	15.13	5.93	3.86	13.06

| | Regional Tourist Board Area | | | | | | | | | | | | | | |
	Cumbria	East Anglia	East Midlands	London	Heart of England	Northumbria	North West	South East	Southern	Thames and Chilterns	West Country	Yorkshire and Humberside	Wales	Scotland	Northern Ireland
theme park	0.00	5.88	11.76	2.94	0.00	2.94	8.82	2.94	2.94	2.94	29.41	11.76	5.88	8.82	2.94
historic house	3.15	6.30	5.12	7.09	9.06	1.97	4.72	8.66	5.91	6.69	11.02	9.84	3.94	13.39	3.15
castle	3.77	3.77	1.89	1.89	5.66	7.55	1.89	13.21	1.89	0.00	9.43	5.66	15.09	22.64	5.66
monument	0.00	10.64	0.00	2.13	6.38	8.51	12.77	8.51	10.64	10.64	10.64	8.51	2.13	4.26	4.26
heritage centre	1.11	1.11	6.67	7.78	4.44	2.22	2.22	10.00	10.00	4.44	10.00	7.78	6.67	18.89	6.67
park/reserve	1.60	8.00	8.00	3.20	3.20	6.40	7.20	4.80	7.20	10.40	10.40	5.60	2.40	16.80	4.80
garden	3.73	3.73	4.15	4.56	5.39	1.24	5.39	10.37	8.30	5.81	17.43	7.47	3.73	15.77	2.90
museum	2.16	7.32	4.99	8.65	6.49	3.83	6.32	6.82	7.15	3.00	13.14	10.48	4.83	12.81	2.00
gallery	2.72	6.12	3.40	10.20	2.04	4.76	12.24	3.40	4.76	3.40	7.48	14.29	9.52	14.97	0.68
zoo, etc.	0.84	7.56	3.36	3.36	1.68	1.68	9.24	7.56	9.24	5.04	19.33	10.08	4.20	12.61	4.20
church, etc.	1.11	7.78	2.22	16.67	6.67	7.78	7.78	2.22	6.67	3.33	10.00	11.11	0.00	13.33	3.33
other	4.45	9.50	5.64	6.23	4.75	3.26	5.04	7.42	6.23	4.15	11.57	9.50	7.12	13.35	1.78

- as trustees our role is to provide the freest possible access to
  the finest possible paintings (gallery), to preserve our heritage
  for future generations to allow access to our national heritage.

Ecclesiastical ownership, perhaps as one would expect, correlated
with some of the best presented and longest missions. The mission
of St Paul's cathedral exemplifies this:

- Our purpose is to proclaim the Christian gospel according to
  the practices and traditions of the Church of England and,
  in an environment of excellence and beauty, to uplift the
  minds of men, women and children to the things of the spirit.

Table 2

UK tourist attraction database: Percentage analysis of entries by region

| | Ownership | | | | | No. of visitors (1992) | | | | | | |
	trust	limited company	plc	local authority	other	under 20,000	20,000–50,000	50,000–100,000	100,000–250,000	250,000–500,000	over 500,000	not known
Cumbria	26.47	14.71	5.88	14.71	38.24	23.53	26.47	5.88	23.53	2.94	0.00	17.65
East Anglia	16.47	16.47	1.18	21.18	44.71	31.76	23.53	9.41	15.29	5.88	4.71	9.41
East Midlands	14.04	14.04	5.26	24.56	42.11	24.56	29.82	10.53	15.79	5.26	3.51	10.53
London	16.85	15.73	2.25	16.85	48.31	40.45	8.99	8.99	6.74	7.87	12.36	14.61
Heart of England	33.85	16.92	1.54	23.08	24.62	43.08	12.31	16.92	6.15	9.23	1.54	10.77
Northumbria	13.04	6.52	2.17	36.96	41.30	47.83	21.74	13.04	6.52	4.35	0.00	6.52
North West	15.58	18.18	3.90	29.87	32.47	24.68	22.08	14.29	12.99	5.19	10.39	10.39
South East	30.00	12.50	1.25	18.75	37.50	33.75	18.75	18.75	13.75	3.75	2.50	8.75
Southern	13.41	21.95	0.00	18.29	46.34	28.05	17.07	14.63	9.76	7.32	1.22	21.95
Thames and Chilterns	15.79	17.54	1.75	31.58	33.33	19.30	17.54	10.30	14.04	10.53	5.26	14.04
West Country	26.75	8.28	1.27	14.65	49.04	42.68	18.47	7.64	10.83	5.73	0.64	14.01
Yorkshire and Humberside	18.18	8.26	2.48	36.36	34.71	34.71	24.79	9.92	14.05	2.48	7.44	6.61
Wales	18.03	21.31	1.64	29.51	29.51	21.31	31.15	14.75	19.67	1.64	0.00	11.48
Scotland	27.38	10.12	0.60	23.21	38.69	45.24	16.67	11.90	9.52	5.95	0.60	10.12
Northern Ireland	17.86	3.57	0.00	35.71	42.86	32.14	35.71	14.29	7.14	3.57	0.00	7.14

| | Type of attraction | | | | | | | | | | | |
	theme park	historic house	castle	monument	heritage centre	park/reserve	garden	museum	gallery	zoo, etc.	church, etc.	other
Cumbria	0.00	14.29	3.57	0.00	1.79	3.57	16.07	23.21	7.14	1.79	1.79	26.79
East Anglia	1.37	10.96	1.37	3.42	0.68	6.85	6.16	30.14	6.16	6.16	4.79	21.92
East Midlands	3.85	12.50	0.96	0.00	5.77	9.62	9.62	28.85	4.81	3.85	1.92	18.27
London	0.67	12.00	0.67	0.67	4.67	2.67	7.33	34.67	10.00	2.67	10.00	14.00
Heart of England	0.00	19.83	2.59	2.59	3.45	3.45	11.21	33.62	2.59	1.72	5.17	13.79
Northumbria	1.30	6.49	5.19	5.19	2.60	10.39	3.90	29.87	9.09	2.60	9.09	14.29
North West	2.19	8.76	0.73	4.38	1.46	6.57	9.49	27.74	13.14	8.03	5.11	12.41
South East	0.64	14.10	4.49	2.56	5.77	3.85	16.03	26.28	3.21	5.77	1.28	16.03
Southern	0.68	10.14	0.68	3.38	6.08	6.08	13.51	29.05	4.73	7.43	4.05	14.19
Thames and Chilterns	1.00	17.00	0.00	5.00	4.00	13.00	14.00	18.00	5.00	6.00	3.00	14.00
West Country	3.66	10.26	1.83	1.83	3.30	4.76	15.38	28.94	4.03	8.42	3.30	14.29
Yorkshire and Humberside	1.94	12.14	1.46	1.94	3.40	3.40	8.74	30.58	10.19	5.83	4.85	15.53
Wales	1.80	9.01	7.21	0.90	5.41	2.70	8.11	26.13	12.61	4.50	0.00	21.62
Scotland	1.01	11.41	4.03	0.67	5.70	7.05	12.75	25.84	7.38	5.03	4.03	15.10
Northern Ireland	1.67	13.33	5.00	3.33	10.00	10.00	11.67	20.00	1.67	8.33	5.00	10.00

- To achieve that purpose, the clergy and lay staff offer daily worship to God; provide pastoral care; serve the Crown, nation, city and diocese; work to fulfil the stewardship of St Paul's heritage; and, subject to maintaining an environment of excellence and beauty, attract as many tourists as possible to uplift their minds and finally to earn sufficient money for the Cathedral to perform all these tasks.

Table 3a

UK tourist attraction database: Percentage analysis of entries by size distribution

Type

	Theme park	Historic house	Castle	Monument	Heritage centre	Park/reserve	Garden	Museum	Gallery	Zoo, etc.	Church, etc.	Other
under 20,000	0.42	14.56	2.08	1.94	4.85	3.05	13.04	34.54	5.69	2.77	4.02	13.04
20,000–50,000	1.59	12.70	2.04	2.27	3.63	4.76	11.11	29.71	8.16	5.44	1.81	16.78
50,000–100,000	1.09	12.04	4.38	2.55	3.28	6.93	13.50	24.45	6.57	6.20	4.01	14.96
100,000–250,000	2.01	6.83	3.61	1.20	4.42	10.04	8.84	23.29	8.03	8.03	3.61	20.08
250,000–500,000	4.80	8.80	0.80	4.00	5.60	12.00	6.40	17.60	5.60	9.60	8.80	16.00
over 500,000	8.89	5.56	3.33	4.44	2.22	10.00	7.78	16.67	7.78	12.22	7.78	13.33
not known	0.88	11.06	1.77	1.77	4.42	6.19	9.73	25.66	7.08	6.19	5.75	19.47

Ownership

	trust	limited company	plc	local authority	Other
under 20,000	27.79	7.60	0.48	20.19	43.94
20,000–50,000	19.01	14.46	1.65	32.23	32.64
50,000–100,000	23.13	12.93	1.36	21.77	40.82
100,000–250,000	14.69	17.48	6.29	32.17	29.37
250,000–500,000	18.18	22.73	3.03	21.21	38.45
over 500,000	9.52	21.43	4.76	26.19	38.10
not known	13.67	18.71	0.72	15.83	51.08

Table 3b

UK tourist attraction database: Percentage analysis of entries by size distribution

Regional tourist board area

	Cumbria	East Anglia	East Midlands	London	Heart of England	Northumbria	North West	South East	Southern	Thames and Chilterns	West Country	Yorkshire and Humberside	Wales	Scotland	Northern Ireland
under 20,000	1.90	6.41	3.33	8.55	6.65	5.23	4.51	6.41	5.46	2.61	15.91	9.74	3.09	18.05	2.14
20,000–50,000	3.72	8.26	7.02	3.31	3.31	4.13	7.02	6.20	5.79	4.13	11.98	12.40	7.44	11.57	3.72
50,000–100,000	1.36	5.44	4.08	5.44	7.48	4.08	7.48	10.20	8.16	7.48	8.16	8.16	6.12	13.61	2.72
100,000–250,000	5.59	8.16	6.29	4.20	2.80	2.10	6.99	7.69	5.59	5.59	11.89	11.89	8.39	11.19	1.40
250,000–500,000	1.52	6.06	4.55	10.61	9.09	3.03	6.06	4.55	9.09	9.09	13.64	4.55	1.52	15.15	1.52
over 500,000	0.00	9.52	4.76	23.81	2.38	0.00	19.05	4.76	2.38	7.14	2.38	21.43	0.00	2.38	0.00
not known	4.32	5.76	4.32	9.35	5.04	2.16	5.76	5.04	12.23	5.76	15.83	5.76	5.04	12.23	1.44

Table 4a

UK tourist attraction database: Percentage analysis of entries by ownership

Type

	Theme park	Historic house	Castle	Monument	Heritage centre	Park/reserve	Garden	Museum	Gallery	Zoo, etc.	Church, etc.	Other
trust	0.20	17.58	2.22	2.22	4.24	5.05	14.75	31.72	5.66	4.85	1.82	9.70
limited company	6.37	6.74	2.25	0.37	5.62	4.12	7.49	23.60	3.00	10.49	1.12	28.84
plc	5.41	2.70	2.70	0.00	5.41	2.70	2.70	27.03	5.41	10.81	0.00	35.14
local authority	0.57	11.41	1.71	1.90	4.37	8.75	8.37	35.55	12.74	2.09	0.19	12.36
other	1.37	10.74	3.25	3.12	3.62	5.24	12.61	22.85	4.99	6.37	9.36	16.48

No. of visitors (1992)

	under 20,000	20,000–50,000	50,000–100,000	100,000–250,000	250,000–500,000	over 500,000	not known
trust	45.70	18.75	13.28	8.20	4.69	1.95	7.42
limited company	19.88	21.74	11.80	15.53	9.32	5.59	16.15
plc	9.09	18.18	9.09	40.91	9.09	9.09	4.55
local authority	29.76	26.99	11.07	15.92	4.84	3.81	7.61
other	38.62	16.49	12.53	8.98	5.01	3.34	15.03

Table 4b

UK tourist attraction database: Percentage analysis of entries by ownership

Regional tourist board area

	Cumbria	East Anglia	East Midlands	London	Heart of England	Northumbria	North West	South East	Southern	Thames and Chilterns	West Country	Yorkshire and Humberside	Wales	Scotland	Northern Ireland
trust	3.56	5.53	3.16	5.53	8.70	2.37	4.74	9.49	4.35	3.56	16.60	8.70	3.95	18.18	1.58
limited company	3.11	8.70	4.97	8.70	6.83	1.86	8.70	6.21	11.18	6.21	8.07	6.21	8.07	10.56	0.62
plc	9.09	4.55	13.64	9.09	4.55	4.55	13.64	4.55	0.00	4.55	9.09	13.64	4.55	4.55	0.00
local authority	1.74	6.25	4.86	5.21	5.21	5.90	7.99	5.21	5.21	6.25	7.99	14.93	6.25	13.54	3.47
other	2.73	7.56	5.04	9.03	3.36	3.99	5.25	6.30	7.77	3.99	16.18	8.82	3.78	13.66	2.52

Another church, in rather terser vein,

- exists to honour God and provide excellent service to visitors at value for money prices.

Government-owned attractions such as English Heritage stressed the need:

- to bring about long term conservation and widespread understanding and enjoyment of the historic environment for the benefit of present and future generations.

Privately owned attractions often stated that running an attraction offered them

- a way of life;
- a chance of meeting people;
- an opportunity to diversify our business and provide enjoyment for visitors;
- a means of developing what had been a hobby for the enjoyment of others.

But perhaps the one that the author liked best for its simplicity and the epitome of enjoyment which was so frequently mentioned in many of the mission statements, regardless of the type or ownership, was

- to make adults feel like children again.

In future editions of the *Directory* it is intended that the coverage of mission statements will be more detailed and recorded against each entry to allow more specific analysis.

Table 5 records admission charges by category and region. As one would expect, theme parks had the highest average charge and churches and galleries the lowest; the lowest highest charge of £6.25 for a heritage centre is somewhat surprising, and it is interesting to reflect on the rationale for the differential between heritage centres, museums and historic houses; there are now very few castles and gardens that do not charge, but 78% of churches are still free. This will be an interesting category to monitor over the next decade. The lowest average admission charging region is Northumbria which, although it has the largest percentage of free entry (54.35%), also has the lowest highest at £3. The south-east has the highest average entry charge and the west country has the lowest entry charge of just 10p to a museum. Wales interestingly joins three other regions with an average admission charge of over £2. The apparent incongruence of London as tenth in the overall averages can be explained by museums with free or low entry being a significant proportion of the sample. Figure 5 demonstrates that tourist boards undertake substantial promotion on behalf of the sector but that radio is of increasing importance.

Details regarding employment and training are presented in Figures 6–9. The average number of employees for the attractions surveyed was 18; the high season average was 25 and low season 11. All-year opening was highest in attractions not affected by adverse weather: 88% of churches and 78% of galleries are open all year but only 42% of gardens. Seasonality also varied according to size. Attractions below 100,000 visitors per annum had a 2:1 ratio for high:low season; this dropped to 1.5:1 for 100,000 to 250,000, while attractions over 500,000 recorded a 3.3:1 ratio. Theme parks and gardens recorded the largest seasonal differentials.

Training, as we have already indicated, is an important facet of effective performance. Figures 7–9 illustrate that over 75% of all attractions offer training to staff. Of these, 92% offered training in-house and 52% used external training. Theme parks, parks/reserves and zoos were the most enthusiastic in-house trainers,

Table 5
UK tourist attractions

(i) Adult admission charges by category

	Average (£)	Highest (£)	Lowest (£)	No charge (%)
Theme park	3.85	12.00	0.50	11.76
Historic house	2.23	12.00	0.30	18.11
Castle	2.27	6.50	0.50	13.21
Monument	1.47	7.80	0.50	25.53
Heritage centre	1.56	6.25	0.50	28.89
Park/reserve	1.78	10.00	0.50	38.40
Garden	2.28	12.00	0.20	14.11
Museum	1.41	7.80	0.10	30.78
Gallery	0.78	7.80	0.20	61.22
Zoo, etc.	2.79	10.75	0.75	17.65
Church, etc.	0.50	6.40	0.50	77.78
Other	1.82	12.50	0.20	30.86

(ii) Adult admission charges by region

	Average (£)	Highest (£)	Lowest (£)	No charge (%)
Cumbria	1.76	5.40	0.90	29.41
East Anglia	1.92	8.50	0.35	24.71
East Midlands	1.97	12.00	0.30	22.81
London	1.62	10.75	1.00	52.81
Heart of England	2.00	7.80	0.40	16.92
Northumbria	0.69	3.00	0.50	54.35
North West	1.24	5.99	0.20	51.95
South East	2.43	6.50	0.80	12.50
Southern	1.72	5.50	0.30	25.61
Thames and Chilterns	2.09	9.50	0.30	28.07
West Country	1.89	10.00	0.10	20.38
Yorkshire and Humberside	1.18	7.99	0.50	46.28
Wales	2.02	12.50	0.50	21.31
Scotland	1.24	5.50	0.50	40.48
Northern Ireland	1.30	4.00	0.50	35.71

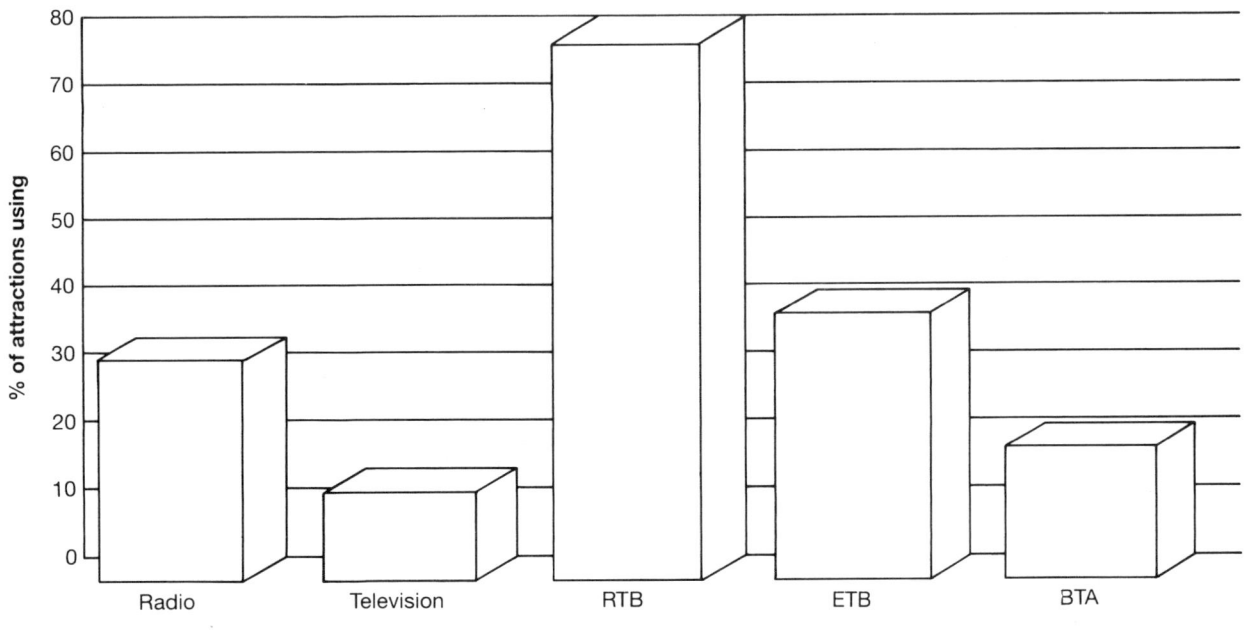

Figure 5

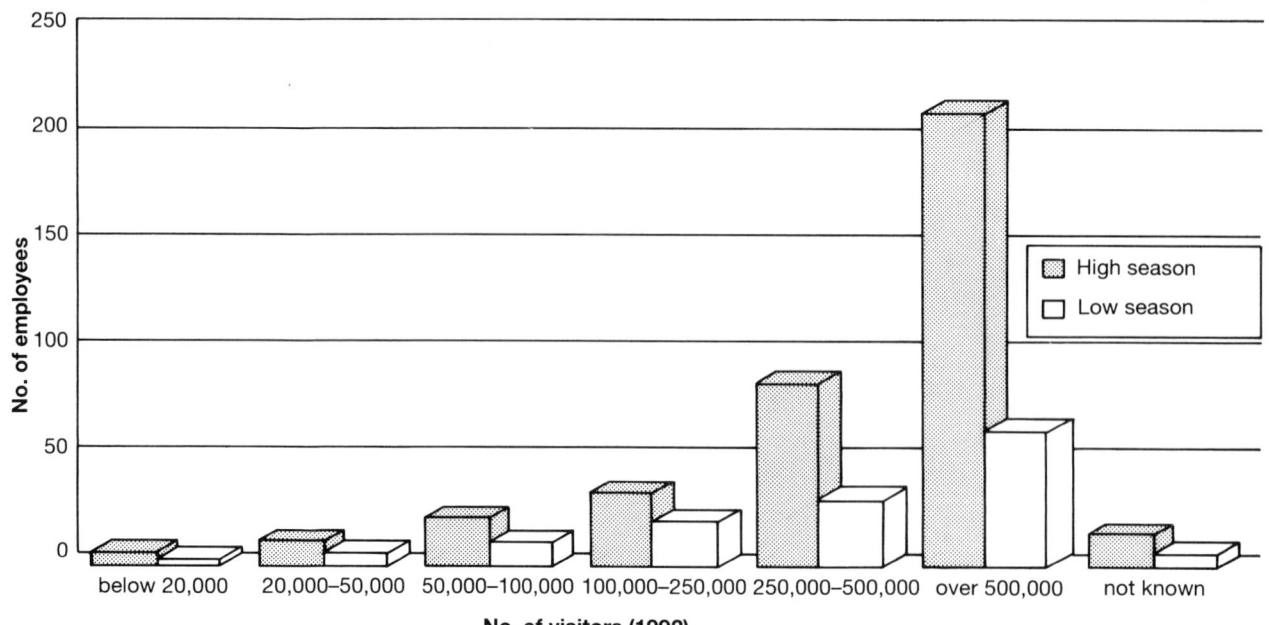

Figure 6a

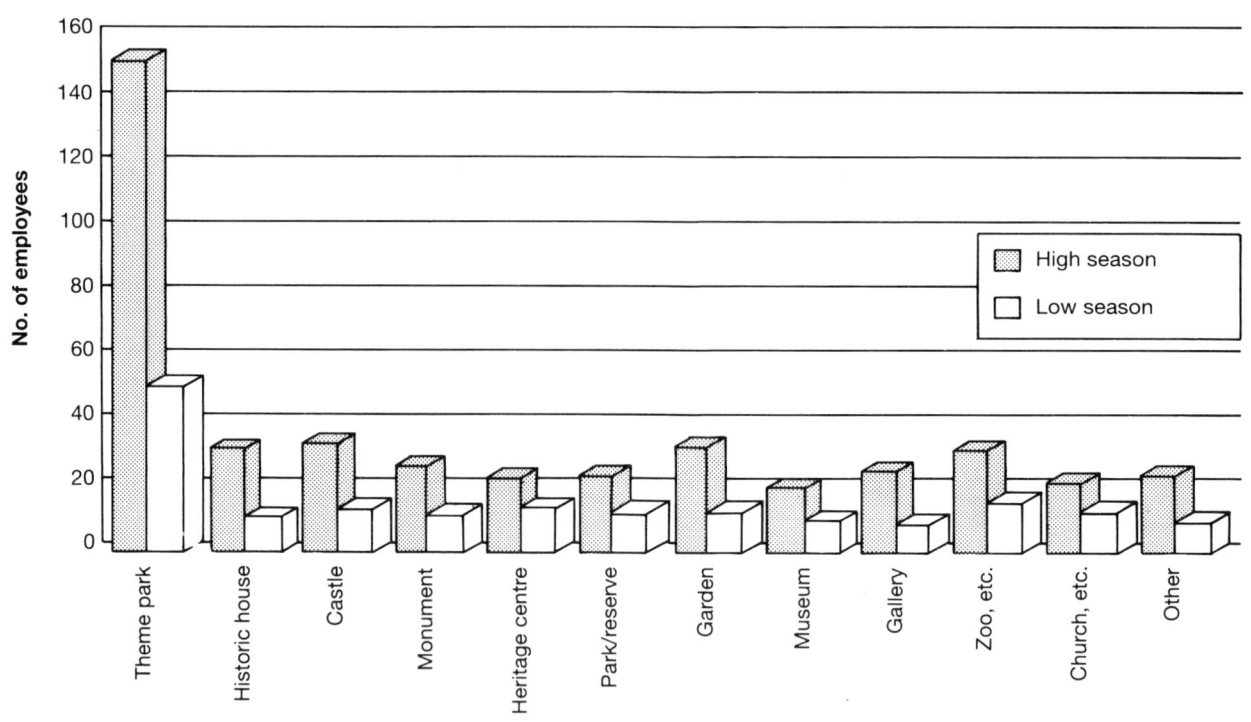

Figure 6b

with 91%, 84% and 82% respectively offering their own training. Ecclesiastical organisations did the least training, which probably reflects their voluntary labour. There is an observable correlation between size and training, the largest attractions being the highest users of external support.

In view of the interest in environmental issues, questions were included on monitoring and auditing aspects of environmental concern. Figure 10 indicates that recycling, waste disposal and energy are given highest priority in attractions as a whole. Theme parks (47%), followed by zoos (33%) and parks (32%) prioritised

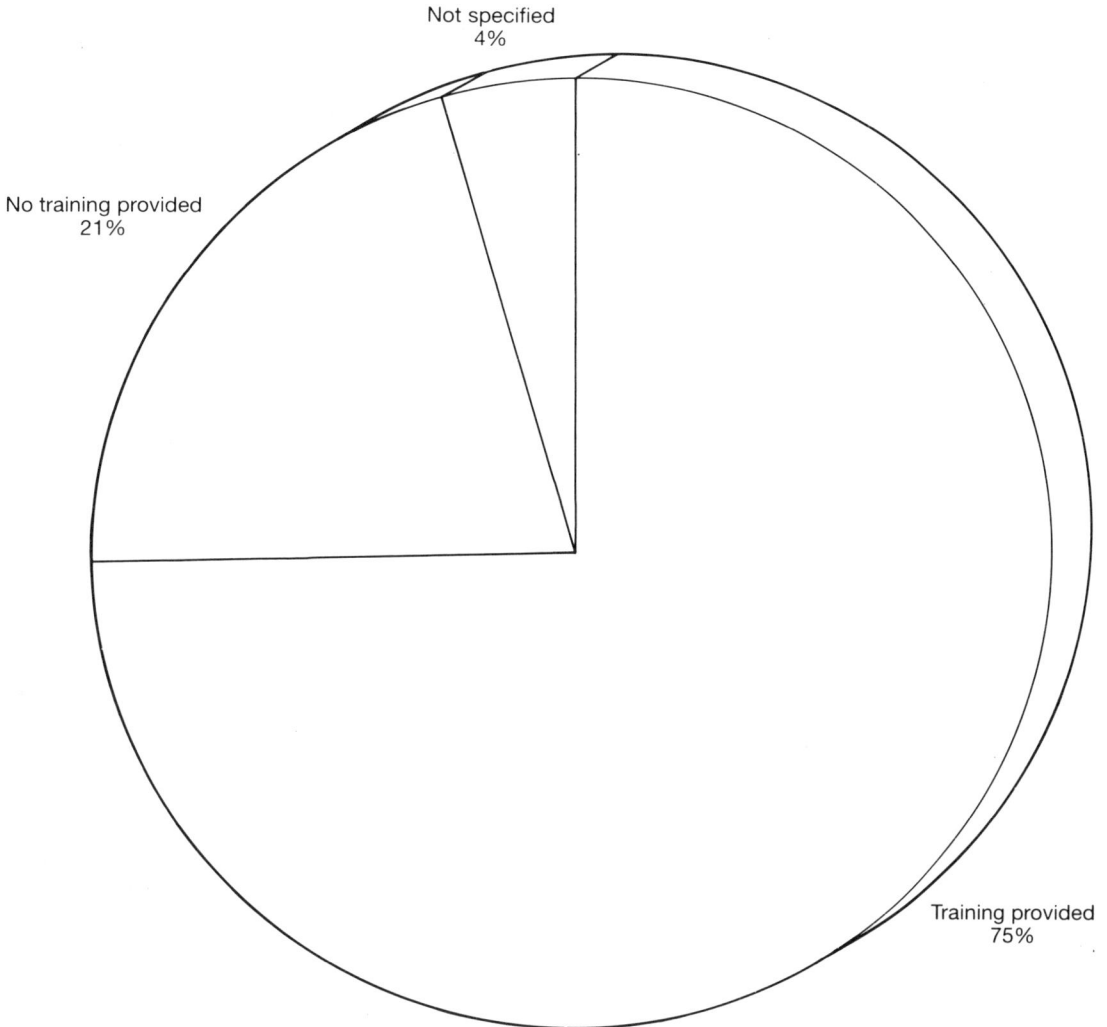

Not specified
4%

No training provided
21%

Training provided
75%

Figure 7

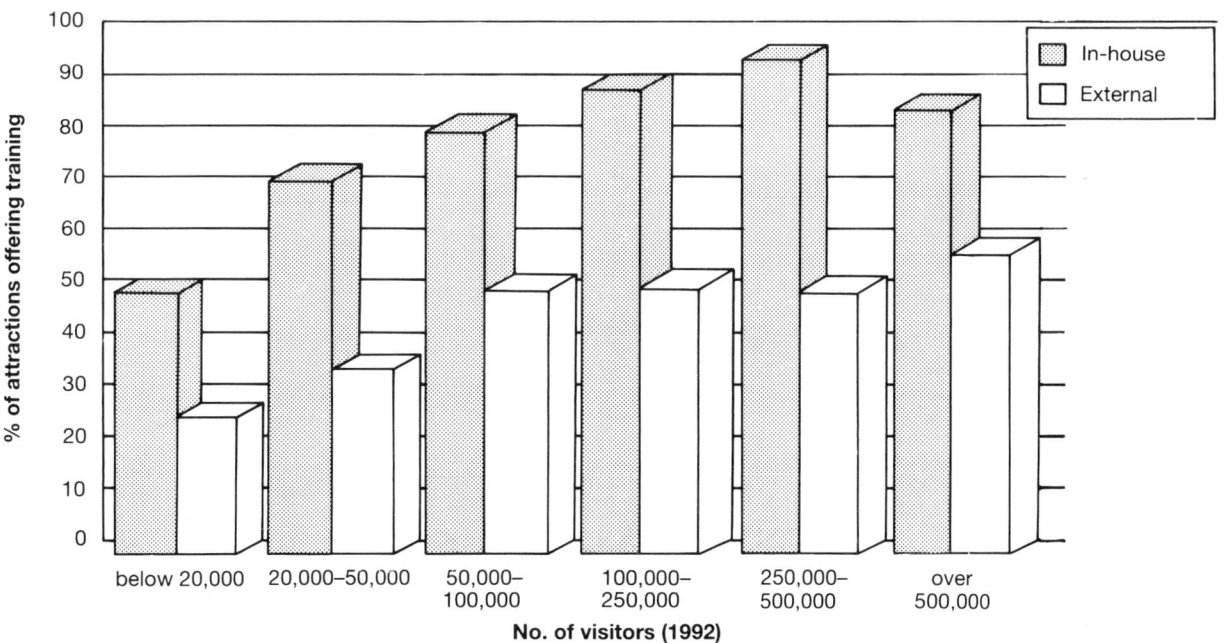

Figure 8

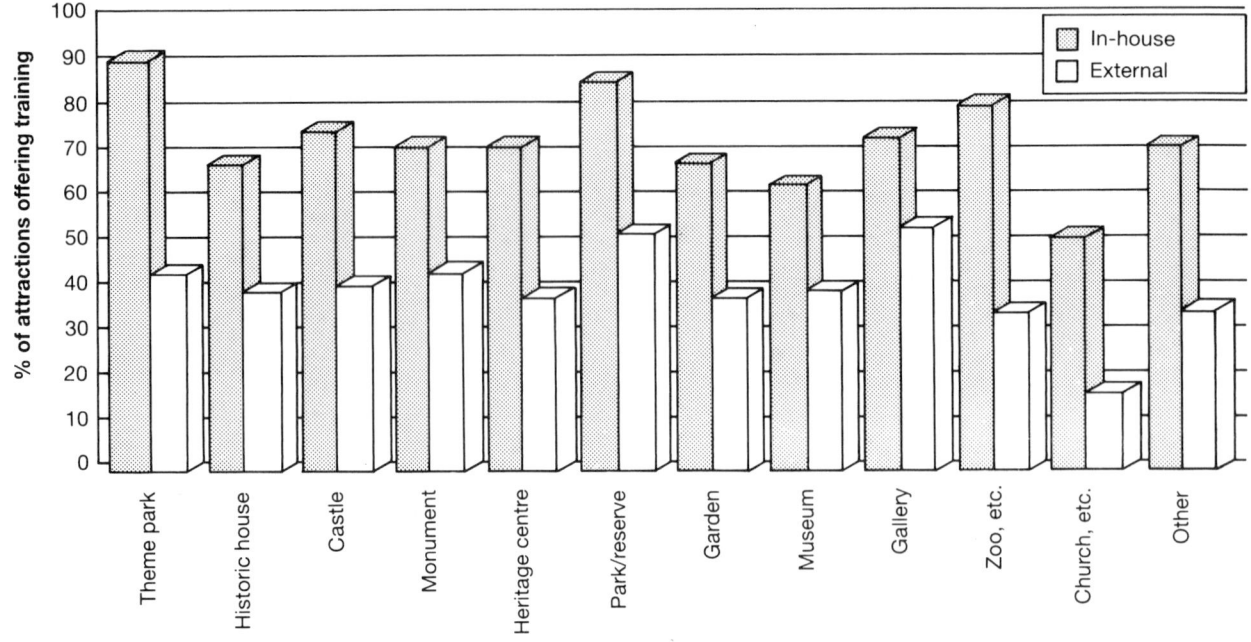

Figure 9

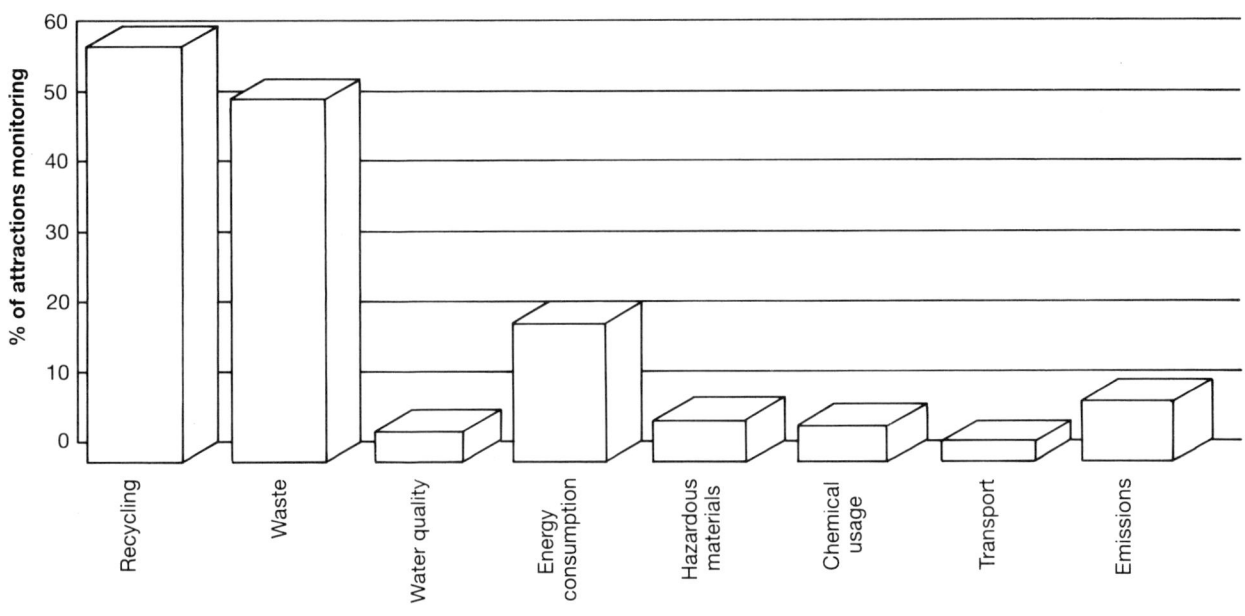

Figure 10

waste disposal. Large seems to mean best in this area, as only
10% of small units monitored waste or paid attention to recycling,
whereas 37–45% of large units (500,000+) monitored regularly.

FACILITIES PROVIDED

A variety of data is presented under the individual entries
regarding the facilities that are provided. Some points of general
interest are highlighted. Space limits the amount of detailed
analysis that can be offered, but a full list of the information held
in the database is recorded in Appendix A.

   All attractions provided a shop or retailing outlet: many
provided more than one. A breakdown of the goods offered for

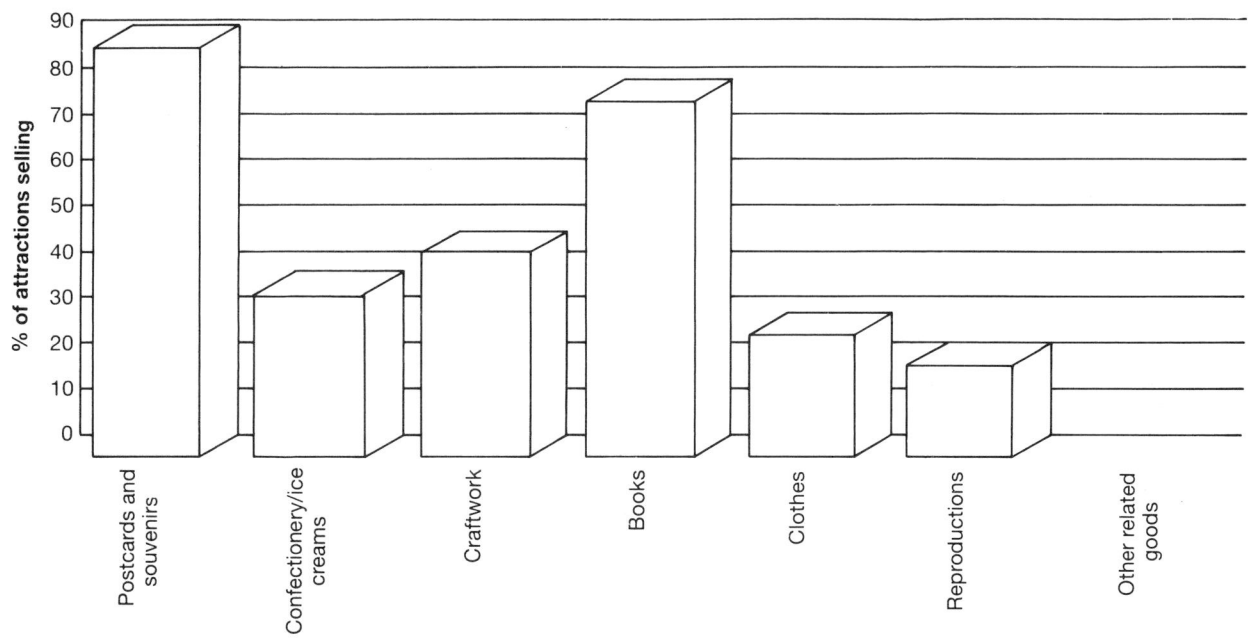

Figure 11

sale is shown in Figure 11 and illustrative detailed tables are presented in Appendix A. Postcards and souvenirs are universal; books are popular everywhere, and, as one would expect, the larger the attraction, the wider the range of goods.

The provision of catering facilities is closely correlated to size of attraction. The following list indicates the progressive rise:

- Below 20,000 = 50%;
- 20,001–50,000 = 80%;
- 50,001–100,000 = 125%;
- 100,001–250,000 = 163%;
- 250,001–500,000 = 365%;
- over 500,000 = 632%

There is little correlation between type or ownership other than ecclesiastical. Licensed restaurants are found in 28% of attractions, although 90% of these are in museums, gardens or historic houses, and surprisingly they do not appear to be correlated to size. Waiter/waitress-served restaurants form 18% of the total and appear evenly distributed; self-service units can be found in 32% of all attractions; snack-bars/foodstalls are found in 46% of units. These averages need to be discounted somewhat by the fact that larger units have multiple outlets, so inflating the overall figures. Bars can be found in 9% of the attractions and 73% offer some sort of picnic area.

Figure 12 presents a picture of the language facilities provided as a percentage of the overall total of units sampled. The languages spoken by staff include French in 37%; German 22%; Italian 9%; Spanish 10%; Japanese 2%; and Chinese 1%. Literature is provided in French by 32%; German 28%; Italian 12%; Spanish 11%; Dutch 10%; Japanese 10%; and other languages 8%. These seem particularly low, allowing for the proportions of overseas visitors. Interpretation plays a major role in determining the level of satisfaction and enjoyment experienced by visitors. Although leaflets, information boards and guide books continue to

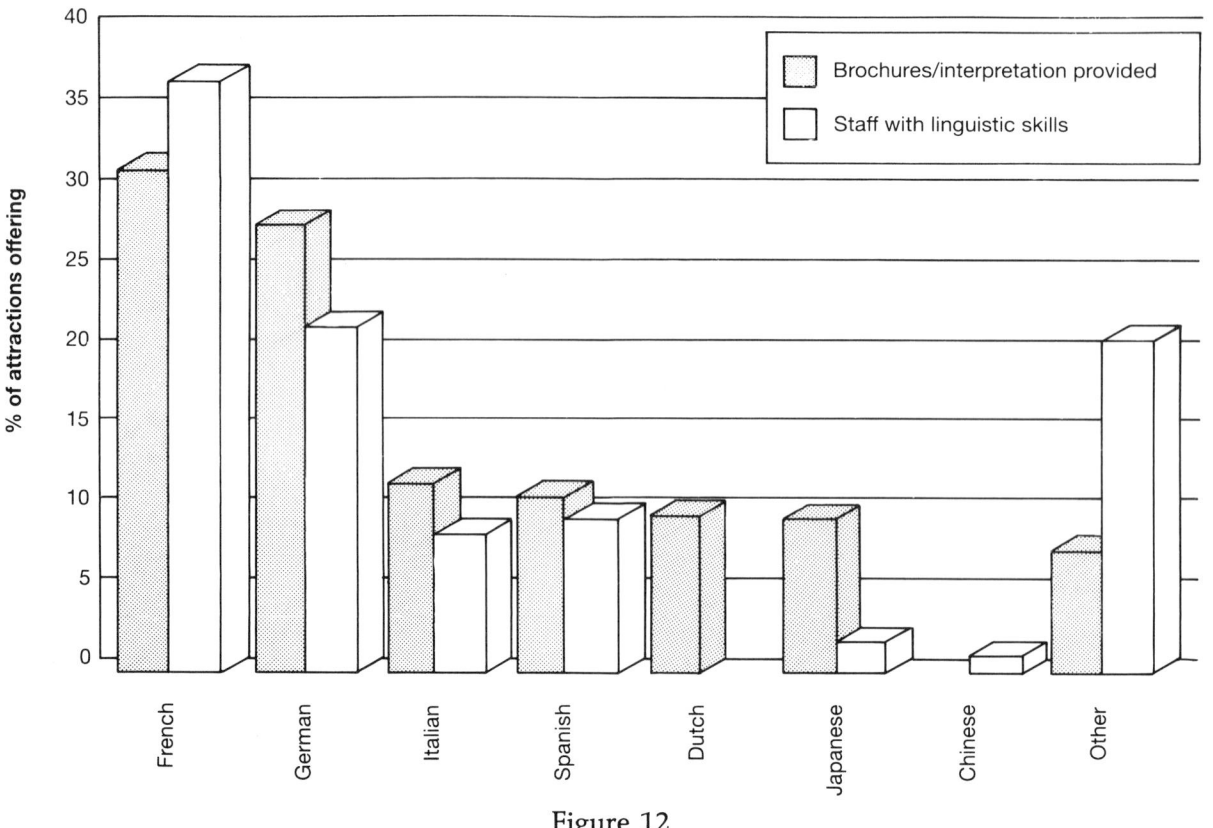

Figure 12

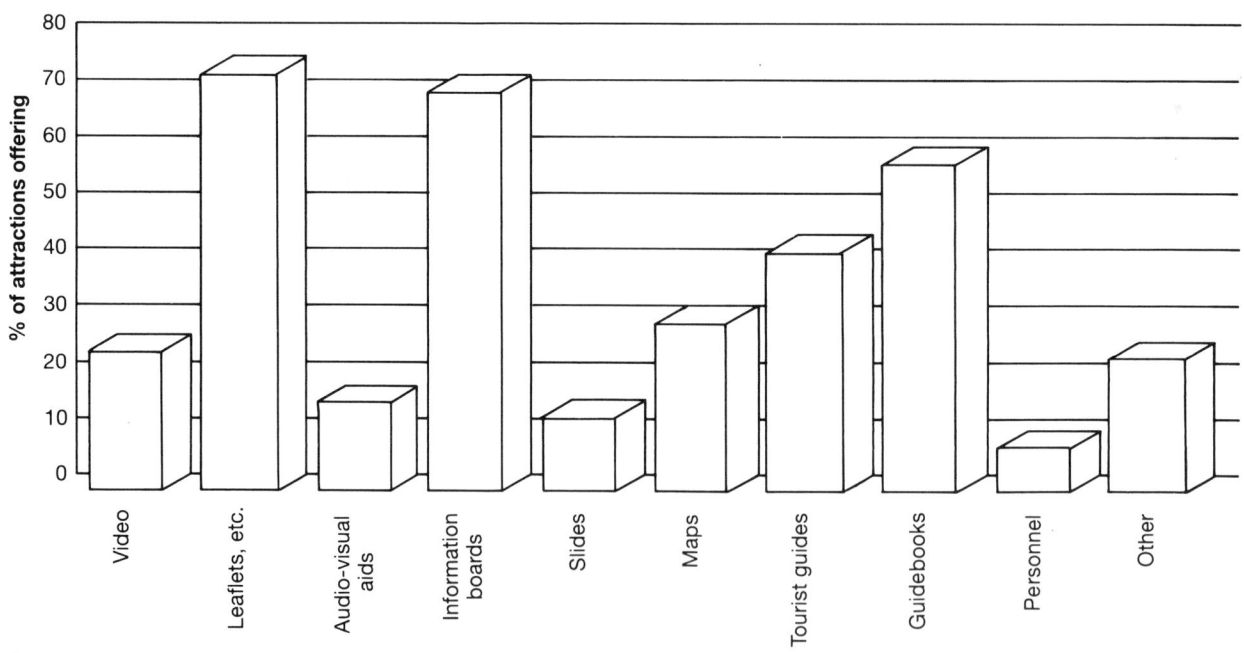

Figure 13

predominate, the role of audio-visual aids will be interesting to monitor (see Figure 13).

We have already observed that children are an important segment of the visitor market. The facilities provided to meet their needs are important (see Figure 14), although 36% of all the attractions surveyed offer no special facilities. Facilities for school-children is an aspect that is well catered for, as indicated in Figure 15.

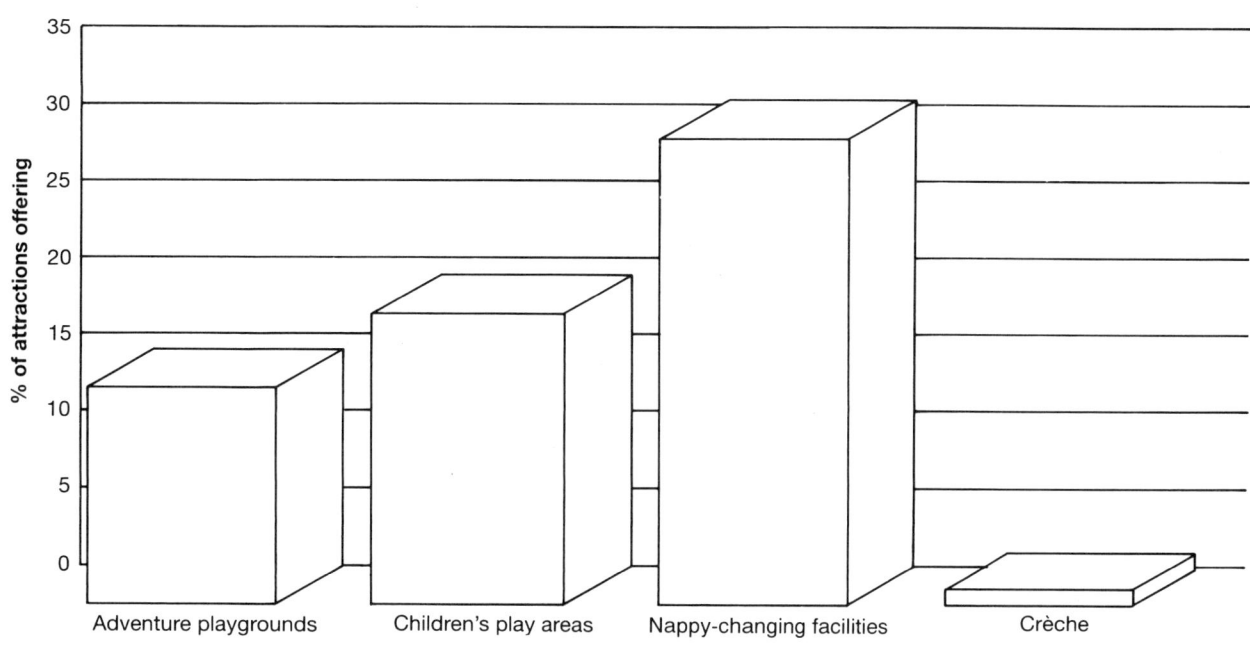

Figure 14

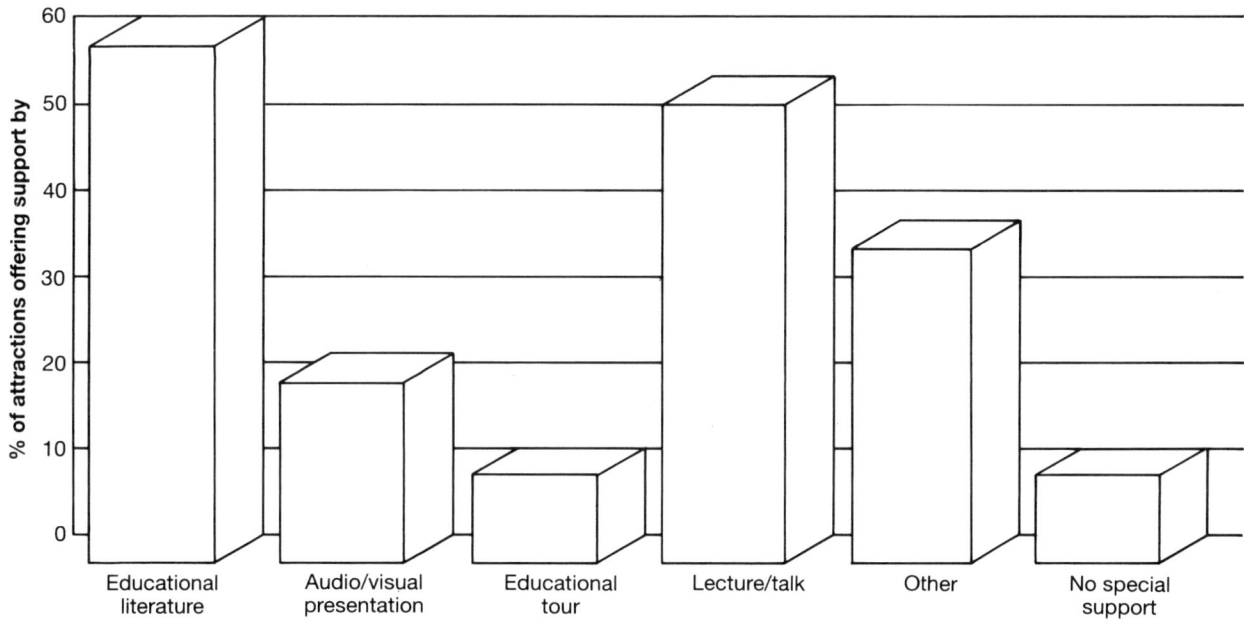

Figure 15

Overall facilities for the disabled are set out in Figure 16. There are some interesting differentials between category and size: theme parks offer by far the best provision of physical facilities, 85% offering easy access and 91% special toilets for the disabled; heritage centres and churches top the league for providing helpers (29% and 28% respectively) and again, 14% of churches provide Braille/sound posts against a 4.5% norm for attractions as a whole.

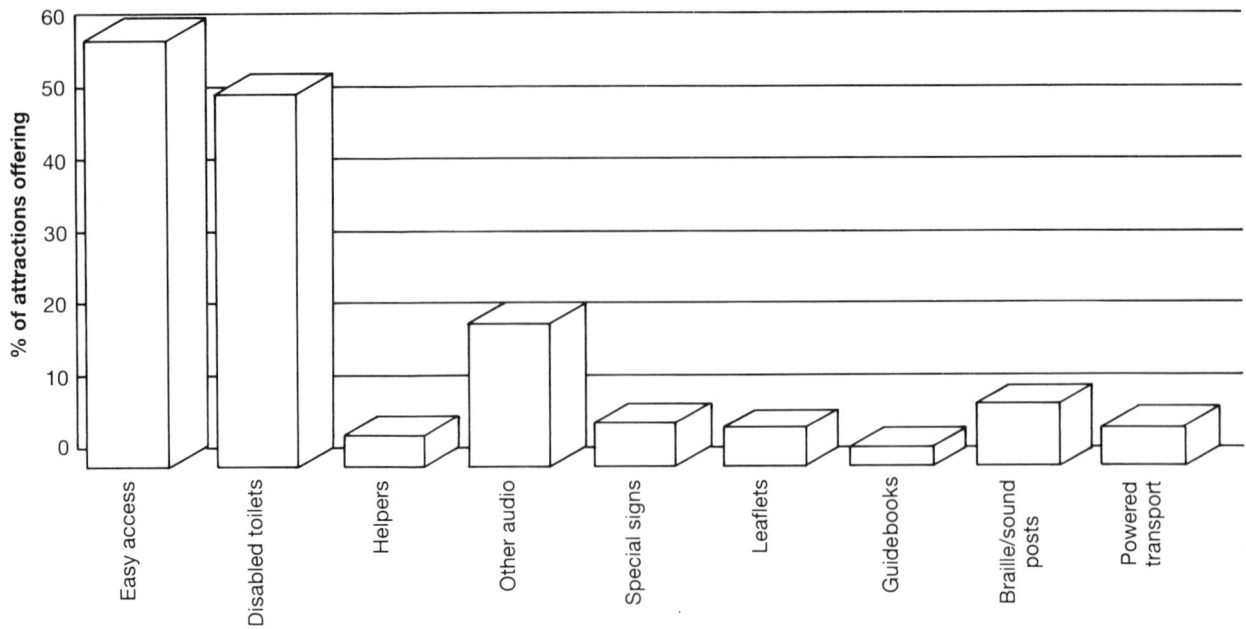

Figure 16

FUTURE DEVELOPMENTS

The commentary has already indicated that future editions will have a wider coverage of the industry and so enable more comprehensive information to be provided. The technical aspects of the database work well, and facilitate analysis of the sector in a way that has not previously been feasible. Individual researchers would find the cost of this type of exercise prohibitively expensive. OCTALS therefore intends to make this information available to researchers and analysts where feasible. The author hopes that the insights provided by this first *Directory* will confirm that continuation of this research and data bank is highly desirable in order to further our understanding of the structure, scope, activity and behaviour of this important segment of the tourism industry.

The success of this initiative will, however, depend on the continuing co-operation of the sector itself in responding to requests for information. We will therefore be pleased to receive suggestions for improvement to the next edition.

H. Anthea Rogers
March 1993

A

A DAY AT THE WELLS
(local authority run)
heritage centre; museum

Established: *1990*
Address: *The Corn Exchange, The Pantiles,*
Tunbridge Wells, Kent, TN2 5QJ
Telephone: *(0892) 546545.* Fax: *(0892) 513857*
Access: (road) *M25/23/A26* (rail) *Tunbridge Wells*
Season: *all year*
Hours: *Apr to Oct – 10am to 5pm daily*
Nov to Mar – 10am to 4pm daily
Admission (1992): *adults £3.20; children £2.50;*
OAP £2.50; student £2.50; school parties £1.75
No. visitors (1992): *60 000 (est.)*

Facilities
Interpretation: *videos; leaflets; audio tapes;*
information boards; guide books; personnel
Languages: *Dutch; French; German; Italian*
Schools: *educational literature; audio/visual*
presentation; educational tour; lecture/
talk; education room available
Disabled: *easy access; helpers; other audio*
facilities; audio tape route
Retailing: *postcards/inexpensive souvenirs;*
confectionery and ice cream; craftwork; books;
historic/Georgian theme items; stationery,
china, jigsaws, etc.
No. shops: *1*

Operations
Contacts: *W S Ferris (Centre Manager); H Bruford*
(Deputy Centre Manager); M Thomas
(Marketing Officer)
No. employees: (high season) *5 full time* (low
season) *5 full time*
Training: *F/T operations staff, F/T management,*
P/T operations staff and casual operations staff
are trained in-house and externally and on
specific courses and day-to-day on job

Marketing
Annual event(s): *Georgian festivities, sedan chair*
Races, lecture series
Sponsor(s): *Borough Council*
Affiliations: *SEETB*
Other: *market research*
UK promotion: *television; national newspapers;*
local newspapers; regional tourist board; other
attractions; leaflets/information packs;
ETB/BTA
Europe/USA Promotion: *leaflets/brochures;*
British Tourist Authority

ABBEYDALE INDUSTRIAL HAMLET
(local authority run)
monument; museum; gallery

Established: *1970*
Address: *Abbeydale Rd Sth, Sheffield, S Yorks,*
S7 2QW
Telephone: *(0742) 367731*
Access: (road) *M1/M18/M62/A1M/A621* (rail)
Sheffield Midland
Parking capacity: (cars) *20* (coaches) *3*
Season: *all year*
Hours: *Tues to Sat – 10am to 5pm; Sun – 11am*
to 5pm; BH – 10am to 5pm; closed Dec 24, 25,
26 and 1 Jan
Admission (1992): *adults £2.00; children £1.00;*
OAP £1.00; student £1.00; ub40s and registered
disabled free, small extra charge for special
events
No. visitors (1992): *35 000*

Facilities
Interpretation: *videos; leaflets; information*
boards; maps; guide books

Languages: *French; German*
Schools: *educational literature*
Disabled: *helpful staff*
Catering: *2 picnic areas*
Franchisees: *Tues to Sat -10am to 5pm Sun -11am*
to 5pm; BH – 10am to 5pm; closed Dec 24, 25,
26, and 1 Jan
Retailing: *postcards/inexpensive souvenirs;*
craftwork; books; clothes; reproductions of
famous artefacts; Sheffield cutlery and st steel
No. shops: *1*

Operations
Contacts: *Ms J Peatman (Keeper of Industrial*
Sites); Mr D O'Grady (Merchandising Officer);
Mr J Castledine (Marketing Officer)
No. employees: (high season) *8 full time; 2 part*
time
Training: *F/T operations staff, F/T management*
and P/T operations staff are trained in-house
and externally and on specific courses and
day-to-day on job
Languages spoken: *French; German*

Marketing
Annual event(s): *working days*
Affiliations: *MA, SPAB*
Other: *press office; market research*
UK promotion: *national newspapers; radio; local*
newspapers; regional tourist board; other
attractions; leaflets/information packs; Coach
Operators Handbook; ETB/BTA
Europe/Asia/Australia/USA promotion:
leaflets/brochures; foreign journals

ABBOT HALL
(trust)
historic house; museum; gallery

Established: *1962*
Address: *Kirkland, Kendal, Cumbria, LA9 5AL*
Telephone: *(0539) 722464*
Access: (road) *M6/A590*
Parking capacity: (cars) *50* (coaches) *3*
Season: *all year*
Hours: *Summer – Mon to Sat – 10.30am to 5pm,*
Sun – 2pm to 5pm; Winter – Mon to Fri – 11am
to 4pm; Saturday and Sunday – 1pm to 4pm
Admission (1992): *adults £2.00; children £1.00;*
OAP £2.00; student £1.00; family tickets £4.00
No. visitors (1992): *20 000 (est.)*

Facilities
Interpretation: *leaflets; information boards; guide*
books
Schools: *educational literature; lecture/talk;*
education officer
Disabled: *easy access; disabled toilets*
Catering: *1 picnic area*
Retailing: *postcards/inexpensive souvenirs;*
confectionery and ice cream; craftwork; books;
clothes
No. shops: *2*

Operations
Contacts: *Vaj Scowe (Director); Mrs J Scarrat*
(Administration Assistant); J P Lyons
(Marketing Consultant)
No. employees (high season) *5 full time; 25 part*
time (low season) *5 full time; 15 part time*
Training: *F/T operations staff, P/T operations*
staff and casual operations staff are trained
in-house and on specific courses and day-to-day
on job
Languages spoken: *French; German*

Marketing
Affiliations: *Historic Houses Association*
Other: *press office; market research*

UK promotion: *local newspapers;*
leaflets/information packs; ETB/BTA
USA/Japan promotion: *British Tourist Authority*

Environmental monitoring: *recycling; waste;*
energy consumption; hazardous materials;
chemical usage; emissions

ABBOTSBURY SUB-TROPICAL GARDENS
(unlimited company)
garden

Address: *Bullers Way, Abbotsbury, Nr*
Weymouth, Dorset
Telephone: *(0305) 871387.* Fax: *(0305) 871688*
Access: (road) *B3157* (rail) *Weymouth*
Parking capacity: (cars) *120* (coaches) *6*
Season: *all year*
Hours: *10am to 5pm daily*
Admission (1992): *adults £2.90; OAP £2.40;*
student £2.90
No. visitors (1992): *60 000*

Facilities
Interpretation: *information boards; maps; guide*
books
Languages: *French; German*
Children: *play area; nappy changing*
Schools: *lecture/talk*
Disabled: *easy access; disabled toilets; special*
signs
Catering: *1 self-service cafeteria*
Franchisees: *10am to 5pm daily*
Retailing: *postcards/inexpensive souvenirs;*
confectionery and ice cream; craftwork; books;
clothes; plants and gardening sundries
No. shops: *1*

Operations
Contacts: *Mr E Green (Estate Agent); Mr M Venn*
(Accountant); Miss J Williams (Manageress); Mr
M Pearson (Information/Tourism Officer)
No. employees: (high season) *9 full time; 6 part*
time (low season) *9 full time*
Training: *F/T operations staff, F/T management*
and P/T operations staff are trained in-house
and on specific courses using tutorials

Marketing
Annual event(s): *N/A*
Other: *press office; market research*
UK promotion: *radio; local newspapers; regional*
tourist board; other attractions;
leaflets/information packs

ABBOTSBURY SWANNERY
(unlimited company)
zoo/wildlife attraction

Address: *New Barn Rd, Abbotsbury,*
Nr Weymouth, Dorset
Telephone: *(0305) 871684.* Fax: *(0305) 871688*
Access: (road) *B3157* (rail) *Weymouth*
Parking capacity: (cars) *120* (coaches) *6*
Hours: *Easter to end of Oct – 9.30am to 5pm*
daily
Admission (1992): *adults £2.90; children £1.00;*
OAP £2.40
No. visitors (1992): *90 000*

Facilities
Interpretation: *videos; leaflets; information*
boards; slides; tour guides; guide books;
children's activity trail
Languages: *French; German*

Schools: *maximum no. 50; educational literature; audio/visual presentation*
Disabled: *easy access; disabled toilets*
Catering: *1 picnic area*
Retailing: *postcards/inexpensive souvenirs; confectionery and ice cream; craftwork; books; environmental and ecological*
No. shops: *1*

Operations
Contacts: *Mr E Green (Estate Agent); Mr M Venn (Accountant); Mrs L Lowe (Manageress); Mr M Pearson (Information/Tourism Officer)*
No. employees: (high season) *10 full time; 6 part time* (low season) *9 full time; 1 part time*
Training: *F/T operations staff and F/T management are trained externally and on specific courses*

Marketing
Annual event(s): *N/A*
Other: *press office; market research*
UK promotion: *radio; local newspapers; regional tourist board; other attractions; leaflets/information packs*

ABBOTSBURY TITHE BARN MUSEUM
(unlimited company)
museum

Established: *1991*
Address: *Church St, Abbotsbury, Nr Weymouth, Dorset*
Telephone: *(0305) 871817.* Fax: *(0305) 871688*
Access: (road) *B3157* (rail) *Weymouth*
Parking capacity: (cars) *120* (coaches) *6*
Hours: *Easter to end of Oct – 10am to 6pm daily*
Admission (1992): *adults £1.50; OAP £1.00; student £1.50*
No. visitors (1992): *20 000*

Facilities
Interpretation: *information boards; tour guides*
Schools: *educational literature*
Disabled: *easy access*

Operations
Contacts: *Mr E Green (Estate Agent); Mr M Venn (Accountant); Mr M Pearson (Information/Tourism Officer)*
No. employees: (high season) *3 part time* (low season) *3 part time*
Training: *P/T operations staff are trained externally and on specific courses*
Languages spoken: *French*

Marketing
Annual event(s): *N/A*
Other: *press office; market research*
UK promotion: *radio; local newspapers; regional tourist board; other attractions; leaflets/information packs*

Environmental monitoring: *waste; water quality; chemical usage*

ABBOTSFORD
(privately owned)
historic house

Established: *1833*
Address: *Melrose, Roxburghshire, TD6 9BQ*
Telephone: *(0896) 2043*
Hours: *N/A*

Facilities
Interpretation: *leaflets; information boards; tour guides; guide books*
Languages: *French; German; Italian*
Schools: *maximum no. 50; lecture/talk*
Disabled: *easy access; disabled toilets*
Catering: *1 self-service cafeteria*
Retailing: *postcards/inexpensive souvenirs; confectionery and ice cream; books*
No. shops: *2*

Operations
Contact: *Mrs P Maxwell-Scott OBE*
No. employees: (high season) *12 full time; 8 part time* (low season) *6 full time; 3 part time*

Marketing
UK promotion: *national newspapers; local newspapers; regional tourist board; leaflets/information packs; STB*

ADLINGTON HALL
(Private)
historic house

Established: *1950*
Address: *Macclesfield, Cheshire, SK10 4LF*
Telephone: *(0625) 829206.* Fax: *(0625) 828756*
Access: (road) *M6 A523* (rail) *Macclesfield*
Parking capacity: (cars) *100* (coaches) *4*
Hours: *Apr to Oct – Sun and BH – 2pm to 5.30pm; Other times by arrangement*
Admission (1992): *adults £2.70; children £1.25; student £1.25; groups £2.00*
No. visitors (1992): *4000*

Facilities
Interpretation: *leaflets; guide books*
Schools: *maximum no. 45; lecture/talk*
Disabled: *easy access*
Catering: *1 waiter/waitress served*
Retailing: *postcards/inexpensive souvenirs*
No. shops: *1*

Operations
Contact: *K Wootton (guide)*
No. employees: (high season) *2 full time; 2 part time*

Marketing
Annual event(s): *craft fairs, antique fairs, organ recitals*
Affiliations: *HHA*
UK promotion: *local newspapers; regional tourist board; leaflets/information packs; NWTB publications*

AEROSPACE MUSEUM, THE
(local authority run)
museum

Established: *1979*
Address: *Cosford, Shifnal, Shropshire, TF11 8UP*
Telephone: *(0902) 374872/374112.* Fax: *(0902) 374813*
Access: (road) *M54/A41* (rail) *Cosford*
Parking capacity: (cars) *2000* (coaches) *50*
Season: *all year*
Hours: *10am to 5pm daily except for Christmas and New Year*
Admission (1992): *adults £4.00; children £2.30; OAP £3.00*
No. visitors (1992): *120 000 (est.)*

Facilities
Interpretation: *videos; leaflets; information boards; tour guides; guide books*
Schools: *educational literature; audio/visual presentation; lecture/talk*
Disabled: *easy access; disabled toilets*
Catering: *1 picnic area*
Retailing: *postcards/inexpensive souvenirs; books; clothes*
No. shops: *1*

Operations
Contact: *J A Francis (Museum Manager)*
No. employees: (high season) *9 full time; 19 part time* (low season) *9 full time; 13 part time*
Training: *F/T operations staff, P/T operations staff and casual operations staff are trained in-house and day-to-day on job*

Marketing
Annual event(s): *RAF Cosford open day*
Affiliations: *MA*
Other: *market research*

UK promotion: *local newspapers; regional tourist board; other attractions; leaflets/information packs; HETB, NWTB; ETB/BTA*
Europe promotion: *European aviation museums*

Environmental monitoring: *recycling; energy consumption*

AGE EXCHANGE REMINISCENCE CENTRE
(limited company)
reminiscence centre; hands on

Established: *1987*
Address: *11 Blackheath Village, Blackheath, London, SE3 9LA*
Telephone: *(081) 318 9105.* Fax: *(081) 318 0060*
Access: (road) *M25/South Circular*
Season: *all year*
Hours: *Mon to Sat – 10am to 5.30pm except BH and Christmas*
Admission (1992): *free; nominal fee for groups*
No. visitors (1992): *20 000 (est.)*

Facilities
Interpretation: *leaflets; tour guides; personnel*
Schools: *maximum no. 30; educational literature; lecture/talk; workshops*
Disabled: *easy access; disabled toilets; helpers*
Catering: *1 snack bar/food stall*
Retailing: *postcards/inexpensive souvenirs; confectionery and ice cream; craftwork; books; clothes; reproductions of famous artefacts; reproduced memorabilia*
No. shops: *1*

Operations
Contact: *Ms P Rossetter (Administrative Director)*
No. employees: (high season) *2 part time* (low season) *2 part time*
Training: *P/T operations staff are trained in-house and day-to-day on job*

Marketing
Annual event(s): *reminiscence theatre/exhibitions*
UK promotion: *radio; local newspapers; regional tourist board; other attractions; leaflets/information packs; ETB/BTA*
Europe promotion: *leaflets/brochures; travel agents' brochures; British Tourist Authority*

ALBERT DOCK
(limited company)
heritage centre; museum; gallery; multi-use visitor attraction

Established: *1984*
Address: *Strand Street, Liverpool 3*
Telephone: *(051) 708 8854.* Fax: *(051) 708 0929*
Access: (road) *M58/M62/A5036* (rail) *Lime Street*
Parking capacity: (cars) *1500*
Season: *all year*
Hours: *All year – Mon to Sun – From 10am*
Admission (1992): *N/A*
No. visitors (1992): *5 800 000 (est.)*

Facilities
Interpretation: *leaflets; information boards; maps; tour guides; guide books*
Children: *nappy changing*
Schools: *educational literature*
Disabled: *easy access; disabled toilets; leaflets; wheelchairs*
Catering: *3 bars/public houses*
Retailing: *postcards/inexpensive souvenirs; confectionery and ice cream; craftwork; books; clothes; reproductions of famous artefacts; 56 retail units*
No. shops: *More than 4*

Operations
Contacts: *R Guy-Jobson (Managing Director)*
No. employees: (high season) *10 full time*
Training: *F/T operations staff and F/T management are trained externally and on specific courses using volunteer induction*
Languages spoken: *French; German; Gaelic*

Marketing
Annual event(s): *varies*
Sponsor(s): *various*
Affiliations: *Liverpool historic waterfront*
Other: *PR Company: Ron Jones Associates, 65 Woodside Business Park, Birkenhead, Merseyside, L41 1EH; press office; market research*
UK promotion: *television; national newspapers; radio; local newspapers; regional tourist board; leaflets/information packs; ETB/BTA*

ALDEBURGH MOOT HALL MUSEUM
(local authority run)
museum; 16thc building

Established: *1964*
Address: *Moot Hall, Market Cross Place, Aldeburgh, Suffolk, IP15 5BT*
Access: (road) *A12*
Hours: *Easter to end of Oct. Easter to June – weekends – 2.30pm to 5pm (6pm Sun); July and Aug – 10.30am to 12.30pm and 2.30pm to 5pm; other times – afternoons only – 2.30pm to 5pm (6pm Sun)*
Admission (1992): *adults £0.35; OAP £0.35;*
No. visitors (1992): *10 000 (est.)*

Facilities
Interpretation: *leaflets; information boards*
Languages: *Dutch; French; German*
Schools: *maximum no. 30; educational literature; audio/visual presentation; lecture/talk; visual aids and models*
Disabled: *access difficult*
Retailing: *postcards/inexpensive souvenirs; books; reproductions of famous artefacts*
No. shops: *1*

Operations
Contacts: *Ms C Foss (Curator/Chairman/ Trustee); Ms C Somerset (Secretary)*
Training: *casual operations staff are trained in-house and day-to-day on job*

Marketing
UK promotion: *regional tourist board*

Environmental monitoring: *recycling; waste; energy consumption; hazardous materials; chemical usage*

ALFRISTON HERITAGE CENTRE AND BLACKSMITH'S
(privately owned)
heritage centre; museum

Established: *1989*
Address: *The Old Forge, Sloe Lane, Alfriston, Polegate, East Sussex*
Telephone: *(0323) 870303*
Access: (road) *M3/A27/A22* (rail) *Berwick*
Parking capacity: (cars) *100* (coaches) *9*
Hours: *Easter to end Oct – 11am to 5pm daily*
Admission (1992): *adults £1.20; children £0.70; OAP £1.00*
No. visitors (1992): *6500 (est.)*

Facilities
Interpretation: *leaflets; information boards; maps; guide books; artefacts and photographs*
Schools: *lecture/talk; questionnaires*
Disabled: *easy access*
Retailing: *postcards/inexpensive souvenirs; craftwork; books*
No. shops: *1*

Operations
Contacts: *Mr J and Mrs S Hernu (joint owners)*

Marketing
UK promotion: *regional tourist board; other attractions; leaflets/information packs*

ALICE IN WONDERLAND VISITOR CENTRE, THE
(trust)
some moving tableaux and commentary on individual cassettes

Established: *1987*
Address: *The Rabbit Hole, 3–4 Trinity Square, Llandudno, Gwynedd, LL30 2PY*
Telephone: *(0492) 860082.* Fax: *(0492) 860082*
Access: (road) *A55/M6/M56* (rail) *Llandudno*
Season: *all year*
Hours: *Easter to Oct – Mon to Sun – 10am to 5pm; Nov to Easter – Mon to Sat – 10am to 5pm. Other times by appointment*
Admission (1992): *adults £2.30; children £1.75; OAP £2.00; family £7.00; schools £1.50*
No. visitors (1992): *30 000 (est.)*

Facilities
Interpretation: *leaflets; audio tapes*
Languages: *Japanese; Dutch; French; German; Italian*
Schools: *maximum no. 60; lecture/talk*
Disabled: *easy access*
Retailing: *postcards/inexpensive souvenirs; craftwork; books; clothes; attraction related goods*
No. shops: *1*

Operations
Contacts: *Mr M A Ratcliffe (Managing Director); Mrs M Ratcliffe (Director)*
No. employees: (high season) *3 full time; 3 part time* (low season) *3 full time; 1 part time*
Training: *F/T operations staff, P/T operations staff and casual operations staff are trained in-house and day-to-day on job using videos*

Marketing
UK promotion: *television; national newspapers; radio; local newspapers; regional tourist board; other attractions; leaflets/information packs; ETB/BTA; VARS*
Europe/Asia/USA/Japan promotion: *television; leaflets/brochures; radio; British Tourist Authority*

Environmental monitoring: *waste; hazardous materials; chemical usage; transport*

ALL SAINTS CHURCH
(church)
church

Established: *1992*
Address: *Daresbury, Warrington, Cheshire, WA4 4AE*
Telephone: *(0925) 740348*
Access: (road) *M56/A56* (rail) *Warrington/ Runcorn*
Parking capacity: (cars) *50*
Season: *all year*
Hours: *Apr to Oct – Weekends and BH; key available from vicarage on request*
Admission (1992): *free*
No. visitors (1992): *5000 (est.)*

Facilities
Interpretation: *leaflets; tour guides; guide books*
Schools: *maximum no. 50; lecture/talk*
Disabled: *easy access*
Retailing: *postcards/inexpensive souvenirs; books; clothes*
No. shops: *1*

Operations
Contacts: *Rev D W Smith (Vicar); R Elliott (Verger)*
Languages spoken: *French*

Marketing
UK promotion: *regional tourist board; leaflets/information packs*

ALLHALLOWS MUSEUM
(trust)
museum

Established: *1946*
Address: *High St, Honiton, Devon, EX13 6DG*
Telephone: *(0404) 44966*
Access: (road) *M5/A303/A30* (rail) *Honiton*
Hours: *May to Sept – Mon to Sat – 10am to 5pm; Oct – Mon to Sat – 10am to 4pm*
Admission (1992): *adults £0.60; children £0.25; OAP £0.60; student £0.60;*
No. visitors (1992): *10 000 (est.)*

Facilities
Interpretation: *leaflets*
Schools: *maximum no. 30; no special support*
Retailing: *postcards/inexpensive souvenirs; books; lace-making accessories*
No. shops: *1*

Operations
Contacts: *M Phillips (Administrator); W Crane (Sales Manager)*
Training: *N/A*

Marketing
Affiliations: *Area Museum Council, SW Fed of Museums and Galleries, MA*
Other: *market research*
UK promotion: *regional tourist board; leaflets/information packs*

ALMOND VALLEY HERITAGE TRUST
(trust and limited co)
heritage centre; museum; zoo/wildlife attraction

Established: *1991*
Address: *Millfield, Kirkton North, Livingston, West Lothian, EH54 7AR*
Telephone: *(0506) 414957*
Access: (road) *M8/A705*
Parking capacity: (cars) *50* (coaches) *10*
Season: *all year*
Hours: *10am to 5pm daily*
Admission (1992): *adults £1.50; children £0.75; OAP £0.75; student £1.50; family ticket £4.00*
No. visitors (1992): *28 000*

Facilities
Interpretation: *leaflets; information boards*
Children: *adventure playground; play area; nappy changing*
Schools: *maximum no. 500; educational literature; demonstrations and pack*
Disabled: *disabled toilets*
Catering: *1 picnic area*
Retailing: *postcards/inexpensive souvenirs; confectionery and ice cream; books*
No. shops: *1*

Operations
Contact: *Mr R Chesters (Curator)*
No. employees: (high season) *4 full time; 3 part time* (low season) *4 full time*

Marketing
Annual event(s): *various*
Sponsor(s): *various*
Other: *market research*
UK promotion: *national newspapers; local newspapers; leaflets/information packs*

Environmental monitoring: *temperature, humidity and light*

ALMONDELL AND CALDERWOOD COUNTRY PARK
(local authority run)
country park with visitor centre

Established: *1969*
Address: *Visitor Centre, Almondell Country Park, Broxburn, West Lothian, EH52 5PE*
Telephone: *0506 882254*
Access: (road) *M8/A89* (rail) *Uphall*
Parking capacity: (cars) *100*
Season: *all year*

Hours: *Park open all year – car parks close sunset; visitor centre – Mon to Thur – Summer 9am to 5pm; Winter 9am to 4pm; Sun – Summer 10am to 6.30pm; Winter 10.30am to 4.30pm*
Admission (1992): *free*
No. visitors (1992): *120 000 (est.)*

Facilities
Interpretation: *leaflets; information boards; slides; maps; park staff*
Children: *adventure playground*
Schools: *maximum no. 15; educational literature; audio/visual presentation; lecture/talk*
Disabled: *disabled toilets; disabled car parking near visitor centre*
Catering: *1 picnic area*
Retailing: *postcards/inexpensive souvenirs; confectionery and ice cream; craftwork; garden furniture made on site*
No. shops: *1*

Operations
Contacts: *Mary Konik (Senior Ranger); Iris Wyper (Receptionist)*
No. employees: *(high season) 7 full time (low season) 5 full time*
Training: *F/T operations staff are trained in-house and externally and on specific courses and day-to-day on job*

Marketing
Annual event(s): *guided walks/activities*
Other: *press office; market research*
UK promotion: *radio; local newspapers; regional tourist board; other attractions; leaflets/information packs*

ALMONRY MUSEUM
(local authority run)
heritage centre; museum

Established: *1957*
Address: *Abbey gate, Evesham, Worcs, WR11 4BG*
Telephone: *(0386) 446944*
Access: *(road) M5/42/A4184 (rail) Evesham*
Season: *all year*
Hours: *all year – Mon to Sat – 10am to 5pm, Sun – 2pm to 5pm (10am in Aug)*
Admission (1992): *adults £1.00*
No. visitors (1992): *10 024*

Facilities
Interpretation: *leaflets; audio tapes*
Schools: *maximum no. 35; educational literature; lecture/talk*
Retailing: *postcards/inexpensive souvenirs; books; films*
No. shops: *1*

Operations
Contacts: *A H Fryer (Custodian); P J Gordon (Town Clerk)*
No. employees: *(high season) 1 full time; 2 part time (low season) 1 full time; 2 part time*

Marketing
Annual event(s): *Almonry open day*
Affiliations: *HETB, Museums and Galleries Commission*
UK promotion: *regional tourist board; leaflets/information packs; local authorities' pulications*

Environmental monitoring: *recycling; energy consumption*

ALTON TOWERS (plc)
theme park; historic house; garden

Established: *1860*
Address: *Alton, Staffs, ST10 4DB*
Telephone: *(0538) 702200. Fax: (0538) 702724*
Access: *(road)*
Parking capacity: *(cars) 8500 (coaches) 500*
Season: *all year*
Hours: *mid Mar to early Nov – 9am to 5pm or later daily; grounds open daily all year except Christmas Day*

Admission (1992): *adults £12.00; children £9.50; OAP £5.50; rates subject to change without notice; under 4s free*
No. visitors (1992): *2 500 000 (est.)*

Facilities
Interpretation: *leaflets; maps*
Languages: *French; German*
Children: *adventure playground; play area; nappy changing*
Schools: *audio/visual presentation; lecture/talk; classroom facility*
Disabled: *easy access; disabled toilets*
Catering: *20 picnic areas*
Retailing: *postcards/inexpensive souvenirs; confectionery and ice cream; craftwork; clothes; videos and cassettes*
No. shops: *More than 4*

Operations
Contacts: *Mr A Hollingsworth (Divisional Director); Ms L Foulkes (Personnel Manager); Mr R Copeman (Retail Director); Mr N Varney (Marketing Director)*
No. employees: *(high season) 200 full time; 1000 part time (low season) 200 full time*
Training: *F/T operations staff, F/T management, P/T operations staff, P/T management, casual operations staff and casual management are trained in-house and externally and on specific courses and day-to-day on job*
Languages spoken: *French*

Marketing
Annual event(s): *various*
Sponsor(s): *various corporate days*
Other: *PR company: Edelman Worldwide, Kingsgate House, 536 Kings Rd, London SW10 OTE; press office; market research*
UK promotion: *television; local newspapers; other attractions*

AMGUEDDFA'R GOGLEDD/MUSEUM OF THE NORTH
(Part of Nat Mus of Wales)
museum

Established: *1989*
Address: *Llanberis, Gwynedd, LL55 4UR*
Telephone: *(0286) 870636. Fax: (0286) 871331*
Access: *(road) A5 A55 (rail) Bangor*
Parking capacity: *(cars) 80 (coaches) 6*
Season: *all year*
Hours: *Dec and Jan – prebooked visits only Feb – 10.30am to 4pm daily; Mar to May – 10am to 5pm daily; June to mid Sept – 9.30am to 6pm daily; Sept to Oct – 10am to 5pm daily; Nov – 10.30am to 4pm daily*
Admission (1992): *adults £5.00; children £2.50; OAP £3.75; student £3.75; prebooked schools £1.70 and 20+ groups 10 per cent discount*
No. visitors (1992): *68 426*

Facilities
Interpretation: *videos; leaflets; information boards; slides; tour guides*
Languages: *Welsh*
Children: *nappy changing*
Schools: *maximum no. 100; educational literature*
Disabled: *easy access; disabled toilets; adapted minibus*
Retailing: *postcards/inexpensive souvenirs; confectionery and ice cream; craftwork; books; reproductions of famous artefacts*
No. shops: *1*

Operations
Contacts: *Dr D Roberts (Keeper); Ms N Williams (Administrative Officer); D Ellis (Shop Manager); Mr J Bevan (Head of Public Services)*
No. employees: *(high season) 5 full time; 20 part time (low season) 5 full time; 20 part time*
Training: *F/T operations staff, F/T management, and P/T operations staff and casual operations staff are trained in-house and on specific courses and day-to-day on job using videos and handbooks*
Languages spoken: *French*

Marketing
Press office; market research

UK promotion: *television; local newspapers; regional tourist board; other attractions; leaflets/information packs; North Wales Tourism*

ANCIENT HIGH HOUSE, THE
(local authority run)
historic house; heritage centre; gallery

Established: *1986*
Address: *Greengate St, Stafford, ST16 2JA*
Telephone: *(0785) 223181 ext 352*
Access: *(road) M6/A34 (rail) Stafford*
Season: *all year*
Hours: *Mon to Fri – 9am to 5pm; Sat – 10am to 4pm (Nov to Mar – to 3pm)*
Admission (1992): *adults £1.20; children £0.60; OAP £0.60; student £0.60*
No. visitors (1992): *6000 (est.)*

Facilities
Interpretation: *videos; leaflets; tour guides; guide books*
Languages: *French; German*
Schools: *maximum no. 35; educational literature; audio/visual presentation*
Retailing: *postcards/inexpensive souvenirs; craftwork; books; clothes; reproductions of famous artefacts; cards, notelets, glassware, etc.; general heritage gifts*
No. shops: *2*

Operations
Contacts: *D Richards (Heritage Manager); J Malpas (TIC Assistant); A Dunne (Heritage Assistant)*
No. employees: *(high season) 2 full time; 7 part time (low season) 2 full time; 6 part time*
Training: *F/T management, P/T operations staff and casual operations staff are trained in-house and externally and on specific courses and day-to-day on job*

Marketing
Annual event(s): *Christmas craft fairs*
Other: *market research*
UK promotion: *local newspapers; regional tourist board; other attractions; leaflets/information packs; HETB accommodation guides, Places to Visit*

Environmental monitoring: *energy consumption*

ANCIENT HOUSE MUSEUM
(registered charity)
museum

Established: *1978*
Address: *High St, Clare, Suffolk, CO10 8NY*
Telephone: *(0787) 277865*
Access: *(road) A45/A113/B1092*
Hours: *Easter to end of Sept – Wed, Fri – 2.30pm to 4.30pm Sun – 11am to 12.30pm and BH*
Admission (1992): *adults £0.60; children £0.30; OAP £0.50; student £0.50*
No. visitors (1992): *2000 (est.)*

Facilities
Interpretation: *leaflets; information boards; maps; guide books*
Schools: *maximum no. 100; lecture/talk*
Disabled: *easy access*
Retailing: *postcards/inexpensive souvenirs; books*
No. shops: *1*

Operations
No. employees: *(high season) 1 full time*
Languages spoken: *Welsh*

Marketing
Affiliations: *Assoc of Suffolk Museums, AIM, AMSSE*
UK promotion: *ETB/BTA; East Anglia Tourist Board*

Environmental monitoring: *recycling; energy consumption; transport*

ANGLESEY ABBEY
(trust)
historic house; garden; gallery

Established: *1967*
Address: *Lode, Cambridge, CB5 9EJ*
Telephone: *(0223) 811200*
Access: (road) *M11/A45* (rail) *Cambridge*
Parking capacity: (cars) *1000* (coaches) *10*
Hours: *End Mar to 18 Oct and BH – Wed to Sun*
Admission (1992): *adults £4.50; children £2.25*
No. visitors (1992): *96 400*

Facilities
Interpretation: *leaflets; information boards; maps; guide books*
Languages: *Japanese; Dutch; French; German*
Children: *nappy changing*
Schools: *maximum no. 100; educational literature; lecture/talk*
Disabled: *easy access; disabled toilets; braille/sound posts; powered transport; leaflets*
Catering: *1 picnic area*
Retailing: *postcards/inexpensive souvenirs; craftwork; books; clothes*
No. shops: *1*

Operations
Contact: *Mr G Moray (Administrator); Head Office*
No. employees: (high season) *19 full time; 85 part time* (low season) *19 full time; 5 part time*
Training: *F/T operations staff and P/T operations staff are trained in-house and externally and on specific courses*
Languages spoken: *French; Russian*

Marketing
Press office; market research
UK promotion: *television; national newspapers; radio; local newspapers; regional tourist board; leaflets/information packs*

ANGLESEY SEA ZOO
(partnership)
zoo/wildlife attraction

Established: *1983*
Address: *Brynsiencyn, Anglesey, Gwynedd, LL61 6TQ*
Telephone: *(0248) 430411. Fax: (0248) 430213*
Access: (road) *M56 to A55/A4080* (rail) *Bangor*
Parking capacity: (cars) *250* (coaches) *5*
Season: *all year*
Hours: *Mar to Oct – Mon to Sun – 10am to 5pm; Nov to Feb – Mon to Sun – 11am to 3pm; closed 21 to 26 Dec and 1 Jan and 4 to 8 Jan*
Admission (1992): *adults £4.00; children £3.00; OAP £3.50; student £3.00; family tickets for four £12.00 and for five £13.00*
No. visitors (1992): *166 729*

Facilities
Interpretation: *videos; leaflets; information boards; maps; tour guides; guide books*
Languages: *French; German; Welsh*
Children: *adventure playground; nappy changing*
Schools: *maximum no. 600; educational literature; audio/visual presentation; lecture/talk*
Disabled: *easy access; disabled toilets*
Catering: *1 picnic area*
Retailing: *postcards/inexpensive souvenirs; confectionery and ice cream; craftwork; books; clothes; pearl/jewellery booth*
No. shops: *2*

Operations
Contacts: *David Lea-Wilson (Partner); Alison Lea-Wilson (Partner); Ian Cruickshank (Marketing Manager/Press Officer)*
No. employees: (high season) *40 full time; 2 part time* (low season) *15 full time; 1 part time*
Training: *F/T operations staff, F/T management, P/T operations staff and P/T management are trained in-house and externally and on specific courses and day-to-day on job using videos and handbooks*

Marketing
Annual event(s): *usually open days for charity*
Affiliations: *Anglesey Attractions Association*

Other: *press office; market research*
UK promotion: *television; national newspapers; local newspapers; regional tourist board; other attractions; leaflets/information packs; Wales Tourist Board; ETB/BTA*
Europe/USA promotion: *travel agents' brochures; British Tourist Authority*

Environmental monitoring: *recycling; waste; hazardous materials; chemical usage*

ANIMAL WORLD
(local authority run)
zoo/wildlife attraction

Established: *1947*
Address: *Moss Bank Park, Bolton*
Telephone: *(0204) 846157*
Access: (road) *M62 A58*
Parking capacity: (cars) *200* (coaches) *20*
Season: *all year*
Hours: *all year – 8am to dusk daily*
Admission (1992): *free*
No. visitors (1992): *40 000 (est.)*

Facilities
Interpretation: *leaflets; information boards*
Children: *play area*
Schools: *educational tour; lecture/talk*
Disabled: *easy access; disabled toilets; helpers; special signs*
Retailing: *confectionery and ice cream*
No. shops: *1*

Operations
Contacts: *H H Ackers (Senior Landscape Manager); J Coleman (Animal Supervisor)*
No. employees: (high season) *2 full time* (low season) *2 full time*
Training: *F/T operations staff and F/T management are trained in-house and on specific courses and day-to-day on job*

Marketing
Annual event(s): *open day*
Other: *press office; market research*
UK promotion: *local newspapers; regional tourist board; ETB/BTA*

Environmental monitoring: *recycling; waste; water quality; chemical usage*

ANNE OF CLEVES HOUSE MUSEUM
(trust)
historic house; museum

Established: *1923*
Address: *52 Southover, High Street, Lewes, E Sussex, BN7 1JA*
Telephone: *(0273) 474610*
Access: (road) *M23/A26/27* (rail) *Lewes*
Hours: *Apr to Oct – Mon to Sat – 10am to 5.30pm; Sun – 2pm to 5.30pm*
Admission (1992): *adults £1.60; children £0.80; OAP £1.60; student £0.80*
No. visitors (1992): *11 956*

Facilities
Interpretation: *leaflets; information boards; guide books*
Schools: *educational literature; educational tour; role play*
Retailing: *postcards/inexpensive souvenirs; craftwork; books*
No. shops: *1*

Operations
Contacts: *H Poole (Administrator); L Steene (Custodian)*
No. employees: (high season) *1 full time; 1 part time* (low season) *1 full time*
Training: *F/T operations staff are trained externally and on specific courses using handbooks and vet training*

Marketing
Annual event(s): *plays, exhibitions, etc.*
UK promotion: *local newspapers; regional tourist board; other attractions; leaflets/information packs; ETB/BTA*

Environmental monitoring: *recycling; energy consumption; hazardous materials; chemical usage*

APPLEBY CASTLE CONSERVATION CENTRE
(plc)
castle; gallery; zoo/wildlife attraction

Established: *1977*
Address: *Appleby Castle, Appleby-in-Westmorland, Cumbria, CA16 6XH*
Telephone: *(07683) 51402. Fax: (07683) 51082*
Access: (road) *M6/A66* (rail) *Settle to Carlisle*
Parking capacity: (cars) *50* (coaches) *3*
Hours: *Easter to Oct – Mon to Sun – 10am to 5pm*
Admission (1992): *on request*
No. visitors (1992): *38 000*

Facilities
Interpretation: *videos; information boards; tour guides; guide books*
Languages: *French; German*
Children: *play area*
Schools: *maximum no. 100; no special support; educational literature*
Catering: *2 picnic areas*
Retailing: *postcards/inexpensive souvenirs; confectionery and ice cream; craftwork; books*
No. shops: *1*

Operations
Contact: *Miss Tessa Edwards (Conservation Centre Manager)*
No. employees: (high season) *6 full time; 5 part time* (low season) *6 full time*

Marketing
Annual event(s): *jazz festival, concerts, displays, etc.*
Sponsor(s): *North West Arts*
Affiliations: *Rare Breeds Survival Trust*
Other: *market research*
UK promotion: *national newspapers; radio; local newspapers; regional tourist board; other attractions; leaflets/information packs; ETB/BTA*

Environmental monitoring: *recycling; bats*

APULDRAM ROSES
(privately owned)
garden; nursery and small garden centre

Established: *1982*
Address: *Apuldram Lane, Dell Quay, Chichester, W Sussex*
Telephone: *(0243) 785769. Fax: (0243) 536973*
Access: (road) *M27/A27* (rail) *Chichester*
Parking capacity: (cars) *50*
Season: *all year*
Hours: *Mon to Sat – 9am to 5pm; Sun and BH – 10.30am to 4.30pm*
Admission (1992): *free*
No. visitors (1992): *20 000 (est.)*

Facilities
Interpretation: *leaflets; catalogue*
Retailing: *postcards/inexpensive souvenirs; craftwork; books; garden ornaments; rustic articles and stoneware*
No. shops: *2*

Operations
Contact: *Ms D Sawday (owner)*
No. employees: (high season) *3 full time; 2 part time* (low season) *3 full time; 2 part time*
Training: *F/T operations staff are trained externally and on specific courses*

Marketing
Annual event(s): *open evenings*
Affiliations: *HTA, local tourist board, Chamber of Comm, H Exhibitors Association and British Association of Rose Growers*
Other: *market research*
UK promotion: *national newspapers; local newspapers; regional tourist board; leaflets/information packs*

ARBEIA ROMAN FORT AND MUSEUM
(local authority run)
monument; museum

Established: 1883
Address: Baring St, South Shields, Tyne and
Wear, NE33 2BB
Telephone: (091) 456 1369. Fax: (091) 427 6862
Access: (road) A1M/A194 (rail) Metro South
Shields
Parking capacity: (cars) 120 (coaches) 20
Season: all year
Hours: Tues to Sat – 10am to 5.30pm (open Sun
Easter to Sept); museum closed Mon but park
open 10am to 4pm; open BH Mon
Admission (1992): free
No. visitors (1992): 70 000 (est.)

Facilities
Interpretation: leaflets; information boards; maps;
tour guides; guide books
Languages: Japanese; French; German; Italian;
Spanish
Schools: maximum no. 120; educational literature;
audio/visual presentation; lecture/talk
Disabled: easy access; helpers
Retailing: postcards/inexpensive souvenirs;
confectionery and ice cream; craftwork;
books; clothes; reproductions of famous
artefacts
No. shops: 1

Operations
Contacts: P T Bidwell (Principal Keeper);
M Twelves (Principal Marketing Officer)
No. employees: (high season) 7 full time (low
season) 7 full time
Training: F/T operations staff and F/T
management are trained in-house and externally
and on specific courses
Languages spoken: French

Marketing
Annual event(s): event days and Roman days
Other: press office; market research
UK promotion: local newspapers; regional tourist
board; other attractions; leaflets/information
packs

Environmental monitoring: hazardous materials

ARBURY HALL
(stately home)
historic house; garden

Established: 1953
Address: Nuneaton, Warwickshire, CV10 7PT
Telephone: (0203) 382804. Fax: (0676) 41671
Access: (road) M6/A444 (rail) Nuneaton
Parking capacity: (cars) 500 (coaches) 4
Hours: Easter Sun to end Sept – Sun and BH –
2pm to 5.30pm
Admission (1992): adults £3.00; children £1.60;
OAP £3.00; student £3.00
No. visitors (1992): 10 000 (est.)

Facilities
Interpretation: leaflets; slides; tour guides; guide
books
Children: nappy changing
Schools: maximum no. 90; educational literature;
lecture/talk; period costumes to try
Disabled: easy access; only ground floor
accessible
Catering: 1 picnic area
Retailing: postcards/inexpensive souvenirs;
craftwork; books
No. shops: 1

Operations
Contact: Major W D Morris-Barker
(Administrator)
No. employees: (high season) 2 full time; 2 part
time (low season) 2 full time; 2 part time
Languages spoken: French; German

Marketing
Annual event(s): craft fair
Affiliations: HHA
UK promotion: Historic Houses and Gardens,
Historic Houses Directory, etc.; ETB/BTA

Environmental monitoring: energy consumption;
hazardous materials; chemical usage

ARDENCRAIG GARDENS
(local authority run)
garden; zoo/wildlife attraction; aviary

Established: 1968
Address: Ardencraig Estate, Eastlands Rd,
Rothesay, Isle of Bute
Telephone: (0700) 504225. Fax: (0700) 504225
Parking capacity: (cars) 10 (coaches) 2
Hours: 1 May to 30 Sept – Mon to Fri – 9am to
4.30pm; Sat and Sun – 1pm to 4.30pm
Admission (1992): free
No. visitors (1992): 2000 (est.)

Facilities
Interpretation: greenhouses, gardens and aviary
Schools: no special support
Disabled: leaflets
Catering: 1 waiter/waitress served
Retailing: postcards/inexpensive souvenirs;
confectionery and ice cream; craftwork
No. shops: 1

Operations

Marketing: N/A

Environmental monitoring: energy consumption

ARDFEARN NURSERY PLANT CENTRE
(partnership)
garden

Established: 1987
Address: Bunchrew, Inverness, IV3 6RH
Telephone: (0463) 243250
Access: (road) A9/A862 (rail) Inverness
Parking capacity: (cars) 20 (coaches) 2
Season: all year
Hours: 9am to 5pm daily – (except Nov to Jan
incl when closed on Sun)
Admission (1992): free
No. visitors (1992): 5000 (est.)

Facilities
Interpretation: leaflets
Schools: maximum no. 15; lecture/talk
Disabled: easy access
Retailing: sales area in centre
No. shops: 1

Operations
Contacts: Mr A Sutherland (Partner); Mr J
Sutherland (Partner)
No. employees: (high season) 4 full time
(low season) 4 full time
Training: F/T operations staff are trained in-house
and externally and on specific courses and day-
to-day on job

Marketing
UK promotion: local newspapers; regional tourist
board

ARDINGTON POTTERY
(private business)
working studio pottery

Established: 1975
Address: 15 Home Farm, School Road,
Ardington, Nr Wantage, Oxon OX12 8PN
Telephone: (0235) 833302
Access: (road) M4/M40/A417 (rail) Didcot
Parking capacity: (cars) 50 (coaches) 3
Season: all year
Hours: all year – Mon to Sat – 10am to 5.30pm;
Sun – 11.30am to 5.30pm
Admission (1992): free
No. visitors (1992): N/A

Facilities
Interpretation: leaflets; by owners/potters
Schools: maximum no. 25; demonstration

Disabled: easy access; leaflets
Retailing: postcards/inexpensive souvenirs;
craftwork
No. shops: 1

Operations
Contacts: L and B Owens (joint partners)
No. employees: (high season) 2 full time
(low season) 2 full time

Marketing
UK promotion: local newspapers; regional tourist
board; leaflets/information packs; Where to Go
by TCTB

Environmental monitoring: energy consumption;
chemical usage

ARGYLL FOREST PARK
(crown commission)
park/reserve; forest and hill walks, picnic sites,
camp sites

Established: 1936
Address: Forest Enterprise, Kilmon, Dunoon,
Argyll, PA23 8SE
Telephone: 036984 666
Access: (road) A83 (rail) Tarbet
Parking capacity: (cars) 110
Season: all year
Hours: N/A
Admission (1992): free
No. visitors (1992): N/A

Facilities
Interpretation: leaflets; information boards; maps;
guide books; recreation ranger
Children: play area
Schools: maximum no. 40; educational literature;
lecture/talk
Disabled: disabled toilets; disabled footpath/trail
Catering: 9 picnic areas
Retailing: postcards/inexpensive souvenirs;
confectionery and ice cream; books
No. shops: 1

Operations
Contact: PD Harrop (District Forester)
No. employees: (high season) 5 full time
(low season) 3 full time
Training: F/T operations staff and F/T
management are trained in-house and externally
and on specific courses and day-to-day on job
Languages spoken: some Danish

Marketing
Annual event(s): forest festival
Other: press office; market research
UK promotion: local newspapers; regional tourist
board; other attractions; leaflets/information
packs; ETB/BTA

ARMAGH COUNTY MUSEUM
(local authority run)
museum

Established: 1935
Address: The Mall East, Armagh
Telephone: (0861) 523070
Access: (road) M1
Season: all year
Hours: open all year – Mon to Sat – 10am to 1pm
and 2pm to 5pm
Admission (1992): free
No. visitors (1992): 25 000 (est.)

Facilities
Interpretation: leaflets; information boards; maps
Schools: maximum no. 50; educational literature;
lecture/talk
Retailing: postcards/inexpensive souvenirs; books
No. shops: 1

Operations
No. employees: (high season) 7 full time
Training: F/T operations staff and F/T
management are trained in-house and on
specific courses and day-to-day on job using
handbooks

Marketing
Annual event(s): *Armagh Art Club annual exhibition*
Sponsor(s): *various – banks, transport cos, etc.*
Other: *PR company: as a branch of the Ulster Museum all national PR would be handled by the marketing officer; press office*
UK promotion: *national newspapers; radio; local newspapers; regional tourist board; leaflets/ information packs; ETB/BTA; Northern Ireland Tourist Board*

Environmental monitoring: *water quality; hazardous materials; chemical usage*

ARMAGH PLANETARIUM
(local authority run)
museum; planetarium/exhibition hall

Established: *1968*
Address: *College Hill, Armagh, Northern Ireland, BT61 9DE*
Telephone: *(0861) 523689.* Fax: *(0861) 526187*
Access: (road) *M1/M12*
Parking capacity: (cars) *100* (coaches) *2*
Season: *all year*
Hours: *open all year – Mon to Sat – 2pm to 4.45pm*
Admission (1992): *adults £2.50; children £1.50; OAP £1.50*
No. visitors (1992): *31 163*

Facilities
Interpretation: *videos; leaflets; presentation/shows*
Children: *nappy changing*
Schools: *maximum no. 117; educational literature*
Disabled: *easy access; disabled toilets; helpers*
Catering: *2 picnic areas*
Retailing: *postcards/inexpensive souvenirs; books; clothes; slide sets,posters,videos*
No. shops: *1*

Operations
Contacts: *Dr Ian Griffen (Director); Eamon Rafferty (Secretary)*
No. employees: (high season) *11 full time; 4 part time* (low season) *11 full time; 1 part time*
Training: *F/T operations staff, P/T operations staff and casual operations staff are trained in-house and day-to-day on job using videos and handbooks*

Marketing
Annual event(s): *telescope nights*
Sponsor(s): *Williams Airfreight, Ulster Travel*
Affiliations: *International Planetarium Society*
Other: *market research*
UK promotion: *television; radio; local newspapers; regional tourist board; other attractions; leaflets/information packs; ETB/BTA; Northern Ireland Tourist Board brochures*

Environmental monitoring: *recycling; energy consumption; hazardous materials; chemical usage*

ARRAN AND ARGYLL TRANSPORT MUSEUM
(independent non-profit)
museum

Established: *1985*
Address: *9 Brathwic Place, Anchor park, Brodick, Isle of Arran*
Telephone: *(07702) 150*
Access: (road) *M74/A78* (rail) *Ardrossan*
Hours: *6 Jan to 20 Dec – Winter – 10am to 4pm and Summer – 11am to sunset*
Admission (1992): *adults £0.75; children £0.50; OAP £0.20; locals and transport workers free*
No. visitors (1992): *N/A*

Facilities
Interpretation: *videos; leaflets; audio tapes; information boards; maps; tour guides; personnel; exhibits*
Languages: *Dutch; French; Gaelic*
Children: *nappy changing*

Schools: *maximum no. 36; educational literature; audio/visual presentation; lecture/talk; pre-booked free*
Disabled: *easy access; helpers; other audio facilities; guide book; sign language and large print guide book*
Catering: *1 bar/public house*
Retailing: *postcards/inexpensive souvenirs; books; reproductions of famous artefacts*
No. shops: *1*

Operations
Contact: *Mr Bernard Mitchell Luker (Curator)*
No. employees: (high season) *2 full time; 3 part time* (low season) *2 full time*
Training: *F/T operations staff, F/T management, P/T operations staff and casual operations staff are trained in-house and externally and on specific courses and day-to-day on job*

Marketing
Market research
UK promotion: *local newspapers; regional tourist board; other attractions; leaflets/information packs; Isle of Arran Tourist Board*

Environmental monitoring: *energy consumption; hazardous materials*

ARRETON MANOR
(privately owned)
historic house; garden; museum

Established: *1957*
Address: *Arreton, Isle of Wight*
Telephone: *(0983) 528134*
Access: (road) *A3056*
Season: *all year*
Hours: *Mon to Fri – 10am to 6pm; closed Sat except BH Sun – 12 noon to 6pm*
Admission (1992): *adults £3.00; children £2.00; OAP £2.50; student £2.00*
No. visitors (1992): *40 000 (est.)*

Facilities
Interpretation: *tour guides; guide books; personnel*
Schools: *maximum no. 60; educational literature; lecture/talk*
Catering: *1 picnic area*
Retailing: *postcards/inexpensive souvenirs; confectionery and ice cream; craftwork; books; clothes*
No. shops: *1*

Operations
Contact: *Mrs J Schroeder (owner)*
No. employees: (high season) *8 full time; 4 part time*
Training: *F/T operations staff, P/T operations staff and casual operations staff are trained in-house and day-to-day on job using handbooks and field studies and classes*
Languages spoken: *French; Italian; Gaelic*

Marketing
Annual event(s): *living history – Arreton Pageant*
UK promotion: *radio; local newspapers; regional tourist board; leaflets/information packs*

Environmental monitoring: *energy consumption; transport; emissions*

ART GALLERY AND MUSEUM
(local authority run)
museum; gallery; glasgow city council museums

Established: *1902*
Address: *Kelvingrove, Glasgow, G3 8AG*
Telephone: *(041) 357 3929.* Fax: *(041) 357 4537*
Access: (road)
Season: *all year*
Hours: *Mon to Sat – 10am to 5pm and Sun – 11am to 5pm*
Admission (1992): *free*
No. visitors (1992): *906 155*

Facilities
Interpretation: *leaflets; information boards; maps; tour guides; guide books*

Languages: *Urdu*
Children: *nappy changing*
Schools: *N/A*
Disabled: *easy access; disabled toilets*
Catering: *1 waiter/waitress served*
Retailing: *postcards/inexpensive souvenirs; craftwork; books; clothes; reproductions of famous artefacts; posters,prints,toys and ceramics*
No. shops: *1*

Operations
Training: *F/T operations staff and F/T management are trained in-house and on specific courses and day-to-day on job*

Marketing
Press office; market research
UK promotion: *local newspapers; regional tourist board; leaflets/information packs*

ARUNDEL TOY AND MILITARY MUSEUM
(privately owned)
museum; tourist attraction

Established: *1978*
Address: *Dolls House, 23 High St, Arundel, W Sussex, BN18 9AD*
Telephone: *(0903) 882908*
Access: (road) *M27/A27* (rail) *Arundel*
Season: *all year*
Hours: *June, July, Aug and Sept – 11am to 5pm daily; every weekend throughout the year, also BH and most Spring days*
Admission (1992): *adults £1.25; children £0.90; OAP £0.90; student £0.90; groups of 20 or more £0.80*
No. visitors (1992): *8000 (est.)*

Facilities
Interpretation: *leaflets; information boards*
Languages: *Spanish*
Schools: *maximum no. 50; no special support; questions answered*
Retailing: *postcards/inexpensive souvenirs; books; model toy soldiers, etc.*
No. shops: *1*

Operations
Contact: *Mrs D Henderson (owner and Administrator)*

Marketing
Affiliations: *AIM*
UK promotion: *local newspapers; regional tourist board; other attractions; leaflets/information packs; s east and southern tourist boards*
Europe/USA promotion: *guide books*

Environmental monitoring: *Glasgow City Council*

ASHMOLEAN MUSEUM
(local authority run)
museum; gallery

Established: *1683*
Address: *Beaumont Street, Oxford, OX1 2PH*
Telephone: *(0865) 278000.* Fax: *(0865) 278018*
Access: (rail) *Oxford*
Season: *all year*
Hours: *all year – Tues to Sat – 10am to 4pm; Sun – 2pm to 4pm; Summer BH – 2pm to 5pm*
Admission (1992): *N/A*
No. visitors (1992): *200 000*

Facilities
Interpretation: *leaflets; information boards; tour guides; guide books*
Languages: *French; German*
Schools: *maximum no. 60; educational literature; educational tour; lecture/talk*
Disabled: *helpers*
Retailing: *postcards/inexpensive souvenirs; confectionery and ice cream; books; reproductions of famous artefacts*
No. shops: *1*

Operations
Contacts: *R M Hobby (Administrator); R I H Charlton (Publications Officer)*

No. employees: (high season) *70 full time; 24 part time* (low season) *70 full time; 24 part time*
Training: *F/T operations staff, F/T management, P/T operations staff and P/T management are trained in-house and externally and on specific courses and day-to-day on job*

Marketing
Affiliations: *MA*
Other: *market research*
UK promotion: *national newspapers; radio; local newspapers; regional tourist board; leaflets/information packs; ETB/BTA*
Worldwide through BTA promotion: *leaflets/brochures; British Tourist Authority*

ASSOCIATION GALLERY
(local authority run)
gallery

Established: *1987*
Address: *9–10 Domingo St, London, EC1*
Telephone: *(071) 608 1445.* Fax: *(071) 253 3007*
Access: (road) *M25* (rail) *Barbican/Old Street*
Season: *all year*
Hours: *Mon to Fri – 9.30am to 6pm; Sat – 11am to 5pm*
Admission (1992): *free*
No. visitors (1992): *11 200 (est.)*

Facilities
Interpretation: *leaflets*
Schools: *maximum no. 25; no special support*
Disabled: *helpers*

Operations
Contacts: *Mr N Davis (Financial Director); Ms J Collier (Services); Ms J Kelly*
No. employees: (high season) *9 full time* (low season) *9 full time*
Training: *F/T operations staff and F/T management are trained in-house and day-to-day on job*

Marketing
Press office; market research
UK promotion: *television; national newspapers; radio; local newspapers*
Europe/USA promotion: *leaflets/brochures*

Environmental monitoring: *hazardous materials; chemical usage; emissions*

ATHELHAMPTON HOUSE AND GARDENS
(private partnership)
historic house; garden

Established: *1960*
Address: *Athelhampton, Dorchester, Dorset, DT2 7 LG*
Telephone: *(0305) 848363.* Fax: *(0305) 848135*
Access: (road) *A35* (rail) *Dorchester*
Parking capacity: (cars) *200* (coaches) *6*
Hours: *Easter to Oct – Wed, Thur, Sun and BH – 12am to 5pm; Open Tue May to Sept and Mon and Fri in August*
Admission (1992): *adults £3.80; children £1.90; OAP £3.80; student £3.80*
No. visitors (1992): *25 000 (est.)*

Facilities
Interpretation: *leaflets; information boards; tour guides; guide books*
Languages: *French; German*
Schools: *maximum no. 40; educational literature; lecture/talk*
Disabled: *easy access; disabled toilets*
Catering: *1 picnic area*
Retailing: *bric-a-brac*
No. shops: *2*

Operations
Contact: *P Cooke*
No. employees: (high season) *5 full time; 10 part time* (low season) *3 full time; 2 part time*
Training: *F/T operations staff, P/T operations staff and casual operations staff are trained in-house and day-to-day on job*
Languages spoken: *French*

Marketing
Annual event(s): *various*
Affiliations: *HHA*
Other: *press office; market research*
UK promotion: *radio; local newspapers; regional tourist board; other attractions; leaflets/information packs; Best of Dorset*

Environmental monitoring: *recycling*

ATWELL WILSON MOTOR MUSEUM
(private)
museum; motor museum

Established: *1989*
Address: *Downside, Stockley Lane, Calne, Wilts, SN11 0NF*
Telephone: *(0249) 813119*
Access: (road) *A4*
Parking capacity: (cars) *50* (coaches) *3*
Season: *all year*
Hours: *Apr to Oct – Mon to Thur – 10am to 5pm, Sun – 11am to 5pm; Nov to Mar – Mon to Thur – 10am to 4pm, Sun – 11am to 4pm*
Admission (1992): *adults £1.50; children £0.75; OAP £1.00; student £0.75*
No. visitors (1992): *3000 (est.)*

Facilities
Interpretation: *videos; leaflets; tour guides*
Schools: *maximum no. 20; educational tour; must book*
Disabled: *easy access; disabled toilets*
Catering: *1 picnic area*
Retailing: *named keyrings*
No. shops: *none*

Operations
Contacts: *R and H Atwell*
Languages spoken: *French; German*

Marketing
Annual event(s): *motor show, motor rally*
Affiliations: *WCTB*
UK promotion: *local newspapers; regional tourist board; leaflets/information packs; WCTB*

AUCHINDRAIN TOWNSHIP OPEN AIR MUSEUM
(trust)
museum; restored township

Established: *1963*
Address: *Inveraray, Argyll, PA32 8XJ*
Telephone: *(0499) 5235*
Access: (road) *A83*
Parking capacity: (cars) *40* (coaches) *4*
Hours: *Apr, May and Sept – Sun to Fri – 10am to 5pm; Jun, Jul and Aug – 10am to 5pm daily*
Admission (1992): *adults £2.20; children £1.40; OAP £1.70; family ticket £6.80*
No. visitors (1992): *17 000*

Facilities
Interpretation: *information boards; maps*
Languages: *Dutch; French; German; Italian; Finnish*
Schools: *no special support*
Catering: *1 picnic area*
Retailing: *postcards/inexpensive souvenirs; confectionery and ice cream; craftwork; books*
No. shops: *1*

Operations
Contact: *J MacDonald (Curator)*
No. employees: (high season) *1 full time; 2 part time* (low season) *1 part time*

Marketing
Annual event(s): *activities day*
Affiliations: *SMC, MA, AIM*
UK promotion: *local newspapers; leaflets/information packs*

AUCKLAND CASTLE
(church commissioners)
historic house; castle; park/reserve; gallery; church

Established: *1983*
Address: *Bishop Auckland, Co Durham, DL14 7NP*
Telephone: *(0388) 601627*
Access: (road) *A1M/A1/A689* (rail) *Bishop Auckland*
Parking capacity: (cars) *100* (coaches) *1*
Hours: *2 May to 19 Sept; Tues – 10am to 12.30pm, Sun, Wed and Thurs – 2pm to 5pm, Sat in Aug – 2pm to 5pm, BH Mon – 2pm to 5pm*
Admission (1992): *adults £1.50; children £0.75; OAP £0.75*
No. visitors (1992): *6000 (est.)*

Facilities
Interpretation: *leaflets; information boards; tour guides; guide books*
Languages: *French; German*
Schools: *maximum no. 40; worksheets*
Retailing: *postcards/inexpensive souvenirs; craftwork; books; reproductions of famous artefacts; honey produced at castle*
No. shops: *1*

Operations
Contact: *A D Yule (Warden)*
No. employees: (high season) *1 full time; 30 part time* (low season) *1 full time*
Training: *F/T management and casual operations staff are trained in-house and on specific courses and day-to-day on job*

Marketing
Affiliations: *HHA*
UK promotion: *regional tourist board; other attractions; leaflets/information packs*

AUTOMOBILIA TRANSPORT MUSEUM
(partnership)
museum

Established: *1981*
Address: *Billy Lane, Old Town, Hebdenbridge, W Yorks, HX7 8RY*
Telephone: *(0422) 844775.* Fax: *(0422) 842884*
Access: (road) *A6033*
Parking capacity: (cars) *150* (coaches) *8*
Season: *all year*
Hours: *Apr to Sept – Tues to Fri – 10am to 5pm, Sat and Sun – 12 noon to 5pm; Oct to Mar – Sat and Sun – 12 noon to 5pm (open BH Mon)*
Admission (1992): *adults £2.20; children £1.10; OAP £1.50; student £1.50; ub40s £1.50; family ticket (2+2) £5.50*
No. visitors (1992): *7000*

Facilities
Interpretation: *videos; tour guides; guide books; exhibition of cars, motorcycles and related items*
Languages: *Dutch*
Children: *nappy changing*
Schools: *educational literature; audio/visual presentation; lecture/talk; demonstrations*
Catering: *1 picnic area*
Retailing: *postcards/inexpensive souvenirs; books*
No. shops: *1*

Operations
Contacts: *Mr B Collins and Ms S Collins (partners); Ms S Sunderland (Secretary)*
No. employees: (high season) *1 part time* (low season) *1 part time*
Languages spoken: *French*

Marketing
Annual event(s): *historic vehicles cavalcade, vintage weekend in Hebdenbridge*
Sponsor(s): *Murt's Motor Centre*
Affiliations: *AIM, MA, Association of British Engineering and Transport Museums*
Other: *market research*
UK promotion: *local newspapers; regional tourist board; other attractions; leaflets/information packs; ETB/BTA*

Europe promotion: *leaflets/brochures; British Tourist Authority*

AVON VALLEY COUNTRY PARK
(private partnership)
theme park; park/reserve; zoo/wildlife attraction

Established: *1989*
Address: *Pixash Lane, Bath Rd, Keynsham, Bristol, BS18 1TS*
Telephone: *(0272) 864929.* Fax: *(0272) 868419*
Access: (road) *M4/A4* (rail) *Bath Spa*
Parking capacity: (cars) *600* (coaches) *100*
Hours: *Easter to end of Oct – Tues to Sat – 10am to 6pm; open BH and every day in Aug*
Admission (1992): *adults £2.75; children £1.75; OAP £2.25; student £2.25; discounts for groups*
No. visitors (1992): *50 000*

Facilities
Interpretation: *leaflets; information boards; maps; guide books*
Children: *adventure playground; play area*
Schools: *educational literature; lecture/talk*
Disabled: *easy access; disabled toilets; helpers; guide book*
Catering: *2 picnic areas*
Retailing: *postcards/inexpensive souvenirs; confectionery and ice cream; books; clothes*
No. shops: *2*

Operations
Contacts: *F Jenkins (Partner); G Dawes (Park Curator); J Douglas (Partner)*
No. employees: (high season) *5 full time; 1 part time* (low season) *2 full time; 1 part time*
Training: *F/T operations staff and F/T management are trained in-house*

Marketing
Affiliations: *ABLE and Wansdyke Tourist Association*
Other: *press office; market research*
UK promotion: *radio; local newspapers; regional tourist board; leaflets/information packs*

Environmental monitoring: *recycling; waste; energy consumption; hazardous materials; chemical usage; transport; emissions*

AVON VALLEY RAILWAY
(limited company)
steam railway

Established: *1970*
Address: *Bitton Station, Bath Rd, Willsbridge, Bristol, BS15 6EH*
Telephone: *(0272) 327296*
Access: (road) *A431* (rail) *Bristol Temple Meads*
Parking capacity: (cars) *50* (coaches) *4*
Season: *all year*
Hours: *Sat and Sun – 11am to 5pm*
Admission (1992): *adults £2.40; children £1.40; OAP £1.60; family ticket (2+2) £6.50; charges are for train ride only*
No. visitors (1992): *25 000 (est.)*

Facilities
Interpretation: *leaflets; slides; guide books*
Disabled: *easy access; special railway carriage*
Catering: *1 picnic area*
Retailing: *postcards/inexpensive souvenirs; books*
No. shops: *1*

Operations
Contact: *K Goodway (Marketing Manager)*

Marketing
Annual event(s): *N/A*
Affiliations: *Association of Railway Preservation*
Other: *market research*
UK promotion: *radio; local newspapers; regional tourist board; leaflets/information packs*

Environmental monitoring: *waste; water quality; hazardous materials; chemical usage*

AVONCROFT MUSEUM OF BUILDINGS
(limited company)
museum; open air museum

Established: *1967*
Address: *Stoke Heath, Bromsgrove, Worcs, B60 4JR*
Telephone: *(0527) 31886*
Access: (road) *M5/M42/A38* (rail) *Bromsgrove*
Parking capacity: (cars) *160* (coaches) *12*
Hours: *June to Aug – Mon to Sun – 11am to 5.30pm; Apr, May, Sept, Oct – Tues to Sun – 11am to 5.30pm; Mar and Nov – Tues to Thurs and Sat to Sun – 11am to 4.30pm*
Admission (1992): *adults £2.80; children £1.40; OAP £1.95; student £1.40; family £7.40*
No. visitors (1992): *59 000*

Facilities
Interpretation: *videos; leaflets; information boards; slides; tour guides; guide books; demonstrations*
Languages: *French; German*
Children: *play area*
Schools: *maximum no. 500; educational literature; lecture/talk; demonstrations*
Disabled: *easy access; wheelchair*
Catering: *1 picnic area*
Retailing: *postcards/inexpensive souvenirs; confectionery and ice cream; craftwork; books; clothes; cards and publications*
No. shops: *1*

Operations
Contact: *M G L Thomas (Director)*
Training: *N/A*

Marketing
Annual event(s): *N/A*
Other: *market research*
UK promotion: *local newspapers; regional tourist board; leaflets/information packs*

Environmental monitroing: *recycling; energy consumption*

AYS COUGHFEE HALL MUSEUM
(trust)
historic house; garden; museum; gallery

Established: *1986*
Address: *Churchgate, Spalding, Lincs, PE11 2RA*
Telephone: *(0775) 761161*
Access: (road) *A1073*
Hours: *Summer – 10.00am to 5.00pm; Winter – 10.00am to 5.00pm*
Admission (1992): *Free*
No. visitors (1992): *38 000 (est.)*

Facilities
Interpretation: *leaflets; information boards; signs*
Children: *play area*
Schools: *maximum no. 25; no special support*
Disabled: *easy access; disabled toilets*
Catering: *1 snack bar/food stall*
Franchisees: *Summer – 10.00am to 5.00pm; Winter – 10.00am to 5.00pm*
Retailing: *postcards/inexpensive souvenirs; books*
No. shops: *1*

Operations
Contacts: *Susanna Davis (Museum and Tourist Information Officer); Dr Douglas Gyte (Leisure and Economic Development Officer)*
No. employees: (high season) *3 full time; 3 part time* (low season) *3 full time*
Training: *F/T operations staff, P/T operations staff and casual operations staff are trained externally and on specific courses*

Marketing
UK promotion: *local newspapers; regional tourist board; leaflets/information packs*

AYTON CASTLE
(privately owned)
castle

Established: *1980*
Address: *Ayton, Berwickshire, TD14 5RD*
Telephone: *(08907) 81212.* Fax: *(08907) 81550*
Access: (road) *A1* (rail) *Berwick on Tweed*
Parking capacity: (cars) *200* (coaches) *20*
Hours: *May to Sept – 2pm to 5pm on Sun only (or by appointment)*
Admission (1992): *adults £2.00; OAP £2.00; student £2.00; children under 15 free*
No. visitors (1992): *2000 (est.)*

Facilities
Interpretation: *leaflets*
Schools: *maximum no. 30; no special support*
Disabled: *disabled toilets; helpers*

Operations
Contact: *Mr D Grainger (Curator)*
No. employees: (high season) *3 part time*
Training: *P/T operations staff are trained in-house and day-to-day on job*

Marketing
Affiliations: *HHA*
Other: *market research*
UK promotion: *local newspapers; regional tourist board; leaflets/information packs*

B

BADDESLEY CLINTON
(trust)
historic house; garden

Established: *1982*
Address: *Knowle, Solihull, B93 0DQ*
Telephone: *(0564) 783294*
Access: (road) *A4141/A41*
Parking capacity: (cars) *500* (coaches) *3*
Hours: *Mar to Sept – Wed to Sun – 12.30am to 6pm; Oct – Wed to Sun – 12.30am to 4.30pm; Nov to Dec – Wed to Sun – 12.30am to 4.30pm (house closed)*
Admission (1992): *adults £3.80; children £1.90; OAP £3.80; student £3.80; group and family tickets*
No. visitors (1992): *85 607*

Facilities
Interpretation: *guide books; room stewards*
Languages: *French; German; Italian*
Children: *nappy changing*
Schools: *maximum no. 60; educational literature; role play*
Disabled: *easy access; disabled toilets; wheelchairs*
Catering: *1 licensed restaurant*
Retailing: *postcards/inexpensive souvenirs; craftwork; books; clothes; reproductions of famous artefacts; National Trust products*
No. shops: *1*

Operations
Contacts: *W R McLeod (Administrator); S Marriott (Personnel Manager); J Pine (Regional Enterprises Manager); D Brown (Regional Public Affairs Manager)*
No. employees: (high season) *5 full time; 30 part time* (low season) *5 full time; 20 part time*
Training: *F/T operations staff, F/T management, P/T operations staff and casual operations staff are trained in-house and externally and on specific courses and day-to-day on job*
Languages spoken: *French; German; Italian*

Marketing
Affiliations: *National Trust*
Other: *press office; market research*
UK promotion: *local newspapers; regional tourist board; other attractions; leaflets/information packs; Historic Houses and Gardens*
USA promotion: *leaflets/brochures; British Tourist Authority*

BADEN POWELL HOUSE HOSTEL
(trust)
museum; hostel for scouts memorial to Baden-Powell

Established: *1962*
Address: *Queens Gate, London, SW7 5JS*
Telephone: *(071) 584 7031.* Fax: *(071) 581 9953*
Access: (road) *A4* (rail) *London Underground*
Parking capacity: (cars) *14*
Season: *all year*
Hours: *7am to 8pm daily except Christmas Day*
Admission (1992): *free*
No. visitors (1992): *100 000 (est.)*

Facilities
Interpretation: *leaflets; information boards; maps*
Children: *nappy changing*
Schools: *maximum no. 112; no special support*
Disabled: *easy access*
Catering: *1 self-service cafeteria*
Retailing: *postcards/inexpensive souvenirs*
No. shops: *1*

Operations
Contact: *W J Mackinnon (Hostel Manager)*

No. employees: (high season) *30 full time*
Training: *F/T management are trained in-house and externally and on specific courses and day-to-day on job using videos, handbooks and slides, flipcharts*
Languages spoken: *French; German; Italian; Japanese*

Marketing
Press office
UK promotion: *regional tourist board; leaflets/information packs*

Environmental monitoring: *recycling; waste; water quality; energy consumption; hazardous materials; chemical usage*

BADSELL FARM PARK
(partnership)
theme park; park/reserve; zoo/wildlife attraction; old breeds of farm animal

Established: *1987*
Address: *Crittenden Road, Hatfield, Tonbridge, Kent, TN12 7EW*
Telephone: *(0892) 832549.* Fax: *(0892) 833436*
Access: (road) *A21/228* (rail) *Paddock Wood*
Parking capacity: (cars) *250* (coaches) *12*
Hours: *Mar to Nov – 10am to 5.30pm daily*
Admission (1992): *adults £3.00; children £2.50; OAP £2.50; student £3.00*
No. visitors (1992): *50 000 (est.)*

Facilities
Interpretation: *leaflets; information boards; tour guides*
Children: *adventure playground; play area; nappy changing*
Schools: *maximum no. 100; educational literature; educational tour; lecture/talk*
Disabled: *easy access; disabled toilets; helpers*
Catering: *2 picnic areas*
Franchisees: *Mar to Nov – 10am to 5.30pm daily*
Retailing: *postcards/inexpensive souvenirs; confectionery and ice cream; craftwork; books; clothes; fruit and veg*
No. shops: *2*

Operations
Contact: *C M Preston (owner/Manager)*
No. employees: (high season) *4 full time; 4 part time* (low season) *2 full time; 1 part time*
Training: *F/T operations staff and P/T operations staff are trained in-house and day-to-day on job*
Languages spoken: *French; German; Spanish; Chinese*

Marketing
Annual event: *Fayre*
Affiliation: *SEETB*
Other: *market research*
UK promotion: *local newspapers; regional tourist board; leaflets/information packs; ETB/BTA; directories*

Environmental monitoring: *recycling; water quality; chemical usage*

BAGSHAW MUSEUM
(local authority run)
historic house; museum; gallery

Established: *1911*
Address: *Wilton Park, Batley, W Yorks, WF17 0AS*
Telephone: *(0924) 472514*
Access: (road) *M62/A62* (rail) *Batley/Dewsbury*
Parking capacity: (cars) *75* (coaches) *10*

Season: *all year*
Hours: *1 Mar to 31 Oct – Mon to Fri – 10am to 5pm, Sat and Sun – 12 noon to 5pm; 1 Nov to 28 Feb – 12 noon to 5pm daily; groups at other times by arrangement*
Admission (1992): *free*
No. visitors (1992): *45 000*

Facilities
Interpretation: *videos; leaflets; audio tapes; information boards; slides; labelling and photographs*
Children: *play area*
Schools: *maximum no. 35; audio/visual presentation; lecture/talk*
Disabled: *easy access; helpers*
Catering: *1 picnic area*
Retailing: *postcards/inexpensive souvenirs; craftwork; books; reproductions of famous artefacts; goods from around the world*
No. shops: *1*

Operations
Contact: *Mr B Haigh (Community Curator)*
No. employees: (high season) *9 full time; 7 part time* (low season) *7 full time; 7 part time*
Training: *F/T operations staff, F/T management, P/T operations staff and casual operations staff are trained in-house and externally and on specific courses and day-to-day on job*

Marketing
Affiliations: *MA, Museums and Galleries Commission, Yorks and Humbs Area Museums Council*
Other: *press office; market research*
UK promotion: *radio; local newspapers; regional tourist board; other attractions; leaflets/information packs*

Environmental monitoring: *water quality*

BAIRD INSTITUTE MUSEUM
(local authority run)
museum

Established: *1891*
Address: *Lugar St, Cummock*
Telephone: *(0290) 22111.* Fax: *(0290) 22461*
Access: (road) *A76*
Parking capacity: (cars) *50* (coaches) *5*
Season: *all year*
Hours: *Fri – 9.30am to 1pm and 1.30pm to 4pm, Sat – 11am to 1pm; other times by appointment*
Admission (1992): *free*
No. visitors (1992): *3500 (est.)*

Facilities
Interpretation: *videos; leaflets; information boards; tour guides*
Schools: *maximum no. 50; educational literature; audio/visual presentation; lecture/talk; worksheets and activities*
Retailing: *postcards/inexpensive souvenirs; books*
No. shops: *1*

Operations
No. employees: (high season) *1 full time; 1 part time* (low season) *1 full time; 1 part time*
Training: *F/T operations staff are trained in-house and day-to-day on job using videos and handbooks*
Languages spoken: *French; German; Spanish*

Environmental monitoring: *recycling; waste; water quality; energy consumption; hazardous materials; chemical usage; transport; emissions*

BALLANCE HOUSE, THE
(limited company)
historic house

Established: *1991*
Address: *118a Lisburn Rd, Glenavy, Co. Antrim, BT29 4NY*
Telephone: *(0846) 64492*
Access: (road) *A30*
Parking capacity: (cars) *24* (coaches) *4*
Season: *all year*
Hours: *April to Sept – Tues to Sun – 2pm to 5pm; Oct to May – Mon to Fri – 2pm to 5pm. Other times by appointment*
No. visitors (1992): *2000 (est.)*

Facilities
Interpretation: *leaflets; information boards; maps; tour guides; exhibitions, period style rooms*
Schools: *maximum no. 50; educational literature; lecture/talk; project leaflets*
Disabled: *easy access; disabled toilets; helpers; leaflets; curator can sign for deaf*
Catering: *1 self-service cafeteria*
Retailing: *postcards/inexpensive souvenirs; books; plants*
No. shops: *1*

Operations
Contacts: *Ms B J Logan (Curator, The Ballance House); Mrs Jill McIvor (Chairman, Ulster New Zealand Trust); Mr John R Cowdy (Treasurer, Ulster New Zealand Trust)*
No. employees: (high season) *1 full time; 2 part time* (low season) *1 full time*
Training: *F/T operations staff and F/T management are trained externally and on specific courses using handbooks*
Languages spoken: *French; German*

Marketing
UK promotion: *radio; local newspapers; regional tourist board; other attractions; leaflets/information packs; NITB literature,* Stop and Visit Lough Neagh
New Zealand promotion: *leaflets/brochures; radio*

Environmental monitoring: *energy consumption; Water consumption*

BALMORAL ESTATES
(Royal household)
castle; garden; exhibitions and country pursuits

Established: *1972*
Address: *The Estate Office, Balmoral, Ballater, Aberdeenshire, AB35 5TB*
Telephone: *(03397) 42334.* Fax: *(03397) 42271*
Access: (road) *A93*
Hours: *1 May to 31 Jul – Mon to Sat – 10am to 5pm*
Admission (1992): *adults £1.75; OAP £1.25*
No. visitors (1992): *90 000 (est.)*

Facilities
Interpretation: *leaflets; information boards; guide books*
Languages: *French; German*
Children: *nappy changing*
Schools: *no special support*
Disabled: *easy access; disabled toilets; helpers; wheelchairs available,special entrances to exhibitions*
Catering: *3 picnic areas*
Retailing: *postcards/inexpensive souvenirs; confectionery and ice cream; craftwork; books; clothes*
No. shops: *3*

Operations
Contact: *Captain J R Wilson (Administrator)*
No. employees: (high season) *30 full time*
Training: *F/T operations staff are trained in-house and externally and on specific courses*

Marketing
Affiliations: *ASVA*
Other: *press office; market research*

UK promotion: *national newspapers; local newspapers; regional tourist board; other attractions; leaflets/information packs*

BANK OF ENGLAND MUSEUM
(independent museum)
museum

Established: *1988*
Address: *Threadneedle St, London, EC2R 8AH*
Telephone: *(071) 601 5545.* Fax: *(071) 601 5808*
Access: (road) *M25* (rail) *Bank*
Season: *all year*
Hours: *Mon to Fri – 10am to 5pm throughout the year; Sun and BH – seasonal variations, please check*
Admission (1992): *free*
No. visitors (1992): *100 000 (est.)*

Facilities
Interpretation: *videos; leaflets; audio tapes; information boards; maps*
Languages: *Japanese; Dutch; French; German; Italian; Spanish; Arabic; Chinese*
Children: *nappy changing*
Schools: *audio/visual presentation; lecture/talk*
Disabled: *disabled toilets; helpers; other audio facilities; portable ramps*
Retailing: *postcards/inexpensive souvenirs; confectionery and ice cream; books*
No. shops: *1*

Operations
Contacts: *Ms D Davies (Manager); Mrs S McHale (Deputy Manager); Ms L Austin/Ms J Greenhalf (Information Officers)*
No. employees: (high season) *8 full time; 7 part time* (low season) *8 full time; 2 part time*
Training: *N/A*
Languages spoken: *French; German; Italian; Spanish*

Marketing
Other: *PR Company: HPS Marketing Comm Ltd, Park House, Desborough Park Rd, High Wycombe, Bucks; press office; market research*
UK promotion: *radio; local newspapers; regional tourist board; other attractions; leaflets/information packs; ETB/BTA*

Environmental monitoring: *waste; water quality; hazardous materials; chemical usage*

BANKFIELD MUSEUM
(local authority run)
museum; gallery

Established: *1889*
Address: *Boothtown Rd, Halifax, W Yorks, HX3 6HG*
Telephone: *(0422) 354823.* Fax: *(0422) 349020*
Access: (road) *M62/A647* (rail) *Halifax*
Parking capacity: (cars) *20* (coaches) *4*
Season: *all year*
Hours: *Tues to Sat – 10am to 5pm Sun – 2pm to 5pm; BH Mon – 10am to 5pm; closed Christmas/New Year*
Admission (1992): *free*
No. visitors (1992): *15 000*

Facilities
Interpretation: *displays and activities*
Children: *play area*
Schools: *maximum no. 40; educational literature; lecture/talk; by pre-booking and workshops*
Disabled: *easy access; helpers; handling collections and activities by arrangement*
Catering: *1 picnic area*
Retailing: *postcards/inexpensive souvenirs; craftwork; books*
No. shops: *1*

Operations
Contacts: *Ms P Millward (Senior Officer); Mr M Hall (Museum Registrar); Ms P Millward*
No. employees: (high season) *6 full time; 2 part time* (low season) *6 full time; 2 part time*

Training: *F/T operations staff, F/T management, P/T operations staff, P/T management and casual operations staff are trained in-house and externally and on specific courses and day-to-day on job using videos and handbooks*

Marketing
Annual event(s): *events, activities, workshops and exhibitions*
Affiliations: *MA, York and Humbs Museums Council, Yorkshire Arts*
Other: *market research*
UK promotion: *national newspapers; radio; local newspapers; regional tourist board; other attractions; leaflets/information packs; ETB/BTA*

BANKSIDE GALLERY
(limited company and trust)
gallery

Established: *1980*
Address: *48 Hopton St, Blackfriars, London, SE1 9JH*
Telephone: *(071) 928 7521.* Fax: *(071) 928 2820*
Access: (road) *A3200* (rail) *London Bridge*
Hours: *Closed Mon, BH and between exhibitions*
Admission (1992): *adults £2.00; children £1.00; OAP £1.00; student £1.00; ub40s £1.00*
No. visitors (1992): *20 000 (est.)*

Facilities
Interpretation: *leaflets; information boards; tour guides*
Disabled: *easy access*
Catering: *1 bar/public house*
Retailing: *postcards/inexpensive souvenirs; books; art materials*
No. shops: *1*

Operations
Contacts: *Mr M Spender (Director); Ms S Read (Shop Manager); Ms S Howall (Assistant Director)*
No. employees: (high season) *3 full time; 6 part time* (low season) *3 full time; 6 part time*
Languages spoken: *French*

Marketing
Annual event(s): *Summer party*
Other: *press office*
UK promotion: *national newspapers; regional tourist board; leaflets/information packs; ETB/BTA*

Environmental monitoring: *light, humidity and temperature*

BARLEYLANDS FARM MUSEUM
(private company)
museum; nature trail and pyo

Established: *1984*
Address: *Barleylands Farm, Barleylands Road, Billericay, Essex*
Telephone: *(0268) 532253.* Fax: *(0268) 532032*
Access: (road) *M25/A127* (rail) *Basildon/Billericay*
Parking capacity: (cars) *30* (coaches) *10*
Hours: *Wed to Sun Summer – 11am to 5pm; Winter – 11am to 5pm*
Admission (1992): *adults £2.00; children £1.00; OAP £1.00; student £1.00*
No. visitors (1992): *6000 (est.)*

Facilities
Interpretation: *information boards; signs*
Schools: *maximum no. 120; educational literature*
Disabled: *easy access; disabled toilets*
Catering: *1 picnic area*
Retailing: *postcards/inexpensive souvenirs; confectionery and ice cream; books; reproductions of famous artefacts*
No. shops: *1*

Operations
Contacts: *P J H Philpot (Director); N Smith (Museum Curator)*
No. employees: (high season) *1 full time; 2 part time* (low season) *1 full time; 2 part time*

Training: *F/T operations staff and P/T operations staff are trained externally and on specific courses*
Languages spoken: *French; German; Italian*

Marketing
Annual event(s): *Essex Steam Rally and Craft Fair*
Affiliations: *AIM*
UK promotion: *local newspapers; regional tourist board; leaflets/information packs*

BARTLEY MILL
(limited company)
heritage centre; museum; working watermill

Established: *1987*
Address: *Bells Yen Green, Frant, Sussex, TN3 8BH*
Telephone: *(0892) 890372. Fax: (0892) 890101*
Access: *(road) M25/A21 (rail) Frant*
Parking capacity: *(cars) 50 (coaches) 2*
Season: *all year*
Hours: *Mar to Oct – 10am to 6pm daily; Oct to Mar – 10am to 5pm daily*
Admission (1992): *adults £1.50; children £1.00; OAP £1.00; student £1.50; family £3.50*
No. visitors (1992): *30 000 (est.)*

Facilities
Interpretation: *leaflets; information boards*
Schools: *maximum no. 30; educational literature; educational tour; lecture/talk*
Catering: *1 picnic area*
Retailing: *postcards/inexpensive souvenirs; confectionery and ice cream; books; clothes; organic and homemade foods*
No. shops: *1*

Operations
Contacts: *P Garnham (owner); A Garnham*
No. employees: *(high season) 5 full time; 5 part time (low season) 3 full time; 1 part time*

Marketing
Press office
UK promotion: *local newspapers; other attractions; leaflets/information packs; ETB/BTA*

BARTON CLAY PITS
(local authority run)
heritage centre; park/reserve; museum; zoo/wildlife attraction

Established: *1987*
Address: *Old Boathouse, Waterside Rd, Barton upon Humber, S Humberside, DN18 5BA*
Telephone: *(0652) 33283*
Access: *(road) A15*
Parking capacity: *(cars) 150 (coaches) 10*
Season: *all year*
Hours: *N/A*
Admission (1992): *free*
No. visitors (1992): *250 000*

Facilities
Interpretation: *leaflets; information boards; slides; maps*
Children: *play area*
Schools: *maximum no. 100; educational literature; lecture/talk*
Disabled: *easy access; disabled toilets*
Catering: *2 picnic areas*
Retailing: *postcards/inexpensive souvenirs; books; reproductions of famous artefacts*
No. shops: *1*

Operations
Contact: *Mr T Allen (Team Leader)*
No. employees: *(high season) 2 full time; 2 part time (low season) 2 full time; 2 part time*
Training: *F/T operations staff and F/T management and casual operations staff are trained in-house and externally and on specific courses and day-to-day on job*
Languages spoken: *French*

Marketing
Annual event(s): *N/A*

UK promotion: *leaflets/information packs*

Environmental monitoring: *recycling; water quality; chemical usage; organic farming/ milling*

BARTON MANOR GARDENS AND VINEYARDS
(limited company)
garden; vineyard

Established: *1976*
Address: *Whippingham, East Cowes, Isle of Wight, PO32 6LB*
Telephone: *(0983) 292835. Fax: (0983) 293923*
Access: *(road) A3021*
Parking capacity: *(cars) 120 (coaches) 6*
Hours: *1 May to second Sun in Oct – 10.30am to 5.30pm daily; weekends in Apr and Easter hols*
Admission (1992): *adults £3.50; OAP £3.00; groups over 15 people £3.00, 1 free child per adult*
No. visitors (1992): *35 000 (est.)*

Facilities
Interpretation: *videos; leaflets; information boards*
Schools: *no special support; £1.50 per head*
Disabled: *easy access; disabled toilets*
Catering: *1 self-service cafeteria*
Franchisees: *1 May to second Sun in Oct – 10.30am to 5.30pm daily*
Retailing: *postcards/inexpensive souvenirs; confectionery and ice cream; craftwork; books; vines*
No. shops: *1*

Operations
Contacts: *Mr P Bywalski (Managing Director); Mr G Patterson (Marketing)*
No. employees: *(high season) 8 full time; 2 part time (low season) 7 full time; 2 part time*
Training: *F/T operations staff, F/T management, P/T operations staff and casual operations staff are trained in-house and day-to-day on job*
Languages spoken: *French*

Marketing
Other: *PR Company: Marriot Design and Advertising, Lower St James St, Newport, Isle of Wight; market research*
UK promotion: *radio; local newspapers; regional tourist board; other attractions; leaflets/ information packs*

Environmental monitoring: *water quality; wildlife and habitats*

BASILDON ZOO
(not known)
zoo/wildlife attraction

Established: *1986*
Address: *Vange, Basildon, Essex, SS16 4QA*
Telephone: *(0268) 553985*
Access: *(road) M25/A13 (rail) Pitsen/Basildon*
Parking capacity: *(cars) 200*
Season: *all year*
Hours: *Summer – 10am to 5pm; Winter – 10am to dusk; Daily except Christmas and Boxing day*
Admission (1992): *adults £2.50; children £1.25*
No. visitors (1992): *40 000 (est.)*

Facilities
Interpretation: *leaflets; information boards*
Children: *adventure playground; play area; nappy changing*
Schools: *lecture/talk; animals meet the children*
Disabled: *easy access; disabled toilets*
Catering: *2 picnic areas*
Franchisees: *Summer – 10am to 5pm*
Retailing: *postcards/inexpensive souvenirs; confectionery and ice cream; books*

Operations
Contact: *Y Surcouf (owner)*
Training: *F/T operations staff and F/T management are trained in-house and on specific courses and day-to-day on job using videos*

Languages spoken: *French; German*

Marketing
Other: *press office*
UK promotion: *local newspapers; regional tourist board; leaflets/information packs; ETB/BTA*

Environmental monitoring: *recycling; hazardous materials; chemical usage*

BASS MUSEUM, VISITOR CENTRE AND SHIRE HORSE STABLES
(plc)
museum; visitor centre and shire horse stables

Established: *1977*
Address: *Horninglow Street, Burton upon Trent, Staffs.*
Telephone: *(0283) 42031. Fax: (0283) 513509*
Access: *(road) M42/A50 (rail) Burton upon Trent*
Parking capacity: *(cars) 200 (coaches) 12*
Season: *all year*
Hours: *all year – Mon to Fri – 10am to 5pm, Sat to Sun – 10.30am to 5pm; closed Christmas, Boxing, New Year's Days*
Admission (1992): *adults £3.45; children £1.85; OAP £2.35; student £2.25; disabled free*
No. visitors (1992): *75 000 (est.)*

Facilities
Interpretation: *videos; leaflets; audio tapes; information boards; slides; maps; tour guides; guide books*
Languages: *Japanese; French; German*
Schools: *educational literature; audio/visual presentation; lecture/talk; pre-trip visit and liaison*
Disabled: *easy access; disabled toilets*
Catering: *3 bars/public houses*
Retailing: *postcards/inexpensive souvenirs; books; clothes; reproductions of famous artefacts; brewery related products; shire horse figures, etc.*
No. shops: *1*

Operations
Contacts: *G McBribe (Museum and Visitor Centre Administrator); S Joyce (Visitor Services Administrator); M Hawksworth (Commercial Manager)*
No. employees: *(high season) 12 full time; 22 part time*
Training: *F/T operations staff, F/T management, P/T operations staff and P/T management are trained in-house and on specific courses and day-to-day on job using handbooks*
Languages spoken: *French*

Marketing
Annual event(s): *Steam events and charity fayre*
UK promotion: *local newspapers; regional tourist board; other attractions; leaflets/information packs; ETB/BTA*
Europe promotion: *British Tourist Authority*

Environmental monitoring: *recycling*

BATEMAN'S (THE NATIONAL TRUST)
(trust)
historic house; garden; working water mill

Established: *1939*
Address: *Bateman's Lane, Burwash, Etchingham, E Sussex, TN19 7DS*
Telephone: *(0435) 882302*
Access: *(road) A265 (rail) Etchingham*
Parking capacity: *(cars) 200 (coaches) 3*
Hours: *Apr to Oct – Sat to Wed – 11am to 5.30pm*
Admission (1992): *adults £3.50; children £1.80; group rates*
No. visitors (1992): *80 000 (est.)*

Facilities
Interpretation: *leaflets; information boards; maps; guide books; room stewards*
Children: *nappy changing*
Schools: *maximum no. 60; educational literature*

Disabled: *easy access; disabled toilets; wheelchairs, additional access on request*
Catering: *1 picnic area*
Retailing: *postcards/inexpensive souvenirs; confectionery and ice cream; craftwork; books; clothes; flour from mill shop*
No. shops: *2*

Operations
Contacts: *D Fox (Administrator); C Taylor (Regional Personnel Manager); R Taylor (Regional Enterprises Manager); L McCracken (Assistant Public Affairs Manager)*
No. employees: *(high season) 7 full time; 25 part time (low season) 6 full time; 2 part time*
Training: *F/T operations staff, F/T management, P/T operations staff and P/T management are trained in-house and externally and on specific courses and day-to-day on job using videos and handbooks*

Marketing
Annual event(s): *Bateman's play, Bateman's concert*
Other: *press office; market research*
UK promotion: *national newspapers; radio; local newspapers; regional tourist board; other attractions; leaflets/information packs; ETB/BTA; Organised by regional office at Scotney Castle, Lamberhurst, Kent*

BATLEY ART GALLERY
(local authority run)
gallery

Address: *Market Place, Batley, W Yorks, WF17 5DA*
Telephone: *(0924) 473141*
Access:(road) *M62/M1* (rail) *Batley*
Season: *all year*
Hours: *Mon, Wed and Fri – 10am to 6pm; Tues – 10am to 5pm; Sat – 10am to 4pm*
Admission (1992): *free*
No. visitors (1992): *6000 (est.)*

Facilities
Interpretation: *videos; leaflets; information boards*
Schools: *educational literature; lecture/talk*

Operations
Contacts: *Ms J Speller (Assistant Curator, Art)*
No. employees: *(high season) 5 full time*
Training: *F/T operations staff and F/T management are trained in-house and externally and on specific courses and day-to-day on job using videos and handbooks*
Languages spoken: *French*

Marketing
Affiliations: *MA*
Other: *press office; market research*
UK promotion: *television; national newspapers; local newspapers; regional tourist board; leaflets/information packs*

Environmental monitoring: *recycling; waste; water quality; energy consumption; hazardous materials; chemical usage; transport; emissions; National Trust Guidelines*

BATTLE ABBEY AND BATTLEFIELD OF HASTINGS
(grant aided by the Government)
monument; park/reserve; museum; battlefield

Established: *1976*
Address: *Head Custodian, Battle Abbey Ticket Office, Battle Abbey, High Street, Battle, E Sussex TN33 0AD*
Telephone: *(04246) 3792*
Access: (road) *A21/A2100* (rail) *Battle*
Parking capacity: *(cars) 250*
Season: *all year*
Hours: *Apr to Sept – 10am to 6pm daily; Oct to Mar – 10am to 4pm daily*
Admission (1992): *adults £2.50; children £1.30; OAP £1.90; student £1.90; ub40 £1.90*
No. visitors (1992): *140 000 (est.)*

Facilities
Interpretation: *videos; leaflets; audio tapes; information boards; guide books*
Languages: *Dutch; French; German; Italian; Spanish*
Schools: *educational literature; audio/visual presentation*
Disabled: *easy access; other audio facilities*
Retailing: *postcards/inexpensive souvenirs; confectionery and ice cream; books; English Heritage range of gifts*
No. shops: *1*

Operations
Contacts: *C Goddard (Head Custodian); J McCrossen/G Lefeure (Personnel Officer/Head of Personnel); E Watkiss/L McNally (Gift and Book Buyers); T Martin (Marketing Officer)*
No. employees: *(high season) 5 full time; 3 part time (low season) 5 full time*
Training: *F/T operations staff, F/T management, P/T operations staff, P/T management, casual operations staff and casual management are trained in-house and on specific courses and day-to-day on job*

Marketing
Annual event(s): *various*
Sponsor(s): *various*
Other: *press office; market research*
UK promotion: *national newspapers; radio; local newspapers; regional tourist board; other attractions; leaflets/information packs; ETB/BTA*

BATTLE OF BRITAIN MEMORIAL FLIGHT (VISITS)
(local authority run)
heritage centre; tour of Battle of Britain aircraft

Established: *1986*
Address: *Royal Air Force, Coningsby, Lincs, LN4 4SY*
Telephone: *(0526) 344041*
Access: (road) *A153*
Parking capacity: *(cars) 50 (coaches) 3*
Season: *all year*
Hours: *Mon to Fri – 10am to 5pm (last tour 3.30pm); closed BH, weekends and 2 weeks over Christmas period*
Admission (1992): *adults £2.50; children £1.25; OAP £1.25; student £1.25; school and cadet groups £1.00*
No. visitors (1992): *20 000 (est.)*

Facilities
Interpretation: *videos; leaflets; tour guides*
Schools: *maximum no. 60; no special support; educational literature; tour adapted to suit age*
Disabled: *easy access*
Catering: *1 snack bar/food stall*
Retailing: *postcards/inexpensive souvenirs; books; pictures*
No. shops: *1*

Operations
Contacts: *Mr G Gallen (Visitor Centre Manager); Ms M Powell (Marketing Manager, Lincolnshire CC)*
No. employees: *(high season) 37 part time (low season) 37 part time*
Training: *F/T management, P/T operations staff and casual operations staff are trained in-house and day-to-day on job using videos and handbooks*
Languages spoken: *French; Chinese*

Marketing
Market research
UK promotion: *radio; local newspapers; regional tourist board; other attractions; leaflets/ information packs; ETB/BTA*
Europe/USA promotion: *leaflets/brochures; travel agents' brochures; British Tourist Authority*

BAYLE MUSEUM
(trust)
museum; historic building – monastic gatehouse

Established: *1923*
Address: *Bayle Gate, Bridlington, E Yorks*
Telephone: *(0262) 603170*
Hours: *June to end Sept – Tues, Wed Thurs – 2pm to 4pm Tues and Thurs - 7pm to 9pm*
Admission (1992): *adults £1.00; children £0.20; OAP £1.00; student £1.00*
No. visitors (1992): *1200 (est.)*

Facilities
Interpretation: *information boards; tour guides; guide books*
Schools: *maximum no. 20*
Disabled: *access difficult*
Retailing: *postcards/inexpensive souvenirs; books*
No. shops: *1*

Operations
Contact: *Mr J Walker (Hon Secretary to the Trustees)*
Training: *casual operations staff are trained in-house and on specific courses*

Marketing
Annual event(s): *Christmas evening for local schools*
Affiliations: *AIM*
UK promotion: *local newspapers; regional tourist board; leaflets/information packs; ETB/BTA*
Europe promotion: *British Tourist Authority*

BEACON COUNTRY PARK
(local authority run)
park/reserve; country park and golf course

Established: *1979*
Address: *Beacon Lane, Upholland, Lancs.*
Telephone: *(0695) 622794*
Access: (road) *M6/M58*
Parking capacity: *(cars) 500 (coaches) 6*
Season: *all year*
Hours: *open access*
Admission (1992): *free*
No. visitors (1992): *200 000 (est.)*

Facilities
Interpretation: *information boards; maps; ranger service*
Children: *play area*
Schools: *educational literature; educational tour; lecture/talk; ranger service*
Disabled: *easy access; disabled toilets*
Catering: *1 bar/public house*
Franchisees: *open access*
Retailing: *clothes; golf equipment*
No. shops: *1*

Operations
Contacts: *R Peters/ P Cooley (Golf Professional/ W Lancs Council); C Rice (W Lancs District Council)*
No. employees: *(high season) 10 full time; 4 part time (low season) 10 full time*
Training: *F/T operations staff and F/T management are trained in-house and externally and on specific courses and day-to-day on job using AIM, MDA courses*

Marketing
Annual event(s): *Beacon Country Show*
Other: *press office; market research*
UK promotion: *radio; local newspapers; regional tourist board; ETB/BTA*

BEACRAIGS COUNTRY PARK
(local authority run)
park/reserve

Established: *1980*
Address: *Nr. Linlithgow, West Lothian, EH49 6PL*
Telephone: *0506 844516*
Access: (road) *M8/M9* (rail) *Linlithgow*
Parking capacity: *(cars) 500 (coaches) 40*
Season: *all year*

Hours: *Summer – Sat, Sun – 9am to 5pm; Mon, Tue – 8.30am to 5pm; Wed – 8.30am to 5pm; Fri – 8.30am to 4pm; closed for lunch 12 noon to 1pm. Winter – Mon to Thur – 8.45am to 4.30pm; Fri – 8.45am to 4pm; Sat – 10am to 4pm; Sun – 9.30am to 4pm*
Admission (1992): *free*
No. visitors (1992): *100 000 (est.)*

Facilities
Interpretation: *leaflets; information boards*
Children: *adventure playground*
Schools: *maximum no. 110; educational literature; audio/visual presentation; lecture/talk*
Disabled: *easy access; disabled toilets; helpers*
Catering: *1 bar/public house*
Franchisees: *Summer – Sat, Sun 9am to 5pm Mon, Tue 8.30am to 5pm*
Retailing: *postcards/inexpensive souvenirs; confectionery and ice cream; craftwork; books; outdoor equipment*
No. shops: *1*

Operations
Contact: *Mr Peter Sunderland (Assistant Director)*
No. employees: (high season) *40 full time* (low season) *35 full time*
Training: *F/T operations staff and P/T operations staff are trained in-house and on specific courses*
Languages spoken: *Italian*

Marketing
Press office; market research
UK promotion: *radio; local newspapers; regional tourist board; leaflets/information packs*

Environmental monitoring: *recycling; waste; water quality; energy consumption; hazardous materials; chemical usage; transport; emissions*

BEAR MUSEUM
(private museum)
museum

Established: *1984*
Address: *38 Dragon St, Petersfield, Hants, GU31 4JJ*
Telephone: *(90730) 265108*
Access: (road) *A3M* (rail) *Petersfield*
Parking capacity: (cars) *3*
Season: *all year*
Hours: *Mon to Sat – 10am to 5pm*
Admission (1992): *free*
No. visitors (1992): *20 000 (est.)*

Facilities
Interpretation: *hands on exhibits*
Children: *play area*
Schools: *maximum no. 30*
Disabled: *helpers; guide book; limited access*
Catering: *1 picnic area*
Retailing: *postcards/inexpensive souvenirs; craftwork; books; reproductions of famous artefacts; bear-related*
No. shops: *1*

Operations
Contacts: *Mr and Mrs J Sparrow (owners)*
Languages spoken: *French*

Marketing
Annual event(s): *teddy bears' parties and picnics*
Affiliations: *Southern Tourist Board*

Environmental monitoring: *recycling; waste; water quality; energy consumption; hazardous materials; chemical usage; transport*

BEATLES STORY, THE
(limited company)
visitor attraction/experience

Established: *1990*
Address: *Britannia Vaults, Albert Dock, Liverpool, L3 4AA*
Telephone: *(051) 709 1963. Fax: (051) 708 0039*
Access: (road) *M62* (rail) *Lime Street*
Parking capacity: (cars) *1500* (coaches) *100*

Season: *all year*
Hours: *summer – 10am to 7pm daily; spring and autumn – 10am to 6pm daily; winter – 10am to 5pm daily. Closed Christmas Day and Boxing Day*
Admission (1992): *adults £3.50; children £2.00; OAP £2.00; student £2.00; ub40s £2.00; family and group discounts available*
No. visitors (1992): *200 000 (est.)*

Facilities
Interpretation: *videos; leaflets; information boards; personnel; tableaux, sound, smells*
Schools: *maximum no. 100; lecture/talk*
Disabled: *easy access; helpers*
Retailing: *postcards/inexpensive souvenirs; confectionery and ice cream; books; clothes; records, tapes, etc.; postcards, film*
No. shops: *1*

Operations
Contact: *M A Byrne (Managing Director)*
No. employees: (high season) *6 full time; 8 part time* (low season) *6 full time; 2 part time*
Training: *F/T operations staff, F/T management and P/T operations staff are trained in-house and externally and on specific courses and day-to-day on job using handbooks and help from Ulster Museum*

Marketing
Annual event(s): *anniversary, 1960s events*
Affiliations: *NWTB, MTB, ETB*
Other: *market research*
UK promotion: *national newspapers; radio; local newspapers; regional tourist board; other attractions; leaflets/information packs; various; ETB/BTA*
Europe/Asia/Australia/USA promotion: *leaflets/brochures; travel agents' brochures; British Tourist Authority*

Environmental monitoring: *recycling; energy consumption*

BEATRIX POTTER GALLERY
(trust)
gallery

Established: *1988*
Address: *Main Street, Hawkshead, Ambleside, Cumbria, LA22 0NS*
Telephone: *(05394) 36355*
Access: (road) *M6/A591* (rail) *Windermere*
Hours: *Easter to Oct – Mon to Fri – 10.30am to 4.30pm*
Admission (1992): *adults £2.40; children £1.20; National Trust members free*
No. visitors (1992): *50 000 (est.)*

Facilities
Interpretation: *leaflets; information boards; guide books*
Languages: *Japanese; French; German*
Schools: *maximum no. 10; lecture/talk*
Disabled: *inaccessible*
Retailing: *postcards/inexpensive souvenirs; craftwork; books; clothes; reproductions of famous artefacts; Beatrix Potter merchandise*
No. shops: *1*

Operations
Contacts: *Fiona Clark (Custodian); Christine Mineham (Shop Manager)*
No. employees: (high season) *1 full time; 8 part time* (low season) *1 full time; 8 part time*
Training: *F/T management and P/T operations staff are trained in-house and externally and on specific courses*

Marketing
Affiliations: *HHA, Cumbria Museums Forum*
Other: *PR Company: Square Advertising PLC, Tempest Court, Broughton, Skipton, BD23 3AE; press office; market research*
UK promotion: *local newspapers; regional tourist board; other attractions; leaflets/information packs; Welcome to Lakeland*

BEAULIEU NATIONAL MOTOR MUSEUM, HOUSE AND ABBEY
(trust)
theme park; historic house; monument; heritage centre; garden; museum

Established: *1952*
Address: *Beaulieu, Hants, SO42 7ZN*
Telephone: *(0590) 612345. Fax: (0590) 612248*
Access: (road) *M3/M27* (rail) *Southampton*
Parking capacity: (cars) *1500* (coaches) *30*
Season: *all year*
No. visitors (1992): *500 000*

Facilities
Interpretation: *videos; leaflets; audio tapes; information boards; slides; maps; tour guides; guide books; personnel*
Languages: *Japanese; Dutch; French; German; Spanish*
Children: *nappy changing*
Schools: *educational literature; audio/visual presentation; educational tour; lecture/talk*
Disabled: *easy access; disabled toilets; other audio facilities; special signs; powered transport; leaflets; free admission, disabled day*
Catering: *1 picnic area*
Retailing: *postcards/inexpensive souvenirs; confectionery and ice cream; craftwork; books; clothes; reproductions of famous artefacts; motoring related items; local products*
No. shops: *More than 4*

Operations
Contacts: *K G Robinson (Managing Director); J Hoy (Personnel Manager); D Knight (Shops Manager); L Harnett (PR Manager)*
No. employees: (high season) *150 full time; 250 part time* (low season) *130 full time; 150 part time*
Training: *F/T operations staff, F/T management, P/T operations staff, P/T management and casual operations staff are trained in-house and on specific courses and day-to-day on job and induction, interpersonal, using videos and handbooks*
Languages spoken: *French; German; Italian*

Marketing
Annual event(s): *various*
Sponsor(s): *various*
Affiliations: *HHA, AIM*
Other: *press office; market research*
UK promotion: *television; national newspapers; radio; local newspapers; regional tourist board; other attractions; leaflets/information packs; GBI; ETB/BTA*
Europe/Asia/Australia/USA promotion: *leaflets/brochures; travel agents' brochures; British Tourist Authority; personal visits*

Environmental monitoring: *recycling; energy consumption*

BEAUMARIS GAOL AND COURT
(local authority run)
historic house; museum

Established: *1974*
Address: *Beaumaris, Anglesey, Gwynedd, North Wales*
Telephone: *(0248) 750262*
Access: (road) *A55/A545* (rail) *Bangor*
Hours: *May to Oct – Mon to Sun – 11am to 6pm; open other times by appointment*
Admission (1992): *adults £2.70; children £2.00; OAP £2.00; family tickets and group discounts available*
No. visitors (1992): *34 000 (est.)*

Facilities
Interpretation: *leaflets; audio tapes; guide books*
Languages: *French; Welsh*
Schools: *maximum no. 120; educational literature; lecture/talk; special events organised*
Disabled: *other audio facilities*
Retailing: *postcards/inexpensive souvenirs; books*
No. shops: *1*

Operations
Contacts: *Gareth Williams (Principal Archivist and Museum Officer); Nest Thomas (Museum Development Officer)*
No. employees: *(high season) 6 part time*
Training: *P/T operations staff are trained in-house and externally and on specific courses and day-to-day on job using videos and handbooks*
Languages spoken: *French; German; Spanish; Japanese*

Marketing
Market research
UK promotion: *radio; local newspapers; regional tourist board; other attractions; leaflets/ information packs; This Week in Wales, Wales in Action, WTB literature*

Environmental monitoring: *waste; energy consumption; hazardous materials; chemical usage; transport*

BECK ISLE MUSEUM OF RURAL LIFE
(trust)
museum

Established: *1967*
Address: *Bridge St, Pickering, N Yorks, YO18 8DU*
Telephone: *(0751) 73653*
Access: *(road) A170*
Hours: *28 Mar to 31 Oct – 10am to 5pm*
Admission (1992): *adults £1.50; children £0.75; OAP £1.25; student £1.50; booked groups: adults £1.25; children £0.65*
No. visitors (1992): *30 000*

Facilities
Interpretation: *leaflets; information boards; maps; guide books*
Schools: *maximum no. 50; worksheets*
Retailing: *postcards/inexpensive souvenirs; books*
No. shops: *1*

Operations
Contacts: *Mr P Glen (Chairman); Mr G Clitheroe (Curator); Mr L Fishpool (Sales); Mr T Johnstone (Advertising)*
Training: *F/T management are trained in-house and externally and on specific courses using videos and handbooks*

Marketing
Affiliations: *MA, museums and art galleries in Yorks and Humbs*
Other: *market research*
UK promotion: *radio; local newspapers; regional tourist board; leaflets/information packs; Museums and Galleries; Museums Alive*

BEDFORD MUSEUM
(local authority run)
museum

Established: *1960*
Address: *Castle Lane, Bedford, MK40 3XD*
Telephone: *(0234) 353323*
Season: *all year*
Hours: *all year – Tues to Sat – 11am to 5pm, Sun and BH – 2pm to 5pm*
Admission (1992): *free*
No. visitors (1992): *39 000*

Facilities
Interpretation: *information boards*
Schools: *maximum no. 90; educational literature; lecture/talk*
Disabled: *easy access; disabled toilets*
Retailing: *postcards/inexpensive souvenirs; craftwork; books*
No. shops: *1*

Operations
Contact: *H J Turner (Curator)*
No. employees: *(high season) 6 full time; 4 part time (low season) 6 full time; 4 part time*

Training: *F/T operations staff, F/T management and P/T operations staff are trained in-house and externally and on specific courses and day-to-day on job*

Marketing
Annual event(s): *Christmas family day*
Other: *market research*
UK promotion: *radio; local newspapers; regional tourist board; leaflets/information packs; ETB/BTA*

BEESTON HALL
(privately owned)
historic house; park/reserve; garden

Established: *1979*
Address: *Beeston St Lawrence, Norwich, NR12 8YS*
Telephone: *(0692) 630771*
Access: *(road) M11/A1151 (rail) Wroxham, Norwich*
Parking capacity: *(cars) 80 (coaches) 2*
Hours: *Easter Sunday to Mid-September – 2pm to 5.30pm.*
Admission (1992): *adults £2.00; children £1.00; OAP £2.00*
No. visitors (1992): *6000 (est.)*

Facilities
Interpretation: *videos; leaflets; guide books; signs*
Children: *play area*
Disabled: *easy access*
Catering: *1 self-service cafeteria*
Retailing: *postcards/inexpensive souvenirs; craftwork; various*
No. shops: *1*

Operations
Contacts: *Sir Ronald Preston (owner); Lady Preston*

Marketing
Annual event(s): *N/A*
Affiliations: *HHA, East Anglia Tourist Board*
UK promotion: *local newspapers; regional tourist board; other attractions; leaflets/information packs*

BEKONSCOT MODEL VILLAGE
(limited company)
model village

Established: *1929*
Address: *Warwick Road, Beaconsfield, Bucks, HP9 2PL*
Telephone: *(0494) 672919*
Access: *(road) M40 A355 (rail) Beaconsfield*
Hours: *Mar to Oct – 10am to 5pm daily*
Admission (1992): *adults £2.50; children £1.25; OAP £1.00; student £1.00; group and family rates*
No. visitors (1992): *220 000*

Facilities
Interpretation: *leaflets; guide books*
Languages: *French; German*
Children: *adventure playground; nappy changing*
Schools: *educational literature*
Disabled: *easy access; disabled toilets; wheelchairs*
Catering: *1 picnic area*
Retailing: *postcards/inexpensive souvenirs; confectionery and ice cream; books; videos of village*
No. shops: *2*

Operations
Contacts: *B Newman (Managing Director); S Falconer (PR Officer)*
No. employees: *(high season) 8 full time; 20 part time (low season) 8 full time; 5 part time*
Training: *F/T operations staff, P/T operations staff and casual operations staff are trained in-house and day-to-day on job*
Languages spoken: *French; German; Russian*

Marketing
Annual event(s): *occasional morris dancers/folk dancers*
Affiliations: *London Tourist Board*

Other: *press office; market research*
UK promotion: *local newspapers; regional tourist board; leaflets/information packs; Where to Go in the Thames and Chilterns*
Europe/TCTB promotion: *leaflets/brochures; British Tourist Authority*

BELLFOUNDRY MUSEUM, THE
(private company)
museum

Established: *1986*
Address: *Freehold Street, Loughborough, Leics LE11 1AR*
Telephone: *(0509) 233414. Fax: (0509) 263305*
Access: *(road) M1/A6/A60/A512 (rail) Loughborough*
Parking capacity: *(cars) 100 (coaches) 12*
Season: *all year*
Hours: *9.30am to 4.30pm daily*
Admission (1992): *adults £0.75; children £0.50; tours – £2.50 (adult) £1.50 (child)*
No. visitors (1992): *15 000 (est.)*

Facilities
Interpretation: *leaflets; tour guides; guide books; signs*
Schools: *maximum no. 150; educational literature; hands on experience*
Disabled: *easy access; disabled toilets*
Retailing: *postcards/inexpensive souvenirs; craftwork; books; numerous but all bell related*
No. shops: *1*

Operations
Contact: *Trevor S Jennings (Curator)*
No. employees: *(high season) 1 full time; 4 part time (low season) 1 full time; 4 part time*

Marketing
Market research
UK promotion: *national newspapers; radio; local newspapers; leaflets/information packs; ETB/BTA; Leics County Council, AIM*
Australia/USA promotion: *leaflets/brochures; travel agents' brochures*

BELVOIR CASTLE
(privately owned)
castle

Established: *1953*
Address: *Belvoir, Nr Grantham, Lincolnshire, NG32 1PD*
Telephone: *(0476) 870262. Fax: (0476) 870443*
Access: *(road) A52/A60M/A1*
Parking capacity: *(cars) 500 (coaches) 25*
Hours: *1 Apr to 30 Sept – Tues, Wed, Thur, Sat, Sun and BH – 11am to 5pm (6pm on Sun and BH)*
Admission (1992): *adults £3.20; children £2.20; OAP £2.20; student £3.20; schools £1.80; adult groups £2.50*
No. visitors (1992): *85 000*

Facilities
Interpretation: *leaflets; information boards; tour guides; guide books*
Languages: *French; German; Italian; Spanish*
Children: *adventure playground*
Schools: *maximum no. 180; educational literature; lecture/talk*
Disabled: *braille guide book*
Catering: *2 picnic areas*
Retailing: *postcards/inexpensive souvenirs; confectionery and ice cream; craftwork*
No. shops: *3*

Operations
No. employees: *(high season) 2 full time; 50 part time (low season) 2 full time; 10 part time*
Training: *P/T operations staff and casual operations staff are trained in-house and day-to-day on job*

Marketing
Annual event(s): *N/A*

Affiliations: *HHA*
Other: *market research*
UK promotion: *radio; local newspapers; regional tourist board; leaflets/information packs; ETB/BTA*

Environmental monitoring: *recycling; waste; energy consumption; hazardous materials*

BENNETTS WATER GARDENS
(private)
garden; zoo/wildlife attraction

Established: *1978*
Address: *Putton Lane, Chickerell, Weymouth, Dorset, DT3 4AF*
Telephone: *(0305) 785150*
Access: (road) *B3157* (rail) *Weymouth*
Parking capacity:(cars) *50* (coaches) *4*
Hours: *Easter to Sept – Tues to Sun – 10am to 5pm*
Admission (1992): *adults £1.80; children £0.80; student £1.80; wheelchairs/under 5s free*
No. visitors (1992): *11 000 (est.)*

Facilities
Interpretation: *leaflets; information boards*
Schools: *maximum no. 50; educational tour*
Disabled: *easy access; disabled toilets; reserved parking*
Catering: *1 snack bar/food stall*
Retailing: *water plants*
No. shops: *1*

Operations
Contacts: *J Bennett (Partner); I A Bennett*
No. employees: (high season) *6 full time; 6 part time* (low season) *4 full time; 1 part time*
Training: *F/T operations staff, P/T operations staff and casual operations staff are trained in-house and day-to-day on job using videos*

Marketing
UK promotion: *national newspapers; radio; local newspapers; regional tourist board; leaflets/information packs*

BENTLEY WILDFOWL AND MOTOR MUSEUM
(local authority run)
historic house; park/reserve; garden; museum; wildfowl

Established: *1970*
Address: *Halland, Nr Lewes, E Sussex, BN8 5AF*
Telephone: *(0825) 840573.* Fax: *(0825) 840573*
Access: (road) *M23/A22/26* (rail) *Lewes*
Season: *all year*
Hours: *Mar to Oct – daily; weekends in Nov, Dec, Feb, mid-Mar*
Admission (1992): *adults £3.10; children £1.50; OAP £2.40*
No. visitors (1992): *59 000 (est.)*

Facilities
Interpretation: *leaflets; audio tapes; information boards; slides; maps; tour guides; guide books*
Languages: *French; German*
Children: *adventure playground; nappy changing*
Schools: *maximum no. 300; educational literature; lecture/talk*
Disabled: *easy access; disabled toilets*
Catering: *1 picnic area*
Franchisees: *Mar to Oct – daily; weekends in Nov, Dec, Feb, mid-Mar*
Retailing: *postcards/inexpensive souvenirs; craftwork; books; clothes; Bentley logo items,bird corn; greetings cards,gift wrap*
No. shops: *1*

Operations
Contacts: *B Sutherland (Manager); C Sutherland/C Keep (shop/birds); P Andrews (Secretary)*
No. employees: (high season) *5 full time; 21 part time* (low season) *5 full time; 6 part time*
Training: *F/T operations staff, F/T management and P/T operations staff are trained in-house and externally and on specific courses and day-to-day on job*

Marketing
Annual event(s): *Vintage transport rally, Wealden potters, craft fairs, falconry*
Affiliations: *Ashdown Forest Association*
Other: *market research*
UK promotion: *national newspapers; radio; local newspapers; regional tourist board; other attractions; leaflets/information packs; ESTTA; ETB/BTA*
Europe promotion: *leaflets/brochures; ESTTA*

BERSHAM HERITAGE CENTRE AND IRONWORKS
(local authority run)
museum

Established: *1983*
Address: *Bersham, Wrexham, Clwyd, LL14 4HT*
Telephone: *(0978) 261529*
Access:(road) *A483* (rail) *Wrexham*
Parking capacity: *(cars) 30*
Season: *all year*
Hours: *Easter to Nov – Mon to Fri – 10am to 5pm; Sat, Sun, BH – 12 noon to 5pm. Nov to Easter – Mon to Fri – 10am to 4pm; Saturday and Sunday – 12 noon to 4pm*
Admission (1992): *adults £1.00; children £0.75; OAP £0.75; student £0.75; heritage centre is free*
No. visitors (1992): *25 000 (est.)*

Facilities
Interpretation: *videos; leaflets; audio tapes; information boards; guide books; personnel*
Languages: *Welsh*
Children: *play area*
Schools: *maximum no. 60; educational literature*
Disabled: *easy access; other audio facilities*
Catering: *1 bar/public house*
Retailing: *postcards/inexpensive souvenirs; confectionery and ice cream; craftwork; books; clothes; reproductions of famous artefacts*
No. shops: *1*

Operations
Contacts: *Ann Williams (Curator); Hilary Williams (Administrator)*
No. employees: (high season) *3 full time; 7 part time* (low season) *3 full time; 1 part time*
Training: *F/T operations staff, F/T management, P/T operations staff and casual operations staff are trained in-house and externally and on specific courses and day-to-day on job*
Languages spoken: *French*

Marketing
Annual event(s): *open day*
Affiliations: *Museums Association*
Other: *market research*
UK promotion: *local newspapers; regional tourist board; other attractions; leaflets/information packs*

Environmental monitoring: *water quality; energy consumption; hazardous materials; chemical usage*

BESSIE SURTEES HOUSE (NDPP)
historic house

Established: *1989*
Address: *41–44 Sandhill, Newcastle upon Tyne, Tyne and Wear, NE1 3JF*
Telephone: *(091) 261 1585.* Fax: *(091) 261 1130*
Access: (road)   (rail) *Newcastle Central*
Hours: *Winter – 10am to 4pm daily. Summer – 10am to 6pm daily*
Admission (1992): *free*
No. visitors (1992): *3942*

Facilities
Interpretation: *videos; leaflets; tour guides*
Languages: *French; German; Italian; Spanish*
Schools: *maximum no. 25; educational literature*
Disabled: *access difficult*
Retailing: *postcards/inexpensive souvenirs; books*
No. shops: *1*

Operations
Contacts: *Ms C Thomson (Head Curator); Mr D Jones (Visitor Services Manager)*
No. employees: (high season) *1 full time; 3 part time* (low season) *1 full time; 3 part time*
Training: *F/T operations staff, F/T management and P/T operations staff are trained in-house and externally and on specific courses and day-to-day on job*
Languages spoken: *Welsh*

Marketing
Press office; market research
UK promotion: *local newspapers; regional tourist board; other attractions; leaflets/information packs; ETB/BTA*

Environmental monitoring: *energy consumption*

BETHNAL GREEN MUSEUM OF CHILDHOOD
(V & A museum and trust)
museum

Established: *1874*
Address: *Cambridge Heath Rd, London, E2 9PA*
Telephone: *(081) 980 2415.* Fax: *(081) 980 4759*
Access: (rail) *Bethnal Green*
Season: *all year*
Hours: *Mon to Thurs and Sat – 10am to 5.45pm; Sun – 2.30pm to 5.45pm Closed 24 – 26 Dec, 1 Jan and May Day*
Admission (1992): *free*
No. visitors (1992): *230 000 (est.)*

Facilities
Interpretation: *leaflets; audio tapes; information boards; maps; guide books*
Languages: *French; German; Italian; Spanish*
Children: *nappy changing*
Schools: *maximum no. 30; lecture/talk; lunch room*
Disabled: *disabled toilets*
Catering: *1 picnic area*
Retailing: *postcards/inexpensive souvenirs*
No. shops: *1*

Operations
Contact: *Mr A Burton (Head of museum)*
Training: *P/T operations staff and P/T management are trained in-house and externally and on specific courses using videos and handbooks*

Marketing
Other: *press office; market research*
UK promotion: *television; national newspapers; radio; local newspapers; regional tourist board; other attractions; leaflets/information packs; ETB/BTA*

Environmental monitoring: *recycling*

BEVERLEY MINSTER
(Parish church)
church

Address: *Beverley, North Humberside, HU17 0DP*
Telephone: *(0482) 868540*
Access: (road) *M62/A164/A1079* (rail) *Beverley*
Season: *all year*
Hours: *Summer – Mon to Sat – 9am to 8pm. Winter – Mon to Sat – 9am to 5pm, Sun – afternoons, services permitting*
Admission (1992): *free*
No. visitors (1992): *100 000 (est.)*

Facilities
Interpretation: *information boards; tour guides; guide books*
Languages: *Dutch; French; German*
Schools: *maximum no. 80; educational literature; by arrangement*
Disabled: *easy access*
Retailing: *postcards/inexpensive souvenirs; books*
No. shops: *1*

Operations
Contact: *Ms R Bannister (Parish Administrator)*

No. employees: (high season) *3 full time; 1 part time* (low season) *3 full time; 1 part time*
Training: *N/A*

Marketing
Annual event(s): *various*
Sponsor(s): *various*
UK promotion: *local newspapers; regional tourist board; other attractions; ETB/BTA*

BEXHILL MUSEUM OF COSTUME AND SOCIAL HISTORY
(registered charity)
museum

Established: *1972*
Address: *Manor Gardens, Bexhill-on-Sea, E Sussex, TN40 1RL*
Telephone: *(0424) 210045*
Access: (road) *A269* (rail) *Bexhill*
Hours: *Apr, May, Sept and Oct – Tues to Fri – 10.30am to 5pm, Sat, Sun and BH – 2pm to 5pm. June to Aug – Mon to Fri – 10.30am to 5pm, Sat and Sun – 2pm to 5pm*
Admission (1992): *adults £1.00; children £0.50; OAP £0.75; student £0.50*
No. visitors (1992): *4000 (est.)*

Facilities
Interpretation: *information boards; tour guides*
Schools: *maximum no. 30; educational literature*
Disabled: *easy access*
Retailing: *postcards/inexpensive souvenirs; books*
No. shops: *1*

Operations
Contacts: *Mrs P Bullock (Associate Chairman); Mr W Trussler; Mrs M Campbell*
No. employees: (high season) *25 part time*
Languages spoken: *Dutch and Flemish*

Marketing
UK promotion: *local newspapers; regional tourist board; other attractions; leaflets/information packs*

BEXLEY MUSEUM
(local authority run)
historic house; heritage centre; garden; museum; gallery

Established: *1980*
Address: *Hall Place, Bourne Rd, Bexley, DA5 1PQ*
Telephone: *(0322) 526574.* Fax: *(0322) 522921*
Access: (road) *A2* (rail) *Bexley*
Parking capacity: (cars) *200* (coaches) *3*
Season: *all year*
Hours: *Mon to Sat – 10am to 5pm (or dusk if earlier), Sun in BST – 2pm to 6pm*
Admission (1992): *free*
No. visitors (1992): *40 000 (est.)*

Facilities
Interpretation: *leaflets; information boards; guide books*
Languages: *French; German*
Schools: *maximum no. 30; educational literature; lecture/talk*
Catering: *1 bar/public house*
Franchisees: *Mon to Sat – 10am to 5pm (or dusk if earlier), Sun in BST – 2pm to 6pm*
Retailing: *postcards/inexpensive souvenirs; books*
No. shops: *2*

Operations
Contact: *Miss J Vale (Museums Curator)*
No. employees: (high season) *1 full time; 6 part time* (low season) *1 full time*
Languages spoken: *French; German*

Marketing
Annual event(s): *N/A*
Sponsor: *Bexley Arts Council*
Affiliations: *MA and HHA*
UK promotion: *local newspapers; regional tourist board; other attractions; leaflets/information packs; BAFM Yearbook*

BICKLEIGH CASTLE
(privately owned)
castle; garden; museum

Established: *1970*
Address: *Bickleigh, Tiverton, Devon, EX16 8RP*
Telephone: *(0884) 855363*
Access: (road) *M5/A396* (rail) *Tiverton Parkway*
Parking capacity: (cars) *55* (coaches) *4*
Hours: *Easter week – Good Friday to Fri and then Wed, Sun and BH to late May BH – 2pm to 5.30pm, then daily to early Oct – except Sat – 2pm to 5.30pm. Groups by arrangement*
Admission (1992): *adults £2.90; children £1.50; student £2.50*
No. visitors (1992): *14 000 (est.)*

Facilities
Interpretation: *leaflets; tour guides; guide books*
Languages: *Dutch; French; German; Italian; Spanish*
Children: *play area*
Schools: *maximum no. 200; educational literature; spotter guides*
Disabled: *easy access; helpers*
Catering: *1 picnic area*
Retailing: *postcards/inexpensive souvenirs; confectionery and ice cream; craftwork; books; reproductions; teddy bears*
No. shops: *2*

Operations
Contacts: *Mr N Boxall; Ms D Dudley*
No. employees: (high season) *14 part time* (low season) *4 part time*

Marketing
Annual event(s): *flower festival in Sept; concerts*
Affiliations: *HHA, WC Tourist Board, Mid Devon Tourist Association*
UK promotion: *radio; local newspapers; regional tourist board; other attractions; leaflets/information packs*
Europe promotion: *leaflets/brochures; British Tourist Authority*

BICTON PARK GARDENS
(trust)
garden; museum

Established: *1963*
Address: *East Budleigh, Budleigh Salterton, Devon, EX9 7DP*
Telephone: *(0395) 68465.* Fax: *(0395) 446126*
Access: (road) *M5/A3052* (rail) *Exmouth*
Parking capacity: (cars) *800* (coaches) *15*
Hours: *Mar to Oct – 10am to 6pm daily*
Admission (1992): *adults £4.70; children £3.70; OAP £3.95; school rates*
No. visitors (1992): *100 000 (est.)*

Facilities
Interpretation: *maps; guide books*
Children: *adventure playground; play area; nappy changing*
Schools: *maximum no. 200; no special support*
Disabled: *easy access; disabled toilets; adapted carriage on woodland railway*
Catering: *1 bar/public house*
Franchisees: *Mar to Oct – 10am to 6pm daily*
Retailing: *postcards/inexpensive souvenirs; confectionery and ice cream; craftwork; books; general gift items*
No. shops: *2*

Operations
Contact: *D Wright (General Manager)*
No. employees: (high season) *14 full time* (low season) *10 full time*
Training: *F/T operations staff and F/T management are trained in-house and day-to-day on job*
Languages spoken: *French*

Marketing
Annual event(s): *International Clowns charity day*
Other: *market research*
UK promotion: *radio; local newspapers; regional tourist board; other attractions; leaflets/information packs*

BIG SHEEP, THE
(sole trader)
theme park; zoo/wildlife attraction

Established: *1988*
Address: *Bideford, Devon, EX39 5AP*
Telephone: *(0237) 472366.* Fax: *(0237) 478800*
Access: (road)
Parking capacity: (cars) *350* (coaches) *9*
Season: *all year*
Hours: *10am to 6pm daily (Nov to Feb – limited programme)*
Admission (1992): *adults £3.00; children £2.00; OAP £3.00;*
No. visitors (1992): *105 000 (est.)*

Facilities
Interpretation: *information boards; maps; tour guides; personnel*
Children: *adventure playground; play area; nappy changing*
Schools: *maximum no. 120; lecture/talk*
Disabled: *easy access; disabled toilets; helpers*
Catering: *1 picnic area*
Retailing: *postcards/inexpensive souvenirs; confectionery and ice cream; craftwork; books; clothes*
No. shops: *2*

Operations
Contact: *Mr R Turner (Manager)*
No. employees: (high season) *25 full time; 13 part time* (low season) *8 full time; 2 part time*
Training: *F/T operations staff, P/T operations staff and casual operations staff are trained in-house and externally and on specific courses and day-to-day on job*
Languages spoken: *French*

Marketing
Annual event(s): *Royal Ascot sheep racing week, international sheepdog trials*
Other: *market research*
UK promotion: *television; national newspapers; radio; local newspapers; regional tourist board; other attractions; leaflets/information packs; ETB/BTA*

BIGNOR ROMAN VILLA
(trust)
museum; Roman villa displaying mosaics

Established: *1812*
Address: *Nr Pulborough, W Sussex, RH20 1PH*
Telephone: *(07987) 259*
Access: (road) *A29/285*
Parking capacity: (cars) *100* (coaches) *10*
Hours: *Mar to May and Oct – Tues to Sun – 10am to 5pm, June to Sept – 10am to 6pm daily*
Admission (1992): *adults £2.25; children £1.15; OAP £1.50; group rates*
No. visitors (1992): *34 000*

Facilities
Interpretation: *information boards; tour guides; guide books; visual displays*
Languages: *French; German*
Schools: *educational literature; educational tour; lecture/talk; hands on activities*
Disabled: *easy access; special signs*
Catering: *1 picnic area*
Retailing: *postcards/inexpensive souvenirs; craftwork; reproductions of famous artefacts; reproduction glassware, coins*
No. shops: *1*

Operations
Contacts: *B and G Compton (Curators)*
No. employees: (high season) *2 full time; 1 part time*

Marketing
Annual event(s): *period activity days*
Other: *market research*
UK promotion: *local newspapers; regional tourist board; other attractions; leaflets/information packs; ETB/BTA*
Europe/USA promotion: *British Tourist Authority*

BILL QUAY COMMUNITY FARM
(local authority run)
park/reserve; farm centre

Established: *1986*
Address: *Hainingwood, Bill Quay, Gateshead*
Telephone: *(091) 438 5340*
Access: (road) *A1M/A185* (rail) *Newcastle upon Tyne*
Season: *all year*
Hours: *9am to 5pm daily*
Admission (1992): *donations requested*
No. visitors (1992): *200 000 (est.)*

Facilities
Interpretation: *leaflets; information boards; personnel*
Children: *adventure playground; play area; nappy changing*
Schools: *educational literature; lecture/talk*
Disabled: *easy access; disabled toilets; helpers; special signs*
Catering: *1 picnic area*
Franchisees: *9am to 5pm daily*
Retailing: *postcards/inexpensive souvenirs*
No. shops: *1*

Operations
Contacts: *Mr D Tuck (Manager); Ms A Roberts (Assistant Manager)*
No. employees: (high season) *6 full time* (low season) *6 full time*
Training: *F/T operations staff and F/T management are trained in-house and on specific courses and day-to-day on job*

Marketing
Annual event: *farm carnival*
Sponsor(s): *various private sector firms*
Affiliations: *Rare Breeds Survival Trust*
Other: *press office; market research*
UK promotion: *television; national newspapers; radio; local newspapers; regional tourist board; leaflets/information packs*

BILLINGHAM BECK VALLEY COUNTRY PARK
(local authority run)
park/reserve; environmental resource centre

Established: *1991*
Address: *The Visitor Centre, Ecology park, Billingham, Cleveland, TS23 1RA*
Telephone: *(0642) 530784*
Access: (road) *A19*
Parking capacity: (cars) *30* (coaches) *3*
Season: *all year*
Hours: *Mon to Fri and Sun – 9am to 4pm*
Admission (1992): *free*

Facilities
Interpretation: *leaflets; information boards; maps; events*
Schools: *maximum no. 30; educational literature; lecture/talk; countryside wardens*
Disabled: *easy access; disabled toilets*
Catering: *2 picnic areas*
Retailing: *postcards/inexpensive souvenirs; books*
No. shops: *1*

Operations
Contact: *Mrs C Raper (Countryside Information Officer)*
No. employees: (high season) *3 full time* (low season) *3 full time*
Training: *N/A*

Marketing
Annual event(s): *various*
Other: *press office; market research*
UK promotion: *radio; local newspapers; regional tourist board; other attractions; leaflets/ information packs*

Environmental monitoring: *recycling; waste; water quality; energy consumption; hazardous materials; chemical usage; transport; emissions*

BINCHESTER ROMAN FORT
(local authority run)
monument

Established: *1981*
Address: *Binchester, Bishop Auckland, Co Durham*
Telephone: *(0388) 663089.* Fax: *(0833) 37163*
Access: (road) *A688* (rail) *Bishop Auckland*
Parking capacity: (cars) *20* (coaches) *3*
Hours: *1 Apr to 30 Sept – Sat to Wed incl – 10.30am to 6pm*
Admission (1992): *adults £0.80; children £0.40*
No. visitors (1992): *3000 (est.)*

Facilities
Interpretation: *leaflets; tour guides*
Schools: *maximum no. 60; educational literature*
Retailing: *postcards/inexpensive souvenirs; books; reproductions of famous artefacts*
No. shops: *1*

Operations
No. employees: (high season) *1 full time*
Training: *N/A*

Marketing
Annual event: *Roman military recreation group*
Other: *press office; market research*
UK promotion: *regional tourist board; leaflets/information packs*

Environmental monitoring: *local authority*

BIRDLAND
(limited company)
zoo/wildlife attraction; bird garden

Established: *1955*
Address: *Riverside, Bourton on the Water, Glos, GL54 2BN*
Telephone: *(0451) 820689/820480.* Fax: *(0451) 822398*
Season: *all year*
Hours: *Apr to Oct – Mon to Sun – 10am to 6pm; Nov to Mar – Mon to Sun – 10am to 4pm*
Admission (1992): *adults £3.00; children £2.00; OAP £2.50*
No. visitors (1992): *N/A*

Facilities
Interpretation: *leaflets*
Schools: *no special support*
Catering: *1 picnic area*
Retailing: *postcards/inexpensive souvenirs; confectionery and ice cream*
No. shops: *1*

Marketing
Affiliation: *HETB*
UK promotion: *regional tourist board; leaflets/information packs*

BIRMINGHAM CATHEDRAL
(church)
church

Established: *1715*
Address: *Colmore Row, Birmingham, B3 2QB*
Telephone: *(021) 236 4333*
Access: (road) *M6/M1/M5* (rail) *New Street*
Season: *all year*
Hours: *All year – Mon to Fri – 7.30am to 6.30pm, Sun – 12.30pm to 3.30pm*
Admission (1992): *free*
No. visitors (1992): *20 000 (est.)*

Facilities
Interpretation: *leaflets; tour guides; guide books*
Languages: *French; German*
Schools: *maximum no. 30; educational literature; lecture/talk; school visits*
Disabled: *easy access; touch and hearing centre*
Retailing: *postcards/inexpensive souvenirs; books*
No. shops: *1*

Operations
Contacts: *P Johnson (Lay Administrator); A G M Lamb (Cathedral Education Advisor)*
No. employees: (high season) *12 full time; 10 part time* (low season) *12 full time; 10 part time*
Training: *F/T operations staff, P/T operations staff and casual operations staff are trained in-house and day-to-day on job*

Marketing
Annual event: *One World*
UK promotion: *regional tourist board; ETB/BTA*

BIRMINGHAM RAILWAY MUSEUM
(trust)
museum; working museum restoring and running locomotives and stock

Established: *1969*
Address: *670 Warwick Road, Tyseley, Birmingham*
Telephone: *(021) 707 4696*
Access: (road) *M5/M6/M42/A41* (rail) *Tyseley*
Parking capacity: (cars) *150*
Season: *all year*
Hours: *All year – Mon to Sun – 10am to 5pm*
Admission (1992): *adults £2.00; children £1.00; OAP £1.00; student £1.00; unemployed rates*
No. visitors (1992): *30 000 (est.)*

Facilities
Interpretation: *videos; leaflets; information boards; tour guides; personnel*
Schools: *maximum no. 65; educational literature; audio/visual presentation; lecture/talk*
Disabled: *easy access*
Catering: *1 picnic area*
Retailing: *postcards/inexpensive souvenirs; confectionery and ice cream; books; clothes; reproductions of famous artefacts; paintings; mugs; prints*
No. shops: *1*

Operations
Contact: *T Thomas (Trustee)*
No. employees: (high season) *9 full time; 2 part time* (low season) *9 full time; 2 part time*

Marketing
Annual event: *Thomas event*
Affiliation: *HETB*
UK promotion: *local newspapers; regional tourist board; leaflets/information packs*

BISHOPS' HOUSE
(local authority run)
historic house; museum

Established: *1976*
Address: *Meersbrook Park, Norton Lees Lane, Sheffield, S8 9BE*
Telephone: *(0742) 557701*
Access: (road) *M1/A61*
Season: *all year*
Hours: *Wed to Sat – 10am to 4.30pm, Sun – 11am to 4.30pm*
Admission (1992): *adults £0.80; children £0.40; OAP £0.40; student £0.80; ub40s free*
No. visitors (1992): *12 000 (est.)*

Facilities
Interpretation: *leaflets; information boards; maps; guide books*
Languages: *French; German*
Schools: *maximum no. 60; educational literature; lecture/talk; educational activities*
Retailing: *postcards/inexpensive souvenirs; books*
No. shops: *1*

Operations
Contacts: *Ms K Streets (Assistant Keeper of Social History); Mr D O'Grady (Merchandising Officer)*
No. employees: (high season) *2 full time* (low season) *2 full time*
Training: *F/T operations staff and F/T management are trained in-house and externally and on specific courses and day-to-day on job*

Marketing
Affiliation: *MA*
Other: *market research*
UK promotion: *national newspapers; radio; local newspapers; regional tourist board; other attractions; leaflets/information packs; Peacock Press Finding Out; ETB/BTA*

Environmental monitoring: *waste; hazardous materials; emissions*

BLACK COUNTRY MUSEUM
(limited company)
museum

Established: *1978*
Address: *Tipton Road, Dudley, West Midlands, DY1 4SQ*
Telephone: *(021) 557 9643.* Fax: *(021) 557 4242*
Access: (road) *M5/A4037* (rail) *Tipton/Sandwell*
Parking capacity: (cars) *200* (coaches) *20*
Season: *all year*
Hours: *Mar to Oct – Mon to Sun – 10am to 5pm. Nov to Jan – Wed to Sun – 10am to 4pm*
Admission (1992): *adults £4.95; children £3.45; OAP £4.45*
No. visitors (1992): *279 000*

Facilities
Interpretation: *videos; leaflets; information boards; tour guides; guide books; personnel*
Languages: *Japanese; French; German; Spanish; Chinese*
Children: *nappy changing*
Schools: *maximum no. 1000; educational literature*
Disabled: *disabled toilets*
Catering: *1 bar/public house*
Retailing: *postcards/inexpensive souvenirs; confectionery and ice cream; craftwork; books; clothes*
No. shops: *2*

Operations
No. employees: (high season) *50 full time; 90 part time* (low season) *50 full time; 30 part time*
Training: *F/T operations staff, F/T management, P/T operations staff, P/T management, casual operations staff and casual management are trained in-house and externally and on specific courses and day-to-day on job*

Marketing
Affiliations: *MA, AIM*
Other: *press office; market research*
UK promotion: *television; national newspapers; radio; local newspapers; regional tourist board; other attractions; leaflets/information packs; ETB/BTA*
USA promotion: *leaflets/brochures; British Tourist Authority*

BLACKBURN CATHEDRAL
(collegiate church)
church

Established: *1926*
Address: *The Cathedral Close, Blackburn, Lancs, BB1 5AA*
Telephone: *(0254) 51491*
Access: (road) *M6* (rail) *Blackburn*
Season: *all year*
Hours: *All year – Mon to Fri – 9am to 5.20pm, Sat – 9am to 4pm, Sun – 8am to 5pm*
Admission (1992): *free*
No. visitors (1992): *12 000 (est.)*

Facilities
Interpretation: *leaflets; information boards; tour guides; guide books*
Schools: *maximum no. 30; educational literature; educational tour*
Disabled: *easy access*
Retailing: *postcards/inexpensive souvenirs; craftwork; books; greetings cards, prayer cards*
No. shops: *1*

Operations
Contact: *D Eccles (Cathedral Secretary)*
No. employees: (high season) *8 full time; 9 part time* (low season) *8 full time; 9 part time*
Languages spoken: *French; German*

BLACKBURN MUSEUM AND ART GALLERY
(local authority run)
museum; gallery

Established: *1874*
Address: *Museum Street, Blackburn, Lancs, BB1 7AJ*
Telephone: *(0254) 667130.* Fax: *(0254) 680870*
Access: (road) *M6/M66/M65/A677/A666* (rail) *Blackburn*
Season: *all year*
Hours: *all year – Tues to Sat – 10am to 5pm*
Admission (1992): *free*
No. visitors (1992): *50 000 (est.)*

Facilities
Interpretation: *leaflets; information boards; guide books*
Languages: *Urdu; Gujarat*
Schools: *maximum no. 30; educational literature; lecture/talk; must book*
Disabled: *easy access; disabled toilets*
Retailing: *postcards/inexpensive souvenirs; guides, posters; guides to local area*
No. shops: *1*

Operations
Contacts: *M Millward (Curator/Manager); A Wallman (Keeper of Art); J Slack (Senior Technician); S Morris (Exhibitions Officer)*
No. employees: (high season) *12 full time; 5 part time* (low season) *12 full time; 5 part time*
Training: *F/T operations staff, F/T management and P/T operations staff are trained in-house and externally and on specific courses and day-to-day on job*

Marketing
Affiliations: *MA; NW Museums Service; NW Museums Federation*
UK promotion: *national newspapers; radio; local newspapers; regional tourist board; other attractions; leaflets/information packs*

BLACKPOOL PLEASURE BEACH
(limited company)
theme park

Established: *1992*
Address: *Ocean Boulevard, Blackpool, Lancs.*
Telephone: *(0253) 41033.* Fax: *(0253) 407609*
Access: (road) *M6/M55* (rail) *own station*
Parking capacity: (cars) *2000* (coaches) *400*
Hours: *March – Sat and Sun – From 10am. April to Nov – Mon to Sun – From 10am*
Admission (1992): *free*
No. visitors (1992): *6 570 000 (est.)*

Facilities
Interpretation: *videos; leaflets; information boards; slides; maps; tour guides; guide books; personnel; exhibitions, sponsorship, etc.*
Children: *adventure playground; play area; nappy changing*
Schools: *maximum no. 200; educational literature; audio/visual presentation*
Disabled: *easy access; disabled toilets; special signs; leaflets; guide book*
Catering: *12 bars/public houses*
Retailing: *postcards/inexpensive souvenirs; confectionery and ice cream; craftwork; books; clothes; reproductions of famous artefacts; perfume; toys; glassware, etc.*
No. shops: *More than 4*

Operations
Contacts: *C Fitton (Personnel Manager); Y Threlfall/D Westgate; D Thornton (Head of Sales and Marketing)*

No. employees: (high season) *300 full time; 1200 part time* (low season) *300 full time; 400 part time*
Training: *F/T operations staff, F/T management, P/T operations staff, P/T management, casual operations staff and casual management are trained in-house and on specific courses*
Languages spoken: *French; Gujarat; Urdu*

Marketing
Sponsor(s): *British Airways, National Express, etc.*
Affiliations: *BALPA, IAAPA, Europarks*
Other: *press office; market research*
UK promotion: *television; national newspapers; radio; local newspapers; regional tourist board; other attractions; leaflets/information packs; Various; ETB/BTA*
Europe/USA/Ireland promotion: *leaflets/brochures; travel agents' brochures; British Tourist Authority; ETB Regional Boards*

BLACKSHAW FARM PARK LTD
(limited company)
park/reserve; farm park

Established: *1986*
Address: *Dalry Road, West Kilbride, North Ayrshire, KA23 9PG*
Telephone: *(0563) 34257*
Access: (road) *B781* (rail) *West Kilbride*
Hours: *End Mar to end Aug – 10.30am to 5pm daily. Sept – Sat, Sun and Mon only*
Admission (1992): *adults £2.50; children £2.00; OAP £2.00; student £2.00; family in car £7.50 and reductions for groups*
No. visitors (1992): *48 000*

Facilities
Interpretation: *leaflets; information boards; slides; maps; tour guides*
Children: *adventure playground; play area; nappy changing*
Schools: *maximum no. 430; slide bank for hire*
Disabled: *easy access; disabled toilets; a few staff attend deaf signing course*
Catering: *7 picnic areas*
Retailing: *postcards/inexpensive souvenirs; confectionery and ice cream; craftwork; books; clothes*
No. shops: *2*

Operations
Contacts: *Mr William Weir (Managing Director); Aileen Todd (Administrator); Rita More and Doreen McIntyre (Shop Manageress and Co-ordinator)*
No. employees: (high season) *15 full time; 5 part time*
Training: *F/T operations staff, F/T management and P/T operations staff are trained in-house and externally and on specific courses and day-to-day on job and local enterprise courses using videos and handbooks*
Languages spoken: *French; German; Italian*

Marketing
Annual event(s): *sheepshearing and lambing*
UK promotion: *radio; local newspapers; regional tourist board; other attractions; leaflets/information packs*

Environmental monitoring: *energy consumption; hazardous materials; chemical usage; transport; emissions*

BLAIR CASTLE
(privately owned)
historic house; castle

Established: *1936*
Address: *Blair Atholl, Pitlochry, Perthshire, PH18 5TL*
Telephone: *(0796) 481207.* Fax: *(0796) 481487*
Access: (road) *A9* (rail) *Blair Atholl*
Parking capacity: (cars) *200* (coaches) *20*
Hours: *1 Apr to last Fri in Oct daily – 10am to 6pm. Last entry 5pm*

Admission (1992): *adults £4.00; children £3.00; OAP £3.00; student £3.00; family (2 adults and up to 5 children) £12.00; disabled £2.00*
No. visitors (1992): *165 000*

Facilities
Interpretation: *information boards; tour guides; guide books*
Languages: *Japanese; French; German; Italian; Spanish*
Schools: *educational literature*
Disabled: *easy access; disabled toilets*
Catering: *1 picnic area*
Retailing: *postcards/inexpensive souvenirs; craftwork; books*
No. shops: *1*

Operations
Contact: *Brian H Nodes (Administrator)*
No. employees: *(high season) 42 full time; 6 part time (low season) 7 full time; 1 part time*
Training: *F/T operations staff, F/T management and P/T operations staff are trained in-house and on specific courses and day-to-day on job*

Marketing
Annual event(s): *Atholl Highlanders parade, horse trials, world piping championships*
Sponsor: *Glenfiddich*
UK promotion: *local newspapers; regional tourist board; other attractions; leaflets/information packs*
Europe/USA promotion: *leaflets/brochures; travel agents' brochures*

BLAIR DRUMMOND SAFARI AND LEISURE PARK
(limited company)
zoo/wildlife attraction; safari and leisure park

Established: *1970*
Address: *Blair Drummond, Nr Stirling, FK9 4UR*
Telephone: *(0786) 841456.* Fax: *(0786) 841491*
Access: *(road) M9/A84 (rail) Stirling*
Parking capacity: *(cars) 2000 (coaches) 50*
Hours: *Apr to Oct – 10am to 5.30pm daily (last admission 4.30pm)*
Admission (1992): *adults £5.50; children £3.00; OAP £3.00; student £5.50; special rates for pre-booked groups and the handicapped; children under 3 free*
No. visitors (1992): *194 848*

Facilities
Interpretation: *leaflets; information boards; guide books; personnel*
Languages: *French; German; Italian; Spanish*
Children: *adventure playground; play area; nappy changing*
Schools: *no special support*
Disabled: *easy access; disabled toilets; powered transport; guide book; necessary helpers free*
Catering: *1 bar/public house*
Franchisees: *Apr to Oct – 10am to 5.30pm daily (last admission 4.30pm)*
Retailing: *postcards/inexpensive souvenirs; confectionery and ice cream; craftwork; books; clothes; toys related to animals; various*
No. shops: *2*

Operations
Contacts: *Ms A Rennick (Manager/Director); Mr M Riddell (Chief Game Warden); Mrs S Keary*
No. employees: *(high season) 33 full time; 2 part time (low season) 10 full time*
Training: *F/T operations staff, P/T operations staff and casual operations staff are trained in-house and day-to-day on job using handbooks*
Languages spoken: *French; German; Italian*

Marketing
Affiliation: *ASVA*
Other: *press office; market research*
UK promotion: *television; national newspapers; radio; local newspapers; regional tourist board; other attractions; leaflets/information packs; ETB/BTA; direct mail and promotions*

BLAISE CASTLE HOUSE MUSEUM
(local authority run)
museum

Established: *1949*
Address: *Henbury, Bristol, BS10 7QS*
Telephone: *(0272) 506759*
Access: *(road) M5*
Parking capacity: *(cars) 150*
Season: *all year*
Hours: *Sat to Wed – 10am to 1pm and 2pm to 5pm all year*
Admission (1992): *free*
No. visitors (1992): *55 000*

Facilities
Interpretation: *leaflets; information boards*
Schools: *maximum no. 50; Victorian role playing*
Disabled: *helpers*
Catering: *1 picnic area*
Franchisees: *Sat to Wed – 10am to 1pm and 2pm to 5pm all year*
Retailing: *postcards/inexpensive souvenirs; books*
No. shops: *1*

Operations
Contacts: *Mr D Eveleigh (Curator); Mr S Aubrey (security and bookings)*
No. employees: *(high season) 6 full time*
Training: *F/T operations staff are trained in-house and on specific courses*
Languages spoken: *French; German; Italian; Spanish*

Marketing
Annual event(s): *craft and activity days*
Sponsor: *Express Dairies*
Other: *press office*
UK promotion: *other attractions; leaflets/information packs; ETB/BTA*

Environmental monitoring: *water quality; tree protection*

BLENHEIM PALACE
(not specified)
historic house; monument; park/reserve; garden; gallery

Established: *1951*
Address: *Woodstock, Oxon*
Telephone: *(0993) 811091*
Access: *(road) M40/A44 (rail) Oxford*
Hours: *Mar to Oct – 10.30am to 5.30pm daily. Park open all year 9am to 5.30pm*
Admission (1992): *adults £6.00; children £3.00; OAP £4.50; student £4.50; group rates*
No. visitors (1992): *500 000*

Facilities
Interpretation: *videos; leaflets; audio tapes; information boards; slides; tour guides; guide books*
Languages: *Japanese; French; German; Italian; Spanish*
Children: *adventure playground*
Schools: *educational literature; audio/visual presentation; educational tour; lecture/talk; full education service*
Disabled: *easy access; disabled toilets; special signs*
Catering: *1 picnic area*
Franchisees: *Mar to Oct – 10.30am to 5.30pm daily*
Retailing: *postcards/inexpensive souvenirs; confectionery and ice cream; craftwork; books; clothes; reproductions of famous artefacts*
No. shops: *4*

Operations
Contact: *P F D Duffie (Administrator)*
Training: *F/T operations staff and P/T operations staff are trained in-house and externally and on specific courses and day-to-day on job using handbooks*
Languages spoken: *French*

Marketing
Annual event(s): *various*
Sponsor: *Audi*
Affiliations: *HHA, Treasure Houses of England*

Other: *market research*
UK promotion: *local newspapers; regional tourist board; other attractions; leaflets/information packs; ETB/BTA*
Europe/Asia/Australia/USA promotion: *leaflets/ brochures; travel agents' brochures; British Tourist Authority*

Environmental monitoring: *energy consumption; internal environment*

BLICKLING HALL
(trust)
historic house; park/reserve; garden

Established: *1956*
Address: *The National Trust, Blickling, Norwich, NR11 6NF*
Telephone: *(0263) 733084.* Fax: *(0263) 734924*
Parking capacity: *(cars) 350 (coaches) 7*
Hours: *(1992) Tues, Wed, Fri, Sat, Sun – restaurant – 11am to 5pm; gardens – 12 noon to 5pm; Hall 1pm to 5pm*
Admission (1992): *adults £4.90; children £2.40; charges include house and gardens, separate prices gardens only*
No. visitors (1992): *112 750*

Facilities
Interpretation: *leaflets; maps; tour guides; guide books*
Children: *nappy changing*
Schools: *maximum no. 60; educational literature; lecture/talk*
Disabled: *easy access; disabled toilets; braille/sound posts; special signs; guide book*
Catering: *1 bar/public house*
Retailing: *postcards/inexpensive souvenirs; craftwork; books; clothes*
No. shops: *1*

Operations
Contact: *Mr H Eaton (Administrator)*
No. employees: *(high season) 20 full time; 60 part time (low season) 20 full time*
Training: *F/T operations staff and P/T operations staff are trained in-house and day-to-day on job using videos and handbooks*
Languages spoken: *French; German; Italian; Spanish; Japanese*

Marketing
Annual event(s): *concerts and fête*
Affiliations: *local tourist association*
Other: *press office; market research*
UK promotion: *local newspapers; regional tourist board; leaflets/information packs; local attraction consortium*
Australia/USA promotion: *leaflets/brochures; radio; British Tourist Authority*

BLUEBELL RAILWAY, THE
(plc)
preserved steam railway

Established: *1960*
Address: *Sheffield Park Station, Nr Uckfield, E Sussex, TN22 3QL*
Telephone: *(0825) 723777.* Fax: *(0825) 724139*
Access: *(road) M23/M25/A275 (rail) Haywards Heath*
Parking capacity: *(cars) 400 (coaches) 20*
Season: *all year*
Hours: *June to Sept – 10am to 5pm daily; Jan and Feb – Sun – 10am to 5pm; weekends in spring and autumn*
Admission (1992): *adults £6.00; children £3.00; OAP £5.20*
No. visitors (1992): *205 000 (est.)*

Facilities
Interpretation: *videos; leaflets; information boards; slides; guide books; society members' input*
Languages: *French*
Children: *nappy changing*
Schools: *maximum no. 50; educational literature; educational tour; lecture/talk*

Disabled: *disabled toilets*
Catering: *1 bar/public house*
Retailing: *postcards/inexpensive souvenirs;
  confectionery and ice cream; books*
No. shops: *4*

Operations
Contacts: *M Miller (Operations Manager); J E
  Potter (Company Secretary)*
No. employees: (high season) *22 full time;
  10 part time* (low season) *21 full time; 3 part
  time*
Training: *F/T operations staff and P/T operations
  staff are trained in-house and on specific
  courses and day-to-day on job*

Marketing
Annual event(s): *steam galas, vintage day*
Affiliations: *AIR*
Other: *press office; market research*
UK promotion: *radio; local newspapers; regional
  tourist board; other attractions;
  leaflets/information packs; SEETB publications*
BTA Offices promotion: *leaflets/brochures;
  British Tourist Authority*

Environmental monitoring: *waste; water quality;
  energy consumption*

BLUE POOL
(sole trader)
heritage centre; park/reserve; museum

Established: *1935*
Address: *Furzebrook, Wareham, Dorset, BH20
  5AT*
Telephone: *(0929) 551408*
Access: (road) *A351* (rail) *Wareham*
Parking capacity: (cars) *200* (coaches) *6*
Hours: *Easter to Oct – 10am to 6pm daily, later
  in high season*
Admission (1992): *adults £1.60; children £0.80;
  OAP £1.20; student £1.60; groups by
  arrangement*
No. visitors (1992): *73 485*

Facilities
Interpretation: *leaflets; guide books*
Children: *adventure playground; nappy changing*
Schools: *maximum no. 100; no special support*
Disabled: *disabled toilets*
Catering: *1 picnic area*
Retailing: *postcards/inexpensive souvenirs;
  confectionery and ice cream; books; general
  gifts; toys*
No. shops: *2*

Operations
Contact: *Miss J Barnard (owner)*
No. employees: (high season) *4 full time; 13 part
  time* (low season) *3 full time; 7 part time*

Marketing
Market research
UK promotion: *local newspapers; regional tourist
  board; leaflets/information packs*

BOAT MUSEUM, THE
(trust)
museum

Established: *1976*
Address: *Dockyard Rd, Ellesmere Port, South
  Wirral, L65 4EF*
Telephone: *(051) 355 5017.* Fax: *(051) 355 4079*
Access: (road) *M53* (rail) *Ellesmere Port*
Parking capacity: (cars) *500* (coaches) *12*
Season: *all year*
Hours: *Apr to Oct – 10am to 5pm daily; Nov to
  Mar – 11am to 4pm daily except Fri*
Admission (1992): *adults £4.00; children £2.70;
  OAP £3.00; student £3.00; family £12.50*
No. visitors (1992): *84 367*

Facilities
Interpretation: *videos; leaflets; information
  boards; maps; tour guides; guide books*
Languages: *French*
Children: *play area; nappy changing*

Schools: *maximum no. 500; educational literature;
  educational tour; lecture/talk*
Disabled: *easy access; disabled toilets; helpers;
  leaflets*
Catering: *1 picnic area*
Retailing: *postcards/inexpensive souvenirs;
  craftwork; books; clothes*
No. shops: *1*

Operations
No. employees: (high season) *9 full time; 24 part
  time* (low season) *8 full time; 20 part time*
Training: *F/T operations staff, F/T management,
  P/T operations staff, P/T management, casual
  operations staff and casual management are
  trained in-house and externally and on specific
  courses and day-to-day on job using handbooks
  and Technical visits*

Marketing
Other: *press office; market research*
UK promotion: *local newspapers; regional tourist
  board; other attractions; leaflets/information
  packs*

Environmental monitoring: *recycling; emissions*

BOD OF GREMISTA
(local authority run)
historic house; museum; reconstructed
  seventeenth-century fishing bod

Established: *1987*
Address: *c/o Shetland Museum, Lower Hillhead,
  Lerwick, ZE1 0EL*
Telephone: *(0595) 5057.* Fax: *(0595) 6729*
Access: (road) *P & O ferry, Aberdeen*
Parking capacity: (cars) *30* (coaches) *7*
Hours: *1 Apr to 30 Sept – daily except Mon and
  Fri*
Admission (1992): *adults £1.00; children £0.50;
  OAP £0.50;*
No. visitors (1992): *700 (est.)*

Facilities
Interpretation: *information boards; tour guides;
  guide books*
Schools: *maximum no. 50; educational literature;
  lecture/talk*
Disabled: *disabled facilities lower floor only*
Retailing: *postcards/inexpensive souvenirs; books*
No. shops: *1*

Operations
Contact: *As for Shetland Museum*
No. employees: (high season) *1 part time*

Marketing
UK promotion: *radio; local newspapers;
  leaflets/information packs*

Environmental monitoring: *designated scientific
  interest*

BODMIN AND WENFORD RAILWAY
(trust)
private railway

Established: *1985*
Address: *General Station, Bodmin, Cornwall,
  PL31 1AQ*
Telephone: *(0208) 73666*
Access: (road) *B3268* (rail) *Bodmin Parkway*
Parking capacity: (cars) *40* (coaches) *3*
Hours: *Easter to Oct and Dec – 10am to 5.30pm
  daily*
Admission (1992): *adults £3.90; children £2.50;
  OAP £3.50; family £11.50*
No. visitors (1992): *30 000 (est.)*

Facilities
Interpretation: *leaflets; tour guides; guide books*
Schools: *maximum no. 100; educational tour;
  lecture/talk*
Disabled: *support for all*
Catering: *2 picnic areas*
Retailing: *postcards/inexpensive souvenirs; books;
  Thomas the Tank Engine items*
No. shops: *1*

Operations
Contacts: *K Searle (General Manager); T Croft
  (Assistant Manager)*
No. employees: (high season) *1 full time; 4 part
  time* (low season) *1 full time; 2 part time*
Training: *F/T operations staff, P/T operations
  staff and casual operations staff are trained
  in-house and on specific courses and day-to-day
  on job*

Marketing
Annual event(s): *various*
Affiliations: *AIR, ARPS, WCTB*
Other: *press office; market research*
UK promotion: *radio; local newspapers; regional
  tourist board; leaflets/information packs; local
  area guides*

BODMIN TOWN MUSEUM
(local authority run)
museum

Established: *1970*
Address: *Mount Folly, Bodmin, Cornwall, PL31
  2HQ*
Telephone: *(0208) 74159*
Access: (road) *A389/30* (rail) *Bodmin Parkway*
Hours: *Easter to Oct – Mon to Sat – 10am to 4pm*
Admission (1992): *free*
No. visitors (1992): *9500*

Facilities
Interpretation: *leaflets; information boards*
Schools: *maximum no. 30; educational literature;
  educational tour*
Retailing: *postcards/inexpensive souvenirs; books;
  minerals*
No. shops: *1*

Operations
Contacts: *M England (Curator); P Davies
  (Chairman, Museum committee); D Watts
  (Shop Manager); S Meads (Museums Officer,
  N Cornwall Council)*
Training: *casual operations staff and casual
  management are trained externally and on
  specific courses*

Marketing
UK promotion: *regional tourist board; other
  attractions; leaflets/information packs; West
  Country Tourist Board*

Environmental monitoring: *transport; habitat
  management on railway*

BODNANT GARDENS
(trust)
garden

Established: *1949*
Address: *Tal-y-Cafn, Nr. Colwyn Bay, Clwyd,
  LL28 5RE*
Telephone: *(0492) 650460.* Fax: *(0492) 650448*
Access: (road) *M6/M56/A470*
Parking capacity: (cars) *250* (coaches) *15*
Hours: *mid-Mar to end Oct daily – 10am to 5pm*
Admission (1992): *adults £3.30; children £1.65;
  groups of 20+ £2.90 each*
No. visitors (1992): *182 672*

Facilities
Interpretation: *leaflets; slides; maps; guide books*
Languages: *Welsh*
Children: *nappy changing*
Schools: *lecture/talk*
Disabled: *easy access; disabled toilets; guide
  book; free use of wheelchairs for visit*
Catering: *1 waiter/waitress served*
Retailing: *postcards/inexpensive souvenirs;
  confectionery and ice cream; craftwork; books;
  plants; horticultural sundries*
No. shops: *3*

Operations
Contacts: *M R Puddle (Head Gardener and
  General Manager); Mrs A Harvey (PA to
  General Manager)*

No. employees: (high season) *24 full time; 20 part
time* (low season) *24 full time; 20 part time*
Training: *F/T operations staff, F/T management,
P/T operations staff and casual operations staff
are trained in-house and externally and on
specific courses and day-to-day on job using
handbooks*

Marketing
Affiliations: *National Trust, Wales Tourist Board*
Other: *press office; market research*
UK promotion: *television; national newspapers;
local newspapers; regional tourist board; other
attractions; leaflets/information packs;
ETB/BTA*
Europe/Australia/USA promotion: *British Tourist
Authority; WTB; gardening societies*

BODRHYDDAN HALL
(private property)
historic house; garden

Established: *1953*
Address: *Rhuddlan, Clwyd, North Wales, LL18
5SB*
Telephone: *(0745) 590414*
Access: (road) *A55*
Parking capacity: (cars) *100* (coaches) *20*
Hours: *June to Sept incl – Tues and Thur – 2pm
to 5.30pm*
Admission (1992): *adults £2.00; children £1.00;*
No. visitors (1992): *5000 (est.)*

Facilities
Interpretation: *leaflets; guides*
Children: *play area*
Schools: *local school parties only*
Disabled: *helpers; guide book*
Catering: *1 waiter/waitress served*
Retailing: *postcards/inexpensive souvenirs;
reproductions of famous artefacts*
No. shops: *1*

Operations
Contacts: *Colonel the Lord Langford (owner)*
No. employees: (high season) *3 full time; 10 part
time* (low season) *3 full time; 2 part time*
Languages spoken: *Welsh*

Marketing
Affiliations: *HHA, CLA*
UK promotion: *other attractions; WTB*

Environmental monitoring: *recycling; water
quality; hazardous materials; chemical usage*

BOLLING HALL
(local authority run)
historic house; museum

Established: *1915*
Address: *Bowling Hall Rd, Bradford, W Yorks,
BD4 7LP*
Telephone: *(0274) 723057*
Access: (road) *M606/A650* (rail) *Bradford*
Parking capacity: (cars) *60* (coaches) *10*
Season: *all year*
Hours: *Tues to Sun – Apr to Sept – 10am to 6pm,
Oct to Mar – 10am to 5pm, closed Christmas
Day, open BH*
Admission (1992): *free*
No. visitors (1992): *40 400*

Facilities
Interpretation: *leaflets; information boards; guide
books*
Children: *nappy changing*
Schools: *maximum no. 100; no special support*
Disabled: *disabled toilets; braille/sound posts*
Retailing: *postcards/inexpensive souvenirs; books*
No. shops: *1*

Marketing
Press office; market research
UK promotion: *other attractions;
leaflets/information packs*

BOLTON ABBEY ESTATE
(trust)
heritage centre; zoo/wildlife attraction; church;
country estate

Established: *1892*
Address: *Bolton Abbey, Skipton, N Yorks, BD23
6EX*
Telephone: *(0756) 710533.* Fax: *(0756) 710535*
Access: (road) *A59*
Parking capacity: (cars) *2500* (coaches) *24*
Season: *all year*
Hours: *Estate open all year. Priory Church –
Summer – 9am to dusk, Winter – 9am to 4pm
(closed 4pm every Fri)*
Admission (1992): *£2.00 per car, £1.00 disabled
drivers, coaches free, 50p motorcycles*
No. visitors (1992): *500 000 (est.)*

Facilities
Interpretation: *leaflets; information boards; maps;
guide books*
Languages: *Japanese; Dutch; French; German;
Italian; Spanish*
Children: *nappy changing*
Schools: *lecture/talk*
Disabled: *easy access; disabled toilets; special
signs; powered transport; leaflets*
Catering: *1 bar/public house*
Retailing: *postcards/inexpensive souvenirs;
confectionery and ice cream; craftwork; books;
clothes; preserves and biscuits*
No. shops: *3*

Operations
Contacts: *Mrs B Allen (Tourism Manager);
Mr J Sheard (Agent)*
No. employees: (high season) *6 full time; 24 part
time* (low season) *6 full time; 4 part time*
Training: *F/T operations staff, F/T management
and P/T operations staff are trained in-house
and externally and on specific courses and
day-to-day on job*

Marketing
Market research
UK promotion: *regional tourist board; other
attractions; leaflets/information packs*

BOOK MUSEUM
(privately owned)
museum

Established: *1977*
Address: *Manvers St, Bath, BA1 1JW*
Telephone: *(0225) 466000.* Fax: *(0225) 482122*
Access: (road) *M4/A4* (rail) *Bath*
Season: *all year*
Hours: *Mon to Fri – 9am to 1pm and 2pm to
5.30pm, Sat – 9.30am to 1pm*
Admission (1992): *free*
No. visitors (1992): *2500 (est.)*

Facilities
Interpretation: *leaflets; information boards*
Retailing: *books; antiquarian books and prints*
No. shops: *2*

Operations
Contacts: *Mr H Bayntun-Coward (owner)*
No. employees: (high season) *2 part time*
(low season) *1 part time*

Marketing
Affiliations: *Antiquarian Booksellers Association*
Other: *press office; market research*
UK promotion: *leaflets/information packs*
Europe/USA promotion: *leaflets/brochures*

Environmental monitoring: *waste; water quality;
hazardous materials; chemical usage; transport*

BORDER HISTORY MUSEUM
(local authority run)
museum

Established: *1980*
Address: *Old Gaol, Nr Market Place, Hexham,
Northumberland*

Telephone: *(0434) 604011.* Fax: *(0434) 601874*
Access: (road) *A69* (rail) *Hexham*
Parking capacity: (cars) *1000* (coaches) *25*
Hours: *Easter to Oct – Mon to Sat – 10am to
4.30pm, May to end Sept – 10am to 4.30pm
daily, Feb to Easter and Nov – Mon, Tues, Sat,
Sun – 10am to 4.30pm. Closed Dec and Jan*
Admission (1992): *adults £1.20; children £0.50;
OAP £0.50; student £0.50;*
No. visitors (1992): *14 500 (est.)*

Facilities
Interpretation: *videos; leaflets; audio tapes;
information boards; maps; tour guides; guides
by appointment*
Languages: *French; German; Danish*
Schools: *educational literature; audio/visual
presentation; lecture/talk; links with other
attractions*
Disabled: *braille/sound posts; leaflets*
Retailing: *postcards/inexpensive souvenirs;
craftwork; books; clothes; reproductions of
famous artefacts; replicas of period objects;
roman items*
No. shops: *2*

Operations
Contacts: *Ms J Goodridge (Museums Officer);
Ms F Fairburn (Museum Development
Assistant); Ms S Wilson (Marketing Officer)*
No. employees: (high season) *2 full time;
4 part time* (low season) *2 full time; 2 part
time*
Training: *F/T operations staff, F/T management,
P/T operations staff, P/T management, casual
operations staff and casual management are
trained in-house and externally and on specific
courses and day-to-day on job using handbooks*
Languages spoken: *French; German*

Marketing
Affiliation: *MA*
Other: *market research*
UK promotion: *radio; local newspapers; regional
tourist board; other attractions; leaflets/
information packs; ETB/BTA*

Environmental monitoring: *recycling; waste;
energy consumption*

BOTANIC CENTRE
(limited company by guarantee)
environmental centre

Established: *1992*
Address: *Ladgate Lane, Acklam, Middlesbrough,
Cleveland*
Telephone: *(0642) 594895.* Fax: *(06420) 596376*
Access: (road) *M1/A19/A1*
Parking capacity: (cars) *200* (coaches) *100*
Season: *all year*
Hours: *Apr to Oct – 11am to 5pm – Wed to Sun,
Nov to Mar – 11am to 3pm – Wed to Sun*
Admission (1992): *adults £2.00; children £0.50;
OAP £1.30; student £1.30; ub40s £1.30*
No. visitors (1992): *15 000 (est.)*

Facilities
Interpretation: *leaflets; information boards; slides;
tour guides; guide books*
Children: *nappy changing*
Schools: *maximum no. 30; lecture/talk; hands on
activities*
Disabled: *easy access; disabled toilets; helpers;
leaflets*
Catering: *1 picnic area*
Retailing: *confectionery and ice cream; craftwork;
books; environmental products*
No. shops: *1*

Operations
Contacts: *Mr S Goldie (Business Manager);
Ms Y Lockwood (PR/Personnel Manager);
Mr I Thompson (Shop and Gardens Manager)*
No. employees: (high season) *8 full time;
8 part time* (low season) *8 full time; 4 part
time*
Training: *P/T operations staff and casual
operations staff are trained in-house and
day-to-day on job using videos and handbooks*
Languages spoken: *German*

Marketing
Annual event: *Help the Earth Week*
Sponsor: *Phillips*
Other: *market research*
UK promotion: *television; national newspapers; radio; local newspapers; regional tourist board; leaflets/information packs; NTB, Gardens of Northumbria and places to visit in Winter*

BOUGHTON HOUSE
(trust)
historic house; park/reserve; working country estate

Established: *1977*
Address: *Boughton House, Kettering, Northamptonshire*
Telephone: *(0536) 515731. Fax: (0536) 417255*
Access: (road) *M1/A43/A14* (rail) *Kettering*
Hours: *Grounds – 1 May to 30 Sept – 1pm to 5pm daily except Fri. House and grounds – 1 Aug to 1 Sept – 2pm to 5pm daily*
Admission (1992): *adults £4.00; children £2.50; OAP £2.50; student £2.50;*

Facilities
Interpretation: *leaflets; information boards; maps; tour guides; guide books; personnel*
Children: *adventure playground; nappy changing*
Schools: *maximum no. 45; educational literature; audio/visual presentation; lecture/talk*
Disabled: *easy access; disabled toilets; helpers*
Catering: *1 picnic area*
Retailing: *postcards/inexpensive souvenirs; confectionery and ice cream; books; reproductions of famous artefacts; garden centre*
No. shops: *2*

Operations
Contacts: *Mr G Fitzpatrick (Director); Ms J Dornan (House manager); Ms E Elwood (Marketing manager)*
No. employees: (high season) *12 full time; 60 part time* (low season) *12 full time; 20 part time*
Training: *F/T operations staff, F/T management, P/T operations staff, P/T management, casual operations staff and casual management are trained in-house and day-to-day on job using slides and guides*
Languages spoken: *French; German; Russian*

Marketing
Annual event(s): *estate open days*
Affiliations: *HHA, Heritage Education Trust, Northants farm attractions and E. Midlands Tourist Board*
Other: *PR Company: Irwin Jordan Ltd, 63 Weekley, Kettering, Northants; market research*
UK promotion: *national newspapers; radio; local newspapers; regional tourist board; other attractions; leaflets/information packs; ETB/BTA; Northants Enterprise Agency*
Europe/USA promotion: *leaflets/brochures; travel agents' brochures; British Tourist Authority*

Environmental monitoring: *recycling; waste; water quality; energy consumption; hazardous materials; chemical usage; transport; emissions*

BOUGHTON MONCHELSEA PLACE
(trust)
historic house

Established: *1960*
Address: *Boughton Monchelsea, Maidstone, Kent, ME17 4BU*
Telephone: *(0622) 743120. Fax: (0622) 743120*
Access: (road) *M20/A274/A299* (rail) *Maidstone*
Parking capacity: (cars) *500*
Hours: *Easter to Oct – Sun and BH – 2.15pm to 6pm. Open Wed also in July and August*
Admission (1992): *adults £3.25; children £2.00; OAP £2.75; student £2.75; disabled £2.75*
No. visitors (1992): *5000*

Facilities
Interpretation: *leaflets; tour guides; guide books*
Languages: *Dutch; French; German*

Children: *play area*
Schools: *maximum no. 52; educational literature*
Disabled: *easy access; disabled toilets*
Catering: *1 licensed restaurant*
Retailing: *postcards/inexpensive souvenirs; craftwork; books*
No. shops: *1*

Operations
Contacts: *C Gooch (Owner); J Harris (Secretary)*
No. employees: (high season) *2 full time; 16 part time* (low season) *2 full time; 6 part time*
Training: *P/T operations staff are trained in-house and day-to-day on job using videos*
Languages spoken: *French; German; Japanese; Welsh*

Marketing
Annual event: *craft fair*
Affiliation: *HHA*
UK promotion: *radio; local newspapers; regional tourist board; other attractions; leaflets/information packs; SEETB*
Europe promotion: *leaflets/brochures; ATAK*

Environmental monitoring: *recycling; waste; water quality; energy consumption; hazardous materials; chemical usage*

BOURNEMOUTH HERITAGE TRANSPORT CENTRE
(trust)
museum

Established: *1979*
Address: *Yellow Buses Depot, Mallard Rd, Bournemouth, Dorset*
Telephone: *(0202) 537011*
Access: (road) *M3/M27* (rail) *Bournemouth*
Parking capacity: (cars) *50* (coaches) *6*
Hours: *May to Sept – Wed – 10am to 4pm, Sat and Sun – 10am to 4pm*
Admission (1992): *adults £1.50; children £0.75; OAP £1.00; student £1.00; family ticket (2+2) £4.00*
No. visitors (1992): *500 (est.)*

Facilities
Interpretation: *leaflets; information boards; tour guides*
Schools: *maximum no. 40; educational literature*
Disabled: *easy access*
Catering: *1 snack bar/food stall*
Retailing: *postcards/inexpensive souvenirs; books; models and transport related*
No. shops: *1*

Operations
Contacts: *Ms V Jeffries (Managing Director); Mr M Peters (Marketing/PR operations)*
No. employees: (high season) *4 full time; 2 part time* (low season) *2 part time*
Training: *F/T operations staff and P/T operations staff are trained externally and day-to-day on job*
Languages spoken: *French; German; Dutch*

Marketing
Affiliations: *National Association of Road Transport Museums*
Other: *press office*
UK promotion: *regional tourist board; other attractions; leaflets/information packs; Bournemouth Tourism Guide*

BOWES RAILWAY CENTRE
(charitable limited co)
monument; heritage centre; unique rope-hauled railway

Established: *1976*
Address: *Springwell Village, Gateshead, Tyne and Wear, NE9 7QJ*
Telephone: *(091) 4161847*
Access: (road) *A1M/B1288* (rail) *Newcastle*
Season: *all year*
Hours: *Easter to Sept – 1st and 3rd Sun and BH – 12 noon to 5pm as working railway (static display every Sat all year round)*

Admission (1992): *adults £2.25; children £1.25; OAP £1.25;*
No. visitors (1992): *5000 (est.)*

Facilities
Interpretation: *information boards; tour guides; guide books*
Schools: *educational literature*
Disabled: *easy access; disabled toilets*
Catering: *1 picnic area*
Retailing: *postcards/inexpensive souvenirs; books*
No. shops: *1*

Operations
Contacts: *Mr H Maddison (Railway Centre Assistant); Mr P Norman (Railway Secretary); Mr A Nicholson (Publicity Officer)*
No. employees: (high season) *1 full time* (low season) *1 full time*

Marketing
Sponsor(s): Local industries
Affiliations: *Association of Railway Preservation Societies, and Northumbria Tourist Board*
Other: *PR Company: HCD Associates, 16 Newbank Walk Winlaton, Tyne and Wear; market research*
UK promotion: *radio; local newspapers; other attractions; leaflets/information packs; local tourist board*

Environmental monitoring: *transport*

BOWHILL HOUSE AND COUNTRY PARK
(trust)
historic house; park/reserve; garden; museum; gallery; theatre

Established: *1975*
Address: *Bowhill, Selkirk, TD7 5ET*
Telephone: *(0750) 20732. Fax: (0750) 22172*
Access: (road) *M6/A7/A708* (rail) *Edinburgh or Berwick*
Parking capacity: (cars) *100* (coaches) *10*
Hours: *country park 28 Apr to 28 Aug – 12 noon to 5pm (not Fridays except in July). House 1 to 31 July – 1pm to 4.30pm*
Admission (1992): *adults £3.00; children £1.00; OAP £2.00; student £2.00; groups 20+ £2.50. Half price for park only*
No. visitors (1992): *11 000 (est.)*

Facilities
Interpretation: *videos; leaflets; information boards; maps; tour guides; guide books*
Children: *adventure playground; play area*
Schools: *educational literature; audio/visual presentation; lecture/talk; education officer*
Disabled: *easy access; disabled toilets; helpers; guided tours for blind*
Catering: *3 picnic areas*
Retailing: *postcards/inexpensive souvenirs; confectionery and ice cream; craftwork; books; clothes; reproductions of famous artefacts; paperweights, prints*
No. shops: *2*

Operations
Contacts: *Mary Carter (House and Theatre Manager)*
No. employees: (high season) *6 full time; 25 part time* (low season) *6 full time; 4 part time*
Training: *F/T operations staff, F/T management, P/T operations staff and casual operations staff are trained in-house and on specific courses and day-to-day on job*

Marketing
Annual event(s): *various*
Affiliations: *HHA, Scotland's border heritage*
Other: *market research*
UK promotion: *radio; local newspapers; regional tourist board; other attractions; leaflets/information packs; local visitor magazines; ETB/BTA*
USA promotion: *leaflets/brochures; USA Scottish games*

BOWOOD HOUSE
(private)
historic house; garden

Established: *1975*
Address: *The Estate Office, Bowood Estates, Calne, Wilts, SN11 0LZ*
Telephone: *(0249) 812102.* Fax: *(0249) 821757*
Access: (road) *M4/A4* (rail) *Chippenham*
Parking capacity: (cars) *1000*
Hours: *Apr to Oct – 11am to 6pm daily*
Admission (1992): *adults £4.50; children £2.25; OAP £3.80*
No. visitors (1992): *150 000 (est.)*

Facilities
Interpretation: *leaflets; information boards; guide books*
Children: *adventure playground; nappy changing*
Schools: *education pack on request*
Disabled: *easy access; disabled toilets; wheelchair*
Catering: *1 picnic area*
Retailing: *postcards/inexpensive souvenirs; craftwork; books; reproductions of famous artefacts; paintings, mugs, pencils, etc; garden centre*
No. shops: *2*

Operations
No. employees: (high season) *14 full time; 60 part time* (low season) *14 full time; 5 part time*
Languages spoken: *French; German*

Marketing
Affiliation:*HHA*
Other: *PR Company: Vincent Chappell and Jackson, 21 Rolle St, Exmouth, Devon; market research*
UK promotion: *television; local newspapers; regional tourist board; other attractions; leaflets/information packs*

Environmental monitoring: *recycling; water quality; energy consumption; chemical usage*

BRADFORD INDUSTRIAL HORSES AT WORK MUSEUM
(local authority run)
museum

Established: *1976*
Address: *Moorside Rd, Bradford, BD2 3HP*
Telephone: *(0274) 631756.* Fax: *(0274) 636362*
Access: (road) *M62/M606/A658*
Parking capacity: (cars) *50* (coaches) *7*
Season: *all year*
Hours: *Tues to Sun – 10am to 5pm, also BH*
Admission (1992): *free*
No. visitors (1992): *120 000 (est.)*

Facilities
Interpretation: *leaflets*
Children: *nappy changing*
Schools: *maximum no. 300; lecture/talk; demos; Victorian school*
Disabled: *easy access; disabled toilets; braille/sound posts; helpers*
Catering: *1 self-service cafeteria*
Retailing: *postcards/inexpensive souvenirs; confectionery and ice cream; books*
No. shops: *1*

Operations
Contacts: *Mr R McHugh (Keeper of Technology); Mr S Kerry (Principal Officer, visitor services); Mrs P Kendal (Administration); Ms J Whittaker/Ms L Killick (Marketing Officers, arts and museums)*
No. employees: (high season) *40 full time*
Training: *F/T operations staff, F/T management, P/T operations staff and casual operations staff are trained externally and on specific courses*

Marketing
Other: *market research*
UK promotion: *local newspapers; regional tourist board; leaflets/information packs*

BRADFORD ON AVON MUSEUM
(trust)
museum

Established: *1990*
Address: *Bridge Street, Bradford on Avon, Wilts, BA15 1BY*
Telephone: *(0225) 863280*
Access: (road) *M4/A363* (rail) *Bradford on Avon*
Parking capacity: (cars) *30*
Season: *all year*
Hours: *Easter to Oct – Mon to Sat – 10.30am to 4pm, Sun – 2pm to 4pm. Oct to Easter – Mon to Fri and Sun – 2pm to 4pm, Sat – 10.30am to 4pm*
Admission (1992): *free*
No. visitors (1992): *17 363*

Facilities
Interpretation: *information boards; maps*
Languages: *French; German*
Schools: *maximum no. 20; no special support*
Disabled: *easy access; disabled toilets; powered transport; lift*
Retailing: *postcards/inexpensive souvenirs*
No. shops: *1*

Operations
Contacts: *R D Clark (Honorary Curator); L Ladd*
Training: *casual operations staff are trained in-house and day-to-day on job using videos*
Languages spoken: *French; German; Ukrainian*

Marketing
Affiliations: *AIM, Area Museum Council For SW*
UK promotion: *local newspapers; regional tourist board; leaflets/information packs; ETB/BTA*

Environmental monitoring: *hazardous materials*

BRAMHAM PARK
(not known)
historic house; garden

Established: *1949*
Address: *Wetherby, W Yorks, LS23 6ND*
Telephone: *(0937) 844265*
Access: (road) *A1*
Parking capacity: (cars) *60* (coaches) *6*
Hours: *Jun to Aug – Sun, Tues, Wed and Thurs*
Admission (1992): *adults £3.00; children £1.00; OAP £2.00*
No. visitors (1992): *3000 (est.)*

Facilities
Interpretation: *leaflets; guide books*
Schools: *no special support*
Disabled: *easy access; disabled toilets*
Catering: *1 picnic area*

Operations
No. employees: (high season) *7 part time*

Marketing
Annual event: *International Three-Day Event*
UK promotion: *local newspapers; regional tourist board; leaflets/information packs; ETB/BTA*

Environmental monitoring: *Temperature and relative humidity*

BRANKLYN GARDEN
(trust)
garden

Established: *1968*
Address: *116 Dundee Rd, Perth, PH2 7BB*
Telephone: *(0738) 25535*
Parking capacity: (cars) *60* (coaches) *2*
Hours: *1 Mar to end Oct – 9.30am to sunset daily*
Admission (1992): *adults £2.00; children £1.00; OAP £1.00; student £1.00; group rates available*
No. visitors (1992): *18 900*

Facilities
Interpretation: *information boards; guide books*
Schools: *maximum no. 20; educational literature; lecture/talk*

Retailing: *postcards/inexpensive souvenirs; books; NT goods*
No. shops: *1*

Operations
Contact: *Mr B Mitchell (Property Administrator)*
No. employees: (high season) *4 full time; 3 part time* (low season) *4 full time*
Training: *F/T operations staff, F/T management, P/T operations staff and casual operations staff are trained in-house and externally and on specific courses*

Marketing
Annual event(s): *Lectures and garden walks*
Affiliations: *ASVA*
Other: *press office; market research*
UK promotion: *national newspapers; local newspapers; regional tourist board; leaflets/information packs; STB*
USA promotion: *British Tourist Authority*

BREAMORE HOUSE AND MUSEUMS
(limited company)
historic house; museum

Established: *1952*
Address: *Breamore, Nr Fordingbridge, Hampshire, SP6 2DF*
Telephone: *(0725) 22468*
Access: (road) *M27/A338* (rail) *Salisbury*
Parking capacity: (cars) *400* (coaches) *10*
Hours: *Apr – Tues, Wed, Sun and Easter holiday, May, Jun, Jul and Sept – Tues, Wed, Thurs, Sat, Sun and all BH, Aug – daily, 2pm to 5.30pm*
Admission (1992): *adults £4.00; children £2.50; OAP £3.50; student £2.50*
No. visitors (1992): *17 742*

Facilities
Interpretation: *leaflets; tour guides; guide books*
Languages: *Dutch; French; German; Italian; Spanish*
Children: *adventure playground*
Schools: *maximum no. 100; educational literature; lecture/talk*
Disabled: *easy access; disabled toilets*
Catering: *1 picnic area*
Franchisees: *Apr – Tues, Wed, Sun and Easter holiday, May, Jun, Jul and Sept – Tues, Wed, Thurs, Sat, Sun and all BH, Aug – daily*
Retailing: *postcards/inexpensive souvenirs; confectionery and ice cream; books; tea towels; gnomes*
No. shops: *1*

Operations
Contacts: *E Hulse (owner); Mrs E Dymott (shop)*
No. employees: (high season) *3 full time; 28 part time* (low season) *3 full time; 5 part time*

Marketing
Annual event: *Breamore rally and craft show*
Sponsor: *H & D Read*
Affiliations: *HHA*
Other: *PR Company: Historic House and Tourist Attractions Marketing, 21 Rolle St, Exmouth, Devon; market research*
UK promotion: *local newspapers; regional tourist board; other attractions; leaflets/information packs*

Environmental monitoring: *chemical usage; Use of peat*

BRECON BEACONS MOUNTAIN CENTRE
(national park authority)
visitor/information centre

Established: *1965*
Address: *Libanus, Nr Brecon, Powys, LD3 8SN*
Telephone: *(0874) 623366*
Access: (road) *A470*
Parking capacity: (cars) *150* (coaches) *2*
Season: *all year*
Hours: *Summer – Mon to Sun – 9.30am to 6pm, Spring/Autumn – Mon to Sun – 9.30am to 5pm, Winter – Mon to Sun – 9.30am to 4.30pm, closed Christmas Day*

Admission (1992): *free*
No. visitors (1992): *133 849*

Facilities
Interpretation: *videos; leaflets; information boards; slides; maps; tour guides; guide books*
Languages: *French; German*
Children: *nappy changing*
Schools: *maximum no. 55; educational literature; audio/visual presentation; lecture/talk*
Disabled: *easy access; disabled toilets; helpers; other audio facilities; wheelchair access to lectures*
Catering: *1 picnic area*
Retailing: *postcards/inexpensive souvenirs; confectionery and ice cream; craftwork; books; clothes; maps, compasses, etc.*
No. shops: *1*

Operations
Contacts: *B R Watkins (Manager); Peter Williams (Assistant Manager)*
No. employees: (high season) *4 full time; 8 part time* (low season) *4 full time; 4 part time*
Training: *F/T operations staff, F/T management, P/T operations staff, P/T management, casual operations staff and casual management are trained in-house and externally and on specific courses and day-to-day on job*
Languages spoken: *French; German*

Marketing
Annual event(s): *theme weekends*
UK promotion: *local newspapers; leaflets/information packs*

BRESSINGHAM STEAM MUSEUM AND GARDENS
(registered charity)
garden; museum

Established: *1968*
Address: *Bressingham, Diss, Norfolk, IP22 2AB*
Telephone: *(037988) 3826.* Fax: *(037988) 8085*
Access: (road) *A1066* (rail) *Diss*
Season: *all year*
Hours: *Summer – 10.00am to 5.30pm, Winter – 10.00am to 4.00pm*
Admission (1992): *adults £3.50; children £2.50; OAP £3.50; student £2.50; under 4 free*
No. visitors (1992): *165 000 (est.)*

Facilities
Interpretation: *leaflets; information boards; guide books; signs*
Children: *play area; nappy changing*
Schools: *lecture/talk*
Disabled: *easy access; disabled toilets*
Catering: *1 picnic area*
Retailing: *postcards/inexpensive souvenirs; confectionery and ice cream; books; clothes; toys; pictures; films; stamps*
No. shops: *2*

Operations
Contacts: *Mervyn Thompson (Manager); Caroline Butler (Assistant Manager)*
No. employees: (high season) *15 full time; 15 part time* (low season) *15 full time; 15 part time*
Training: *F/T operations staff and F/T management are trained in-house and on specific courses*

Marketing
Annual event: *annual fire engine rally*
Other: *press office; market research*
UK promotion: *television; local newspapers; regional tourist board; leaflets/information packs; ETB/BTA*
Europe promotion: *British Tourist Authority*

Environmental monitoring: *recycling; waste; hazardous materials*

BRIGHTON SEA LIFE CENTRE
(limited company)
zoo/wildlife attraction

Established: *1991*

Address: *Marine Parade, Brighton, E Sussex, BN2 1TB*
Telephone: *(0273) 604234.* Fax: *(0273) 681840*
Access: (road) *A27* (rail) *Brighton*
Season: *all year*
Hours: *All year – 10am to 6pm daily*
Admission (1992): *adults £4.25; children £3.25; OAP £3.75; student £2.45; disabled £2.80*

Facilities
Interpretation: *videos; leaflets; information boards; tour guides; guide books*
Languages: *French; German*
Children: *nappy changing*
Schools: *educational literature; audio/visual presentation; educational tour; lecture/talk; touch pools; follow up*
Disabled: *easy access; disabled toilets*
Catering: *1 picnic area*
Retailing: *postcards/inexpensive souvenirs; craftwork; books; clothes; reproductions of famous artefacts*
No. shops: *1*

Operations
Contacts: *C Scurrah (Manager); H Stewart-Laidlaw (Shop Supervisor); C Billen (Marketing officer, central office)*
Training: *F/T operations staff, F/T management, P/T operations staff and casual operations staff are trained in-house and on specific courses and day-to-day on job using handbooks*

Marketing
Affiliation: *SEETB*
Other: *press office; market research*
UK promotion: *television; national newspapers; radio; local newspapers; regional tourist board; other attractions; leaflets/information packs; ETB/BTA*

BRISTOL CATHEDRAL
(charity)
church

Established: *1140*
Address: *College Green, Bristol, BS1 5TJ*
Telephone: *(0272) 250692.* Fax: *(0272) 253678*
Access: (road) *M4/M5*
Season: *all year*
Hours: *8am to 6pm*
Admission (1992): *free*
No. visitors (1992): *20 000 (est.)*

Facilities
Interpretation: *leaflets; information boards; tour guides; guide books*
Languages: *Japanese; Dutch; French; German; Italian; Spanish*
Schools: *maximum no. 60; educational literature*
Catering: *1 snack bar/food stall*
Franchisees: *8.00am to 6pm*
Retailing: *postcards/inexpensive souvenirs; books; tea towels; spoons; pictures; greetings cards*
No. shops: *1*

Operations
Contacts: *Canon P F Johnson (Canon Treasurer); Mrs Joy Coupe (Administrator)*
No. employees: (high season) *7 full time; 4 part time* (low season) *7 full time; 4 part time*
Training: *F/T operations staff, F/T management and P/T operations staff are trained in-house and day-to-day on job using videos and handbooks*

Marketing
Sponsor(s): *many local and national companies*
Affiliations: *English Heritage*
UK promotion: *local newspapers; regional tourist board; other attractions; leaflets/information packs*
Europe/USA promotion: *leaflets/brochures; visits*

Environmental monitoring: *recycling; waste; water quality; energy consumption; hazardous materials; chemical usage; transport; emissions*

BRISTOL INDUSTRIAL MUSEUM
(local authority run)
museum

Established: *1978*
Address: *Princes Wharf, City Docks, Bristol, BS1 4RN*
Telephone: *(0272) 251470*
Access: (road) *M4/M32* (rail) *Temple Meads*
Parking capacity: (cars) *30*
Season: *all year*
Hours: *all year – Sat to Wed – 10am to 5pm*
Admission (1992): *adults £2.00; OAP £2.00; student £2.00; leisure card holders and children free*
No. visitors (1992): *140 000 (est.)*

Facilities
Interpretation: *leaflets; information boards*
Schools: *maximum no. 50; educational literature; education officer*
Disabled: *easy access; disabled toilets*
Retailing: *postcards/inexpensive souvenirs; books*
No. shops: *1*

Operations
Contact: *A King (Assistant Curator)*
No. employees: (high season) *7 full time*
Training: *F/T operations staff, F/T management, P/T operations staff, P/T management, casual operations staff and casual management are trained in-house and externally and on specific courses*
Languages spoken: *French; German; Italian*

Marketing
Other: *press office*

BRISTOL ZOO GARDENS
(charity)
zoo/wildlife attraction

Established: *1836*
Address: *Guthrie Road, Clifton, Bristol, BS8 3HA*
Telephone: *(0272) 738951.* Fax: *(0272) 736814*
Access: (road) *M5/A4176* (rail) *Bristol Temple Meads*
Parking capacity: (cars) *200*
Season: *all year*
Hours: *all year – 9am to 6pm (5pm in Winter)*
Admission (1992): *adults £4.80; children £2.50; OAP £4.80; concession on mondays £2.50*
No. visitors (1992): *400 000 (est.)*

Facilities
Interpretation: *leaflets; information boards; maps; guide books*
Children: *adventure playground; nappy changing*
Schools: *maximum no. 30; educational literature; educational tour; lecture/talk; education co-ordinators*
Disabled: *easy access; disabled toilets*
Catering: *1 bar/public house*
Retailing: *postcards/inexpensive souvenirs; confectionery and ice cream; books; clothes*
No. shops: *2*

Operations
Contacts: *G R Greed (Director); C Cattle (Retail Manageress); J Palmer (Marketing Manager)*
No. employees: (high season) *140 full time* (low season) *75 full time; 6 part time*
Training: *F/T operations staff are trained in-house and externally and on specific courses and day-to-day on job*
Languages spoken: *French; Italian*

Marketing
Annual event(s): *various*
Affiliation: *Federation of Zoo Gardens of Great Britain*
Other: *press office; market research*
UK promotion: *television; radio; local newspapers; regional tourist board; other attractions; leaflets/information packs; ETB/BTA*

Environmental monitoring: *recycling; waste; energy consumption; hazardous materials.*

BRITISH ENGINEERIUM STEAM MUSEUM
(trust)
museum

Established: *1975*
Address: *Nevill Road, Hove, Sussex, BN3 7QA*
Telephone: *(0273) 559583.* Fax: *(0273) 566403*
Access: (road) *A23/A27* (rail) *Brighton/Hove*
Parking capacity: (cars) *40* (coaches) *2*
Season: *all year*
Hours: *all year – 10am to 5pm daily*
Admission (1992): *adults £3.00; children £2.00;
OAP £2.00; student £2.00; family £8.00*
No. visitors (1992): *15 000 (est.)*

Facilities
Interpretation: *leaflets; tour guides; guide books*
Languages: *French; guides available*
Schools: *maximum no. 600; educational literature;
educational tour; lecture/talk*
Disabled: *helpers; help available on request*
Retailing: *postcards/inexpensive souvenirs;
confectionery and ice cream; books*
No. shops: *1*

Operations
Contacts: *S Wadbrook (Museum Administrator);
C McCarthy (Business Development Manager)*
No. employees: (high season) *7 full time;
4 part time* (low season) *7 full time; 4 part
time*
Training: *F/T operations staff and P/T operations
staff are trained in-house and day-to-day on job
using HND*

Marketing
Affiliation: *AMSSEE*
Other: *press office; market research*
UK promotion: *local newspapers; regional tourist
board; other attractions; leaflets/information
packs; ETB/BTA*

BRITISH IN INDIA MUSEUM
(limited company)
museum

Established: *1972*
Address: *Newtown St, Colne, Lancashire, BB8 0JJ*
Telephone: *(0282) 870215.* Fax: *(0282) 870215*
Access: (road) *M65/A682/A56*
Parking capacity: (cars) *10*
Hours: *Mon to Sat (not Tues) – 10am to 4pm.
Closed Dec and Jan, all BH, 7 to 16 Jul and 7 to
13 Sept. Groups welcome throughout the year
by appointment*
Admission (1992): *adults £1.20; children £0.50;
OAP £1.20; student £0.50*

Facilities
Interpretation: *leaflets*
Schools: *maximum no. 40; no special support*
Retailing: *postcards/inexpensive souvenirs;
books*
No. shops: *1*

Operations
Contacts: *Mr H Nelson (Director); Mrs D Nelson
(Director)*
No. employees: (high season) *1 part time*
Languages spoken: *French*

Marketing
UK promotion: *local newspapers;
leaflets/information packs*

Environmental monitoring: *recycling; waste;
water quality*

BRIXHAM MUSEUM and HISTORY SOCIETY
(society and registered charity)
museum

Established: *1958*
Address: *Bolton Cross, Brixham, TQ5 8LZ*
Telephone: *(0803) 856267*
Access: (road) *M5/A3022* (rail) *Paignton*
Hours: *Easter to end of Oct – Mon to Sat – 10am
to 5pm*

Admission (1992): *adults £1.20; children £0.60;
OAP £0.60; student £0.60; pre-booked groups
£0.80 and £0.45 each*
No. visitors (1992): *6427*

Facilities
Interpretation: *videos; information boards; guides
for groups by arrangement*
Schools: *maximum no. 30; educational literature;
school liaison officer*
Disabled: *ground floor access, majority of
museum*
Retailing: *postcards/inexpensive souvenirs; books;
local photographs*
No. shops: *1*

Operations
Contacts: *Mrs W Salter (Curator and Secretary to
Executive Committee); Mrs J Bishop (shop);
Committee*
No. employees: (high season) *3 part time* (low
season) *1 part time*
Languages spoken: *French*

Marketing
Affiliations: *MA, Area Museum Council SW,
Devonshire Association, Devon Wildlife Trust*
Other: *press office*
UK promotion: *radio; local newspapers; regional
tourist board; leaflets/information packs;
Torbay tourist boards*

BROADLEAS GARDENS CHARITABLE TRUST
(trust)
garden

Established: *1984*
Address: *Broadleas, Devizes, Wilts, SN10 5JQ*
Telephone: *(0380) 722035*
Access:(road) *A360*
Hours: *Apr to Oct – Sun, Wed and Thur – 2pm
to 6pm*
Admission (1992): *adults £1.50; children £0.50;
group rates*
No. visitors (1992): *1500 (est.)*

Facilities
Interpretation: *leaflets; information boards*
Retailing: *plants*
No. shops: *1*

Operations
Contacts: *Lady Anne Cowdray (Curator)*
No. employees: (high season) *2 full time;
2 part time* (low season) *2 full time; 2 part
time*
Languages spoken: *French*

Marketing
Annual event(s): *NGS openings*
UK promotion: *national newspapers; radio; local
newspapers; regional tourist board;
leaflets/information packs*

Environmental monitoring: *internal conditions*

BROADS MUSEUM
(privately owned)
museum; Britain's tallest windmill

Established: *1976*
Address: *Sutton Windmill, Stalham, Norwich,
NR12 9RZ*
Telephone: *(0692) 581195*
Access: (road) *A149*
Parking capacity: (cars) *50* (coaches) *3*
Hours: *1 Apr to 30 Sept – 10am to 5.30pm*
Admission (1992): *adults £2.00; children £1.00;*

Facilities
Interpretation: *leaflets; tour guides; guide books*
Schools: *educational literature*
Catering: *1 picnic area*
Retailing: *postcards/inexpensive souvenirs*
No. shops: *1*

Operations
Contacts: *Mr C Nunn*

No. employees: (high season) *2 full time; 3 part
time* (low season) *2 full time*

Marketing
Affiliations: *AIM, E Anglia Tourist Board*
Other: *market research*
UK promotion: *local newspapers; regional tourist
board; other attractions; leaflets/information
packs*

BRODICK CASTLE AND COUNTRY PARK AND GOATFELL
(trust)
castle; park/reserve; garden; zoo/wildlife
attraction

Established: *1958*
Address: *Isle of Arran, KA27 8HY*
Telephone: *(0770) 2202*
Access: (road) *Ferry Ardrossan* (rail) *Glasgow to
Ardrossan*
Season: *all year*
Hours: *Park and Goatfell open all year*
Admission (1992): *N/A*
No. visitors (1992): *68 000 (est.)*

Facilities
Interpretation: *leaflets; information boards; maps;
tour guides; guide books; ranger, garden and
mountain-guided walks*
Languages: *French; German; Italian; Braille*
Children: *adventure playground; nappy changing*
Schools: *educational literature; lecture/talk;
guided walks and trails*
Disabled: *easy access; disabled toilets; special
signs; special level car-park*
Catering: *2 picnic areas*
Retailing: *postcards/inexpensive souvenirs;
confectionery and ice cream; craftwork; books*
No. shops: *1*

Operations
Contact: *Ms O Raymond (Administrator)*
No. employees: (high season) *12 full time; 46 part
time* (low season) *12 full time*
Training: *F/T operations staff, F/T management
and P/T operations staff are trained in-house
and externally and on specific courses and
day-to-day on job*

Marketing
Annual event(s): *musical concerts and open day*
Other: *press office*

BROMHAM MILL
(local authority run)
heritage centre; museum; gallery

Established: *1984*
Address: *Bromham, Beds. Postal Address: Leisure
Services Dept, Bedfordshire County Council,
County Hall, Beds MK42 9AP*
Telephone: *(0234) 228330.* Fax: *(0234) 228921*
Access: (road) *A428* (rail) *Bedford Midland Rd*
Parking capacity: (cars) *30* (coaches) *4*
Hours: *Apr to Oct – Wed to Fri – 10.30am to
4.30pm, Sat, Sun, BH – 11.30am to 6pm*
Admission (1992): *adults £0.60; children £0.30;
OAP £0.30*
No. visitors (1992): *10 219*

Facilities
Interpretation: *leaflets; information boards; tour
guides; guide books*
Schools: *educational literature; educational tour;
lecture/talk; milling demos*
Catering: *1 picnic area*
Retailing: *postcards/inexpensive souvenirs;
confectionery and ice cream; craftwork;
books*
No. shops: *1*

Operations
Contacts: *S Wileman (Cultural and Community
Services Assistant); H McMahon (Marketing
and Publicity Officer)*
No. employees: (high season) *4 part time* (low
season) *1 part time*

Training: *F/T management and P/T operations staff are trained in-house and externally and on specific courses and day-to-day on job using videos and handbooks*
Languages spoken: *French; German; Italian; Spanish*

Marketing
Annual event: *National Apple Day*
Affiliation: *regional tourist board*
Other: *press office; market research*
UK promotion: *local newspapers; regional tourist board; leaflets/information packs; ETB/BTA*

BROMLEY MUSEUM
(local authority run)
historic house; garden; museum; Roman villa and bath house on separate sites

Established: *1965*
Address: *The Priory, Church Hill, Orpington, Kent, BR6 0HH*
Telephone: *(0689) 873826*
Access: *(road) M25/A224 (rail) Orpington*
Parking capacity: *(cars) 15*
Season: *all year*
Admission (1992): *free*
No. visitors (1992): *12 000 (est.)*

Facilities
Interpretation: *information boards; tour guides*
Schools: *maximum no. 30; educational literature; lecture/talk*
Disabled: *easy access; access only to ground floor*

Operations
Contacts: *Dr A Tyler (Curator); Mr P Beale/Ms M McCullough (marketing assistants)*
No. employees: *(high season) 2 full time (low season) 2 full time*
Training: *F/T management are trained in-house and externally and on specific courses using videos and lectures, workshops*
Languages spoken: *Danish*

Marketing
Other: *PR Company: Edward Harvey Associates, Maidstone; press office; market research*
UK promotion: *radio; local newspapers; other attractions; leaflets/information packs; LTB*

Environmental monitoring: *recycling; waste; energy consumption; transport*

BROOKLANDS MUSEUM
(trust)
museum; historic site

Established: *1990*
Address: *Brooklands Road, Weybridge, Surrey, KT13 0QN*
Telephone: *(0932) 857381. Fax: (0932) 855465*
Access: *(road) M25/B374 (rail) Weybridge*
Parking capacity: *(cars) 400 (coaches) 10*
Season: *all year*
Hours: *May to Sept – Sat, Sun and BH – 10am to 5pm, Oct to Mar – Sat, Sun and BH – 10am to 4pm*
Admission (1992): *adults £4.00; children £2.00; OAP £3.00; student £3.00*
No. visitors (1992): *60 000 (est.)*

Facilities
Interpretation: *videos; leaflets; tour guides; guide books; personnel*
Children: *nappy changing*
Schools: *maximum no. 60; educational literature; audio/visual presentation; educational tour*
Disabled: *easy access; disabled toilets*
Catering: *1 bar/public house*
Retailing: *postcards/inexpensive souvenirs; confectionery and ice cream; craftwork; books; clothes; reproductions of famous artefacts*
No. shops: *1*

Operations
Contacts: *M E Barton (Museum Director); A Watson (PA to Director); V Denney (Retail Manager (Shop)); R Wilkes (Marketing Manager)*
No. employees: *(high season) 11 full time; 3 part time (low season) 11 full time; 3 part time*
Training: *F/T operations staff, F/T management, P/T operations staff and casual operations staff are trained in-house and externally and on specific courses and day-to-day on job and MA training courses using videos and handbooks*

Marketing
Annual event(s): *various*
Sponsor(s): *various*
Affiliations: *MA, AMSSEE, AIM, Royal Aeronautical Society, British Aircraft Preservation Council*
Other: *press office; market research*
UK promotion: *national newspapers; radio; local newspapers; regional tourist board; other attractions; leaflets/information packs; ETB/BTA*
Europe/USA/Japan promotion: *television; leaflets/brochures; British Tourist Authority*

Environmental monitoring: *recycling; waste; water quality; energy consumption; hazardous materials; chemical usage; transport; emissions; land contamination*

BROOKSIDE MINIATURE RAILWAY
(limited company)
garden; museum; miniature railway

Established: *1989*
Address: *Macclesfield Road, Poynton, Cheshire, SK12 1BY*
Telephone: *(0625) 812919. Fax: (0625) 859119*
Access: *(road) M63/A523 (rail) Hazel Grove, Poynton*
Parking capacity: *(cars) 400 (coaches) 10*
Season: *all year*
Hours: *Apr to Sept – Wed and Sun – 11.30am to 5pm, July to Aug – Tues to Thur and Sun – 11.30am to 5pm, Oct to Mar – Sun – 11.30am to 5pm*
Admission (1992): *adults £0.20; children £0.20; student £0.20*
No. visitors (1992): *50 000 (est.)*

Facilities
Interpretation: *leaflets*
Children: *play area*
Schools: *maximum no. 50; no special support*
Disabled: *easy access; disabled toilets*
Catering: *1 picnic area*
Franchisees: *Apr to Sept – Wed and Sun – 11.30am to 5pm*
Retailing: *clothes*
No. shops: *More than 4*

Operations
Contacts: *C E M Halsall (owner operator); D McFarlane (General Manager)*
No. employees: *(high season) 1 full time; 3 part time*
Languages spoken: *French; German*

Marketing
Annual event: *transport gala*
Other: *market research*
UK promotion: *local newspapers; regional tourist board; other attractions; leaflets/information packs*

Environmental monitoring: *hazardous materials; chemical usage*

BROUGHTON CASTLE
(private home)
historic house; garden

Established: *1962*
Address: *Banbury, Oxon, OX15 5EB*
Telephone: *(0295) 262624*
Access: *(road) M40/A4260 (rail) Banbury*
Parking capacity: *(cars) 60*

Hours: *May to Sept – Wed and Sun – 2pm to 5pm, also Thur in July and Aug and BH*
Admission (1992): *adults £3.00; children £1.30; OAP £2.30; student £2.30*
No. visitors (1992): *20 000 (est.)*

Facilities
Interpretation: *leaflets; tour guides; guide books*
Languages: *Japanese; Dutch; French; German; Italian; Spanish*
Schools: *maximum no. 100; educational literature; educational tour; lecture/talk*
Catering: *1 snack bar/food stall*
Retailing: *postcards/inexpensive souvenirs; craftwork; books*
No. shops: *1*

Operations
Contact: *C J George (Administrator)*
No. employees: *(high season) 2 part time (low season) 2 part time*

Marketing
Affiliation: *HHA*
UK promotion: *local newspapers; regional tourist board; leaflets/information packs; ETB/BTA*

BROWHOUSE YARD MUSEUM
(local authority run)
historic house; garden; museum

Established: *1977*
Address: *Castle Boulevard, Nottingham*
Telephone: *(0602) 483504*
Access: *(road) M1 (rail) Nottingham*
Season: *all year*
Hours: *10am to 5pm daily except Christmas Day*
Admission (1992): *free*
No. visitors (1992): *132 000 (est.)*

Facilities
Interpretation: *information boards*
Languages: *French; German*
Schools: *maximum no. 30; educational literature; lecture/talk; by arrangement*
Disabled: *easy access; disabled toilets; powered transport*
Retailing: *postcards/inexpensive souvenirs; books; reproductions of famous artefacts; local history material*
No. shops: *1*

Operations
Contacts: *Mr S Voe (Service Manager, Operations); Mr B Playle (Assistant Director of Museums); Mr N Milner (Sales); Mr R Sandwell (Marketing)*
No. employees: *(high season) 5 full time*
Training: *F/T management are trained in-house and externally and on specific courses and day-to-day on job*
Languages spoken: *French; German*

Marketing
Other: *press office; market research*
UK promotion: *regional tourist board; leaflets/information packs; ETB/BTA*

BRUCE CASTLE MUSEUM
(local authority run)
historic house; museum

Established: *1906*
Address: *Lordship Lane, London, N17 8NU*
Telephone: *(081) 808 8772*
Access: *(road) A10 (rail) Bruce Grove*
Season: *all year*
Hours: *Tues to Sun – 1pm to 5pm, except 25, 26 Dec, 1 Jan and Good Friday*
Admission (1992): *free*

Facilities
Interpretation: *information boards*
Schools: *maximum no. 30; no special support*
Retailing: *postcards/inexpensive souvenirs; books*
No. shops: *1*

Operations
Contact: *Ms P Wheatcroft (Curator)*

No. employees: (high season) *6 full time; 1 part time*
Training: *F/T operations staff, F/T management and P/T operations staff are trained in-house and day-to-day on job using videos and handbooks*

Marketing
Affiliations: *MA*
UK promotion: *leaflets/information packs*

Environmental monitoring: *recycling; waste; water quality; energy consumption; hazardous materials; chemical usage; emissions*

BRYN BRAS CASTLE
(private)
historic house; garden

Established: *1967*
Address: *Llanrug, Nr Caernarfon, North Wales, LL55 4RE*
Telephone: *(0286) 870210*
Access: (road) *A4086* (rail) *Bangor*
Parking capacity: (cars) *50* (coaches) *3*
Hours: *May to July – Sun to Fri – 1pm to 5pm, July to Aug – Sun to Fri – 10.30am to 5pm, Sept – Sun to Fri – 1pm to 5pm. Closed all Saturdays*
Admission (1992): *adults £2.80; children £1.40*

Facilities
Interpretation: *information boards; tour guides; guide books*
Catering: *1 picnic area*
Retailing: *postcards/inexpensive souvenirs; confectionery and ice cream; craftwork; books*
No. shops: *1*

Operations
Contacts: *Mrs M Gray-Parry*
No. employees: (high season) *3 full time; 6 part time* (low season) *3 full time; 2 part time*
Training: *F/T operations staff, F/T management, P/T operations staff, P/T management, casual operations staff and casual management are trained in-house and day-to-day on job*

Marketing
Affiliations: *HHA, WTB, NFU, Federation of Small Businesses, Welsh Gardens Trust*
Other: *market research*
UK promotion: *national newspapers; local newspapers; regional tourist board; other attractions; leaflets/information packs; ETB/BTA*

Environmental monitoring: *temperature and humidity*

BUCKFAST BUTTERFLIES AND DARTMOOR OTTER SANCTUARY
(private)
zoo/wildlife attraction

Established: *1984*
Address: *Buckfastleigh, Devon, TQ11 0DZ*
Access: (road) *A38*
Parking capacity: (cars) *200* (coaches) *50*
Hours: *Easter to Oct – 10am to 5.30pm daily*
Admission (1992): *adults £3.25; children £2.00; OAP £2.75*
No. visitors (1992): *100 000 (est.)*

Facilities
Interpretation: *videos; leaflets; information boards; tour guides; guide books*
Languages: *French; German*
Children: *nappy changing*
Schools: *maximum no. 200; educational literature; audio/visual presentation; educational tour; lecture/talk*
Disabled: *easy access; disabled toilets; helpers*
Catering: *1 bar/public house*

Retailing: *postcards/inexpensive souvenirs; confectionery and ice cream; craftwork; books; clothes*
No. shops: *2*

Operations
Contact: *D J Field (Director)*
No. employees: (high season) *4 full time; 4 part time* (low season) *4 full time*
Training: *F/T operations staff, F/T management, P/T operations staff and P/T management are trained in-house and externally and on specific courses and day-to-day on job*

Marketing
Press office; market research
UK promotion: *television; radio; local newspapers; regional tourist board; other attractions; leaflets/information packs; ETB/BTA*
Europe promotion: *leaflets/brochures; travel agents' brochures; British Tourist Authority*

BUCKLERS HARD VILLAGE AND MARITIME MUSEUM
(limited company)
museum; historic shipbuilding village

Established: *1963*
Address: *Bucklers Hard, Beaulieu, Hants, SO42 7XB*
Telephone: *(0590) 616203*
Access: (road) *M3/M27/M271/B3054* (rail) *Brockenhurst*
Parking capacity: (cars) *600* (coaches) *16*
Season: *all year*
Hours: *Winter – 10am to 4.30pm, Easter to Spring BH – 10am to 6pm, Spring BH to 1 Sept – 10am to 9pm*
Admission (1992): *adults £2.40; children £1.60; OAP £1.95; student £1.95; group rates £1.95 adults, £1.20 children; also coach rates*
No. visitors (1992): *180 000 (est.)*

Facilities
Interpretation: *leaflets; information boards; tour guides; guide books; personnel*
Schools: *educational literature; lecture/talk; guides in period costume*
Disabled: *special signs; leaflets; guide book*
Catering: *1 bar/public house*
Retailing: *postcards/inexpensive souvenirs; confectionery and ice cream; craftwork; books; clothes; reproductions of famous artefacts*
No. shops: *3*

Operations
Contacts: *Mr E Walters (Manager); Mrs J Hoy (Personnel Manager); Ms L Harnet (Publicity Manager)*
No. employees: (high season) *4 full time; 21 part time* (low season) *4 full time; 14 part time*
Training: *F/T operations staff, F/T management, P/T operations staff, P/T management, casual operations staff and casual management are trained in-house and on specific courses and day-to-day on job using videos*
Languages spoken: *French; German*

Marketing
Annual event: *village festival*
Other: *press office; market research*
UK promotion: *regional tourist board; other attractions; leaflets/information packs; ETB/BTA*
USA/BTA schemes promotion: *leaflets/brochures; British Tourist Authority*

Environmental monitoring: *recycling; waste*

BUCKLEYS YESTERDAY'S WORLD
(private)
museum

Established: *1983*
Address: *Next to Battle Abbey, High Street, Battle, Nr Hastings, E Sussex TN33 0AQ*
Telephone: *(042477) 4269. Fax: (042477) 5378*

Access: (road) *M25/A21* (rail) *Hastings*
Parking capacity: (cars) *1000* (coaches) *12*
Season: *all year*
Hours: *all year – 10am to 6pm daily*
Admission (1992): *adults £3.25; children £1.95; OAP £2.75; student £2.75; family £9.50, disabled £1.00*
No. visitors (1992): *100 000*

Facilities
Interpretation: *videos; information boards; push-button commentaries, discovery sheet for each visitor*
Languages: *Japanese; Dutch; French; German; Spanish*
Children: *play area; nappy changing; creche*
Schools: *maximum no. 120; educational literature; audio/visual presentation; video*
Disabled: *not suitable for wheelchairs*
Catering: *2 picnic areas*
Franchisees: *all year – 10am to 6pm daily*
Retailing: *postcards/inexpensive souvenirs; confectionery and ice cream; books; clothes; reproductions of famous artefacts; old fashioned tins and toys*
No. shops: *1*

Operations
Contacts: *A Buckley (owner/Curator); B Buckley (owner); R Buckley (Promotions Manager)*
No. employees: (high season) *10 full time; 3 part time* (low season) *5 full time; 2 part time*
Training: *F/T operations staff, F/T management, P/T operations staff and P/T management are trained in-house and on specific courses and day-to-day on job using videos and handbooks*

Marketing
Affiliations: *AIM, Top Attractions in E Sussex Association, tourist board*
Other: *press office; market research*
UK promotion: *television; local newspapers; regional tourist board; other attractions; leaflets/information packs*
Europe promotion: *leaflets/brochures; British Tourist Authority; direct mail*

Environmental monitoring: *water quality; hazardous materials*

BUDE MUSEUM
(local authority run)
museum

Established: *1976*
Address: *c/o The Castle, Bude, Cornwall, EX23 8LF*
Telephone: *(0288) 353576. Fax: (0288) 353576*
Access: (road) *A39/3072*
Hours: *Easter to Sept – 11am to 4pm daily*
Admission (1992): *adults £0.50; children £0.25; OAP £0.25; student £0.25;*
No. visitors (1992): *5000 (est.)*

Facilities
Interpretation: *videos*
Schools: *maximum no. 30; educational literature*
Disabled: *easy access*
Catering: *1 self-service cafeteria*
Retailing: *postcards/inexpensive souvenirs; books*
No. shops: *1*

Operations
Contact: *F H C Kendall (Curator)*
No. employees: (high season) *1 full time*
Languages spoken: *Spanish*

BUFFERS
(family-run)
zoo/wildlife attraction; model railway and working dairy farm

Established: *1989*
Address: *Backoth Hill Farm, Storiths, Bolton Abbey, Skipton, N Yorks*
Telephone: *(0756) 710253*
Access: (road) *A59*

Parking capacity: (cars) 20 (coaches) 1
Season: *all year*
Hours: *10.30am to 5pm daily, closed Mon – Nov to Easter*
Admission (1992): *no admission charges when using cafe; otherwise £0.50 per person*
No. visitors (1992): *10 000 (est.)*

Facilities
Interpretation: *leaflets; information boards*
Languages: *French*
Children: *nappy changing*
Schools: *maximum no. 30; educational literature; lecture/talk*
Disabled: *easy access; disabled toilets*
Catering: *1 waiter/waitress served*
Retailing: *postcards/inexpensive souvenirs; confectionery and ice cream; craftwork; books; model railways and vehicles*
No. shops: *1*

Operations
Contacts: *Mr and Mrs K Blackburn (owners)*
No. employees: (high season) *8 part time* (low season) *10 part time*
Training: *F/T operations staff, F/T management, P/T operations staff and casual operations staff are trained in-house and externally and on specific courses and day-to-day on job*

Marketing
Market research
UK promotion: *local newspapers; leaflets/information packs*

BUILDING OF BATH MUSEUM, THE
(trust and charity)
museum; chapel

Established: *1992*
Address: *The Countess of Huntingdon's Chapel, The Vineyards, The Paragon, Bath, BA1 5NA*
Telephone: *(0225) 333895*
Access: (road) *M4/A4* (rail) *Bath Spa*
Hours: *Tues to Sun – 11.30am to 5.30pm. Closed 16 Dec to 1 Mar*
Admission (1992): *adults £2.00; children £1.00; OAP £1.50; student £1.50; groups by prior arrangement*
No. visitors (1992): *13 000 (est.)*

Facilities
Interpretation: *leaflets; information boards; tour guides*
Schools: *maximum no. 50; educational literature; lecture/talk*
Retailing: *postcards/inexpensive souvenirs; books; posters*
No. shops: *1*

Operations
Contacts: *Mr C Woodward (Curator/Director); Ms B Nash (Administrator)*
No. employees: (high season) *2 full time; 2 part time* (low season) *2 full time; 2 part time*
Training: *F/T operations staff, F/T management, P/T operations staff and P/T management are trained in-house and on specific courses and day-to-day on job using videos and handbooks*
Languages spoken: *French*

Marketing
Affiliation: *Association of Bath Leisure Enterprises*
UK promotion: *local newspapers; regional tourist board; other attractions; leaflets/information packs; ABLE; ETB/BTA*
USA promotion: *British Tourist Authority; video outlet (promotions)*

BUNGAY CASTLE
(trust)
castle

Established: *1945*
Address: *Bungay, Suffolk*
Access: (road) *A143* (rail) *Norwich/Beccles*
Season: *all year*
Hours: *9am to 6pm all year*

Admission (1992): *free*
No. visitors (1992): *3000 (est.)*

Facilities
Interpretation: *guide books*
Schools: *maximum no. 30; lecture/talk*

Operations
Contacts: *Mr P Murrow (clerk of the trust)*
Languages spoken: *French; German; Urdu*

Marketing
Annual event: *Bungay festival*
Sponsor(s): *various*
UK promotion: *regional tourist board*

Environmental monitoring: *recycling; waste; energy consumption; chemical usage*

BURE VALLEY RAILWAY
(limited company)
steam railway

Established: *1990*
Address: *Norwich Rd, Aylsham, Norfolk, NR11 6BW*
Telephone: *(0263) 733858. Fax: (0263) 733814*
Access: (road) *A140* (rail) *Hoveton*
Parking capacity: (cars) *70* (coaches) *10*
Hours: *Easter to Oct – every day in Jul, Aug and Sept plus Santa Specials*
Admission (1992): *adults £6.00; children £3.50; OAP £5.00*
No. visitors (1992): *44 000*

Facilities
Interpretation: *leaflets; information boards; maps; guide books*
Children: *nappy changing*
Schools: *maximum no. 200; educational literature; lecture/talk*
Disabled: *easy access; disabled toilets*
Catering: *2 picnic areas*
Retailing: *postcards/inexpensive souvenirs; confectionery and ice cream; craftwork; books; clothes*
No. shops: *2*

Operations
Contacts: *Mr P Hart (Managing Director); Ms J Hall (Retail Manager)*
No. employees (high season) *6 full time; 8 part time* (low season) *6 full time*
Training: *F/T operations staff, F/T management, P/T operations staff and casual operations staff are trained in-house and day-to-day on job*

Marketing
Annual event(s): *fundays, Santa Specials, etc.*
Other: *market research*
UK promotion: *local newspapers; regional tourist board; other attractions; leaflets/information packs; ETB/BTA*

BURNBY HALL GARDENS AND MUSEUM
(trust)
garden; museum; national collection of water-lilies

Established: *1964*
Address: *The Balk, Pocklington, Nr York, YO4 2QF*
Telephone: *(0759) 302068*
Access: (road) *A1079*
Parking capacity: (cars) *60* (coaches) *5*
Hours: *Apr to mid Oct – 10am to 6pm daily*
Admission (1992): *adults £1.80; children £0.50; OAP £1.50; under 5s free, special rates for groups over 20*
No. visitors (1992): *37 000 (est.)*

Facilities
Interpretation: *leaflets; information boards; tour guides; guide books*
Children: *nappy changing*
Schools: *maximum no. 100; educational literature*
Disabled: *easy access; disabled toilets; wheelchairs available free of charge*
Catering: *1 picnic area*
Franchisees: *Apr to mid Oct – 10am to 6pm daily*

Retailing: *postcards/inexpensive souvenirs; books; plants; pottery; films and balls*
No. shops: *1*

Operations
Contacts: *Mr D Hughes (Warden Resident); Mr J Grainger (Administrator)*
No. employees: (high season) *4 full time; 6 part time* (low season) *4 full time; 2 part time*
Training: *F/T operations staff are trained in-house and day-to-day on job*

Marketing
Annual event(s): *band concerts*
UK promotion: *local newspapers; regional tourist board; leaflets/information packs; ETB/BTA*
North Sea Ferries promotion: *leaflets/brochures*

Environmental monitoring: *recycling*

BURNS COTTAGE AND MUSEUM
(trust)
historic house; garden; museum

Address: *Alloway, Ayr, KA7 4PY*
Telephone: *0292 441215*
Access: (road) *A77* (rail) *Ayr*
Parking capacity: (cars) *200* (coaches) *20*
Season: *all year*
Hours: *Summer – 9am to 7pm (Sun – 10am), Spring and Autumn – 10am to 5pm (Sun – 2pm to 5pm), Winter – 10am to 4pm (closed Sun)*
Admission (1992): *adults £1.80; children £0.90; OAP £0.90; family ticket (2 adults, 3 children) £4.25; disabled £0.90*
No. visitors (1992): *75 000*

Facilities
Interpretation: *leaflets; information boards; tour guides; guide books*
Languages: *French; German*
Schools: *maximum no. 100; lecture/talk; school worksheet*
Disabled: *easy access; disabled toilets; leaflets*
Catering: *1 licensed restaurant*
Retailing: *postcards/inexpensive souvenirs; craftwork; books; reproductions of famous artefacts*
No. shops: *1*

Operations
Contacts: *John Manson (Curator); C. Kilpatrick (Secretary/Treasurer)*
No. employees: (high season) *2 full time; 6 part time* (low season) *2 full time; 2 part time*
Training: *F/T operations staff and P/T operations staff are trained in-house and day-to-day on job*

Marketing
Other: *market research*
UK promotion: *local newspapers; regional tourist board; other attractions; leaflets/information packs; Scottish Tourist Board*
Europe/Asia/Australia/USA promotions: *Scottish Tourist Board*

BURNS MONUMENT AND GARDENS
(trust)
monument; garden

Established: *1830*
Address: *Alloway, Ayr, KA7 4PQ*
Telephone: *(0292) 441321*
Access: (road) *A77* (rail) *Ayr*
Parking capacity: (cars) *200* (coaches) *20*
Season: *all year*
Hours: *Summer – 9am to 7pm (Sun – 10am to 7pm), Spring and Autumn – 10am to 5pm (Sun – 2am to 5pm), (BH – 10am to 5pm), Winter – 10am to 4pm*
Admission (1992): *adults £1.80; children £0.90; OAP £0.90; student £1.80; family ticket (2+2) £4.25*
No. visitors (1992): *50 000*

Facilities
Interpretation: *leaflets; information boards; guide books*

Languages: *French; German*
Schools: *lecture/talk*
Retailing: *postcards/inexpensive souvenirs; books; reproductions of famous artefacts*
No. shops: *1*

Operations
Contact: *John Manson (Curator)*
No. employees: (high season) *1 full time; 2 part time* (low season) *1 full time*
Languages spoken: *French*

BURRELL COLLECTION
(local authority run)
museum

Established: *1983*
Address: *Pollock Country Park, Glasgow, G43 1AT*
Telephone: *(041) 649 7151.* Fax: *(041) 636 0086*
Access: (road) *M8*
Season: *all year*
Admission (1992): *free*
No. visitors (1992): *486 085*

Facilities
Interpretation: *leaflets; audio tapes; information boards; maps; tour guides; guide books*
Languages: *Urdu*
Children: *nappy changing*
Schools: *museum education officer*
Disabled: *easy access; disabled toilets; special signs; audio guide and taped commentary*
Catering: *1 bar/public house*

Marketing
Other: *press office; market research*
UK promotion: *national newspapers; local newspapers; regional tourist board; leaflets/information packs*

BURTON AGNES HALL
(trust and limited company)
historic house; garden; gallery

Established: *1949*
Address: *Burton Agnes, Driffield, YO25 0ND*
Telephone: *(0262) 490324.* Fax: *(0262) 490513*
Access: (road) *M62/A166* (rail) *Driffield*
Parking capacity: (cars) *100* (coaches) *6*
Hours: *Apr to Oct – 11am to 5pm daily, guaranteed number of groups at other times by arrangement*
Admission (1992): *adults £3.00; children £2.00; OAP £2.50; student £3.00*
No. visitors (1992): *27 023*

Facilities
Interpretation: *leaflets; tour guides; guide books*
Languages: *French; German*
Children: *play area*
Schools: *maximum no. 200; educational literature; lecture/talk; children's guide book*
Disabled: *easy access; disabled toilets; leaflets; guide book; scented garden for partially sighted*
Catering: *1 picnic area*
Franchisees: *Apr to Oct – 11am to 5pm daily, guaranteed number groups at other times by arrangement*
Retailing: *postcards/inexpensive souvenirs; confectionery and ice cream; craftwork; books; garden produce; items for home and garden*
No. shops: *1*

Operations
Contact: *M Wilson (Company Secretary)*
No. employees: (high season) *2 full time; 15 part time* (low season) *2 full time; 6 part time*
Training: *P/T operations staff and casual operations staff are trained in-house and day-to-day on job*
Languages spoken: *French*

Marketing
Annual event: *Flower festival in aid of St Catherine's Hospice, Scarborough*
Affiliation: *HHA*
Other: *market research*
UK promotion: *local newspapers; regional tourist board; other attractions; leaflets/information packs; Destination Humberside; directories; Coach Drivers' Club Yearbook*

Environmental monitoring: *Glasgow City Council*

BURTON CONSTABLE HALL
(trust)
historic house

Established: *1968*
Address: *The Estate Office, Burton Constable, Nr Hull, HU11 4LN*
Telephone: *(0964) 562400.* Fax: *(0964) 563229*
Hours: *Easter to Sept – Sun to Wed – 1pm to 5pm, groups at other times by prior arrangement*
Admission (1992): *adults £3.00; children £1.50; OAP £2.25*
No. visitors (1992): *4199*

Facilities
Interpretation: *tour guides; guide books*
Children: *adventure playground*
Disabled: *access facilities in progress for 1993*
Catering: *1 picnic area*
Franchisees: *Easter to Sept – Sun to Wed – 1pm to 5pm*
Retailing: *postcards/inexpensive souvenirs*
No. shops: *1*

Operations
Contacts: *Mr D Wrench (Director)*
No. employees: (high season) *5 full time; 11 part time* (low season) *5 full time; 2 part time*

Marketing
Affiliation: *HHA*
Other: *market research*
UK promotion: *local newspapers; leaflets/ information packs*

BUTE MUSEUM
(trust)
museum

Established: *1903*
Address: *Stuart St, Rothesay, Isle of Bute, PA20 9JT*
Telephone: *(0700) 502248*
Access: (road) *ferry*
Season: *all year*
Hours: *Oct to Mar – 2.30pm to 4.30pm (except Mon and Sun), Apr to Sept – Mon to Sat – 10.30am to 4.30pm and Sun – 2.30pm to 4.30pm*
Admission (1992): *adults £0.70; children £0.20; OAP £0.40; free admission for school groups*
No. visitors (1992): *9000*

Facilities
Interpretation: *leaflets; information boards; maps; tour guides; guide books*
Schools: *maximum no. 40; lecture/talk; teachers and competitions*
Disabled: *touch table for blind*
Retailing: *postcards/inexpensive souvenirs; craftwork; books*
No. shops: *1*

Operations
Contact: *Miss A Montgomery (Organising Secretary (Hon.))*
Languages spoken: *French; German*

Marketing
Affiliations: *SMC and M and G Commission*
Other: *press office; market research*

UK promotion: *local newspapers; regional tourist board; leaflets/information packs; STB and local regional boards*

Environmental monitoring: *recycling; waste*

BUTTERFLY AND FALCONRY PARK, THE
(private company)
wildlife attraction

Established: *1987*
Address: *Long Sutton, Nr Spalding, Lincs, PE12 9LE*
Telephone: *(0406) 363833.* Fax: *(0406) 363182*
Access: (road) *A17*
Parking capacity: (cars) *400* (coaches) *50*
Hours: *Mid Mar to end Oct; summer – 10am to 6pm*
Admission (1992): *adults £2.80; children £1.80; OAP £2.50;*
No. visitors (1992): *85 000 (est.)*

Facilities
Interpretation: *leaflets; information boards; signs*
Children: *adventure playground; play area; nappy changing*
Schools: *maximum no. 300; educational literature*
Disabled: *easy access; disabled toilets; special signs*
Catering: *1 picnic area*
Retailing: *postcards/inexpensive souvenirs; confectionery and ice cream; craftwork; books; clothes; various*
No. shops: *2*

Operations
Contacts: *Peter Worth (Director); Julie Worth (Director)*
No. employees: (high season) *10 full time; 20 part time* (low season) *6 full time; 6 part time*
Training: *F/T operations staff are trained externally and on specific courses*
Languages spoken: *Spanish*

Marketing
Affiliations: *EATB, EMTB, Lincs and Humberside TA*
Other: *press office; market research*
UK promotion: *local newspapers; regional tourist board; other attractions; leaflets/information packs; ETB/BTA*
Europe promotion: *travel agents' brochures*

BUTTERFLY WORLD
(local authority run)
garden; zoo/wildlife attraction; live butterfly flight house

Established: *1989*
Address: *Queens Park, Chorley New Road, Bolton*
Telephone: *(0204) 363528*
Access: (road) *M62/A673* (rail) *Bolton Trinity St.*
Parking capacity: (cars) *30* (coaches) *6*
Hours: *Apr to Oct – 10am to 5pm daily, Nov – 12am to 4pm daily*
Admission (1992): *adults £1.30; children £0.55; OAP £0.60; group rates*
No. visitors (1992): *10 000 (est.)*

Facilities
Interpretation: *leaflets; audio tapes; information boards; tour guides*
Languages: *French; German*
Children: *play area*
Schools: *educational tour; lecture/talk*
Disabled: *easy access; disabled toilets; helpers*
Catering: *1 picnic area*
Retailing: *postcards/inexpensive souvenirs; confectionery and ice cream; craftwork; books; clothes*
No. shops: *1*

Operations
Contacts: *H H Ackers (Senior Landscape Manager); D Hall (Butterfly Supervisor)*
No. employees: (high season) *1 full time; 2 part time* (low season) *1 full time; 2 part time*

Training: *F/T operations staff, F/T management and P/T operations staff are trained in-house and externally and day-to-day on job using videos and SMC information*

Marketing
Annual event: *open day*
Affiliation: *ETB*
Other: *press office; market research*
UK promotion: *television; national newspapers; radio; local newspapers; regional tourist board; leaflets/information packs; ETB/BTA*

BUTTERFLY WORLD AND FOUNTAIN WORLD
(limited company)
zoo/wildlife attraction

Established: *1983*
Address: *Staplers Rd, Wooton, Isle of Wight, PO33 4RW*
Telephone: *(0983) 883430*
Parking capacity: (cars) *150* (coaches) *4*
Hours: *Good Friday to 31 Oct – 10am to 5.30pm*
Admission (1992): *adults £2.60; children £1.80; OAP £2.20;*
No. visitors (1992): *71 000 (est.)*

Facilities
Interpretation: *information boards; tour guides; guide books*
Children: *play area*
Schools: *maximum no. 70; educational literature*
Disabled: *easy access*
Catering: *1 picnic area*
Retailing: *postcards/inexpensive souvenirs; confectionery and ice cream; books; butterfly themes; Japanese/Italian themes*
No. shops: *2*

Operations
Contacts: *Mr P Griffith (Director); Ms C Griffith (Director)*
No. employees: (high season) *6 full time; 11 part time* (low season) *6 full time; 7 part time*
Training: *F/T operations staff, F/T management and P/T operations staff are trained in-house and day-to-day on job*
Languages spoken: *French*

Marketing
Affiliations: *Isle of Wight Places of Interest Association, Southern Tourist Board*
Other: *market research*
UK promotion: *leaflets/information packs*

Environmental monitoring: *recycling; energy consumption; chemical usage*

BUXTON MICRARIUM
(private company)
unique, hands on microscopes. The natural world exhibition.

Established: *1981*
Address: *The Crescent, Buxton, Derbyshire*
Telephone: *(0290) 78662*
Access: (road) *A6* (rail) *Buxton*
Hours: *Easter to end Sept – 10am to 5pm*
Admission (1992): *adults £2.25; children £1.25; OAP £1.75; student £1.75*
No. visitors (1992): *35 000 (est.)*

Facilities
Interpretation: *microscopes*
Languages: *French; German*
Schools: *maximum no. 60; microscopes demonstration*
Disabled: *easy access*
Retailing: *postcards/inexpensive souvenirs; books; microscopes and slides*
No. shops: *1*

Operations
Contacts: *Mrs Janet Carter (Director); Mr Gerben Oppermans (Manager); Mrs Nicki Oppermans (Manager)*

No. employees: (high season) *3 full time; 3 part time* (low season) *3 full time*

Marketing
UK promotion: *national newspapers; local newspapers; regional tourist board; other attractions; leaflets/information packs; local map; ETB/BTA*

BUXTON MUSEUM AND ART GALLERY
(local authority run)
museum; gallery

Established: *1928*
Address: *Terrace Road, Buxton, SK17 6DU*
Telephone: *(0298) 24658*
Access:(road) *A52*
Season: *all year*
Hours: *Summer – 9.30am to 5.30pm, Winter – closes 5pm Sat*
No. visitors (1992): *50 000 (est.)*

Facilities
Languages: *Japanese*
Schools: *maximum no. 60; educational literature; working with teachers*
Disabled: *easy access; disabled toilets*
Retailing: *postcards/inexpensive souvenirs; books; reproductions of famous artefacts; archaeological reproductions, minerals*
No. shops: *1*

Operations
Contact: *Richard Malliwell (Assistant Curator)*
No. employees: (high season) *7 full time* (low season) *7 full time*
Training: *F/T operations staff and F/T management are trained in-house and externally and on specific courses and day-to-day on job*
Languages spoken: *French; Chinese; Dutch, sign language*

Marketing
Press office; market research
UK promotion: *leaflets/information packs; various*

Environmental monitoring: *Awareness of environment*

C

C M BOOTH COLLECTION OF HISTORIC VEHICLES, THE
(privately owned)
museum

Established: *1972*
Address: *Falstaff Antiques, 63–67 High St, Rolveden, Cranbrook, Kent*
Telephone: *(0580) 241234*
Access: (road) *A28* (rail) *Ashford*
Season: *all year*
Hours: *Mon to Sat – 10am to 5.30pm; open occasional Sundays. Closed Christmas Day and Boxing Day*
Admission (1992): *adults £1.20; children £0.60; OAP £1.20*
No. visitors (1992): *8000 (est.)*

Facilities
Interpretation: *leaflets; information boards*
Children: *play area*
Schools: *maximum no. 20; no special support*
Disabled: *access by wheelchair not possible*
Retailing: *postcards/inexpensive souvenirs; books; antiques and lifts*
No. shops: *1*

Operations
Contacts: *Mr C Booth (Owner)*
No. employees: (high season) *2 full time* (low season) *2 full time*

Marketing
Market research
UK promotion: *local newspapers; regional tourist board; other attractions; leaflets/information packs*

Environmental monitoring: *recycling; waste*

CADBURY WORLD
(limited company)
visitor centre

Established: *1990*
Address: *PO Box 1958, Bournville, Birmingham*
Telephone: *(021) 433 4334.* Fax: *(021) 451 1366*
Access: (road) *M5/A38* (rail) *Bournville*
Parking capacity: (cars) *390* (coaches) *20*
Season: *all year*
Hours: *please ring for details*
Admission (1992): *adults £4.50; children £3.00; OAP £3.95; family £13.00*
No. visitors (1992): *400 000 (est.)*

Facilities
Interpretation: *videos; leaflets; audio tapes; information boards; slides; maps; tour guides; guide books*
Children: *play area; nappy changing*
Schools: *maximum no. 60; educational literature*
Disabled: *easy access; disabled toilets*
Catering: *2 picnic areas*
Retailing: *postcards/inexpensive souvenirs; confectionery and ice cream; books; clothes; reproductions of famous artefacts; handmade chocolates*
No. shops: *2*

Operations
Contacts: *S Pearsall (Operations Manager); P Powell (Centre Services Manager); J Tilt (Retail Manager); G Baldwin (Marketing Manager)*
Training: *F/T operations staff, F/T management, P/T operations staff, P/T management, casual operations staff and casual management are trained in-house and externally and on specific courses and day-to-day on job*
Languages spoken: *French*

Marketing
Affiliations: *BCUB, HETB, ETOA*
Other: *press office; market research*
UK promotion: *national newspapers; radio; local newspapers; regional tourist board; leaflets/information packs; various*
USA promotion: *British Tourist Authority*

Environmental monitoring: *energy consumption*

CADHAY
(not specified)
historic house; garden

Established: *1958*
Address: *Ottery St Mary, Devon, EX11 1QT*
Telephone: *(040481) 2435*
Access: (road) *A30*
Parking capacity: (cars) *200* (coaches) *15*
Hours: *July and Aug – Tues to Thur and BH – 2pm to 5.30pm*
Admission (1992): *adults £2.50; children £1.00; OAP £2.50;*
No. visitors (1992): *2000 (est.)*

Facilities
Interpretation: *tour guides; guide books*
Retailing: *postcards; inexpensive souvenirs; books*
No. shops: *unknown*

Operations
Contact: *W Powlett (Lady)*
Languages spoken: *French; German; Spanish*

Marketing
UK promotion: *local newspapers; regional tourist board; leaflets/information packs*

CALDERGLEN COUNTRY PARK
(local authority run)
park/reserve; garden; gallery; zoo/wildlife attraction; golf-course

Established: *1982*
Address: *Strathaven Rd, East Kilbride, G75 0QZ*
Telephone: *(03552) 36644*
Access: (road) *M74* (rail) *Glasgow - E Kilbride*
Parking capacity: (cars) *225* (coaches) *2*
Season: *all year*
Hours: *park open all year; visitor centre open at certain times*
Admission (1992): *free*
No. visitors (1992): *300 000 (est.)*

Facilities
Interpretation: *leaflets; audio tapes; information boards; slides; maps; tour guides; guide books; ranger service*
Children: *adventure playground; play area*
Schools: *maximum no. 40; educational literature; audio/visual presentation; lecture/talk*
Disabled: *easy access*
Catering: *1 bar/public house*
Franchisees: *Park open all year*
Retailing: *postcards/inexpensive souvenirs; confectionery and ice cream; craftwork; books; clothes*
No. shops: *1*

Operations
Contacts: *Mr A Collins (Park Manager/District Ranger)*
No. employees: (high season) *23 full time; 3 part time* (low season) *12 full time; 2 part time*
Training: *F/T operations staff, F/T management and P/T operations staff are trained in-house and externally and on specific courses and day-to-day on job*

Marketing
Annual event: *country fair*
Sponsor(s): *various*
Affiliations: *SNH*
Other: *press office; market research*
UK promotion: *local newspapers; regional tourist board; other attractions; leaflets/information packs; Clyde Valley Tourist Board*

CALKE ABBEY
(trust)
historic house; park/reserve; garden

Established: *1989*
Address: *The National Trust, Ticknall, Derby, DE73 1LE*
Telephone: *(0332) 863822*
Access: (road) *M1/M42/A514* (rail) *Derby or Burton*
Parking capacity: (cars) *150* (coaches) *3*
Hours: *house – 1st Apr to end Oct – Sat to Wed – 1pm to 5.30pm; garden – as above – 11am to 5.30pm; park – throughout the year; restaurant and house – as the house and weekends 12 noon to 4pm – Nov to 20 Dec*
Admission (1992): *adults £4.20; children £2.10; NT members free*
No. visitors (1992): *100 000*

Facilities
Interpretation: *videos; leaflets; information boards; maps; guide books; personnel*
Languages: *French; German*
Children: *nappy changing*
Schools: *maximum no. 50; educational literature*
Disabled: *easy access; disabled toilets; helpers; powered transport*
Catering: *1 snack bar/food stall*
Retailing: *postcards/inexpensive souvenirs; craftwork; books; clothes; NT gifts*
No. shops: *1*

Operations
Contact: *K Usher (Administrator)*
No. employees: (high season) *13 full time; 25 part time* (low season) *10 full time; 4 part time*
Training: *F/T operations staff, F/T management, P/T operations staff, P/T management, casual operations staff and casual management are trained in-house and on specific courses and day-to-day on job*

Marketing
Other: *press office; market research*
UK promotion: *local newspapers; regional tourist board; other attractions; leaflets/information packs; ETB/BTA*

Environmental monitoring: *recycling; waste; energy consumption; River pollution*

CAMBO COUNTRY PARK
(private/sole trader)
park/reserve

Established: *1982*
Address: *Kingsbarns, St Andrews, Fife, KY6 8QE*
Telephone: *(0333) 50810*
Access: (road) *M90/A91/A917* (rail) *Leuchars*
Parking capacity: (cars) *200* (coaches) *20*
Hours: *Easter to Sept daily 10am to 6pm*
Admission (1992): *adults £2.10; children £1.40; OAP £1.75; family ticket £6.70*
No. visitors (1992): *23 300*

Facilities
Interpretation: *leaflets; information boards; maps*

Children: *play area; nappy changing*
Schools: *maximum no. 10; educational literature*
Disabled: *easy access; disabled toilets*
Catering: *1 bar/public house*
Retailing: *postcards/inexpensive souvenirs; confectionery and ice cream*
No. shops: *1*

Operations
Contact: *Grant Fraser-Tytler (Proprietor)*
No. employees: (high season) *6 part time* (low season) *2 part time*
Training: *P/T operations staff and casual operations staff are trained in-house and day-to-day on job using videos and handbooks*

Marketing
Annual event(s): *Easter egg hunts; teddy bears' picnic*
Europe promotion: *Scottish Tourist Board*

CAMBORNE SCHOOL OF MINES GEOLOGICAL MUSEUM
(university museum)
museum; gallery

Established: *1888*
Address: *Pool, Redruth, Cornwall, TR15 3SE*
Telephone: *(0209) 714866 X3032. Fax: (0209) 716977*
Access: (road) *A30* (rail) *Redruth*
Season: *all year*
Hours: *all year – Mon to Fri – 9am to 5pm*
Admission (1992): *free*
No. visitors (1992): *10 000 (est.)*

Facilities
Interpretation: *information boards; maps*
Schools: *maximum no. 75; educational literature; audio/visual presentation; lecture/talk; work sheets*
Catering: *1 picnic area*
Retailing: *postcards/inexpensive souvenirs; books*
No. shops: *1*

Operations
Contact: *Dr R L Atkinson (Curator)*
No. employees: (high season) *1 part time* (low season) *1 part time*

Marketing
UK promotion: *regional tourist board; other attractions*

Environmental monitoring: *recycling; water quality*

CAMBRIAN RAILWAY SOCIETY AND OSWESTRY CYCLE MUSEUM
(limited company)
museum

Established: *1991*
Address: *Oswald Road, Oswestry, Shropshire*
Telephone: *(0691) 671749*
Access: (road) *A5*
Parking capacity: (cars) *80* (coaches) *2*
Season: *all year*
Hours: *all year – Mon to Sun – 10am to 4pm; closed Christmas, New Year's days and Good Friday*
Admission (1992): *adults £1.50; children £0.60*
No. visitors (1992): *6000 (est.)*

Facilities
Interpretation: *leaflets; information boards; maps; tour guides; guide books*
Schools: *maximum no. 30; educational literature*
Disabled: *helpers*
Retailing: *postcards/inexpensive souvenirs; books*
No. shops: *1*

Operations
Contact: *H Higman (Museum Administrator)*

Marketing
Annual event(s): *special steam up days*
Other: *press office*

UK promotion: *radio; local newspapers; regional tourist board; leaflets/information packs; ETB/BTA*

CAMBRIDGE AND COUNTY FOLK MUSEUM
(limited company)
museum

Established: *1936*
Address: *2/3 Castle St, Cambridge, CB3 0AQ*
Telephone: *(0223) 355159*
Access: (road) *M11/A604* (rail) *Cambridge*
Season: *all year*
Hours: *Apr to Sept – Mon to Sat – 10.30am to 5pm and Sun – 2pm to 5pm; Oct to Mar – Tues to Sat – 10.30am to 5pm and Sun – 2pm to 5pm*
Admission (1992): *adults £1.00; children £0.50; OAP £0.50; student £0.50; ub40s £0.50*
No. visitors (1992): *20 000 (est.)*

Facilities
Interpretation: *leaflets; information boards; guide books*
Languages: *Japanese; French; German*
Schools: *educational literature*
Disabled: *other audio facilities*
Retailing: *postcards/inexpensive souvenirs; books*
No. shops: *1*

Operations
No. employees: (high season) *3 full time* (low season) *3 full time*
Training: *F/T operations staff, F/T management, P/T operations staff and P/T management and casual operations staff are trained in-house and externally and on specific courses and day-to-day on job*

Marketing
Other: *market research*
UK promotion: *radio; local newspapers; leaflets/information packs*

Environmental monitoring: *recycling*

CAMERA OBSCURA
(limited company)
heritage centre

Established: *1853*
Address: *Castle Hill, Royal Mile, Edinburgh, EH1 2LZ*
Telephone: *(031) 226 3704*
Fax: *(031) 225 4239*
Season: *all year*
Hours: *Apr to Oct – 9.30am to 6pm (later July and Aug), Nov to Mar – 10am to 5pm (open every day except 25 Dec and 1 Jan)*
Admission (1992): *adults £2.75; children £1.40; OAP £1.80; student £2.20; family ticket £7.95*
No. visitors (1992): *100 000 (est.)*

Facilities
Interpretation: *leaflets; information boards; maps; tour guides*
Languages: *Japanese; French; German; Italian; Spanish; Swedish*
Schools: *maximum no. 100; educational literature*
Retailing: *postcards/inexpensive souvenirs; confectionery and ice cream; craftwork; books; clothes; reproductions of famous artefacts*
No. shops: *1*

Operations
Contacts: *Mr A Johnson (Manager); Ms S Pattpay (Assistant manager)*
No. employees: (high season) *5 full time; 10 part time* (low season) *5 full time; 5 part time*
Training: *F/T operations staff, F/T management, P/T operations staff and casual operations staff are trained in-house and externally and on specific courses and day-to-day on job using handbooks*
Languages spoken: *French; German*

Marketing
Affiliations: *ASVA*
Other: *market research*
UK promotion: *local newspapers; regional tourist board; other attractions; leaflets/information packs*

Environmental monitoring: *recycling*

CANONGATE KIRK
(church)
church

Address: *Royal Mile, Edinburgh*
Hours: *June to Sept – 10.30am to 4.30pm*
Admission (1992): *free*
No. visitors (1992): *10 000 (est.)*

Facilities
Interpretation: *leaflets; slides; guide books*
Languages: *Japanese; Dutch; French; German; Italian; Spanish; many others*
Disabled: *easy access*
Catering: *1 snack bar/food stall*
Retailing: *postcards/inexpensive souvenirs*
No. shops: *1*

Operations
Contact: *Rev C Robertson (Minister)*
Training: *casual operations staff are trained in-house and day-to-day on job using handbooks*
Languages spoken: *French; German; Italian*

Environmental monitoring: *recycling; waste; water quality; energy consumption; transport*

CANTERBURY CATHEDRAL
(trust)
church

Established: *597*
Address: *Cathedral House, 11 The Precincts, Canterbury, Kent, CT1 2EH*
Telephone: *(0227) 762862. Fax: (0227) 762897*
Access: (road) *M2/A2* (rail) *Canterbury East/West*
Season: *all year*
Hours: *N/A*
Admission (1992): *free*
No. visitors (1992): *2 250 000 (est.)*

Facilities
Interpretation: *videos; leaflets; audio tapes; information boards; slides; tour guides; guide books*
Languages: *Japanese; Dutch; French; German; Italian; Spanish; Russian; Swedish*
Schools: *educational literature; audio/visual presentation; educational tour; lecture/talk; project room*
Disabled: *easy access; disabled toilets; helpers; special signs; leaflets; touch and hearing centre*
Retailing: *postcards/inexpensive souvenirs; confectionery and ice cream; craftwork; books; clothes; reproductions of famous artefacts*
No. shops: *1*

Operations
Contact: *Lt Col D P Earlam (Director of visits)*
Training: *F/T operations staff, F/T management, P/T operations staff, P/T management, casual operations staff and casual management are trained in-house and on specific courses*

Marketing
Annual event(s): *various*
Sponsor(s): *various*
Affiliations: *ALVA, SEETB, Pilgrims Association*
Other: *press office; market research*
UK promotion: *regional tourist board; leaflets/information packs; ETB/BTA*
Europe promotion: *British Tourist Authority*

CAPEL MANOR
(College of Horticulture)
park/reserve; garden; zoo/wildlife attraction;
gardens and farm centre – 2 sites

Established: *1970*
Address: *Bullsmoor Lane, Enfield, Middlesex, EN1*
4QR
Telephone: *(0992) 763849*. Fax: *(0992) 717544*
Access: (road) *M25/A10*
Parking capacity: (cars) *350* (coaches) *20*
Hours: *Apr to Oct – 10am to 5.30pm daily; Nov*
to Mar – Mon to Fri – 10am to 5.30pm
Admission (1992): *adults £2.00; children £1.00;*
OAP £1.50; student £1.50; disabled and ub40s
£1.50
No. visitors (1992): *60 000 (est.)*

Facilities
Interpretation: *information boards; maps; tour*
guides
Schools: *educational literature*
Disabled: *easy access; disabled toilets*
Catering: *1 snack bar/food stall*

Operations
Contacts: *Dr S Dowbiggin (Principal); Mr D*
Byrne (Assistant Principal); Ms J Rushton
(Marketing)
Training: *F/T operations staff, F/T management*
and casual operations staff are trained in-house
and on specific courses using handbooks
Languages spoken: *French; German; Italian;*
Spanish; Russian; Dutch; Swedish

Marketing
Annual event(s): *various*
Sponsor: *NatWest*
Affiliations: *Royal Horticultural Society, LTB*
Other: *market research*
UK promotion: *national newspapers; radio; local*
newspapers; regional tourist board; other
attractions; leaflets/information packs; local
tourist boards

CAPESTHORNE HALL
(limited company)
historic house; garden

Established: *1962*
Address: *Siddington, Macclesfield, Cheshire, SK11*
9JY
Telephone: *(0625) 861221/861779*. Fax: *(0625)*
861619
Access: (road) *M6/A34* (rail) *Macclesfield*
Parking capacity: (cars) *1000* (coaches) *30*
Hours: *Apr to Sept – 12 noon to 6pm (hall 2pm*
to 4pm)
Admission (1992): *adults £3.70; children £1.00;*
OAP £3.20; family £8.00
No. visitors (1992): *60 000 (est.)*

Facilities
Interpretation: *leaflets; tour guides; guide books;*
corporate brochures
Languages: *Italian*
Children: *play area; nappy changing*
Schools: *maximum no. 50; educational tour;*
lecture/talk
Disabled: *easy access; disabled toilets*
Catering: *2 picnic areas*
Retailing: *postcards/inexpensive souvenirs;*
confectionery and ice cream; craftwork; books
No. shops: *2*

Operations
Contacts: *J D Hegarty (Administrator);*
E Centelleche (Catering Manager)
No. employees: (high season) *10 full time; 20 part*
time (low season) *10 full time; 10 part time*
Training: *P/T operations staff and casual*
operations staff are trained in-house and
externally and on specific courses and
day-to-day on job
Languages spoken: *French; German*

Marketing
Annual event(s): *various*
Sponsor(s): *various*
Affiliations: *HHA*
Other: *market research*

UK promotion: *national newspapers; local*
newspapers; regional tourist board; other
attractions; leaflets/information packs; various;
ETB/BTA

Environmental monitoring: *recycling; energy*
consumption; hazardous materials; peat in
garden

CAPTAIN COOK SCHOOLROOM MUSEUM
(trust)
historic house; museum

Established: *1928*
Address: *101 High St, Great Ayton, N Yorks, TS9*
6NB
Access: (road) *A19/A172/A173*
Hours: *Apr to Oct – 2pm to 4.30pm daily*
Admission (1992): *adults £0.80; children £0.40;*
OAP £0.40; student £0.40; family ticket £2.00
No. visitors (1992): *3845*

Facilities
Interpretation: *information boards; maps;*
artefacts and photographs
Schools: *maximum no. 24; lecture/talk*
Retailing: *postcards/inexpensive souvenirs*
No. shops: *1*

Operations
Contacts: *Mr R Spinks (Secretary); Mr I Sproates*
(Treasurer)
No. employees: (high season) *5 part time*
Languages spoken: *Italian*

Marketing
UK promotion: *regional tourist board; other*
attractions; leaflets/information packs

Environmental monitoring: *water quality; energy*
consumption

CAREW CASTLE AND TIDAL MILL
(local authority run)
castle; mill

Established: *1984*
Address: *Carew, Nr. Tenby, Dyfed*
Telephone: *(0646) 651782*
Access: (road) *A477*
Parking capacity: (cars) *200* (coaches) *3*
Hours: *Easter to Nov – Mon to Sun – 10am to*
5pm
Admission (1992): *adults £2.00; children £1.00;*
OAP £1.00; student £0.90; family ticket £5.00
No. visitors (1992): *50 000 (est.)*

Facilities
Interpretation: *leaflets; audio tapes; information*
boards; slides; tour guides; guide books
Schools: *maximum no. 50; educational literature;*
audio/visual presentation
Retailing: *postcards/inexpensive souvenirs;*
craftwork; books; clothes
No. shops: *2*

Operations
Contact: *G M Candler (Site Co-ordinator)*
No. employees: (high season) *8 full time; 3 part*
time (low season) *6 full time*
Training: *F/T operations staff, F/T management,*
P/T operations staff, P/T management, casual
operations staff and casual management are
trained in-house and on specific courses and
day-to-day on job

Marketing
Annual event(s): *Theatre interpretation; schools*
programme; holiday activities; battle
re-enactments
Affiliations: *CADW/Wales Tourist Board*
Other: *press office; market research*
UK promotion: *television; national newspapers;*
radio; local newspapers; regional tourist board;
other attractions; leaflets/information packs

CARFAX TOWER
(local authority run)
church tower

Established: *1992*
Address: *Carfax, Oxford*
Telephone: *(0865) 792653*. Fax: *(0865) 252592*
Access: (road) *M40* (rail) *Oxford*
Hours: *Mar to Oct – daily*
Admission (1992): *adults £0.70; children £0.40*
No. visitors (1992): *44 529*

Facilities
Interpretation: *leaflets; information boards*
Languages: *French; German; Italian; Spanish*
Schools: *maximum no. 15; no special support*
Disabled: *not suitable for disabled*
Retailing: *postcards/inexpensive souvenirs*
No. shops: *1*

Operations
Contacts: *H Armitage (Information Officer, City*
of Oxford)
No. employees: (high season) *3 part time*
Training: *P/T operations staff are trained*
in-house and prior to commencement
Languages spoken: *French; Welsh*

Marketing
Other: *market research*
UK promotion: *radio; regional tourist board;*
leaflets/information packs
Europe/Asia/Australia/USA promotions: *British*
Tourist Authority

Environmental monitoring: *recycling; waste;*
water quality; Wildlife

CARISBROOKE CASTLE
(commission)
castle

Established: *1836*
Address: *Carisbrooke, Nr Newport, Isle of Wight*
Telephone: *(0983) 522107*
Parking capacity: (cars) *200* (coaches) *15*
Season: *all year*
Hours: *1 Apr to 30 Sept – 10am to 6pm daily;*
1 Oct to 31 Mar – 10am to 4pm daily,
except Christmas Day, Boxing Day, New Year's
Day
Admission (1992): *adults £3.20; children £1.60;*
OAP £2.50; student £2.50; ub40 £2.50
No. visitors (1992): *120 000 (est.)*

Facilities
Interpretation: *leaflets; audio tapes; information*
boards; guide books
Schools: *maximum no. 1000; audio/visual*
presentation
Disabled: *disabled toilets*
Catering: *2 picnic areas*
Franchisees: *1 Apr to 30 Sept – 10am to 6pm*
daily; 1 Oct to 31 Mar – 10am to 4pm daily
except Christmas Day, Boxing Day, New Year's
Day
Retailing: *postcards/inexpensive souvenirs; books*
No. shops: *1*

Operations
Contacts: *J Evans (Head Custodian); Ms S Smith*
(Department Head personnel); Ms S Fellows
(Trading); Mr J Paton/Mr D Lane (Managers)
No. employees: (high season) *10 full time; 2 part*
time (low season) *4 full time*
Training: *F/T operations staff, F/T management,*
P/T operations staff, casual operations staff and
casual management are trained in-house and on
specific courses and day-to-day on job
Languages spoken: *French; Arabic; Urdu*

Marketing
Annual event(s): *various*
Other: *press office; market research*
UK promotion: *national newspapers; radio; local*
newspapers; regional tourist board;
leaflets/information packs; ETB/BTA
USA promotion: *leaflets/brochures; travel agents'*
brochures; British Tourist Authority

Environmental monitoring: *recycling; waste; water quality; energy consumption; hazardous materials; chemical usage; transport; emissions*

CARLISLE CATHEDRAL
(Part of Carlisle Cathedral)
museum; church

Established: *1122*
Address: *Cathedral Office, 7 The Abbey, Carlisle, CA3 8TZ*
Telephone: *(0228) 48151.* Fax: *(0228) 48769*
Access: (rail) *Carlisle*
Season: *all year*
Hours: *throughout the year – 7.30am to 6.30pm. Parties not able to view cathedral during service times*
Admission (1992): *donations of £1.00 per head requested on voluntary basis*
No. visitors (1992): *215 000 (est.)*

Facilities
Interpretation: *leaflets; information boards; tour guides; guide books*
Languages: *Dutch; French; German*
Schools: *maximum no. 25; educational literature; lecture/talk; education centre/packs*
Disabled: *easy access; helpers; wheelchair available, loop hearing system*
Catering: *1 self-service cafeteria*
Retailing: *postcards/inexpensive souvenirs; craftwork; books; clothes; reproductions of famous artefacts; general gifts and crafts*
No. shops: *1*

Operations
Contacts: *Ellis T Amos (Chapter Clerk); Mrs C E Baines (Administrative Officer)*
Languages spoken: *French*

Marketing
Annual event(s): *art exhibition*
Affiliations: *Cumbria Tourist Board*
Other: *press office*
UK promotion: *local newspapers; regional tourist board; leaflets/information packs; ETB/BTA*

Environmental monitoring: *recycling; hazardous materials; chemical usage*

CARRICK-A-REDE ROPE BRIDGE
(trust)
historic house; castle; monument; heritage centre; park/reserve; garden; museum; church

Established: *1986*
Address: *121a White Park Rd, Ballintoy, Ballycastle, Co Antrim, N. Ireland*
Parking capacity: (cars) *150* (coaches) *5*
Hours: *17 to 21 Apr – Mon to Sun – 11am to 6pm; May and June – Sat, Sun and BH – 11am to 6pm; July and Aug – Mon to Sun – 11am to 6pm*
Admission (1992): *car and coach parking fees*
No. visitors (1992): *75 000 (est.)*

Facilities
Interpretation: *leaflets; information boards; maps; guide books*
Languages: *French; German*
Schools: *maximum no. 60; educational literature; lecture/talk*
Disabled: *easy access; disabled toilets*
Catering: *1 picnic area*
Franchisees: *17 to 21 Apr – Mon to Sun – 11am to 6pm*

Operations
Contacts: *Jim Taylor (warden in charge); Diane Forbes (Regional Park Affairs Manager)*
Training: *F/T operations staff and P/T operations staff are trained in-house and day-to-day on job*
Languages spoken: *French; German*

Marketing
Other: *market research*

CARRICKFERGGUS CASTLE
(public sector)
castle; monument

Established: *1928*
Address: *Marine Highway, Carrickferggus, Co Antrim, Northern Ireland, BT38 7BG*
Telephone and fax: *(09603) 65190*
Access: (road) *M5* (rail) *York Road*
Season: *all year*
Hours: *Apr to Sept – Mon to Sat – 10am to 6pm, Sun – 2pm to 6pm; Oct to Mar – Mon to Sat – 10am to 4pm, Sun – 2pm to 4pm*
Admission (1992): *adults £1.50; children £0.75; OAP £0.75; group discounts, under 5s free*
No. visitors (1992): *58 000 (est.)*

Facilities
Interpretation: *information boards; tour guides; guide books; audio visual theatre*
Languages: *Dutch; French*
Schools: *educational literature; audio/visual presentation*
Disabled: *easy access; disabled toilets*
Catering: *1 snack bar/food stall*
Retailing: *postcards/inexpensive souvenirs; books*
No. shops: *1*

Operations
Contact: *David Steele (Castle Manager)*
No. employees: (high season) *6 full time* (low season) *6 full time*
Training: *F/T management are trained in-house and on specific courses and day-to-day on job*
Languages spoken: *French; German*

Marketing
Other: *press office; market research*
UK promotion: *local newspapers; regional tourist board; leaflets/information packs*

Environmental monitoring: *recycling; waste; water quality; energy consumption; hazardous materials*

CARTWRIGHT HALL
(local authority run)
gallery

Established: *1904*
Address: *Lister Park, Bradford*
Telephone: *(0274) 493313.* Fax: *(0274) 481045*
Access: (road) *A650*
Season: *all year*
Hours: *Tues to Sun – 10am to 6pm (Winter 10am to 5pm); open BH Mon*
Admission (1992): *free*
No. visitors (1992): *115 019*

Facilities
Interpretation: *interactive video guide*
Children: *nappy changing*
Schools: *maximum no. 100; educational literature; workshops by arrangement*
Disabled: *easy access; disabled toilets; lift*
Catering: *1 self-service cafeteria*
Franchisees: *Tues to Sun – 10am to 6pm (Winter 10am to 5pm); open BH Mon*
Retailing: *postcards/inexpensive souvenirs; confectionery and ice cream; books; posters; toys*
No. shops: *1*

Operations
Contacts: *Ms C Krzesinka (Senior Officer, arts and exhibitions); Mr S Kerry; Ms K Jones (Administration); Ms J Whittaker (Arts Marketing Officer)*
No. employees: (high season) *20 full time; 2 part time*
Training: *F/T operations staff and F/T management are trained in-house and on specific courses*

Marketing
Annual event(s): *Bradford Festival*

Sponsor(s): *various*
Affiliations: *MA, YHAB, VAGA*
Other: *press office; market research*
UK promotion: *local newspapers; regional tourist board; other attractions; leaflets/information packs*

Environmental monitoring: *energy consumption*

CASTLE EDEN WALKWAY COUNTRY PARK
(local authority run)
park/reserve; environmental education resource centre

Established: *1989*
Address: *Station House Visitor Centre, Thorpe Thewles, Stockton on Tees, Cleveland*
Telephone: *(0740) 30011*
Access: (road) *A177*
Parking capacity: (cars) *150* (coaches) *5*
Season: *all year*
Hours: *Mon to Fri and Sun – 9am to 4pm*
Admission (1992): *free*
No. visitors (1992): *165 000*

Facilities
Interpretation: *leaflets; information boards; maps; events*
Children: *adventure playground; play area*
Schools: *maximum no. 30; educational literature; lecture/talk; rangers and activities*
Disabled: *easy access; disabled toilets*
Catering: *2 picnic areas*
Retailing: *postcards/inexpensive souvenirs; books*
No. shops: *1*

Operations
Contacts: *Mrs M Clough (Countryside Information Assistant); Mrs C Raper (Countryside Information Officer)*
No. employees: (high season) *3 full time; 2 part time* (low season) *3 full time*
Training: *F/T operations staff and F/T management are trained in-house and externally and on specific courses and day-to-day on job using council training department*
Languages spoken: *Hindi; Gujerati; Punjabi*

Marketing
Annual event(s): *various*
Other: *press office; market research*
UK promotion: *radio; local newspapers; regional tourist board; other attractions; leaflets/information packs*

CASTLE HOWARD
(limited company)
historic house; museum

Established: *1700*
Address: *York, YO6 7DA*
Telephone: *(065) 384 333.* Fax: *(065) 384 462*
Access: (road) *A64* (rail) *York*
Parking capacity: (cars) *300* (coaches) *20*
Hours: *Mar to Oct – gardens – 10am, castle – 11am, last admission 4.30pm*
No. visitors (1992): *200 000 (est.)*

Facilities
Interpretation: *leaflets; information boards; tour guides; guide books*
Languages: *French; German*
Children: *adventure playground*
Schools: *lecture/talk; by arrangement*
Disabled: *easy access; disabled toilets; powered transport; wheelchairs*
Catering: *2 self-service cafeterias*
Retailing: *postcards/inexpensive souvenirs; craftwork; books; clothes; reproductions of famous artefacts*
No. shops: *3*

Operations
Contact: *M Carmichael (Administrator)*
No. employees: (high season) *150 part time* (low season) *150 part time*
Training: *P/T operations staff are trained in-house and on specific courses*

Marketing
Annual event(s): *various*
Affiliation: *HHA*
Other: *market research*
UK promotion: *television; radio; local newspapers; regional tourist board; leaflets/information packs*
USA promotion: *leaflets/brochures; travel agents' brochures*

CATHEDRAL CHURCH OF ST NICHOLAS
(Place of worship)
church

Established: *1400*
Address: *St Nicholas Churchyard, Newcastle Upon Tyne, NE1 1PF*
Telephone: *(091) 232 1939. Fax: (091) 230 0735*
Access: *(road) A1M/A69*
Season: *all year*
Hours: *Sun – 7am to 12pm and 4pm to 7.30pm; Mon to Fri – 7am to 6pm; Sat – 8am to 4pm; BH – 8am to 4pm*
Admission (1992): *free*
No. visitors (1992): *48 500 (est.)*

Facilities
Interpretation: *leaflets; information boards; slides; tour guides; guide books*
Languages: *French*
Children: *nappy changing*
Schools: *maximum no. 50; educational literature; lecture/talk*
Disabled: *easy access; disabled toilets*
Catering: *1 snack bar/food stall*
Retailing: *postcards/inexpensive souvenirs; craftwork; books; reproductions of famous artefacts; slides and music tapes*
No. shops: *1*

Operations
Contacts: *Mrs B Bailes (Gift Shop Manageress); Mr D Govler (Chapter Clerk)*
No. employees: *(high season) 6 full time; 5 part time (low season) 6 full time; 5 part time*
Training: *F/T operations staff, F/T management and P/T operations staff are trained in-house and day-to-day on job using videos and handbooks*
Languages spoken: *French; German*

Marketing
Press office
UK promotion: *regional tourist board; leaflets/information packs; Northumbria Tourist Board*

CAWDOR CASTLE
(limited company)
historic house; garden

Established: *1976*
Address: *Nairn, Scotland, IV12 5RD*
Telephone: *(06677) 615. Fax: (06677) 674*
Access: *(road) A96*
Parking capacity: *(cars) 200 (coaches) 20*
Hours: *1 May to first Sun in Oct – 10am to 5.30pm daily (last admission 5pm)*
Admission (1992): *adults £3.50; children £1.90; OAP £2.80; student £2.80; family ticket £10.00 (2 adults and up to 5 children)*
No. visitors (1992): *107 000 (est.)*

Facilities
Interpretation: *information boards; guide books*
Languages: *Japanese; French; German*
Children: *nappy changing*
Schools: *educational literature; ranger service*
Disabled: *easy access; disabled toilets*
Catering: *1 picnic area*
Retailing: *postcards/inexpensive souvenirs; confectionery and ice cream; craftwork; books; clothes*
No. shops: *3*

Operations
Contact: *Countess Cawdor (Director)*
No. employees: *(high season) 25 full time; 20 part time (low season) 7 full time; 3 part time*

Training: *F/T operations staff, P/T operations staff and casual operations staff are trained in-house and day-to-day on job*

Marketing
Affiliations: *HHA and local tourist boards*
Other: *market research*
UK promotion: *local newspapers; regional tourist board; other attractions; leaflets/information packs*
Europe/USA/Japan promotion: *leaflets/brochures; British Tourist Authority*

CECIL HIGGINS ART GALLERY AND MUSEUM
(trust)
historic house; museum; gallery

Established: *1949*
Address: *Castle Close, Bedford, MK40 3NY*
Telephone: *(0234) 211222*
Access: *(road) M1/A428/1 (rail) Bedford*
Season: *all year*
Hours: *all year – Tues to Fri – 12.30am to 5pm, Sat – 11am to 5pm, Sun – 2pm to 5pm*
Admission (1992): *free*
No. visitors (1992): *28 000 (est.)*

Facilities
Interpretation: *leaflets; information boards; tour guides; guide books*
Schools: *maximum no. 35; educational literature; lecture/talk*
Disabled: *easy access; disabled toilets*
Catering: *1 picnic area*
Retailing: *postcards/inexpensive souvenirs; books*
No. shops: *1*

Operations
Contact: *H Graham (Curator)*
No. employees: *(high season) 11 full time; 9 part time (low season) 11 full time; 7 part time*
Training: *F/T operations staff, F/T management and P/T operations staff are trained in-house and on specific courses using handbooks*
Languages spoken: *French; German; Japanese*

Marketing
Annual event(s): *river festival*
Sponsor(s): *Bedford Tourist Association*
Other: *press office*
UK promotion: *radio; local newspapers; regional tourist board; other attractions; leaflets/information packs; ETB/BTA*

Environmental monitoring: *waste; energy consumption; hazardous materials; chemical usage*

CEFN COED COLLIERY MUSEUM
(local authority run)
museum

Established: *1980*
Address: *Crynant, Neath, West Glamorgan, SA1D 8SN*
Telephone: *(0639) 750556*
Access: *(road) M4/A4109 (rail) Neath*
Parking capacity: *(cars) 50 (coaches) 4*
Season: *all year*
Hours: *Apr to Sept – Mon to Sun – 10.30am to 6pm; Oct to Mar – Mon to Sun – 10.30am to 4pm; closed Christmas Day and New Year's Day*
Admission (1992): *adults £1.25; children £0.80; OAP £0.80; student £1.25; under 5s free*
No. visitors (1992): *16 500 (est.)*

Facilities
Interpretation: *videos; audio tapes; information boards; tour guides; guide books*
Schools: *maximum no. 45; educational literature*
Disabled: *easy access; disabled toilets*
Catering: *2 picnic areas*
Retailing: *postcards/inexpensive souvenirs; confectionery and ice cream; books; souvenir lamps, brassware, etc*
No. shops: *1*

Operations
Contacts: *Mr Robert Merrill (Manager); Marlene Adams (Deputy Manager)*
No. employees: *(high season) 4 full time; 1 part time (low season) 4 full time*
Training: *F/T operations staff and F/T management are trained in-house and on specific courses using videos and handbooks*
Languages spoken: *French; German; Italian*

Marketing
Other: *market research*
UK promotion: *television; local newspapers; regional tourist board; other attractions; leaflets/information packs*

Environmental monitoring: *energy consumption; hazardous materials; chemical usage*

CENTRAL CHURCH OF THE ROYAL AIR FORCE
(church)
church

Established: *1958*
Address: *St Clement Danes, Strand, London, WC2R 1DH*
Telephone: *(071) 242 8282*
Season: *all year*
Hours: *8am to 5pm except Boxing Day, closing after service on Christmas Day*
Admission (1992): *free*

Facilities
Interpretation: *guide books*
Schools: *maximum no. 30; no special support; lecture/talk*
Disabled: *wheelchair*
Retailing: *postcards/inexpensive souvenirs*
No. shops: *none*

Operations
No. employees: *(high season) 2 full time; 2 part time*

Marketing
UK promotion: *ETB/BTA*

CENTRE FOR ALTERNATIVE TECHNOLOGY
(plc and charity)
theme park; garden; energy and lifestyle exhibitions

Established: *1975*
Address: *Machynlleth, Powys, SY20 9AZ*
Telephone: *(0654) 702400. Fax: (0654) 702782*
Access: *(road) A487 (rail) Machynlleth*
Parking capacity: *(cars) 150 (coaches) 6*
Season: *all year*
Hours: *10am to 5pm or dusk, which ever is earlier (phone for Winter opening)*
Admission (1992): *adults £4.20; children £2.00; OAP £3.20; student £3.20; family ticket £12.20*
No. visitors (1992): *90 000*

Facilities
Interpretation: *videos; leaflets; information boards; maps; tour guides; guide books*
Languages: *French; Spanish*
Children: *adventure playground; play area; nappy changing*
Schools: *maximum no. 30; educational literature; audio/visual presentation; lecture/talk; residential facilities*
Disabled: *easy access; disabled toilets*
Catering: *2 picnic areas*
Retailing: *postcards/inexpensive souvenirs; craftwork; books; clothes; technology related and plants*
No. shops: *1*

Operations
Contacts: *Mr R Dance (Administrator); Ms S Stubbins; Mr D Jenkins and Mr M Baldwin (Publicity and Marketing)*
No. employees: *(high season) 30 full time; 20 part time (low season) 20 full time*

Training: *F/T operations staff, F/T management, P/T operations staff and P/T management are trained in-house and externally and on specific courses and day-to-day on job. Also technical knowledge*
Languages spoken: *French*

Marketing
Other: *press office; market research*
UK promotion: *local newspapers; regional tourist board; other attractions; leaflets/information packs; ETB/BTA; Tourism brochures*
Europe/editorial worldwide promotions: *leaflets/brochures; British Tourist Authority*

CEREDIGION MUSEUM
(local authority run)
museum

Established: *1973*
Address: *Coliseum, Terrace Road, Aberystwyth, Dyfed, SY23 2AQ*
Telephone: *(0920) 634210/1/2/3*
Access: (road) *A44*
Season: *all year*
Hours: *all year – Mon to Sat – 10am to 5pm, open Sun during school holidays; closed 25 Dec to 1 Jan*
Admission (1992): *free*
No. visitors (1992): *37 000*

Facilities
Languages: *Welsh*
Schools: *maximum no. 30; lecture/talk; quiz sheets, etc.*
Disabled: *easy access; disabled toilets; lift*
Retailing: *postcards/inexpensive souvenirs; books*
No. shops: *1*

Operations
Contacts: *Michael Freeman (Curator)*
No. employees: (high season) *6 full time; 3 part time* (low season) *6 full time*
Training: *F/T management are trained in-house and on specific courses and day-to-day on job*
Languages spoken: *French*

Marketing
UK promotion: *local newspapers; leaflets/information packs; bedroom browsers*

Environmental monitoring: *recycling; waste; water quality; energy consumption; hazardous materials; chemical usage; transport; emissions*

CHAMBERCOMBE MANOR
(trust)
historic house; garden; museum; zoo/wildlife attraction

Established: *1972*
Address: *Ilfracombe, Devon, EX34 9RJ*
Telephone: *(0271) 862624*
Access: (road) *M5/A361* (rail) *Barnstaple*
Parking capacity: (cars) *30* (coaches) *5*
Season: *all year*
Hours: *gardens open all year, Manor – Apr to end Sept – Mon to Fri – 10am to 4.30pm, Sun – 10am to 5pm; Winter tours by prior arrangement*
Admission (1992): *adults £3.00; children £2.00; OAP £2.50; student £2.00; group rates available*
No. visitors (1992): *10 000 (est.)*

Facilities
Interpretation: *leaflets; information boards; maps; tour guides; guide books*
Children: *adventure playground; nappy changing*
Schools: *maximum no. 60; educational literature; lecture/talk; nature trail*
Disabled: *helpers; leaflets; guide book*
Catering: *1 picnic area*
Retailing: *postcards/inexpensive souvenirs; plants*
No. shops: *1*

Operations
Contact: *Ms L Harris (Manageress)*
No. employees: (high season) *6 part time* (low season) *2 part time*

Training: *P/T operations staff, P/T management and casual operations staff are trained in-house and externally and day-to-day on job*

Marketing
Annual event(s): *Victorian fête, banquets, etc.*
UK promotion: *local newspapers; regional tourist board; other attractions; leaflets/information packs; WC Tourist Board; ETB/BTA*
Europe promotion: *farm and cottage holidays*

CHARD AND DISTRICT MUSEUM
(trust)
museum

Established: *1970*
Address: *Godworthy House, High St, Chard, TA20 1QL*
Telephone: *(0460) 65091*
Access: (road) *M5/A30/A303*
Hours: *Early May to mid Oct – Mon to Sat – 10.30am to 4.30pm, Jul and Aug – Sun – 10.30am to 4.30pm*
Admission (1992): *adults £1.50; children £0.50; OAP £1.00;*
No. visitors (1992): *3000*

Facilities
Interpretation: *information boards; exhibits*
Schools: *maximum no. 30; educational literature; lecture/talk; advisor*
Disabled: *easy access; disabled toilets*
Catering: *1 picnic area*
Retailing: *postcards/inexpensive souvenirs*
No. shops: *1*

Operations
Contact: *Mr B Knight (Chairman)*

Marketing
Sponsor(s): *local businesses*
Affiliations: *SW Museums Federation, SW Area Museum Council*
Other: *market research*
UK promotion: *local newspapers; leaflets/information packs*

Environmental monitoring: *recycling; water quality; energy consumption; conservation trust*

CHARLES DICKENS BIRTHPLACE MUSEUM
(local authority run)
historic house; museum

Established: *1970*
Address: *393 Old Commercial Rd, Portsmouth, Hants, PO1 4QL*
Telephone: *(0705) 827261.* Fax: *(0705) 875267*
Access: (road) *M275* (rail) *Portsmouth/Southsea*
Hours: *Mar to Oct – 10.30am to 5.30pm daily*
Admission (1992): *adults £1.00; children £0.70; OAP £0.75; student £0.70; family ticket £2.25*
No. visitors (1992): *8000*

Facilities
Interpretation: *leaflets; information boards; guide books*
Languages: *Dutch; French; German; Italian; Spanish*
Schools: *maximum no. 12; talks by arrangement*
Retailing: *postcards/inexpensive souvenirs; books; videos; ceramics*
No. shops: *1*

Operations
Contacts: *Ms R Hardiman (Keeper of Art); Mr R Thorne (Administrative Officer); Mr P Stone (Trading Manager); Ms D Ralpus (Publicity Officer)*
No. employees: (high season) *2 full time; 4 part time*
Training: *F/T operations staff, F/T management and P/T operations staff are trained in-house and externally and day-to-day on job and by induction using one day courses*

Marketing
Annual event(s): *birthday event, death anniversary*

Affiliation: *MA*
Other: *market research*
UK promotion: *radio; local newspapers; regional tourist board; other attractions; leaflets/information packs; ETB/BTA*

Environmental monitoring: *hazardous materials; conservation of exhibits*

CHARLES MANNING'S AMUSEMENT PARK
(partnership)
amusement park

Established: *1933*
Address: *Felixstowe, Suffolk*
Telephone: *(0394) 282370.* Fax: *(0394) 671622*
Access: (road) *A12/A45*
Season: *all year*
Hours: *arcade open all year; rides open Easter to end Sept (weekends and school holidays)*
Admission (1992): *free*
No. visitors (1992): *300 000 (est.)*

Facilities
Interpretation: *information boards*
Children: *adventure playground; play area; nappy changing*
Schools: *no special support*
Disabled: *easy access; disabled toilets*
Catering: *20 snack bars/food stalls*
Retailing: *postcards/inexpensive souvenirs; confectionery and ice cream; craftwork*
No. shops: *1*

Operations
Contact: *Mr C Manning (partner)*
No. employees: (high season) *20 full time; 10 part time* (low season) *10 full time; 2 part time*
Training: *F/T operations staff, P/T operations staff and casual operations staff are trained in-house and day-to-day on job using handling collections*
Languages spoken: *French*

Marketing
UK promotion: *local newspapers; regional tourist board; leaflets/information packs; ETB/BTA*

Environmental monitoring: *recycling; energy consumption; hazardous materials; chemical usage; humidity percentage*

CHARLES RENNIE MACKINTOSH SOCIETY
(charitable status)
church

Established: *1976*
Address: *Queens Cross, 870 Garscube Rd, Glasgow, G20 7EL*
Telephone: *(041) 946 6600*
Access: (road) *M8* (rail) *Glasgow*
Season: *all year*
Hours: *Throughout the year – Tues, Thurs and Fri – 12 noon to 5.30pm and 2.30pm to 5pm on Sun (also limited access at other times)*
Admission (1992): *free*
No. visitors (1992): *3000 (est.)*

Facilities
Interpretation: *leaflets; information boards; guide books*
Schools: *maximum no. 50; educational literature; lecture/talk*
Disabled: *leaflets; guide book; access difficult*
Catering: *1 snack bar/food stall*
Retailing: *postcards/inexpensive souvenirs; books*
No. shops: *1*

Operations
Contact: *Ms P Douglas (Director)*
Training: *casual operations staff are trained in-house and day-to-day on job using safety rules for rides*

Marketing
Annual event(s): *tours, conferences and lectures*
Sponsor(s): *various*
Affiliations: *Scottish Civic Trust*
Other: *market research*

UK promotion: *national newspapers; radio; regional tourist board; leaflets/information packs; STB*

Environmental monitoring: *energy consumption*

CHATELHERAULT COUNTRY PARK
(local authority run)
historic house; park/reserve

Established: *1987*
Address: *Ferniegair, Hamilton, ML3 7UE*
Telephone: *(0698) 426213.* Fax: *(0698) 421532*
Access: (road) *M74 (Junct 6)/A72* (rail) *Hamilton*
Parking capacity: (cars) *400* (coaches) *8*
Season: *all year*
Hours: *Apr to Sept – 10.30am to 6pm; Oct to Mar – 10.30am to 5pm; House – 11am to 4.30pm*
Admission (1992): *adults £1.15; children £0.60; OAP £0.60; student £0.60; ub40 £0.60*
No. visitors (1992): *300 000 (est.)*

Facilities
Interpretation: *videos; leaflets; audio tapes; information boards; slides; maps; tour guides; guide books; personnel*
Languages: *French; German*
Children: *adventure playground*
Schools: *educational literature; audio/visual presentation; lecture/talk*
Disabled: *easy access; disabled toilets*
Catering: *1 picnic area*
Franchisees: *Apr to Sept – 10.30am to 6pm; Oct to Mar 10.30am to 5pm. House – 11am to 4.30pm*
Retailing: *postcards/inexpensive souvenirs; craftwork; books*
No. shops: *1*

Operations
Contacts: *Mr J I Brockie MBE (Park Manager); Mr T J McCormack (Project Officer)*
No. employees: (high season) *9 full time; 4 part time* (low season) *9 full time*
Training: *F/T operations staff, F/T management and P/T operations staff are trained in-house and externally and on specific courses using handbooks*
Languages spoken: *French; German*

Marketing
Other: *press office; market research*
UK promotion: *local newspapers; regional tourist board; other attractions; leaflets/information packs; STB, Group Organisers and Travel Trade Guide; Clyde Valley Tourist Board*

CHATSWORTH
(trust)
historic house; garden; farmyard

Established: *1949*
Address: *Bakewell, Derbyshire, DE45 1PP*
Telephone: *(0246) 582204.* Fax: *(0246) 583536*
Access: (road) *M1* (rail) *Chesterfield*
Hours: *Easter to end Oct daily*
Admission (1992): *adults £4.75; children £2.25; OAP £4.00; student £4.00; family ticket £12.00*
No. visitors (1992): *340 000*

Facilities
Interpretation: *leaflets; audio tapes; guide books*
Languages: *Japanese; French; German*
Children: *adventure playground; nappy changing*
Schools: *educational literature; lecture/talk*
Disabled: *easy access; disabled toilets; leaflets; garden only*
Catering: *1 picnic area*
Retailing: *postcards/inexpensive souvenirs; confectionery and ice cream; craftwork; books; clothes; china; jumpers; pottery*
No. shops: *3*

Operations
Contacts: *Mr E Oliver; Mrs V Edwards (Shop Manager)*
No. employees: (high season) *40 full time; 130 part time* (low season) *40 full time*

Training: *F/T operations staff, P/T operations staff and casual operations staff are trained in-house and day-to-day on job*
Languages spoken: *French*

Marketing
Annual event: *angling and country fair*
Other: *press office; market research*
UK promotion: *national newspapers; radio; local newspapers; regional tourist board; other attractions; leaflets/information packs; ETB/BTA; local tourist boards*
Europe/USA promotion: *leaflets/brochures; travel agents' brochures; British Tourist Authority*

Environmental monitoring: *water quality; hazardous materials; chemical usage*

CHATTERLEY WHITFIELD MINING MUSEUM
(trust)
museum

Established: *1979*
Address: *Tunstall, Stoke on Trent, ST6 8UN*
Telephone: *(0782) 813337*
Access: (road) *M6/A527* (rail) *Stoke on Trent*
Parking capacity: (cars) *1000* (coaches) *200*
Season: *all year*
Hours: *Mar to Oct – Mon to Sun – 10am to 5pm; Nov to Feb – Tues to Sun – 11am to 4pm*
Admission (1992): *adults £4.15; children £3.10; OAP £3.10; student £3.10; family £12.50*
No. visitors (1992): *40 000*

Facilities
Interpretation: *leaflets; information boards; maps; tour guides; personnel*
Schools: *maximum no. 1000; educational literature; audio/visual presentation; lecture/talk; drama presentations*
Disabled: *disabled toilets; helpers; object handling sessions pit tours*
Catering: *1 picnic area*
Retailing: *postcards/inexpensive souvenirs; confectionery and ice cream; craftwork; books*
No. shops: *1*

Operations
Contacts: *J Hutchinson (Director); P Gifford (Reception and Retail Services Manager)*
No. employees: (high season) *6 full time; 8 part time* (low season) *6 full time; 8 part time*
Training: *F/T operations staff, F/T management, P/T operations staff, P/T management and casual operations staff are trained in-house and externally and on specific courses and day-to-day on job and pit visits using videos*

Marketing:
Annual event(s): *various*
Sponsor(s): *PMT Ltd, etc.*
Affiliations: *HETB, NSTA, NSMA, etc.*
Other: *market research*
UK promotion: *national newspapers; radio; local newspapers; regional tourist board; other attractions; leaflets/information packs; HETB Guides; ETB/BTA*
Europe/Australia/USA promotion: *leaflets/brochures; British Tourist Authority*

CHAVENAGE
(trust)
historic house

Established: *1971*
Address: *Chavenage, Tetbury, Glos, GL8 8XP*
Telephone: *(0666) 502329*
Access: (road) *M4/M5/A46* (rail) *Kemble*
Parking capacity: (cars) *50* (coaches) *3*
Hours: *May to Sept – Thurs and Sun – 2pm to 5pm also BH and Easter Sun. Parties of 20 or more at other times by arrangement*
Admission (1992): *adults £2.50; children £1.25; OAP £2.50; student £2.50; friends of HHA free*
No. visitors (1992): *3000 (est.)*

Facilities
Interpretation: *tour guides*

Schools: *maximum no. 50; educational literature; lecture/talk*
Catering: *1 picnic area*

Operations
Contact: *Mr D Lowsley-Williams (owner)*
No. employees: (high season) *1 part time* (low season) *1 part time*
Languages spoken: *French*

Marketing
Annual event: *Gloucester Drama Association*
Affiliation: *HHA*
UK promotion: *regional tourist board; leaflets/information packs; ETB/BTA; Heart of England and Thanetdown Tourist Boards*
USA promotion: *British Tourist Authority*

CHELMSFORD AND ESSEX, ESSEX REGIMENT MUSEUMS
(local authority run)
historic house; museum

Established: *1835*
Address: *Oaklands Park, Moulsham Street, Chelmsford, Essex, CM2 9AQ*
Telephone: *(0245) 353066/260614*
Access: (road) *M25/A12* (rail) *Chelmsford*
Parking capacity: (cars) *15*
Season: *all year*
Hours: *Summer – 10am to 5pm; Winter – 10am to 5pm – Mon to Sat, Sun 2pm to 5pm*
Admission (1992): *N/A*
No. visitors (1992): *40 000 (est.)*

Facilities
Interpretation: *videos; leaflets; information boards; signs*
Languages: *French; German*
Children: *play area*
Schools: *educational literature; audio/visual presentation*
Disabled: *easy access; tactile objects for blind groups*
Retailing: *postcards/inexpensive souvenirs; books; various*
No. shops: *1*

Operations
Contacts: *Ian Hook (Site Manager); Katharine Chant (Head of Museums Service)*
No. employees: (high season) *13 full time; 5 part time*
Training: *F/T operations staff, F/T management and P/T operations staff are trained in-house and externally and on specific courses and day-to-day on job*

Marketing
Annual event(s): *annual lecture; founders day; lecture; event*
Affiliations: *Museums Association, area museums service for SE England and others*
Other: *press office; market research*
UK promotion: *local newspapers; other attractions; leaflets/information packs*

CHELMSFORD CATHEDRAL
(cathedral)
church

Address: *New St, Chelmsford, Essex, CM1 1AT*
Telephone: *(0245) 263660.* Fax: *(0245) 496802*
Access: (road) *M25/A12* (rail) *Liverpool St*
Season: *all year*
Hours: *weekdays – 8am to 5.45pm*
Admission (1992): *free*
No. visitors (1992): *15 000 (est.)*

Facilities
Interpretation: *leaflets; information boards; guide books*
Languages: *French; German*
Schools: *maximum no. 40; educational literature; lecture/talk*
Disabled: *easy access*
Catering: *1 picnic area*

Retailing: *postcards/inexpensive souvenirs; craftwork; books*
No. shops: *1*

Operations
Contact: *Canon T Thompson (Vice-provost)*
Training: *casual operations staff are trained in-house and day-to-day on job using videos and handbooks*

Marketing
Annual event(s): *concerts*
Sponsor(s): *various*
Affiliations: *East Anglian Tourist Board*
Other: *press office*
UK promotion: *local newspapers; regional tourist board*

CHELSEA PHYSIC GARDEN
(limited company)
garden

Established: *1983*
Address: *66 Royal Hospital Rd, London, SW3 4HS*
Telephone: *(071) 352 5646*
Access: (road) *M4/M40/A3212* (rail) *Victoria*
Hours: *Apr to Oct – Sun and Wed – 2pm to 5pm; Chelsea Show week – 12 noon to 5pm; Chelsea Festival week – 12 noon to 5pm*
Admission (1992): *adults £2.50; children £1.30; OAP £2.50; student £1.30*
No. visitors (1992): *10 000*

Facilities
Interpretation: *leaflets; information boards; maps; tour guides; guide books; exhibition area*
Languages: *French; German; Italian*
Children: *nappy changing*
Schools: *maximum no. 15; educational literature; lecture/talk; workshops*
Disabled: *easy access; disabled toilets; helpers*
Catering: *1 licensed restaurant*
Franchisees: *Apr to Oct – Sun and Wed – 2pm to 5pm; Chelsea Show week – 12 noon to 5pm; Chelsea Festival week – 12 noon to 5pm*
Retailing: *postcards/inexpensive souvenirs; confectionery and ice cream; craftwork; books; clothes*
No. shops: *1*

Operations
Contact: *Ms S Minter (Curator)*
No. employees: (high season) *7 full time; 3 part time* (low season) *7 full time; 2 part time*
Training: *F/T operations staff, F/T management, P/T operations staff and casual operations staff are trained externally and on specific courses and day-to-day on job*
Languages spoken: *French; German*

Marketing
Annual event: *exhibition, Chelsea Flower Show week*
Affiliations: *NCCPE, BGCI*
Other: *market research*
UK promotion: *local newspapers; regional tourist board; other attractions; leaflets/information packs; ETB/BTA; in flight magazine*

CHESIL GALLERY
(private gallery)
museum; gallery; residential art gallery and studio

Established: *1985*
Address: *Chiswell, Portland, Dorset, DT5 1AW*
Telephone: *(0305) 822738*
Access: (road) *A354*
Parking capacity: (cars) *20* (coaches) *5*
Hours: *May to Sept; open for two months every day 2pm to 7pm (pay exhibitions); residential exhibitions Fri, Sat and Sun*
Admission (1992): *adults £1.50*
No. visitors (1992): *5000 (est.)*

Facilities
Interpretation: *leaflets; information boards; maps*
Languages: *French; German*
Children: *nappy changing*

Schools: *educational literature; lecture/talk; when appropriate*
Disabled: *easy access; helpers*
Catering: *1 picnic area*
Retailing: *postcards/inexpensive souvenirs; books; works of art*
No. shops: *1*

Operations
Contact: *Ms M Somerville (Organiser)*
No. employees: (high season) *1 part time*
Languages spoken: *French; German*

Marketing
Annual event(s): *special exhibitions loan from South Bank Centre or Henry Moore Foundation*
Sponsor(s): *various*
UK promotion: *national newspapers; local newspapers; regional tourist board; leaflets/information packs*
Europe promotion: *leaflets/brochures; travel agents' brochures*

Environmental monitoring: *recycling; waste; hazardous materials; chemical usage*

CHESSINGTON WORLD OF ADVENTURES
(plc)
theme park; zoo/wildlife attraction

Established: *1932*
Address: *Chessington, Surrey, KT9 2NE*
Telephone: *(0372) 729560.* Fax: *(0372) 725050*
Access: (road) *M25/A243/A3* (rail) *Chessington South*
Parking capacity: (cars) *10 000* (coaches) *110*
Hours: *zoo only – 1 Jan to 26 Mar, theme park – 27 Mar to 7 Nov; zoo only – 8 Nov to 19 Dec*
Admission (1992): *adults £10.75; children £9.75; OAP £5.00; student £5.50; group rates available*
No. visitors (1992): *1 250 000 (est.)*

Facilities
Interpretation: *leaflets; information boards; maps; guide books*
Children: *adventure playground; play area; nappy changing*
Schools: *maximum no. 6000; audio/visual presentation; lecture/talk; teachers booklet*
Disabled: *easy access; disabled toilets; leaflets; guide book*
Catering: *1 bar/public house*
Retailing: *postcards/inexpensive souvenirs; confectionery and ice cream; craftwork; clothes*
No. shops: *more than 4*

Operations
Contacts: *Mr D Attwood (Deputy General Manager, Operations); Ms R McEwan (Personnel); Ms C Grant (Merchandising); Mr B Sedgley (Sales)*
Training: *F/T operations staff, F/T management, P/T operations staff, P/T management, casual operations staff and casual management are trained in-house and externally and on specific courses and day-to-day on job*
Languages spoken: *French; German; Spanish; Chinese*

Marketing
Annual event(s): *fireworks*
Affiliations: *various tourist boards*
Other: *press office; market research*
UK promotion: *television; national newspapers; radio; local newspapers; regional tourist board; other attractions; leaflets/information packs; LTB, STB, SEETB*
Europe promotion: *leaflets/brochures; British Tourist Authority*

Environmental monitoring: *recycling; waste; water quality; energy consumption*

CHESTER CATHEDRAL
(cathedral)
church

Established: *1092*
Address: *1 Abbey Square, Chester, CH1 2HU*
Telephone: *(0244) 324756*

Access: (road) *M53/A41* (rail) *Chester*
Season: *all year*
Hours: *7.30am to 6.30pm daily*
Admission (1992): *free*
No. visitors (1992): *750 000*

Facilities
Interpretation: *videos; leaflets; information boards; tour guides; guide books; personnel*
Languages: *Japanese; French; German; Italian; Spanish; Welsh*
Schools: *maximum no. 50; educational literature; audio/visual presentation*
Disabled: *easy access; disabled toilets; helpers; guide book*
Catering: *1 licensed restaurant*
Retailing: *postcards/inexpensive souvenirs; craftwork; books; reproductions of famous artefacts; music tapes*
No. shops: *1*

Operations
Contacts: *Mr D Burrows (Cathedral Administrator)*
No. employees: (high season) *35 full time; 10 part time* (low season) *35 full time; 5 part time*

Environmental monitoring: *recycling; waste; water quality; energy consumption; hazardous materials; chemical usage; transport; emissions*

CHESTER VISITOR CENTRE
(limited company)
museum; tourist information centre with exhibition and video presentation

Established: *1984*
Address: *Vicars Lane, Chester, CH1 1QX*
Telephone: *(0244) 351609.* Fax: *(0244) 319819*
Access: (road) *M53/A56* (rail) *Chester General*
Season: *all year*
Hours: *Oct to Mar – 9am to 7pm; Apr to Sept – 9am to 9pm*
Admission (1992): *free*
No. visitors (1992): *300 000 (est.)*

Facilities
Interpretation: *videos; information boards; maps; tour guides; guide books*
Languages: *Japanese; Dutch; French; German; Italian; Spanish*
Schools: *maximum no. 100; educational literature; audio/visual presentation*
Disabled: *easy access*
Catering: *1 picnic area*
Retailing: *postcards/inexpensive souvenirs; confectionery and ice cream; craftwork; books; clothes; reproductions of famous artefacts; giftware*
No. shops: *2*

Operations
Contacts: *Mr K Wilson (Director); Ms V Pickering (Director); Mr D Walker*
No. employees: (high season) *8 full time; 10 part time* (low season) *7 full time; 3 part time*
Training: *F/T operations staff, P/T operations staff and casual operations staff are trained in-house and day-to-day on job*
Languages spoken: *French; German*

Marketing
Annual event(s): *craft fairs*
UK promotion: *national newspapers; local newspapers; regional tourist board; other attractions; leaflets/information packs; ETB/BTA*
BTA promotion: *leaflets/brochures; British Tourist Authority*

Environmental monitoring: *recycling*

CHESTER ZOO
(charity)
garden; zoo/wildlife attraction

Established: *1934*
Address: *Upton by Chester, Cheshire, CH2 1LH*

Telephone: *(0244) 380280*. Fax: *(0244) 371273*
Access: (road) *M56/M53/A41* (rail) *Chester*
Parking capacity: (cars) *6000* (coaches) *200*
Season: *all year*
Hours: *all year – from 10am daily*
Admission (1992): *adults £5.50; children £3.00;
   OAP £3.00;*
No. visitors (1992): *900 000*

Facilities
Interpretation: *information boards; maps; tour
   guides; guide books*
Languages: *Dutch; French; German; Chinese*
Children: *adventure playground; play area; nappy
   changing*
Schools: *maximum no. 100; educational literature;
   audio/visual presentation; educational tour;
   lecture/talk*
Disabled: *easy access; disabled toilets*
Catering: *1 bar/public house*
Retailing: *postcards/inexpensive souvenirs;
   confectionery and ice cream; craftwork; books;
   clothes; animal related toys and items*
No. shops: *3*

Operations
Contacts: *Dr M Brambell (Director); P Rudd
   (Personnel Officer); A Jones (Retail Sales
   Manager); C Vere (Marketing Manager)*
No. employees: (high season) *200 full time; 50
   part time* (low season) *140 full time*
Training: *F/T operations staff, P/T operations
   staff and casual operations staff are trained in-
   house and on specific courses and day-to-day
   on job using videos and handbooks*
Languages spoken: *French; Spanish; Japanese;
   Dutch*

Marketing
Affiliation: *National Federation of Zoological
   Gardens of Britain and Ireland*
Other: *press office; market research*
UK promotion: *television; radio; local
   newspapers; regional tourist board; other
   attractions; leaflets/information packs*

CHESTNUT CENTRE
(partnership)
park/reserve; zoo/wildlife attraction

Established: *1985*
Address: *Castleton Rd, Chapel-En-Le Frith,
   Derbyshire*
Telephone: *(0298) 814099*. Fax: *(0298) 816213*
Access: (road) *A625*
Parking capacity: (cars) *80* (coaches) *3*
Season: *all year*
Hours: *1 Mar to 1 Jan – 10.30am to 5.30pm or
   dusk daily; open weekends only – 2 Jan to end
   Feb*
Admission (1992): *adults £3.00; children £2.00;
   OAP £3.00; student £3.00*
No. visitors (1992): *50 000 (est.)*

Facilities
Interpretation: *information boards; guide books*
Children: *nappy changing*
Schools: *maximum no. 90; educational literature;
   lecture/talk; prior booking only*
Catering: *2 picnic areas*
Retailing: *postcards/inexpensive souvenirs;
   confectionery and ice cream; craftwork; books;
   clothes*
No. shops: *1*

Operations
Contact: *Mr R Heap (partner)*
No. employees: (high season) *4 full time; 4 part
   time* (low season) *2 full time; 1 part time*
Training: *F/T operations staff, F/T management,
   P/T operations staff and casual operations staff
   are trained in-house and day-to-day on job
   using videos and handbooks*
Languages spoken: *French; German*

Marketing
UK promotion: *leaflets/information packs*

Environmental monitoring: *energy consumption*

CHETTLE HOUSE
(privately owned)
historic house; garden

Established: *1984*
Address: *Chettle, Blandford Forum, Dorset*
Telephone: *(025889) 209*. Fax: *(025889) 380*
Access: (road) *A354*
Parking capacity: (cars) *100* (coaches) *4*
Hours: *Good Friday to 2nd Sun in Oct – 11am to
   5pm, not Sat and Tues*
Admission (1992): *adults £1.80; OAP £1.80*
No. visitors (1992): *8000 (est.)*

Facilities
Interpretation: *leaflets; guide books*
Schools: *maximum no. 40; educational literature*
Disabled: *helpers*
Catering: *1 picnic area*

Operations
Contact: *Mr P Bourke*
Languages spoken: *French*

Marketing
Annual event(s): *craft fair*
Other: *press office*
UK promotion: *local newspapers;
   leaflets/information packs*

Environmental monitoring: *recycling; water
   quality; energy consumption*

CHICHELEY HALL
(trust)
historic house; garden

Established: *1976*
Address: *Newport Pagnell, Bucks, MK16 9JJ*
Telephone: *(023065) 252*. Fax: *(023065) 388*
Access: (road) *M1/A422*
Parking capacity: (cars) *60* (coaches) *2*
Hours: *Easter to May and August – Sun and
   BH – 2.30pm to 5pm*
Admission (1992): *adults £3.00; children £1.50;
   student £1.50; groups £2.40*
No. visitors (1992): *3000 (est.)*

Facilities
Interpretation: *tour guides; guide books*
Schools: *maximum no. 40; lecture/talk*
Disabled: *easy access*
Catering: *1 self-service cafeteria*
Retailing: *postcards/inexpensive souvenirs;
   keyrings, etc.*
No. shops: *1*

Operations
Contacts: *J Ro*
Languages spoken: *French; Italian*

Marketing
Affiliations: *HHA*
UK promotion: *national newspapers; local
   newspapers; leaflets/information packs*
USA promotion: *travel agents' brochures*

Environmental monitoring: *recycling; waste;
   energy consumption; hazardous materials;
   chemical usage; transport; emissions*

CHILD-BEALE WILDLIFE PARK
(trust)
park/reserve; garden; zoo/wildlife attraction

Established: *1956*
Address: *Church Farm, Lower Basildon, Reading,
   Berks, RG8 9NH*
Telephone: *(0734) 845172*. Fax: *(0734) 845171*
Access: (road) *M4/A329* (rail) *Pangbourne*
Parking capacity: (cars) *1000* (coaches) *30*
Hours: *Mar to Dec – 10am to 6pm daily*
Admission (1992): *adults £4.00; children £2.00;
   OAP £3.00; disabled £2.00*
No. visitors (1992): *150 000 (est.)*

Facilities
Interpretation: *leaflets; information boards; maps;
   guide books; education and teacher packs*

Children: *adventure playground; play area; nappy
   changing*
Schools: *maximum no. 25; educational literature*
Disabled: *easy access; disabled toilets*
Catering: *6 picnic areas*
Franchisees: *Mar to Dec – 10am to 6pm daily*
Retailing: *postcards/inexpensive souvenirs;
   confectionery and ice cream; craftwork; books;
   clothes; souvenirs*
No. shops: *2*

Operations
Contacts: *A Howard (Manager); R Pratt (Shop
   Manager)*
No. employees: (high season) *12 full time; 13 part
   time* (low season) *12 full time; 2 part time*
Training: *F/T operations staff, P/T operations
   staff are trained in-house and day-to-day on job*

Marketing
Annual event(s): *craft fair, model boat fair, horse
   shows, etc.*
Sponsor(s): *Marine Modelling Magazine*
Other: *market research*
UK promotion: *national newspapers; radio; local
   newspapers; regional tourist board;
   leaflets/information packs; ETB/BTA; Beautiful
   Berkshire*
Europe promotion: *leaflets/brochures; British
   Tourist Authority*

Environmental monitoring: *recycling; waste;
   energy consumption*

CHILDREN'S FARM, THE
(family business)
open farm

Established: *1981*
Address: *Ash End House Farm, Middleton Lane,
   Middleton, Nr Tamworth, Staffs*
Telephone: *(021) 329 3240*
Access: (road) *M42/A4091*
Parking capacity: (cars) *200* (coaches) *8*
Season: *all year*
Hours: *10am to 6pm daily*
Admission (1992): *adults £1.10; children £2.20;
   OAP £1.10; student £1.10; teachers and
   disabled carers £1.10*
No. visitors (1992): *87 000 (est.)*

Facilities
Interpretation: *leaflets; information boards; tour
   guides*
Children: *adventure playground; play area; nappy
   changing*
Schools: *maximum no. 120; educational literature;
   pre-tour guide*
Disabled: *disabled toilets*
Catering: *2 picnic areas*
Retailing: *postcards/inexpensive souvenirs;
   confectionery and ice cream; craftwork; books*
No. shops: *1*

Operations
Contacts: *R G Rawlins (Farmer); J M Rawlins
   (Visits Coordinator); P Rawlins (Shop Manager)*
No. employees: (high season) *5 full time;
   19 part time* (low season) *4 full time; 12 part
   time*
Training: *F/T operations staff, P/T operations
   staff and casual operations staff are trained
   in-house and day-to-day on job*

Marketing
Market research
UK promotion: *local newspapers; regional tourist
   board; other attractions; leaflets/information
   packs*

CHILHAM CASTLE
(local authority run)
historic house; castle; garden

Established: *1950*
Address: *Chilham, Nr Canterbury, Kent,
   CT4 8DB*
Telephone: *(0227) 730319*

Access: (road) M2/M20/A252 (rail)
Chilham/Faversham
Hours: banqueting facilities open 11am to 5pm
daily
Admission (1992): adults £2.80; children £1.40;
OAP £2.20; group rates

Facilities
Interpretation: leaflets; information boards; maps;
guide books
Children: play area
Catering: 1 bar/public house
Retailing: postcards/inexpensive souvenirs
No. shops: 1

Operations
Contacts: Miss Martin; Mrs Stratford

Marketing
Affiliation: HHA
Other: market research
UK promotion: television; national newspapers;
radio; local newspapers; regional tourist board;
leaflets/information packs; ETB/BTA
Europe promotion: leaflets/brochures; travel
agents' brochures; British Tourist Authority

Environmental monitoring: waste; water quality;
hazardous materials; chemical usage

CHILLINGHAM CASTLE
(limited company)
castle; garden; museum

Established: 1986
Address: Chillingham, Alnwick, Northumberland,
NE66 5NJ
Telephone: (06685) 359. Fax: (06685) 463
Access: (road) A1/A697
Parking capacity: (cars) 60 (coaches) 10
Hours: Easter weekend and 1 May to 30 Sept –
1.30pm to 5pm, every day except Tues
Admission (1992): adults £3.00; children
£2.00; OAP £2.50; booked groups over 20
£2.00
No. visitors (1992): 18 000 (est.)

Facilities
Interpretation: leaflets; information boards; tour
guides; guide books
Schools: maximum no. 50; educational literature;
lecture/talk; tour on request
Disabled: disabled toilets
Catering: 1 self-service cafeteria
Retailing: antiques and curios
No. shops: 2

Operations
Contact: Mr B Bailles (Administrator)
No. employees: (high season) 2 full time;
9 part time (low season) 2 full time; 2 part
time

Marketing
Affiliations: HHA
Other: market research
UK promotion: national newspapers; local
newspapers; regional tourist board; other
attractions; leaflets/information packs; Coach
Drivers' Club

CHILLINGHAM WILD CATTLE ASSOCIATION LTD
(limited company and charity)
zoo/wildlife attraction

Established: 1939
Address: Estate House, Chillingham, Alnwick,
Northumberland, NE66 5NW
Telephone: (06685) 250
Access: (road) A1/A697
Parking capacity: (cars) 40 (coaches) 2
Hours: 1 Apr to 31 Oct – Sun – 2pm to 5pm;
Mon to Sat except Tues – 10am to noon and
2pm to 5pm (other times by arrangement)
Admission (1992): adults £2.00; children £0.50;
OAP £1.50; groups of 20 or more £1.50
No. visitors (1992): 7000 (est.)

Facilities
Interpretation: tour guides
Schools: maximum no. 50; no special support
Catering: 1 picnic area
Retailing: postcards/inexpensive souvenirs;
Chillingham bull mugs
No. shops: 1

Operations
Contacts: Mrs A Widdows (Secretary/Treasurer);
Mr A Widdows (Warden)
No. employees: (high season) 1 full time; 1 part
time (low season) 2 part time

Marketing
UK promotion: local newspapers; regional tourist
board; other attractions; leaflets/information
packs; local guides and NTB

CHILTERN OPEN AIR MUSEUM
(charity)
historic house; garden; museum; open air museum
of buildings

Established: 1981
Address: Newland park, Gorelands Lane,
Chalfont St Giles, Bucks, HP8 4AD
Telephone: (0494) 871117
Access: (road) M25/A413/A412
Parking capacity: (cars) 200 (coaches) 4
Hours: Apr to Oct – Wed to Sun – 2pm to 6pm
Admission (1992): adults £2.50; children £2.00;
OAP £2.00; student £2.00;
No. visitors (1992): 50 800

Facilities
Interpretation: information boards; maps; guide
books; personnel
Children: adventure playground
Schools: maximum no. 200; educational literature;
lecture/talk; activity sessions
Disabled: easy access; disabled toilets;
braille/sound posts; other audio facilities
Catering: 1 picnic area
Retailing: postcards/inexpensive souvenirs;
confectionery and ice cream; craftwork; books;
clothes; reproductions of famous artefacts;
models of buildings
No. shops: 1

Operations
Contacts: J & M Moir (Project Directors);
P Shreeve (Shop Manager)
No. employees: (high season) 4 full time; 152 part
time (low season) 4 full time; 80 part time
Training: F/T operations staff, F/T management,
casual operations staff and casual management
are trained externally and on specific courses
and day-to-day on job

Marketing
Annual event(s): children's Day, transport festival,
sheepdog trials, harvest celebrations, Victorian
Christmas
Sponsor: Trebor Bassett
Affiliations: AIM
Other: market research
UK promotion: local newspapers; regional tourist
board; other attractions; leaflets/information
packs

Environmental monitoring: chemical usage; No
fertilisers or sprays

CHINGLE HALL
(private)
historic house

Established: 1960
Address: Whittingham Lane, Goosnargh, Preston,
Lancs, PR3 2JJ
Telephone: (0772) 861082
Access: (road) M6/A6 (rail) Preston
Parking capacity: (cars) 60 (coaches) 2
Hours: Easter to Oct – Mon to Sat – 12 noon to
4pm, Sun – 10am to 5pm
Admission (1992): adults £2.50; children £1.50;
OAP £2.00; student £2.00;
No. visitors (1992): 12 000

Facilities
Interpretation: tour guides
Languages: German
Schools: maximum no. 50; work sheet
Disabled: easy access
Catering: 1 picnic area
Retailing: postcards/inexpensive souvenirs;
confectionery and ice cream
No. shops: 1

Operations
Contacts: S Bruce; D Burn
No. employees: (high season) 25 part time (low
season) 25 part time
Training: P/T operations staff are trained
in-house and on specific courses using
handbooks
Languages spoken: French; German

Marketing
Annual event(s): Hallowe'en candlelit tours
UK promotion: local newspapers;
leaflets/information packs

CHOLDERTON RARE BREEDS FARM PARK
(family business)
garden; farm park

Established: 1987
Address: Amesbury Road, Cholderton, Salisbury,
Wilts, SP4 0EW
Telephone: (0980) 64438
Access: (road) A303
Parking capacity: (cars) 100 (coaches) 10
Hours: Mar to Oct – 10am to 6pm daily
Admission (1992): adults £3.00; children £1.50;
OAP £2.50;
No. visitors (1992): 30 000 (est.)

Facilities
Interpretation: information boards; maps
Children: adventure playground; play area
Schools: educational literature; educational tour;
lecture/talk
Disabled: easy access
Catering: 3 picnic areas
Retailing: postcards/inexpensive souvenirs;
confectionery and ice cream; craftwork; books;
clothes
No. shops: 1

Operations
Contacts: D W and P R Sydenham (proprietors)
No. employees: (high season) 4 full time; 5 part
time (low season) 3 full time
Training: F/T operations staff, P/T operations
staff and casual operations staff are trained in-
house and day-to-day on job using handbooks

Marketing
Market research
UK promotion: local newspapers; regional tourist
board; other attractions; leaflets/information
packs; Welcome to Wiltshire, Best of
Hampshire, Best of Salisbury; ETB/BTA;
Winchester Guide, Southampton Guide,
Discover Dorset
Europe promotion: leaflets/brochures; Dorset
County Council

Environmental monitoring: energy consumption

CHRIST CHURCH CATHEDRAL
(charity)
church

Established: 1546
Address: St Aldates, Oxford
Telephone: (0865) 276154
Access: (road) M40 (rail) Oxford
Season: all year
Hours: all year – 9am to 4.30pm daily (open from
1pm Sun)
Admission (1992): adults £1.50; children £0.50;
OAP £0.50; student £0.50;
No. visitors (1992): 239 000

Facilities
Interpretation: videos; leaflets; information
boards; tour guides; guide books

Languages: *Japanese; Dutch; French; German; Italian; Spanish; Chinese*
Schools: *maximum no. 100; audio/visual presentation; lecture/talk*
Disabled: *easy access*
Retailing: *postcards/inexpensive souvenirs*
No. shops: *1*

Operations
Contacts: *E Evans (Dean Verger)*
Languages spoken: *French*

CHRISTCHURCH PRIORY
(place of worship)
church

Established: *1000*
Address: *Christchurch, Dorset, BH23 1BU*
Telephone: *(0202) 485804*
Access: *(road) M27/A35 (rail) Christchurch*
Season: *all year*
Hours: *Weekdays – 9.30am to 5.30pm subject to service times, Sun – 2.15pm to 5.30pm*
Admission (1992): *£1.00 donation requested, visit to tower £0.50 and museum £0.50*
No. visitors (1992): *175 000 (est.)*

Facilities
Interpretation: *leaflets; information boards; tour guides; guide books*
Languages: *Japanese; French; German; Italian; Spanish*
Schools: *maximum no. 25; educational literature; lecture/talk*
Disabled: *easy access; leaflets; guide book; large typed plan*
Retailing: *postcards/inexpensive souvenirs; books*
No. shops: *2*

Operations
Contacts: *G Piper, (Chairman, Priory Pilgrims and tourism); Mrs H Denton (bookstall and gift shop)*
No. employees: *(high season) 1 full time; 1 part time (low season) 1 full time; 1 part time*

Marketing
Annual event(s): *concerts on Wednesdays in Summer, organ recitals most Thursdays*
Sponsor(s): *various local firms*
Affiliations: *STB*
UK promotion: *regional tourist board; other attractions; leaflets/information packs*

CHRISTCHURCH SPITALFIELDS
(Church of England)
church

Established: *1987*
Address: *2 Fournier St, London, E1 6QE*
Telephone: *(071) 247 7202*
Access: *(road) Inner Ring Road A501 (rail) Aldgate East*
Season: *all year*
Hours: *Mon to Fri – 12 noon to 2.30pm, Sun – service times 10.30am and 6.30pm*
Admission (1992): *N/A*

Facilities
Interpretation: *tour guides*
Disabled: *easy access; lifts*

Operations
Contacts: *H Garraway (Parish Assistant)*
Languages spoken: *French; German; Spanish*

Marketing
Annual event(s): *music festival*
UK promotion: *ETB/BTA*

CHRISTCHURCH TRICYCLE MUSEUM
(private and local authority)
museum

Established: *1985*
Address: *Quay Rd, Christchurch, Dorset, BH23 1BY*
Telephone: *(0202) 479849*
Access: *(road) A35 (rail) Christchurch*
Hours: *Jun, Jul, Aug, Sept – 10am to 5pm daily – weekends only Easter, Apr, May, Oct*
Admission (1992): *adults £1.00; children £0.60; OAP £0.80; student £0.80; family ticket £2.50, group; rates*
No. visitors (1992): *9000 (est.)*

Facilities
Interpretation: *leaflets; audio tapes; information boards*
Schools: *maximum no. 20; lecture/talk; talk if required; questionnaire*
Retailing: *postcards/inexpensive souvenirs*
No. shops: *1*

Operations
Contacts: *Ms B Derby/Mr S Black (Curators); Mr R Street (Director and owner)*
No. employees: *(high season) 1 full time; 1 part time*

Marketing
Annual event(s): *tricycle cavalcade*
Affiliations: *AIM, Southern Tourist Board*
Other: *market research*
UK promotion: *other attractions; leaflets/information packs*

CHURCH OF ST CUTHBERT AND TURNER MAUSOLEUM
(parochial church council)
church

Established: *1982*
Address: *Kirkleatham Village, Redcar, Cleveland*
Telephone: *(0642) 475198*
Access: *(road) A1M/A174/A1042 (rail) Redcar*
Parking capacity: *(cars) 25 (coaches) 2*
Hours: *Apr to Oct – Sat, Sun and BH – 2pm to 5pm*
Admission (1992): *free*
No. visitors (1992): *3000 (est.)*

Facilities
Interpretation: *leaflets; tour guides; guide books*
Schools: *maximum no. 50; lecture/talk*
Disabled: *helpers*
Retailing: *postcards/inexpensive souvenirs*
No. shops: *1*

Operations
Contacts: *Mrs D Cook (Church Warden/Verger); R S Ramsdale (Administrator)*
No. employees: *(high season) 20 part time*
Training: *P/T operations staff are trained in-house and on specific courses and day-to-day on job*

Marketing
Annual event(s): *various concerts*
Affiliations: *Northumbria Tourist Board, HHA*
UK promotion: *regional tourist board*

CHURCH OF ST MARTIN-WITHIN-LUDGATE
(trust and Church of England)
church

Established: *1685*
Address: *Ludgate Hill, London, EC4*
Telephone: *(071) 628 0478*
Season: *all year*
Hours: *Tues to Sun morning and afternoon*
Admission (1992): *free*
No. visitors (1992): *10 000 (est.)*

Facilities
Interpretation: *leaflets; tour guides*
Schools: *maximum no. 12; educational literature; lecture/talk*

Retailing: *postcards/inexpensive souvenirs; books*
No. shops: *none*

Operations
Contacts: *Mr J Prentice (Church Warden)*

Marketing
Annual event(s): *music recitals*
Affiliations: *St Paul's Cathedral*
UK promotion: *leaflets/information packs; ETB/BTA*

CHURCH OF THE HOLYRUDE STIRLING
(Church of Scotland)
church

Established: *1600*
Address: *St John St, Stirling*
Telephone: *(0786) 74154*
Season: *all year*
Hours: *For public worship on all Sundays throughout the year. Open to visitors May to Sept – Mon to Fri – 10am to 5pm*
Admission (1992): *offering plate*
No. visitors (1992): *7500 (est.)*

Facilities
Interpretation: *leaflets; information boards; tour guides; guide books*
Languages: *French; German; Italian; Spanish*

CHURCHILL GARDENS MUSEUM
(local authority run)
garden; museum

Established: *1967*
Address: *Venns Lane, Hereford*
Telephone: *(0432) 267409. Fax: (0432) 342662*
Parking capacity: *(cars) 25 (coaches) 2*
Season: *all year*
Admission (1992): *adults £0.75; children £0.40; OAP £0.40*
No. visitors (1992): *6000 (est.)*

Facilities
Interpretation: *leaflets; tour guides*
Schools: *maximum no. 50; educational literature; lecture/talk*
Disabled: *easy access; helpers*
Retailing: *postcards/inexpensive souvenirs; craftwork; books; reproductions of famous artefacts; straw work*
No. shops: *1*

Operations
No. employees: *(high season) 2 full time; 2 part time (low season) 2 full time*
Training: *F/T operations staff and P/T operations staff are trained in-house and day-to-day on job*

Marketing
Annual event: *Victoria Christmas event*
Affiliations: *West Midlands Area Museum Service, Museum and Galleries Commission, MA*
Other: *market research*
UK promotion: *local newspapers; regional tourist board; leaflets/information packs; ETB/BTA*

CIDER MUSEUM AND KING OFFA DISTILLERY
(trust)
museum; working cider brandy distillery

Established: *1981*
Address: *21 Ryelands Street, Hereford, HR4 0LW*
Telephone: *(0423) 354207*
Access: *(road) M50/A49/A438 (rail) Shrewsbury*
Parking capacity: *(cars) 30 (coaches) 2*
Season: *all year*

Hours: *Apr to Oct – Mon to Sun – 10am to 5.30pm; Nov to Mar – Mon to Sat – 1pm to 5pm; closed Christmas, Boxing, New Year's Day*
Admission (1992): *adults £1.80; children £1.25; OAP £1.25; student £1.25; group discounts*
No. visitors (1992): *22 447*

Facilities
Interpretation: *leaflets; audio tapes; information boards; slides; displays and exhibits*
Schools: *maximum no. 50*
Retailing: *postcards/inexpensive souvenirs; confectionery and ice cream; craftwork; books; cider products*
No. shops: *1*

Operations
Contacts: *K Bradbury (Curator); P Dabbs (Museum Assistant); T Carr (Promotions Consultant)*
No. employees: *(high season) 2 full time; 13 part time (low season) 2 full time; 12 part time*
Training: *F/T management are trained in-house and externally and on specific courses using videos*
Languages spoken: *French*

Marketing
Annual event(s): *apple day celebrations*
Affiliations: *Museums Association, Association of Independent Museums*
Other: *market research*
UK promotion: *local newspapers; regional tourist board; other attractions; leaflets/information packs; ETB/BTA; Association of promotion for Herefordshire Handbook*
Europe/USA promotion: *leaflets/brochures; travel agents' brochures*

Environmental monitoring: *recycling; energy consumption; hazardous materials; chemical usage*

CILGWYN CANDLES WORKSHOP AND MINI MUSEUM
(partnership)
museum; gallery; craft workshop

Established: *1976*
Address: *Trefelin, Cilgwyn, Newport, Pembs, Dyfed SA42 0QN*
Telephone: *(0239) 820470. Fax: (0239) 820470*
Access: *(road) M4/A487 (rail) Haverfordwest*
Parking capacity: *(cars) 8*
Season: *all year*
Hours: *all year – 10am to 6pm*
Admission (1992): *free*
No. visitors (1992): *13 000*

Facilities
Interpretation: *leaflets; information boards*
Schools: *maximum no. 20; lecture/talk; candle making demonstration*
Disabled: *easy access*
Retailing: *postcards/inexpensive souvenirs; craftwork; books; candles and related goods; local books*
No. shops: *1*

Operations
Contacts: *Mrs Inger John (Proprietor); Dr Brian John*
No. employees: *(high season) 1 full time; 1 part time*
Languages spoken: *French*

Marketing
Affiliations: *Origin Dyfed, Pembrokeshire craft markets, Newport Chamber of Trade*
Other: *market research*
UK promotion: *radio; local newspapers; regional tourist board; other attractions; leaflets/information packs; Dyfed Craft Trail; WTB and South Wales Tourism Council*

Environmental monitoring: *recycling; hazardous materials*

CLAN MACPHERSON MUSEUM
(trust)
museum

Established: *1952*
Address: *Newtonmore, Inverness-shire*
Telephone: *(0540) 673 332*
Access: *(road) A9*
Parking capacity: *(cars) 10*
Hours: *1 May to 30 Sept – Mon to Sat – 10am to 5.30pm; Sun – 2.30pm to 5.30pm*
Admission (1992): *free*
No. visitors (1992): *5000 (est.)*

Facilities
Interpretation: *slides*
Schools: *maximum no. 30; no special support; talks by arrangement*
Disabled: *easy access*
Retailing: *postcards/inexpensive souvenirs; books; clothes; personalised museum items*
No. shops: *1*

Operations
Contacts: *Mr A Macpherson (Museum Curator); Ms S Macpherson (Secretary - Trustees)*
No. employees: *(high season) 1 full time*
Training: *F/T operations staff are trained externally and on specific courses*

Marketing
UK promotion: *local newspapers; leaflets/information packs; ETB/BTA*

Environmental monitoring: *recycling; waste; energy consumption; hazardous materials*

CLANDON PARK
(trust)
historic house; garden; museum

Established: *1970*
Address: *West Clandon, Guildford, Surrey, GU4 7RQ*
Telephone: *(0483) 222482*
Access: *(road) A247/A246*
Parking capacity: *(cars) 200 (coaches) 4*
Hours: *Apr to Oct – Sat to Wed – 1.30pm to 5.30pm*
Admission (1992): *adults £3.60; children £1.80; OAP £3.60; student £3.60; groups £3.00*
No. visitors (1992): *50 943*

Facilities
Interpretation: *leaflets; information boards; guide books*
Languages: *Dutch; French; German*
Children: *nappy changing*
Schools: *lecture/talk*
Disabled: *disabled toilets; braille/sound posts; special signs*
Catering: *1 picnic area*
Franchisees: *Apr to Oct – Sat to Wed – 1.30pm to 5.30pm*
Retailing: *postcards/inexpensive souvenirs; craftwork; books; clothes; china*
No. shops: *1*

Operations
Contact: *D Asquith (Administrator)*
No. employees: *(high season) 19 full time; 2 part time (low season) 15 full time*
Training: *F/T operations staff and F/T management are trained in-house and externally and on specific courses*

Marketing
Annual event(s): *recitals and concerts*
Sponsor(s): *various*
Affiliations: *National Trust*
Other: *press office; market research*
UK promotion: *centrally through National Trust*

CLAPTON COURT GARDENS
(privately owned)
garden; plant centre

Established: *1979*
Address: *Crewkerne, Somerset, TA18 8PT*

Telephone: *(0460) 73220*
Access: *(road) A30/B3165*
Hours: *Mar to Oct – Mon to Fri – 10.30am to 5pm; Sun – 2pm to 5pm, Easter Sat – 2pm to 5pm*
Admission (1992): *adults £3.00; children £1.00; OAP £3.00; student £1.50; under 4s free*
No. visitors (1992): *25 000 (est.)*

Facilities
Catering: *1 waiter/waitress served*
Retailing: *unusual plants, shrubs and trees*
No. shops: *1*

Operations
Contacts: *Captain S Loder (Proprietor); Mrs P Cox (Stock Manager)*
No. employees: *(high season) 3 full time; 5 part time (low season) 3 full time; 2 part time*
Training: *P/T operations staff are trained in-house and day-to-day on job using videos and handbooks*

Marketing
Annual event: *rare plant sale in aid of NCCPG*
Affiliations: *HHA, STB, West Country Tourist Board*
UK promotion: *national newspapers; local newspapers; regional tourist board; other attractions; leaflets/information packs*

Environmental monitoring: *chemical usage*

CLUANIE DEER FARM PARK
(limited company)
theme park; zoo/wildlife attraction

Established: *1987*
Address: *Near Beauly, Inverness-shire, IV4 7AE*
Telephone: *(0463) 782415. Fax: (0463) 782415*
Parking capacity: *(cars) 90 (coaches) 3*
Hours: *mid May to mid Oct – 10am to 5pm daily*
Admission (1992): *adults £2.75; children £1.75; OAP £2.25; student £2.75*
No. visitors (1992): *29 000*

Facilities
Interpretation: *videos; information boards; maps; guide books; personnel*
Children: *play area*
Schools: *maximum no. 200; educational literature; audio/visual presentation; lecture/talk*
Disabled: *easy access; disabled toilets; helpers*
Catering: *2 picnic areas*
Retailing: *postcards/inexpensive souvenirs; confectionery and ice cream; craftwork; books; clothes; farm produce; tapes and CDs*
No. shops: *1*

Operations
Contacts: *Mr W Crawford (Manager); Mr A Crawford (Director)*
No. employees: *(high season) 3 full time; 3 part time (low season) 2 full time*
Training: *F/T operations staff, F/T management and P/T operations staff are trained in-house and externally and on specific courses and day-to-day on job using handbooks*

Marketing
Annual event(s): *gourmet food fair, wool fair, wood fair, etc.*
UK promotion: *national newspapers; radio; local newspapers; regional tourist board; other attractions; leaflets/information packs; ETB/BTA*

COACH HOUSE MUSEUM
(trust)
heritage centre; museum

Established: *1981*
Address: *St George's Close, Langton Matravers, Swanage, Dorset*
Telephone: *(0929) 423168*
Access: *(road) A351/B3069 (rail) Wareham*
Parking capacity: *(cars) 8*
Hours: *1 Apr to 31 Oct – Mon to Sat – 10am to 12 noon and 2pm to 4pm. At other times by appointment*

Admission (1992): *adults £0.50; children £0.20; OAP £0.50; student £0.20*
No. visitors (1992): *2600*

Facilities
Interpretation: *leaflets; audio tapes; slides; maps; tour guides*
Languages: *French; German; Italian; Spanish*
Schools: *maximum no. 16; audio/visual presentation; lecture/talk; work sheets and activities*
Disabled: *easy access*
Retailing: *postcards/inexpensive souvenirs; books*
No. shops: *1*

Operations
Contacts: *R Saville (Curator); M Harrison (Treasurer); H Roe (Publicity Officer)*
No. employees: *(high season) 24 part time*
Languages spoken: *French; German; Turkish; Russian; Gaelic*

Marketing
Affiliations: *AIM, AMC, ABA*
UK promotion: *radio; local newspapers; other attractions; leaflets/information packs*

COATS OBSERVATORY
(local authority run)
museum; observatory

Established: *1883*
Address: *49 Oakshaw St West, Paisley, PA1 2DR*
Telephone: *(041) 889 2013.* Fax: *(041) 889 9240*
Access: *(road) M8 (rail) Paisley Gilmour St*
Season: *all year*
Hours: *Mon, Tues, Thurs – 2pm to 8pm; Wed, Fri, Sat – 10am to 5pm (closed Sun and Public Holidays)*
Admission (1992): *free*
No. visitors (1992): *12 000 (est.)*

Facilities
Interpretation: *videos; leaflets; information boards; slides; tour guides*
Languages: *French; German*
Schools: *maximum no. 25; educational literature; audio/visual presentation; lecture/talk*
Retailing: *postcards/inexpensive souvenirs*
No. shops: *1*

Operations
Contacts: *Mr P McCormack (Observatory Officer)*
No. employees: *(high season) 3 full time; 1 part time*
Training: *F/T operations staff and P/T operations staff are trained in-house and on specific courses and day-to-day on job*
Languages spoken: *French; German; Italian*

Marketing
UK promotion: *local newspapers; regional tourist board; leaflets/information packs*

COBHAM MANOR RIDING CENTRE AND COUNTRY PURSUITS
(local authority run)
equestrian centre, base for circular walks

Established: *1992*
Address: *Water Lane, Thurnham, Maidstone, Kent, ME14 3LU*
Telephone: *(0622) 38497/38871*
Access: *(road) M20/A20*
Parking capacity: *(cars) 120 (coaches) 40*
Season: *all year*
Hours: *all year – Tues to Sun – 9am to 6pm*
Admission (1992): *free*
No. visitors (1992): *20 000 (est.)*

Facilities
Interpretation: *leaflets; information boards; maps; tour guides*
Schools: *maximum no. 20; no special support*
Disabled: *easy access*
Catering: *1 picnic area*
Retailing: *postcards/inexpensive souvenirs; confectionery and ice cream; books; clothes*

No. shops: *1*

Operations
Contacts: *Mr and Mrs J Brumer (proprietors)*
No. employees: *(high season) 6 full time; 6 part time (low season) 6 full time; 6 part time*
Training: *F/T operations staff are trained in-house and on specific courses and day-to-day on job*

Marketing
Affiliations: *British Horse Society*
Other: *press office*
UK promotion: *local newspapers; regional tourist board; leaflets/information packs*

COCKLEY CLEY ICENI VILLAGE AND MUSEUMS
(limited company)
historic house; museum; church; reconstucted iceni village, medieval and Saxon buildings

Established: *1971*
Address: *The Estate Office, Cockley Cley, Swaffham, Norfolk, PE37 8AG*
Telephone: *(0760) 721339*
Access: *(road) A1065*
Parking capacity: *(cars) 150 (coaches) 10*
Hours: *1 Apr to 31 Oct – 11am to 5pm daily*
Admission (1992): *adults £2.50; children £1.00; OAP £1.50; student £1.50; 10% discount for groups of 10 or more*
No. visitors (1992): *30 000 (est.)*

Facilities
Interpretation: *leaflets; information boards; maps; guide books*
Schools: *maximum no. 200; educational literature; lecture/talk*
Disabled: *disabled toilets; braille/sound posts*
Catering: *1 picnic area*
Retailing: *postcards/inexpensive souvenirs; confectionery and ice cream; books; reproductions of famous artefacts*
No. shops: *1*

Operations
Contact: *Group Captain T Ferguson OBE (Director)*
No. employees: *(high season) 6 part time (low season) 3 part time*

Marketing
UK promotion: *local newspapers; regional tourist board; other attractions; leaflets/information packs; ETB/BTA; school publications*
Europe promotion: *British Tourist Authority*

Environmental monitoring: *waste; energy consumption*

COCKTHORPE HALL TOY MUSEUM
(private company)
museum

Established: *1987*
Address: *Cockthorpe, Wells, Norfolk, NR23 1QS*
Telephone: *(0328) 830293*
Access: *(road) A149*
Parking capacity: *(cars) 20*
Season: *all year*
Hours: *Summer – 10.00am to 5.00pm, Winter – 11.00am to 4.00pm*
Admission (1992): *adults £2.00; children £1.00; OAP £1.75*
No. visitors (1992): *30 000 (est.)*

Facilities
Interpretation: *videos; leaflets; audio tapes; information boards; guide books; signs*
Schools: *maximum no. 100; lecture/talk; demonstrations*
Catering: *1 snack bar/food stall*
Retailing: *postcards/inexpensive souvenirs; books; toys*
No. shops: *1*

Operations
Contact: *David Kidd (Proprietor)*
No. employees: *(high season) 1 full time; 2 part time (low season) 1 full time*

Training: *F/T operations staff and P/T operations staff are trained in-house and day-to-day on job*

Marketing
Annual event(s): *Father Christmas in Toyland*
Other: *market research*
UK promotion: *local newspapers; leaflets/information packs*

COLCHESTER ZOO
(limited company)
zoo/wildlife attraction

Established: *1963*
Address: *Maldon Rd, Stanway, Colchester, Essex, CO3 5SL*
Telephone: *(0206) 331292.* Fax: *(0206) 331392*
Access: *(road) A604/A12 (rail) Colchester*
Parking capacity: *(cars) 3000*
Season: *all year*
Hours: *9.30am daily – last admissions 5.30pm or 1 hour before dusk if earlier*
Admission (1992): *adults £4.70; children £2.60; OAP £4.00; disabled £1.90, under 3s free*
No. visitors (1992): *302 000*

Facilities
Interpretation: *leaflets; audio tapes; information boards; maps; tour guides; guide books; personnel*
Children: *adventure playground; nappy changing*
Schools: *educational literature; projects and work sheets*
Disabled: *easy access; disabled toilets; special signs; zoo is very hilly – easier route is provided*
Catering: *3 picnic areas*
Retailing: *postcards/inexpensive souvenirs; confectionery and ice cream; books; clothes*
No. shops: *4*

Operations
Contacts: *Mr D Tropeano (Director); Mrs A Tropeano (Director); Ms A Burr (Marketing Director)*
No. employees: *(high season) 60 full time; 40 part time (low season) 30 full time; 20 part time*
Training: *F/T operations staff, P/T operations staff and casual operations staff are trained in-house and day-to-day on job*

Marketing
Annual event(s): *special interest days including Santa's Grotto*
Other: *press office; market research*
UK promotion: *local newspapers; regional tourist board; other attractions; leaflets/information packs; ETB/BTA*
Europe promotion: *British Tourist Authority*

COLLECTION OF THE WORSHIPFUL COMPANY OF CLOCKMAKERS
(trust)
museum

Established: *1873*
Address: *The Clock Room, Guildhall Library, Aldermanbury, London, EC2P 2EJ*
Access: *(rail) Moorgate*
Season: *all year*
Hours: *Mon to Fri – 9.30am to 4.30pm except BH (often closed for 2 hours Mon am)*
Admission (1992): *free*

Facilities
Interpretation: *guide books*
Disabled: *easy access*

Operations
No. employees: *(high season) 2 part time*

COLLIFORD LAKE PARK
(private)
park/reserve; museum; zoo/wildlife attraction

Established: *1984*
Address: *St Neot, Liskeard, Cornwall, PL14 6PZ*
Telephone: *(020882) 469*
Access: (road) *A30*
Parking capacity: (cars) *100* (coaches) *4*
Hours: *Easter to Oct - 10.30am to 5pm daily (open until 6pm in mid season)*
Admission (1992): *adults £3.50; children £2.50; OAP £3.00; family ticket available*

Facilities
Interpretation: *leaflets; information boards*
Children: *adventure playground; play area; nappy changing*
Schools: *no special support; educational literature; handling sessions*
Disabled: *easy access; disabled toilets*
Catering: *2 picnic areas*
Retailing: *postcards/inexpensive souvenirs; confectionery and ice cream; craftwork; books; clothes; animal ornaments*
No. shops: *1*

Operations
Contacts: *W F Harper (Owner)*
No. employees: (high season) *3 full time; 2 part time* (low season) *3 full time; 2 part time*

Marketing
UK promotion: *local newspapers; regional tourist board; other attractions; leaflets/information packs; ETB/BTA*

COLNE VALLEY MUSEUM
(trust)
museum; listed building

Established: *1970*
Address: *Cliffe ash, Golcar, Huddersfield, W Yorks, HD7 4PY*
Telephone: *(0484) 659762*
Access: (road) *M62/A62*
Season: *all year*
Hours: *Sat, Sun, and BH - 2pm to 5pm except Christmas and New Year*
Admission (1992): *adults £0.80; children £0.40; OAP £0.40; student £0.40; groups by arrangement*
No. visitors (1992): *10 000 (est.)*

Facilities
Interpretation: *leaflets; information boards; tour guides; guide books; stewards*
Schools: *maximum no. 35; lecture/talk; craft activities*
Disabled: *2 out of 3 floors accessible, assistance by arrangement*
Catering: *1 snack bar/food stall*
Retailing: *postcards/inexpensive souvenirs; craftwork; books; clogs, cloth woven on site*
No. shops: *1*

Operations
Contacts: *Mrs L Ellis (Secretary); Mrs M Haywood (Membership Secretary); Mr B Kilner (Executive Committee Member)*

Marketing
Annual event(s): *craft and working weekends*
Affiliations: *Yorks and Humbs Tourist Board, Yorks and Humbs Museums Council*
UK promotion: *radio; local newspapers; regional tourist board; leaflets/information packs; ETB/BTA; posters*

COLNE VALLEY RAILWAY
(limited company and preservation society)
museum; tourist steam railway

Established: *1972*
Address: *Castle Hedingham, Halstead, Essex, CO9 3DZ*
Telephone: *(0787) 61174*
Access: (road) *A604* (rail) *Braintree*

Parking capacity: (cars) *200* (coaches) *20*
Hours: *Closed 23 Dec to 1 Feb and Mon; otherwise 10am to 5pm or dusk if earlier*
Admission (1992): *adults £4.00; children £2.00; OAP £2.00; student £4.00; prices include steam train rides; also family tickets and static display prices*
No. visitors (1992): *60 000 (est.)*

Facilities
Interpretation: *information boards; guide books; personnel; tours by arrangement*
Schools: *maximum no. 1000; educational literature; lecture/talk; specially organised visit*
Disabled: *easy access; helpers; helpers by arrangement, some trains suitable for wheelchairs*
Catering: *1 picnic area*
Franchisees: *Closed 23 Dec to 1 Feb and Mon; otherwise 10am to 5pm or dusk if earlier*
Retailing: *postcards/inexpensive souvenirs; confectionery and ice cream; books*
No. shops: *2*

Operations
Contact: *Mr D Humas (Manager)*

Marketing
Annual event(s): *Santa special and themed special interest events*
Sponsor(s): *Eastern Electricity*
Affiliations: *Association of Railway Press Societies, Association of Independent Railways, Transport Trust*
Other: *press office; market research*
UK promotion: *other attractions; leaflets/information packs*

COLOUR MUSEUM
(registered charity)
museum; educational centre of a professional society

Established: *1978*
Address: *Perkin House, 82 Grattan Rd, Bradford, W Yorks, BD1 2JB*
Telephone: *(0274) 390955.* Fax: *(0274) 392888*
Access: (road) *M1/M62/M606/A650/B6144*
Season: *all year*
Hours: *Tues to Fri - 2pm to 5pm, Sat - 10am to 4pm. Groups by arrangement - Tues to Fri am*
Admission (1992): *adults £0.80; children £0.40; OAP £0.40; student £0.40; family ticket £1.95; group rate for educational visits £0.25*
No. visitors (1992): *18 209*

Facilities
Interpretation: *videos; audio tapes; information boards; slides; guide books*
Schools: *maximum no. 60; audio/visual presentation; work sheets*
Retailing: *postcards/inexpensive souvenirs; books*
No. shops: *1*

Operations
Contact: *S Burge (Curator)*
No. employees: (high season) *2 full time; 4 part time* (low season) *2 full time; 4 part time*
Training: *F/T operations staff and F/T management are trained externally and on specific courses*

Marketing
Affiliation: *National Heritage*
Other: *market research*
UK promotion: *national newspapers; local newspapers; regional tourist board; other attractions; leaflets/information packs*

Environmental monitoring: *recycling*

COMBE MARTIN WILDLIFE AND DINOSAUR PARK
zoo/wildlife attraction; dinosaur park

Established: *1985*
Address: *Combe Martin, N Devon, EX34 0NG*
Telephone: *(0271) 882486.* Fax: *(0271) 883342*

Access: (road) *M5/A399* (rail) *Barnstaple*
Hours: *Mar to Nov - 10am to 4.30pm daily*
Admission (1992): *adults £4.50; children £3.00; OAP £4.00*
No. visitors (1992): *80 000 (est.)*

Facilities
Interpretation: *leaflets; information boards; tour guides*
Children: *adventure playground; play area; nappy changing*
Schools: *educational literature; educational tour; lecture/talk; handling sessions*
Disabled: *transport service*
Catering: *1 bar/public house*
Franchisees: *Mar to Nov - 10am to 4.30pm daily*
Retailing: *postcards/inexpensive souvenirs; confectionery and ice cream; books; clothes; toy dinosaurs; wildlife items*
No. shops: *1*

Operations
Contacts: *S Eddy (Head Keeper); Mr and Mrs R Butcher (proprietors); T Wray (Secretary)*
No. employees: (high season) *2 full time; 6 part time* (low season) *1 full time; 1 part time*
Training: *F/T operations staff, F/T management, P/T operations staff, P/T management, casual operations staff and casual management are trained externally and on specific courses and day-to-day on job*
Languages spoken: *French; German*

Marketing
Other: *market research*
UK promotion: *television; national newspapers; radio; local newspapers; regional tourist board; other attractions; leaflets/information packs; ETB/BTA*

COMMONWEALTH INSTITUTE
(registered charity)
museum; educational resource

Established: *1962*
Address: *Kensington High St, London, W8 6NR*
Telephone: *(071) 603 4535.* Fax: *(071) 602 7374*
Access: (road) *Kensington High St* (rail) *High St Kensington*
Season: *all year*
Hours: *Mon to Sat - 10am to 5pm, Sun - 2pm to 5pm, closed 24-26 Dec, 1 Jan, Good Friday and May Day*
Admission (1992): *free*
No. visitors (1992): *300 000 (est.)*

Facilities
Interpretation: *leaflets; information boards; maps; guide books*
Languages: *French; Spanish; Chinese; Commonwealth*
Schools: *must book, and activities*
Disabled: *easy access; disabled toilets; special signs*
Catering: *1 bar/public house*
Franchisees: *Mon to Sat - 10am to 5pm, Sun - 2pm to 5pm*
Retailing: *postcards/inexpensive souvenirs; confectionery and ice cream; craftwork; books; clothes from commonwealth countries; food; wine; arts and crafts*
No. shops: *1*

Operations
Contacts: *Mr S Cox (Director-General); Mr P Kennedy (Chief Administrative Officer); S Dugal (Finance); Ms H Sewell (Marketing and Publicity)*
No. employees: (high season) *90 full time*
Training: *F/T operations staff and F/T management are trained in-house and externally and on specific courses and day-to-day on the job*

Marketing
Annual event(s): *Indian Miniatures Exhibition*
Sponsor(s): *London Catering Services*
Other: *press office; market research*

UK promotion: *national newspapers; local newspapers; leaflets/information packs; LTB; ETB/BTA*
Europe promotion: *British Tourist Authority*

COMPTON ACRES GARDENS
(limited company)
garden

Established: *1952*
Address: *Canford Cliffs Rd, Poole, Dorset, BH13 7ES*
Telephone: *(0202) 700778.* Fax: *(0202) 707537*
Access: (road) *M27* (rail) *Bournemouth/Poole*
Parking capacity: (cars) *110* (coaches) *11*
Hours: *1 Mar to end Oct – 10.30am to 6.30pm daily*
Admission (1992): *adults £3.50; children £1.00; OAP £2.50; student £2.50*

Facilities
Interpretation: *leaflets; guide books*
Languages: *French*
Children: *nappy changing*
Schools: *maximum no. 100; no special support*
Disabled: *easy access; disabled toilets; leaflets; guide book; wheelchairs available*
Catering: *2 snack bars/food stalls*
Retailing: *postcards/inexpensive souvenirs; confectionery and ice cream; garden centre*
No. shops: *3*

Operations
Contact: *Mr P Willsher (General Manager)*
No. employees: (high season) *8 full time; 35 part time* (low season) *8 full time*
Training: *F/T operations staff and P/T operations staff are trained in-house and day-to-day on job using videos*
Languages spoken: *French; Spanish; Chinese; Commonwealth*

Marketing
Other: *market research*
UK promotion: *television; radio; local newspapers; regional tourist board; other attractions; leaflets/information packs; ETB/BTA*
Europe/USA promotion: *leaflets/brochures; British Tourist Authority*

CONISTON BOATING CENTRE
(local authority run)
boating centre

Established: *1978*
Address: *Lake Rd, Coniston, Cumbria, LA21 8AN*
Telephone: *(05394) 41366*
Access: (road) *M6/A593/A5084/A590* (rail) *Foxfield*
Parking capacity: (cars) *70*
Hours: *Easter to Oct – 9.30am to 5.30pm daily, Nov to Easter – 10am to 5pm launching only*
Admission (1992): *fees for launching/hire*
No. visitors (1992): *45 000 (est.)*

Facilities
Interpretation: *leaflets; information boards*
Languages: *Japanese; Dutch; French; German; Italian; Spanish; on boat hire only*
Schools: *maximum no. 20; no special support*
Disabled: *disabled toilets*
Catering: *1 picnic area*
Franchisees: *Easter to Oct – 9.30am to 5.30pm daily, Nov to Easter – 10am to 5pm launching only*
Retailing: *postcards/inexpensive souvenirs; confectionery and ice cream*
No. shops: *1*

Operations
Contacts: *Mr H Carroll (Head Boatman); Mr A Lovett (Senior Officer)*
No. employees: (high season) *2 full time; 4 part time* (low season) *1 full time; 1 part time*
Training: *F/T operations staff and P/T operations staff are trained in-house and externally and on specific courses and day-to-day on job*

Marketing
Annual event: *Coniston Water Festival*
Sponsor(s): *Small local companies*
Other: *press office; market research*
UK promotion: *local newspapers; regional tourist board; leaflets/information packs; ETB/BTA*

CONWY CASTLE
(government executive agency)
castle

Address: *Conwy Castle, Conwy, Gwynedd, LL32 8LD*
Access: (road) *A55* (rail) *North Wales Line*
Season: *all year*
Hours: *Apr to Oct – Mon to Sun – 9.30am to 6.30pm, Oct to Apr – Mon to Sat – 9.30am to 4pm, Sun - 2pm to 4pm*
Admission (1992): *adults £2.50; children £1.50; OAP £1.50; student £1.50*
No. visitors (1992): *180 000*

Facilities
Interpretation: *leaflets; information boards; tour guides; guide books*
Languages: *French; German*
Schools: *maximum no. 100; educational literature*
Disabled: *disabled toilets*
Retailing: *postcards/inexpensive souvenirs; craftwork; books; reproductions of famous artefacts*
No. shops: *1*

Operations
Contact: *Paul Meredith (Head Custodian)*
No. employees: (high season) *3 full time; 3 part time* (low season) *2 full time; 1 part time*
Training: *F/T operations staff, P/T operations staff and casual operations staff are trained in-house and externally and on specific courses and day-to-day on job*

Environmental monitoring: *water quality; chemical usage; emissions; noise*

CONWY VISITOR CENTRE
(limited company)
heritage centre

Established: *1979*
Address: *Rosehill Street, Conwy, Gwynedd, LL32 8LD*
Telephone: *(0492) 596288*
Access: (road) *M56/A55/A470* (rail) *Holyhead*
Parking capacity: (cars) *500* (coaches) *25*
Hours: *Mar to Dec – Thurs to Tues – 9.30am to 5.30pm*
Admission (1992): *adults £0.50; children £0.30*
No. visitors (1992): *200 000 (est.)*

Facilities
Interpretation: *videos; leaflets; audio tapes; information boards; maps; tour guides; guide books*
Languages: *French; German; Welsh*
Schools: *maximum no. 120; audio/visual presentation; lecture/talk*
Disabled: *easy access; helpers; leaflets; guide book*
Catering: *1 self-service cafeteria*
Retailing: *postcards/inexpensive souvenirs; confectionery and ice cream; craftwork; books; clothes; reproductions of famous artefacts; video/audio tapes; brass items*
No. shops: *2*

Operations
Contacts: *Mr G Seimann (Managing Director); Ms H Wright (Manager); Mr G Seimann (Managing Director)*
No. employees: (high season) *6 full time; 20 part time* (low season) *2 full time; 4 part time*
Training: *F/T operations staff, F/T management and P/T operations staff are trained in-house and day-to-day on job*

Marketing
Annual event: *Conwy Carnival*
Affiliations: *Conwy Tourist Association*
Other: *market research*
UK promotion: *radio; local newspapers; regional tourist board; leaflets/information packs; This Week in North Wales*
Europe/USA promotion: *British Tourist Authority*

COOPER GALLERY
(local authority Cooper Trustees)
gallery

Established: *1913*
Address: *Church St, Barnsley, S Yorks, S70 2AH*
Telephone: *(0226) 242905*
Access: (road) *M1*
Season: *all year*
Hours: *Tues – 1pm to 5.30pm, Wed to Sat – 10am to 5.30pm*
Admission (1992): *free*
No. visitors (1992): *20 000 (est.)*

Facilities
Interpretation: *leaflets; information boards*
Schools: *maximum no. 30; some touring workshops*
Disabled: *access to ground floor galleries, assistance by prior arrangement*
Retailing: *postcards/inexpensive souvenirs*
No. shops: *none*

Operations
No. employees: (high season) *4 full time*

Marketing
UK promotion: *local newspapers; regional tourist board; other attractions; leaflets/information packs*

Environmental monitoring: *recycling; waste; water quality; energy consumption; chemical usage*

CORINIUM MUSEUM
(local authority run)
museum

Established: *1856*
Address: *Park Street, Cirencester, Glos, GL7 2BX*
Telephone: *(0285) 655611*
Access: (road) *M5/M4* (rail) *Kemble*
Season: *all year*
Hours: *Apr to Oct – Mon to Sat – 10am to 5.30pm, Sun – 2pm to 5.30pm, Nov to Mar – Tues to Sat – 10am to 5pm, Sun – 2pm to 5pm*
Admission (1992): *adults £1.00; children £0.50; OAP £0.75; student £0.75*
No. visitors (1992): *70 000 (est.)*

Facilities
Interpretation: *leaflets; information boards; maps; guide books*
Languages: *French; German*
Children: *nappy changing*
Schools: *maximum no. 60; educational literature; lecture/talk*
Disabled: *easy access; disabled toilets; braille/sound posts; guide book*
Retailing: *postcards/inexpensive souvenirs; books; reproductions of famous artefacts*
No. shops: *1*

Operations
Contacts: *D Viner (Curator); J Pyzer (Shop Manager)*
No. employees: (high season) *4 full time; 4 part time* (low season) *4 full time; 3 part time*
Training: *F/T operations staff, F/T management and P/T operations staff are trained in-house and externally and on specific courses and day-to-day on job*

Marketing
Annual event(s): *various*
Sponsor(s): *various*
Affiliations: *Area Museum Council, HETB, etc.*
Other: *press office; market research*

UK promotion: *radio; local newspapers; regional tourist board; other attractions; leaflets/information packs*
Europe/USA promotion: *leaflets/brochures*

CORNISH SEAL SANCTUARY
(plc)
zoo/wildlife attraction; marine animal rescue centre

Established: *1957*
Address: *Gweek, Nr Helston, Cornwall, TR12 6UG*
Telephone: *(0326) 22361*. Fax: *(0326) 22210*
Access: (road) *A394/3083*
Parking capacity: (cars) *350* (coaches) *8*
Season: *all year*
Hours: *all year – 9.30am to 6pm daily (closed 4.30pm from Nov to Easter)*
Admission (1992): *adults £4.00; children £2.00; OAP £3.00*
No. visitors (1992): *160 000 (est.)*

Facilities
Interpretation: *videos; leaflets; information boards; slides; tour guides; guide books; exhibitions, seal hospital*
Languages: *French; German*
Children: *play area; nappy changing*
Schools: *educational literature; audio/visual presentation; lecture/talk; talk on request*
Disabled: *easy access; disabled toilets; helpers; powered transport; leaflets; guide book*
Catering: *1 picnic area*
Retailing: *postcards/inexpensive souvenirs; confectionery and ice cream; craftwork; books; clothes; reproductions of famous artefacts; seal and marine related goods*
No. shops: *3*

Operations
Contacts: *M Thomas (Managing Director); M Tonkins (PA); B Roper (Director)*
No. employees: (high season) *14 full time; 20 part time* (low season) *14 full time*
Training: *F/T operations staff, F/T management, P/T management and casual management are trained in-house and day-to-day on job using videos*

Marketing
Other: *market research*
UK promotion: *national newspapers; radio; local newspapers; regional tourist board; other attractions; leaflets/information packs; ETB/BTA*
Europe promotion: *leaflets/brochures; British Tourist Authority*

Environmental monitoring: *recycling; waste; energy consumption; hazardous materials; chemical usage*

CORNWALL DONKEY AND PONY SANCTUARY
(limited company and trust)
donkey sanctuary and craft centre

Established: *1991*
Address: *Lower Maidenland, St Kew, Nr Bodmin, Cornwall, PL30 3HA*
Telephone: *(0208) 84 242*
Access: (road) *A39*
Parking capacity: (cars) *150* (coaches) *4*
Season: *all year*
Hours: *week preceding Easter to mid Oct – 10am to 5pm daily; throughout the year – Sun – 10am to 4.30pm except Christmas*
Admission (1992): *adults £3.00; children £2.00; OAP £2.50; student £3.00; above were friendship payments valid until 31 Mar 1993*
No. visitors (1992): *20 000 (est.)*

Facilities
Interpretation: *videos*
Children: *adventure playground; play area; nappy changing*
Schools: *maximum no. 150; by arrangement*
Disabled: *easy access; disabled toilets*

Catering: *1 picnic area*
Retailing: *craftwork; jams, cakes and produce*
No. shops: *more than 4*

Operations
Contact: *Ms C Belton*
No. employees: (high season) *9 full time; 7 part time* (low season) *5 full time*
Training: *F/T operations staff, P/T operations staff and casual operations staff are trained in-house and day-to-day on job*
Languages spoken: *French; German*

Marketing
Annual event(s): *various*
Other: *press office; market research*
UK promotion: *national newspapers; local newspapers; regional tourist board; leaflets/information packs*

Environmental monitoring: *recycling; waste; water quality; hazardous materials; chemical usage; emissions*

CORSHAM COURT
(trust)
historic house; garden; museum

Established: *1900*
Address: *Corsham Court, Wilts, SN13 0BZ*
Telephone: *(0249) 712214*. Fax: *(0249) 444556*
Access: (road) *M4*
Parking capacity: (cars) *400* (coaches) *5*
Hours: *Apr to Sept – Tues to Sun – 2pm to 6pm; Jan to Mar and Oct to Nov – 2pm to 4.30pm (closed Mon and Fri)*
Admission (1992): *adults £3.00; children £1.50; OAP £3.00; student £3.00; group rates*
No. visitors (1992): *17 000*

Facilities
Interpretation: *tour guides; guide books*
Schools: *maximum no. 50; educational tour*
Disabled: *helpers; wheelchair*
Retailing: *postcards/inexpensive souvenirs; books*
No. shops: *1*

Operations
Contacts: *P Peach (Curator); C Walthe (Assistant Land Agent)*
No. employees: (high season) *2 full time; 6 part time* (low season) *2 full time; 3 part time*
Languages spoken: *French*

Marketing
Affiliations: *HHA, WCTB, Thamesdown and District Tourist Association*
UK promotion: *radio; local newspapers; regional tourist board; leaflets/information packs; various; ETB/BTA*

COTON MANOR GARDENS
(privately owned)
garden

Established: *1968*
Address: *Coton Manor, Northampton, NN6 8RQ*
Telephone: *(0604) 740219*. Fax: *(0604) 740838*
Access: (road) *M1/A428/A50* (rail) *Northampton*
Parking capacity: (cars) *150* (coaches) *5*
Hours: *Easter to end Sept – Wed, Sun and BH – 2pm to 6pm, also Thurs in Jul and Aug*
Admission (1992): *adults £2.50; children £0.50; OAP £2.00; student £2.00*

Facilities
Interpretation: *guide books*
Schools: *maximum no. 50; no special support*
Disabled: *easy access*
Catering: *1 picnic area*
Retailing: *postcards/inexpensive souvenirs; confectionery and ice cream; books; pottery and garden items*
No. shops: *2*

Operations
No. employees: (high season) *2 full time; 4 part time* (low season) *2 full time; 1 part time*

Marketing
UK promotion: *local newspapers; leaflets/information packs*

COTSWOLD COUNTRYSIDE COLLECTION
(local authority run)
historic house; museum

Established: *1981*
Address: *Northleach, Glos, GL54 3JH*
Telephone: *(0451) 860715*
Access: (road) *A40* (rail) *Moreton in Marsh*
Parking capacity: (cars) *50* (coaches) *5*
Hours: *Apr to Oct – Mon to Sat – 10am to 5.30am, Sun – 2pm to 5.30pm*
Admission (1992): *adults £1.00; children £0.50; OAP £0.75; student £0.75*
No. visitors (1992): *20 000 (est.)*

Facilities
Interpretation: *leaflets; information boards; guide books*
Languages: *Dutch*
Schools: *maximum no. 60; educational literature; audio/visual presentation*
Disabled: *easy access; disabled toilets; leaflets; guide book*
Catering: *1 picnic area*
Retailing: *postcards/inexpensive souvenirs; confectionery and ice cream; craftwork; books*
No. shops: *1*

Operations
Contacts: *A R Harwood (Keeper of Social History); D Viner (Curator of Museums)*
No. employees: (high season) *2 full time; 4 part time*
Training: *F/T management and P/T operations staff are trained in-house and externally and on specific courses and day-to-day on job*

Marketing
Annual event(s): *various*
Sponsor(s): *various*
Affiliations: *Area Museum Council, HETB, etc.*
Other: *press office; market research*
UK promotion: *local newspapers; regional tourist board; other attractions; leaflets/information packs*
Europe/USA promotion: *leaflets/brochures; travel agents' brochures*

COTSWOLD MOTOR MUSEUM
(private collection)
museum

Established: *1978*
Address: *The Old Mill, Bourton on the Water, GL54 2BY*
Telephone: *(0451) 821255*
Access: (road) *A429* (rail) *Moreton in the Marsh*
Hours: *Feb to Nov – 10am to 6pm daily*
Admission (1992): *adults £1.20; children £0.60*

Facilities
Schools: *maximum no. 100; educational literature; lecture/talk*
Disabled: *easy access*

Operations
Contact: *Mr M Cavanagh (owner)*

Environmental monitoring: *recycling; waste; energy consumption; hazardous materials; chemical usage*

COUGHTON COURT
(local authority run)
historic house; garden

Established: *1947*
Address: *Nr Alcester, Warwickshire, B49 5JA*
Telephone: *(0789) 400777*. Fax: *(0789) 765544*

Access: (road) M40/M42/M5/A435 (rail)
Birmingham International
Parking capacity: (cars) 250 (coaches) 5
Hours: Easter to Sept – Sat to Wed – 1.30pm to
5pm, grounds – 12am to 6pm; Oct – Sat to
Sun – 1.30 to 5pm, grounds – 12am to 5pm
Admission (1992): adults £3.50; children £1.75;
National Trust members free
No. visitors (1992): 33 000

Facilities
Interpretation: leaflets; audio tapes; information
boards; maps; guide books
Children: play area
Schools: maximum no. 50; educational literature
Disabled: easy access; disabled toilets
Catering: 1 self-service cafeteria
Retailing: postcards/inexpensive souvenirs; books;
tea towels
No. shops: 1

Operations
Contacts: C McLaren-Throckmorton (Managing
Partner); A McLaren (Partner)
No. employees: (high season) 4 full time; 25 part
time (low season) 4 full time; 3 part time

Marketing
Annual event(s): music concerts
Sponsor(s): Lloyds Music Trust, David D Brown
Affiliations: National Trust, HHA, Warwick
Garden Trust
UK promotion: local newspapers; regional tourist
board; leaflets/information packs; Heart of
England

Environmental monitoring: recycling

**COUNCIL FOR THE PORT OF RURAL
ENGLAND**
(registered charity)
conservation visitor centre

Established: 1987
Address: Derby Wing, Worden Hall, Worden
Park, Leyland, Lancs
Telephone: (0772) 456181
Access: (road) M6/B5248 (rail) Leyland
Hours: Feb to Mar and Nov to Dec – 12 noon to
4pm; Apr to Oct – 11.30am to 5pm; closed
Mon
Admission (1992): free
No. visitors (1992): 30 000 (est.)

Facilities
Interpretation: leaflets; audio tapes; information
boards; slides
Schools: maximum no. 60; audio/visual
presentation; lecture/talk
Retailing: postcards/inexpensive souvenirs;
craftwork; books
No. shops: 1

Operations
Contact: Ms R Whitlock (Visitor Centre Manager)

Marketing
Other: press office

COUNTY AND REGIMENTAL MUSEUM
(local authority run)
monument; museum; gallery

Established: 1987
Address: Stanley Street, Preston, PR1 4YP
Telephone: (0772) 264075
Access: (road) M6 (rail) Preston
Parking capacity: (cars) 30 (coaches) 5
Season: all year
Hours: all year – 10am to 5pm daily (except
Thurs and Sun)
Admission (1992): adults £1.00; OAP £1.00;
student £1.00
No. visitors (1992): 20 000

Facilities
Interpretation: videos; leaflets; audio tapes;
information boards; maps

Schools: maximum no. 100; educational literature;
audio/visual presentation; lecture/talk
Disabled: disabled toilets; braille/sound posts
Retailing: postcards/inexpensive souvenirs; books
No. shops: 1

Operations
Contact: Dr S Bull (Curator)
No. employees: (high season) 5 full time; 6 part
time (low season) 5 full time; 7 part time
Training: F/T operations staff and F/T
management are trained in-house and externally
and on specific courses and day-to-day on job

Marketing
Market research
UK promotion: television; radio; local
newspapers; regional tourist board; other
attractions; leaflets/information packs;
ETB/BTA

Environmental monitoring: recycling; waste;
water quality; energy consumption; hazardous
materials; chemical usage; transport; emissions;
land use and conservation

COURAGE SHIRE HORSE CENTRE
(plc)
museum

Established: 1977
Address: Cherry Garden Lane, Maidenhead
Thicket, Maidenhead, Berks
Telephone: (0628) 824848
Access: (road) M4/M40/A4
Parking capacity: (cars) 100 (coaches) 10
Hours: Mar to Oct – 10.30am to 5pm
Admission (1992): adults £2.80; children £2.00;
OAP £2.00; student £2.00
No. visitors (1992): 75 000

Facilities
Interpretation: videos; leaflets; tour guides; guide
books
Children: adventure playground; play area; nappy
changing
Schools: maximum no. 50; educational literature;
audio/visual presentation; lecture/talk
Disabled: easy access; disabled toilets; helpers;
leaflets; guide book
Catering: 1 picnic area
Retailing: postcards/inexpensive souvenirs;
confectionery and ice cream; craftwork; books;
clothes; reproductions of famous artefacts
No. shops: 1

Operations
Contact: I B Fisher (Director)
No. employees: (high season) 12 full time; 18 part
time (low season) 12 full time; 2 part time
Training: F/T operations staff, P/T operations
staff and casual operations staff are trained
in-house and externally and on specific courses
and day-to-day on job
Languages spoken: German

Marketing
Annual event(s): vintage day, dog show, heavy
horse show
Other: market research
UK promotion: radio; local newspapers; regional
tourist board; leaflets/information packs
Europe/USA promotion: leaflets/brochures

Environmental monitoring: energy consumption;
hazardous materials; chemical usage; transport;
emissions

COURTAULD INSTITUTE GALLERIES
(university)
historic house; museum; gallery

Established: 1990
Address: Somerset House, Strand, London,
WC2R 0RN
Telephone: (071) 873 2526. Fax: (071) 873 2772
Access: (rail) Temple/Covent Garden
Season: all year
Hours: Mon to Sat – 10am to 6pm, Sun – 2pm to
6pm except 24, 25, 26 Dec and 1 Jan

Admission (1992): adults £3.00; children £1.50;
OAP £1.50; student £1.50;
No. visitors (1992): 108 526

Facilities
Interpretation: leaflets; information boards; maps;
guide books
Languages: French
Schools: maximum no. 25; educational literature;
lecture/talk
Disabled: easy access; disabled toilets; stairlift
Catering: 1 self-service cafeteria
Franchisees: Mon to Sat – 10am to 6pm, Sun –
2pm to 6pm
Retailing: postcards/inexpensive souvenirs;
craftwork; books; reproductions of famous
artefacts
No. shops: 1

Operations
Contacts: Dr D Farr, CBE (Director); Ms B Farr
(Manager A Zwemmer at Courtauld)
No. employees: (high season) 20 full time; 4 part
time
Training: F/T operations staff are trained in-house
and day-to-day on job

Marketing
Annual event(s): art exhibitions
Sponsor(s): various
Other: PR company; Bolton and Quinn
UK promotion: national newspapers; regional
tourist board; leaflets/information packs

Environmental monitoring: waste; hazardous
materials; chemical usage

COVENTRY CATHEDRAL
(Church of England)
church

Established: 1962
Address: 7 Priory Row, Coventry, CV1 5ES
Telephone: (0203) 227517. Fax: (0203) 631448
Access: (road) M1/M45/M69/M6/M42/A45/A46
(rail) Coventry
Season: all year
Hours: Easter to Sept – Mon to Sun – 9.30am to
7pm; Oct to Easter – Mon to Sun – 9.30am to
5.30pm
Admission (1992): £2.00 donation, £1.50 for
groups
No. visitors (1992): 300 000 (est.)

Facilities
Interpretation: videos; leaflets; audio tapes;
information boards; tour guides; guide books;
visitors centre
Languages: Dutch; French; German; Italian;
Spanish; Swedish; Hindi; Gujarati
Schools: educational literature; audio/visual
presentation; lecture/talk; must arrange visit
Disabled: braille/sound posts; helpers; other audio
facilities; touch and hearing centre
Catering: 1 self-service cafeteria
Franchisees: Easter to Sept – Mon to Sun –
9.30am to 7pm
Retailing: postcards/inexpensive souvenirs; books;
reproductions of famous artefacts
No. shops: 3

Operations
Contacts: D Mead (Bursar); B Mabbs (Visitor
Centre Manager (AV)); M Ford (Visitor Centre
Bookshop Manager); D Mead (Bursar)
Languages spoken: French; German; Italian

Marketing
Annual event(s): regular concerts, mystery plays
Sponsor(s): various
Affiliations: Pilgrims Association
Other: press office
UK promotion: regional tourist board;
leaflets/information packs; ETB/BTA;
Warwickshire Entertainments Bulletin

Environmental monitoring: collections
environment

COVENTRY TOY MUSEUM, THE
(private)
historic house; museum

Established: *1972*
Address: *Whitefriars Gate, Much Park St,
   Coventry, CV1 2LT*
Telephone: *(0203) 227560*
Access: (road) *M6/A45* (rail) *Coventry*
Season: *all year*
Hours: *12am to 6pm daily*
Admission (1992): *adults £1.00; children £0.50;
   OAP £0.50; student £1.00*
No. visitors (1992): *8000 (est.)*

Facilities
Interpretation: *leaflets*
Schools: *maximum no. 30*
Catering: *1 picnic area*
Retailing: *postcards/inexpensive souvenirs*
No. shops: *1*

Operations
Contact: *R Morgan (owner)*
No. employees: (high season) *1 full time* (low
   season) *1 full time*

Marketing
Press office
UK promotion: *regional tourist board; ETB/BTA*

CRABBLE CORN MILL
(limited company)
museum; working mill

Established: *1990*
Address: *Lower Rd, River, Dover, Kent, CT17
   0UY*
Telephone: *(0304) 823292*
Access: (road) *M2/A2* (rail) *Kearsney*
Parking capacity: (cars) *30*
Season: *all year*
Hours: *Easter to Oct – Wed to Mon – 10am to
   5pm (daily in Aug – Sun – 12am to 5pm); Nov
   to Mar – weekends – 10am to 5pm*
Admission (1992): *adults £2.50; children £1.25;
   OAP £1.75; student £1.75; family £7.00*
No. visitors (1992): *8648*

Facilities
Interpretation: *videos; leaflets; information
   boards; tour guides; guide books*
Languages: *French*
Schools: *maximum no. 200; educational literature;
   audio/visual presentation; educational tour*
Catering: *1 licensed restaurant*
Retailing: *postcards/inexpensive souvenirs;
   confectionery and ice cream; craftwork; books;
   flour and flour products*
No. shops: *1*

Operations
Contacts: *A Denyer (Manager); J Taylor
   (Assistant Manager)*
No. employees: (high season) *2 full time; 5 part
   time* (low season) *2 full time; 1 part time*
Languages spoken: *German*

Marketing
Annual event(s): *Victorian theme day*
Affiliations: *AIM, SEETB, ATAK*
Other: *market research*
UK promotion: *local newspapers; regional tourist
   board; other attractions; leaflets/information
   packs*

CRANMORE TOWER
(privately owned)
theme park; historic house; monument; museum;
   gallery; zoo/wildlife attraction; nature interest

Established: *1989*
Address: *Cranmore, Shepton Mallet, Somerset,
   BA4 4LY*
Telephone: *(0747) 880742*
Access: (road) *A37* (rail) *Frome*
Parking capacity: (cars) *100* (coaches) *3*
Season: *all year*
Hours: *Summer – 10am to 8pm daily;
   Winter – 10am to 5pm daily*

Admission (1992): *adults £1.50; children £0.75;
   OAP £0.75; student £1.00*
No. visitors (1992): *5000 (est.)*

Facilities
Interpretation: *leaflets; audio tapes; information
   boards; maps; tour guides; guide books*
Languages: *Japanese; Dutch; French; German;
   Italian; Spanish*
Children: *adventure playground; play area; nappy
   changing; creche*
Schools: *maximum no. 30; educational literature;
   audio/visual presentation; lecture/talk*
Disabled: *easy access; disabled toilets; helpers;
   special signs; leaflets; guide book*
Catering: *3 picnic areas*
Retailing: *postcards/inexpensive souvenirs;
   confectionery and ice cream; craftwork; books;
   reproductions of famous artefacts*
No. shops: *3*

Operations
Contact: *F Shahbahrami (Proprietor)*
No. employees: (high season) *10 part time* (low
   season) *5 part time*
Training: *F/T management and P/T operations
   staff and casual operations staff are trained
   in-house and externally and on specific courses
   and day-to-day on job*
Languages spoken: *German*

Marketing
Annual event(s): *mushroom month, festivals and
   barbecues*
Affiliation: *Folly Fellowship*
UK promotion: *radio; local newspapers; regional
   tourist board; leaflets/information packs;
   ETB/BTA*

CROMBIE COUNTRY PARK
(local authority run)
park/reserve

Established: *1983*
Address: *Monikie, Broughty Ferry, Dundee, DD5
   3QL*
Telephone: *(02416) 360*

Facilities
Schools: *maximum no. 50; audio/visual
   presentation; lecture/talk*
Disabled: *easy access; disabled toilets; guide book*
Catering: *3 picnic areas*

Operations
Contact: *Mr M Pawley (Countryside Officer)*
No. employees: (high season) *4 full time; 3 part
   time* (low season) *4 full time*
Training: *F/T operations staff and P/T operations
   staff are trained in-house and on specific
   courses and day-to-day on job using videos and
   handbooks and Courses*
Languages spoken: *French; German; Italian;
   Spanish*

Marketing
Annual event(s): *mini Highland games, nature fun
   week for children*
Other: *press office*
UK promotion: *national newspapers; local
   newspapers; regional tourist board;
   leaflets/information packs*

Environmental monitoring: *recycling; waste;
   water quality; energy consumption; hazardous
   materials; chemical usage; transport*

CROMER LIFEBOAT MUSEUM
(charity)
museum

Established: *1970*
Address: *The Gangway, Cromer, Norfolk, NR27
   0HY*
Telephone: *Cromer 512503*

Access: (road) *A140/A148/A149* (rail) *Cromer*
Hours: *Easter BH and 1 May to Oct*
Admission (1992): *free*
No. visitors (1992): *50 000 (est.)*

Facilities
Interpretation: *leaflets; information boards; maps;
   tour guides*
Schools: *maximum no. 30; educational literature;
   audio/visual presentation; lecture/talk*
Disabled: *easy access; helpers; leaflets*
Catering: *1 snack bar/food stall*
Retailing: *postcards/inexpensive souvenirs;
   craftwork; books; clothes*
No. shops: *1*

Operations
Contact: *J Smith (Hon Secretary)*
No. employees: (high season) *10 part time* (low
   season) *2 part time*
Languages spoken: *French*

Marketing
Annual event(s): *Lifeboat Day*
Affiliations: *Museums in Norfolk Group*
Other: *press office*
UK promotion: *local newspapers;
   leaflets/information packs; ETB/BTA*

Environmental monitoring: *recycling; waste;
   water quality; chemical usage*

CROMER MUSEUM
(local authority run)
museum

Established: *1978*
Address: *East Cottages, Tucker St, Cromer,
   Norfolk, NR27 9HB*
Telephone: *(0263) 513543*
Access: (road) *A140* (rail) *Norwich*
Season: *all year*
Hours: *Mon – 10am to 1pm and 2pm to 5pm;
   Tues to Sat – 10am to 5pm; Sun – 2pm to 5pm*
Admission (1992): *adults £0.80; children £0.40;
   OAP £0.50; student £0.50; unemployed £0.50,
   groups of over 10 £0.50*
No. visitors (1992): *22 688*

Facilities
Interpretation: *leaflets; information boards*
Languages: *Dutch; French*
Schools: *maximum no. 20; educational literature;
   lecture/talk; living history events*
Retailing: *postcards/inexpensive souvenirs; books;
   clothes; reproductions of famous artefacts;
   maps; minerals and fossils*
No. shops: *1*

Operations
Contact: *Mr M Warren (Curator)*
No. employees: (high season) *1 full time; 2 part
   time* (low season) *1 full time; 2 part time*
Training: *F/T management and P/T operations
   staff are trained externally and on specific
   courses and day-to-day on job*

Marketing
Annual event(s): *various*
Other: *press office; market research*
UK promotion: *regional tourist board; other
   attractions; leaflets/information packs*

Environmental monitoring: *recycling; waste*

CROXTETH HALL AND COUNTRY PARK
(local authority run)
historic house; park/reserve; garden; museum;
   rare breeds farm

Established: *1979*
Address: *Croxteth Hall Lane, Liverpool, L12 0HB*
Telephone: *(051) 228 5311*
Access: (road) *M57*
Parking capacity: (cars) *3000* (coaches) *20*
Season: *all year*
Hours: *Easter to Sept – 10am to 5pm daily*
Admission (1992): *adults £2.00; children £1.00;
   OAP £1.00; student £1.00*

No. visitors (1992): *200 000*

Facilities
Interpretation: *videos; leaflets; audio tapes; information boards; slides; maps; tour guides; guide books; personnel; displays*
Children: *adventure playground*
Schools: *maximum no. 1000; educational literature; audio/visual presentation; educational tour; lecture/talk; national curriculum programmes*
Disabled: *easy access; disabled toilets*
Catering: *6 picnic areas*
Franchisees: *Easter to Sept – 10am to 5pm daily*
Retailing: *postcards/inexpensive souvenirs; confectionery and ice cream; craftwork; books; numerous gift items*
No. shops: *4*

Operations
Contact: *E E Jackson (Head of Croxteth Hall)*
No. employees: (high season) *70 full time; 20 part time* (low season) *70 full time; 10 part time*
Training: *F/T operations staff, F/T management, P/T operations staff, P/T management, casual operations staff and casual management are trained in-house and externally and on specific courses and day-to-day on job*

Marketing
Annual event(s): *various*
Other: *press office; market research*
UK promotion: *radio; local newspapers; regional tourist board; other attractions; leaflets/information packs; numerous*

Environmental monitoring: *light dust temperature control*

CUMBERLAND PENCIL MUSEUM AND EXHIBITION CENTRE
(limited company)
museum

Established: *1981*
Address: *Southey Works, Greta Bridge, Keswick, Cumbria, CA12 5NG*
Telephone: *(07687) 73626*
Access: (road) *M6/A66* (rail) *Penrith*
Parking capacity: (cars) *50*
Season: *all year*
Hours: *all year – Mon to Sat – 9.30am to 4pm; closed 25 and 26 Dec and 1 Jan*
Admission (1992): *adults £2.00; children £1.00; OAP £1.00; family ticket £4.00*
No. visitors (1992): *105 000 (est.)*

Facilities
Interpretation: *videos; audio tapes; information boards*
Schools: *maximum no. 25; no special support; educational literature*
Retailing: *postcards/inexpensive souvenirs; confectionery and ice cream; books; pencils, stationery, etc.*
No. shops: *1*

Operations
Contacts: *Mrs Yvonne Gray (Museum Supervisor); Mrs B Reynolds (Personnel Manager)*
No. employees: (high season) *4 full time; 2 part time* (low season) *3 full time; 2 part time*
Training: *F/T operations staff, F/T management and P/T operations staff are trained in-house and externally and on specific courses and day-to-day on job using videos*

Marketing
Press office
UK promotion: *regional tourist board; other attractions; leaflets/information packs; ETB/BTA*

CUMBRIA CRYSTAL LTD
(limited company)
craft workshop; crystal manufacture by hand

Established: *1975*

Address: *Lightburn Road, Ulverston, Cumbria, CA12 0DA*
Telephone: *(0229) 54400.* Fax: *(0229) 581132*
Access: (road) *M6/A590* (rail) *Ulverston*
Parking capacity: (cars) *100* (coaches) *4*
Season: *all year*
Hours: *open throughout year. Factory: Mon to Thurs – 9am to 4pm, Fri – 9am to 3pm; shop: Mon to Fri – 9am to 5pm, Sat – 10am to 4pm, Sun – 12am to 4pm (June to Sept inc), all BH except Christmas and New Year*
Admission (1992): *adults £0.90; children £0.40; OAP £0.40; student £0.40*
No. visitors (1992): *50 000 (est.)*

Facilities
Interpretation: *leaflets; information boards; maps*
Schools: *educational literature*
Disabled: *easy access; leaflets*
Retailing: *craftwork*
No. shops: *1*

Operations
Contacts: *Mr Len England (Managing Director); June Hewitt (Retail/Factory Shop Manager)*
No. employees: (high season) *25 full time; 9 part time* (low season) *25 full time; 8 part time*
Training: *F/T operations staff, P/T operations staff and casual operations staff are trained in-house and day-to-day on job using videos and handbooks*

Marketing
UK promotion: *national newspapers; local newspapers; regional tourist board; other attractions; leaflets/information packs; ETB/BTA*

CUMING MUSEUM
(local authority run)
museum

Established: *1902*
Address: *155–7 Walworth Rd, London, SE17 1RS*
Telephone: *(071) 701 1342*
Access: (road) *A215* (rail) *Elephant and Castle*
Season: *all year*
Hours: *Tues to Sat – 10am to 5pm*
Admission (1992): *free*
No. visitors (1992): *10 000 (est.)*

Facilities
Interpretation: *leaflets; information boards*
Schools: *maximum no. 40; educational literature; lecture/talk; activity sessions*
Retailing: *postcards/inexpensive souvenirs; books; cards; stamps*
No. shops: *1*

Operations
Contact: *Ms C Ellis (keeper)*
No. employees: (high season) *4 full time* (low season) *4 full time*
Training: *F/T operations staff and F/T management are trained in-house and externally and on specific courses*

Marketing
Press office; market research
UK promotion: *local newspapers*

Environmental monitoring: *recycling; waste; energy consumption; hazardous materials; chemical usage*

CYFARTHFA CASTLE MUSEUM, ART GALLERY AND PARK
(local authority run)
historic house; park/reserve; museum; gallery

Established: *1910*
Address: *Brecon Road, Merthyr Tydfil, Mid Glamorgan, CF47 8RE*
Telephone: *(0685) 723112.* Fax: *(0865) 723112*
Access: (road) *M4/A470* (rail) *Cardiff–Merthyr*
Parking capacity: (cars) *100* (coaches) *20*
Season: *all year*

Hours: *Apr to Sept – Mon to Sat – 10am to 6pm, Sun – 2pm to 5pm; Oct to Mar – Mon to Sat – 10am to 5pm, Sun – 2pm to 5pm*
Admission (1992): *adults £0.50; children £0.30; OAP £0.30; students free if booked in advance*
No. visitors (1992): *32 000*

Facilities
Interpretation: *leaflets; information boards*
Children: *play area*
Schools: *maximum no. 60; educational literature; lecture/talk; must book in advance*
Disabled: *easy access; stairlift and wheelchairs*
Catering: *1 picnic area*
Franchisees: *Apr to Sept – Mon to Sat – 10am to 6pm, Sun – 2pm to 5pm; Oct to Mar – Mon to Sat – 10am to 5pm, Sun – 2pm to 5pm*
Retailing: *postcards/inexpensive souvenirs; books*
No. shops: *1*

Operations
Contact: *Stephen Done (Curator)*
No. employees: (high season) *4 full time; 2 part time*
Training: *F/T operations staff, F/T management and P/T operations staff are trained in-house and externally and on specific courses and day-to-day on job using videos and handbooks and council training centre*

Marketing
Annual event(s): *Heritage Day and Merthyr Show*
Sponsor(s): *various locals, e.g. Hoover*
Affiliations: *Museums Association, Welsh Federal Museums and Art Galleries, National Heritage*
Other: *market research*
UK promotion: *television; radio, local newspapers; regional tourist board; other attractions; leaflets/information packs; ETB/BTA*
Europe/USA promotion: *leaflets/brochures; travel agents' brochures*

Environmental monitoring: *recycling; council policy*

D

D H LAWRENCE BIRTHPLACE MUSEUM
(local authority run)
historic house; museum

Established: *1975*
Address: *8A Victoria St, Eastwood, Nottingham, NG16 3AW*
Telephone: *(0773) 763312*
Access: (road) *M1* (rail) *Nottingham Midland*
Season: *all year*
Hours: *Apr to Oct – 10am to 5pm; Nov to Mar – 10am to 4pm*
Admission (1992): *adults £1.50; children £0.75; OAP £0.75; student £0.75; ub40s £0.75*
No. visitors (1992): *10 700*

Facilities
Interpretation: *videos; leaflets; information boards; maps; tour guides*
Languages: *Japanese; Dutch; French; German; Italian*
Schools: *maximum no. 50; audio/visual presentation; lecture/talk*
Retailing: *postcards/inexpensive souvenirs; craftwork; books; quality gifts*
No. shops: *1*

Operations
Contacts: *Mrs J Lillystone (Museum Manager); Mrs J Wildgust (Leisure Development Officer)*
No. employees: (high season) *1 full time; 7 part time* (low season) *1 full time; 5 part time*
Training: *F/T operations staff, P/T operations staff and casual operations staff are trained in-house and day-to-day on job*

Marketing
Affiliations: *Museums and Galleries Commission, EMMS*
UK promotion: *radio; local newspapers; regional tourist board; other attractions; leaflets/information packs; ETB/BTA*
Europe/Asia/USA promotion: *leaflets/brochures; travel agents' brochures; British Tourist Authority*

Environmental monitoring: *recycling; energy consumption; transport*

DALEMAIN HISTORIC HOUSE
(private business)
historic house

Established: *1977*
Address: *Dalemain, Cumbria, CA11 0NB*
Telephone: *(07684) 86450*
Access: (road) *M6/A592* (rail) *Penrith*
Parking capacity: (cars) *200* (coaches) *10*
Hours: *Apr to Oct – Sun to Thur – 11.15am to 5pm*
Admission (1992): *adults £3.80; children £2.80; OAP £3.80; student £3.80; wheelchairs free*
No. visitors (1992): *20 000 (est.)*

Facilities
Interpretation: *tour guides; guide books; information sheets*
Languages: *French; German*
Children: *adventure playground*
Schools: *maximum no. 50; lecture/talk*
Disabled: *easy access; disabled toilets*
Catering: *1 picnic area*
Retailing: *postcards/inexpensive souvenirs; confectionery and ice cream; books; china, etc.*
No. shops: *1*

Operations
Contact: *Mrs S L Blaylock (Personal Assistant)*

No. employees: (high season) *2 full time; 40 part time* (low season) *2 full time; 11 part time*
Training: *casual operations staff are trained in-house and day-to-day on job*

Marketing
Annual event: *Rainbow Craft Fair*
Affiliation: *Historic Houses Association*
UK promotion: *regional tourist board; other attractions; leaflets/information packs*

Environmental monitoring: *recycling; energy consumption*

DALES COUNTRYSIDE MUSEUM
(local authority run)
museum; national park and tourist information centre

Established: *1979*
Address: *Station Yard, Hawes, Wensleydale, N Yorks, DL8 3NT*
Telephone: *(0969) 667494*
Access: (road) *M6/A1M/A685* (rail) *Northallerton*
Parking capacity: (cars) *200* (coaches) *8*
Hours: *Apr to Oct – 10am to 5pm daily; Nov and Mar – weekends – 11am to 4pm; Boxing Day to New Year's Eve and Feb half term – 11am to 4pm daily*
Admission (1992): *adults £1.00; children £0.50; OAP £0.50; student £0.50*
No. visitors (1992): *25 000*

Facilities
Interpretation: *leaflets; information boards; maps*
Schools: *maximum no. 30; educational literature; lecture/talk*
Disabled: *disabled toilets; helpers*
Catering: *1 picnic area*
Retailing: *postcards/inexpensive souvenirs; craftwork; books; clothes*
No. shops: *1*

Operations
Contact: *Mr M Gresswell (Curator)*
No. employees: (high season) *1 full time; 4 part time* (low season) *1 full time; 4 part time*
Training: *F/T management, P/T operations staff and P/T management are trained in-house and externally and on specific courses and day-to-day on job*

Marketing
Annual event(s): *various*
Other: *market research*
UK promotion: *national newspapers; radio; local newspapers; regional tourist board; other attractions; leaflets/information packs; ETB/BTA*

DALMENY HOUSE
(privately owned)
historic house

Established: *1981*
Address: *South Queensferry, West Lothian, EH30 9TQ*
Telephone: *(031) 331 1888.* Fax: *(031) 331 1788*
Access: (road) *A90* (rail) *Dalmeny Station*
Parking capacity: (cars) *100* (coaches) *4*
Hours: *May to Sept – Sun – 1pm to 5.30pm, Mon and Tues – 12 noon to 5.30pm*
Admission (1992): *adults £3.20; children £1.50; student £2.50*
No. visitors (1992): *8000 (est.)*

Facilities
Interpretation: *tour guides*
Languages: *French; German*
Disabled: *easy access; disabled toilets*
Catering: *1 self-service cafeteria*

Operations
Contacts: *Mrs L Morison (Administrator); Mrs M Chapman (Marketing Consultant)*
No. employees: (high season) *1 full time; 15 part time* (low season) *1 full time*
Languages spoken: *French*

Marketing
Affiliations: *HHA, ASVA*
Other: *PR Company: Charisma c/o Dalmeny House; market research*
UK promotion: *regional tourist board; other attractions; leaflets/information packs; STB, BTA*

DAMSIDE GARDEN HERBS
(privately owned)
garden

Established: *1990*
Address: *By Johnshaven, Montrose, Angus*
Telephone: *(0561) 61498.* Fax: *(0561) 61498*
Access: (road) *A92*
Parking capacity: (cars) *30* (coaches) *5*
Hours: *Easter Fri to Christmas Eve – 10am to 5pm daily (closed Mon)*
Admission (1992): *adults £1.00; children £0.80; OAP £0.80; student £0.80*
No. visitors (1992): *4000 (est.)*

Facilities
Interpretation: *information boards; maps; tour guides*
Languages: *Gaelic; Latin (plants)*
Children: *nappy changing*
Schools: *maximum no. 28; educational literature*
Disabled: *easy access; disabled toilets; helpers; special signs*
Catering: *1 waiter/waitress served*
Retailing: *postcards/inexpensive souvenirs; craftwork; books; clothes; potpourri and aromatherapy oils*
No. shops: *1*

Operations
Contacts: *Mr and Mrs S Cruickshank (joint owners)*
No. employees: (high season) *3 full time; 8 part time* (low season) *3 full time; 4 part time*
Training: *F/T operations staff, F/T management, P/T operations staff and casual operations staff are trained in-house and externally and on specific courses and day-to-day on job*
Languages spoken: *French*

Marketing
UK promotion: *local newspapers; regional tourist board; other attractions; leaflets/information packs; Kincardine and Deeside Publications*

DAN-YR-OGOF SHOWCAVES
(limited company)
showcaves

Established: *1939*
Address: *Glyntawe, Abercraf, Upper Swansea Valley*
Telephone: *(0639) 730284*
Access: (road) *M4/A4067* (rail) *Neath/Swansea*
Parking capacity: (cars) *1000* (coaches) *40*

Hours: *Apr to Nov – Mon to Sun – 10am; all
year round for booked school groups*
Admission (1992): *adults £4.75; children £3.00*
No. visitors (1992): *100 000*

Facilities
Interpretation: *videos; leaflets; audio tapes;
information boards; tour guides; guide
books*
Languages: *French; Welsh*
Children: *nappy changing*
Schools: *maximum no. 200; educational literature;
lecture/talk*
Disabled: *disabled toilets; caves unsuitable for
wheelchairs*
Catering: *2 picnic areas*
Retailing: *postcards/inexpensive souvenirs;
confectionery and ice cream; craftwork; books;
reproductions of famous artefacts*
No. shops: *1*

Operations
Contacts: *Ian Gwilim (Manager); Simon Daniel
(Retail Manager)*
No. employees: (high season) *7 full time; 35 part
time* (low season) *7 full time; 4 part time*
Training: *F/T operations staff, F/T management
and P/T operations staff are trained in-house
and externally and on specific courses and
day-to-day on job*
Languages spoken: *German; Italian*

Marketing
Annual event(s): *music in the mountains*
Affiliations: *British Association of Showcaves*
Other: *market research*
UK promotion: *television; regional tourist
board; other attractions; leaflets/information
packs*

Environmental monitoring: *recycling; water
quality; hazardous materials; chemical
usage*

DARLINGTON MUSEUM
(local authority run)
museum

Established: *1921*
Address: *Tubwell row, Darlington, Co Durham,
DL1 1PD*
Telephone: *(0325) 463795*
Access: (road) *A1M* (rail) *Darlington*
Season: *all year*
Hours: *Mon, Tues, Wed and Fri – 10am to 1pm
and 2pm to 6pm, Thurs – 10am to 1pm only,
Sat – 10am to 1pm and 2pm to 5.30pm; closed
Christmas and New year, Good Friday and
May BH*
Admission (1992): *free*
No. visitors (1992): *22 000*

Facilities
Interpretation: *displays*
Schools: *maximum no. 40; lecture/talk; talk if
required*
Disabled: *easy access; access for wheelchairs to
ground floor only, service call system*
Retailing: *postcards/inexpensive souvenirs; books;
local history items and ceramics*
No. shops: *1*

Operations
Contacts: *Mr A Suddes (Curator)*
No. employees: (high season) *2 full time;
2 part time* (low season) *2 full time; 2 part
time*
Training: *F/T operations staff and
F/T management are trained in-house and
day-to-day on job*

Marketing
Affiliations: *MA, North of England Museum
Service*
Other: *market research*
UK promotion: *local newspapers; regional tourist
board; leaflets/information packs*

DARNAWAY FARM VISITOR CENTRE
(private company)
historic house; castle; museum; farm visitor centre

Established: *1980*
Address: *Tearie, Darnaway, Forres, Moray,
IV36 0ET*
Telephone: *(03094) 469*
Access: (road) *A96* (rail) *Forres–Aberdeen*
Parking capacity: (cars) *40* (coaches) *3*
Hours: *1 May to mid Sept – 10am to 5pm daily;
tours in July and Aug – 3 afternoons per week*
No. visitors (1992): *10 000 (est.)*

Facilities
Interpretation: *information boards; slides; tour
guides*
Children: *play area*
Schools: *maximum no. 100; educational literature;
audio/visual presentation; lecture/talk; estate
ranger*
Disabled: *easy access; disabled toilets; helpers*
Catering: *2 picnic area*
Retailing: *postcards/inexpensive souvenirs;
confectionery and ice cream; craftwork; books*
No. shops: *1*

Operations
Contacts: *Mr V Thomson (Estates Ranger); Mr D
McConnell (Estates Manager)*
No. employees: (high season) *1 full time; 3 part
time* (low season) *1 full time*
Training: *F/T management and P/T operations
staff are trained in-house and externally and on
specific courses and day-to-day on job*
Languages spoken: *French*

Marketing
Affiliations: *ASVA*
Other: *market research*
UK promotion: *regional tourist board; other
attractions; leaflets/information packs*

DARNOCH CATHEDRAL
(private – Kirk Session)
church

Established: *1214*
Address: *The Square, Dornoch, Sutherland*
Access: (road) *A9*
Parking capacity: (cars) *2* (coaches) *2*
Season: *all year*
Hours: *dawn to dusk*
Admission (1992): *free*

Facilities
Interpretation: *leaflets; guide books*
Languages: *French; German*
Schools: *lecture/talk*
Disabled: *easy access; leaflets; guide book*

Environmental monitoring: *rural heritage
husbandry*

DARTMOUTH MUSEUM
(charity)
historic house; museum

Established: *1949*
Address: *The Butterwalk, Dartmouth, Devon,
TQ6 9P2*
Telephone: *(0803) 832923*
Access: (road) *M6*
Season: *all year*
Hours: *Apr to Oct – 11am to 5pm; Nov to
Mar – 1.15pm to 4pm*
Admission (1992): *adults £0.70; children £0.20;
OAP £0.50*
No. visitors (1992): *13 000 (est.)*

Facilities
Interpretation: *leaflets; information boards; maps;
guide books*

Schools: *maximum no. 20; no special support*
Retailing: *postcards/inexpensive souvenirs; books*
No. shops: *1*

Operations
Contact: *R Cawthorne (Curator)*

Marketing
Affiliations: *Area Museum Council*
UK promotion: *local newspapers; regional tourist
board*

DEAL CASTLE
(government)
castle

Address: *Victoria Road, Deal, Kent, CT14 7BA*
Telephone: *(0304) 372762*
Access: (road) *A2*
Season: *all year*
Hours: *Apr to Oct – 10am to 6pm daily; Oct to
Mar – Tues to Sun – 10am to 4pm*
Admission (1992): *adults £1.80; children £0.90;
OAP £1.40; student £1.40; ub40 £1.40*
No. visitors (1992): *32 000 (est.)*

Facilities
Interpretation: *leaflets; audio tapes; information
boards; maps; guide books*
Languages: *French; German*
Schools: *maximum no. 500; educational literature;
teachers handbook*
Disabled: *guide book*
Catering: *1 picnic area*
Retailing: *postcards/inexpensive souvenirs;
confectionery and ice cream; books;
reproductions of famous artefacts*
No. shops: *1*

Operations
No. employees: (high season) *2 full time; 1 part
time* (low season) *1 full time; 1 part time*
Training: *F/T operations staff, F/T management,
P/T operations staff, P/T management and
casual operations staff and casual management
are trained in-house and on specific courses and
day-to-day on job*

Marketing
Other: *press office*
UK promotion: *national newspapers; local
newspapers; regional tourist board; other
attractions; leaflets/information packs*
Europe promotion: *leaflets/brochures; travel
agents' brochures*

DEAN CASTLE and COUNTRY PARK
(local authority run)
castle; park/reserve; museum; gallery;
zoo/wildlife attraction

Established: *1976*
Address: *Dean Rd, Kilmarnock, Ayrshire, KA1
3BU*
Telephone: *(0563) 22702.* Fax: *(0563) 29661*
Access: (road) *A77/A71* (rail)
Glasgow–Kilmarnock
Parking capacity: (cars) *100* (coaches) *6*
Season: *all year*
Hours: *castle – 12pm to 5pm daily; park – dawn
to dusk daily (closed 25, 26 Dec and 1, 2 Jan).
Organised groups by arrangement*
Admission (1992): *adults £1.00; children £0.75;
OAP £1.00; student £1.00*
No. visitors (1992): *145 000 (est.)*

Facilities
Interpretation: *leaflets; information boards; slides;
maps; tour guides; guide books*
Languages: *French; German*
Children: *adventure playground; play area; nappy
changing*
Schools: *maximum no. 100; educational literature*
Disabled: *easy access; disabled toilets; only
ground floors accessible*
Catering: *3 picnic areas*
Franchisees: *castle – 12pm to 5pm daily*

Retailing: *postcards/inexpensive souvenirs;
confectionery and ice cream; craftwork; books;
reproductions of famous artefacts*
No. shops: 2

Operations
Contacts: *Mr J Homer (Curator); Ms E Sutherland
(Administrator); Ms M Gallacher (Senior
Receptionist)*
No. employees: (high season) *20 full time; 7 part
time* (low season) *20 full time; 3 part time*
Training: *F/T operations staff, F/T management,
P/T operations staff and casual operations staff
are trained in-house and externally and on
specific courses and day-to-day on job using
videos and handbooks*
Languages spoken: *French; German*

Marketing
Annual event(s): *jazz festival*
Affiliations: *ASVA, MA, SMC, SAC and M & G
Commission*
Other: *market research*
UK promotion: *national newspapers; radio; local
newspapers; regional tourist board; other
attractions; leaflets/information packs;
ETB/BTA; STB*
USA promotion: *leaflets/brochures; STB
Strathclyde Region*

Environmental monitoring: *recycling*

DENMANS GARDEN
(limited company)
garden

Established: *1984*
Address: *Clock House, Fontwell, W Sussex, BN18
0SU*
Telephone: *(0243) 542808.* Fax: *(0243) 544064*
Access: (road) *A27* (rail) *Barnham*
Hours: *Mar to Dec – 9am to 5pm daily*
Admission (1992): *adults £2.25; children £1.25;
OAP £1.85; group rates £1.65*
No. visitors (1992): *21 000 (est.)*

Facilities
Interpretation: *leaflets; tour guides*
Schools: *maximum no. 50; lecture/talk*
Disabled: *easy access*
Catering: *1 self-service cafeteria*
Retailing: *postcards/inexpensive souvenirs; books;
plants; gifts*
No. shops: 2

Operations
Contact: *M J Neve (Managing Director)*
Training: *F/T operations staff, P/T operations
staff and casual operations staff are trained
in-house and day-to-day on job using
handbooks and In House manuals*
Languages spoken: *French*

Marketing
UK promotion: *regional tourist board; other
attractions; leaflets/information packs;
ETB/BTA*
Europe/USA promotion: *leaflets/brochures*

Environmental monitoring: *water quality; energy
consumption; hazardous materials; Wildlife
monitoring*

DERBY CATHEDRAL
(cathedral)
church

Address: *Irongate, Derby*
Telephone: *(0332) 41201*
Season: *all year*
Hours: *daily from 9am*
Admission (1992): *discretionary donation*
No. visitors (1992): *40 000 (est.)*

Facilities
Interpretation: *leaflets; guide books; guided tours
by appointment*
Languages: *French; German; Italian; Spanish*

Schools: *educational literature; audio/visual
presentation; lecture/talk; by arrangement to fit
requirements*
Disabled: *easy access*
Retailing: *postcards/inexpensive souvenirs; books*
No. shops: 1

Operations
Contacts: *The Very Rev B H Lewers (Provost);
Mrs M Pittman (Publicity Officer)*

Marketing
Annual event(s): *flower festivals; organ recitals*
Other: *market research*
UK promotion: *radio; local newspapers; regional
tourist board; other attractions;
leaflets/information packs; city council
publications*

DERBY INDUSTRIAL MUSEUM
(local authority run)
museum

Established: *1974*
Address: *Silk Mill Lane, Off Full St, Derby,
DE1 3AR*
Telephone: *(0332) 255308*
Access: (road) *M1/A52* (rail) *Derby Midland*
Season: *all year*
Hours: *Mon – 11am to 5pm; Tues to Sat – 10am
to 5pm; Sun and BH – 2pm to 5pm. All year;
closed Christmas Day and New Year's Day*
Admission (1992): *adults £0.30; children £0.10;
OAP £0.10; student £0.10*
No. visitors (1992): *20 282*

Facilities
Interpretation: *leaflets; information boards*
Schools: *maximum no. 35; lecture/talk; by
appointment and activities*
Disabled: *easy access; disabled toilets*
Retailing: *postcards/inexpensive souvenirs; books*
No. shops: 1

Operations
Contact: *Mr J Platt (Senior Keeper of Industry)*
No. employees: (high season) *5 full time; 5 part
time* (low season) *5 full time; 5 part time*
Training: *F/T operations staff, F/T management,
P/T operations staff, P/T management, casual
operations staff and casual management are
trained in-house and externally and on specific
courses and day-to-day on job*

Marketing
Annual event(s): *family days and holiday
activities*
Sponsor(s): *various*
Affiliations: *East Midlands Museums Service*
Other: *PR company: Welding Woodhead,
44 George St, Edgbaston, Birmingham; market
research*
UK promotion: *radio; local newspapers; regional
tourist board; leaflets/information packs;
ETB/BTA*

DERBY MUSEUM AND ART GALLERY
(local authority run)
museum; gallery

Established: *1879*
Address: *The Strand, Derby, DE1 1BS*
Telephone: *(0332) 255586*
Access: (road) *M1/A52* (rail) *Derby Midland*
Season: *all year*
Hours: *Mon – 11am to 5pm; Tues to Sat – 10am
to 5pm; Sun and BH – 2pm to 5pm; closed
Christmas Day and Boxing Day*
Admission (1992): *free*
No. visitors (1992): *100 547*

Facilities
Interpretation: *leaflets; information boards*
Schools: *maximum no. 35; lecture/talk; by
appointment and activities*
Disabled: *easy access; disabled toilets*
Retailing: *postcards/inexpensive souvenirs;
craftwork; books; reproductions of famous
artefacts*

No. shops: 1

Operations
Contact: *Mr D Fraser (Museums and Arts Officer)*
No. employees: (high season) *40 full time; 10 part
time* (low season) *40 full time; 10 part time*
Training: *F/T operations staff, F/T management,
P/T operations staff, P/T management, casual
operations staff and casual management are
trained in-house and externally and on specific
courses and day-to-day on job using videos*

Marketing
Annual event(s): *family days and holiday
activities*
Sponsor(s): *various*
Affiliations: *East Midlands Museum Service*
Other: *PR company: Welding Woodhead,
44 George Rd, Edgbaston, Birmingham; market
research*
UK promotion: *radio; local newspapers; regional
tourist board; leaflets/information packs;
ETB/BTA*

DERWENT WALK COUNTRY PARK
(local authority run)
park/reserve

Established: *1970*
Address: *Thornley Woodlands Centre, Rowlands
Gill, Tyne and Wear, NE40 3SY*
Telephone: *(0207) 545212*
Access: (road) *A694*
Parking capacity: (cars) *80*
Season: *all year*
Hours: *open at all times*
Admission (1992): *free*
No. visitors (1992): *16 000*

Facilities
Interpretation: *leaflets; information boards*
Schools: *maximum no. 60; educational literature*
Disabled: *easy access; disabled toilets; leaflets*
Catering: *3 picnic areas*
Retailing: *postcards/inexpensive souvenirs*
No. shops: 1

Operations
Contacts: *Mr T Weston (Conservation Officer);
Mr J Hemstock (Interpretation Officer)*
No. employees: (high season) *8 full time; 2 part
time* (low season) *8 full time; 2 part time*
Training: *F/T operations staff, F/T management
and P/T operations staff are trained in-house
and externally and on specific courses using
videos*
Languages spoken: *French*

Marketing
Annual event(s): *various*
Other: *press office; market research*
UK promotion: *local newspapers; regional tourist
board; other attractions; leaflets/information
packs*

DEVONSHIRE REGIMENT MUSEUM
(trust)
museum

Established: *1946*
Address: *Wyvern Barracks, Barrack Road, Exeter,
EX2 6AE*
Telephone: *(0392) 218178*
Access: (road) *M5/A30* (rail) *Exeter*
Parking capacity: (cars) *100* (coaches) *20*
Season: *all year*
Hours: *all year – Mon to Fri – 9am to 4.30pm*
Admission (1992): *free*
No. visitors (1992): *453*

Facilities
Interpretation: *information boards*
Schools: *maximum no. 30; no special support*
Retailing: *postcards/inexpensive souvenirs*
No. shops: 1

Operations
Contacts: *Lt Col D R Roberts (Assistant Curator);
Major J Carroll (Curator)*

No. employees: (high season) *1 full time* (low season) *1 full time*

Marketing
Affiliation: *Area Museum Council South West*

Environmental monitoring: *water quality*

DEWEY MUSEUM, THE
(trust)
museum

Established: *1972*
Address: *The Public Library, 3 Horse Shoes Mall, Warminster, Wilts*
Telephone: *(0985) 215640*
Access: (road) *A36* (rail) *Warminster*
Season: *all year*
Hours: *Mon and Tues – 10am to 5pm; Thur and Fri – 10am to 8pm*
Admission (1992): *free*
No. visitors (1992): *10 000 (est.)*

Facilities
Interpretation: *information boards; displays*
Schools: *maximum no. 20; educational literature; lecture/talk*
Disabled: *easy access*
Retailing: *postcards/inexpensive souvenirs; books*
No. shops: *1*

Operations
Contacts: *Mr R Field (Hon Curator); Mr D Howell (Assistant Curator)*
No. employees: (high season) *3 part time* (low season) *3 part time*
Training: *P/T operations staff are trained in-house and day-to-day on job and seminars*

Marketing
UK promotion: *local newspapers*

DEWSBURY MUSEUM
(local authority run)
museum; gallery

Established: *1896*
Address: *Crow Nest Park, Heckmondwike Rd, Dewsbury, W Yorks, WF13*
Telephone: *(0924) 468171*
Access: (road) *M62/M1/A652* (rail) *Dewsbury*
Parking capacity: (cars) *40* (coaches) *10*
Season: *all year*
Hours: *1 Mar to 31 Oct – Mon to Fri – 10am to 5pm; Sat and Sun – 12 noon to 5pm; 1 Nov to 28 Feb – 12 noon to 5pm daily. Groups at other times by arrangement*
Admission (1992): *free*
No. visitors (1992): *32 000*

Facilities
Interpretation: *videos; leaflets; audio tapes; information boards; slides; labelling and photographs*
Children: *play area*
Schools: *maximum no. 35; audio/visual presentation; lecture/talk*
Catering: *1 picnic area*
Retailing: *postcards/inexpensive souvenirs; books; quality toys and games*
No. shops: *1*

Operations
Contact: *Mr B Haigh (Community Curator)*
No. employees: (high season) *9 full time; 7 part time* (low season) *7 full time; 7 part time*
Training: *F/T operations staff, F/T management, P/T operations staff and casual operations staff are trained in-house and externally and on specific courses and day-to-day on job*

Marketing
Annual event(s): *historic vehicles rally*
Sponsor(s): *Sainsbury plc*
Affiliations: *MA, Museums and Galleries Commission, Yorks and Humbs Area Museums Council*
Other: *press office; market research*

UK promotion: *radio; local newspapers; regional tourist board; other attractions; leaflets/information packs*

DICK INSTITUTE
(local authority run)
museum; gallery; library

Established: *1903*
Address: *Kilmarnock and Loudoun, Kilmarnock, KA1 3BU*
Telephone: *(0563) 29661*
Access: (road) *A77/A71* (rail) *Glasgow–Kilmarnock*
Parking capacity: (cars) *50* (coaches) *4*
Season: *all year*
Hours: *Mon, Tues, Thur and Fri – 9am to 8pm; Wed and Sat – 9am to 5pm; closed Sun and BH*
Admission (1992): *free*
No. visitors (1992): *60 000 (est.)*

Facilities
Interpretation: *information boards*
Schools: *maximum no. 60; educational literature; workshops and activities*
Disabled: *easy access; disabled toilets*
Retailing: *postcards/inexpensive souvenirs; craftwork; books; reproductions of famous artefacts; contemporary paintings and prints*
No. shops: *1*

Operations
Contacts: *Mr J Hunter (Curator); Ms E Sutherland (Administration Officer); Ms M Gallagher (Senior Receptionist); Mr D Bett (Exhibitions Officer)*
No. employees: (high season) *5 full time; 5 part time*
Training: *F/T operations staff, F/T management, P/T operations staff and casual operations staff are trained in-house and externally and on specific courses and day-to-day on job using videos and handbooks*
Languages spoken: *German; Spanish*

Marketing
Affiliations: *SMC and Scottish Arts Council*
Other: *market research*
UK promotion: *radio; local newspapers; regional tourist board; other attractions; leaflets/information packs*

Environmental monitoring: *recycling; waste; water quality; energy consumption; hazardous materials; chemical usage; transport; emissions*

DICKENS HOUSE MUSEUM
(trust)
historic house; museum

Established: *1925*
Address: *48 Doughty Street, London, WC1N 2LX*
Telephone: *(071) 405 2127.* Fax: *(071) 831 5175*
Season: *all year*
Hours: *Mon to Sat – 10am to 5pm; closed BH and Christmas week*
Admission (1992): *adults £2.00; children £1.00; OAP £1.50; student £1.50; family ticket £4.00*
No. visitors (1992): *24 955*

Facilities
Interpretation: *information boards; guide books*
Languages: *Japanese; Dutch; French; German; Italian; Spanish; and more*
Schools: *maximum no. 80; educational literature; lecture/talk*
Retailing: *postcards/inexpensive souvenirs; craftwork; books; clothes; reproductions of famous artefacts*
No. shops: *1*

Operations
Contacts: *Mr B Perkins (Shop Manager); Mr D Parker (Curator)*
No. employees: (high season) *2 full time; 8 part time* (low season) *2 full time; 8 part time*

Training: *F/T operations staff, P/T operations staff and casual operations staff are trained in-house and day-to-day on job using handbooks and in-house manuals*

Marketing
UK promotion: *national newspapers; regional tourist board; other attractions; leaflets/information packs; ETB/BTA*
Europe/USA promotion: *British Tourist Authority*

Environmental monitoring: *energy consumption; hazardous materials*

DICKENS HOUSE MUSEUM BROADSTAIRS
(local authority run)
historic house; museum

Established: *1973*
Address: *Victoria Parade, Broadstairs, Kent*
Telephone: *(0643) 861232*
Access: (road) *M2/A229* (rail) *Victoria Broadstairs*
Hours: *Apr to Oct – 2.30pm to 5.30pm daily*
Admission (1992): *adults £0.80; children £0.40; student £0.60*
No. visitors (1992): *10 000 (est.)*

Facilities
Interpretation: *leaflets; tour guides; guide books*
Languages: *French; German*
Schools: *maximum no. 30; lecture/talk*
Retailing: *postcards/inexpensive souvenirs*
No. shops: *1*

Operations
Contact: *Ms J Smith (Hon Curator)*
No. employees: (high season) *3 part time*
Languages spoken: *French; German; Punjabi*

Marketing
UK promotion: *regional tourist board; leaflets/information packs; ETB/BTA; Museums and Galleries*

DIDCOT RAILWAY CENTRE
(local authority run)
museum

Established: *1967*
Address: *Didcot, Oxon, OX11 7WJ*
Telephone: *(0235) 817200.* Fax: *(0235) 510621*
Access: (road) *M4/A34* (rail) *Didcot Parkway*
Parking capacity: (cars) *600* (coaches) *12*
Season: *all year*
Hours: *Apr to Sept – 11am to 5pm daily*
Admission (1992): *adults £4.50; children £4.00; OAP £4.00; family £14.50*
No. visitors (1992): *100 000 (est.)*

Facilities
Interpretation: *leaflets; information boards; tour guides; guide books*
Languages: *French; German*
Children: *nappy changing*
Schools: *maximum no. 100; educational literature; educational tour; lecture/talk; follow up visit for child*
Disabled: *easy access; disabled toilets; helpers*
Catering: *1 picnic area*
Retailing: *postcards/inexpensive souvenirs; confectionery and ice cream; books; clothes; reproductions of famous artefacts; original railway items*
No. shops: *2*

Operations
Contacts: *M Dean (General Manager); J Howse (Marketing Executive)*
No. employees: (high season) *4 full time; 6 part time* (low season) *4 full time; 13 part time*
Training: *F/T operations staff, F/T management, P/T operations staff, P/T management and casual operations staff are trained in-house and externally and on specific courses and day-to-day on job*

Marketing
Annual event(s): *various*
Other: *press office; market research*

UK promotion: *national newspapers; radio; local newspapers; regional tourist board; other attractions; leaflets/information packs; ETB/BTA*
Europe/USA/Japan promotion: *leaflets/brochures; British Tourist Authority*

DINMORE MANOR AND GARDENS
(limited company)
historic house; garden; church

Established: *1932*
Address: *Dinmore Manor, Hereford, HR4 8EE*
Telephone: *(0432) 830322.* Fax: *(0432) 830503*
Access: (road) *A49*
Parking capacity: (cars) *30*
Season: *all year*
Hours: *9.30am to 5.30pm daily; evening visits by arrangement*
Admission (1992): *adults £2.00; OAP £2.00; student £2.00*

Facilities
Interpretation: *leaflets; guide books*
Disabled: *easy access*

Operations
Contact: *Mr R Murphy (Chairman)*
Languages spoken: *French*

Marketing
Annual event(s): *National Gardens Open Day Scheme*
Affiliations: *Associated Promotion of Herefordshire and HHA*
UK promotion: *local newspapers; regional tourist board; leaflets/information packs; Hereford and Worcs Countryside Service*

Environmental monitoring: *waste; water quality; energy consumption; hazardous materials; emissions*

DINOSAUR MUSEUM
(privately owned)
museum

Established: *1984*
Address: *Icen Way, Dorchester, Dorset*
Telephone: *(0305) 269880.* Fax: *(0305) 268885*
Access: (road) *A35/A37*
Season: *all year*
Hours: *9.30am to 5.30pm daily; closed 24–26 Dec*
Admission (1992): *adults £2.95; children £1.95; OAP £2.50; student £2.50; family ticket (2 + 2) £8.95*
No. visitors (1992): *155 000 (est.)*

Facilities
Interpretation: *videos; audio tapes; information boards; maps; guide books; reconstructions*
Schools: *maximum no. 100; audio/visual presentation; lecture/talk; handling facilities*
Disabled: *low displays and labelling*
Retailing: *postcards/inexpensive souvenirs; craftwork; books; dinosaurian*
No. shops: *1*

Operations
Contacts: *Mr T Batty (General Manager); Ms J Ridley (Director); Ms T McDonald (Merchandising Manager)*
No. employees: (high season) *11 full time; 12 part time* (low season) *8 full time; 9 part time*
Training: *F/T operations staff, P/T operations staff and casual operations staff are trained in-house and day-to-day on job*

Marketing
Annual event(s): *special exhibitions*
Sponsor(s): *Royal Mail*
Other: *press office; market research*
UK promotion: *radio; local newspapers; regional tourist board; other attractions; leaflets/information packs*
Europe/USA promotion: *British Tourist Authority*

Environmental monitoring: *water quality*

DINOSAUR SAFARI
(privately owned)
museum

Established: *1991*
Address: *The Dinosaurium, Old Christchurch Lane, Bournemouth, Dorset, BH1 1NE*
Telephone: *(0202) 293544.* Fax: *(0305) 268885*
Access: (road) *M27/A338* (rail) *Bournemouth*
Season: *all year*
Hours: *9.30am to 5.30pm daily all year*
Admission (1992): *adults £2.95; children £1.95; OAP £2.50; student £2.50; family ticket (2 + 2) £8.95*
No. visitors (1992): *95 000 (est.)*

Facilities
Interpretation: *videos; leaflets; audio tapes; information boards; reconstructions and computers*
Schools: *maximum no. 70; audio/visual presentation; lecture/talk*
Retailing: *postcards/inexpensive souvenirs; books; dinosaurs*
No. shops: *1*

Operations
Contacts: *Mr T Batty (General Manager); Ms J Ridley (Director); Ms T McDonald (Merchandising Manager)*
No. employees: (high season) *11 full time; 12 part time* (low season) *8 full time; 9 part time*
Training: *F/T operations staff, P/T operations staff and casual operations staff are trained in-house and day-to-day on job using handbooks*
Languages spoken: *French*

Marketing
Press office; market research
UK promotion: *radio; local newspapers; regional tourist board; other attractions; leaflets/information packs*

DINTON PASTURES COUNTRY PARK
(local authority run)
park/reserve

Established: *1978*
Address: *Davis St, Hurst, Reading, RG10 0TH*
Telephone: *(0734) 342016*
Access: (road) *M4/A429*
Parking capacity: (cars) *500*
Season: *all year*
Hours: *dawn to dusk daily*
Admission (1992): *free*
No. visitors (1992): *650 000*

Facilities
Interpretation: *leaflets; information boards; maps; guide books*
Children: *adventure playground; play area; nappy changing*
Schools: *maximum no. 400; educational literature; educational tour; assisted*
Disabled: *easy access; disabled toilets*
Catering: *3 picnic areas*
Franchisees: *dawn to dusk daily*

Operations
Contact: *C Buggy (Countryside Officer)*
No. employees: (high season) *5 full time; 7 part time* (low season) *5 full time; 1 part time*
Training: *F/T operations staff, F/T management, P/T operations staff and casual operations staff are trained in-house and externally and on specific courses and day-to-day on job*

Marketing
Annual event: *countryside day*
Other: *press office; market research*
UK promotion: *local newspapers; leaflets/information packs*

DOCHFOUR GARDENS
(private garden)
garden

Established: *1980*
Address: *Dochfour Estate, Dochgarroch, Inverness, IV3 6JY*
Telephone: *(046) 386 218.* Fax: *(046) 386 366*
Access: (road) *A82*
Parking capacity: (cars) *40*
Season: *all year*
Hours: *Apr to Oct – 9am to 5pm weekdays – 2pm to 5pm weekends; winter closed – weekends only*
Admission (1992): *adults £1.50*
No. visitors (1992): *4000 (est.)*

Facilities
Interpretation: *leaflets*
Schools: *maximum no. 20; lecture/talk*
Retailing: *postcards/inexpensive souvenirs; plants, trees and shrubs*
No. shops: *1*

Operations
Contacts: *Lady Burton; Mr D Robb (Gardener)*
No. employees: (high season) *2 full time* (low season) *2 full time*
Training: *F/T operations staff are trained in-house and day-to-day on job*
Languages spoken: *French*

Marketing
UK promotion: *national newspapers; local newspapers; regional tourist board; STB*

Environmental monitoring: *recycling; water quality; energy consumption; transport*

DODDINGTON PLACE GARDENS
(privately owned)
garden

Established: *1989*
Address: *Doddington Place, Doddington, Nr Sittingbourne, Kent, ME9 0BB*
Telephone: *(0795) 86385*
Access: (road) *A20/A2* (rail) *Sittingbourne*
Parking capacity: (cars) *300*
Hours: *Easter to Sept – Wed, BH and Sun in May – 11am to 6pm. Other times for groups by appointment*
Admission (1992): *adults £1.50; children £0.25; OAP £1.50; student £1.50; disabled £1.10*
No. visitors (1992): *6000 (est.)*

Facilities
Interpretation: *leaflets*
Schools: *maximum no. 40*
Disabled: *easy access; disabled toilets*
Catering: *1 waiter/waitress served*
Retailing: *wide range of gifts*
No. shops: *1*

Operations
Contact: *Mrs Oldfield (owner)*
No. employees: (high season) *1 full time; 6 part time* (low season) *1 full time; 3 part time*
Training: *F/T operations staff and P/T operations staff are trained externally and on specific courses*

Marketing
Affiliations: *HHA, CLA, SETB, ATAK, S Wales Tourism*
Other: *market research*
UK promotion: *local newspapers; regional tourist board; other attractions; leaflets/information packs; National Gardens Scheme Yearbook*

DONKEY SANCTUARY, THE
(charity)
sanctuary for donkeys

Established: *1973*
Address: *Sidmouth, Devon, EX10 0NU*
Telephone: *(0395) 578222.* Fax: *(0395) 579266*
Access: (road) *M5/A3052* (rail) *Exeter/Honiton*

Parking capacity: (cars) *100* (coaches) *6*
Season: *all year*
Hours: *from 9am daily*
Admission (1992): *free*
No. visitors (1992): *90 000 (est.)*

Facilities
Interpretation: *videos; leaflets; information boards; maps; tour guides*
Schools: *educational tour; lecture/talk*
Disabled: *easy access; disabled toilets; helpers*
Catering: *1 picnic area*

Operations
Contacts: *Dr E D Svendsen (Administrator); R Barnes (Personnel Manager); P Svendsen (Assistant Administrator)*
No. employees: (high season) *130 full time; 20 part time*
Training: *F/T operations staff, F/T management and P/T operations staff are trained in-house and externally and on specific courses and day-to-day on job*

Marketing
Annual event(s): *donkey week and Slade Centre festival*
UK promotion: *television; national newspapers; leaflets/information packs*
Newsletter promotion: *leaflets/brochures*

DORSET COUNTY MUSEUM
(trust)
museum

Established: *1884*
Address: *High West St, Dorchester, DT1 1XA*
Telephone: *(0305) 262735*
Access: (road) *A37/A35* (rail) *Dorchester*
Season: *all year*
Hours: *Mon to Sat – 10am to 5pm except Christmas Day, Boxing day and Good Friday*
Admission (1992): *adults £2.00; children £1.00; OAP £1.00; student £1.00; society members free*
No. visitors (1992): *55 562*

Facilities
Interpretation: *leaflets; information boards; guide books*
Schools: *educational literature; lecture/talk; by arrangement and activities*
Retailing: *postcards/inexpensive souvenirs; craftwork; books; reproductions of famous artefacts*
No. shops: *1*

Operations
Contact: *Mr R De Peyer (Curator)*
No. employees: (high season) *7 full time; 2 part time* (low season) *7 full time; 2 part time*
Training: *F/T management are trained externally and on specific courses*
Languages spoken: *French*

Marketing
Annual event(s): *various*
Affiliations: *MA, Area Museum Council, Association of IM, etc.*
Other: *market research*
UK promotion: *television; radio; regional tourist board; other attractions; leaflets/information packs; Best of Dorset; ETB/BTA*

Environmental monitoring: *recycling; energy consumption; hazardous materials; chemical usage*

DORSET HEAVY HORSE CENTRE
(limited company)
heavy horse and shetland centre

Established: *1984*
Address: *Edmondsham Rd, Verwood, Dorset, BH21 5RJ*
Telephone: *(0202) 824040*
Access: (road) *M27/A31/B3081*
Hours: *Good Friday to 31 Oct – 10am to 5.30pm*
Admission (1992): *adults £2.95; children £1.95; OAP £2.25; special prices for groups, under 3s free*

No. visitors (1992): *35 000 (est.)*

Facilities
Interpretation: *videos; leaflets; information boards; tour guides; commentaries*
Children: *play area*
Schools: *maximum no. 50; educational literature; audio/visual presentation; lecture/talk; schools pack*
Disabled: *easy access; disabled toilets*
Catering: *1 picnic area*
Retailing: *postcards/inexpensive souvenirs; confectionery and ice cream; craftwork; books; clothes*
No. shops: *1*

Operations
Contacts: *Mrs R Mercer (Director and General Manager); Ms P Spooner (Marketing Consultant)*
No. employees: (high season) *6 full time; 4 part time*
Training: *F/T operations staff, P/T operations staff and casual operations staff are trained in-house and day-to-day on job*
Languages spoken: *French; Italian*

Marketing
Affiliations: *Shire Horse Society, Suffolk Society, etc.*
Other: *PR company: SOS, 2 Mill St, Corfe Mullen, Wimborne, Dorset; press office; market research*
UK promotion: *national newspapers; radio; local newspapers; regional tourist board; other attractions; leaflets/information packs; Dorset tourism, Bournemouth and Poole guides; ETB/BTA*

Environmental monitoring: *recycling; waste; water quality; energy consumption; hazardous materials; chemical usage; transport; emissions*

DORSET MILITARY MUSEUM
(trust)
museum

Established: *1927*
Address: *The Keep, Bridport Road, Dorchester, Dorset, DT1 1RN*
Telephone: *(0305) 264066*
Access: (road) *A35* (rail) *Dorchester*
Parking capacity: (cars) *10*
Season: *all year*
Hours: *all year – Mon to Sat – 9am to 5pm*
Admission (1992): *adults £1.00; children £0.50; OAP £0.50; groups £0.25*
No. visitors (1992): *10 310*

Facilities
Interpretation: *information boards*
Schools: *maximum no. 30; no special support*
Retailing: *postcards/inexpensive souvenirs*
No. shops: *1*

Operations
Contact: *Major J Carroll (Curator)*
No. employees: (high season) *2 full time* (low season) *2 full time*

Marketing
UK promotion: *radio; local newspapers; leaflets/information packs; Discover Dorset; West Dorset brochure*

DOWN COUNTY MUSEUM
(local authority run)
heritage centre; museum

Established: *1984*
Address: *The Mall, Downpatrick, Co. Down, BT30 6AH*
Telephone: *(0396) 615218.* Fax: *(0396) 615590*
Access: (road) *A7*
Season: *all year*
Hours: *July to mid Sept – Mon to Fri – 11am to 5pm, Sat and Sun – 2pm to 5pm; mid Sept to July – Tues to Fri – 11am to 5pm, Sat – 2pm to 5pm*

Admission (1992): *free*
No. visitors (1992): *39 608*

Facilities
Interpretation: *leaflets; reception staff*
Languages: *Japanese; French; German; Italian; Spanish*
Children: *nappy changing*
Schools: *maximum no. 50; educational literature; audio/visual presentation; lecture/talk; activities by arrangement*
Disabled: *disabled toilets; helpers*
Retailing: *postcards/inexpensive souvenirs; confectionery and ice cream; craftwork; books; clothes; linen tablecloths, tea towels*
No. shops: *1*

Operations
Contacts: *Mrs Patricia Bardon (Museum Administrator); Ms Leslie Simpson (Assistant Curator); Gerard Lennon (Community Education Officer)*
No. employees: (high season) *10 full time; 8 part time* (low season) *10 full time; 4 part time*
Training: *F/T operations staff, F/T management, casual operations staff and casual management are trained in-house and day-to-day on job*

Marketing
Annual event(s): *St Patrick's Day Activities*
Affiliations: *NI Museums Advisory Committee, Museums and Galleries Commission, Irish Museums Association*
Other: *PR company: Heritage Island, 37 Main St, Donnybrook, Dublin; market research*
UK promotion: *national newspapers; radio; local newspapers; regional tourist board; other attractions; leaflets/information packs; Holiday UK, Holidays and Leisure Guide*
Europe/USA/Marketing by Heritage Island promotion: *leaflets/brochures; NI Tourist Board*

DRUMMOND CASTLE GARDENS
(limited co and trust)
garden

Established: *1960*
Address: *Muthill, Nr Crieff, Perthshire, PH7 4HZ*
Telephone: *(076481) 257.* Fax: *(076481) 550*
Access: (road) *A822*
Parking capacity: (cars) *60* (coaches) *3*
Hours: *1 May to 30 Sept – 2pm to 6pm daily (last entry 5pm)*
Admission (1992): *adults £2.00; children £1.00; OAP £1.00; student £2.00;*
No. visitors (1992): *8530*

Facilities
Interpretation: *maps*
Schools: *maximum no. 100; educational literature; lecture/talk*
Retailing: *postcards/inexpensive souvenirs*
No. shops: *1*

Operations

Contacts: *Mr M Aldridge (Factor); J Buchanan (Custodian)*
No. employees: (high season) *5 full time; 3 part time*
Languages spoken: *French; Spanish; Irish*

Marketing
Annual event(s): *Scotland's Gardens Scheme open day*
Affiliations: *Scotland's Garden Scheme*
Other: *market research*
UK promotion: *local newspapers; regional tourist board; other attractions; leaflets/information packs; Perthshire Tourist Board*

DRUSILLAS PARK
(partnership)
park/reserve; garden; zoo/wildlife attraction

Established: *1925*
Address: *Alfriston, E Sussex, BN26 5QS*
Telephone: *(0323) 870656.* Fax: *(0323) 870846*
Access: (road) *M23/A27* (rail) *Polegate*

Parking capacity: (cars) *1000* (coaches) *50*
Season: *all year*
Hours: *all year – 10am to 4pm daily*
Admission (1992): *adults £4.50; children £3.95; OAP £3.25; under 3s free*
No. visitors (1992): *330 000 (est.)*

Facilities
Interpretation: *videos; leaflets; information boards; maps; tour guides; guide books*
Children: *adventure playground; nappy changing*
Schools: *maximum no. 600; educational literature; educational tour; lecture/talk*
Disabled: *easy access; disabled toilets; braille/ sound posts; helpers; special signs; leaflets; guide book*
Catering: *1 bar/public house*
Retailing: *craftwork; conservatories*
No. shops: *more than 4*

Operations
Contacts: *M and K Ann (Managing Partners, Purchasing Managers, and Publicity and PR Managers); C Coles (Personnel and Training)*
No. employees: *(high season) 60 full time; 100 part time (low season) 35 full time; 20 part time*
Training: *F/T operations staff, F/T management, P/T operations staff, P/T management, casual operations staff and casual management are trained in-house and externally and on specific courses and day-to-day on job*

Marketing
Annual event(s): *N/A*
Affiliations: *National Federation of Zoos, Rare Breeds Survival Trust*
Other: *press office; market research*
UK promotion: *television; national newspapers; radio; local newspapers; regional tourist board; other attractions; leaflets/information packs; 100s of Places to Visit, Group Organisers Guide; ETB/BTA; Day Out of London, SEETB*
Europe promotion: *leaflets/brochures; travel agents' brochures; British Tourist Authority*

DUART CASTLE
(partnership)
castle

Established: *1970*
Address: *Isle of Mull, Argyll, PA64 6AP*
Telephone: *(06802) 309*
Access: (road) *ferry from Oban*
Parking capacity: (cars) *60* (coaches) *6*
Hours: *1 May to 30 Sept – 10.30am to 6pm*
Admission (1992): *adults £3.00; children £1.50; OAP £2.00*
No. visitors (1992): *25 000 (est.)*

Facilities
Interpretation: *information boards; tour guides; guide books*
Languages: *French; German; Italian*
Disabled: *not suitable for wheelchairs*
Catering: *1 self-service cafeteria*
Retailing: *postcards/inexpensive souvenirs; craftwork; crystal and china; Maclean tartans*
No. shops: *1*

Operations
Contacts: *Sir L Maclean (owner); Lady Maclean*
No. employees: *(high season) 7 full time; 2 part time (low season) 5 full time; 2 part time*
Training: *F/T operations staff and P/T operations staff are trained in-house and day-to-day on job using videos and handbooks*
Languages spoken: *French; German; Spanish*

Marketing
Affiliations: *HHA, ASVA*
Other: *market research*
UK promotion: *local newspapers; regional tourist board; other attractions; leaflets/information packs; STB, West Highland holidays, Landmark and Waterfront Connection*
Europe promotion: *British Tourist Authority*

Environmental monitoring: *recycling; waste; water quality; energy consumption; hazardous materials*

DUKE OF CORNWALL'S LIGHT INFANTRY MUSEUM
(trust)
museum

Established: *1923*
Address: *The Keep, Bodmin, Cornwall, PL31 1EG*
Telephone: *(0208) 72810*
Access: (road) *B3268*
Season: *all year*
Hours: *all year – Mon to Fri – 8am to 5pm*
Admission (1992): *adults £1.00; children £1.00; OAP £1.00; student £1.00*
No. visitors (1992): *5274*

Facilities
Interpretation: *leaflets; information boards; maps; guide books*
Schools: *educational tour; lecture/talk*
Retailing: *postcards/inexpensive souvenirs; books; clothes; model soldiers, badges, books, etc.*
No. shops: *1*

Operations
Contact: *Major W H White (Light Infantry County Secretary)*
No. employees: *(high season) 1 full time (low season) 1 full time*
Languages spoken: *various*

Marketing
Affiliation: *Army Museums Ogilby Trust*
Other: *market research*
UK promotion: *regional tourist board; other attractions; leaflets/information packs*

Environmental monitoring: *recycling*

DULWICH PICTURE GALLERY
(trust)
garden; museum

Established: *1813*
Address: *College Rd, London, SE21 7AD*
Telephone: *(081) 693 5254.* Fax: *(081) 693 0923*
Access: (road) *A205* (rail) *Dulwich*
Season: *all year*
Hours: *Tues to Fri – 10am to 1pm and 2pm to 5pm; Sat – 11am to 5pm; Sun – 2pm to 5pm; closed Mon and PH*
Admission (1992): *adults £2.00; OAP £1.00; student £1.00; ub40s £1.00; NACF members and under 16s free*
No. visitors (1992): *40 000*

Facilities
Interpretation: *leaflets; information boards; slides; tour guides; guide books*
Schools: *maximum no. 30; educational literature; lecture/talk*
Disabled: *easy access; helpers*
Retailing: *postcards/inexpensive souvenirs; books; catalogues; prints*
No. shops: *1*

Operations
Contacts: *Ms S Gair (Administrator); Dr A Sumner (Keeper); Ms C MacDonald (Shop Manager); Mr J Spicer (Sponsorship and Development)*
No. employees: *(high season) 12 full time; 4 part time (low season) 12 full time; 4 part time*

Marketing
Annual event(s): *exhibitions*
Sponsor(s): *various*
Other: *press office*
UK promotion: *leaflets/information packs*

DUNAVERIG FARM LIFE CENTRE
(private partnership)
heritage centre; museum; farm animals; nature walks

Established: *1993*
Address: *Dunaverig, Ruskie, Thornhill, Stirling, FK8 3QW*
Telephone: *(078) 685 277.* Fax: *(078) 685 404*
Access: (road) *M8/A84/A873* (rail) *Stirling*
Parking capacity: (cars) *40* (coaches) *2*
Hours: *Apr to Oct – 10am to 6pm daily*
Admission (1992): *adults £1.80; children £1.00*
No. visitors (1992): *30 000 (est.)*

Facilities
Interpretation: *leaflets; information boards; maps; tour guides; guide books*
Children: *adventure playground*
Schools: *maximum no. 50; educational literature*
Disabled: *easy access; disabled toilets*
Catering: *2 picnic areas*
Retailing: *postcards/inexpensive souvenirs; confectionery and ice cream; craftwork; books; old farm tools and horseshoes*
No. shops: *1*

Operations
Contacts: *Mrs S Stewart (Director/Partner); Mr P Stewart (Director/Partner)*
No. employees: *(high season) 1 full time; 3 part time*
Training: *F/T operations staff, F/T management, P/T operations staff and casual operations staff are trained in-house and on specific courses and day-to-day on job*
Languages spoken: *French; German*

Marketing
UK promotion: *local newspapers; regional tourist board; other attractions; leaflets/information packs*

DUNCOMBE PARK
(local authority partnership)
historic house; garden

Established: *1990*
Address: *Helmsley, York, N Yorks, YO6 5EB*
Telephone: *(0439) 70213.* Fax: *(0439) 71114*
Access: (road) *A170*
Parking capacity: (cars) *250* (coaches) *5*
Hours: *May to Oct – Sun to Thurs – 11am to 6pm; Apr – open Sun and also Easter weekend and Sat before BH; open at other times by arrangement*
Admission (1992): *adults £4.00; children £2.00; OAP £3.50; student £3.50; grounds only £2.50; groups £3.00*
No. visitors (1992): *30 000 (est.)*

Facilities
Interpretation: *videos; leaflets; information boards; tour guides; guide books*
Languages: *Dutch; French; German*
Children: *play area; nappy changing*
Schools: *maximum no. 50; educational literature*
Disabled: *easy access; disabled toilets; there are steep inclines and gravel paths*
Catering: *1 picnic area*
Retailing: *postcards/inexpensive souvenirs; craftwork; books; gifts made at the estate; quality gifts*
No. shops: *1*

Operations
Contact: *Ms H Cameron (Administrator)*
No. employees: *(high season) 2 full time; 15 part time (low season) 2 full time; 2 part time*
Training: *F/T operations staff, F/T management, P/T operations staff and casual operations staff are trained in-house and externally and on specific courses and day-to-day on job*

Marketing
Annual event(s): *concerts, craft country and steam fairs, motor events*
Sponsor(s): *Digital and local companies*
Affiliations: *HHA*
Other: *market research*

UK promotion: *national newspapers; local newspapers; regional tourist board; other attractions; leaflets/information packs; ETB/BTA*
Europe/USA promotion: *leaflets/brochures; British Tourist Authority*

DUNHAM MASSEY HALL AND PARK
(trust)
historic house; park/reserve; garden

Established: *1981*
Address: *The National Trust, Altrincham, Cheshire, WA14 4SJ*
Telephone: *(061) 941 1025.* Fax: *(061) 941 2815*
Access: (road) *M56/A56*
Parking capacity: (cars) *500* (coaches) *10*
Season: *all year*
Hours: *Apr to Oct – 12am to 5pm daily (house open Sat to Wed only); deer park open all year*
Admission (1992): *adults £4.00; children £2.00; OAP £4.00; student £2.00; family £10.00*
No. visitors (1992): *54 000*

Facilities
Interpretation: *leaflets; information boards; guide books*
Languages: *French; German*
Schools: *maximum no. 60; educational tour*
Disabled: *easy access; disabled toilets; braille/sound posts; helpers; powered transport; leaflets; guide book*
Catering: *1 picnic area*
Retailing: *postcards/inexpensive souvenirs; books; national trust goods*
No. shops: *1*

Operations
Contacts: *J Strickson (Administrator); C Alford (Assistant Administrator); B Morley (Regional Public Affairs Manager)*
No. employees: (high season) *19 full time* (low season) *19 full time*

Marketing
Annual event(s): *concerts*
Other: *press office*

Environmental monitoring: *conservation*

DUNROBIN CASTLE
(trust)
castle; garden; museum

Address: *Golspie, Sutherland, KW10 6RR*
Telephone: *(0408) 633 177.* Fax: *(0408) 633 800*
Access: (road) *A9* (rail) *Own railway station*
Parking capacity: (cars) *300* (coaches) *10*
Season: *all year*
Hours: *May – Mon to Thurs – 10.30am to 12.30pm, June to Sept – Mon to Sat – 10.30am to 5.30pm and Sun – 1pm to 5.30pm, 1 to 15 Oct – Mon to Sat – 10.30am to 4.30pm and Sun – 1pm to 4.30pm. Groups by appointment out of season*
Admission (1992): *adults £3.20; children £1.60; OAP £2.10; groups £3.00*
No. visitors (1992): *51 775*

Facilities
Interpretation: *leaflets; information boards; tour guides; guide books*
Languages: *French; German*
Schools: *no special support*
Catering: *1 picnic area*
Retailing: *postcards/inexpensive souvenirs; craftwork; clothes; art nouveau, china and silver*
No. shops: *1*

Operations
Contacts: *Lord Strathnaver and Mrs S Broad (Director and Administrator); Mr K Jones and Mr R Riley (Curator and semi-retired Curator)*
No. employees: (high season) *12 full time; 2 part time* (low season) *5 full time; 1 part time*

Training: *F/T operations staff, P/T operations staff and casual operations staff are trained in-house and day-to-day on job*
Languages spoken: *French; German; Dutch*

Marketing
Annual event(s): *vintage car rally, concerts*
Sponsor: *Local Police Dependants' Fund*
Affiliations: *Grand Tour of Scotland, HHA, ASVA, Sutherland and Ross and Cromarty Tourist Boards and STB*
Other: *market research*
UK promotion: *regional tourist board; leaflets/information packs; ETB/BTA; castles and gardens, Scots, coaches and parties welcome, etc.*

DUNSTABLE DOWNS COUNTRY PARK
(local authority run)
monument; park/reserve; common land

Address: *Whipsnade Road, Dunstable, Beds*
Telephone: *(0582) 608489*
Access: (road) *M1/A5* (rail) *Leagrave*
Parking capacity: (cars) *600* (coaches) *30*
Season: *all year*
Hours: *Oct to Mar – Sun – 12 noon to 4pm, Apr to Sept – Tues to Sat – 1pm to 4.30pm, Sun and BH – 12 noon to 6pm*
Admission (1992): *free*
No. visitors (1992): *900 000*

Facilities
Interpretation: *leaflets; information boards; slides; maps; guide books*
Schools: *maximum no. 25; educational literature; audio/visual presentation; educational tour; lecture/talk*
Disabled: *easy access; disabled toilets; leaflets*
Catering: *3 picnic areas*
Franchisees: *Oct to Mar – Sun – 12 noon to 4pm*
Retailing: *postcards/inexpensive souvenirs; craftwork; books*
No. shops: *1*

Operations
Contacts: *D Hillyard (Chief Ranger); H McMahon (Marketing and Publicity Officer)*
No. employees: (high season) *2 full time; 2 part time* (low season) *2 full time; 1 part time*
Training: *F/T operations staff, P/T operations staff and casual operations staff are trained in-house and externally and on specific courses and day-to-day on job*
Languages spoken: *French; German*

Marketing
Annual event(s): *Countryside Day*
Other: *press office; market research*
UK promotion: *ETB/BTA*

DURHAM HERITAGE CENTRE
(limited company and trust)
monument; heritage centre; museum; church

Established: *1976*
Address: *St Mary-le-Bow, North Bailey, Durham, DH1 3ET*
Access: (road) *M1/A167/A690* (rail) *Durham*
Hours: *Holy Saturday and Easter week, then Sat and Sun until 2 May BH, then daily until last weekend of Sept – 2pm to 4.30pm (also some mornings in July and Aug or by arrangement)*
Admission (1992): *adults £0.60; children £0.30; OAP £0.40; student £0.40*
No. visitors (1992): *3000 (est.)*

Facilities
Interpretation: *leaflets; audio tapes; information boards; slides; maps*
Schools: *maximum no. 50; educational literature; audio/visual presentation; lecture/talk*
Disabled: *easy access*
Catering: *1 picnic area*
Retailing: *postcards/inexpensive souvenirs; books; reproductions of famous artefacts*
No. shops: *1*

Operations
Contacts: *Dr A I Doyle (Chairman/Secretary of Trust/Company); Mrs J M Jones (Honorary Curator)*
No. employees: (high season) *16 part time*

Marketing
Affiliations: *AIM and North of England Museums Service*
Other: *market research*
UK promotion: *other attractions; leaflets/information packs; NTB, Durham County Council Museums and Galleries*

Environmental monitoring: *recycling; waste; hazardous materials; chemical usage; transport*

DURHAM LIGHT INFANTRY MUSEUM AND ART GALLERY
(trust)
museum; gallery; park

Established: *1968*
Address: *Aykley Heads, Durham, DH1 5TU*
Telephone: *(091) 384 2214.* Fax: *(091) 386 1700*
Access: (road) *M1/A690* (rail) *Durham*
Parking capacity: (cars) *80* (coaches) *20*
Season: *all year*
Hours: *Tues to Sat – 10am to 5pm and Sun – 2pm to 5pm; closed Mon but open BH; closed Christmas and New Year*
Admission (1992): *adults £0.75; children £0.35; OAP £0.35; season ticket holders and students free*
No. visitors (1992): *40 000 (est.)*

Facilities
Interpretation: *leaflets; information boards; guide books*
Children: *nappy changing*
Schools: *maximum no. 100; lecture/talk; workshops and activities*
Disabled: *easy access; disabled toilets; lift to art gallery*
Catering: *1 picnic area*
Franchisees: *Tues to Sat – 10am to 5pm and Sun – 2pm to 5pm; closed Mon but open BH; closed Christmas and New Year*
Retailing: *postcards/inexpensive souvenirs; books; exhibition catalogues; tourist literature*
No. shops: *1*

Operations
Contacts: *T Deary (Arts Development Manager); Mr D Hardingham (Art Gallery Assistant); Mr S Shannon (Regimental Assistant)*
No. employees: (high season) *8 full time; 3 part time*
Languages spoken: *French*

Marketing
Annual event(s): *military vehicle rally and concerts*
Other: *press office; market research*
UK promotion: *local newspapers; regional tourist board; other attractions; leaflets/information packs; ETB/BTA*

DUXFORD AIRFIELD
(national museum)
museum

Established: *1976*
Address: *Duxford, Cambridge, CB2 4QR*
Telephone: *(0223) 835000.* Fax: *(0223) 837267*
Access: (road) *M11/A505* (rail) *Cambridge*
Parking capacity: (cars) *1500* (coaches) *150*
Season: *all year*
Hours: *mid Mar to Oct – 10am to 6pm daily; end Oct to mid Mar – 10am to 4pm daily; closed 24 to 26 Dec and 1 Jan*
Admission (1992): *adults £5.50; children £2.75; OAP £3.80; student £2.75; unemployed/disabled £2.75*
No. visitors (1992): *400 000 (est.)*

Facilities
Interpretation: *leaflets; audio tapes; maps; guide books*

Languages: *French; German*
Children: *adventure playground; nappy changing*
Schools: *educational literature; audio/visual
  presentation; lecture/talk; quiz sheets*
Disabled: *easy access; disabled toilets; leaflets*
Catering: *3 picnic areas*
Retailing: *postcards/inexpensive souvenirs;
  confectionery and ice cream; books;
  reproductions of famous artefacts; model kits
  and paintings*
No. shops: *2*

Operations
Contacts: *Mr E Inman (Director); Mrs L Dobson
  (Personnel Officer); Ms C Mahon (Head of
  Visitor Services/Marketing)*
No. employees: (high season) *91 full time; 17 part
  time* (low season) *89 full time; 14 part time*
Training: *F/T operations staff, F/T management,
  P/T operations staff and casual operations staff
  are trained in-house and externally and on
  specific courses and day-to-day on job using
  Seminars and courses*
Languages spoken: *French; German; Italian;
  Spanish*

Marketing
Annual event(s): *air shows*
Affiliation: *East Anglia Tourist Board*
Other: *PR company: MBS Advertising, 100 South
  St, Bishops Stortford, Herts; press office;
  market research*
UK promotion: *television; national newspapers;
  radio; local newspapers; regional tourist board;
  other attractions; leaflets/information packs;
  ETB/BTA*
Europe promotion: *British Tourist Authority*

**DYFFRYN HOUSE CONFERENCE CENTRE AND
GARDENS**
(local authority run)
garden

Established: *1945*
Address: *St Nicholas, Cardiff*
Telephone: *(0222) 593328.* Fax: *(0222) 591966*
Access: (road) *M4/A48*
Season: *all year*
Admission (1992): *adults £2.00; children £1.50;
  OAP £1.50; student £1.50*

Facilities
Interpretation: *videos; leaflets; slides*
Languages: *French; German; Welsh*
Children: *play area*
Schools: *maximum no. 100; educational literature;
  lecture/talk*
Disabled: *easy access; disabled toilets; reserved
  car parking*
Catering: *2 bars/public houses*
Retailing: *postcards/inexpensive souvenirs;
  confectionery and ice cream; craftwork; books;
  plants*

Operations
Contacts: *Miss Helen Kennedy (Director);
  Miss Moira Pratt (Personnel and Wages); June
  Davies/Nichola Walby Roberts (Conference and
  Marketing Officers)*
Training: *P/T operations staff, P/T management
  and casual operations staff are trained in-house
  and externally and on specific courses and
  day-to-day on job using videos and handbooks*

Marketing
Annual event(s): *various*
Other: *market research*
UK promotion: *national newspapers; radio; local
  newspapers; regional tourist board; other
  attractions; leaflets/information packs*
Global promotion: *leaflets/brochures; British
  Tourist Authority; WTB and Cardiff Marketing
  Ltd*

Environmental monitoring: *recycling; waste;
  water quality; energy consumption; hazardous
  materials; chemical usage*

DYSON PERRINS MUSEUM
(trust)
museum

Established: *1951*
Address: *Severn Street, Worcs, WR1 2NE*
Telephone: *(0905) 23221.* Fax: *(0905) 23601*
Access: (road) *M5/A44* (rail) *Shrub Hill*
Season: *all year*
Hours: *all year – Mon to Fri – 9.30am to 5pm,
  Sat – 10am to 5pm*
Admission (1992): *free*
No. visitors (1992): *50 000 (est.)*

Facilities
Interpretation: *guide books*
Schools: *lecture/tour on request*
Disabled: *no steps in museum*
Retailing: *postcards/inexpensive souvenirs;
  craftwork; books*
No. shops: *1*

Operations
Contact: *H E Frost (Curator and Company
  Secretary)*
No. employees: (high season) *4 full time;
  4 part time* (low season) *4 full time; 4 part
  time*

Marketing
Affiliations: *AIM, MA, West Midlands Area
  Museum Service*
UK promotion: *local newspapers; regional tourist
  board; other attractions; leaflets/information
  packs*
Australia/USA/Japan/Saudi Arabia promotion:
  television; leaflets/brochures; radio

Environmental monitoring: *recycling*

E

EARLSHALL CASTLE AND GARDENS
(privately owned)
historic house; castle; park/reserve; garden

Established: *1983*
Address: *Earlshall Castle, Leuchars By St Andrews, Fife, KY16 0DP*
Telephone: *(0334 839205)*
Parking capacity: (cars) *100* (coaches) *4*
Hours: *1 Apr to 31 Oct – 1pm to 6pm daily. Groups at any time by arrangement*
Admission (1992): *adults £2.90; children £1.00; OAP £2.30; group rates available*
No. visitors (1992): *10 500*

Facilities
Interpretation: *tour guides; guide books*
Schools: *maximum no. 70; educational literature*
Disabled: *free admission for those confined to wheelchair*
Catering: *2 picnic areas*
Retailing: *postcards/inexpensive souvenirs; confectionery and ice cream; craftwork; books; pottery and silver items*
No. shops: *1*

Operations
Contacts: *The Baron of Earlshall (owner); The Baroness of Earlshall; Mrs L Snowdon (PA)*
No. employees: (high season) *5 full time; 18 part time* (low season) *5 full time; 1 part time*
Training: *F/T operations staff, P/T operations staff and casual operations staff are trained in-house and day-to-day on job*

Marketing
Annual event: *Craft Festival*
Affiliations: *HHA, ASVA and HIFI*
Other: *market research*
UK promotion: *leaflets/information packs*
Europe/USA promotion: *leaflets/brochures*

EASDALE ISLAND FOLK MUSEUM
(private)
museum

Established: *1980*
Address: *Easdale Island, By Oban, Argyll, PA34 4TB*
Telephone: *(08523) 370*
Access: (road) *A816* (rail) *Oban*
Hours: *1 April to end September – Weekdays 10.30am to 5.30pm, Sundays 10.30am to 4.30pm*
Admission (1992): *adults £1.00; children £0.25; OAP £0.75; student £0.25*
No. visitors (1992): *8000 (est.)*

Facilities
Interpretation: *leaflets; information boards; guide books*
Languages: *French; German; Spanish*
Schools: *maximum no. 15; lecture/talk*

Operations
Contacts: *Jean Adams (Museum Curator); Mary Withall and Anna Davidson (Assistant Curators)*
No. employees: (high season) *1 full time; 3 part time* (low season) *1 full time; 3 part time*
Training: *P/T operations staff and casual operations staff are trained in-house and day-to-day on job using videos and handbooks*
Languages spoken: *French*

Marketing
Affiliations: *Scottish Museums Council, Association of Independent Museums, SSIA*

Other: *market research*
UK promotion: *local newspapers; regional tourist board; Oban Mull and District Tourist Board*

Environmental monitoring: *chemical usage; Planting trees*

EAST ANGLIAN RAILWAY MUSEUM
(limited company)
museum; railway

Established: *1969*
Address: *Chappel and Wakes Colne Station, Colchester, Essex, CO6 2DS*
Telephone: *(0206) 242524*
Access: (road) *A12/A604* (rail) *Chappel and Wakes Colne*
Parking capacity: (cars) *100* (coaches) *10*
Season: *all year*
Hours: *9.30am to 5pm daily*
Admission (1992): *adults £2.00; children £1.00; OAP £1.00; student £2.00; under 5s free*
No. visitors (1992): *30 000 (est.)*

Facilities
Interpretation: *videos; information boards; guide books*
Children: *play area; nappy changing*
Schools: *maximum no. 60; educational literature*
Disabled: *disabled toilets; helpers; ramp on to trains*
Catering: *1 picnic area*
Retailing: *postcards/inexpensive souvenirs; confectionery and ice cream; books*
No. shops: *2*

Operations
Contacts: *M Stanbury (Chairman); C Johnson (Sales Manager); M Miller (Marketing Trustee)*
No. employees: (high season) *1 full time* (low season) *1 full time*
Languages spoken: *French*

Marketing
Annual event: *beer festival*
Sponsor(s): *Alan Chapman and James*
Affiliations: *Association of Railway Preservation Societies, AIM, East Anglian Tourist Board, Transport Trust*
Other: *market research*
UK promotion: *local newspapers; regional tourist board; other attractions; leaflets/information packs; East Anglian Tourist Board; railway magazines*

EAST HAM NATURE RESERVE
(local authority run)
park/reserve

Established: *1979*
Address: *Norman Rd, London, E6 4HN*
Telephone: *(081) 470 4525*
Access: (road) *A13* (rail) *East Ham*
Season: *all year*
Hours: *reserve – 9am to 5pm or dusk daily; visitor centre – schools during week, general visitors Sat and Sun – 2pm to 5pm*
Admission (1992): *free*

Facilities
Interpretation: *information boards; maps; tour guides; guide books*
Children: *nappy changing*
Schools: *must book in advance*
Disabled: *easy access; other audio facilities; wheelchair trail, raised planting, tape and braille guide*

Retailing: *postcards/inexpensive souvenirs; books*
No. shops: *1*

Operations
Contact: *Mr B Graham (Chief Museum Assistant)*
No. employees: (high season) *4 full time* (low season) *4 full time*

Marketing
Other: *press office; market research*
UK promotion: *local newspapers; regional tourist board; other attractions; leaflets/information packs*

EAST LAMBROOK MANOR GARDEN
(privately owned)
garden

Established: *1950*
Address: *East Lambrook, South Petherton, Somerset, TA13 5HL*
Telephone: *(0460) 40328. Fax: (0460) 42344*
Access: (road) *M5/A303* (rail) *Yeovil/Taunton*
Parking capacity: (cars) *100* (coaches) *2*
Hours: *1 Mar to 31 Oct – Mon to Sat – 10am to 5pm*
Admission (1992): *adults £2.00; children £0.50; OAP £1.80; student £0.50*
No. visitors (1992): *14 000 (est.)*

Facilities
Interpretation: *leaflets; information boards; maps*
Schools: *maximum no. 50; lecture/talk*
Catering: *1 bar/public house*
Retailing: *postcards/inexpensive souvenirs; confectionery and ice cream; books; clothes; plants*
No. shops: *2*

Operations
No. employees: (high season) *2 full time; 8 part time* (low season) *2 full time; 7 part time*
Training: *F/T operations staff and P/T operations staff are trained in-house and externally and on specific courses and day-to-day on job*

Marketing
UK promotion: *leaflets/information packs; ETB/BTA; RHS Journal*

EAST LANCASHIRE RAILWAY
(limited company)
preserved railway

Established: *1987*
Address: *Bolton Street Station, Bolton Street, Bury, Lancs.*
Telephone: *(061) 764 7790*
Access: (road) *M62/A56* (rail) *Metrolink*
Parking capacity: (cars) *200* (coaches) *40*
Season: *all year*
Hours: *all year – Weekends and BH – 10am to 5pm*
No. visitors (1992): *110 000*

Facilities
Interpretation: *videos; leaflets; information boards; maps; tour guides; guide books*
Schools: *maximum no. 350; audio/visual presentation; lecture/talk*
Disabled: *easy access; disabled toilets; helpers*
Catering: *1 picnic area*
Retailing: *postcards/inexpensive souvenirs; confectionery and ice cream; books; railway related goods*

No. shops: *4*

Operations
Contact: *G Vevers (Publicity Director)*

Marketing
Annual event(s): *various*
Other: *market research*
UK promotion: *national newspapers; radio; local newspapers; regional tourist board; other attractions; leaflets/information packs; ETB/BTA*

Environmental monitoring: *waste; energy consumption; chemical usage*

EAST RIDDLESDEN HALL
(national trust)
historic house

Established: *1934*
Address: *Bradford Rd, Keighley, W Yorks, BD20 5EL*
Telephone: *(0535) 607075*
Access:(road) *A650* (rail) *Keighley*
Hours: *Apr to Oct – Sat to Wed – 12 noon to 5pm*
Admission (1992): *adults £2.80; children £1.30*
No. visitors (1992): *40 000*

Facilities
Interpretation: *leaflets; guide books*
Languages: *French; German*
Children: *nappy changing*
Schools: *maximum no. 60; educational literature; briefing and teachers' session*
Disabled: *braille/sound posts; helpers; leaflets*
Catering: *1 picnic area*
Retailing: *postcards/inexpensive souvenirs; craftwork; books*
No. shops: *1*

Operations
Contact: *Ms D Owen (Administrator)*
No. employees: (high season) *5 full time; 20 part time* (low season) *3 full time; 2 part time*
Training: *F/T operations staff, F/T management and P/T operations staff are trained in-house and externally and on specific courses and induction*

Marketing
Annual event(s): *activities, special interest, musical and themed events*
Other: *PR Company: BRAHM, Leeds*
UK promotion: *radio; local newspapers; regional tourist board; other attractions; leaflets/information packs; ETB/BTA*

Environmental monitoring: *recycling; waste; energy consumption; chemical usage; transport; emissions*

EDEN CAMP MODERN HISTORY THEME MUSEUM
(privately-owned limited company)
museum

Established: *1987*
Address: *Malton, N Yorks, YO17 0SD*
Telephone: *(0653) 697777.* Fax: *(0653) 698243*
Access: (road) *A64* (rail) *Malton*
Parking capacity: (cars) *400* (coaches) *40*
Hours: *14 Feb to 23 Dec – 10am to 5pm daily*
Admission (1992): *adults £3.00; children £2.00; OAP £2.00; special rates for groups*
No. visitors (1992): *250 000 (est.)*

Facilities
Interpretation: *videos; leaflets; audio tapes; information boards*
Children: *adventure playground; nappy changing*
Schools: *maximum no. 400; educational literature; lecture/talk; by arrangement*
Disabled: *easy access; disabled toilets; braille/sound posts; other audio facilities; special signs; leaflets; guide book*
Catering: *1 bar/public house*

Retailing: *postcards/inexpensive souvenirs; confectionery and ice cream; craftwork; books; reproductions of famous artefacts; toys, posters and films; jams and biscuits*
No. shops: *1*

Operations
Contacts: *Mr S Jaques (Managing Director); Mr R Postill (Assistant Manager)*
No. employees: (high season) *25 full time; 36 part time* (low season) *14 full time; 15 part time*
Training: *F/T operations staff, P/T operations staff and casual operations staff are trained in-house and day-to-day on job using videos and handbooks*

Marketing
Press office; market research
UK promotion: *television; radio; local newspapers; regional tourist board; leaflets/ information packs; ETB/BTA*

Environmental monitoring: *recycling; waste; energy consumption; hazardous materials; chemical usage*

EDINBURGH CANAL CENTRE
(limited company)
museum; canal boats for sightseeing, hire and educational cruises

Established: *1989*
Address: *27 Baird Rd, Ratho, Midlothian, EH28 8RA*
Telephone: *(031) 333 1320.* Fax: *(031) 333 3480*
Access: (road) *M8/M9/A8/A71* (rail) *Edinburgh Waverley*
Parking capacity: (cars) *50*
Season: *all year*
Hours: *open all year*
Admission (1992): *prices vary according to facilities used*

Facilities
Interpretation: *leaflets*
Children: *play area; nappy changing*
Schools: *maximum no. 36; educational literature*
Disabled: *easy access; disabled toilets*
Catering: *2 bars/public houses*
Retailing: *postcards/inexpensive souvenirs; confectionery and ice cream*
No. shops: *1*

Operations
Contacts: *Mr R Rusack (Managing Director); Mrs P Doherty (Marketing Co-ordinator)*
Training: *F/T operations staff, F/T management, P/T operations staff and casual operations staff are trained in-house and externally and on specific courses and day-to-day on job*

Marketing
Annual event(s): *Scottish Open Canal Jump Competition and cruises to visit Santa*
Affiliations: *STB, Edinburgh Marketing and Forth Valley Tourist Board*
Other: *market research*
UK promotion: *national newspapers; local newspapers; regional tourist board; other attractions; leaflets/information packs; All STB publications*

EDINBURGH MUSEUM OF CHILDHOOD
(local authority run)
museum

Established: *1986*
Address: *42 High St, Edinburgh*
Telephone: *(031) 225 2424.* Fax: *(031) 557 3346*
Access: (road) *M8/A1/A9M* (rail) *Edinburgh Waverley*
Season: *all year*
Hours: *Mon to Sat – 10am to 6pm (Oct to May – 10am to 5pm); Edinburgh Festival – Sun – 2pm to 5pm*
Admission (1992): *free*
No. visitors (1992): *241 006*

Facilities
Interpretation: *videos; audio tapes; information boards; guide books; displays and objects*
Children: *play area; nappy changing*
Schools: *maximum no. 50*
Disabled: *easy access; disabled toilets*
Retailing: *postcards/inexpensive souvenirs; books; reproduction traditional toys*
No. shops: *1*

Operations
Contacts: *Mr J Heyes (Keeper, childhood collections); Mr D Janes (Deputy City Curator); Ms L Stotners (Sales Administration Assistant); Ms L Fraser (Marketing Manager)*
No. employees: (high season) *12 full time; 2 part time* (low season) *15 full time; 2 part time*
Training: *F/T operations staff and F/T management are trained in-house and externally and on specific courses and day-to-day on job*
Languages spoken: *French; Italian*

Marketing
Affiliations: *MA*
Other: *press office; market research*
UK promotion: *local newspapers; regional tourist board; leaflets/information packs; What's on in Edinburgh, Edinburgh for Under 5s; ETB/BTA*

EDINBURGH ZOO
(charity)
zoo/wildlife attraction

Established: *1913*
Address: *Corstorphine Rd, Edinburgh, EH12 6TS*
Telephone: *(031) 334 9171.* Fax: *(031) 316 4050*
Access: (road) *A8* (rail) *Edinburgh*
Parking capacity: (cars) *540* (coaches) *110*
Season: *all year*
Hours: *Apr to Sept – 9am to 6pm; Mar and Oct – 9am to 5pm; Nov to Feb – 9am to 4.30pm (all hours daily except Sun open 9.30am)*
Admission (1992): *adults £4.30; children £2.30; OAP £2.30; student £4.30; ub40 £2.30, family ticket £12.00 (2 + 2)*
No. visitors (1992): *486 324*

Facilities
Interpretation: *videos; leaflets; audio tapes; information boards; slides; maps; guide books; special information talks at feeding times, etc.*
Children: *adventure playground; play area; nappy changing*
Schools: *maximum no. 200; educational literature; audio/visual presentation; lecture/talk*
Disabled: *easy access; disabled toilets*
Catering: *2 bars/public houses*
Retailing: *postcards/inexpensive souvenirs; confectionery and ice cream; craftwork; books; clothes*
No. shops: *2*

Operations
Contacts: *Mr R J Wheater (Director); Mr S Selvester (Marketing Assistant)*
No. employees: (high season) *160 full time; 20 part time* (low season) *100 full time; 10 part time*
Training: *F/T operations staff and F/T management are trained in-house and on specific courses and day-to-day on job using videos*
Languages spoken: *French; German*

Marketing
Annual event(s): *various*
Sponsor(s): *various*
Affiliations: *ASVA, Federation of Zoological Gardens of Great Britain and Ireland*
Other: *press office; market research*
UK promotion: *television; local newspapers; regional tourist board; other attractions; leaflets/information packs; ETB/BTA; STB*
Europe/USA promotion: *STB*

Environmental monitoring: *recycling; energy consumption; hazardous materials*

EDMONDSHAM HOUSE AND GARDEN
(privately owned)
historic house; garden

Established: *1987*
Address: *Edmondsham House, Edmondsham,
    Wimborne, Dorset, BH21 5RE*
Telephone: *(07254) 207*
Access:*(road) B3081*
Parking capacity: *(cars) 80 (coaches) 2*
Hours: *house and garden – Easter Sun, BH Mon
    and Weds in Apr and Oct – 2pm to 5pm;
    garden only – Wed and Sun Apr to Oct – 2pm
    to 5pm*
Admission (1992): *adults £2.00; children £1.00;
    £1.00/£0.50p garden only*
No. visitors (1992): *1000 (est.)*

Facilities
Interpretation: *leaflets; personal guided tour of
    house*
Languages: *French; for arranged visit*
Schools: *maximum no. 20; personal attention*
Disabled: *easy access; personal attention*
Catering: *1 picnic area*

Operations
Contact: *Mrs J Smith (owner)*
No. employees: *(high season) 6 full time; 1 part
    time (low season) 6 full time; 1 part time*

Marketing
Affiliations: *HHA, CLA and TGA*
UK promotion: *radio; local newspapers; regional
    tourist board*

ELIZABETHAN EXHIBITION GALLERY
(local authority run)
exhibition gallery

Established: *1979*
Address: *Brook St, Wakefield*
Telephone: *(0924) 295797. Fax: (0924) 295632*
Access: *(road) M62 (rail) Wakefield Westgate*
Season: *all year*
Hours: *Mon to Sat – 10.30am to 5pm,
    Sun – 2.30pm to 5pm; open during exhibitions,
    closing for re-hanging; open BH except
    Christmas and New Year*
Admission (1992): *free*
No. visitors (1992): *15 000 (est.)*

Facilities
Interpretation: *depends on type of exhibition*
Schools: *education officer*
Disabled: *helpers*
Retailing: *postcards/inexpensive souvenirs; books;
    reproductions of famous artefacts; posters and
    prints*
No. shops: *1*

Operations
Contact: *Ms M Sanderson (Administrator)*
No. employees: *(high season) 2 full time; 2 part
    time*
Training: *F/T operations staff, P/T operations
    staff and casual operations staff are trained
    in-house and externally and on specific courses
    and day-to-day on job*
Languages spoken: *French*

Marketing
Other: *press office*
UK promotion: *local newspapers; regional tourist
    board; leaflets/information packs*

Environmental monitoring: *organic garden*

ELSHAM HALL COUNTRY AND WILDLIFE PARK
(partnership)
historic house; garden; zoo/wildlife attraction

Established: *1970*
Address: *Brigg, N Lincs*
Telephone: *(0652) 688698*
Access: *(road) M180 (rail) Barnetby*
Parking capacity: *(cars) 150 (coaches) 20*
Season: *all year*

Hours: *Easter Sun to mid Sept – 11am to 5pm
    daily; mid Sept to Easter – Sun only – 11am to
    4pm; closed all Winter BHs*
Admission (1992): *adults £3.00; children £2.00;
    OAP £2.00; student £3.00; schools £1.00*
No. visitors (1992): *47 000*

Facilities
Interpretation: *videos; leaflets; information
    boards; slides; maps; tour guides; guide books;
    personnel*
Languages: *Dutch; French; German*
Children: *adventure playground; play area; nappy
    changing*
Schools: *maximum no. 400; educational literature;
    lecture/talk; trails*
Disabled: *easy access; disabled toilets; special
    signs; leaflets; guide book*
Catering: *2 picnic areas*
Retailing: *postcards/inexpensive souvenirs;
    confectionery and ice cream; craftwork; books;
    clothes; reproductions of famous artefacts*
No. shops: *More than 4*

Marketing
Affiliations: *HHA*
Other: *press office; market research*
UK promotion: *television; national newspapers;
    radio; local newspapers; regional tourist board;
    other attractions; leaflets/information packs;
    YHTB, EMTB*

Environmental monitoring: *recycling; hazardous
    materials*

ELSTOW MOOT HALL
(local authority run)
museum

Established: *1950*
Address: *Elstow Green, Church End, Elstow,
    Beds.*
Telephone: *(0234) 228330. Fax: (0234) 228921*
Access: *(road) A6*
Parking capacity: *(cars) 8 (coaches) 1*
Hours: *Apr to Oct – Tues to Sat and BH – 2pm
    to 5pm, Sun – 2pm to 5.30pm*
Admission (1992): *adults £0.60; children £0.30;
    OAP £0.30; school parties free*
No. visitors (1992): *3775*

Facilities
Interpretation: *leaflets; information boards; tour
    guides; guide books*
Schools: *educational literature; educational tour;
    lecture/talk*
Catering: *1 picnic area*
Retailing: *postcards/inexpensive souvenirs; books;
    reproductions of famous artefacts*
No. shops: *1*

Operations
Contacts: *S Wileman (Cultural and Community
    Services Assistant)*
No. employees: *(high season) 3 part time (low
    season) 1 part time*
Training: *F/T management and P/T operations
    staff are trained in-house and externally and on
    specific courses and day-to-day on job*

Marketing
Annual event: *Heritage Day*
Affiliation: *Regional Tourist Board*
Other: *press office; market research*
UK promotion: *local newspapers; regional tourist
    board; leaflets/information packs; ETB/BTA*

Environmental monitoring: *education*

ELVISLY YOURS CENTRE
(limited company)
Elvis Presley souvenir shop

Established: *1982*
Address: *107 Shoreditch High St, London, E1 6JN*
Telephone: *(071) 739 2001. Fax: (071) 739 2001*

Access:*(rail) Liverpool St*
Season: *all year*
Hours: *Mon to Fri – 10am to 6pm except PH,
    most Sats – 10am to 4pm (phone first)*
Admission (1992): *free*
No. visitors (1992): *1000 (est.)*

Facilities
Interpretation: *videos; leaflets*

Operations
Contacts: *Mr S Shaw (Director); Mr D Griffiths
    (Manager)*
Training: *casual operations staff using videos,
    lectures and workshops*

Marketing
Annual event(s): *birthday and commemorative
    party*
UK promotion: *national newspapers;
    leaflets/information packs*
Europe promotion: *overseas wholesale*

Environmental monitoring: *recycling; waste;
    energy consumption; transport*

ELY CATHEDRAL
(cathedral/charity)
church

Established: *1189*
Address: *The College, Ely, Cambs, CB7 4DN*
Telephone: *(0353) 667735. Fax: (0353) 665658*
Season: *all year*
Hours: *Summer – 7am to 7pm daily; Winter – Mon
    to Fri – 7.30am to 6pm, Sun – 7.30am to 5pm*
Admission (1992): *adults £2.60; OAP £2.10;
    student £2.10; special rates for groups*
No. visitors (1992): *250 000 (est.)*

Facilities
Interpretation: *leaflets; information boards; tour
    guides; guide books*
Languages: *Dutch; French; German; Italian*
Schools: *educational literature; lecture/talk*
Disabled: *easy access*
Catering: *1 self-service cafeteria*
Retailing: *postcards/inexpensive souvenirs; books;
    cathedral related*
No. shops: *2*

Operations
Contacts: *Canon D Green; Ms C Douglas
    (Personnel Officer); Ms J Pye/Mr J Simmons
    (visitors/shops)*
No. employees: *(high season) 30 full time; 44 part
    time (low season) 30 full time; 30 part time*
Training: *N/A*
Languages spoken: *Russian*

Marketing
Annual event(s): *recitals and concerts*
Other: *market research*
UK promotion: *local newspapers; regional tourist
    board; other attractions; leaflets/information
    packs*
Europe/USA promotion: *leaflets/brochures*

ELY MUSEUM
(trust)
museum

Established: *1989*
Address: *28c High St, Ely, Cambs, CB7 4LH*
Telephone: *(0353) 666655*
Access: *(road) M11/A10 (rail) Ely*
Season: *all year*
Hours: *Summer – Tues to Sat – 10.30am to 1pm
    and 2.15pm to 5pm Sun – 2.15pm to 5pm;
    Winter – Tues to Sat – 11.30am to 4pm*
Admission (1992): *adults £1.00; children £0.50;
    OAP £0.50; student £0.50; concessions £0.50p,
    groups £0.80p; school groups £0.30p*
No. visitors (1992): *8500*

Facilities
Interpretation: *videos; leaflets; information
    boards; maps; personnel; curator*

Schools: *maximum no. 80; educational literature; lecture/talk; certain materials available*
Retailing: *postcards/inexpensive souvenirs; books*
No. shops: *1*

Operations
Contact: *R Carman (Hon Curator)*
No. employees: (high season) *3 part time* (low season) *3 part time*
Training: *P/T operations staff and P/T management are trained in-house and day-to-day on job*
Languages spoken: *French; German; Spanish; Dutch*

Marketing
Affiliations: *MGC, AMSSEE*
UK promotion: *radio; local newspapers; regional tourist board; other attractions; leaflets/information packs; ETB/BTA*

Environmental monitoring: *recycling*

EMBSAY STEAM RAILWAY
(Trust)
heritage centre; museum; steam railway

Established: *1968*
Address: *The Station, Embsay, Nr Skipton, N Yorks*
Telephone: *(0756) 794727*
Access: (road) *M1/M6/M62/A59* (rail) *Skipton*
Parking capacity: (cars) *200* (coaches) *20*
Season: *all year*
Hours: *every Sun throughout the year and BH except 25 and 26 Dec; Jul – Tues and Sat; Aug – Tues to Thur, Sat and Sun; also special event days*
Admission (1992): *adults £2.70; children £1.35; OAP £2.00; student £2.00*
No. visitors (1992): *84 000*

Facilities
Interpretation: *videos; leaflets; information boards; maps; tour guides; guide books; evening dining train*
Schools: *maximum no. 200; audio/visual presentation; lecture/talk*
Disabled: *easy access; helpers*
Catering: *3 bars/public houses*
Retailing: *postcards/inexpensive souvenirs; confectionery and ice cream; craftwork; books; clothes*
No. shops: *1*

Operations
Contact: *Mr S Walker (Business and Marketing Manager)*
No. employees: (high season) *1 full time* (low season) *1 full time*
Training: *F/T operations staff, F/T management, P/T operations staff, P/T management, casual operations staff and casual management are trained in-house and externally and on specific courses and day-to-day on job*

Marketing
Annual event(s): *Mother's day, Easter, Santa, Hallowe'en, etc.*
Affiliations: *AIR, ARPS, AIM*
Other: *press office; market research*
UK promotion: *national newspapers; radio; local newspapers; regional tourist board; other attractions; leaflets/information packs; ETB/BTA*
Europe/USA promotion: *leaflets/brochures; British Tourist Authority*

EPPING FOREST DISTRICT MUSEUM
(local authority run)
museum

Established: *1981*
Address: *39/41 Sun St, Waltham Abbey, Essex, EN9 1EL*
Telephone: *(0992) 716882*
Access: (road) *M25/A121* (rail) *Waltham Cross*
Season: *all year*

Hours: *Mon, Fri, Sat and Sun – 2pm to 5pm; Tues – 12 noon to 5pm; closed Christmas Day, Boxing day and New Year's Day*
Admission (1992): *free*
No. visitors (1992): *25 000 (est.)*

Facilities
Interpretation: *leaflets; information boards*
Schools: *maximum no. 30; educational literature; lecture/talk; workshops and exhibitions*
Catering: *1 snack bar/food stall*
Retailing: *postcards/inexpensive souvenirs; books; local society publications*
No. shops: *1*

Operations
Contacts: *Miss K Carver (Museum Officer); Mrs J Stephens (Administrative and Education manager)*
No. employees: (high season) *3 full time; 7 part time* (low season) *3 full time; 7 part time*

Marketing
UK promotion: *local newspapers; other attractions; leaflets/information packs*

Environmental monitoring: *recycling; waste; water quality; energy consumption; hazardous materials; chemical usage; transport; emissions*

ERDDIG HALL
(Trust)
historic house; garden

Established: *1977*
Address: *Erddig, Wrexham, Clwyd, LL13 0YT*
Telephone: *(0978) 355314*
Access: (road) *A483/A525*
Parking capacity: (cars) *300* (coaches) *6*
Hours: *April to end Sept – Sat to Wed – 11am to 4pm*
Admission (1992): *adults £5.00; children £2.50*
No. visitors (1992): *90 000*

Facilities
Interpretation: *guide books*
Languages: *Dutch; French; German*
Children: *nappy changing*
Schools: *educational literature; audio/visual presentation; lecture/talk; hands on programme*
Disabled: *disabled toilets*
Catering: *1 picnic area*
Retailing: *postcards/inexpensive souvenirs; confectionery and ice cream; craftwork; books; clothes; reproductions of famous artefacts*
No. shops: *1*

Operations
Contacts: *Robert Dillon (Administrator); Carys Howell (Regional Public Affairs Manager)*
No. employees: (high season) *12 full time; 25 part time* (low season) *12 full time; 5 part time*
Training: *F/T operations staff, F/T management, P/T operations staff and casual operations staff are trained in-house and externally and on specific courses and day-to-day on job*

Marketing
Annual event(s): *open-air play; concerts; apple festival*
Other: *press office; market research*
UK promotion: *national newspapers; local newspapers; regional tourist board; other attractions; leaflets/information packs*
USA promotion: *British Tourist Authority; Royal Oak Foundation*

ERITH MUSEUM
(local authority run)
museum

Established: *1932*
Address: *Erith Library, Walnut Tree Rd, Erith, Kent, DA8 1RS*
Telephone: *(0322) 336582*
Access: (rail) *Erith*
Season: *all year*
Hours: *Mon and Wed – 2.15pm to 5.15pm, Sat – 2.15pm to 5pm*

Admission (1992): *free*
No. visitors (1992): *2000 (est.)*

Facilities
Interpretation: *leaflets; audio tapes; information boards; maps*
Schools: *maximum no. 30; no special support*
Retailing: *postcards/inexpensive souvenirs; information sheets*
No. shops: *1*

Operations
Contact: *Miss J Vale (Curator)*
No. employees: (high season) *4 part time*
Languages spoken: *Welsh*

Marketing
Affiliations: *MA, registered museum*
UK promotion: *local newspapers; regional tourist board; other attractions; leaflets/information packs; Museums and Galleries; Historic Houses; BAFM Yearbook*

Environmental monitoring: *recycling; waste; water quality; hazardous materials; chemical usage*

ESCOT AQUATIC CENTRE AND GARDENS
(limited company)
garden; zoo/wildlife attraction; pet and aquatic retail centre

Established: *1984*
Address: *Parklands Farm, Escot, Ottery St Mary, Devon, EX11 1LU*
Telephone: *(0404) 822188.* Fax: *(0404) 822903*
Access: (road) *M5/A30*
Season: *all year*
Hours: *10am to 6pm daily including BH; closed 25 to 31 Dec incl*
Admission (1992): *adults £1.95; children £1.65; OAP £1.65; under 5s free*
No. visitors (1992): *50 000 (est.)*

Facilities
Interpretation: *information boards; maps*
Children: *play area; nappy changing*
Schools: *maximum no. 60; no special support; talk if required*
Disabled: *disabled toilets*
Catering: *1 picnic area*
Retailing: *postcards/inexpensive souvenirs; confectionery and ice cream; craftwork; aquatic goods; pets and accessories*
No. shops: *4*

Operations
Contacts: *Mr and Mrs Kennaway (Managing Directors)*
No. employees: (high season) *7 full time; 3 part time* (low season) *7 full time; 3 part time*
Training: *F/T operations staff and F/T management are trained in-house and day-to-day on job and City and Guild Petshop Man*

Marketing
Annual event(s): *concerts, dog shows and fun days*
Affiliations: *PTIA (Pet Trade Industry Association), HHA*
UK promotion: *local newspapers; regional tourist board; other attractions; leaflets/information packs; Town and County Guides; ETB/BTA*

ESKDALE CORN MILL
(local authority run)
working Elizabethan mill

Established: *1976*
Address: *The Mill, Boot, Eskdale, Cumbria, CA19 1TG*
Telephone: *(09467) 23335*
Access: (road) *M6 (Hardknott Pass)* (rail) *Ravenglass/Eskdale*
Hours: *Easter to Oct – Tues to Sun – 11am to 6pm*
Admission (1992): *adults £1.00; children £0.50; OAP £0.80; student £0.50*

No. visitors (1992): 7000 (est.)

Facilities
Interpretation: *information boards; tour guides; guide books*
Languages: *French; German*
Schools: *maximum no. 50; educational literature; audio/visual presentation; educational quiz*
Disabled: *mill situated on steep hillside*
Catering: *1 picnic area*
Retailing: *postcards/inexpensive souvenirs; confectionery and ice cream; craftwork; books; corn dollies, mugs, etc.*
No. shops: *1*

Operations
Contact: *David King (Manager)*
No. employees: (high season) *1 full time; 1 part time*
Languages spoken: *French*

Marketing
Affiliation: *North West Mills*
UK promotion: *radio; local newspapers; regional tourist board; leaflets/information packs; educational visit handbook, journalists handbook*

ETHNIC DOLL AND TOY MUSEUM
(private museum)
museum

Established: *1985*
Address: *Castlegate House, 1 Tankerton Road, Whitstable, Canterbury, Kent CT5 2AB*
Telephone: *(0227) 771456/769877*
Access: (road) *M2/A299* (rail) *Whitstable*
Parking capacity: (cars) *2000* (coaches) *5*
Season: *all year*
Hours: *all year – 10am to 5pm daily; closed Christmas to end Jan*
Admission (1992): *adults £1.60; children £0.80; OAP £1.30; student £1.60; group rates*
No. visitors (1992): *12 000 (est.)*

Facilities
Interpretation: *leaflets; tour guides; talks*
Languages: *German*
Schools: *maximum no. 50; educational literature; educational tour; lecture/talk*
Disabled: *disabled toilets; access to ground floor only*
Retailing: *postcards/inexpensive souvenirs; books; toys, magazines, posters, dolls, etc.*
No. shops: *1*

Operations
Contact: *B Pickering (Curator and Director)*
Languages spoken: *French*

Marketing
Market research
UK promotion: *radio; local newspapers; regional tourist board; other attractions; leaflets/information packs; What's On and Where in Kent; Coach Tour Handbook; ETB/BTA; specialist magazines*
Europe/USA promotion: *leaflets/brochures; British Tourist Authority; personal contacts*

ETRURIA INDUSTRIAL MUSEUM
(local authority run)
museum; working steam-powered mill

Established: *1991*
Address: *Lower Bedford Street, Shelton, Stoke-on-Trent, ST4 7AF*
Telephone: *(0782) 287557*
Access: (road) *M6/A500/B5045* (rail) *Stoke*
Parking capacity: (cars) *20* (coaches) *2*
Season: *all year*
Hours: *all year – Wed to Sun – 10am to 4pm; closed Christmas week and Good Friday*
Admission (1992): *free*
No. visitors (1992): *11 500 (est.)*

Facilities
Interpretation: *information boards; tour guides; guide books*

Schools: *maximum no. 50; educational literature*
Disabled: *disabled toilets; access difficult for disabled*

Operations
Contacts: *A Nuttall (Manager); R Gwynne (Promotions Officer)*
Training: *F/T operations staff and F/T management are trained in-house and on specific courses and day-to-day on job*
Languages spoken: *German*

Marketing
Press office; market research
UK promotion: *radio; local newspapers; regional tourist board; other attractions; leaflets/information packs; local initiatives*

EUREKA! THE MUSEUM FOR CHILDREN
(private charity)
museum

Established: *1992*
Address: *Discovery Rd, Halifax, W Yorks, HX1 2NE*
Telephone: *(0422) 330069.* Fax: *(0422) 330275*
Access: (road) *M62/A629/A58*
Parking capacity: (cars) *300* (coaches) *6*
Season: *all year*
Hours: *Oct to Jun – Mon and Tues – 10am to 2pm Wed – 10am to 7pm, Thurs to Sun – 10am to 5pm; Jul to Sept – Mon and Tues opening hours extended to 5pm*
Admission (1992): *adults £3.50; children £2.50; OAP £3.50; student £3.50; under 3s free*

Facilities
Interpretation: *leaflets; information boards; museum floor staff – enablers and hands on experience for children*
Children: *nappy changing*
Schools: *maximum no. 300; activities in development*
Disabled: *easy access; disabled toilets*
Catering: *1 picnic area*
Franchisees: *Oct to Jun – Mon and Tues – 10am to 2pm Wed – 10am to 7pm, Thurs to Sun – 10am to 5pm; July to Sept – Mon and Tues opening hours extended to 5pm*
Retailing: *postcards/inexpensive souvenirs; confectionery and ice cream; books; clothes; puzzles and toys*
No. shops: *1*

Operations
Contacts: *Ms G Thomas (Director); Mr A Bates (Administration Director); Ms M Rowland (Buyer); Ms R Smith (Marketing)*
No. employees: (high season) *67 full time; 9 part time* (low season) *51 full time; 4 part time*
Training: *F/T operations staff, F/T management, P/T operations staff, P/T management, casual operations staff and casual management are trained in-house and externally and on specific courses and day-to-day on job using handbooks and guest lecturers, visits*

Marketing
Annual event(s): *to be decided*
Other: *press office; market research*
UK promotion: *national newspapers; regional tourist board; leaflets/information packs; Tetley Guide and Family Fun in Britain Guide; ETB/BTA; education publications*

EXBURY GARDENS
(limited company and charity)
garden

Established: *1955*
Address: *Exbury, Southampton, Hants*
Telephone: *(0703) 891203.* Fax: *(0703) 243380*
Access: (road) *M27/A326/B3054* (rail) *Southampton*
Parking capacity: (cars) *2500* (coaches) *40*
Hours: *Mar to Oct incl – 10am to 5.30pm daily*

Admission (1992): *adults £3.50; children £2.50; OAP £3.00; student £3.50; group rates £3.00 over 15 people, reductions at some other times*
No. visitors (1992): *140 000 (est.)*

Facilities
Interpretation: *videos; leaflets; maps; tour guides; guide books*
Children: *nappy changing*
Disabled: *easy access; disabled toilets*
Catering: *1 picnic area*
Franchisees: *Mar to Oct incl - 10am to 5.30pm daily*
Retailing: *postcards/inexpensive souvenirs; confectionery and ice cream; craftwork; books; honey; videos; paintings*
No. shops: *1*

Operations
Contact: *Mr C Orr-Ewing (Managing Agent)*
No. employees: (high season) *9 full time; 20 part time* (low season) *9 full time; 6 part time*
Training: *F/T operations staff are trained externally and on specific courses using handbooks*
Languages spoken: *French; German; Italian; Spanish; Urdu; Dutch*

Marketing
Other: *market research*
UK promotion: *television; national newspapers; local newspapers; regional tourist board; other attractions; leaflets/information packs*

Environmental monitoring: *recycling; waste*

EXETER CATHEDRAL
(charity)
church

Established: *1107*
Address: *Exeter, EX1 1HS*
Telephone: *(0392) 55573*
Access: (road) *M5* (rail) *Exeter St Davids*
Season: *all year*
Hours: *all year – 7.30am to 6.30pm daily*
Admission (1992): *donations £1.00*
No. visitors (1992): *400 000 (est.)*

Facilities
Interpretation: *videos; leaflets; audio tapes; information boards; tour guides; guide books*
Languages: *Japanese; Dutch; French; German; Italian; Spanish; Russian; Swedish*
Schools: *educational literature; audio/visual presentation; educational tour*
Disabled: *easy access; disabled toilets; braille/sound posts; helpers; leaflets; guide book*
Catering: *1 self-service cafeteria*
Retailing: *postcards/inexpensive souvenirs; craftwork; books; reproductions of famous artefacts*
No. shops: *1*

Operations
Contacts: *Col. M J Woodcock (Chapter Clerk); D Hanson (Shop Manager)*
No. employees: (high season) *15 full time; 15 part time* (low season) *15 full time; 15 part time*
Training: *F/T operations staff and P/T operations staff are trained in-house and day-to-day on job*

Marketing
Annual event(s): *concerts*
Sponsor(s): *Exeter City Council*
UK promotion: *local newspapers*

EXMOOR BIRD GARDENS
(partnership)
zoo/wildlife attraction

Established: *1981*
Address: *Bratton Fleming, Barnstaple, North Devon, EX31 4SG*
Telephone: *(05983) 352.* Fax: *(05983) 412*
Access: (road) *M5/A399*
Parking capacity: (cars) *200* (coaches) *5*

Season: *all year*
Hours: *Nov to Mar – 10am to 4pm; Apr to Oct – 10am to 6pm*
Admission (1992): *adults £3.50; children £2.25; OAP £3.50*
No. visitors (1992): *48 000 (est.)*

Facilities
Interpretation: *leaflets*
Children: *adventure playground*
Schools: *maximum no. 1000; lecture/talk*
Disabled: *easy access; disabled toilets*
Catering: *1 picnic area*
Retailing: *postcards/inexpensive souvenirs; confectionery and ice cream; books; clothes*
No. shops: *1*

Operations
Contact: *M Clark (Director of Zoological gardens)*
No. employees: (high season) *3 full time; 6 part time* (low season) *3 full time; 2 part time*
Training: *F/T operations staff, P/T operations staff and casual operations staff are trained in-house and day-to-day on job*
Languages spoken: *French; German; Spanish; Dutch*

Marketing
Affiliation: *Federation of Zoological Gardens of Great Britain and Ireland*
UK promotion: *local newspapers; regional tourist board; other attractions; leaflets/information packs*

EYEMOUTH MUSEUM
(trust)
museum

Established: *1982*
Address: *Auld Kirk, Market Place, Eyemouth, Berwickshire, TD14 5HE*
Telephone: *(08907) 50678*
Access: (road) *A1107*
Hours: *Easter to end Oct – Apr, May, June and Sept – Mon to Sat – 10am to 5pm; Jul and Aug – 9.30am to 6pm and 1pm to 5.30pm on Sun*
Admission (1992): *adults £1.00; children £0.50; OAP £0.50; student £0.50; groups 10 or more £0.80p adult and £0.40p child/OAP*
No. visitors (1992): *5000 (est.)*

Facilities
Interpretation: *audio tapes; information boards*
Schools: *maximum no. 40; educational literature*
Disabled: *easy access*
Retailing: *postcards/inexpensive souvenirs; books; tourist information centre stock*
No. shops: *1*

Operations
Contacts: *Mrs Jean Bowe (Hon Curator); Mr D Aitchison (Chairman)*
No. employees: (high season) *2 part time* (low season) *1 part time*

Marketing
Affiliation: *Borders Museums Forum and SMC*
UK promotion: *radio; local newspapers; regional tourist board; leaflets/information packs*

Environmental monitoring: *water quality*

F

FAIR MAID'S HOUSE
(private retail outlet)
historic house

Established: *1968*
Address: *North Port, Perth, PH1 5LU*
Telephone: *(0798) 25976*
Access: *(road) M90*
Season: *all year*
Hours: *daily 10.00am to 5.00pm. except Sundays, Christmas and first week in January*
Admission (1992): *free*
No. visitors (1992): *15 000 (est.)*

Facilities
Interpretation: *leaflets; information boards; maps; tour guides; guide books*
Languages: *French; German; Italian; Arabic*
Disabled: *easy access; helpers*
Retailing: *postcards/inexpensive souvenirs; craftwork; clothes*
No. shops: *1*

Operations
Contact: *Eva McDonald (Proprietor)*
No. employees: *(high season) 6 part time (low season) 6 part time*
Training: *P/T operations staff and P/T management are trained in-house and externally and day-to-day on job and trade fair participation*
Languages spoken: *French*

Marketing
Market research
UK promotion: *regional tourist board; other attractions; leaflets/information packs; STB and Tayside*

FALLS OF CLYDE NATURE RESERVE
(trust)
park/reserve; zoo/wildlife attraction

Established: *1984*
Address: *Scottish Wildlife Trust Visitor Centre, The Dye Works, New Lanark, Lanark, ML11 9DB*
Telephone: *(0555) 665262*
Access: *(road) A73*
Hours: *reserve open all year; centre open Mon to Fri 11am to 5pm and Sat and Sun 1pm to 5pm (centre closed Jan and only open weekends Nov, Dec, Feb and Mar)*
Admission (1992): *free*
No. visitors (1992): *48 000 (est.)*

Facilities
Interpretation: *videos; leaflets; information boards; slides; maps; tour guides; guide books*
Children: *adventure playground*
Schools: *maximum no. 80; educational literature; games and having fun*
Catering: *3 picnic areas*
Retailing: *postcards/inexpensive souvenirs; craftwork; books; clothes; recycled goods*
No. shops: *1*

Operations
Contacts: *Mr J Darbyshire (Head Ranger); Mr E Third (Seasonal Ranger); Ms S Wilson (Sales and Information Assistant)*
No. employees: *(high season) 3 full time (low season) 1 full time*
Languages spoken: *French; German; Italian; Arabic*

Marketing
Affiliation: *British Society for Nature Preservation*

Other: *press office; market research*
UK promotion: *local newspapers; regional tourist board; leaflets/information packs*

Environmental monitoring: *recycling; energy consumption*

FALMOUTH MARITIME MUSEUM
(limited company)
museum

Established: *1981*
Address: *2 Bell's Court, off Market St, Falmouth, Cornwall*
Telephone: *(0326) 250507*
Access: *(rail) Falmouth*
Season: *all year*
Hours: *1 Apr to 31 Oct – Mon to Sat – 10am to 4pm; 1 Nov to 31 Mar – Mon to Sat – 10am to 3pm*
Admission (1992): *adults £1.10; children £0.70; OAP £1.10; student £1.10*
No. visitors (1992): *5000 (est.)*

Facilities
Interpretation: *leaflets; information boards; artefacts and displays*
Schools: *maximum no. 30; educational literature*
Retailing: *postcards/inexpensive souvenirs; books*
No. shops: *1*

Operations
Contacts: *Lieutenant Commander J Beck (Trustee Secretary and Curator); Commander K England (Trustee)*

Marketing
Affiliation: *AIM*
UK promotion: *local newspapers; regional tourist board; leaflets/information packs*

FAMILY HERITAGE MUSEUM
(privately owned)
heritage centre; museum

Established: *1990*
Address: *Farnaght, Tamlaght, Enniskillen, Co Fermanagh, BT74 NN*
Telephone: *(0365) 87278*
Access: *(road) M1/B514/A4*
Parking capacity: *(cars) 30 (coaches) 3*
Season: *all year*
Hours: *Spring and Summer – 10am to 10pm; Winter – 10am to 5pm*
Admission (1992): *adults £1.50; children £0.50; OAP £1.50; student £1.50*
No. visitors (1992): *400 (est.)*

Facilities
Schools: *maximum no. 40; lecture/talk*
Disabled: *easy access; helpers*
Retailing: *postcards/inexpensive souvenirs; craftwork; books*
No. shops: *1*

Operations
Contacts: *D S and I M Carrothers (owners)*

Environmental monitoring: *humidity, temperature and light*

FAMOUS OLD BLACKSMITHS SHOP CENTRE
(limited company)
museum; shops and arts centre

Established: *1880*
Address: *Gretna Green, Carlisle, CA6 5EA*
Telephone: *(0461) 38441. Fax: (0461) 38442*
Access: *(road) M74*
Parking capacity: *(cars) 200 (coaches) 60*
Season: *all year*
Hours: *Jan, Feb, Mar, Nov and Dec – 9am to 5pm; Apr, May and Oct – 9am to 6pm; June and Sept – 9am to 7pm; July and Aug – 9am to 8pm*
Admission (1992): *£0.50p entrance for museum, may be reviewed*

Facilities
Interpretation: *leaflets; information boards*
Languages: *Japanese; Dutch; French; German; Italian; Spanish; Swedish,Danish and more*
Children: *play area; nappy changing*
Schools: *maximum no. 50; educational literature; lecture/talk*
Disabled: *easy access; disabled toilets*
Catering: *1 bar/public house*
Retailing: *postcards/inexpensive souvenirs; craftwork; books; reproductions of famous artefacts; sculptures and paintings*
No. shops: *More than 4*

Operations
Contact: *Ms S Clark (Director)*
No. employees: *(high season) 30 full time; 30 part time (low season) 13 full time*
Training: *F/T operations staff, F/T management, P/T operations staff and casual operations staff are trained in-house and externally and on specific courses*

Marketing
Market research
UK promotion: *television; national newspapers; local newspapers; regional tourist board; leaflets/information packs*

FARMWORLD
(limited company)
theme park; farm park

Established: *1989*
Address: *Stoughton Farm Park, Gartree Rd, Oadby, Leicester*
Telephone: *(0583) 710355. Fax: (0533) 713211*
Access: *(road) M69/A47 (rail) Leicester*
Parking capacity: *(cars) 500 (coaches) 20*
Season: *all year*
Hours: *Easter to Oct – 10am to 5.30pm daily; Nov to Easter – 10am to 5pm daily*
Admission (1992): *adults £3.75; children £2.00; OAP £2.75; discounts for groups and younger children,family ticket £9.50*
No. visitors (1992): *120 000*

Facilities
Interpretation: *leaflets; information boards; slides; tour guides*
Children: *adventure playground; play area; nappy changing*
Schools: *maximum no. 600; educational literature; audio/visual presentation; lecture/talk*
Disabled: *easy access; disabled toilets; parking spaces*
Catering: *1 bar/public house*
Franchisees: *Easter to Oct – 10am to 5.30pm daily; Nov to Easter – 10am to 5pm daily*
Retailing: *postcards/inexpensive souvenirs; confectionery and ice cream; craftwork; books; organic vegetables*

No. shops: *4*

Operations
Contact: *Mr C Tabiner (Manager)*
No. employees: (high season) *12 full time; 6 part time* (low season) *12 full time; 2 part time*
Training: *F/T operations staff, F/T management, P/T operations staff and casual operations staff are trained in-house and externally and on specific courses and day-to-day on job using handbooks*

Marketing
Affiliation: *East Midlands Tourist Board*
Other: *market research*
UK promotion: *local newspapers; regional tourist board; other attractions; leaflets/information packs; Cream of Leicestershire*

Environmental monitoring: *waste; energy consumption; chemical usage*

FASQUE
(trust)
historic house; red deer park

Established: *1978*
Address: *Fettercairn, Kincardineshire, Scotland, AB30 1DJ*
Telephone: *(05614) 569. Fax: (05614) 325*
Access: (road) *A94/B966* (rail) *Montrose*
Parking capacity: (cars) *100* (coaches) *5*
Hours: *1 May to 30 Sept – 1.30pm to 5.30pm daily except Fri*
Admission (1992): *adults £2.00; children £1.00; OAP £1.50; adult groups £1.50*
No. visitors (1992): *9000 (est.)*

Facilities
Interpretation: *information boards; tour guides; guide books*
Languages: *French; German; Italian*
Children: *adventure playground*
Schools: *maximum no. 60; educational literature*
Disabled: *helpers; touch tours for the blind*
Catering: *1 picnic area*
Retailing: *postcards/inexpensive souvenirs; confectionery and ice cream; craftwork*
No. shops: *1*

Operations
Contact: *J Smith (Curator)*
No. employees: (high season) *2 full time; 3 part time* (low season) *1 full time; 1 part time*
Training: *casual operations staff are trained in-house and day-to-day on job and 2 days' familiarisation using videos and handbooks*
Languages spoken: *French*

Marketing
Annual event: *Victorian fair*
Affiliations: *HHA and STB*
Other: *market research*
UK promotion: *television; local newspapers; regional tourist board; other attractions; leaflets/information packs*

Environmental monitoring: recycling; water quality; energy consumption; hazardous materials; chemical usage; wildlife conservation

---

FELBRIGG HALL
(Trust)
historic house; park/reserve; garden

Address: *National Trust, Roughton, Norwich, Norfolk, NR11 8PR*
Telephone: *(0263) 837444*
Access: (road) *A148/A140*
Parking capacity: (cars) *600* (coaches) *10*
Hours: *April to end October. Summer – gardens 11.00am to 5.30pm; hall opens 1.30pm*
Admission (1992): *adults £4.30; children £2.00*
No. visitors (1992): *62 000 (est.)*

Facilities
Interpretation: *leaflets; guide books; signs*
Children: *nappy changing*

Schools: *maximum no. 60*
Disabled: *easy access; disabled toilets; helpers; powered transport; guide book; braille on halls and walls*
Catering: *2 picnic areas*
Retailing: *postcards/inexpensive souvenirs; confectionery and ice cream; craftwork; books; clothes; various*
No. shops: *1*

Operations
Contact: *Graham Hicks (Administrator)*
No. employees: (high season) *12 full time; 110 part time* (low season) *12 full time; 30 part time*
Training: *F/T operations staff, F/T management, P/T operations staff and casual operations staff are trained in-house and externally and on specific courses and day-to-day on job*
Languages spoken: *French; German; Italian*

Marketing
Affiliations: *National Trust*
Other: *PR Company; press office; market research*
UK promotion: *local newspapers; regional tourist board; other attractions; leaflets/information packs; ETB/BTA*
Europe promotion: *leaflets/brochures; travel agents' brochures; British Tourist Authority*

FELIN CREWI WORKING WATERMILL
(partnership)
heritage centre; working watermill

Established: *1985*
Address: *Penegoes, Machynlleth, Powys, SY20 8N4*
Telephone: *(0654) 703113*
Access: (road) *M54/A4889* (rail) *Machynlleth*
Parking capacity: (cars) *40* (coaches) *2*
Season: *all year*
Hours: *Easter to Sept – Mon to Sun – 10.30am to 5.30pm; Winter – normally open 3 days per week*
Admission (1992): *adults £1.40; children £0.70; OAP £1.20*
No. visitors (1992): *30 000 (est.)*

Facilities
Interpretation: *leaflets; information boards; tour guides*
Languages: *French*
Children: *nappy changing*
Schools: *maximum no. 50; educational literature; lecture/talk; working models*
Disabled: *easy access; disabled toilets; helpers; special signs; all except second floor*
Catering: *1 licensed restaurant*
Franchisees: *Easter to Sept – Mon to Sun – 10.30am to 5.30pm; Winter – normally open 3 days per week*
Retailing: *postcards/inexpensive souvenirs; books; flour, muesli, other foodstuffs*
No. shops: *1*

Operations
Contacts: *Patti Partridge (Partner); Philip Lewis (Miller)*
No. employees: (high season) *4 full time; 9 part time* (low season) *2 full time; 1 part time*
Training: *F/T operations staff, F/T management, P/T operations staff, P/T management, casual operations staff and casual management are trained in-house and externally and on specific courses and day-to-day on job using videos and handbooks*

Marketing
Annual event(s): *National Mills Day demonstrations*
Affiliations: *Traditional Cornmillers Guild*
Other: *market research*
UK promotion: *radio; local newspapers; regional tourist board; other attractions; leaflets/information packs; ETB/BTA*
Europe/USA promotion: *British Tourist Authority*

Environmental monitoring: *recycling; waste; energy consumption; hazardous materials; chemical usage*

FELSTED VINEYARDS
(partnership/local authority)
vineyard with winery

Established: *1960*
Address: *The Vineyards, Crix Green, Felsted, Essex, CM6 3JT*
Telephone: *(0245) 361 504*
Access: (road) *M11/A131/A130/A120* (rail) *Braintree*
Parking capacity: (cars) *50*
Season: *all year*
Hours: *1 Apr to 30 Sept – Tues to Fri – 10am to 7pm; all year round – Sat – 10am to 7pm and Sun – 12 noon to 3pm*
Admission (1992): *adults £0.75; conducted tours by arrangement – £2.50 min 12 people*

Facilities
Interpretation: *videos; leaflets*
Children: *play area*
Schools: *maximum no. 30; educational literature; audio/visual presentation; lecture/talk*
Catering: *2 picnic areas*
Retailing: *confectionery and ice cream; craftwork; books; vineyard's wines; local produce*
No. shops: *1*

Operations
Contacts: *Mrs B Cole (Partner); Mr M Lilley (Partner)*
No. employees: (high season) *2 full time; 2 part time* (low season) *2 full time; 2 part time*
Training: *F/T management are trained externally and on specific courses and day-to-day on job*

Marketing
Affiliation: *East Anglian Wine Growers Association*
UK promotion: *television; radio; local newspapers; regional tourist board; leaflets/information packs; coach tours; Essex over 200 Places to Visit*

Environmental monitoring: *recycling; waste; water quality; energy consumption; hazardous materials; chemical usage; transport; emissions*

FENNY LODGE GALLERY
(limited company)
gallery

Established: *1983*
Address: *Simpson Road, Fenny Stratford, Bletchley, Milton Keynes*
Telephone: *(0908) 642207. Fax: (0908) 647840*
Access: (road) *M1/A421* (rail) *Bletchley*
Parking capacity: (cars) *8*
Hours: *Mon to Fri – 9am to 5pm, Sat – 9am to 4pm; closed all BH Mon, Christmas and New Year*
Admission (1992): *free*
No. visitors (1992): *6000 (est.)*

Facilities
Interpretation: *leaflets*
Disabled: *disabled toilets*
Retailing: *craftwork; British craft; paintings; prints*
No. shops: *1*

Operations
Contact: *Mrs Miller*
No. employees: (high season) *2 full time; 4 part time* (low season) *2 full time; 4 part time*
Languages spoken: *French; German; Italian; Spanish*

Marketing
Annual event(s): *Spring and Christmas exhibitions*
Other: *PR Company: Lucinda Rathbach, 10 Raynham Rd, London, W6; market research*
UK promotion: *local newspapers; regional tourist board; other attractions; leaflets/information packs*

Environmental monitoring: *recycling; waste; hazardous materials; chemical usage*

FERENS ART GALLERY
(local authority run)
gallery

Established: *1928*
Address: *Queen Victoria Sq, Hull, HU1 3RA*
Telephone: *(0482) 593902.* Fax: *(0482) 593913*
Access: (road) *M62/A63* (rail) *Hull Paragon*
Season: *all year*
Hours: *Mon to Sat – 10am to 5pm, Sun – 1.30pm
to 4.30pm; closed New Year's Day, Christmas
and Boxing Day and Good Friday*
Admission (1992): *free*
No. visitors (1992): *200 000 (est.)*

Facilities
Interpretation: *guide books*
Languages: *Dutch*
Children: *nappy changing*
Schools: *maximum no. 200; educational literature;
lecture/talk; project based workshops*
Disabled: *easy access; disabled toilets; helpers*
Catering: *1 waiter/waitress served*
Retailing: *postcards/inexpensive souvenirs;
craftwork; books; clothes; greetings cards*
No. shops: *1*

Operations
Contact: *Ms L Karlsen (Principal Keeper)*
No. employees (high season) *21 full time*
Training: *F/T operations staff and F/T
management are trained in-house and externally
and on specific courses and day-to-day on job*

Marketing
Sponsor(s): *various*
Other: *press office; market research*
UK promotion: *radio; regional tourist board;
leaflets/information packs*

FFESTINIOG RAILWAY
(public railway supported by trust)
heritage centre; museum; operating railway

Established: *1836*
Address: *Harbour Station, Portmadog, Gwynedd,
LL49 9NF*
Telephone: *(0766) 512340.* Fax: *(0766) 514576*
Access: (road) *A487* (rail) *Blaenau Ffestiniog*
Parking capacity: (cars) *55* (coaches) *4*
Season: *all year*
Hours: *timetabled service*
Admission (1992): *fares vary according to routes,
discounts for groups, OAPs and children*
No. visitors (1992): *190 000 (est.)*

Facilities
Interpretation: *videos; leaflets; guide books*
Languages: *Dutch; French; German*
Children: *nappy changing*
Schools: *educational literature*
Disabled: *easy access; disabled toilets; other audio
facilities*
Catering: *1 bar/public house*
Retailing: *postcards/inexpensive souvenirs;
confectionery and ice cream; craftwork; books;
clothes; model railway supplies*
No. shops: *3*

Operations
Contacts: *Mr A Heywood (Traffic and
Commercial Manager); Mr G Rushton (General
Manager); Mrs G Shephard (Sales Supervisor)*
No. employees: (high season) *40 full time; 60 part
time* (low season) *40 full time; 5 part time*
Training: *F/T operations staff, F/T management,
P/T operations staff and casual operations staff
are trained in-house and day-to-day on job
using videos and handbooks and information
sheets*
Languages spoken: *French; Italian*

Marketing
Annual event: *steam gala*
Affiliations: *The Transport Trust, Great Little
Trains of Wales, etc*
Other: *PR company: details on request; market
research*

UK promotion: *national newspapers; local
newspapers; regional tourist board; other
attractions; leaflets/information packs;
ETB/BTA; WTB*
Europe/WTB promotion: *leaflets/brochures;
travel agents' brochures; British Tourist
Authority*

Environmental monitoring: *energy consumption;
hazardous materials*

FILEY MUSEUM
(board of trustees)
museum

Established: *1971*
Address: *8–10 Queen St, Filey, N Yorks*
Access: (road) *A64/A165*
Hours: *late May to mid Sept - Sun to Fri - 2pm to
5pm*
Admission (1992): *adults £0.50; children £0.25;
OAP £0.50; student £0.50*
No. visitors (1992): *2600 (est.)*

Facilities
Interpretation: *leaflets; information boards; guide
books*
Schools: *maximum no. 30; lecture/talk*
Disabled: *easy access*

Operations
Contact: *Mr M Fearon (Honorary Curator)*
Languages spoken: *Welsh*

Marketing
UK promotion: *regional tourist board*

Environmental monitoring: *energy consumption;
hazardous materials; chemical usage; transport;
emissions*

FISHBOURNE ROMAN PALACE AND MUSEUM
(charity)
museum; archaeological site

Established: *1968*
Address: *Salthill Road, Fishbourne, Chichester, W
Sussex, PO19 3QR*
Telephone: *(0243) 785859*
Access: (road) *A25/A259* (rail) *Chichester*
Parking capacity: (cars) *80* (coaches) *17*
Season: *all year*
Hours: *Mar, Apr, Oct – 10am to 5pm daily, May
to Sept – 10am to 6pm daily, Nov, Dec,
Feb – 10am to 4pm daily, Dec to Feb – Sun
only – 10am to 4pm*
Admission (1992): *adults £3.20; children £1.50;
OAP £2.60; student £2.60; family £8.00,groups
£2.60*
No. visitors (1992): *84 433*

Facilities
Interpretation: *audio tapes; information boards;
slides; guide books*
Languages: *French; German; Italian*
Schools: *maximum no. 250; educational literature;
audio/visual presentation; lecture/talk;
workshops*
Disabled: *easy access; disabled toilets; other audio
facilities; tape guided tour*
Catering: *1 picnic area*
Franchisees: *Mar, Apr, Oct – 10am to 5pm daily,
May to Sept – 10am to 6pm daily*
Retailing: *postcards/inexpensive souvenirs; books;
reproductions of famous artefacts*
No. shops: *2*

Operations
Contacts: *D J Rudkin (Director); P Biffen (Shop
Manager)*
No. employees: (high season) *4 full time; 9 part
time* (low season) *4 full time; 4 part time*
Training: *F/T operations staff, F/T management,
P/T operations staff and casual operations staff
are trained in-house and day-to-day on job*

Marketing
Annual event: *Roman activities weekend*

Other: *market research*
UK promotion: *local newspapers; regional tourist
board; other attractions; leaflets/information
packs*
Europe promotion: *British Tourist Authority*

FITZWILLIAM MUSEUM
(university museum)
museum; gallery

Established: *1846*
Address: *Trumpington St, Cambridge, CB2 1RB*
Telephone: *(0223) 332900.* Fax: *(0223) 332923*
Access: (road) *M11/A45/A1* (rail) *Cambridge*
Season: *all year*
Hours: *Tues to Sat – 10am to 5pm, Sun – 2.15pm
to 5pm; closed Spring and Summer BH, also
closed Good Friday, May Day and 24 Dec to 1
Jan incl*
Admission (1992): *free*
No. visitors (1992): *220 000*

Facilities
Interpretation: *leaflets; tour guides*
Schools: *maximum no. 30; educational officer*
Disabled: *disabled toilets; level entry to ground
floor*
Catering: *1 snack bar/food stall*
Franchisees: *Tues to Sat – 10am to 5pm,
Sun – 2.15pm to 5pm*
Retailing: *postcards/inexpensive souvenirs; books;
clothes; reproductions of famous artefacts;
posters*
No. shops: *2*

Operations
Contacts: *W Northam/R Maddicott (museum/
FME Ltd)*
No. employees: (high season) *60 full time; 15 part
time* (low season) *60 full time; 15 part time*
Training: *F/T operations staff and P/T operations
staff are trained in-house and on specific
courses and day-to-day on job*
Languages spoken: *French*

Marketing
Annual event(s): *exhibitions*
Sponsor(s): *various*
Affiliations: *MA, National Arts Collection Fund*
Other: *press office*
UK promotion: *local newspapers; other
attractions; leaflets/information packs*

FLAMBARDS VILLAGE THEME PARK
(limited company)
theme park; museum

Established: *1976*
Address: *Helston, Cornwall, TR13 0GA*
Telephone: *(0326) 573404.* Fax: *(0326) 575344*
Access: (road) *A3093*
Hours: *Easter to end of Oct -10am to 5.30pm
daily*
Admission (1992): *adults £7.50; children £6.50;
OAP £3.95*

Facilities
Interpretation: *videos; leaflets; audio tapes;
information boards; maps; guide books*
Children: *adventure playground; nappy
changing*
Schools: *maximum no. 5000*
Disabled: *easy access; disabled toilets; leaflets;
guide book*
Catering: *2 picnic areas*
Retailing: *postcards/inexpensive souvenirs;
confectionery and ice cream; craftwork; books;
clothes*
No. shops: *More than 4*

Operations
Contact: *Mr J Hale (Managing Director)*
Training: *F/T operations staff, F/T management,
P/T operations staff, P/T management, casual
operations staff and casual management are
trained in-house and on specific courses and
day-to-day on job using videos*
Languages spoken: *French; German; Italian*

Marketing
Other: *press office; market research*
UK promotion: *television; national newspapers;
radio; local newspapers; regional tourist board;
other attractions; leaflets/information packs;
ETB/BTA*

FLETCHER MOSS BOTANICAL GARDEN
(local authority run)
garden

Established: *1914*
Address: *Stenner Lane, Didsbury, Manchester,
M20*
Telephone: *(061) 434 1877*
Access: (road) *M63/A5145*
Parking capacity: (cars) *12*
Season: *all year*
Hours: *all year – dawn to dusk*
Admission (1992): *free*
No. visitors (1992): *18 000 (est.)*

Facilities
Interpretation: *leaflets; information boards; tour
guides; guide books*
Schools: *maximum no. 20; no special support;
lecture/talk*
Disabled: *disabled toilets*
Catering: *1 self-service cafeteria*

Operations
No. employees: (high season) *8 full time* (low
season) *8 full time*
Training: *F/T operations staff are trained in-house
and on specific courses using videos and
handbooks*
Languages spoken: *French; German; Italian;
Spanish*

Marketing
Press office
UK promotion: *regional tourist board;
leaflets/information packs; ETB/BTA*

Environmental monitoring: *recycling; waste;
water quality; energy consumption; hazardous
materials; chemical usage; emissions*

FLEUR DE LIS HERITAGE CENTRE
(local society)
heritage centre; museum

Established: *1977*
Address: *13 Preston Street, Faversham, Kent,
ME13 8NS*
Telephone: *(0795) 534542*
Access: (road) *M2/A2/A2041* (rail) *Faversham*
Season: *all year*
Hours: *10am to 4pm daily; closed Sun from Nov
to Mar*
Admission (1992): *adults £1.00; children £0.50;
OAP £0.50; student £0.50*
No. visitors (1992): *4500 (est.)*

Facilities
Interpretation: *audio tapes; information boards*
Languages: *Dutch; French; German*
Schools: *maximum no. 50; educational literature;
lecture/talk*
Disabled: *easy access; building for the most part
unsuitable*
Retailing: *postcards/inexpensive souvenirs; books;
facsimiles of maps, slides, books and maps*
No. shops: *1*

Operations
Contacts: *M Sifford (Honorary Manager); A
Percival (Honorary Director)*
No. employees: (high season) *20 part time* (low
season) *20 part time*
Training: *P/T operations staff and P/T
management are trained in-house and externally
and on specific courses and day-to-day on job
using handbooks*

Marketing
Annual event(s): *Faversham open house scheme*

Affiliations: *various*
UK promotion: *local newspapers; regional tourist
board*

FLIMWELL BIRD PARK
(private)
zoo/wildlife attraction

Established: *1990*
Address: *Hawkhurst Road, Flimwell, Wadhurst,
E Sussex, TN5 7GP*
Telephone: *(0580) 87202*
Access: (road) *A268/A21*
Parking capacity: (cars) *50* (coaches) *6*
Hours: *Apr to Sept – 10.30am to 5pm daily,
weekends in Oct*
Admission (1992): *adults £2.50; children
£1.75; OAP £1.75; disabled £1.10, groups
£1.10*
No. visitors (1992): *6500*

Facilities
Interpretation: *leaflets*
Children: *play area; nappy changing*
Schools: *maximum no. 80; educational literature*
Disabled: *disabled toilets; powered transport*
Catering: *2 picnic areas*
Franchisees: *Apr to Sept – 10.30am to 5pm daily,
weekends in Oct*
Retailing: *postcards/inexpensive souvenirs;
confectionery and ice cream; books*
No. shops: *1*

Operations
Contact: *V Frearson (Manager)*
No. employees: (high season) *2 full time* (low
season) *2 part time*
Languages spoken: *French; German*

Marketing
Annual event: *Easter egg hunt*
UK promotion: *local newspapers; regional
tourist board; leaflets/information packs;
SEETB*

Environmental monitoring: *transport; tree/coastal
protection*

FLOORS CASTLE
(privately owned)
historic house; castle

Established: *1977*
Address: *Kelso, Roxburghshire, TD5 7SF*
Telephone: *0573 223333. Fax: 0573 226056*
Access: (road) *A6089* (rail) *Berwick on Tweed*
Hours: *Easter and from 25 April to end October,
May, June and September – Sun to Thurs
10.30am to 5.30pm, July and Aug – daily
10.30am to 5.30pm, Oct – Sun and Wed
10.30am to 4pm*
Admission (1992): *adults £3.20; children £1.60;
OAP £2.50*
No. visitors (1992): *60 000 (est.)*

Facilities
Interpretation: *tour guides; guide books*
Languages: *French; German; Italian*
Children: *play area; nappy changing*
Schools: *maximum no. 30; no special support*
Disabled: *helpers*
Catering: *1 picnic area*
Retailing: *postcards/inexpensive souvenirs*
No. shops: *1*

Marketing
Annual event(s): *massed pipe bands*
Affiliations: *Historic Houses Association,
Association of Scottish Visitor Attractions*
UK promotion: *local newspapers; regional tourist
board; other attractions; leaflets/information
packs*

FLORENCECOURT HOUSE
(trust)
historic house; park/reserve; garden

Established: *1960*
Address: *Florencecourt, Enniskillen, County
Fermanagh, Northern Ireland*
Telephone: *(036582) 249*
Access: (road) *A4/A32*
Parking capacity: (cars) *300* (coaches) *20*
Hours: *Apr, May, Sept – Sat, Sun, BH – 1pm to
6pm, Easter week – Mon to Sun – 1pm to 6pm,
June to Aug – Wed to Mon – 12 noon to 6pm;
estate open daily all year round from 10am to
6pm*
Admission (1992): *adults £2.30; children £1.20;
OAP £2.30; student £1.20; group discounts
available*
No. visitors (1992): *14 520*

Facilities
Interpretation: *leaflets; information boards; maps;
tour guides; guide books*
Languages: *French; German; Italian; Spanish*
Children: *play area; nappy changing*
Schools: *educational literature*
Disabled: *easy access; disabled toilets; helpers;
special signs; leaflets; guide book; easy
parking*
Catering: *1 picnic area*
Retailing: *postcards/inexpensive souvenirs;
confectionery and ice cream; craftwork;
books; reproductions of famous artefacts;
National Trust products; tin flutes, games,
etc.*
No. shops: *1*

Operations
Contacts: *Christopher Corry-Thomas
(Administrator); Mr W Boyd (Regional
Personnel Manager); Miss H Bermingham
(Regional Enterprises Manager); Mrs D Forbes
(Regional Marketing Manager)*
No. employees: (high season) *3 full time;
16 part time* (low season) *3 full time; 4 part
time*
Training: *F/T operations staff, F/T management,
P/T operations staff, P/T management
and casual operations staff are trained in-house
and externally and on specific courses and
day-to-day on job*

Marketing
Annual event(s): *craft fairs, country fair*
Affiliations: *Irish Heritage Properties*
Other: *press office; market research*
UK promotion: *television; national newspapers;
radio; local newspapers; regional tourist board;
other attractions; leaflets/information packs;
Northern Ireland Tourist Board*
Europe/Southern Ireland promotion:
leaflets/brochures; travel agents' brochures

FORD GREEN HALL
(local authority run)
historic house

Established: *1952*
Address: *Ford Green Road, Smallthorne, Stoke on
Trent, Staffs.*
Telephone: *(0782) 534771*
Access: (road) *M6/A500/A53/A50* (rail) *Stoke on
Trent*
Parking capacity: (cars) *80* (coaches) *1*
Season: *all year*
Hours: *all year – Sun to Thur – 1pm to 5pm;
closed 25 Dec to 1 Jan and Good Friday*
Admission (1992): *free*
No. visitors (1992): *11 000*

Facilities
Interpretation: *information boards; tour guides;
guide books*
Languages: *German*
Schools: *maximum no. 30; educational literature;
education room, handling*
Disabled: *disabled toilets*
Catering: *1 waiter/waitress served*
Retailing: *postcards/inexpensive souvenirs; books;
potpourri, spices, cut flowers*
No. shops: *1*

Operations
Contacts: J Franklin (Branch Manager); Stoke on Trent City Council; A Townsend (Shop Manager); B Gwynne (Promotions Officer)
No. employees: (high season) 1 full time; 3 part time (low season) 1 full time; 3 part time
Training: P/T operations staff are trained in-house and day-to-day on job using videos and handbooks
Languages spoken: French; German; Swahili

Marketing
Annual event(s): various
Other: market research
UK promotion: local newspapers; other attractions; leaflets/information packs

Environmental monitoring: waste; energy consumption; hazardous materials; chemical usage; forestry; meadows

---

FORGE MILL MUSEUM AND BORDESLEY ABBEY VISITORS' CENTRE
(local authority run)
heritage centre; park/reserve; museum

Established: 1983
Address: Needle Mill Lane, Riverside, Redditch, Worcs, B97 6RR
Telephone: (0527) 62509
Access: (road) M42/A441 (rail) Redditch
Parking capacity: (cars) 100 (coaches) 4
Hours: Easter to Sept – Mon to Thur – 11am to 4.30pm, Sat to Sun – 2pm to 5pm
Admission (1992): adults £1.50; children £0.50; OAP £1.00; student £0.50; family £3.50
No. visitors (1992): 10 000

Facilities
Interpretation: videos; leaflets; information boards; tour guides; guide books
Languages: French; German; Spanish
Schools: maximum no. 60; educational literature; lecture/talk; school visits
Disabled: easy access; disabled toilets; helpers
Catering: 2 picnic areas
Retailing: postcards/inexpensive souvenirs; books; needles; threads
No. shops: 1

Operations
Contact: B Mead (Manager)
No. employees: (high season) 4 full time; 6 part time (low season) 4 full time; 3 part time
Training: F/T operations staff, F/T management and P/T operations staff are trained in-house and externally and on specific courses and day-to-day on job
Languages spoken: French; German

Marketing
Annual event: craft fayre
Affiliations: HETB, MA, West Midlands Area Museum Service
Other: market research
UK promotion: local newspapers; regional tourist board; other attractions; leaflets/information packs

---

FORMAKIN ESTATE
(trust)
historic house; garden; zoo/wildlife attraction

Established: 1988
Address: Formakin Estate, Millhill Road, Bishopton, PA7 5NX
Telephone: (0505) 863400
Access: (road) M8/A9 (rail) Bishopton
Parking capacity: (cars) 150 (coaches) 6
Season: all year
Hours: daily 11am to 5pm; closed Christmas and New Year
Admission (1992): adults £1.50; children £0.50; OAP £1.50; student £1.50
No. visitors (1992): 45 000 (est.)

Facilities
Interpretation: leaflets; information boards; tour guides

Children: adventure playground; play area
Schools: educational literature; lecture/talk
Disabled: disabled toilets; helpers; leaflets
Catering: 4 picnic areas
Franchisees: daily 11am to 5pm; closed Christmas and New Year
Retailing: postcards/inexpensive souvenirs; confectionery and ice cream; craftwork; books; clothes
No. shops: More than 4

Operations
Contact: Mr J Tonner (Estate Manager)
No. employees: (high season) 40 full time; 6 part time (low season) 20 full time; 4 part time
Training: F/T operations staff, F/T management, P/T operations staff, P/T management, casual operations staff and casual management are trained in-house and day-to-day on job

Marketing
Annual event(s): various
Sponsor(s): various
UK promotion: national newspapers; local newspapers; regional tourist board; other attractions; leaflets/information packs

Environmental monitoring: energy consumption

FORNCETT INDUSTRIAL STEAM MUSEUM
(private collection)
museum

Established: 1982
Address: Low Rd, Forncett St Mary, Norwich, Norfolk
Telephone: (050841) 8277
Access: (road) A140 (rail) Spooner Row
Parking capacity: (cars) 100 (coaches) 4
Hours: 1st Sun in month, May to Dec; also scheduled steam days and special event days
Admission (1992): adults £2.50; 2 children free with every paying adult

Facilities
Interpretation: leaflets; information boards; guide books; live steam demonstrations during opening times
Children: play area
Schools: maximum no. 100; educational literature; lecture/talk; live steam demonstrations
Disabled: easy access; disabled toilets
Catering: 1 snack bar/food stall
Retailing: postcards/inexpensive souvenirs; confectionery and ice cream; books
No. shops: 1

Operations
Contacts: Dr R Francis (Director)
Training: N/A

Marketing
Annual event(s): live steam demonstrations
Other: market research
UK promotion: national newspapers; radio; local newspapers; regional tourist board; other attractions; leaflets/information packs

---

FOXFIELD STEAM RAILWAY
(limited company)
museum; preserved railway

Established: 1967
Address: Caverswall Road Station, Blythe Bridge, Stoke on Trent, Staffs.
Telephone: (0782) 396210
Access: (road) M6/A50 (rail) Blythe Bridge
Parking capacity: (cars) 200 (coaches) 4
Hours: Easter to Sept – Sat to Sun – 11am to 5.30pm
Admission (1992): adults £2.70; children £1.40; OAP £1.40; group discounts
No. visitors (1992): 13 000 (est.)

Facilities
Interpretation: leaflets; guide books
Disabled: easy access; helpers
Catering: 1 bar/public house

Retailing: postcards/inexpensive souvenirs; confectionery and ice cream; toys
No. shops: 2

Operations
Contacts: L J Reed (Secretary); B Allen (Treasurer); D M Scragg (Press/Publicity Officer)
Training: P/T operations staff are trained in-house and day-to-day on job using practical training

Marketing
Annual event(s): Friends of Thomas the Tank Engine weekends, Gala weekend
Other: market research
UK promotion: national newspapers; radio; local newspapers; regional tourist board; other attractions; leaflets/information packs; North Staffs Tourism Association Publications

---

FREUD MUSEUM
(trust)
historic house; museum

Established: 1986
Address: 20 Haresfield Gardens, London, NW3 5SX
Telephone: (071) 435 2002. Fax: (071) 431 5452
Access: (road) Finchley Road
Parking capacity: (cars) 2
Season: all year
Hours: Wed to Sun – 12 noon to 5pm
Admission (1992): adults £2.50; OAP £1.50; student £1.50; group tours outside normal hours £3.00, ub40s £1.50; under12s free
No. visitors (1992): 12 000 (est.)

Facilities
Interpretation: videos; leaflets; information boards
Schools: maximum no. 40; educational literature; outside normal hours
Retailing: postcards/inexpensive souvenirs; craftwork; books; reproductions of famous artefacts
No. shops: 1

Operations
Contacts: Ms E Davies (Director); Ms S O'Cleary; Ms A Green (PR)
No. employees: (high season) 7 full time; 2 part time (low season) 7 full time; 2 part time

Marketing
Press office; market research
UK promotion: regional tourist board; other attractions; leaflets/information packs; ETB/BTA

Environmental monitoring: hazardous materials

FREWEN COLLEGE
(trust)
historic house; garden

Established: 1970
Address: Brickwall House, Northam, E Sussex, TN31 6NL
Telephone: (07974) 2494. Fax: (07974) 2567
Access: (road) A21/B2088 (rail) Rye
Parking capacity: (cars) 50 (coaches) 10
Hours: Apr to end Sept – Sat – 2pm to 5pm
Admission (1992): adults £1.50
No. visitors (1992): 1000 (est.)

Facilities
Interpretation: leaflets; tour guides; guide books
Languages: French
Schools: maximum no. 50; educational literature
Disabled: easy access; guide book
Retailing: postcards/inexpensive souvenirs; books; school choir tapes
No. shops: none

Operations
Contacts: Mrs M Frewen Parsons (Curator); Mrs Pemberton (Bursar); Mrs A Frewen (Advertising Manager)
No. employees: (high season) 2 full time

Languages spoken: *French; German; Spanish; Russian*

Marketing
Annual event(s): *art and crafts fair and concerts*
Sponsor(s): *Musical Trust and Brickwall Arts Society*
UK promotion: *radio; local newspapers; regional tourist board; leaflets/information packs; S East England Tourist Board*

FRIGATE UNICORN
(company limited by guarantee)
historic ship

Established: *1975*
Address: *Victoria Dock, Dundee, DD1 3JA*
Telephone: *(0382) 200900.* Fax: *(0382) 202555*
Access: (road) *A85*
Parking capacity: (cars) *30* (coaches) *10*
Season: *all year*
Hours: *daily 10am to 5pm excluding Christmas Day, Boxing Day and New Year's Day*
Admission (1992): *adults £2.00; children £1.50; OAP £1.50; student £1.50*
No. visitors (1992): *34 400*

Facilities
Interpretation: *leaflets; information boards; tour guides; guide books; schools educational pack*
Languages: *Dutch; French; German*
Schools: *maximum no. 100; educational literature; lecture/talk; schools educational pack*
Disabled: *easy access*
Catering: *1 snack bar/food stall*
Retailing: *postcards/inexpensive souvenirs; confectionery and ice cream; books; items showing unicorns*
No. shops: *1*

Operations
Contacts: *Hamish Robertson (Development Manager); Gwen Clarke (Administrator)*
No. employees: (high season) *5 full time; 17 part time* (low season) *5 full time; 17 part time*
Training: *F/T operations staff and P/T operations staff are trained in-house and externally and on specific courses and day-to-day on job*
Languages spoken: *French*

Marketing
Annual event: *pirates' fun day*
Affiliations: *Scottish Museums Council, Dundee Tourist Board, Scottish Tourist Board*
Other: *market research*
UK promotion: *regional tourist board; other attractions; leaflets/information packs*

FROME MUSEUM
(trust)
museum; gallery

Established: *1966*
Address: *1 North Parade, Frome, BA11*
Access: (road) *A361*
Season: *all year*
Hours: *Wed to Sat – 10am to 4pm – closed Jan and PH*
Admission (1992): *adults £0.30; children £0.10*
No. visitors (1992): *3000 (est.)*

Facilities
Interpretation: *leaflets; information boards; show cases*
Schools: *maximum no. 50; educational literature; lecture/talk*
Retailing: *postcards/inexpensive souvenirs; craftwork; books*
No. shops: *1*

Operations
Contact: *Mrs E Atkinson (Secretary)*

Marketing
Affiliations: *Area Museums Council for the South West, Museums Federation for the South West*
UK promotion: *local newspapers*

FRONTIERLAND WESTERN THEME PARK
(limited company)
theme park

Established: *1986*
Address: *Morecambe, Lancs, LA4 4DG*
Telephone: *(0524) 410024.* Fax: *(0524) 831399.*
Access: (road) *M6/A683* (rail) *Morecambe*
Parking capacity: (cars) *500* (coaches) *50*
Hours: *Mar to May – Weekends – 11am to 10pm; May to Aug – 11am to 10pm daily; Sept – weekends*
Admission (1992): *adults £5.99; children £3.50; group and family discounts available*
No. visitors (1992): *1 200 000 (est.)*

Facilities
Interpretation: *leaflets; information boards; maps*
Children: *play area; nappy changing*
Schools: *maximum no. 1000; no special support; lecture/talk*
Disabled: *easy access; disabled toilets*
Catering: *2 bars/public houses*
Retailing: *postcards/inexpensive souvenirs; confectionery and ice cream; clothes; T-shirts; key rings; toys; games; hats, etc.*
No. shops: *4*

Operations
Contacts: *M Rothwell (Park Manager); F Formby (Personnel and Retail manager); A Kirkhope (Marketing Manager)*
No. employees: (high season) *20 full time; 110 part time* (low season) *20 full time*
Training: *F/T operations staff, F/T management, P/T operations staff and P/T management are trained in-house and externally and on specific courses*

Marketing
Market research
UK promotion: *television; national newspapers; radio; local newspapers; regional tourist board; other attractions; leaflets/information packs; NWTB,Local County; ETB/BTA; Various advertisements in publications*

G

GAINSBOROUGH'S HOUSE
(trust)
historic house; gallery

Established: *1961*
Address: *46 Gainsborough St, Sudbury, Suffolk, CO10 6EU*
Telephone: *(0787) 372958*
Access: (road) *A134* (rail) *Sudbury*
Season: *all year*
Hours: *Tues to Sat – 10am to 5pm, Sun and BH Mon – 2pm to 5pm (closed at 4pm from Nov to Easter)*
Admission (1992): *adults £2.00; children £1.00; OAP £1.50; student £1.00;*
No. visitors (1992): *18 000*

Facilities
Interpretation: *leaflets; information boards*
Languages: *French; German*
Schools: *no special support; lecture/talk*
Disabled: *disabled toilets; helpers*
Retailing: *postcards/inexpensive souvenirs; confectionery and ice cream; books*
No. shops: *1*

Operations
Contact: *H Belsey (Curator)*
No. employees: (high season) *3 full time; 4 part time* (low season) *3 full time; 4 part time*
Training: *F/T management and P/T operations staff are trained in-house and externally and on specific courses using videos and handbooks*
Languages spoken: *French; German*

Marketing
Annual event(s): *temporary exhibitions*
Other: *market research*
UK promotion: *local newspapers; regional tourist board; leaflets/information packs*
Europe promotion: *British Tourist Authority*

Environmental monitoring: *waste; water quality; energy consumption; transport*

GAIRLOCH HERITAGE MUSEUM
(trust)
museum

Established: *1978*
Address: *Achtercairn, Gairloch, Ross-shire*
Access: (road) *A832*
Parking capacity: (cars) *20* (coaches) *2*
Hours: *Easter to end Sept – 10am to 5pm daily except Sun*
Admission (1992): *adults £1.00; children £0.20; OAP £1.00; student £1.00*
No. visitors (1992): *17 540*

Facilities
Interpretation: *leaflets; information boards; tour guides; guide books*
Languages: *French; German; Italian*
Schools: *maximum no. 20; educational literature; lecture/talk*
Disabled: *easy access*
Catering: *1 self-service cafeteria*
Retailing: *postcards/inexpensive souvenirs; books; gaelic related articles*
No. shops: *1*

Operations
Contact: *Mr R Wentworth (Curator)*
No. employees: (high season) *1 full time; 20 part time*
Languages spoken: *French*

Marketing
Affiliation: *SMC*
Other: *market research*
UK promotion: *regional tourist board; other attractions; leaflets/information packs; STB and Ross and Cromarty Tourist Board*

GALLOWAY FOREST PARK
(government body)
forest shop and visitor centre

Established: *1991*
Address: *Kirroughtree Visitor Centre, Stronord, Palnure, Newton Stewart, Wigtownshire*
Telephone: *(0671) 2165*
Access: (road) *A75*
Parking capacity: (cars) *60* (coaches) *3*
Hours: *Easter to end of Sept – 10.30am to 5pm daily*
Admission (1992): *free*
No. visitors (1992): *10 000 (est.)*

Facilities
Interpretation: *videos; leaflets; audio tapes; information boards; maps; guide books*
Children: *adventure playground*
Schools: *maximum no. 40; educational literature; audio/visual presentation; lecture/talk*
Disabled: *easy access; disabled toilets*
Catering: *1 picnic area*
Retailing: *postcards/inexpensive souvenirs; confectionery and ice cream; craftwork; books*
No. shops: *1*

Operations
Contact: *Mr J Livingstone (Recreation Officer)*
No. employees: (high season) *3 part time*
Training: *P/T operations staff and P/T management are trained in-house and externally and on specific courses and day-to-day on job*

Marketing
Press office; market research
UK promotion: *national newspapers; local newspapers; regional tourist board; leaflets/information packs; Dumfries and Galloway Tourist Board*

GARDEN HOUSE, THE
(trust)
garden

Established: *1892*
Address: *Buckland Monachorum, Yelverton, Devon*
Telephone: *(0822) 854769*
Access: (road) *M5/A386* (rail) *Plymouth*
Parking capacity: (cars) *70* (coaches) *1*
Hours: *Mar to Oct – 10.30am to 5pm daily*
Admission (1992): *adults £2.50; children £0.50; OAP £2.25*
No. visitors (1992): *16 000 (est.)*

Facilities
Interpretation: *leaflets; maps*
Schools: *maximum no. 35; guided tour*
Catering: *1 picnic area*
Retailing: *plants*
No. shops: *1*

Operations
Contact: *K Wiley (Manager)*
No. employees: (high season) *4 full time; 3 part time* (low season) *4 full time; 2 part time*

Training: *F/T operations staff, F/T management, P/T operations staff, P/T management, casual operations staff and casual management are trained in-house and day-to-day on job using videos and handbooks*
Languages spoken: *French; German; Spanish*

Marketing
UK promotion: *other attractions; leaflets/information packs*

Environmental monitoring: *maintaining Devon banks*

GEM ROCK MUSEUM
(privately owned)
museum

Established: *1972*
Address: *Chain Rd, Creetown, Newton Stewart, Galloway, DG8 7HJ*
Telephone: *(0671) 82 357.* Fax: *(0671) 82 554*
Access: (road) *A75*
Parking capacity: (cars) *50* (coaches) *2*
Season: *all year*
Hours: *1 Mar to 31 Oct – 9.30am to 6pm daily, 1 Nov to 24 Dec – 10am to 4pm – closed Thur and Fri; closed 25 Dec to 7 Jan; 8 Jan to 28 Feb – 10am to 4pm weekends only (or by appointment during the week)*
Admission (1992): *adults £2.00; children £1.00; OAP £1.50; student £1.50; special group rates and season tickets*
No. visitors (1992): *60 000*

Facilities
Interpretation: *videos; leaflets; audio tapes; information boards; talks by arrangement, workshop viewings*
Languages: *French*
Children: *nappy changing*
Schools: *maximum no. 30; educational literature; audio/visual presentation; lecture/talk; quiz*
Disabled: *easy access; disabled toilets*
Catering: *1 self-service cafeteria*
Retailing: *postcards/inexpensive souvenirs; confectionery and ice cream; craftwork; books; gemstone items and specimens; shortbread, etc*
No. shops: *1*

Operations
Contacts: *Mr T Stephenson FGA (Proprietor); Mrs R Stephenson (Joint Proprietor); Mrs K Stephenson (Joint Buyer)*
No. employees: (high season) *6 full time; 7 part time* (low season) *5 full time; 1 part time*

Marketing
Other: *market research*
UK promotion: *television; radio; local newspapers; regional tourist board; other attractions; leaflets/information packs; Dumfries and Galloway Tourist Board*
Europe promotion: *area tourist boards*

Environmental monitoring: *recycling; water quality; hazardous materials*

GIBRALTAR POINT NATIONAL NATURE RESERVE
(trust)
park/reserve

Established: *1949*
Address: *Gibraltar Point Field Station, Gibraltar Road, Skegness, PE24 4SU*

Telephone: *(0754) 762677*
Access: *(road) A52*
Parking capacity: *(cars) 70 (coaches) 2*
Season: *all year*
Hours: *Residential – Mar to Nov incl; day
    visits – all year; visitor centre – Summer – all
    week; – Oct to Apr – weekends only*
Admission (1992): *free. Car parking £1.50 peak
    £0.50p low season*
No. visitors (1992): *200 000 (est.)*

Facilities
Interpretation: *leaflets; information boards; maps;
    tour guides; guide books; personnel*
Schools: *maximum no. 60; educational literature;
    audio/visual presentation; lecture/talk; teachers'
    pack*
Disabled: *easy access; disabled toilets*
Catering: *2 picnic areas*
Retailing: *postcards/inexpensive souvenirs;
    craftwork; books; clothes*
No. shops: *1*

Operations
Contact: *Mr C Hawke (Senior warden)*
No. employees: *(high season) 6 full time; 1 part
    time (low season) 3 full time; 1 part time*
Training: *F/T operations staff, F/T management
    and P/T operations staff are trained in-house
    and externally and on specific courses and
    day-to-day on job using handbooks*
Languages spoken: *French*

Marketing
Affiliations: *Royal Society for Nature Conservation*
UK promotion: *national newspapers; regional
    tourist board; other attractions; leaflets/
    information packs*

Environmental monitoring: *recycling; waste;
    energy consumption; transport*

GLADSTONE'S LAND
(National Trust for Scotland)
historic house

Established: *1980*
Address: *4776 Lawnmarket, Edinburgh, EH1 2NT*
Telephone: *(031) 226 5856*
Access: *(road) A1 (rail) Edinburgh Waverley*
Hours: *1 Apr to 31 Oct – Mon to Sat – 10am to
    4.30pm and Sun – 2pm to 4.30pm*
Admission (1992): *adults £2.20; children £1.10;
    OAP £1.10; student £1.10; UB40 £1.10*
No. visitors (1992): *43 627*

Facilities
Interpretation: *leaflets; information boards; maps;
    tour guides; guide books; volunteer room and
    school guides*
Languages: *Japanese; Dutch; French; German;
    Italian; Spanish*
Schools: *maximum no. 33; educational literature;
    audio/visual presentation; lecture/talk; dressing
    up costumes*
Disabled: *special guided tour for blind visitors by
    arrangement*
Retailing: *postcards/inexpensive souvenirs;
    confectionery and ice cream; books; NT for
    Scotland goods*
No. shops: *1*

Operations
Contacts: *Mrs A Butler (Representative); Mr D
    Cameron (Director of Administration); Mrs E
    Renwick (Head of Central Buying); M Lockhart
    (Regional Information Officer)*
No. employees: *(high season) 3 full time; 2 part
    time (low season) 1 full time; 1 part time*
Training: *F/T operations staff, F/T management
    and P/T operations staff and casual operations
    staff are trained in-house and on specific
    courses and day-to-day on job*

Marketing
Affiliations: *Association of Scottish Visitor
    Attractions*
Other: *press office; market research*
UK promotion: *regional tourist board; other
    attractions; leaflets/information packs;
    Edinburgh Marketing*

Environmental monitoring: *recycling; waste;
    water quality; energy consumption; hazardous
    materials; chemical usage*

GLASGOW BOTANIC GARDENS
(local authority run)
garden

Established: *1841*
Address: *730 Great Western Road, Glasgow, G12
    0UE*
Telephone: *041 334 2422*
Access: *(road) M8*
Season: *all year*
Hours: *grounds – daily 7am to dusk;
    glasshouses – Kibble Palace Summer – 10am to
    4.45pm, Winter – 10am to 4.15pm; main range
    Summer – 1pm to 4.45pm, Winter – 1pm to
    4.15pm (opens 12 noon Sun)*
No. visitors (1992): *250 000 (est.)*

Facilities
Interpretation: *leaflets; information boards; guide
    books*
Children: *play area*
Schools: *maximum no. 100; educational literature*
Disabled: *easy access; disabled toilets*

Operations
Contact: *EG Donaldson (Acting Curator)*
Languages spoken: *German*

Marketing
Annual event: *open week*
Other: *press office; market research*
UK promotion: *leaflets/information packs*

GLASGOW VENNEL MUSEUM
(local authority run)
museum; gallery

Established: *1988*
Address: *10 Glasgow Vennel, Irvine, KA12 0BD*
Telephone: *(0294) 75059*
Access: *(road) A71/A736/A78 (rail) Glasgow to
    Ayr*
Season: *all year*
Hours: *1 June to 30 Sept – Mon, Tues, Thur, Fri
    and Sat – 10am to 1pm and 2pm to 5pm – Sun
    2pm to 5pm; 1 Oct to 31 May – Tues, Thur, Fri
    and Sat – 10am to 1pm and 2pm to 5pm; other
    times by appointment*
Admission (1992): *free*
No. visitors (1992): *4500 (est.)*

Facilities
Interpretation: *videos; leaflets; information
    boards; displays and exhibitions*
Schools: *maximum no. 40; educational literature;
    audio/visual presentation; lecture/talk*
Disabled: *easy access; disabled toilets; helpers*
Retailing: *postcards/inexpensive souvenirs; books*
No. shops: *1*

Operations
Contacts: *Ms D Keasal (District Curator); Ms L
    McAuley (District Council Marketing Officer)*
No. employees (high season) *2 full time; 8 part
    time (low season) 2 full time; 3 part time*
Training: *F/T operations staff, F/T management,
    P/T operations staff and casual operations staff
    are trained in-house and externally and on
    specific courses and day-to-day on job using
    videos*

Marketing
Annual event: *annual schools exhibition*
Sponsor(s): *ASDA and Harry Fairburn Motors*
Affiliations: *Burns Industry group*
Other: *press office; market research*
UK promotion: *local newspapers; regional tourist
    board; other attractions; leaflets/information
    packs; Cunningham Coasts Ahead; ETB/BTA;
    STB and magazines*

Environmental monitoring: *energy consumption*

GLASGOW ZOO PARK
(trust)
zoo/wildlife attraction

Established: *1946*
Address: *Calderpark, Uddington, Glasgow, G71
    7RZ*
Telephone: *(041) 771 1185*
Access: *(road) M73/M74/A74 (rail) Uddington*
Parking capacity: *(cars) 200 (coaches) 50*
Season: *all year*
Hours: *10am to 5pm daily*
Admission (1992): *adults £3.45; children £2.10;
    OAP £2.10; student £2.10; family ticket £9.00*
No. visitors (1992): *140 000 (est.)*

Facilities
Interpretation: *leaflets; information boards; slides;
    maps; guide books*
Children: *play area; nappy changing*
Schools: *educational literature; lecture/talk*
Disabled: *easy access; disabled toilets; wheelchairs
    available*
Catering: *3 picnic areas*
Franchisees: *10am to 5pm daily*
Retailing: *postcards/inexpensive souvenirs;
    confectionery and ice cream; animal-related
    gifts*
No. shops: *2*

Operations
Contacts: *R J P O'Grady (Director–Secretary)*
No. employees: *(high season) 30 full time; 4 part
    time (low season) 30 full time; 4 part time*
Training: *F/T operations staff, F/T management,
    P/T operations staff and casual operations staff
    are trained in-house and externally and on
    specific courses and day-to-day on job and
    correspondence courses using videos and
    handbooks*
Languages spoken: *French; Norwegian*

Marketing
Affiliations: *Federation of Zoos of Great Britain
    and Ireland*
Other: *press office; market research*
UK promotion: *local newspapers; regional tourist
    board; leaflets/information packs*

Environmental monitoring: *recycling; water
    quality; energy consumption; hazardous
    materials; chemical usage; transport*

GLEN TROOL VISITOR CENTRE
(government body)
forest shop; visitor centre

Established: *1992*
Address: *Galloway Forest Park, Bargrennan,
    Newton Stewart, Wigtownshire*
Telephone: *(067184) 302*
Access: *(road) A714*
Parking capacity: *(cars) 60 (coaches) 3*
Hours: *Easter to end Sept – 10.30am to 5pm daily*
Admission (1992): *free*
No. visitors (1992): *20 000 (est.)*

Facilities
Interpretation: *leaflets; information boards; maps;
    guide books*
Schools: *maximum no. 40; educational literature;
    lecture/talk*
Disabled: *easy access; disabled toilets*
Catering: *1 picnic area*
Retailing: *postcards/inexpensive souvenirs;
    confectionery and ice cream; craftwork; books*
No. shops: *1*

Operations
Contact: *Mr J Livingstone (Recreation Officer)*
No. employees: *(high season) 3 part time*
Training: *P/T operations staff and P/T
    management are trained in-house and externally
    and on specific courses and day-to-day on job*

Marketing
Other: *press office; market research*
UK promotion: *national newspapers; local
    newspapers; regional tourist board;
    leaflets/information packs; Dumfries and
    Galloway Tourist Board*

Environmental monitoring: *recycling*

GLENBARR ABBEY VISITORS CENTRE
(trust)
historic house; museum

Established: *1986*
Address: *Glenbarr Abbey, Glenbarr by Tarbert, Argyll*
Telephone: *(05832) 247*. Fax: *(05832) 255*
Access: *(road) A83*
Parking capacity: *(cars) 25 (coaches) 2*
Hours: *Easter to mid Oct – 10am to 6pm except Tues; open by arrangement in the Winter*
Admission (1992): *adults £2.00; children £1.00; OAP £1.50;*
No. visitors (1992): *2300 (est.)*

Facilities
Interpretation: *personal tour by A Macalister, 5th Laird of Glenbarr*
Schools: *maximum no. 25; no special support*
Catering: *1 snack bar/food stall*
Retailing: *postcards/inexpensive souvenirs; craftwork; books; clothes*
No. shops: *1*

Operations
Contacts: *A Macalister, 5th Laird of Glenbarr (Curator); Ms J Macalister (Curator)*
No. employees: *(high season) 2 full time; 1 part time*
Training: *P/T operations staff are trained in-house and day-to-day on job*
Languages spoken: *French; German; Italian*

Marketing
Annual event: *clan gathering of Macalisters, Macdonalds and McSporrans*
UK promotion: *local newspapers; regional tourist board; leaflets/information packs; STB, 1001 Things to See in Scotland*
Australia/USA promotion: *Macalister Society*

Environmental monitoring: *hazardous materials*

GLENGOULANDIE DEER PARK
(private partnership)
park/reserve; zoo/wildlife attraction

Established: *1966*
Address: *Glengoulandie, Foss, By Pitlochry, Perthshire, PH16 5NL*
Telephone: *(0887) 830261*
Access: *(road) M90/B846 (rail) Pitlochry*
Parking capacity: *(cars) 20 (coaches) 3*
Hours: *May to Sept – 9am to 5pm daily*
Admission (1992): *adults £0.95; children £0.65; cars £3.00*
No. visitors (1992): *7000 (est.)*

Facilities
Interpretation: *leaflets*
Children: *play area*
Schools: *maximum no. 60; no special support*
Catering: *1 picnic area*
Retailing: *postcards/inexpensive souvenirs; confectionery and ice cream; craftwork; clothes*
No. shops: *1*

Operations
Contact: *Mrs H McAdam (Secretary)*
No. employees: *(high season) 4 part time*

Marketing
UK promotion: *local newspapers; regional tourist board; leaflets/information packs*

Environmental monitoring: *recycling; water quality; hazardous materials*

GLOUCESTER CATHEDRAL
(charity under statute)
church

Established: *1089*
Address: *Chapter Office, College Green, Gloucester, GL1 2LR*
Telephone: *(0452) 528095*
Access: *(road) M5*
Season: *all year*
Hours: *Summer – 10am to 6pm; Winter – 10am to 5pm*
Admission (1992): *donations*
No. visitors (1992): *300 000 (est.)*

Facilities
Interpretation: *leaflets; information boards; tour guides; guide books*
Languages: *French; German; Spanish*
Children: *nappy changing*
Schools: *educational literature; lecture/talk*
Disabled: *easy access; disabled toilets; braille/sound posts; helpers; other audio facilities; leaflets; touch and hearing centre for visually handicapped*
Catering: *1 self-service cafeteria*
Retailing: *postcards/inexpensive souvenirs; craftwork; books; reproductions of famous artefacts*
No. shops: *2*

Operations
Contact: *Mr S Ward (Chapter Steward)*

Marketing
Annual event: *Three Choirs festival*

GOD'S HOUSE TOWER MUSEUM
(local authority run)
museum; museum of archaeology

Established: *1960*
Address: *Winkle St, Town Quay, Southampton*
Telephone: *(0703) 220007*
Access: *(road) M27 (rail) Southampton*
Season: *all year*
Hours: *Tues to Fri – 10am to 12 noon and 1pm to 5pm, Sat – 10am to 12 noon and 1pm to 4pm, Sun – 2pm to 5pm; closed all day Mon*
Admission (1992): *free; hire by arrangement*
No. visitors (1992): *14 000*

Facilities
Interpretation: *leaflets; information boards*
Schools: *maximum no. 40; school visits and workshops*
Retailing: *postcards/inexpensive souvenirs; books; reproductions of famous artefacts*
No. shops: *1*

Operations
Contacts: *Mr S Hardy (Southampton Heritage Manager); Mrs H Spillett (Research Officer)*
No. employees: *(high season) 2 full time (low season) 2 full time*
Training: *F/T operations staff are trained in-house and externally and on specific courses*
Languages spoken: *French; German; Italian; Spanish; Cantonese and Mandarin*

Marketing
Press office; market research
UK promotion: *local newspapers; regional tourist board*

Environmental monitoring: *energy consumption; precinct enhancement*

GOLDEN HILL FORT
(privately owned)
monument; museum

Established: *1986*
Address: *Hill Lane, Freshwater, Isle of Wight, PO40 9TF*
Telephone: *(0983) 753380*
Access: *(road) M3*
Parking capacity: *(cars) 100 (coaches) 12*
Season: *all year*
Hours: *10am to 5pm daily except Christmas day*

Admission (1992): *adults £1.10; children £0.60; OAP £0.60; student £0.60; group rates available*
No. visitors (1992): *32 000*

Facilities
Interpretation: *leaflets; audio tapes; tour guides; guide books*
Children: *play area*
Schools: *maximum no. 50; educational literature; audio/visual presentation; lecture/talk*
Disabled: *easy access; disabled toilets; powered transport*
Catering: *1 bar/public house*
Retailing: *postcards/inexpensive souvenirs; confectionery and ice cream; craftwork; stitchcraft geo-gems paintings*
No. shops: *More than 4*

Operations
Languages spoken: *Dutch*

Marketing
Affiliations: *English Heritage*
UK promotion: *national newspapers; radio; local newspapers; regional tourist board; other attractions; leaflets/information packs; ETB/BTA*

Environmental monitoring: *hazardous materials*

GOOSEDALE MODEL AVIATION CENTRE
(limited company)
museum; boating lake and area for large aviation models

Established: *1990*
Address: *Goosedale Farm; Moor Rd, Bestwood, Nottingham, NG6 8UJ*
Telephone: *(0602) 632175*
Access: *(road) M1/A611/B683 (rail) Nottingham*
Parking capacity: *(cars) 500 (coaches) 200*
Season: *all year*
Hours: *1 Apr to 30 Sept – 10am to 6pm daily (evenings by appointment); 1 Oct to 31 Mar – as above but closed Tues*
Admission (1992): *adults £2.50; children £1.20; OAP £1.20; student £1.20; unemployed and disabled £1.20; groups of children £1.00*
No. visitors (1992): *10 000 (est.)*

Facilities
Interpretation: *videos; leaflets; tour guides; guides by appointment*
Children: *nappy changing*
Schools: *maximum no. 100; educational literature; lecture/talk; demonstrations*
Disabled: *easy access; disabled toilets; helpers*
Catering: *1 picnic area*
Retailing: *postcards/inexpensive souvenirs; confectionery and ice cream; craftwork; books; model aeroplanes and equipment*
No. shops: *1*

Operations
Contacts: *Mr M Ward (Director); L Russell (Restaurant Manager); V Ward (Director)*
No. employees: *(high season) 8 full time; 8 part time (low season) 8 full time; 2 part time*
Training: *F/T operations staff, P/T operations staff and casual operations staff are trained in-house and day-to-day on job*

Marketing
Annual event: *European flying show*
UK promotion: *television; national newspapers; radio; local newspapers; regional tourist board; leaflets/information packs*
Europe promotion: *leaflets/brochures; modelling magazines*

Environmental monitoring: *recycling*

GORSE BLOSSOM RAILWAY AND WOODLAND PARK
(limited company)
theme park; miniature railway and woodland park

Established: *1984*
Address: *Bickington, Newton Abbot, Devon, TQ12 6JD*

Telephone: (0626) 821361
Access: (road) M5 A38 (rail) Newton Abbot
Parking capacity: (cars) 180 (coaches) 4
Hours: Easter to 1st Sun in Oct – 10am to 5pm
daily
Admission (1992): adults £3.50; children £2.50;
OAP £3.00;
No. visitors (1992): 45 382

Facilities
Interpretation: leaflets; information boards
Children: adventure playground; play area; nappy
changing
Schools: maximum no. 120; lecture/talk; steam
demonstrations
Disabled: easy access; disabled toilets
Catering: 3 picnic areas
Retailing: postcards/inexpensive souvenirs;
confectionery and ice cream; craftwork; books;
clothes; railway and nature related; local jams
and honey, etc.
No. shops: 1

Operations
Contacts: G Kichenside (Managing Director);
P Kichenside (Commercial Director)
No. employees (high season) 10 full time; 12 part
time (low season) 4 full time
Languages spoken: Norwegian

Marketing
Affiliations: 7 1/4 Gauge Railway Society;
Heywood Society; Association of Railway
Preservation Societies
Other: market research
UK promotion: television; national newspapers;
radio; local newspapers; regional tourist board;
other attractions; leaflets/information packs;
WCTB; local authority

Environmental monitoring: water quality;
chemical usage

GOSFORD FOREST PARK
(dept. of agriculture)
castle; park/reserve; zoo/wildlife attraction

Established: 1958
Address: 54 Gosford Rd, Markethill, County
Armagh, BT60 1UG
Telephone: (0861) 551277
Access: (road) M1/A28
Season: all year
Hours: open all year
Admission (1992): adults £0.80; children £0.40;
coach £15.00; car £1.50
No. visitors (1992): 40 000 (est.)

Facilities
Interpretation: leaflets; information boards; slides;
maps; tour guides; guide books
Schools: educational literature; lecture/talk
Disabled: disabled toilets; special signs
Catering: 1 picnic area

Operations
Contact: Mr P G Duffy (Forestry Officer)
No. employees: (high season) 8 full time;
1 part time (low season) 8 full time; 1 part
time
Training: F/T operations staff, F/T management,
P/T operations staff and P/T management are
trained externally and on specific courses using
demonstrations
Languages spoken: French; German

Marketing
Annual event: poultry fair
UK promotion: television; radio; local
newspapers; regional tourist board;
leaflets/information packs

Environmental monitoring: recycling; waste;
energy consumption; emissions

GOSFORD HOUSE
(private limited company and trust)
historic house; garden; gallery

Established: 1984
Address: Longniddry, East Lothian, EH32 0PX
Telephone: (08757) 201. Fax: (08757) 620
Access: (road) A198 (rail) Longniddry
Parking capacity: (cars) 25 (coaches) 5
Hours: June and July – Sat, Sun and Wed – 2pm
to 5pm
Admission (1992): adults £1.00; children £0.50;
OAP £0.75; groups by arrangement
No. visitors (1992): 1250

Facilities
Interpretation: leaflets
Schools: maximum no. 50; no special support

Operations
Contact: Mr R R Gledson (Factor)
No. employees: (high season) 3 full time

Marketing
Affiliations: HHA; East Lothian Tourist Board
UK promotion: regional tourist board;
leaflets/information packs

Environmental monitoring: conservation forest

GOSS AND CRESTED CHINA LTD
(limited company)
heritage centre; showroom for antique heraldic
china

Established: 1980
Address: 62 Murray Rd, Horndean, Waterlooville,
Hants, PO8 9JL
Telephone: (0705) 597440. Fax: (0705) 591975
Access: (road) A3M/A3 (rail) Petersfield/Havant
Season: all year
Hours: all year except BH – Mon to Sat – 8.30am
to 5.30pm, open some Sundays
Admission (1992): free
No. visitors (1992): 1000 (est.)

Facilities
Interpretation: leaflets; publications
Retailing: books; antique heraldic china; coffee
and tea available
No. shops: 1

Operations
Contacts: Mr N Pine (Managing Director
(Publications)); Miss C Owen (Manageress) Mrs
L Pine (Director (Porcelain))
No. employees: (high season) 5 full time;
1 part time (low season) 5 full time; 1 part
time
Training: F/T operations staff, F/T management,
P/T operations staff and P/T management are
trained in-house and day-to-day on job
Languages spoken: German

Marketing
Annual event: Goss and Crested China Club open
day
Other: PR company: Midas Public Relations, 109
Stephendale Rd, Fulham, London SW4
UK promotion: radio; local newspapers; leaflets/
information packs; ETB/BTA

Environmental monitoring: recycling

GRAHAM SUTHERLAND GALLERY
(National Museum of Wales)
museum; gallery

Established: 1976
Address: The Rhos, Haverfordwest, Dyfed,
SA62 4AS
Telephone: (0437) 751296. Fax: (0437) 751322
Access: (road) M4/A40 (rail) Haverfordwest
Hours: end Mar – End September, Tuesday to
Sunday and BH 10.30am to 12.30pm/1.30pm to
5pm; Oct for schools/colleges/groups
Admission (1992): adults £1.00; children £0.50;
OAP £0.75; student £0.75
No. visitors (1992): 20000

Facilities
Interpretation: videos; leaflets; information
boards; tour guides
Languages: Welsh
Schools: maximum no. 25; educational literature;
audio/visual presentation; lecture/talk;
workshops
Disabled: easy access; disabled toilets
Catering: 1 picnic area
Franchisees: end Mar – end Sept, Tues to Sun and
BH 10.30am to 12.30pm/1.30pm to 5pm; Oct
for schools/colleges/groups
Retailing: postcards/inexpensive souvenirs;
craftwork; books
No. shops: 2

Operations
Contact: Mrs S E Moss (Officer in Charge)
No. employees: (high season) 2 full time; 7 part
time (low season) 2 full time; 2 part time
Training: F/T operations staff, F/T management
and casual operations staff are trained in-house
and externally and on specific courses and
day-to-day on job using publications
Languages spoken: French

Marketing
Annual event(s): monthly lecture/concerts
Other: press office; market research
UK promotion: television; national newspapers;
local newspapers; regional tourist board; other
attractions; leaflets/information packs

GRAMPIAN TRANSPORT MUSEUM
(trust)
museum

Established: 1983
Address: Alford, Aberdeenshire, AB33 8AD
Telephone: (09755) 62292. Fax: 09755 62180
Access: (road) A944
Parking capacity: (cars) 200 (coaches) 7
Hours: April to Oct daily 10am to 5pm
Admission (1992): adults £2.30; children £0.80;
OAP £1.50
No. visitors (1992): 62 320

Facilities
Interpretation: videos; audio tapes; information
boards; guide books
Children: adventure playground
Schools: maximum no. 2; educational literature;
lecture/talk
Disabled: disabled toilets
Catering: 1 picnic area
Retailing: postcards/inexpensive souvenirs;
craftwork; books
No. shops: 1

Operations
Contact: Mike Ward (Curator)
No. employees: (high season) 3 full time; 4 part
time (low season) 1 full time; 1 part time
Training: F/T operations staff are trained in-house
and externally and on specific courses and
day-to-day on job
Languages spoken: French; Spanish; Welsh

Marketing
Annual event(s): various
Sponsor(s): various
Other: market research
UK promotion: national newspapers; radio; local
newspapers; regional tourist board; other
attractions; leaflets/information packs

GRANTHAM MUSEUM
(local authority run)
museum

Established: 1926
Address: St Peter's Hill, Grantham, Lincs, NG31
6PY
Telephone: (0476) 68783
Access: (road) A1 (rail) London–Grantham
Hours: closed Sun, Oct to Mar; Summer – 10am
to 5pm, Winter – 10am to 5pm.
Admission (1992): adults £0.40; children £0.20
No. visitors (1992): 8000 (est.)

Facilities
Interpretation: *leaflets; information boards; maps; guide books; signs*
Schools: *maximum no. 40; educational literature; special workshops*
Disabled: *easy access; helpers; special signs; leaflets; guide pamphlet*
Retailing: *postcards/inexpensive souvenirs; books; clothes*
No. shops: *1*

Operations
Contact: *L M Budreau-Ross (Curator)*
No. employees: (high season) *1 full time; 5 part time* (low season) *1 full time; 5 part time*
Training: *F/T management, P/T operations staff and casual operations staff are trained in-house and on specific courses*

Marketing
Sponsor(s): *Melton Mowbray Building Society*
Affiliations: *Museums Association*
Other: *PR Company: Lincolnshire County Council; press office; market research*
UK promotion: *radio; local newspapers; regional tourist board; leaflets/information packs; East Midlands, South Kesteven District Council publications; ETB/BTA*
USA promotion: *leaflets/brochures*

GRAVES ART GALLERY
(local authority run)
gallery

Established: *1934*
Address: *Surrey St, Sheffield, S1 1XZ*
Telephone: *(0742) 735158.* Fax: *(0742) 735994*
Access: (road) *M1*
Season: *all year*
Hours: *Mon to Sat – 10am to 6pm, BH Mon and Tues – 10am to 5pm, closed Christmas*
Admission (1992): *free*
No. visitors (1992): *150 000 (est.)*

Facilities
Interpretation: *leaflets*
Children: *nappy changing*
Schools: *maximum no. 25; educational literature; lecture/talk; materials trolley*
Disabled: *helpers; special signs; access to goods lift*
Catering: *1 licensed restaurant*
Retailing: *postcards/inexpensive souvenirs; books*
No. shops: *1*

Operations
Contacts: *Mr D Alston/Ms A Goodchild (Director of Arts); Ms S Young (Personnel)*
No. employees: (high season) *63 full time; 110 part time*
Training: *F/T operations staff, F/T management, P/T operations staff and P/T management are trained in-house and externally and on specific courses using videos and handbooks*
Languages spoken: *French*

Marketing
Annual event: *children's art exhibition*
Other: *market research*
UK promotion: *national newspapers; radio; local newspapers; regional tourist board; leaflets/information packs*

Environmental monitoring: *air quality*

GRAY ART GALLERY
(local authority run)
museum; gallery

Established: *1921*
Address: *Clarence Rd, Hartlepool, TS24 8BT*
Telephone: *(0429) 268916.* Fax: *(0429) 869625*
Access: (road) *A189*
Parking capacity: (cars) *20* (coaches) *3*
Season: *all year*
Hours: *Mon to Sat – 10am to 5.30pm, Sun – 2pm to 5pm*

Admission (1992): *free*
No. visitors (1992): *40 000*

Facilities
Interpretation: *videos; leaflets; information boards; maps; real artefacts*
Children: *nappy changing*
Schools: *maximum no. 30; as requested by school*
Disabled: *easy access; disabled toilets; helpers*
Retailing: *postcards/inexpensive souvenirs; books*
No. shops: *1*

Operations
Contact: *Mr F Savage Caldwell (Curator)*
No. employees: (high season) *8 full time; 5 part time* (low season) *8 full time; 5 part time*
Training: *F/T operations staff, F/T management, P/T operations staff and P/T management are trained in-house and externally and on specific courses and day-to-day on job*
Languages spoken: *French; Italian*

Marketing
Annual event(s): *programme of concerts, craft days and special events*
Other: *market research*
UK promotion: *radio; local newspapers; other attractions; leaflets/information packs*
Europe promotion: *leaflets/brochures*

GRAYTHWAITE HALL GARDENS
(trust)
garden

Address: *Graythwaite, Ulverston, Cumbria, LA12 8BA*
Telephone: *(05395) 31248.* Fax: *(05395) 30060*
Access: (road) *M6/A590*
Parking capacity: (cars) *50* (coaches) *5*
Hours: *Spring/early Summer – 10am to 6pm daily*
Admission (1992): *adults £2.00; OAP £2.00; student £2.00*
No. visitors (1992): *2000 (est.)*

Facilities
Interpretation: *leaflets*
Catering: *1 picnic area*

Operations
Contact: *Mr O Pearson (Estate Secretary)*
No. employees: (high season) *1 full time* (low season) *1 full time*
Languages spoken: *French; German; Russian; Polish*

Marketing
UK promotion: *regional tourist board; other attractions; leaflets/information packs*

Environmental monitoring: *recycling; energy consumption*

GREAT ORME TRAMWAY
(local authority run)
cable-hauled tramway

Established: *1902*
Address: *Grwp, Aberconwy, Maesdu, Llandudno*
Telephone: *(0492) 870870.* Fax: *(0492) 860821*
Access: (road) *A55* (rail) *Llandudno*
Hours: *Easter to Oct – Mon to Sun – 10am to 6pm*
Admission (1992): *adults £3.00; child and family tickets*
No. visitors (1992): *140 000*

Facilities
Interpretation: *information boards; guide books*
Schools: *no special support*
Disabled: *easy access; disabled toilets*
Catering: *1 picnic area*
Retailing: *postcards/inexpensive souvenirs; confectionery and ice cream; craftwork; books; clothes; mugs, pens*
No. shops: *1*

Operations
Contacts: *Dereck Roberts (Transport Manager); Rosemary Sutton (Marketing Officer)*

No. employees: (high season) *12 full time; 1 part time* (low season) *3 full time*
Training: *F/T operations staff and P/T operations staff are trained in-house and day-to-day on job*

Marketing
Press office; market research
UK promotion: *local newspapers; regional tourist board; other attractions; leaflets/information packs; Bedroom Browser Attractions Flyer; Welsh Tourist Board*

Environmental monitoring: *chemical usage*

GREAT WESTERN RAILWAY MUSEUM
(local authority run)
museum

Established: *1962*
Address: *Faringdon Rd, Swindon, SN1 5BJ*
Telephone: *(0793) 493189.* Fax: *(0793) 541685*
Access: (road) *M4/A420/A419/A3102* (rail) *Swindon*
Season: *all year*
Hours: *all year – Mon to Sat – 10am to 5pm, Sun – 2pm to 5pm*
Admission (1992): *adults £1.80; children £0.90; OAP £0.90; student £0.90; under 5s free*
No. visitors (1992): *37 790*

Facilities
Interpretation: *videos; leaflets; audio tapes; information boards; maps*
Schools: *maximum no. 100; educational literature; lecture/talk*
Disabled: *handling/touch table*
Retailing: *postcards/inexpensive souvenirs; confectionery and ice cream; books; clothes; reproductions of famous artefacts*
No. shops: *1*

Operations
Contacts: *T Bryan (Museum Keeper); Personnel Department (Thamesdown BC); L Crennell (Administrative Officer); B McDavitt (Marketing and Promotions Manager)*
No. employees: (high season) *5 full time; 3 part time* (low season) *5 full time*
Training: *F/T operations staff and F/T management are trained in-house and externally and on specific courses and day-to-day on job*
Languages spoken: *Welsh*

Marketing
Annual event(s): *various*
Affiliations *MA*
Other: *market research*
UK promotion: *radio; local newspapers; regional tourist board; leaflets/information packs; ETB/BTA*

GREENWICH BOROUGH MUSEUM
(local authority run)
museum

Established: *1919*
Address: *232 Plumstead High St, London, SE18 1JT*
Telephone: *(081) 855 3240*
Access: (road) *A102M* (rail) *Plumstead*
Season: *all year*
Hours: *Tues, Thur, Fri and Sat – 10am to 1pm and 2pm to 5pm; Mon – 2pm to 7pm*
Admission (1992): *free*
No. visitors (1992): *25 000*

Facilities
Interpretation: *videos; leaflets; information boards*
Children: *nappy changing*
Schools: *maximum no. 50; educational literature; audio/visual presentation; lecture/talk; workshops and object handling*
Disabled: *helpers*
Retailing: *postcards/inexpensive souvenirs; books*
No. shops: *1*

Operations
Contacts: *B Gillow (Curator); B Burford (Education Service/Assistant Curator)*

Training: *F/T operations staff, F/T management,
P/T operations staff and P/T management are
trained in-house and externally and on specific
courses and day-to-day on job*

Marketing
Sponsor(s): *local firms*
Affiliations: *MA, AMSSEE*
Other: *press office; market research*
UK promotion: *radio; local newspapers; regional
tourist board; other attractions; leaflets/
information packs; ETB/BTA*

Environmental monitoring: *recycling; waste;
energy consumption*

GREYFRIARS, THE
(trust)
historic house; garden

Established: *1966*
Address: *Friar St, Worcester, WR1 2LZ*
Telephone: *(0905) 23571*
Access: (road) *M5*
Hours: *Apr to Oct – Wed and Thur – 2pm to
5pm*
Admission (1992): *adults £1.60; children £0.80;
family £4.25*
No. visitors (1992): *3500 (est.)*

Facilities
Interpretation: *leaflets; tour guides; guide books*

Operations
Contact: *V Hemingway (Administrator)*
No. employees: (high season) *25 part time*
Training: *P/T operations staff are trained
in-house and on specific courses and day-to-day
on job using handbooks*

Marketing
Affiliation: *NT*
Other: *press office; market research*
UK promotion: *national newspapers; local
newspapers; regional tourist board; other
attractions; leaflets/information packs; ETB/
BTA*

GREYFRIARS KIRK
(Society of Friends)
church

Established: *1955*
Address: *Greyfriars Place, (off Candlemaker
Row), Edinburgh, EH1 2QQ*
Telephone: *(031) 225 1900*
Access: (road) *M8/A1* (rail) *Edinburgh Waverley*
Hours: *Easter to end Sept – 10am to 4pm
weekdays and 10am to 2pm Sat*
Admission (1992): *free*
No. visitors (1992): *7000*

Facilities
Interpretation: *leaflets; tour guides; guide books*
Languages: *Japanese; Dutch; French; German;
Italian; Spanish; Gaelic*
Schools: *maximum no. 50; educational literature;
lecture/talk; special leaflets*
Disabled: *easy access; disabled toilets; other audio
facilities*
Retailing: *postcards/inexpensive souvenirs;
reproductions of famous artefacts*
No. shops: *1*

Operations
Contacts: *Miss J Laidlan (Co-ordinator); Mrs P
Mathieson (Honorary Secretary, Society of
Friends); Miss I Stewart (Stock Controller); Mrs
C McWilliam (Publications Convener)*
No. employees: (high season) *40 part time*
Training: *P/T operations staff are trained
in-house and on specific courses*
Languages spoken: *French*

Marketing
Affiliations: *Old Town Renewal Trust; Cockburn
Association*
Other: *market research*

UK promotion: *regional tourist board; other
attractions; leaflets/information packs; STB*

Environmental monitoring: *heat, light, humidity*

GRIZEDALE FOREST PARK
(government department)
visitor centre/forest recreation

Established: *1987*
Address: *Grizedale, Ambleside, Cumbria, LA22
0QJ*
Telephone: *(0229) 860373.* Fax: *(0229) 860273*
Access: (road) *M6/A590*
Parking capacity: (cars) *120*
Hours: *Apr to Oct – Mon to Sun – 10am to 5pm;
Nov to Mar – Sat and Sun – 10am to 5pm;
closed Jan*
No. visitors (1992): *180 000 (est.)*

Facilities
Interpretation: *leaflets; information boards; maps;
guide books*
Children: *play area; nappy changing*
Schools: *maximum no. 30; educational literature;
lecture/talk*
Disabled: *easy access; disabled toilets*
Catering: *1 picnic area*
Franchisees: *Apr to Oct – Mon to Sun – 10am to
5pm*
Retailing: *postcards/inexpensive souvenirs;
craftwork; books; clothes*
No. shops: *1*

Operations
Contact: *Paul Burke (Head Recreation Ranger)*
No. employees: (high season) *2 full time; 4 part
time* (low season) *2 full time; 4 part time*
Training: *F/T operations staff and P/T operations
staff are trained in-house and on specific
courses*
Languages spoken: *French; German; Gaelic*

Marketing
Affiliation: *Cumbria Tourist Board*
Other: *press office; market research*
UK promotion: *regional tourist board; leaflets/
information packs; STB*

GROAM HOUSE MUSEUM TRUST
(trust)
heritage centre; museum

Established: *1989*
Address: *High Street, Rosemarkie, Ross-shire,
IV10 8UF*
Telephone: *0381 20961*
Access: (road) *A9/A832* (rail) *Inverness, Dingwall*
Parking capacity: (cars) *100* (coaches) *20*
Season: *all year*
Hours: *1 May to 1 Oct – Mon to Sat – 11am to
5pm, Sun 2.30pm to 4.30pm; every winter
weekend*
Admission (1992): *adults £1.50; OAP £0.75;*
No. visitors (1992): *5665*

Facilities
Interpretation: *videos; leaflets; audio tapes;
information boards; maps; tour guides; guide
books; annually published academic lectures*
Languages: *Japanese; French; German; Italian*
Schools: *maximum no. 28; educational literature;
audio/visual presentation; lecture/talk;
hands-on exhibits*
Disabled: *easy access; guided tours and hands-on
exhibits for blind*
Retailing: *postcards/inexpensive souvenirs;
confectionery and ice cream; craftwork; books;
clothes; reproductions of famous artefacts; scale
models of pictish stones; tapes*
No. shops: *1*

Operations
Contacts: *Elizabeth Marshall (Honorary Curator);
Susan Seright (Assistant to Curator)*
No. employees (high season) *1 full time; 1 part
time* (low season) *1 part time*

Training: *F/T operations staff and P/T operations
staff are trained externally and on specific
courses and day-to-day on job using videos*

Marketing
Annual event(s): *academic lecture, childrens'
week, harp concerts, 3 other talks*
Sponsor: *Scottish Arts Council*
Affiliations: *Scottish Museums Council; Highlands
and Islands Museum Council; Ross and Cromarty
Museum*
Other: *market research*
UK promotion: *radio; local newspapers; regional
tourist board; other attractions;
leaflets/information packs; ETB/BTA; Ross and
Cromarty Tourist Board*

Environmental monitoring: *waste; water quality;
hazardous materials; chemical usage*

GROSVENOR MUSEUM
(local authority run)
museum

Established: *1885*
Address: *27 Grosvenor Street, Chester, CH1 2DD*
Telephone: *(0244) 321616*
Access: (road) *A420*
Season: *all year*
Hours: *all year – Mon to Sat – 10.30am to 5pm,
Sun – 2pm to 5pm; closed Christmas, New
Year's Day and Good Friday*
Admission (1992): *free*
No. visitors (1992): *100 000 (est.)*

Facilities
Interpretation: *videos; leaflets; information
boards; maps; tour guides; guide books*
Schools: *maximum no. 50; educational literature;
audio/visual presentation; lecture/talk*
Disabled: *helpers*
Retailing: *postcards/inexpensive souvenirs;
craftwork; books; clothes; reproductions of
famous artefacts*
No. shops: *1*

Operations
Contacts: *M Lindop/S Matthews (Support
Officer/Curatorial Officer); S Rogers
(Administrative Officer)*
No. employees: (high season) *37 full time; 11 part
time* (low season) *37 full time; 11 part time*
Training: *F/T operations staff and F/T management
are trained in-house and externally and on
specific courses using videos*
Languages spoken: *French; German*

Marketing
Affiliations: *Museums Association*
Other: *market research*
UK Promotion: *local newspapers; regional tourist
board; other attractions; leaflets/information
packs; NWTB*

GUILDFORD CATHEDRAL
(dean and chapter)
church

Established: *1961*
Address: *Stag Hill, Guildford, Surrey, GU2 5UP*
Telephone: *(0483) 65287.* Fax: *(0483) 303350*
Access: (road) *M25/A3* (rail) *Guildford*
Parking capacity: (cars) *200* (coaches) *20*
Season: *all year*
Hours: *all year – 8.30am to 5.30pm daily*
Admission (1992): *free*
No. visitors (1992): *80 000 (est.)*

Facilities
Interpretation: *videos; leaflets; information
boards; tour guides; guide books*
Languages: *Dutch; French; German; Italian*
Children: *creche*

Schools: *maximum no. 4; educational literature; educational tour*
Disabled: *easy access; disabled toilets; helpers; other audio facilities; loop system*
Catering: *1 picnic area*
Franchisees: *all year – 8.30am to 5.30pm daily*
Retailing: *postcards/inexpensive souvenirs; craftwork; books; religious artefacts, tapes, cassettes, CDs*
No. shops: *2*

Operations
Contacts: *J W A Fleming (Cathedral Administrator); F Shipton/J Lawson (Giftshop/Bookshop Managers)*
No. employees: (high season) *150 part time* (low season) *150 part time*
Languages spoken: *French; German; Italian; Spanish; Greek*

Marketing
Annual event(s): *Concerts, recitals, special services*
Sponsor(s): *BBC, Vienna Boys' Choir, GPCS*
Affiliations: *Association of English Cathedrals, Pilgrims Association*
UK promotion: *radio; local newspapers; regional tourist board; other attractions; leaflets/information packs; Surrey Group Visitors' Guide, 100s of Places to Visit in SE; SEETB*
Europe promotion: *Valley of Wey Attraction Group*

Environmental Monitoring: *recycling; chemical usage*

GUILDHALL BEVERLEY, THE
(local authority run)
historic house; heritage centre

Established: *1700*
Address: *Register Sq, Beverley, Humberside, HU17 9AU*
Telephone: *(0482) 867430.* Fax: *(0482) 883913*
Access: (road) *M62/A1079/A63/A164* (rail) *Beverley*
Season: *all year*
Hours: *Mon to Fri – 9am to 5.30pm; Sat – 9am to 4.30pm; Sun – 11am to 3pm*
Admission (1992): *free*
No. visitors (1992): *73 000 (est.)*

Facilities
Interpretation: *leaflets; information boards; slides; maps; tour guides; guide books*
Languages: *Japanese; Dutch; French; German; Italian*
Schools: *maximum no. 50; educational literature; lecture/talk*
Disabled: *easy access; helpers; leaflets*

Operations
Contact: *Mr R Grange (Tourism Promotion Manager)*
No. employees: (high season) *1 full time; 3 part time* (low season) *1 full time; 3 part time*
Training: *F/T operations staff and P/T operations staff are trained in-house and externally and on specific courses and day-to-day on job using videos and talks/discussions*
Languages spoken: *French; German*

Marketing
Annual event(s): *music festival and folk festival*
Other: *press office; market research*
UK promotion: *television; national newspapers; radio; local newspapers; regional tourist board; other attractions; leaflets/information packs; ETB/BTA*
Europe/USA promotion: *leaflets/brochures; travel agents' brochures*

Environmental monitoring: *recycling; waste; hazardous materials*

GUINNESS WORLD OF RECORDS EXHIBITION
(limited company)
exhibition

Established: *1984*
Address: *The Trocadero, Piccadilly, London, W1V 7FD*
Telephone: *(071) 439 7381.* Fax: *(071) 494 1266*
Access: (rail) *Piccadilly Circus*
Season: *all year*
Hours: *10am to 10pm daily, closed Christmas Day*
Admission (1992): *adults £5.00; children £3.20; OAP £3.95 student £3.95*
No. visitors (1992): *500 000 (est.)*

Facilities
Interpretation: *videos; leaflets; audio tapes; information boards; slides; maps; guide books; personnel; computers*
Languages: *French; German; Italian; Spanish*
Children: *nappy changing*
Schools: *maximum no. 250*
Disabled: *easy access; disabled toilets; helpers; other audio facilities*
Catering: *1 snack bar/food stall*
Retailing: *postcards/inexpensive souvenirs; confectionery and ice cream; craftwork; clothes*
No. shops: *More than 4*

Operations
Contacts: *Mr H Gledhill (General Manager); Mr R Stamford (General Manager); Ms E Bunurrti (Sales and Public Relations)*
No. employees: (high season) *33 full time; 8 part time* (low season) *33 full time; 4 part time*
Training: *F/T operations staff and P/T operations staff are trained in-house and on specific courses*

Marketing
Annual event: *beat the record*
Affiliations: *LTB*
Other: *press office; market research*
UK promotion: *radio; local newspapers; regional tourist board; leaflets/information packs; ETB/BTA; London Underground*
Europe/Asia/Australia promotion: British Tourist Authority

GULLIVER'S KINGDOM
(private company)
theme park

Established: *1977*
Address: *Temple Walk, Matlock, Bath, Derbyshire, DE4 3PG*
Telephone: *(0629) 58054.* Fax: *(0629) 57710*
Access: (road) *M1/M6/A6* (rail) *Matlock/Derby*
Parking capacity: (cars) *400* (coaches) *30*
Hours: *Easter to October – Summer – 10.30am to 5.30pm*
Admission (1992): *adults £4.25; children £4.25; OAP £3.75; under 3 feet free*

Facilities
Interpretation: *leaflets; information boards; signs*
Children: *adventure playground; play area; nappy changing*
Schools: *no special support*
Disabled: *disabled toilets*
Catering: *1 picnic area*
Retailing: *postcards/inexpensive souvenirs; confectionery and ice cream; craftwork; clothes; personalised goods*
No. shops: *More than 4*

Operations
Training: *F/T management, P/T management and casual management are trained in-house and on specific courses and day-to-day on job using videos and handbooks and lectures*
Languages spoken: *French; German*

Marketing
Other: *press office; market research*
UK promotion: *television; local newspapers; other attractions; leaflets/information packs*

GURKHA MUSEUM
(limited company)
museum

Established: *1990*
Address: *Peninsula Barracks, Romsey Rd, Winchester, Hants, SO23 8TS*
Telephone: *(0962) 842832.* Fax: *(0962) 880880*
Season: *all year*
Hours: *10am to 5pm, Tues to Sat and BH*
Admission (1992): *adults £1.50; children £0.75; OAP £0.75; student £0.75; group prices available*
No. visitors (1992): *15 000 (est.)*

Facilities
Interpretation: *leaflets; audio tapes; information boards; tour guides; dioramas and tableaux*
Languages: *Nepali*
Children: *nappy changing*
Schools: *maximum no. 40; educational literature; lecture/talk*
Disabled: *easy access; disabled toilets; helpers; leaflets*
Retailing: *postcards/inexpensive souvenirs; confectionery and ice cream; craftwork; books; clothes; reproductions of famous artefacts; Nepalese jewellery*
No. shops: *1*

Operations
Contacts: *J Lamond (Curator); Mrs F Haitto (Shop Manager)*

Marketing
Other: *market research*
UK promotion: *national newspapers; local newspapers; regional tourist board; other attractions; leaflets/information packs; ETB/BTA*
Europe/Asia/Australia/USA/South Africa New Zealand promotion: *leaflets/brochures; travel agents' brochures*

H

HAGGS CASTLE
(local authority run)
museum; museum specifically for children

Established: *1976*
Address: *St Andrews Drive, Glasgow, G41 4RB*
Telephone: *(041) 427 2725*
Season: *all year*
Hours: *Mon to Sat – 10am to 5pm, Sun – 11am to 5pm*
Admission (1992): *free*
No. visitors (1992): *37 518*

Facilities
Languages: *Urdu*
Disabled: *helpers*
Retailing: *postcards/inexpensive souvenirs; books; posters*
No. shops: *1*

Operations
Languages spoken: *French; Spanish; Hindi; Polish and more*

Marketing
Other: *press office; market research*
UK promotion: *leaflets/information packs*

Environmental monitoring: *waste; energy consumption; hazardous materials; transport; emissions*

HALIFAX PIECE HALL
(local authority run)
monument; museum; gallery

Established: *1976*
Address: *Halifax, W Yorks, HX1 1RE*
Telephone: *(0422) 358087.* Fax: *(0422) 349310*
Access: (road) *M62/A646/A58*
Parking capacity: (cars) *600*
Season: *all year*
Hours: *Piece Hall – Mon to Sat – 8.30am to 6.30pm, Sun – 10am to 6.15pm; Museum and Art Gallery – Tues to Sun – 10am to 5pm*
Admission (1992): *adults £1.00; children £0.50; OAP £0.50; student £0.50; above charges are for industrial museum, piece hall and gallery are free*
No. visitors (1992): *1 000 000 (est.)*

Facilities
Interpretation: *leaflets; information boards; tour guides; guide books; guides by arrangement*
Languages: *Dutch; French; German*
Children: *play area; nappy changing*
Schools: *educational literature; to suit requirements*
Disabled: *disabled toilets; lift*
Catering: *1 picnic area*
Franchisees: *Piece Hall – Mon to Sat – 8.30am to 6.30pm, Sun – 10am to 6.15pm*
Retailing: *postcards/inexpensive souvenirs; confectionery and ice cream; craftwork; books; clothes; reproductions of famous artefacts; antiques and stamps*
No. shops: *More than 4*

Operations
Contacts: *Ms P Eastwood (Administration Officer); Mr P Todd/Mr S Underhay (Supervisors); Mr M Hull/Ms P Eastwood (Registrar/Administrator); Mr C Aldred (Events Officer)*
No. employees: (high season) *17 full time; 18 part time* (low season) *17 full time; 18 part time*

Training: *F/T operations staff, F/T management, P/T operations staff and casual operations staff are trained in-house and externally and on specific courses and day-to-day on job*

Marketing
Annual event(s): *events, fun days, exhibitions, concerts and plays*
Sponsor(s): *BBC Radio Leeds and local companies*
Affiliations: *MA, Yorks and Humbs Tourist Board*
Other: *market research*
UK promotion: *local newspapers; regional tourist board; other attractions; leaflets/information packs; ETB/BTA*
Council Tourism Section promotion: *Council Tourism Section*

HAMERTON WILDLIFE CENTRE
(privately owned)
zoo/wildlife attraction

Established: *1990*
Address: *Hamerton, Huntingdon, Cambs*
Telephone: *(08323) 362.* Fax: *(08323) 677*
Access: (road) *A1/A14*
Parking capacity: (cars) *500* (coaches) *10*
Season: *all year*
Hours: *Summer – 10.30am to 6pm, Winter – 10.30am to 4pm (changes with the clocks) except Christmas Day*
Admission (1992): *adults £3.50; children £2.00; OAP £3.00; under 5s free*
No. visitors (1992): *35 000*

Facilities
Interpretation: *information boards; maps; guide books*
Children: *play area; nappy changing*
Schools: *maximum no. 400; educational literature*
Disabled: *easy access; disabled toilets*
Catering: *2 picnic areas*
Retailing: *postcards/inexpensive souvenirs; confectionery and ice cream; books; wildlife related*
No. shops: *1*

Operations
No. employees: (high season) *4 full time* (low season) *3 full time*
Languages spoken: *French; German*

Marketing
Annual event(s): *various*
Affiliation: *Federation of Zoological gardens of Great Britain and Ireland*
UK promotion: *radio; local newspapers; regional tourist board; other attractions; leaflets/information packs; East Anglia guide and AA 2000 Days Out*

Environmental monitoring: *recycling; waste; energy consumption; chemical usage*

HAMILTON DISTRICT MUSEUM
(local authority run)
historic house; museum

Established: *1967*
Address: *129 Muir St, Hamilton, ML3 6BJ*
Telephone: *(0698) 283981*
Access: (road) *M74* (rail) *Hamilton*
Parking capacity: (cars) *20* (coaches) *2*
Season: *all year*
Hours: *all Year – Mon to Sat – 10am to 5pm – closed 12 noon to 1pm, Wed and Sat*
Admission (1992): *free*

No. visitors (1992): *22 593*

Facilities
Interpretation: *leaflets; information boards; slides; maps; guide books*
Schools: *maximum no. 35*
Disabled: *helpers*
Retailing: *postcards/inexpensive souvenirs; books*
No. shops: *1*

Operations
Contacts: *T F Mackenzie (Museum Curator); J J R Brown (Deputy Curator and Education Officer)*
No. employees: (high season) *8 full time; 5 part time* (low season) *7 full time; 5 part time*

Marketing
Annual event(s): *concert and activities*
Sponsor: *SAC*
Affiliations: *MA, SMC, SMF, CVTB, SMAS, SAMS*
Other: *market research*
UK promotion: *radio; local newspapers; regional tourist board; other attractions; leaflets/information packs; AA, etc*

HAMMERWOOD PARK
(private)
historic house

Established: *1983*
Address: *Hammerwood Park, Nr East Grinstead, Sussex, RH19 3QE*
Telephone: *(0342) 850594.* Fax: *(0342) 850864*
Access: (road) *A264*
Parking capacity: (cars) *60*
Season: *all year*
Hours: *Easter to Sept – Wed, Sat and BH – 2pm to 5.30pm*
Admission (1992): *adults £3.50; children £1.50; OAP £3.50; student £3.50*
No. visitors (1992): *6000 (est.)*

Facilities
Interpretation: *videos; tour guides; guide books*
Languages: *French; Italian*
Schools: *maximum no. 50; educational tour; lecture/talk*
Disabled: *easy access; disabled toilets*
Retailing: *postcards/inexpensive souvenirs*
No. shops: *1*

Operations
Contacts: *Pinmegar Family*
No. employees: (high season) *10 full time; 4 part time* (low season) *4 full time; 2 part time*
Training: *F/T operations staff, F/T management, P/T operations staff, P/T management, casual operations staff and casual management are trained in-house and day-to-day on job*
Languages spoken: *French; Italian*

Marketing
Annual event(s): *concerts*
Affiliations: *IBI, HHA, etc.*
UK promotion: *leaflets/information packs*

Environmental monitoring: *Environment of collection*

HAMPTON COURT PALACE
(government)
historic royal palace

Established: *1840*
Address: *East Molesley, Surrey, KT8 9AV*
Telephone: *(081) 977 8441.* Fax: *(081) 977 8318*

Access: (road) M3/M25 (rail) *Hampton Court*
Parking capacity: (cars) *200*
Season: *all year*
Hours: *Summer – Mon – 10.15am to 6pm, Tues to Sun – 9.30am to 6pm; Winter – Mon – 10.15am to 4.30pm, Tues to Sun – 9.30am to 4.30pm*
Admission (1992): *adults £5.90; children £3.90; OAP £4.50; student £4.50*
No. visitors (1992): *502 000*

Facilities
Interpretation: *audio tapes; maps; tour guides; guide books; personnel; models*
Languages: *Japanese; French; German; Italian; Spanish*
Children: *nappy changing*
Schools: *maximum no. 100; no special support*
Disabled: *easy access; disabled toilets; free entry for helpers; wheelchairs*
Catering: *2 self-service cafeterias*
Franchisees: *Summer – Mon – 10.15am to 6pm, Tues to Sun – 9.30am to 6pm*
Retailing: *postcards/inexpensive souvenirs; craftwork; books; clothes; reproductions of famous artefacts*
No. shops: *More than 4*

Operations
Contacts: *Mr C MacDonald (Palace Director); Mr M Bridger (Personnel); Mr M McVay (Retail Trading); Ms L Shead (Marketing)*
No. employees: *(high season) 250 full time (low season) 180 full time*
Training: *F/T operations staff, F/T management, P/T operations staff, P/T management and casual operations staff are trained externally and on specific courses*
Languages spoken: *French; Italian*

Marketing
Other: *PR Company: Anne Scott Association; press office; market research*
UK promotion: *television; radio; regional tourist board; other attractions; leaflets/information packs*

HANBURY HALL (NATIONAL TRUST)
(limited company and trust)
historic house

Established: *1978*
Address: *Droitwich, Worcs, WR9 7EA*
Telephone: *(0527) 821214. Fax: (0527) 821251*
Access: (road) *M5*
Parking capacity: (cars) *100* (coaches) *5*
Hours: *Apr to Oct – Sat, Sun and Mon – 2pm to 6pm*
Admission (1992): *adults £2.80; children £1.40; OAP £2.80; student £2.80; family ticket £7.70*
No. visitors (1992): *23 000 (est.)*

Facilities
Interpretation: *leaflets; tour guides; guide books; room stewards*
Languages: *Japanese; French; German*
Children: *nappy changing*
Schools: *maximum no. 25; educational literature; lecture/talk*
Disabled: *easy access; disabled toilets; braille/sound posts; guide book; wheelchairs*
Catering: *1 picnic area*
Retailing: *postcards/inexpensive souvenirs; confectionery and ice cream; craftwork; books; clothes*
No. shops: *1*

Operations
Contact: *J Blades (Administrator)*
No. employees: *(high season) 3 full time; 42 part time (low season) 3 full time; 22 part time*
Training: *F/T operations staff, F/T management, P/T operations staff and casual operations staff are trained in-house and externally and on specific courses and day-to-day on job using handbooks*
Languages spoken: *French; German; Spanish*

Marketing
Annual event(s): *craft fairs, rallies, outdoor plays, fete, etc.*
Affiliations: *through the NT*

Other: *press office; market research*
UK promotion: *national newspapers; radio; local newspapers; regional tourist board; other attractions; leaflets/information packs*
NT promotion: *leaflets/brochures; NT*

Environmental monitoring: *energy consumption*

HANCOCK MUSEUM
(local authority and university)
museum

Established: *1884*
Address: *Barras Bridge, Newcastle Upon Tyne, NE2 4PT*
Telephone: *(091) 222 7418. Fax: (091) 222 6753*
Access: (road) *A1* (rail) *Metro – Haymarket Nole*
Parking capacity: (cars) *24*
Season: *all year*
Hours: *Mon to Sat – 10am to 5pm and Sun – 2pm to 5pm (except Christmas Day, Boxing Day, New Year's Day and Good Friday)*
Admission (1992): *adults £1.50; children £0.75; OAP £0.75; group rates £1.00 adult and £0.50p child*
No. visitors (1992): *100 000 (est.)*

Facilities
Interpretation: *leaflets; information boards; guide books*
Schools: *educational literature; events and activities*
Disabled: *easy access; helpers*
Catering: *1 self-service cafeteria*
Retailing: *postcards/inexpensive souvenirs; confectionery and ice cream; books; clothes; toys and natural history items*
No. shops: *1*

Operations
Contacts: *Mr A Coles (Principal Keeper); Mr P Cartman (Administrative and Personnel Officer); Ms V Faulkner (Commercial Officer); M Twelves (Principal Marketing/Commercial)*
No. employees: *(high season) 8 full time; 7 part time*
Training: *F/T operations staff, F/T management and P/T operations staff are trained externally and on specific courses using videos and handbooks*

Marketing
Annual event(s): *events and activities for families and children*
Affiliation: *Natural History Society*
Other: *press office*
UK promotion: *television; radio; local newspapers; regional tourist board; leaflets/information packs; Northumbria Tourist Board*

Environmental monitoring: *recycling; waste; water quality; hazardous materials; chemical usage*

HARDYS WESSEX EXHIBITION
(privately owned)
exhibition

Established: *1990*
Address: *56 Icen Way, Dorchester, Dorset*
Telephone: *(0305) 250525*
Access: (road) *A35* (rail) *Dorchester*
Hours: *Apr to Oct – 10am to 3pm daily*
Admission (1992): *adults £2.30; children £1.15; OAP £1.15; student £1.15*
No. visitors (1992): *5000 (est.)*

Facilities
Interpretation: *leaflets; information boards*
Schools: *maximum no. 50*
Retailing: *postcards/inexpensive souvenirs; craftwork; books*
No. shops: *1*

Operations
Contact: *M Amey (owner)*
No. employees: *(high season) 2 part time*
Languages spoken: *French; German*

Marketing
Annual event: *Father Christmas visit*
Other: *market research*
UK promotion: *radio; local newspapers; regional tourist board; other attractions; leaflets/information packs; ETB/BTA*
Europe promotion: *leaflets/brochures*

Environmental monitoring: *recycling; hazardous materials; chemical usage*

HARLOW CARR BOTANICAL GARDENS
(limited company)
garden

Established: *1951*
Address: *Crag Lane, Harrogate, HG3 1QB*
Telephone: *(0423) 565418*
Access: (road) *B6162*
Parking capacity: (cars) *250* (coaches) *12*
Season: *all year*
Hours: *daily – 9.30am to 6pm or dusk if earlier*
Admission (1992): *adults £3.00; OAP £2.40; children free*
No. visitors (1992): *106 000*

Facilities
Interpretation: *leaflets; audio tapes; information boards; maps; tour guides; guide books*
Languages: *Japanese*
Children: *play area; nappy changing*
Schools: *lecture/talk*
Disabled: *easy access; disabled toilets; other audio facilities; powered transport*
Catering: *1 picnic area*
Franchisees: *daily – 9.30am to 6pm or dusk if earlier*
Retailing: *postcards/inexpensive souvenirs; confectionery and ice cream; craftwork; books; plants; gifts*
No. shops: *1*

Operations
Contact: *Mr B Nuttall (Administrator)*
No. employees: *(high season) 18 full time (low season) 18 full time*
Training: *N/A*

Marketing
Other: *press office*
UK promotion: *local newspapers; regional tourist board; other attractions; leaflets/information packs*

HARRIS MUSEUM AND ART GALLERY
(local authority run)
museum; gallery

Established: *1893*
Address: *Market Square, Preston, Lancs, PR1 2PP*
Telephone: *(0772) 58248. Fax: (0772) 266195*
Access: (road) *M62/A6/A59* (rail) *Preston*
Season: *all year*
Hours: *all year – Mon to Sat – 10am to 5pm*
Admission (1992): *free*
No. visitors (1992): *150 000 (est.)*

Facilities
Interpretation: *leaflets; audio tapes; information boards; tour guides*
Schools: *maximum no. 60*
Disabled: *easy access; disabled toilets; other audio facilities*
Catering: *1 waiter/waitress served*
Retailing: *postcards/inexpensive souvenirs; craftwork; books; reproductions of famous artefacts*
No. shops: *1*

Operations
Contacts: *A Walker (Museum and Art Officer); E Anderson (Senior Exhibitions Officer); J Regan (Development Officer)*
No. employees: *(high season) 20 full time (low season) 20 full time*
Training: *F/T operations staff and F/T management are trained in-house and externally and on specific courses and day-to-day on job*
Languages spoken: *French; German*

Marketing
Annual event(s): *official openings and exhibitions*
Sponsor(s): *various*
Affiliations: *various*
Market research
UK promotion: *other attractions; leaflets/ information packs*

HARROLD ODELL COUNTRY PARK
(local authority run)
park/reserve

Established: *1982*
Address: *Harrold, Beds.* Postal Address: *Leisure Services Dept, County Hall, Bedford, MK42 9AP*
Telephone: *(0234) 228330* Fax: *(0234) 228921*
Access: (road) *M1/A428*
Parking capacity: (cars) *50* (coaches) *3*
Season: *all year*
Hours: *Oct to Mar – Sat to Sun and BH – 1pm to 4pm, Apr to Sept – Tues to Sat – 1pm to 4.30pm, Sun – 1pm to 6pm*
Admission (1992): *free*
No. visitors (1992): *17 500*

Facilities
Interpretation: *leaflets; audio tapes; information boards; slides*
Schools: *maximum no. 25; educational literature; audio/visual presentation; educational tour; lecture/talk; conservation projects*
Disabled: *easy access; disabled toilets*
Catering: *1 picnic area*
Franchises: *Oct to Mar – Sat to Sun and BH – 1pm to 4pm*
Retailing: *postcards/inexpensive souvenirs; craftwork; books*
No. shops: *1*

Operations
Contacts: *D Hillyard (Chief Ranger); H McMahon (Marketing and Publicity Officer)*
No. employees: (high season) *1 full time; 2 part time* (low season) *1 full time; 2 part time*
Training: *F/T operations staff, F/T management and P/T operations staff are trained in-house and externally and on specific courses and day-to-day on job*
Languages spoken: *French*

Marketing
Other: *press office; market research*
UK promotion: *leaflets/information packs; ETB/BTA*

Environmental monitoring: *recycling; waste; hazardous materials; chemical usage; emissions*

HARROW MUSEUM AND HERITAGE CENTRE
(trust)
historic house; museum

Established: *1986*
Address: *Headstone Manor, Pinner View, Harrow, HA2 6PX*
Telephone: *(081) 861 2626.* Fax: *(081) 863 6407*
Access: (road) *M40/M1* (rail) *Harrow and Wealdstone*
Parking capacity: (cars) *50* (coaches) *1*
Season: *all year*
Hours: *Wed to Fri – 12.30pm to 5pm or dusk; Sat, Sun and BH – 10.30am to 5pm; closed Christmas week*
Admission (1992): *free*
No. visitors (1992): *100 000*

Facilities
Interpretation: *leaflets; information boards; voluntary staff*
Children: *play area*
Schools: *maximum no. 90; educational literature; lecture/talk*
Disabled: *easy access; disabled toilets*
Catering: *1 picnic area*
Retailing: *postcards/inexpensive souvenirs; confectionery and ice cream; books; models of historic buildings; childrens activities*
No. shops: *1*

Operations
Contacts: *Ms H Smith (Curator); Mrs J Strode (Harrow Arts Council)*
No. employees: (high season) *2 full time; 1 part time*
Training: *F/T operations staff and casual operations staff are trained externally and on specific courses using AVs, OHPs*

Marketing
Annual event: *May Day at the Manor*
Affiliations: *AIM, Area Museums Service, SE England*
Other: *market research*
UK promotion: *local newspapers; other attractions; leaflets/information packs; museums and galleries*

Environmental monitoring: *recycling; waste; water quality; energy consumption; hazardous materials; chemical usage; transport; emissions*

HARTLEPOOL MARITIME MUSEUM
(local authority run)
museum

Established: *1974*
Address: *Northgate, Hartlepool, Cleveland*
Telephone: *(0429) 272814.* Fax: *(0429) 869265*
Access: (road) *A189*
Season: *all year*
Hours: *Mon to Sat – 10am to 5pm*
Admission (1992): *free*
No. visitors (1992): *10 000*

Facilities
Interpretation: *information boards; real artefacts*
Schools: *maximum no. 30; as required by schools*
Disabled: *access difficult*
Retailing: *postcards/inexpensive souvenirs; books*
No. shops: *1*

Operations
Contact: *Mr F Savage Caldwell (Curator)*
No. employees: (high season) *1 full time; 2 part time*
Training: *F/T operations staff, F/T management, P/T operations staff and P/T management are trained in-house and externally and on specific courses and day-to-day on job*
Languages spoken: *French; German; Italian*

Marketing
Other: *market research*
UK promotion: *radio; local newspapers; regional tourist board; other attractions; leaflets/information packs; ETB/BTA*
Europe promotion: *leaflets/brochures*

HARVEYS WINE MUSEUM
(Harveys of Bristol Ltd)
museum; historic building

Established: *1965*
Address: *12 Denmark St, Bristol, BS1 5DQ*
Telephone: *(0272) 277661.* Fax: *(0272) 253378*
Access: (road) *M32/A4* (rail) *Bristol Temple Meads*
Season: *all year*
Hours: *weekdays – 10am to 1pm and 2pm to 5pm; weekends – 2pm to 5pm*
Admission (1992): *adults £2.50; children £1.50; OAP £1.50; student £1.50; from £3.50 for guided tours with tutored tasting*
No. visitors (1992): *20 000 (est.)*

Facilities
Interpretation: *videos; leaflets; information boards; maps*
Languages: *French; Spanish*
Schools: *maximum no. 30; educational literature; audio/visual presentation; lecture/talk*
Disabled: *access difficult*
Catering: *1 waiter/waitress served*
Retailing: *postcards/inexpensive souvenirs; confectionery and ice cream; craftwork; reproduction posters and glasses*
No. shops: *2*

Operations
Contacts: *Mr R Compton (General Manager); Ms M Pigott (Curator); Ms T Spencer (Sales Executive); Ms J Hawkes (Publicity and promotions Executive)*
No. employees: (high season) *3 full time; 12 part time* (low season) *3 full time; 12 part time*
Training: *F/T operations staff, P/T operations staff and casual operations staff are trained in-house and externally and on specific courses and day-to-day on job*
Languages spoken: *French; German; Russian and Polish*

Marketing
Annual event(s): *various*
Affiliations: *British Tourist Attractions Association, WC Tourist Board*
Other: *press office; market research*
UK promotion: *local newspapers; regional tourist board; other attractions; leaflets/information packs; ETB/BTA*
Europe/USA promotion: *leaflets/brochures; travel agents' brochures; British Tourist Authority*

HARWICH REDOUBT
(charity)
monument; museum; fort

Established: *1970*
Address: *Main Rd, Harwich, Essex*
Telephone: *(0255) 503429.* Fax: *(0255) 240404*
Access: (road) *A120* (rail) *Harwich*
Season: *all year*
Hours: *Sun – 10am to 12 noon and 2pm to 5pm throughout the year; Sat – 2pm to 5pm in June and Sept; daily – 2pm to 5pm in July and Aug*
Admission (1992): *adults £1.00; OAP £1.00; student £1.00; accompanied children free*
No. visitors (1992): *10 000 (est.)*

Facilities
Interpretation: *leaflets; audio tapes; slides; tour guides; guide books*
Languages: *Japanese; Dutch; French; German; Italian; Spanish; Danish*
Schools: *educational literature; audio/visual presentation; lecture/talk*
Disabled: *access difficult*
Catering: *1 snack bar/food stall*
Retailing: *postcards/inexpensive souvenirs; confectionery and ice cream; guide books*
No. shops: *1*

Operations
Contact: *Mr A Rutter (Secretary)*
No. employees: (high season) *1 part time*
Training: *P/T operations staff are trained in-house and day-to-day on job using videos*
Languages spoken: *French; German; Spanish*

Marketing
Annual event: *Redoubt Fete*
Affiliations: *Civic Trust*
UK promotion: *regional tourist board; Historic Houses, Castles and Gardens; ETB/BTA*

Environmental monitoring: *recycling; waste; energy consumption*

HASELEY MANOR
(privately owned)
historic house; park/reserve; garden; craft centre and sweet factory

Established: *1977*
Address: *Arreton, Nr Newport, Isle of Wight, PO30 3AN*
Telephone: *(09838) 65420.* Fax: *(09838) 67547*
Parking capacity: (cars) *150* (coaches) *6*
Hours: *Easter to 31 Oct – 10am to 5.30pm daily; Winter by appointment only*
Admission (1992): *adults £3.00; children £2.50; OAP £2.60*
No. visitors (1992): *100 000*

Facilities
Interpretation: *videos; leaflets; audio tapes; information boards; guide books*
Children: *adventure playground; nappy changing*
Schools: *educational literature; audio/visual presentation; lecture/talk*
Disabled: *disabled toilets; special signs; no charge for single wheelchair visitors*
Catering: *1 picnic area*
Franchisees: *Easter to 31 Oct – 10am to 5.30pm daily; Winter by appointment only*
Retailing: *postcards/inexpensive souvenirs; confectionery and ice cream; craftwork; books; clothes*
No. shops: *4*

Operations
Contacts: *Miss S Bishop (Sales/Reception); R Young (Principal)*
No. employees: *(high season) 3 full time; 36 part time (low season) 2 full time*
Training: *F/T operations staff, P/T operations staff and casual operations staff are trained in-house and day-to-day on job*
Languages spoken: *French; German; Dutch*

Marketing
PR Company: *Brian Marriot Advertising Newport, I of W; market research*
UK promotion: *regional tourist board; other attractions; leaflets/information packs*

Environmental monitoring: *recycling; waste; water quality; energy consumption; hazardous materials; chemical usage; transport; emissions*

HASTINGS MUSEUM AND ART GALLERY
(local authority run)
museum

Established: *1892*
Address: *Johns Place, Cambridge Road, Hastings, E Sussex, TN34 1ET*
Telephone: *(0424) 721202*
Access: *(road) A21*
Parking capacity: *(cars) 15*
Season: *all year*
Hours: *all year – Mon to Sat – 10am to 5pm, Sun – 3pm to 5pm*
Admission (1992): *free*
No. visitors (1992): *28 000*

Facilities
Interpretation: *leaflets; information boards; guide books*
Languages: *Dutch; French; German*
Schools: *maximum no. 60; educational literature*
Catering: *1 picnic area*
Retailing: *postcards/inexpensive souvenirs; books*
No. shops: *1*

Operations
Contacts: *V Williams (Curator)*
No. employees: *(high season) 8 full time; 1 part time (low season) 7 full time; 1 part time*
Training: *F/T operations staff, F/T management, P/T operations staff and P/T management are trained externally and on specific courses*

Marketing
Annual event(s): *concerts*
Affiliation: *Museums and Galleries Commission*
Other: *market research*
UK promotion: *national newspapers; radio; local newspapers; regional tourist board; other attractions; leaflets/information packs*
Europe promotion: *leaflets/brochures*

HASTINGS SEA LIFE CENTRES
(limited company)
zoo/wildlife attraction

Established: *1990*
Address: *Rock-A-Nore Rd, Hastings, E Sussex, TN34 3DW*
Telephone: *(0424) 718776. Fax: (0424) 718757*
Access: *(road) A27 (rail) Hastings*
Parking capacity: *(cars) 600 (coaches) 40*
Season: *all year*

Hours: *10am to 6pm daily except Christmas Day and open later in Summer*
Admission (1992): *adults £3.95; children £2.75; OAP £3.45; student £2.10; disabled £2.10*
No. visitors (1992): *235 000 (est.)*

Facilities
Interpretation: *videos; leaflets; audio tapes; information boards; tour guides; guide books*
Languages: *Dutch; French*
Children: *adventure playground; nappy changing*
Schools: *maximum no. 400; educational literature; audio/visual presentation; lecture/talk; touch pools and projects*
Disabled: *easy access; disabled toilets*
Catering: *1 picnic area*
Retailing: *postcards/inexpensive souvenirs; confectionery and ice cream; craftwork; books; clothes; reproductions of famous artefacts; marine related goods; chocolate and china*
No. shops: *1*

Operations
Contacts: *Mr N Wild (Manager); Ms L Gabriels (Shop Supervisor); Ms C Billen (Marketing Officer (Central office))*
No. employees: *(high season) 12 full time; 25 part time (low season) 12 full time; 4 part time*
Training: *F/T operations staff, F/T management and P/T operations staff are trained in-house and externally and on specific courses and day-to-day on job*
Languages spoken: *French; German; Spanish; Dutch*

Marketing
Affiliation: *Regional Tourist Board*
Other: *press office; market research*
UK promotion: *television; national newspapers; radio; local newspapers; regional tourist board; other attractions; leaflets/information packs; ETB/BTA; local tourist guides*

Environmental monitoring: *Council policy*

HATCH COURT
(not known)
historic house; park/reserve; garden; museum

Established: *1975*
Address: *Hatch Beauchamp, Taunton, Somerset, TA3 6AA*
Telephone: *(0823) 480120. Fax: (0823) 480058*
Access: *(road) M5/A358 (rail) Taunton*
Parking capacity: *(cars) 150 (coaches) 10*
Hours: *June to Sept – house and garden – Thur – 2.30pm to 5.30pm; garden – Fri – 2.30pm to 5.30pm*
Admission (1992): *adults £2.50; children £1.00; under 12s free*
No. visitors (1992): *2000 (est.)*

Facilities
Interpretation: *tour guides*
Schools: *maximum no. 50; lecture/talk*
Catering: *1 picnic area*
Retailing: *postcards/inexpensive souvenirs; confectionery and ice cream*
No. shops: *none*

Operations
Contacts: *Dr and Mrs R Odgers (owners)*
No. employees: *(high season) 1 full time; 3 part time*
Training: *N/A*

Marketing
Affiliation: *HHA*
UK promotion: *regional tourist board; other attractions; leaflets/information packs*

Environmental monitoring: *recycling; waste; water quality; energy consumption; hazardous materials; chemical usage; transport; emissions*

HATCHLANDS PARK
(trust)
historic house; garden

Established: *1982*
Address: *East Clandon, Guildford, Surrey, GU4 7RT*
Telephone: *(0483) 222787*
Access: *(road) A246*
Parking capacity: *(cars) 200*
Hours: *1 Apr to 18 Oct – Tues, Wed, Thur, Sun and BH Mon – 2pm to 5.30pm; also open Sat during Aug*
Admission (1992): *adults £3.20; children £1.60; OAP £3.20; student £3.20*
No. visitors (1992): *26 297*

Facilities
Interpretation: *leaflets; information boards; guide books*
Children: *nappy changing*
Schools: *maximum no. 20; lecture/talk; talk on request*
Disabled: *disabled toilets; special signs*
Catering: *1 waiter/waitress served*
Franchisees: *1 Apr to 18 Oct – Tues, Wed, Thur, Sun and BH Mon*
Retailing: *postcards/inexpensive souvenirs; craftwork; books; clothes; china*
No. shops: *1*

Operations
Contact: *Mr D Asquith (Administrator)*
No. employees: *(high season) 12 full time (low season) 5 full time*
Training: *F/T operations staff and F/T management are trained in-house and externally and on specific courses*

Marketing
Annual event(s): *music recitals and concerts*
Sponsor(s): *various*
Affiliation: *National Trust*
Other: *press office*
UK promotion: *National Trust*

Environmental monitoring: *recycling; energy consumption; chemical usage*

HATFIELD FOREST
(charity)
park/reserve

Established: *1924*
Address: *No. 1 Takeley Hill Cottages, Takeley, Bishops Stortford, Herts, CM22 6NE*
Telephone: *(0279) 870678*
Access: *(road) M11/A120 (rail) Bishops Stortford*
Parking capacity: *(cars) 1000 (coaches) 3*
Season: *all year*
Hours: *Easter to Oct – 10am to 5pm daily*
Admission (1992): *cars £2.20*
No. visitors (1992): *200 000 (est.)*

Facilities
Interpretation: *leaflets; information boards; maps; guide books; weekend information centre*
Schools: *maximum no. 120; educational literature; lecture/talk*
Disabled: *disabled toilets*
Catering: *1 snack bar/food stall*

Operations
Contact: *J Wisenfeld (Head Warden)*
No. employees: *(high season) 4 full time; 20 part time (low season) 4 full time; 10 part time*
Training: *F/T operations staff, F/T management, P/T operations staff and casual operations staff are trained in-house and externally and on specific courses and day-to-day on job using videos and handbooks*
Languages spoken: *French*

Marketing
Annual event: *children's fun day*
Other: *press office; market research*
UK promotion: *television; national newspapers; radio; local newspapers; regional tourist board; other attractions; leaflets/information packs; ETB/BTA*

Environmental monitoring: *chemical usage*

HATFIELD HOUSE
(privately owned)
historic house; park/reserve; garden

Established: *1947*
Address: *Hatfield, Herts, AL9 5NQ*
Telephone: *(0707) 262823.* Fax: *(0707) 275719*
Access: (road) *M25/A1* (rail) *Hatfield*
Hours: *Mar to Oct – Tues to Sat – 12 noon to 4pm, Sun – 1.30pm to 5pm; park and gardens open daily*
Admission (1992): *adults £4.50; children £3.00; OAP £3.70; group rates*
No. visitors (1992): *167 771*

Facilities
Interpretation: *information boards; tour guides; guide books*
Languages: *Japanese; French; German; Italian; Spanish*
Children: *adventure playground; nappy changing*
Schools: *educational literature; educational tour; tailored guided tours*
Disabled: *easy access; disabled toilets; lift to first floor*
Catering: *1 self-service cafeteria*
Franchisees: *Mar to Oct – Tues to Sat – 12 noon to 4pm, Sun – 1.30pm to 5pm; park and gardens open daily*
Retailing: *postcards/inexpensive souvenirs; craftwork; books; reproductions of famous artefacts; variety of gifts, preserves, etc.*
No. shops: *3*

Operations
Contacts: *Col D G McCord (Curator); M O'Lone (Estate Agent); E Smith (Shop Manageress);*
Languages spoken: *French*

Marketing
Annual event(s): *various*
Affiliation: *East Anglia and London Tourist Board*
Other: *PR Company: Judith Patten Public Relations, Neville House, 55 Eden Street, Kingston Upon Thames, Surrey, KT1 1BW.; press office; market research*
UK promotion: *radio; local newspapers; regional tourist board; other attractions; leaflets/ information packs; Tourist Board publications; ETB/BTA; national magazines, mailing list, etc.*
Europe/USA promotion: *leaflets/brochures; British Tourist Authority*

Environmental monitoring: *recycling; waste; water quality; energy consumption; hazardous materials; chemical usage; transport; emissions; environmental audit*

HAVANT MUSEUM
(local authority run)
museum

Established: *1978*
Address: *East St, Havant, Hants, PO9 1BS*
Telephone: *(0705) 451155*
Access: (road) *A27* (rail) *Havant*
Season: *all year*
Hours: *Tues to Sat – 10am to 5pm all year*
Admission (1992): *free*
No. visitors (1992): *16 600*

Facilities
Interpretation: *videos; leaflets; information boards*
Schools: *maximum no. 35; lecture/talk*
Retailing: *postcards/inexpensive souvenirs; books; reproductions of famous artefacts; videos*
No. shops: *1*

Operations
Contact: *Dr C Palmer (Curator)*
No. employees: (high season) *3 full time; 1 part time* (low season) *3 full time; 1 part time*
Languages spoken: *French; German; Italian; Spanish; Japanese*

Marketing
Affiliation: *MA*
Other: *press office; market research*
UK promotion: *local newspapers; leaflets/ information packs*

HAVERFORDWEST CASTLE MUSEUM AND ART GALLERY
(local authority run)
castle; museum; gallery

Established: *1967*
Address: *The Castle, Haverfordwest, Pembrokeshire, SA61 2EF*
Telephone: *(0437) 763708*
Access: (road) *A40*
Parking capacity: (cars) *30* (coaches) *3*
Season: *all year*
Hours: *Mon to Sat – 10am to 4.30pm, closed Sun, Christmas Day, New Year's Day and Good Friday*
Admission (1992): *adults £0.50; OAP £0.25; student £0.25; unemployed £0.25, children free*
No. visitors (1992): *10 000 (est.)*

Facilities
Interpretation: *leaflets; information boards; guide books*
Languages: *Welsh*
Schools: *maximum no. 30; educational literature; lecture/talk*
Catering: *1 picnic area*
Retailing: *postcards/inexpensive souvenirs; books*
No. shops: *1*

Operations
Contacts: *Mrs T J Morris (Museums Officer); Personnel Department (County Hall, Camarthen); Mr P Simmonds (Senior Museums Officer)*
No. employees: (high season) *3 full time; 2 part time* (low season) *3 full time; 2 part time*
Training: *F/T operations staff and F/T management are trained in-house and day-to-day on job*

Marketing
Annual event(s): *exhibition openings*
Sponsor(s): *various*
Affiliations: *Museums Association*
Other: *market research*
UK promotion: *local newspapers; regional tourist board; leaflets/information packs*

HEALE GARDENS AND PLANT CENTRE
(private partnership)
historic house; garden; plant centre

Established: *1984*
Address: *Heale House, Woodford, Salisbury, Wilts., SP4 6NT*
Telephone: *(0722) 73504*
Access: (road) *A345/A360* (rail) *Salisbury*
Parking capacity: (cars) *80* (coaches) *6*
Season: *all year*
Hours: *all year – 10am to 7pm daily*
Admission (1992): *adults £2.00; OAP £2.00; student £2.00*
No. visitors (1992): *13 000*

Facilities
Interpretation: *guide books*
Disabled: *easy access; special signs*
Catering: *1 picnic area*
Retailing: *postcards/inexpensive souvenirs; confectionery and ice cream; craftwork; books; clothes; garden gifts and tools*
No. shops: *1*

Operations
Contact: *M Taylor (Manageress)*
No. employees: (high season) *1 full time; 2 part time* (low season) *1 full time; 2 part time*

Marketing
Annual event(s): *garden seminars*
Affiliations: *HHA*

UK promotion: *local newspapers; regional tourist board; other attractions; leaflets/information packs*

Environmental monitoring: *hazardous materials; chemical usage; emissions*

HEAVEN FARM
(private)
museum; zoo/wildlife attraction; nature trail

Established: *1986*
Address: *Heaven Farm, Danehill, Uckfield, E Sussex, TN22 3RG*
Telephone: *(0825) 790226*
Access: (road) *A275*
Parking capacity: (cars) *100* (coaches) *4*
Season: *all year*
Admission (1992): *adults £1.80; children £0.80; OAP £1.00*
No. visitors (1992): *20 000 (est.)*

Facilities
Interpretation: *leaflets; information boards; slides; maps; tour guides; guide books*
Languages: *German*
Children: *nappy changing*
Schools: *maximum no. 60; educational literature; educational tour; lecture/talk*
Disabled: *easy access; disabled toilets; leaflets; guide book*
Catering: *1 picnic area*
Retailing: *postcards/inexpensive souvenirs; confectionery and ice cream; craftwork; books; reproductions of famous artefacts*
No. shops: *1*

Operations
Contact: *J W Butler (Managing Director)*
No. employees: (high season) *7 part time* (low season) *1 part time*

Marketing
Annual event: *vintage farming*
Sponsor: *SEVAC*
UK promotion: *radio; local newspapers; regional tourist board; other attractions; leaflets/ information packs; ETB/BTA*

HEBDEN CRYPT
(limited company)
house of legends and horrors

Established: *1990*
Address: *38 Hanging Royd Lane, Hebden Bridge, W Yorks, HX7 7DD*
Telephone: *(0422) 845690*
Access: (road) *M62* (rail) *Hebden Bridge*
Season: *all year*
Hours: *Tues to Sun – 10am to 5pm (Jan to Mar – 11am to 3pm)*
Admission (1992): *adults £2.20; children £1.50; OAP £1.50; student £1.50*
No. visitors (1992): *30 000 (est.)*

Facilities
Interpretation: *leaflets; information boards; personnel*
Schools: *maximum no. 30; no special support*
Catering: *1 snack bar/food stall*
Retailing: *postcards/inexpensive souvenirs; confectionery and ice cream; books; clothes; skulls, posters; crystals, etc*
No. shops: *1*

Operations
Contact: *W Gricks (Director)*
No. employees: (high season) *3 full time* (low season) *1 full time; 2 part time*

Marketing
UK promotion: *local newspapers; regional tourist board; leaflets/information packs; ETB/BTA*

HELMSHORE TEXTILE MUSEUMS
(local authority run)
museum

Established: 1968
Address: Holcombe Road, Helmshore,
  Rossendale, Lancs, BB4 4NP
Telephone: (0706) 226459
Access: (road) M66/M65/A56 (rail) East
  Lancashire
Parking capacity: (cars) 45 (coaches) 3
Hours: Apr to June and Oct – Mon to Fri – 2pm
  to 5pm, Sun – 11am to 5pm; July to
  Sept – Mon to Fri – 12 noon to 5pm, Sat – 2pm
  to 5pm, Sun 11am to 5pm
Admission (1992): adults £1.50; children £0.60;
  OAP £1.50; student £0.60; family £3.70
No. visitors (1992): 25 000 (est.)

Facilities
Interpretation: videos; leaflets; information
  boards; attendants
Schools: maximum no. 100; educational literature;
  audio/visual presentation; educational tour;
  lecture/talk
Disabled: easy access; disabled toilets
Catering: 1 picnic area
Retailing: postcards/inexpensive souvenirs;
  confectionery and ice cream; books
No. shops: 1

Operations
No. employees: (high season) 8 full time; 10 part
  time (low season) 8 full time; 5 part time
Training: P/T operations staff and casual
  operations staff are trained in-house and on
  specific courses

Marketing
Annual event(s): various
Affiliation: MA
Other: press office
UK promotion: local newspapers; regional tourist
  board; other attractions; leaflets/information
  packs

HERB FARM AND SAXON MAZE, THE
(private company)
garden; herb garden and maze

Established: 1986
Address: Peppard Rd, Sonning Common,
  Reading, Berks, RG4 9NJ
Telephone: (0734) 724220
Access: (road) M4/B481 (rail) Reading
Parking capacity: (cars) 100 (coaches) 10
Season: all year
Hours: Tues to Sun – 10am to 5pm
Admission (1992): adults £0.50; children £0.25;
  OAP £0.25; charge for maze only
No. visitors (1992): 30 000 (est.)

Facilities
Schools: maximum no. 60; lecture/talk; must
  book
Catering: 1 snack bar/food stall
Retailing: postcards/inexpensive souvenirs;
  confectionery and ice cream; craftwork; books;
  herb plants and products
No. shops: 1

Operations
Contacts: R Scott (owner)
No. employees: (high season) 2 full time; 4 part
  time (low season) 2 full time; 1 part time
Training: P/T operations staff and casual
  operations staff are trained in-house and
  day-to-day on job using videos and handbooks
Languages spoken: French; German

Marketing
Annual event: country fayre
Affiliations: HTA Tourist Board, Beautiful
  Berkshire
Other: market research
UK promotion: local newspapers; regional tourist
  board; leaflets/information packs

Environmental monitoring: transport; emissions

HEREFORD CATHEDRAL
(body corporate unlimited)
museum; church

Address: 5 College Cloisters, Cathedral Close,
  Hereford, HR1 2NG
Telephone: (0432) 359880. Fax: (0432) 352952.
Access: (road) M5/A49 (rail) Hereford
Season: all year
Hours: Summer – 10am to 4.15pm;
  Winter – 10.30am to 3.15pm
Admission (1992): charges for Mappa Mundi
  exhibition and chained library
No. visitors (1992): 75 000

Facilities
Interpretation: leaflets; audio tapes; information
  boards; slides; maps; tour guides; guide books
Languages: Japanese; Dutch; French; German;
  Italian; Spanish
Schools: maximum no. 100; educational literature;
  audio/visual presentation; lecture/talk
Disabled: braille/sound posts; helpers; other audio
  facilities; leaflets; guide book
Catering: 3 picnic areas
Retailing: postcards/inexpensive souvenirs;
  confectionery and ice cream; craftwork; books;
  clothes; reproductions of famous artefacts;
  Mappa Mundi goods; cards, pottery and
  jewellery
No. shops: 1

Operations
Contacts: Miss M Martin (Shop Manager); Mr D
  Harding (Cathedral Steward)
No. employees: (high season) 20 full time; 20 part
  time (low season) 20 full time; 10 part time
Training: F/T management are trained in-house
  and day-to-day on job using photocopied
  handouts

Marketing
Annual event(s): orchestral/choral concerts,
  recitals, exhibitions, Mappa Mundi day
Other: PR Company: Association for the
  promotion of Herefordshire; press office;
  market research
UK promotion: radio; local newspapers; regional
  tourist board; other attractions;
  leaflets/information packs
Europe promotion: leaflets/brochures

HEREFORDSHIRE WATERWORKS MUSEUM
(trust)
museum; working museum displaying Broomy
  Hill engines

Established: 1975
Address: Lower Pumping Station, Broomy Hill,
  Hereford
Telephone: (0432) 273635
Access: (road) M50/A49 (rail) Hereford
Parking capacity: (cars) 20 (coaches) 2
Hours: Easter to Aug – Mon to Sun – 2pm to 5pm
Admission (1992): adults £1.50; children £0.75;
  OAP £0.75
No. visitors (1992): 1500

Facilities
Interpretation: leaflets; tour guides; guide books
Schools: maximum no. 70; educational literature;
  lecture/talk
Disabled: easy access; helpers
Catering: 1 picnic area
Retailing: postcards/inexpensive souvenirs; books;
  refreshments
No. shops: 1

Operations
Contacts: R J Benson (Honorary Secretary); R E
  Morgan (Honorary Treasurer)
Languages spoken: French; Welsh

Marketing
Affiliations: MA, Association of Independent
  Museums, Association for promotion of
  Herefordshire
Other: market research
UK promotion: radio; local newspapers; regional
  tourist board; other attractions; leaflets/
  information packs; visitor's Handbook to
  Herefordshire

Europe promotion: leaflets/brochures

HERITAGE FARM PARK
(private)
historic house; heritage centre; park/reserve;
  garden; museum; zoo/wildlife attraction; open
  farm

Established: 1990
Address: Leslie Hill, Ballymoney, Co. Antrim
Telephone: (02656) 66803/63109
Access: (road) A26 (rail) Ballymoney
Parking capacity: (cars) 100 (coaches) 8
Hours: Easter to Apr, Sept and BH – 2pm
  to 6pm; June – Sat, Sun and BH – 2pm to 6pm;
  July, Aug – Mon to Fri – 11am to 6pm,
  Sun – 2pm to 6pm; other times by arrangement
Admission (1992): adults £1.90; children £1.30;
  OAP £1.30; student £1.00; groups £1.30
No. visitors (1992): 11 100

Facilities
Interpretation: videos; leaflets; information
  boards; guide books
Languages: French
Children: adventure playground; play area
Schools: maximum no. 150; educational literature;
  lecture/talk
Catering: 1 picnic area
Retailing: postcards/inexpensive souvenirs;
  confectionery and ice cream; craftwork;
  books
No. shops: 1

Operations
Contacts: John Leslie (Manager); James Leslie
  (Proprietor)
No. employees: (high season) 1 full time; 4 part
  time
Training: F/T operations staff and P/T operations
  staff are trained in-house and day-to-day on job
Languages spoken: German

Marketing
Annual event: Threshing Day
Other: market research
UK promotion: local newspapers; regional tourist
  board; other attractions; leaflets/information
  packs; ETB/BTA
USA promotion: leaflets/brochures; travel agents'
  brochures; British Tourist Authority

Environmental monitoring: waste; hazardous
materials

HERITAGE MOTOR CENTRE
(trust)
park/reserve; museum; gallery; support and
  operation of motoring events

Established: 1993
Address: British Motor Industry Heritage Trust,
  Banbury Rd, Gaydon, Warwick, CV35 0BJ
Telephone: (0926) 641188. Fax: (0926) 641555
Access: (road) M40/B4100
Parking capacity: (cars) 400 (coaches) 36
Season: all year
Hours: 10am to 5.30pm daily Mar to Nov; closed
  Christmas Day and Boxing Day
Admission (1992): adults £5.00; children £3.00;
  OAP £3.00; family ticket £12.00
No. visitors (1992): 300 000 (est.)

Facilities
Interpretation: videos; leaflets; audio tapes;
  information boards; slides; tour guides; guide
  books
Children: adventure playground; play area; nappy
  changing; creche
Schools: educational literature; lecture/talk;
  education officer
Disabled: easy access; disabled toilets; helpers;
  special provision by prior arrangement
Catering: 1 picnic area
Franchisees: 10am to 5.30pm daily, Mar to Nov
Retailing: postcards/inexpensive souvenirs; books;
  clothes; models, diecast and kit form
No. shops: 1

Operations

Contacts: *Mr P Mitchell (Managing Director);
Mr F Turner (Operations Manager); Mr R Shah
(Finance Manager); Mr P Wall (Marketing
Manager)*

No. employees: (high season) *45 full time; 20 part
time* (low season) *45 full time; 5 part time*

Training: *F/T operations staff, F/T management,
P/T operations staff and P/T management and
casual operations staff are trained in-house
and externally and on specific courses and
day-to-day on job*

Languages spoken: *French*

Marketing

Other: *PR Company: under discussion; press
office; market research*

UK promotion: *regional tourist board;
leaflets/information packs; ETB/BTA*

HERON CORN MILL AND MUSEUM OF PAPERMAKING

(trust)
museum; working water-driven corn mill

Established: *1975*

Address: *c/o Henry Cooke Makin, Waterhouse
Mills, Beetham, Milnthorpe, Cumbria LA7 7AR*

Telephone: *(05395) 63363*. Fax: *(05395) 63869*

Access: (road) *M6/A6* (rail) *Lancaster/Carnforth*

Parking capacity: (cars) *40* (coaches) *4*

Hours: *Apr to Sept – Tues to Sun – 11am to 5pm*

Admission (1992): *adults £1.25; children £0.80;
OAP £0.80; group discounts*

No. visitors (1992): *5015*

Facilities

Interpretation: *leaflets; information boards; maps;
tour guides; guide books; actual machinery*

Languages: *Japanese; Dutch; French; German;
Italian; Spanish*

Schools: *educational literature; lecture/talk;
papermaking demonstration*

Disabled: *assistance for wheelchairs*

Catering: *1 picnic area*

Retailing: *postcards/inexpensive souvenirs;
confectionery and ice cream; books; cereal
paper products*

No. shops: *1*

Operations

Contact: *N T Stobbs (Administrator)*

No. employees: (high season) *3 part time* (low
season) *1 part time*

Languages spoken: *French; German; Danish*

Marketing

Annual event(s): *National Mills Day*

Affiliations: *Association of Independent Museums,
SPAB*

UK promotion: *local newspapers; regional tourist
board; other attractions; leaflets/information
packs*

Environmental monitoring: *waste; water quality;
energy consumption; hazardous materials;
emissions*

HEVER CASTLE

(limited company)
historic house; castle; garden

Established: *1963*

Address: *Hever, Edenbridge, Kent, TN8 7NG*

Telephone: *(0732) 865224*. Fax: *(0732) 866796*

Access: (road) *M25/A21* (rail) *Edenbridge*

Hours: *Mar to Nov – 12 noon to 6pm daily
(gardens open at 11am)*

Admission (1992): *adults £5.00; children £2.50;
OAP £4.50; family ticket £12.50*

No. visitors (1992): *300 000 (est.)*

Facilities

Interpretation: *leaflets; information boards; tour
guides; guide books*

Languages: *Dutch; French; German; Italian;
Spanish*

Children: *adventure playground; nappy changing*

Schools: *educational literature; educational tour*

Disabled: *easy access; disabled toilets; transport
for entry into castle*

Catering: *1 bar/public house*

Retailing: *postcards/inexpensive souvenirs;
confectionery and ice cream; books;
reproductions of famous artefacts; china,
toiletries, stationery*

No. shops: *3*

Operations

Contacts: *R A Pullin (Managing Director); D A
James (Financial Administrator); C Prout (Sales
and Publicity Officer)*

No. employees: (high season) *37 full time; 111
part time* (low season) *37 full time; 36 part time*

Training: *F/T operations staff, F/T management,
P/T operations staff and casual operations staff
are trained in-house and externally and on
specific courses and day-to-day on job*

Marketing

Annual event(s): *jousting, dancing, flower
festival, quilting exhibition*

Affiliations: *HHA, ETB, SEETB, M25 Meetings
Group, ATAK, etc.*

Other: *market research*

UK promotion: *television; national newspapers;
radio; local newspapers; regional tourist board;
other attractions; leaflets/information packs;
ETB/BTA*

Europe promotion: *leaflets/brochures; travel
agents' brochures; British Tourist Authority*

HEXHAM ABBEY

(Church of England)
church

Established: *674*

Address: *Beaumont St, Hexham,
Northumberland, NE46 2HD*

Telephone: *(0434) 602031*

Access: (road) *A69*

Season: *all year*

Hours: *May to Sept – 9am to 7pm, Oct to
Apr – 9am to 5pm*

Admission (1992): *free*

No. visitors (1992): *100 000 (est.)*

Facilities

Interpretation: *leaflets; guide books*

Schools: *maximum no. 30; educational literature*

Disabled: *easy access*

Retailing: *postcards/inexpensive souvenirs*

No. shops: *1*

Operations

Contact: *Mrs J. Burlton (Administrator)*

No. employees: (high season) *1 full time* (low
season) *1 full time*

Training: *casual operations staff are trained
volunteers*

Languages spoken: *French; German; Italian;
Spanish; Japanese*

Marketing

UK promotion: *local tourist boards*

Environmental monitoring: *recycling; waste;
water quality; energy consumption*

HIGH BEECHES GARDENS

(trust)
garden

Established: *1988*

Address: *The High Beeches, Handcross, W
Sussex, RH17 6HQ*

Telephone: *(0444) 400589*

Access: (road) *M23*

Parking capacity: (cars) *80* (coaches) *6*

Admission (1992): *adults £2.50; OAP £2.50;
student £2.50; guided groups £3.50*

No. visitors (1992): *4356*

Facilities

Interpretation: *leaflets; information boards; maps;
tour guides; guide books; catering on event
days and by appointment only*

Languages: *Japanese; French; German; Spanish*

Schools: *maximum no. 60; educational literature;
lecture/talk*

Disabled: *disabled toilets*

Catering: *1 picnic area*

Retailing: *postcards and guide books at gate*

No. shops: *none*

Operations

Contacts: *Ms A Boscawen and Ms S Bray*

No. employees: (high season) *2 full time; 1 part
time* (low season) *2 full time; 2 part time*

Training: *F/T operations staff are trained in-house
and day-to-day on job*

Languages spoken: *sometimes available*

Marketing

Annual event(s): *special seasonal flower days and
events*

Affiliations: *HHA and SE England Tourist Board*

Other: *market research*

UK promotion: *national newspapers; radio; local
newspapers; regional tourist board; other
attractions; leaflets/information packs;
ETB/BTA*

Europe/USA promotion: *leaflets/brochures;
British Tourist Authority*

HIGHCLERE CASTLE

(private)
historic house

Established: *1988*

Address: *Highclere Park, Nr Newbury, Berks,
RG15 9RN*

Telephone: *(0635) 253210*. Fax: *(0635) 254051*

Access: (road) *M4/A34* (rail) *Newbury*

Parking capacity: (cars) *500* (coaches) *8*

Hours: *July to Sept – Wed to Sun – 2pm to 6pm;
BH – 11am to 6pm*

Admission (1992): *adults £4.00; children £2.50;
OAP £3.50; student £2.50; gardens only £2.00*

No. visitors (1992): *30 000 (est.)*

Facilities

Interpretation: *leaflets; tour guides; guide books*

Languages: *French*

Schools: *maximum no. 100; educational literature;
lecture/talk; out of season visits only*

Disabled: *easy access; disabled toilets*

Catering: *1 picnic area*

Retailing: *postcards/inexpensive souvenirs;
craftwork; books; reproductions of famous
artefacts*

No. shops: *1*

Operations

No. employees: (high season) *5 full time; 30 part
time* (low season) *5 full time; 4 part time*

Languages spoken: *French; Spanish*

Marketing

Annual event(s): *various*

Affiliation: *HHA*

UK promotion: *television; radio; local
newspapers; regional tourist board; other
attractions; leaflets/information packs; Various;
ETB/BTA*

Environmental monitoring: *waste; chemical usage;
Conservation*

HIRSEL, THE

(private company)
park/reserve; garden; museum; craft centre with
workshops

Address: *Coldstream, Berwickshire, TD12 4LP*

Telephone: *0890 2834*

Access: (road) *M1/M6/A697* (rail) *Berwick upon
Tweed*

Parking capacity: (cars) *100* (coaches) *10*

Season: *all year*

Hours: *park open all reasonable daylight hours.
Museum, craft shops, etc. – 9.30am to 5pm
approx*

Admission (1992): *parking charge £2.00 per car*

No. visitors (1992): *21 000 (est.)*

Facilities
Interpretation: *leaflets; information boards*
Children: *play area; nappy changing*
Disabled: *easy access; disabled toilets; leaflets*
Catering: *1 picnic area*
Franchisees: *park open all reasonable daylight hours. Museum, craft shops, etc. – 9.30am to 5pm approx*
Retailing: *postcards/inexpensive souvenirs; craftwork*
No. shops: *more than 4*

Operations
Contacts: *Hon Caroline Douglas-Home (Estate Factor)*
No. employees: (high season) *1 full time* (low season) *1 full time*

Marketing
Annual event(s): *craft fairs*
Sponsor(s): *local banks or businesses*
Affiliations: *HHA, Scottish Borders Tourist Board, Scottish Museum Council*
Other: *market research*
UK promotion: *national newspapers; radio; local newspapers; regional tourist board; leaflets/information packs*

HISTORIC DOCKYARD CHATHAM, THE
(trust)
heritage centre

Established: *1985*
Address: *Chatham, Kent, ME4 4TE*
Telephone: *(0634) 812551.* Fax: *(0634) 826918*
Access: (road) *M2/A229* (rail) *Chatham*
Parking capacity: (cars) *2000* (coaches) *30*
Season: *all year*
Hours: *Mar to Oct – Wed to Sun – 10am to 6pm; Nov to Mar – Wed, Sat and Sun – 10am to 4.30pm*
Admission (1992): *adults £5.20; children £2.60; OAP £4.50; student £4.50; half price for return visit in one year*
No. visitors (1992): *120 000 (est.)*

Facilities
Interpretation: *videos; leaflets; information boards; maps; tour guides; guide books; audio visual displays, sight-sound-smells gallery*
Languages: *French*
Children: *play area; nappy changing*
Schools: *maximum no. 600; educational literature; educational tour; lecture/talk*
Disabled: *easy access; disabled toilets; helpers; special signs; leaflets*
Catering: *1 bar/public house*
Franchisees: *Mar to Oct – Wed to Sun – 10am to 6pm*
Retailing: *postcards/inexpensive souvenirs; confectionery and ice cream; craftwork; books; clothes; reproductions of famous artefacts; games, lamps, videos, film stock*
No. shops: *4*

Operations
Contacts: *B Robertson (Chief Executive); Major P Dare (Company Secretary); S Hudson (Marketing Manager)*
No. employees: (high season) *54 full time; 56 part time* (low season) *54 full time; 48 part time*
Training: *F/T operations staff, F/T management, P/T operations staff, P/T management, casual operations staff and casual management are trained in-house and externally and on specific courses and day-to-day on job*
Languages spoken: *French; German*

Marketing
Annual event(s): *various*
Sponsor: *Lloyds Bank*
Affiliations: *MA, AIM, International Congress of Maritime Museums, Kent Museums Group, Area Museums Service*
Other: *market research*
UK promotion: *national newspapers; local newspapers; regional tourist board; other attractions; leaflets/information packs; ETB/ BTA*

Europe promotion: *leaflets/brochures; British Tourist Authority*

Environmental monitoring: *recycling; waste; water quality*

HM TOWER OF LONDON
(government agency)
castle; museum; church

Address: *London, EC3N 4AB*
Telephone: *(071) 709 0765.* Fax: *(071) 480 5350*
Access: (rail) *Tower Hill*
Season: *all year*
Hours: *Mar to Oct – Mon to Sat – 9.30am to 6pm, Sun – 10am to 6pm; Nov to Feb – Mon to Sat – 9.30am to 5pm, Sun – closed*
Admission (1992): *adults £6.40; children £3.90; OAP £4.80; student £4.80; disabled £4.80 (helper free); ub40s £4.80; family ticket (2+ up to 5) £17.50*
No. visitors (1992): *2 000 000 (est.)*

Facilities
Interpretation: *videos; leaflets; information boards; tour guides; guide books; yeoman warders*
Languages: *Japanese; French; German; Italian; Spanish*
Children: *nappy changing*
Schools: *maximum no. 650; lecture/talk; on request*
Disabled: *disabled toilets; leaflets; guide book*
Catering: *1 picnic area*
Retailing: *postcards/inexpensive souvenirs; confectionery and ice cream; books; clothes; reproductions of famous artefacts; toys and china*
No. shops: *4*

Operations
Contacts: *Major General C Tyler (Resident Governor); Ms K Derbyshire (Personnel); Mrs M Sivyer (Public Relations)*
No. employees: (high season) *232 full time*
Training: *F/T operations staff, F/T management, P/T operations staff, P/T management, casual operations staff and casual management are trained externally and on specific courses*

Marketing
Affiliation: *Historic Royal Palaces Agency*
Other: *press office; market research*
UK promotion: *television; national newspapers; local newspapers; regional tourist board; leaflets/information packs; ETB/BTA*
Tourist Boards promotion: *travel agents' brochures; British Tourist Authority*

HMS BELFAST
(government funded)
museum

Established: *1971*
Address: *Morgan's Lane, Tooley St, London, SE1 2JH*
Telephone: *(071) 407 6434.* Fax: *(071) 403 0719*
Access: (rail) *London Bridge*
Season: *all year*
Hours: *Summer – 10am to 5.20pm daily; Winter – 10am to 4.30pm daily; closed 25, 26 Dec and 1 Jan*
Admission (1992): *adults £3.80; children £1.90; OAP £1.90; student £1.90; family ticket (2+2) £10.00*
No. visitors (1992): *200 000 (est.)*

Facilities
Interpretation: *videos; leaflets; audio tapes; information boards; slides; maps; guide books; dioramas*
Languages: *French; German; Italian*
Schools: *maximum no. 52; audio/visual presentation; lecture/talk*
Disabled: *easy access; disabled toilets; other audio facilities; leaflets*
Catering: *1 picnic area*

Franchisees: *Summer – 10am to 5.20pm daily; Winter – 10am to 4.30pm daily*
Retailing: *postcards/inexpensive souvenirs; confectionery and ice cream; books; clothes; reproductions of famous artefacts; naval related*
No. shops: *1*

Operations
Contacts: *Captain F Collins (Director); Commander C Le Quezenec (Deputy Director); Mr J Muir (Shop Manager); Ms S Hogben (Publicity and Exhibitions)*
No. employees: (high season) *40 full time; 3 part time* (low season) *40 full time; 3 part time*
Languages spoken: *French; German*

Marketing
Other: *press office; market research*
UK promotion: *radio; local newspapers; regional tourist board; other attractions; leaflets/information packs; ETB/BTA; Posters*
Europe/USA promotion: *leaflets/brochures; travel agents' brochures; British Tourist Authority*

Environmental monitoring: *recycling; waste; energy consumption; hazardous materials; chemical usage; transport; emissions*

HMS VICTORY
(commissioned warship)
commissioned warship

Established: *1922*
Address: *College Rd, HM Naval Base, Portsmouth*
Telephone: *(0705) 839766*
Access: (road) *M27/M275* (rail) *Portsmouth harbour*
Parking capacity: (cars) *500*
Season: *all year*
Hours: *1 Mar to 1 Oct – 10am to 6pm (7pm July and Aug), 1 Nov to 28 Feb – 10am to 5pm except Christmas Day*
Admission (1992): *adults £4.00; children £2.50; OAP £3.50; student £2.50; educational £1.50*
No. visitors (1992): *400 000 (est.)*

Facilities
Interpretation: *information boards; maps; tour guides*
Languages: *Japanese; Dutch; French; German; Italian; Spanish; Polish; Russian and more*
Children: *nappy changing*
Schools: *educational literature; information sheets*
Disabled: *easy access; guide book*
Catering: *1 picnic area*
Franchisees: *1 Mar to 1 Oct – 10am to 6pm (7pm July and Aug)*
Retailing: *postcards/inexpensive souvenirs; confectionery and ice cream; craftwork; books; clothes; reproductions of famous artefacts*
No. shops: *3*

Operations
Contacts: *Commanding Officer HMS Victory; 1st LT HMS Victory*
No. employees: (high season) *26 full time*
Training: *F/T operations staff and F/T management are trained in-house and on specific courses and language training*

Marketing
Annual event(s): *N/A*
Other: *press office; market research*
UK promotion: *television; national newspapers; radio; local newspapers; regional tourist board; other attractions; leaflets/information packs; ETB/BTA*
Europe/USA promotion: *leaflets/brochures; travel agents' brochures; British Tourist Authority*

HOGARTH'S HOUSE
(local authority run)
historic house; garden; museum; gallery

Established: *1903*
Address: *Hogarth Lane, Great West Rd, Chiswick, W4 2QN*
Telephone: *(081) 994 6757*

Access: (road) *M4/A4* (rail) *Chiswick*
Parking capacity: (cars) *20*
Season: *all year*
Hours: *Summer - Mon, Wed to Sat - 11am to 6pm, Sun - 2pm to 6pm; Winter - Mon, Wed to Sat - 11am to 4pm, Sun - 2pm to 4pm; closed 1st 2 weeks in Sept and last 3 weeks in Dec and 1 Jan*
Admission (1992): *free*
No. visitors (1992): *5751*

Facilities
Interpretation: *guide books*
Schools: *maximum no. 30; lecture/talk*
Retailing: *postcards/inexpensive souvenirs; books; reproductions of famous artefacts*
No. shops: *1*

Operations
Contacts: *Mr L Channer (Custodian); Mr A Downend (Principal Librarian)*
No. employees: (high season) *1 full time* (low season) *1 full time*
Languages spoken: *French*

Marketing
Other: *press office*
UK promotion: *local newspapers; regional tourist board; other attractions; leaflets/information packs; ETB/BTA*

HOLBURNE MUSEUM AND CRAFTS STUDY CENTRE
(trust)
historic house; garden; museum; gallery; crafts study centre

Established: *1916*
Address: *Gt Pulteney St, Bath, Avon, BA2 4DB*
Telephone: *(0225) 466669*
Access: (road) *M4/A4/A367/A431* (rail) *Bath Spa*
Parking capacity: (cars) *32* (coaches) *2*
Hours: *end Feb to mid Dec - Mon to Sat - 11am to 5pm, Sun - 2.30pm to 6pm; check on opening at other times of the year*
Admission (1992): *adults £2.50; children £1.00; OAP £2.00; student £2.00; family ticket £6.00, reduction of £0.50p for groups*
No. visitors (1992): *22 297*

Facilities
Interpretation: *leaflets; information boards; slides; maps; tour guides; guide books*
Schools: *maximum no. 50; educational literature; lecture/talk; educational programme*
Disabled: *easy access; disabled toilets; lift to all floors*
Catering: *1 picnic area*
Franchisees: *end Feb to mid Dec - Mon to Sat - 11am to 5pm, Sun - 2.30pm to 6pm*
Retailing: *postcards/inexpensive souvenirs; craftwork; books; to complement exhibitions*
No. shops: *1*

Operations
Contacts: *Ms B Roscoe (Curator); Ms B Milner (Assistant Curator); Ms J Naismith (Administrator and Publicity Officer)*
No. employees: (high season) *4 full time; 10 part time*

Marketing
Sponsor(s): *Friends of the Holburne Museum*
Affiliations: *Area Museums Council for the SW*
Other: *press office; market research*
UK promotion: *television; national newspapers; radio; local newspapers; regional tourist board; other attractions; leaflets/information packs; AMCSW; ETB/BTA; W Country Tourist Board*
Europe/USA promotion: *leaflets/brochures*

HOLKER HALL AND GARDENS
(limited company)
historic house; park/reserve; garden; museum

Established: *1952*
Address: *Cark-in-Cartmel, Grange-Over-Sands, Cumbria, LA11 7PL*

Telephone: *(05395) 58328.* Fax: *(05395) 58776*
Access: (road) *M6/A590* (rail) *Cark and Cartmel*
Parking capacity: (cars) *5000* (coaches) *40*
Hours: *Apr to Nov - Sun to Fri - 10.30am to 6pm*
Admission (1992): *various*
No. visitors (1992): *75 000 (est.)*

Facilities
Interpretation: *leaflets; tour guides; guide books*
Languages: *French; German; Spanish*
Children: *adventure playground; nappy changing*
Schools: *maximum no. 100; educational literature; guides; teachers' notes*
Disabled: *easy access; disabled toilets*
Catering: *1 picnic area*
Retailing: *postcards/inexpensive souvenirs; confectionery and ice cream; books; clothes; china; glassware; silk flowers*
No. shops: *1*

Operations
Contacts: *Mrs C Johnson (Administrator); Lady Cavendish (Owner); Mrs C Johnson (Administrator)*
No. employees: (high season) *5 full time; 32 part time* (low season) *5 full time; 32 part time*
Training: *F/T operations staff, F/T management, P/T operations staff and P/T management are trained in-house and on specific courses*
Languages spoken: *French; Spanish*

Marketing
Annual event: *Great Garden and Countryside Festival, MG Rally*
Sponsor(s): *varies from year to year*
Affiliation: *HHA*
Other: *market research*
UK promotion: *national newspapers; local newspapers; regional tourist board; other attractions; leaflets/information packs*

HOLKHAM HALL
(limited company)
historic house; park/reserve; museum

Established: *1950*
Address: *Wells-Next-The-Sea, Norfolk, NR23 1AB*
Telephone: *(0328) 710227.* Fax: *(0328) 711707*
Access: (road) *A149*
Parking capacity: (cars) *1000* (coaches) *20*
Hours: *May to Sept - Sun to Thur - 1.30pm to 5pm*
Admission (1992): *adults £2.70; children £1.20; OAP £2.70; student £2.70*
No. visitors (1992): *30 000 (est.)*

Facilities
Interpretation: *leaflets; guide books*
Schools: *no special support*
Disabled: *disabled toilets; limited access to first floor*
Catering: *1 picnic area*
Retailing: *postcards/inexpensive souvenirs; confectionery and ice cream; craftwork; books; pottery*
No. shops: *2*

Operations
No. employees: (high season) *3 full time; 25 part time* (low season) *3 full time; 5 part time*
Languages spoken: *French; German; Spanish*

Marketing
Affiliation: *HHA*
UK promotion: *local newspapers; regional tourist board; other attractions; leaflets/information packs; district council leaflets*

Environmental monitoring: *water quality; energy consumption*

HOLLINGWORTH LAKE COUNTRY PARK
(local authority run)
park/reserve

Established: *1975*
Address: *Littleborough, Lancs, OL15 0AQ*
Telephone: *(0706) 373421*

Access: (road) *M62/B6225* (rail) *Littleborough*
Parking capacity: (cars) *650*
Season: *all year*
Hours: *Apr to Sept - 10.30am to 7pm daily (open until 8pm at weekends); Oct to Mar - 11am to 4pm daily (open until 5.30pm at weekends)*
Admission (1992): *car park charges*
No. visitors (1992): *130 000 (est.)*

Facilities
Interpretation: *leaflets; audio tapes; information boards; slides; maps; guide books*
Children: *adventure playground; play area*
Schools: *educational literature; audio/visual presentation; educational tour; lecture/talk*
Disabled: *easy access; disabled toilets; powered transport; parking*
Catering: *6 picnic areas*
Franchisees: *Apr to Sept - 10.30am to 7pm daily (open until 8pm at weekends); Oct to Mar - 11am to 4pm daily (open until 5.30pm at weekends)*
Retailing: *postcards/inexpensive souvenirs; books*
No. shops: *1*

Operations
Contact: *E Dale (Senior Warden)*
No. employees: (high season) *6 full time; 3 part time* (low season) *6 full time; 3 part time*
Training: *F/T operations staff, F/T management and P/T operations staff are trained in-house and externally and on specific courses*

Marketing
Annual event(s): *'Go Wild' events programme, volunteer and junior events*
UK promotion: *local newspapers; other attractions; leaflets/information packs*

HORNSEA FREEPORT
(limited company)
theme park; museum; zoo/wildlife attraction; discount retail shopping centre

Established: *1949*
Address: *Hornsea Pottery Retail and Leisure Park, Hornsea, E Yorks*
Telephone: *(0964) 534211.* Fax: *(0964) 535077*
Access: (road) *M62/B1238* (rail) *Hull*
Parking capacity: (cars) *1200* (coaches) *16*
Season: *all year*
Hours: *Easter to Oct - 10am to 5pm daily (Aug BH 10am to 6pm); Nov to Easter - 10am to 4pm daily; closed 24 to 26 Dec incl*
Admission (1992): *adults £3.99; children £2.99; OAP £2.50; charges are for attraction; free entry to retail park*
No. visitors (1992): *800 000*

Facilities
Interpretation: *leaflets; information boards; maps*
Children: *adventure playground; play area; nappy changing*
Schools: *maximum no. 200; lecture/talk; birds of prey display*
Disabled: *easy access; disabled toilets*
Catering: *1 picnic area*
Retailing: *postcards/inexpensive souvenirs; confectionery and ice cream; craftwork; books; clothes; clothing and footwear*
No. shops: *More than 4*

Operations
Contacts: *Mr K Sellwood (Manager); Ms J Achroyd (PA to MD); Mr K Sellwood/ Mr T Pearce (Manager/Director); Ms L Ellingham (PR Executive)*
No. employees: (high season) *60 full time; 140 part time* (low season) *60 full time; 20 part time*
Training: *F/T operations staff, F/T management, P/T operations staff and casual operations staff are trained in-house and on specific courses and day-to-day on job using handbooks*

Marketing
Annual event(s): *car clubs and caravan rallies, craft fairs*
Other: *PR Company: Fountainhead, High St, Hull; press office; market research*

UK promotion: *television; national newspapers;
radio; local newspapers; regional tourist board;
other attractions; leaflets/information packs;
ETB/BTA*
Europe/Japan promotion: *leaflets/brochures*

Environmental monitoring: *countryside
conservation*

HORNSEA MUSEUM
(trust)
historic house; museum

Established: *1978*
Address: *11 Newbegin, Hornsea, N Humbs, HU18
1AB*
Telephone: *(0964) 533443*
Access: (road) *M62/B1244*
Season: *all year*
Hours: *Easter to end Oct – Mon to Sat – 10am to
5pm, Sun – 2pm to 5pm; other times by
appointment*
Admission (1992): *adults £1.25; children £0.85;
OAP £0.85; student £0.85; family ticket
(up to 6) £4.50*
No. visitors (1992): *10 000 (est.)*

Facilities
Interpretation: *leaflets; information boards; tour
guides*
Languages: *Dutch; French; German*
Schools: *maximum no. 45; educational literature;
lecture/talk; Victorian activities*
Disabled: *easy access; disabled toilets; about half
total area accessible*
Catering: *1 picnic area*
Retailing: *postcards/inexpensive souvenirs; books;
original watercolours*
No. shops: *1*

Operations
Contacts: *Ms C Walker (Honorary Curator); Ms
M Kennedy (Honorary Administrator)*
Training: *casual operations staff are trained in-
house and day-to-day on job using handbooks*

Marketing
Annual event(s): *craft days*
Affiliations: *Yorks and Humbs Museums Council*
Other: *market research*
UK promotion: *radio; local newspapers; regional
tourist board; other attractions; leaflets/
information packs*

Environmental monitoring: *recycling; waste;
hazardous materials*

HOSKINS BREWERY
(plc)
museum; brewery

Established: *1983*
Address: *Beaumanor Brewery, Beaumanor Rd,
Leicester, LEA 5QE*
Telephone: *(0533) 661122.* Fax: *(0533) 610150*
Access: (road) *M1* (rail) *Leicester*
Parking capacity: (cars) *30* (coaches) *1*
Season: *all year*
Hours: *10am to 3.30pm*
No. visitors (1992): *5000 (est.)*

Facilities
Interpretation: *videos; leaflets; tour guides*
Catering: *1 bar/public house*
No. shops: *1*

Operations
Contact: *Mrs D Wood (Tour Organiser)*
No. employees: (high season) *3 full time* (low
season) *3 full time*

Marketing
UK promotion: *local newspapers; leaflets/
information packs*

HOUGHTON HALL
(private estate)
historic house

Established: *1976*
Address: *Houghton, King's Lynn, Norfolk, PE31
6UE*
Telephone: *(0485) 528569.* Fax: *(0485) 528167*
Access: (road) *A148*
Hours: *Easter Sunday to last Sunday in Sept on
various days; Summer – 12.30pm to 5.30 pm*
Admission (1992): *adults £4.00; children £2.00;
OAP £3.50*
No. visitors (1992): *16 000 (est.)*

Facilities
Interpretation: *tour guides; guide books; signs*
Languages: *French; German*
Children: *play area*
Schools: *educational literature*
Disabled: *easy access; disabled toilets; lift*
Catering: *1 picnic area*
Retailing: *postcards/inexpensive souvenirs;
craftwork; books*
No. shops: *1*

Operations
Contact: *Miss S M Cleaver (Administrator)*
No. employees: (high season) *1 full time; 25 part
time*

Marketing
Annual event: *military band concert*
Affiliation: *HHA*
Other: *market research*
UK promotion: *local newspapers; regional tourist
board; leaflets/information packs; ETB/BTA*

HOUGHTON LODGE GARDEN AND
HYDROPONICUM
(family farm)
historic house; garden; hydroponicum (soil-less
horticulture)

Established: *1980*
Address: *Stockbridge, Hampshire, SO20 6LQ*
Telephone: *(0264) 810502.* Fax: *(071) 352 7478*
Access: (road) *M3/A30* (rail) *Winchester/Andover*
Parking capacity: (cars) *100* (coaches) *3*
Hours: *Mar to Sept – Mon, Tues, Fri – 2pm to
5pm weekends and BH 10am to 5pm; other
times by appointment*
Admission (1992): *adults £2.50; OAP £2.50;
student £2.50; children free if with parents*
No. visitors (1992): *4000 (est.)*

Facilities
Interpretation: *leaflets; audio tapes; information
boards; guide books; guides booked in advance*
Children: *nappy changing*
Disabled: *easy access; disabled toilets; wheelchair
available*
Catering: *1 picnic area*
Retailing: *books; plants, flowers, hydronic kits*
No. shops: *1*

Operations
Contacts: *Mr and Mrs M Busk (owners); Mr N
Glossop (Head Gardener)*
No. employees: (high season) *1 full time; 3 part
time* (low season) *1 full time; 2 part time*
Languages spoken: *French; German*

Marketing
Affiliations: *HHA, Southern Tourist Board*
UK promotion: *local newspapers; regional tourist
board; other attractions; leaflets/information
packs; ETB/BTA*

HOUGHTON MILL
(trust)
historic house; gallery; 17th-century watermill

Established: *1984*
Address: *The National Trust, Houghton,
Huntingdon, Cambs, PE17 2AZ*
Telephone: *(0480) 301494*
Access: (road) *A1123/A1* (rail) *Huntingdon*

Parking capacity: (cars) *50*
Hours: *27 Mar to 10 Oct – Sat, Sun and BH
Mon – 2pm to 5.30pm; July and Aug – Mon,
Tues and Wed – afternoons*
Admission (1992): *adults £1.80; children £0.90;
student £1.80; milling days on Sun and BH
£2.20 adults*
No. visitors (1992): *11 000*

Facilities
Interpretation: *leaflets; information boards; guide
books; miniature millstones to turn by hand*
Schools: *maximum no. 50; educational literature;
trail around village*
Retailing: *postcards/inexpensive souvenirs;
wholemeal flour*
No. shops: *1*

Operations
Contact: *Mr R Forrest (Custodian (Miller))*
No. employees: (high season) *1 full time; 1 part
time* (low season) *1 full time*

Marketing
Annual event(s): *guided tours*
Other: *press office*
UK promotion: *radio; local newspapers; regional
tourist board; leaflets/information packs; E
Anglia Tourist Board; Directory of Educational
Visits*

ENVIRONMENTAL MONITORING: *water
quality; chemical usage*

HOVE MUSEUM AND ART GALLERY
(local authority run)
museum; gallery

Established: *1927*
Address: *19 New Church Road, Hove, E Sussex,
BN3 4AB*
Telephone: *(0273) 779410*
Access: (road) *A27/A23* (rail) *Hove*
Season: *all year*
Hours: *all year – Tues to Fri – 10am to 5pm,
Sat – 10am to 4.30pm, Sun – 2pm to 5pm*
Admission (1992): *free*
No. visitors (1992): *25 000*

Facilities
Interpretation: *videos; leaflets; information boards*
Languages: *Japanese; French; Italian*
Schools: *maximum no. 20; educational literature;
educational tour; lecture/talk; quiz sheets*
Disabled: *easy access; disabled toilets*
Catering: *1 picnic area*
Retailing: *postcards/inexpensive souvenirs; books;
catalogues*
No. shops: *1*

Operations
Contacts: *T Wilcox (Curator); L Orams
(Secretary)*
No. employees: (high season) *2 full time; 9 part
time* (low season) *2 full time; 9 part time*
Training: *F/T operations staff, P/T operations
staff and casual operations staff are trained
externally and on specific courses and
day-to-day on job using videos and mill guide*

Marketing
Annual event: *fun day*
Sponsor(s): *AMEX, local companies*
Other: *market research*
UK promotion: *radio; local newspapers; regional
tourist board; other attractions; leaflets/
information packs; SETB publications*
Europe promotion: *leaflets/brochures; Draveil
Tourist Information*

HOW WE LIVED THEN MUSEUM OF SHOPS
(privately owned)
museum

Established: *1988*
Address: *20 Cornfield Terrace, Eastbourne, E
Sussex, BN21 4NS*
Telephone: *(0323) 737143*

Access: (road) *A22/A27* (rail) *Eastbourne*
Hours: *10am to 5.30pm daily; closed in Jan for maintenance*
Admission (1992): *adults £2.00; children £1.00; OAP £1.50; student £1.50; disabled entry to ground floor free*

Facilities
Interpretation: *tour guides; tour guides by arrangement only*
Schools: *maximum no. 30; educational literature; lecture/talk; talks and worksheets*
Disabled: *ground-floor access only free*
Retailing: *postcards/inexpensive souvenirs; confectionery and ice cream; books; Victorian and traditional*
No. shops: *1*

Operations
Contacts: *Mr G and Mrs J Upton (owners)*
No. employees: (high season) *4 part time* (low season) *4 part time*
Training: *P/T operations staff are trained in-house and day-to-day on job*
Languages spoken: *French; German; Italian*

Marketing
Market research
UK promotion: *local newspapers; regional tourist board; other attractions; leaflets/information packs; ETB/BTA; SE England Tourist Board*
Europe promotion: *leaflets/brochures; British Tourist Authority*

HOWLETTS ZOO PARK
(trust)
zoo/wildlife attraction

Established: *1975*
Address: *Bekesbourne, Nr Canterbury, Kent*
Telephone: *(0227) 721286.* Fax: *(0227) 721853*
Access: (road) *A2* (rail) *Bekesbourne*
Season: *all year*
Hours: *all year – 10am to 5pm daily*
Admission (1992): *adults £6.50; children £4.50; OAP £4.50; student £2.25*
No. visitors (1992): *150 000 (est.)*

Facilities
Interpretation: *videos; leaflets; information boards; tour guides; guide books; personnel*
Languages: *Dutch; French; Spanish*
Children: *nappy changing*
Schools: *educational literature; audio/visual presentation; lecture/talk*
Disabled: *easy access; disabled toilets*
Catering: *1 picnic area*
Retailing: *postcards/inexpensive souvenirs; confectionery and ice cream; craftwork; books; clothes*
No. shops: *2*

Operations
Contacts: *R Boutwood/M Lockyer (Administrative Director/Animal Director); S Sheather (Wages and Personnel Manager); F Stringer/J Carauna (Gift Shop Manager/Catering Manager); S Duff (Marketing Officer)*
No. employees: (high season) *47 full time; 23 part time* (low season) *45 full time; 10 part time*
Training: *F/T operations staff, P/T operations staff and casual operations staff are trained in-house and externally and day-to-day on job*
Languages spoken: *French*

Marketing
PR Company: *Boutwood Advertising, 37 Terminus Road, Eastbourne, E Sussex; press office; market research*
UK promotion: *television; national newspapers; radio; local newspapers; regional tourist board; other attractions; leaflets/information packs; ETB/BTA*
Europe promotion: *leaflets/brochures; British Tourist Authority*

Environmental monitoring: *recycling; waste; energy consumption*

HUDDERSFIELD ART GALLERY
(local authority run)
gallery

Established: *1945*
Address: *Princess Alexandra Walk, Huddersfield, HD1 2SU*
Telephone: *(0484) 513808.* Fax: *(0484) 531983*
Access: (road) *M62/M1/A62/A629/A616* (rail) *Huddersfield*
Season: *all year*
Hours: *Mon to Fri – 10am to 6pm, Sat – 10am to 4pm*
Admission (1992): *free*
No. visitors (1992): *49 000*

Facilities
Interpretation: *videos; leaflets; information boards; exhibitions and displays*
Schools: *maximum no. 40; educational literature; lecture/talk*
Disabled: *easy access; disabled toilets*
Retailing: *postcards/inexpensive souvenirs; books*
No. shops: *1*

Operations
Contacts: *Mr R Hall (Senior Curator, Art Galleries); Ms J Speller (Assistant Curator, Art); Mr A Mitha (Curator, Multicultural Services)*
No. employees: (high season) *5 full time*
Training: *F/T operations staff and F/T management are trained in-house and externally and on specific courses and day-to-day on job using videos*
Languages spoken: *French; German*

Marketing
Affiliations: *MA*
Other: *press office; market research*
UK promotion: *television; national newspapers; local newspapers; regional tourist board; leaflets/information packs*

Environmental monitoring: *recycling; water quality; hazardous materials*

HUGHENDEN MANOR
(trust)
historic house; park/reserve

Established: *1939*
Address: *Hughenden Valley, High Wycombe, Bucks, HP14 4LA*
Telephone: *(0494) 532580*
Access: (road) *M40/A4128* (rail) *High Wycombe*
Parking capacity: (cars) *80* (coaches) *1*
Hours: *Mar – Sat to Sun – 2pm to 6pm; Apr to Oct – Wed to Sat – 2pm to 6pm, Sun – 12am to 6pm*
Admission (1992): *adults £3.30; children £1.65; OAP £3.30; student £3.30; NT members free*
No. visitors (1992): *26 000*

Facilities
Interpretation: *leaflets; guide books*
Languages: *French; German*
Schools: *maximum no. 60; educational literature*
Disabled: *disabled toilets; braille/sound posts; other audio facilities*
Catering: *1 picnic area*
Retailing: *postcards/inexpensive souvenirs; craftwork; books; clothes*
No. shops: *1*

Operations
Contacts: *D Gordon (Custodian); S Walker (Land Agent); S Evitt (Regional Enterprises Manager); S Forrester (Regional Public Affairs Manager)*
No. employees: (high season) *2 full time; 8 part time* (low season) *2 full time; 2 part time*
Training: *F/T operations staff, F/T management, P/T operations staff and casual operations staff are trained in-house and externally and on specific courses and day-to-day on job*
Languages spoken: *French; Italian; Urdu; Gujarati*

Marketing
Press office
UK promotion: *leaflets/information packs; ETB/BTA*

HULL AND EAST RIDING MUSEUM
(local authority run)
museum

Established: *1928*
Address: *High St, Hull*
Telephone: *(0482) 593902.* Fax: *(0482) 595062*
Access: (road) *M62/A63* (rail) *Hull Paragon*
Parking capacity: (cars) *30*
Season: *all year*
Hours: *Mon to Sat – 10am to 5pm, Sun – 1.30pm to 4.30pm; closed New Year's Day, Christmas and Boxing Day and Good Friday*
Admission (1992): *free*
No. visitors (1992): *80 875 (est.)*

Facilities
Interpretation: *videos; audio tapes; information boards; slides*
Languages: *Dutch*
Schools: *maximum no. 100; educational literature; audio/visual presentation; lecture/talk*
Retailing: *postcards/inexpensive souvenirs; craftwork; books; Roman and Celtic items; greetings cards, etc.*
No. shops: *1*

Operations
Contact: *Dr A Foxon (Keeper of Archaeology)*
No. employees: (high season) *11 full time*
Training: *F/T operations staff and F/T management are trained in-house and externally and on specific courses and day-to-day on job using videos and handbooks*

Marketing
Sponsor(s): *various*
Other: *press office; market research*
UK promotion: *local newspapers; regional tourist board; other attractions*

Environmental monitoring: *recycling; water quality*

HUNTERIAN ART GALLERY
(university)
historic house; gallery

Established: *1980*
Address: *University of Glasgow, 82 Hillhead Street, Glasgow, G12 8QQ*
Telephone: *(041) 330 5431.* Fax: *(041) 307 8017*
Access: (road) *M8* (rail) *Glasgow*
Season: *all year*
Hours: *Monday to Saturday 9.30am to 5pm (Mackintosh House closed 12.30pm to 1.30pm); closed local public holidays, Christmas and New Year*
Admission (1992): *free*
No. visitors (1992): *97 748*

Facilities
Interpretation: *leaflets; information boards; guide books*
Schools: *no special support*
Disabled: *easy access; disabled toilets; wheelchairs provided*
Catering: *1 bar/public house*
Retailing: *postcards/inexpensive souvenirs; books; art boards, framed prints*
No. shops: *1*

Operations
Contacts: *Mr. C.J. Allan (Deputy Director); Ms. J. Barrie (Shop only) (Administrative Assistant)*
No. employees: (high season) *18 full time; 8 part time* (low season) *18 full time; 8 part time*
Training: *F/T operations staff, F/T management, P/T operations staff and P/T management are trained in-house and externally and on specific courses and day-to-day on job using videos and handbooks*

Marketing
Annual event(s): *special annual programme*
Sponsor(s): *various*
Affiliations: *HAA, CAS, NACF, SMC, GGTB*
Other: *market research*

UK promotion: *local newspapers; regional tourist board; other attractions; leaflets/information packs; Scottish Tourist Board, GGTB publications; ETB/BTA; listings in national visual arts publications*

Environmental monitoring: *energy consumption; hazardous materials*

HUTTON-IN-THE-FOREST
(privately owned)
historic house; garden

Established: *1980*
Address: *Penrith, Cumbria, CA11 9TH*
Telephone: *(07684) 84449.* Fax: *(07684) 84571*
Access: (road) *M6/B5305* (rail) *Penrith 5miles*
Parking capacity: (cars) *50* (coaches) *7*
Hours: *house and tea room: end May to Nov – Thur, Fri and Sun – 1pm to 4pm; the gardens, grounds and forest walk are open 11am to 5pm every day except Saturdays*
Admission (1992): *adults £3.00; children £1.00; student £2.50*
No. visitors (1992): *14 000 (est.)*

Facilities
Interpretation: *leaflets; information boards; tour guides; guide books*
Languages: *French; German*
Schools: *maximum no. 50; educational literature; Victorian experience*
Catering: *1 licensed restaurant*
Retailing: *postcards/inexpensive souvenirs; confectionery and ice cream; antiques*
No. shops: *1*

Operations
Contact: *Mr Andrew Plane (Administrator)*
No. employees: (high season) *1 full time; 32 part time* (low season) *1 full time; 20 part time*
Training: *P/T operations staff and casual operations staff are trained in-house and externally and on specific courses and day-to-day on job*

Marketing
Annual event(s): *Meet the Gardener, Hutton Experience*
Affiliation: *HHA*
Other: *market research*
UK promotion: *local newspapers; regional tourist board; other attractions; leaflets/information packs;* Historic Houses, Castles and Gardens

I

IDEN CROFT HERBS
(partnership)
garden; herb centre with plant collections

Established: *1971*
Address: *Frittenden Road, Staplehurst, Kent,*
TN12 0DH
Telephone: *(0580) 891432.* Fax: *(0580) 892416*
Access: (road) *M20/A229* (rail) *Staplehurst*
Parking capacity: (cars) *80* (coaches) *1*
Season: *all year*
Hours: *all year – Mon to Sat – 9am to 5pm; open*
Sun from Mar to Sept – 11am to 5pm
Admission (1992): *donation box for gardens,*
coaches £10.00, tours £2.00 per person
No. visitors (1992): *17 000 (est.)*

Facilities
Interpretation: *leaflets; information boards; maps;*
tour guides; guide books
Languages: *Braille*
Children: *play area; nappy changing*
Schools: *maximum no. 50; no special support;*
educational literature; audio/visual
presentation; educational tour; lecture/talk
Disabled: *easy access; disabled toilets; braille/*
sound posts; helpers; leaflets; guide book
Catering: *1 picnic area*
Retailing: *postcards/inexpensive souvenirs;*
confectionery and ice cream; craftwork; books;
clothes; plants
No. shops: *1*

Operations
Contacts: *R and D Titterington (owner/Manager);*
M Browne (Secretary); A Wickens (Nursery
Manager)
No. employees: (high season) *5 full time; 6 part*
time (low season) *5 full time; 3 part time*
Training: *F/T operations staff, F/T management,*
P/T operations staff and casual operations staff
are trained in-house and day-to-day on job
Languages spoken: *French*

Marketing
Annual event: *National Heritage Week*
Affiliations: *British Herb Trade Association,*
Horticultural Trades Association
Other: *market research*
UK promotion: *national newspapers; local*
newspapers; regional tourist board; other
attractions; leaflets/information packs; SETB,
Maps and Guides; ETB/BTA; AA, Access
Guides, Plantfinder, National Collections Letter
Europe/USA promotion: *leaflets/brochures; travel*
agents' brochures; British Tourist Authority

IFORD MANOR GARDENS
(privately owned)
garden

Established: *1984*
Address: *Iford Manor, Bradford on Avon, Wilts,*
BA15 2BA
Telephone: *(0225) 863146*
Access: (road) *M4/A36* (rail) *Bradford on Avon*
Parking capacity: (cars) *100* (coaches) *2*
Hours: *Apr – Sun – 2pm to 5pm and Easter Mon;*
May to Sept – Tues, Wed, Thur, Sat and
Sun – 2pm to 5pm and BH; Oct – Sun – 2pm to
5pm
Admission (1992): *adults £2.00; children £1.50;*
OAP £1.50; student £1.50
No. visitors (1992): *10 000 (est.)*

Facilities
Interpretation: *tour guides; guide books; tour*
guides for groups only
Languages: *French; German; Italian*

Disabled: *easy access*
Catering: *1 self-service cafeteria*

Operations
Contact: *Mrs E Cartwright–Hignett (owner)*
No. employees: (high season) *4 full time; 4 part*
time
Training: *F/T operations staff are trained*
externally and on specific courses using videos
and courses designed as necessary

Marketing
Affiliations: *HHA, WCTB, ABLE*
UK promotion: *national newspapers; local*
newspapers; regional tourist board; other
attractions; leaflets/information packs; Official
Bath Guide, Blue Guide

Environmental monitoring: *recycling; water*
quality; Garden conservation

ILFRACOMBE MUSEUM
(trust)
museum

Established: *1932*
Address: *Wilder Rd, Ilfracombe, N Devon, EX34*
8AF
Telephone: *(0271) 863541*
Access: (road) *M5/A361* (rail) *Barnstaple*
Season: *all year*
Hours: *Easter to Nov – 10am to 5.30pm daily;*
Nov to Easter – Mon to Sat – 10am to 12.30pm
Admission (1992): *adults £0.60; children £0.20;*
OAP £0.40; student £0.20; under 5s and
disabled free
No. visitors (1992): *43 000*

Facilities
Interpretation: *leaflets; information boards; maps;*
guide books
Schools: *maximum no. 50; free admission*
Disabled: *easy access; helpers*
Retailing: *postcards/inexpensive souvenirs; books;*
reproductions of famous artefacts
No. shops: *1*

Operations
Contact: *Mrs J Slocombe (Curator)*
No. employees: (high season) *1 full time; 9 part*
time (low season) *1 full time*
Languages spoken: *German*

Marketing
UK promotion: *local publicity department*

INCREDIBLY FANTASTIC OLD TOY SHOW
(privately owned)
museum

Established: *1989*
Address: *26 Westgate, Lincoln, LN1 3BD*
Telephone: *(0522) 520534*
Access: (road) *M1/A46* (rail) *Lincoln*
Hours: *closed Christmas Eve to Easter; Easter to*
end Sept – Tues to Sat – 11am to 5pm, Sun and
BH, Mon – 12 noon to 4pm, Oct to Christmas
eve; open weekends and school holidays as
above; group visits at other times by
arrangement
Admission (1992): *adults £1.50; children £0.75;*
OAP £1.00; student £1.50
No. visitors (1992): *21 000 (est.)*

Facilities
Interpretation: *videos; information boards;*
demonstrations and talks

Children: *nappy changing*
Schools: *maximum no. 60; educational literature;*
lecture/talk; displays many aspects
Disabled: *easy access; helpers*
Retailing: *postcards/inexpensive souvenirs; books;*
old toys and collectors' items
No. shops: *1*

Operations
Contacts: *Mr and Mrs R Hutchinson (joint*
owners)
No. employees: (high season) *2 part time* (low
season) *2 part time*

Marketing
UK promotion: *television; national newspapers;*
radio; local newspapers; regional tourist board;
other attractions; leaflets/information packs;
ETB/BTA
USA/articles promotion: *British Tourist*
Authority

INTERNATIONAL HELICOPTER MUSEUM, THE
(trust)
museum

Established: *1989*
Address: *Weston Airport, Locking Moor Rd,*
Weston-Super-Mare, Avon, BS22 8PP
Telephone: *(0934) 635227.* Fax: *(0934) 822400*
Access: (road) *M5/A371* (rail) *Milton Halt*
Parking capacity: (cars) *100* (coaches) *10*
Season: *all year*
Hours: *Mar to Nov – 10am to 6pm daily; Nov to*
Feb – 10am to 4pm daily
Admission (1992): *adults £2.50; children £1.50;*
OAP £1.50; family £6.50
No. visitors (1992): *20 000 (est.)*

Facilities
Interpretation: *information boards*
Children: *nappy changing*
Schools: *maximum no. 100; educational literature;*
educational tour; lecture/talk
Disabled: *easy access; disabled toilets; helpers*
Catering: *1 picnic area*
Retailing: *postcards/inexpensive souvenirs;*
confectionery and ice cream; books; clothes;
model helicopters, toys, etc.
No. shops: *1*

Operations
Contacts: *W Cowlin (Manageress); E Rees*
(Founder/Trustee)
No. employees: (high season) *2 full time; 2 part*
time (low season) *2 full time*
Languages spoken: *French; German*

Marketing
Annual event(s): *Holidays*
Sponsor: *Helicopter International*
Affiliations: *WCTB, AMC, British Aviation*
Preservation Council
Other: *press office; market research*
UK promotion: *local newspapers; regional tourist*
board; other attractions; leaflets/information
packs
Europe/Asia/Australia/USA promotion:
helicopter publications

Environmental monitoring: *recycling; energy*
consumption; chemical usage; transport; use
electric vehicles

INVERARAY JAIL
(limited company)
museum; courthouse and prisons

Established: 1989
Address: Church Square, Inveraray, Argyll
Telephone: (0449) 2381. Fax: (0449) 2195
Access: (road) A83
Season: all year
Hours: Apr to Oct – 9.30am to 6pm daily; Nov to
   Mar – 10am to 5pm daily (last admission 1 hr
   before closing; some extended Summer opening
   hours)
Admission (1992): adults £3.60; children £1.75;
   OAP £1.90; student £2.85; special group rates
   £1.45 to £2.85 on request
No. visitors (1992): 110 000 (est.)

Facilities
Interpretation: leaflets; information boards; tour
   guides; guide books; personnel
Languages: French; German; Italian
Schools: educational literature; various activities
Disabled: disabled toilets; access may be difficult;
   free admission to ground floor
Retailing: postcards/inexpensive souvenirs;
   craftwork; books
No. shops: 1

Operations
Contacts: J Linley (Governor); M Dando
   (Assistant Governor)
No. employees: (high season) 12 full time; 5 part
   time (low season) 9 full time; 4 part time
Training: F/T operations staff, F/T management
   and P/T operations staff are trained in-house
   and externally and on specific courses and
   day-to-day on job
Languages spoken: French; German; Spanish

Marketing
Market research
UK promotion: television; national newspapers;
   radio; local newspapers; regional tourist board;
   other attractions; leaflets/information packs;
   ETB/BTA; Local publications
Europe/Asia/Australia/USA promotion:
   leaflets/brochures; travel agents' brochures

Environmental monitoring: recycling; energy
   consumption

INVEREWE GARDEN
(National Trust, Scotland)
garden

Established: 1952
Address: Poolewe, Wester Ross, IV22 2LQ
Telephone: Poolewe 200
Access: (road) A832
Parking capacity: (cars) 80 (coaches) 10
Season: all year
Hours: gardens – daily 9.30am to sunset; visitor
   centre and restaurant – Easter to Oct 10am to
   5pm
Admission (1992): adults £2.80; children £1.40;
   OAP £1.40; student £1.00; half price for
   parties
No. visitors (1992): 130 000

Facilities
Interpretation: information boards; tour guides;
   guide books; information centre
Languages: French; German
Schools: garden tour
Disabled: easy access; disabled toilets
Catering: 1 self-service cafeteria
Retailing: postcards/inexpensive souvenirs;
   craftwork; books; clothes
No. shops: 1

Operations
No. employees: (high season) 16 full time; 24 part
   time (low season) 16 full time
Training: F/T operations staff and P/T operations
   staff are trained in-house and externally and on
   specific courses and day-to-day on job using
   handbooks
Languages spoken: French; German; Italian

Marketing
Market research
UK promotion: regional tourist board

IRONBRIDGE GORGE MUSEUM
(trust)
historic house; monument; museum; gallery

Established: 1973
Address: Ironbridge, Telford, Shropshire
Telephone: (0952) 433522/432166. Fax: (0952)
   432204
Access: (road) M6/M54/A442 (rail) Telford
   Central
Season: all year
Hours: Sept to May – Mon to Sun – 10am to
   5pm; June to Aug – Mon to Sun – 10am to 6pm
Admission (1992): adults £7.80; children £5.00;
   OAP £6.80; student £5.00; family £23.50
No. visitors (1992): 315 000

Facilities
Interpretation: leaflets; audio tapes; information
   boards; slides; maps; tour guides; guide books;
   personnel
Languages: Japanese; French; German; Italian;
   Spanish
Children: play area; nappy changing
Schools: maximum no. 500; educational literature;
   audio/visual presentation; lecture/talk; school
   loan service, etc.
Disabled: easy access; disabled toilets; other audio
   facilities; leaflets; wheelchairs
Catering: 1 bar/public house
Franchisees: Sept to May – Mon to Sun – 10am to
   5pm; June to Aug – Mon to Sun – 10am to 6pm
Retailing: postcards/inexpensive souvenirs;
   confectionery and ice cream; craftwork; books;
   reproductions of famous artefacts; handmade
   goods and toys; food, toiletries
No. shops: More than 4

Operations
Contacts: G Lawes (Chief Executive); J Nicholls
   (Personnel Officer); P Jennings (General
   Manager, Trading Company); K Foster (Head
   of Public Relations)
No. employees: (high season) 153 full time; 88
   part time (low season) 153 full time
Training: F/T operations staff, F/T management,
   P/T operations staff, P/T management, casual
   operations staff and casual management are
   trained in-house and externally and on specific
   courses and day-to-day on job

Marketing
Annual event(s): various
Other: press office; market research
UK promotion: national newspapers; local
   newspapers; regional tourist board; other
   attractions; leaflets/information packs;
   ETB/BTA
Europe/Asia/Australia/USA promotions:
   leaflets/brochures; travel agents' brochures;
   British Tourist Authority

Environmental monitoring: chemical usage

ISLE OF ARRAN HERITAGE MUSEUM
(trust)
heritage centre; museum

Established: 1979
Address: Rosaburn, Brodick, Isle of Arran, KA27
   8DP
Telephone: (0770) 2636
Access: (road) Ferry and A841
Parking capacity: (cars) 20 (coaches) 1
Hours: Easter to end Oct – Mon to Sat – 10am to
   5pm (open on certain Sun for special events)
Admission (1992): adults £1.50; children £0.75;
   OAP £1.00; 25 per cent reduction for pre-
   booked groups
No. visitors (1992): 14 150

Facilities
Interpretation: leaflets; information boards; guide
   books
Schools: no special support

Catering: 1 picnic area
Retailing: postcards/inexpensive souvenirs;
   confectionery and ice cream; craftwork; books
No. shops: 1

Operations
Contacts: Mrs G Small (Chairperson); Mrs J
   Johnson (Secretary); Mrs M Alexander
   (Treasurer)
No. employees: (high season) 6 part time (low
   season) 6 part time
Languages spoken: French; German; Italian;
   Swedish

Marketing
Annual event(s): sheepshearing and horseshoeing
   demonstrations
Affiliations: SMC and Association of Independent
   Museums
UK promotion: local newspapers; regional tourist
   board; leaflets/information packs; Isle of Arran
   Tourist Board and Natural History Journal

Environmental monitoring: recycling; waste;
   energy consumption

ISLE OF GIGHA
(limited company)
historic house; heritage centre; park/reserve;
   garden; an island

Established: 1946
Address: Achamore House, Isle of Gigha, Argyll,
   Scotland, PA41 7AD
Telephone: (05835) 275. Fax: (05835) 244
Access: (road) Ferry Tayinloan
Season: all year
Hours: all year
Admission (1992): adults £2.00; children £1.00;
   OAP £1.00; student £1.00
No. visitors (1992): 14 000

Facilities
Interpretation: maps; tour guides; guide books
Children: adventure playground; play area; nappy
   changing
Schools: educational literature
Disabled: helpers; leaflets
Catering: 1 bar/public house
Retailing: postcards/inexpensive souvenirs;
   confectionery and ice cream; craftwork; books;
   clothes; reproductions of famous artefacts; fish
   and cheese
No. shops: 2

Marketing
UK promotion: television; national newspapers;
   radio; local newspapers; regional tourist board;
   leaflets/information packs; STB

ISLE OF WIGHT RARE BREEDS AND
WATERFOWL PARK
(privately owned)
park/reserve; zoo/wildlife attraction; rare breeds
   and domestic farm animals

Established: 1990
Address: Undercliff Drive, St Lawrence, Ventnor,
   Isle of Wight
Telephone: (0983) 852582
Access: (road) A3055 (rail) Shanklin
Parking capacity: (cars) 80 (coaches) 8
Season: all year
Hours: Easter to 31 Oct – 10am to 5.30pm daily;
   Winter – Sat and Sun – 10am to 4pm
Admission (1992): adults £2.30; children £1.30;
   OAP £1.80; student £2.30
No. visitors (1992): 32 000

Facilities
Interpretation: leaflets; information boards; maps;
   tour guides; guide books
Children: play area
Schools: educational literature; lecture/talk;
   teachers packs
Disabled: easy access; disabled toilets
Catering: 3 picnic areas

Retailing: *postcards/inexpensive souvenirs;
confectionery and ice cream; craftwork; books;
clothes; bird tables and models*
No. shops: *1*

Operations
Contacts: *Mr and Mrs H Noyes (joint owners)*
No. employees: (high season) *3 full time; 10 part
time* (low season) *3 full time*
Training: *P/T operations staff are trained in-house
and day-to-day on job*

Marketing
Annual event: *sheepshearing*
Affiliation: *Rare Breeds Survival Trust*
UK promotion: *local newspapers; regional tourist
board; leaflets/information packs*

ITCHEN VALLEY COUNTRY PARK
(local authority run)
park/reserve; visitor centre

Established: *1988*
Address: *High Wood Barn, Allington Lane, West
End, Southampton, SO3 3HQ*
Telephone: *(0703) 466091*
Access: (road) *M27/A27* (rail) *Southampton
Parkway*
Parking capacity: (cars) *200*
Season: *all year*
Hours: *open all year – Sat and Sun – 1pm to
5.30pm; Wed to Fri – 11am to 5.30pm, closing
earlier in Winter (4.30pm)*
Admission (1992): *free*
No. visitors (1992): *200 000 (est.)*

Facilities
Interpretation: *leaflets; audio tapes; information
boards; maps; guided walks*
Children: *adventure playground; play area*
Schools: *maximum no. 35; audio/visual
presentation*
Disabled: *easy access; disabled toilets; leaflets;
levelled walk and tapping trail*
Catering: *1 picnic area*
Retailing: *postcards/inexpensive souvenirs;
confectionery and ice cream; craftwork;
books*
No. shops: *1*

Operations
Contact: *Miss F Chalmers (Countryside Officer)*
No. employees: (high season) *5 full time;
1 part time* (low season) *5 full time; 1 part
time*
Training: *F/T operations staff, F/T management,
P/T operations staff, P/T management and
casual operations staff are trained in-house and
externally and on specific courses and day-to-day
on job*

Marketing
Annual event(s): *May Day festival, Eastleigh
Town and Country show*
Sponsor: Echo *newspaper*
Other: *market research*
UK promotion: *local newspapers; regional tourist
board; other attractions; leaflets/information
packs; ETB/BTA; Let's go with the children,
Places to Visit*

IZAAK WALTON'S COTTAGE
(local authority run)
historic house; garden; museum

Established: *1920*
Address: *Worsten Lane, Shallowford, Nr. Stone,
Staffs*
Telephone: *(0785) 760278*
Access: (road) *M6/A5013* (rail) *Norton Bridge*
Parking capacity: (cars) *10*
Hours: *Apr to Oct – Tues to Sun – 11am to
4.30pm; Nov and Mar – Sat to Sun – 11am to
4pm; closed Dec to Feb*
Admission (1992): *adults £1.00; children £0.50;
OAP £0.50; student £0.50;*
No. visitors (1992): *3000 (est.)*

Facilities
Interpretation: *leaflets; tour guides*
Retailing: *postcards/inexpensive souvenirs;
craftwork; books; reproductions of famous
artefacts; fishing permits*
No. shops: *1*

Operations
Contacts: *D Richards (Heritage Manager);
J Malpas (TIC Assistant); A Dunne (Heritage
Assistant)*
No. employees: (high season) *2 full time; 4 part
time* (low season) *2 full time*
Training: *F/T management and P/T operations
staff are trained in-house and day-to-day
on job*

Marketing
Annual event(s): *garden party, angling fete*
UK promotion: *local newspapers; regional tourist
board; other attractions; leaflets/information
packs*

Environmental monitoring: *recycling; water
quality*

J

J M BARRIE'S BIRTHPLACE
(National Trust, Scotland)
museum

Established: *1963*
Address: *9 Brechin Road, Kirriemuir, Angus,
  DD8 4BX*
Telephone: *(0575) 72646*
Access: (road) *A926*
Hours: *Easter Weekend, 1 May to 30 Sept –
  Mon to Sat 11am to 5.30pm, Sun 2pm to
  5.30pm*
Admission (1992): *adults £1.50; children £0.80;
  OAP £0.80; student £0.80; booked parties over
  20 – £1.20 or £0.60 (concessions)*
No. visitors (1992): *10 500 (est.)*

Facilities
Interpretation: *leaflets; audio tapes; information
  boards; tour guides; guide books*
Languages: *French; German; Italian; Spanish*
Children: *nappy changing; creche*
Schools: *maximum no. 35; educational literature;
  audio/visual presentation*
Catering: *1 snack bar/food stall*
Retailing: *postcards/inexpensive souvenirs;
  books*
No. shops: *1*

Operations
Contact: *Mrs. Karen Gilmour (Property
  Representative)*
No. employees: (high season) *1 full time; 10 part
  time* (low season) *1 full time; 10 part time*
Training: *F/T operations staff, P/T operations
  staff and casual operations staff, trained in-house
  and on specific courses and day-to-day on job
  using handbooks*

Marketing
Press office; market research
UK promotion: *leaflets/information packs;
  ETB/BTA*
Europe/USA promotion: *British Tourist
  Authority*

JANE WELSH CARLYLE MUSEUM
(trust)
museum

Established: *1984*
Address: *Lodge St, Haddington, East Lothian*
Telephone: *(062) 082 3738.* Fax: *(062) 082 4216*
Access: (road) *A1*
Hours: *Apr to Sept – Wed, Thur, Fri and
  Sat – 2pm to 5pm*
Admission (1992): *adults £0.75; OAP £0.50;
  student £0.50; children free if accompanied by
  adults*
No. visitors (1992): *600 (est.)*

Facilities
Interpretation: *leaflets; maps; guide books*
Schools: *maximum no. 20; educational literature*
Disabled: *access difficult for disabled*

Operations
Contact: *Mrs P Roberts (organiser)*
No. employees: (high season) *2 part time*
Languages spoken: *French; Spanish*

Marketing
Affiliation: *SMC*
UK promotion: *national newspapers; local
  newspapers; regional tourist board; leaflets/
  information packs; East Lothian Tourist
  Guide*

JENNER MUSEUM
(trust)
historic house; garden; museum

Established: *1985*
Address: *The Chantry, Church Lane, High Street,
  Berkeley, Glos, GL13 9BH*
Telephone: *(0453) 810631*
Access: (road) *M5/A38*
Parking capacity: (cars) *30* (coaches) *2*
Hours: *Apr to Sept – Tues to Sat – 12.30am to
  5.30pm, Sun – 1pm to 5.30pm; Oct – Sun
  only – 1pm to 5.30pm*
Admission (1992): *adults £1.20; children £0.30;
  OAP £0.90; student £0.50*
No. visitors (1992): *7000 (est.)*

Facilities
Interpretation: *videos; leaflets; information
  boards; maps; guide books; artefacts,
  reconstructed room*
Languages: *Japanese; French; German*
Schools: *maximum no. 40; educational literature;
  audio/visual presentation; lecture/talk*
Disabled: *easy access; disabled toilets; helpers*
Catering: *1 picnic area*
Retailing: *postcards/inexpensive souvenirs; books;
  prints of medical papers; grapes and vines*
No. shops: *1*

Operations
Contacts: *D Rawlinson (Custodian); G Hannam
  (Deputy Custodian); M Lennox (Deputy
  Custodian)*
No. employees: (high season) *8 part time* (low
  season) *5 part time*
Training: *P/T operations staff and P/T
  management are trained in-house and externally
  and on specific courses and day-to-day on job*

Marketing
Affiliation: *Area Museum Council*
Other: *market research*
UK promotion: *local newspapers; regional tourist
  board; other attractions; leaflets/information
  packs; ETB/BTA*
USA promotion: *USA Friends of Jenner
  Association*

JERVAULX ABBEY
(limited company)
monument

Established: *1960*
Address: *Nr Ripon, N Yorks, H64 4PH*
Access: (road) *A6108*
Parking capacity: (cars) *55* (coaches) *4*
Season: *all year*
Hours: *open daily*
Admission (1992): *adults £1.00; children £5.00*
No. visitors (1992): *20 000 (est.)*

Facilities
Interpretation: *guide books*
Children: *play area; nappy changing*
Schools: *maximum no. 30; no special support*
Disabled: *disabled toilets*
Catering: *1 picnic area*
Retailing: *postcards/inexpensive souvenirs*
No. shops: *1*

Operations
Contact: *Mr I Burdon (partner)*
No. employees: (high season) *4 full time* (low
  season) *3 full time*

Marketing
UK promotion: *regional tourist board*

Environmental monitoring: *recycling; energy
  consumption; hazardous materials*

JOHN MOORE COUNTRYSIDE MUSEUM, THE
(trust)
historic house; garden; museum

Established: *1980*
Address: *41 Church St, Tewkesbury, Glos,
  GL20 5SN*
Telephone: *(0684) 297174*
Access: (road) *M5/M50/A38* (rail) *Gloucester or
  Cheltenham*
Parking capacity: (cars) *50*
Hours: *Easter to Oct – Tues to Sat – 10am to 1pm
  and 2pm to 5pm*
Admission (1992): *adults £0.40; children
  £0.20; OAP £0.20; student £0.20; group
  rates*
No. visitors (1992): *5604*

Facilities
Interpretation: *leaflets; information boards; maps*
Schools: *maximum no. 25; lecture/talk*
Retailing: *postcards/inexpensive souvenirs*
No. shops: *1*

Operations
Contact: *Dr R J King (Curator)*
No. employees: (high season) *1 full time*

Marketing
Annual event(s): *live animals conservation*
Affiliations: *MA, Glos Museums Group, Area
  Museums Council for SW, Museums
  Federation*
UK promotion: *local newspapers; regional tourist
  board; leaflets/information packs; ETB/BTA*

Environmental monitoring: *recycling; hazardous
  materials; chemical usage*

JOHN WESLEY'S CHAPEL
(trust)
heritage centre; church

Established: *1930*
Address: *The New Room, 36 Horsefair, Bristol,
  BS1 3JE*
Telephone: *(0272) 264740*
Access: (road) *M32* (rail) *Bristol Temple Meads*
Parking capacity: (cars) *10*
Season: *all year*
Hours: *Mon to Sat – 10am to 1pm and 2pm to
  4pm; closed BH and Wed, Oct to Apr*
Admission (1992): *free*
No. visitors (1992): *9750*

Facilities
Interpretation: *leaflets; information boards; tour
  guides; guide books*
Schools: *lecture/talk*
Retailing: *postcards/inexpensive souvenirs; books;
  reproductions of famous artefacts*
No. shops: *1*

Operations
Contacts: *Mr L Gunn (Custodian); Rev A George
  (Warden)*
No. employees: (high season) *3 part time* (low
  season) *3 part time*
Training: *P/T operations staff are trained
  in-house and day-to-day on job*

Marketing
Annual event: *Wesley day*
Affiliation: *Methodist Church Heritage Committee*

UK promotion: *regional tourist board;
leaflets/information packs; ETB/BTA*
USA promotion: *British Tourist Authority*

JONAH'S JOURNEY
(church)
theme park; heritage centre; museum

Established: *1987*
Address: *Rosemount Celebration Centre, 120
Rosemount Place, Aberdeen*
Telephone: *(0224) 647614*
Season: *all year*
Hours: *Mon to Fri – 10am to 4pm, Sat/Sun by
arrangement; Oct to Mar – 10am to 2pm;
closed on PH*
Admission (1992): *adults £0.50; children £1.00;
OAP £0.50; student £0.50; group – £10.00 for
12 children*
No. visitors (1992): *8000 (est.)*

Facilities
Interpretation: *leaflets; information boards; tour
guides; personnel*
Languages: *French*
Schools: *maximum no. 35; educational literature;
activities and drama*
Catering: *1 snack bar/food stall*
Retailing: *books*
No. shops: *1*

Operations
Contacts: *Rev D. Graham (Parish Minister); Mrs.
A.M. Gaffron (Supervisor)*
No. employees: (high season) *3 full time* (low
season) *3 full time*
Training: *F/T operations staff are trained in-house
and externally and on specific courses and
day-to-day on job*
Languages spoken: *German*

Marketing
Annual event(s): *drama: Christmas and Easter
story*
Affiliation: *Aberdeen Tourist Board*
UK promotion: *local newspapers; regional tourist
board; leaflets/information packs; Aberdeen
Tourist Board*

JORVIK VIKING CENTRE
(trust)
museum

Established: *1984*
Address: *Coppergate Sq, York, N Yorks, YO1
1NT*
Telephone: *(0904) 613711.* Fax: *(0904) 640028*
Access: (road) *M1/A1* (rail) *York*
Season: *all year*
Hours: *1 Apr to 31 Oct – 9am to 7pm; 1 Nov to
31 Mar – 9am to 5.30pm*
Admission (1992): *adults £3.80; children £1.90;
OAP £2.85*
No. visitors (1992): *900 853*

Facilities
Interpretation: *leaflets; audio tapes; information
boards; slides; tour guides; guide books*
Languages: *Japanese; Dutch; French; German;
Italian; Spanish; Swedish; Norwegian*
Schools: *maximum no. 30; lecture/talk*
Disabled: *easy access; disabled toilets; helpers;
lifts*
Retailing: *postcards/inexpensive souvenirs;
craftwork; books; reproductions of famous
artefacts*
No. shops: *1*

Operations
Contacts: *Mr R Armstrong (Centre Manager);
Ms A Gemmell (Shop Manager); Ms R Bowden
(Marketing Manager)*
No. employees: (high season) *36 full time;
12 part time* (low season) *36 full time; 2 part
time*
Training: *F/T operations staff are trained in-house
and day-to-day on job using handbooks*
Languages spoken: *French*

Marketing
Annual event: *Jorvick Viking Festival*
Sponsor(s): *various*
Other: *press office; market research*
UK promotion: *regional tourist board;
leaflets/information packs; ETB/BTA*
Europe/Asia/USA promotion: *leaflets/brochures;
travel agents' brochures; British Tourist
Authority*

Environmental monitoring: *recycling*

K

KAILZIE GARDENS
(privately owned)
garden; gallery; plant centre

Established: *1977*
Address: *Kailzie, Peebles, EH45 9HT*
Telephone: *0721 720007*
Access: (road) *M10/A1* (rail) *Endinburgh*
Parking capacity: (cars) *50* (coaches) *3*
Season: *all year*
Hours: *Easter to end October – 11am to 5.30pm; other times – 10am to 5pm with honesty box*
Admission (1992): *adults £1.80; children £0.50; OAP £1.80*
No. visitors (1992): *20 000 (est.)*

Facilities
Interpretation: *leaflets; maps*
Children: *play area*
Schools: *maximum no. 40*
Disabled: *easy access; disabled toilets*
Catering: *1 picnic area*
Franchisees: *Easter to end Oct – 11am to 5.30pm; other times – 10am to 5pm with honesty box*
Retailing: *postcards/inexpensive souvenirs; craftwork; books*
No. shops: *1*

Operations
No. employees: (high season) *2 full time; 1 part time*
Languages spoken: *French; Spanish*

Marketing
Other: *market research*
UK promotion: *national newspapers; radio; local newspapers; regional tourist board; other attractions; leaflets/information packs; ETB/BTA; Borders Tourist Office*
Europe promotion: *leaflets/brochures*

Environmental monitoring: *recycling; waste; energy consumption; hazardous materials*

KEIGHLEY AND WORTH VALLEY RAILWAY
(preservation society and limited company)
independent railway

Established: *1968*
Address: *The Railway Station, Haworth, Keighley, BD22 8NJ*
Telephone: *(0535) 645214*
Access: (road) *A629* (rail) *Keighley*
Parking capacity: (cars) *300* (coaches) *10*
Season: *all year*
Hours: *weekends all year – 9.20am to 5pm; daily in Summer – 11am to 5pm*
Admission (1992): *adults £4.00; children £2.00; OAP £2.00; student £4.00;*
No. visitors (1992): *155 000 (est.)*

Facilities
Interpretation: *leaflets; information boards; maps; guide books*
Languages: *Japanese*
Schools: *maximum no. 350; no special support*
Disabled: *easy access; disabled toilets; helpers*
Catering: *2 picnic areas*
Retailing: *postcards/inexpensive souvenirs; books*
No. shops: *3*

Operations
Contacts: *Mr C Ogilvie (Secretary)*
No. employees: (high season) *1 full time; 8 part time* (low season) *1 full time; 2 part time*
Training: *F/T operations staff are trained in-house and day-to-day on job*

Marketing
Annual event(s): *Rail enthusiasts' events and Santa specials*
Affiliations: *Association of Railway Preservation Societies*
Other: *press office; market research*
UK promotion: *regional tourist board; other attractions; leaflets/information packs*

Environmental monitoring: *recycling; waste*

KELBURN COUNTRY CENTRE
(private business)
theme park; historic house; garden; riding school and trekking centre

Established: *1977*
Address: *Fairlie, Ayrshire, KA29 0BE*
Telephone: *(0475) 568685.* Fax: *(0475) 568328*
Access: (road) *A78* (rail) *Largs*
Parking capacity: (cars) *500* (coaches) *50*
Season: *all year*
Hours: *Easter to mid Oct – 10am to 6pm; Winter months – 11am to 5pm*
Admission (1992): *adults £3.00; children £1.50; OAP £1.50; student £1.50; groups £1.50*
No. visitors (1992): *75 000*

Facilities
Interpretation: *leaflets; information boards; maps; guide books*
Children: *adventure playground; play area; nappy changing*
Schools: *maximum no. 1000; educational literature; lecture/talk; ranger service*
Disabled: *helpers; special guided walks*
Catering: *1 picnic area*
Retailing: *postcards/inexpensive souvenirs; confectionery and ice cream; craftwork; books; crafts*
No. shops: *3*

Operations
Contacts: *Earl of Glasgow (owner/Manager); Countess of Glasgow; Ms I Patterson (publicity and special events)*
No. employees: (high season) *12 full time; 22 part time* (low season) *6 full time; 2 part time*

Marketing
Annual event(s): *Woodcraft and Forestry Fair, Noah's Ark carnival and Viking day*
Affiliations: *HHA, ASVA*
Other: *market research*
UK promotion: *national newspapers; radio; local newspapers; regional tourist board; leaflets/information packs; STB*

Environmental monitoring: *water quality; energy consumption; hazardous materials; chemical usage; transport; emissions*

KELLIE CASTLE
(trust)
historic house; castle; garden

Established: *1971*
Address: *Pittenweem, Fife, KY10 2RF*
Telephone: *(03338) 271*
Parking capacity: (cars) *50* (coaches) *2*
Hours: *Apr – weekends only – 2pm to 6pm; 1 May to 30 Sept – 2pm to 6pm daily; Easter – Fri to Mon – 2pm to 6pm; 1 to 31 Oct – 2pm to 5pm daily*

Admission (1992): *adults £2.80; children £1.40; OAP £1.40; student £1.40; NTS and NT members free*
No. visitors (1992): *20 000 (est.)*

Facilities
Interpretation: *videos; leaflets; tour guides; guide books*
Languages: *Dutch; French; German; Italian; Spanish; Danish; Swedish*
Children: *adventure playground*
Schools: *maximum no. 50; no special support*
Disabled: *other audio facilities; wheelchair*
Catering: *1 picnic area*
Retailing: *postcards/inexpensive souvenirs*
No. shops: *1*

Operations
Contacts: *Dr S Blackden (Resident Representative); Mrs M Lockhart (Regional Information Officer)*
No. employees: (high season) *2 full time; 8 part time* (low season) *2 full time; 1 part time*
Training: *P/T operations staff are trained in-house and day-to-day on job and pre-season on site*

Marketing
Annual event(s): *garden open day and children's day*
Affiliations: *NTS*

Environmental monitoring: *conservation*

KELMSCOTT MANOR
(trust)
historic house

Established: *1960*
Address: *Kelmscott, Nr Lechlade, Glos, GL7 3DA*
Telephone: *(0367) 52486*
Access: (road) *A420*
Parking capacity: (cars) *75* (coaches) *1*
Hours: *Apr to Sept – Wed – 11am to 1pm and 2pm to 5pm; Thur and Fri by special appointment*
Admission (1992): *adults £4.00; children £2.00; student £2.00*
No. visitors (1992): *7000 (est.)*

Facilities
Interpretation: *leaflets; information boards; guide books; tour guides by appointment*
Schools: *maximum no. 50; educational literature; lecture/talk*
Catering: *1 picnic area*
Retailing: *postcards/inexpensive souvenirs; confectionery and ice cream; books; clothes; reproductions of famous artefacts*
No. shops: *1*

Operations
Contacts: *H Webb (Administrator); D Chapman (House Steward)*
No. employees: (high season) *3 full time; 5 part time* (low season) *3 full time; 2 part time*
Training: *casual operations staff are trained in-house and day-to-day on job using videos*
Languages spoken: *French; German*

Marketing
UK promotion: *regional tourist board; leaflets/information packs*

Environmental monitoring: *recycling; organic gardening*

KENILWORTH CASTLE
(English Heritage)
castle; monument

Established: *1930*
Address: *Kenilworth, Warwickshire, CV8 1NE*
Telephone: *(0926) 52078*
Access: (road) *M40/M42/M6/A46* (rail) *Coventry*
Parking capacity: (cars) *300* (coaches) *4*
Season: *all year*
Hours: *Easter to Oct – Mon to Sun – 10am to 6pm; Oct to Easter – Tues to Sun – 10am to 4pm*
Admission (1992): *adults £1.50; children £0.75; OAP £1.10; student £1.10; ub40 £1.10*
No. visitors (1992): *100 000 (est.)*

Facilities
Interpretation: *leaflets; audio tapes; information boards; guide books*
Schools: *maximum no. 100*
Catering: *1 picnic area*
Retailing: *postcards/inexpensive souvenirs; confectionery and ice cream; books; middle ages military history; sweets*
No. shops: *1*

Operations
Contact: *M Oarden (Group Custodian)*
No. employees: (high season) *6 full time* (low season) *3 full time; 2 part time*
Training: *F/T operations staff, F/T management, P/T operations staff, P/T management, casual operations staff and casual management are trained in-house and externally and on specific courses and day-to-day on job using handbooks*
Languages spoken: *French*

Marketing
Annual event(s): *various*
Affiliation: *HHA*
Other: *PR Company: Central Office of Information Midlands Area; press office; market research*
UK promotion: *national newspapers; local newspapers; regional tourist board; leaflets/information packs; various; ETB/BTA*
USA promotion: *leaflets/brochures; travel agents' brochures; British Tourist Authority*

KENNET HORSE BOAT COMPANY
(family business)
canal boat trips

Established: *1969*
Address: *32 West Mills, Newbury, Berks*
Telephone: *(0635) 44154*
Access: (road) *M4/A34/A4* (rail) *Newbury/ Kintbury*
Parking capacity: (cars) *20* (coaches) *2*
Hours: *Easter to Sept – daily*
Admission (1992): *varies*

Facilities
Interpretation: *leaflets*
Schools: *maximum no. 100; no special support; literature sent to school*
Disabled: *disabled toilets; wheelchairs accommodated if prior notice*
Catering: *1 bar/public house*
Retailing: *postcards/inexpensive souvenirs; confectionery and ice cream; craftwork; books; canal painted items*
No. shops: *1*

Operations
Contacts: *B and J Butler (proprietors)*
No. employees: (high season) *3 full time; 3 part time*

Marketing
Market research
UK promotion: *national newspapers; local newspapers; regional tourist board; other attractions; leaflets/information packs; Where to Go in Thames and Chilterns*

Environmental monitoring: *recycling; hazardous materials; chemical usage; transport; emissions*

KEW BRIDGE STEAM MUSEUM
(trust)
museum

Established: *1975*
Address: *Green Dragon Lane, Brentford, Middlesex, TW8 0EN*
Telephone: *9081) 568 4757*
Access: (road) *M4/A315* (rail) *Kew Bridge*
Parking capacity: (cars) *41* (coaches) *5*
Season: *all year*
Hours: *11am to 5pm daily – steam engines operate weekends only*
Admission (1992): *adults £2.50; children £1.40; OAP £1.40; student £1.40; disabled £1.40 (£0.90 to £1.70 Mon to Fri – no steam demonstration)*
No. visitors (1992): *23 122*

Facilities
Interpretation: *leaflets; audio tapes; information boards; tour guides; guide books; volunteers*
Schools: *maximum no. 60; educational literature; audio/visual presentation; lecture/talk; must pre-book*
Disabled: *easy access; special tours by arrangement*
Catering: *1 licensed restaurant*
Franchisees: *11am to 5pm daily – steam engines operate weekends only*
Retailing: *postcards/inexpensive souvenirs; books; sewing kits of engines*
No. shops: *1*

Operations
Contacts: *Mr A Condick (Manager); Ms L Bossine (Assistant Manager)*
No. employees: (high season) *6 full time; 5 part time* (low season) *6 full time; 5 part time*
Training: *F/T operations staff, P/T operations staff and casual operations staff are trained in-house and day-to-day on job*

Marketing
Annual event(s): *steam interest and teddy bear day*
Sponsor(s): *local companies*
Affiliations: *AIM, AMSSEE*
Other: *market research*
UK promotion: *local newspapers; regional tourist board; other attractions; leaflets/information packs; ETB/BTA*

Environmental monitoring: *recycling; waste; emissions*

KIELDER FOREST AND CASTLE
(Forestry Commission)
castle; forest

Established: *1926*
Address: *C/O Forest Enterprise, Eals Burn, Bellingham, Hexham, Northumberland*
Telephone: *(0434) 220242. Fax: (0434) 220756*
Access: (road) *A68*
Parking capacity: (cars) *800* (coaches) *20*
Season: *all year*
Hours: *forest open all year; castle open Easter to Oct*
Admission (1992): *free*

Facilities
Interpretation: *videos; leaflets; information boards; maps; tour guides; guide books; personnel*
Children: *adventure playground; play area; nappy changing*
Schools: *maximum no. 52; educational literature; lecture/talk*
Disabled: *easy access; disabled toilets; other audio facilities; guide book*
Catering: *6 picnic areas*
Franchisees: *forest open all year; castle open Easter to Oct*

Retailing: *postcards/inexpensive souvenirs; craftwork; books; clothes*
No. shops: *1*

Operations
Contact: *Mr C Probert (Recreation and Information Officer)*
Training: *F/T operations staff are trained in-house and externally and on specific courses and day-to-day on job*

Marketing
Annual event(s): *various*
Other: *press office; market research*
UK promotion: *local newspapers; regional tourist board; other attractions; leaflets/information packs; ETB/BTA; caravan and camping guides*

Environmental monitoring: *recycling; waste; energy consumption*

KIELDER WATER
(plc)
park/reserve; museum; Europe's largest manmade lake

Established: *1982*
Address: *Yarrow Moor, Falstone, Hexham, Northumberland*
Telephone: *(0434) 240475*
Access: (road) *A68*
Parking capacity: (cars) *300* (coaches) *10*
Season: *all year*
Hours: *visitor centre Apr to Oct – 10am to 6pm; park open all year round*
Admission (1992): *depends on activities*
No. visitors (1992): *300 000*

Facilities
Interpretation: *videos; leaflets; information boards; tour guides; guide books; audio visual and hands on participation*
Children: *adventure playground; play area; nappy changing*
Schools: *educational literature; audio/visual presentation; lecture/talk*
Disabled: *easy access; disabled toilets*
Catering: *1 snack bar/food stall*
Retailers: *postcards/inexpensive souvenirs; confectionery and ice cream; craftwork; books; clothes*
No. shops: *2*

Operations
Contact: *Mr J Lackenby (Reservoir Manager)*
No. employees: (high season) *21 full time; 5 part time* (low season) *15 full time; 3 part time*
Training: *F/T operations staff, F/T management, P/T operations staff, P/T management and casual operations staff are trained in-house and on specific courses and day-to-day on job using handbooks*

Marketing
Sponsor(s): *various*
Other: *press office; market research*
UK promotion: *national newspapers; radio; local newspapers; regional tourist board; other attractions; leaflets/information packs; ETB/BTA*
Europe promotion: *leaflets/brochures; British Tourist Authority*

Environmental monitoring: *recycling*

KING'S LYNN MUSEUMS
(local authority run)
museum

Established: *1904*
Address: *Lynn Museum, Old Market Street, King's, Lynn, Norfolk and Town House Museum,, Queen Street, King's Lynn, Norfolk*
Telephone: *(0553) 775001*
Access: (road) *A49*
Season: *all year*
Hours: *Summer – 10am to 5pm. Winter – 10am to 5pm*

Admission (1992): *adults £0.60; children £0.30;
OAP £0.40; student £0.40*
No. visitors (1992): *18 000 (est.)*

Facilities
Interpretation: *videos; leaflets; information
boards; maps; signs*
Schools: *maximum no. 30; educational literature;
audio/visual presentation; handling sessions*
Disabled: *easy access*
Retailing: *postcards/inexpensive souvenirs; books;
reproductions of famous artefacts*
No. shops: *1*

Operations
Contact: *Katherine Brown (Curator)*
No. employees: (high season) *5 full time; 4 part
time* (low season) *5 full time; 4 part time*
Training: *F/T operations staff, F/T management,
P/T operations staff and casual operations staff
are trained in-house and externally and on
specific courses and day-to-day on job using
videos and handbooks*

Marketing
Annual event(s): *Living History*
Affiliations: *Museums Association*
Other: *market research*
UK promotion: *local newspapers; regional tourist
board; other attractions; leaflets/information
packs*

Environmental monitoring: *recycling; waste;
water quality; energy consumption; hazardous
materials; chemical usage; transport; emissions*

KINGDOM OF THE SEA
(limited company)
aquarium

Established: *1990*
Address: *Marine Parade, Great Yarmouth,
Norfolk, NR30 3AH*
Telephone: *(0493) 330631.* Fax: *(0493) 330442*
Access: (road) *A12 from M25* (rail) *Great
Yarmouth*
Season: *all year*
Hours: *Summer – 10am to dusk; Winter – 10am
to Dusk*
Admission (1992): *adults £4.25; children £3.25;
OAP £3.25; student £2.20; disabled £3.25;
(child) £2.50*
No. visitors (1992): *259 000 (est.)*

Facilities
Interpretation: *videos; leaflets; information
boards; guide books; signs*
Children: *nappy changing*
Schools: *maximum no. 150; educational literature;
audio/visual presentation; lecture/talk*
Disabled: *easy access; disabled toilets*
Catering: *1 picnic area*
Retailing: *postcards/inexpensive souvenirs;
confectionery and ice cream; craftwork; books;
clothes*
No. shops: *1*

Operations
Contacts: *Ms J Jawaskyi (General Manager);
Andrew Larter, Martin Wilson (Catering
Manager, Retail Manager); Tony Shorthose
(Marketing Director)*
No. employees: (high season) *22 full time; 40 part
time* (low season) *22 full time*
Training: *F/T operations staff, F/T management,
P/T operations staff and P/T management are
trained in-house and day-to-day on job using
videos and handbooks*
Languages spoken: *Dutch*

Marketing
Other: *PR Company: Mike Salter
Communications, 3 Hall Rd, Wramplingham,
Norwich NR18 0RX*
UK promotion: *radio; local newspapers; regional
tourist board; other attractions; leaflets/
information packs; holiday guides; ETB/BTA*

Environmental monitoring: *hazardous materials;
transport*

KINGDOM OF THE SEA GT YARMOUTH
(limited company)
marine attraction

Established: *1990*
Address: *Marine Parade, Gt Yarmouth, Norfolk,
NR30 3AH*
Telephone: *(0493) 330631.* Fax: *(0493) 330442*
Access: (road) *A12*
Season: *all year*
Hours: *daily from 10am except Christmas and
Boxing Day*
Admission (1992): *adults £3.99; children £2.99;
OAP £2.99; handicapped from £2.50*
No. visitors (1992): *200 000 (est.)*

Facilities
Interpretation: *videos; leaflets; audio tapes;
information boards; maps; guide books*
Schools: *educational literature; audio/visual
presentation; lecture/talk*
Disabled: *easy access; disabled toilets*
Catering: *1 self-service cafeteria*
Retailing: *postcards/inexpensive souvenirs;
confectionery and ice cream; craftwork; books;*
No. shops: *1*

Operations
Contacts: *Ms J Jawaskyi (Manager); Ms S
Attanson; Mr M Wilson; Ms M Kidner
(Marketing Executives)*
No. employees: (high season) *20 full time; 10 part
time* (low season) *10 full time; 2 part time*
Training: *F/T operations staff, P/T operations
staff and casual operations staff are trained
in-house and day-to-day on job*

Marketing
PR Company: *Mike Salter Communications,
3 Hall Rd, Wramplingham, Norfolk; market
research*
UK promotion: *radio; local newspapers; regional
tourist board; other attractions;
leaflets/information packs*

Environmental monitoring: *waste; water quality;
energy consumption; hazardous materials*

KINGDOM OF THE SEA HUNSTANTON
(limited company)
marine attraction

Established: *1989*
Address: *Southern Promenade, Hunstanton,
Norfolk, PE3 5BH*
Telephone: *(0485) 533576.* Fax: *(0485) 533531*
Access: (road) *A17*
Season: *all year*
Hours: *10am daily except Christmas and Boxing
Day*
Admission (1992): *adults £3.99; children £2.99;
OAP £2.99; handicapped from £2.50*
No. visitors (1992): *160 000 (est.)*

Facilities
Interpretation: *videos; leaflets; audio tapes;
information boards; maps; guide books*
Children: *nappy changing*
Schools: *educational literature; audio/visual
presentation; lecture/talk*
·Disabled: *easy access; disabled toilets*
Catering: *1 self-service cafeteria*
Retailing: *postcards/inexpensive souvenirs;
confectionery and ice cream; craftwork; books;*
No. shops: *1*

Operations
Contacts: *Mr I Foster (Manager); Ms B
Kingwood; Mr M Wilson; Ms M Kidner
(Marketing Executive)*
No. employees: (high season) *20 full time;
10 part time* (low season) *10 full time; 2 part
time*
Training: *F/T operations staff, P/T operations
staff and casual operations staff are trained
in-house and day-to-day on job*

Marketing
PR Company: *Mike Salter Communications,
3 Hall Rd, Wramplingham, Norwich; NR18
0RX; press office; market research*

UK promotion: *national newspapers; radio; local
newspapers; regional tourist board; other
attractions; leaflets/information packs;
ETB/BTA*

Environmental monitoring: *water quality;
hazardous materials*

**KINGS OWN SCOTTISH BORDERS
REGIMENTAL MUSEUM**
(trust)
museum

Established: *1955*
Address: *The Barracks, Berwick upon Tweed,
TD15 1DG*
Telephone: *(0289) 307426.* Fax: *(0289) 331928*
Access: (road) *A1* (rail) *Berwick*
Hours: *Mon to Fri – 10am to 4pm, Sat – 9.30am
to 11.30am; closed on Sun and certain PH*
Admission (1992): *free*

Facilities
Interpretation: *videos; displays*
Schools: *maximum no. 20; educational literature*
Disabled: *disabled toilets; helpers*
Retailing: *postcards/inexpensive souvenirs; books*
No. shops: *1*

Operations
Contact: *Lt Col C G O Hogg (Regimental
Secretary)*
No. employees: (high season) *1 full time* (low
season) *1 full time*
Training: *F/T operations staff are trained
externally and on specific courses using
videos*

Marketing
UK promotion: *leaflets/information packs;
ETB/BTA*

Environmental monitoring: *water quality*

KINGSTON BAGPUIZE HOUSE AND GARDEN
(private)
historic house; garden

Established: *1980*
Address: *Kingston House, Kingston Bagpuize, Nr
Abingdon, Oxfordshire, OX13 5AL*
Telephone: *(0865) 820259*
Access: (road) *A420/A415*
Parking capacity: (cars) *40* (coaches) *1*
Hours: *Apr to Sept – Sun and BH – 2.30pm to
5.30pm, groups at other times by appointment*
Admission (1992): *adults £2.50; children £1.50;
OAP £2.00;*
No. visitors (1992): *2650*

Facilities
Interpretation: *leaflets; maps; tour guides; guide
books*
Children: *nappy changing*
Disabled: *wheelchairs*
Catering: *1 waiter/waitress served*
Retailing: *postcards/inexpensive souvenirs;
books*
No. shops: *1*

Operations
Contact: *T Muir (The Lady)*
No. employees: (high season) *4 part time* (low
season) *5 part time*
Training: *P/T operations staff and casual
operations staff are trained in-house and
day-to-day on job*

Marketing
Annual event: *garden fete*
Affiliation: *HHA*
UK promotion: *national newspapers; local
newspapers; regional tourist board; leaflets/
information packs; Historic Houses Castles and
Gardens; Goldeneye Cotswold Map Guide, etc.;
Tourist Information Centre Leaflets, formerly
TCTB publications*

KINGSTON MAURWARD GARDENS AND FARM
(local authority run)
garden; farm animal park

Established: *1990*
Address: *Dorset College of Agriculture, Kingston Maurward, Dorchester, Dorset, DT2 8PY*
Telephone: *(0305) 264738. Fax: (0305) 250059*
Access: (road) *A35/A356/A354*
Parking capacity: (cars) *100* (coaches) *6*
Hours: *Easter to Oct – 1pm to 5pm daily*
Admission (1992): *adults £2.50; children £1.50*
No. visitors (1992): *10 000*

Facilities
Interpretation: *leaflets; information boards; maps; tour guides*
Children: *play area*
Schools: *maximum no. 30; educational tour*
Disabled: *easy access; disabled toilets*
Catering: *1 picnic area*
Retailing: *postcards/inexpensive souvenirs; confectionery and ice cream; posters*
No. shops: *1*

Operations
Contacts: *T Loasby (Manager); J Grant (Warden); A Grant (Warden)*
No. employees: (high season) *3 part time*
Training: *P/T operations staff are trained in-house and day-to-day on job*

Marketing
Annual event: *open day*
Affiliation: *Dorset Tourism*
Other: *market research*
UK promotion: *local newspapers; regional tourist board; leaflets/information packs; ETB/BTA*

KIRK OF ST NICHOLAS
(parish church)
church

Established: *1160*
Address: *Union Street, Aberdeen, AB1 1JL*
Telephone: *(0224) 643494*
Access: (road) *A92* (rail) *Aberdeen*
Season: *all year*
Hours: *May to Sept – Mon to Fri – 12pm to 4pm and Sat 1pm to 3pm by ringing door bell – Mon to Fri 10am to 1pm*
Admission (1992): *free*
No. visitors (1992): *5000 (est.)*

Facilities
Interpretation: *information boards; tour guides; guide books*
Languages: *French; German*
Schools: *maximum no. 30; educational literature*
Disabled: *easy access; disabled toilets*
Retailing: *postcards/inexpensive souvenirs*
No. shops: *1*

Operations
Contacts: *Rev James C Stewart (Minister); Miss Sheila O Wright (Convener of Wardens); Mr Tom Anderson (Publicity Convener)*

Marketing
Annual event(s): *Aberdeen International Youth Festival performances*
Sponsor: *AIYF*
UK promotion: *leaflets/information packs*

KIRKCALDY MUSEUM AND ART GALLERY
(local authority run)
museum; gallery

Established: *1925*
Address: *War Memorial Gardens, Kirkcaldy, Fife, KY1 1YG*
Telephone: *(0592) 260732*
Access: (road) *M90* (rail) *Kirkcaldy*
Parking capacity: (cars) *20* (coaches) *1*
Season: *all year*
Hours: *Mon to Sat 11am to 5pm, Sun 2pm to 5pm; closed PH*

Admission (1992): *free*
No. visitors (1992): *52 000 (est.)*

Facilities
Interpretation: *videos; information boards; tour guides*
Schools: *maximum no. 30; educational literature; lecture/talk; drama, artefact handling*
Disabled: *easy access; disabled toilets*
Catering: *1 licensed restaurant*
Retailing: *postcards/inexpensive souvenirs; craftwork; books; reproductions of famous artefacts; reproduction Wemyss ware*
No. shops: *1*

Operations
Contacts: *Ms Dallas Mechan (Curator); Gavin Grant (Assistant Curator); Fiona McQuarrie (Secretary/Shop Manager); Vicki Seymour (Exhibition Officer)*
No. employees: (high season) *12 full time; 2 part time*
Training: *P/T operations staff and P/T management are trained in-house and externally and on specific courses and day-to-day on job*
Languages spoken: *French; Italian*

Marketing
Market research
UK promotion: *national newspapers; radio; local newspapers; regional tourist board; other attractions; leaflets/information packs; AA*
Europe promotion: *artist directories*

KIRKLEES LIGHT RAILWAY
(limited company)
theme park; narrow gauge steam railway,miniature fairground rides and working model vehicles

Established: *1991*
Address: *The Railway Station, Clayton West, Nr Huddersfield, W Yorks, HD8 9PE*
Telephone: *(0484) 865727*
Access: (road) *M1/A636* (rail) *Huddersfield*
Parking capacity: (cars) *400* (coaches) *10*
Season: *all year*
Hours: *Whitsun to Sept – Mon to Sat – 1pm, Sun – 11am; Oct to Whitsun – weekends only – Sat – 1pm, Sun – 11am; open all BH except Christmas Day*
Admission (1992): *adults £3.00; children £2.00*
No. visitors (1992): *50 000 (est.)*

Facilities
Interpretation: *leaflets; information boards; maps*
Children: *play area*
Schools: *maximum no. 80; lecture/talk; on request*
Disabled: *easy access; helpers*
Catering: *1 picnic area*

Operations
Contact: *Mr B Taylor (Managing Director)*
No. employees: (high season) *3 full time*
Training: *F/T operations staff are trained in-house and on specific courses and day-to-day on job*
Languages spoken: *German*

Marketing
Annual event(s): *Hallowe'en and Santa specials, also teddy bears' picnic*
Other: *market research*
UK promotion: *television; radio; local newspapers; regional tourist board; other attractions; leaflets/information packs*

Environmental monitoring: *recycling*

KNARESBOROUGH CASTLE AND COURTHOUSE MUSEUM
(local authority run)
castle; museum

Established: *1974*
Address: *Castle Yard, Knaresborough, N Yorks*
Telephone: *(0423) 503340*
Access: (road) *A61* (rail) *Knaresborough*

Season: *all year*
Hours: *grounds open all year; castle and museum – Easter holiday weekend, then 1 May BH to end Sept – 10.30am to 5pm daily*
Admission (1992): *adults £0.80; children £0.40; OAP £0.40; local residents and schools free*
No. visitors (1992): *18 472*

Facilities
Interpretation: *leaflets; information boards; tour guides; guide books*
Languages: *German*
Schools: *maximum no. 60; educational literature; lecture/talk*
Retailing: *postcards/inexpensive souvenirs; craftwork*
No. shops: *1*

Operations
Contact: *Mrs M Kershaw (Curator)*
No. employees: (high season) *4 full time; 8 part time* (low season) *4 full time*
Training: *F/T management, P/T operations staff and casual operations staff are trained in-house and externally and on specific courses and day-to-day on job*

Marketing
Affiliation: *MA*
UK promotion: *leaflets/information packs*

Environmental monitoring: *recycling; water quality; energy consumption; transport; emissions*

KNOLE
(National Trust)
historic house

Established: *1946*
Address: *The National Trust, Knole, Sevenoaks, Kent, TN15 0RP*
Telephone: *(0732) 450608*
Access: (road) *M25*
Parking capacity: (cars) *350* (coaches) *10*
Hours: *Apr to Oct – Wed and Fri to Sun – 11am to 5pm, Thur – 2pm to 5pm*
Admission (1992): *adults £4.00; children £2.00; OAP £4.00; student £2.00; car park £2.50*
No. visitors (1992): *90 000 (est.)*

Facilities
Interpretation: *guide books*
Languages: *French; German*
Children: *nappy changing*
Schools: *maximum no. 100; educational tour*
Disabled: *disabled toilets*
Catering: *1 snack bar/food stall*
Retailing: *postcards/inexpensive souvenirs; books; clothes; gifts,china,linen, etc.*
No. shops: *1*

Operations
Contact: *F C Downer (Administrator)*
No. employees: (high season) *3 full time; 37 part time* (low season) *3 full time; 7 part time*

Marketing
Annual event(s): *operetta, piano recital*
Sponsor(s): *various*
UK promotion: *local newspapers; regional tourist board; leaflets/information packs*

KNOWSLEY SAFARI PARK
(private)
park/reserve; zoo/wildlife attraction

Established: *1971*
Address: *Prescot, Merseyside, L34 4AN*
Telephone: *(051) 430 9009. Fax: (051) 426 3677*
Access: (road) *M57*
Parking capacity: (cars) *3000* (coaches) *100*
Hours: *Mar to Nov – 10am to 4pm*
Admission (1992): *£8.00 per car*
No. visitors (1992): *300 000 (est.)*

Facilities
Interpretation: *guide books*
Languages: *French; German; Spanish*

Children: *nappy changing*
Schools: *maximum no. 6000; educational
  literature*
Disabled: *easy access; disabled toilets*
Catering: *1 bar/public house*
Retailing: *postcards/inexpensive souvenirs;
  craftwork; clothes*
No. shops: *3*

Operations
Contact: *D H Ross*
No. employees: (high season) *45 full time; 20 part
  time* (low season) *18 full time*
Training: *F/T operations staff, P/T operations
  staff and casual operations staff are trained
  in-house and day-to-day on job*
Languages spoken: *French*

Marketing
UK promotion: *television; radio; local
  newspapers; regional tourist board;
  leaflets/information packs*

L

LACE CENTRE, THE
(limited company)
museum; exhibition and retail

Established: *1980*
Address: *Severns Building, Castle Rd,*
Nottingham, NG1 6AA
Telephone: *(0602) 413539*
Access: (road) *M1/A52* (rail) *Nottingham*
Season: *all year*
Hours: *Mar to Dec – 10am to 5pm; Jan and*
Feb – 10am to 4pm. Closed Christmas Day
Admission (1992): *free*
No. visitors (1992): *120 000 (est.)*

Facilities
Interpretation: *leaflets; slides; lectures*
Languages: *Japanese*
Schools: *maximum no. 30; no special support*
Disabled: *helpers*
Retailing: *postcards/inexpensive souvenirs;*
craftwork; books; Nottingham lace
No. shops: *1*

Operations
Contacts: *Mr J Richards (Chairman); Mrs J King*
(Director/Manageress)
No. employees: (high season) *1 full time; 6 part*
time (low season) *1 full time; 6 part time*
Training: *P/T operations staff are trained*
in-house and day-to-day on job

Marketing
Market research
UK promotion: *local newspapers; regional tourist*
board; leaflets/information packs; ETB/BTA
Europe/USA promotion: *leaflets/brochures;*
British Tourist Authority

Environmental monitoring: *recycling; waste;*
water quality; energy consumption; hazardous
materials; chemical usage; transport; emissions

LACE HALL, THE
(limited company)
heritage centre; museum

Established: *1988*
Address: *High Pavement, The Lace Market,*
Nottingham, NG1 1HN
Telephone: *(0602) 484221*
Access: (road) *M1*
Season: *all year*
Hours: *summer – 10am to 5.30pm daily; winter –*
10am to 5pm daily. Closed Christmas Day and
Boxing Day
Admission (1992): *adults £2.00; children £1.00;*
OAP £1.00; student £1.00
No. visitors (1992): *30 500*

Facilities
Interpretation: *videos; leaflets; audio tapes;*
information boards; slides; maps; tour guides;
guide books; personnel; working lace machines
Languages: *French; German*
Children: *nappy changing*
Schools: *maximum no. 60; educational literature;*
audio/visual presentation
Disabled: *easy access; disabled toilets*
Catering: *1 snack bar/food stall*
Retailing: *postcards/inexpensive souvenirs;*
craftwork; books; lace items; pottery and quilts
No. shops: *2*

Operations
Contacts: *Ms E Baxter and Ms V Ford (Duty*
Managers); Mr A James (Director); Ms E Baxter
(Exhibition/Marketing Manager)
No. employees: (high season) *7 full time; 10 part*
time (low season) *7 full time; 7 part time*

Training: *F/T operations staff and P/T operations*
staff are trained in-house and day-to-day on job

Marketing
Annual event(s): *fashion shows and bobbin lace*
weekends
Other: *market research*
UK promotion: *radio; local newspapers; regional*
tourist board; other attractions; leaflets/
information packs; ETB/BTA

LACKHAM GARDENS AND AGRICULTURAL MUSEUM
(trust)
park/reserve; garden; museum; zoo/wildlife
attraction

Established: *1988*
Address: *Lackham House, Lacock, Chippenham,*
Wilts, SN15 2NY
Telephone: *(0249) 443111.* Fax: *(0249) 444474*
Access: (road) *M4/A350* (rail) *Chippenham*
Parking capacity: (cars) *50* (coaches) *5*
Hours: *Mar to Nov – 11am to 5pm daily*
Admission (1992): *adults £3.15; children £1.00;*
OAP £2.00
No. visitors (1992): *20 000 (est.)*

Facilities
Interpretation: *leaflets; guide books*
Children: *adventure playground; play area*
Schools: *maximum no. 5000; by arrangement*
Disabled: *easy access; disabled toilets; 2*
wheelchairs
Catering: *1 picnic area*
Retailing: *postcards/inexpensive souvenirs;*
books
No. shops: *1*

Operations
Contacts: *Mr P Morris (Principal); O Menhinick*
(Horticulture Department Manager); A
Menhinick (Gardens and Museum Reception);
D Tucker (Museum Curator)
No. employees: (high season) *6 full time; 2 part*
time (low season) *6 full time; 2 part time*

Marketing
Annual event(s): *country day, National Gardens*
Scheme Open Day
Other: *PR Company: OATS Ltd, 701/702 Delta*
Business Park, Gt Weston Way, Swindon;
market research
UK promotion: *radio; local newspapers; regional*
tourist board; other attractions;
leaflets/information packs

LADY LEVER ART GALLERY
(national museum)
monument; museum; gallery

Established: *1922*
Address: *Port Sunlight Village, Bebbington,*
Wirral, L62 5EQ
Telephone: *(051) 645 3623.* Fax: *(051) 643 1694*
Access: (road) *M53/A41*
Season: *all year*
Hours: *all year – Mon to Sat – 10am to 5pm,*
Sun – 12 noon to 5pm
Admission (1992): *free*
No. visitors (1992): *89 065*

Facilities
Interpretation: *videos; leaflets; audio tapes;*
information boards; slides; maps; tour guides;
guide books
Languages: *French; German*

Schools: *educational literature; audio/visual*
presentation; lecture/talk; must book prior to
visit
Disabled: *easy access; disabled toilets; car parking*
Retailing: *postcards/inexpensive souvenirs; books;*
slides, posters, cards, pictures, etc.
No. shops: *1*

Operations
Contacts: *R Foster (Director of NMGM) (J Treuherz*
(Keeper of Art Galleries)); A Archard (Head of
Personnel); C Hitchins (General Manager
(NMGM Enterprises)); B Hope (Marketing
Manager)
No. employees: (high season) *23 full time*
Training: *F/T operations staff, F/T management,*
P/T operations staff, P/T management, casual
operations staff and casual management are
trained in-house and externally and on specific
courses and day-to-day on job
Languages spoken: *French*

Marketing
Annual event: *ongoing temporary exhibition and*
events programme
Sponsor(s): *organised by NMGM's development*
officer
Affiliation: *Museums Association*
Other: *press office; market research*
UK promotion: *television; national newspapers;*
radio; local newspapers; regional tourist board;
other attractions; leaflets/information packs;
ETB/BTA
Europe/USA promotion: *leaflets/brochures;*
British Tourist Authority

Environmental monitoring: *hazardous materials;*
chemical usage

LAIDHAY CROFT MUSEUM
(trust)
museum

Established: *1974*
Address: *Laidhay, Dunbeath, Caithness*
Telephone: *(059) 33 244*
Access: (road) *A9* (rail) *Helmsdale or Wick*
Parking capacity: (cars) *14* (coaches) *4*
Hours: *Easter Sun to end Oct – 10am to*
6pm daily (groups by appointment at other
times)
Admission (1992): *adults £0.50; children £0.20*
No. visitors (1992): *14 200 (est.)*

Facilities
Interpretation: *leaflets*
Schools: *maximum no. 20; educational literature;*
lecture/talk
Disabled: *easy access*
Catering: *1 snack bar/food stall*
Franchisees: *Easter Sun to end Oct – 10am to 6pm*
daily (groups by appointment at other times)
Retailing: *postcards/inexpensive souvenirs*
No. shops: *none*

Operations
Contact: *Ms E Cameron (Secretary/Curator)*
No. employees: (high season) *1 part time* (low
season) *1 part time*
Languages spoken: *French; German; Spanish;*
Japanese; Russian

Marketing
UK promotion: *other attractions*

Environmental monitoring: *recycling; energy*
consumption; hazardous materials

LAKE DISTRICT NATIONAL PARK VISITOR CENTRE
(local authority run)
national park visitor centre

Established: *1969*
Address: *Brockhole, Windermere, Cumbria, LA23 1LJ*
Telephone: *(05394) 46601.* Fax: *(05394) 45555*
Access: (road) *M6/A590/A591* (rail) *Oxenholme/ Windermere*
Parking capacity: (cars) *250* (coaches) *8*
Hours: *Easter to Oct – Mon to Sun – 10am to 5pm*
Admission (1992): *free. Car and coach parking charge*
No. visitors (1992): *150 000*

Facilities
Interpretation: *videos; leaflets; audio tapes; information boards; slides; maps; events*
Languages: *Japanese; French*
Children: *adventure playground; nappy changing*
Schools: *educational literature; audio/visual presentation; lecture/talk; role play, educational cruises*
Disabled: *easy access; disabled toilets; special signs; powered transport*
Catering: *3 picnic areas*
Retailing: *postcards/inexpensive souvenirs; craftwork; books; hallmarked gifts*
No. shops: *1*

Operations
Contact: *Tim Haley (Brockhole Centre Manager)*
No. employees: (high season) *5 full time; 20 part time* (low season) *5 full time*
Training: *F/T operations staff, F/T management, P/T operations staff, P/T management and casual operations staff are trained in-house and externally and on specific courses and day-to-day on job*

Marketing
Annual event(s): *various*
Sponsor(s): *various*
Other: *press office; market research*
UK promotion: *local newspapers; other attractions; leaflets/information packs*

LAND FARM GARDEN
(privately owned)
garden; gallery

Address: *Colden, Nr Hebden Bridge, W Yorks, HX7 7PJ*
Telephone: *(0422) 842260*
Access: (road) *M62* (rail) *Hebden Bridge*
Parking capacity: (cars) *20*
Hours: *1st weekend in May to last weekend in Aug – open weekends and BH*
Admission (1992): *adults £1.50; OAP £1.50; student £1.50; £2.50 for conducted groups including refreshments*
No. visitors (1992): *1400*

Facilities
Interpretation: *tour guides; refreshments only for conducted tours*
Schools: *maximum no. 30; educational literature*
Catering: *1 picnic area*
Retailing: *plants*
No. shops: *1*

Operations
Contact: *Mr J Williams (owner)*
No. employees: (high season) *2 part time*
Training: *P/T operations staff are trained in-house and day-to-day on job using videos and handbooks*

Marketing
Annual event(s): *art and sculpture exhibitions and concerts*
UK promotion: *Yorkshire Tourist Board*

LAND'S END
(limited company)
heritage centre; landmark

Established: *1988*
Address: *Land's End, Sennen, Penzance, Cornwall, TR19 7AA*
Telephone: *(0736) 871501.* Fax: *(0736) 871812*
Access: (road) *M5/A30* (rail) *Penzance*
Parking capacity: (cars) *2000* (coaches) *20*
Season: *all year*
Hours: *10am to dusk daily except Christmas Day*
Admission (1992): *adults £4.95; OAP £4.45; student £4.45; under 15s free*
No. visitors (1992): *500 000 (est.)*

Facilities
Interpretation: *videos; leaflets; information boards; slides; maps; guide books; audio visual exhibition*
Languages: *French; German*
Children: *play area; nappy changing*
Schools: *educational literature; by arrangement*
Disabled: *easy access; disabled toilets; ramp on land train*
Catering: *1 bar/public house*
Retailing: *postcards/inexpensive souvenirs; confectionery and ice cream; craftwork; books; clothes; reproductions of famous artefacts; art*
No. shops: *More than 4*

Operations
Contacts: *J Boston (Managing Director)*
No. employees: (high season) *100 full time; 80 part time* (low season) *30 full time; 20 part time*
Training: *F/T operations staff, F/T management and P/T operations staff are trained in-house and externally and on specific courses and day-to-day on job*

Marketing
Affiliations: *CATA, WCTB, ETB*
Other: *press office; market research*
UK promotion: *television; local newspapers; regional tourist board; other attractions; leaflets/information packs; ETB/BTA*

LANDMARK HIGHLAND HERITAGE AND ADVENTURE PARK
(limited company)
park/reserve; heritage and adventure park

Established: *1970*
Address: *Carrbridge, Inverness-shire, (047984) 613*
Telephone: *(047984) 384*
Access: (road) *A9* (rail) *Carrbridge*
Parking capacity: (cars) *300* (coaches) *8*
Hours: *Sept, Oct, June, Apr and May – 9.30am to 6pm; Jul and Aug – 9.30am to 8pm; Nov to Mar – 9.30am to 5pm*
Admission (1992): *adults £4.50; children £3.00; OAP £3.00; student £4.50; group prices on application*

Facilities
Interpretation: *leaflets; information boards; slides; maps; demonstrations and multivision show*
Languages: *French; German; Italian*
Children: *adventure playground; play area; nappy changing*
Schools: *maximum no. 200; special centre*
Disabled: *easy access; disabled toilets*
Catering: *1 picnic area*
Retailing: *postcards/inexpensive souvenirs; confectionery and ice cream; craftwork; books; pottery; food; wine; games*
No. shops: *1*

Operations
Contact: *Danny Fullerton (General Manager)*
No. employees: (high season) *40 full time; 20 part time* (low season) *15 full time; 5 part time*
Training: *F/T operations staff and F/T management are trained in-house and externally and on specific courses and day-to-day on job using videos*
Languages spoken: *French; German; Italian*

Marketing
Affiliations: *ASVA, AIM, SIBM, MA and 3 Area Tourist Boards*
Other: *market research*
UK promotion: *television; radio; local newspapers; regional tourist board; other attractions; leaflets/information packs*

Environmental monitoring: *recycling; waste; energy consumption; chemical usage*

LANREATH FOLK FARM MUSEUM
(private)
museum

Established: *1973*
Address: *Churchtown, Lanreath, Looe, Cornwall, PL13 2NX*
Telephone: *(0503) 220321*
Access: (road) *B3359*
Parking capacity: (cars) *20* (coaches) *1*
Hours: *Easter to Oct – 10am to 6pm daily*
Admission (1992): *adults £2.00; children £1.00; OAP £2.00; student £1.50; group rates*
No. visitors (1992): *7500 (est.)*

Facilities
Interpretation: *leaflets; information boards; tour guides; guide books*
Children: *adventure playground; play area*
Schools: *maximum no. 60; educational literature; educational tour; lecture/talk*
Disabled: *helpers; leaflets; guide book*
Catering: *1 picnic area*
Retailing: *postcards/inexpensive souvenirs; confectionery and ice cream; craftwork; books*
No. shops: *1*

Operations
Contact: *J Facey (Owner)*
No. employees: (high season) *1 full time; 1 part time*

LARGS MUSEUM
(independent)
museum

Established: *1975*
Address: *Kirkgate House, Manse Court, Largs, Ayrshire, KA30 8AW*
Access: (road) *A8*
Hours: *May (usually last week) until mid Sept – 2pm to 5pm daily*
Admission (1992): *free*
No. visitors (1992): *2000 (est.)*

Facilities
Interpretation: *information boards; photographs and displays*
Schools: *maximum no. 40; lecture/talk*
Disabled: *easy access*

Operations
Contact: *Miss Hall (Curator)*

Marketing
UK promotion: *regional tourist board; leaflets/information packs*

LARNE TOURIST INFORMATION AND INTERPRETATION CENTRE
(local authority run)
information and interpretation centre

Established: *1992*
Address: *Narrow Gauge Road, Larne, Co. Antrim, N. Ireland*
Telephone: *(0574) 260088.* Fax: *(0574) 260660*
Season: *all year*
Hours: *Winter – 10am to 5pm; Summer – 9am to 7.30pm*
Admission (1992): *free*
No. visitors (1992): *12 750 (est.)*

Facilities
Interpretation: *videos; leaflets; information boards; maps; guide books*

Languages: *Dutch; French; German; Italian; Spanish*
Children: *nappy changing*
Schools: *maximum no. 30; educational literature; audio/visual presentation; lecture/talk*
Disabled: *easy access; disabled toilets*
Retailing: *postcards/inexpensive souvenirs; confectionery and ice cream; craftwork; books; clothes; reproductions of famous artefacts; maps, jewellery, linen*
No. shops: *1*

Operations
Contacts: *Catherine Vance (Tourist Information Supervisor); Mr H Francis*
No. employees: *(high season) 2 full time; 3 part time (low season) 2 full time; 1 part time*
Training: *F/T operations staff and P/T operations staff are trained in-house and day-to-day on job*

Marketing
Market research
UK promotion: *regional tourist board; leaflets/information packs*
Europe/USA promotion: *leaflets/brochures; travel agents' brochures*

LEA GARDENS
(private company)
garden

Established: *1959*
Address: *Lea, Matlock, Derbyshire, DE4 5GH*
Telephone: *(0629) 534380*
Access: (road) *A6*
Parking capacity: (cars) *100* (coaches) *2*
Hours: *20 Mar to 31 July – 10am to 7.00pm.*
Admission (1992): *adults £2.00; children £0.50; OAP £2.00; season ticket £3.00*
No. visitors (1992): *15 000 (est.)*

Facilities
Interpretation: *leaflets; guide books*
Children: *play area*
Disabled: *disabled in wheelchairs admitted free*
Catering: *1 self-service cafeteria*
Retailing: *postcards/inexpensive souvenirs; craftwork; colour brochure*
No. shops: *1*

Operations
Contacts: *Jon Tye (Managing Director); Peter Tye (Assistant Manager); Jenny Tye*
No. employees: *(high season) 3 full time; 3 part time (low season) 3 full time; 1 part time*
Training: *F/T operations staff and P/T operations staff are trained in-house and externally and day-to-day on job*
Languages spoken: *French; German; Italian; Spanish*

Marketing
UK promotion: *radio; local newspapers; regional tourist board; other attractions; leaflets/ information packs; EMTB – Invitation to Visit*

LEE VALLEY PARK FARMS
(public authority)
sport and leisure park

Established: *1968*
Address: *Stubbins Hall Lane, Crooked Mile, Waltham Abbey, Essex*
Telephone: *(0992) 892291*
Access: (road) *M25*
Parking capacity: (cars) *500* (coaches) *50*
Season: *all year*
Hours: *10am to 4.30pm*
Admission (1992): *adults £2.00; children £1.20; OAP £1.20; groups £1.10 or £0.90*
No. visitors (1992): *37 000 (est.)*

Facilities
Interpretation: *videos; leaflets; information boards; maps; tour guides; guide books*
Children: *play area; nappy changing*
Schools: *educational literature; audio/visual presentation*

Disabled: *easy access; disabled toilets*
Catering: *2 picnic areas*
Retailing: *postcards/inexpensive souvenirs; confectionery and ice cream*
No. shops: *1*

Operations
Contacts: *Mr P Nangle (Director of Leisure Facilities); Ms P Cleaver (Director of Finances and Personnel); Mr C Stringer/Ms C Brooke (Publicity/Promotions)*
Training: *F/T operations staff, F/T management, P/T operations staff, P/T management, casual operations staff and casual management are trained in-house and externally and on specific courses and day-to-day on job using discussion, open forum*
Marketing: *Press office, market research*
UK promotion: *local newspapers; regional tourist board, other attractions; leaflets/information packs*

Environmental monitoring: *recycling; waste; water quality; chemical usage; emissions*

LEEDS CASTLE
(trust)
historic house; castle; garden; museum; zoo/wildlife attraction

Established: *1975*
Address: *Nr Maidstone, Kent, ME17 1PL*
Telephone: *(0622) 765400.* Fax: *(0622) 735616*
Access: (road) *M20/A20* (rail) *Bearsted*
Parking capacity: (cars) *2500* (coaches) *30*
Season: *all year*
Hours: *Mar to Oct – 11am to 5pm daily; Nov to Mar – Mon to Fri (guided tours) – 11am to 4pm; weekends – 11am to 4pm; open by appointment only at other times*
Admission (1992): *adults £6.50; children £4.50; OAP £5.50; student £5.50; family £18.00; disabled £3.50; group rates*
No. visitors (1992): *511 429*

Facilities
Interpretation: *leaflets; information boards; slides; maps; tour guides; guide books*
Languages: *Japanese; Dutch; French; German; Italian; Spanish*
Children: *nappy changing*
Schools: *educational literature; educational tour*
Disabled: *easy access; disabled toilets; braille/sound posts; powered transport; leaflets; guide book; minibus, stair lift, wheelchairs*
Catering: *1 bar/public house*
Retailing: *postcards/inexpensive souvenirs; confectionery and ice cream; craftwork; books; clothes; reproductions of famous artefacts; plants, stationery, pewter; toys*
No. shops: *3*

Operations
Contacts: *G Jackson (Managing Director); D Devlin (Personnel Manager); S White (Merchandising Manager and Marketing); J Oswin (Marketing Manager)*
No. employees: *(high season) 137 full time; 171 part time (low season) 107 full time; 20 part time*
Training: *F/T operations staff, F/T management, P/T operations staff and casual operations staff are trained in-house and externally and on specific courses and day-to-day on job and visitor care training using videos and handbooks*

Marketing:
Annual event(s): *various*
Affiliations: *MHA, BTA, ETB, ATAK, LTB, SEETB, AMCHAM, AWTE, BITOA, SAGTA, EAPS*
Other: *PR Company: Edwards Harvey Associates, Bank Street, Maidstone, Kent, ME14 1PZ; press office; market research*
UK promotion: *national newspapers; radio; local newspapers; regional tourist board; other attractions; leaflets/information packs; ETB/BTA*

Europe/USA/Worldwide via BTA promotion: *leaflets/brochures; British Tourist Authority*

LEEDS CITY MUSEUM
(local authority run)
museum

Established: *1820*
Address: *Calverley St, Leeds, LS1 3AA*
Telephone: *(0532) 478279*
Access: (rail) *Leeds City*
Season: *all year*
Hours: *Tues to Fri – 9.30am to 5.30pm, Sat – 9.30am to 4pm*
Admission (1992): *free*
No. visitors (1992): *120 000*

Facilities
Interpretation: *information boards; guide books; objects*
Schools: *maximum no. 40; no special support*
Disabled: *easy access*
Retailing: *postcards/inexpensive souvenirs; craftwork; books; reproductions of famous artefacts; model kits*
No. shops: *1*

Operations
Contacts: *Mr P Brears (Director); Mrs M Petty; Mr P Brears*
Training: *F/T operations staff are trained externally and on specific courses using videos and role playing*
Languages spoken: *French; German; Italian; Spanish; Japanese; Dutch, Russian*

Marketing
Annual event(s): *various*
Other: *market research*
UK promotion: *leaflets/information packs*

Environmental monitoring: *waste; water quality; energy consumption; hazardous materials; chemical usage; Conservation of grounds*

LEEDS INDUSTRIAL MUSEUM
(local authority run)
heritage centre; museum; historic textile mill

Established: *1982*
Address: *Armley Mills, Canal Rd, Leeds, LS12 2QF*
Telephone: *(0532) 637861*
Access: (road) *A65/A647* (rail) *Leeds*
Parking capacity: (cars) *100* (coaches) *8*
Season: *all year*
Hours: *Tues to Sat – 10am to 5pm; Sun – 2pm to 5pm; open BH Mon*
Admission (1992): *adults £1.10; children £0.50; OAP £0.50; student £0.50; ub40s £0.50, under 5s free*
No. visitors (1992): *40 000 (est.)*

Facilities
Interpretation: *videos; leaflets; audio tapes; information boards; slides; guide books*
Schools: *educational literature; audio/visual presentation; in role experiences*
Disabled: *easy access; disabled toilets; helpers; wheelchair and standard lifts*
Catering: *2 picnic areas*
Retailing: *postcards/inexpensive souvenirs; craftwork; books; clothes; reproductions of famous artefacts; educational materials; gifts*
No. shops: *1*

Operations
Contacts: *Mr P Kelly (Curator); Leisure Services Personnel; Ms M Petty (Purchasing and Stock Controller); Leisure Services Marketing*
No. employees: *(high season) 17 full time; 1 part time*
Training: *F/T operations staff and F/T management are trained in-house and externally and on specific courses and day-to-day on job*

Marketing
Annual event(s): *steam demonstrations, working weekends and exhibitions*

Sponsor(s): *TDAP*
Affiliations: *Y and H Museums Council, MA, Museums Federation*
Other: *market research*
UK promotion: *radio; local newspapers; regional tourist board; other attractions; leaflets/ information packs; Travel Trade News; ETB/BTA; Yorks Tourist Board*

LEGBOURNE RAILWAY MUSEUM
(private company)
museum

Established: *1989*
Address: *The Old Station, Legbourne, Louth, Lincs, LN11 8LH*
Telephone: *(0507) 603116*
Access: (road) *A157*
Parking capacity: (cars) *6*
Hours: *Easter to end Sept – 10.30am to 5pm or later*
Admission (1992): *adults £1.25; children £0.50; OAP £0.75*
No. visitors (1992): *4000 (est.)*

Facilities
Interpretation: *leaflets; information boards; tour guides; guide books; signs*
Children: *play area; nappy changing*
Schools: *maximum no. 50; educational literature*
Disabled: *easy access; disabled toilets; access to signal box, not suitable for severe disabled*
Catering: *1 picnic area*
Retailing: *postcards/inexpensive souvenirs; confectionery and ice cream; books; toys*
No. shops: *1*

Operations
Contacts: *S A Legge (Co-owner); M Legge (Co-owner)*
No. employees: (high season) *1 full time; 1 part time*

Marketing
UK promotion: *local newspapers; regional tourist board; other attractions; leaflets/information packs; ETB/BTA*

Environmental monitoring: *water quality; energy consumption; hazardous materials; chemical usage; emissions; conservation*

LEIGHTON BUZZARD RAILWAY
(limited company)
museum; steam railway

Established: *1967*
Address: *Pages Park Station, Billington Road, Leighton Buzzard, Beds, LU7 8TN*
Telephone: *(0525) 373888*
Access: (road) *M1/A4146/A505* (rail) *Leighton Buzzard*
Parking capacity: (cars) *70* (coaches) *3*
Hours: *Easter to Sept – Sun and BH – 11am to 4.30pm; Dec – Sat to Sun – 10am to 3pm*
Admission (1992): *adults £3.50; children £1.75; OAP £2.75*
No. visitors (1992): *14 000 (est.)*

Facilities
Interpretation: *leaflets; information boards; maps; guide books; personnel; trains*
Schools: *maximum no. 120; video, publicity*
Disabled: *easy access; disabled toilets*
Catering: *1 picnic area*
Retailing: *postcards/inexpensive souvenirs; confectionery and ice cream; books; clothes; souvenirs; railway related items*
No. shops: *1*

Operations
Contacts: *J Horsley (General Manager); N Read (Sales Manager); G Stroud (Marketing, PR Manager)*

Marketing
Annual event(s): *various*
Sponsor(s): *various*

Affiliations: *Transport Trust; TCTB; South Beds Tourist Association; Railway Preservation Society*
Other: *press office; market research*
UK promotion: *radio; local newspapers; regional tourist board; other attractions; leaflets/information packs; various*
Europe/USA promotion: *leaflets/brochures; travel agents' brochures*

LEIGHTON HOUSE
(local authority run)
historic house; museum; gallery

Established: *1896*
Address: *12 Holland Park Rd, London, W14 8LZ*
Telephone: *(071) 602 3316.* Fax: *(071) 371 2467*
Access: (road) *Kensington High St* (rail) *High St Kensington*
Season: *all year*
Hours: *Mon to Sat – 11am to 5.30pm except PH and BH gardens open 31 Mar to 30 Sept*
Admission (1992): *free*
No. visitors (1992): *36 000 (est.)*

Facilities
Interpretation: *leaflets; audio tapes; tour guides; guide books*
Schools: *maximum no. 25; educational literature; lecture/talk; resource packs*
Catering: *1 picnic area*
Franchisees: *Mon to Sat – 11am to 5.30pm except PH and BH; gardens open 31 Mar to 30 Sept*
Retailing: *postcards/inexpensive souvenirs*
No. shops: *1*

Operations
Contacts: *Ms J Banham (Curator); Mr M Volpe (Marketing and Publicity)*
No. employees: (high season) *4 full time; 5 part time*
Training: *F/T operations staff, F/T management and P/T management are trained in-house and externally and on specific courses using handbooks*

Marketing
Annual event(s): *lectures, concerts, study days and receptions*
Affiliations: *MA, Area Museum Service*
Other: *press office; market research*
UK promotion: *local newspapers; regional tourist board; leaflets/information packs; ETB/BTA*
USA promotion: *specialist magazines*

LEITH HALL
(trust)
historic house

Established: *1953*
Address: *Kennethmont, Huntly, Aberdeenshire, AB54 4NQ*
Telephone: *(04643) 216*
Access: (road) *A96*
Parking capacity: (cars) *50* (coaches) *4*
Hours: *1 May to 30 Sept – daily 2pm to 6pm; Oct Sat/Sun – 2pm to 6pm*
Admission (1992): *adults £3.00; children £1.50; OAP £1.50; student £1.50*
No. visitors (1992): *14 000*

Facilities
Interpretation: *guide books; guided tours*
Languages: *French; German; Italian; Spanish*
Children: *nappy changing*
Schools: *maximum no. 50; educational literature*
Disabled: *disabled toilets*
Catering: *1 waiter/waitress served*
Retailing: *postcards/inexpensive souvenirs; confectionery and ice cream; books; NTS products*
No. shops: *1*

Operations
Contacts: *Mrs. Steve Le Gassick (Resident Representative)*
No. employees: (high season) *2 full time; 20 part time* (low season) *2 full time; 1 part time*

Training: *F/T management and P/T operations staff are trained in-house and externally and day-to-day on job and National Trust training*
Languages spoken: *French; Spanish*

Marketing
Press office
UK promotion: *radio; local newspapers; regional tourist board; leaflets/information packs; Local tourist board publications; Scottish Tourist Board*
Europe/Asia/USA promotion: *NESCOT*

Environmental monitoring: *energy consumption; hazardous materials; chemical usage; temperature and humidity*

LENNOXLOVE HOUSE
(trust)
historic house

Established: *1982*
Address: *Lennoxlove Estate, Haddington, East Lothian, EH41 4NZ*
Telephone: *(062) 082 3720.* Fax: *(062) 082 5112*
Access: (road) *A1* (rail) *Edinburgh*
Parking capacity: (cars) *40* (coaches) *6*
Hours: *Easter weekend and May to Sept – 2pm to 5pm – Wed, Sat and Sun*
Admission (1992): *adults £2.50; children £1.50; OAP £2.50; student £2.50; special group rates*
No. visitors (1992): *3000 (est.)*

Facilities
Interpretation: *tour guides; guide books*
Languages: *French; German*
Schools: *maximum no. 100; no special support*
Retailing: *postcards/inexpensive souvenirs; books*
No. shops: *1*

Operations
No. employees: (high season) *14 part time* (low season) *1 part time*
Training: *casual operations staff are trained in-house and day-to-day on job*
Languages spoken: *French; German*

Marketing
Affiliation: *Association of Scottish Visitor Attractions*
UK promotion: *regional tourist board; other attractions; leaflets/information packs*

Environmental monitoring: *water quality; hazardous materials; chemical usage*

LEONARDSLEE GARDENS
(private)
garden

Established: *1920*
Address: *Lower Beeding, Horsham, Sussex*
Telephone: *(0403) 891212*
Access: (road) *M23/A279* (rail) *Horsham*
Parking capacity: (cars) *2500* (coaches) *30*
Hours: *Apr to Oct – 10am to 6pm daily*
Admission (1992): *adults £4.00; children £2.00; OAP £4.00; student £4.00*
No. visitors (1992): *65 000 (est.)*

Facilities
Interpretation: *guide books*
Disabled: *not suitable for disabled*
Catering: *1 picnic area*
Retailing: *postcards/inexpensive souvenirs; confectionery and ice cream; craftwork; books; clothes; plants*
No. shops: *3*

Operations
Contact: *R R Loder (Manager)*
No. employees: (high season) *6 full time; 40 part time* (low season) *4 full time; 4 part time*
Training: *F/T operations staff, P/T operations staff and casual operations staff are trained in-house and day-to-day on job*
Languages spoken: *French; German; Danish*

Marketing
Annual event: *craft fair*
Other: *market research*
UK promotion: *television; national newspapers; radio; local newspapers; regional tourist board; other attractions; leaflets/information packs*

LEVENS HALL AND TOPIARY GARDENS
(sole proprietor)
historic house; garden

Established: *1955*
Address: *Kendal, Cumbria, LA8 0PD*
Telephone: *(05395) 60321*
Access: (road) *M6/A6*
Parking capacity: (cars) *100* (coaches) *10*
Hours: *1 Apr to 30 Sept – Sun to Thur – 11am to 5pm*
Admission (1992): *adults £3.80; children £2.20; OAP £3.30; group discounts available*
No. visitors (1992): *45 000*

Facilities
Interpretation: *tour guides*
Languages: *Dutch; French; German*
Children: *play area; nappy changing*
Schools: *educational literature*
Disabled: *easy access; disabled toilets; only gardens suitable for disabled*
Catering: *1 picnic area*
Retailing: *postcards/inexpensive souvenirs; confectionery and ice cream; craftwork; books*
No. shops: *1*

Operations
Contacts: *Mr P Milner (Accountant/ Administrator); Mrs S E Bagot (owner)*
No. employees: (high season) *7 full time; 24 part time* (low season) *6 full time; 6 part time*
Training: *F/T operations staff, F/T management, P/T operations staff and casual operations staff are trained in-house and externally and on specific courses and day-to-day on job*

Marketing
Affiliation: *HHA*
UK promotion: *local newspapers; regional tourist board; other attractions; leaflets/information packs; Cumbria Magazine, Coach Drivers Club, etc.; ETB/BTA*

Environmental monitoring: *water quality; energy consumption; hazardous materials; chemical usage*

LEWES CASTLE AND MUSEUMS
(trust)
historic house; castle; museum

Established: *1850*
Address: *Barbican House, 169 High Street, Lewes, E Sussex, BN7 1YE*
Telephone: *(0273) 486290*
Access: (road) *M23/A26/A27* (rail) *Lewes*
Season: *all year*
Hours: *Mon to Sat – 10am to 5.30pm, Sun – 11am to 5.30pm*
Admission (1992): *adults £2.50; children £1.25; OAP £2.50; student £1.25*
No. visitors (1992): *31 138*

Facilities
Interpretation: *leaflets; information boards; maps; guide books; personnel; some role plays*
Languages: *French; German*
Schools: *maximum no. 33; educational literature; educational tour; lecture/talk; role play, road show*
Disabled: *none*
Catering: *1 snack bar/food stall*
Retailing: *postcards/inexpensive souvenirs; craftwork; books; reproductions of famous artefacts*
No. shops: *2*

Operations
Contacts: *H Poole (Administrator); J Bleach/J Rix (Senior Custodians)*

No. employees: (high season) *4 full time; 4 part time* (low season) *4 full time; 4 part time*
Training: *F/T operations staff, F/T management and P/T operations staff are trained in-house and externally and on specific courses and day-to-day on job using handbooks*
Languages spoken: *French; German*

Marketing
Annual event(s): *theatrical performances*
Other: *market research*
UK promotion: *radio; local newspapers; regional tourist board; other attractions; leaflets/information packs; ETB/BTA*
Europe promotion: *leaflets/brochures; British Tourist Authority*

LICHFIELD CATHEDRAL
(trust)
church

Established: *1195*
Address: *The Close, Lichfield, Staffs, WS13 7LD*
Telephone: *(0543) 256120*
Access: (road) *M6/M42/A38* (rail) *Birmingham*
Season: *all year*
Hours: *7.30am to 6.15pm daily*
Admission (1992): *booked groups £2.00; otherwise donations*
No. visitors (1992): *200 000 (est.)*

Facilities
Interpretation: *leaflets; information boards; slides; tour guides; guide books*
Languages: *Japanese; French; German; Italian*
Schools: *maximum no. 300; educational literature; audio/visual presentation; lecture/talk; as required*
Disabled: *easy access; disabled toilets; braille/sound posts; other audio facilities; guide book*
Catering: *1 picnic area*
Retailing: *postcards/inexpensive souvenirs; craftwork; books; reproductions of famous artefacts*
No. shops: *2*

Operations
Contacts: *The Dean and Chapter*
No. employees: (high season) *8 full time; 20 part time*
Languages spoken: *French; German; Italian; Spanish; Dutch*

Marketing
Annual event: *Lichfield Festival*
Sponsor(s): *various*
Affiliation: *Heritage Education Trust*
Other: *press office; market research*
UK promotion: *radio; local newspapers; regional tourist board; leaflets/information packs; ETB/BTA*

Environmental monitoring: *recycling*

LIGHTWATER VALLEY THEME PARK
(limited company)
theme park

Established: *1979*
Address: *North Stainley, Ripon, N Yorks, HG4 3HT*
Telephone: *(0765) 635321.* Fax: *(0765) 635359*
Access: (road) *A1/A6108*
Parking capacity: (cars) *1500* (coaches) *250*
Hours: *Easter to Oct – 10am to 5/6pm daily in Jun, July and Aug; other times – weekends, BH and school holidays*
Admission (1992): *adults £7.99; children £6.99; OAP £5.50; student £7.99; special group rates*
No. visitors (1992): *500 000 (est.)*

Facilities
Interpretation: *leaflets; information boards; maps*
Children: *adventure playground; play area; nappy changing*
Schools: *maximum no. 1000; lecture/talk; by arrangement*

Disabled: *easy access; disabled toilets; helpers; helpers admitted free*
Catering: *1 bar/public house*
Retailing: *postcards/inexpensive souvenirs; confectionery and ice cream; craftwork; books; clothes; games, china and glass; gifts*
No. shops: *More than 4*

Operations
Contacts: *Mr G Blades (Operations Director); Mr T Browbridge/Mr T Silver (Operation/ Retail); Ms P Knowson (Sales and Marketing)*
No. employees: (high season) *220 full time; 80 part time* (low season) *21 full time; 25 part time*
Training: *F/T operations staff, F/T management, P/T operations staff, P/T management, casual operations staff and casual management are trained in-house and on specific courses and day-to-day on job*

Marketing
Annual event(s): *various*
Affiliations: *BALPPA*
Other: *PR Company: Lynx PR, The Cookery, Roaley Lane, Leeds LS13 1AA; press office; market research*
UK promotion: *television; regional tourist board; leaflets/information packs; ETB/BTA*

LINCOLN CATHEDRAL
(Dean and Chapter, Lincoln)
historic house; church

Established: *1092*
Address: *Lincoln, LN2 1PX*
Telephone: *(0522) 544544.* Fax: *(0522) 523113*
Access: (road) *A46* (rail) *Lincoln*
Season: *all year*
Hours: *Sept to May – 7.15am to 6pm (5pm Sun); June to Aug – 7.15am to 8pm (6pm Sun)*
Admission (1992): *adults £2.50; OAP £1.00; student £1.00; suggested donations above*
No. visitors (1992): *350 000 (est.)*

Facilities
Interpretation: *leaflets; information boards; tour guides; guide books; personnel*
Languages: *Japanese; Dutch; French; German; Italian; Spanish; Swahili; Arabic*
Schools: *maximum no. 40; educational literature; audio/visual presentation; lecture/talk; pre-visits for teachers*
Disabled: *easy access; disabled toilets; braille/ sound posts; special signs; powered transport*
Catering: *1 self-service cafeteria*
Retailing: *postcards/inexpensive souvenirs; craftwork; books; clothes; reproductions of famous artefacts; prints, tapes and videos*
No. shops: *3*

Operations
Contacts: *Mr R Pond, Mrs C Key (Chapter Clerk/Marketing Officer); The Chapter Clerk; Ms L Tilbury (Visitor Officer); Mr R Parsons (Director of Fabric Fund)*
No. employees: (high season) *45 full time; 100 part time* (low season) *45 full time; 80 part time*
Training: *F/T operations staff, F/T management and P/T operations staff are trained in-house and externally and on specific courses using videos and handbooks*

Marketing
Sponsor(s): *many*
Affiliations: *HHA English Cathedrals Association*
Other: *press office; market research*
UK promotion: *local newspapers; regional tourist board; leaflets/information packs; ETB/BTA; E Mids Tourist Board*

Environmental monitoring: *waste; water quality; energy consumption; hazardous materials; chemical usage; transport; emissions*

LINCOLNSHIRE LIGHT RAILWAY AND HERITAGE CENTRE
(private partnership)
heritage centre; museum

Established: *1973*
Address: *Station Yard, Burgh Le Marsh, Near Skegness, Lincolnshire, PE24 5EZ*
Telephone: *(075) 485 347*
Access: (road) *A158* (rail) *Skegness*
Parking capacity: (cars) *30*
Hours: *Apr, May, Sept – 11am to 5pm – closed Fri and Sat (open Easter); June, July, Aug – 10.30am to 5pm – closed Sat; Oct – Sun, Mon, Tues and Wed – 11am to 5pm; Nov – Sun only; Dec – Santa specials – certain days – 2pm to 4pm*
Admission (1992): *adults £1.50; children £0.75; OAP £1.00; student £0.75; ub40 £1.00; railway ride £0.70 all classes*
No. visitors (1992): *10 000*

Facilities
Interpretation: *information boards; tour guides; personnel; original full size exhibits*
Schools: *maximum no. 50; educational literature; lecture/talk; demonstrations*
Disabled: *easy access; disabled toilets; helpers; leaflets*
Retailing: *postcards/inexpensive souvenirs; books; reproductions of famous artefacts; railway related*
No. shops: *1*

Operations
Contacts: *Mr A Turner/Mrs S Turner (co-Directors)*
Languages spoken: *French; Italian; Swedish*

Marketing
Annual event(s): *Hallowe'en and Christmas events*
Affiliations: *E Mids area Museums Service, AIM, Lincolnshire Museums Forum*
Other: *market research*
UK promotion: *radio; regional tourist board; other attractions; leaflets/information packs; ETB/BTA; museum and railway publications*

Environmental monitoring: *emissions*

LINCOLNSHIRE POULTRY PARK, THE
(partnership)
park/reserve; museum; breeds of domestic poultry from around the world

Established: *1990*
Address: *Lakeside, Barlings Lane, Langworth, Lincoln*
Telephone: *(0522) 682400*
Access: (road) *A158*
Season: *all year*
Hours: *10am to 6pm or dusk daily most of the year*
Admission (1992): *adults £1.50; children £0.50; OAP £1.00; Mencap £0.50 and reductions for disabled and groups*
No. visitors (1992): *1100 (est.)*

Facilities
Interpretation: *information boards; tour guides*
Children: *adventure playground; play area; nappy changing*
Schools: *maximum no. 40; educational literature; projects and eggs*
Disabled: *easy access; disabled toilets; helpers*
Catering: *1 picnic area*
Retailing: *postcards/inexpensive souvenirs; confectionery and ice cream; craftwork; fertile hatching eggs*
No. shops: *2*

Operations
Contacts: *Mr J Sutton (Partner); Mrs D Holmes (Partner)*
No. employees: (high season) *1 full time; 4 part time* (low season) *1 full time; 2 part time*
Training: *casual operations staff are trained in-house and day-to-day on job*
Languages spoken: *French*

Marketing
Market research
UK promotion: *local newspapers; regional tourist board; other attractions; leaflets/information packs; Batemans Guide to Best Attractions*

Environmental monitoring: *recycling; energy consumption*

LIVERPOOL CATHEDRAL
(cathedral)
church

Established: *1978*
Address: *St James Mount, Liverpool, L1*
Telephone: *(051) 709 6271. Fax: (051) 709 1112*
Access: (road) *M62* (rail) *Liverpool Lime St*
Parking capacity: (cars) *150* (coaches) *30*
Season: *all year*
Hours: *8.30am to 6.30pm daily*
Admission (1992): *donations*
No. visitors (1992): *350 000 (est.)*

Facilities
Interpretation: *information boards; slides; tour guides; guide books; guides*
Languages: *Japanese; French; German; Italian*
Schools: *educational tour; lecture/talk; education officer*
Disabled: *easy access; disabled toilets; helpers; other audio facilities; special signs*
Catering: *1 picnic area*
Retailing: *postcards/inexpensive souvenirs; craftwork; books; reproductions of famous artefacts; goods with cathedral insignia; fancy goods*
No. shops: *1*

Operations
Contacts: *H Wilson (Cathedral Secretary); Canon H Thomas (Canon Treasurer); F Munro (Marketing Manageress)*
No. employees: (high season) *70 full time; 30 part time* (low season) *70 full time; 30 part time*
Training: *F/T operations staff, F/T management, P/T operations staff and P/T management are trained in-house and externally and on specific courses and day-to-day on job*

Marketing
Annual event(s): *festival and music*
Sponsor(s): *various*
Affiliation: *NWTB*
UK promotion: *local newspapers; regional tourist board; leaflets/information packs; various; ETB/BTA*

LIVERPOOL MUSEUM
(national museum)
monument; museum; zoo/wildlife attraction; planetarium, aquarium and natural history centre

Established: *1861*
Address: *William Brown Street, Liverpool, L3 8EN*
Telephone: *(051) 207 0001. Fax: (051) 207 3759*
Access: (road) *M62/A59/A57/A580/A5038* (rail) *Lime Street*
Parking capacity: (cars) *20* (coaches) *4*
Season: *all year*
Hours: *all year – Mon to Sat – 10am to 5pm, Sun – 12 noon to 5pm; closed Christmas, New Year's day and Good Friday*
Admission (1992): *admission to museum free, charges to planetarium £1.20 and £0.60*
No. visitors (1992): *526 670*

Facilities
Interpretation: *videos; leaflets; audio tapes; information boards; slides; maps; guide books*
Languages: *French; German*
Children: *nappy changing*
Schools: *educational literature; audio/visual presentation; lecture/talk; teachers courses available*
Disabled: *easy access; disabled toilets; leaflets; 1 wheelchair and car parking spaces available*
Catering: *1 self-service cafeteria*

Franchisees: *all year – Mon to Sat – 10am to 5pm, Sun – 12 noon to 5pm*
Retailing: *postcards/inexpensive souvenirs; craftwork; books; models of dinosaurs, posters; NMGM designer gift collection*
No. shops: *1*

Operations
Contacts: *R Foster (Director of NMGM) E Greenwood (Keeper of Museum); A Archard (Head of Personnel); C Hitchins (General Manager (NMGM Enterprises)); B Hope (Marketing Manager)*
No. employees: (high season) *136 full time; 26 part time*
Training: *F/T operations staff, F/T management, P/T operations staff, P/T management, casual operations staff and casual management are trained in-house and externally and on specific courses and day-to-day on job using videos and handbooks*
Languages spoken: *French; German*

Marketing
Sponsor(s): *Contact NMGM's Development Officer*
Affiliation: *Museums Association*
Other: *press office; market research*
UK promotion: *television; national newspapers; radio; local newspapers; regional tourist board; other attractions; leaflets/information packs; ETB/BTA*
Europe/USA promotion: *leaflets/brochures; British Tourist Authority*

Environmental monitoring: *hazardous materials; chemical usage; emissions*

LLANGOLLEN MOTOR MUSEUM
(private partnership)
museum

Established: *1981*
Address: *Pentrefelin, Llangollen, Clwyd, LL20 8EE*
Telephone: *(0978) 860324*
Access: (road) *A542*
Season: *all year*
Hours: *Easter to Oct – daily 10am to 5pm; Winter – Mon to Fri, 10am to 5pm*
Admission (1992): *adults £1.25; children £0.75; OAP £0.75; student £1.25; family ticket £2.50*
No. visitors (1992): *4500*

Facilities
Interpretation: *information boards*
Schools: *educational literature; lecture/talk*
Disabled: *easy access*
Catering: *1 picnic area*
Retailing: *postcards/inexpensive souvenirs; confectionery and ice cream; spares for collectors' vehicles*
No. shops: *1*

Operations
Contacts: *A. Broadhurst and A. Broadhurst Jr (partners)*
No. employees: (high season) *2 full time; 2 part time* (low season) *2 full time*
Training: *P/T operations staff and casual operations staff are trained in-house and day-to-day on job using videos and handbooks*
Languages spoken: *French; German; Spanish; Japanese; Russian*

Marketing
Annual event: *annual driving rally*
Affiliations: *Museums Association, Wales Tourist Board*
UK promotion: *other attractions; leaflets/ information packs; specialist magazines*

Environmental monitoring: *recycling; energy consumption; hazardous materials*

LLEWELLYN ALEXANDER (FIRE PAINTINGS) LTD
(limited company)
gallery

Established: *1988*
Address: *124–6 The Cut, Waterloo, London, SE1 8LN*
Telephone: *(071) 620 1322. Fax: (071) 928 9469*
Access: *(rail) Waterloo*
Season: *all year*
Hours: *Mon to Fri – 10am to 7.30pm; Sat – 1.30pm to 7.30pm*
Admission (1992): *free*
No. visitors (1992): *10 000 (est.)*

Facilities
Disabled: *easy access*

Operations
Contact: *Ms M Szabo (PA to Managing Director)*
No. employees: *(high season) 6 part time*
Training: *F/T operations staff and P/T operations staff*
Languages spoken: *French*

Marketing
Annual event(s): *private views for new exhibitions*
Affiliations: *London Chamber of Commerce; American Chamber of Commerce*
Other: *press office*
UK promotion: *national newspapers*

LLOYD GEORGE MUSEUM AND HIGHGATE HIS HOME, THE
(local authority run)
historic house; garden; museum

Established: *1948*
Address: *Llanystumdwy, Criccieth, Gwynedd*
Telephone: *(0766) 522071. Fax: (0286) 679637*
Access: *(road) A497 (rail) Porthmadog*
Parking capacity: *(cars) 15 (coaches) 10*
Season: *all year*
Hours: *Easter to Sept – Mon to Sun – 10am to 5pm; Oct – Mon to Fri – 11am to 4pm. Other times by appointment only*
Admission (1992): *adults £2.00; children £1.30; OAP £1.30; family tickets £5.00; group reductions*
No. visitors (1992): *10 000 (est.)*

Facilities
Interpretation: *leaflets; tour guides; guide books*
Languages: *French; Welsh*
Schools: *maximum no. 50; educational literature; audio/visual presentation; lecture/talk; special events organised*
Disabled: *easy access; disabled toilets*
Catering: *1 picnic area*
Retailing: *postcards/inexpensive souvenirs; craftwork; books*
No. shops: *1*

Operations
Contact: *Nest Thomas (Museums Development Officer)*
No. employees: *(high season) 1 full time; 9 part time (low season) 1 full time; 2 part time*
Training: *F/T operations staff and P/T operations staff are trained in-house and externally and on specific courses and day-to-day on job*
Languages spoken: *French*

Marketing
UK promotion: *radio; local newspapers; regional tourist board; other attractions; leaflets/ information packs*

Environmental monitoring: *recycling; waste*

LOCAL INTEREST MUSEUM, THE
(local authority run)
museum

Established: *1972*
Address: *Greaves Street, Oldham, Lancs.*
Telephone: *(061) 678 4657. Fax: (061) 627 1025*
Access: *(road) M62/A627 (rail) Oldham*

Parking capacity: *(cars) 200*
Season: *all year*
Hours: *all year – Mon and Wed to Fri – 10am to 5pm, Sat 10am to 4pm; closed Tues at 1pm*
Admission (1992): *free*
No. visitors (1992): *25 000 (est.)*

Facilities
Interpretation: *videos; leaflets; information boards; activity guide for sale*
Languages: *Urdu; Bengali; Punjabi*
Schools: *maximum no. 35; educational literature; educational tour; lecture/talk; education officer*
Disabled: *easy access; disabled toilets*
Catering: *1 licensed restaurant*
Retailing: *postcards/inexpensive souvenirs; books*
No. shops: *1*

Operations
Contacts: *A McEvoy (Principal Museum Officer); C Mamion (Marketing and Promotions Officer)*
No. employees: *(high season) 12 full time; 2 part time (low season) 12 full time; 2 part time*
Training: *F/T operations staff are trained in-house and day-to-day on job using videos and handbooks*

Marketing
Annual event(s): *various*
UK promotion: *radio; local newspapers; leaflets/ information packs*

LOCHORE MEADOWS COUNTRY PARK
(local authority run)
park/reserve

Established: *1976*
Address: *Ballingry, Fife, KY5 8BA*
Telephone: *(0592) 860086. Fax: (0592) 860093*
Access: *(road) M90*
Parking capacity: *(cars) 120 (coaches) 10*
Season: *all year*
Hours: *park centre – Summer – 9am to 9pm; Winter – 9am to 5pm*
No. visitors (1992): *400 000 (est.)*

Facilities
Interpretation: *leaflets; information boards; slides; tour guides*
Children: *adventure playground; nappy changing*
Schools: *maximum no. 300; educational literature; audio/visual presentation; lecture/talk; school visits*
Disabled: *easy access; disabled toilets; special signs; leaflets; trained staff*
Catering: *3 picnic areas*

Operations
Contacts: *N Donaldson (Deputy Park ranger); M Davidson (Administration Assistant)*
No. employees: *(high season) 42 full time; 30 part time (low season) 42 full time*
Training: *F/T operations staff, F/T management and P/T operations staff are trained in-house and externally and on specific courses and day-to-day on job using handbooks*

Marketing
Annual event(s): *various*
Other: *PR Company: Hodge Associates, Fife House; press office*
UK promotion: *local newspapers; regional tourist board; leaflets/information packs*
Europe promotion: *leaflets/brochures*

LOCHWINNOCH COMMUNITY MUSEUM
(local authority run)
museum; gallery

Established: *1984*
Address: *High St, Lochwinnoch, Renfrewshire, Scotland, PA12 4AB*
Telephone: *(0505) 842615*
Access: *(road) M8/A37 (rail) Lochwinnoch*
Parking capacity: *(cars) 5 (coaches) 1*

Season: *all year*
Hours: *open all year except PH; Mon, Wed and Fri – 10am to 1pm, 2pm to 5pm and 6pm to 8pm; Tues and Sat – 10am to 1pm and 2pm to 5pm; closed Thur and Sun*
Admission (1992): *free*
No. visitors (1992): *12 000 (est.)*

Facilities
Interpretation: *leaflets; information boards; maps*
Schools: *maximum no. 30; educational literature; lecture/talk*
Disabled: *easy access*

Operations
Contacts: *Mr C Lee (Community Museums Officer); Mr P Wetherall (Department of Arts and Libraries)*
No. employees: *(high season) 2 full time*

Marketing
Annual event(s): *annual art exhibition*
Affiliations: *MA*
UK promotion: *national newspapers; radio; local newspapers; leaflets/information packs*

Environmental monitoring: *recycling; water quality; energy consumption; hazardous materials*

LOCHWINNOCH NATURE CENTRE
(charity)
park/reserve

Established: *1980*
Address: *Largs Road, Lochwinnoch, Renfrewshire*
Telephone: *0505 842663*
Access: *(road) M8*
Parking capacity: *(cars) 40 (coaches) 2*
Season: *all year*
Hours: *10am to 5pm daily*
Admission (1992): *adults £1.00; members free*
No. visitors (1992): *35 000 (est.)*

Facilities
Schools: *maximum no. 50; educational literature; audio/visual presentation; lecture/talk*
Disabled: *easy access*
Retailing: *postcards/inexpensive souvenirs; craftwork; books; clothes*
No. shops: *1*

Operations
Contacts: *G. Christer (Manager); J. Shaw (Shop Manageress)*
No. employees: *(high season) 4 full time; 2 part time*
Training: *F/T operations staff, F/T management and P/T operations staff are trained in-house and on specific courses*
Languages spoken: *French*

Marketing
Press office; market research
UK promotion: *national newspapers; regional tourist board; other attractions; leaflets/ information packs*

Environmental monitoring: *energy consumption*

LOGAN BOTANIC GARDEN
(trust)
garden

Established: *1969*
Address: *Port Logan, Stranraer, Wigtownshire, DG9 9ND*
Telephone: *077686 231. Fax: 077686 333*
Access: *(road) A75/A716 (rail) Stranraer*
Parking capacity: *(cars) 50 (coaches) 5*
Hours: *15 March to 31 Oct – 10am to 6pm daily*
Admission (1992): *adults £1.50; children £0.50; OAP £1.00; student £1.00; 10 per cent discount for parties of 15 or more*
No. visitors (1992): *35 000*

Facilities
Interpretation: *guide books; information centre*
Schools: *maximum no. 50; educational literature*
Disabled: *easy access; disabled toilets; free use of wheelchair*
Catering: *1 licensed restaurant*
Franchisees: *15 March to 31 Oct – 10am to 6pm daily*
Retailing: *postcards/inexpensive souvenirs; craftwork; books; plants*
No. shops: *1*

Operations
Contacts: *Mr B Unwin (Assistant Curator)*
No. employees: (high season) *7 full time; 4 part time* (low season) *7 full time; 2 part time*
Training: *F/T operations staff are trained in-house and externally and on specific courses and day-to-day on job using videos and handbooks*

Marketing
UK promotion: *local newspapers; other attractions; leaflets/information packs*

Environmental monitoring: *water quality; energy consumption*

LONDON BUTTERFLY HOUSE
(limited company)
garden; zoo/wildlife attraction

Established: *1981*
Address: *Syon Park, Brentford, Middx, TW8 8JF*
Telephone: *(081) 560 7272.* Fax: *(081) 560 0378*
Access: (road) *A4* (rail) *Gunnersbury Park*
Parking capacity: (cars) *600* (coaches) *20*
Season: *all year*
Hours: *BST – 10am to 5pm; BWT – 10am to 3.30pm except 25, 26 Dec*
Admission (1992): *adults £2.20; children £1.40; OAP £1.40; student £2.20; family ticket (2 + 4) £6.50*
No. visitors (1992): *110 000 (est.)*

Facilities
Interpretation: *leaflets; information boards; guide books*
Schools: *maximum no. 100; lecture/talk*
Disabled: *easy access*
Catering: *4 picnic areas*
Retailers: *postcards/inexpensive souvenirs; confectionery and ice cream; craftwork; books; clothes*
No. shops: *More than 4*

Operations
Contact: *Mr J Burgess (Manager)*
No. employees: (high season) *3 full time; 3 part time* (low season) *2 full time; 1 part time*
Training: *F/T operations staff and P/T operations staff are trained in-house and day-to-day on job*

Marketing
UK promotion: *regional tourist board; other attractions; leaflets/information packs; ETB/BTA*
Europe promotion: *leaflets/brochures; British Tourist Authority*

Environmental monitoring: *Conservation*

LONDON CANAL MUSEUM
(trust)
heritage centre; museum

Established: *1992*
Address: *12/13 New Wharf Rd, King's cross, London, N1 9RT*
Telephone: *(071) 713 0836*
Access: (rail) *King's Cross*
Season: *all year*
Hours: *Tues to Sun – 10am to 4.30pm, open BH; closed 24–26 Dec, 1 and 2 Jan and 14–21 Feb*
Admission (1992): *adults £2.50; children £1.25; OAP £1.25; student £1.25; unwaged £1.25, groups £1.00; £2.00*
No. visitors (1992): *10 000 (est.)*

Facilities
Interpretation: *videos; information boards; maps; tour guides*
Schools: *maximum no. 30; educational literature; lecture/talk; classroom*
Disabled: *ground floor access at the moment*
Retailing: *postcards/inexpensive souvenirs; craftwork; books; canal art*
No. shops: *1*

Operations
Contact: *Mr N Sadler (Curator/Director)*
No. employees: (high season) *1 full time; 3 part time* (low season) *1 full time; 2 part time*
Languages spoken: *Thai; Philippino*

Marketing
UK promotion: *local newspapers; other attractions; leaflets/information packs*

LONDON ECOLOGY CENTRE
(trust)
gallery; ecology centre

Established: *1985*
Address: *45 Shelton St, Covent Garden, London, WC2H 9HJ*
Telephone: *(071) 379 4324*
Access: (rail) *Covent Garden*
Season: *all year*
Hours: *Mon to Sat – 10am to 6pm (8pm in Dec)*
Admission (1992): *free*
No. visitors (1992): *45 000 (est.)*

Facilities
Interpretation: *leaflets; information boards; personnel*
Schools: *maximum no. 50; no special support*
Catering: *1 snack bar/food stall*
Franchisees: *Mon to Sat – 10am to 6pm (8pm in Dec)*
Retailing: *postcards/inexpensive souvenirs; craftwork; books; energy saving goods*
No. shops: *1*

Operations
Contact: *Ms D Cripps (Manager)*
No. employees: (high season) *2 full time* (low season) *2 full time*
Training: *F/T operations staff, F/T management and casual operations staff are trained in-house and externally and on specific courses and day-to-day on job*

Marketing
Annual event(s): *various*
Other: *market research*
UK promotion: *national newspapers; radio; local newspapers; leaflets/information packs; ETB/BTA*

LONDON TOY AND MODEL MUSEUM
(limited company)
museum

Established: *1982*
Address: *21/23 Craven Hill, London, W2 3EN*
Telephone: *(071) 262 9450.* Fax: *(071) 724 9111*
Access: (road) *Bayswater Rd* (rail) *Paddington*
Season: *all year*
Hours: *Tues to Sat – 10am to 5.30pm, Sun and BH – 11am to 5.30pm*
Admission (1992): *adults £3.00; children £1.50; OAP £2.00; student £2.00; reductions for groups*
No. visitors (1992): *67 902*

Facilities
Interpretation: *leaflets; information boards; tour guides; guide books*
Languages: *Japanese; French; German; Italian; Spanish*
Children: *play area; nappy changing*
Schools: *maximum no. 80; educational literature*
Disabled: *easy access; to be developed*
Catering: *1 picnic area*
Retailing: *postcards/inexpensive souvenirs; craftwork; books; clothes*
No. shops: *1*

Operations
Contacts: *Mr H Macgillivray (Curator); Ms J Rayner (Operations); Mr T Hayward (Maintenance)*
No. employees: (high season) *10 full time; 5 part time*
Training: *F/T operations staff, F/T management, P/T operations staff and casual operations staff are trained in-house and on specific courses and day-to-day on job*
Languages spoken: *French; Italian; Spanish; Portuguese*

Marketing
Annual event(s): *Toy boat regatta*
Affiliations: *SAGTA, British Toy Makers' Guild*
Other: *press office; market research*
UK promotion: *television; national newspapers; radio; local newspapers; regional tourist board; other attractions; leaflets/information packs*

Environmental monitoring: *recycling*

LONGDALE CRAFT CENTRE AND MUSEUM
(limited company)
museum; gallery; craft village and workshops

Established: *1974*
Address: *Longdale Lane, Ravenshead, Nottinghamshire, NG15 9AH*
Telephone: *(0623) 794858.* Fax: *(0623) 794858*
Parking capacity: (cars) *70* (coaches) *6*
Season: *all year*
Hours: *9am to 6pm – craft village and museum; 9am to 10pm – restaurant*
Admission (1992): *adults £1.20; children £1.00; OAP £1.00; student £1.00*
No. visitors (1992): *100 000 (est.)*

Facilities
Interpretation: *leaflets; information boards; maps; tour guides; guide books; artists as guides*
Children: *nappy changing*
Schools: *maximum no. 56; educational literature; lecture/talk*
Disabled: *easy access; disabled toilets; leaflets; guide book*
Catering: *1 picnic area*
Retailing: *postcards/inexpensive souvenirs; craftwork; books; clothes; crafts by resident artists*
No. shops: *2*

Operations
Contacts: *Mr G Brown FRSA (Director); Ms J Purcell (Manager)*
No. employees: (high season) *5 full time; 20 part time* (low season) *5 full time; 20 part time*
Training: *F/T operations staff, P/T operations staff and casual operations staff are trained in-house and day-to-day on job*
Languages spoken: *French; Italian*

Marketing
Annual event(s): *exhibitions*
UK promotion: *television; national newspapers; radio; local newspapers; regional tourist board; other attractions; leaflets/information packs; ETB/BTA*
Coach operators promotion: *leaflets/brochures; travel agents' brochures; British Tourist Authority*

LONGDOWN DAIRY FARM
(limited company)
zoo/wildlife attraction; working dairy farm

Established: *1984*
Address: *Longdown, Ashurst, Nr Southampton, Hants*
Telephone: *(0703) 293326.* Fax: *(0703) 293376*

Facilities
Interpretation: *leaflets; information boards; maps; tour guides; guide books*

Children: *adventure playground; play area; nappy changing*
Schools: *maximum no. 100; educational literature; lecture/talk*
Disabled: *easy access; disabled toilets*
Retailing: *postcards/inexpensive souvenirs; confectionery and ice cream; craftwork; books; clothes*
No. shops: *1*

Operations
Contacts: *Mr B Pass (Farm Manager); Ms A Todhunter (Marketing Manager)*
No. employees: *(high season) 7 full time; 6 part time (low season) 7 full time; 2 part time*
Training: *F/T operations staff and P/T operations staff are trained in-house and externally and on specific courses and day-to-day on job*
Languages spoken: *French; German*

Marketing
Press office; market research
UK promotion: *local newspapers; regional tourist board; other attractions; leaflets/information packs*

Environmental monitoring: *no smoking*

LONGLEAT HOUSE AND SAFARI PARK
(trust)
historic house; park/reserve; garden; zoo/wildlife attraction

Established: *1949*
Address: *Warminster, Wilts*
Telephone: *(0985) 844551.* Fax: *(0985) 844838*
Access: *(road) M3/M4/A303/A36 (rail) Westbury/Warminster*
Parking capacity: *(cars) 700 (coaches) 80*
Season: *all year*
Hours: *Summer – 10.30am to 6pm daily; Winter – 10.30am to 4pm daily*
Admission (1992): *adults £10.00; children £8.00; OAP £8.00; group rates*
No. visitors (1992): *500 000 (est.)*

Facilities
Interpretation: *leaflets; audio tapes; information boards; tour guides; guide books*
Languages: *French; German*
Children: *adventure playground; play area; nappy changing*
Schools: *educational literature*
Disabled: *easy access; disabled toilets*
Catering: *1 bar/public house*
Franchisees: *Summer – 10.30am to 6pm daily*
Retailing: *postcards/inexpensive souvenirs; confectionery and ice cream; craftwork; books; toys,china,novelty goods, etc.*
No. shops: *More than 4*

Operations
Contact: *T R W Moore (Land Agent)*
No. employees: *(high season) 125 full time; 117 part time (low season) 72 full time; 8 part time*
Training: *F/T operations staff, F/T management, P/T operations staff, P/T management, casual operations staff and casual management are trained in-house and day-to-day on job*

Marketing
Other: *press office; market research*
UK promotion: *television; local newspapers; regional tourist board; other attractions; leaflets/information packs; various; ETB/BTA*

Environmental monitoring: *waste; water quality; hazardous materials; chemical usage; emissions*

LONGSTONE HERITAGE CENTRE
(partnership)
heritage centre

Established: *1986*
Address: *St Mary's, Isles of Scilly, Cornwall, TR21 0NW*

Telephone: *(0702) 22924* Fax: *(0702) 22924*
Parking capacity: *(cars) 10*
Hours: *Apr to Oct – 9am to 5pm daily*
Admission (1992): *adults £1.75; children £0.90; OAP £1.50; student £1.75*
No. visitors (1992): *10 000 (est.)*

Facilities
Interpretation: *leaflets; audio tapes; information boards; maps; animated models*
Children: *play area; nappy changing*
Schools: *maximum no. 55; no special support*
Disabled: *helpers*
Catering: *1 picnic area*
Retailing: *postcards/inexpensive souvenirs; books; birthdate newspapers to order*
No. shops: *1*

Operations
Contact: *I Willsher (owner)*
No. employees: *(high season) 3 full time (low season) 2 full time*
Languages spoken: *French; German; Italian*

Marketing
Affiliations: *IOS Tourism Association*
UK promotion: *local newspapers; regional tourist board; leaflets/information packs*

Environmental monitoring: *waste; water quality; energy consumption; hazardous materials; chemical usage*

LOOK OUT, THE
(local authority run)
heritage centre

Established: *1991*
Address: *Nine Mile Ride, Bracknell, Berks*
Telephone: *(0344) 868222.* Fax: *(0344) 869343*
Access: *(road) M3/A322 (rail) Bracknell*
Parking capacity: *(cars) 250 (coaches) 10*
Season: *all year*
Hours: *10am to 5pm daily*
Admission (1992): *adults £1.50; children £1.00; OAP £1.00; student £1.00*
No. visitors (1992): *300 000*

Facilities
Interpretation: *leaflets; information boards; slides; maps; guide books*
Children: *nappy changing*
Schools: *maximum no. 30; educational literature; educational tour; lecture/talk*
Disabled: *easy access; disabled toilets*
Catering: *1 picnic area*
Retailing: *postcards/inexpensive souvenirs; craftwork; books*
No. shops: *1*

Operations
Contacts: *A Swinney (Centre Manager); H Sussex (Support Services Officer); C Warren (Marketing Officer)*
No. employees: *(high season) 4 full time; 14 part time (low season) 4 full time; 14 part time*
Training: *F/T operations staff, F/T management, P/T operations staff and P/T management are trained in-house and on specific courses and day-to-day on job*

Marketing
Annual event(s): *various*
Other: *market research*
UK promotion: *local newspapers; regional tourist board; other attractions; leaflets/information packs; Places to Visit in Winter, Let's Go with the Children, etc.; ETB/BTA*

LOST GARDENS OF HELIGAN, THE
(limited company)
park/reserve; garden; museum

Established: *1992*
Address: *Heligan Gardens, Pentewan, St Austell, Cornwall, PL26 5EN*
Telephone: *(0726) 844157.* Fax: *(0726) 843023*
Access: *(road) B3273 (rail) St Austell*
Parking capacity: *(cars) 120 (coaches) 5*

Season: *all year*
Hours: *10.30am to 5pm daily except Christmas Day*
Admission (1992): *adults £2.50; children £1.50; OAP £2.00; Friends of Heligan £12.00 to admit 2 persons for a year*
No. visitors (1992): *10 000*

Facilities
Interpretation: *leaflets; information boards; maps; tour guides; guide books*
Children: *nappy changing*
Schools: *maximum no. 50; educational literature; lecture/talk; wildlife warden and forester*
Disabled: *disabled toilets; special signs*
Catering: *1 picnic area*
Retailing: *postcards/inexpensive souvenirs; confectionery and ice cream; craftwork; books; plants*
No. shops: *1*

Operations
Contacts: *Mr T Smit (Project Director); Mr J Nelson (Restoration of Buildings); Mr R Poole (Marketing Director)*
No. employees: *(high season) 12 full time; 2 part time (low season) 12 full time; 2 part time*
Training: *F/T operations staff are trained in-house and externally and on specific courses and day-to-day on job*

Environmental monitoring: *recycling; waste; chemical usage*

LOTHERTON HALL BIRD GARDEN
(local authority run)
zoo/wildlife attraction

Established: *1979*
Address: *Towton Rd, Nr Aberford, Leeds, W Yorks, LS25 3EB*
Telephone: *(0532) 813723*
Access: *(road) M1/A1 (rail) Garforth, Leeds*
Season: *all year*
Hours: *Mar to Oct – Mon to Fri – 10am to 5pm, Sat and Sun – 11am to 6pm, Oct to Mar – Mon to Fri – 10am to 4pm, Sat and Sun – 11am to 4pm*
Admission (1992): *free*
No. visitors (1992): *600 000 (est.)*

Facilities
Interpretation: *information boards; slides; tour guides; guide books*
Schools: *educational literature; audio/visual presentation; lecture/talk*
Disabled: *easy access; disabled toilets*
Catering: *1 picnic area*
Retailing: *postcards/inexpensive souvenirs; books*
No. shops: *1*

Operations
Contact: *Mr W Timmis (Curator)*
No. employees: *(high season) 5 full time (low season) 5 full time*
Training: *F/T management are trained in-house and on specific courses*
Languages spoken: *French*

Marketing
Press office; market research
UK promotion: *leaflets/information packs*

LULWORTH COVE HERITAGE
(privately owned)
heritage centre

Established: *1991*
Address: *The Coach House, Lulworth Cove, Nr Wareham, Dorset, BH20 5RQ*
Telephone: *(092) 941 587*
Access: *(road) A31/A35/B3071 (rail) Wool*
Season: *all year*
Hours: *Summer – 10am to 6pm, Winter – 11am to 4pm*

Admission (1992): *adults £1.50; children £0.80;
OAP £0.80; student £0.80; family ticket (2 + 2)
£4.00*
No. visitors (1992): *20 000 (est.)*

Facilities
Interpretation: *videos; information boards*
Schools: *maximum no. 25; educational
literature; audio/visual presentation;
questionnaire*
Disabled: *easy access; disabled toilets*
Catering: *1 bar/public house*
Retailing: *postcards/inexpensive souvenirs;
craftwork; books; clothes*
No. shops: *1*

Operations
Contacts: *Mrs S Hallett (Manageress);
Ms P Spooner (Marketing)*
No. employees: (high season) *1 full time* (low
season) *1 full time*

Marketing
Affiliation: *National Heritage*
Other: *PR Company: SOS, 2 Mill St, Corfe
Mullen, Wimborne, Dorset; press office; market
research*
UK promotion: *national newspapers; local
newspapers; regional tourist board; other
attractions; leaflets/information packs;
ETB/BTA*

LUTON MUSEUM AND ART GALLERY
(local authority run)
museum

Established: *1931*
Address: *Wardown Park, Luton, Beds, LU2 7HA*
Telephone: *(0582) 36941.* Fax: *(0582) 483178*
Access: (road) *M1/A6* (rail) *Luton*
Parking capacity: (cars) *100* (coaches) *5*
Season: *all year*
Hours: *all year – Mon to Sat – 10am to 5pm,
Sun – 1pm to 5pm*
Admission (1992): *free*
No. visitors (1992): *57 000*

Facilities
Interpretation: *leaflets; audio tapes; information
boards; guide books*
Children: *adventure playground; play area*
Schools: *maximum no. 100; educational literature;
pre-visit; handling collection*
Disabled: *easy access*
Catering: *1 picnic area*
Retailing: *postcards/inexpensive souvenirs;
craftwork; books; reproductions of famous
artefacts; stationery; giftware*
No. shops: *1*

Operations
Contact: *L Burgess (Sales and Administration
Officer)*
No. employees: (high season) *21 full time; 7 part
time*
Training: *F/T operations staff, F/T management,
P/T operations staff and P/T management are
trained in-house and externally and on specific
courses and day-to-day on job*

Marketing
Annual event(s): *various*
Other: *PR Company: Arranged by Luton Borough
Council; press office; market research*
UK promotion: *radio; local newspapers; regional
tourist board; other attractions; leaflets/
information packs; ETB/BTA*
Europe promotion: *leaflets/brochures; British
Tourist Authority*

LYME REGIS EXPERIENCE
(limited company)
historic experience

Established: *1990*
Address: *Marine Parade, Lyme Regis, Dorset,
DT7 3JH*
Telephone: *(0297) 443039*
Access: (road) *A3052*

Hours: *Mar to June – 10am to 6pm, July to
Sept – 10am to 10pm, Sept to Oct – 10am to
6pm*
Admission (1992): *adults £2.20; children £1.00;
OAP £1.90*
No. visitors (1992): *8000 (est.)*

Facilities
Interpretation: *videos; audio tapes; information
boards; slides*
Schools: *maximum no. 30; educational literature;
audio/visual presentation*
Disabled: *easy access; helpers*
Retailing: *postcards/inexpensive souvenirs;
craftwork; books*
No. shops: *1*

Operations
Contacts: *Mr R Fox (Director); Ms M Fox
(Director); Mr M Simpson FBIPP (Director)*
No. employees: (high season) *2 full time* (low
season) *2 full time*
Languages spoken: *French; German; Italian*

Marketing
Press office
UK promotion: *radio; local newspapers; regional
tourist board; other attractions;
leaflets/information packs; ETB/BTA*
USA promotion: *British Tourist Authority*

LYMPNE CASTLE
(limited company)
castle

Established: *1965*
Address: *Hythe, Kent, CT21 4LQ*
Telephone: *(0303) 267571*
Access: (road) *M20/A20* (rail) *Sandling*
Parking capacity: (cars) *50* (coaches) *4*
Hours: *Easter to early Oct – 10.30am to 6pm;
closed occasional Sundays*
Admission (1992): *adults £2.00; children £0.50*
No. visitors (1992): *12 000 (est.)*

Facilities
Interpretation: *leaflets; guide books*
Schools: *maximum no. 100; talk on request*
Retailing: *postcards/inexpensive souvenirs; books*
No. shops: *1*

Operations
Contact: *Mr H Margary (Director)*
No. employees: (high season) *3 full time* (low
season) *3 full time*
Languages spoken: *French*

Marketing
Affiliation: *HHA*
UK promotion: *leaflets/information packs;
ETB/BTA; SE England Tourist Board*

M

MAES ASTRO TOURIST ATTRACTION
(partnership)
museum; zoo/wildlife attraction

Established: *1988*
Address: *Llanbedr, Barmouth, Gwynedd, LL45 2PZ*
Telephone: *(0341) 23467.* Fax: *(0341) 280827*
Access: (road) *A496* (rail) *Llanbedr*
Parking capacity: (cars) *100* (coaches) *6*
Hours: *Easter to Nov – 10am to 5.30pm daily*
Admission (1992): *adults £2.50; children £1.90; OAP £1.90*
No. visitors (1992): *50 000 (est.)*

Facilities
Interpretation: *videos; leaflets; audio tapes; information boards*
Children: *adventure playground; nappy changing*
Schools: *maximum no. 120; educational literature*
Disabled: *easy access; disabled toilets*
Catering: *1 picnic area*
Retailing: *postcards/inexpensive souvenirs; confectionery and ice cream; craftwork; clothes*
No. shops: *More than 4*

Operations
Contact: *Mr M Valizadeh (owner)*
No. employees: (high season) *5 full time; 5 part time* (low season) *1 full time; 1 part time*

Marketing
UK promotion: *regional tourist board; other attractions; leaflets/information packs*

MALL GALLERIES
(limited company registered charity)
gallery

Established: *1971*
Address: *The Mall, London, SW1*
Telephone: *(071) 930 6844.* Fax: *(071) 839 7830*
Access: (rail) *Charing Cross*
Season: *all year*
Hours: *10am to 5pm daily except 23 Dec to 5 Jan and when changing exhibitions*
Admission (1992): *adults £2.00; children £1.00; OAP £1.00; student 1.00;*
No. visitors (1992): *60 000 (est.)*

Facilities
Interpretation: *art exhibitions*
Disabled: *chair lift down steps*

Operations
Contact: *Mr J Sayers (Company Accountant/ Secretary)*
Training: *F/T operations staff, P/T operations staff and casual operations staff are trained in-house and day-to-day on job*

Marketing
UK promotion: *national newspapers; regional tourist board; leaflets/information packs*

MALTON MUSEUM
(trust)
museum

Established: *1982*
Address: *Old Town Hall, Market Place, Malton, N Yorks*
Telephone: *(0653) 695136*
Access: (road) *A64* (rail) *Malton*
Hours: *Easter Sat to 31 Oct – Mon to Sat – 10am to 4pm, Sun – 2pm to 4pm*

Admission (1992): *adults £0.85; children £0.55; OAP £0.55; student £0.55; family ticket £2.50*
No. visitors (1992): *6000 (est.)*

Facilities
Interpretation: *leaflets; information boards*
Schools: *maximum no. 50; teacher resource pack*
Disabled: *easy access*
Retailing: *postcards/inexpensive souvenirs; books; Roman reproduction items*
No. shops: *1*

Operations
Contact: *Mrs P Wiggle (Senior Assistant)*
No. employees: (high season) *6 part time* (low season) *3 part time*
Training: *P/T operations staff are trained in-house and day-to-day on job*
Languages spoken: *Dutch*

Marketing
Affiliations: *museums and art galleries*
UK promotion: *leaflets/information packs; Ryedale Top Attractions*

MALVERN MUSEUM
(limited company, registered charity)
museum; scheduled ancient monument

Established: *1981*
Address: *Abbey Gateway, Abbey Rd, Malvern, Worcs, WR14 3ES*
Telephone: *(0684) 567811*
Access: (road) *M5/A449* (rail) *Great Malvern*
Hours: *Easter to end Oct – 10.30am to 5pm daily except Wed in school term time*
Admission (1992): *adults £0.50; children £0.10; OAP £0.50*
No. visitors (1992): *5000 (est.)*

Facilities
Interpretation: *leaflets; information boards*
Languages: *Dutch; French; German*
Schools: *maximum no. 30; lecture/talk; talk by arrangement*
Retailing: *postcards/inexpensive souvenirs; books*
No. shops: *1*

Operations: *N/A*

Marketing
UK promotion: *local newspapers; regional tourist board; ETB/BTA*

MANCHESTER CATHEDRAL
(Church of England)
church

Established: *1400*
Address: *The Cathedral, Manchester, M3 1SX*
Telephone: *(061) 833 2220.* Fax: *(061) 839 6226*
Season: *all year*
Hours: *8am to 6.30pm daily*
Admission (1992): *free*
No. visitors (1992): *100 000 (est.)*

Facilities
Interpretation: *leaflets; information boards; maps; tour guides; personnel*
Schools: *educational literature; lecture/talk*
Disabled: *easy access; disabled toilets; helpers; leaflets*
Retailing: *postcards/inexpensive souvenirs; craftwork; books; brass rubbings; cards (birthday etc.)*
No. shops: *1*

Operations
Contacts: *Dean Waddington (Dean); K Petch/M Stephen (Secretaries); G Robinson (Head Verger); G Albison (Publicity Officer)*
No. employees: (high season) *15 full time; 4 part time*
Training: *F/T operations staff, F/T management, P/T operations staff and P/T management are trained in-house and on specific courses and day-to-day on job*

Marketing
Annual event(s): *concerts, recitals, literary events, religious services*
Affiliations: *Arts About Manchester Ltd., NWTB, Pilgrims Association*
Other: *market research*
UK promotion: *radio; local newspapers; regional tourist board; other attractions; leaflets/ information packs; Wales in Action, Capital Breaks, Great British Holidays, Holiday for Disabled, Place; ETB/BTA; NWTB, Yorks and Humberside Tourist Board, Wales*
Europe/Toulouse Association promotion: *leaflets/ brochures; British Tourist Authority*

MANCHESTER UNITED MUSEUM AND TOUR CENTRE
(plc)
museum

Established: *1986*
Address: *Old Trafford, Manchester, M16 0RA*
Telephone: *(061) 877 4002*
Access: (road) *M62/A56* (rail) *Old Trafford*
Parking capacity: (cars) *1000* (coaches) *50*
Season: *all year*
Hours: *Tues to Sun – 9.30am to 4pm*
Admission (1992): *adults £4.95; children £2.95; OAP £2.95; student £4.95; families £11.95*
No. visitors (1992): *45 000*

Facilities
Interpretation: *videos; leaflets; information boards; tour guides*
Schools: *maximum no. 55; educational literature; educational tour*
Disabled: *easy access; disabled toilets; sign language for deaf*
Catering: *1 snack bar/food stall*
Retailing: *postcards/inexpensive souvenirs*
No. shops: *2*

Operations
Contact: *M Maxfield (Manager)*
No. employees: (high season) *6 full time; 10 part time* (low season) *6 full time; 10 part time*
Training: *F/T operations staff, P/T operations staff and casual operations staff are trained in-house and day-to-day on job using handbooks*
Languages spoken: *French*

Marketing
Affiliation: *AIM*
UK promotion: *national newspapers; local newspapers; regional tourist board; leaflets/ information packs*

Environmental monitoring: *recycling; waste*

MANDERSTON
(private company)
historic house; garden; museum

Established: *1979*
Address: *Duns, Berwickshire, TD11 3PP*
Telephone: *(0361) 83450.* Fax: *(0361) 82010*

Access: (road) *A1/A6105* (rail) *Berwick upon Tweed*
Parking capacity: (cars) *300* (coaches) *12*
Hours: *mid May to Sept – Sun and Thur – from 2pm*
Admission (1992): *adults £3.75; children £1.00; OAP £3.75; gardens only £2.00 (adults) £0.50 (children) £2.00 (OAP)*
No. visitors (1992): *14 000*

Facilities
Interpretation: *leaflets; tour guides; guide books*
Schools: *maximum no. 100; educational literature; lecture/talk*
Disabled: *easy access; helpers*
Catering: *1 picnic area*
Retailing: *postcards/inexpensive souvenirs; confectionery and ice cream; craftwork; monogrammed souvenirs*
No. shops: *1*

Operations
Contacts: *The Lord Palmer; Julie Bareham (Secretary/PA); Valerie Dyamond (Gift Shop Manageress)*
No. employees: (high season) *2 full time; 20 part time* (low season) *2 full time; 3 part time*
Training: *P/T operations staff are trained in-house and day-to-day on job using videos*

Marketing
Affiliation: *HHA*
Other: *market research*
UK promotion: *radio; local newspapers; regional tourist board; other attractions; leaflets/information packs; Scottish Borders Tourist Board, Scottish Border Heritage*

MANNINGFORD GARDENS AND NURSERY
(privately owned)
garden

Established: *1991*
Address: *Manningford Abbots, Nr Pewsey, Wilts, SN9 5PB*
Telephone: *(0672) 62232*
Access: (road) *M4/A345* (rail) *Pewsey*
Parking capacity: (cars) *40*
Season: *all year*
Hours: *Mon, Tues and Thur to Sat – 8.30am to 5pm; Sun – 10.30am to 1pm and 2pm to 5pm. Closed 25 Dec to 2 Jan*
Admission (1992): *free but donations welcome*
No. visitors (1992): *20 000 (est.)*

Facilities
Languages: *French*
Children: *adventure playground*
Schools: *maximum no. 36; lecture/talk; visits to schools*
Disabled: *easy access*
Catering: *1 picnic area*
Retailing: *craftwork; 18th and 19th century plants*
No. shops: *1*

Operations
Contact: *Mr P Jones (owner)*
No. employees: (high season) *3 full time; 2 part time* (low season) *3 full time*
Training: *F/T operations staff are trained in-house and on specific courses and day-to-day on job*
Languages spoken: *French*

Marketing
Annual event(s): *classes and plant days*
UK promotion: *local newspapers; regional tourist board; ETB/BTA*

MANNINGTON GARDENS AND COUNTRYSIDE
(privately owned)
historic house; park/reserve; garden

Established: *1972*
Address: *Mannington Hall, Norwich*
Telephone: *(026387) 4175. Fax: (026761) 214*
Access: (road) *A140/A148*
Parking capacity: (cars) *200* (coaches) *50*
Season: *all year*

Hours: *countryside – 9am to dusk daily; gardens – Apr to Oct – Sun – 12 noon to 5pm, May to Aug – Wed, Thur and Fri – 11am to 5pm. Hall by appointment only*
Admission (1992): *adults £2.00; OAP £1.50; student £1.50; disabled £1.50; car park for walks £1.00*
No. visitors (1992): *10 000 (est.)*

Facilities
Interpretation: *leaflets; information boards; maps; guide books*
Children: *adventure playground; nappy changing*
Schools: *educational literature; lecture/talk*
Disabled: *easy access; disabled toilets; wheelchairs*
Catering: *1 picnic area*
Retailing: *postcards/inexpensive souvenirs; confectionery and ice cream; books; plants*
No. shops: *2*

Operations
Contact: *Lord Walpole*
No. employees: (high season) *1 full time; 5 part time* (low season) *1 full time*
Languages spoken: *French*

Marketing
Annual event(s): *various*
Affiliation: *HHA*
Other: *market research*
UK promotion: *radio; local newspapers; regional tourist board; other attractions; leaflets/information packs; ETB/BTA*

Environmental monitoring: *organic nursery*

MANOR FARM COUNTRY PARK
(local authority run)
historic house; park/reserve; garden; museum; zoo/wildlife attraction; church; working farmstead

Established: *1984*
Address: *Plylands Lane, Bursledon, Soton, Hants*
Telephone: *(0489) 787055. Fax: (0489) 790357*
Access: (road) *M27/A27/A334* (rail) *Botley*
Parking capacity: (cars) *370*
Season: *all year*
Hours: *farm – Easter to end Oct – 10am to 5.30pm daily, Nov to Easter – Sun and half term – 10am to dusk. Park – daylight hours daily*
Admission (1992): *adults £2.50; children £1.20; OAP £2.00; student £1.20; family £7.20; season tickets; car parking £1.00/£1.25*
No. visitors (1992): *250 000 (est.)*

Facilities
Interpretation: *videos; leaflets; information boards; maps; guide books; personnel*
Children: *play area; nappy changing*
Schools: *maximum no. 400; audio/visual presentation; Victorian activities*
Disabled: *easy access; disabled toilets*
Catering: *3 picnic areas*
Franchisees: *farm – Easter to end Oct – 10am to 5.30pm daily, Nov to Easter – Sun and half term – 10am to dusk*
Retailing: *postcards/inexpensive souvenirs; confectionery and ice cream; craftwork; books; blacksmith and woodcraft*
No. shops: *1*

Operations
Contacts: *Ms B Newbury (Park Manager); Mr K Sanders (Administrator)*
No. employees: (high season) *11 full time; 5 part time* (low season) *8 full time; 3 part time*
Training: *F/T operations staff, F/T management, P/T operations staff and casual operations staff are trained in-house and externally and on specific courses and day-to-day on job*
Languages spoken: *Italian*

Marketing
Annual event: *Victorian fair*
Sponsor(s): *local suppliers*
Other: *press office; market research*
UK promotion: *national newspapers; radio; local newspapers; regional tourist board; other attractions; leaflets/information packs*

Environmental monitoring: *recycling; waste; water quality; energy consumption; hazardous materials; chemical usage; transport; emissions*

MANOR HOUSE MUSEUM/ALFRED EAST ART GALLERY
(local authority run)
museum; gallery

Established: *1989*
Address: *Sheep St, Kettering, Northants*
Telephone: *(0536) 410333. Fax: (0536) 410333*
Access: (road) *A14 (Al/Ml link)* (rail) *Kettering*
Season: *all year*
Hours: *9.30am to 5pm daily*
Admission (1992): *N/A*
No. visitors (1992): *18 000 (est.)*

Facilities
Interpretation: *videos; leaflets; audio tapes; information boards; personnel; signs*
Schools: *maximum no. 100; educational literature; lecture/talk; handling sessions*
Disabled: *easy access; other audio facilities*
Catering: *4 picnic areas*
Retailing: *postcards/inexpensive souvenirs; craftwork; books; prints from art collection*
No. shops: *2*

Operations
Contact: *Su Davies (Museum, Gallery and TIC Manager)*
No. employees: (high season) *3 full time; 8 part time*
Training: *F/T operations staff, F/T management and P/T operations staff are trained in-house and externally and on specific courses and day-to-day on job*

Marketing
Annual event(s): *living history, talks, music, dance*
Other: *press office*
UK promotion: *radio; local newspapers; regional tourist board; other attractions; leaflets/information packs*
Europe promotion: *travel agents' brochures*

Environmental monitoring: *waste; water quality; energy consumption; hazardous materials; chemical usage; flora and birds*

MAPLEDURHAM HOUSE AND WATERMILL
(partnership)
historic house; watermill and country park

Established: *1967*
Address: *The Estate Office, Mapledurham, Reading, RG4 7TR*
Telephone: *(0734) 723350. Fax: (0734) 724016*
Access: (road) *M4/A4074* (rail) *Reading*
Parking capacity: (cars) *1500*
Hours: *Easter to Sept – weekends and BH – park 12.30am to 7pm, watermill 1pm to 5pm, house 2.30pm to 5pm*
Admission (1992): *adults £4.00; children £2.00; OAP £4.00*
No. visitors (1992): *20 000 (est.)*

Facilities
Interpretation: *audio tapes; tour guides; guide books; guides*
Languages: *French*
Schools: *maximum no. 100; educational literature; educational tour; lecture/talk*
Catering: *2 picnic areas*
Retailing: *postcards/inexpensive souvenirs; confectionery and ice cream; craftwork; books; clothes; toys and gifts*
No. shops: *2*

Operations
Contact: *J R Emary (Administrator)*
No. employees: (high season) *2 full time; 30 part time* (low season) *2 full time; 2 part time*
Training: *F/T operations staff, P/T operations staff and casual operations staff are trained in-house and day-to-day on job*
Languages spoken: *French; German*

Marketing
Annual event(s): *craft fairs*
Sponsor: *H D promotions*
Other: *market research*
UK promotion: *national newspapers; radio; local newspapers; regional tourist board; other attractions; leaflets/information packs; ETB/BTA*
Europe/Asia/Australia/USA promotion: *leaflets/brochures; travel agents' brochures; British Tourist Authority*

MARAZION MARINE AQUARIUM
(sole proprietor)
zoo/wildlife attraction

Established: *1982*
Address: *The Square, Marazion, Cornwall*
Telephone: *(0736) 710456*
Access: (road) *A30* (rail) *Penzance*
Hours: *May to Sept – daily*
Admission (1992): *adults £0.75; children £0.50; disabled free*
No. visitors (1992): *17 000*

Facilities
Interpretation: *leaflets; information boards; guide books*
Schools: *maximum no. 40; lecture/talk; reduced rates*
Retailing: *books*
No. shops: *none*

Operations
Contact: *D Whybrow*
No. employees: (high season) *2 full time; 1 part time*

Marketing
UK promotion: *local newspapers; leaflets/information packs; ETB/BTA*

MARBLE ARCH CAVES
(local authority run)
show cave

Established: *1985*
Address: *Marlbank, Co. Fermanagh, BT9 1EW*
Telephone: *(036582) 8855*
Access: (road) *A4/A32*
Parking capacity: (cars) *150* (coaches) *6*
Hours: *Mar to Nov – from 11am daily*
Admission (1992): *adults £4.00; children £2.00; OAP £3.00; student £3.00; family tickets £10.00*
No. visitors (1992): *56 012*

Facilities
Interpretation: *videos; leaflets; information boards; tour guides*
Languages: *French; German*
Children: *nappy changing*
Schools: *educational literature; audio/visual presentation; lecture/talk*
Disabled: *easy access; disabled toilets*
Catering: *1 picnic area*
Franchisees: *Mar to Nov – from 11am daily*
Retailing: *postcards/inexpensive souvenirs; confectionery and ice cream; craftwork; books; rock samples, fossil replicas*
No. shops: *1*

Operations
Contact: *Mr Richard Watson (Principal Officer)*
No. employees: (high season) *6 full time; 36 part time* (low season) *5 full time*
Training: *F/T operations staff, F/T management, P/T operations staff and casual operations staff are trained in-house and on specific courses and day-to-day on job using handbooks*
Languages spoken: *French; Italian*

Marketing
Market research
UK promotion: *national newspapers; radio; local newspapers; regional tourist board; other attractions; leaflets/information packs*

Environmental monitoring: *water quality*

MARGAM PARK
(local authority run)
theme park; historic house; castle; heritage centre; park/reserve; garden; gallery

Established: *1978*
Address: *Margam, Port Talbot, W Glamorgan*
Telephone: *(0639) 881635. Fax: (0639) 895897*
Access: (road) *M4*
Parking capacity: (cars) *3000* (coaches) *100*
Season: *all year*
Hours: *Apr to Sept – 10am to 5.30pm daily; Oct to Mar – Wed to Sun – 10am to 5pm. No attractions open during winter*
Admission (1992): *adults £3.00; children £2.00; OAP £2.00; student £3.00*
No. visitors (1992): *220 000*

Facilities
Interpretation: *leaflets; information boards; maps; guide books; audio visual presentation*
Languages: *Welsh*
Children: *adventure playground; nappy changing*
Schools: *maximum no. 100; educational literature; audio/visual presentation; lecture/talk*
Disabled: *easy access; disabled toilets; 2 wheelchairs*
Catering: *9 picnic areas*
Franchisees: *Apr to Sept – 10am to 5.30pm daily; Oct to Mar – Wed to Sun – 10am to 5pm. No attractions open during winter*
Retailing: *postcards/inexpensive souvenirs; craftwork; books; clothes; many personalised products*
No. shops: *1*

Operations
Contacts: *Ian Cadogan (Park Director); Judith Collins (Senior Administrator); Neil Perry (Commercial Manager)*
No. employees: (high season) *36 full time; 20 part time* (low season) *26 full time; 10 part time*
Training: *F/T operations staff, F/T management, P/T operations staff, P/T management, casual operations staff and casual management are trained in-house and externally and on specific courses and day-to-day on job using videos and handbooks*
Languages spoken: *French; German*

Marketing
Annual event(s): *beautiful homes and gardens, craft fairs, vintage car rallies, antique fair, plays, etc.*
Sponsor(s): various
Affiliations: *HHA*
Other: *press office; market research*
UK promotion: *television; national newspapers; radio; local newspapers; regional tourist board; other attractions; leaflets/information packs; coaching Magazines, WTB and Tourism South Wales Initiatives; ETB/BTA*
Europe/USA promotion: *British Tourist Authority; WTB*

Environmental monitoring: *recycling; water quality; chemical usage; conservation code*

MARGARET WAUDBY ORIENTAL GARDEN
(trust)
garden

Established: *1989*
Address: *11 Beech Grove, Upper Poppleton, Nr York, N Yorks, YO2 6DS*
Telephone: *(0904) 797372*
Access: (road) *M1/A59* (rail) *Poppleton*
Parking capacity: (cars) *50* (coaches) *4*
Season: *all year*
Hours: *9am to 5pm daily*
No. visitors (1992): *4000 (est.)*

Facilities
Interpretation: *leaflets*
Languages: *Japanese*
Children: *play area; nappy changing*

Schools: *maximum no. 50; educational literature; lecture/talk*
Disabled: *easy access; Braille/sound posts; helpers; leaflets*
Catering: *1 picnic area*

Operations
Training: *F/T operations staff and P/T operations staff are trained externally and day-to-day on job*

Marketing
UK promotion: *regional tourist board; leaflets/information packs; ETB/BTA; Yorks and Humbs Tourist Board*

Environmental monitoring: *recycling*

MARGATE OLD TOWN HALL LOCAL HISTORY MUSEUM
(local authority run)
museum

Established: *1987*
Address: *Thanet District Council, Council Offices, Cecil St, Margate, Kent CT9 1XZ*
Telephone: *(0843) 225511 ext 2520. Fax: (0843) 226289*
Access: (road) *M25/M2/A299/M28* (rail) *Margate*
Hours: *May to Sept – Mon to Sat – 10am to 5pm*
Admission (1992): *adults £0.80; children £0.50; OAP £0.50; student £0.60;*
No. visitors (1992): *3927*

Facilities
Interpretation: *leaflets; information boards; maps; tour guides; guide books*
Languages: *French; German*
Schools: *maximum no. 20; educational literature; educational tour; lecture/talk; activity sessions*
Disabled: *helpers*
Retailing: *postcards/inexpensive souvenirs; books; posters, copy prints*
No. shops: *1*

Operations
Contacts: *C Wilson (Museum Officer); J Williams (Museum Assistant)*
No. employees: (high season) *2 full time; 2 part time* (low season) *2 full time*
Training: *F/T operations staff, F/T management, P/T operations staff and P/T management are trained in-house and externally and on specific courses and day-to-day on job*
Languages spoken: *Japanese; Chinese*

Marketing
Annual event: *Margate – A Political History Exhibition*
Other: *PR company: arranged by Thanet District Council; press office; market research*
UK promotion: *national newspapers; radio; local newspapers; regional tourist board; other attractions; leaflets/information packs; Kent Holiday Guide; ETB/BTA*
Europe promotion: *leaflets/brochures; British Tourist Authority; SEETB*

Environmental monitoring: *recycling*

MARITIME MUSEUM
(private partnership)
museum

Established: *1974*
Address: *19 Chapel St, Penzance, Cornwall*
Telephone: *(0736) 68890*
Access: (road) *A30*
Hours: *Easter to end Oct – Mon to Sat – 10am to 5pm*
Admission (1992): *adults £1.50; children £0.75; OAP £1.50; student £0.75; family ticket (2 + 2) £4.00*
No. visitors (1992): *7000 (est.)*

Facilities
Interpretation: *leaflets; guide books*
Schools: *maximum no. 20*

Retailing: *postcards/inexpensive souvenirs;
artefacts*
No. shops: *1*

Operations
Contact: *R Morris (Partner)*
No. employees: (high season) *7 part time*

Environmental monitoring: *energy consumption;
chemical usage; emissions*

MARITIME MUSEUM RAMSGATE
(trust)
museum; historic vessels

Established: *1984*
Address: *Clock House, Pier Yard, Royal Harbour,
Ramsgate, Kent, CT11 8LS*
Telephone: *(0843) 587765*
Access: (road) *M2/A299/A253* (rail) *Ramsgate*
Parking capacity: (cars) *50*
Season: *all year*
Hours: *Easter to Sept – Mon to Fri – 9.30am to
4.30pm, Sat – 2pm to 5pm, Sun – 1pm to 6pm;
Oct to Easter – Mon to Fri – 9.30am to 4.30pm*
Admission (1992): *adults £0.80; children £0.40;
OAP £0.40; student £0.50*
No. visitors (1992): *20 000 (est.)*

Facilities
Interpretation: *videos; leaflets; audio tapes;
information boards; slides; tour guides;
personnel; model theatre shows*
Languages: *French; German*
Schools: *maximum no. 120; educational literature;
audio/visual presentation; educational tour;
lecture/talk; model theatre, guided tour*
Catering: *1 picnic area*
Retailing: *postcards/inexpensive souvenirs; books;
models, fossils, nauticalia*
No. shops: *1*

Operations
Contacts: *M Cates (Director); D Chamberlain
(Administrator)*
No. employees: (high season) *4 full time; 3 part
time* (low season) *4 full time; 1 part time*
Training: *F/T operations staff, F/T management,
P/T operations staff and casual operations staff
are trained in-house and externally and on
specific courses and day-to-day on job*

Marketing
Annual event: *children's open day*
Sponsor(s): *various*
Affiliations: *MA, AMSEE, AIM*
Other: *market research*
UK promotion: *local newspapers; other
attractions; leaflets/information packs; free
advertising in media as news item*

MARK HALL CYCLE MUSEUM AND GARDENS
(local authority run)
garden; museum

Established: *1982*
Address: *Muskham Rd, Harlow, Essex, CM20 2LF*
Telephone: *(0279) 439680*
Access: (road) *M11/A414* (rail) *Harlow*
Parking capacity: (cars) *12* (coaches) *2*
Season: *all year*
Hours: *Sun to Thur – 10am to 1pm and 2pm to
5pm*
Admission (1992): *free*
No. visitors (1992): *28 000 (est.)*

Facilities
Interpretation: *leaflets; information boards; guide
books*
Schools: *maximum no. 100; educational literature*
Disabled: *easy access; disabled toilets*
Catering: *1 picnic area*
Retailing: *postcards/inexpensive souvenirs;
books*
No. shops: *1*

Operations
Contact: *Mr J Collins (Assistant Curator,
Transport)*
No. employees: (high season) *3 full time* (low
season) *3 full time*
Languages spoken: *French; German*

Marketing
Affiliation: *MA*
Other: *press office*
UK promotion: *local newspapers; regional tourist
board; leaflets/information packs*

MARLE PLACE GARDENS AND NURSERY
(private)
garden

Established: *1990*
Address: *Marle Place, Brenchley, Kent, TN12 7HS*
Telephone: *(0892) 722304.* Fax: *(0732) 464466*
Access: (road) *M25/A21* (rail) *Paddock Wood*
Parking capacity: (cars) *4* (coaches) *1*
Hours: *Apr to Oct – 10am to 5.30pm daily*
Admission (1992): *adults £2.00; children £1.50;
OAP £1.50; student £2.00*
No. visitors (1992): *12 000 (est.)*

Facilities
Interpretation: *information boards; tour guides*
Languages: *French*
Disabled: *easy access*
Catering: *1 picnic area*
Retailing: *craftwork; books; garden produce,
plants; paintings*
No. shops: *1*

Operations
Contact: *L Williams*
No. employees: (high season) *3 full time; 1 part
time* (low season) *3 full time; 1 part time*
Training: *P/T operations staff and casual
operations staff are trained in-house and
day-to-day on job*

Marketing
Market research
UK promotion: *radio; local newspapers; regional
tourist board; other attractions; leaflets/
information packs; SEETB; ETB/BTA*
Europe promotion: *travel agents' brochures*

MARSH FARM COUNTRY PARK
(local authority run)
working farm

Established: *1984*
Address: *Marsh Farm Rd, South Woodham
Ferrers, Chelmsford, Essex, CM3 5LD*
Telephone: *(0245) 321552.* Fax: *(0245) 324191*
Access: (road) *M25/A132/A13/A127* (rail) *South
Woodham Ferrers*
Parking capacity: (cars) *1000* (coaches) *50*
Hours: *Feb half term to end Nov – Mon to Fri –
10am to 4.30pm, Sat and Sun – 10am to
5.30pm (also BH and school holidays)*
Admission (1992): *adults £1.95; children £1.45;
OAP £1.45; groups 15+ £1.75 (adults) and
£1.25 (children); disabled/special needs helpers
free*
No. visitors (1992): *110 000 (est.)*

Facilities
Interpretation: *information boards; tour guides;
guide books; interactive educational games*
Children: *adventure playground; play area; nappy
changing*
Schools: *maximum no. 200; educational literature;
tour for extra charge*
Disabled: *easy access; disabled toilets; hands on
experience by arrangement in advance*
Catering: *3 picnic areas*
Franchisees: *Feb half term to end Nov – Mon to
Fri – 10am to 4.30pm, Sat and Sun – 10am to
5.30pm (also BH and school holidays)*
Retailing: *postcards/inexpensive souvenirs; books;
clothes; farm related giftware; china*
No. shops: *1*

Operations
Contacts: *Ms K Latham/Mr H Rudge (Visitor
Services/Farm Manager); Ms A Leigh/Ms J
Warner (Gift Shop/Farm Secretary)*
No. employees: (high season) *9 full time; 10 part
time* (low season) *8 full time; 3 part time*
Training: *F/T operations staff, F/T management,
P/T operations staff, P/T management and
casual operations staff are trained in-house and
externally and on specific courses and
day-to-day on job and annual in-house week
using demonstration*

Marketing
Annual event(s): *farm interest activities and fayres*
Other: *press office; market research*
UK promotion: *radio; local newspapers; regional
tourist board; other attractions; leaflets/
information packs; ETB/BTA; booklets*

Environmental monitoring: *recycling; waste;
energy consumption; chemical usage*

MARWELL ZOOLOGICAL PARK
(trust)
zoo/wildlife attraction

Established: *1972*
Address: *Colden Common, Winchester, Hants*
Telephone: *(90962) 777407.* Fax: *(0962) 777511*
Access: (road) *M3/M27* (rail) *Eastleigh*
Parking capacity: (cars) *800* (coaches) *100*
Season: *all year*
Hours: *Apr to Oct – 10am to 6pm; Nov to Mar –
10am to 5pm*
Admission (1992): *adults £5.50; children £4.30;
OAP £5.00; group rates available*
No. visitors (1992): *280 000*

Facilities
Interpretation: *leaflets; information boards; maps;
guide books*
Children: *adventure playground; play area; nappy
changing*
Schools: *educational literature; audio/visual
presentation; lecture/talk*
Disabled: *easy access; disabled toilets; Braille/
sound posts; helpers; special signs; powered
transport; leaflets; guide book*
Catering: *1 bar/public house*
Franchisees: *Apr to Oct – 10am to 6pm; Nov to
Mar – 10am to 5pm*
Retailing: *postcards/inexpensive souvenirs;
confectionery and ice cream; craftwork; books;
clothes; general giftware*
No. shops: *3*

Operations
Contacts: *P Hickman (General Manager); Miss L
Stafford (PA to Director)*
No. employees: (high season) *55 full time; 12 part
time* (low season) *55 full time; 4 part time*
Training: *F/T operations staff, P/T operations
staff and casual operations staff are trained
in-house and day-to-day on job using videos*
Languages spoken: *French*

Marketing
Annual event: *winter wonderland*
Affiliations: *National Federation of Zoological
Parks*
Other: *press office; market research*
UK promotion: *television; local newspapers;
regional tourist board; other attractions;
leaflets/information packs; ETB/BTA*

Environmental monitoring: *recycling; waste;
water quality; energy consumption; hazardous
materials; chemical usage; transport;
environmental audit*

MARX MEMORIAL LIBRARY
(charity)
heritage centre; library

Established: *1933*
Address: *37a Clerkenwell Green, London,
EC1R 0DU*
Telephone: *(071) 253 1485*

Hours: *Mon – 1pm to 6pm; Tues, Wed and Thur – 1pm to 8pm; Sat – 10am to 1pm. Closed Aug and BH*
Admission (1992): *groups £1.00, otherwise donations*
No. visitors (1992): *500 (est.)*

Facilities
Interpretation: *leaflets; tour guides*
Languages: *Russian*
Schools: *maximum no. 60; educational literature; lecture/talk*
Disabled: *easy access*
Retailing: *postcards/inexpensive souvenirs; books*

Operations
Contact: *Ms T Newland BA MSc (Librarian)*
Training: *F/T operations staff and casual operations staff are trained in-house and day-to-day on job*
Languages spoken: *French*

Marketing
Annual event(s): *anniversary of death of Karl Marx*
UK promotion: *national newspapers; regional tourist board; leaflets/information packs; ETB/BTA*

Environmental monitoring: *recycling; energy consumption; chemical usage; transport*

MAXWELTON HOUSE
(trust)
historic house; garden; museum; church

Established: *1973*
Address: *Maxwelton House, Moniaive, Bythornhill, Dumfriesshire, DG3 4DX*
Telephone: *(08482) 385*
Access: (road) *B729*
Parking capacity: (cars) *28* (coaches) *9*
Hours: *Easter to Sept daily*
Admission (1992): *adults £3.00; children £1.50; OAP £2.50; parties £2.00*
No. visitors (1992): *7000 (est.)*

Facilities
Interpretation: *leaflets; tour guides; guide books*
Schools: *maximum no. 52; educational literature; lecture/talk*
Disabled: *disabled toilets; helpers; guide book*
Catering: *1 picnic area*
Retailing: *postcards/inexpensive souvenirs; craftwork*
No. shops: *1*

Operations
Contact: *Roderick Stenhouse (Estate Administrator)*
No. employees: (high season) *3 full time; 6 part time* (low season) *3 full time; 6 part time*
Languages spoken: *French; German; Italian; Spanish; Russian – all by arrangement*

Marketing
UK promotion: *local newspapers; regional tourist board; other attractions; leaflets/information packs; Dumfries and Galloway*

MCLELLAN GALLERIES
(local authority run)
gallery

Established: *1990*
Address: *270 Sauchiehall St, Glasgow, G2 3EH*
Telephone: *(041) 331 1854. Fax: (041) 332 9957*
Access: (road) *M8*
Season: *all year*
Hours: *during exhibitions – Mon to Sat – 10am to 5pm, Sun – 11am to 5pm*
Admission (1992): *free*
No. visitors (1992): *84 418*

Facilities
Interpretation: *leaflets; information boards*
Languages: *Urdu*

Children: *nappy changing*
Schools: *museum education dept*
Retailing: *postcards/inexpensive souvenirs; craftwork; books*
No. shops: *1*

Operations
Training: *F/T operations staff and F/T management are trained in-house and on specific courses and day-to-day on job*

Marketing
Press office; market research
UK promotion: *television; national newspapers; local newspapers; leaflets/information packs*

MCLEAN MUSEUM AND ART GALLERY
(local authority run)
museum; gallery

Established: *1876*
Address: *15 Kelly St, Greenock, PA16 8JX*
Telephone: *(0475) 23741*
Access: (road) *M8* (rail) *Greenock West*
Season: *all year*
Hours: *Mon to Thur except local and public holidays – 10am to 12 noon and 1pm to 5pm*
Admission (1992): *free*
No. visitors (1992): *21 122*

Facilities
Interpretation: *leaflets; information boards*
Schools: *maximum no. 40; educational literature; lecture/talk*
Disabled: *easy access*
Retailing: *postcards/inexpensive souvenirs; books*
No. shops: *1*

Operations
Contact: *Valerie Boa (Curator)*
No. employees: (high season) *5 full time; 2 part time* (low season) *5 full time; 1 part time*
Training: *F/T operations staff and F/T management are trained externally and on specific courses*

Marketing
Market research
UK promotion: *national newspapers; local newspapers; regional tourist board; leaflets/information packs*

Environmental monitoring: *Glasgow city policies*

MERCER ART GALLERY
(local authority run)
gallery

Established: *1991*
Address: *31 Swan Rd, Harrogate, N Yorks, HG1 2SA*
Telephone: *(0423) 503340*
Access: (road) *A61*
Season: *all year*
Hours: *Tues to Sat – 10am to 5pm, Sun – 2pm to 5pm. Open BH Mon. Closed 25 and 26 Dec and 1 Jan*
Admission (1992): *free*
No. visitors (1992): *15 331*

Facilities
Schools: *maximum no. 40; lecture/talk*
Disabled: *easy access; disabled toilets*
Retailing: *postcards/inexpensive souvenirs; catalogues of exhibitions; prints of paintings*
No. shops: *1*

Operations
Contact: *Mrs M Kershaw (Curator)*
No. employees: (high season) *7 full time; 6 part time* (low season) *7 full time; 6 part time*
Training: *F/T operations staff, F/T management, P/T operations staff and casual operations staff are trained in-house and externally and on specific courses and day-to-day on job*
Languages spoken: *French; German*

Marketing
Affiliations: *Yorks and Humbs Arts*

UK promotion: *leaflets/information packs*

MERCHANT'S HOUSE (LITTLE MUSEUM)
(trust)
historic house

Established: *1980*
Address: *45 Church St, Tewkesbury, Glos, GL20 5SN*
Telephone: *(0684) 297174*
Access: (road) *M5/M50/A38* (rail) *Gloucester*
Parking capacity: (cars) *50*
Hours: *Easter to 31 Oct – Tues to Sat – 10am to 5pm*
Admission (1992): *donations box*
No. visitors (1992): *5000 (est.)*

Facilities
Interpretation: *information boards*
Schools: *maximum no. 25; no special support*

Operations
Contact: *Dr R King (Curator)*
No. employees: (high season) *1 full time*

Environmental monitoring: *humidity and light levels*

METROLAND
(limited company)
theme park

Established: *1988*
Address: *39 Garden Walk, Metro Centre, Gateshead, Tyne and Wear*
Telephone: *(091) 493 2048. Fax: (091) 493 2904*
Access: (road) *A1* (rail) *Metro*
Parking capacity: (cars) *12 000*
Season: *all year*
Hours: *Mon, Tues and Wed – 10am to 8pm; Thur Fri and Sat – 10am to 10pm; Sun – 12 noon to 6pm. Closed Christmas Day*
Admission (1992): *adults £4.95; children £3.95; entry only (no rides) adults £1.00, small children free; after 6pm £3.00 entry and all rides free*
No. visitors (1992): *400 000*

Facilities
Interpretation: *leaflets; information boards; maps; tour guides; guide books*
Children: *adventure playground; play area; nappy changing*
Schools: *reduction for schools*
Disabled: *easy access; disabled toilets*
Catering: *4 picnic areas*
Retailing: *postcards/inexpensive souvenirs; confectionery and ice cream; craftwork; books; clothes*
No. shops: *More than 4*

Operations
Contacts: *Mr S Woolf (General Manager); Mr K Goodrick (Park Supervisor); Mr A Stewart (Retail/Catering Manager); Ms V Connell (Marketing Manager)*
No. employees: (high season) *60 full time; 30 part time* (low season) *60 full time; 10 part time*
Training: *F/T operations staff, F/T management, P/T operations staff, P/T management, casual operations staff and casual management are trained in-house and externally and on specific courses and day-to-day on job*

Marketing
Annual event(s): *various*
Other: *press office; market research*
UK promotion: *television; national newspapers; radio; local newspapers; regional tourist board; other attractions; leaflets/information packs; ETB/BTA*

MICHELHAM PRIORY
(limited company)
historic house; garden; museum

Established: *1960*
Address: *Upper Dicker, Hailsham, E Sussex,
BN27 3QS*
Telephone: *(0323) 844224*
Access: (road) *A22/A27* (rail) *Berwick/Polegate*
Parking capacity: (cars) *800* (coaches) *10*
Hours: *Mar to Oct – 11am to 5.30pm daily; Mar
and Nov – Sun only – 11am to 4pm*
Admission (1992): *adults £3.30; children £1.90;
OAP £2.90; student £2.50; family ticket
£9.00*
No. visitors (1992): *53 600*

Facilities
Interpretation: *leaflets; audio tapes; slides; tour
guides; guide books*
Languages: *Dutch; French; German; Italian;
Spanish; Russian, Esperanto*
Children: *play area*
Schools: *maximum no. 150; educational literature;
educational tour; lecture/talk*
Disabled: *easy access; disabled toilets; Braille/
sound posts*
Catering: *1 picnic area*
Franchisees: *Mar to Oct – 11am to 5.30pm daily;
Mar and Nov – Sun only – 11am to 4pm*
Retailing: *postcards/inexpensive souvenirs;
confectionery and ice cream; books*
No. shops: *2*

Operations
Contact: *A C Gottlieb (Director)*
No. employees: (high season) *5 full time;
2 part time* (low season) *5 full time; 2 part
time*
Training: *F/T operations staff are trained in-house
and day-to-day on job using videos and
handbooks*
Languages spoken: *Spanish*

Marketing
Annual event(s): *various*
Affiliations: *HHA, ESTA, SEETB*
Other: *market research*
UK promotion: *national newspapers; radio; local
newspapers; regional tourist board; other
attractions; leaflets/information packs;
SEETB publications, other magazines;
ETB/BTA*
Europe/USA promotion: *leaflets/brochures; travel
agents' brochures; British Tourist Authority*

Environmental monitoring: *energy consumption;
hazardous materials*

MIDLAND MOTOR MUSEUM
(limited company)
museum

Established: *1978*
Address: *Stourbridge Rd, Bridgworth, Shropshire,
WV15 6DT*
Telephone: *(0746) 761761.* Fax: *(0746) 762992*
Access: (road) *A458*
Parking capacity: (cars) *50* (coaches) *3*
Hours: *July to Sept – daily; Mar to Oct – Sat and
Sun*
Admission (1992): *adults £3.50; children £1.75;
OAP £2.80; student £2.80; family £9.95*
No. visitors (1992): *22 000 (est.)*

Facilities
Interpretation: *information boards*
Schools: *maximum no. 100; educational literature*
Disabled: *easy access*
Catering: *1 picnic area*
Retailing: *postcards/inexpensive souvenirs;
books*
No. shops: *1*

Operations
Contacts: *M Barker (Curator); D Goddard
(Director)*
No. employees: (high season) *6 part time* (low
season) *2 part time*
Languages spoken: *French; German*

Marketing
UK promotion: *local newspapers; regional tourist
board; other attractions; leaflets/information
packs*

MILL GREEN MUSEUM AND MILL
(local authority run)
museum; working watermill

Established: *1976*
Address: *Mill Green, Hatfield, Herts, AL9 5PD*
Telephone: *(0707) 271362*
Access: (road) *M1/A1000/A414* (rail) *Hatfield*
Parking capacity: (cars) *10* (coaches) *1*
Season: *all year*
Hours: *Tues to Fri – 10am to 5pm; Sat and Sun –
2pm to 5pm*
Admission (1992): *free*
No. visitors (1992): *24 000*

Facilities
Interpretation: *leaflets; information boards; guide
books; personnel*
Languages: *French; German*
Schools: *maximum no. 35; educational literature*
Disabled: *helpers*
Catering: *1 picnic area*
Retailing: *postcards/inexpensive souvenirs*
No. shops: *1*

Operations
Contact: *S Kirby (Curator)*
No. employees: (high season) *4 full time; 13 part
time* (low season) *4 full time; 4 part time*
Training: *F/T operations staff, F/T management,
P/T operations staff and casual operations staff
are trained in-house and externally and on
specific courses and day to day on job*

Marketing
Affiliations: *MA, AMSSEE, SPAB, etc.*
Other: *market research*
UK promotion: *local newspapers; regional tourist
board; other attractions; leaflets/information
packs; ETB/BTA*

MILL OF TOWIE
(trust)
heritage centre; working water mill

Established: *1987*
Address: *Auchindachy, Nr Keith, Banffshire*
Telephone: *(054281) 307*
Access: (road) *A96/B9014* (rail) *Keith*
Parking capacity: (cars) *40* (coaches) *4*
Hours: *May to Sept – 10am to 4pm – Wed to
Mon*
Admission (1992): *adults £1.00; children £0.50;
OAP £0.50; student £0.50*
No. visitors (1992): *3000 (est.)*

Facilities
Interpretation: *leaflets; information boards; tour
guides*
Children: *play area; nappy changing*
Schools: *maximum no. 35; educational literature*
Disabled: *disabled toilets*
Catering: *3 picnic areas*
Retailing: *postcards/inexpensive souvenirs;
craftwork; books; clothes; goods made at the
mill*
No. shops: *1*

Operations
Contact: *Mr I Dempster (Development Manager)*
No. employees: (high season) *4 full time; 2 part
time* (low season) *3 full time*
Training: *F/T operations staff are trained
externally and on specific courses using videos
and handbooks*

Marketing
UK promotion: *local newspapers; regional tourist
board; leaflets/information packs*

Environmental monitoring: *recycling; energy
consumption; temperature and humidity*

MILTON'S COTTAGE
(trust)
historic house; museum

Established: *1887*
Address: *Deanway, Chalfont St Giles, Bucks,
HP8 4JH*
Telephone: *(0494) 872313*
Access: (road) *M40/M25/A413* (rail) *Gerrards
Cross*
Parking capacity: (cars) *20*
Hours: *Mar to Oct – Tues to Sat – 10am to 1pm
and 2pm to 6pm; Sun – 2pm to 6pm*
Admission (1992): *adults £1.50; children £0.60;
OAP £1.50; student £1.50; groups over 20
adults £1.20*
No. visitors (1992): *5059*

Facilities
Interpretation: *tour guides; guide books*
Schools: *lecture/talk*
Retailing: *postcards/inexpensive souvenirs;
craftwork; books; guides, craft books, maps*
No. shops: *1*

Operations
Contact: *T G May (Curator)*
No. employees: (high season) *1 full time; 1 part
time* (low season) *1 full time; 1 part time*

Marketing
Affiliations: *ETB/BTA, BCG, MGC*
UK promotion: *local newspapers; regional tourist
board; other attractions; leaflets/information
packs; Historic Houses, Castles and Gardens,
etc.; ETB/BTA*

Environmental monitoring: *energy consumption;
organic production*

MINIATURE PONY CENTRE
(privately owned)
zoo/wildlife attraction; working stud of miniature
Shetland ponies

Established: *1987*
Address: *Wormhill Farm, North Bovey, Nr
Newton Abbot, Devon, TQ13 8RG*
Telephone: *(0647) 432400.* Fax: *(0647) 433662*
Access: (road) *B3212*
Parking capacity: (cars) *100* (coaches) *6*
Season: *all year*
Hours: *10am to 5pm daily*
Admission (1992): *adults £3.95; children £2.95;
OAP £3.50*
No. visitors (1992): *56 000 (est.)*

Facilities
Interpretation: *videos; leaflets; information
boards; guide books*
Children: *adventure playground; play area; nappy
changing*
Schools: *no special support*
Disabled: *easy access; disabled toilets; guide book*
Catering: *1 picnic area*
Retailing: *postcards/inexpensive souvenirs;
confectionery and ice cream; craftwork; books;
clothes*
No. shops: *1*

Operations
Contacts: *Mr and Mrs A Dennis (owners)*
No. employees: (high season) *10 full time; 10 part
time* (low season) *5 full time*
Training: *F/T operations staff, P/T operations
staff and casual operations staff are trained
in-house and day-to-day on job*

Marketing
Market research
UK promotion: *regional tourist board; other
attractions; leaflets/information packs;
ETB/BTA*

MINSMERE RSPB NATURE RESERVE
(charity)
park/reserve

Established: *1947*
Address: *Westleton, Nr Saxmundham, Suffolk,
IP17 3BY*

Telephone: *(072) 873 298*
Access: (road) *A12* (rail) *Saxmundham*
Parking capacity: (cars) *200*
Season: *all year*
Hours: *Wed to Mon – 9am to 9pm or dusk if earlier*
Admission (1992): *adults £3.00; children £1.50; OAP £2.00; student £2.00; RSPB members free*
No. visitors (1992): *70 000 (est.)*

Facilities
Interpretation: *leaflets; information boards; maps; tour guides*
Schools: *maximum no. 50; educational literature; lecture/talk*
Disabled: *easy access; disabled toilets*
Catering: *1 picnic area*
Retailing: *postcards/inexpensive souvenirs; confectionery and ice cream; craftwork; books; clothes; bird related products*
No. shops: *1*

Operations
Contact: *Mr G Welch (Reserve Manager)*
No. employees: (high season) *7 full time; 2 part time* (low season) *6 full time; 2 part time*
Training: *F/T operations staff, F/T management and P/T operations staff are trained in-house and externally and on specific courses and day-to-day on job*

Marketing
Annual event(s): *Discover Minsmere Reserve*
Other: *press office; market research*
UK promotion: *national newspapers; regional tourist board; other attractions; leaflets/information packs; Day Out in East Anglia; ETB/BTA*

MINSTER CHURCH OF ST CUTHBERGA
(parochial church council)
church

Established: *1120*
Address: *High St, Wimborne Minster, Dorset, BH21*
Telephone: *(0202) 884753*
Access: (road) *M27/A31* (rail) *Bournemouth/Poole*
Parking capacity: (cars) *30*
Season: *all year*
Hours: *9.30am to 5.30pm daily*
Admission (1992): *free*
No. visitors (1992): *100 000 (est.)*

Facilities
Interpretation: *leaflets; tour guides; guide books*
Languages: *French; German; Italian; Spanish*
Schools: *educational literature*
Disabled: *easy access; helpers; leaflets; guide book*
Retailing: *postcards/inexpensive souvenirs; books; bibles and prayer books*
No. shops: *1*

Operations
Contacts: *Rev Canon D Price (Rector); Mrs C Oliver (Shop Manager)*
No. employees: (high season) *3 full time; 3 part time*

Marketing
Press office; market research
UK promotion: *radio; local newspapers; regional tourist board; ETB/BTA; Southern Tourist Board*

Environmental monitoring: *water quality; chemical usage; related to reserve*

MINTERNE GARDENS
(private)
garden

Established: *1928*
Address: *Minterne Magna, Dorchester, Dorset, DT2 7AU*
Telephone: *(0300) 341370*
Access: (road) *A352*
Parking capacity: (cars) *30* (coaches) *5*
Hours: *Apr to Oct – 10am to 7pm daily*

Admission (1992): *adults £2.00*
No. visitors (1992): *5000*

Operations
No. employees: (high season) *2 full time; 1 part time* (low season) *2 full time*

Marketing
Affiliation: *HHA*
UK promotion: *local newspapers; regional tourist board; ETB/BTA*

MODEL FARM AND FOLK MUSEUM
(limited company)
museum; farm attraction, craft centre

Established: *1972*
Address: *Wolvesnewton, Chepstow, Gwent, NP6 6NZ*
Telephone: *(02915) 231*
Access: (road) *M4/A449* (rail) *Newport*
Parking capacity: (cars) *120* (coaches) *4*
Hours: *Easter to end Oct – 11am to 6pm daily*
Admission (1992): *adults £2.50; children £1.50; OAP £2.25; student £1.50*
No. visitors (1992): *20 000 (est.)*

Facilities
Children: *adventure playground; play area*
Schools: *maximum no. 150; educational literature*
Disabled: *easy access; helpers*
Catering: *1 picnic area*
Retailing: *postcards/inexpensive souvenirs; confectionery and ice cream; craftwork; books; pocket money items, giftware*
No. shops: *1*

Operations
Contacts: *R J W Greenland (Director); P M Greenland*
No. employees: (high season) *2 full time; 15 part time* (low season) *2 full time*
Training: *F/T operations staff and P/T operations staff are trained in-house and on specific courses and day-to-day on job*

Marketing
Annual event(s): *crafts for Christmas*
Other: *market research*
UK promotion: *national newspapers; local newspapers; regional tourist board; other attractions; leaflets/information packs*

MODEL HOUSE CRAFT AND DESIGN CENTRE
(limited company)
gallery; royal mint display and open craft studios

Established: *1989*
Address: *Bull Ring, Llantrisant, Mid Glamorgan, CF7 8EB*
Telephone: *(0443) 237758*
Access: (road) *M4*
Parking capacity: (cars) *100* (coaches) *5*
Season: *all year*
Hours: *May to Dec – Tues to Sun – 10am to 5pm; Jan to Apr – Wed to Sun – 12am to 5pm*
Admission (1992): *free*
No. visitors (1992): *50 034*

Facilities
Interpretation: *leaflets; maps*
Languages: *Welsh*
Children: *nappy changing*
Schools: *maximum no. 35; educational literature*
Disabled: *easy access; disabled toilets; disabled lift facility*
Catering: *1 snack bar/food stall*
Franchisees: *May to Dec – Tues to Sun – 10am to 5pm; Jan to Apr – Wed to Sun – 12am to 5pm*
Retailing: *postcards/inexpensive souvenirs; craftwork; books; craft and design items*
No. shops: *1*

Operations
Contacts: *Mr J G Hughes (Director); J Rolfe (Administration Manager); John Birmingham (Marketing Manager)*

No. employees: (high season) *4 full time; 2 part time* (low season) *4 full time; 1 part time*
Training: *P/T operations staff, casual operations staff and casual management are trained in-house and day-to-day on job*

Marketing
Annual event(s): *various*
Sponsor(s): *various*
Affiliations: *Welsh Arts Council, South East Wales Arts Council*
Other: *press office; market research*
UK promotion: *regional tourist board; leaflets/information packs; Wales Tourist Board*
Europe promotion: *leaflets/brochures*

MODEL VILLAGE
(limited company)
model village

Established: *1937*
Address: *Bourton on the Water, Glos*
Telephone: *(0451) 820467.* Fax: *(0451) 810236*
Access: (road) *M40/A429*
Parking capacity: (cars) *30*
Season: *all year*
Hours: *summer – 9am to 6.30pm daily; winter – 9.30am to dusk daily*
Admission (1992): *adults £1.20; children £0.75; OAP £1.10; student £1.10*

Facilities
Interpretation: *leaflets; guide books*
Schools: *maximum no. 60; no special support*
Catering: *1 bar/public house*
Retailing: *postcards/inexpensive souvenirs*
No. shops: *1*

Operations
Contact: *P Morris (Director)*
No. employees: (high season) *8 full time* (low season) *4 full time*
Languages spoken: *French; German; Welsh*

Marketing
UK promotion: *leaflets/information packs; Heart of England; ETB/BTA*
Europe/USA promotion: *British Tourist Authority*

Environmental monitoring: *recycling; energy consumption*

MONKEY SANCTUARY, THE
(partnership)
garden; zoo/wildlife attraction; education centre

Established: *1964*
Address: *Murrayton, Looe, Cornwall, PL13 1NE*
Telephone: *(0503) 262532*
Access: (road) *A38* (rail) *Looe*
Parking capacity: (cars) *120*
Hours: *Easter to Sept – Sun to Thur – 10.30am to 5pm*
Admission (1992): *adults £3.50; children £1.50; OAP £2.50*
No. visitors (1992): *50 000 (est.)*

Facilities
Interpretation: *videos; leaflets; information boards; maps; tour guides; personnel*
Children: *play area*
Schools: *educational literature; educational tour; lecture/talk; workshops*
Disabled: *disabled toilets; staff willing to help*
Catering: *1 picnic area*
Retailing: *postcards/inexpensive souvenirs; craftwork; clothes*
No. shops: *1*

Operations
Contact: *P Neaves (Administrator/Secretary)*
No. employees: (high season) *8 full time; 5 part time* (low season) *8 full time; 5 part time*
Training: *F/T operations staff, P/T operations staff and casual operations staff are trained in-house and day-to-day on job*
Languages spoken: *French; German; Dutch*

Marketing
UK promotion: *local newspapers; regional tourist board; other attractions; leaflets/information packs; The Tourist Handbook*

MOORS VALLEY COUNTRY PARK
(local authority run)
park/reserve; gallery; coniferous plantations

Established: *1986*
Address: *Horton Rd, Ashley Heath, Ringwood, Hants, BH24 2ET*
Telephone: *(0425) 470721.* Fax: *(0425) 471656*
Access: (road) *M27/A31* (rail) *Bournemouth*
Parking capacity: (cars) *400* (coaches) *6*
Season: *all year*
Hours: *dawn to dusk daily*
Admission (1992): *car parking charges*
No. visitors (1992): *1 000 000 (est.)*

Facilities
Interpretation: *leaflets; information boards; maps*
Languages: *French*
Children: *adventure playground; nappy changing*
Schools: *educational literature; education officer*
Disabled: *easy access; disabled toilets; powered transport*
Catering: *3 picnic areas*
Franchisees: *dawn to dusk daily*
Retailing: *postcards/inexpensive souvenirs; confectionery and ice cream; craftwork; books; railway memorabilia*
No. shops: *2*

Operations
Contact: *Mr D Crompton (Head Warden)*
No. employees: (high season) *10 full time; 8 part time* (low season) *10 full time*
Training: *F/T operations staff, F/T management and P/T operations staff are trained in-house and externally and on specific courses and day-to-day on job*

Marketing
Annual event(s): *various*
Other: *market research*
UK promotion: *local newspapers; regional tourist board; leaflets/information packs*

MORPETH CHANTRY BAGPIPE MUSEUM
(local authority run)
museum

Established: *1987*
Address: *Bridge St, Morpeth, Northumberland, NE61 1PJ*
Telephone: *(0670) 519466.* Fax: *(0670) 510348*
Access: (road) *A1*
Season: *all year*
Hours: *Mar to Dec – 9.30am to 5.30pm; Jan and Feb – 10am to 4pm. Closed between Christmas and New Year*
Admission (1992): *adults £0.65; children £0.35; OAP £0.35; student £0.35; groups £0.10, minimum £3.60*
No. visitors (1992): *10 000 (est.)*

Facilities
Interpretation: *audio tapes; information boards*
Schools: *audio/visual presentation; lecture/talk*
Disabled: *disabled toilets; helpers; other audio facilities*
Retailing: *postcards/inexpensive souvenirs; books; music cassettes*
No. shops: *1*

Operations
Contact: *Ms A Moore (Museum Curator)*
No. employees: (high season) *1 full time; 1 part time* (low season) *1 full time; 1 part time*
Training: *F/T management and P/T operations staff are trained in-house and externally and on specific courses and day-to-day on job using handbooks*
Languages spoken: *French*

Marketing
Annual event(s): *concerts*
Sponsor: *Morpeth Gathering Company, Morpeth*

UK promotion: *local newspapers; regional tourist board; leaflets/information packs; ETB/BTA*

MORWELLHAM QUAY
(trust)
heritage centre; museum; copper river port

Established: *1970*
Address: *The Morwellham and Tamar Valley Trust, Morwellham, Tavistock, Devon, PL19 8JL*
Telephone: *(0822) 832766*
Access: (road) *A390*
Parking capacity: (cars) *700* (coaches) *15*
Season: *all year*
Hours: *10am to 5.30pm daily*
Admission (1992): *adults £6.25; children £4.25; OAP £5.25; student £5.25; group rates*
No. visitors (1992): *125 000*

Facilities
Interpretation: *leaflets; audio tapes; information boards; slides; maps; tour guides; guide books; personnel; hands on*
Languages: *Dutch; French; German*
Children: *play area; nappy changing*
Schools: *maximum no. 300; no special support; educational literature; school visits in winter*
Disabled: *easy access; disabled toilets*
Catering: *1 picnic area*
Retailing: *postcards/inexpensive souvenirs; confectionery and ice cream; craftwork; books; clothes*
No. shops: *4*

Operations
Contacts: *G Emerson (Director); C Lawrence-King (Deputy Director); A Emerson (Shops Director)*
No. employees: (high season) *20 full time; 80 part time* (low season) *15 full time*
Training: *F/T operations staff, F/T management, P/T operations staff, P/T management, casual operations staff and casual management are trained in-house and externally and on specific courses and day-to-day on job*
Languages spoken: *French; Italian; Russian; Swedish*

Marketing
Affiliations: *AIM, Museums and Galleries Commission*
Other: *market research*
UK promotion: *television; local newspapers; regional tourist board; other attractions; leaflets/information packs; AA 2000 Days Out, Where to Go What to Do, Cream of Devon, Coach Drivers Handbook; ETB/BTA*

Environmental monitoring: *recycling*

MOULDSWORTH MOTOR MUSEUM
(privately owned)
museum

Established: *1975*
Address: *Smithy Lane, Mouldsworth, Ches, CH3 8AR*
Telephone: *(0928) 31781*
Access: (road) *M56/M6/B5393* (rail) *Mouldsworth*
Parking capacity: (cars) *100* (coaches) *10*
Hours: *Mar to Nov – Sun and BH weekends – 12 noon to 5pm; July and Aug – 1pm to 5pm. School visits and guided tours by appointment*
Admission (1992): *adults £2.00; children £1.50; OAP £1.50; student £1.50*

Facilities
Interpretation: *leaflets; information boards; maps; tour guides; guide books*
Schools: *maximum no. 100; educational literature; lecture/talk*
Disabled: *easy access*

Operations
Contact: *Mr J Peacop (Director)*
No. employees: (high season) *2 part time*
Languages spoken: *French*

Marketing
Market research
UK promotion: *national newspapers; local newspapers; regional tourist board; other attractions; leaflets/information packs; Vale Royal Chester Tourism*
Europe/USA/Japan promotion: *magazine articles*

Environmental monitoring: *recycling; waste; water quality; energy consumption; hazardous materials; chemical usage; emissions*

MOUNT EDGCUMBE HOUSE AND COUNTRY PARK
(local authority run)
historic house; park/reserve; garden

Established: *1971*
Address: *Cremyll, Torpoint, Cornwall, PL10 1HZ*
Telephone: *(0752) 822236.* Fax: *(0752) 822199*
Access: (road) *A374/B3247* (rail) *Plymouth*
Parking capacity: (cars) *320* (coaches) *6*
Season: *all year*
Hours: *gardens and park – all year – dawn to dusk. House – Apr to Oct – Wed to Sun and BH – 11am to 5.30pm. Restaurant and shop – Apr to Oct – 10am to 5.30pm daily*
Admission (1992): *adults £3.00; children £1.50; OAP £2.15; student £2.15; group rates*
No. visitors (1992): *300 000 (est.)*

Facilities
Interpretation: *leaflets; information boards; maps; guide books*
Languages: *Japanese; Dutch; French; German; Spanish; Russian; Polish*
Children: *nappy changing*
Schools: *maximum no. 100; educational literature; educational tour; lecture/talk*
Disabled: *easy access; disabled toilets; 2 wheelchairs, lift to first floor*
Catering: *1 picnic area*
Franchisees: *gardens and park – all year – dawn to dusk.*
Retailing: *postcards/inexpensive souvenirs; craftwork; books; West Country goods*
No. shops: *2*

Operations
No. employees: (high season) *12 full time; 6 part time* (low season) *9 full time; 1 part time*
Training: *F/T operations staff, F/T management, P/T operations staff and P/T management are trained in-house and externally and on specific courses and day-to-day on job*

Marketing
Affiliations: *Cornwall Association of Tourist Attractions, Plymouth Attractions Group*
Other: *market research*
UK promotion: *local newspapers; regional tourist board; other attractions; leaflets/information packs; ETB/BTA; articles in national newspapers and magazines*

MOUNT EPHRAIM GARDENS
(partnership)
garden

Established: *1984*
Address: *Mount Ephraim, Faversham, Kent, ME13 9TX*
Telephone: *(0227) 751496*
Access: (road) *M2/A2/A299* (rail) *Faversham*
Parking capacity: (cars) *100* (coaches) *4*
Hours: *Apr to Sept – 2pm to 6pm daily*
Admission (1992): *adults £1.75; children £0.25; OAP £1.75; student £1.75; groups £1.50*
No. visitors (1992): *10 500*

Facilities
Interpretation: *leaflets; information boards*
Languages: *French*
Catering: *1 waiter/waitress served*
Retailing: *craftwork; homemade preserves and sweets*
No. shops: *1*

Operations
Contacts: *L and M Dawes (Manager/owner)*
No. employees: *(high season) 2 full time; 4 part
time (low season) 2 full time*
Training: *P/T operations staff are trained on
specific courses and day-to-day on job*
Languages spoken: *French*

Marketing
Annual event(s): *outdoor Shakespeare, outdoor
classical concert*
Sponsor(s): *Swale Borough Council and others*
Other: *market research*
UK promotion: *local newspapers; regional tourist
board; other attractions; leaflets/information
packs*
Europe promotion: *leaflets/brochures*

Environmental monitoring: *water quality;
hazardous materials; chemical usage; Landscape*

MOUNT STEWART HOUSE AND GARDENS
(trust)
historic house; garden

Established: *1957*
Address: *Newtownards, Co. Down, BT22 2AD*
Telephone: *(024774) 387/487*
Access: *(road) A20*
Parking capacity: *(cars) 250 (coaches) 10*
Hours: *house – May to Sept – Wed to Mon – 1pm
to 6pm, Apr and Oct – Sat and Sun – 1pm to
6pm. Gardens – Apr to Sept – Mon to Sun –
10.30am to 6pm*
Admission (1992): *adults £3.30; children £1.65;
group discounts available*
No. visitors (1992): *40 000*

Facilities
Interpretation: *leaflets; information boards; slides;
maps; tour guides; guide books*
Languages: *French; German*
Children: *nappy changing*
Schools: *maximum no. 100; educational literature;
lecture/talk*
Disabled: *easy access; disabled toilets; helpers;
leaflets*
Catering: *1 self-service cafeteria*
Retailing: *postcards/inexpensive souvenirs;
confectionery and ice cream; books*
No. shops: *1*

Operations
Contacts: *Mr H R Hutchman (Administrator); Ms
Maire Bermingham (Regional Enterprises
Manager); Ms Diane Forbes (Regional Public
Affairs Manager)*
No. employees: *(high season) 11 full time; 23 part
time (low season) 11 full time; 2 part time*
Training: *F/T operations staff, F/T management,
P/T operations staff, P/T management and
casual operations staff are trained in-house and
externally and on specific courses and
day-to-day on job*
Languages spoken: *French*

Marketing
Affiliations: *Irish Heritage Properties*
Other: *press office; market research*
UK promotion: *local newspapers; regional tourist
board; other attractions; leaflets/information
packs*
Europe/USA promotion: *leaflets/brochures;
travel agents' brochures; British Tourist
Authority*

MUCH WENLOCK MUSEUM
(local authority run)
museum

Established: *1968*
Address: *High St, Much Wenlock, Shropshire,
TF13 6HR*
Telephone: *(0952) 727773*
Access: *(road) M54/A458*
Hours: *Apr to Oct – 10am to 1pm and 2pm to
5pm daily*
Admission (1992): *adults £0.50; others free*
No. visitors (1992): *6000*

Facilities
Interpretation: *leaflets; information boards;
displays*
Schools: *maximum no. 30; educational literature;
lecture/talk; activity/handling session*
Disabled: *easy access; helpers*
Retailing: *postcards/inexpensive souvenirs; books;
dinosaurs*
No. shops: *1*

Operations
Contacts: *J Bishop (Museum Assistant); J
Goodson/N Nixon (Marketing Officer/Senior
Curator)*
No. employees: *(high season) 1 full time; 1 part
time*
Training: *F/T operations staff and F/T
management are trained in-house and on
specific courses and day-to-day on job using
videos and handbooks and courses*
Languages spoken: *French; German*

Marketing
Annual event(s): *various*
Affiliations: *MA, etc.*
Other: *market research*
UK promotion: *radio; local newspapers; regional
tourist board; leaflets/information packs; Heart
of England, etc.*

MULL AND WEST HIGHLAND NARROW
GAUGE RAILWAY
(limited company)
tourist railway

Established: *1983*
Address: *Old Pier Station, Craignure, Isle of
Mull, PA65 6AY*
Telephone: *(06802) 494*
Access: *(road) A849 (rail) Oban*
Parking capacity: *(cars) 20 (coaches) 3*
Hours: *Easter and May to mid Oct – 11am to
5pm daily*
Admission (1992): *adults £1.75; children £1.20;
family ticket (2 adults + 2 children) £4.70*
No. visitors (1992): *30 000*

Facilities
Interpretation: *leaflets; guide books*
Languages: *French; German; Italian*
Schools: *maximum no. 54*
Disabled: *easy access; 2 coaches able to take
wheelchairs*
Retailing: *postcards/inexpensive souvenirs;
confectionery and ice cream; craftwork;
books*
No. shops: *1*

Operations
Contacts: *Graham F. Ellis (Director); Roger
Nicholas (Operations Manager)*
No. employees: *(high season) 2 full time; 6 part
time (low season) 1 full time; 3 part time*
Training: *F/T operations staff, F/T management
and P/T operations staff are trained in-house
and day-to-day on job using handbooks and in
house materials*

Marketing
Affiliation: *Association of Independent Railways*
Other: *market research*
UK promotion: *local newspapers; regional tourist
board; other attractions; leaflets/information
packs*
Europe/Australia/USA promotion: *British Tourist
Authority*

Environmental monitoring: *internal environment*

MULLAGHBAWN FOLK MUSEUM
(community business)
historic house; museum

Established: *1969*
Address: *Tullymacrieve, Mullaghbawn, Co.
Armagh*
Telephone: *(0693) 888278. Fax: (0693) 830208*
Access: *(road) B29 (rail) Newry*
Parking capacity: *(cars) 20 (coaches) 4*

Hours: *Easter to Oct – Mon to Sat – 11am to
7pm; Rest of year – Sun – 2pm to 7pm*
Admission (1992): *adults £1.00; children and OAP
free*
No. visitors (1992): *1500*

Facilities
Interpretation: *leaflets*
Children: *adventure playground*
Schools: *maximum no. 50; educational literature*
Disabled: *easy access; disabled toilets*
Catering: *1 picnic area*
Retailing: *postcards/inexpensive souvenirs;
confectionery and ice cream; craftwork*
No. shops: *1*

Operations
Contact: *Micheal McCoy*
No. employees: *(high season) 1 full time; 2 part
time*
Training: *F/T operations staff are trained
externally and on specific courses using
handbooks*
Languages spoken: *French*

Environmental monitoring: *waste; water quality;
energy consumption; hazardous materials;
chemical usage*

MUMMIES AND MAGIC
(privately owned)
museum

Established: *1989*
Address: *Bournemouth Exhibition Centre, Old
Christchurch Lane, Bournemouth, BH1 1NE*
Telephone: *(0202) 293544. Fax: (0305) 268885*
Access: *(road) M27/A338 (rail) Bournemouth*
Hours: *Easter onwards – 9.30am to 5.30pm daily*
Admission (1992): *adults £2.95; children £1.95;
OAP £2.50; student £2.50; family ticket
(2 adults + 2 children) £8.95*

Facilities
Interpretation: *videos; leaflets; audio tapes;
information boards; guide books;
reconstructions*
Schools: *maximum no. 100; educational literature;
lecture/talk*
Retailing: *postcards/inexpensive souvenirs;
craftwork; books; reproductions of famous
artefacts; Egyptian style*
No. shops: *1*

Operations
Contacts: *Mr T Batty (General Manager);
Ms J Ridley (Director); Ms T McDonald
(Merchandising Manager)*
No. employees: *(high season) 11 full time; 12 part
time (low season) 8 full time; 9 part time*
Training: *F/T operations staff, P/T operations
staff and casual operations staff are trained
in-house and day-to-day on job*

Marketing
Press office; market research
UK promotion: *national newspapers; radio; local
newspapers; regional tourist board; other
attractions; leaflets/information packs*
Europe/USA promotion: *British Tourist Authority*

MUSEUM OF ARMY FLYING
(limited company)
museum

Established: *1984*
Address: *Middle Wallop, Stockbridge, Hants,
SO20 8DY*
Telephone: *(0264) 384421*
Access: *(road) M3/A343/A303 (rail) Grateley/
Andover*
Parking capacity: *(cars) 80 (coaches) 20*
Season: *all year*
Hours: *10am to 4.30pm daily*
Admission (1992): *adults £3.50; children £2.00;
OAP £2.50; student £2.00; group rates available*

No. visitors (1992): *52 000 (est.)*

Facilities
Interpretation: *videos; leaflets; audio tapes; information boards; maps; tour guides; guide books*
Children: *play area; nappy changing*
Schools: *maximum no. 100; educational literature; audio/visual presentation; lecture/talk; talks if required*
Disabled: *easy access; disabled toilets*
Catering: *1 picnic area*
Franchisees: *10am to 4.30pm daily*
Retailing: *postcards/inexpensive souvenirs; confectionery and ice cream; craftwork; books; clothes; reproductions of famous artefacts; model kits and aviation books*
No. shops: *1*

Operations
Contacts: *M Andrews (Museum Director); D Armitage (Curator); Mrs K Thirsk (Accountant/Shop Manager); R Davies (Business and Publicity Manager)*
No. employees: (high season) *6 full time; 5 part time* (low season) *6 full time; 4 part time*

Marketing
Annual event(s): *various*
Sponsor(s): *various*
Affiliations: *Southern TB, Defence of the Realm, Museums and Galleries Commission*
Other: *press office; market research*
UK promotion: *radio; local newspapers; regional tourist board; other attractions; leaflets/ information packs; various; ETB/BTA*

MUSEUM OF ARMY TRANSPORT
(trust)
museum

Established: *1983*
Address: *Flemingate, Beverley, Humberside*
Telephone: *(0482) 860445.* Fax: *(0482) 866459*
Access: (road) *M62* (rail) *Beverley*
Parking capacity: (cars) *100*
Season: *all year*
Hours: *10am to 5pm daily except 24–26 Dec*
Admission (1992): *adults £2.50; children £1.50; OAP £1.50; student £1.50; ub40s £1.50*
No. visitors (1992): *90 000 (est.)*

Facilities
Interpretation: *videos; leaflets; information boards; maps; tour guides; guide books; tour guides on request*
Children: *adventure playground; nappy changing*
Schools: *maximum no. 100; educational literature; audio/visual presentation; lecture/talk; activity days*
Disabled: *easy access; disabled toilets; wheelchairs*
Catering: *1 bar/public house*
Franchisees: *10am to 5pm daily except 24–26 Dec*
Retailing: *postcards/inexpensive souvenirs; confectionery and ice cream; books; toys and videos*
No. shops: *1*

Operations
Contacts: *L Jordan (Marketing Manager); Ms L Wright (Finance Officer); Ms H Cole (Shop Manager)*
Languages spoken: *German*

Marketing
Annual event: *Northern Model EXPO*
Affiliation: *Destination Humberside*
Other: *press office; market research*
UK promotion: *radio; local newspapers; regional tourist board; other attractions; leaflets/ information packs; ETB/BTA*
Europe promotion: *leaflets/brochures; travel agents' brochures; British Tourist Authority*

Environmental monitoring: *waste; water quality; energy consumption*

MUSEUM OF BRITISH ROAD TRANSPORT
(trust)
museum

Established: *1980*
Address: *St Agnes Lane, Hales St, Coventry, CV1 1PN*
Telephone: *(0203) 932425.* Fax: *(0203) 832465*
Season: *all year*
Hours: *10am to 4.30pm daily*
Admission (1992): *adults £2.50; children £1.50; OAP £1.50; student £1.50*
No. visitors (1992): *87 000*

Facilities
Interpretation: *videos; leaflets; audio tapes; information boards; slides; maps; tour guides; guide books*
Children: *nappy changing*
Schools: *educational literature; audio/visual presentation*
Disabled: *easy access; disabled toilets*
Catering: *1 picnic area*
Retailing: *postcards/inexpensive souvenirs*
No. shops: *1*

Operations
Contacts: *B Littlewood (Managing Director); A Morritt (Shop Supervisor); C Boyce (Development Manager)*
No. employees: (high season) *23 full time; 3 part time*
Training: *F/T operations staff, F/T management, P/T operations staff, P/T management and casual operations staff using handbooks*
Languages spoken: *French; German*

Marketing
Annual event: *Coventry car run*
Sponsor(s): various
Affiliation: *MA, Association of British Transport and Engineering Museums*
Other: *PR company: Leader Communications, 7th Floor, Chamber of Commerce House, Harburns Rd, Edgbaston, Birmingham; press office; market research*
UK promotion: *television; radio; local newspapers; regional tourist board; other attractions; leaflets/information packs; various; ETB/BTA*
Europe/USA promotion: *British Tourist Authority; trade shows*

Environmental monitoring: *recycling*

MUSEUM OF CHILDHOOD
(independent)
museum

Established: *1973*
Address: *1 Castle St, Beaumaris, Anglesey, Gwynedd, LL58 8AP*
Telephone: *(0248) 712498*
Access: (road) *M56/A55* (rail) *Bangor*
Season: *all year*
Hours: *Easter to Nov – Mon to Sat – 10am to 5pm, Sun – 12am to 5pm*
Admission (1992): *adults £2.00; children £1.00; OAP £1.00; under 16s £1.00; disabled free*
No. visitors (1992): *28 752*

Facilities
Interpretation: *leaflets; information boards; guide books*
Schools: *maximum no. 60; audio/visual presentation; lecture/talk*
Disabled: *only ground floor accessible*
Retailing: *postcards/inexpensive souvenirs; craftwork; books; reproductions of famous artefacts; reproduction antique toys; dolls, teddy bears, etc.*
No. shops: *1*

Operations
Contacts: *Robert Brown (owner); Mrs Joan Brown (Director)*
No. employees: (high season) *6 part time* (low season) *4 part time*
Training: *P/T operations staff are trained in-house and day-to-day on job using videos and handbooks*

Languages spoken: *French; German; Italian; Spanish; Japanese*

Marketing
Market research
UK promotion: *television; national newspapers; radio; local newspapers; regional tourist board; other attractions; leaflets/information packs; ETB/BTA*
Europe promotion: *leaflets/brochures; British Tourist Authority*

MUSEUM OF CHILDHOOD, THE
(partnership)
museum

Established: *1986*
Address: *Church St, Ribchester, Lancs, PR3 3YE*
Telephone: *(0254) 878520.* Fax: *(0254) 823977*
Access: (road) *M6/A59*
Parking capacity: (cars) *50*
Season: *all year*
Hours: *Tues to Sun – 10.30am to 5pm*
Admission (1992): *adults £1.95; children £1.25; OAP £1.75*
No. visitors (1992): *50 000 (est.)*

Facilities
Interpretation: *leaflets; information boards*
Children: *play area*
Schools: *maximum no. 75; educational tour; lecture/talk*
Catering: *1 snack bar/food stall*
Retailing: *postcards/inexpensive souvenirs; teddies, dolls houses, dolls, toys*
No. shops: *1*

Operations
Contacts: *A Wild; D Wild*
No. employees: (high season) *2 full time; 5 part time* (low season) *2 full time; 3 part time*
Training: *P/T operations staff and casual operations staff are trained in-house and day-to-day on job*
Languages spoken: *French; Italian; Spanish; Portuguese*

Marketing
Market research
UK promotion: *radio; local newspapers; regional tourist board; leaflets/information packs; ETB/BTA; collectors magazines*
Worldwide promotion: *collectors magazines*

Environmental monitoring: *recycling; waste; water quality; energy consumption; chemical usage*

MUSEUM OF COSTUME
(local authority run)
museum

Established: *1963*
Address: *Assembly Rooms, Bennett St, Bath, BA1 2EW*
Telephone: *(0225) 461111.* Fax: *(0225) 444793*
Access: (road) *M4/A4* (rail) *Bath Spa*
Season: *all year*
Hours: *Mar to Oct – 9.30am to 6pm, Sun – 10am to 6pm; Nov to Feb – 10am to 5pm; Sun – 11am to 5pm*
Admission (1992): *adults £2.40; children £1.35; OAP £2.40; student £2.40*
No. visitors (1992): *177 000*

Facilities
Interpretation: *information boards; tour guides; guide books*
Schools: *maximum no. 50; educational literature*
Disabled: *easy access; disabled toilets; helpers*
Catering: *1 waiter/waitress served*
Franchisees: *Mar to Oct – 9.30am to 6pm, Sun – 10am to 6pm; Nov to Feb – 10am to 5pm, Sun – 11am to 5pm*
Retailing: *postcards/inexpensive souvenirs; books*
No. shops: *1*

Operations
Contacts: *Mrs P Ruddock (Senior Keeper and Keeper of Costume); Mrs K Dyer (Retail Services Manager); Ms S Bird (Museums Curator)*
No. employees: (high season) *11 full time; 19 part time* (low season) *11 full time; 13 part time*
Training: *F/T operations staff, F/T management, P/T operations staff, P/T management and casual operations staff are trained in-house and on specific courses and day-to-day on job using handbooks*
Languages spoken: *Welsh*

Marketing
UK promotion: *local newspapers; regional tourist board; leaflets/information packs; ETB/BTA*
Europe/Asia/USA promotion: *leaflets/brochures; British Tourist Authority*

Environmental monitoring: *waste; energy consumption*

MUSEUM OF EAST ANGLIAN LIFE
(limited company charitable trust)
museum

Established: *1967*
Address: *Stowmarket, Suffolk, IP14 1DL*
Telephone: *(0449) 612 229*
Access: (road) *A45* (rail) *Stowmarket*
Hours: *Apr to Oct – 10am to 5pm*
Admission (1992): *adults £3.25; children £1.60; OAP £2.00; student £2.00; family ticket £9.00; special rates for groups*
No. visitors (1992): *35 000*

Facilities
Interpretation: *leaflets; guide books*
Children: *nappy changing*
Schools: *educational literature; education centre*
Disabled: *easy access; disabled toilets*
Catering: *2 picnic areas*
Retailing: *postcards/inexpensive souvenirs; confectionery and ice cream; craftwork; books*
No. shops: *1*

Operations
Contacts: *R Walding (Director); C Kent (Visitor Services Manager)*
No. employees: (high season) *8 full time; 10 part time* (low season) *8 full time; 2 part time*
Training: *F/T operations staff and F/T management are trained externally and on specific courses*

Marketing
Annual event(s): *craft, transport and countryside special interest events*
Sponsor(s): *various*
Affiliations: *AIM*
Other: *market research*
UK promotion: *local newspapers; regional tourist board; leaflets/information packs; county and district authorities*

Environmental monitoring: *energy consumption*

MUSEUM OF ENGLISH NAIVE ART
(trust)
museum

Established: *1987*
Address: *The Countess of Huntingdon Chapel, The Paragon, Bath, BA1 5NA*
Telephone: *(0225) 446020*
Access: (road) *M4/A4* (rail) *Bath Spa*
Hours: *Apr to Dec – Mon to Sat – 10.30am to 5pm, Sun – 2pm to 6pm*
Admission (1992): *adults £2.00; children £1.50; OAP £1.50; student £1.50*
No. visitors (1992): *9000*

Facilities
Interpretation: *leaflets; guide books*
Children: *nappy changing*
Schools: *maximum no. 50; educational literature; educational tour; lecture/talk*

Retailing: *postcards/inexpensive souvenirs; craftwork; books; reproductions of famous artefacts*
No. shops: *1*

Operations
Contact: *M Brewster (Curator)*
No. employees: (high season) *1 full time; 5 part time*
Languages spoken: *French*

Marketing
Annual event(s): *concerts*
Other: *market research*
UK promotion: *local newspapers; leaflets/information packs; ETB/BTA*
Europe/USA promotion: *leaflets/brochures*

MUSEUM OF FIRE
(local authority run)
museum

Established: *1988*
Address: *Lothian and Borders Fire Brigade, Lauriston Place, Edinburgh, EH3 9DC*
Telephone: *(031) 228 2401.* Fax: *(031) 228 6662*
Hours: *Mon to Fri – 9am to 4.30pm. Closed 1st 2 weeks in Aug and 2 weeks over Christmas and New Year*
Admission (1992): *free*
No. visitors (1992): *3500*

Facilities
Interpretation: *tour guides*
Schools: *maximum no. 30; educational literature; project*
Disabled: *easy access; disabled toilets; leaflets*

Operations
Contacts: *Mr R Virtue (Divisional Officer); Mr R Skorupa (Station Officer)*
No. employees: (high season) *16 full time*
Training: *F/T operations staff and F/T management are trained in-house and externally and on specific courses*

Marketing
Affiliations: *SMC, MA*
Other: *press office*
UK promotion: *local newspapers; regional tourist board; leaflets/information packs*

Environmental monitoring: *recycling*

MUSEUM OF FLIGHT
(National Museum of Scotland)
museum

Established: *1975*
Address: *East Fortune, North Berwick, E Lothian, EH39 5LF*
Telephone: *(0620) 88308*
Access: (road) *A7* (rail) *Drem*
Parking capacity: (cars) *800* (coaches) *60*
Hours: *Easter to end Sept – 10.30am to 4.30pm daily. Otherwise by appointment*
No. visitors (1992): *40 000 (est.)*

Facilities
Interpretation: *videos; leaflets; information boards; slides; maps; tour guides; guide books*
Languages: *French; German*
Children: *nappy changing*
Schools: *maximum no. 70; lecture/talk; work sheets*
Disabled: *easy access; disabled toilets*
Catering: *1 snack bar/food stall*
Franchisees: *Easter to end Sept – 10.30am to 4.30pm daily.*
Retailing: *postcards/inexpensive souvenirs; confectionery and ice cream; books; aero models*
No. shops: *1*

Operations
Contacts: *Sqn Ldr R J Major (Rtd) (Curator); B Buchan (Publicity)*

No. employees: (high season) *14 full time* (low season) *4 full time*
Training: *F/T operations staff and F/T management are trained in-house and externally and on specific courses using videos and handbooks*

Marketing
Annual event(s): *rallies*
Affiliations: *National Museum of Scotland*
UK promotion: *radio; local newspapers; regional tourist board; leaflets/information packs*

Environmental monitoring: *recycling; waste*

MUSEUM OF INSTALLATION
(limited company)
museum

Established: *1990*
Address: *33 Great Sutton St, London, EC1 0LR*
Telephone: *(071) 253 0802.* Fax: *(071) 582 7022*
Access: (road) *Barbican*
Hours: *Wed to Sat – 2pm to 6pm at Exhibition times*
Admission (1992): *free*
No. visitors (1992): *2000 (est.)*

Facilities
Interpretation: *videos; audio tapes; slides; artists' exhibitions*
Languages: *French; German; Spanish; depends on exhibits*
Schools: *maximum no. 20; educational literature; audio/visual presentation; lecture/talk; colleges*
Retailing: *books; catalogues and prints*
No. shops: *None*

Operations
Contacts: *N Oliveira/N Oxley/M Petry (Directors)*
No. employees: (high season) *1 part time*
Training: *P/T operations staff are trained in-house and day-to-day on job*

MUSEUM OF KENT LIFE
(limited company)
museum; open air museum

Established: *1984*
Address: *Lock Lane, Sandling, Maidstone, Kent*
Telephone: *(0622) 763936.* Fax: *(0622) 662024*
Access: (road) *M20/A229* (rail) *Maidstone East*
Parking capacity: (cars) *200* (coaches) *3*
Hours: *Easter to Sept – 10.30am to 5.30pm daily*
Admission (1992): *adults £3.00; children £1.50; OAP £1.50; student £1.50*
No. visitors (1992): *28 000 (est.)*

Facilities
Interpretation: *videos; leaflets; audio tapes; information boards; maps; tour guides*
Children: *nappy changing*
Schools: *maximum no. 40; educational literature; workshops demonstrations*
Disabled: *easy access; disabled toilets*
Catering: *1 licensed restaurant*
Franchisees: *Easter to Sept – 10.30am to 5.30pm daily*
Retailing: *postcards/inexpensive souvenirs; craftwork; books; clothes*
No. shops: *1*

Operations
Contacts: *V Carslaw (Acting Manager); N Yates (Acting Director); J Amey (Shop Supervisor)*
No. employees: (high season) *5 full time; 4 part time* (low season) *3 full time*
Training: *F/T operations staff, F/T management, P/T operations staff, P/T management, casual operations staff and casual management are trained externally and on specific courses*
Languages spoken: *French; German; Spanish*

Marketing
Sponsor(s): *various*

Affiliations: *ETB*
Other: *market research*
UK promotion: *national newspapers; radio; local newspapers; regional tourist board; other attractions; leaflets/information packs; ETB/BTA*
Europe promotion: *British Tourist Authority*

Environmental monitoring: *recycling; waste; energy consumption; hazardous materials; chemical usage; emissions*

MUSEUM OF LEAD MINING
(trust)
museum

Established: *1974*
Address: *Goldscaur Row, Wanlockhead, By Biggar, ML12 6UT*
Telephone: *(0659) 74387*
Access: (road) *M74/A76* (rail) *Kirkconnel*
Parking capacity: (cars) *40* (coaches) *2*
Hours: *Easter to Oct – 11am to 4.30pm daily. Oct to Mar by appointment*
Admission (1992): *adults £2.50; children £1.00; OAP £2.00; student £2.00; family ticket available*
No. visitors (1992): *30 000 (est.)*

Facilities
Interpretation: *videos; leaflets; audio tapes; information boards; maps; tour guides; guide books*
Languages: *French; German*
Children: *nappy changing*
Schools: *maximum no. 70; educational literature; slide collection*
Disabled: *easy access; disabled toilets; helpers; special objects to hold for the blind*
Catering: *2 picnic areas*
Retailing: *postcards/inexpensive souvenirs; craftwork; books; clothes*
No. shops: *1*

Operations
Contacts: *Ms J Orr (Manager); Ms A Cadd (Administration Officer); Ms C Davis (Curatorial Assistant)*
No. employees: (high season) *3 full time; 15 part time* (low season) *3 full time; 1 part time*
Training: *F/T operations staff, F/T management, P/T operations staff and casual operations staff are trained in-house and externally and on specific courses*

Marketing
Market research
UK promotion: *national newspapers; radio; local newspapers; regional tourist board; other attractions; leaflets/information packs*
Europe promotion: *British Tourist Authority*

MUSEUM OF LONDON
(Department of National Heritage, trust)
museum

Established: *1976*
Address: *150 London Wall, London, EC2Y 5HN*
Telephone: *(071) 600 3699.* Fax: *(071) 600 1058*
Access: (rail) *St Paul's/Barbican*
Season: *all year*
Hours: *Tues to Sat – 10am to 6pm; Sun – 12 noon to 6pm. Closed Christmas period but open other BH*
Admission (1992): *adults £3.00; children £1.50; OAP £1.50; student £1.50*
No. visitors (1992): *412 403*

Facilities
Interpretation: *leaflets; audio tapes; information boards; slides; guide books*
Children: *nappy changing*
Schools: *educational literature; lecture/talk*
Disabled: *easy access; disabled toilets; Braille/sound posts; taped guides, objects to feel*
Catering: *2 self-service cafeterias*
Franchisees: *Tues to Sat – 10am to 6pm; Sun – 12 noon to 6pm*

Retailing: *postcards/inexpensive souvenirs; books; clothes; reproductions of famous artefacts*
No. shops: *1*

Operations
Contact: *Mr W Tayleur (Head of Marketing)*
Languages spoken: *French*

Marketing
Annual event(s): *various*
Other: *press office; market research*
UK promotion: *national newspapers; leaflets/information packs; Holiday London*
USA/leaflets over the world promotion: *leaflets/brochures; British Tourist Authority*

Environmental monitoring: *waste; energy consumption; hazardous materials*

MUSEUM OF MECHANICAL MUSIC
(private limited company)
theme park; museum; indoor musical theme park

Established: *1990*
Address: *Bradley Grange, Bradley Lane, Rufforth, York, YO2 3QW*
Telephone: *(0904) 83773.* Fax: *(0904) 83659*
Access: (road) *A64/B1224/A1*
Parking capacity: (cars) *150* (coaches) *8*
Season: *all year*
Hours: *June to end Sept – Tues, Wed, Thur and Sun – 2pm; winter – every Sun. Christmas – special bookings*
Admission (1992): *adults £3.99; children £2.20; reductions for groups*
No. visitors (1992): *13 000 (est.)*

Facilities
Interpretation: *tour guides; mechanical organs and musical instruments*
Schools: *educational literature; special live show*
Disabled: *easy access; disabled toilets; special signs*
Catering: *1 bar/public house*
Retailing: *video, cassettes, pictures, books*
No. shops: *none*

Operations
Contact: *Mrs S Harrison (Director)*

Marketing
Annual event(s): *cinema organ concerts*
UK promotion: *television; national newspapers; radio; local newspapers; regional tourist board; other attractions; leaflets/information packs; Yorks and Humbs Tourist Board*
Europe/Australia/USA promotion: *leaflets/ brochures; specialist publications*

MUSEUM OF STAFFORDSHIRE REGIMENT
(Ministry of Defence sponsored)
museum; regimental

Established: *1963*
Address: *c/o RHQ Staffs, Whittington Barracks, Lichfield, Staffs*
Telephone: *(021) 311 3229.* Fax: *(021) 311 3205*
Access: (road) *M6/M42/A51/A5* (rail) *Lichfield/ Tamworth*
Parking capacity: (cars) *200* (coaches) *20*
Season: *all year*
Hours: *Mon to Fri – 9am to 4.30pm*
Admission (1992): *donations only*
No. visitors (1992): *9500 (est.)*

Facilities
Interpretation: *leaflets; audio tapes; information boards; maps*
Schools: *maximum no. 40; no special support*
Disabled: *easy access; other audio facilities*
Retailing: *postcards/inexpensive souvenirs; regimental memorabilia*
No. shops: *1*

Operations
Contacts: *Major R McLean (Curator); N Ferris (Attendant)*

No. employees: (high season) *1 full time; 1 part time* (low season) *1 full time; 1 part time*
Languages spoken: *French; German*

Marketing
Affiliations: *West Midlands Area Museums Services*
Other: *market research*
UK promotion: *regional tourist board; other attractions; leaflets/information packs; ETB/BTA; HETB*

Environmental monitoring: *water quality; energy consumption; transport*

MUSEUM OF THE CUMBRAES
(local authority run)
museum; gallery

Established: *1978*
Address: *Garrison House, Millport, Cumbrae*
Telephone: *(0475) 530741*
Access: (road) *A78 & ferry*
Hours: *1 June to 30 Sept – Mon to Sat – 11am to 1pm and 1.30pm to 5pm*
Admission (1992): *free*
No. visitors (1992): *10 000 (est.)*

Facilities
Interpretation: *leaflets; information boards; slides; displays and exhibitions*
Schools: *maximum no. 40; educational literature; audio/visual presentation; lecture/talk*
Disabled: *easy access; helpers*
Retailing: *postcards/inexpensive souvenirs; books*
No. shops: *1*

Operations
Contacts: *Ms D Keasal (District Curator); Ms L McAuley (District Council Marketing Officer)*
No. employees: (high season) *2 full time; 8 part time* (low season) *2 full time; 3 part time*
Training: *F/T operations staff, F/T management, P/T operations staff and casual operations staff are trained in-house and externally and on specific courses and day-to-day on job*

Marketing
Press office; market research
UK promotion: *local newspapers; regional tourist board; other attractions; leaflets/information packs; ETB/BTA; STB and magazines*

MUSEUM OF THE HOME
(privately owned)
private collection

Established: *1986*
Address: *Castle Hill Museum, 7 Westgate Hill, Pembroke, Dyfed, SA71 4LB*
Telephone: *(0646) 681200*
Access: (road) *M4/A477/A40*
Hours: *Easter to end Oct – 10.30am to 5.30pm. Closed some Thur and Sat*
Admission (1992): *adults £1.00; children £0.70; OAP £0.70; student £0.70;*
No. visitors (1992): *7948*

Facilities
Interpretation: *personal welcome*
Schools: *maximum no. 15; educational literature*
Disabled: *not suitable for wheelchairs, other disabilities personal attention*

Operations
Contacts: *St John and J Stimson (owners)*
No. employees: (high season) *2 full time* (low season) *2 full time*
Languages spoken: *French; Norwegian*

Marketing
Affiliation: *AIM*
UK promotion: *leaflets/information packs; district council tourism office and local publications*

Environmental monitoring: *recycling; water quality; energy consumption; hazardous materials; chemical usage*

MUSEUM OF THE MOVING IMAGE
(British Film Institute)
museum

Established: *1988*
Address: *South Bank, Waterloo, London, SE1 8XT*
Telephone: *(071) 928 3535. Fax: (071) 633 9323*
Access: *(rail) Waterloo*
Season: *all year*
Hours: *10am to 6pm daily. Closed 24–26 Dec*
Admission (1992): *adults £5.50; children £4.00; OAP £4.00; student £4.70; family ticket (2 + 4) £16.00; UB40s £4.00; BFI members £4.00; group rates available*
No. visitors (1992): *451 586*

Facilities
Interpretation: *videos; leaflets; audio tapes; information boards; slides; maps; guide books; personnel; film clips*
Languages: *Japanese; French; German; Italian; Spanish*
Schools: *audio/visual presentation; lecture/talk; themed seminars*
Disabled: *easy access; disabled toilets; helpers; other audio facilities; leaflets; telephone links*
Catering: *1 bar/public house*
Retailing: *postcards/inexpensive souvenirs; books; reproductions of famous artefacts; videos*
No. shops: *2*

Operations
Contacts: *Mr P Cullard (Deputy Controller); Mr C Flower (Personnel); Mr L Hardcastle (Curator); Ms P Owens (Marketing)*
Training: *F/T operations staff, F/T management, P/T operations staff, P/T management, casual operations staff and casual management are trained in-house and on specific courses and day-to-day on job*

Marketing
Annual event(s): *grandparents day, animator in residence award and exhibitions*
Sponsor(s): *various*
Affiliations: *LTB, Tourism Society*
Other: *PR Company: Freud Communications, 7 Berners Mews, London, W1P 8PG; press office; market research*
UK promotion: *national newspapers; radio; local newspapers; regional tourist board; leaflets/information packs; Underground*
Europe/Asia/Australia/USA promotion: *leaflets/brochures; travel agents' brochures; British Tourist Authority; LTB*

MUSEUM OF THE ORDER OF ST JOHN
(charity)
historic house; museum; church

Established: *1970*
Address: *St John's Gate, St John's Lane, Clerkenwell, London, EC1M 4DA*
Telephone: *(071) 253 6644*
Access: *(rail) Farringdon*
Season: *all year*
Hours: *Mon to Fri – 10am to 5pm; Sat – 10am to 4pm. Closed BH, Christmas and New Year*
Admission (1992): *free but £2.00 donation requested for tour*
No. visitors (1992): *17 000 (est.)*

Facilities
Interpretation: *leaflets; tour guides; guide books*
Languages: *French; German*
Schools: *maximum no. 35*
Disabled: *disabled toilets*
Retailing: *postcards/inexpensive souvenirs; books; St John Ambulance equipment and uniforms*
No. shops: *1*

Operations
Contacts: *Ms P Willis (Curator); Mr P Reader (Purchasing Manager); Ms A Devonshire (Deputy Curator)*
No. employees: (high season) *5 full time; 3 part time* (low season) *5 full time; 3 part time*
Training: *F/T management are trained externally and on specific courses and day-to-day on job using handbooks*

Languages spoken: *French; German; Italian; Spanish*

Marketing
Press office
UK promotion: *local newspapers; other attractions; leaflets/information packs*
Europe promotion: *leaflets/brochures; British Tourist Authority; with Medical Museum, London*

MUSEUM OF TRANSPORT
(trust)
museum

Established: *1980*
Address: *Boyle St, Cheetham, Manchester, M8 8UW*
Telephone: *(061) 205 2122*
Access: *(road) M602/A665 (rail) Manchester Victoria*
Season: *all year*
Hours: *Wed, Sat, Sun and BH – 10am to 5pm*
Admission (1992): *adults £1.25; children £0.75; OAP £0.75; student £1.25*
No. visitors (1992): *12 500*

Facilities
Interpretation: *leaflets; slides; tour guides; guide books*
Schools: *educational literature; audio/visual presentation; lecture/talk*
Disabled: *easy access; disabled toilets; Braille/sound posts; helpers*
Catering: *1 self-service cafeteria*
Retailing: *postcards/inexpensive souvenirs; confectionery and ice cream; books; clothes; models/transport related items*
No. shops: *2*

Operations
Contacts: *D Talbot (Chairman); S Lord (Publicity Officer); J Pollock (Merchandising); P Williams (Publicity Officer)*
No. employees: (high season) *3 part time*
Training: *P/T operations staff and P/T management are trained in-house and day-to-day on job*
Languages spoken: *French; German; Italian*

Marketing
Annual event(s): *special weekends, weekend for disabled*
Affiliation: *NWTB*
Other: *press office; market research*
UK promotion: *local newspapers; regional tourist board; leaflets/information packs*

MUSEUM OF TRANSPORT
(local authority run)
museum

Established: *1964*
Address: *Kelvin Hall, 1 Bunhouse Rd, Glasgow, G3 1DP*
Telephone: *(041) 357 3929. Fax: (041) 357 4537*
Season: *all year*
Hours: *Mon to Sat – 10am to 5pm; Sun – 11am to 5pm*
Admission (1992): *free*
No. visitors (1992): *493 239*

Facilities
Interpretation: *leaflets; information boards; tour guides; guide books*
Languages: *Urdu*
Children: *nappy changing*
Schools: *museum education dept*
Disabled: *disabled toilets*
Catering: *1 self-service cafeteria*
Retailing: *postcards/inexpensive souvenirs; books; toys, posters and prints*
No. shops: *1*

Operations
Training: *F/T operations staff are trained in-house and on specific courses and day-to-day on job*

Marketing
Annual event(s): *special weekends, weekend for disabled*
Affiliation: *NWTB*
Other: *press office; market research*
UK promotion: *local newspapers; regional tourist board; leaflets/information packs*

Environmental monitoring: *hazardous materials; transport; emissions*

MUSICAL MUSEUM
(trust)
museum

Established: *1963*
Address: *368 High St, Brentford, Middx*
Telephone: *(081) 560 8108*
Access: *(rail) Kew Bridge*
Hours: *Apr to Oct – Sat and Sun – 2pm to 5pm; also July and Aug – Wed to Fri – 2pm to 4pm*
Admission (1992): *adults £2.00; children £1.50; OAP £1.50;*
No. visitors (1992): *5000 (est.)*

Facilities
Interpretation: *tour guides*
Schools: *maximum no. 50; educational literature*
Disabled: *easy access*
Retailing: *postcards/inexpensive souvenirs; books*
No. shops: *1*

Operations
Contacts: *Mr M Ryder (Chairman); Mr O Cooper (Retail Sales)*
Training: *casual operations staff and casual management are trained in-house and on specific courses and day-to-day on job*

Marketing
Annual event(s): *concerts*
Affiliations: *AIM, AMSSEE, etc.*
Other: *market research*
UK promotion: *local newspapers; leaflets/information packs*
USA promotion: *leaflets/brochures*

Environmental monitoring: *hazardous materials; transport; emissions*

MYDDELTON HOUSE GARDENS
(local authority run)
garden

Address: *Myddelton House, Bulls Cross, Enfield, Middx, EN2 9HG*
Telephone: *(0992) 717711. Fax: (0992) 719937*
Access: *(road) M25/A10*
Parking capacity: *(cars) 50 (coaches) 8*
Season: *all year*
Hours: *Mon to Fri – 10am to 3.30pm*
Admission (1992): *adults £1.00; children £0.50; OAP £0.50*
No. visitors (1992): *2000 (est.)*

Facilities
Interpretation: *leaflets; information boards; maps*
Schools: *maximum no. 100; lecture/talk*
Disabled: *easy access; disabled toilets*

MYRETON MOTOR MUSEUM
(privately owned)
museum

Established: *1966*
Address: *Aberlady, E Lothian, EH32 OPZ*
Telephone: *(08757) 288*
Access: *(road) A1/A198 (rail) Edinburgh Drem*
Parking capacity: *(cars) 60 (coaches) 12*
Season: *all year*

Hours: *Easter to Oct – 10am to 6pm daily; Oct to Easter – 10am to 5pm daily except Christmas Day and New Year's Day*
Admission (1992): *adults £2.00; children £0.50*

Facilities
Interpretation: *leaflets; information boards; guide books*
Children: *nappy changing*
Schools: *maximum no. 70; no special support; work sheets*
Disabled: *easy access; disabled toilets*
Catering: *1 picnic area*
Retailing: *postcards/inexpensive souvenirs; books*
No. shops: *1*

Operations
Contact: *M Mutch (Curator)*

Marketing
Affiliations: *AIM*
UK promotion: *regional tourist board; other attractions; leaflets/information packs*

N

NATIONAL AMBULANCE MUSEUM
(limited company and trust)
heritage centre; museum

Established: *1988*
Address: *Waterloo Close, Stonehouse, Plymouth, Devon, PL1 3ST*
Telephone: *(0752) 266851*
Access: (road) *A38* (rail) *Plymouth*
Parking capacity: (cars) *14*
Season: *all year*
Hours: *10am to 5pm daily except 24–26 Dec and 1 Jan*
Admission (1992): *free but donations welcome*
No. visitors (1992): *12 500 (est.)*

Facilities
Interpretation: *tour guides; displays*
Schools: *maximum no. 40; lecture/talk*
Disabled: *easy access; helpers; powered transport*
Retailing: *postcards/inexpensive souvenirs; model ambulances*
No. shops: *1*

Operations
Contacts: *Mr T Hall (Director)*
No. employees: (high season) *14 full time* (low season) *14 full time*
Training: *F/T operations staff and F/T management are trained in-house and externally and on specific courses and day-to-day on job*

Marketing
Annual event(s): *Ubrooke House rally and autojumble*
Other: *press office; market research*
UK promotion: *television; national newspapers; radio; local newspapers; regional tourist board; other attractions; leaflets/information packs; West of England; ETB/BTA*
Europe/USA/Channel Islands promotion: *leaflets/brochures; British Tourist Authority*

NATIONAL ARMY MUSEUM
(non dept public body)
museum

Established: *1971*
Address: *Royal Hospital Rd, Chelsea, London, SW3 4HT*
Telephone: *(071) 730 0717.* Fax: *(071) 823 6573*
Access: (rail) *Sloane Square*
Season: *all year*
Hours: *10am to 5.30pm daily except 24–26 Dec, 1 Jan, Good Friday and May BH*
Admission (1992): *free*

Facilities
Interpretation: *videos; leaflets; information boards; slides; maps; audio/visual displays*
Children: *nappy changing*
Schools: *audio/visual presentation; lecture/talk; must book in advance*
Disabled: *easy access; disabled toilets*
Catering: *1 self-service cafeteria*
Franchisees: *10am to 5.30pm daily except 24–26 Dec, 1 Jan, Good Friday and May BH*
Retailing: *postcards/inexpensive souvenirs; confectionery and ice cream; books; clothes; reproductions of famous artefacts; toys models*
No. shops: *1*

Operations
Contacts: *M Millo (Head of Commercial Activities); D Langham (Museum Secretary); J Humphreys (PR)*
Training: *F/T operations staff and F/T management are trained in-house and externally and on specific courses and day-to-day on job using videos and handbooks*
Languages spoken: *French; Chinese*

Marketing
Annual event(s): *summer activities for young people*
Other: *press office; market research*
UK promotion: *national newspapers; local newspapers; regional tourist board; other attractions; leaflets/information packs; ETB/BTA; London Underground*
USA promotion: *leaflets/brochures; British Tourist Authority*

NATIONAL CYCLE MUSEUM
(trust)
museum

Established: *1984*
Address: *Brayford Wharf North, Lincoln, LN1 1YW*
Telephone: *(0552) 545091*
Access: (road) *A46/A57/A15* (rail) *Newark/Lincoln*
Season: *all year*
Hours: *10am to 5pm*
Admission (1992): *adults £0.80; children £0.40*
No. visitors (1992): *25 000 (est.)*

Facilities
Interpretation: *leaflets; information boards; guide books; signs*
Schools: *maximum no. 30; no special support*
Retailing: *postcards/inexpensive souvenirs; books; clothes; posters*
No. shops: *1*

Operations
Contacts: *Mrs S Beeley, Mr L James (Curator, Secretary); G Edgar, D Stephenson, T Ward (Reception/Shop, Restorer, General Assistant)*
No. employees: (high season) *4 full time; 2 part time* (low season) *4 full time*
Languages spoken: *French; German*

Marketing
Market research
UK promotion: *national newspapers; radio; local newspapers; regional tourist board; leaflets/information packs; Lincolnshire County Council*

NATIONAL GALLERY
(government funded trust)
gallery

Established: *1838*
Address: *Trafalgar Square, London, WC2N 5DN*
Telephone: *(071) 839 3321.* Fax: *(071) 930 4764*
Access: (rail) *Charing Cross*
Season: *all year*
Hours: *Mon to Sat – 10am to 6pm; Sun – 2pm to 6pm. Closed 24–26 Dec, 1 Jan, Good Friday and May Day*
Admission (1992): *free except special exhibitions*
No. visitors (1992): *4 441 000 (est.)*

Facilities
Interpretation: *videos; leaflets; audio tapes; information boards; slides; maps; tour guides; guide books*
Languages: *Japanese; French; German; Italian; Spanish*
Children: *nappy changing*
Schools: *maximum no. 50; educational literature; audio/visual presentation; lecture/talk*
Disabled: *easy access; disabled toilets; leaflets; wheelchairs induction loop in lecture theatre*
Catering: *1 snack bar/food stall*
Franchisees: *Mon to Sat – 10am to 6pm; Sun – 2pm to 6pm*
Retailing: *postcards/inexpensive souvenirs; books*
No. shops: *2*

Operations
Contacts: *Mr N MacGregor (Director); Ms L Grew (Personnel); Mr W Silver (Managing Director, National Gallery Publications); Ms J Liddiard (Press and PR)*
Training: *F/T operations staff and F/T management are trained in-house and externally and on specific courses and day-to-day on job*

Marketing
Annual event(s): *3 major exhibitions*
Sponsor(s): *various*
Other: *press office; market research*
UK promotion: *television; national newspapers; radio; local newspapers; regional tourist board; leaflets/information packs; ETB/BTA*
worldwide promotion: *leaflets/brochures; British Tourist Authority*

NATIONAL HORSERACING MUSEUM
(limited company and trust)
museum

Established: *1983*
Address: *99 High St, Newmarket, Suffolk, CB8 8JL*
Telephone: *(0638) 667333*
Access: (road) *M11/A45* (rail) *Newmarket*
Parking capacity: (cars) *100* (coaches) *4*
Hours: *Apr to June and Sept to Dec – Tues to Sat – 10am to 5pm, Sun – 2pm to 5pm (BH Mon – 10am to 5pm); July and Aug – Mon to Sat – 10am to 5pm, Sun – 12 noon to 5pm*
Admission (1992): *adults £2.50; children £0.75; OAP £1.50; student £1.50*
No. visitors (1992): *27 000*

Facilities
Interpretation: *videos; information boards; maps; tour guides; guide books; showcases*
Schools: *maximum no. 30; educational literature; lecture/talk; quiz sheets*
Disabled: *easy access; disabled toilets; helpers*
Catering: *1 picnic area*
Franchisees: *Apr to June and Sept to Dec – Tues to Sat – 10am to 5pm, Sun – 2pm to 5pm (BH Mon – 10am to 5pm); July and Aug – Mon to Sat – 10am to 5pm, Sun – 12 noon to 5pm*
Retailing: *postcards/inexpensive souvenirs; confectionery and ice cream; craftwork; books; clothes; reproductions of famous artefacts; glass, leatherware and tablemats*
No. shops: *1*

Operations
Contacts: *Mr J Round Turner (Director); Mr G Snelling (Curator); Ms J Haynes (Secretary)*
No. employees: (high season) *3 full time; 16 part time* (low season) *3 full time; 3 part time*
Training: *F/T operations staff, F/T management, P/T operations staff and casual operations staff are trained in-house and on specific courses and day-to-day on job using videos and handbooks*
Languages spoken: *French; German; Italian; Spanish*

Marketing
Annual event: *Christmas fair*
Affiliations: *MA, Association of Suffolk Museums*

Other: *PR Company: Mr R Chapman, 24
Amberley, Bury Rd, Newmarket, Suffolk;
market research*
UK promotion: *national newspapers; local
newspapers; regional tourist board; other
attractions; leaflets/information packs; coach
tour directories; ETB/BTA*
Europe/USA promotion: *leaflets/brochures; travel
agents' brochures; British Tourist Authority*

Environmental monitoring: *recycling; water
quality; energy consumption; hazardous
materials*

NATIONAL MARITIME MUSEUM
(national museum)
monument; museum

Established: *1980*
Address: *Albert Dock, Liverpool, L3 4AA*
Telephone: *(051) 207 0001.* Fax: *(051) 709 3003*
Access: (road) *M62/A57*
Parking capacity: (cars) *1300* (coaches) *8*
Season: *all year*
Hours: *10.30am to 5.30pm daily*
Admission (1992): *adults £1.50; children £0.75;
OAP £0.75; student £0.75; group and family
discounts available*
No. visitors (1992): *326 492*

Facilities
Interpretation: *videos; leaflets; audio tapes;
information boards; slides; maps; guide books;
personnel; role players*
Languages: *French; German*
Children: *nappy changing*
Schools: *educational literature; lecture/talk*
Disabled: *easy access; disabled toilets; other audio
facilities; special signs; wheelchairs; transcripts,
link system in lecture theatre, car parking*
Catering: *1 snack bar/food stall*
Franchisees: *10.30am to 5.30pm daily*
Retailing: *postcards/inexpensive souvenirs;
craftwork; books; reproductions of famous
artefacts; posters, souvenirs; NMGM designer
gift collection*
No. shops: *1*

Operations
Contacts: *Richard Foster (Director, NMGM);
Michael Stammers (Keeper); Mr A Archard
(Head of Personnel); Ms C Hitchins (General
Manager); Mrs B Hope (Marketing Manager)*
No. employees: (high season) *135 full time; 7 part
time*
Training: *F/T operations staff, F/T management,
P/T operations staff, P/T management, casual
operations staff and casual management are
trained in-house and externally and on specific
courses and day-to-day on job*

Marketing
Annual event(s): *exhibition and events programme*
Sponsor(s): *Organised by NMGM*
Affiliations: *Museums Association*
Other: *press office; market research*
UK promotion: *television; national newspapers;
radio; local newspapers; regional tourist board;
other attractions; leaflets/information packs;
ETB/BTA*
Europe/USA promotion: *leaflets/brochures;
British Tourist Authority*

NATIONAL MARITIME MUSEUM
GREENWICH
(statutory body)
museum

Established: *1937*
Address: *Romney Rd, Greenwich, London, SE10
9NF*
Telephone: *(081) 858 4422.* Fax: *(081) 312 6632*
Access: (road) *M25/A2/A200/A206* (rail)
Greenwich
Hours: *Apr to Sept – Mon to Sat – 10am to 6pm,
Sun – 12 noon to 6pm; Oct to Mar – Mon to
Sat – 10am to 5pm, Sun – 2pm to 5pm. Closed
24–26 Dec*

Admission (1992): *adults £6.95; children £4.95;
OAP £4.95; student £4.95; youth cards;
disabled student rate*
No. visitors (1992): *560 000 (est.)*

Facilities
Interpretation: *videos; leaflets; information
boards; slides; maps; guide books; tour guides
by arrangement*
Languages: *Japanese; French; German; Spanish*
Children: *adventure playground; play area; nappy
changing*
Schools: *educational literature; audio/visual
presentation; lecture/talk; education dept;
curriculum related*
Disabled: *easy access; disabled toilets; other audio
facilities; leaflets; occasional signed and touch
tours*
Catering: *1 picnic area*
Retailing: *postcards/inexpensive souvenirs;
confectionery and ice cream; craftwork; books;
clothes; reproductions of famous artefacts;
nautical goods*
No. shops: *4*

Operations
Contacts: *P Roper (Development Director);
S Mennell*
No. employees: (high season) *300 full time* (low
season) *250 full time*
Training: *F/T operations staff, F/T management,
P/T operations staff and P/T management are
trained in-house and externally and on specific
courses and day-to-day on job using videos and
handbooks*
Languages spoken: *French; German; Spanish;
Japanese*

Marketing
Annual event(s): *wooden boat show*
Sponsor(s): *Classic Boat magazine*
Affiliations: *MA, LTB, British Incoming Tour
Operators Association*
Other: *press office; market research*
UK promotion: *national newspapers; radio; local
newspapers; regional tourist board; other
attractions; leaflets/information packs;
ETB/BTA*

Environmental monitoring: *recycling; energy
consumption; hazardous materials*

NATIONAL MOTORCYCLE MUSEUM, THE
(trust)
museum

Established: *1984*
Address: *Coventry Rd, Bickenhill, Solihull,
W Midlands, B92 0EJ*
Telephone: *(0675) 443311.* Fax: *(021) 711 3153*
Access: (road) *M42/A45*
Parking capacity: (cars) *800* (coaches) *20*
Season: *all year*
Hours: *Mon to Sun – 10am to 6pm*
Admission (1992): *adults £3.75; children £2.50;
OAP £2.50*
No. visitors (1992): *200 000 (est.)*

Facilities
Interpretation: *leaflets; information boards; guide
books; exhibits*
Schools: *maximum no. 40; project packs*
Disabled: *easy access; disabled toilets*
Catering: *1 self-service cafeteria*
Retailing: *postcards/inexpensive souvenirs;
confectionery and ice cream; books; clothes;
reproductions of famous artefacts*
No. shops: *1*

Operations
Contacts: *W R Richards (Founding Trustee);
K Jones (Manager); K Wilson (PR Officer)*
No. employees: (high season) *15 full time;
2 part time* (low season) *15 full time; 2 part
time*
Training: *F/T operations staff, F/T management
and P/T operations staff are trained in-house
and day-to-day on job*
Languages spoken: *Swedish*

Marketing
PR company: *The Publicity Dept Ltd, Benson
House, Lomard St, Birmingham,
B12 0QR*
UK promotion: *local newspapers; regional tourist
board; leaflets/information packs; local and
national guides; ETB/BTA*
Europe/USA promotion: *British Tourist
Authority; special interest magazine*

NATIONAL MUSEUM OF LABOUR HISTORY
(limited company)
museum; archive

Established: *1990*
Address: *103 Princess St, Manchester, M1 6DD*
Telephone: *(061) 228 7212.* Fax: *(061) 237 5965*
Access: (road) *M56* (rail) *Manchester
Piccadilly/Oxford Road*
Season: *all year*
Hours: *Tues to Sat – 10am to 5pm*
Admission (1992): *free*
No. visitors (1992): *12 000*

Facilities
Interpretation: *leaflets; information boards*
Schools: *educational literature; lecture/talk*
Disabled: *disabled toilets; other audio facilities*
Retailing: *postcards/inexpensive souvenirs;
books; clothes; posters of trade union
banners*
No. shops: *1*

Operations
Contacts: *Siobhan Harpur (Commercial
Manager); Cath Birchall (Administrator); Kapila
Mistry (Administrative Officer); Dorothy
Fenton (Marketing Officer)*
No. employees: (high season) *13 full time; 3 part
time* (low season) *13 full time; 3 part time*
Training: *F/T operations staff, F/T management,
P/T operations staff, P/T management, casual
operations staff and casual management are
trained in-house and externally and on specific
courses and day-to-day on job using videos and
handbooks*
Languages spoken: *French; German; Italian;
Spanish*

Marketing
Market research
UK promotion: *national newspapers; local
newspapers; other attractions; leaflets/
information packs; Manchester City Council
Visitors Guide*
Europe/USA promotion: *direct mail*

Environmental monitoring: *recycling; energy
consumption; hazardous materials*

NATIONAL PINETUM, THE (BEDGEBURY)
(local authority run)
park/reserve; garden; tree collection

Established: *1960*
Address: *Forest Enterprise, Goudhurst,
Cranbrook, Kent, TN17 2SL*
Telephone: *(0580) 211044.* Fax: *(0580) 212423*
Access: (road) *M25/A21*
Parking capacity: (cars) *600* (coaches) *6*
Season: *all year*
Hours: *10am to 8pm daily. Visitor centre closed
Oct to Apr*
Admission (1992): *adults £1.50; children £0.75;
OAP £1.00*
No. visitors (1992): *50 000 (est.)*

Facilities
Interpretation: *leaflets; information boards; maps;
tour guides; guide books*
Schools: *maximum no. 40; educational tour;
lecture/talk*
Disabled: *disabled toilets*
Retailing: *postcards/inexpensive souvenirs;
craftwork; books; leaflets, technical notes;
refreshments*
No. shops: *1*

Operations
Contacts: *C Morgan (Curator); S Colley (Office Manager)*
No. employees: *(high season) 7 full time; 2 part time (low season) 7 full time*
Training: *F/T operations staff, F/T management and casual operations staff are trained in-house and externally and on specific courses and day-to-day on job*
Languages spoken: *French; German*

Marketing
Affiliations: *IUCN, BGEN, Arb Association, RHS*
Other: *press office; market research*
UK promotion: *national newspapers; local newspapers; regional tourist board; leaflets/ information packs; ETB/BTA*
Europe promotion: *British Tourist Authority*

NATIONAL POSTAL MUSEUM
(royal mail)
museum

Established: *1966*
Address: *King Edward Building, King Edward St, London, EC1A 1LP*
Telephone: *(071) 239 5426*. Fax: *(071) 600 3021*
Access: *(rail) St Paul's*
Season: *all year*
Hours: *Mon to Fri – 9.30am to 4.30pm*
Admission (1992): *free*
No. visitors (1992): *30 000 (est.)*

Facilities
Interpretation: *leaflets; maps; tour guides; guide books*
Languages: *Japanese; French; German*
Schools: *maximum no. 60; educational literature; audio/visual presentation; lecture/talk*
Retailing: *postcards/inexpensive souvenirs; books; reproductions of famous artefacts; stamps*
No. shops: *1*

Operations
Contacts: *Mr S Guron (Manager); Mr B Ilett (Administrator)*
No. employees: *(high season) 15 full time (low season) 15 full time*
Languages spoken: *French; Danish; Dutch; Urdu*

Marketing
Press office
UK promotion: *regional tourist board; other attractions; leaflets/information packs; ETB/BTA*

Environmental monitoring: *water quality; energy consumption; chemical usage; emissions; humidity levels*

NATIONAL RAILWAY MUSEUM
(national museum, government funded)
museum

Established: *1975*
Address: *Leeman Rd, York, YO2 4XJ*
Telephone: *(0904) 621261*. Fax: *(0904) 631319*
Access: *(road) M62/M1/A64/A59/A1239/A19*
Parking capacity: *(cars) 90 (coaches) 7*
Season: *all year*
Hours: *Mon to Sat – 10am to 6pm, Sun – 11am to 6pm*
Admission (1992): *adults £3.80; children £1.90; OAP £2.50; student £2.50; under 5s free*
No. visitors (1992): *550 000 (est.)*

Facilities
Interpretation: *leaflets; information boards; maps; guide books*
Children: *nappy changing*
Schools: *maximum no. 40; pre-book educational area*
Disabled: *easy access; disabled toilets; helpers; lift and wheelchairs*
Catering: *1 self-service cafeteria*
Franchisees: *Mon to Sat – 10am to 6pm, Sun – 11am to 6pm*

Retailing: *postcards/inexpensive souvenirs; craftwork; books; clothes; reproductions of famous artefacts; locomotive name plates, posters*
No. shops: *1*

Operations
Contacts: *C Allender (Museum Manager); Ms C Alderson (Retail Manager); Mr R Wardroper (Head of Public Affairs)*
No. employees: *(high season) 90 full time; 6 part time (low season) 85 full time*
Training: *F/T operations staff, F/T management, P/T operations staff, P/T management, casual operations staff and casual management are trained in-house and on specific courses and day-to-day on job*
Languages spoken: *French; German*

Marketing
Annual event(s): *various*
Sponsor(s): *occasionally*
Other: *press office; market research*
UK promotion: *television; national newspapers; radio; local newspapers; regional tourist board; leaflets/information packs; various; ETB/BTA*
Europe/Asia/Australia/USA promotion: *leaflets/ brochures; British Tourist Authority*

NATIONAL SHIRE HORSE CENTRE
(limited company)
theme park; park/reserve; museum; zoo/wildlife attraction; farm animal attraction

Established: *1978*
Address: *Yealmpton, Plymouth, PL8 2EL*
Telephone: *(0752) 880268*. Fax: *(0752) 881014*
Access: *(road) M5/A38/A379 (rail) Plymouth*
Parking capacity: *(cars) 1000 (coaches) 30*
Season: *all year*
Hours: *10am to 5pm daily except 24–26 Dec*
Admission (1992): *adults £4.95; children £3.30; OAP £4.45; student £4.95*
No. visitors (1992): *300 000 (est.)*

Facilities
Interpretation: *leaflets; information boards; guide books; personnel*
Children: *adventure playground; play area; nappy changing*
Schools: *educational literature; lecture/talk*
Disabled: *easy access; disabled toilets*
Catering: *2 bars/public houses*
Retailing: *postcards/inexpensive souvenirs; confectionery and ice cream; craftwork; books; clothes*
No. shops: *4*

Operations
No. employees: *(high season) 45 full time; 35 part time (low season) 20 full time; 10 part time*
Training: *F/T operations staff, P/T operations staff and casual operations staff are trained in-house and day-to-day on job using videos and handbooks and courses*
Languages spoken: *French; German*

Marketing
Other: *press office; market research*
UK promotion: *television; radio; local newspapers; regional tourist board; other attractions; leaflets/information packs; ETB/BTA*

Environmental monitoring: *energy consumption*

NATIONAL SOUND ARCHIVE (BRITISH LIBRARY)
(dept of British Library)
museum; sound archive

Established: *1955*
Address: *29 Exhibition Rd, London, SW7 2AS*
Telephone: *(071) 589 6603*. Fax: *(071) 823 8970*
Access: *(road) A4/A315; (rail) South Kensington*
Season: *all year*
Hours: *Mon to Fri – 10am to 5pm except PH*
Admission (1992): *free*

No. visitors (1992): *N/A*

Facilities
Interpretation: *leaflets; audio tapes*
Schools: *maximum no. 25; lecture/talk; by appointment*
Retailing: *postcards/inexpensive souvenirs; books*
No. shops: *1*

Operations
Contacts: *C Jewitt (Acting Director); M Loftus (Administrative Officer); A Bamford (Education and Publications)*
No. employees: *(high season) 38 full time; 2 part time*
Training: *N/A*
Languages spoken: *French; German; Spanish*

Marketing
Press office; market research
UK promotion: *leaflets/information packs*

Environmental monitoring: *recycling; waste*

NATURAL HISTORY MUSEUM
(dept of National Heritage trust)
museum

Established: *1881*
Address: *Cromwell Rd, London, SW7 5BD*
Telephone: *(071) 938 9123*. Fax: *(071) 938 9290*
Access: *(road) M4/A4 (rail) South Kensington*
Season: *all year*
Hours: *Mon to Sat – 10am to 5.50pm, Sun – 11am to 5.50pm*
Admission (1992): *adults £4.00; children £2.00; OAP £2.30; student £2.30; family ticket £10.50*
No. visitors (1992): *1 700 000*

Facilities
Interpretation: *videos; leaflets; audio tapes; information boards; maps; guide books*
Children: *nappy changing*
Schools: *audio/visual presentation; lecture/talk; discovery and activity centre*
Disabled: *easy access; disabled toilets; helpers*
Catering: *1 picnic area*
Franchisees: *Mon to Sat – 10am to 5.50pm, Sun – 11am to 5.50pm*
Retailing: *postcards/inexpensive souvenirs; confectionery and ice cream; craftwork; books; clothes; reproductions of famous artefacts*
No. shops: *More than 4*

Operations
Contacts: *Dr N Chalmers (Director); Mrs P Orchard (Personnel); Mrs S Lasson (Retail and Buying); Mrs J Batchelor (Marketing)*
Training: *F/T operations staff, F/T management, P/T operations staff, P/T management, casual operations staff and casual management are trained in-house and externally and on specific courses and day-to-day on job*

Marketing
Annual event: *Christmas crackers*
Other: *press office; market research*
UK promotion: *television; national newspapers; radio; local newspapers; regional tourist board; leaflets/information packs; ETB/BTA*
Europe/USA/worldwide promotion: *television; leaflets/brochures; radio; British Tourist Authority*

NATURAL WORLD
(trust)
zoo/wildlife attraction

Established: *1978*
Address: *The Quay, Poole, Dorset, BH15 1JH*
Telephone: *(0202) 686712*. Fax: *(0202) 681100*
Access: *(road) M27/A35 (rail) Poole*
Parking capacity: *(cars) 100 (coaches) 5*
Season: *all year*
Hours: *summer – 9am to 9pm; autumn – 10am to 6pm; winter – 10am to 5pm*
Admission (1992): *adults £2.95; children £2.00; OAP £2.50; student £2.25; under 4s free*

No. visitors (1992): *130 000*

Facilities
Interpretation: *leaflets; information boards; maps; guide books*
Schools: *maximum no. 100; audio/visual presentation; lecture/talk; quiz specimen handling*
Disabled: *easy access; helpers; other audio facilities; leaflets; guide book*
Catering: *1 licensed restaurant*
Retailing: *postcards/inexpensive souvenirs; confectionery and ice cream; books; posters*
No. shops: *2*

Operations
Contact: *Mr Stephens (Chairman)*
No. employees: (high season) *4 full time; 6 part time* (low season) *4 full time; 2 part time*
Training: *F/T operations staff, F/T management, P/T operations staff, P/T management, casual operations staff and casual management are trained in house and day-to-day on job*
Languages spoken: *French; German; Italian; Spanish; Japanese; Chinese*

Marketing
Press office; market research
UK promotion: *radio; local newspapers; regional tourist board; other attractions; leaflets/ information packs; holiday guides*

Environmental monitoring: *recycling; waste; hazardous materials; chemical usage; transport; emissions*

NAWORTH CASTLE
(private home)
castle

Established: *1984*
Address: *Brampton, Cumbria*
Telephone: *(06977) 41156/3666*
Access: (road) *M6/A69* (rail) *Carlisle*
Parking capacity: (cars) *50* (coaches) *12*
Hours: *Easter to Nov – Wed, Sat, Sun and BH – 12 noon to 5pm; Aug – Wed to Sun – 12 noon to 5pm*
Admission (1992): *adults £2.50; children £1.50; OAP £1.50; student £1.50; family £6.00*
No. visitors (1992): *7500 (est.)*

Facilities
Interpretation: *leaflets; information boards; tour guides; guide books*
Languages: *French; German; Italian; Spanish*
Schools: *maximum no. 100; lecture/talk; half price admission*
Disabled: *none*
Catering: *1 picnic area*
Retailing: *postcards/inexpensive souvenirs; books*
No. shops: *1*

Operations
Contact: *Paul S MacDonald (Administrator)*
Training: *F/T operations staff and casual operations staff are trained in-house and day-to-day on job using recommended procedure*

Marketing
Annual event(s): *concert series*
Sponsor(s): *Arts Council, city council*
Affiliations: *HHA, Cumbria Tourist Board*
UK promotion: *radio; local newspapers; regional tourist board; other attractions; leaflets/ information packs; CTB Leisure Guide; Historic Houses, Castles and Gardens*

Environmental monitoring: *water quality; energy consumption; hazardous materials; chemical usage*

NEIDPATH CASTLE
(limited company)
castle; garden; museum

Established: *1900*
Address: *Peebles, Tweeddale, EH45 8NN*

Telephone: *(0721) 720333*
Access: (road) *A72*
Parking capacity: (cars) *40*
Hours: *Thur before Easter to 30 Sept – Mon to Sat – 11am to 5pm, Sun 1pm to 5pm; Oct – Tues – 11am to 4pm*
Admission (1992): *adults £1.50; children £0.75; OAP £1.00; student £1.00;*
No. visitors (1992): *15 000 (est.)*

Facilities
Interpretation: *leaflets; information boards; tour guides; guide books*
Schools: *lecture/talk*
Retailing: *postcards/inexpensive souvenirs; craftwork*
No. shops: *1*

Operations
Contacts: *Mr A J MacDonald (Custodian); Mrs H B MacDonald (Assistant Custodian)*
No. employees: (high season) *1 full time; 1 part time* (low season) *2 part time*

Marketing
Annual event(s): *Peebles art festival*
Sponsor(s): *Peebles art festival*
Affiliations: *HHA*
Other: *market research*
UK promotion: *local newspapers; regional tourist board; other attractions; leaflets/information packs; Scottish Borders Tourist Board*
USA promotion: *travel agents' brochures; British Tourist Authority; Great British Heritage Pass*

NELSON MUSEUM AND LOCAL HISTORY CENTRE, THE
(local authority run)
museum; gallery

Established: *1924*
Address: *Priory St, Monmouth, Gwent, NP5 3XA*
Telephone: *(0600) 713519*
Access: (road) *A40*
Season: *all year*
Hours: *Mon to Sat – 10am to 1pm and 2pm to 5pm; Sun – 2pm to 5pm*
Admission (1992): *adults £1.00; OAP £0.50; student £0.50*
No. visitors (1992): *25 000 (est.)*

Facilities
Interpretation: *museum display*
Schools: *maximum no. 40; educational literature*
Disabled: *easy access*
Retailing: *postcards/inexpensive souvenirs; books*
No. shops: *1*

Operations
Contacts: *A Helme (Curator)*
No. employees: (high season) *2 full time; 2 part time* (low season) *2 full time; 2 part time*
Training: *F/T operations staff, F/T management and P/T operations staff are trained in-house and on specific courses and day-to-day on job using videos and handbooks*

Marketing
Other: *market research*
UK promotion: *local newspapers; regional tourist board; other attractions; leaflets/information packs; local consortium*

NESS GARDENS
(local authority run)
garden

Address: *Ness, Neston, Ches, L64 4AY*
Telephone: *(051) 336 8733.* Fax: *(051) 353 1004*
Access: (road) *M56/M53*
Parking capacity: (cars) *1000* (coaches) *10*
Season: *all year*
Hours: *Nov to Feb – 9.30am to 4pm daily; Mar to Oct – 9.30am to dusk daily*
Admission (1992): *adults £3.00; children £2.00; OAP £2.00; student £2.00*
No. visitors (1992): *130 000*

Facilities
Interpretation: *leaflets; information boards; maps; tour guides; guide books*
Children: *adventure playground*
Schools: *maximum no. 60; educational literature; educational tour*
Disabled: *easy access; disabled toilets; Braille/ sound posts; guide book*
Catering: *1 picnic area*
Retailing: *postcards/inexpensive souvenirs; craftwork; books; toys, plants*
No. shops: *2*

Operations
Contacts: *Dr E J Sharples (Business Administrator); Prof R Marrs (Director)*
No. employees: (high season) *30 full time; 90 part time* (low season) *30 full time; 60 part time*
Training: *F/T operations staff, F/T management, P/T operations staff, P/T management and casual operations staff are trained in-house and externally and on specific courses*
Languages spoken: *German*

Marketing
Affiliation: *Royal Horticultural Society*
Other: *market research*
UK promotion: *national newspapers; local newspapers; regional tourist board; other attractions; leaflets/information packs; ETB/BTA*

Environmental monitoring: *recycling; energy consumption*

NEW FOREST BUTTERFLY FARM
(limited company)
zoo/wildlife attraction; butterfly farm

Established: *1981*
Address: *Longdown, Ashurst, Nr Southampton*
Telephone: *(0703) 292166.* Fax: *(0703) 293376*
Access: (road) *M271 A35*
Parking capacity: (cars) *150* (coaches) *30*
Hours: *1 Apr to 31 Oct – 10am to 5pm daily*
Admission (1992): *adults £3.50; children £2.50; OAP £3.20*

Facilities
Interpretation: *leaflets; information boards; tour guides; guide books*
Children: *adventure playground; play area; nappy changing*
Schools: *maximum no. 100; educational literature; lecture/talk*
Disabled: *easy access; disabled toilets*
Catering: *1 picnic area*
Retailing: *postcards/inexpensive souvenirs; confectionery and ice cream; craftwork; books*
No. shops: *2*

Operations
Contact: *Ms A Todhunter (Marketing Manager)*
No. employees: (high season) *6 full time; 15 part time* (low season) *6 full time; 3 part time*
Training: *F/T operations staff and F/T management are trained externally and on specific courses*

Marketing
Press office; market research
UK promotion: *local newspapers; regional tourist board; other attractions; leaflets/information packs*

NEW FOREST MUSEUM AND VISITOR CENTRE
(limited company and trust)
heritage centre; museum

Established: *1988*
Address: *High St, Lyndhurst, Hants*
Telephone: *(0703) 283914.* Fax: *(0703) 284236*
Access: (road) *M27* (rail) *Brockenhurst*
Parking capacity: (cars) *700* (coaches) *9*
Season: *all year*
Hours: *summer – 10am to 6pm daily; winter – 10am to 5pm daily*

Admission (1992): *adults £2.50; children £1.50; OAP £2.00*
No. visitors (1992): *70 000*

Facilities
Interpretation: *audio tapes; information boards; slides; maps; guide books; life sized models, audio/visual show*
Languages: *French; German*
Schools: *maximum no. 50; educational literature; lecture/talk*
Disabled: *easy access; disabled toilets*
Retailing: *postcards/inexpensive souvenirs; confectionery and ice cream; craftwork; books*
No. shops: *1*

Operations
Contacts: *Ms J Edom (Centre Manager); Ms D Marriott (Shop Supervisor)*
No. employees: (high season) *5 full time; 3 part time* (low season) *5 full time; 8 part time*
Training: *F/T operations staff, P/T operations staff and casual operations staff are trained in-house and on specific courses and day-to-day on job*
Languages spoken: *French*

Marketing
Other: *market research*
UK promotion: *television; local newspapers; regional tourist board; other attractions; leaflets/information packs*

NEW LANARK VILLAGE
(trust)
monument; heritage centre; park/reserve; museum

Established: *1785*
Address: *New Lanark, Lanarkshire ML11 9DB*
Telephone: *(0555) 661345.* Fax: *(0555) 665738*
Access: (road) *M6/M74/A73* (rail) *Lanark*
Parking capacity: (cars) *400* (coaches) *12*
Season: *all year*
Hours: *11am to 5pm*
Admission (1992): *adults £2.45; children £1.60; OAP £1.60; student £1.60*
No. visitors (1992): *300 000*

Facilities
Interpretation: *videos; leaflets; audio tapes; information boards; slides; maps; tour guides; guide books; Annie McCleod experience*
Languages: *Japanese; French; German; Italian; Spanish*
Children: *play area; nappy changing*
Schools: *maximum no. 200; educational literature; school study room*
Disabled: *easy access; disabled toilets*
Catering: *1 picnic area*
Retailing: *postcards/inexpensive souvenirs; confectionery and ice cream; craftwork; books; clothes; reproductions of famous artefacts*
No. shops: *3*

Operations
Contacts: *Mr J Arnold (Managing Director); Mrs A Hamilton (Personnel Officer); Mrs G Strathie (Visitor Centre Supervisor); Mrs A Bell (Development Officer)*
No. employees: (high season) *30 full time; 20 part time* (low season) *30 full time; 10 part time*
Training: *F/T operations staff, F/T management, P/T operations staff and P/T management are trained in-house and externally and on specific courses and day-to-day on job*

Marketing
Annual event(s): *various*
Sponsor(s): *CWS Ltd*
Affiliations: *Association of Independent Museums and Heritage Sites*
Other: *market research*
UK promotion: *national newspapers; radio; local newspapers; regional tourist board; other attractions; leaflets/information packs; Scottish Tourist Board*

Environmental monitoring: *recycling; waste; energy consumption*

NEW WORLD TAPESTRY CENTRES
(personally run)
tapestry production centres

Established: *1976*
Address: *Contact Mr T Mor for Devon Sites, 125 Thornton Road, Girton, Cambridge, CB3 0NE*
Telephone: *(0223) 277794.* Fax: *(0223) 277794*
Hours: *Sites at Bideford, Topsham, Plymouth, Tiverton, Totnes and Lyme Regis. Contact as above for opening times*
Admission (1992): *£1.00 to make a stitch*

Facilities
Interpretation: *watch work in progress and make a stitch*
Schools: *maximum no. 35; briefing prior to visit*
Catering: *1 waiter/waitress served*
Retailing: *postcards/inexpensive souvenirs*
No. shops: *1*

Operations
Contact: *Mr T Mor (designer and owner)*
Languages spoken: *French; German; Italian; Spanish*

Marketing
UK promotion: *attend exhibitions*
USA/lecture tours promotion: *lecture tours*

NEWARK AIR MUSEUM
(limited company)
heritage centre; museum; aviation museum

Established: *1973*
Address: *The Airfield, Winthorpe, Newark, Notts, NG24 2NY*
Telephone: *(0636) 707170*
Access: (road) *A1/A17/A46* (rail) *Newark*
Parking capacity: (cars) *100* (coaches) *20*
Season: *all year*
Hours: *Apr to Oct – weekdays – 10am to 5pm, weekends – 10am to 6pm; Nov to Mar – 10am to 4pm daily except 24–26 Dec*
Admission (1992): *adults £2.50; children £1.50; OAP £1.50; student £1.50; group rates on application*
No. visitors (1992): *32 000 (est.)*

Facilities
Interpretation: *leaflets; information boards; slides; maps; tour guides; guide books*
Schools: *maximum no. 100; educational literature; lecture/talk; by arrangement*
Disabled: *easy access; disabled toilets*
Catering: *2 picnic areas*
Retailing: *postcards/inexpensive souvenirs; confectionery and ice cream; books; aviation kits and videos*
No. shops: *1*

Operations
Contacts: *Ms R Blackmore (Shop Manager); Mr H Heeley (Publicity Director)*
No. employees: (high season) *4 full time; 2 part time* (low season) *4 full time; 2 part time*

Marketing
Annual event(s): *gala days*
Affiliation: *British Aviation Preservation Council*
Other: *press office; market research*
UK promotion: *local newspapers; regional tourist board; other attractions; leaflets/information packs*
Europe promotion: *leaflets/brochures; local tourist board*

NEWARK MUSEUM
(local authority run)
museum

Established: *1912*
Address: *Appleton Gate, Newark, Notts*
Telephone: *(0636) 702358*
Access: (road) *A46/A1* (rail) *Newark Northgate*
Season: *all year*

Hours: *Mon to Sat – 10am to 1pm and 2pm to 5pm, closed Thurs; Apr to Sept – Sun – 2pm to 5pm*
Admission (1992): *free*
No. visitors (1992): *12 000 (est.)*

Facilities
Interpretation: *information boards; displays*
Schools: *maximum no. 30; lecture/talk; handling objects*
Retailing: *postcards/inexpensive souvenirs; books; reproductions of famous artefacts*
No. shops: *1*

Operations
Contact: *J Milford (Museums and Heritage Manager)*
No. employees: (high season) *3 full time; 2 part time* (low season) *3 full time; 2 part time*
Training: *F/T operations staff, F/T management and P/T operations staff are trained in-house and externally and on specific courses and day-to-day on job*
Languages spoken: *French*

Marketing
Press office
UK promotion: *local newspapers; regional tourist board; leaflets/information packs*

Environmental monitoring: *recycling; transport*

NEWHAM GRANGE LEISURE FARM
(local authority run)
museum; leisure farm

Established: *1973*
Address: *Newham Way, Newham, Middlesbrough, Cleveland*
Telephone: *(0642) 300261.* Fax: *(0642) 300276*
Access: (road) *A19/A174/B1365*
Parking capacity: (cars) *40* (coaches) *4*
Season: *all year*
Hours: *Mar to Sept – Tues to Sun – 9am to 5pm; Sept to Mar – Sun – 9am to 5pm or dusk*
Admission (1992): *adults £1.10; children £0.60; OAP £0.60; student £1.10; special rates for group bookings*
No. visitors (1992): *35 000 (est.)*

Facilities
Interpretation: *leaflets; information boards; maps; guide books; personnel; farm guide on request*
Children: *adventure playground; play area; nappy changing*
Schools: *maximum no. 200; educational literature; lecture/talk; farm guide on request*
Disabled: *easy access; disabled toilets*
Catering: *1 picnic area*
Retailing: *postcards/inexpensive souvenirs; confectionery and ice cream; books*
No. shops: *2*

Operations
Contacts: *J Moody (Landscape Manager); Mr D David (Marketing Officer)*
No. employees: (high season) *2 full time; 4 part time* (low season) *2 full time; 1 part time*
Training: *F/T operations staff, F/T management and P/T operations staff are trained in-house and on specific courses and day-to-day on job using videos*
Languages spoken: *French*

Marketing
Annual event: *family fun day*
Affiliation: *NFU*
Other: *press office; market research*
UK promotion: *local newspapers; regional tourist board; other attractions; leaflets/information packs; ETB/BTA*

NEWHAVEN FORT
(local authority run)
monument; museum

Established: *1988*
Address: *Fort Rd, Newhaven, E Sussex*
Telephone: *(0273) 517622*

Access: (road) *A259* (rail) *Newhaven Town*
Parking capacity: (cars) *300* (coaches) *10*
Hours: *Easter to Oct – Wed to Sun – 10.30am to 6pm (and daily during July and Aug)*
Admission (1992): *adults £2.50; children £1.50; OAP £1.75; student £1.75*
No. visitors (1992): *26 500*

Facilities
Interpretation: *videos; leaflets; information boards; guide books*
Languages: *French*
Children: *adventure playground*
Schools: *maximum no. 50; educational literature; educational tour; lecture/talk*
Catering: *1 picnic area*
Franchisees: *Easter to Oct – Wed to Sun – 10.30am to 6pm*
Retailing: *postcards/inexpensive souvenirs; confectionery and ice cream; books*
No. shops: *1*

Operations
Contact: *I Everett (Fort Manager)*
No. employees: (high season) *2 full time; 1 part time* (low season) *2 full time; 1 part time*
Training: *F/T operations staff and F/T management are trained in-house and on specific courses*

Marketing
Annual event(s): *battles, car rallies, etc.*
Other: *market research*
UK promotion: *local newspapers; regional tourist board; other attractions; leaflets/information packs*

Environmental monitoring: *hazardous materials; chemical usage*

NEWLYN ART GALLERY
(educational charity)
gallery

Established: *1895*
Address: *Newlyn, Penzance, Cornwall, TR18 5PZ*
Telephone: *(0736) 63715*
Access: (rail) *Penzance*
Season: *all year*
Hours: *Mon to Sat – 10am to 5pm (July and Aug – to 6pm)*
Admission (1992): *free*
No. visitors (1992): *28 000 (est.)*

Facilities
Interpretation: *leaflets; information boards; guide books; newsletter*
Schools: *maximum no. 40; educational literature; lecture/talk; with the artist by arrangement*
Disabled: *helpers*
Retailing: *postcards/inexpensive souvenirs; craftwork; books; reproductions of famous artefacts; original artwork ceramics; jewellery*
No. shops: *1*

Operations
Contact: *Ms J Bennette (Gallery Manager)*
No. employees: (high season) *2 full time; 4 part time* (low season) *2 full time; 4 part time*
Training: *F/T operations staff and P/T operations staff are trained in-house and day-to-day on job using videos*

Marketing
Market research
UK promotion: *television; national newspapers; radio; local newspapers; regional tourist board; other attractions; leaflets/information packs; Penwith Guide; ETB/BTA; Cornwall Tourist Board, art magazines*

NEWPORT MUSEUM AND ART GALLERY
(local authority run)
museum; gallery

Established: *1967*
Address: *John Frost Square, Newport, Gwent, NP9 1HZ*
Telephone: *(0633) 840064.* Fax: *(0633) 222615*

Access: (road) *M4/A48/A449* (rail) *Newport*
Season: *all year*
Hours: *Mon to Thur – 9.30am to 5pm, Fri – 9.30am to 4.30pm, Sat – 9.30am to 4pm. Closed on BH and local government holidays*
No. visitors (1992): *115 663*

Facilities
Interpretation: *videos; leaflets; audio tapes; information boards; slides; maps; tour guides; guide books*
Languages: *Welsh*
Schools: *educational literature; lecture/talk; school workshops*
Disabled: *other audio facilities; lifts to most floors*
Retailing: *postcards/inexpensive souvenirs; craftwork; books; clothes; reproductions of famous artefacts; Welsh souvenirs*
No. shops: *1*

Operations
Contact: *R Trelt (Curator)*
No. employees: (high season) *32 full time; 3 part time* (low season) *31 full time; 3 part time*
Training: *F/T operations staff, F/T management, P/T operations staff, P/T management, casual operations staff and casual management are trained in-house and externally and on specific courses and day-to-day on job*
Languages spoken: *French; German*

Marketing
Affiliation: *Museums Association*
Other: *market research*
UK promotion: *local newspapers; regional tourist board; other attractions; leaflets/information packs; Welsh Tourist Board*

NEWSTEAD ABBEY
(local authority run)
historic house; park/reserve; garden; museum

Established: *1931*
Address: *Linby, Notts, NG15 8GE*
Telephone: *(0623) 793557*
Access: (road) *M1/A60* (rail) *Newstead*
Parking capacity: (cars) *500* (coaches) *100*
Hours: *1 Apr to 1st Sun in Oct daily. Gardens – 10am to dusk all year. House – 12 noon to 6pm*
Admission (1992): *adults £3.50; children £1.90; OAP £1.90; student £1.90; groups £2.50; concessions £1.50*
No. visitors (1992): *100 000 (est.)*

Facilities
Interpretation: *videos; leaflets; audio tapes; information boards; tour guides; guide books*
Languages: *French; German*
Children: *adventure playground*
Schools: *maximum no. 100; educational literature; lecture/talk; education officer*
Disabled: *disabled toilets; other audio facilities; special signs*
Catering: *1 snack bar/food stall*
Retailing: *postcards/inexpensive souvenirs; craftwork; books; clothes; reproductions of famous artefacts; prints*
No. shops: *1*

Operations
Contacts: *Mr B Ayres (Custodian/Team Leader); Mr G Clay (Head Guide); Mr N Milner (Teamleader Trading); Mr R Sandell (Marketing Officer)*
No. employees: (high season) *4 full time; 13 part time* (low season) *4 full time*
Training: *F/T operations staff, F/T management, P/T operations staff and casual operations staff are trained in-house and day-to-day on job using videos and handbooks*

Marketing
Annual event(s): *various*
Sponsor: *VW on occasions*
Affiliations: *MA, HHA*
Other: *press office; market research*
UK promotion: *radio; local newspapers; regional tourist board; other attractions; leaflets/information packs; ETB/BTA*
USA promotion: *British Tourist Authority*

Environmental monitoring: *energy consumption; hazardous materials; chemical usage; emissions*

NIDDERDALE MUSEUM
(trust)
museum

Established: *1975*
Address: *Council Offices, King St, Pateley Bridge, Harrogate, N Yorks, HG3 5AY*
Telephone: *(0423) 711225*
Access: (road) *B6165/B6265*
Parking capacity: (cars) *12* (coaches) *1*
Season: *all year*
Hours: *Easter to end Sept – 2pm to 5pm daily; winter – Sun – 2pm to 5pm. Groups throughout the year at any time by arrangement*
Admission (1992): *adults £0.80; children £0.40; OAP £0.40*
No. visitors (1992): *10 000 (est.)*

Facilities
Interpretation: *guide books*
Schools: *maximum no. 60; quiz sheets*
Retailing: *postcards/inexpensive souvenirs; books*
No. shops: *1*

Operations
Contacts: *Mrs E Burgess (Hon Secretary); Mrs M Hanley (Buyer); Mrs M Blacker (Publicity Officer)*
Languages spoken: *French; German*

Marketing
Affiliations: *Yorks and Humbs Museums Service, AIM*
UK promotion: *leaflets/information packs*

NORFOLK RURAL LIFE MUSEUM AND UNION FARM
(local authority run)
museum; working farm

Established: *1976*
Address: *Gressenhall, Dereham, Norfolk, NR20 4DR*
Telephone: *(0362) 860563.* Fax: *(0362) 860951*
Access: (road) *A47/B1110*
Parking capacity: (cars) *200* (coaches) *10*
Hours: *summer – 10am to 5pm*
Admission (1992): *adults £3.00; children £0.60; OAP £1.80; student £1.80; groups and other concessions £1.80*
No. visitors (1992): *35 000 (est.)*

Facilities
Interpretation: *leaflets; information boards; guide books; signs*
Children: *nappy changing*
Schools: *maximum no. 300; educational literature; resources and handling*
Disabled: *easy access; disabled toilets; other audio facilities; free for helpers*
Catering: *1 picnic area*
Retailing: *postcards/inexpensive souvenirs; confectionery and ice cream; books; local produce*
No. shops: *1*

Operations
Contacts: *Bridget Yates (Curator); Hilary Slater (Sales Officer); Doug Chinnem (Assistant Director, Business)*
No. employees: (high season) *10 full time; 11 part time* (low season) *10 full time; 1 part time*
Training: *F/T operations staff, F/T management, P/T operations staff and P/T management are trained in-house and externally and on specific courses and day-to-day on job*

Marketing
UK promotion: *local newspapers; regional tourist board; other attractions; leaflets/information packs*

NORMANBY HALL COUNTRY PARK
(local authority run)
historic house; park/reserve; garden; museum;
farming museum

Established: *1964*
Address: *Normanby, Scunthorpe, Humberside,
DN15 9HU*
Telephone: *(0724) 720588*
Access: (road) *B1430* (rail) *Scunthorpe*
Parking capacity: (cars) *1000* (coaches) *10*
Season: *all year*
Hours: *park – 8am to 8pm or dusk daily. House
and museum – 1 Apr to 30 Sept – 1pm to 5pm
daily*
Admission (1992): *free*
No. visitors (1992): *130 000*

Facilities
Interpretation: *leaflets; information boards; maps;
guide books; personnel*
Children: *play area; nappy changing*
Schools: *maximum no. 30; educational literature;
lecture/talk; must pre-book*
Disabled: *disabled toilets; portable ramps for hall*
Catering: *1 picnic area*
Franchisees: *Park – 8am to 8pm or dusk daily.
House and museum – 1 Apr to 30 Sept – 1pm
to 5pm daily*
Retailing: *postcards/inexpensive souvenirs;
craftwork; books*
No. shops: *3*

Operations
Contacts: *Mr N Jacques (Park Manager);
Ms E Webster (Clerk/Typist)*
No. employees: (high season) *8 full time; 8 part
time* (low season) *8 full time; 2 part time*
Training: *F/T operations staff, F/T management,
P/T operations staff and casual operations staff
are trained in-house and externally and on
specific courses and day-to-day on job using
videos*
Languages spoken: *French; German*

Marketing
Annual event(s): *various*
Sponsor(s): *Kimberly Clark – horse trials*
Affiliations: *MA*
Other: *PR Company: Newman Walker
Associates, 16 East Acridge, Barton,
Humberside; market research*
UK promotion: *local newspapers; regional tourist
board; other attractions; leaflets/information
packs*

NORTH AYRSHIRE MUSEUM
(local authority run)
museum; gallery

Established: *1959*
Address: *Manse St, Kirkgate, Saltcoats, KA21
5AA*
Telephone: *(0294) 64174*
Access: (road) *A78* (rail) *Glasgow–Largs*
Season: *all year*
Hours: *1 June to 30 Sept – Mon, Tues and Thur
to Sat – 10am to 1pm and 2pm to 5pm; 1 Oct
to 31 May – Tues and Thur to Sat – 10am to
1pm and 2pm to 5pm*
Admission (1992): *free*
No. visitors (1992): *11 000 (est.)*

Facilities
Interpretation: *leaflets; information boards; maps;
displays and exhibitions*
Schools: *maximum no. 40; educational literature;
audio/visual presentation; lecture/talk*
Disabled: *easy access; disabled toilets; helpers*
Retailing: *postcards/inexpensive souvenirs; books*
No. shops: *1*

Operations
Contacts: *Ms D Keasal (District Curator); Ms L
McAuley (District Council Marketing Officer)*
No. employees: (high season) *2 full time; 8 part
time* (low season) *2 full time; 3 part time*
Training: *F/T operations staff, F/T management,
P/T operations staff and casual operations staff
are trained in-house and externally and on
specific courses and day-to-day on job*

Marketing
Annual event(s): *camera club exhibition and
youth workshops*
Sponsor(s): *ASDA, Harry Fairburn Motors Ltd*
Affiliations: *Friends of the Museum Association*
Other: *press office; market research*
UK promotion: *local newspapers; regional tourist
board; other attractions; leaflets/information
packs; ETB/BTA; STB and magazines*

Environmental monitoring: *recycling*

NORTH CARR LIGHTSHIP ANSTRUTHER HARBOUR
(limited company managing agent)
historic ship

Established: *1992*
Address: *51 High St, Pittenweem, Fife*
Telephone: *(0333) 310589.* Fax: *(0333) 310589*
Access: (road) *M90/A92/A915/A917* (rail)
Kirkcaldy
Season: *all year*
Hours: *Easter to Oct – 11am to 5pm daily; Nov
to Easter – 1pm to 4.30pm weekends. Open at
other times by appointment*
Admission (1992): *adults £1.90; children £0.80;
OAP £0.80; student £0.80*
No. visitors (1992): *10 000 (est.)*

Facilities
Interpretation: *leaflets; information boards; tour
guides; guide books*
Schools: *maximum no. 50; educational literature;
lecture/talk*
Disabled: *easy access*
Retailing: *postcards/inexpensive souvenirs; clothes*
No. shops: *1*

Operations
Contact: *Mr R Macalindin (Ships Manager)*
No. employees: (high season) *2 full time; 1 part
time* (low season) *1 full time; 1 part time*
Training: *F/T operations staff are trained in-house
and day-to-day on job using videos and
handbooks*
Languages spoken: *French; Norwegian*

Marketing
Market research
UK promotion: *radio; local newspapers; regional
tourist board; other attractions; leaflets/
information packs; ETB/BTA*

Environmental monitoring: *recycling; water
quality; energy consumption; hazardous
materials; chemical usage*

NORTH CORNWALL MUSEUM AND GALLERY
(private)
museum; gallery

Established: *1973*
Address: *The Clease, Camelford, Cornwall,
PL32 9PL*
Telephone: *(0840) 212954*
Access: (road) *A39* (rail) *Bodmin Parkway*
Hours: *Apr to Sept – Mon to Sat – 10am to 5pm*
Admission (1992): *adults £1.00; children £0.50;
OAP £0.75; student £0.75; group rates*
No. visitors (1992): *3000 (est.)*

Facilities
Interpretation: *labels and books*
Schools: *maximum no. 40; no special support*
Disabled: *access to ground floor, helpers for blind
by arrangement*
Retailing: *postcards/inexpensive souvenirs;
books*

Operations
Contacts: *S A Holden (Curator, owner and TIC
Manager)*

Marketing
Affiliation: *AIM*
UK promotion: *leaflets/information packs*

NORTH DEVON MARITIME MUSEUM
(trust)
museum

Established: *1976*
Address: *Odun House, Odun Rd, Appledore,
Bideford, Devon, EX39 1PT*
Access: (road) *A39*
Hours: *Easter to Oct – 2pm to 5.30pm (May to
Sept – Mon to Fri – 11am to 1pm)*
Admission (1992): *adults £1.00; children £0.30;
OAP £0.70; student £0.30*
No. visitors (1992): *6160*

Facilities
Interpretation: *videos; information boards; guide
books*
Schools: *audio/visual presentation; lecture if
asked for*
Retailing: *postcards/inexpensive souvenirs; books*
No. shops: *1*

Operations
Contacts: *P Wiggett (Secretary); B F Virgo (Shop
Organiser)*

Marketing
UK promotion: *leaflets/information packs*

Environmental monitoring: *recycling*

NORTH DOWN HERITAGE CENTRE
(local authority run)
museum

Established: *1984*
Address: *Town Hall, Castle Park Avenue,
Bangor, Co. Down, BT2 4BT*
Telephone: *(0247) 270371.* Fax: *(0247) 271370*
Parking capacity: (cars) *30* (coaches) *2*
Season: *all year*
Hours: *Sept to June – Mon to Sat – 10.30am to
4.30pm, Sun – 2pm to 4.30pm (July and Aug –
Mon to Sat – 10.30am to 5.30pm, Sun – 2pm to
5.30pm)*
Admission (1992): *free*
No. visitors (1992): *50 000*

Facilities
Interpretation: *videos; leaflets; information
boards; slides*
Languages: *French; German*
Schools: *maximum no. 50; educational literature;
lecture/talk*
Disabled: *easy access; disabled toilets; Braille/
sound posts; special lifts*
Catering: *1 self-service cafeteria*
Franchisees: *Sept to June – Mon to Sat – 10.30am
to 4.30pm, Sun – 2pm to 4.30pm*
Retailing: *postcards/inexpensive souvenirs;
craftwork; books*
No. shops: *1*

Operations
Contacts: *I A Wilson (Manager); W James
(Personnel Officer, Borough Council);
S Bossence (Clerk)*
No. employees: (high season) *5 full time; 1 part
time* (low season) *4 full time; 1 part time*

Marketing
Affiliation: *Irish Museums Association*
UK promotion: *national newspapers; local
newspapers; regional tourist board; leaflets/
information packs*

NORTH EAST AIRCRAFT MUSEUM
(trust)
museum

Established: *1976*
Address: *Old Washington Rd, Sunderland, Tyne
and Wear, SR5 3HZ*
Telephone: *(091) 519 0662*
Access: (road) *A19*
Parking capacity: (cars) *50*
Season: *all year*

Hours: *10am to 5pm daily*
Admission (1992): *adults £1.25; children £0.75; OAP £0.75*
No. visitors (1992): *24 000*

Facilities
Interpretation: *information boards; tour guides*
Schools: *maximum no. 30; educational literature*
Catering: *1 snack bar/food stall*
Retailing: *postcards/inexpensive souvenirs; confectionery and ice cream; books*
No. shops: *1*

Operations
Contacts: *Mr I Bowes (Museum Manager); Mr P Hunt (Treasurer); Mr D Charles (Publicity Manager)*
No. employees: (high season) *1 full time* (low season) *1 full time*

Marketing
Annual event(s): *open day*
Affiliations: *AIM, Transport Trust, British Aviation Preservation Council*
Other: *market research*
UK promotion: *local newspapers; leaflets/ information packs*

NORTH NORFOLK RAILWAY
(plc)
preserved railway

Established: *1968*
Address: *The Station, Sheringham, Norfolk*
Telephone: *(0263) 822045*
Access: (road) *A149* (rail) *Sheringham*
Parking capacity: (cars) *200* (coaches) *8*
Hours: *summer – 10am to 6pm*
Admission (1992): *various*
No. visitors (1992): *125 000 (est.)*

Facilities
Interpretation: *tour guides; guide books*
Schools: *educational literature*
Disabled: *easy access; adapted railway carriage*
Catering: *1 picnic area*
Retailing: *postcards/inexpensive souvenirs; books*
No. shops: *3*

Operations
Contacts: *D Madden (General Manager); R Millett (Marketing Manager)*
No. employees: (low season) *8 full time*
Training: *F/T operations staff are trained in-house and day-to-day on job*

Marketing
Annual event(s): *Easter egg specials, Thomas the Tank specials*
Other: *market research*
UK promotion: *radio; local newspapers; leaflets/ information packs; ETB/BTA*

NORTH WOOLWICH OLD STATION MUSEUM
(local authority run)
museum; railway station

Established: *1984*
Address: *Pier Rd, London, E16 2JJ*
Telephone: *(071) 474 7244*
Season: *all year*
Hours: *Mon, Tues, Wed and Sat – 10am to 5pm; Sun and BH – 2pm to 5pm*
Admission (1992): *free*
No. visitors (1992): *27 080*

Facilities
Interpretation: *guide books; original railway material*
Children: *play area; nappy changing*
Schools: *maximum no. 30; by arrangement*
Disabled: *easy access; disabled toilets*
Retailing: *postcards/inexpensive souvenirs; books; reproductions of famous artefacts*
No. shops: *1*

Operations
No. employees: (high season) *7 full time* (low season) *7 full time*
Training: *N/A*

Marketing
Annual event(s): *steam days, model railway days, films and talks*
Other: *press office; market research*
UK promotion: *other attractions; leaflets/ information packs; railway journals*

Environmental monitoring: *waste; hazardous materials; emissions*

NORTHBOURNE COURT GARDENS
(partnership)
historic house; garden; mediaeval barn and stables

Established: *1950*
Address: *Northbourne, Deal, Kent, CT14 0LW*
Telephone: *(0304) 611281.* Fax: *(0304) 614512*
Access: (road) *M2/A258/A256* (rail) *Canterbury*
Parking capacity: (cars) *300* (coaches) *50*
Hours: *various charity garden openings. All other access by appointment only*
Admission (1992): *adults £2.50; children £1.50; OAP £1.50; student £1.50*
No. visitors (1992): *3000 (est.)*

Facilities
Interpretation: *leaflets; tour guides; personnel*
Languages: *French*
Children: *play area*
Schools: *maximum no. 40; educational tour*

Operations
Contact: *Hon C James (owner/General Manager)*
No. employees: (high season) *3 full time; 1 part time* (low season) *3 full time*
Training: *F/T operations staff and casual operations staff are trained in-house and day-to-day on job*

Marketing
Affiliations: *HHA, National Gardens Scheme, ETB*
Other: *market research*
UK promotion: *local newspapers; regional tourist board; leaflets/information packs; ETB/BTA*

Environmental monitoring: *recycling; hazardous materials*

NORTHERN IRELAND AQUARIUM, THE
(local authority run)
public aquarium

Established: *1988*
Address: *The Ropewalk, Castle St, Portaferry, Co. Down*
Telephone: *(02477) 28062.* Fax: *(02477) 28936*
Access: (road) *A20*
Parking capacity: (cars) *80*
Season: *all year*
Hours: *winter – Tues to Sat – 10.30am to 5pm, Sun – 1pm to 5pm; summer – Mon to Sat – 10am to 6pm, Sun – 1pm to 6pm*
Admission (1992): *adults £1.50; children £0.85; OAP £0.85; group discounts*
No. visitors (1992): *71 452*

Facilities
Interpretation: *leaflets; information boards; tour guides*
Children: *adventure playground; play area*
Schools: *maximum no. 50; educational literature; lecture/talk*
Disabled: *easy access; disabled toilets; helpers*
Catering: *2 picnic areas*
Retailing: *postcards/inexpensive souvenirs; marine theme souvenirs*
No. shops: *2*

Operations
Contacts: *Billy Ried (Manager) Alistair Davison (Assistant Manager)*
No. employees: (high season) *5 full time; 18 part time* (low season) *5 full time; 10 part time*

Training: *F/T operations staff, P/T operations staff and casual operations staff are trained in-house and on specific courses and day-to-day on job*

Marketing
Annual event(s): *various – usually arts based*
Other: *market research*
UK promotion: *radio; local newspapers; regional tourist board; other attractions; leaflets/ information packs*

Environmental monitoring: *hazardous materials; chemical usage*

NORTON CONYERS
(privately owned)
historic house; garden

Established: *1976*
Address: *Nr Ripon, N Yorks, HG4 5EH*
Telephone: *(0765) 640 333*
Access: (road) *A1/A61*
Parking capacity: (cars) *100* (coaches) *3*
Hours: *House – BH Sun and daily from 9 May to 12 Sept – 2pm to 5.30pm; 26–31 July – 2pm to 5.30pm daily. Garden – all year – Mon to Fri – 9am to 5pm (and 6 Mar to 5 Sept – Sat and Sun – 2pm to 5.30pm)*
Admission (1992): *adults £2.30; children £1.00; OAP £1.50; student £1.50; ub40s and disabled £1.50*
No. visitors (1992): *2740*

Facilities
Interpretation: *leaflets; tour guides; refreshments by arrangement and BH*
Schools: *maximum no. 25; no special support*
Disabled: *disabled toilets; ground floor accessible*
Catering: *1 picnic area*
Retailing: *postcards/inexpensive souvenirs; maps and marmalade*
No. shops: *1*

Operations
Contact: *Miss M Beston (Administrator)*
No. employees: (high season) *15 part time*
Languages spoken: *French*

Marketing
Affiliations: *HHA, Yorks and Humbs Tourist Board*
Other: *market research*
UK promotion: *local newspapers; regional tourist board; other attractions; leaflets/information packs*
Europe promotion: *leaflets/brochures*

NORTON PRIORY MUSEUM AND GARDENS
(trust)
monument; garden; museum; sculpture park

Established: *1982*
Address: *Tudor Rd, Manor Park, Runcorn, Ches, WA7 1SX*
Telephone: *(0928) 569895*
Access: (road) *M56*
Parking capacity: (cars) *120* (coaches) *10*
Season: *all year*
Hours: *Apr to Oct – Mon to Fri – 12am to 5pm, weekends – 12am to 6pm; Nov to Mar – 12am to 4pm daily*
Admission (1992): *adults £2.40; children £1.20; OAP £1.20; student £1.20; ub40s £1.20*
No. visitors (1992): *28 767*

Facilities
Interpretation: *videos; leaflets; audio tapes; information boards; slides; maps; guide books; models*
Schools: *maximum no. 100; educational literature; audio/visual presentation; educational tour; lecture/talk*
Disabled: *easy access; disabled toilets; other audio facilities; special signs*
Catering: *1 picnic area*

Retailing: *postcards/inexpensive souvenirs;
confectionery and ice cream; craftwork; books;
pottery, plants from garden; greetings cards*
No. shops: *2*

Operations
Contact: *M Warhurst (Museum Director)*
No. employees: (high season) *11 full time; 9 part
time* (low season) *11 full time; 2 part time*
Training: *F/T operations staff, P/T operations
staff and casual operations staff are trained
in-house and externally and on specific courses
and day-to-day on job*

Marketing
Annual event(s): *sculpture workshops*
Sponsor(s): *various*
Affiliations: *AIM, NWTB, NW Museums Service,
NW Museums Federation, National Heritage,
Vale Royal Tourism*
Other: *market research*
UK promotion: *other attractions; leaflets/
information packs*

NORWICH CASTLE MUSEUM
(local authority run)
castle; museum; gallery

Established: *1894*
Address: *Norwich, Norfolk, NR1 3JU*
Telephone: *(0603) 223624.* Fax: *(0603) 765651*
Season: *all year*
Hours: *Mon to Sat – 10am to 5pm; Sun – 2pm to
5pm*
Admission (1992): *adults £1.60; children £0.60;
OAP £1.20; student £1.20*
No. visitors (1992): *250 000 (est.)*

Facilities
Interpretation: *videos; leaflets; information
boards; tour guides; guide books; signs*
Children: *nappy changing*
Schools: *handling sessions*
Disabled: *easy access; disabled toilets*
Catering: *1 self-service cafeteria*
Franchisees: *Mon to Sat – 10am to 5pm; Sun –
2pm to 5pm*
Retailing: *postcards/inexpensive souvenirs;
craftwork; books; reproductions of famous
artefacts; reproduction jewellery; various*
No. shops: *1*

Operations
Contacts: *D Chinnery (Assistant Director);
B McWilliams (Principal Assistant Director);
H Slater (Sales Manager)*
No. employees: (high season) *30 full time; 10 part
time* (low season) *30 full time; 10 part time*
Training: *F/T operations staff, F/T management
and P/T operations staff are trained in-house
and externally and on specific courses and
day-to-day on job using videos and handbooks
and Pro forma sheets*

Marketing
Annual event(s): *various, craft and painting
workshops*
Sponsor(s): *local companies*
Affiliations: *Museums Association*
Other: *market research*
UK promotion: *local newspapers; regional tourist
board; other attractions; leaflets/information
packs*

Environmental monitoring: *recycling; waste;
energy consumption; hazardous materials;
chemical usage*

NORWICH CATHEDRAL
(private company)
historic house; monument; heritage centre;
garden; museum; gallery; church

Established: *1096*
Address: *62 The Close, Norwich, NR1 4EH*
Telephone: *(0603) 626290.* Fax: *(0603) 620715*
Access: *(road) M11/A11/A47 (rail) Norwich*
Season: *all year*

Hours: *summer – 7.30am to 7pm, winter –
7.30am to 6pm*
Admission (1992): *free*
No. visitors (1992): *590 000*

Facilities
Interpretation: *leaflets; information boards; slides;
tour guides; guide books; signs*
Languages: *Japanese; French; German*
Children: *nappy changing*
Schools: *maximum no. 120; educational literature;
audio/visual presentation; schools room*
Disabled: *easy access; disabled toilets; Braille/
sound posts; helpers; other audio facilities;
leaflets; touch and hearing centre*
Catering: *1 picnic area*
Retailing: *postcards/inexpensive souvenirs;
craftwork; books; reproductions of famous
artefacts; videos, slides, music tapes, etc.; jams,
biscuits, jewellery, glass*
No. shops: *1*

Operations
Contacts: *The Dean; Rita Thompson (Shop
Manageress); Lucy Paton (visitors Officer)*
No. employees: (high season) *18 full time;
3 part time* (low season) *18 full time; 3 part
time*
Languages spoken: *French*

Marketing
Annual event(s): *concerts, exhibitions, dance
programmes*
Sponsor(s): *various*
Affiliations: *East Anglia TB, Pilgrims Association*
Other: *market research*
UK promotion: *national newspapers; radio; local
newspapers; regional tourist board; leaflets/
information packs; EATB; ETB/BTA; hotels,
libraries, etc.*

Environmental monitoring: *waste; energy
consumption; hazardous materials; chemical
usage*

NORWICH GALLERY
(local authority run)
gallery

Established: *1972*
Address: *Norfolk Institute of Art and Design,
St George St, Norwich, NR3 1BB*
Telephone: *(0603) 610561.* Fax: *(0603) 615728*
Access: *(road) M11/A11/A47 (rail) Norwich*
Parking capacity: (cars) *3*
Season: *all year*
Hours: *Mon to Fri – 10am to 6pm; Sat – 10am to
4pm*

Facilities
Interpretation: *leaflets; information boards; signs*
Schools: *maximum no. 50; educational literature*
Retailing: *gallery publications*
No. shops: *1*

Operations
Contact: *Lynda Checketts (Curator)*
No. employees: (high season) *1 full time; 2 part
time*
Training: *P/T operations staff, P/T management
and casual operations staff are trained in-house
and externally and on specific courses and
day-to-day on job*
Languages spoken: *French; German; Italian;
Spanish*

Marketing
Annual event(s): *East national open art exhibition,
workshops, lectures, masterclasses*
Affiliation: *Visual Arts Galleries Association*
Other: *market research*
UK promotion: *national newspapers; local
newspapers; regional tourist board; other
attractions; leaflets/information packs;
ETB/BTA; art press*

NOTHE FORT
(Weymouth Civic Society)
museum

Established: *1980*
Address: *Barrack Rd, Weymouth, Dorset,
DT4 8TY*
Telephone: *(0305) 787243*
Access: *(road) A354*
Parking capacity: (cars) *100*
Season: *all year*
Hours: *May to Sept – 10.30am to 5.30pm;
winter – Sun – 2pm to dusk*
Admission (1992): *adults £2.00; OAP £1.00;
student £1.00*
No. visitors (1992): *50 000 (est.)*

Facilities
Interpretation: *leaflets; information boards; tour
guides*
Children: *adventure playground*
Schools: *maximum no. 40; educational literature;
educational tour; lecture/talk*
Disabled: *easy access; disabled toilets*
Catering: *1 snack bar/food stall*
Retailing: *postcards/inexpensive souvenirs; books;
films and batteries*
No. shops: *1*

Operations
Contacts: *A Murray (Curator); E Webb
(Custodian); G Watts (Publicity Officer)*
No. employees: (high season) *3 full time;
30 part time* (low season) *3 full time; 5 part
time*

Marketing
UK promotion: *local newspapers; other
attractions; leaflets/information packs*

NUMBER ONE THE ROYAL CRESCENT
(trust)
historic house

Established: *1970*
Address: *1 Royal Crescent, Bath, BA1 2LR*
Telephone: *(0225) 428126*
Hours: *Mar to end Oct – Tues to Sun and BH –
11am to 5pm; Nov to 12 Dec – Tues to Sun –
11am to 4pm*
Admission (1992): *adults £3.00; children £2.50;
OAP £2.50; student £2.50; educational groups
of children £2.00, family ticket £7.00*
No. visitors (1992): *50 000 (est.)*

Facilities
Interpretation: *leaflets; tour guides; guide books*
Languages: *Japanese; Dutch; French; German;
Italian; Spanish; Danish; Chinese; Norwegian*
Schools: *maximum no. 50; no special support;
talk on request*
Retailing: *postcards/inexpensive souvenirs;
craftwork; books*
No. shops: *1*

Operations
Contact: *Mrs C Salt (Administrator)*
No. employees: (high season) *17 part time* (low
season) *17 part time*

Marketing
Affiliations: *Area Museums Council for the
SW, HHA, Association of Bath Leisure
Enterprises*
Other: *market research*
UK promotion: *local newspapers; other
attractions; leaflets/information packs*

NUNNINGTON HALL
(NT charity)
historic house; garden

Established: *1979*
Address: *Nunnington, Nr Helmsley, York,
YO6 5UY*
Telephone: *(04395) 283*

Hours: *Easter or Apr to Oct – Tues, Wed, Thur,
Sun and BH – 12 noon to 6pm, Sat – 2pm to
6pm*
Admission (1992): *adults £3.30; children £1.50;
OAP £3.30; student £3.30*
No. visitors (1992): *45 000 (est.)*

Facilities
Interpretation: *leaflets; guide books*
Children: *nappy changing*
Schools: *maximum no. 50; educational literature*
Disabled: *easy access; disabled toilets*
Catering: *1 self-service cafeteria*
Retailing: *postcards/inexpensive souvenirs;
craftwork; books; clothes; toiletries*
No. shops: *1*

Operations
Contact: *Mrs J Franklin (Administrator)*
No. employees: (high season) *3 full time; 16 part
time* (low season) *3 full time; 4 part time*
Training: *F/T operations staff and P/T operations
staff are trained in-house and externally and on
specific courses*
Languages spoken: *French; German; Italian;
Spanish; Danish*

Marketing
Annual event(s): *Christmas and spring concerts*
Other: *press office; market research*
UK promotion: *local newspapers; regional tourist
board; other attractions; leaflets/information
packs*

Environmental monitoring: *humidity*

NUNWELL HOUSE and GARDENS
(privately owned)
historic house; garden; museum

Established: *1984*
Address: *Nunwell House, Brading, Isle of Wight*
Telephone: *(0983) 407240*
Hours: *July, Aug and Sept – Sun to Thur – 10am
to 5pm*
Admission (1992): *adults £2.30; children £0.60;
OAP £1.80*

Facilities
Interpretation: *leaflets; information boards; maps;
tour guides; guide books*
Languages: *French; German*
Schools: *educational literature*
Catering: *1 picnic area*
Retailing: *postcards/inexpensive souvenirs*
No. shops: *none*

Marketing
Affiliations: *Defence of the Realm (Portsmouth),
Historic Houses Association*
UK promotion: *local newspapers; regional tourist
board; leaflets/information packs*

Environmental monitoring: *recycling; waste;
hazardous materials; chemical usage*

OAKWELL HALL COUNTRY PARK
(local authority run)
historic house; garden; country park

Established: *1928*
Address: *Nutter Lane, Birstall, Batley, W Yorks*
Telephone: *(0924) 474926. Fax: (0924) 420536*
Access: (road) *M62/A652*
Parking capacity: (cars) *150* (coaches) *5*
Season: *all year*
Hours: *Mar to Oct – Mon to Fri – 10am to 5pm,
Sat and Sun – 12 noon to 5pm; Nov to Feb – 12
noon to 5pm daily*
Admission (1992): *adults £0.70; children £0.35;
OAP £0.70; student £0.70; charge for hall, site
free, passport holders £0.35*
No. visitors (1992): *85 000 (est.)*

Facilities
Interpretation: *leaflets; information boards; maps;
guide books*
Languages: *German*
Children: *adventure playground; nappy changing*
Schools: *maximum no. 30; full education support*
Disabled: *disabled toilets; initiatives in progress*
Catering: *2 picnic areas*
Retailing: *postcards/inexpensive souvenirs;
confectionery and ice cream; craftwork; books;
reproductions of famous artefacts; seeds,
needlework kits and toys; stamps, jams, etc*
No. shops: *1*

Operations
No. employees: (high season) *14 full time; 8 part
time* (low season) *14 full time; 5 part time*
Training: *F/T operations staff, F/T management,
P/T operations staff and P/T management are
trained in-house and externally and on specific
courses and day-to-day on job*
Languages spoken: *French*

Marketing
Affiliations: *MA, YHTB*
Other: *market research*
UK promotion: *local newspapers; regional tourist
board; leaflets/information packs*

OBAN SEA LIFE CENTRE
(limited company)
zoo/wildlife attraction

Established: *1979*
Address: *Barcaldine, Connel, Oban, Argyll, PA37
1SE*
Telephone: *(063) 172 386. Fax: (063) 172 529*
Access: (road) *A828* (rail) *Oban*
Season: *all year*
Hours: *Feb to Nov – 10am to 6pm daily; Dec and
Jan – weekends*
Admission (1992): *adults £3.95; children £2.95;
OAP £3.25; student £1.95; disabled £3.35*

Facilities
Interpretation: *videos; leaflets; information
boards; maps; tour guides; guide books*
Languages: *French; German*
Children: *adventure playground; play area; nappy
changing*
Schools: *educational literature; audio/visual
presentation; lecture/talk; touch pools and
projects*
Disabled: *easy access; disabled toilets*
Catering: *1 picnic area*
Retailing: *postcards/inexpensive souvenirs;
craftwork; books; clothes; reproductions of
famous artefacts*
No. shops: *1*

Operations
Contacts: *Mr G Stenhouse (Manager); Ms P
Reeve (Shop Supervisor); Ms C Billen
(Marketing Officer)*
Training: *F/T operations staff, F/T management,
P/T operations staff and casual operations staff
are trained in-house and on specific courses and
day-to-day on job using videos and handbooks*

Marketing
Affiliation: *ASVA*
Other: *press office; market research*
UK promotion: *television; national newspapers;
radio; local newspapers; regional tourist board;
other attractions; leaflets/information packs;
ETB/BTA*

Environmental monitoring: *recycling; energy
consumption; hazardous materials*

OCEANARIUM
(limited company)
zoo/wildlife attraction; seawater aquarium

Established: *1988*
Address: *42 New St, St David's, Dyfed, SA62 6SS*
Telephone: *(0437) 720453*
Access: (road) *A487* (rail) *Fishguard/
Haverfordwest*
Parking capacity: (cars) *40* (coaches) *2*
Season: *all year*
Hours: *summer – 10am till late; winter – 10.30am
to 4pm*
Admission (1992): *adults £2.25; children £1.50;
OAP £2.25; student £2.25; family tickets with 2
children £7.00 and 3 children £7.50*
No. visitors (1992): *50 000 (est.)*

Facilities
Interpretation: *tour guides; guide books; visual
displays*
Schools: *maximum no. 45; educational literature;
audio/visual presentation*
Disabled: *easy access; access to ground floor only*
Catering: *1 picnic area*
Retailing: *postcards/inexpensive souvenirs; books;
shells*
No. shops: *1*

Operations
Contact: *Mr K Cross (Business Manager/Director)*
No. employees: (high season) *2 full time; 2 part
time* (low season) *2 full time*

Marketing
Affiliation: *corporate member – Dyfed Wildlife
Trust*
Other: *market research*
UK promotion: *local newspapers; other
attractions; leaflets/information packs; Coast to
Coast*

Environmental monitoring: *recycling; waste;
water quality; energy consumption; hazardous
materials; chemical usage; transport; emissions*

OFFA'S DYKE ASSOCIATION
(association)
monument; museum

Established: *1971*
Address: *West St, Knighton, Powys*
Telephone: *(0547) 528753*
Access: (rail) *Knighton*
Parking capacity: (cars) *10*
Season: *all year*

Hours: *Apr to Oct – 9am to 5.30pm daily; Nov to
Mar – Mon to Fri – 9am to 5pm*
No. visitors (1992): *20 000 (est.)*

Facilities
Interpretation: *videos; leaflets; maps; guide books*
Languages: *Dutch; Welsh*
Schools: *maximum no. 30; educational literature;
audio/visual presentation; lecture/talk*
Disabled: *easy access*
Catering: *1 picnic area*
Retailing: *postcards/inexpensive souvenirs;
craftwork; books; clothes*
No. shops: *1*

Operations
Contacts: *Rebe Brick (Correspondence Secretary);
Miss Mary Cadwallader (Hon Secretary); Ernie
Kary*
No. employees: (high season) *1 full time; 3 part
time* (low season) *1 full time*
Training: *F/T operations staff are trained
externally and on specific courses*

Marketing
UK promotion: *regional tourist board; leaflets/
information packs*
Europe/Holland promotion: *leaflets/brochures*

Environmental monitoring: *recycling; water
quality; energy consumption*

OLD BYRE
(local authority run)
heritage centre; the heritage of Mull

Established: *1986*
Address: *Dervaig, Isle of Mull, Argyll*
Telephone: *(06884) 229*
Parking capacity: (cars) *18* (coaches) *1*
Hours: *Palm Sun to mid Oct – 10.30am to
6.30pm daily*
Admission (1992): *adults £2.00; children £1.00;
OAP £1.50; student £1.50*
No. visitors (1992): *4060*

Facilities
Interpretation: *leaflets; audio tapes; information
boards; slides; maps; guide books*
Schools: *audio/visual presentation*
Catering: *1 licensed restaurant*
Retailing: *postcards/inexpensive souvenirs;
confectionery and ice cream; craftwork; books;
clothes; related to Mull and its wildlife*
No. shops: *1*

Operations
Contact: *Mrs U Bradley*
No. employees: (high season) *2 full time; 1 part
time* (low season) *2 full time*

Marketing
Market research
UK promotion: *local newspapers; regional tourist
board; other attractions; leaflets/information
packs; STB*
Europe/USA promotion: *leaflets/brochures*

Environmental monitoring: *planning applications*

OLD CROWN COURT AND CELLS
(local authority run)
historic building

Established: *1956*
Address: *58 High West St, Dorchester, Dorset,
DT1 1YZ*

Telephone: *(0305) 252408.* Fax: *(0305) 251481*
Access: *(road) A35 (rail) Dorchester*
Season: *all year*
Hours: *Jan to Dec – Mon to Fri – 10am to 1pm
and 2pm to 5pm. Closed BH and Tues
following*
Admission (1992): *groups by appointment £12.00,
maximum 25 people for tour*
No. visitors (1992): *2000 (est.)*

Facilities
Interpretation: *audio tapes; guide books;
personnel*
Languages: *Dutch; French; German; Italian;
Spanish; Danish*
Schools: *maximum no. 50; educational literature;
audio/visual presentation; lecture/talk*

Operations
Contacts: *Ms J Knatt (Tourism Officer); Ms S
Clarke (Tourism Assistant)*
Training: *P/T operations staff are trained
externally and on specific courses*
Languages spoken: *French*

Marketing
UK promotion: *regional tourist board*

OLD DAIRY FARM CENTRE
(private company)
farm and craft centre

Established: *1986*
Address: *Upper Stowe, Nr Weedon, Northants,
NN7 4SH*
Telephone: *(0327) 40525*
Access: *(road) A5*
Parking capacity: *(cars) 70 (coaches) 6*
Season: *all year*
Hours: *summer – 10am to 5.30pm; winter – 10am
to 4.30pm*
No. visitors (1992): *60 000 (est.)*

Facilities
Interpretation: *leaflets; maps; signs*
Languages: *French; German*
Children: *nappy changing*
Schools: *maximum no. 60; educational literature;
audio/visual presentation; lecture/talk;
demonstrations, samples*
Disabled: *easy access; disabled toilets; helpers*
Catering: *1 picnic area*
Retailing: *postcards/inexpensive souvenirs;
confectionery and ice cream; craftwork; books;
clothes*
No. shops: *3*

Operations
Contacts: *H S Brodie (owner); A C Moss
(Administrator)*
No. employees: (high season) *3 full time; 14 part
time* (low season) *3 full time; 8 part time*

Marketing
Annual event(s): *lambing, shearing, farm open
craft fair*
Other: *market research*
UK promotion: *national newspapers; radio; local
newspapers; leaflets/information packs; EMYB;
ETB/BTA*

OLD GRAMMAR SCHOOL
(local authority run)

Established: *1988*
Address: *South Church Side, Market Place, Hull*
Telephone: *(0482) 593902.* Fax: *(0482) 595062*
Access: *(road) M62/A63 (rail) Hull Paragon*
Season: *all year*
Hours: *Mon to Sat – 10am to 5pm; Sun – 1.30pm
to 4.30pm. Closed Christmas Day, Boxing Day,
New Year's Day and Good Friday*
No. visitors (1992): *82 204 (est.)*

Facilities
Interpretation: *videos; audio tapes; information
boards*

Languages: *Dutch*
Schools: *maximum no. 100; educational literature;
audio/visual presentation; lecture/talk*
Disabled: *easy access; disabled toilets; lift*
Retailing: *postcards/inexpensive souvenirs; books*
No. shops: *1*

Operations
Contact: *Ms J Tyler (Keeper of Social History)*
No. employees: (high season) *8 full time*
Training: *F/T operations staff and F/T
management are trained in-house and externally
and on specific courses and day-to-day on job*
Languages spoken: *French; German*

Marketing
Sponsor(s): *various*
Other: *press office; market research*
UK promotion: *local newspapers; regional tourist
board; other attractions*

OLD OPERATING THEATRE MUSEUM
(trust)
museum

Address: *9a St Thomas St, Southwark, London,
SE1 9RY*
Telephone: *(071) 955 4791*
Access: *(rail) London Bridge*
Season: *all year*
Hours: *first Sun in month, Mon, Wed and Fri –
12.30pm to 4pm*
Admission (1992): *adults £1.50; children £1.00;
OAP £1.00; student £1.00; unwaged £1.00*
No. visitors (1992): *6500 (est.)*

Facilities
Interpretation: *information boards*
Schools: *maximum no. 50; lecture/talk*
Retailing: *postcards/inexpensive souvenirs; books*
No. shops: *1*

Operations
Contact: *Mr K Flude (Curator)*
No. employees: (high season) *1 part time* (low
season) *1 part time*

Marketing
Affiliation: *AMSSEE*

Environmental monitoring: *energy consumption;
hazardous materials*

OLD RECTORY, THE
(trust)
historic house; garden; museum; gallery; reference
library for scholars

Established: *1957*
Address: *1 Rectory St, Epworth, Doncaster, S
Yorks, DN9 1HX*
Telephone: *(0427) 872268*
Access: *(road) M180/A161 (rail) Doncaster*
Parking capacity: *(cars) 12 (coaches) 3*
Hours: *1 Mar to 31 Oct – Mon to Sat – 10am to
12 noon and 2pm to 4pm; Sun – 2pm to 4pm*
Admission (1992): *adults £1.50; children £0.75;
student £0.75*
No. visitors (1992): *7000 (est.)*

Facilities
Interpretation: *information boards; tour guides;
tape/slide show for groups*
Languages: *French; German*
Schools: *maximum no. 30; educational literature;
audio/visual presentation; lecture/talk*
Disabled: *easy access; helpers*
Catering: *1 picnic area*
Retailing: *postcards/inexpensive souvenirs; books;
prints, honey and ties; souvenirs of pilgrim
fathers*
No. shops: *1*

Operations
Contact: *Mr C Barton (Warden)*
No. employees: (high season) *1 full time; 4 part
time* (low season) *1 full time; 2 part time*

Training: *F/T management, P/T operations staff
and casual operations staff are trained in-house
and day-to-day on job using council training
schemes*

Marketing
Affiliation: *Church Shops Association*
UK promotion: *regional tourist board; other
attractions; leaflets/information packs; Historic
Houses, Castles and Gardens*

Environmental monitoring: *waste; water quality;
energy consumption; hazardous materials;
chemical usage*

OLD SEMEIL HERB GARDEN
(sole trader)
garden

Established: *1981*
Address: *Strathdon, Aberdeenshire, AB36 8XJ*
Telephone: *(09756) 51343*
Access: *(road) A944/A97*
Parking capacity: *(cars) 10 (coaches) 2*
Hours: *Easter to mid Oct – Apr – weekends, May
to Aug – 10am to 5pm daily, Sept and Oct –
10am to 5pm daily (except Thur)*
Admission (1992): *free*
No. visitors (1992): *5000 (est.)*

Facilities
Interpretation: *leaflets; information boards; maps;
guide books*
Children: *play area*
Schools: *maximum no. 50; no special support*
Disabled: *easy access; disabled toilets*
Catering: *1 waiter/waitress served*
Retailing: *postcards/inexpensive souvenirs;
confectionery and ice cream; craftwork; books;
herbal items and oils*
No. shops: *1*

Operations
Contact: *Mrs G Cook (Owner)*
No. employees: (high season) *1 full time; 3 part
time* (low season) *1 part time*
Training: *P/T operations staff and casual
operations staff are trained in-house and
day-to-day on job*

Marketing
UK promotion: *local newspapers; regional tourist
board; other attractions; leaflets/information
packs; Gordon District Tourist Board, STB*

OLD SMITHY TOURIST CENTRE
(partnership)
garden

Established: *1948*
Address: *Godshill, Nr Ventnor, Isle of Wight,
PO38 3JE*
Telephone: *(0983) 840364*
Parking capacity: *(cars) 250 (coaches) 50*
Hours: *Easter to end Oct – 10am to 5pm daily*
Admission (1992): *adults £0.70; children £0.40;
group rates £0.40*
No. visitors (1992): *60 000 (est.)*

Facilities
Interpretation: *leaflets*
Schools: *maximum no. 50; no special support*
Disabled: *easy access*
Catering: *1 picnic area*
Retailing: *postcards/inexpensive souvenirs;
confectionery and ice cream; craftwork; books;
clothes*
No. shops: *4*

Operations
Contacts: *Miss D Andrews/Mrs R Brooks
(Partners)*
No. employees: (high season) *6 full time;
20 part time* (low season) *4 full time; 6 part
time*
Training: *F/T operations staff, P/T operations
staff and casual operations staff are trained
in-house and day-to-day on job*

Marketing
Affiliation: *Southern Tourist Board*
UK promotion: *radio; local newspapers; leaflets/ information packs; ETB/BTA*

Environmental monitoring: *recycling; waste; water quality; organic gardening*

OLDWAY MANSION
(local authority run)
historic house; heritage centre; garden

Established: *1947*
Address: *Torquay Rd, Paignton, Devon*
Telephone: *(0803) 296244.* Fax: *(0803) 292677*
Access: (road) *A379* (rail) *Paignton*
Parking capacity: (cars) *60* (coaches) *3*
Season: *all year*
Hours: *Mon to Fri – 9am to 5pm, Sat – 9am to 1pm (and in summer – Sun – 2pm to 5pm)*
Admission (1992): *free*

Facilities
Interpretation: *leaflets; tour guides; guide books*
Schools: *maximum no. 20; no special support*
Disabled: *easy access; disabled toilets; lift to 1st floor*
Catering: *1 self-service cafeteria*
Retailing: *sales by hallkeeper*
No. shops: *none*

Operations
Contact: *Mr P Carpenter (Property Administrative Officer)*
No. employees: (high season) *3 full time*
Training: *F/T operations staff are trained in-house and on specific courses*

Marketing
Annual event(s): *flower shows and exhibitions*
Other: *press office; market research*
UK promotion: *regional tourist board; leaflets/ information packs; ETB/BTA*

ONCE BREWED NATIONAL PARK VISITOR CENTRE
(local authority run)
park/reserve; national park exhibition and interpretation

Established: *1968*
Address: *Military Rd, Nr Bardon Mill, Hexham, Northumberland, NE47 7AN*
Telephone: *(0434) 344396*
Access: (road) *A69/B6318*
Parking capacity: (cars) *60* (coaches) *4*
Hours: *13 Mar to 31 Aug – 10am to 6pm; 1 Sept to 31 Oct – 10am to 5pm; Nov – weekends – 10am to 3pm*
Admission (1992): *free*
No. visitors (1992): *59 000 (est.)*

Facilities
Interpretation: *videos; leaflets; information boards; slides; maps; guide books*
Languages: *Japanese; Dutch; French; German; Italian; Swedish; Danish; Norwegian*
Schools: *educational literature; audio/visual presentation*
Disabled: *easy access; disabled toilets; leaflets*
Catering: *1 picnic area*
Retailing: *postcards/inexpensive souvenirs; confectionery and ice cream; craftwork; books; clothes; reproductions of famous artefacts*
No. shops: *1*

Operations
No. employees: (high season) *4 part time* (low season) *2 part time*
Training: *F/T management and P/T operations staff are trained in-house and externally and on specific courses and day-to-day on job using videos and handbooks*

Marketing
Press office; market research
UK promotion: *radio; local newspapers; regional tourist board; leaflets/information packs; ETB/BTA*

Europe promotion: *leaflets/brochures; British Tourist Authority*

ORIEL MOSTYN
(limited company)
gallery

Established: *1978*
Address: *12 Vaughan St, Llandudno, Gwynedd, LL30 1AB*
Telephone: *(0492) 879201.* Fax: *(0492) 878869*
Access: (road) *A55* (rail) *Llandudno*
Season: *all year*
Hours: *Mon to Sat – 10.30am to 5pm*
No. visitors (1992): *30 000 (est.)*

Facilities
Languages: *Welsh*
Schools: *maximum no. 30; educational literature; lecture/talk; workshops*
Disabled: *easy access; disabled toilets*
Retailing: *craftwork; books*
No. shops: *1*

Operations
Contact: *Mary Heathcote (Administrator)*
No. employees: (high season) *5 full time; 5 part time*
Languages spoken: *French; Spanish*

Marketing
UK promotion: *national newspapers; local newspapers; leaflets/information packs; art magazines*
Europe promotion: *leaflets/brochures; art magazines*

Environmental monitoring: *recycling; transport*

ORIENTAL MUSEUM
(university dept)
museum

Established: *1960*
Address: *University of Durham, Elvet Hill, Durham, DH1 3TH*
Telephone: *(091) 374 2911.* Fax: *(091) 374 3242*
Access: (road) *A1(M)/A167* (rail) *Durham*
Season: *all year*
Hours: *Mon to Fri – 9.30am to 1pm and 2pm to 5pm, Sat and Sun – 2pm to 5pm. Closed between Christmas and New Year*
Admission (1992): *adults £1.00; children £0.50; OAP £0.50; student £0.50*
No. visitors (1992): *15 000 (est.)*

Facilities
Interpretation: *information boards; guide books*
Schools: *maximum no. 50; educational literature; lecture/talk; schools officer*
Disabled: *only part of the museum accessible by wheelchair*
Retailing: *postcards/inexpensive souvenirs; confectionery and ice cream; craftwork; books; clothes*
No. shops: *1*

Operations
Contacts: *J Ruffle (Keeper); Mrs F Navabpour (Custodian)*
No. employees: (high season) *5 full time; 3 part time* (low season) *5 full time; 3 part time*

Marketing
Annual event: *kite day*
Affiliations: *NEMS, NTB*
Other: *market research*
UK promotion: *regional tourist board; other attractions; leaflets/information packs*

OTTER TRUST, THE
(trust)
wildlife attraction

Established: *1977*
Address: *Earsham, Nr Bungay, Suffolk, NR35 2AF*

Telephone: *(0986) 893470*
Access: (road) *A143*
Hours: *1 Apr to 31 Oct – 10.30am to 6pm*
Admission (1992): *adults £3.00; children £1.50; OAP £2.50*
No. visitors (1992): *50 000 (est.)*

Facilities
Interpretation: *leaflets; information boards; maps; guide books; signs*
Children: *play area; nappy changing*
Schools: *maximum no. 28; educational literature; audio/visual presentation; lecture/talk*
Disabled: *easy access; disabled toilets*
Catering: *6 picnic areas*
Retailing: *postcards/inexpensive souvenirs; books; various*
No. shops: *1*

Operations
Contact: *Jeanne Wayre (Director)*
No. employees: (high season) *15 full time* (low season) *8 full time*

Marketing
UK promotion: *leaflets/information packs*

OUR LITTLE FARM
(privately owned)
park/reserve; farm park and nature trail

Established: *1990*
Address: *Lodge Farm, Harby Lane, Plungar, Notts, NG13 0JH*
Telephone: *(0949) 60349*
Access: (road) *A52*
Parking capacity: (cars) *150* (coaches) *3*
Hours: *20 Mar to 1 Nov – Tues to Sun – 10.30am to 5.30pm; open BH Mon*
Admission (1992): *adults £1.95; children £1.10; OAP £1.50*
No. visitors (1992): *30 000 (est.)*

Facilities
Interpretation: *leaflets; information boards*
Children: *adventure playground; nappy changing*
Schools: *maximum no. 120; educational literature*
Disabled: *easy access; disabled toilets*
Catering: *2 picnic areas*
Retailing: *postcards/inexpensive souvenirs; books; toys*
No. shops: *1*

Operations
Contacts: *Mr and Mrs A Brierley (owners)*
No. employees: (high season) *5 part time*
Training: *P/T operations staff are trained in-house and day-to-day on job*
Languages spoken: *French*

Marketing
Annual event: *vintage threshing and ploughing weekend*
Other: *market research*
UK promotion: *regional tourist board; other attractions; leaflets/information packs; shires of middle England*

OXBURGH HALL
(charity)
historic house; garden

Established: *1953*
Address: *Oxborough, King's Lynn, Norfolk, PE33 9PS*
Telephone: *(036) 621 258*
Access: (road) *A134* (rail) *Downham Market*
Parking capacity: (cars) *250* (coaches) *6*
Hours: *27 Mar to 31 Oct – daily except Thur and Fri – 1.30pm to 5.30pm, BH Mon – 11am to 5.30pm*
Admission (1992): *adults £3.60; children £1.80; group rates £2.80 (adults) £1.40 (children) minimum no. 15*
No. visitors (1992): *51 700*

Facilities
Interpretation: *leaflets; slides; tour guides; guide books; guides by arrangement*

Schools: *maximum no. 80*
Disabled: *easy access; disabled toilets; Braille/ sound posts; leaflets; guide book; wheelchairs*
Catering: *1 licensed restaurant*
Retailing: *postcards/inexpensive souvenirs; confectionery and ice cream; craftwork; books*
No. shops: *1*

Operations
Contacts: *Mr B Carter (Administrator); Ms S Carter (Shop Manageress); Mr P Dickson (Reg Public Affairs Manager)*
No. employees: (high season) *4 full time; 20 part time* (low season) *4 full time; 2 part time*
Training: *F/T operations staff, F/T management, P/T operations staff and P/T management are trained in-house and externally and on specific courses and day-to-day on job*

Marketing
Annual event(s): *musical concerts*
Affiliation: *Norfolk Tourist Attractions Association*
Other: *PR company: Foster, Seligman and Wright, Norwich, Norfolk*
UK promotion: *national newspapers; local newspapers; regional tourist board; other attractions; leaflets/information packs; ETB/BTA*

OXFORD STORY, THE
(limited company)
heritage centre

Established: *1988*
Address: *6 Broad St, Oxford, OX1 3AJ*
Telephone: *(0865) 728822.* Fax: *(0865) 791716*
Access: (road) *M40/A4144/A4165/A420* (rail) *Oxford*
Season: *all year*
Hours: *Apr to Oct – Mon to Sun – 9.30am to 5pm; Nov to Mar – Mon to Sun – 10am to 4pm. Closed Christmas Day*
Admission (1992): *adults £3.95; children £2.95; OAP £3.55; student £3.55*

Facilities
Interpretation: *videos; leaflets; audio tapes; information boards; slides; guide books; exhibition*
Languages: *Japanese; French; German; Italian; Spanish*
Children: *nappy changing*
Schools: *educational literature; audio/visual presentation; lecture/talk*
Disabled: *easy access; disabled toilets; other audio facilities*
Retailing: *postcards/inexpensive souvenirs; confectionery and ice cream; books; clothes; reproductions of famous artefacts; university merchandise, gifts; gift items*
No. shops: *2*

Operations
Contacts: *A Leonard (Centre Manager); E Feeney (Deputy Manager); C Dee (Marketing Executive)*
No. employees: (high season) *9 full time; 30 part time* (low season) *9 full time; 16 part time*
Training: *F/T operations staff, F/T management, P/T operations staff and casual operations staff are trained in-house and externally and on specific courses and day-to-day on job*

Marketing
Affiliation: *Destination Oxford*
Other: *market research*
UK promotion: *television; local newspapers; regional tourist board; other attractions; leaflets/information packs; most major ones; ETB/BTA; Southern Tourist Board*
Europe/Asia/Australia/USA promotion: *leaflets/ brochures; British Tourist Authority; direct mail*

Environmental monitoring: *water quality*

OXFORDSHIRE COUNTY MUSEUM
(local authority run)
historic house; museum

Established: *1965*
Address: *Fletchers House, Park St, Woodstock, Oxon, OX20 1SN*
Telephone: *(0993) 811456*
Access: (road) *A3400*
Season: *all year*
Hours: *May to Sept – Mon to Fri – 10am to 5pm, Sat – 10am to 6pm, Sun – 2pm to 6pm; Oct to Apr – Tues to Fri – 10am to 4pm, Sat – 10am to 5pm, Sun – 2pm to 5pm*
No. visitors (1992): *64 000*

Facilities
Interpretation: *information boards*
Schools: *maximum no. 30; teacher support*
Catering: *1 picnic area*
Retailing: *postcards/inexpensive souvenirs; craftwork; books; reproductions of famous artefacts; local artwork*
No. shops: *1*

Operations
Contacts: *K Dunning (Museum Manager); J Pomfret (Bookshop Manageress); C Anderson (Senior Museum Officer)*
No. employees: (high season) *2 full time; 10 part time* (low season) *2 full time; 10 part time*
Training: *F/T operations staff, F/T management, P/T operations staff, P/T management and casual operations staff are trained in-house and externally and on specific courses and day-to-day on job using videos*

Marketing
Affiliations: *MA*
Other: *market research*
UK promotion: *radio; local newspapers; other attractions; leaflets/information packs*

P

PADSTOW SHIPWRECK MUSEUM
(sole proprietor)
museum

Established: *1991*
Address: *South Quay, Padstow, Cornwall*
Telephone: *(0841) 532663*
Hours: *Apr to Oct – 10am to 5pm daily*
Admission (1992): *adults £1.00; children £0.50; OAP £0.85; student £0.60*
No. visitors (1992): *20 000 (est.)*

Facilities
Interpretation: *information boards; maps; guide books*
Schools: *maximum no. 35*
Disabled: *easy access*
Retailing: *small number of artefacts*
No. shops: *none*

Operations
Contact: *R J Davis (Owner)*
No. employees: (high season) *3 part time* (low season) *3 part time*
Languages spoken: *French*

Marketing
UK promotion: *local newspapers; regional tourist board*

PAIGNTON AND DARTMOUTH STEAM RAILWAY
(plc)
preserved steam railway

Established: *1973*
Address: *Queen's Park Station, Torbay Rd, Paignton, Devon, TQ4 6AF*
Telephone: *(0803) 555872.* Fax: *(0803) 664313*
Access: (road) *A380* (rail) *Paignton*
Hours: *Easter to Oct – 10am to 5.30pm (also certain days in Dec)*
Admission (1992): *adults £5.80; children £4.00; OAP £5.30; discount for groups of 20 or more*
No. visitors (1992): *157 000*

Facilities
Interpretation: *leaflets; information boards; maps; guide books*
Children: *nappy changing*
Schools: *maximum no. 100*
Disabled: *easy access*
Catering: *1 snack bar/food stall*
Franchisees: *Easter to Oct – 10am to 5.30pm*
Retailing: *postcards/inexpensive souvenirs; confectionery and ice cream; craftwork; books; clothes*
No. shops: *2*

Operations
Contacts: *J Cobar (Director and General Manager); M Henderson (Marketing)*
No. employees: (high season) *45 full time; 3 part time* (low season) *30 full time; 2 part time*
Training: *F/T operations staff, P/T operations staff and casual operations staff are trained in-house and on specific courses and day-to-day on job*

Marketing
Annual event(s): *diesel gala*
Other: *press office; market research*
UK promotion: *radio; local newspapers; regional tourist board; other attractions; leaflets/ information packs; ETB/BTA*

PAIGNTON ZOO
(trust)
zoo/wildlife attraction

Established: *1923*
Address: *Totnes Rd, Paignton, Devon, TQ4 7EU*
Telephone: *(0803) 557479.* Fax: *(0803) 523457*
Access: (road) *M4/A3022* (rail) *Paignton*
Parking capacity: (cars) *1000* (coaches) *20*
Season: *all year*
Hours: *summer – 10am to 6pm daily; winter – 10am to 5pm daily except Christmas Day*
Admission (1992): *adults £5.40; children £3.00; OAP £4.50; student £3.00; family ticket (2 + 2) £15.30*
No. visitors (1992): *250 000*

Facilities
Interpretation: *videos; audio tapes; information boards; guide books; personnel*
Children: *adventure playground; play area; nappy changing*
Schools: *maximum no. 350; audio/visual presentation; lecture/talk*
Disabled: *easy access; disabled toilets; leaflets; free admission for wheelchairs*
Catering: *1 bar/public house*
Retailing: *postcards/inexpensive souvenirs; confectionery and ice cream; craftwork; books; clothes, animal related; film*
No. shops: *more than 4*

Operations
Contacts: *Mr P Stevens (Executive Director); Ms D Holloway (Marketing Manager)*
No. employees: (high season) *70 full time; 30 part time* (low season) *50 full time; 10 part time*
Training: *F/T operations staff are trained in-house and on specific courses and day-to-day on job using handbooks*

Marketing
Annual event(s): *various*
Sponsor(s): *various*
Affiliation: *National Federation of Zoos*
Other: *press office; market research*
UK promotion: *television; local newspapers; other attractions; leaflets/information packs; various*

PAISLEY MUSEUM AND ART GALLERIES
(local authority run)
museum; gallery

Established: *1871*
Address: *High St, Paisley, Renfrewshire, PA1 2BA*
Telephone: *(041) 889 3151.* Fax: *(041) 889 9240*
Access: (rail) *Paisley*
Season: *all year*
Hours: *10am to 5pm – Mon to Sat except PH*
Admission (1992): *free*
No. visitors (1992): *71 000 (est.)*

Facilities
Interpretation: *leaflets; information boards; tour guides; guide books*
Languages: *French*
Schools: *maximum no. 50; educational literature; lecture/talk*
Disabled: *disabled toilets*
Retailing: *postcards/inexpensive souvenirs; craftwork; books; reproductions of famous artefacts; prints from art collection*
No. shops: *1*

Operations
Contact: *Mr P Wetherall (Deputy Director, Arts and Libraries)*

No. employees: (high season) *35 full time; 5 part time*
Training: *F/T operations staff, F/T management, P/T operations staff and casual operations staff are trained in-house and externally and on specific courses and day-to-day on job using videos and handbooks*
Languages spoken: *French; German*

Marketing
Annual event(s): *Paisley festival and Sma' Shot Day*
Sponsor(s): *various*
Affiliations: *MA, SMC and Scottish Museums Federation*
Other: *press office; market research*
UK promotion: *local newspapers; regional tourist board; other attractions; leaflets/information packs; museum and visitor attraction directories*

Environmental monitoring: *recycling; waste; water quality; energy consumption; chemical usage*

PALACE OF HOLYROODHOUSE
(royal household)
historic house; royal palace

Established: *1857*
Address: *Edinburgh, EH8 8DX*
Telephone: *(031) 556 7371.* Fax: *(031) 556 5256*
Access: (rail) *Edinburgh*
Parking capacity: (cars) *150* (coaches) *15*
Season: *all year*
Hours: *summer – Mon to Sat – 9.30am to 5.15pm, Sun – 10.30am to 4.30pm; winter – Mon to Sat – 9.30am to 3.45pm. Closed late May 2 weeks and late June/July 3 weeks*
Admission (1992): *adults £3.00; children £1.50; OAP £2.50; student £3.00; family ticket £7.50*
No. visitors (1992): *300 000 (est.)*

Facilities
Interpretation: *leaflets; information boards; tour guides; guide books*
Languages: *Japanese; French; German; Italian; Spanish*
Schools: *maximum no. 40; educational literature; free Nov to Mar inclusive*
Catering: *1 self-service cafeteria*
Franchisees: *Summer – Mon to Sat – 9.30am to 5.15pm, Sun – 10.30am to 4.30pm*
Retailing: *postcards/inexpensive souvenirs; confectionery and ice cream; craftwork; books; silver and jewellery*
No. shops: *1*

Operations
Contacts: *Mr D Wickes (Superintendent); Miss M Cochrane (Supervisor, Public Enterprises)*
No. employees: (high season) *26 full time; 2 part time* (low season) *14 full time; 2 part time*
Training: *F/T operations staff and F/T management are trained in-house and externally and on specific courses and day-to-day on job and in-house lectures using videos and handbooks*

Marketing
Market research
UK promotion: *local newspapers; regional tourist board; leaflets/information packs; STB, Edinburgh marketing*
Europe/Asia/USA promotion: *leaflets/brochures*

Environmental monitoring: *energy consumption*

PALACE STABLES HERITAGE CENTRE, THE
(local authority run)
heritage centre

Established: *1992*
Address: *The Palace Demesne, Armagh, Co. Armagh, BT60 4EL*
Telephone: *(0861) 522722.* Fax: *(0861) 524246*
Access: (road) *M1/A3*
Parking capacity: (cars) *50* (coaches) *2*
Season: *all year*
Hours: *Apr to Sept – Mon to Sat – 10am to 7pm, Sun – 1pm to 7pm; Sept to Mar – Mon to Sat – 10am to 5pm, Sun – 2pm to 5pm*
Admission (1992): *adults £2.50; children £1.50; OAP £2.00; student £2.00; family ticket £7.00*
No. visitors (1992): *N/A*

Facilities
Interpretation: *videos; leaflets; audio tapes; information boards; slides; maps; tour guides; guide books; personnel; models, murals, artefacts*
Children: *adventure playground; play area*
Schools: *educational literature; audio/visual presentation; lecture/talk; work books, information packs*
Disabled: *easy access; disabled toilets; Braille/ sound posts; helpers; other audio facilities; leaflets; lift to upper floor*
Catering: *1 picnic area*
Franchisees: *Apr to Sept – Mon to Sat – 10am to 7pm, Sun – 1pm to 7pm; Sept to Mar – Mon to Sat – 10am to 5pm, Sun – 2pm to 5pm*
Retailing: *postcards/inexpensive souvenirs; confectionery and ice cream; craftwork; books; clothes; reproductions of famous artefacts; pens, pencils, etc.*
No. shops: *1*

Operations
Contact: *Sandra E Matchett (Supervisor)*
No. employees: (high season) *7 full time; 3 part time* (low season) *7 full time; 3 part time*
Training: *F/T operations staff, F/T management and P/T operations staff are trained in-house and externally and on specific courses using handbooks*
Languages spoken: *French; Japanese; Turkish*

Environmental monitoring: *hazardous materials; emissions*

PALLANT HOUSE
(trust)
historic house; garden; gallery

Established: *1982*
Address: *9 North Pallant, Chichester, W Sussex, PO19 1TJ*
Telephone: *(0243) 774557*
Access: (road) *A27* (rail) *Chichester*
Season: *all year*
Hours: *Thur to Sat – 10am to 5.30pm*
Admission (1992): *adults £2.50; children £1.00; OAP £1.70; student £1.70*
No. visitors (1992): *14 064*

Facilities
Interpretation: *leaflets; information boards; tour guides; guide books*
Languages: *Japanese; Dutch; French; German; Italian*
Schools: *maximum no. 30; educational literature; educational tour; lecture/talk; school visits, training*
Disabled: *helpers; disabled access not possible*
Retailing: *postcards/inexpensive souvenirs; craftwork; books*
No. shops: *1*

Operations
Contacts: *D Coke (Curator); J Powell (Administrator); L Purchase (Shop Manager); G Traynor (Press Officer)*
No. employees: (high season) *4 full time; 5 part time* (low season) *4 full time*
Languages spoken: *German*

Marketing
Annual event(s): *concerts and exhibitions*
Sponsor: *Chandos Records Ltd.*
Other: *press office; market research*
UK promotion: *local newspapers; regional tourist board; other attractions; leaflets/information packs; various; Chichester visitors Group*

Environmental monitoring: *temperature and relative humidity*

PARADISE MILL
(trust)
museum

Established: *1984*
Address: *Park Lane, Macclesfield, Ches, SK11 6TJ*
Telephone: *(0625) 618228*
Access: (road) *M6/A523* (rail) *Macclesfield*
Season: *all year*
Hours: *Tues to Sun – 1pm to 5pm. Closed Christmas, New Year and Good Friday*
Admission (1992): *adults £1.80; children £1.10; OAP £1.10; student £1.10*
No. visitors (1992): *13 000 (est.)*

Facilities
Interpretation: *leaflets; information boards; maps; guide books; restored silk mill*
Children: *nappy changing*
Schools: *maximum no. 30*
Disabled: *easy access; disabled toilets; lift*
Retailing: *postcards/inexpensive souvenirs; craftwork; books; silk items, wooden toys; wrapping paper, etc.*
No. shops: *1*

Operations
Contacts: *M Stevenson (Museum Director); C Wasche (Administrative Assistant); A Beard/C Wasche (Shop Manager)*
Training: *F/T operations staff, F/T management, P/T operations staff, P/T management, casual operations staff and Casual management are trained in-house and externally and on specific courses and day-to-day on job*
Languages spoken: *French; Italian*

Marketing
Annual event(s): *Christmas cheer*
Sponsor(s): *various art groups*
Other: *press office; market research*
UK promotion: *local newspapers; regional tourist board; other attractions; leaflets/information packs; NWTB, Cheshire County Tourism*

PARADISE WILDLIFE PARK
(limited company)
zoo/wildlife attraction

Established: *1985*
Address: *White Stubbs Lane, Broxbourne, Herts, EN10 7QA*
Telephone: *(0992) 468001.* Fax: *(0992) 440525*
Access: (road) *M25/A10* (rail) *Broxbourne*
Parking capacity: (cars) *270* (coaches) *10*
Season: *all year*
Hours: *Apr to Sept – 10am to 6pm; Oct to Mar – 10am to dusk*
Admission (1992): *adults £3.50; children £2.50; OAP £3.00; disabled £2.00*
No. visitors (1992): *90 000 (est.)*

Facilities
Interpretation: *leaflets; information boards; slides; tour guides; guide books*
Children: *adventure playground; play area; nappy changing*
Schools: *maximum no. 300; educational literature; audio/visual presentation; educational tour; lecture/talk*
Disabled: *easy access; disabled toilets*
Catering: *1 bar/public house*
Franchisees: *Apr to Sept – 10am to 6pm; Oct to Mar – 10am to dusk*
Retailing: *postcards/inexpensive souvenirs; confectionery and ice cream; craftwork; books; clothes; T-shirts; garden ornaments*
No. shops: *3*

Operations
Contacts: *S Sampson (Manager); M Goodchild (Office Manager)*
No. employees: (high season) *13 full time; 6 part time* (low season) *8 full time; 4 part time*
Training: *F/T operations staff, P/T operations staff and casual operations staff are trained in-house and on specific courses and day-to-day on job using videos*
Languages spoken: *French; German; Spanish*

Marketing
PR company: *Hertfordshire Marketing; market research*
UK promotion: *local newspapers; regional tourist board; other attractions; leaflets/information packs; ETB/BTA*

PARCEVALL HALL GARDENS
(charitable company)
garden; Bradford diocesan retreat house on site

Established: *1963*
Address: *Skyreholme, Skipton, N Yorks, BD23 6DE*
Telephone: *(0756) 720311*
Access: (road) *B6265/B6160*
Parking capacity: (cars) *23*
Season: *all year*
Hours: *Easter to 31 Oct – 10am to 6pm. At other times by appointment*
Admission (1992): *adults £2.00; children £0.50*
No. visitors (1992): *12 000 (est.)*

Facilities
Interpretation: *maps; guide books; guided tours by arrangement*
Disabled: *access difficult*
Catering: *1 picnic area*
Retailing: *postcards/inexpensive souvenirs*
No. shops: *none*

Operations
Contact: *J Makin (Garden Administrator)*
No. employees: (high season) *3 full time; 2 part time* (low season) *3 full time; 2 part time*
Training: *F/T operations staff, F/T management and P/T operations staff are trained in-house and externally and on specific courses and day-to-day on job using handbooks*
Languages spoken: *French*

Marketing
UK promotion: *local newspapers; other attractions; leaflets/information packs*

PARHAM ELIZABETHAN HOUSE AND GARDENS
(charity)
historic house; garden

Established: *1948*
Address: *Nr Pulborough, W Sussex, RH20 4HS*
Telephone: *(0903) 742021.* Fax: *(0903) 746557*
Access: (road) *A283* (rail) *Pulborough*
Parking capacity: (cars) *200* (coaches) *10*
Hours: *House – Easter to Oct – Wed, Thur, Sun and BH – 2pm to 6pm. Gardens – 1pm to 6pm*
Admission (1992): *adults £3.50; children £2.00; OAP £3.00*
No. visitors (1992): *30 000*

Facilities
Interpretation: *audio tapes; tour guides; guide books*
Languages: *French; German*
Children: *play area*
Schools: *maximum no. 150; educational tour*
Disabled: *easy access; access to gardens only*
Catering: *1 picnic area*
Retailing: *postcards/inexpensive souvenirs; confectionery and ice cream; craftwork; books; mugs, bookmarks, tour tapes; soaps, cards, etc.*
No. shops: *2*

Operations
Contact: *P Kennedy (Administrator)*
No. employees: (high season) *9 full time; 40 part time* (low season) *9 full time; 1 part time*

Training: *casual operations staff are trained in-house and day-to-day on job using handbooks and gardening equipment*

Marketing
Affiliations: *HHA*
UK promotion: *local newspapers; regional tourist board; other attractions; leaflets/information packs*

Environmental monitoring: *conservation*

PARKE RARE BREEDS FARM
(private)
zoo/wildlife attraction; rare breeds farm

Established: *1983*
Address: *Parke Estate, Bovey Tracey, Devon, TQ13 9JQ*
Telephone: *(0626) 833909*
Access: (road) *A382/B3387* (rail) *Newton Abbot*
Parking capacity: (cars) *80* (coaches) *4*
Hours: *Apr to Oct – 10am to 6pm*
Admission (1992): *adults £3.50; children £1.75; OAP £3.00; student £3.00*
No. visitors (1992): *23 320*

Facilities
Interpretation: *leaflets; information boards; guide books*
Schools: *maximum no. 100; educational literature; pre-booked guided tour*
Disabled: *not suitable for disabled*
Catering: *1 picnic area*
Retailing: *postcards/inexpensive souvenirs; confectionery and ice cream; craftwork; animal/wildlife items*
No. shops: *1*

Operations
Contact: *T Ash (owner)*
No. employees: (high season) *2 full time; 8 part time* (low season) *2 full time; 1 part time*
Training: *P/T operations staff and casual operations staff are trained in-house and day-to-day on job*
Languages spoken: *French; German*

Marketing
Affiliation: *Rare Breeds Survival Trust*
Other: *market research*
UK promotion: *local newspapers; regional tourist board; other attractions; leaflets/information packs*

PARRACOMBE GARDEN RAILWAY
(private)
garden; model railway on historic site

Established: *1987*
Address: *Fair View, Church Town, Parracombe, Devon, EX31 4RJ*
Telephone: *(05983) 478*
Access: (road) *A39*
Hours: *Easter to Oct – Sat to Thur – 10am to 6pm*
Admission (1992): *adults £1.50; children £1.00; OAP £1.00*
No. visitors (1992): *1500 (est.)*

Facilities
Interpretation: *leaflets; information boards; tour guides; guide books*
Disabled: *easy access*
Catering: *1 waiter/waitress served*
Retailing: *postcards/inexpensive souvenirs*

Operations
Contact: *L A Wooder (owner)*

Marketing
UK promotion: *regional tourist board; leaflets/information packs; Railway Modeller*

PARSONAGE FARM RURAL HERITAGE CENTRE
(partnership)
heritage centre; museum; farm

Established: *1989*
Address: *North Elham, Canterbury, Kent, CT4 6UY*
Telephone: *(0303) 840356/840766*
Access: (road) *M20/M2/A20/A2* (rail) *Canterbury East*
Parking capacity: (cars) *100* (coaches) *3*
Hours: *Easter to Sept – Tues to Sun and BH Mon – 10.30am to 5pm*
Admission (1992): *adults £2.30; children £1.40; OAP £1.60; disabled £1.60*
No. visitors (1992): *6800*

Facilities
Interpretation: *information boards; guide books*
Schools: *maximum no. 30; educational literature*
Disabled: *easy access; disabled toilets*
Catering: *1 picnic area*
Retailing: *postcards/inexpensive souvenirs; confectionery and ice cream; craftwork; books*
No. shops: *1*

Operations
No. employees: (high season) *2 full time; 1 part time*

Marketing
Annual event(s): *Easter egg hunt, sheep and wool weekend, vintage harvest weekend, harvest treasure*
UK promotion: *local newspapers; regional tourist board; other attractions; leaflets/information packs*

Environmental monitoring: *preservation of nature*

PASSMORE EDWARDS MUSEUM
(local authority run)
museum

Established: *1900*
Address: *Romford Rd, London, E15 4BZ*
Telephone: *(081) 534 0276. Fax: (081) 519 4296*
Access: (rail) *Stratford*
Season: *all year*
Hours: *Wed to Fri – 11am to 5pm, Sat – 1pm to 5pm, Sun and BH – 2pm to 5pm*
Admission (1992): *free*
No. visitors (1992): *17 256*

Facilities
Interpretation: *exhibitions*
Children: *nappy changing*
Schools: *maximum no. 30; by arrangement*
Disabled: *easy access; disabled toilets; powered transport*
Retailing: *postcards/inexpensive souvenirs; books; reproductions of famous artefacts*
No. shops: *1*

Operations
Contact: *Mr T McAllister (Chief Museum Assistant)*
No. employees: (high season) *5 full time* (low season) *5 full time*

Marketing
Annual event(s): *national archaeology day, women's history and talks*
Sponsor(s): *various*
Other: *press office; market research*
UK promotion: *local newspapers; regional tourist board; other attractions; leaflets/information packs*

PAULTON'S PARK
(limited company)
theme park

Established: *1983*
Address: *Ower, Romsey, Hants, SO22 6ND*
Telephone: *(0703) 814442. Fax: (0703) 813025*
Access: (road) *M27/A31/A36*
Parking capacity: (cars) *700*

Hours: *Mar to Oct – 10am to 6.30pm daily. Closes earlier spring and autumn*
No. visitors (1992): *375 000*

Facilities
Interpretation: *information boards; guide books*
Children: *play area; nappy changing*
Disabled: *easy access; disabled toilets*
Catering: *5 picnic area*
Retailing: *postcards/inexpensive souvenirs; confectionery and ice cream; craftwork; books; clothes; reproductions of famous artefacts*
No. shops: *4*

Operations
Contacts: *Mr R Mancey (Director/General Manager); Mr J Mancey (Managing Director); Mr S Ray (Retail and Admissions); Ms A Ruffell (Marketing)*
No. employees: (high season) *35 full time; 250 part time* (low season) *25 full time*
Training: *F/T operations staff, F/T management, P/T operations staff and casual operations staff are trained in-house and externally and on specific courses and day-to-day on job*

Marketing
Affiliations: *New Forest Tourism, South Hants Tourism Group, British Association of Leisure Parks, STB*
Other: *press office; market research*
UK promotion: *television; local newspapers; regional tourist board; other attractions; leaflets/information packs*

Environmental monitoring: *recycling; hazardous materials*

PAXTON HOUSE
(trust)
historic house; park/reserve; garden; gallery

Established: *1992*
Address: *Berwick upon Tweed, TD15 1SZ*
Telephone: *(0289) 86291. Fax: (0289) 86660*
Access: (road) *A1* (rail) *Berwick upon Tweed*
Parking capacity: (cars) *60* (coaches) *3*
Hours: *Easter to 31 Oct – 10am to 5pm daily*
Admission (1992): *adults £3.50; children £1.75; OAP £3.00*
No. visitors (1992): *20 000 (est.)*

Facilities
Interpretation: *tour guides*
Children: *adventure playground; nappy changing*
Schools: *maximum no. 50; no special support*
Disabled: *easy access; disabled toilets*
Catering: *1 self-service cafeteria*
Retailing: *postcards/inexpensive souvenirs; craftwork*
No. shops: *1*

Operations
Contact: *Mr K Scotland (Executive Director)*
No. employees: (high season) *3 full time; 17 part time* (low season) *3 full time; 1 part time*
Training: *P/T operations staff are trained in-house and day-to-day on job using videos and handbooks*

Marketing
Affiliations: *HHA, Scotland's Border Heritage, ASVA*
Other: *market research*
UK promotion: *local newspapers; regional tourist board; other attractions; leaflets/information packs; Holiday Guide*

Environmental monitoring: *water quality; breeding projects*

PEATLANDS PARK
(local authority run)
park/reserve

Established: *1990*
Address: *Derryhubbert Rd, Dungannon, Co. Tyrone*

Telephone: *(0762) 851102.* Fax: *(0762) 851821*
Access: (road) *M1*
Parking capacity: (cars) *250*
Season: *all year*
Hours: *May to Sept – 9am to 8pm; Mar, Apr and Oct – 9am to 7pm; Nov to Feb – 9am to 5pm. Daily except Christmas Day*
Admission (1992): *free*
No. visitors (1992): *110 000 (est.)*

Facilities
Interpretation: *videos; leaflets; information boards; slides; maps; tour guides*
Schools: *maximum no. 50; educational literature; audio/visual presentation; lecture/talk*
Disabled: *easy access; disabled toilets*
Catering: *3 picnic areas*
Retailing: *postcards/inexpensive souvenirs; craftwork; books*
No. shops: *1*

Operations
Contact: *Mr K Stanfield (Warden)*
No. employees: (high season) *8 full time; 4 part time* (low season) *8 full time; 1 part time*
Training: *F/T management, P/T management and casual management are trained in-house and externally and on specific courses and day-to-day on job*

Marketing
Annual event(s): *seasonal programmes*
Other: *press office; market research*
UK promotion: *television; national newspapers; radio; local newspapers; regional tourist board; other attractions; leaflets/information packs*

PECKFORTON CASTLE
(limited company)
historic house; castle; film and television location

Established: *1990*
Address: *Stone House Lane, Peckforton, Tarporley, Ches*
Telephone: *(0829) 260930.* Fax: *(0829) 261230*
Access: (road) *M6/M56/M53/A49/A41/A534* (rail) *Chester/Crewe*
Parking capacity: (cars) *400* (coaches) *20*
Hours: *Easter to Sept – 10am to 6pm daily*
Admission (1992): *adults £2.50; children £1.50; OAP £1.50; student £1.50; group rate £1.00*
No. visitors (1992): *30 000 (est.)*

Facilities
Interpretation: *videos; leaflets; information boards; slides; personnel*
Children: *nappy changing*
Schools: *maximum no. 100; general history tour*
Disabled: *disabled toilets*
Catering: *1 bar/public house*
Retailing: *postcards/inexpensive souvenirs; confectionery and ice cream; craftwork; books*
No. shops: *2*

Operations
Contacts: *G Lyndon Jones (Operations Manager); L Bond (PA to owner); E Graybill (owner/Director)*
No. employees: (high season) *10 full time; 3 part time* (low season) *5 full time; 2 part time*
Training: *F/T operations staff, F/T management, P/T operations staff and casual operations staff are trained in-house and day-to-day on job using videos and lectures and seminars*

Marketing
Market research
UK promotion: *national newspapers; local newspapers; regional tourist board; other attractions; leaflets/information packs; numerous; ETB/BTA*

Environmental monitoring: *waste; energy consumption; hazardous materials; chemical usage*

PECORAMA
(limited company)
theme park; garden; broadly based tourist attraction centred around railway theme

Established: *1974*
Address: *Underleys, Beer, Nr Seaton, Devon, EX12 3NA*
Telephone: *(0297) 21542.* Fax: *(0297) 20229*
Access: (road) *M5/A3052* (rail) *Axminster*
Parking capacity: (cars) *400* (coaches) *6*
Season: *all year*
Hours: *Easter to Oct – Mon to Fri – 10am to 5.30pm, Sat – 10am to 1pm*
Admission (1992): *adults £2.60; children £1.10; OAP £2.35*
No. visitors (1992): *77 000 (est.)*

Facilities
Interpretation: *leaflets; guide books*
Children: *adventure playground; play area; nappy changing*
Schools: *maximum no. 200; educational literature*
Disabled: *easy access; disabled toilets; wheelchair*
Catering: *1 bar/public house*
Retailing: *postcards/inexpensive souvenirs; confectionery and ice cream; books; clothes; railway related goods; film, glass items, toys*
No. shops: *3*

Operations
Contacts: *S C Pritchard (Chairman); V Quick (Personnel Manager); M Ridgers (Tourism Site Manager)*
No. employees: (high season) *18 full time; 21 part time* (low season) *8 full time*
Training: *F/T operations staff, F/T management and P/T operations staff are trained in-house and externally and on specific courses and day-to-day on job*
Languages spoken: *French; German*

Marketing
Affiliations: *WCTB*
Other: *market research*
UK promotion: *local newspapers; regional tourist board; other attractions; leaflets/information packs*
Europe/Australia/USA promotion: Continental Modeller

PEMBROKE CASTLE
(trust)
castle

Established: *1900*
Address: *Pembroke, Dyfed, SA71 4LA*
Telephone: *(0646) 681510*
Access: (road) *A477/A4139/A4075* (rail) *Pembroke*
Season: *all year*
Hours: *1 Apr to 30 Sept – 9.30am to 6.00pm; Mar and Oct 10am to 5pm; Nov to Feb 10am to 4pm. Closed Christmas Day, Boxing Day and New Year's Day*
Admission (1992): *adults £2.00; children £1.20; OAP £1.20; family ticket (2 + 2) £6.00*
No. visitors (1992): *120 000*

Facilities
Interpretation: *videos; tour guides; guide books*
Languages: *Dutch; French; German; Italian*
Children: *nappy changing*
Schools: *educational literature*
Disabled: *disabled toilets*
Catering: *1 picnic area*
Retailing: *postcards/inexpensive souvenirs; confectionery and ice cream; books; reproductions of famous artefacts*
No. shops: *1*

Operations
Contact: *I B Ramsden (Sec/Manager)*
No. employees: (high season) *6 full time; 3 part time* (low season) *2 full time; 5 part time*
Languages spoken: *French*

Marketing
Annual event(s): *British Legion days, army days*
UK promotion: *local newspapers; regional tourist board; leaflets/information packs*

Environmental monitoring: *recycling; waste; water quality*

PENCARROW
(trust)
historic house; garden

Established: *1974*
Address: *Bodmin, Cornwall, PL30 3AG*
Telephone: *(020884) 449*
Access: (road) *M4/M5/A389/A30/B3266* (rail) *Bodmin Parkway*
Parking capacity: (cars) *120* (coaches) *3*
Hours: *Easter to 15 Oct – 1.30pm to 5pm daily except Fri and Sat (1 June to 10 Sept and BH – open at 11am)*
Admission (1992): *adults £3.00; children £1.50; price includes house and garden*
No. visitors (1992): *16 000 (est.)*

Facilities
Interpretation: *tour guides; guide books*
Languages: *Dutch; French; German; Italian; Spanish*
Children: *play area*
Schools: *maximum no. 80; educational literature*
Disabled: *easy access; disabled toilets; helpers; special tours for partially sighted and blind*
Catering: *1 picnic area*
Retailing: *postcards/inexpensive souvenirs; confectionery and ice cream; craftwork; books; plants*
No. shops: *1*

Operations
Contacts: *Mr D Russell (Administrator); Mrs Russell; Lady Molesworth-St Aubyn*
No. employees: (high season) *4 full time; 19 part time* (low season) *4 full time; 19 part time*
Training: *casual operations staff are trained in-house and day-to-day on job*

Marketing
Affiliations: *HHA, Cornwall Association of Tourist Attractions*
Other: *market research*
UK promotion: *local newspapers; other attractions; leaflets/information packs*

PENDLE HERITAGE CENTRE
(trust)
historic house; heritage centre

Established: *1977*
Address: *Park Hill, Barrowford, Nelson, Lancs, BB9 6JQ*
Telephone: *(0282) 695366.* Fax: *(0282) 611718*
Access: (road) *M65* (rail) *Nelson*
Parking capacity: (cars) *100* (coaches) *3*
Season: *all year*
Hours: *10am to 5pm daily*
No. visitors (1992): *19 000*

Facilities
Interpretation: *videos; leaflets; information boards; slides; maps; tour guides; guide books*
Languages: *by request*
Schools: *maximum no. 100; educational literature; educational tour; lecture/talk*
Disabled: *easy access; disabled toilets*
Catering: *1 picnic area*
Retailing: *postcards/inexpensive souvenirs; confectionery and ice cream; craftwork; books*
No. shops: *1*

Operations
Contact: *E M J Miller (Director)*
No. employees: (high season) *7 full time; 8 part time* (low season) *7 full time; 8 part time*
Training: *F/T operations staff, F/T management, P/T operations staff, P/T management, casual operations staff and casual management are trained in-house and externally and on specific courses and day-to-day on job using special notes*
Languages spoken: *French*

Marketing
Annual event(s): *open gardens*
Other: *market research*
UK promotion: *local newspapers; regional
tourist board; leaflets/information packs;
ETB/BTA*

PENNYARCADIA
(limited company)
museum

Established: *1982*
Address: *Market Place, Pocklington, York,
YO4 2AR*
Telephone: *(0759) 303420*
Access: (road) *A1079*
Hours: *June to Aug – 10am to 5pm; May and
Sept – 12.30pm to 5pm; open at other times by
arrangement*
Admission (1992): *adults £3.00; children £2.00;
OAP £2.00; student £3.00; group rates £2.00
(adults) £1.50 (OAP and children)*
No. visitors (1992): *4000 (est.)*

Facilities
Interpretation: *slides; tour guides; personnel;
audio/visual presentation*
Schools: *maximum no. 150; audio/visual
presentation; lecture/talk*
Disabled: *easy access; helpers*
Retailing: *postcards/inexpensive souvenirs;
confectionery and ice cream; books*
No. shops: *1*

Operations
Contacts: *P Gresnam (Managing Director);
J Gresnam (Secretary)*
No. employees: (high season) *6 part time*
Training: *P/T operations staff are trained
in-house and day-to-day on job using
handbooks*
Languages spoken: *French*

Marketing
Affiliations: *AIM, Destination Humberside*
Other: *market research*
UK promotion: *local newspapers; regional tourist
board; other attractions; leaflets/information
packs*
Europe promotion: *leaflets/brochures*

Environmental monitoring: *recycling*

PENRHYN CASTLE
(trust)
historic house; castle; museum; gallery; industrial
railway museum

Established: *1952*
Address: *Bangor, Gwynedd, LL57 4HN*
Telephone: *(0248) 353084*
Access: (road) *A55/A5*
Parking capacity: (cars) *300* (coaches) *8*
Hours: *Apr to Oct – 12 noon to 5pm daily
(July and Aug –from 11am). Grounds – 10am
to 6pm*
Admission (1992): *adults £4.20; children
£2.10; family ticket £10.50; group rates
available*
No. visitors (1992): *78 586*

Facilities
Interpretation: *leaflets; audio tapes; guide books;
Braille guide and room stewards*
Languages: *Dutch; French; German; Welsh*
Children: *adventure playground; nappy changing*
Schools: *maximum no. 30; educational literature*
Disabled: *easy access; disabled toilets; Braille/
sound posts; special signs; powered transport;
leaflets; loop tape guide*
Catering: *6 picnic areas*
Retailing: *postcards/inexpensive souvenirs;
confectionery and ice cream; craftwork; books;
clothes; castle design products*
No. shops: *2*

Operations
No. employees: (high season) *11 full time; 85 part
time* (low season) *11 full time*

Training: *F/T operations staff, F/T management,
P/T operations staff, P/T management and
casual operations staff are trained in-house and
externally and on specific courses and
day-to-day on job*
Languages spoken: *French*

Marketing
Annual event(s): *Penllaw, country fair, remote
control model day*
Affiliations: *Spectators Guide to Snowdonia*
Other: *press office; market research*
UK promotion: *local newspapers; regional tourist
board; other attractions; leaflets/information
packs; Wales Tourist Board leaflets; Wales
Tourist Board*

PENSTHORPE WATERFOWL TRUST
(trust)
park/reserve; zoo/wildlife attraction

Established: *1988*
Address: *Fakenham, Norfolk, NR21 0LN*
Telephone: *(0328) 851465*. Fax: *(0328) 855905*
Access: (road) *A1067*
Parking capacity: (cars) *200* (coaches) *6*
Hours: *Apr to Dec – daily; Jan to Mar – Sat and
Sun. Summer – 11am to 5pm; winter – 11am to
5pm*
Admission (1992): *adults £3.50; children £1.60;
OAP £3.00; parties £2.50 (adults) £1.30
(children)*
No. visitors (1992): *60 000 (est.)*

Facilities
Interpretation: *videos; leaflets; information
boards; maps; tour guides; guide books;
signs*
Children: *adventure playground; nappy changing*
Schools: *maximum no. 120; educational literature;
audio/visual presentation; school room*
Disabled: *easy access; disabled toilets; Braille/
sound posts; helpers; other audio facilities;
special signs; wheelchairs on loan*
Catering: *1 picnic area*
Franchisees: *Apr to Dec – daily; Jan to Mar – Sat
and Sun*
Retailing: *postcards/inexpensive souvenirs;
craftwork; books; decoy ducks; paintings,
prints, china*
No. shops: *1*

Operations
Contacts: *David North (Director, Education and
Conservation); W M Matins (Director)*
No. employees: (high season) *7 full time;
12 part time* (low season) *7 full time; 4 part
time*
Training: *F/T operations staff and F/T
management are trained in-house and externally
and on specific courses*

Marketing
Annual event(s): *various*
Sponsor(s): *various*
Other: *market research*
UK promotion: *local newspapers; regional tourist
board; other attractions; leaflets/information
packs*
Europe promotion: *twinned with Belgium site*

Environmental monitoring: *recycling; energy
consumption; chemical usage; transport; diesel
vehicles*

PEOPLE'S PALACE MUSEUM
(local authority run)
museum

Established: *1898*
Address: *Glasgow Green, Glasgow*
Telephone: *(041) 554 0223*. Fax: *(041) 550 0892*
Season: *all year*
Hours: *Mon to Sat – 10am to 5pm; Sun – 11am
to 5pm*
Admission (1992): *free*
No. visitors (1992): *298 668*

Facilities
Interpretation: *leaflets; information boards; guide
books*
Languages: *Urdu*
Children: *nappy changing*
Schools: *museum education dept services*
Disabled: *easy access*
Catering: *1 self-service cafeteria*
Retailing: *postcards/inexpensive souvenirs; books;
posters*
No. shops: *1*

Operations
Training: *F/T operations staff and F/T
management are trained in-house and on
specific courses and day-to-day on job*
Languages spoken: *French*

Marketing
Press office

Environmental monitoring: *recycling; waste;
water quality; energy consumption;
various*

PERCIVAL DAVID FOUNDATION OF CHINESE
ART
(university museum)
museum; University of London School of Oriental
and African Studies

Established: *1952*
Address: *53 Gordon Square, London, WC1H 0PD*
Telephone: *(071) 387 3909*. Fax: *(071) 383 5163*
Access: (rail) *Russell Square*
Hours: *Mon to Fri – 10.30am to 5pm. Closed
Maundy Thur to Easter Mon and Christmas to
New Year*
No. visitors (1992): *6000 (est.)*

Facilities
Interpretation: *leaflets; guide books; exhibitions*
Languages: *Chinese*
Schools: *maximum no. 20; no special support;
must be booked*
Disabled: *disabled toilets; lift to galleries*
Retailing: *postcards/inexpensive souvenirs; books;
clothes; slides of exhibits*
No. shops: *1*

Operations
Contact: *Ms R Scott (Curator)*
No. employees: (high season) *10 full time; 1 part
time*

Marketing
UK promotion: *leaflets/information packs*

PETER PAN'S PLAYGROUND
(limited company)
theme park

Established: *1976*
Address: *Western Esplanade, Southend on Sea,
Essex, SS1 1EE*
Telephone: *(0702) 468023*. Fax: *(0702) 601044*
Access: (road) *M25/A127/A13* (rail) *Southend*
Hours: *Jan, Feb and Mar – weekends – 11am to
5pm weather permitting; Apr to Sept – 11am to
10pm daily; Oct and Nov – weekends – 11am
to 5pm*
Admission (1992): *free*
No. visitors (1992): *1 000 000 (est.)*

Facilities
Interpretation: *leaflets; information boards; guide
books*
Children: *adventure playground; play area*
Schools: *lecture/talk*
Disabled: *easy access; disabled toilets*
Catering: *2 picnic areas*
Retailing: *postcards/inexpensive souvenirs;
confectionery and ice cream; T-shirts; soft toys
and novelties*
No. shops: *1*

Operations
Contacts: *Mr P Miller (Managing Director);
Mr M Miller (Manager); Mrs M Melvin
(Administration); Mrs S Morris (PR
promotions)*
No. employees: *(high season) 150 full time; 50
part time (low season) 25 full time; 25 part time*
Training: *F/T operations staff, F/T management
and P/T operations staff are trained in-house
and day-to-day on job*
Languages spoken: *French; Italian; Spanish;
Chinese*

Marketing
Market research
UK promotion: *national newspapers; radio; local
newspapers; regional tourist board; leaflets/
information packs; ETB/BTA*

PETER SCOTT GALLERY
(university funded)
gallery

Established: *1988*
Address: *Lancaster University, Lancaster, LA1
4YW*
Telephone: *(0524) 65201 ext 3182. Fax: (0524)
63806*
Access: *(road) M6/A6 (rail) Lancaster*
Hours: *termtime only – Mon to Fri – 11am to
5pm (also Thur – 6pm to 8.30pm)*
Admission (1992): *free*
No. visitors (1992): *13 000 (est.)*

Facilities
Interpretation: *leaflets; information boards; maps*
Schools: *maximum no. 30; lecture/talk;
occasional worksheets*
Disabled: *easy access; disabled toilets; chairlift to
upper gallery*
Catering: *10 snack bars/food stalls*
Retailing: *postcards/inexpensive souvenirs;
confectionery and ice cream; books*
No. shops: *more than 4*

Operations
Contacts: *M Gavagan/A Rawlings (Gallery
Director/Gallery Assistant)*
No. employees: *(high season) 2 full time; 1 part
time (low season) 2 full time*
Training: *F/T operations staff, F/T management
and P/T operations staff are trained in-house
and externally and on specific courses and
day-to-day on job using special courses*

Marketing
Affiliation: *NW Museum Service*
Other: *press office*
UK promotion: *local newspapers; regional tourist
board; ETB/BTA; specialist art publications;
British Tourist Authority*

PETERBOROUGH CATHEDRAL
(cathedral)
church; visitor centre

Established: *655*
Address: *Minster Precincts, Peterborough,
PE1 1XX*
Telephone: *(0733) 343342. Fax: (0733) 52465*
Access: *(road) M11/A1/A47/A15 (rail)
Peterborough*
Season: *all year*
Hours: *cathedral – May to Sept – 7am to 8pm,
Oct to Apr – 7am to 6pm. Visitor centre –
Easter to end Oct – 11am to 3pm (Nov to
Easter – Sat only)*
Admission (1992): *adults £1.00; children £0.75;
OAP £0.75; student £0.75; charges for
visitor centre, cathedral free, group rates
available*
No. visitors (1992): *200 000*

Facilities
Interpretation: *leaflets; audio tapes; information
boards; maps; tour guides; guide books; hands
on models in visitor centre*
Languages: *French; German; Italian; Spanish*

Schools: *maximum no. 200; educational literature;
audio/visual presentation; lecture/talk;
experience day as a monk*
Disabled: *easy access; disabled toilets; Braille/
sound posts; helpers*
Catering: *1 picnic area*
Retailing: *postcards/inexpensive souvenirs;
confectionery and ice cream; craftwork; books;
reproductions of famous artefacts*
No. shops: *2*

Operations
Contacts: *Mr S Hession (Chapter Clerk); Mrs S
Gower (Shop Manageress)*
No. employees: *(high season) 15 full time; 26 part
time (low season) 15 full time; 26 part time*

Marketing
Annual event: *annual music festival*
Sponsor(s): *various*
Other: *market research*
UK promotion: *local newspapers; regional tourist
board; other attractions; leaflets/information
packs; ETB/BTA; Peterborough Tourism*

PETRIE MUSEUM OF EGYPTIAN
ARCHAEOLOGY
(university)
museum

Established: *1988*
Address: *University College London, Gower St,
London, WC1E 6BT*
Telephone: *(071) 387 7050. Fax: (071) 387 8057*
Hours: *Mon to Fri – 10am to 12 noon and 1.15pm
to 5pm. Closed Christmas, Easter and 4 weeks
in Summer*
Admission (1992): *free*
No. visitors (1992): *2000 (est.)*

Facilities
Interpretation: *guide books*
Retailing: *postcards/inexpensive souvenirs;
craftwork; books; reproductions of famous
artefacts*

Operations
Contacts: *Ms B Adams (Curator); Ms R Janssen
(Assistant Curator)*
No. employees: *(high season) 3 full time; 10 part
time*
Languages spoken: *French; German*

Marketing
Annual event(s): *Sat morning lectures, friends
activities*
Affiliations: *MA, Area Museums Council*
UK promotion: *national newspapers; local
newspapers; regional tourist board; leaflets/
information packs*
Europe/USA promotion: *leaflets/brochures*

Environmental monitoring: *environment and
ecology*

PETTITT'S FEATHERCRAFT AND ANIMAL
ADVENTURE PARK
(partnership)
zoo/wildlife attraction; childrens adventure park

Established: *1921*
Address: *Camphill, Reedham, Norwich, Norfolk,
NR13 3UA*
Telephone: *(0493) 700094. Fax: (0493) 701403*
Access: *(road) A47*
Parking capacity: *(cars) 500 (coaches) 20*
Hours: *Easter to end Oct – Sun to Fri – 10am to
5.30pm*
Admission (1992): *adults £4.50; children £3.50;
OAP £2.95; student £3.50*
No. visitors (1992): *110 000 (est.)*

Facilities
Interpretation: *videos; leaflets; information
boards; maps; guide books*
Children: *adventure playground; play area; nappy
changing*

Schools: *maximum no. 200; treasure hunt and
activities*
Disabled: *easy access; disabled toilets; helpers;
special signs; leaflets*
Catering: *1 picnic area*
Retailing: *postcards/inexpensive souvenirs;
confectionery and ice cream; craftwork; books;
feathercraft, candles, carving*
No. shops: *4*

Operations
Contacts: *Mr T Kay (Director); Ms H Wright
(Company Secretary)*
No. employees: *(high season) 20 full time; 32 part
time (low season) 10 full time; 4 part time*
Training: *F/T operations staff, F/T management
and P/T operations staff are trained in-house
and day-to-day on job*
Languages spoken: *French*

Marketing
Annual event(s): *classic car shows, treasure hunts,
etc.*
Other: *market research*
UK promotion: *radio; local newspapers; regional
tourist board; other attractions;
leaflets/information packs*

Environmental monitoring: *chemical usage;
temperature and humidity*

PICKFORD'S HOUSE MUSEUM
(local authority run)
historic house; museum

Established: *1988*
Address: *41 Friar St, Derby, DE1 1DA*
Telephone: *(0332) 255363*
Access: *(road) M1/A52 (rail) Derby Midland*
Parking capacity: *(cars) 20*
Season: *all year*
Hours: *Mon – 11am to 5pm, Tues to Sat – 10am
to 5pm, Sun and BH – 2pm to 5pm. Closed
Christmas holidays*
Admission (1992): *adults £0.30; children £0.10;
OAP £0.10; student £0.10*
No. visitors (1992): *20 282*

Facilities
Interpretation: *leaflets; information boards*
Schools: *maximum no. 35; lecture/talk; by
appointment and activities*
Disabled: *easy access; ground floor only*
Retailing: *postcards/inexpensive souvenirs*
No. shops: *1*

Operations
Contact: *Ms D Moss (Keeper of Decorative Arts)*
No. employees: *(high season) 3 full time; 2 part
time (low season) 3 full time; 2 part time*
Training: *F/T operations staff, F/T management,
P/T operations staff, P/T management, casual
operations staff and casual management are
trained in-house and externally and on specific
courses and day-to-day on job using videos and
handbooks*

Marketing
Annual event(s): *family days, carnival day and
holiday activities*
Sponsor(s): *various*
Affiliation: *E Mids Museums Service*
Other: *PR company: Welding Woodhead, 44
George St, Edgbaston, Birmingham; market
research*
UK promotion: *radio; local newspapers; regional
tourist board; leaflets/information packs; ETB/
BTA*

PILKINGTON GLASS MUSEUM
(plc)
museum; gallery

Established: *1964*
Address: *Prescot Rd, St Helens, Lancs, WA10
3TT*
Telephone: *(0744) 692499*
Access: *(road) M6/M62/A58 (rail) St Helens
Central*

Season: *all year*
Hours: *Mon to Fri – 10am to 5pm, Sat, Sun and BH – 2pm to 4.30pm*
Admission (1992): *free*
No. visitors (1992): *35 000 (est.)*

Facilities
Interpretation: *videos; leaflets; information boards; maps*
Languages: *French; German*
Schools: *maximum no. 50; educational literature*
Disabled: *disabled toilets*
Catering: *1 picnic area*
Franchisees: *all year – Mon to Fri – 10am to 5pm, Sat, Sun and BH – 2pm to 4.30pm*
Retailing: *postcards/inexpensive souvenirs; craftwork; books*
No. shops: *1*

Operations
Contact: *I M Burgoyne (Curator)*
No. employees: *(high season) 3 full time; 5 part time (low season) 3 full time; 5 part time*

Marketing
Annual event(s): *exhibitions*
Affiliation: *Museums Association*
Other: *press office*
UK promotion: *local newspapers; regional tourist board; other attractions; leaflets/information packs*

PLAS NEWYDD
(trust)
historic house; garden; museum; gallery

Established: *1976*
Address: *Llanfairpwll, Anglesey, Gwynedd*
Telephone: *(0248) 714795*
Access: *(road) A4080 (rail) Llanfairpwll*
Parking capacity: *(cars) 100 (coaches) 4*
Hours: *Apr to Sept – Sun to Fri – 12am to 5pm; Oct – Fri to Sun – 12am to 5pm*
Admission (1992): *adults £3.50; children £1.75; groups of 20 and over £2.80*
No. visitors (1992): *53 000*

Facilities
Interpretation: *leaflets; guide books*
Languages: *Dutch; French; German*
Children: *adventure playground; nappy changing*
Schools: *maximum no. 60; educational literature*
Disabled: *easy access; disabled toilets; Braille/ sound posts; guide book*
Catering: *1 picnic area*
Retailing: *postcards/inexpensive souvenirs; craftwork; books*
No. shops: *1*

Operations
Training: *casual operations staff are trained in-house and day-to-day on job*

Marketing
Annual event(s): *various*
Other: *market research*
UK promotion: *local newspapers; regional tourist board; leaflets/information packs; Wales Tourist Board*
Europe/USA promotion: *leaflets/brochures; travel agents' brochures; British Tourist Authority*

Environmental monitoring: *recycling; waste; energy consumption; hazardous materials*

PLEASURE BEACH
(private limited company)
leisure amusement park

Established: *1930*
Address: *South Beach Parade, Great Yarmouth, Norfolk, NR30 3EH*
Telephone: *(0493) 844585.* Fax: *(0493) 853483*
Access: *(road) M11/M12/A11/A47*
Hours: *Apr – Sun and BH; May – Aug – 11am to 10pm, Sept – 11am to 6pm (open later at weekends)*
Admission (1992): *ride by tokens, all day passes £10.00 or £6.00*
No. visitors (1992): *2 000 000 (est.)*

Facilities
Interpretation: *leaflets; information boards*
Children: *play area; nappy changing*
Schools: *no special support*
Disabled: *easy access; disabled toilets; helpers; leaflets*
Catering: *3 snack bars/food stalls*
Retailing: *postcards/inexpensive souvenirs; confectionery and ice cream; clothes*
No. shops: *2*

Operations
Contacts: *Mr J Jones (Managing Director); Mr J Caldon (General Manager); Mr J Ashton (Head of Administration and Marketing)*
No. employees: *(high season) 200 full time (low season) 20 full time*
Training: *F/T operations staff, F/T management and casual operations staff are trained in-house and day-to-day on job using videos and handbooks*
Languages spoken: *French; Welsh*

Marketing
Affiliations: *Association of Leading Attractions, Norfolk Tourist Attractions Association, British Association of Leisure Parks*
Other: *press office; market research*
UK promotion: *national newspapers; radio; local newspapers; other attractions; leaflets/ information packs; ETB/BTA*

Environmental monitoring: *hazardous materials; chemical usage; environmental control*

PLEASUREWOOD HILLS AMERICAN THEME PARK
(limited company)
theme park

Established: *1982*
Address: *Corton, Lowestoft, Suffolk, NR32 5DZ*
Telephone: *(0502) 508200.* Fax: *(0502) 567393*
Access: *(road) A12*
Parking capacity: *(cars) 5000 (coaches) 100*
Hours: *May to Oct, Easter and BH – from 10am daily*
Admission (1992): *adults £8.50; children £8.50; OAP £5.00; student £8.50; disabled £5.00*
No. visitors (1992): *450 000 (est.)*

Facilities
Interpretation: *leaflets; information boards; maps; guide books*
Children: *adventure playground; play area; nappy changing*
Schools: *educational literature*
Disabled: *easy access; disabled toilets*
Catering: *5 picnic areas*
Retailing: *postcards/inexpensive souvenirs; confectionery and ice cream; craftwork; books; clothes*
No. shops: *more than 4*

Operations
Contacts: *Mr P Hadden (Operations Director); Ms S Fitzgerald; Mr M Wilson; Ms M Kidner (Marketing Executive)*
No. employees: *(high season) 300 full time; 50 part time (low season) 10 full time*
Training: *F/T operations staff, P/T operations staff and casual operations staff are trained in-house and day-to-day on job using videos*
Languages spoken: *French*

Marketing
Annual event(s): *Wood's airshow, birthday and firework finale*
Sponsor(s): *charity events*
Affiliations: *BACPA*
Other: *PR company: Mike Salter Communications, 3 Hall lane, Wramplington, Norfolk; market research*
UK promotion: *television; radio; local newspapers; regional tourist board; other attractions; leaflets/information packs; ETB/ BTA*

Environmental monitoring: *recycling; waste; water quality; energy consumption*

PLYMOUTH DOME
(local authority run)
heritage centre

Established: *1989*
Address: *The Hoe, Plymouth, Devon, PL1 2NZ*
Telephone: *(0752) 603300.* Fax: *(0752) 600608*
Access: *(road) M5/A38 (rail) Plymouth*
Season: *all year*
No. visitors (1992): *180 000*

Facilities
Interpretation: *videos; leaflets; audio tapes; information boards; slides; maps; guide books; personnel; audio/visual*
Languages: *French; German; Spanish*
Children: *nappy changing*
Schools: *maximum no. 200; teachers packs*
Disabled: *easy access; disabled toilets; helpers; other audio facilities; leaflets; guide book*
Catering: *1 self-service cafeteria*
Retailing: *postcards/inexpensive souvenirs; craftwork; books; clothes; reproductions of famous artefacts; pictures*
No. shops: *1*

Operations
Contact: *Mr J Ford (Manager)*
No. employees: *(high season) 26 full time; 4 part time (low season) 18 full time; 2 part time*
Training: *F/T operations staff, F/T management, P/T operations staff and casual operations staff are trained in-house and on specific courses and day-to-day on job using handbooks*

Marketing
PR Company: *Chris Neal Consultancy, Quayside House, Newham Rd, Truro, Cornwall, TR1 2DP; market research*
UK promotion: *television; radio; local newspapers; regional tourist board; other attractions; leaflets/information packs; local tourist boards; ETB/BTA*
Europe promotion: *British Tourist Authority*

POLESDEN LACEY
(trust)
historic house

Established: *1944*
Address: *The National Trust, Polesden Lacey, Dorking, Surrey, RH5 6BD*
Telephone: *(0372) 452046/458203*
Access: *(road) M25/A246 (rail) Great Bookham/ Boxhill and West Humble*
Parking capacity: *(cars) 900 (coaches) 5*
Season: *all year*
Hours: *Apr to Oct – Wed to Sun – 1.30pm to 5.30pm, BH – 11am to 5.30pm; Mar and Nov – Sat and Sun – 1.30pm to 4.30pm, BH – 11am to 5.30pm. Grounds – 11am to 6pm daily*
Admission (1992): *adults £2.50; children £1.25; OAP £2.50; student £2.50; group rates*
No. visitors (1992): *205 000*

Facilities
Interpretation: *leaflets; information boards; maps; guide books*
Languages: *Dutch; French; German*
Children: *nappy changing*
Schools: *maximum no. 30; educational literature; children's quiz*
Disabled: *easy access; disabled toilets; Braille/ sound posts; powered transport; leaflets*
Catering: *1 picnic area*
Retailing: *postcards/inexpensive souvenirs; confectionery and ice cream; craftwork; books; clothes; reproductions of famous artefacts; tea towels, china, toys, etc.; local crafts*
No. shops: *2*

Operations
Contact: *J F V Vandelever-Boorer (Administrator)*
No. employees: *(high season) 15 full time; 2 part time (low season) 15 full time; 2 part time*
Training: *F/T operations staff, F/T management, P/T operations staff and casual operations staff are trained in-house and on specific courses*
Languages spoken: *French; German; Italian; Spanish*

Marketing
Annual event(s): *open air theatre*
Other: *press office; market research*
UK promotion: *radio; local newspapers; regional tourist board; other attractions; leaflets/ information packs; ETB/BTA*

Environmental monitoring: *energy consumption; water consumption*

POLLOCK'S TOY MUSEUM
(trust)
museum

Established: *1955*
Address: *1 Scala St, London, W1P 1LT*
Telephone: *(071) 636 3452*
Access: (road) *Tottenham Court Road* (rail) *Goodge Street*
Season: *all year*
Hours: *Mon to Sat – 10am to 5pm. Closed BH*
Admission (1992): *adults £1.50; children £0.50; OAP £1.50; student £1.50*

Facilities
Interpretation: *videos; leaflets; information boards*
Children: *nappy changing*
Schools: *maximum no. 30; no special support*
Retailing: *postcards/inexpensive souvenirs; books; toy theatres*
No. shops: *1*

Operations
Contacts: *Mr J Fawdry (Director); Ms V Sheppard (Curator); Ms G Warden (Manager)*
No. employees: (high season) *3 full time; 2 part time* (low season) *3 full time; 2 part time*

Marketing
Annual event(s): *toy theatre performances*
Affiliation: *MA*
UK promotion: *leaflets/information packs; ETB/ BTA*
Europe/USA promotion: *British Tourist Authority*

Environmental monitoring: *recycling; waste*

POLLOK HOUSE
(local authority run)
historic house

Established: *1967*
Address: *Pollok Country Park, Glasgow, G43 1AT*
Telephone: *(041) 632 0274*
Access: (road) *M8*
Season: *all year*
Admission (1992): *free*
No. visitors (1992): *148 250*

Facilities
Interpretation: *leaflets; information boards; tour guides; guide books*
Languages: *Urdu*
Children: *nappy changing*
Schools: *museum education dept services*
Catering: *1 picnic area*
Retailing: *postcards/inexpensive souvenirs; craftwork; books; reproductions of famous artefacts; stationery and jewellery*
No. shops: *1*

Operations
Training: *F/T operations staff and F/T management are trained in-house and on specific courses and day-to-day on job*
Languages spoken: *French; German; Italian; Spanish*

Marketing
Press office; market research
UK promotion: *leaflets/information packs*

PONSONBY FARM PARK
(partnership)
open working farm

Established: *1988*
Address: *Cumrey Kitchen, Ponsonby, Seascale, Cumbria*
Telephone: *(0946) 841426*
Access: (road) *M6/A595* (rail) *Seascale*
Parking capacity: (cars) *60* (coaches) *4*
Hours: *May to Nov – Tues to Sun – 10.30am to 5pm*
Admission (1992): *adults £1.80; children £0.90; group discounts*
No. visitors (1992): *9000 (est.)*

Facilities
Interpretation: *leaflets; information boards; maps; tour guides; guide books*
Children: *play area*
Schools: *maximum no. 80; educational literature*
Catering: *2 picnic areas*
Retailing: *postcards/inexpensive souvenirs; confectionery and ice cream; craftwork*
No. shops: *1*

Operations
Contacts: *David Stanley (Partner); Miss Cathy Miller (Partner)*
No. employees: (high season) *1 full time; 3 part time* (low season) *1 full time*

Marketing
UK promotion: *local newspapers; regional tourist board; other attractions; leaflets/information packs*

PONTEFRACT CASTLE
(local authority run)
castle

Address: *The Chain, Pontefract*
Telephone: *(0977) 600208*
Access: (road) *M62* (rail) *Pontefract*
Season: *all year*
Hours: *times seasonal*
Admission (1992): *free*
No. visitors (1992): *35 000 (est.)*

Facilities
Interpretation: *visitor centre*
Schools: *maximum no. 40; educational literature; lecture/talk; activities and sports*
Disabled: *easy access; disabled toilets*
Retailing: *postcards/inexpensive souvenirs; books; reproductions of famous artefacts; prints and posters*
No. shops: *1*

Operations
Contact: *Ms M Sanderson (Administrator)*
No. employees: (high season) *1 full time; 3 part time* (low season) *1 full time; 1 part time*
Training: *F/T operations staff, P/T operations staff and casual operations staff are trained in-house and on specific courses and day-to-day on job*

Marketing
Annual event(s): *venue for events*
Other: *press office*
UK promotion: *local newspapers; regional tourist board; other attractions; leaflets/information packs; ETB/BTA*

PONTEFRACT MUSEUM
(local authority run)
museum

Established: *1979*
Address: *Salter Row, Pontefract*
Telephone: *(0977) 797289*
Access: (road) *M62* (rail) *Pontefract*
Season: *all year*
Hours: *Mon to Sat – 10.30am to 5pm, Sun – 2.30pm to 5pm, open BH except Christmas and New Year*
Admission (1992): *free*

No. visitors (1992): *35 000 (est.)*

Facilities
Interpretation: *leaflets; information boards; displays and exhibitions*
Languages: *French; German*
Children: *nappy changing*
Schools: *maximum no. 40; educational literature; audio/visual presentation; lecture/talk; projects and animators*
Retailing: *postcards/inexpensive souvenirs; books; reproductions of famous artefacts; prints*
No. shops: *1*

Operations
Contacts: *Ms M Sanderson (Administrator)*
No. employees: (high season) *3 full time; 3 part time* (low season) *3 full time; 3 part time*
Training: *F/T operations staff, F/T management, P/T operations staff, P/T management, casual operations staff and casual management are trained in-house and externally and on specific courses*

Marketing
Annual event(s): *acts as a venue*
Other: *press office*
UK promotion: *local newspapers; other attractions; leaflets/information packs; ETB/ BTA*

Environmental monitoring: *recycling; hazardous materials*

PONTYPOOL AND BLAENAVON RAILWAY
(limited company)
preserved railway

Established: *1984*
Address: *c/o Council Offices, Lion St, Blaenavon, Gwent*
Access: (road) *M4/A4043* (rail) *Abergavenny*
Parking capacity: (cars) *70* (coaches) *30*
Hours: *Apr to Sept – Sun and BH Mon; also Santa specials in Dec*
Admission (1992): *adults £1.50; children £0.80; family ticket £4.00*
No. visitors (1992): *7000 (est.)*

Facilities
Catering: *1 snack bar/food stall*
Retailing: *postcards/inexpensive souvenirs; books; pens, pencils, bookmarks, etc.*
No. shops: *1*

Operations
Languages spoken: *French; Dutch*

Marketing
Annual event(s): *Thomas the Tank Engine weekends and Santa special weekends*
Affiliation: *Association of Railway Preservation Societies*
Other: *press office*
UK promotion: *local newspapers; regional tourist board; other attractions; leaflets/information packs*

Environmental monitoring: *recycling; hazardous materials*

POOLE POTTERY
(limited company)
heritage centre

Established: *1925*
Address: *The Quay, Poole, Dorset, BH15 1RF*
Telephone: *(0202) 668681.* Fax: *(0202) 682894*
Access: (road) *A350*
Hours: *Mar, Oct, Nov and Dec – 10am to 4pm daily; Apr to Sept – 10am to 4.30pm daily*
Admission (1992): *free*
No. visitors (1992): *330 806*

Facilities
Interpretation: *videos; information boards; personnel*

Schools: *maximum no. 100; no special support*
Catering: *1 self-service cafeteria*
Retailing: *postcards/inexpensive souvenirs;*
pottery seconds
No. shops: *1*

Operations
Contact: *Mr K Childs (Retail Manager)*
No. employees: (high season) *15 full time;*
30 part time (low season) *9 full time; 18 part*
time
Training: *F/T operations staff, P/T operations*
staff and casual operations staff are trained
in-house and day-to-day on job

Marketing
Market research
UK promotion: *leaflets/information packs*
Europe promotion: *British Tourist Authority*

POOLE'S CAVERN
(limited company)
park/reserve; museum; show cave and country
park

Established: *1977*
Address: *Green Lane, Buxton, Derbys, SK17 9DH*
Telephone: *(0298) 26918*
Access: (road) *M6/A515/A54*
Parking capacity: (cars) *60* (coaches) *6*
Hours: *Easter to end Oct – 10am to 5pm. Closed*
Wed – Apr, May and Oct
Admission (1992): *adults £3.00; children £1.50;*
OAP £2.40; student £2.40; reductions for
booked parties
No. visitors (1992): *45 000*

Facilities
Interpretation: *videos; information boards; tour*
guides; guide books
Languages: *Dutch; French; German; Spanish*
Schools: *educational literature; audio/visual*
presentation; tour with guide
Disabled: *disabled toilets; wheelchairs available*
Catering: *2 picnic areas*
Retailing: *postcards/inexpensive souvenirs;*
confectionery and ice cream; books;
reproductions of famous artefacts
No. shops: *1*

Operations
Contact: *Mr D Allsop (Country Park Warden)*
No. employees: (high season) *2 full time; 10 part*
time (low season) *2 full time*
Training: *F/T operations staff and P/T operations*
staff are trained externally and on specific
courses and day-to-day on job

Marketing
Affiliations: *various including natural history –*
conservation
Other: *market research*
UK promotion: *national newspapers; local*
newspapers; regional tourist board; other
attractions; leaflets/information packs; E Mids
Tourist Board; ETB/BTA; leaflet and brochure
distribution
Europe promotion: *leaflets/brochures; British*
Tourist Authority

Environmental monitoring: *hazardous materials;*
chemical usage; emissions

PORT LYMPNE ZOO PARK, MANSION AND
GARDENS
(trust)
zoo/wildlife attraction

Established: *1976*
Address: *Port Lympne, Lympne, Nr Hythe, Kent,*
CT21 4PD
Telephone: *(0303) 264647*. Fax: *(0303) 264944*
Access: (road) *M20/A20* (rail) *Ashford*
Season: *all year*
Hours: *10am to 5pm daily*
Admission (1992): *adults £6.50; children £4.50;*
OAP £4.50; student £2.25
No. visitors (1992): *100 000 (est.)*

Facilities
Interpretation: *videos; leaflets; information*
boards; tour guides; guide books; personnel
Languages: *Dutch; French; Spanish*
Children: *nappy changing*
Schools: *educational literature; audio/visual*
presentation; lecture/talk
Disabled: *disabled toilets*
Catering: *1 bar/public house*
Retailing: *postcards/inexpensive souvenirs;*
confectionery and ice cream; craftwork; books;
clothes
No. shops: *2*

Operations
Contacts: *R Boutwood/M Lockyer*
(Administrative Director/Animal Director);
S Sheather (Wages and Personnel Manager);
F Stringer/J Carauna (Gift Shop Manager/
Catering Manager); S Duff (Marketing Officer)
No. employees: (high season) *71 full time; 28 part*
time (low season) *64 full time; 10 part time*
Training: *F/T operations staff, P/T operations*
staff and casual operations staff are trained
in-house and externally and day-to-day on job
using handbooks
Languages spoken: *French*

Marketing
Other: *PR company: Boutwood Advertising, 37*
Terminus Road, Eastbourne, E Sussex; press
office; market research
UK promotion: *television; national newspapers;*
radio; local newspapers; regional tourist board;
other attractions; leaflets/information packs;
ETB/BTA
Europe promotion: *leaflets/brochures; British*
Tourist Authority

Environmental monitoring: *conservation of 8*
woods

PORT OF HARWICH MARITIME MUSEUM
(charity)
monument; museum

Established: *1972*
Address: *Harbour Crescent, Harwich, Essex*
Telephone: *(0255) 503429*. Fax: *(0255) 240404*
Access: (road) *A120* (rail) *Harwich*
Hours: *Easter to Oct – Sun – 10am to 12 noon*
and 2pm to 5pm
Admission (1992): *adults £0.50; OAP £0.50;*
student £0.50; accompanied children free
No. visitors (1992): *5000 (est.)*

Facilities
Interpretation: *leaflets; information boards; tour*
guides; guide books
Schools: *maximum no. 30; lecture/talk*
Disabled: *access difficult*

Operations
Contact: *Mr A Rutter (Secretary)*
Languages spoken: *French; German*

Marketing
Affiliation: *Civic Trust*
UK promotion: *regional tourist board; museum*
guides

Environmental monitoring: *recycling; water*
quality; hazardous materials

PORTLAND CASTLE
(quango)
castle; monument

Established: *1960*
Address: *Castle Town, Portland, Dorset,*
DT5 1AZ
Telephone: *(0305) 820539*
Access: (rail) *Weymouth*
Parking capacity: (cars) *40* (coaches) *5*
Hours: *Good Friday or 1 Apr to 30 Sept – 10am*
to 6pm daily
Admission (1992): *adults £1.10; children £0.55;*
OAP £0.85; student £0.85

No. visitors (1992): *16 500 (est.)*

Facilities
Interpretation: *leaflets; audio tapes; information*
boards; guide books
Languages: *Japanese; French; German*
Schools: *maximum no. 50; role playing materials*
Retailing: *postcards/inexpensive souvenirs;*
confectionery and ice cream; books;
reproductions of famous artefacts
No. shops: *1*

Operations
Contacts: *Ms N Turner/Ms C White (Custodian/*
Group Custodian); Ms M Davies (Personnel);
Ms S Fellows (Head of Trading); Mr N Weiss/
Mr J Griffin (Marketing/Marketing Director)
No. employees: (high season) *1 full time; 1 part*
time (low season) *1 full time; 1 part time*
Training: *F/T operations staff, F/T management,*
P/T operations staff, P/T management, casual
operations staff and casual management are
trained in-house and externally and on specific
courses and day-to-day on job and role playing
courses
Languages spoken: *French; German; Dutch*

Marketing
Annual event(s): *Elizabethan life school weeks,*
jazz festival
Sponsor(s): *jazz, local crime prevention panel*
Affiliations: *CADW, Historic Scotland, American*
Friends of English Heritage
Other: *press office; market research*
UK promotion: *national newspapers; local*
newspapers; regional tourist board; other
attractions; leaflets/information packs

Environmental monitoring: *recycling; waste;*
water quality; energy consumption; hazardous
materials; chemical usage; transport; emissions

PORTSMOUTH CATHEDRAL
(cathedral)
church

Established: *1188*
Address: *St Thomas's St, Portsmouth, Hants, PO1*
2HH
Telephone: *(0705) 823300*
Access: (road) *M27/M275*
Season: *all year*
Hours: *Sun to Fri – 6.30am to 6.30pm, Sat –*
9.30am to 6.30pm
Admission (1992): *free*
No. visitors (1992): *15 000 (est.)*

Facilities
Interpretation: *leaflets; information boards; guide*
books
Languages: *French; German*
Schools: *maximum no. 40; educational literature*
Disabled: *easy access*
Retailing: *postcards/inexpensive souvenirs; books*
No. shops: *1*

Operations
Contacts: *Mr B Jones (Administrator);*
Ms R Fairfax (Visitors Officer)

Marketing
Annual event(s): *concerts*

Environmental monitoring: *conservation of*
building

PORTSMOUTH SEA LIFE CENTRE
(limited company)
zoo/wildlife attraction

Established: *1986*
Address: *Clarence Esplanade, Southsea,*
Portsmouth, PO5 3PB
Telephone: *(0705) 734461*. Fax: *(0705) 294443*
Access: (road) *M27/M275* (rail) *Portsmouth*
Season: *all year*
Hours: *10am to 6pm daily (later in summer).*
Closed Christmas Day

Admission (1992): adults £3.95; children £2.85; OAP £3.10; disabled and schools £2.10

Facilities
Interpretation: videos; leaflets; audio tapes; information boards; tour guides; guide books
Languages: French; German
Children: adventure playground; play area; nappy changing
Schools: educational literature; audio/visual presentation; lecture/talk; projects touch pools
Disabled: easy access; disabled toilets
Catering: 1 picnic area
Retailing: postcards/inexpensive souvenirs; craftwork; books; clothes; fish related
No. shops: 1

Operations
Contacts: Mr G Smith (Manager); Ms J Ebdon (Shop Supervisor); Ms B Oakley (Publicity/ Promotions)
Training: F/T operations staff, F/T management, P/T operations staff and casual operations staff are trained in-house and on specific courses and day-to-day on job

Marketing
Affiliation: regional tourist board
Other: press office; market research
UK promotion: television; national newspapers; radio; local newspapers; regional tourist board; other attractions; leaflets/information packs; ETB/BTA

POTTERS MUSEUM OF CURIOSITY
(limited company)
museum

Established: 1987
Address: Jamaica Inn Court, Bolventor, Launceston, Cornwall
Telephone: (0566) 86838
Access: (road) A30
Parking capacity: (cars) 200 (coaches) 10
Hours: Easter to Oct – 9.30am to 4pm daily (June to Sept – to 6pm)
Admission (1992): adults £2.25; children £1.50; OAP £1.50; student £2.25; group rates
No. visitors (1992): 32 000 (est.)

Facilities
Interpretation: information boards; guide books
Children: adventure playground; play area; nappy changing
Schools: maximum no. 50; no special support
Disabled: easy access; disabled toilets
Catering: 1 bar/public house
Retailing: postcards/inexpensive souvenirs; confectionery and ice cream; craftwork; books; clothes
No. shops: 2

Operations
Contacts: R Mullins (Curator/Manageress); A J Watts (Director)
No. employees: (high season) 1 full time; 2 part time (low season) 1 full time

Marketing
UK promotion: regional tourist board; other attractions; leaflets/information packs

Environmental monitoring: recycling; waste; water quality; energy consumption; hazardous materials; chemical usage; transport; emissions

---

POWYSLAND MUSEUM AND MONTGOMERY CANAL CENTRE
(local authority run)
historic house; museum

Established: 1990
Address: The Canal Wharf, Welshpool, Powys, SY21 7AQ
Telephone: (0938) 554656
Access: (road) A483
Season: all year

Hours: Mon, Tues, Thur and Fri – 11am to 1pm and 2pm to 5pm; Whitsun to 30 Sept – Sat and Sun – 10am to 1pm and 2pm to 5pm; 1 Oct to Whitsun – Sat – 2pm to 5pm
Admission (1992): free
No. visitors (1992): 13 000

Facilities
Interpretation: videos; leaflets; information boards; maps; tour guides
Languages: Welsh
Schools: maximum no. 100; lecture/talk; quiz sheets
Disabled: easy access; disabled toilets; powered transport

Operations
Contacts: Ms E Bredsdorff (Museum Curator)
No. employees: (high season) 2 full time; 4 part time (low season) 2 full time; 2 part time

Marketing
Annual event(s): open evenings
Sponsor(s): various
UK promotion: radio; local newspapers; regional tourist board; leaflets/information packs
Europe promotion: leaflets/brochures

PRESTON TOWER
(privately owned)
14thc border pele tower

Established: 1976
Address: Chathill, Northumberland, NE67 5DH
Telephone: (066589) 227
Access: (road) A1
Parking capacity: (cars) 10 (coaches) 1
Season: all year
Hours: Daylight hours
Admission (1992): adults £1.00; children £0.50; OAP £0.50; student £0.50; groups of 10 or more £0.50
No. visitors (1992): 12 000 (est.)

Facilities
Interpretation: leaflets; information boards; maps; 2 rooms furnished in contemporary style
Schools: maximum no. 40; educational pack

Operations
Contact: Major T H Baker Cresswell
Languages spoken: French; German; Danish; Swedish; Norwegian

Marketing
Affiliation: HHA
UK promotion: local newspapers; regional tourist board; leaflets/information packs; NTB

PRIDEAUX PLACE
(partnership)
historic house

Established: 1987
Address: Padstow, Cornwall, PL28 8RP
Telephone: (0841) 532411
Access: (road) A389
Parking capacity: (cars) 30
Hours: Easter 2 weeks and Whitsun to end of Sept – Sun to Thur – 1.30pm to 5pm, BH – 11am to 5pm
Admission (1992): adults £3.50; OAP £3.50; student £3.50; under 14s free
No. visitors (1992): 13 000 (est.)

Facilities
Interpretation: leaflets; information boards; tour guides; guide books
Languages: French; German; Italian; Spanish
Schools: maximum no. 40; educational literature; lecture/talk
Disabled: helpers
Catering: 1 waiter/waitress served
Retailing: postcards/inexpensive souvenirs; craftwork; books
No. shops: 1

Operations
Contact: Ms S Major (Administrator)

No. employees: (high season) 4 full time; 24 part time (low season) 4 full time; 4 part time
Training: P/T operations staff are trained in-house and on specific courses

Marketing
Annual event(s): opera
Sponsor(s): Barclays Bank, Phillips Auctioneers
Affiliations: HHA, CTB, WCTB, CATA
Other: market research
UK promotion: local newspapers; regional tourist board; other attractions; leaflets/information packs; ETB/BTA

PRIEST'S MILL
(privately owned)
watermill visitor centre

Established: 1986
Address: Caldbeck, Via Wigton, Cumbria, CA7 8DR
Telephone: (06998) 369
Parking capacity: (cars) 20
Hours: mid Mar to Nov – Tues to Sun – 11am to 5pm; Nov and Dec – weekends
Admission (1992): free
No. visitors (1992): 20 000 (est.)

Facilities
Interpretation: leaflets
Children: nappy changing
Disabled: easy access; disabled toilets
Catering: 1 picnic area
Retailing: postcards/inexpensive souvenirs; craftwork; books; clothes; countryside gifts, mining books
No. shops: 4

Operations
Contact: Miss Coryn E Clarke (owner/Manager)
No. employees: (high season) 3 full time; 10 part time (low season) 2 full time; 8 part time
Training: P/T operations staff are trained in-house and day-to-day on job using videos and handbooks
Languages spoken: French; German; Italian; Spanish

Marketing
UK promotion: regional tourist board; other attractions; leaflets/information packs

---

PROBUS COUNTY DEMONSTRATION GARDEN
(local authority run)
garden

Established: 1970
Address: Probus, Truro, Cornwall, TR2 4HQ
Telephone: (0872) 74282. Fax: (0872) 222490
Access: (road) A390
Parking capacity: (cars) 80 (coaches) 2
Season: all year
Hours: May to Sept – 10am to 5pm daily; Oct to Apr – Mon to Fri – 10am to 4pm
Admission (1992): adults £2.00; OAP £2.00; student £2.00
No. visitors (1992): 24 000 (est.)

Facilities
Interpretation: leaflets; information boards; maps; tour guides
Schools: maximum no. 100; educational literature
Disabled: easy access; disabled toilets
Catering: 1 picnic area
Franchisees: May to Sept – 10am to 5pm daily; Oct to Apr – Mon to Fri – 10am to 4pm
Retailing: books
No. shops: 1

Operations
Contact: P McMillan Browse (Principal Horticultural Officer)
No. employees: (high season) 6 full time; 2 part time

Marketing
Annual event(s): *exhibitions and shows*
UK promotion: *local newspapers; regional tourist board; other attractions; leaflets/information packs*

Environmental monitoring: *recycling; energy consumption*

PROVAND'S LORDSHIP
(local authority run)
historic house

Established: *1984*
Address: *3 Castle St, Glasgow, G4 0RB*
Telephone: *(041) 552 8819*
Season: *all year*
Admission (1992): *free*
No. visitors (1992): *96 749*

Facilities
Interpretation: *leaflets; information boards; maps*
Languages: *Urdu*
Schools: *museum education dept services*
Retailing: *postcards/inexpensive souvenirs; books; reproductions of famous artefacts; stationery*
No. shops: *1*

Operations
Training: *F/T operations staff and F/T management are trained in-house and on specific courses and day-to-day on job*

Marketing
Press office; market research
UK promotion: *national newspapers; local newspapers; regional tourist board; leaflets/information packs*

Environmental monitoring: *recycling; waste; energy consumption; hazardous materials; chemical usage; local authority policy*

PUGNEY'S COUNTRY PARK
(local authority run)
park/reserve; water sports centre

Established: *1985*
Address: *Asdale Rd, Wakefield, W Yorks, WF2 7EQ*
Telephone: *(0924) 386782. Fax: (0924) 200456*
Access: (road) *M1*
Parking capacity: (cars) *1000*
Season: *all year*
Hours: *9am to dusk daily except Christmas Day*
Admission (1992): *free admission, charges for hire and use of facilities*
No. visitors (1992): *350 000 (est.)*

Facilities
Interpretation: *leaflets*
Languages: *French; German*
Schools: *maximum no. 50; educational literature; lecture/talk*
Disabled: *disabled toilets*
Catering: *6 picnic areas*
Franchisees: *9am to dusk daily except Christmas Day*

Operations
Contact: *Mr D Hillman (Principal Outdoor Manager)*
Training: *F/T operations staff, F/T management, P/T operations staff, P/T management, casual operations staff and casual management are trained in-house and externally and on specific courses and day-to-day on job*

Marketing
Annual event(s): *triathlon and charity events*
Other: *press office; market research*
UK promotion: *radio; local newspapers; regional tourist board; leaflets/information packs; ETB/BTA*
Europe promotion: *British Tourist Authority*

PUMPHOUSE EDUCATIONAL MUSEUM
(company limited by guarantee and trust)
heritage centre; park/reserve; museum; zoo/wildlife attraction

Established: *1991*
Address: *Lavender Pond Nature Reserve, Lavender Rd, Rotherhithe, London, SE16 1DZ*
Telephone: *(071) 231 2976*
Parking capacity: (cars) *20*
Season: *all year*
Hours: *Mon to Fri – 10am to 4pm and by special arrangement*
Admission (1992): *adults £2.00; children £1.50; OAP £1.50; student £1.50*
No. visitors (1992): *3432*

Facilities
Interpretation: *videos; leaflets; audio tapes; information boards; slides; maps*
Languages: *Norwegian*
Schools: *maximum no. 60; educational literature; audio/visual presentation; lecture/talk; education officer*
Disabled: *easy access; disabled toilets; Braille/sound posts; lift*
Catering: *1 picnic area*
Retailing: *postcards/inexpensive souvenirs; books*
No. shops: *1*

Operations
Contact: *Ms C Roberts (Community and Development)*
No. employees: (high season) *5 full time*
Training: *F/T operations staff and F/T management are trained in-house and externally and on specific courses and day-to-day on job using videos and handbooks*

Marketing
Annual event(s): *various*
Affiliations: *AIM, AMSSEE, NMRS*
Other: *PR company: G Mansell Inc; press office; market research*
UK promotion: *national newspapers; local newspapers; regional tourist board; other attractions; leaflets/information packs; ETB/BTA; Scandinavian press*
Europe promotion: *leaflets/brochures*

Environmental monitoring: *water quality*

PUPPET CENTRE TRUST
(trust and limited company)
gallery; information and resource centre

Established: *1974*
Address: *BAC, 176 Lavender Hill, London*
Telephone: *(071) 228 5335*
Access: (road) *A3* (rail) *Clapham*
Season: *all year*
Hours: *Mon to Fri – 2pm to 6pm. Closed Christmas and New Year*
Admission (1992): *free*
No. visitors (1992): *3000*

Facilities
Interpretation: *videos; leaflets; information boards; personnel*
Languages: *French; Italian*
Children: *nappy changing*
Schools: *educational literature; educational pack*
Disabled: *easy access; disabled toilets*
Retailing: *mail order service; puppets and materials*

Operations
Contacts: *Ms C March (Development Director); Ms A Ledgard (Education Officer); Ms A Ditum (Administrator)*
No. employees: (high season) *3 full time*
Training: *F/T operations staff and F/T management are trained in-house and externally and on specific courses and day-to-day on job*
Languages spoken: *French; Italian; Swedish; Danish; Norwegian*

Marketing
Annual event(s): *puppeteers day and projects*
Sponsor(s): *various*
Other: *market research*

UK promotion: *television; national newspapers; radio; leaflets/information packs*

Environmental monitoring: *recycling; waste; water quality; energy consumption; hazardous materials; chemical usage*

PUPPET THEATRE MUSEUM, THE
(private independent)
museum

Established: *1984*
Address: *Edinburgh House, Bagot St, Abbots Bromley, Rugeley, Staffs, WS15 3DA*
Telephone: *(0285) 840348*
Access: (road) *M6/B5014* (rail) *Rugeley*
Parking capacity: (cars) *5* (coaches) *1*
Season: *all year*
Hours: *Sun – 2pm to 6pm. Other times by arrangement*
Admission (1992): *adults £0.50; children £0.25; OAP £0.50; student £0.50*
No. visitors (1992): *1731*

Facilities
Interpretation: *information boards; slides; tour guides; lecture demonstrations*
Schools: *maximum no. 30; lecture/talk; treasure hunt*
Disabled: *easy access; disabled toilets*
Catering: *1 snack bar/food stall*
Retailing: *postcards/inexpensive souvenirs*
No. shops: *1*

Operations
Contact: *D S E Hayward (Director)*
No. employees: (high season) *1 part time* (low season) *1 part time*

Marketing
Annual event: *horn dance day*
Affiliation: *AIM*
UK promotion: *local newspapers; regional tourist board*

Q

QUAY ARTS
(limited company)
heritage centre; museum; gallery

Established: *1977*
Address: *Little London, Newport, Isle of Wight*
Telephone: *528825*
Season: *all year*
Hours: *Mon to Sat – 10am to 5pm, Sun – 12 noon to 6pm*
Admission (1992): *free*
No. visitors (1992): *20 000 (est.)*

Facilities
Interpretation: *leaflets; information boards; maps*
Catering: *1 picnic area*
Retailing: *postcards/inexpensive souvenirs; confectionery and ice cream; craftwork; frames, ceramics printing*
No. shops: *3*

Operations
Contacts: *Mr S Walworth (Administrator); Ms A Toms (Director)*
No. employees: (high season) *3 full time; 2 part time* (low season) *3 full time; 2 part time*
Languages spoken: *French; Italian*

Marketing
Annual event(s): *dance, drama and art workshops*
Sponsor(s): *local businesses*
UK promotion: *national newspapers; radio; local newspapers; regional tourist board; leaflets/ information packs; ETB/BTA*
Europe promotion: *community arts centres*

Environmental monitoring: *recycling; waste; energy consumption*

QUEEN ELIZABETH COUNTRY PARK
(local authority run)
country park

Established: *1976*
Address: *Gravel Hill, Horndean, Waterlooville, Hants, PO8 0QE*
Telephone: *(0705) 595040.* Fax: *(0705) 592409*
Access: (road) *A3*
Parking capacity: (cars) *500* (coaches) *12*
Season: *all year*
Hours: *park centre – Mar to Oct – 10am to 6pm daily, Nov and Dec – weekends – 10am to 6pm, Jan and Feb – Sun – 10am to 6pm*
Admission (1992): *£1.50 per car*
No. visitors (1992): *340 000 (est.)*

Facilities
Interpretation: *videos; leaflets; information boards; maps; guide books; guided walks and activities*
Children: *nappy changing*
Schools: *educational literature; audio/visual presentation; lecture/talk*
Disabled: *easy access; disabled toilets; wheelchairs*
Catering: *8 picnic areas*
Franchisees: *park centre – Mar to Oct – 10am to 6pm daily, Nov and Dec – weekends – 10am to 6pm, Jan and Feb – Sun – 10am to 6pm*
Retailing: *postcards/inexpensive souvenirs; craftwork; books*
No. shops: *1*

Operations
Contacts: *M Guy (Park Manager); Mrs A Francis (Area Administrative Officer)*
No. employees: (high season) *8 full time; 5 part time* (low season) *8 full time; 5 part time*
Training: *F/T operations staff, F/T management and P/T operations staff are trained in-house*

and externally and on specific courses and day-to-day on job
Languages spoken: *French; Spanish*

Marketing
Annual event(s): *Hampshire country fair and sheep dog trials*
Other: *market research*
UK promotion: *local newspapers; regional tourist board; other attractions; leaflets/information packs*

QUEEN'S OWN HIGHLANDERS REGIMENTAL MUSEUM
(trust)
museum

Established: *1967*
Address: *Fort George, Ardersier, By Inverness*
Telephone: *(0463) 224380*
Access: (road) *A9/A96* (rail) *Inverness*
Season: *all year*
Hours: *1 Apr to 30 Sept – Mon to Fri – 10am to 6pm, Sun – 2pm to 6pm; 1 Oct to 31 Mar – Mon to Fri – 10am to 4pm*
Admission (1992): *free*
No. visitors (1992): *50 000 (est.)*

Facilities
Interpretation: *leaflets; information boards*
Schools: *maximum no. 24; no special support*
Retailing: *postcards/inexpensive souvenirs; books*
No. shops: *1*

Operations
Contact: *Regimental Secretary*
No. employees: (high season) *2 full time* (low season) *2 full time*

Marketing
Affiliations: *various museum associations*
Other: *market research*
UK promotion: *regional tourist board*

Environmental monitoring: *recycling; hazardous materials; countryside conservation*

QUEX HOUSE AND GARDENS AND POWELL-COTTON MUSEUM
(trust)
historic house; garden; museum

Established: *1927*
Address: *Quex Park, Birchington, Kent*
Telephone: *(0843) 42168*
Access: (road) *M2/M20/M25/A28* (rail) *Birchington*
Parking capacity: (cars) *60* (coaches) *6*
Season: *all year*
Hours: *Apr to Sept – Wed, Thur and Sun – 2.15pm to 6pm (also open Fri in Aug); Sept to Dec – Wed and Sun – 2.15pm to 6pm; Jan to Apr – Sun – 2.15pm to 6pm*
Admission (1992): *adults £1.50; children £1.00; OAP £1.00*
No. visitors (1992): *18 000*

Facilities
Interpretation: *guide books*
Children: *nappy changing*
Schools: *maximum no. 250; lecture/talk; demonstrations*
Disabled: *easy access; disabled toilets*
Catering: *1 snack bar/food stall*
Retailing: *postcards/inexpensive souvenirs; craftwork; books; clothes; reproductions of famous artefacts*
No. shops: *1*

Operations
Contact: *D R Howlett (Curator)*
No. employees: (high season) *3 full time; 15 part time* (low season) *3 full time; 5 part time*

Marketing
Market research
UK promotion: *national newspapers; local newspapers; regional tourist board; other attractions; leaflets/information packs*

R

RADSTOCK MIDSOMER NORTON MUSEUM
(independent)
museum

Established: *1989*
Address: *Barton Meade House, Haydon,
  Radstock, Bath, BA3 3QS*
Telephone: *(0761) 437722*
Access: (road) *M4/A4* (rail) *Bath*
Parking capacity: (cars) *25*
Season: *all year*
Hours: *Sat – 10am to 4pm; Sun – 2pm to 5pm;
  BH Mon – 2pm to 5pm*
Admission (1992): *adults £1.50; children £0.50;
  OAP £0.50; student £0.50*
No. visitors (1992): *6000 (est.)*

Facilities
Interpretation: *leaflets; information boards; tour
  guides; guide books*
Schools: *maximum no. 50; educational literature;
  lecture/talk; Victorian lessons*
Disabled: *helpers*
Catering: *1 picnic area*
Retailing: *postcards/inexpensive souvenirs;
  confectionery and ice cream; books*
No. shops: *1*

Operations
Contacts: *Mrs M Rowe (Hon Treasurer); Mrs V
  Ashman*
Languages spoken: *French; German*

Marketing
Annual event(s): *Easter and Christmas fayres*
Other: *market research*
UK promotion: *national newspapers; radio; local
  newspapers; regional tourist board; other
  attractions; leaflets/information packs;
  Wansdyke Tourist Association*

Environmental monitoring: *recycling*

RAGGED SCHOOL MUSEUM
(limited company and charity)
museum

Established: *1990*
Address: *46–48 Copperfield Rd, London, E3 4RR*
Telephone: *(081) 980 6405*
Access: (road) *A12* (rail) *Mile End*
Season: *all year*
Hours: *Wed and Thur – 10am to 5pm; 1st Sun in
  every month – 2pm to 5pm*
Admission (1992): *adults £1.00; children £1.00*
No. visitors (1992): *11 000 (est.)*

Facilities
Interpretation: *leaflets; information boards;
  maps; tour guides; guide books; personnel;
  exhibits*
Schools: *maximum no. 75; educational literature;
  lecture/talk; recreation of Victorian lessons*
Catering: *1 snack bar/food stall*
Retailing: *postcards/inexpensive souvenirs;
  confectionery and ice cream; books*
No. shops: *2*

Operations
Contact: *Ms P Plumb (Administrator)*
No. employees: (high season) *1 full time;
  1 part time* (low season) *1 full time; 1 part
  time*

Marketing
Affiliations: *AIM, M and G Association*
Other: *market research*

UK promotion: *local newspapers; other
  attractions; leaflets/information packs*

RAGLEY HALL
(private)
historic house; park/reserve

Established: *1959*
Address: *Alcester, Warks., B49 5NJ*
Telephone: *(0789) 762090.* Fax: *(0789) 764791*
Access: (road) *M40/M42/A46/A435* (rail)
  Birmingham/Stratford
Parking capacity: (cars) *1000* (coaches) *30*
Hours: *Easter to Sept – Sat to Sun – 12 noon to
  5pm, park – 10am to 6pm*
Admission (1992): *adults £4.50; children £3.50;
  OAP £3.50; student £3.50*
No. visitors (1992): *98 000*

Facilities
Interpretation: *leaflets; information boards; tour
  guides; guide books*
Languages: *French; German*
Children: *adventure playground; play area*
Schools: *maximum no. 60; educational literature*
Disabled: *easy access; disabled toilets; helpers; lift*
Catering: *1 picnic area*
Retailing: *postcards/inexpensive souvenirs;
  confectionery and ice cream; craftwork; books;
  reproductions of famous artefacts*
No. shops: *2*

Operations
Contact: *M Barbour (Business Manager)*
No. employees: (high season) *4 full time; 30 part
  time* (low season) *4 full time; 6 part time*
Training: *F/T operations staff, F/T management,
  P/T operations staff and P/T management are
  trained in-house and externally and on specific
  courses*

Marketing
Annual event(s): *various*
Other: *market research*
UK promotion: *national newspapers; radio; local
  newspapers; regional tourist board; other
  attractions; leaflets/information packs; ETB/
  BTA*
Europe/USA promotion: *leaflets/brochures; travel
  agents' brochures; British Tourist Authority;
  SCATA*

Environmental monitoring: *recycling*

RARE FARM ANIMALS OF HOLLANDEN
(sole trader)
park/reserve; farm park and shop

Established: *1985*
Address: *Mill Lane, Hildenborough, Nr
  Sevenoaks, Kent, TN15 0SQ*
Telephone: *(0732) 832276.* Fax: *(0732) 838011*
Access: (road) *A21* (rail) *Hildenborough*
Parking capacity: (cars) *500* (coaches) *20*
Hours: *Mar to Oct – 10.30am to 5pm daily*
Admission (1992): *adults £3.40; children £2.20;
  OAP £2.75; disabled £1.60*
No. visitors (1992): *82 000 (est.)*

Facilities
Interpretation: *information boards; slides; guide
  books*
Children: *adventure playground; play area; nappy
  changing*
Schools: *maximum no. 400; educational literature;
  educational tour; lecture/talk*
Disabled: *easy access; leaflets; guide book*

Catering: *1 picnic area*
Retailing: *postcards/inexpensive souvenirs;
  confectionery and ice cream; craftwork; books;
  clothes*
No. shops: *3*

Operations
No. employees: (high season) *4 full time; 14 part
  time*
Languages spoken: *French*

Marketing
Annual event(s): *wool day, craft day*
Affiliations: *Rare Breeds Survival Trust*
Other: *press office; market research*
UK promotion: *radio; local newspapers; regional
  tourist board; other attractions; leaflets/
  information packs*

Environmental monitoring: *recycling; waste*

RAVENGLASS AND ESKDALE RAILWAY, THE
(limited company)
museum; railway

Established: *1876*
Address: *Ravenglass, Cumbria, CA18 1SW*
Telephone: *(0229) 717171.* Fax: *(0229) 717011*
Access: (road) *M6/A595* (rail) *Ravenglass*
Parking capacity: (cars) *250* (coaches) *6*
Season: *all year*
Hours: *Apr to Oct – Mon to Sun; 26 Dec to 1
  Jan. Reduced service at other times, special
  trains any time*
Admission (1992): *adults £5.40; children £2.70;
  OAP £4.90; family £13.50*
No. visitors (1992): *170 000 (est.)*

Facilities
Interpretation: *videos; leaflets; information
  boards; slides; maps; guide books*
Languages: *Japanese; French; German; Norwegian*
Children: *play area; nappy changing*
Schools: *maximum no. 100; educational literature;
  audio/visual presentation*
Disabled: *easy access; disabled toilets*
Catering: *1 bar/public house*
Retailing: *postcards/inexpensive souvenirs;
  confectionery and ice cream; books; clothes*
No. shops: *2*

Operations
Contact: *Douglas Ferreira (General Manager)*
No. employees: (high season) *27 full time; 7 part
  time* (low season) *20 full time*
Training: *F/T operations staff, P/T operations
  staff and casual operations staff are trained
  in-house and day-to-day on job*

Marketing
Annual event(s): *various*
Affiliations: *Association of Independent Railways*
Other: *market research*
UK promotion: *local newspapers; regional tourist
  board; leaflets/information packs*

RED HOUSE MUSEUM ART GALLERY AND GARDENS
(local authority run)
garden; museum; gallery

Established: *1951*
Address: *Quay Rd, Christchurch, Dorset*
Telephone: *(0202) 482860.* Fax: *(0962) 869836*
Access: (road) *M27/A35/A31*
Season: *all year*

Hours: *Tues to Sat – 10am to 5pm; Sun – 2pm to 5pm*
Admission (1992): *adults £1.00; children £0.60; OAP £0.60; student £0.60*
No. visitors (1992): *25 000 (est.)*

Facilities
Interpretation: *leaflets; information boards*
Schools: *maximum no. 30*
Retailing: *postcards/inexpensive souvenirs; craftwork; books; reproductions of famous artefacts*
No. shops: *1*

Operations
Contacts: *Mr S Locke (Director); Ms A Carter (Curator); Ms C Taylor (Assistant Curator); Ms J Bailey*
No. employees: *(high season) 3 full time; 7 part time (low season) 3 full time; 7 part time*
Training: *F/T operations staff, F/T management, P/T operations staff and P/T management are trained in-house and externally and on specific courses and day-to-day on job*

Marketing
Annual event(s): *craft fairs*
Affiliations: *MA*
Other: *press office; market research*
UK promotion: *television; national newspapers; radio; local newspapers; regional tourist board; other attractions; leaflets/information packs*

Environmental monitoring: *water quality; chemical usage*

RED LODGE
(local authority run)
historic house; museum

Established: *1920*
Address: *Park Row, Bristol, BS1*
Telephone: *(0272) 211360*
Season: *all year*
Hours: *Mon to Sat – 10am to 1pm and 2pm to 5pm*
Admission (1992): *adults £2.00; OAP £2.00; student £2.00; under 16s free; concessions for Bristol residents*
No. visitors (1992): *20 000 (est.)*

Facilities
Interpretation: *guide books*
Schools: *maximum no. 30*
Retailing: *postcards/inexpensive souvenirs*
No. shops: *none*

Operations
Contacts: *Bristol Museums and Art Gallery (Curator of Applied Art)*
No. employees: *(high season) 2 full time (low season) 2 full time*
Training: *F/T operations staff and F/T management are trained in-house and on specific courses and day-to-day on job using videos and handbooks*
Languages spoken: *French; German*

Marketing
Press office
UK promotion: *regional tourist board; leaflets/ information packs; ETB/BTA*

REGIMENTS OF GLOUCESTERSHIRE MUSEUM
(trust)
museum

Established: *1990*
Address: *Custom House, Gloucester Docks, Gloucester, GL1 2HE*
Telephone: *(0452) 522682*
Access: *(road) M5/A34 (rail) Gloucester*
Parking capacity: *(cars) 500 (coaches) 20*
Season: *all year*
Hours: *Tues to Sun – 10am to 5pm*
Admission (1992): *adults £2.50; children £1.25; OAP £1.50; family £6.25*
No. visitors (1992): *13 000*

Facilities
Interpretation: *videos; audio tapes; information boards; exhibitions*
Languages: *French; German; Italian*
Schools: *maximum no. 35; educational literature; lecture/talk*
Disabled: *easy access; disabled toilets; helpers; lift*
Retailing: *postcards/inexpensive souvenirs; books; clothes*
No. shops: *1*

Operations
Contact: *C Beresford (Curator)*
No. employees: *(high season) 2 full time; 17 part time (low season) 2 full time; 17 part time*
Training: *F/T operations staff, F/T management and P/T operations staff are trained in-house and externally and day-to-day on job*

Marketing
Affiliations: *MA, AIM, HETB*
Other: *market research*
UK promotion: *radio; local newspapers; regional tourist board; other attractions; leaflets/ information packs*

Environmental monitoring: *recycling; waste; energy consumption; hazardous materials; chemical usage; emissions*

RHONDDA HERITAGE PARK
(local authority run)
heritage centre; colliery attraction

Established: *1987*
Address: *Lewis Merthyr, Coed Cae Rd, Trehafod, Mid Glamorgan, CF37 7NP*
Telephone: *(0443) 682036. Fax: (0443) 687420*
Access: *(road) M4/A470 (rail) Treherbert*
Parking capacity: *(cars) 200 (coaches) 5*
Season: *all year*
Hours: *all Year – Mon to Sun – 10am to 6pm*
Admission (1992): *adults £3.50; children £2.50; OAP £2.50; student £2.50*
No. visitors (1992): *33 000*

Facilities
Interpretation: *audio tapes; information boards; slides; maps; tour guides; guide books*
Children: *play area; nappy changing*
Schools: *maximum no. 150; educational literature; audio/visual presentation*
Disabled: *easy access; disabled toilets; helpers; guide book*
Catering: *1 picnic area*
Franchisees: *all Year – Mon to Sun – 10am to 6pm*
Retailing: *postcards/inexpensive souvenirs; craftwork; books; clothes; reproductions of famous artefacts; mining souvenirs*
No. shops: *1*

Operations
Contacts: *Catherine Hill (Director); Caroline Mortimer (Administrative Officer); Mary Scourfield (Marketing Assistant)*
No. employees: *(high season) 14 full time; 9 part time (low season) 14 full time; 9 part time*
Training: *F/T operations staff, P/T operations staff and casual operations staff are trained in-house and day-to-day on job*
Languages spoken: *French; German; Italian*

Marketing
Annual event(s): *Christmas celebrations*
Affiliation: *Council of Museums in Wales*
Other: *press office; market research*
UK promotion: *television; national newspapers; radio; local newspapers; regional tourist board; other attractions; leaflets/information packs; ETB/BTA*
Europe/Asia/Australia/USA promotion: *leaflets/ brochures; travel agents' brochures; British Tourist Authority*

RHYL SEA LIFE CENTRE
(limited company)
zoo/wildlife attraction

Established: *1992*
Address: *East Parade, Rhyl, Clwyd, LL18 3AF*
Telephone: *(0745) 344660. Fax: (0745) 332991*
Access: *(road) M6/A55/A548 (rail) Rhyl*
Season: *all year*
Hours: *10am to 6pm daily except Christmas Day; open later in summer*
Admission (1992): *adults £3.85; children £2.75; OAP £2.75; school groups £1.95; disabled £3.35*
No. visitors (1992): *N/A*

Facilities
Interpretation: *videos; leaflets; information boards; tour guides; guide books*
Languages: *French; German*
Children: *adventure playground; play area; nappy changing*
Schools: *educational literature; audio/visual presentation; lecture/talk; projects and touch pools*
Disabled: *easy access; disabled toilets*
Catering: *1 picnic area*
Retailing: *postcards/inexpensive souvenirs; craftwork; books; clothes; reproductions of famous artefacts*
No. shops: *1*

Operations
Contacts: *Mr T Forer (Manager); Ms R Andrews (Shop Supervisor); Mr D Sturdy (Publicity/ Promotions Officer)*
Training: *F/T operations staff, F/T management, P/T operations staff and casual operations staff are trained in-house and on specific courses and day-to-day on job using videos and handbooks*
Languages spoken: *French; Spanish; Welsh*

Environmental monitoring: *recycling*

RIBER CASTLE WILDLIFE PARK
(private company)
wildlife attraction

Established: *1962*
Address: *Riber Castle, Matlock, Derbyshire*
Telephone: *(0629) 582073*
Access: *(road) M1/A615 (rail) Matlock*
Parking capacity: *(cars) 1000 (coaches) 100*
Season: *all year .*
Hours: *summer – 10.00am to 5.00pm, winter – 10.00am to between 3.00pm and 4.30pm*
Admission (1992): *adults £3.50; children £2.00; OAP £3.00*
No. visitors (1992): *150 000 (est.)*

Facilities
Interpretation: *leaflets; information boards; maps; signs*
Children: *play area; nappy changing*
Schools: *liaison with teachers*
Disabled: *easy access*
Catering: *1 bar/public house*
Retailing: *postcards/inexpensive souvenirs; confectionery and ice cream; craftwork*
No. shops: *1*

Operations: *N/A*

Marketing
UK promotion: *national newspapers; local newspapers*

RIPLEY'S BELIEVE IT OR NOT
(limited company)
oditorium

Established: *1992*
Address: *9 Marine Parade, Great Yarmouth, Norfolk, NR30 3AH*
Telephone: *(0493) 332217. Fax: (0493) 332217*
Access: *(road) A12*
Hours: *1 Apr to 31 Oct – from 10am; also weekends and school holidays during winter*

Admission (1992): *adults £2.99; children £1.99; OAP £2.20; handicapped £1.99; school groups £1.50*

Facilities
Interpretation: *videos; leaflets; information boards; maps; guide books; personnel*
Children: *nappy changing; creche*
Schools: *educational literature*
Disabled: *easy access*
Retailing: *postcards/inexpensive souvenirs; confectionery and ice cream; craftwork; books; reproductions of famous artefacts*
No. shops: *1*

Operations
Contacts: *Mr M McDonald (Manager); Ms C Hannant; Ms M Wilson; Ms M Kidner (Marketing Executive)*
No. employees: *(high season) 5 full time; 5 part time (low season) 3 full time; 3 part time*

Marketing
PR company: *Mike Salter Communications, 3 Hall Rd, Wramplingham, Norfolk; market research*
UK promotion: *local newspapers; regional tourist board; other attractions; leaflets/information packs; ETB/BTA*

Environmental monitoring: *recycling; waste; energy consumption; hazardous materials; transport*

RIPON CATHEDRAL
(cathedral)
church

Established: *656*
Address: *Ripon, N Yorks*
Telephone: *(0765) 604108*
Access: *(road) A1 (rail) Harrogate*
Parking capacity: *(cars) 50*
Season: *all year*
Hours: *all year – Mon to Sat – 7.30am to 6.30pm; winter – Sun – 7.30am to 5pm; summer – Sun – 7.30am to 8pm*
Admission (1992): *free, but a donation of £1.50 is requested*
No. visitors (1992): *170 000 (est.)*

Facilities
Interpretation: *leaflets; audio tapes; information boards; tour guides; guide books*
Languages: *Japanese; Dutch; French; German; Italian; Spanish; Russian*
Schools: *maximum no. 40; educational literature; lecture/talk; pre visit for teachers*
Disabled: *easy access; disabled toilets; helpers; other audio facilities*
Catering: *1 waiter/waitress served*
Franchisees: *all year – Mon to Sat – 7.30am to 6.30pm; winter – Sun – 7.30am to 5pm; summer – Sun – 7.30am to 8pm*
Retailing: *postcards/inexpensive souvenirs; craftwork; books*
No. shops: *1*

Operations
Contacts: *The Revd Canon D Ford (Visitors Canon); Mr R Lambie (Administrator); Mrs C Benson (Manager)*
No. employees: *(high season) 22 full time; 10 part time (low season) 22 full time; 10 part time*
Training: *F/T operations staff, P/T operations staff and casual operations staff are trained in-house and day-to-day on job*

Marketing
Annual event(s): *various*
Sponsor(s): *various*
Other: *press office*

RIPON PRISON and POLICE MUSEUM
(trust)
museum

Established: *1984*
Address: *St Marygate, Ripon, N Yorks, HG4 1LX*

Telephone: *(0765) 690799*
Access: *(road) M1/A61/B6265 (rail) Harrogate*
Hours: *Easter or 1 Apr to 31 Oct – 1pm to 5pm daily (July and Aug weekdays 11am to 5pm)*
Admission (1992): *adults £0.80; children £0.40; OAP £0.60; student £0.60*
No. visitors (1992): *11 963*

Facilities
Schools: *maximum no. 25; lecture/talk*
Retailing: *postcards/inexpensive souvenirs*
No. shops: *1*

Operations
Contact: *M Morton (Hon Deputy Curator)*
No. employees: *(high season) 4 part time (low season) 5 part time*
Languages spoken: *German; Italian; Spanish; Japanese; Dutch; Russian*

Marketing
UK promotion: *regional tourist board; leaflets/information packs*

ROBERT OWEN MUSEUM
(limited company)
museum

Established: *1983*
Address: *The Cross, Broad Street, Newtown, Powys, SY16 2BB*
Telephone: *(0686) 626345*
Access: *(road) M54/A483 (rail) Aberystwyth*
Season: *all year*
Hours: *all Year – Mon to Fri – 9.45am to 11.45am, 2pm to 3.30pm, Sat – 10am to 11.30am; closed Christmas week and Good Friday*
Admission (1992): *free*
No. visitors (1992): *2000 (est.)*

Facilities
Interpretation: *videos; information boards*
Schools: *maximum no. 30; lecture/talk*
Disabled: *access difficult*
Retailing: *postcards/inexpensive souvenirs; books*
No. shops: *1*

Operations
Contact: *John Hatton Davidson (Hon Curator)*
No. employees: *(high season) 1 full time (low season) 1 full time*

Marketing
Affiliations: *AIM, Council of Museums in Wales*
UK promotion: *regional tourist board; leaflets/information packs; museums and galleries; sundry museums directories*

ROCHDALE ART GALLERY
(local authority run)
gallery

Established: *1901*
Address: *Esplanade, Rochdale, Lancs*
Telephone: *(0706) 342154. Fax: (0706) 59475*
Access: *(road) M62 (rail) Rochdale*
Season: *all year*
Hours: *all year – Mon, Tues, Thur and Fri – 10am to 5pm, Wed – 10am to 1pm, Sat – 10am to 4pm*
Admission (1992): *free*
No. visitors (1992): *29 899*

Facilities
Interpretation: *leaflets; information boards; slides; guide books*
Languages: *Urdu*
Children: *creche*
Schools: *maximum no. 25; educational tour; lecture/talk; slide packs*
Retailing: *postcards/inexpensive souvenirs; books*
No. shops: *1*

Operations
Contact: *M Sulter (Art Gallery Services Officer)*
No. employees: *(high season) 2 full time; 4 part time (low season) 2 full time; 4 part time*

Training: *F/T operations staff, F/T management, P/T operations staff and P/T management are trained in-house and externally and on specific courses and day-to-day on job*

Marketing
Annual event: *Rochdale Festival*
Sponsor(s): *various*
Affiliations: *Art Galleries Association, National Art Collection Fund, MA, NWMAGS, Contemporary Art Society*
Other: *market research*
UK promotion: *national newspapers; radio; local newspapers; regional tourist board; other attractions; leaflets/information packs*
Europe/USA promotion: *art magazines*

Environmental monitoring: *humidity in museum*

ROCHESTER CASTLE
(English Heritage)
castle; monument

Established: *1800*
Address: *The Keep, Rochester Castle, Rochester, Kent, ME1 1SX*
Telephone: *(0634) 402276*
Access: *(road) M2/A2 (rail) Strood/Rochester*
Season: *all year*
Hours: *Nov to Mar – Tues to Sun – 10am to 4pm; Apr to Sept – 10am to 6pm daily*
Admission (1992): *adults £1.70; children £0.80; OAP £1.20; student £1.20; group discounts*
No. visitors (1992): *79 995*

Facilities
Interpretation: *audio tapes; guide books*
Schools: *maximum no. 500; educational literature*
Disabled: *disabled toilets*
Catering: *1 picnic area*
Retailing: *postcards/inexpensive souvenirs; books*
No. shops: *1*

Operations
Contacts: *E H Barfoot (Regional Visitor Services Manager); C E Blott (Group Custodian); English Heritage (Buying Office, London); M Brunier (Regional Development Officer)*
No. employees: *(high season) 3 full time; 1 part time (low season) 3 full time*
Training: *F/T operations staff, F/T management, P/T operations staff and casual operations staff are trained in-house and on specific courses and day-to-day on job using videos and handbooks*
Languages spoken: *French; Spanish*

Marketing
Press office; market research
UK promotion: *local newspapers; regional tourist board; other attractions; leaflets/information packs*
Europe/Australia/USA promotion: *British Tourist Authority*

Environmental monitoring: *recycling; waste; water quality; energy consumption; hazardous materials; chemical usage*

ROCK CIRCUS
(plc)
museum; tourist attraction

Established: *1989*
Address: *London Pavilion, Piccadilly Circus, London, W1V 9LA*
Telephone: *(071) 734 7203. Fax: (071) 734 8023*
Access: *(rail) Piccadilly Circus*
Season: *all year*
Hours: *summer – 10am to 10pm; winter – 11am to 9pm; midday every Tues*
Admission (1992): *adults £6.25; children £4.25; OAP £5.25; student £5.25; reduced rates for groups*
No. visitors (1992): *500 000 (est.)*

Facilities
Interpretation: *videos; leaflets*
Languages: *Japanese; Dutch; French; German; Italian; Spanish*

Children: *nappy changing*
Schools: *educational literature; lecture/talk*
Disabled: *easy access; disabled toilets; helpers*
Catering: *2 snack bars/food stalls*
Retailing: *postcards/inexpensive souvenirs;
  confectionery and ice cream; books*
No. shops: *1*

Operations
Contacts: *Mr C Bishop (Exhibition Manager); Ms
  F Baigent (Personnel); Mr R Coe (Front of
  House); Ms H Redwood (Press)*
Training: *F/T operations staff and F/T
  management are trained in-house and externally
  and on specific courses and day-to-day on job
  using videos and handbooks*

Marketing
Press office; market research
UK promotion: *radio; regional tourist board;
  leaflets/information packs; ETB/BTA*

ROCK GARDEN AND CAVE
(family business)
park/reserve; garden

Established: *1986*
Address: *Rock House, Chudleigh, Newton Abbot,
  Devon, TQ13 0EE*
Telephone: *(0626) 852134*
Access: (road) *M5/A38/B3344* (rail) *Newton
  Abbot*
Parking capacity: (cars) *50* (coaches) *2*
Hours: *nursery open all year; gardens – Easter to
  end of Oct – 9.30am to 4.30pm daily*
Admission (1992): *adults £1.50; children £0.75;
  OAP £0.75*

Facilities
Interpretation: *leaflets; guide books*
Schools: *maximum no. 50*
Catering: *1 picnic area*
Retailing: *confectionery and ice cream; plants,
  nursery stock and shrubs*
No. shops: *2*

Operations
Contacts: *Mr B Boulton; Ms D Dale; Mrs D
  Boulton*
No. employees: (high season) *4 full time; 2 part
  time* (low season) *4 full time; 1 part time*
Languages spoken: *French; German; Italian;
  Spanish*

Marketing
UK promotion: *local newspapers; other
  attractions; leaflets/information packs*

Environmental monitoring: *recycling; waste;
  water quality*

ROCKINGHAM CASTLE
(privately owned)
historic house; garden

Address: *Market Harborough, Leics, LE16 8TH*
Telephone: *(0536) 770240*
Access: (road) *M1/A6003* (rail) *kettering*
Parking capacity: (cars) *500* (coaches) *6*
Hours: *1 Apr or Easter to 30 Sept – Sun, Thur,
  BH Mon and Tues following – 1.30pm to
  5.30pm (also Tues during Aug). At other times
  by appointment*
Admission (1992): *adults £3.50; children £2.00;
  OAP £2.80; groups £2.80*
No. visitors (1992): *30 000 (est.)*

Facilities
Interpretation: *leaflets; information boards; maps;
  tour guides; guide books*
Languages: *French; German*
Schools: *educational literature; slides and video*
Disabled: *easy access*
Catering: *1 picnic area*
Retailing: *postcards/inexpensive souvenirs;
  craftwork; books; clothes; lithographs; pottery*
No. shops: *1*

Operations
Contacts: *Cdr L M M Saunders Watson (owner);
  Mrs G Saunders Watson; Mr N Hudson
  (Consultant)*
No. employees: (high season) *5 full time; 30 part
  time* (low season) *5 full time; 10 part time*
Training: *P/T operations staff and casual
  operations staff are trained in-house and
  day-to-day on job*

Marketing
Annual event(s): *living history and craft fair*
Affiliations: *HHA*
Other: *PR Company: N Hudson and Co, High
  Wardington House, Upper Wardington,
  Banbury, Oxon; market research*
UK promotion: *local newspapers; regional tourist
  board; other attractions; leaflets/information
  packs; ETB/BTA*

Environmental monitoring: *conservation of area*

ROMAN BATHS MUSEUM
(local authority run)
museum

Established: *1897*
Address: *Pump Room, Stall St, Bath, Avon*
Telephone: *(0225) 461111. Fax: (0225) 448521*
Access: (road) *M4/A4/A46/A36*
Season: *all year*
Admission (1992): *adults £3.80; children £1.80;
  OAP £3.80; student £3.80; under 8s and local
  residents free*
No. visitors (1992): *825 000*

Facilities
Interpretation: *information boards; slides; tour
  guides; guide books; infobars*
Languages: *Japanese; Dutch; French; German;
  Italian; Spanish; many more*
Children: *nappy changing*
Schools: *lecture/talk*
Disabled: *disabled toilets; helpers; guide trained in
  sign language*
Catering: *1 waiter/waitress served*
Retailing: *postcards/inexpensive souvenirs;
  confectionery and ice cream; books; clothes;
  reproductions of famous artefacts; education
  related publications; gifts*
No. shops: *3*

Operations
Contacts: *Mr S Clews (Keeper of Local History);
  Mr N Smith (Personnel Officer); Mrs K Dyer
  (Shops Manageress); Mr S Bird (Assistant
  Director Museums)*
No. employees: (high season) *19 full time; 37 part
  time* (low season) *19 full time; 23 part time*
Training: *F/T operations staff, F/T management,
  P/T operations staff and P/T management are
  trained in-house and externally and on specific
  courses and day-to-day on job*

Marketing
Annual event: *open week*
Affiliations: *Council for British Archaeology,
  Museums Association*
Other: *market research*
UK promotion: *regional tourist board; leaflets/
  information packs*
Worldwide city marketing promotion: *British
  Tourist Authority*

ROMAN VILLA BRADING
(privately owned)
monument; museum

Address: *Isle of Wight, c/o agents: Dreweatt
  Neate, Staple Chambers, Winchester*
Telephone: *(0962) 842233. Fax: (0962) 841349*
Hours: *1 Apr to 30 Sept – 10am to 5.30pm daily.
  By arrangement Oct to Mar*
No. visitors (1992): *20 000 (est.)*

Facilities
Interpretation: *leaflets; tour guides*
Schools: *lecture/talk*
Catering: *1 picnic area*
Retailing: *postcards/inexpensive souvenirs; books;
  reproductions of famous artefacts*
No. shops: *1*

Operations
Contacts: *Ms J Bagnall (Curator); Mr D Bashford
  (Assistant); Dreweatt Neate (agents)*
No. employees: (high season) *4 part time* (low
  season) *1 part time*
Languages spoken: *French; German; Italian;
  Spanish*

Marketing
UK promotion: *regional tourist board; other
  attractions; leaflets/information packs; ETB/
  BTA*

Environmental monitoring: *water quality;
  energy consumption; humidity and
  temperature*

**ROMANY FOLKLORE MUSEUM AND
WORKSHOP**
(privately owned)
museum; working museum

Established: *1975*
Address: *Limes End Yard, High St, Selborne,
  Hants*
Telephone: *(042050) 486*
Access: (road) *B3006* (rail) *Alton*
Season: *all year*
Hours: *10.30am to 5.30pm*
Admission (1992): *adults £1.50; children £0.75*

Facilities
Interpretation: *personally conducted tour*
Schools: *maximum no. 40; educational literature;
  lecture/talk*
Disabled: *easy access*
Retailing: *postcards/inexpensive souvenirs;
  craftwork; books; clothes*
No. shops: *1*

Operations
Contact: *Mr P Ingram (owner)*

Marketing
Annual event(s): *Afternoon of live folk music*
UK promotion: *local newspapers; regional tourist
  board; leaflets/information packs*

**ROMNEY, HYTHE AND DYMCHURCH
RAILWAY**
(plc)
tourist railway

Established: *1927*
Address: *New Romney Station, New Romney,
  Kent, TN28 8PL*
Telephone: *(0679) 62353. Fax: (0679) 63591*
Access: (road) *M20/A259*
Parking capacity: (cars) *340*
Hours: *Easter to Sept – daily; Mar and Oct –
  weekends only*
Admission (1992): *depends on length of journey*
No. visitors (1992): *150 000 (est.)*

Facilities
Interpretation: *leaflets; information boards; guide
  books*
Children: *adventure playground; nappy changing*
Schools: *educational literature; educational tour;
  video loan before visit*
Disabled: *easy access*
Catering: *2 picnic areas*
Retailing: *postcards/inexpensive souvenirs;
  confectionery and ice cream; books; models, die
  cast, toys, videos*
No. shops: *4*

Operations

Contacts: *J B Snell (Managing Director); J Roberts (Administrative Manager); B Smith (Commercial Manager); D Smith (Marketing Manager)*
No. employees: *(high season) 35 full time; 25 part time (low season) 35 full time*
Training: *F/T operations staff, P/T operations staff and casual operations staff are trained in-house and day-to-day on job*
Languages spoken: *Romany*

Marketing

Annual event(s): *steam and diesel gala, bus rally, On Parade*
Sponsor(s): *Kodak, Eastbourne buses*
Affiliations: *AIR, AMR*
Other: *press office*
UK promotion: *radio; local newspapers; regional tourist board; other attractions; leaflets/ information packs; ETB/BTA*

ROTHER VALLEY COUNTRY PARK
(local authority run)
park/reserve

Established: *1983*
Address: *Mansfield Rd, Wales Bar, Sheffield, S31 8PE*
Telephone: *(0742) 471452.* Fax: *(0742) 481251*
Access: (road) *M1/A618* (rail) *Kiveton Bridge*
Parking capacity: (cars) *5000* (coaches) *15*
Season: *all year*
Hours: *8.30am to dusk*
Admission (1992): *£1.50 per car May to Sept*
No. visitors (1992): *750 000 (est.)*

Facilities

Interpretation: *videos; leaflets; information boards; maps*
Children: *adventure playground; play area; nappy changing*
Schools: *maximum no. 40; educational literature; audio/visual presentation; lecture/talk*
Disabled: *easy access; disabled toilets*
Catering: *1 picnic area*
Franchisees: *8.30am to dusk*
Retailing: *postcards/inexpensive souvenirs; confectionery and ice cream; craftwork; books; clothes*
No. shops: *more than 4*

Operations

Contacts: *P Middleton (Manager); R Lunghi (Administrator)*
No. employees: *(high season) 45 full time; 2 part time (low season) 20 full time; 2 part time*
Training: *F/T operations staff, F/T management, P/T operations staff, P/T management, casual operations staff and casual management are trained in-house and externally and on specific courses and day-to-day on job*

Marketing

Annual event(s): *various*
Sponsor(s): *various*
Affiliations: *Tourist Board, MNOEA, LLAM*
Other: *press office; market research*
UK promotion: *radio; local newspapers; regional tourist board; leaflets/information packs; ETB/ BTA; public transport*

ROTHERFIELD PARK
(privately owned)
historic house; garden

Established: *1988*
Address: *East Tisted, Alton, Hampshire, GU34 3QL*
Telephone: *(0420) 58204.* Fax: *(0420) 587312*
Access: (road) *M3/A32* (rail) *Alton*
Parking capacity: (cars) *300*
Hours: *Easter, Spring and Summer BH and 1st 7 days in June, July and Aug – 2pm to 5pm (teas available). Garden only – Thur and Sun, Easter to end Sept – 2pm to 5pm (no teas)*
Admission (1992): *adults £2.50; OAP £2.50; student £2.50; charges for garden only £1.00*
No. visitors (1992): *2500*

Facilities

Interpretation: *leaflets; maps; guide books*
Schools: *maximum no. 50; educational literature*
Disabled: *easy access; disabled toilets; guide book*
Catering: *1 picnic area*
Retailing: *postcards/inexpensive souvenirs*
No. shops: *1*

Operations

Contacts: *Sir James Scott (owner); Lady Scott*

Marketing

Annual event(s): *fairs and horse trials*
Affiliations: *HHA*
UK promotion: *local newspapers; regional tourist board; leaflets/information packs; ETB/BTA*

Environmental monitoring: *recycling; waste; water quality; energy consumption; hazardous materials; chemical usage*

ROUGEMONT HOUSE MUSEUM
(local authority run)
historic house; museum

Established: *1988*
Address: *Castle St, Exeter*
Telephone: *(0392) 265858.* Fax: *(0392) 421252*
Access: (road) *M5* (rail) *Exeter Central/Exeter St David's*
Hours: *Easter to Oct – Mon to Sat – 10am to 5.30pm*
Admission (1992): *adults £1.50; children £0.75; OAP £0.75; student £0.75; family ticket £3.50*
No. visitors (1992): *30 000 (est.)*

Facilities

Interpretation: *videos; leaflets; audio tapes; information boards*
Schools: *maximum no. 50; educational literature; lecture/talk*
Catering: *1 waiter/waitress served*
Retailing: *postcards/inexpensive souvenirs; books; relevant to temporary exhibits*
No. shops: *1*

Operations

Contacts: *Ms J Simpson (Museum Services Manager); Ms L Adamson (Personnel, Exeter City Council) Ms R Randall (Press and Public Events Officer)*
No. employees: *(high season) 4 full time; 4 part time*
Training: *F/T operations staff are trained in-house and day-to-day on job*
Languages spoken: *French*

Marketing

Press office; market research
UK promotion: *regional tourist board; leaflets/ information packs; local publications, coach operators H/BK; ETB/BTA*

Environmental monitoring: *recycling; waste*

ROYAL AIR FORCE MUSEUM
(trust)
museum

Established: *1972*
Address: *Grahame Park Way, Hendon, London, NW9 5LL*
Telephone: *(081) 205 2266.* Fax: *(081) 200 1751*
Access: (road) *M25/M1/A1/A41/A5* (rail) *Colindale*
Parking capacity: (cars) *250* (coaches) *15*
Season: *all year*
Hours: *10am to 6pm daily except 24 to 26 Dec and 1 Jan*
Admission (1992): *adults £4.50; children £2.25; OAP £2.25; student £2.25; ub40 £2.25; registered disabled free*
No. visitors (1992): *180 000*

Facilities

Interpretation: *videos; information boards; slides; tour guides; guide books*
Children: *nappy changing*

Schools: *audio/visual presentation; lecture/talk*
Disabled: *easy access; disabled toilets; Braille/ sound posts; wheelchairs*
Catering: *1 picnic area*
Franchisees: *10am to 6pm daily except 24 to 26 Dec and 1 Jan*
Retailing: *postcards/inexpensive souvenirs; books; clothes; reproductions of famous artefacts; prints; videos; model kits*
No. shops: *1*

Operations

Contacts: *Dr M Fopp (Director); Mr R Craig (Secretary); Mr M Barry (Marketing)*
No. employees: *(high season) 90 full time*
Training: *F/T operations staff and F/T management are trained in-house and on specific courses and day-to-day on job using Council issues*

Marketing

Affiliations: *LTB, ETB, MA*
Other: *press office; market research*
UK promotion: *national newspapers; local newspapers; regional tourist board; other attractions; leaflets/information packs; ETB/ BTA*
Europe/USA promotion: *leaflets/brochures; British Tourist Authority; LTB*

ROYAL ALBERT MEMORIAL MUSEUM
(local authority run)
museum

Established: *1869*
Address: *Queen St, Exeter, EX4 3RX*
Telephone: *(0392) 265858.* Fax: *(0392) 421252*
Access: (road) *M5* (rail) *Exeter Central/Exeter St Davids*
Season: *all year*
Hours: *Tues to Sat – 10am to 5.30pm*
Admission (1992): *free*
No. visitors (1992): *130 327*

Facilities

Interpretation: *leaflets; information boards*
Schools: *maximum no. 60; educational literature; lecture/talk*
Retailing: *postcards/inexpensive souvenirs; craftwork; books; reproductions of famous artefacts; models and colouring sheets; gifts*
No. shops: *1*

Operations

Contacts: *Ms J Simpson (Museums Services Manager); Ms L Adamson (Personnel, Exeter City Council); Ms R Randall (Press and Public Events Officer)*
No. employees: *(high season) 25 full time; 5 part time (low season) 25 full time; 5 part time*
Training: *F/T operations staff, F/T management, P/T operations staff and P/T management are trained in-house and externally and on specific courses and day-to-day on job using videos*

Marketing

Press office; market research
UK promotion: *regional tourist board; leaflets/ information packs; hand books and local publications; ETB/BTA*

Environmental monitoring: *energy consumption; hazardous materials; temperature and humidity*

ROYAL ANCIENT AND MONASTIC CHURCH OF ST PAUL
(church)
church

Established: *685*
Address: *Church Bank, Jarrow, Tyne and Wear*
Telephone: *(489) 7052*
Access: (rail) *metro station*
Season: *all year*
Hours: *Mon to Sat – 10am to 4.30pm; Sun – 10am to 12 noon and 2.30pm to 4.30pm*
Admission (1992): *free*
No. visitors (1992): *30 000 (est.)*

Facilities
Interpretation: *leaflets; guide books*
Languages: *French; German; Italian*
Schools: *maximum no. 60; with local museum*
Disabled: *building easily accessible*
Retailing: *postcards/inexpensive souvenirs; craftwork; books*
No. shops: *1*

Marketing
Annual event(s): *Jarrow lecture and concerts*

ROYAL BOTANIC GARDENS KEW
(trust)
historic house; garden; gallery; scientific research centre

Established: *1840*
Address: *Kew, Richmond, Surrey, TN9 3AB*
Telephone: *(081) 940 1171.* Fax: *(081) 332 5197*
Access: (road) *M4/A307* (rail) *Kew*
Parking capacity: (cars) *300*
Season: *all year*
Hours: *9.30am and closing according to season. Closed Christmas Day and New Year's Day*
Admission (1992): *adults £3.30; children £1.10; OAP £1.70; student £1.70; ub40s £1.70; season tickets*
No. visitors (1992): *1 000 000 (est.)*

Facilities
Interpretation: *videos; leaflets; information boards; slides; maps; tour guides; guide books*
Languages: *Japanese; French; German; Spanish*
Children: *nappy changing*
Schools: *maximum no. 800; free entry during term time*
Disabled: *easy access; disabled toilets; wheelchairs*
Catering: *1 snack bar/food stall*
Franchisees: *9.30am and closing according to season*
Retailing: *postcards/inexpensive souvenirs; books; clothes; reproductions of famous artefacts; Kew publications; china glassware*
No. shops: *2*

Operations
Contacts: *Mr J Lavin (Deputy Director, Operations); Ms M Long (Personnel); Mr C Shillito (Retail); Mr R Joiner (Marketing)*
Training: *F/T operations staff, F/T management, P/T operations staff, P/T management, casual operations staff and casual management are trained in-house and externally and on specific courses and day-to-day on job*
Languages spoken: *French; German; Italian; Spanish; Portuguese; Russian*

Marketing
Annual event(s): *jazz concerts and Christmas events*
Other: *press office; market research*
UK promotion: *regional tourist board; other attractions; leaflets/information packs; ETB/ BTA*
Europe/Asia/PR activity promotion: *television; leaflets/brochures; radio; British Tourist Authority*

ROYAL CORNWALL MUSEUM
(charity)
museum; gallery

Established: *1818*
Address: *River St, Truro, Cornwall, TR1 25J*
Telephone: *(0872) 72205*
Access: (rail) *Truro*
Season: *all year*
Hours: *Mon to Sat – 9am to 5pm; closed BH*
Admission (1992): *adults £1.00; children £0.50; OAP £0.50; accompanied children, RIC, NACF and MA members, and school parties free*
No. visitors (1992): *40 000 (est.)*

Facilities
Interpretation: *leaflets; information boards; maps; guide books; signs*
Languages: *French; German; Spanish*

Schools: *maximum no. 60; educational literature; lecture/talk*
Disabled: *easy access; disabled toilets; other audio facilities; leaflets*
Catering: *1 self-service cafeteria*
Retailing: *postcards/inexpensive souvenirs; craftwork; books; reproductions of famous artefacts*
No. shops: *1*

Operations
Contacts: *Ms C Dudley (Director); Mr R Penhallwrick (Curator); Ms H Phillips (Buyer)*
No. employees: (high season) *11 full time; 14 part time* (low season) *11 full time; 12 part time*
Training: *F/T operations staff, F/T management, P/T operations staff and P/T management are trained in-house and externally and on specific courses and day-to-day on job using handbooks*
Languages spoken: *French; German; Italian; Spanish; Portuguese; Russian*

Marketing
Market research
UK promotion: *radio; local newspapers; regional tourist board; leaflets/information packs; district tourist board, CTB and WCTB; ETB/ BTA*

Environmental monitoring: *recycling; waste; water quality; energy consumption; hazardous materials; chemical usage; transport*

ROYAL ENGINEERS MUSEUM
(trust)
museum

Established: *1986*
Address: *Brompton Barracks, Chatham, Kent, ME4 4UG*
Telephone: *(0634) 406397.* Fax: *(0634) 822371*
Access: (road) *M2/A2*
Parking capacity: (cars) *40* (coaches) *3*
Season: *all year*
Hours: *all year – Mon to Thur – 10am to 5pm, weekends – 11.30am to 5pm*
Admission (1992): *adults £2.00; children £1.00; OAP £1.00; student £2.00; family £4.50*
No. visitors (1992): *18 000 (est.)*

Facilities
Interpretation: *videos; leaflets*
Languages: *French; German*
Schools: *maximum no. 30; no special support*
Disabled: *easy access; disabled toilets*
Catering: *1 picnic area*
Retailing: *postcards/inexpensive souvenirs; books; clothes; Royal Engineers' ties and badges*
No. shops: *1*

Operations
Contacts: *Col G W Napier (Director); J P Ellender (Administrative Officer); J Hoare (Staff Sgt); R Skinner (Marketing Manager)*
No. employees: (high season) *6 full time; 5 part time* (low season) *6 full time; 5 part time*
Training: *F/T operations staff, P/T operations staff and casual operations staff are trained in-house and day-to-day on job*
Languages spoken: *French; German*

Marketing
Market research
UK promotion: *local newspapers; regional tourist board; leaflets/information packs*
Europe promotion: *leaflets/brochures; British Tourist Authority*

ROYAL GREEN JACKETS MUSEUM
(trust)
museum

Established: *1926*
Address: *Peninsula Barracks, Romsey Rd, Winchester, Hants, SO23 8QS*
Telephone: *(0962) 863846*
Access: (road) *M3/A34* (rail) *Winchester*
Parking capacity: (cars) *300* (coaches) *50*

Season: *all year*
Hours: *Mon to Sat – 10am to 5pm; Sun – 12 noon to 4pm; closed 2 weeks at Christmas*
Admission (1992): *adults £2.00; children £1.00; OAP £1.00*

Facilities
Interpretation: *videos; leaflets; information boards; maps; tour guides; guide books; visual displays and artefacts*
Languages: *French*
Retailing: *postcards/inexpensive souvenirs; books*
No. shops: *1*

Operations
Contacts: *Major R Cannidy (Curator)*
No. employees: (high season) *10 full time* (low season) *10 full time*
Training: *F/T operations staff and F/T management are trained in-house and externally and on specific courses and day-to-day on job*

Marketing
Affiliation: *Museums and Galleries Commission*
Other: *market research*
UK promotion: *national newspapers; radio; local newspapers; regional tourist board; other attractions; leaflets/information packs; Defence Heritage, Southern Tourist Board; ETB/BTA*
Europe/USA promotion: *leaflets/brochures*

ROYAL HORTICULTURAL SOCIETY GARDEN
(trust)
garden

Established: *1989*
Address: *Rosemoor, Great Torrington, Devon, EX38 8PH*
Telephone: *(0805) 24067.* Fax: *(0805) 24717*
Access: (road) *M5/B3220*
Season: *all year*
Admission (1992): *adults £2.50; children £0.50; OAP £2.50; groups of 20+ £2.00; under 6s free*
No. visitors (1992): *90 000 (est.)*

Facilities
Interpretation: *leaflets; guide books*
Children: *nappy changing*
Disabled: *easy access; disabled toilets; guide book*
Catering: *1 picnic area*
Retailing: *postcards/inexpensive souvenirs; books; clothes*
No. shops: *1*

Operations
Contacts: *Mr C Rougier (Director, Rosemoor); Mr C Bailes (Curator)*
No. employees: (low season) *14 full time; 2 part time*
Training: *F/T operations staff, F/T management, P/T operations staff and casual operations staff are trained in-house and externally and on specific courses and day-to-day on job using handbooks and courses*
Languages spoken: *French*

Marketing
Press office; market research
UK promotion: *television; national newspapers; radio; local newspapers; regional tourist board; other attractions; leaflets/information packs*

Environmental monitoring: *energy consumption; hazardous materials; emissions*

ROYAL LONDON HOSPITAL ARCHIVES AND MUSEUM
(NHS trust)
museum; church

Established: *1989*
Address: *St Augustine with St Phillip's Church, Newark St, London, E1 2AA*
Telephone: *(071) 377 7000*
Access: (road) *M25/M11/A11* (rail) *Liverpool St*
Season: *all year*

Hours: *Mon to Fri – 10am to 4.30pm; closed BH and Christmas to New year*
Admission (1992): *free, but guided tours £1.00*
No. visitors (1992): *5000 (est.)*

Facilities
Interpretation: *videos; leaflets; audio tapes; information boards; slides; maps; tour guides; tour by booking*
Schools: *maximum no. 20; educational literature; lecture/talk*
Disabled: *easy access*
Catering: *1 snack bar/food stall*
Franchisees: *Mon to Fri – 10am to 4.30pm; closed BH and Christmas to New year*
Retailing: *postcards/inexpensive souvenirs; confectionery and ice cream; books*
No. shops: *4*

Operations
Contact: *Mr J Evans (Archivist)*
No. employees: (high season) *1 full time; 1 part time* (low season) *1 full time; 1 part time*
Training: *P/T operations staff and casual operations staff are trained in-house and externally and on specific courses and day-to-day on job*
Languages spoken: *French; German*

Marketing
Affiliations: *AIM, AMSEE, London Medical Museums Group, MA*
Other: *press office; market research*
UK promotion: *other attractions; leaflets/information packs*

Environmental monitoring: *recycling; energy consumption; hazardous materials; chemical usage*

ROYAL MARINES MUSEUM
(limited company and trust)
museum

Established: *1975*
Address: *Southsea, Hampshire, PO4 9PX*
Telephone: *(0705) 819385.* Fax: *(0705) 838420*
Access: (road) *M27/A2030* (rail) *Portsmouth*
Parking capacity: (cars) *300* (coaches) *50*
Season: *all year*
Hours: *Whitsun to Aug – 9.30am to 5pm; Sept to May – 9.30am to 4.30pm; closed for a few days over Christmas*
Admission (1992): *adults £2.50; children £1.25; OAP £1.50; student £1.25; Royal Navy and Royal Marines free*
No. visitors (1992): *38 000 (est.)*

Facilities
Interpretation: *videos; leaflets; audio tapes; information boards; slides; maps; guide books*
Children: *adventure playground*
Schools: *maximum no. 30; educational literature; lecture/talk*
Catering: *1 picnic area*
Retailing: *postcards/inexpensive souvenirs; confectionery and ice cream; craftwork; books; clothes; photoframes, etc.*
No. shops: *1*

Operations
Contacts: *Mr K Wilkins (Director); Ms L Coote (Finance); Mr A Lane (Curator); Ms J Hodgkins (Marketing)*
No. employees: (high season) *18 full time; 14 part time* (low season) *18 full time; 10 part time*
Training: *F/T operations staff, F/T management, P/T operations staff, P/T management, casual operations staff and casual management are trained in-house and day-to-day on job*

Marketing
Press office; market research
UK promotion: *television; local newspapers; regional tourist board; other attractions; leaflets/information packs*

Environmental monitoring: *hazardous materials*

ROYAL MUSEUM OF SCOTLAND
(trust)
museum

Established: *1892*
Address: *Chambers St, Edinburgh, EH14 1RZ*
Telephone: *(031) 225 7534.* Fax: *(031) 220 4819*
Season: *all year*
Hours: *Mon to Sat – 10am to 5pm; Sun – 12pm to 5pm*
Admission (1992): *free*
No. visitors (1992): *457 207*

Facilities
Interpretation: *leaflets; information boards; maps; guide books*
Children: *nappy changing*
Schools: *educational literature*
Disabled: *easy access; disabled toilets*
Catering: *1 self-service cafeteria*
Retailing: *postcards/inexpensive souvenirs; craftwork; books*
No. shops: *2*

Operations
Contacts: *Mr M Jones (Director); Ms B Buchan (Press/Advertising Officer)*
No. employees: (high season) *263 full time; 54 part time*
Training: *F/T operations staff, F/T management, P/T operations staff and P/T management are trained externally and on specific courses*

Marketing
Annual event(s): *Clydesdale Bank concerts*
Sponsor: *Clydesdale Bank*
Other: *press office; market research*
UK promotion: *national newspapers; local newspapers; regional tourist board; leaflets/information packs*

ROYAL NAVY SUBMARINE MUSEUM
(trust)
museum

Established: *1982*
Address: *Haslar Jetty Rd, Gosport, Hampshire, PO12 2AS*
Telephone: *(0705) 510354.* Fax: *(0705) 511349*
Access: (road) *M27/A32* (rail) *Portsmouth*
Parking capacity: (cars) *30* (coaches) *10*
Season: *all year*
Hours: *Nov to Mar – 10am to 3.30pm daily; Apr to Oct – 10am to 4.30pm daily*
Admission (1992): *adults £3.00; children £2.00; OAP £2.00; student £2.00*
No. visitors (1992): *83 000*

Facilities
Interpretation: *videos; information boards; tour guides; personnel*
Languages: *French; German; Braille*
Schools: *educational literature*
Disabled: *Braille/sound posts; access difficult*
Catering: *1 self-service cafeteria*
Franchisees: *Nov to Mar – 10am to 3.30pm daily; Apr to Oct – 10am to 4.30pm daily*
Retailing: *postcards/inexpensive souvenirs; books; clothes*
No. shops: *1*

Operations
Contact: *Mr G Doban (Deputy Director)*
No. employees: (high season) *6 full time; 44 part time* (low season) *6 full time; 40 part time*
Training: *F/T operations staff, F/T management, P/T operations staff and P/T management are trained externally and on specific courses*

Marketing
Annual event(s): *fun day*
Affiliations: *MA*
Other: *PR company: Aylesworth Fleming, 20 Poole Hill, Bournemouth; market research*
UK promotion: *television; local newspapers; regional tourist board; other attractions; leaflets/information packs*
Europe promotion: *leaflets/brochures; British Tourist Authority*

Environmental monitoring: *recycling; waste; water quality; hazardous materials; chemical usage*

ROYAL OBSERVATORY VISITOR CENTRE
(trust)
museum; science centre

Established: *1981*
Address: *Blackford Hill, Edinburgh, EH9 3HJ*
Telephone: *(031) 668 8405.* Fax: *(031) 668 8864*
Parking capacity: (cars) *50* (coaches) *2*
Season: *all year*
Hours: *1 Apr to 30 Sept – Mon to Fri – 10am to 4pm, Sat to Sun – 12 noon to 5pm; 1 Oct to 30 Mar – 1pm to 5pm daily*
Admission (1992): *adults £1.50; children £0.75; OAP £0.75; student £0.75; ub40s £0.75*
No. visitors (1992): *12 500 (est.)*

Facilities
Interpretation: *videos; information boards; interactive exhibits*
Languages: *French; German; Italian; Spanish*
Schools: *maximum no. 35; educational literature; lecture/talk*
Disabled: *easy access; disabled toilets; lift*
Retailing: *postcards/inexpensive souvenirs; books; clothes; charts, planispheres, photos*
No. shops: *1*

Operations
Contacts: *Richard Ellam (Development Manager); Chris Davis (Shop Manager)*
No. employees: (high season) *3 full time* (low season) *3 full time*
Languages spoken: *French; Chinese; Welsh*

Marketing
Annual event(s): *open evenings, lectured open days*
Affiliations: *Scottish Museums Council, Edinburgh Marketing*
UK promotion: *local newspapers; regional tourist board; other attractions; leaflets/information packs*

ROYAL PAVILION, ART GALLERY AND MUSEUM
(local authority run)
historic house; museum; gallery

Established: *1850*
Address: *Brighton, E Sussex, BN1 1UE*
Telephone: *(0273) 603005.* Fax: *(0273) 779108*
Access: (road) *M25/M23/A23* (rail) *Brighton*
Season: *all year*
Hours: *Oct to May – 10am to 5pm daily; June to Sept – 10am to 6pm daily*
Admission (1992): *adults £3.30; children £1.70; OAP £2.50; student £2.50; group rate £2.90*
No. visitors (1992): *315 000*

Facilities
Interpretation: *leaflets; information boards; tour guides; guide books*
Languages: *Japanese; French; German; Italian; Spanish*
Children: *nappy changing*
Schools: *maximum no. 50; educational tour; lecture/talk*
Disabled: *easy access; disabled toilets; helpers; Braille maps on request*
Catering: *1 self-service cafeteria*
Retailing: *postcards/inexpensive souvenirs; craftwork; books; clothes; reproductions of famous artefacts*
No. shops: *1*

Operations
Contacts: *J Rutherford (Director and Head of Museums); D Brever/H Jackson (Principal Marketing Manager)*
No. employees: (high season) *110 full time; 10 part time*
Training: *F/T operations staff, F/T management, P/T operations staff and P/T management are trained in-house and externally and on specific courses and day-to-day on job*

Marketing
Annual event(s): *Freeday*
Other: *market research*
UK promotion: *local newspapers; regional tourist board; other attractions; leaflets/information packs; ETB/BTA*

ROYAL PHOTOGRAPHIC SOCIETY
(registered charity loyal authority)
museum; gallery

Established: *1980*
Address: *Milsom St, Bath, BA2 6AH*
Telephone: *(0225) 462841.* Fax: *(0225) 448688*
Access: (road) *M4/A4* (rail) *Bath*
Season: *all year*
Hours: *9.30am to 5.30pm daily except Christmas Day and Boxing Day*
Admission (1992): *adults £3.00; children £1.75; OAP £1.75; student £1.75; members, under 7s and disabled visitors free*
No. visitors (1992): *100 000*

Facilities
Interpretation: *videos; leaflets; information boards; maps; tour guides; guide books*
Children: *nappy changing*
Schools: *maximum no. 60; lecture/talk; workshops by arrangement*
Disabled: *easy access; disabled toilets; powered transport*
Catering: *1 waiter/waitress served*
Franchisees: *9.30am to 5.30pm daily except Christmas Day and Boxing Day*
Retailing: *postcards/inexpensive souvenirs; books; clothes; frames, posters and prints*
No. shops: *1*

Operations
Contacts: *Ms A Nevill (Secretary) Mr S Blake (Finance); Ms D Ireland (Merchandising)*
No. employees: (high season) *30 full time; 10 part time*
Languages spoken: *French; German*

Environmental monitoring: *recycling*

ROYAL PUMP ROOM MUSEUM
(local authority run)
museum

Established: *1954*
Address: *Crown Place, Harrogate, N Yorks, HG1 2RY*
Telephone: *(0423) 503340*
Access: (road) *A61*
Season: *all year*
Hours: *Tues to Sat – 10am to 5pm; Sun – 2pm to 5pm; open BH Mon; closed 25 and 26 Dec and 1 Jan*
Admission (1992): *adults £1.00; children £0.60; OAP £0.60; local residents: adults £0.50, children £0.25*
No. visitors (1992): *40 000 (est.)*

Facilities
Interpretation: *information boards*
Schools: *maximum no. 40; educational literature; lecture/talk; object handling sessions*
Disabled: *easy access; disabled toilets*
Retailing: *postcards/inexpensive souvenirs; reproductions of famous artefacts; sulphur water*
No. shops: *1*

Operations
Contact: *Mrs M Kershaw (Curator)*
No. employees: (high season) *7 full time; 6 part time* (low season) *7 full time; 6 part time*
Training: *F/T operations staff, F/T management, P/T operations staff and casual operations staff are trained in-house and externally and on specific courses and day-to-day on job*

Marketing
Affiliation: *MA*
UK promotion: *leaflets/information packs*

ROYAL SCOTTISH ACADEMY
(charity)
gallery

Established: *1826*
Address: *The Mound, Edinburgh, EH2 2EL*
Telephone: *(031) 225 6671.* Fax: *(031) 225 2349*
Access: (rail) *Edinburgh Waverley*
Hours: *during exhibitions – Mon to Sat – 10am to 5pm, Sun – 2pm to 5pm*
Admission (1992): *charges vary*

Facilities
Interpretation: *information boards; art exhibitions*
Schools: *by prior arrangement*
Disabled: *easy access; disabled toilets*
Retailing: *postcards/inexpensive souvenirs; craftwork; books*
No. shops: *1*

Operations
Contacts: *Mr W T Meikle (Administrative Secretary); Shop Manager, RSA Enterprises*
No. employees: (high season) *3 full time; 11 part time* (low season) *3 full time; 5 part time*

Marketing
Annual event: *annual exhibition*
Sponsor(s): *various*
UK promotion: *national newspapers; local newspapers*

Environmental monitoring: *humidity and light levels*

ROYAL SIGNALS MUSEUM
(trust)
museum

Established: *1967*
Address: *Blandford Camp, Dorset, DT11 8RH*
Telephone: *(0258) 482267.* Fax: *(0258) 482603*
Access: (road) *B3082*
Parking capacity: (cars) *10* (coaches) *2*
Season: *all year*
Hours: *Mon to Fri – all year – 10am to 5pm; Sat and Sun – June to Sept only – 10am to 4pm*
Admission (1992): *free*
No. visitors (1992): *12 000 (est.)*

Facilities
Interpretation: *leaflets; guide books*
Schools: *educational literature*
Disabled: *easy access*
Retailing: *postcards/inexpensive souvenirs; books; glass; posters; signal corps items*
No. shops: *1*

Operations
Contacts: *Dr P Thwaites (Deputy Director); Major R Pickard (Curator)*
No. employees: (high season) *6 full time; 12 part time* (low season) *6 full time*
Training: *F/T operations staff and F/T management are trained externally and on specific courses*

Marketing
UK promotion: *local newspapers; regional tourist board; leaflets/information packs; ETB/BTA*
Europe promotion: *leaflets/brochures*

ROYAL VICTORIA COUNTRY PARK
(local authority run)
heritage centre; park/reserve; museum

Established: *1980*
Address: *Netley, Nr Southampton, Hampshire, SO3 5GA*
Telephone: *(0703) 455157.* Fax: *(0703) 452451*
Access: (road) *M27* (rail) *Netley*
Parking capacity: (cars) *250* (coaches) *10*
Season: *all year*
Hours: *park – Apr to Sept – 8am to 9pm, Oct to Mar – 8am to 5pm. Centre – Easter to Sept – Mon to Sat – 11am to 5pm, Sun – 10am to 5pm; 3 Oct to 12 Dec – Sun – 11am to 4pm*
Admission (1992): *on application*

Facilities
Interpretation: *videos; leaflets; audio tapes; information boards; slides*
Children: *adventure playground; play area; nappy changing*
Schools: *maximum no. 50; educational literature*
Disabled: *easy access; disabled toilets*
Catering: *1 picnic area*
Franchisees: *park – Apr to Sept – 8am to 9pm, Oct to Mar – 8am to 5pm*
Retailing: *postcards/inexpensive souvenirs; confectionery and ice cream; books*
No. shops: *1*

Operations
No. employees: (high season) *5 full time; 8 part time* (low season) *5 full time; 2 part time*
Training: *F/T operations staff, F/T management, P/T operations staff and casual operations staff are trained in-house and externally and on specific courses and day-to-day on job*

Marketing
Sponsor(s): *several*
Affiliations: *several*
Other: *press office; market research*
UK promotion: *local newspapers; regional tourist board; other attractions; leaflets/information packs*

Environmental monitoring: *hazardous materials*

ROYALTY AND EMPIRE
(limited company)
museum

Established: *1983*
Address: *Windsor and Eton Central Station, Thames St, Windsor, Berks, SL4 1PJ*
Telephone: *(0753) 857837.* Fax: *(0753) 830028*
Access: (road) *M4/M3*
Season: *all year*
Hours: *summer – 9.30am to 5.30pm daily; winter – 9.30am to 4.30pm daily*
Admission (1992): *adults £3.95; children £2.45; OAP £2.95; student £2.95; family £10.50*
No. visitors (1992): *250 000 (est.)*

Facilities
Interpretation: *videos; leaflets; information boards; slides; maps; tour guides; guide books*
Languages: *Japanese; Dutch; French; German; Italian; Spanish*
Schools: *maximum no. 200; educational literature; educational tour*
Disabled: *easy access; disabled toilets; helpers*
Catering: *2 snack bars/food stalls*
Retailing: *postcards/inexpensive souvenirs; confectionery and ice cream; craftwork; books; Royal Doulton china, Victorian gifts*
No. shops: *more than 4*

Operations
Contacts: *S Mansfield (General Manager); J Hilder (Front of House Manager); C Bretherton (Buyer); J Procter (Sales and Marketing Manager)*
No. employees: (high season) *30 full time; 30 part time* (low season) *25 full time; 15 part time*
Training: *F/T operations staff, F/T management, P/T operations staff, P/T management, casual operations staff and casual management are trained in-house and on specific courses and day-to-day on job using videos and handbooks*

Marketing
PR company: *Beer Davies Publicity, 50 Margaret St, London, W1N 7FD; market research*
UK promotion: *local newspapers; regional tourist board; leaflets/information packs; Group Travel Organiser, Coach Tours UK; ETB/BTA; operators brochures*
Europe promotion: *British Tourist Authority*

Environmental monitoring: *recycling; energy consumption*

RSPB NORTH CLIFFS AND WEST LIGHT PLATFORM
(charity)
park/reserve; zoo/wildlife attraction

Established: *1976*
Address: *c/o Warden Liam McFaul, South Cleggan, Rathlin Island, Co. Antrim, BT54 6RT*
Telephone: *(02657) 63935.* Fax: *(02657) 63952*
Access: *(road) A44 (rail) Rathlin Ferry Port*
Hours: *Apr to Sept – Mon to Sun – by prior arrangement*
Admission (1992): *free*
No. visitors (1992): *5665*

Facilities
Interpretation: *leaflets; information boards; tour guides; telescope*
Schools: *lecture/talk*
Retailing: *RSPB membership packs*

Operations
No. employees: (high season) *1 full time*
Training: *F/T management and P/T operations staff are trained in-house and on specific courses using videos and handbooks*
Languages spoken: *French; German; Italian; Spanish; Dutch*

Marketing
Annual event(s): *Around the island boat trip*
Other: *press office; market research*
UK promotion: *television; national newspapers; radio; local newspapers; leaflets/information packs*
Europe promotion: *leaflets/brochures; sister organisations*

RURAL LIFE CENTRE
(trust)
garden; museum; arboretum

Established: *1973*
Address: *Old Kiln Museum, Reeds Rd, Tilford, Farnham, Surrey*
Telephone: *(025) 125 5571 2300*
Access: *(road) M25/M3/A287 (rail) Farnham*
Parking capacity: (cars) *150* (coaches) *8*
Hours: *1 Apr to 30 Sept – Wed to Sun – 11am to 6pm*
Admission (1992): *adults £2.50; children £1.25; OAP £2.00; student £2.50; disabled £2.00*
No. visitors (1992): *8000*

Facilities
Interpretation: *leaflets; information boards; slides; guide books*
Children: *nappy changing*
Schools: *maximum no. 100; educational literature; lecture/talk; blacksmith demonstration*
Disabled: *easy access; disabled toilets; leaflets; guide book*
Catering: *1 picnic area*
Retailing: *postcards/inexpensive souvenirs; confectionery and ice cream; craftwork; books*
No. shops: *1*

Operations
Contacts: *Mr H Jackson (owner)*
No. employees: (high season) *1 part time*

Marketing
Annual event: *rustic Sunday*
UK promotion: *regional tourist board; other attractions; leaflets/information packs; ETB/BTA; Southern and SE Tourist Boards*

Environmental monitoring: *recycling; waste; water quality; energy consumption; hazardous materials; chemical usage; transport; emissions; all threats to wildlife*

RUSKIN MUSEUM
(trust)
museum

Established: *1900*
Address: *Ywedale Road, Coniston, Cumbria, LA21 8DU*

Telephone: *(05394) 41164*
Access: *(road) A590*
Hours: *Easter to Nov – Sun to Fri – 11am to 1pm, 2pm to 5pm*
Admission (1992): *adults £1.00; children £0.50; OAP £1.00; student £1.00*
No. visitors (1992): *4000 (est.)*

Facilities
Interpretation: *leaflets*
Schools: *maximum no. 10; lecture/talk*
Disabled: *easy access*

Operations
Contact: *J. Dawson (Hon Curator)*
No. employees: (high season) *2 part time*

Marketing
Market research
UK promotion: *leaflets/information packs; museum related publications*

RUSSELL-COTES ART GALLERY AND MUSEUM
(local authority run)
historic house; garden; museum; gallery

Established: *1923*
Address: *East Cliff, Bournemouth, Dorset, BH1 3AA*
Telephone: *(0202) 551009.* Fax: *(0202) 294677*
Access: *(road) A338 (rail) Bournemouth*
Season: *all year*
Hours: *Tues to Sun – 10am to 5pm except Christmas Day, New Year's Day, Good Friday, and May and Aug BH*
Admission (1992): *adults £1.00; children £0.50; OAP £0.50; student £0.50*
No. visitors (1992): *38 027*

Facilities
Interpretation: *leaflets; information boards; displays*
Children: *nappy changing*
Schools: *maximum no. 60; educational literature; lecture/talk; customised approach*
Disabled: *easy access; disabled toilets; helpers*
Catering: *1 self-service cafeteria*
Retailing: *postcards/inexpensive souvenirs; books; posters*
No. shops: *1*

Operations
Contacts: *Mr S Olding (Head of Museums Service); Ms C Easton (Administration Officer); Ms V Pirie (Keeper of Interpretation)*
No. employees: (high season) *23 full time; 5 part time*

Marketing
Annual event(s): *Bournemouth arts festival*
Sponsor(s): *local businesses*
Affiliations: *MA*
Other: *market research*
UK promotion: *local newspapers; regional tourist board; leaflets/information packs; ETB/BTA; BTA galleries leaflet*

RUTHERGLEN MUSEUM
(local authority run)
museum

Established: *1981*
Address: *King St, Rutherglen, G73 1DG*
Telephone: *(041) 647 0837*
Season: *all year*
Hours: *Mon to Sat – 10am to 5pm; Sun – 11am to 5pm*
Admission (1992): *free*
No. visitors (1992): *8662*

Facilities
Interpretation: *leaflets; information boards*
Languages: *Urdu*
Disabled: *easy access*
Retailing: *postcards/inexpensive souvenirs; books*
No. shops: *1*

Operations
Languages spoken: *French; German*

RUTHIN CRAFT CENTRE
(local authority run)
gallery; craft studios

Established: *1982*
Address: *Park Rd, Ruthin, Clwyd, LL15 1BB*
Telephone: *(08242) 4774*
Access: *(road) M54/A525/A494 (rail) Chester*
Parking capacity: (cars) *100* (coaches) *5*
Season: *all year*
Hours: *Whitsun to 30 Sept – 10am to 5.30pm daily; 1 Oct to Whitsun – Mon to Sat – 10am to 5pm, Sun – 12 noon to 5pm*
Admission (1992): *N/A*
No. visitors (1992): *200 000 (est.)*

Facilities
Interpretation: *leaflets; information boards; maps; tour guides; guide books*
Languages: *Welsh*
Schools: *lecture by special arrangement*
Disabled: *easy access; disabled toilets; leaflets*
Catering: *1 waiter/waitress served*
Retailing: *postcards/inexpensive souvenirs; confectionery and ice cream; craftwork; books; clothes; designer makers*
No. shops: *more than 4*

Operations
Contact: *Carole Netting (Craft Development Officer)*
No. employees: (high season) *3 full time; 3 part time* (low season) *3 full time; 3 part time*
Training: *F/T management and P/T management are trained in-house and externally and on specific courses and day-to-day on job*

Marketing
UK promotion: *local newspapers; regional tourist board; other attractions; leaflets/information packs*
Europe/USA promotion: *leaflets/brochures; Wales Tourist Board*

RYDAL MOUNT
(trust)
historic house; garden

Established: *1970*
Address: *Ambleside, Cumbria, LA22 9LU*
Telephone: *(05394) 33002*
Access: *(road) M6/A591 (rail) Oxenholme/Windermere*
Parking capacity: (cars) *20* (coaches) *3*
Season: *all year*
Hours: *Mar to Oct – Mon to Sun – 9.30am to 5pm; Nov to Feb – Wed to Mon – 10am to 4pm*
Admission (1992): *adults £2.00; children £0.80; group discounts*
No. visitors (1992): *40 000 (est.)*

Facilities
Interpretation: *information boards; tour guides*
Languages: *Japanese; Dutch; French; German; Italian; Spanish; many others*

Operations
Contacts: *Gordon H Brookes (Curator); Miss M Bennett (Assistant Curator); Mrs M Henderson (owner)*
No. employees: (high season) *3 full time; 11 part time* (low season) *3 full time*
Training: *F/T operations staff and P/T operations staff are trained in-house and day-to-day on job*
Languages spoken: *Welsh*

Marketing
Affiliations: *HHA*
UK promotion: *regional tourist board; other attractions; leaflets/information packs; ETB/BTA*
USA promotion: *leaflets/brochures; British Tourist Authority*

Environmental monitoring: *recycling; waste; energy consumption*

RYHOPE ENGINES MUSEUM
(trust)
museum

Established: *1972*
Address: *Sunderland, SR2 0ND*
Telephone: *(091) 565 0219*
Access: (road) *A1018*
Parking capacity: (cars) *50* (coaches) *10*
Hours: *Easter to end of year – Sat and Sun – 2pm to 5pm (also open BH and other days as announced or by arrangement)*
Admission (1992): *adults £0.50; children £0.30; OAP £0.30*
No. visitors (1992): *5000 (est.)*

Facilities
Interpretation: *leaflets; tour guides; guide books*
Schools: *maximum no. 50; educational literature*
Disabled: *helpers*
Catering: *1 snack bar/food stall*
Retailing: *postcards/inexpensive souvenirs; books; reproductions of famous artefacts*
No. shops: *1*

Marketing
Affiliations: *AIM, AIA, N of England Museums Service*
UK promotion: *radio; local newspapers; regional tourist board; leaflets/information packs; ETB/ BTA*

S

SAFFRON WALDEN MUSEUM
(local authority and museum society)
museum

Established: 1835
Address: Museum St, Saffron Walden, Essex,
CB10 1JL
Telephone: (0799) 522494
Access: (road) M11/A11 (rail) Audley End
Parking capacity: (cars) 20
Season: all year
Hours: 1 Apr to 31 Oct – Mon to Sat – 10am to
5pm, Sun and BH – 2.30pm to 5pm; 1 Nov to
31 Mar – Tues to Sat – 11am to 4pm, Sun and
BH – 2.30pm to 4.30pm
Admission (1992): adults £1.00; OAP £0.50;
student £0.50; ub40s £0.50

Facilities
Interpretation: leaflets; information boards
Schools: maximum no. 36; educational literature;
audio/visual presentation; lecture/talk;
handling sessions
Disabled: easy access; disabled toilets
Catering: 1 picnic area
Retailing: postcards/inexpensive souvenirs; books;
reproductions of famous artefacts; saffron
crocus in season
No. shops: 1

Operations
Contacts: Mr L Pole (Curator); Ms M Evans
(Visitor Services)
No. employees: (high season) 3 full time; 5 part
time (low season) 3 full time; 5 part time

Marketing
Annual event(s): exhibitions and craft events
Affiliations: E Anglia Tourist Board, MA
Other: press office; market research
UK promotion: local newspapers; regional tourist
board; other attractions; leaflets/information
packs

SALCOMBE MARITIME AND LOCAL HISTORY MUSEUM
(trust)
museum

Established: 1992
Address: Town Hall Basement, Market St,
Salcombe, Devon
Access: (road) A381 (rail) Plymouth
Hours: Easter to Oct – 10.30am to 4.30pm daily
Admission (1992): adults £1.00; OAP £1.00;
student £1.00
No. visitors (1992): 3500 (est.)

Facilities
Interpretation: information boards
Schools: maximum no. 50; lecture/talk

Marketing
UK promotion: regional tourist board; leaflets/
information packs

SALFORD MUSEUM AND ART GALLERY
(local authority run)
museum; gallery

Established: 1850
Address: Peel Park, Salford, M5 4WH

Telephone: (061) 736 2649. Fax: (061) 745 9490
Access: (road) M602/A6 (rail) Salford Crescent
Parking capacity: (cars) 60 (coaches) 6
Season: all year
Hours: all year – Mon to Fri – 10am to 4.45pm,
Sun – 2pm to 5pm
No. visitors (1992): 68 570

Facilities
Interpretation: leaflets; information boards; guide
books
Languages: French; German
Children: nappy changing
Schools: maximum no. 60; educational literature;
school resource area
Disabled: easy access; disabled toilets
Catering: 1 self-service cafeteria
Retailing: postcards/inexpensive souvenirs;
confectionery and ice cream; craftwork; books;
clothes; reproductions of famous artefacts;
audio cassettes, CDs, etc.
No. shops: 1

Operations
Contacts: M Leber (Principal Officer – Museum
and Heritage); A Core (Senior Administrative
Assistant)
No. employees: (high season) 19 full time; 2 part
time
Training: F/T operations staff, F/T management,
P/T operations staff, P/T management, casual
operations staff and casual management are
trained in-house and externally and on specific
courses and day-to-day on job

Marketing
Market research
UK promotion: local newspapers; regional
tourist board; leaflets/information packs;
NWTB

SALISBURY AND SOUTH WILTSHIRE MUSEUM
(trust)
museum

Established: 1981
Address: The Kings House, 65 The Close,
Salisbury, Wilts, SP1 2EN
Telephone: (0722) 332151
Access: (road) M3/M4/A30/A36 (rail) Salisbury
Season: all year
Hours: all year – Mon to Sat – 10am to 5pm
Admission (1992): adults £2.25; children £0.50;
OAP £1.50; student £1.50; groups £1.50; school
rates
No. visitors (1992): 43 000 (est.)

Facilities
Interpretation: leaflets; information boards; guide
books
Languages: French; German
Children: nappy changing
Schools: maximum no. 50; educational literature
Disabled: easy access; disabled toilets
Catering: 1 self-service cafeteria
Retailing: postcards/inexpensive souvenirs;
craftwork; books; clothes; reproductions of
famous artefacts; pictures, posters, publications;
speciality foods
No. shops: 1

Operations
Contacts: P R Saunders (Curator); J Reeve
(Secretary); T Fallon (Shop Manager); R Wilson
(Publicity Officer)
No. employees: (high season) 6 full time; 13 part
time (low season) 6 full time; 13 part time

Training: F/T operations staff, P/T operations
staff and casual operations staff are trained
in-house and externally and on specific courses
and day-to-day on job using videos and
handbooks
Languages spoken: French; German; Spanish

Marketing
Annual event(s): various
Sponsor(s): various
Affiliations: MA, AIM, STB, WCTB, Salisbury
and S Wiltshire Tourism Association, etc.
Other: press office; market research
UK promotion: local newspapers; regional tourist
board; other attractions; leaflets/information
packs; Open in Winter
Europe promotion: leaflets/brochures

Environmental monitoring: energy consumption

SALISBURY CATHEDRAL
(trust)
church

Address: The Close, Salisbury, Wilts
Telephone: (0722) 328726
Access: (road) M3/A30
Parking capacity: (cars) 100
Season: all year
Hours: Mon to Sat – 8am to 6.30pm extended to
8.30pm May to Aug; Sun – 12.30pm to 2.30pm
and 4pm to 6.30pm
Admission (1992): adults £1.50; children £0.50;
OAP £1.00; student £0.50 – these are
donations; booked school groups £0.35
No. visitors (1992): 500 000 (est.)

Facilities
Interpretation: leaflets; information boards; tour
guides; guide books; audio telephones
Languages: Japanese; Dutch; French; German;
Italian; Spanish
Children: nappy changing
Schools: educational literature; education centre
Disabled: easy access; disabled toilets; Braille/
sound posts; helpers; wheelchairs, interpretative
facilities for blind
Catering: 1 picnic area
Franchisees: Mon to Sat – 8am to 6.30pm
extended to 8.30pm May to Aug; Sun –
12.30pm to 2.30pm and 4pm to 6.30pm
Retailing: postcards/inexpensive souvenirs;
craftwork; books; reproductions of famous
artefacts
No. shops: 1

Operations
Training: P/T operations staff and casual
operations staff are trained in-house and day-to-
day on job and by heads of department
Languages spoken: French

Marketing
Press office; market research
UK promotion: local newspapers; regional tourist
board; other attractions; leaflets/information
packs
Europe/USA promotion: leaflets/brochures;
British Tourist Authority

SALLY LUNN'S REFRESHMENT HOUSE AND MUSEUM
(limited company)
historic house

Established: 1985
Address: 4 North Parade, Bath, Avon, BA1 1NX

Telephone: *(0225) 461634*
Access: (road) *M4* (rail) *Bath Spa*
Season: *all year*
Hours: *Mon to Sat – 10am to 5pm; Sun – 12 noon to 6pm*
Admission (1992): *adults £0.30*
No. visitors (1992): *48 000 (est.)*

Facilities
Interpretation: *audio tapes; information boards; tour guides; guide books*
Languages: *Japanese; French; German*
Schools: *maximum no. 15; lecture/talk; by arrangement*
Catering: *1 waiter/waitress served*
Retailing: *postcards/inexpensive souvenirs; books*
No. shops: *1*

Operations
Contacts: *Mr J Abraham (General Manager); Mr M Overton (owner)*
No. employees: (high season) *10 full time; 40 part time* (low season) *10 full time; 30 part time*
Training: *F/T operations staff, F/T management, P/T operations staff and casual operations staff are trained in-house and externally and on specific courses and day-to-day on job using handbooks*
Languages spoken: *French; German; Italian; Spanish*

Marketing
Affiliations: *Bath Chamber of Commerce, Bath Hotels and Restaurants Association, Association of Bath Leisure*
Other: *market research*
UK promotion: *regional tourist board; other attractions; leaflets/information packs; ETB/BTA*
Bath publications promotion: *British Tourist Authority*

Environmental monitoring: *energy consumption; hazardous materials; transport*

SALT MUSEUM, THE
(local authority run)
museum

Established: *1981*
Address: *162 London Rd, Northwich, Ches, CW9 8AB*
Telephone: *(0606) 41331.* Fax: *(0606) 350420*
Access: (road) *M6/A556*
Parking capacity: (cars) *40* (coaches) *2*
Season: *all year*
Hours: *Tues to Fri – 10am to 5pm; Sat and Sun – 2pm to 5pm*
Admission (1992): *adults £0.80; children £0.40; family £2.00*
No. visitors (1992): *20 000 (est.)*

Facilities
Interpretation: *videos; information boards; slides; exhibits, models, reconstructions*
Schools: *maximum no. 60; educational literature; audio/visual presentation; lecture/talk; handling sessions, labs*
Catering: *1 snack bar/food stall*
Retailing: *postcards/inexpensive souvenirs; confectionery and ice cream; craftwork; books; clothes; range of salt related gifts*
No. shops: *1*

Operations
Contacts: *S Penney (Curator); P Horrocks (Personnel and Training Officer)*
No. employees: (high season) *5 full time; 5 part time* (low season) *5 full time; 5 part time*
Training: *F/T operations staff, F/T management, P/T operations staff and casual operations staff are trained in-house and externally and on specific courses and day-to-day on job*

Marketing
Annual event(s): *Theatre in Education events*
Sponsor(s): *various*
Affiliation: *Museums Association*
Other: *market research*

UK promotion: *local newspapers; regional tourist board; other attractions; leaflets/information packs*

SALVATION ARMY INTERNATIONAL HERITAGE CENTRE
(charity)
heritage centre; museum

Established: *1988*
Address: *117–121 Judd St, King's Cross, London, WC1H 9NN*
Telephone: *(071) 387 1656.* Fax: *(071) 387 3768*
Access: (rail) *King's Cross*
Season: *all year*
Hours: *Mon to Fri – 9.30am to 3.30pm except PH; Sat – 9.30am to 12.30pm*
Admission (1992): *free*
No. visitors (1992): *2200 (est.)*

Facilities
Interpretation: *leaflets; information boards; tour guides; displays*
Children: *nappy changing*
Disabled: *easy access; disabled toilets; helpers; helpers on request*
Retailing: *postcards/inexpensive souvenirs; books; Salvation Army supplies*
No. shops: *1*

Operations
Contact: *Major J Fairbank (Archivist/Director)*
No. employees: (high season) *6 full time; 1 part time* (low season) *6 full time; 1 part time*
Training: *F/T operations staff, P/T operations staff and casual operations staff are trained in-house and day-to-day on job*
Languages spoken: *French; Spanish*

Marketing
UK promotion: *leaflets/information packs; ETB/BTA*

SAND
(private)
historic house; garden

Established: *1981*
Address: *Sidbury, Sidmouth, Devon, EX10 0QN*
Telephone: *(03957) 230*
Access: (road) *A375*
Parking capacity: (cars) *100* (coaches) *1*
Admission (1992): *adults £2.00; children £0.40; OAP £2.00; student £0.40*
No. visitors (1992): *664*

Facilities
Interpretation: *tour guides*
Schools: *maximum no. 40; guided tour*
Catering: *1 waiter/waitress served*
Retailing: *postcards/inexpensive souvenirs; books*
No. shops: *1*

Marketing
Affiliation: *HHA*
Other: *market research*
UK promotion: *local newspapers; regional tourist board; leaflets/information packs; ETB/BTA*

SANDTOFT TRANSPORT CENTRE
(charitable status)
museum

Established: *1971*
Address: *Belton Rd, Sandtoft, Nr Doncaster, DN18*
Telephone: *(0724) 711391*
Access: (road) *M180/A161* (rail) *Doncaster*
Parking capacity: (cars) *60* (coaches) *5*
Hours: *Contact direct for dates of trolleybus rides. Centre open on Sat and Sun afternoons – Apr to Oct*

Admission (1992): *trolleybus rides – adults £2.50; children £1.00; OAP £1.00. Centre only – adults £1.00, others £0.50*
No. visitors (1992): *5000 (est.)*

Facilities
Interpretation: *videos; leaflets; information boards; slides; personnel*
Children: *play area*
Schools: *educational literature; audio/visual presentation; lecture/talk; experience of trolleybus*
Disabled: *easy access; helpers; leaflets*
Catering: *1 picnic area*
Retailing: *postcards/inexpensive souvenirs; confectionery and ice cream; books*
No. shops: *1*

Operations
Contact: *Mr D Brown (Publicity Officer)*
Training: *casual operations staff and casual management are trained in-house and day-to-day on job and driving and conducting*

Marketing
Annual event(s): *trolleybus rides; July – Sandtoft Gathering*
Affiliation: *Destination Humberside*
Other: *market research*
UK promotion: *national newspapers; local newspapers; regional tourist board; other attractions; leaflets/information packs; ETB/BTA*

SATROSHERE
(limited company, charitable status)
hands on science centre

Established: *1990*
Address: *19 Justice Mill Lane, Aberdeen, AB1 2EQ*
Telephone: *(0224) 213232.* Fax: *(0224) 211685*
Access: (road) *A92/A96* (rail) *Aberdeen*
Season: *all year*
Hours: *weekdays – 10am to 5pm (closed Tues during term time); Sun – 1.30pm to 5pm*
Admission (1992): *adults £3.00; children £1.50; OAP £1.50; student £1.50; school groups or children with family £1.00*
No. visitors (1992): *60 000 (est.)*

Facilities
Interpretation: *information boards; guide books*
Children: *play area; nappy changing*
Schools: *maximum no. 150; educational literature; lecture/talk; lectures on request*
Disabled: *easy access; disabled toilets; helpers*
Catering: *1 snack bar/food stall*
Retailing: *postcards/inexpensive souvenirs; books; science toys*
No. shops: *1*

Operations
Contacts: *Dr A Flett (General Manager); Mr E Goodall (Floor Manager); Mrs A Butler (Shop Supervisor); Ms J Traynor (Development Officer)*
No. employees: (high season) *10 full time; 8 part time* (low season) *10 full time; 4 part time*
Training: *P/T operations staff and casual operations staff are trained in-house and day-to-day on job*

Marketing
Annual event(s): *various*
Sponsor(s): *various*
Other: *press office; market research*
UK promotion: *television; radio; local newspapers; regional tourist board; other attractions; leaflets/information packs*

Environmental monitoring: *energy consumption; transport; air cleanliness*

SAVILL GARDEN, THE
(government department)
garden

Established: *1950*
Address: *Wick Lane, Englefield Green, Egham, Surrey*
Telephone: *(0753) 860222.* Fax: *(0753) 859617*
Access: (road) *M25/A30* (rail) *Egham*
Parking capacity: (cars) *700* (coaches) *20*
Season: *all year*
Hours: *10am to 6pm daily (weekends – to 7pm)*
Admission (1992): *adults £3.00; OAP £2.50; groups of 20+ £2.50*
No. visitors (1992): *75 000 (est.)*

Facilities
Interpretation: *leaflets; tour guides; guide books*
Disabled: *easy access; disabled toilets; special signs*
Catering: *1 picnic area*
Retailing: *postcards/inexpensive souvenirs; craftwork; books*
No. shops: *1*

Operations
Contact: *J D Bond (Keeper of the Gardens)*

Marketing
Market research
UK promotion: *local newspapers; regional tourist board; national horticultural magazines*

Environmental monitoring: *hazardous materials*

SAXON TOWER CHURCH OF ST MICHAEL
(church)
church

Established: *1986*
Address: *Cornmarket St, Oxford, OX1 3EY*
Telephone: *(0865) 726543*
Season: *all year*
Hours: *Apr to Oct – 10am to 5pm; Nov to Mar – 10am to 4pm*
Admission (1992): *adults £1.00; children £0.30; OAP £0.60; student £0.60*
No. visitors (1992): *20 000 (est.)*

Facilities
Interpretation: *leaflets; guide books*

Operations
Contacts: *P W Beavis (Church Administrator)*
No. employees: (high season) *1 full time; 2 part time* (low season) *1 full time; 2 part time*

Marketing
UK promotion: *regional tourist board; leaflets/information packs; Welcome to Oxford*

SCAPLEN'S COURT MUSEUM
(local authority run)
museum

Address: *High St, Poole, Dorset, BH15 1BW*
Telephone: *(0202) 683138.* Fax: *(0202) 660896*
Access: (road) *A35* (rail) *Poole*
Season: *all year*
Hours: *Mar to Oct – Mon to Sat – 10am to 5pm, Sun – 2pm to 5pm; Nov to Feb – Sat – 10am to 5pm, Sun – 2pm to 5pm*
Admission (1992): *adults £0.75; children £0.30*
No. visitors (1992): *36 000*

Facilities
Interpretation: *leaflets; information boards*
Schools: *maximum no. 30; 2 advisory teachers*
Disabled: *access difficult*
Retailing: *postcards/inexpensive souvenirs; books*
No. shops: *1*

Operations
Contacts: *Mr G Smith (Curator); Mr C Fisher (Visitor Services)*
No. employees: (high season) *2 full time* (low season) *2 full time*
Training: *F/T operations staff, F/T management, P/T operations staff, P/T management, casual operations staff and casual management are trained in-house and externally and on specific courses and day-to-day on job*

Marketing
Annual event: *Victorian and Second World War cooking*
Affiliations: *MA, Area Museum Council for SW*
Other: *market research*
UK promotion: *local newspapers; regional tourist board; other attractions; leaflets/information packs; Bournemouth Tourism, Southern Tourist Board, Poole Tourism*

SCONE PALACE
(trust)
historic house; garden

Established: *1966*
Address: *Scone Palace, Perth, PH2 6BD*
Telephone: *(0738) 52300.* Fax: *(0738) 52588*
Access: (road) *M90/A93* (rail) *Perth*
Parking capacity: (cars) *200* (coaches) *14*
Hours: *Good Friday to mid Oct – Mon to Sat – 9.30am to 5pm, Sun – 1.30pm to 5pm (July and Aug 10am). Open at other times by appointment*
Admission (1992): *adults £4.00; children £2.20; OAP £3.20; group and student rates available*
No. visitors (1992): *108 962*

Facilities
Interpretation: *tour guides; guide books*
Languages: *Japanese; Dutch; French; German; Italian; Spanish; Hebrew; Arabic*
Children: *adventure playground; play area; nappy changing*
Schools: *maximum no. 50; educational literature; quiz, guide book and guide*
Disabled: *disabled toilets; helpers; leaflets*
Catering: *1 picnic area*
Retailing: *postcards/inexpensive souvenirs; confectionery and ice cream; craftwork; books; clothes; family tartan*
No. shops: *2*

Operations
Contact: *A R Robinson (Administrator)*
No. employees: (high season) *14 full time; 44 part time* (low season) *7 full time; 3 part time*

Marketing
Annual event(s): *horse trials, concerts, corporate hospitality, game fair, pageants*
Sponsor(s): *various*
Affiliations: *HHA, BITOA, Association of Scottish Visitor Attractions*
Other: *market research*
UK promotion: *television; national newspapers; radio; local newspapers; regional tourist board; other attractions; leaflets/information packs; ETB/BTA; STB, HH and garden directories*
Europe/Asia/Australia/USA promotion: *leaflets/brochures; British Tourist Authority*

Environmental monitoring: *collections*

SCOTLAND STREET SCHOOL MUSEUM
(local authority run)
museum; architecturally significant building

Established: *1990*
Address: *225 Scotland St, Glasgow, G5 8QB*
Telephone: *(041) 429 1202*
Access: (road) *M8* (rail) *Shield Road*
Parking capacity: (cars) *30* (coaches) *4*
Season: *all year*
Hours: *Mon – Sat – 10am to 5pm; Sun – 2pm to 5pm. Closed public and local holidays*
Admission (1992): *free*
No. visitors (1992): *68 289*

Facilities
Interpretation: *videos; leaflets; information boards; maps; tour guides*
Children: *play area; nappy changing*
Schools: *maximum no. 35; educational literature; audio/visual presentation; lecture/talk*
Disabled: *disabled toilets; disabled access to ground floor only*
Catering: *1 self-service cafeteria*

Franchisees: *Mon to Sat – 10am to 5pm; Sun – 2pm to 5pm. Closed public and local holidays*
Retailing: *postcards/inexpensive souvenirs; craftwork; books*
No. shops: *1*

Operations
No. employees: (high season) *13 full time; 4 part time* (low season) *13 full time; 4 part time*
Training: *F/T operations staff, F/T management and P/T operations staff are trained in-house and externally and on specific courses and visits to similar sites*
Language spoken: *French; German; Spanish*

Marketing
Press office; market research
UK promotion: *radio; local newspapers; regional tourist board; other attractions; leaflets/information packs; Greater Glasgow Tourist Office, STB guides and EMN*

Environmental monitoring: *energy consumption*

SCOTTISH AGRICULTURAL MUSEUM
(National Museums of Scotland)
museum

Established: *1980*
Address: *Royal Highland Centre, Ingliston, Edinburgh*
Telephone: *(031) 333 2674*
Access: (road) *A8*
Parking capacity: (cars) *5* (coaches) *3*
Hours: *May and Sept – Mon to Fri – 10am to 5pm; June, July and Aug – Mon to Sat – 10am to 5pm; winter – every Wed in school term time – 10am to 5pm*
Admission (1992): *free*
No. visitors (1992): *33 000*

Facilities
Interpretation: *leaflets; information boards; guide books*
Schools: *maximum no. 50; educational literature; audio/visual presentation*
Disabled: *easy access; disabled toilets; helpers; chair lift to 1st floor and adjacent parking*
Catering: *1 picnic area*
Retailing: *postcards/inexpensive souvenirs; craftwork; books*
No. shops: *1*

Operations
Contacts: *Mr G Sprott (Curator); Ms B Buchan (PR Officer, National Museums of Scotland)*
No. employees: (high season) *3 full time; 1 part time* (low season) *2 full time*
Training: *F/T operations staff and P/T operations staff are trained in-house and day-to-day on job*
Languages spoken: *French; German*

Marketing
Annual event(s): *Royal Highland Show*
Sponsor(s): *Royal Highland and Agricultural Society*
Other: *market research*
UK promotion: *regional tourist board; other attractions; leaflets/information packs; STB, Edinburgh Marketing and Forth Valley Tourist Board*
Europe/USA promotion: *leaflets/brochures*

SCOTTISH INDUSTRIAL RAILWAY CENTRE
(limited company)
museum; live steam centre

Established: *1984*
Address: *Minnivey Colliery, Burnton, Dalmellington, Ayrshire*
Access: (road) *A713* (rail) *Ayr*
Parking capacity: (cars) *50* (coaches) *2*
Hours: *last Sun in May, last weekends June, July and Aug, all Sun in July and Aug, and last Sun in Sept – 11am to 4pm*

Admission (1992): *adults £1.00; children £0.50; OAP £0.50; student £1.00; family ticket £2.50 maximum*
No. visitors (1992): *2350*

Facilities
Interpretation: *leaflets; maps; tour guides; guide books*
Disabled: *easy access; helpers*
Catering: *1 snack bar/food stall*
Retailing: *postcards/inexpensive souvenirs; books*
No. shops: *1*

Operations
Languages spoken: *French; German*

Marketing
Affiliations: *AIM, Transport Trust, Association of Railway Preservation Societies*
UK promotion: *radio; local newspapers; regional tourist board; other attractions; leaflets/information packs; Ayrshire Tourist Board and STB*
Europe/USA promotion: *British Tourist Authority*

SCOTTISH MARITIME MUSEUM
(limited company)
heritage centre; museum

Established: *1984*
Address: *Laird Forge, Gottries Rd, Irvine, Ayrshire, KA12 8QE*
Telephone: *(0294) 78283*
Access: (road) *A78/A71/A736* (rail) *Glasgow–Ayr*
Parking capacity: (cars) *40* (coaches) *4*
Hours: *1 Apr to 31 Oct – 10am to 5pm daily*
Admission (1992): *adults £1.75; children £0.90; OAP £0.90; student £1.75; family ticket £3.50*
No. visitors (1992): *22 500 (est.)*

Facilities
Interpretation: *leaflets; information boards; tour guides*
Schools: *maximum no. 75; educational literature; lecture/talk*
Disabled: *easy access*
Catering: *1 picnic area*
Retailing: *postcards/inexpensive souvenirs; confectionery and ice cream; craftwork; books*
No. shops: *1*

Operations
No. employees: (high season) *28 full time; 2 part time* (low season) *28 full time; 2 part time*
Training: *F/T operations staff, F/T management and P/T operations staff are trained in-house and externally and on specific courses and day-to-day on job*

Marketing
Annual event(s): *pop concert and harbour festival*
Affiliations: *SMC, Toccata*
Other: *PR company: Proscot; market research*
UK promotion: *national newspapers; radio; local newspapers; regional tourist board; other attractions; leaflets/information packs; Ayrshire Tourist Board*

SCOTTISH MINING MUSEUM
(trust) museum

Established: *1984*
Address: *Lady Victoria Colliery, Newtongrange, Midlothian, EH22 4QN*
Telephone: *(031) 663 7519.* Fax: *(031) 654 1618*
Access: (road) *A7*
Parking capacity: (cars) *70*
Hours: *1 Apr to 30 Sept – 11am to 4pm daily*
Admission (1992): *adults £1.95; children £1.00; OAP £1.00; student £1.00; unemployed £1.00; disabled £1.00*
No. visitors (1992): *17 000*

Facilities
Interpretation: *videos; leaflets; audio tapes; information boards; tour guides*
Children: *nappy changing*
Schools: *maximum no. 60; educational literature; audio/visual presentation*

Disabled: *disabled toilets*
Catering: *2 self-service cafeterias*
Retailing: *postcards/inexpensive souvenirs; replica miners lamps*
No. shops: *1*

Operations
Contacts: *Mr C McLean (Director); Ms J Gillies (Administrator); Ms V Donaldson (Marketing Manager)*
No. employees: (high season) *15 full time; 1 part time* (low season) *7 full time*
Training: *F/T operations staff and F/T management are trained in-house and externally and on specific courses using videos and handbooks*
Languages spoken: *French; German*

Marketing
Annual event(s): *open day and quoits competition*
Other: *market research*
UK promotion: *national newspapers; local newspapers; regional tourist board; other attractions; leaflets/information packs; ETB/BTA*

Environmental monitoring: *waste; energy consumption; hazardous materials; chemical usage*

SCOTTISH WHISKY HERITAGE CENTRE
(plc)
heritage centre

Established: *1988*
Address: *354 Castle Hill, The Royal Mile, Edinburgh, EH1 2NE*
Telephone: *(031) 220 0441.* Fax: *(031) 220 6288*
Access: (rail) *Edinburgh*
Season: *all year*
Hours: *10am to 5pm daily; open later during summer*
Admission (1992): *adults £3.20; children £1.75; OAP £2.00; student £2.70; family ticket (2 adults and 4 children) £8.75*
No. visitors (1992): *150 000 (est.)*

Facilities
Interpretation: *videos; audio tapes; information boards; slides; tour guides; guide books; dark ride*
Languages: *Japanese; Dutch; French; German; Italian; Spanish; Swedish*
Children: *nappy changing*
Schools: *educational literature*
Disabled: *easy access; disabled toilets; helpers by arrangement; lift*
Catering: *1 waiter/waitress served*
Retailing: *postcards/inexpensive souvenirs; books; clothes; whisky*
No. shops: *1*

Operations
Contact: *Mr G Melville (General Manager)*
No. employees: (high season) *18 full time; 15 part time* (low season) *18 full time; 10 part time*
Training: *F/T operations staff, F/T management, P/T operations staff and casual operations staff are trained in-house and externally and on specific courses and day-to-day on job using videos*

Marketing
Market research
UK promotion: *radio; regional tourist board; other attractions; leaflets/information packs; Edinburgh Marketing*

Environmental monitoring: *water quality; energy consumption*

SCOTTISH WILDLIFE TRUST
(trust)
heritage centre; park/reserve; zoo/wildlife attraction; observation hide

Established: *1969*
Address: *Loch of Lowes Visitor Centre, Dunkeld, Perthshire, PH8 0HH*

Telephone: *(0350) 727337*
Access: (road) *A9/A923* (rail) *Dunkeld*
Parking capacity: (cars) *24* (coaches) *2*
Season: *all year*
Hours: *visitor centre – Apr to Sept – 10am to 5pm daily; observation hide open all year*
Admission (1992): *free, but donation boxes*
No. visitors (1992): *40 000*

Facilities
Interpretation: *leaflets; information boards; slides; rangers and displays*
Schools: *maximum no. 30; educational literature; audio/visual presentation; lecture/talk; by arrangement*
Disabled: *helpers*
Catering: *3 picnic areas*
Retailing: *postcards/inexpensive souvenirs; books; clothes*
No. shops: *1*

Operations
Contact: *Dr A Barclay (Ranger)*
No. employees: (high season) *3 full time* (low season) *1 full time*
Training: *F/T operations staff and casual operations staff are trained in-house and day-to-day on job*
Languages spoken: *French; German; Italian; Spanish; Japanese; Chinese; Dutch; Russian; and more*

Marketing
Annual event(s): *various*
UK promotion: *regional tourist board; leaflets/information packs; Perthshire Tourist Board*

SCUNTHORPE MUSEUM
(local authority run)
museum

Established: *1909*
Address: *Oswald Rd, Scunthorpe, DN20 0HY*
Telephone: *(0724) 843533*
Access: (road) *M180* (rail) *Scunthorpe*
Parking capacity: (cars) *20* (coaches) *1*
Season: *all year*
Hours: *Mon to Sat – 10am to 5pm; Sun – 2pm to 5pm*
Admission (1992): *free*
No. visitors (1992): *30 000 (est.)*

Facilities
Interpretation: *videos; information boards; exhibits*
Schools: *maximum no. 30; education officer*
Disabled: *disabled toilets; helpers; 1st floor access difficult*
Retailing: *craftwork; books*
No. shops: *1*

Operations
No. employees: (high season) *10 full time; 1 part time* (low season) *10 full time; 1 part time*
Training: *F/T operations staff and F/T management are trained in-house and externally and on specific courses and day-to-day on job*

Marketing
Affiliation: *MA*
Other: *market research*
UK promotion: *local newspapers; leaflets/information packs*

Environmental monitoring: *water quality*

SEA LIFE CENTRE
(limited company)
zoo/wildlife attraction

Established: *1990*
Address: *The Promenade, Blackpool, Lancs, FY1 5AA*
Telephone: *(0253) 22445.* Fax: *(0253) 751647*
Access: (road) *M55/A583* (rail) *Blackpool North*
Season: *all year*
Hours: *all year – 10am to 6pm daily (open until 10pm in peak season)*

Admission (1992): *adults £3.95; children £2.75; OAP £3.25; student £1.95; disabled £2.40*
No. visitors (1992): *650 000*

Facilities
Interpretation: *videos; leaflets; audio tapes; information boards; tour guides; guide books*
Children: *nappy changing*
Schools: *maximum no. 400; educational literature; audio/visual presentation; educational tour; lecture/talk; interactive touchpools*
Disabled: *easy access; disabled toilets*
Catering: *1 self-service cafeteria*
Retailing: *postcards/inexpensive souvenirs; craftwork; books; clothes; branded gifts,toys*
No. shops: *1*

Operations
Contacts: *M Stephenson and R Haynes (Deputy General Managers) D M Sturdy (Marketing Officer)*
No. employees: *(high season) 45 full time (low season) 15 full time; 2 part time*
Training: *F/T operations staff, F/T management, P/T operations staff and casual operations staff are trained in-house and externally and on specific courses and day-to-day on job*

Marketing
Affiliation: *National Zoological Association*
Other: *press office; market research*
UK promotion: *television; local newspapers; regional tourist board; leaflets/information packs; Bedroom Browsers; ETB/BTA*

Environmental monitoring: *recycling; hazardous materials; chemical usage*

SEA LIFE CENTRE
(plc)
zoo/wildlife attraction; marine aquarium

Established: *1991*
Address: *Scalby Mills Rd, Scarborough, N Yorks, YO12 6RP*
Telephone: *(0723) 376125. Fax: (0723) 376285*
Access: *(road) A165 (rail) Scarborough*
Parking capacity: *(cars) 180 (coaches) 6*
Season: *all year*
Hours: *10am to 6pm daily except Christmas Day; open until 9pm mid July to 1st week in Sept*
Admission (1992): *adults £3.95; children £2.95; OAP £2.95; disabled £2.45; schools £2.10*
No. visitors (1992): *250 000 (est.)*

Facilities
Interpretation: *videos; leaflets; information boards; maps; guide books; personnel*
Languages: *French; German*
Children: *nappy changing*
Schools: *lecture/talk*
Disabled: *easy access; disabled toilets; lift to 1st floor*
Catering: *1 picnic area*
Retailing: *postcards/inexpensive souvenirs; confectionery and ice cream; craftwork; books; clothes; marine and sea related*
No. shops: *2*

Operations
Contacts: *Mr K Thomas (General Manager); Ms R Pearson (Deputy Manager); Ms L Swales (Retail); Ms D Remm (Catering); Ms S Burke (Press and Publicity Officer)*
No. employees: *(high season) 11 full time; 30 part time (low season) 11 full time; 5 part time*
Training: *F/T operations staff, F/T management, P/T operations staff and casual operations staff are trained in-house and externally and on specific courses and day-to-day on job using videos and Internal courses*

Marketing
Affiliation: *National Zoological Association*
Other: *press office; market research*
UK promotion: *television; local newspapers; regional tourist board; leaflets/information packs; Bedroom Browsers; ETB/BTA*

Environmental monitoring: *water quality*

SEAFORD TROPICAL BUTTERFLY HOUSE/GARDENS/MAZE
(private ownership)
garden; zoo/wildlife attraction

Established: *1988*
Address: *Seaford, Down Patrick, Co. Down, BT30 8PG*
Telephone: *(039687) 225. Fax: (039687) 370*
Access: *(road) A24*
Parking capacity: *(cars) 350 (coaches) 20*
Season: *all year*
Hours: *butterfly house open Easter to Oct – Mon to Sat – 10am to 5pm, Sun – 2pm to 6pm. Gardens open all year round*
Admission (1992): *adults £2.00; children £1.20; OAP £1.20; student £1.00*
No. visitors (1992): *31 000*

Facilities
Interpretation: *tour guides*
Children: *play area*
Schools: *maximum no. 50; educational literature; lecture/talk*
Disabled: *easy access; disabled toilets*
Catering: *1 picnic area*
Franchisees: *butterfly house – Easter to Oct – Mon to Sat – 10am to 5pm, Sun – 2pm to 6pm*
Retailing: *postcards/inexpensive souvenirs; confectionery and ice cream; craftwork; books; clothes*
No. shops: *1*

Operations
Contact: *Mr Patrick Forde (owner)*
No. employees: *(high season) 2 full time; 2 part time (low season) 1 full time; 1 part time*
Training: *F/T operations staff, P/T operations staff and casual operations staff are trained in-house and day-to-day on job using videos and Internal courses*

Marketing
Affiliation: *HHA*
Other: *market research*
UK promotion: *national newspapers; radio; local newspapers; regional tourist board; other attractions; leaflets/information packs; ETB/BTA; Northern Ireland Tourist Board*
Via NITB promotion: *leaflets/brochures; travel agents' brochures; British Tourist Authority*

Environmental monitoring: *water quality*

SEATON DELAVAL HALL
(private house)
historic house; garden

Established: *1950*
Address: *Seaton Sluice, Whitley Bay, Northumberland, NE26 4QR*
Telephone: *(091) 237 3040*
Access: *(road) A190*
Parking capacity: *(cars) 200 (coaches) 4*
Hours: *1 May to 30 Sept – Wed, Sun and BH – 2pm to 6pm*
Admission (1992): *adults £1.50; children £0.50; OAP £1.50; student £0.50; groups of over 30 people £1.00*
No. visitors (1992): *3000*

Facilities
Interpretation: *leaflets; tour guides; guide books*
Schools: *maximum no. 40; lecture/talk*
Catering: *1 picnic area*
Retailing: *postcards/inexpensive souvenirs*
No. shops: *1*

Operations
Contact: *F Hetherington (Agent)*
No. employees: *(high season) 2 full time; 3 part time*

Marketing
Annual event(s): *piano recital and antique fair*
Affiliations: *HHA*
UK promotion: *local newspapers; leaflets/information packs*

SELBY ABBEY
(parish church)
church

Established: *1069*
Address: *Selby Abbey, The Crescent, Selby, N Yorks, YO8 0PU*
Telephone: *(0757) 703123*
Access: *(road) M1/A1/A19 (rail) Selby*
Season: *all year*
Hours: *Sept to May – 9am to 4pm daily, June to Aug – 9am to 7pm daily*
Admission (1992): *free*
No. visitors (1992): *30 000 (est.)*

Facilities
Interpretation: *leaflets; information boards; tour guides; guide books*
Languages: *French; German*
Schools: *maximum no. 100; educational literature; lecture/talk*
Disabled: *easy access; wheelchair*
Retailing: *postcards/inexpensive souvenirs; books*
No. shops: *1*

Operations
Contacts: *Mr C Walters (Verger); Mr H Croxford (Guiding Manager); Mrs M Simpson (Bookshop Manager)*
No. employees: *(high season) 1 full time*
Training: *F/T operations staff are trained in-house and day-to-day on job*

Marketing
Affiliation: *Great Churches Association*
UK promotion: *regional tourist board; leaflets/information packs; ETB/BTA*
Europe promotion: *leaflets/brochures; British Tourist Authority*

SELLAFIELD VISITORS CENTRE
(plc)
industrial tourism related to nuclear industry

Established: *1988*
Address: *British Nuclear Fuels, Sellafield, Seascale, Cumbria, CA20 1PG*
Telephone: *(09467) 27027. Fax: (09467) 27021*
Access: *(road) M6/A595 (rail) Sellafield*
Parking capacity: *(cars) 100 (coaches) 10*
Hours: *Nov to Mar – Mon to Sun – 10am to 4pm, Apr to Oct – Mon to Sun – 10am to 6pm*
No. visitors (1992): *150 000 (est.)*

Facilities
Interpretation: *videos; leaflets; audio tapes; information boards; slides; tour guides; guide books*
Languages: *Japanese; French; German*
Children: *nappy changing*
Schools: *maximum no. 50; educational literature; lecture/talk; pre-school visit*
Disabled: *easy access; disabled toilets; helpers*
Catering: *1 picnic area*
Retailing: *postcards/inexpensive souvenirs; confectionery and ice cream; craftwork; books; clothes; toy models, logo items, etc.; local craftware*
No. shops: *1*

Operations
Contacts: *P M Cater (Visitors Centre Manager); Mrs C Giel (Marketing Coordinator)*
No. employees: *(high season) 12 full time; 21 part time (low season) 12 full time; 21 part time*
Training: *F/T operations staff, F/T management and P/T operations staff are trained in-house and externally and on specific courses and day-to-day on job and visits to other sites*

Marketing
Affiliations: *Cumbria Tourist Board, West Lakes TTA*
Other: *press office; market research*
UK promotion: *television; national newspapers; radio; local newspapers; regional tourist board; other attractions; leaflets/information packs; What's On in Cumbria*

SELLET HALL GARDENS
(sole trader)
garden

Established: *1985*
Address: *Sellet Hall, Kirkby, Lonsdale, Lancs, LA6 2QF*
Telephone: *(05242) 71865.* Fax: *(05242) 72208*
Access: *(road) M6/A65 (rail) Lancaster/ Oxenholme*
Parking capacity: *(cars) 20 (coaches) 2*
Season: *all year*
Hours: *all year – 10am to 5pm daily*
Admission (1992): *adults £0.70; groups £0.50*
No. visitors (1992): *10 000 (est.)*

Facilities
Interpretation: *leaflets; maps; tour guides*
Children: *nappy changing*
Schools: *maximum no. 20; educational tour; lecture/talk*
Disabled: *easy access*
Catering: *1 picnic area*
Retailing: *postcards/inexpensive souvenirs; confectionery and ice cream; books; bonsai, tools, plants, etc.; preserves, chutneys, tea, etc.*
No. shops: *1*

Operations
Contact: *J Gray*
No. employees: (high season) *2 full time; 3 part time* (low season) *1 full time; 2 part time*

Marketing
Affiliation: *HHA, British Herb Traders Association*
Other: *market research*
UK promotion: *national newspapers; radio; local newspapers; regional tourist board; other attractions; leaflets/information packs*

Environmental monitoring: *recycling; waste; hazardous materials; transport; emissions*

SELLY MANOR MUSEUM
(trust)
historic house; garden; museum

Established: *1917*
Address: *Corner of Maple Rd and Sycamore Rd, Bournville, Birmingham, B30 1UB*
Telephone: *(021) 472 0199.* Fax: *(021) 414 1348*
Access: *(road) M42/M5/A38 (rail) Bournville*
Hours: *Jan to Dec – Tues to Fri – 10am to 5pm*
Admission (1992): *adults £1.00; children £0.50; booked schools free*
No. visitors (1992): *20 000*

Facilities
Interpretation: *leaflets; information boards; maps; tour guides; guide books*
Schools: *maximum no. 50; educational literature*
Disabled: *disabled toilets; leaflets; guide book*
Retailing: *postcards/inexpensive souvenirs; craftwork; books*
No. shops: *1*

Operations
Contact: *E M Henslowe (Curator/Manager)*
No. employees: (high season) *1 full time; 4 part time* (low season) *1 full time; 4 part time*
Training: *F/T operations staff, F/T management and P/T operations staff are trained in-house and externally and on specific courses and day-to-day on job*
Languages spoken: *French; German; Italian; Spanish*

Marketing
Annual event: *craft fair*
Other: *market research*
UK promotion: *radio; local newspapers; regional tourist board; other attractions; leaflets/information packs*

Environmental monitoring: *recycling; hazardous materials; chemical usage*

SHAFTESBURY ABBEY MUSEUM AND RUINS
(limited company and trust)
monument; garden; museum; abbey ruins

Established: *1985*
Address: *Park Walk, Shaftesbury, Dorset, SP7 8JR*
Telephone: *(0747) 52910*
Access: *(road) A350*
Hours: *Easter to end of Sept – 9.30am to 5.30pm daily; Oct – weekends only*
Admission (1992): *adults £0.90; children £0.30; OAP £0.60; children in school party £0.25*
No. visitors (1992): *8000 (est.)*

Facilities
Interpretation: *leaflets*
Retailing: *postcards/inexpensive souvenirs; books; historical books*
No. shops: *1*

Operations
No. employees: (high season) *4 part time*
Training: *P/T operations staff are trained in-house and day-to-day on job*
Languages spoken: *French; German; Irish*

Marketing
Annual event: *St Edward's Supper*
Affiliation: *Area Museum Council for the SW*
Other: *press office*
UK promotion: *regional tourist board; other attractions; leaflets/information packs; heritage*

Environmental monitoring: *recycling*

SHAKESPEARE GLOBE MUSEUM
(limited company and trust)
monument; heritage centre; museum

Established: *1972*
Address: *The Shakespeare Globe Trust, Bear Gardens, Bankside, Southwark, London SE1 9EB*
Telephone: *(071) 928 6342.* Fax: *(071) 928 7968*
Access: *(rail) London Bridge*
Season: *all year*
Hours: *Mon to Sat – 10am to 5pm; Sun – 2pm to 5.30pm*
Admission (1992): *adults £3.00; children £2.00; OAP £2.00; student £2.00; group rates available*
No. visitors (1992): *15 000 (est.)*

Facilities
Interpretation: *videos; leaflets; information boards; maps*
Schools: *maximum no. 100; lecture/talk; theatrical workshops*
Disabled: *easy access; access to museum only*
Retailing: *postcards/inexpensive souvenirs; books; model of theatre*
No. shops: *1*

Operations
Contacts: *Mr R Jackson (Administrator); Mr M Abbott (PR); Mr G Gilbey (Marketing)*
No. employees: (high season) *17 full time; 8 part time* (low season) *17 full time; 8 part time*
Languages spoken: *French*

Marketing
Annual event(s): *plays*
UK promotion: *national newspapers; regional tourist board; other attractions; leaflets/ information packs*

SHALDON WILDLIFE TRUST
(trust)
zoo/wildlife attraction

Established: *1964*
Address: *Ness Drive, Shaldon, Devon, TQ14 0HP*
Telephone: *(0626) 872234.* Fax: *(0626) 872234*
Access: *(road) M5/B3199 (rail) Teignmouth*
Season: *all year*
Hours: *Mar to Sept – 10am to 6pm; Oct to Feb – 11am to 4pm*

Admission (1992): *adults £2.30; children £1.45; OAP £1.45; group rates*
No. visitors (1992): *15 000 (est.)*

Facilities
Interpretation: *leaflets; information boards; tour guides*
Schools: *maximum no. 50; educational literature; educational tour; lecture/talk*
Disabled: *disabled toilets; helpers*
Catering: *1 snack bar/food stall*
Retailing: *postcards/inexpensive souvenirs; confectionery and ice cream; books; T-shirts, tea towels, badges, etc.; beach goods*
No. shops: *2*

Operations
Contacts: *M Moore (Executive Director); S Muir (Director); C Ford (Retail Manager)*
No. employees: (high season) *3 full time; 1 part time* (low season) *3 full time; 1 part time*
Training: *F/T operations staff, P/T operations staff, casual operations staff are trained in-house and externally and on specific courses and day-to-day on job and City and Guilds 763*

Marketing
Affiliation: *Federation of Zoos*
Other: *market research*
UK promotion: *television; national newspapers; radio; local newspapers; regional tourist board; other attractions; leaflets/information packs; District Council*

SHANDY HALL
(registered charitable trust)
historic house; garden; museum

Established: *1973*
Address: *Coxwold, York, YO6 4AD*
Telephone: *(03476) 465*
Access: *(road) A19*
Parking capacity: *(cars) 12*
Hours: *June to Sept – 2pm to 4.30pm; Sun – 2.30pm to 4.30pm; groups at other times by arrangement*
Admission (1992): *adults £2.00; children £1.00; student £1.00*
No. visitors (1992): *3500*

Facilities
Interpretation: *leaflets; tour guides; guide books*
Disabled: *wheelchair possible with attendant*
Retailing: *postcards/inexpensive souvenirs; craftwork; books; unusual plants*
No. shops: *1*

Operations
Contact: *Mrs J Monkman (Hon Curator)*
No. employees: (high season) *3 part time* (low season) *3 part time*

Marketing
UK promotion: *regional tourist board; leaflets/information packs; Hambleton District Council leaflet*

Environmental monitoring: *recycling; waste; energy consumption; hazardous materials; chemical usage*

SHEFFIELD BOTANICAL GARDENS
(local authority run)
garden

Established: *1936*
Address: *Clarkenhouse Rd, Sheffield, S Yorks, S10 2LN*
Telephone: *(0742) 671115*
Access: *(road) M1/A57 (rail) Sheffield Central*
Season: *all year*
Hours: *Mon to Fri – 7.30am to dusk (max 8pm); Sat – 9am to dusk; Sun – 10am to dusk*
Admission (1992): *free*
No. visitors (1992): *50 000 (est.)*

Facilities
Schools: *maximum no. 30*

Disabled: *easy access; disabled toilets; garden for organised disabled gardens association*

Operations
Contact: *Mr D Williams (Horticultural Education Officer)*

Marketing
Annual event(s): *various*

Environmental monitoring: *chemical usage; organic garden*

SHERBORNE ABBEY
(Diocese of Salisbury)
church; abbey

Established: *927*
Address: *Sherborne, Dorset, DT9 3LX*
Telephone: *(0935) 812452*
Access: (road) *M5/M3/A30* (rail) *Sherborne*
Season: *all year*
Hours: *summer – 9am to 6pm; winter – 9am to 4pm*

Facilities
Interpretation: *leaflets; information boards; tour guides; guide books*
Languages: *Dutch; French; German; Italian; Spanish*
Schools: *educational literature; educational tour; lecture/talk; 12 expert guides*
Disabled: *helpers; loop for hard of hearing, 2 wheelchairs*
Retailing: *postcards/inexpensive souvenirs; books; guide books*

Operations
No. employees: (high season) *5 full time; 6 part time* (low season) *5 full time; 6 part time*

Marketing
Annual event(s): *concerts*
Sponsor(s): *various*
Other: *press office*
UK promotion: *local newspapers; regional tourist board; leaflets/information packs; ETB/BTA*

SHERIFF HUTTON PARK
(trust)
historic house; acting school

Address: *Sheriff Hutton, York, YO6 1RH*
Telephone: *(03477) 442.* Fax: *(03477) 442*
Access: (road) *A64* (rail) *York*
Hours: *mid Jan to mid Dec – Mon to Fri – 10am to 4.30pm*
Admission (1992): *adults £3.00; children £2.00; OAP £2.50; student £2.50; family ticket £6.00*

Facilities
Interpretation: *leaflets; personnel*
Schools: *educational literature; theatre performances*
Disabled: *disabled toilets; helpers; leaflets*
Catering: *1 picnic area*

Operations
Contact: *Mrs C Feakins (Administrator)*

Marketing
Affiliations: *HHA, Yorks and Humbs Tourist Board*
UK promotion: *local newspapers; regional tourist board; leaflets/information packs*
Europe/Australia/USA promotion: *British Council*

SHERLOCK HOLMES MUSEUM
(limited company)
museum

Established: *1990*
Address: *221b Baker St, London, NW1 6XE*
Telephone: *(071) 935 8866.* Fax: *(071) 738 1269*
Access: (rail) *Baker St*
Season: *all year*
Hours: *10am to 6pm daily*
Admission (1992): *adults £5.00; children £3.00; OAP £5.00; student £5.00*
No. visitors (1992): *70 000 (est.)*

Facilities
Interpretation: *leaflets; personnel*
Languages: *French; German; Italian; Japanese; Spanish*
Schools: *maximum no. 100; guided tour*
Catering: *1 waiter/waitress served*

Operations
Contact: *J Aidiniantz (Director)*
No. employees: (high season) *4 full time; 2 part time* (low season) *4 full time; 1 part time*
Training: *F/T operations staff, P/T operations staff and casual operations staff are trained in-house and day-to-day on job*

Marketing
overseas guide books promotion: *British Tourist Authority*

SHERWOOD FOREST VISITOR CENTRE
(local authority run)
park/reserve

Address: *Edwinstowe, Mansfield, Notts, NG21 9HN*
Telephone: *(0623) 823202*
Access: (road) *M1/A614* (rail) *Nottingham/Newark*
Season: *all year*
Hours: *summer – 10.30am to 5pm, winter – 10.30am to 4.30pm*
Admission (1992): *£1.00 car parking fee weekends and BH – Apr to Sept*
No. visitors (1992): *1 000 000 (est.)*

Facilities
Interpretation: *leaflets; information boards; maps; personnel; signs*
Languages: *Dutch; French; German; Japanese*
Schools: *maximum no. 50; educational literature; audio/visual presentation*
Disabled: *disabled toilets; other audio facilities; powered transport; wheelchairs*
Catering: *1 picnic area*
Retailing: *postcards/inexpensive souvenirs; confectionery and ice cream; craftwork; books; clothes*
No. shops: *1*

Operations
No. employees: (high season) *6 full time; 20 part time* (low season) *5 full time; 10 part time*
Training: *F/T operations staff, F/T management, P/T operations staff, P/T management, casual operations staff and casual management are trained in-house and externally and on specific courses and day-to-day on job*
Languages spoken: *Spanish*

Marketing
Annual event: *Robin Hood Festival*
Other: *press office; market research*
UK promotion: *national newspapers; local newspapers; regional tourist board; other attractions; leaflets/information packs; ETB/BTA*
Europe/USA/Canada promotion: *leaflets/brochures; British Tourist Authority*

SHETLAND CROFT HOUSE MUSEUM
(local authority run)
museum; reconstructed 19th century crofthouse

Established: *1971*

Address: *c/o Shetland Museum, Lower Hillhead, Lerwick, ZE2 0EL*
Telephone: *(0595) 5057.* Fax: *(0595) 6729*
Access: (road) *ferry*
Parking capacity: (cars) *10* (coaches) *2*
Hours: *1 May to 30 Sept – 9am to 1pm and 2pm to 5pm daily*
Admission (1992): *adults £1.00; children £0.50; OAP £0.50*
No. visitors (1992): *6000 (est.)*

Facilities
Interpretation: *leaflets; tour guides; guide books*
Schools: *maximum no. 50; educational literature; audio/visual presentation*
Retailing: *postcards/inexpensive souvenirs; books*
No. shops: *1*

Operations
Contacts: *Mr T Watt (Curator); Mr I Tait (Assistant Curator); Ms C Anderson (Museum Assistant)*
No. employees: (high season) *2 part time*

Marketing
Affiliations: *MA, SMF*
UK promotion: *radio; local newspapers; leaflets/information packs; Shetlands guides*

Environmental monitoring: *site is SSSI Conservation*

SHETLAND MUSEUM
(local authority run)
museum

Established: *1965*
Address: *Lower Hillhead, Lerwick, Shetland, ZE1 0EL*
Telephone: *(0595) 5057.* Fax: *(0595) 6729*
Access: (road) *ferry*
Season: *all year*
Hours: *Mon, Wed and Fri – 10am to 7pm; Tues, Thur and Sat – 10am to 5pm*
Admission (1992): *free*
No. visitors (1992): *36 000 (est.)*

Facilities
Interpretation: *general display*
Schools: *maximum no. 50; educational literature; lecture/talk*
Disabled: *disabled toilets; helpers; powered transport; chair lift*
Retailing: *postcards/inexpensive souvenirs; craftwork; books; clothes*
No. shops: *1*

Operations
Contacts: *Mr T Watt (Curator); Mr I Tait (Assistant Curator); Ms C Anderson (Museum Assistant)*
No. employees: (high season) *5 full time (low season) 3 full time*
Training: *F/T operations staff, F/T management and P/T operations staff are trained in-house and externally and on specific courses and day-to-day on job*

Marketing
Affiliations: *MA, SMF*
UK promotion: *radio; local newspapers; regional tourist board; Shetland Visitor, Shetland Guide book*

SHIBDEN HALL
(local authority run)
historic house; garden; museum

Established: *1935*
Address: *Lister's Rd, Halifax, W Yorks*
Telephone: *(0422) 352246.* Fax: *(0422) 348440*
Access: (road) *M62/A58* (rail) *Halifax*
Parking capacity: (cars) *100* (coaches) *10*
Hours: *Mar to Nov – Mon to Sat – 10am to 5pm, Sun – 12 noon to 5pm; Feb – Sun – 2pm to 5pm*
Admission (1992): *adults £1.50; children £0.75; OAP £0.75; student £0.75*
No. visitors (1992): *35 000*

Facilities
Interpretation: *leaflets; tour guides*
Children: *adventure playground; play area; nappy changing*
Schools: *educational literature; lecture/talk; specialist visits, education room*
Disabled: *assistance from staff*
Catering: *2 picnic areas*
Franchisees: *Mar to Nov – Mon to Sat – 10am to 5pm, Sun – 12 noon to 5pm; Feb – Sun – 2pm to 5pm*
Retailing: *postcards/inexpensive souvenirs; craftwork; books; cards*
No. shops: *1*

Operations
Contact: *Ms R Westwood (Museums Officer)*
No. employees: *(high season) 4 full time; 7 part time (low season) 4 full time; 4 part time*
Training: *F/T operations staff, F/T management, P/T operations staff, P/T management and casual operations staff are trained in-house and externally and on specific courses and day-to-day on job*

Marketing
Annual event(s): *craft weekends and Yorkshire Day*
Affiliation: *MA*
Other: *market research*
UK promotion: *radio; local newspapers; regional tourist board; other attractions; leaflets/information packs; ETB/BTA*

SHIPWRECK AND HERITAGE CENTRE
(partnership)
heritage centre; museum; shipwreck, diving exhibitions

Established: *1966*
Address: *Quay Rd, Charlestown, Cornwall, PL25 3NJ*
Telephone: *(0726) 69897.* Fax: *(0726) 815511*
Access: *(road) A390 (rail) St Austell*
Parking capacity: *(cars) 200 (coaches) 10*
Hours: *Mar to Oct – 10am daily, closing times according to season 5pm to 7pm*
Admission (1992): *adults £2.50; children £1.25; OAP £2.50; student £1.50; family ticket (2 + 2) £5.00; group booking £1.50*
No. visitors (1992): *40 000 (est.)*

Facilities
Interpretation: *videos; leaflets; audio tapes; information boards; slides; maps; tour guides; guide books; exhibits*
Children: *nappy changing*
Schools: *educational literature; audio/visual presentation; lecture/talk; quiz and pupil pack*
Disabled: *easy access; disabled toilets; special signs; guide book*
Catering: *1 licensed restaurant*
Retailing: *postcards/inexpensive souvenirs; confectionery and ice cream; craftwork; books; clothes; reproductions of famous artefacts; shipwreck artefacts*
No. shops: *1*

Operations
Contacts: *Mr J Kneale (owner); Ms R Kneale (owner)*
No. employees: *(high season) 15 full time; 15 part time (low season) 7 full time; 5 part time*
Training: *F/T operations staff, F/T management, P/T operations staff, P/T management, and casual operations staff and casual management are trained in-house and day-to-day on job using videos and handbooks*

Marketing
Affiliations: *museums*
Other: *market research*
UK promotion: *local newspapers; regional tourist board; other attractions; leaflets/information packs; Discover Cornwall; ETB/BTA*

Environmental monitoring: *energy consumption*

SHIREHALL MUSEUM
(local authority run)
museum

Established: *1992*
Address: *Common Place, Little Walsingham, Norfolk, NR22 6BP*
Telephone: *(0328) 820510*
Access: *(road) B1105*
Hours: *Easter Maundy Thur to 30 Sept – Mon to Sat – 10am to 5pm (closed Mon 1pm to 2pm); open weekends only in Oct*
Admission (1992): *adults £0.80; children £0.40; OAP £0.50; student £0.50*
No. visitors (1992): *9367*

Facilities
Interpretation: *leaflets; information boards*
Schools: *maximum no. 20; educational literature; lecture/talk; living history events*
Retailing: *postcards/inexpensive souvenirs; books; clothes; reproductions of famous artefacts; maps*
No. shops: *1*

Operations
Contact: *Mr M Warren (Curator)*
No. employees: *(high season) 1 full time; 2 part time (low season) 1 full time*
Training: *F/T management and P/T operations staff are trained externally and on specific courses and day-to-day on job using experience*
Languages spoken: *French; guided tour in French*

Marketing
Press office; market research
UK promotion: *regional tourist board; other attractions; leaflets/information packs*

Environmental monitoring: *recycling; waste*

SHUGBOROUGH
(trust)
historic house; monument; park/reserve; garden; museum; farm

Established: *1966*
Address: *Milford, Nr Stafford, ST17 0XB*
Telephone: *(0889) 881388.* Fax: *(0889) 881323*
Access: *(road) M6/A513*
Parking capacity: *(cars) 500 (coaches) 60*
Hours: *Mar to Oct – Mon to Sun – 11am to 5pm; open to booked parties at other times*
Admission (1992): *adults £3.00; children £2.00; OAP £2.00; these prices refer to house; there are other charges for museum and farm*
No. visitors (1992): *225 000 (est.)*

Facilities
Interpretation: *leaflets; audio tapes; information boards; slides; tour guides; guide books; personnel*
Languages: *French; German; Spanish*
Children: *adventure playground; nappy changing*
Schools: *educational literature; various demonstrations*
Disabled: *easy access; disabled toilets; other audio facilities*
Catering: *2 picnic areas*
Franchisees: *Mar to Oct – Mon to Sun – 11am to 5pm*
Retailing: *postcards/inexpensive souvenirs; confectionery and ice cream; craftwork; books; clothes*
No. shops: *1*

Operations
Contacts: *P Arnott (Operations Manager); G Elkin (Deputy Director); A Wood (Office Manager); J Spier (Marketing Manager)*
No. employees: *(high season) 30 full time; 100 part time (low season) 30 full time; 40 part time*
Training: *F/T operations staff, F/T management, P/T operations staff and casual operations staff are trained in-house and externally and on specific courses and day-to-day on job*

Marketing
Annual event(s): *enquire for details*
Sponsor: *Performing Arts*
Affiliation: *National Trust*

Other: *press office; market research*
UK promotion: *television; national newspapers; radio; local newspapers; regional tourist board; other attractions; leaflets/information packs; ETB/BTA*

Environmental monitoring: *Light, humidity and temperature*

SHUTTLEWORTH COLLECTION, THE
(trust)
heritage centre; museum; working collection of aeroplanes and road vehicles

Established: *1963*
Address: *Old Warden Aerodrome, Nr Biggleswade, Beds, SG18 9ER*
Telephone: *(0767) 627288.* Fax: *(0767) 627745*
Access: *(road) M1/A1 (rail) Biggleswade*
Parking capacity: *(cars) 3000 (coaches) 50*
Season: *all year*
Hours: *Apr to Oct – 10am to 5pm daily; Nov to Mar – 10am to 4pm daily*
Admission (1992): *adults £4.00; children £2.50; OAP £2.50; student £2.50*
No. visitors (1992): *82 618*

Facilities
Interpretation: *videos; leaflets; information boards; tour guides; guide books*
Children: *play area*
Schools: *maximum no. 100; educational literature; audio/visual presentation; lecture/talk; three action days*
Disabled: *easy access; disabled toilets*
Catering: *2 picnic areas*
Franchisees: *Apr to Oct – 10am to 5pm daily; Nov to Mar – 10am to 4pm daily*
Retailing: *postcards/inexpensive souvenirs; confectionery and ice cream; craftwork; books; clothes*
No. shops: *1*

Operations
Contacts: *P Symes (General Manager); K Ward (Administrative Assistant)*
No. employees: *(high season) 10 full time; 8 part time (low season) 10 full time; 8 part time*

Marketing
Annual event(s): *various*
Sponsor(s): *Argus Specialist Exhibitions/ Publications.*
Affiliations: *AIM, AMSSEE, TBD*
Other: *PR company: Cambridge Marketing Ltd, Century House, Market St, Swavesey, Cambs, CB4 5QG; press office; market research*
UK promotion: *national newspapers; radio; local newspapers; regional tourist board; other attractions; leaflets/information packs; various; ETB/BTA; national aviation and motoring magazines*
Europe/USA promotion: *British Tourist Authority*

SIDMOUTH MUSEUM
(Sid Vale Association)
museum

Established: *1971*
Address: *Hope Cottage, Church St, Sidmouth, Devon*
Telephone: *(0395) 516139*
Access: *(road) B3175*
Hours: *Apr to Oct – Tues to Sat – 10am to 4.30pm, Sun – 2pm to 4.30pm*
Admission (1992): *adults £0.50; children £0.20; OAP £0.50; student £0.20*
No. visitors (1992): *7630*

Facilities
Interpretation: *displays and exhibitions*
Schools: *maximum no. 20; educational tour; lecture/talk; by appointment only*
Retailing: *postcards/inexpensive souvenirs; books*
No. shops: *1*

Operations
Contacts: *J Connolly (Administration); B Websdale (Sales Manager)*

Languages spoken: *French; German; Japanese; Spanish*

Marketing
Affiliations: *AIM, AMCSW*
UK promotion: *regional tourist board; leaflets/information packs; ETB/BTA*

SILK MUSEUM, THE
(trust)
museum

Established: *1987*
Address: *The Heritage Centre, Roest, Macclesfield, Ches*
Telephone: *(0625) 613210*
Access: (road) *M6/A523* (rail) *Manchester/Stoke*
Season: *all year*
Hours: *Tues to Sat – 11am to 5pm; Sun – 1pm to 5pm*
Admission (1992): *adults £1.80; children £1.10; OAP £1.10; student £1.10*
No. visitors (1992): *16 000 (est.)*

Facilities
Interpretation: *leaflets; information boards; slides; maps; guide books*
Schools: *maximum no. 90; educational literature; Victorian school lesson*
Disabled: *easy access; disabled toilets; chair lift and lift*
Catering: *1 waiter/waitress served*
Franchisees: *all year – Tues to Sat – 11am to 5pm; Sun – 1pm to 5pm*
Retailing: *postcards/inexpensive souvenirs; craftwork; books; silk goods, pictures, toys; paper goods*
No. shops: *1*

Operations
Contacts: *M Stevenson (Museum Director); C Wasche (Administration Assistant); A Beard/ C Wasche (Shop Manageress)*
No. employees: (high season) *5 full time; 9 part time* (low season) *5 full time*
Training: *F/T operations staff, F/T management, P/T operations staff, P/T management, casual operations staff and casual management are trained in-house and externally and on specific courses and day-to-day on job*

Marketing
Annual event: *Christmas cheer*.
Sponsor(s): *various art and community groups*
Other: *press office; market research*
UK promotion: *local newspapers; regional tourist board; other attractions; leaflets/ information packs; NWTB, Cheshire County Tourism*
USA promotion: *leaflets/brochures*

SION HILL HALL
(trust)
historic house; museum

Established: *1982*
Address: *Kirby Wiske, Thirsk, N Yorks, YO7 4EU*
Telephone: *(0845) 587206*
Access: (road) *A167* (rail) *Thirsk*
Parking capacity: (cars) *200* (coaches) *2*
Hours: *May to Oct – 1st Sun in month – 2pm to 5pm; at other times by arrangement*
Admission (1992): *adults £3.00; OAP £2.50; student £2.50; children free*
No. visitors (1992): *2500 (est.)*

Facilities
Interpretation: *information boards; tour guides*
Schools: *maximum no. 30; educational literature*
Catering: *1 self-service cafeteria*
Retailing: *postcards/inexpensive souvenirs; confectionery and ice cream; craftwork*
No. shops: *1*

Operations
Contacts: *Mr J Bridges (Administrator); Mrs B Bridges (Curator)*
No. employees: (high season) *3 full time; 3 part time* (low season) *3 full time; 3 part time*

Marketing
Affiliation: *HHA*
UK promotion: *local newspapers; other attractions; leaflets/information packs; Hambleton BC Heritage and Tradition leaflet*

SIR JOHN SOANE'S MUSEUM
(trust and charity)
historic house; museum

Established: *1837*
Address: *13 Lincoln's Inn Fields, London, WC2A 3BP*
Telephone: *(071) 405 2107.* Fax: *(071) 831 3957*
Season: *all year*
Hours: *Tues to Sat – 10am to 5pm, 1st Tues in month – 6pm to 9pm. Closed BH*
Admission (1992): *free*
No. visitors (1992): *53 000*

Facilities
Interpretation: *leaflets; guide books*
Schools: *maximum no. 20; introductory talk*
Disabled: *helpers*
Retailing: *postcards/inexpensive souvenirs; books; slides*
No. shops: *1*

Operations
Contacts: *Mr P Thornton (Curator); Ms J Maher (Resident Warden)*
No. employees: (high season) *20 full time* (low season) *20 full time*

Marketing
UK promotion: *ETB/BTA*

SKIPTON CASTLE
(division of Fattorini Ltd)
castle

Established: *1956*
Address: *Skipton, N Yorks, BD23 1AQ*
Telephone: *(0756) 792442*
Access: (road) *M65/M6/M62/A1/A59/A65/ A629/A650* (rail) *Skipton*
Season: *all year*
Hours: *Mon to Sat – 10am to 6pm (Oct to Feb – 4pm); Sun – 2pm to 6pm. Closed on Christmas Day*
Admission (1992): *adults £2.60; children £1.30; under 5s free*
No. visitors (1992): *116 011*

Facilities
Interpretation: *leaflets; information boards; tour guides; guide books*
Languages: *Japanese; Dutch; French; German; Italian; Spanish; Esperanto*
Schools: *educational literature; information pack for purchase*
Disabled: *access difficult*
Retailing: *postcards/inexpensive souvenirs; books*
No. shops: *1*

Operations
Contacts: *Mr H Fattorini (Administrator)*
No. employees: (high season) *6 full time; 20 part time* (low season) *6 full time; 20 part time*
Training: *F/T operations staff and P/T operations staff are trained in-house and day-to-day on job*
Languages spoken: *Italian; Spanish*

Marketing
Market research
UK promotion: *local newspapers; regional tourist board; other attractions; leaflets/information packs; ETB/BTA*
Europe/Asia/Australia/USA promotion: *leaflets/brochures; British Tourist Authority*

SKIPTON HOLY TRINITY PARISH CHURCH
(parochial church council)
church

Address: *Skipton, N Yorks*
Telephone: *(0756) 700773*
Access: (road) *M62/M606/A650/A629* (rail) *Skipton*
Season: *all year*
Hours: *9am to 5pm daily*
Admission (1992): *free*
No. visitors (1992): *80 000 (est.)*

Facilities
Interpretation: *information boards; guide books; guide boards*
Languages: *Dutch; French; German; Italian; Spanish*
Disabled: *wheelchair available*
Retailing: *postcards/inexpensive souvenirs; books*
No. shops: *1*

Operations
Contact: *Revd A Botwright*

Marketing
UK promotion: *leaflets/information packs; educational visit handbook*

Environmental monitoring: *recycling; waste; energy consumption*

SMUGGLERS ADVENTURE
(limited company)
heritage centre; museum; smugglers museum

Established: *1989*
Address: *Hastings Heritage Ltd, St Clements Caves, West Hill, Hastings, E Sussex, TN34 1HY*
Telephone: *(0424) 422964.* Fax: *(0424) 717747*
Access: (road) *M25/A21/259* (rail) *Hastings*
Season: *all year*
Hours: *Sept to Easter – 11am to 4.30pm daily; Easter to Sept – 10am to 5.30pm daily*
Admission (1992): *adults £3.50; children £2.25; OAP £2.75; student £2.75; family and group rates*
No. visitors (1992): *140 000 (est.)*

Facilities
Interpretation: *audio tapes; information boards; guide books*
Languages: *Dutch; French; German; Italian; Japanese; Spanish*
Schools: *maximum no. 200; educational literature; audio/visual presentation; lecture/talk; smugglers roadshow*
Retailing: *postcards/inexpensive souvenirs; confectionery and ice cream; craftwork; books; clothes; reproductions of famous artefacts; personalised goods, toys, etc.*
No. shops: *1*

Operations
Contacts: *D Hartley (General Manager); A Donnelly (Assistant Manager); S Dickson (Retail Manager)*
No. employees: (high season) *12 full time; 6 part time* (low season) *9 full time*
Training: *F/T operations staff, P/T operations staff and casual operations staff are trained in-house and day-to-day on job*

Marketing
Annual event(s): *Hallowe'en, smugglers day*
Other: *market research*
UK promotion: *television; national newspapers; radio; local newspapers; regional tourist board; other attractions; leaflets/information packs; Group Travel Organiser; ETB/BTA*
Europe promotion: *leaflets/brochures; Hastings Tourism Department*

SMUGGLING EXPERIENCE, THE
(privately owned)
museum

Established: *1988*
Address: *The Warehouse, Cliff Top, Robin
Hood's Bay, N Yorks, YO22 4RE*
Telephone: *(0947) 880010.* Fax: *(0947) 880781*
Access: *(road) A171 (rail) Scarborough*
Hours: *Easter to Oct – 10am to 6pm*
Admission (1992): *adults £1.50; children £0.75;
OAP £0.75*
No. visitors (1992): *7909*

Facilities
Interpretation: *audio tapes; personnel; scenes and
animations*
Retailing: *postcards/inexpensive souvenirs; books*
No. shops: *1*

Operations
Contacts: *Mr R Leak/Mrs P Edwards (Partners)*
No. employees: *(high season) 1 full time*
Training: *F/T operations staff, P/T operations
staff and casual operations staff are trained
in-house and day-to-day on job using
videos*
Languages spoken: *French; German; Spanish*

Marketing
*PR company: Leawood Marketing, Winston
House, Robin Hood's Bay, N Yorks, YO22 4RL;
press office; market research*
UK promotion: *regional tourist board; other
attractions; leaflets/information packs; Out and
About; ETB/BTA*

SNIBSTON DISCOVERY PARK
(local authority run)
heritage centre; park/reserve; museum

Established: *1992*
Address: *Ashby Rd, Coalville, Leics, LE6 2LN*
Telephone: *(0530) 510851.* Fax: *(0530) 813301*
Access: *(road) M1/M42/M69/A50*
Parking capacity: *(cars) 250 (coaches) 40*
Season: *all year*
Hours: *summer – 10am to 6pm; winter – 10am to
6pm*
Admission (1992): *adults £3.00; children £2.00;
OAP £2.00; student £2.00; groups adults £2.25;
concessions £1.25*

Facilities
Interpretation: *leaflets; information boards; guide
books; signs*
Children: *play area; nappy changing*
Schools: *maximum no. 300; education room,
pre-visit*
Disabled: *easy access; disabled toilets;
Braille/sound posts; other audio facilities;
special signs; wheelchairs for hire*
Catering: *1 picnic area*
Franchisees: *summer – 10am to 6pm;
winter – 10am to 6pm*
Retailing: *postcards/inexpensive souvenirs;
confectionery and ice cream; craftwork; books;
various*
No. shops: *1*

Operations
Contacts: *Heather Broughton (Project Director);
Norman Proctor (Administrative Officer);
Steven Carrington (Retail Manager); Frances
Wortley (Marketing Officer)*
No. employees: *(high season) 48 full time; 6 part
time*
Training: *F/T operations staff, F/T management,
P/T operations, and P/T management and
casual operations staff are trained in-house and
externally and on specific courses and
day-to-day on job*
Languages spoken: *French; German*

Marketing
Other: *PR company: Lynne Butt PR, Gardeners
Cottage, School Hill, Walton on the Wolds,
Leics, LE12 8JE*

UK promotion: *local newspapers;
leaflets/information packs; Travel GB, Cocah
Tours UK, Coach Monthly*

SNOWDON MOUNTAIN RAILWAY
(plc)
tourist railway

Established: *1896*
Address: *Llanberis, Caernarfon, Gwynedd,
LL5 4TY*
Telephone: *(0286) 870227.* Fax: *(0286) 872518*
Access: *(road) A4086 (rail) Bank*
Hours: *Mar to Oct – 9am to 5pm; BH, mid July
to early Sept – 8.30am to 5pm*
Admission (1992): *adults £12.50; children £9.00;
economy return (2 + 2) £34.50*
No. visitors (1992): *125 000*

Facilities
Interpretation: *videos; leaflets; information
boards; guide books*
Schools: *no special support*
Disabled: *easy access; disabled toilets; helpers*
Catering: *1 bar/public house*
Retailing: *postcards/inexpensive souvenirs;
craftwork; books*
No. shops: *2*

Operations
No. employees: *(high season) 75 full time;
2 part time (low season) 39 full time; 1 part
time*
Training: *F/T operations staff and P/T operations
staff are trained in-house and externally and on
specific courses and day-to-day on job using
videos and handbooks*
Languages spoken: *French; Spanish*

Marketing
Market research
UK promotion: *regional tourist board; other
attractions; leaflets/information packs;
ETB/BTA*

Environmental monitoring: *energy consumption;
hazardous materials; chemical usage; transport;
emissions*

SOBRIETY WATERWAYS ADVENTURE
CENTRE AND MUSEUM
(limited company charitable trust)
museum; waterways adventure centre

Established: *1989*
Address: *Dutch Riverside, Goole, Humberside*
Telephone: *(0405) 768730.* Fax: *(0405) 768730*
Access: *(road) M62*
Parking capacity: *(cars) 20 (coaches) 2*
Season: *all year*
Hours: *Mon to Fri – 8.30am to 4.30pm*
Admission (1992): *arranged groups including
activities £1.50 per head, otherwise free*
No. visitors (1992): *3000 (est.)*

Facilities
Interpretation: *videos; leaflets; information
boards; slides; tour guides; guide books*
Children: *creche*
Schools: *maximum no. 60; educational literature;
lecture/talk; inset days and pre visits*
Disabled: *easy access; disabled toilets; helpers*
Retailing: *postcards/inexpensive souvenirs;
craftwork; books; clothes; tankards*
No. shops: *1*

Operations
Contacts: *Mr R Watson (Project Director);
Mrs L Thornton (Administration Officer);
Mrs I Kitt (Arts and Museum Officer)*
Training: *F/T operations staff and P/T operations
staff are trained in-house and externally and on
specific courses and day-to-day on job using
videos and handbooks*
Languages spoken: *French; Spanish; Welsh*

Marketing
Annual event(s): *folk concerts, exhibitions, art
weeks*

Affiliations: *Museums Federation Yorks and
Humbs, Yorks and Humbs Arts*
Other: *market research*
UK promotion: *local newspapers;
leaflets/information packs*

Environmental monitoring: *waste; water quality*

SOMERSET RURAL LIFE MUSEUM
(local authority run)
monument; museum; gallery

Established: *1976*
Address: *Abbey Farm, Chilkwell St, Glastonbury,
Somerset, BA6 8DB*
Telephone: *(0458) 831197*
Access: *(road) M5/A361/A39 (rail)
Bath/Taunton/Castle Cary*
Parking capacity: *(cars) 60*
Season: *all year*
Hours: *1 Apr to 31 Oct – weekdays – 10am to
5pm, weekends – 2pm to 6pm; 1 Nov to 31
Mar – weekdays – 10am to 5pm, Sat – 11am to
4pm*
Admission (1992): *adults £1.20; children £0.30;
OAP £0.80*
No. visitors (1992): *29 980*

Facilities
Interpretation: *leaflets; audio tapes; information
boards; guide books*
Languages: *French*
Schools: *activities by booking*
Disabled: *easy access; disabled toilets*
Catering: *2 picnic areas*
Retailing: *postcards/inexpensive souvenirs;
confectionery and ice cream; craftwork; books*
No. shops: *1*

Operations
Contacts: *Ms M Gryspeerdt (Keeper, Rural Life);
Ms A Davis (Clerical Assistant); Ms J Sparkes
(Shop Manager)*
No. employees: *(high season) 5 full time; 5 part
time*
Training: *F/T operations staff, F/T management,
P/T operations staff and casual operations staff
are trained in-house and externally and on
specific courses and day-to-day on job*
Languages spoken: *French*

Marketing
Affiliations: *MA, SW Federation for Museums*
Other: *market research*
UK promotion: *television; national newspapers;
radio; local newspapers; regional tourist board;
other attractions; leaflets/information packs;
WCTB*

Environmental monitoring: *recycling; waste*

SOOTY'S WORLD
(limited company)
historic house; museum; animated exhibition

Established: *1987*
Address: *Windhill Manor, Leeds Rd, Shipley,
W Yorks, BD18 1BP*
Telephone: *(0274) 592955.* Fax: *(0274) 531122*
Access: *(road) M606/A657 (rail) Leeds*
Parking capacity: *(cars) 50 (coaches) 4*
Season: *all year*
Hours: *Mon to Thur – 10.30am to 4.30pm, Sat
and Sun – 10am to 5pm; open Fri in school
holidays. Closed 25 and 26 Dec and 1 Jan*
Admission (1992): *adults £2.00; children £1.50;
OAP £2.00; student £1.50; disabled £1.50*
No. visitors (1992): *45 000 (est.)*

Facilities
Interpretation: *leaflets; personnel*
Schools: *maximum no. 30; no special support*
Disabled: *easy access; lift and toilet to be installed*
Catering: *1 picnic area*
Retailing: *postcards/inexpensive souvenirs; books;
clothes; toys, games, videos and cassettes*
No. shops: *1*

Operations
Contacts: Ms P Redmonds (Managing Director);
Ms S Dent (Sales Administrator); Mr B
Redmonds (Director)
No. employees: (high season) 4 full time;
5 part time (low season) 4 full time; 5 part
time
Training: F/T operations staff are trained in-house
and externally and on specific courses and
day-to-day on job using handbooks
Languages spoken: German

Marketing
Affiliation: AIM
Other: market research
UK promotion: television; local newspapers;
regional tourist board; leaflets/information
packs; ETB/BTA

Environmental monitoring: recycling; waste;
energy consumption; hazardous materials;
chemical usage

SOUTH LONDON ART GALLERY
(local authority run)
gallery

Established: 1891
Address: 65 Peckham Rd, London, SE5 8UH
Telephone: (071) 703 6120
Access: (rail) Elephant and Castle
Season: all year
Hours: Tues, Wed and Fri – 10am to 5pm;
Thur – 10am to 7pm; Sun – 2pm to 5pm.
Closed for 2 weeks between exhibitions
Admission (1992): free
No. visitors (1992): 10 000 (est.)

Facilities
Interpretation: leaflets; information boards
Schools: maximum no. 30; educational literature;
lecture/talk; workshops
Retailing: postcards/inexpensive souvenirs;
books
No. shops: 1

Operations
Contact: Mr D Thorpe (Manager)
No. employees: (high season) 4 full time (low
season) 4 full time
Training: F/T operations staff and F/T
management are trained in-house and externally
and on specific courses

Marketing
Press office; market research
UK promotion: local newspapers; leaflets/
information packs

SOUTH SHIELDS MUSEUM AND ART GALLERY
(local authority run)
museum; gallery

Established: 1976
Address: Ocean Rd, South Shields, Tyne and
Wear, NE38 0PQ
Telephone: (091) 456 8740
Access: (rail) metro station
Season: all year
Hours: Tues to Fri – 10am to 5.30pm; Sat – 10am
to 4.30pm; Sun – 2pm to 5pm
Admission (1992): free
No. visitors (1992): 205 442

Facilities
Interpretation: videos; audio tapes; information
boards; slides
Schools: maximum no. 70; education room
activities
Disabled: easy access; disabled toilets; Braille/
sound posts; other audio facilities
Catering: 1 snack bar/food stall
Retailing: postcards/inexpensive souvenirs;
confectionery and ice cream; craftwork; books;
reproductions of famous artefacts
No. shops: 2

Operations
Contacts: Mr J Wilks (Senior Curator);
Mr P Cartman (Personnel Officer);
Ms V Faulkner (Commercial Officer);
M Twelves (Principal Marketing Officer)
No. employees: (high season) 8 full time (low
season) 8 full time
Training: F/T operations staff and F/T
management are trained externally and on
specific courses

Marketing
Annual event: friends of the museum
Other: press office; market research
UK promotion: national newspapers; local
newspapers; regional tourist board;
leaflets/information packs; ETB/BTA

Environmental monitoring: Temperature and
humidity

SOUTH WALES BORDERERS MUSEUM, THE
(trust)
museum

Established: 1934
Address: The Barracks, Brecon, Powys, LD3 7EB
Telephone: (0874) 623111
Access: (road) A40 (rail) Newport
Parking capacity: (cars) 6
Hours: Apr to Sept – Mon to Sat – 9am to 1pm,
2pm to 5pm; Oct to Mar – daily – 9am to 1pm,
2pm to 5pm
Admission (1992): adults £0.70; OAP £0.70;
student £0.70
No. visitors (1992): 12 500 (est.)

Facilities
Interpretation: videos; leaflets
Schools: maximum no. 25; educational literature;
audio/visual presentation
Disabled: easy access; disabled toilets
Retailing: postcards/inexpensive souvenirs;
books; clothes; reproductions of famous
artefacts
No. shops: 1

Operations
Contacts: Major R P Smith (Curator);
Mrs C Green
No. employees: (high season) 3 full time; 7 part
time (low season) 3 full time; 7 part time
Training: F/T operations staff, P/T operations
staff and casual operations staff are trained
in-house and day-to-day on job

Marketing
PR company: Quadrant PR, Cardiff
UK promotion: local newspapers; regional tourist
board; leaflets/information packs; Welsh
Tourist Board

Environmental monitoring: recycling; energy
consumption

SOUTHEND CENTRAL MUSEUM AND PLANETARIUM
(local authority run)
museum; planetarium

Established: 1981
Address: Victoria Avenue, Southend on Sea,
SS2 6EW
Telephone: (0702) 330214. Fax: (0702) 355110
Access: (road) M25/A127 (rail) Southend
Season: all year
Hours: Mon – 1pm to 5pm; Tues to Sat – 10am to
5pm. Planetarium – Wed to Sat – shows
between 10am and 4pm
Admission (1992): adults £1.80; children £1.00;
OAP £1.00; museum free, charges as stated for
planetarium, discounts for groups
No. visitors (1992): 38 300

Facilities
Interpretation: videos; leaflets; audio tapes;
information boards
Schools: maximum no. 60; no special support;
talks by arrangement

Disabled: easy access; other audio facilities; no
access to planetarium or toilets but wheelchair
available
Catering: 1 picnic area
Retailing: postcards/inexpensive souvenirs; books;
video and audio tapes
No. shops: 1

Operations
Contacts: Mr A Wright (Curator); Mrs E Manning
(Clerical Officer); Mr P Dibdon (Senior
Supervisor); Mr K Crowe (Keeper, Human
History)
No. employees: (high season) 18 full time; 2 part
time
Languages spoken: German; Spanish

Marketing
Market research
UK promotion: radio; local newspapers;
leaflets/information packs; ETB/BTA

SOUTHPORT RAILWAY CENTRE
(limited company)
museum; railway centre with running line

Established: 1971
Address: The Old Engine Shed, Derby Rd,
Southport, Merseyside, PR9 0TY
Telephone: (0704) 530693
Access: (road) M6/M57/M58/A565/A59 (rail)
Southport
Parking capacity: (cars) 250 (coaches) 10
Season: all year
Hours: June – Mon to Fri – 1pm to 5pm,
weekends – 11am to 5pm; July and Aug – Mon
to Fri – 10.30am to 4.30pm, weekends – 11am
to 5pm; winter – weekends – 1pm to 5pm
Admission (1992): adults £2.00; children £1.00;
OAP £1.50; student £2.00; group rates available
No. visitors (1992): 21 500 (est.)

Facilities
Interpretation: leaflets; information boards; guide
books
Schools: maximum no. 999; educational literature;
audio/visual presentation; educational tour;
lecture/talk
Disabled: easy access; disabled toilets; helpers
Catering: 1 picnic area
Retailing: postcards/inexpensive souvenirs;
confectionery and ice cream; books
No. shops: 1

Operations
Contacts: D W Watkins (Chairman and
Treasurer); H Royden (Secretary); C S Mills
(Sales and Publicity Director)
Training: P/T operations staff are trained
in-house and day-to-day on job

Marketing
Annual event(s): various
Other: press office
UK promotion: national newspapers; radio; local
newspapers; regional tourist board; other
attractions; leaflets/information packs; Pocket
Guides and Maps; Merseyside Tourist Board
leaflets

SOUTHPORT ZOO AND CONSERVATION TRUST
(trust)
zoo/wildlife attraction

Established: 1967
Address: Princes Park, Southport, Merseyside,
PR8 1RX
Telephone: (0704) 538102
Access: (road) M6/M58 (rail) Southport
Season: all year
Hours: summer – 10am to 6pm daily; winter –
10am to 4pm daily
Admission (1992): adults £2.40; children £1.40;
OAP £1.90; group rates
No. visitors (1992): 80 000 (est.)

Facilities
Interpretation: leaflets; audio tapes; slides; guide
books; talks by volunteers

Children: *play area; nappy changing*
Schools: *maximum no. 500; lecture/talk*
Disabled: *easy access; disabled toilets; guide book*
Catering: *2 picnic areas*
Retailing: *postcards/inexpensive souvenirs; confectionery and ice cream; books; clothes*
No. shops: *1*

Operations
Contacts: *Mr and Mrs Petrie (Directors); P Robinson (Curator)*
No. employees: (high season) *8 full time; 6 part time* (low season) *8 full time; 2 part time*
Training: *F/T operations staff and P/T operations staff are trained in-house and day-to-day on job using handbooks*

Marketing
Annual event(s): *various*
Affiliation: *National Federation of Zoological Gardens*
Other: *press office*
UK promotion: *national newspapers; radio; local newspapers; other attractions; leaflets/information packs*

SOUTHWARK CATHEDRAL
(cathedral)
church

Address: *Montague Close, London, SE1 9DA*
Telephone: *(071) 407 3708.* Fax: *(071) 357 7389*
Access: (rail) *London Bridge*
Season: *all year*
Hours: *8am to 6pm daily*
Admission (1992): *donations*
No. visitors (1992): *15 000 (est.)*

Facilities
Interpretation: *leaflets; information boards; guide books*
Languages: *French; German; Italian; Spanish*
Schools: *educational literature; lecture/talk*
Disabled: *disabled toilets; other audio facilities*
Catering: *1 waiter/waitress served*
Franchisees: *8am to 6pm daily*
Retailing: *postcards/inexpensive souvenirs; books; reproductions of famous artefacts; giftware*
No. shops: *1*

Operations
Contact: *Canon R White (Vice-Provost)*

Marketing
Annual event: *Southwark Festival*
Other: *press office*
UK promotion: *leaflets/information packs; ETB/BTA; Southwark Heritage Centre*

SOUTHWICK COUNTRY HERB CENTRE
(privately owned)
park/reserve; garden; herb garden and shop

Established: *1990*
Address: *Southwick Farm, Nomansland, Nr Tiverton, Devon, EX16 8NW*
Telephone: *(0884) 861099*
Access: (road) *M5/A361/B3137* (rail) *Tiverton Parkway*
Parking capacity: (cars) *50* (coaches) *2*
Season: *all year*
Hours: *Mon to Sat – 10.30am to 5.30pm; Sun – 11am to 5.30pm*
Admission (1992): *free*
No. visitors (1992): *25 000 (est.)*

Facilities
Interpretation: *leaflets; tour guides*
Children: *nappy changing*
Schools: *maximum no. 30; educational literature; lecture/talk*
Disabled: *helpers*
Catering: *1 self-service cafeteria*
Retailing: *postcards/inexpensive souvenirs; confectionery and ice cream; craftwork; books; herbs, plants; garden accessories*
No. shops: *1*

Operations
Contacts: *Mr and Mrs M Menist (owners)*
No. employees: (high season) *7 part time*
Languages spoken: *French; German*

Marketing
UK promotion: *local newspapers; regional tourist board; leaflets/information packs; ETB/BTA*

SPEKE HALL, THE
(trust)
historic house; garden

Established: *1944*
Address: *The Walk, Liverpool, L24 1XD*
Telephone: *(051) 427 7231.* Fax: *(051) 427 9860*
Access: (road) *M56/M62* (rail) *Liverpool Hunts Cross*
Parking capacity: (cars) *150* (coaches) *5*
Hours: *Apr to Oct – Tues to Sun – 1pm to 5.30pm; Nov – weekends – 1pm to 4.30pm*
Admission (1992): *adults £3.00; children £1.50; OAP £3.00; student £3.00; group rate £2.40*
No. visitors (1992): *83 000 (est.)*

Facilities
Interpretation: *leaflets; information boards; maps; guide books; stewards*
Languages: *Japanese; French; German*
Schools: *maximum no. 70; educational literature; educational tour*
Disabled: *easy access; disabled toilets; Braille/ sound posts; helpers; special signs; leaflets; guide book*
Catering: *1 picnic area*
Retailing: *postcards/inexpensive souvenirs; books; clothes*
No. shops: *1*

Operations
Contact: *C Davidson (Administrator)*
No. employees: (high season) *12 full time; 14 part time* (low season) *12 full time*
Training: *F/T operations staff, F/T management, P/T operations staff and casual operations staff are trained in-house and externally and on specific courses and day-to-day on job*

Marketing
Sponsor(s): *BT, HP Chomie Pelzer*
Other: *press office; market research*
UK promotion: *local newspapers; regional tourist board; other attractions; leaflets/information packs; NWTB; ETB/BTA*

Environmental monitoring: *conserving tree species*

SPENCER HOUSE
(limited company)
historic house

Established: *1991*
Address: *27 St James's Place, London, SW1A 1NR*
Telephone: *(071) 499 8620.* Fax: *(071) 493 5765*
Access: (rail) *Green Park*
Hours: *Sun – 11.30am to 5.30pm except Aug and Jan*
Admission (1992): *adults £5.00; children £4.00; OAP £4.00; student £4.00; NT or V & A members £4.00 with card; under 10s not admitted*
No. visitors (1992): *12 500 (est.)*

Facilities
Interpretation: *leaflets; tour guides; guide books*
Languages: *Japanese; French; German; Italian; Spanish*
Disabled: *easy access; disabled toilets*
Retailing: *postcards/inexpensive souvenirs*
No. shops: *None*

Operations
Contacts: *Mr S Jones (Director); Cadogan Management*
No. employees: (high season) *15 full time*

Marketing
PR company: *Cadogan Management, 27 Albemarle St, London, W1X 3FA; press office; market research*
UK promotion: *leaflets/information packs; ETB/BTA*
Europe/Asia/Australia/USA promotion: *leaflets/brochures; British Tourist Authority*

SPEYSIDE HEATHER/GARDEN VISITOR CENTRE
(partnership)
heritage centre; garden
Established: *1972*
Address: *Skye of Curr, Dulnain Bridge, Inverness-shire, PH26 3PA*
Telephone: *(047) 985 359.* Fax: *(047) 985 396*
Access: (road) *A95* (rail) *Aviemore*
Parking capacity: (cars) *70* (coaches) *6*
Season: *all year*
Hours: *Apr to Oct – 9am to 5.30pm daily, Nov to Mar – Mon to Sat – 9am to 5pm*
Admission (1992): *adults £0.70; children £0.45; OAP £0.45; student £0.45; family ticket £1.60*
No. visitors (1992): *80 000 (est.)*

Facilities
Interpretation: *leaflets; information boards*
Languages: *Dutch; French; German; Italian; Spanish; Russian; Swedish*
Children: *adventure playground; nappy changing*
Schools: *educational literature*
Disabled: *easy access; disabled toilets*
Catering: *1 picnic area*
Retailing: *postcards/inexpensive souvenirs; confectionery and ice cream; craftwork; books; clothes; garden plants and sundries*
No. shops: *2*

Operations
Contacts: *Ms E Lambie (owner); Mr D A Lambie (owner)*
No. employees: (high season) *15 full time; 10 part time* (low season) *6 full time; 5 part time*
Training: *F/T operations staff, F/T management, P/T operations staff, P/T management, casual operations staff and casual management are trained in-house and day-to-day on job*

Marketing
Market research
UK promotion: *regional tourist board; other attractions; local tourist office*

Environmental monitoring: *water quality; humidity*

SPITBANK FORT
(privately owned)
monument; museum

Established: *1984*
Address: *1 mile from Portsmouth Harbour, postal: 15 Hillhead Rd, Fareham, Hants*
Telephone: *(0329) 664286*
Access: *Cowes/Southsea ferry* (rail) *Gosport*
Hours: *Easter to 30 Sept – 11am to 5pm. Closed Mon except BH, weather permitting*
Admission (1992): *adults £4.00; children £2.50; OAP £4.00; student £2.50*
No. visitors (1992): *15 000 (est.)*

Facilities
Interpretation: *videos; leaflets; information boards; guide books*
Schools: *maximum no. 70; educational literature*
Disabled: *not suitable*
Catering: *1 picnic area*
Retailing: *postcards/inexpensive souvenirs; confectionery and ice cream; books*
No. shops: *1*

Operations
Contacts: *Mr S Maguire (owner); Mr P Gough (owner)*
Languages spoken: *French; German*

Marketing
Annual event(s): *various*
UK promotion: *local newspapers; regional tourist board; Defence of Realm*

SPITTING IMAGE RUBBERWORKS
(limited company)
museum; tourist attraction

Established: *1990*
Address: *Cubitts Yard, James St, Covent Garden, London, WC2E 8PA*
Telephone: *(071) 240 0393. Fax: (071) 240 0719*
Access: (rail) *Charing Cross*
Season: *all year*
Hours: *Mon to Fri – 11am to 5.30pm; Sat and Sun – 11am to 6.30pm. Closed 25 and 26 Dec and 1 Jan*
Admission (1992): *adults £3.95; children £2.95; OAP £2.95; student £2.95; family ticket £11.50; group rates £1.50/£2.50*
No. visitors (1992): *186 000 (est.)*

Facilities
Interpretation: *leaflets; information boards; maps; tour guides; guide books; personnel*
Languages: *French; German*
Schools: *maximum no. 50; educational literature; audio/visual presentation; lecture/talk*
Disabled: *easy access; helpers*
Retailing: *postcards/inexpensive souvenirs; confectionery and ice cream; books; clothes; cards answer tape; TV related*
No. shops: *1*

Operations
Contacts: *Ms D Baker (Manager); Ms K McCusker (Assistant Manager); Ms N Balamash (Retail)*
No. employees: *(high season) 12 full time; 3 part time (low season) 6 full time; 2 part time*
Training: *F/T operations staff, F/T management, P/T operations staff and casual operations staff are trained in-house and day-to-day on job*

Marketing
Press office; market research
UK promotion: *national newspapers; local newspapers; regional tourist board; other attractions; leaflets/information packs; LTB*
Europe promotion: *leaflets/brochures; British Tourist Authority*

Environmental monitoring: *recycling*

SPRINGBURN MUSEUM TRUST
(trust)
museum; gallery

Established: *1986*
Address: *Atlas Square, Ayr St, Springburn, G21 4BW*
Telephone: *(041) 557 1405*
Access: (road) *M8/A803* (rail) *Springburn*
Season: *all year*
Hours: *Mon to Fri – 10.30am to 5pm; Sat – 10am to 4.30pm, Sun – 2pm to 5pm. Closed Christmas and New Year*
Admission (1992): *free*
No. visitors (1992): *220 000 (est.)*

Facilities
Interpretation: *videos; information boards; touring and temporary exhibitions*
Schools: *educational literature*
Disabled: *easy access*
Retailing: *postcards/inexpensive souvenirs; books*
No. shops: *1*

Operations
Contact: *Alison Cutforth (Curator)*
No. employees: *(high season) 5 full time; 1 part time (low season) 5 full time; 1 part time*
Training: *F/T operations staff, F/T management, P/T operations staff and P/T management are trained externally and on specific courses*
Languages spoken: *French*

Marketing
Market research
UK promotion: *local newspapers; regional tourist board; other attractions; leaflets/information packs*
USA promotion: *specialist journals*

Environmental monitoring: *recycling; waste*

SPRINGHILL
(trust)
historic house; garden; museum

Established: *1957*
Address: *Moneymore, Co. Londonderry, BT45 7NQ*
Telephone: *(06487) 48210*
Access: (road) *M2/B18*
Parking capacity: (cars) *50* (coaches) *6*
Hours: *July and Aug – Fri to Wed – 2pm to 6pm; Apr to Sept – weekends and BH – 2pm to 6pm*
Admission (1992): *adults £2.00; children £1.00; OAP £2.00; student £1.00*
No. visitors (1992): *10 000*

Facilities
Interpretation: *leaflets; tour guides; guide books*
Children: *play area*
Schools: *maximum no. 120; educational literature; trails, games, dressing up*
Disabled: *easy access; disabled toilets; guide book*
Catering: *1 snack bar/food stall*
Retailing: *postcards/inexpensive souvenirs; confectionery and ice cream*
No. shops: *1*

Operations
Contacts: *Mrs H P Law (Property Manager); Ms Diane Forbes (Public Affairs Manager)*
No. employees: *(high season) 3 full time; 20 part time (low season) 3 full time; 3 part time*
Training: *F/T operations staff, F/T management, P/T operations staff and casual operations staff are trained in-house and externally and on specific courses and day-to-day on job*

SPURN LIGHTSHIP
(local authority run)
lightship

Established: *1987*
Address: *Hull Marina, Castle St, Hull*
Telephone: *(0482) 593902. Fax: (0482) 595062*
Access: (road) *M62/A63* (rail) *Hull Paragon*
Hours: *Mon to Sat – 10am to 5pm (closed Mon and Tues in winter months); Sun – 1.30pm to 4.30pm. Closed New Year's Day, Christmas Day, Boxing Day and Good Friday*
Admission (1992): *free*
No. visitors (1992): *66 418 (est.)*

Facilities
Interpretation: *information boards*
Languages: *Dutch*
Schools: *maximum no. 30; educational literature*
Retailing: *postcards/inexpensive souvenirs*
No. shops: *1*

Operations
Contact: *Mr D Northmore (Education Officer)*
No. employees: *(high season) 3 full time*
Training: *F/T operations staff and F/T management are trained in-house and externally and on specific courses and day-to-day on job*

Marketing
Press office; market research
UK promotion: *local newspapers; regional tourist board; other attractions*

SS GREAT BRITAIN
(trust)
museum

Established: *1970*
Address: *Great Western Dock, Bristol, BS1 6TY*
Telephone: *(0272) 260680. Fax: (0272) 255788*
Access: (road) *M4/M5/M32* (rail) *Bristol Temple Meads*
Parking capacity: (cars) *120* (coaches) *10*
Season: *all year*
Hours: *summer – 10am to 6pm daily; winter – 10am to 5pm daily*
Admission (1992): *adults £2.80; children £1.90; OAP £1.90*
No. visitors (1992): *150 000 (est.)*

Facilities
Interpretation: *videos; audio tapes; tour guides; guide books*
Languages: *French; German*
Schools: *maximum no. 65; educational literature; audio/visual presentation; educational tour*
Disabled: *disabled toilets*
Catering: *1 picnic area*
Retailing: *postcards/inexpensive souvenirs; books*
No. shops: *1*

Operations
Contact: *B H Wheddon (Commercial Director)*
No. employees: *(high season) 25 full time; 4 part time (low season) 25 full time*
Training: *F/T operations staff, P/T operations staff and casual operations staff are trained in-house and day-to-day on job using videos and handbooks*

Marketing
Affiliations: *AIM, Maritime Trust*
Other: *press office*
UK promotion: *national newspapers; radio; local newspapers; regional tourist board; leaflets/information packs; ETB/BTA*
Europe/Australia/USA promotion: *leaflets/brochures; British Tourist Authority*

Environmental monitoring: *hazardous materials*

SS SHIELDHALL
(society, charitable status)
historic steamship

Established: *1988*
Address: *Ocean Village, Canute Rd, Southampton, SO1 1JS*
Telephone: *(0703) 790876*
Access: (road) *M3/M27* (rail) *Southampton*
Season: *all year*
Hours: *11am to 5pm daily except Christmas Day and Boxing Day*
Admission (1992): *donation requested, 50p suggested*
No. visitors (1992): *40 000 (est.)*

Facilities
Interpretation: *leaflets; information boards; guide books*
Schools: *maximum no. 40; educational literature; lecture/talk; schools by arrangement*
Catering: *1 snack bar/food stall*
Retailing: *postcards/inexpensive souvenirs; confectionery and ice cream; craftwork; books; nautical*
No. shops: *1*

Operations
Contacts: *Mr L White (Chairman); Ms G Robinson (Shop); Mr N Robinson (Publicity)*
Languages spoken: *French; German*

Marketing
Annual event: *steam weekend*
Affiliations: *relations with maritime preservation societies*
UK promotion: *local newspapers; other attractions; leaflets/information packs; guide books*

Environmental monitoring: *waste; energy consumption; hazardous materials*

ST ANDREW'S CATHEDRAL (EPISCOPAL)
(church)
church

Established: *1914*
Address: *King St, Aberdeen, Grampian*
Telephone: *(0224) 640119*
Access: (road) *A92*
Parking capacity: (cars) *10*
Hours: *May to Sept – 10am to 4pm*
Admission (1992): *free*
No. visitors (1992): *7500*

Facilities
Interpretation: *leaflets; information boards; guide books*
Languages: *Japanese; Dutch; French; German; Italian; Spanish*
Schools: *maximum no. 30; no special support*
Disabled: *easy access; disabled toilets; other audio facilities*
Retailing: *postcards/inexpensive souvenirs; craftwork; books; reproductions of famous artefacts*
No. shops: *1*

Marketing
Affiliation: *SMC*
Other: *market research*
UK promotion: *local newspapers; regional tourist board; leaflets/information packs; STB*
USA promotion: *travel agents' brochures; British Tourist Authority*

Environmental monitoring: *waste; water quality; hazardous materials; chemical usage; emissions; pollution*

ST ANDREW'S CATHEDRAL INVERNESS
(charity)
church

Established: *1869*
Address: *Ardross St, Ness Walk, Inverness*
Telephone: *(0463) 233535*
Access: (road) *A9/A82/A96*
Season: *all year*
Hours: *8.30am to 6.00pm daily (later in evening June to Sept)*
Admission (1992): *free but donations welcome*
No. visitors (1992): *N/A*   .

Facilities
Interpretation: *guide books*
Languages: *French; German; Italian; Spanish*
Schools: *educational literature; lecture/talk*
Catering: *1 snack bar/food stall*
Retailing: *postcards/inexpensive souvenirs; craftwork; books*
No. shops: *1*

Operations
Contact: *Very Revd Malcolm E Grant (Provost and Rector)*
Training: *N/A*
Languages spoken: *French; German; Spanish; Greek*

Marketing
Annual event(s): *concerts and recitals*
UK promotion: *regional tourist board; leaflets/information packs; Friends of Cathedral Music*

Environmental monitoring: *hazardous materials; chemical usage; internal environmental conditions*

ST ANDREWS BOTANIC GARDEN
(local authority run)
garden

Established: *1889*
Address: *The Canongate, St Andrews*
Telephone: *(0334) 76452*
Parking capacity: (cars) *38*
Season: *all year*

Hours: *Oct to Mar – 10am to 4pm; Apr to Sept – 10am to 7pm*
Admission (1992): *adults £0.60; children £0.60; OAP £0.60; student £0.60*
No. visitors (1992): *10 000 (est.)*

Facilities
Interpretation: *leaflets; guide books*
Schools: *no special support; junior horticultural base*
Catering: *1 picnic area*
Retailing: *postcards/inexpensive souvenirs; plants*
No. shops: *1*

Operations
Contacts: *Mr R J Mitchell (Hon Curator); A Kydd (Director Leisure and Recreation, NEFDC)*
No. employees: (high season) *10 full time* (low season) *8 full time*
Training: *F/T operations staff and F/T management are trained in-house and on specific courses*

Marketing
Press office
UK promotion: *regional tourist board; leaflets/information packs*

ST ANDREWS PRESERVATION TRUST MUSEUM
(trust)
museum

Established: *1977*
Address: *12 North St, St Andrews, Fife, KY16 9PW*
Telephone: *(0334) 77629*
Access: (road) *M90/A91/A915* (rail) *Leuchars*
Hours: *Easter weekend and mid June to mid Sept – 2pm to 4.30pm daily*
Admission (1992): *free*
No. visitors (1992): *4500 (est.)*

Facilities
Interpretation: *information boards*
Retailing: *postcards/inexpensive souvenirs; books; reproduced maps and postcards*
No. shops: *1*

Operations
Contacts: *Ms E Proudfoot (Chairman of Trust); Ms R Neave (Curator)*
No. employees: (high season) *1 full time; 1 part time* (low season) *1 full time; 1 part time*
Training: *F/T operations staff are trained externally and on specific courses*

Marketing
Affiliation: *SMC*
UK promotion: *local newspapers; regional tourist board; other attractions; leaflets/information packs*

Environmental monitoring: *chemical usage*

ST ANDREWS SEA LIFE CENTRE
(limited company)
zoo/wildlife attraction

Established: *1988*
Address: *The Scores, St Andrews, Fife, KY16 9AS*
Telephone: *(0334) 74786.* Fax: *(0334) 72950*
Access: (road) *M90/A91* (rail) *St Andrews*
Season: *all year*
Hours: *10am to 6pm daily except Christmas Day (open later in summer)*
Admission (1992): *adults £3.90; children £2.75; OAP £3.35; student £1.95; disabled £2.75 (wheelchair bound visitors free)*

Facilities
Interpretation: *videos; leaflets; information boards; maps; tour guides; guide books*
Languages: *French; German*
Children: *nappy changing*
Schools: *educational literature; audio/visual presentation; lecture/talk; touch pool and projects*

Disabled: *easy access; disabled toilets*
Catering: *1 licensed restaurant*
Retailing: *postcards/inexpensive souvenirs; confectionery and ice cream; craftwork; books; clothes; reproductions of famous artefacts*
No. shops: *1*

Operations
Contacts: *Ms L Sword (Manager); Ms E Roche (Shop Supervisor); Ms H Long (Publicity and promotions Officer)*
Training: *F/T operations staff, F/T management, P/T operations staff and casual operations staff are trained in-house and on specific courses and day-to-day on job*

Marketing
Affiliation: *ASVA*
Other: *press office; market research*
UK promotion: *television; national newspapers; radio; local newspapers; regional tourist board; other attractions; leaflets/information packs; ETB/BTA*

ST ANN'S CHURCH
(parish church)
church

Established: *1712*
Address: *St Ann's Street, Manchester, M2*
Telephone: *(061) 834 0239*
Access: (rail) *Manchester*
Season: *all year*
Hours: *all year – Mon to Sat – 9.30am to 4.45pm, Sun – 9am to 6.30pm*
Admission (1992): *free*
No. visitors (1992): *35 000 (est.)*

Facilities
Interpretation: *leaflets; information boards; tour guides; personnel*
Schools: *maximum no. 20; educational tour*
Disabled: *easy access; disabled toilets; helpers*
Retailing: *postcards/inexpensive souvenirs; books; literature*
No. shops: *1*

Operations
Contacts: *C Longley (Verger); Canon M Arundel (Rector)*
No. employees: (high season) *1 full time*
Training: *N/A*

Marketing
Annual event: *St Ann's festival*
UK promotion: *local newspapers; regional tourist board; NWTB*

Environmental monitoring: *recycling; waste; water quality; energy consumption; hazardous materials; chemical usage; transport; emissions*

ST COLUMB'S CATHEDRAL
(church)
museum; church

Established: *1633*
Address: *London St, Londonderry*
Telephone: *(0504) 262746*
Access: (rail) *Waterside*
Season: *all year*
Hours: *all Year – Mon to Sun – 9am to 1pm, 2pm to 5pm*
Admission (1992): *£0.50 to charter house museum*
No. visitors (1992): *20 000 (est.)*

Facilities
Interpretation: *leaflets; audio tapes; information boards; slides; tour guides; guide books*
Languages: *French; German; Spanish*
Schools: *educational literature; audio/visual presentation; lecture/talk*
Disabled: *easy access; helpers*
Retailing: *postcards/inexpensive souvenirs; craftwork*
No. shops: *1*

Operations
Contacts: *Very Revd D C Orr (Dean); Mrs Hazel Wright (Sexton); Mrs E Fielding*

No. employees: (high season) *1 full time; 2 part time* (low season) *1 full time; 2 part time*
Training: *P/T operations staff are trained in-house and day-to-day on job*

Marketing
Annual event: *Two Cathedrals festival*
Sponsor(s): *Derry City Council, M and S*
UK promotion: *radio; local newspapers; regional tourist board*

Environmental monitoring: *waste; chemical usage*

ST EDMUNDSBURY CATHEDRAL
(registered charity)
monument; gallery; church; venue for arts events

Established: *1500*
Address: *Angel Hill, Bury St Edmunds, Suffolk, IP33 1LS*
Telephone: *(0284) 754933.* Fax: *(0284) 768655*
Access: (road) *A45* (rail) *Bury St Edmunds*
Season: *all year*
Hours: *BS Time – June, July and Aug – 8am to 8pm; at other BST times – 8am to 6pm (Fri – 7pm); GMT – 8am to 5.30pm*
Admission (1992): *20p charge for treasury; suggested donations £1.00*
No. visitors (1992): *80 000 (est.)*

Facilities
Interpretation: *videos; leaflets; information boards; maps; tour guides; guide books*
Languages: *Dutch; French; German; Spanish*
Schools: *maximum no. 100; educational literature; audio/visual presentation; lecture/talk; talks available on request*
Disabled: *easy access; disabled toilets; helpers; other audio facilities*
Catering: *1 waiter/waitress served*
Retailing: *postcards/inexpensive souvenirs; craftwork; books; reproductions of famous artefacts; cassettes and arts programmes*
No. shops: *1*

Operations
Contacts: *Mr C Borthwick (Office Manager); Mr M Cousins (Arts Administrator); Mrs S Furnell (Shop Manager)*
No. employees: (high season) *9 full time; 8 part time* (low season) *9 full time; 8 part time*
Training: *F/T operations staff, F/T management, P/T operations staff, P/T management, casual operations staff and casual management are trained in-house and externally and on specific courses and day-to-day on job using audio-visuals*

Marketing
Annual event: *Bury St Edmunds festival*
Sponsor(s): *various*
Affiliations: *various church/arts/music organisations*
Other: *press office; market research*
UK promotion: *television; national newspapers; radio; local newspapers; regional tourist board; other attractions; leaflets/information packs; ETB/BTA*

ST FIN BARRE'S CATHEDRAL
(cathedral)
church

Established: *600*
Address: *Bishop St, Cork*
Telephone: *(021) 962286*
Parking capacity: (cars) *30*
Season: *all year*
Hours: *Mon to Sat – 10am to 1pm and 2pm to 5.30pm (winter 5pm)*
Admission (1992): *adults £0.50*
No. visitors (1992): *24 292*

Facilities
Interpretation: *leaflets; tour guides*
Languages: *French; German; Italian; Spanish*
Schools: *educational literature; lecture/talk*
Disabled: *easy access*

Operations
Languages spoken: *French*

Environmental monitoring: *energy consumption; hazardous materials*

ST GEORGE'S CATHEDRAL
(Roman Catholic – trust)
historic house; heritage centre; church

Established: *1848*
Address: *Westminster Bridge Rd, London, SE1 7HY*
Telephone: *(071) 928 5256*
Access: (rail) *Waterloo*
Season: *all year*
Hours: *6.30am to 8pm daily*
Admission (1992): *free*

Facilities
Interpretation: *leaflets; tour guides*
Schools: *maximum no. 60; educational literature; lecture/talk*
Disabled: *easy access; disabled toilets*
Retailing: *postcards/inexpensive souvenirs; books; religious artefacts*
No. shops: *1*

Operations
Contacts: *Very Revd Canon J Pannett; Assistant Priests*
No. employees: (high season) *2 full time; 6 part time*
Training: *F/T management and P/T operations staff are trained in-house and on specific courses*

Marketing
Annual event(s): *liturgical*
Other: *press office; market research*
UK promotion: *national newspapers; local newspapers; ETB/BTA*

ST GEORGE'S CHAPEL
(charity)
church

Established: *1348*
Address: *Windsor Castle, Berks*
Telephone: *(0753) 865538*
Access: (road) *M4* (rail) *Windsor*
Season: *all year*
Hours: *Mon to Sat – 10am to 4pm, Sun – 2pm to 4pm*
Admission (1992): *adults £3.00; children £1.80; OAP £1.80*
No. visitors (1992): *300 000 (est.)*

Facilities
Interpretation: *leaflets; information boards; tour guides; guide books*
Languages: *Japanese; Dutch; French; German; Italian; Spanish*
Schools: *maximum no. 50; educational literature; educational tour; lecture/talk*
Disabled: *easy access; other audio facilities; wheelchair*
Retailing: *postcards/inexpensive souvenirs; books; reproductions of famous artefacts*
No. shops: *3*

Operations
Contacts: *Lt Col N J Newman (Chapter Clerk); P Coleman (Manageress, Bookshop)*
Training: *P/T operations staff and P/T management are trained in-house and on specific courses*
Languages spoken: *French; Italian; Spanish*

Marketing
Annual event(s): *Windsor festival, concerts, exhibitions*
Sponsor(s): *various*
Other: *market research*

UK promotion: *local newspapers; regional tourist board; other attractions; leaflets/information packs; ETB/BTA*

Environmental monitoring: *recycling*

ST GILES' CATHEDRAL
(church)
church

Established: *1120*
Address: *High St, Edinburgh, EH1 1RE*
Telephone: *(031) 225 9442*
Access: (road) *M8/M90/M9/A1* (rail) *Edinburgh Waverley*
Season: *all year*
Hours: *winter – Mon to Sat – 9am to 5pm; summer – Mon to Sat – 9am to 7pm; Sun – 1pm to 5pm*
Admission (1992): *free*
No. visitors (1992): *80 000 (est.)*

Facilities
Interpretation: *leaflets; information boards; tour guides; guide books*
Languages: *Japanese; French; German; Italian; Spanish*
Schools: *maximum no. 100; educational literature*
Catering: *1 self-service cafeteria*
Retailing: *postcards/inexpensive souvenirs; craftwork; books; reproductions of famous artefacts*
No. shops: *1*

Operations
Contacts: *Very Revd G Macmillan (Minister of St Giles', Dean of Thistle); Ms D Boulton (Shop Manager); Ms B Stirrat (Restaurant Manager); Ms A Thomson (Visitor Services Manager)*
No. employees: (high season) *12 full time; 4 part time* (low season) *10 full time*
Training: *F/T operations staff and casual operations staff are trained in-house and on specific courses and day-to-day on job using handbooks*

Marketing
Annual event(s): *organ recitals*
Affiliations: *Church of Scotland*
Other: *market research*
UK promotion: *regional tourist board; other attractions; leaflets/information packs; STB*
USA promotion: *STB*

ST IVES SOCIETY OF ARTISTS
(trust)
gallery

Established: *1927*
Address: *Old Mariner's Church, Norway Square, St Ives, Cornwall*
Telephone: *(0736) 795582*
Hours: *Mar to Nov and mid Dec to mid Jan*
Admission (1992): *adults £0.20; OAP £0.10; student £0.10*
No. visitors (1992): *20 000 (est.)*

Facilities
Interpretation: *leaflets*
Schools: *educational literature; lecture/talk*
Retailing: *original paintings and etchings; sculptures*
No. shops: *none*

Operations
Contact: *Ms I Lang (Secretary/Curator)*
No. employees: (high season) *1 full time; 1 part time* (low season) *1 full time; 1 part time*

Marketing
Annual event(s): *Christmas exhibition*
UK promotion: *local newspapers; leaflets/information packs; ETB/BTA; Who is Who in Art, Magic*

ST MARTIN-IN-THE-FIELDS
(charity)
gallery; church

Established: *1726*
Address: *Trafalgar Square, London, WC2N 4JS*
Telephone: *(071) 930 0089*. Fax: *(071) 839 5163*
Access: (rail) *Charing Cross*
Season: *all year*

Facilities
Interpretation: *leaflets; information boards; guide books*
Languages: *French; German; Italian; Spanish*
Schools: *maximum no. 35; educational literature; lecture/talk; by arrangement*
Disabled: *easy access; disabled toilets; other audio facilities*
Catering: *1 snack bar/food stall*
Retailing: *postcards/inexpensive souvenirs; craftwork; books; reproductions of famous artefacts; T-shirts*
No. shops: *2*

Operations
Contacts: *Ms C Graham-Brown (Chief Executive); Ms A Hargreaves (Restaurant)*
No. employees: (high season) *20 full time; 25 part time* (low season) *20 full time; 15 part time*
Training: *F/T operations staff, F/T management, P/T operations staff, P/T management, casual operations staff and casual management are trained in-house and externally and on specific courses and day-to-day on job and professional MBA catering*
Languages spoken: *French; German*

Marketing
Annual event(s): *Concerts, Messiah*
Other: *market research*
UK promotion: *other attractions; leaflets/ information packs*
Europe/USA promotion: *television; leaflets/ brochures*

Environmental monitoring: *recycling; waste; energy consumption; hazardous materials; emissions*

ST MARY REDCLIFFE CHURCH BRISTOL
(church)
church

Established: *1300*
Address: *The Vicar's Office, 11 Redcliffe Parade West, Bristol, BS1 6SP*
Telephone: *(0272) 291 487*
Access: (road) *M32* (rail) *Bristol Temple Meads*
Season: *all year*
Hours: *8am to 6pm daily; 8am to 8pm during June, July and Aug; 8am to 12 noon – Boxing Day and Easter Monday*
Admission (1992): *free*
No. visitors (1992): *10 000 (est.)*

Facilities
Interpretation: *leaflets; information boards; tour guides; guide books*
Languages: *French; German; Spanish*
Schools: *maximum no. 40; educational literature; lecture/talk*
Disabled: *easy access; deaf loop for services*
Retailing: *postcards/inexpensive souvenirs; slides*
No. shops: *1*

Operations
Contact: *Vicar*
No. employees: (high season) *2 full time*
Languages spoken: *French; German; Italian; Spanish; Chinese; Portuguese*

Marketing
Annual event(s): *concerts, organ recitals*
Sponsor(s): *various*

Other: *press office*
UK promotion: *other attractions; leaflets/ information packs*

ST MARY'S EPISCOPAL CATHEDRAL
(cathedral)
church

Established: *1879*
Address: *Palmerston Place, Edinburgh*
Telephone: *(031) 225 6293*. Fax: *(031) 225 3181*
Season: *all year*
Hours: *7.30am to 6.15pm daily*
Admission (1992): *free*
No. visitors (1992): *6000 (est.)*

Facilities
Interpretation: *leaflets; information boards; tour guides; guide books*
Languages: *Japanese; Dutch; French; German; Italian; Spanish*
Children: *creche*
Schools: *educational literature*
Disabled: *easy access; disabled toilets; other audio facilities*
Retailing: *postcards/inexpensive souvenirs*
No. shops: *1*

Marketing
Affiliations: *Edinburgh Marketing*
UK promotion: *regional tourist board; leaflets/ information packs*

ST MARY'S PARISH CHURCH
(church council)
church

Established: *1390*
Address: *Nantwich, Ches, CW5 5RQ*
Telephone: *(0829) 625268*
Access: (road) *M6/A534/A530/A529/A500/A51* (rail) *Crewe*
Season: *all year*
Hours: *8.30am to 5.30pm daily*
Admission (1992): *free*
No. visitors (1992): *50 000 (est.)*

Facilities
Interpretation: *leaflets; tour guides; guide books*
Schools: *maximum no. 90; educational tour; lecture/talk; guides free; exhibitions*
Disabled: *easy access; disabled toilets*
Retailing: *postcards/inexpensive souvenirs; paintings, sketches, books, stationery*
No. shops: *1*

Operations
Contact: *Canon R Price (Rector)*

Marketing
Annual event(s): *concerts*
Sponsor: *Wellcome Foundation*
UK promotion: *local newspapers; regional tourist board; other attractions; leaflets/information packs; local tourist information office, local libraries*

ST MARY'S PRIORY OLD MALTON
(church)
church

Established: *1150*
Address: *The Gannock House, Old Malton, N Yorks, YO17 0HB*
Telephone: *(0653) 692121*
Access: (rail) *Malton*
Parking capacity: (cars) *100* (coaches) *4*
Season: *all year*
Hours: *dawn to dusk*
Admission (1992): *donations*
No. visitors (1992): *2000 (est.)*

Facilities
Interpretation: *guide books*
Languages: *French*
Schools: *maximum no. 30; educational literature; lecture/talk*
Disabled: *easy access*

Operations
Contact: *Revd J Manchester*
No. employees: (high season) *1 full time* (low season) *1 full time*

Marketing
Annual event(s): *concerts and exhibitions*
Sponsor(s): *local businesses*
UK promotion: *regional tourist board; leaflets/ information packs; ETB/BTA*

ST MICHAEL THE ARCHANGEL CHURCH
(church)
church

Established: *1490*
Address: *Kirkby Malham, Skipton, N Yorks*
Telephone: *(0729) 830215*
Access: (road) *A65*
Parking capacity: (cars) *30* (coaches) *1*
Season: *all year*
Hours: *dawn to dusk daily*
Admission (1992): *free*
No. visitors (1992): *7000 (est.)*

Facilities
Interpretation: *leaflets; information boards; tour guides; guide books*
Schools: *maximum no. 30; educational literature*
Retailing: *postcards/inexpensive souvenirs; books*

Operations
Contact: *Revd B Newth*
No. employees: (high season) *1 full time* (low season) *1 full time*
Languages spoken: *French*

Marketing
Annual event: *mediaeval market*
UK promotion: *local newspapers; regional tourist board; ETB/BTA*

Environmental monitoring: *recycling*

ST MICHAEL'S PARISH CHURCH
(trust)
church

Established: *1242*
Address: *Kirkgate, Linlithgow*
Telephone: *(0506) 842195*
Access: (road) *M9* (rail) *Glasgow–Edinburgh*
Parking capacity: (cars) *50*
Season: *all year*
Hours: *Oct to May – Mon to Fri – 10am to 12 noon and 2pm to 4pm; June to Sept – Mon to Sat – 10am to 12 noon and 2pm to 4pm*
Admission (1992): *free*
No. visitors (1992): *12 000 (est.)*

Facilities
Interpretation: *leaflets; information boards; tour guides; guide books*
Languages: *Dutch; French; German*
Schools: *maximum no. 50; educational literature; lecture/talk*

Operations
Contact: *Revd I Paterson (Minister)*
No. employees: (high season) *2 part time* (low season) *2 part time*

Marketing
UK promotion: *regional tourist board; leaflets/ information packs; STB*

ST MUNGO'S 13TH CENTURY CHURCH
(church)
church

Established: *1200*
Address: *Simonburn, Hexham, Northumberland*
Access: (road) *B6320* (rail) *Hexham*
Parking capacity: (cars) *20* (coaches) *10*
Season: *all year*
Hours: *during daylight*
Admission (1992): *offertory box*
No. visitors (1992): *1500*

Facilities
Interpretation: *leaflets; information boards; guide books*
Schools: *educational literature; lecture/talk; acting story of St Mungo*
Retailing: *postcards/inexpensive souvenirs; books*
No. shops: *1*

Operations
Contacts: *Revd Canon S V Prins (Rector)*
Languages spoken: *French; Italian*

ST NICHOLAS PRIORY
(local authority run)
historic house; museum

Address: *The Mint, Off Fore St, Exeter*
Telephone: *(0392) 265858*. Fax: *(0392) 421252*
Access: (road) *M5* (rail) *Exeter Central/Exeter St David's*
Hours: *Easter to Oct – Tues to Sat – 10am to 1pm and 2pm to 5.30pm*
Admission (1992): *adults £0.50*
No. visitors (1992): *N/A*

Facilities
Interpretation: *information boards; guide books*
Schools: *maximum no. 50; educational literature*

Operations
Contacts: *Ms J Simpson (Museums Services Manager); Ms L Adamson (Personnel, Exeter City Council); Ms R Randall (Press and Public Events Officer)*
Training: *F/T operations staff, F/T management, P/T operations staff and casual operations staff are trained in-house and on specific courses and day-to-day on job*

Marketing
Annual event(s): *children's Christmas activities*
Other: *press office; market research*
UK promotion: *regional tourist board; leaflets/ information packs; Coach Operators Handbook, local publications; ETB/BTA*

ST OLAVE'S CHURCH
(Anglican church)
church

Established: *1952*
Address: *8 Hart St, London, EC3R 7NB*
Telephone: *(071) 488 4318*
Access: (rail) *Tower Hill*
Season: *all year*
Hours: *9am to 5pm daily*
Admission (1992): *free*
No. visitors (1992): *3000 (est.)*

Facilities
Interpretation: *tour guides; guide books*
Schools: *maximum no. 30; lecture/talk*

Operations
Contacts: *Revd J Cowling (Rector); Mr W Shepherd (Administrator)*

ST PAUL'S CATHEDRAL
(cathedral church)
church

Established: *1710*
Address: *St Paul's Churchyard, London, EC4M 8AD*
Telephone: *(071) 236 4128*. Fax: *(071) 248 3104*
Parking capacity: (cars) *400* (coaches) *12*
Season: *all year*
Hours: *9am to 4.30pm daily. Galleries closed Sun*
Admission (1992): *adults £2.50; children £1.50; student £2.00; OAP prices under review, also charges for gallery*
No. visitors (1992): *2 500 000 (est.)*

Facilities
Interpretation: *videos; leaflets; information boards; tour guides; guide books*
Languages: *Japanese; French; German; Italian; Spanish*
Children: *nappy changing*
Schools: *maximum no. 25; educational literature; audio/visual presentation; lecture/talk*
Disabled: *easy access; disabled toilets; helpers; powered transport*
Retailing: *postcards/inexpensive souvenirs; books; glass and silverware*
No. shops: *3*

Operations
Contacts: *Mr R Milliam (Visits Officer); Mrs H Matthews (Administration); Mr E Newton (Shop Manager)*
No. employees: (high season) *8 full time; 4 part time*
Training: *F/T operations staff, F/T management and casual operations staff are trained in-house and externally and on specific courses and day-to-day on job*

Marketing
Annual event(s): *recitals and concerts*
Affiliations: *AVLA, Association of English Cathedrals*
Other: *press office; market research*
UK promotion: *regional tourist board; leaflets/ information packs; ETB/BTA*

ST WILFRID'S CHURCH
(church)
church

Established: *1300*
Address: *Burnsall, Skipton, N Yorks*
Telephone: *(0756) 720331*
Season: *all year*
Hours: *7.30am to 7pm daily*
Admission (1992): *free*

Facilities
Interpretation: *leaflets*
Schools: *maximum no. 150; no special support*
Disabled: *easy access*

Operations
Contact: *Revd D Clarke (Rector)*
Languages spoken: *by arrangement*

Marketing
Affiliation: *Bradford Diocese*
Other: *PR company: Revd B Newith, The Vicarage, Kirby Malham, Skipton, N Yorks; market research*
UK promotion: *regional tourist board; leaflets/ information packs; ETB/BTA*

STAGS HOLT FARM AND STUD
(privately owned)
museum; working farm dedicated to Suffolk punches

Established: *1989*
Address: *Stags Holt, March, Cambs, PE14 0BJ*
Telephone: *(0354) 52406*

Access: (road) *A141*
Parking capacity: (cars) *400* (coaches) *30*
Hours: *Good Friday to end of Oct – every day except Mon (open BH Mon)*
Admission (1992): *adults £2.30; children £1.20; OAP £1.50*
No. visitors (1992): *12 000 (est.)*

Facilities
Interpretation: *videos; tour guides; personnel*
Children: *adventure playground; play area; nappy changing*
Schools: *maximum no. 150; educational literature; lecture/talk*
Disabled: *easy access; disabled toilets*
Catering: *1 picnic area*
Retailing: *postcards/inexpensive souvenirs; confectionery and ice cream; craftwork; clothes*
No. shops: *1*

Operations
Contact: *Mr P Crockford (owner)*
No. employees: (high season) *7 full time; 2 part time* (low season) *4 full time; 2 part time*
Training: *F/T operations staff are trained in-house and day-to-day on job*

Marketing
Annual event(s): *vintage tractor ploughing and horse working days*
Sponsor(s): *various*
Other: *market research*
UK promotion: *radio; local newspapers; regional tourist board; other attractions; leaflets/ information packs; Fen Tourism Group; ETB/ BTA*

STAINED GLASS MUSEUM
(trust)
museum

Established: *1979*
Address: *The North Triforium Gallery, Ely Cathedral, Ely*
Access: (road) *A10*
Parking capacity: (cars) *150* (coaches) *10*
Hours: *1 Mar to 31 Oct – Mon to Fri – 10.30am to 4pm; throughout the year – Sat 10.30am to 4.30pm, Sun – 12 noon to 3pm; BH and school holidays 10.30am to 4.30pm*
Admission (1992): *adults £1.50; children £0.70; OAP £0.70; student £0.70; schoolchildren £0.35*
No. visitors (1992): *13 000*

Facilities
Interpretation: *leaflets; information boards*
Languages: *French; German; Italian*
Children: *play area*
Schools: *maximum no. 30; educational literature; lecture/talk; activities*
Retailing: *postcards/inexpensive souvenirs; craftwork; books; reproductions of famous artefacts; stationery*
No. shops: *2*

Operations
Contacts: *Mrs S Reynolds (Supervisor); Mrs S Matthews*
No. employees: (high season) *6 part time* (low season) *6 part time*
Training: *P/T operations staff are trained in-house and day-to-day on job*

Marketing
Affiliations: *museums and galleries, AMSSEE*
Other: *market research*
UK promotion: *radio; local newspapers; regional tourist board; other attractions; leaflets/ information packs; ETB/BTA; via cathedral*
Europe/USA promotion: *leaflets/brochures*

STAINTONDALE SHIRE HORSE FARM
(family ownership)
heritage centre; park/reserve; zoo/wildlife attraction; local rural history and conservation

Established: *1985*
Address: *Staintondale, Scarborough, N Yorks, YO13 0EY*

Telephone: *(0723) 870458*
Access: (road) *A171*
Parking capacity: (cars) *100*
Hours: *Easter Sun to Wed then 2 May to 26 Sept – Sun, Tues, Wed and Fri – 10.30am to 4.30pm*
Admission (1992): *adults £2.50; children £1.50; OAP £2.00; student £1.50*
No. visitors (1992): *20 000 (est.)*

Facilities
Interpretation: *videos; leaflets; information boards; slides; free activity guide*
Children: *play area; nappy changing*
Schools: *maximum no. 50; educational literature; audio/visual presentation; lecture/talk; nature trail*
Disabled: *disabled toilets; helpers; special signs*
Catering: *1 picnic area*
Retailing: *postcards/inexpensive souvenirs; confectionery and ice cream; craftwork; books; farm video tape*
No. shops: *1*

Operations
Contacts: *Mr T Jenkins (owner); Mr M Noble (P/A to Mr Jenkins); Ms A Jenkins (Retail Proprietor)*
No. employees: (high season) *2 full time; 4 part time* (low season) *1 full time; 2 part time*
Training: *F/T operations staff, P/T operations staff and casual operations staff are trained in-house and day-to-day on job*

Marketing
Annual event: *Christmas Experience for Save the Children Fund*
Other: *market research*
UK promotion: *local newspapers; regional tourist board; other attractions; leaflets/information packs; local guides; ETB/BTA*

STAMFORD MUSEUM
(local authority run)
museum

Established: *1980*
Address: *Broad St, Stamford, Leics, PE9 1PJ*
Telephone: *(0780) 66317.* Fax: *(0780) 480363*
Access: (road) *A1* (rail) *Stamford*
Season: *all year*
Hours: *Apr to Sept – Mon to Sat – 10am to 5pm, Sun – 2pm to 5pm; Oct to Mar – Mon to Sat – 10am to 12.30pm and 1.30pm to 5pm*
Admission (1992): *adults £0.40; children £0.20; OAP £0.40; student £0.40*
No. visitors (1992): *12 000*

Facilities
Interpretation: *videos; leaflets; tour guides; displays*
Schools: *maximum no. 30; educational literature; lecture/talk; guided tour on request*
Disabled: *access to ground floor*
Retailing: *postcards/inexpensive souvenirs; books; local interest literature*
No. shops: *1*

Operations
Contact: *Mr J Smith (Curator/Manager)*
No. employees: (high season) *2 full time; 4 part time* (low season) *2 full time; 2 part time*
Training: *F/T operations staff, F/T management, P/T operations staff and casual operations staff are trained in-house and externally and on specific courses and day-to-day on job*

Marketing
Annual event(s): *winter lecture series*
Affiliations: *MA*
Other: *press office; market research*
UK promotion: *local newspapers; regional tourist board; other attractions; leaflets/information packs; ETB/BTA; E Mids Tourist Board*

Environmental monitoring: *conservation of farm*

STAMFORD SHAKESPEARE COMPANY
(registered charity)
open air theatre

Established: *1992*
Address: *Rutland Open Air Theatre, Tolethorpe Hall, Stamford, Lincs, PE9 4BH*
Telephone: *(0780) 54381.* Fax: *(0780) 53354*
Access: (road) *A1*
Parking capacity: (cars) *150* (coaches) *8*
Hours: *June to Sept – 4pm to 12 midnight*
Admission (1992): *student £5.00; £6.50 to £9.00, £1.00 off all prices except Fri and Sat*
No. visitors (1992): *24 000 (est.)*

Facilities
Interpretation: *leaflets; signs*
Schools: *maximum no. 100; no special support*
Disabled: *easy access; disabled toilets; helpers*
Catering: *1 bar/public house*
Retailing: *postcards/inexpensive souvenirs; confectionery and ice cream; craftwork; books; clothes*
No. shops: *1*

Operations
Contacts: *D Harrison (General Manager); Ann Hoyles (Part-time Secretary)*
No. employees: (high season) *1 full time; 15 part time*
Languages spoken: *French*

Marketing
Affiliations: *E Mids Tourist Board, E Mids Arts Board, Stamford Tourist Association*
Other: *press office*
UK promotion: *radio; local newspapers; regional tourist board; leaflets/information packs; ETB/BTA; tourism section, Leicester CC*
Europe/USA promotion: *leaflets/brochures; radio; British Tourist Authority*

STANBOROUGH PARK
(local authority run)
park/reserve; water based attraction

Established: *1970*
Address: *Stanborough Rd, Welwyn Garden City, Herts, AL8 6DQ*
Telephone: *(0707) 327655.* Fax: *(0707) 339664*
Access: (road) *M1/A414* (rail) *Welwyn Garden City*
Parking capacity: (cars) *2000*
Season: *all year*
Hours: *sailing lake – Mar to Dec – Mon to Fri – from 9am. Boating lake – Apr to Oct – Sat to Sun – 12 noon to 4pm. General park always open*
Admission (1992): *cars £2.00*
No. visitors (1992): *300 000 (est.)*

Facilities
Interpretation: *leaflets*
Children: *adventure playground*
Schools: *no special support*
Disabled: *disabled toilets*
Catering: *1 picnic area*
Franchisees: *sailing lake – Mar to Dec – Mon to Fri – from 9am*

Operations
Contact: *C Kitts (Manager)*
No. employees: (high season) *14 full time; 30 part time* (low season) *6 full time; 15 part time*
Training: *F/T operations staff, F/T management, P/T operations staff and casual operations staff are trained in-house and on specific courses and day-to-day on job*

Marketing
Annual event(s): *firework spectacular*
Sponsor(s): *Capital Radio*
Affiliations: *East Anglian Tourist Board*
Other: *market research*
UK promotion: *local newspapers; regional tourist board; leaflets/information packs; Royal Yachting Association, educational trips handbooks*

Environmental monitoring: *Conservation*

STANFORD HALL
(partnership of the family)
historic house

Established: *1958*
Address: *Stanford Hall, Lutterworth, Leics, LE17 6DH*
Telephone: *(0788) 860250*
Access: (road) *M1/M6*
Parking capacity: (cars) *1000* (coaches) *6*
Hours: *Easter to end Sept – 2.30pm to 6pm*
Admission (1992): *adults £2.80; children £1.30; OAP £2.50*
No. visitors (1992): *40 000 (est.)*

Facilities
Interpretation: *information boards; tour guides; guide books*
Schools: *maximum no. 60; no special support*
Disabled: *disabled toilets*
Catering: *1 picnic area*
Franchisees: *Easter to end Sept – 2.30pm to 6pm*
Retailing: *postcards/inexpensive souvenirs; book marks, key rings, pens*
No. shops: *1*

Operations
Contact: *Lt Col E H L Aubrey-Fletcher (Administrator)*
No. employees: (high season) *2 full time; 32 part time* (low season) *2 full time; 4 part time*

Marketing
Annual event(s): *various*
Affiliation: *HHA*
UK promotion: *local newspapers; regional tourist board; Historic Houses, Castle and Gardens, Historic House Directory*

Environmental monitoring: *water quality; energy consumption; hazardous materials; chemical usage*

STANFORD HALL MOTORCYCLE MUSEUM
museum

Established: *1962*
Address: *Stanford Hall, Lutterworth, Leics, LE17 6DH*
Telephone: *(0788) 860250*
Access: (road) *M1/M6*
Parking capacity: (cars) *1000* (coaches) *6*
Hours: *Easter to end Sept – 2.30pm to 6pm*
Admission (1992): *adults £0.90; children £0.20*
No. visitors (1992): *2500 (est.)*

Facilities
Disabled: *disabled toilets*

Operations
Contact: *Lt Col E H L Aubrey-Fletcher (Administrator)*
No. employees: (low season) *1 part time*
Training: *N/A*

Marketing
UK promotion: *local newspapers; museums and galleries*

STANSTEAD PARK
(trust)
historic house; garden; church

Established: *1985*
Address: *Rowlands Castle, Hampshire, PO9 6DX*
Telephone: *(0705) 412265*
Access: (road) *A3/A27*
Parking capacity: (cars) *3000* (coaches) *15*
Hours: *Easter Sun and Mon; 1 Sun in May to last Tues in Sept – Sun, Mon and Tues – 2pm to 5.30pm*
Admission (1992): *adults £3.50; children £1.50; OAP £3.50; student £3.50; charges include house and grounds, grounds only £2.00/£1.00, group rates £3.00/£1.00*
No. visitors (1992): *10 000 (est.)*

Facilities
Interpretation: *leaflets; information boards; maps; tour guides; guide books*
Languages: *French; German; all Scandinavian*
Children: *nappy changing*
Schools: *maximum no. 150; educational literature; lecture/talk*
Disabled: *access difficult, steep steps*
Catering: *2 picnic areas*
Retailing: *postcards/inexpensive souvenirs; confectionery and ice cream; craftwork; books; clothes; plants*
No. shops: *2*

Operations
Contacts: *Captain J Gowen RN (Agent); Ms B Andersen (Events Manager)*
No. employees: *(high season) 11 full time; 60 part time (low season) 11 full time; 5 part time*
Training: *F/T operations staff, F/T management and P/T operations staff are trained in-house and externally and on specific courses and day-to-day on job*

Marketing
Annual event(s): *country and western, celebrity fair, craft fair and charity cricket matches*
Sponsor(s): *Portsmouth News, Portsmouth Hospice*
Affiliations: *HHA, Southern Tourist Board*
Other: *PR company: M Masson, Masson Rayner Co, 15 Moreton Rd, Bosham, W Sussex; press office; market research*
UK promotion: *national newspapers; radio; local newspapers; regional tourist board; other attractions; leaflets/information packs; ETB/BTA*
Europe promotion: *leaflets/brochures; British Tourist Authority*

STANWAY HOUSE
(trust)
historic house; garden

Established: *1981*
Address: *Stanway, Cheltenham, Glos*
Telephone: *(0386) 73469.* Fax: *(0386) 73688*
Access: (road) *M5/B4077* (rail) *Cheltenham*
Parking capacity: (cars) *100* (coaches) *20*
Hours: *June to Sept – Tues and Thur – 2pm to 5pm. Other times by appointment*
Admission (1992): *adults £2.00; children £1.00; OAP £1.75*
No. visitors (1992): *10 000 (est.)*

Facilities
Interpretation: *guide books; guide in each room*
Catering: *1 waiter/waitress served*
Franchisees: *June to Sept – Tues and Thur – 2pm to 5pm. Other times by appointment*

Operations
Contact: *Ms L Poley (Administrator)*
No. employees: *(high season) 7 part time (low season) 4 part time*
Languages spoken: *French; German; Danish Swedish*

Marketing
Affiliation: *HHA*
UK promotion: *regional tourist board; leaflets/ information packs; ETB/BTA*

Environmental monitoring: *tree planting*

STAR COTTAGE GARDEN
(privately owned)
garden; gallery

Established: *1992*
Address: *Star Cottage, 8 Roman Way, Cowgrove, Wimborne, Dorset*
Telephone: *(0202) 885130*
Access: (road) *B3082*
Parking capacity: (cars) *8* (coaches) *2*
Season: *all year*
Hours: *Easter to end of Oct – Sat and Sun – 2pm to 6pm; end of Oct to Easter – Sun – 2pm to 4pm*

Admission (1992): *adults £0.75; children £0.40; OAP £0.75; student £0.40*

Facilities
Interpretation: *leaflets*
Schools: *maximum no. 40; no special support*
Retailing: *postcards/inexpensive souvenirs; books; prints and original paintings*
No. shops: *1*

Operations
Contact: *Lys De Bray (owner)*

Marketing
UK promotion: *regional tourist board; leaflets/ information packs; ETB/BTA*

STEAM BREWERY MUSEUM
(leasehold by Samuel Smith)
museum

Established: *1978*
Address: *All Saints St, Stamford, Lincs, PE9 2PA*
Telephone: *(0780) 52186*
Access: (road) *A1* (rail) *Stamford*
Hours: *1 Apr to 10 Oct – Wed to Fri – 10am to 4pm, Sat and Sun – 10am to 6pm; open BH*
Admission (1992): *adults £1.30; children £0.70; OAP £0.70; student £0.70*
No. visitors (1992): *4000 (est.)*

Facilities
Interpretation: *leaflets; audio tapes; information boards; maps; guide books; guides if required*
Children: *nappy changing*
Disabled: *easy access; disabled toilets; helpers*
Catering: *1 bar/public house*
Retailing: *postcards/inexpensive souvenirs; books; clothes; woodwork by coopers*
No. shops: *1*

Operations
Contacts: *Mr and Mrs Brown (Managers); Miss B Galvin (Curator)*
No. employees: *(high season) 2 full time*

Marketing
Annual event(s): *coopering*
UK promotion: *national newspapers; local newspapers; regional tourist board; leaflets/ information packs; ETB/BTA*
Europe/USA promotion: *leaflets/brochures; travel agents' brochures*

STEAMTOWN RAILWAY CENTRE
(limited company)
museum

Established: *1968*
Address: *Warton Rd, Carnforth, Lancs, LA5 9HX*
Telephone: *(0524) 732100.* Fax: *(0524) 735518*
Access: (road) *M6/A6* (rail) *Carnforth*
Parking capacity: (cars) *500* (coaches) *10*
Season: *all year*
Hours: *Easter to Sept – 9am to 5pm daily; Oct to Easter – 10am to 4pm daily*
Admission (1992): *adults £3.50; children £2.30; OAP £2.30; range of prices available for each category*
No. visitors (1992): *55 000 (est.)*

Facilities
Interpretation: *leaflets; information boards; tour guides*
Children: *adventure playground*
Schools: *educational literature; audio/visual presentation; educational tour; lecture/talk*
Disabled: *easy access; leaflets*
Catering: *1 picnic area*
Retailing: *postcards/inexpensive souvenirs; confectionery and ice cream; books*
No. shops: *2*

Operations
Contact: *P Marshall (Manager)*
No. employees: *(high season) 2 full time; 6 part time (low season) 2 full time; 2 part time*

Marketing
UK promotion: *television; radio; local newspapers; regional tourist board; leaflets/ information packs; ETB/BTA*

STEWARTRY MUSEUM
(local authority run)
museum

Established: *1893*
Address: *St Mary St, Kirkcudbright, DG6 4AQ*
Telephone: *(0557) 31643.* Fax: *(0557) 30005*
Access: (road) *A711*
Hours: *Easter to 30 Apr – Mon to Sat – 11am to 4pm; 1 May to 30 June – Mon to Sat – 11am to 5pm; 1 July to 31 Aug – Mon to Sat – 11am to 7.30pm, Sun – 2pm to 5pm; 1 to 30 Sept – Mon to Sat – 11am to 5pm; 1 to 31 Oct – Mon to Sat – 11am to 4pm; 1 Nov to Easter – Sat only – 11am to 4pm*
Admission (1992): *adults £1.00; OAP £0.50; season tickets; children free*
No. visitors (1992): *6000*

Facilities
Interpretation: *museum exhibition*
Schools: *no special support*
Retailing: *postcards/inexpensive souvenirs; books*
No. shops: *1*

Operations
Contact: *Dr D F Devereux (Curator)*
No. employees: *(high season) 1 full time; 3 part time (low season) 1 full time; 2 part time*

Marketing
Affiliation: *SMC*
Other: *market research*
UK promotion: *regional tourist board; other attractions; leaflets/information packs*

STEWARTS GARDEN–LANDS
(limited company)
garden; garden leisure centre

Established: *1962*
Address: *Lyndhurst Rd, Christchurch, Dorset, BH23 4SA*
Telephone: *(04252) 72244.* Fax: *(04252) 79723*
Access: (road) *M27/A35*
Parking capacity: (cars) *400* (coaches) *2*
Season: *all year*
Hours: *Mon to Sat – 9am to 6pm; Sun – 10am to 6pm. Closed Christmas Day and Boxing Day*
Admission (1992): *free*

Facilities
Interpretation: *leaflets*
Children: *play area; nappy changing*
Schools: *maximum no. 30; lecture/talk*
Disabled: *easy access, disabled toilets*
Catering: *1 picnic area*

Operations
Contacts: *Mr M Stewart (Managing Director); Mrs J Thorne (Personnel Administration); Mr D Wills (Garden Centre Manager); Mr R Loader (Garden Centre Manager)*
No. employees: *(high season) 65 full time; 110 part time (low season) 60 full time; 100 part time*
Training: *F/T operations staff, F/T management, P/T operations staff, P/T management, casual operations staff and casual management are trained in-house and externally and on specific courses and day-to-day on job*

Marketing
PR company: *P Dowding PR, 36 Warland Way, Corfe Mullen, Wimborne, Dorset; market research*
UK promotion: *local newspapers; leaflets/ information packs*

STOCKGROVE COUNTRY PARK
(local authority run)
park/reserve

Established: *1972*
Address: *Nr Heath and Reach, Leighton Buzzard, Beds*
Telephone: *(0525) 237760*
Access: *(road) M1/A5 (rail) Leighton Buzzard*
Parking capacity: *(cars) 70 (coaches) 2*
Season: *all year*
Hours: *Oct to Mar – Sat and Sun – 12 noon to 4pm; Apr to Sept – Tues to Sat – 1pm to 4.30pm, Sun – 12 noon to 6pm*
Admission (1992): *free*
No. visitors (1992): *360 000*

Facilities
Interpretation: *videos; leaflets; audio tapes; information boards; slides; guide books*
Schools: *maximum no. 25; educational literature; audio/visual presentation; lecture/talk*
Disabled: *easy access; disabled toilets; other audio facilities; leaflets*
Catering: *1 picnic area*
Franchisees: *Oct to Mar – Sat and Sun – 12am to 4pm*
Retailing: *postcards/inexpensive souvenirs; craftwork; books*
No. shops: *1*

Operations
Contacts: *D Hillyard (Chief Ranger); H McMahon (Marketing and Publicity Officer)*
No. employees: *(high season) 1 full time; 2 part time (low season) 1 full time; 1 part time*
Training: *F/T operations staff, P/T operations staff and casual operations staff are trained in-house and externally and on specific courses and day-to-day on job using videos and handbooks*
Languages spoken: *French*

Marketing
Press office; market research
UK promotion: *ETB/BTA*

Environmental monitoring: *recycling; waste; energy consumption*

STOCKPORT WAR MEMORIAL AND ART GALLERY
(local authority run)
gallery

Established: *1925*
Address: *Wellington Rd South, Stockport, SK3 8AB*
Telephone: *(061) 474 4453. Fax: (061) 429 0335*
Access: *(road) M63/A6 (rail) Stockport*
Season: *all year*
Hours: *Mon to Fri – 11am to 5pm (Wed to 7pm); Sat – 10am to 5pm*
Admission (1992): *free*
No. visitors (1992): *27 000 (est.)*

Facilities
Interpretation: *videos; leaflets; information boards; personnel*
Schools: *maximum no. 35; educational tour; lecture/talk; workshops*
Disabled: *easy access; disabled toilets; access to ground floor only*
Retailing: *postcards/inexpensive souvenirs; craftwork; books; original artwork, paintings, etc.*
No. shops: *1*

Operations
Contacts: *J Sculley (Senior Visual Arts Officer); M Brennan (Gallery Assistant)*
No. employees: *(high season) 4 full time; 1 part time (low season) 4 full time; 1 part time*
Training: *F/T operations staff and F/T management are trained in-house and externally and on specific courses and day-to-day on job using videos and handbooks and projectors, videos, OHPs*

Marketing
Annual event(s): *art exhibitions and craft show*

Sponsor: *Omega Print and Design*
Affiliations: *Stockport Heritage Services*
Other: *press office; market research*
UK promotion: *radio; local newspapers; regional tourist board; other attractions; leaflets/ information packs; ETB/BTA*

Environmental monitoring: *recycling; waste; water quality; hazardous materials; chemical usage*

STOCKWOOD CRAFT MUSEUM AND GARDENS
(local authority run)
garden; museum

Established: *1986*
Address: *Farley Hill, Luton, Beds*
Telephone: *(0582) 38714. Fax: (0582) 483178*
Access: *(road) M1 (rail) Luton*
Parking capacity: *(cars) 60 (coaches) 5*
Season: *all year*
Hours: *Mar to Oct – Wed to Sat – 10am to 5pm, Sun – 10am to 6pm; Nov to Mar – Fri to Sun – 10am to 4pm*
Admission (1992): *Mossman collection chargeable, rest of site free*
No. visitors (1992): *60 000*

Facilities
Interpretation: *leaflets; information boards; maps; tour guides; guide books*
Children: *play area; nappy changing*
Schools: *maximum no. 100; educational literature; educational tour*
Disabled: *easy access; disabled toilets*
Catering: *2 picnic areas*
Retailing: *postcards/inexpensive souvenirs; craftwork; books; quality giftware, stationery*
No. shops: *1*

Operations
Contact: *L Burgess (Sales and Administrative Officer)*
No. employees: *(high season) 3 full time; 7 part time (low season) 3 full time; 5 part time*
Training: *F/T operations staff, F/T management, P/T operations staff and P/T management are trained in-house and externally and on specific courses and day-to-day on job*

Marketing
Annual event: *Easter craft fair*
Other: *PR company: Luton Borough Council agencies; press office; market research*
UK promotion: *radio; local newspapers; regional tourist board; leaflets/information packs; ETB/ BTA*
Europe promotion: *leaflets/brochures; travel agents' brochures; British Tourist Authority*

Environmental monitoring: *energy consumption*

STOTT PARK BOBBIN MILL
(English Heritage)
working mill

Established: *1983*
Address: *Low Stott Park, Ulverston, Cumbria, LA12 8AX*
Telephone: *(05395) 31087*
Access: *(road) M6/A590 (rail) Ulverston*
Parking capacity: *(cars) 40 (coaches) 6*
Hours: *Apr to Nov – 10am to 6pm daily*
Admission (1992): *adults £1.80; children £0.90; OAP £1.40; under 5s free*
No. visitors (1992): *20 000 (est.)*

Facilities
Interpretation: *tour guides; guide books; bobbin makers*
Languages: *French*
Schools: *maximum no. 100; lecture/talk; special guided tour*
Disabled: *disabled toilets*
Catering: *1 picnic area*
Retailing: *postcards/inexpensive souvenirs; confectionery and ice cream; books; bobbins*
No. shops: *1*

Operations
Contacts: *Mr M J Nield (Chief Technician/Mill Manager); Mrs P Tinning (Custodian)*
No. employees: *(high season) 7 full time (low season) 2 full time*
Training: *F/T operations staff are trained in-house and on specific courses and day-to-day on job using videos and handbooks*

STOURTON HOUSE GARDEN
(privately owned)
garden

Established: *1983*
Address: *Stourton, Warminster, Wilts, BA12 6QF*
Telephone: *(0747) 840417*
Access: *(road) A303/B3092*
Parking capacity: *(cars) 2000 (coaches) 20*
Hours: *1 Apr to 30 Nov – Wed, Thur, Sun and BH – 11am to 6pm*
Admission (1992): *adults £2.00; children £0.50; OAP £2.00; student £2.00*
No. visitors (1992): *10 000*

Facilities
Interpretation: *gardens*
Disabled: *easy access*
Catering: *1 self-service cafeteria*
Retailing: *postcards/inexpensive souvenirs; dried flowers, bouquet bags*

Operations
Contacts: *Col and Mrs Bullivant (owners)*
No. employees: *(high season) 3 full time; 3 part time*
Languages spoken: *French*

Marketing
Annual event(s): *Special flower days, e.g. daffodils, hydrangeas*
Affiliations: *HHA, WC Tourist Board, Southern Tourist Board, National Gardens Scheme*
UK promotion: *radio; local newspapers; regional tourist board; leaflets/information packs; ETB/ BTA*

STOW MILL
(privately owned)
windmill

Established: *1828*
Address: *Paston, North Walsham, Norfolk*
Telephone: *(0263) 720298*
Season: *all year*
Hours: *dawn to dusk*
Admission (1992): *adults £0.50; children £0.30*
No. visitors (1992): *5000 (est.)*

Facilities
Interpretation: *information boards*
Schools: *maximum no. 40*
Retailing: *postcards/inexpensive souvenirs; books*
No. shops: *1*

Operations
No. employees: *(high season) 1 part time (low season) 1 part time*

Marketing
UK promotion: *ETB/BTA*

Environmental monitoring: *organic gardening*

STOWE LANDSCAPE GARDENS
(trust)
historic house; monument; garden

Established: *1989*
Address: *Stowe, Buckingham, MK18 5EH*
Telephone: *(0280) 822850*
Access: *(road) A422*
Parking capacity: *(cars) 600 (coaches) 6*

Admission (1992): *adults £3.50; family ticket £9.00, NT members free*
No. visitors (1992): *50 000 (est.)*

Facilities
Interpretation: *leaflets; information boards; maps; tour guides; guide books*
Children: *nappy changing*
Disabled: *easy access; disabled toilets; powered transport*
Catering: *4 picnic areas*

Operations
Contact: *R Jury (Administrator)*

Marketing
Annual event(s): *music and fireworks, opera*
UK promotion: *local newspapers; regional tourist board; leaflets/information packs*

STRANGERS' HALL MUSEUM
(local authority run)
historic house; museum

Established: *1922*
Address: *Charing Cross, Norwich, Norfolk, NR2 4AL*
Telephone: *(0603) 667229*
Access: (road) *A11* (rail) *Norwich*
Season: *all year*
Hours: *Mon to Sat – 10am to 5pm except Good Friday and a few days over Christmas*
Admission (1992): *adults £0.80; children £0.40; OAP £0.50; student £0.50; ub40s £0.50*
No. visitors (1992): *27 000*

Facilities
Interpretation: *videos; leaflets; information boards; guide books*
Schools: *maximum no. 60; lecture/talk*
Retailing: *postcards/inexpensive souvenirs; books*
No. shops: *1*

Operations
Contacts: *Mr D Chinery (Assistant Director); Mr B McWilliam (Assistant Director); Ms H Slater (Publication Officer)*
No. employees: (high season) *3 full time; 5 part time* (low season) *3 full time; 5 part time*

Marketing
Annual event: *Christmas children's day*
UK promotion: *television; radio; local newspapers; regional tourist board; leaflets/information packs; ETB/BTA*

STRANRAER MUSEUM
(local authority run)
museum; gallery

Established: *1990*
Address: *55 George St, Stranraer, DG9 7JP*
Telephone: *(0776) 5088.* Fax: *(0776) 4819*
Access: (road) *A75/A77* (rail) *Stranraer*
Season: *all year*
Hours: *Mon to Sat – 10am to 5pm*
Admission (1992): *free*
No. visitors (1992): *16 294*

Facilities
Interpretation: *videos; leaflets; information boards; exhibitions*
Languages: *French*
Schools: *maximum no. 50; educational literature; loan packs*
Disabled: *easy access; disabled toilets*
Retailing: *postcards/inexpensive souvenirs; books*
No. shops: *1*

Operations
Contact: *Ms A Reid (Curator)*
No. employees: (high season) *7 full time; 2 part time* (low season) *5 full time; 1 part time*
Training: *F/T operations staff, F/T management, P/T operations staff, P/T management, casual operations staff and casual management are trained in-house and externally and on specific courses and day-to-day on job*

Languages spoken: *French; Spanish*

Marketing
Market research
UK promotion: *radio; local newspapers; regional tourist board; other attractions; leaflets/information packs; STB*

STRATFORD BUTTERFLY FARM
(limited company)
zoo/wildlife attraction

Established: *1985*
Address: *Tramway Walk, Swans Nest Lane, Stratford-upon-Avon, Warks, W37 7LS*
Telephone: *(0789) 299288*
Access: (road) *M40/A34* (rail) *Stratford-upon-Avon*
Season: *all year*
Hours: *Mon to Sun – from 10am*
Admission (1992): *adults £3.00; children £2.25; OAP £2.25; student £2.25; family £8.50; schools £1.75*
No. visitors (1992): *70 000 (est.)*

Facilities
Interpretation: *videos; leaflets; information boards; guide books*
Schools: *maximum no. 200; educational literature; lecture/talk*
Disabled: *easy access*
Retailing: *postcards/inexpensive souvenirs; confectionery and ice cream; craftwork; books; clothes*
No. shops: *1*

Operations
Contacts: *R Lamb (Manager); R Farrell (Shop Buyer); S Regan (Publicity Executive)*
No. employees: (high season) *6 full time; 4 part time* (low season) *6 full time; 3 part time*
Training: *F/T operations staff, P/T operations staff and casual operations staff are trained in-house and day-to-day on job using videos and handbooks and courses*

Marketing
Affiliations: *Butterfly Conservation, Warks Nature Conservation Trust, amateur entomologists*
Other: *press office; market research*
UK promotion: *local newspapers; regional tourist board; other attractions; leaflets/information packs; Heart of England Guide*
Europe/Asia/Australia/USA promotion: *leaflets/brochures*

Environmental monitoring: *Environmental, humidity, etc.*

STRAWBERRY HILL
(limited company)
historic house

Established: *1992*
Address: *St Mary's College, Waldegrave Rd, Twickenham, Middx, TW12 3YF*
Telephone: *(081) 892 0051.* Fax: *(081) 744 2080*
Access: (road) *M25/M3/A316* (rail) *Strawberry Hill*
Parking capacity: (cars) *250* (coaches) *5*
Season: *all year*
Hours: *June to Sept – Sun – 2pm to 5pm; Oct to May – Sun by arranged tours only*
Admission (1992): *adults £3.00; children £2.20; OAP £1.50; student £2.20; under 10s free*
No. visitors (1992): *1300 (est.)*

Facilities
Interpretation: *tour guides*
Schools: *maximum no. 20; 14 years+*
Catering: *1 picnic area*
Retailing: *postcards/inexpensive souvenirs*
No. shops: *1*

Operations
Contact: *Ms C Green (Marketing Director)*
No. employees: (high season) *14 part time* (low season) *12 part time*

Training: *P/T operations staff are trained in-house and on specific courses*

Marketing
Affiliations: *HHA, English Heritage*
Other: *press office; market research*
UK promotion: *local newspapers; regional tourist board; other attractions; leaflets/information packs*

STREETLIFE – HULL MUSEUM OF TRANSPORT
(local authority run)
museum

Established: *1989*
Address: *High St, Hull*
Telephone: *(0482) 593902.* Fax: *(0482) 595062*
Access: (road) *M62/A63* (rail) *Hull Paragon*
Season: *all year*
Hours: *Mon to Sat – 10am to 5pm; Sun – 1.30pm to 4.30pm. Closed Christmas Day, Boxing Day, New Year's Day and Good Friday*
Admission (1992): *free*
No. visitors (1992): *64 427*

Facilities
Interpretation: *videos; audio tapes; information boards*
Languages: *Dutch*
Children: *nappy changing*
Schools: *maximum no. 100; educational literature; audio/visual presentation; lecture/talk*
Disabled: *easy access; disabled toilets*
Catering: *1 picnic area*
Retailing: *postcards/inexpensive souvenirs; craftwork; books; transport items; greetings cards, etc.*
No. shops: *1*

Operations
Contact: *Mr S Goodhard (Keeper of Transport)*
No. employees: (high season) *6 full time*
Training: *F/T operations staff and F/T management are trained in-house and externally and on specific courses and day-to-day on job using in house course*

Marketing
Sponsor(s): *various*
Other: *press office; market research*
UK promotion: *local newspapers; regional tourist board; other attractions*

STROMNESS MUSEUM
(trust)
museum

Established: *1838*
Address: *52 Alfred St, Stromness, Orkney*
Telephone: *(0856) 850025*
Access: *Caithnes ferry*
Season: *all year*
Hours: *May to Sept – Mon to Sat – 10.30am to 5pm; Oct to Apr – Mon to Sat – 10.30am to 12.30pm and 1.30pm to 5pm*
Admission (1992): *adults £0.50; children £0.20; OAP £0.50; student £0.50*
No. visitors (1992): *13 230*

Facilities
Interpretation: *displays*
Languages: *German*
Schools: *maximum no. 30; no special support*
Retailing: *postcards/inexpensive souvenirs; books*
No. shops: *1*

Operations
Contacts: *Mr J Troup (Hon Secretary); B Wilson (Hon Curator)*
No. employees: (high season) *3 part time* (low season) *3 part time*

Marketing
UK promotion: *radio; local newspapers; Orkney Tourist Board*

Environmental monitoring: *energy consumption; hazardous materials*

STRUMPSHAW HALL STEAM MUSEUM
(limited company)
museum

Established: *1975*
Address: *Low Rd, Strumpshaw, Norwich,*
Norfolk, NR13 4HR
Telephone: *(0603) 712339*
Access: (road) *A47*
Parking capacity: (cars) *400*
Hours: *14 May to 2 Oct – 2pm to 5pm*
Admission (1992): *adults £2.00; children £1.00;*
OAP £1.50; student £1.00
No. visitors (1992): *4000 (est.)*

Facilities
Interpretation: *leaflets; guide books; signs*
Children: *play area*
Schools: *maximum no. 50; audio/visual*
presentation
Disabled: *easy access*
Catering: *1 picnic area*
Retailing: *postcards/inexpensive souvenirs; books*
No. shops: *1*

Operations
Contact: *Ann Abramson (Curator)*
No. employees: (high season) *1 full time; 2 part*
time

Marketing
Market research
UK promotion: *local newspapers; leaflets/*
information packs; ETB/BTA

Environmental monitoring: *relative humidity*

SUDBURY HALL AND MUSEUM OF CHILDHOOD
(trust)
historic house; garden; museum

Established: *1971*
Address: *Sudbury, Ashbourne, Derbyshire, DE6*
5HT
Telephone: *(0283) 585305*
Access: (road) *A50/A516*
(rail) *Tutbury and Hatton*
Parking capacity: (cars) *170* (coaches) *5*
Hours: *1 Apr to 31 Oct – Wed to Sun and BH*
Mon – 1pm to 5.30pm
Admission (1992): *adults £2.00; children £1.00;*
NT members free
No. visitors (1992): *40 000 (est.)*

Facilities
Interpretation: *leaflets; information boards; guide*
books
Children: *nappy changing*
Schools: *maximum no. 60; educational literature;*
lecture/talk; role play
Disabled: *easy access; disabled toilets; helpers;*
museum only
Catering: *1 licensed restaurant*
Retailing: *postcards/inexpensive souvenirs;*
confectionery and ice cream; craftwork; books;
clothes; reproductions of famous artefacts; NT
goods
No. shops: *2*

Operations
No. employees: (high season) *6 full time;*
50 part time (low season) *6 full time; 1 part*
time
Training: *F/T operations staff, F/T management,*
P/T operations staff and casual operations staff
are trained in-house and externally and on
specific courses

Marketing
Annual event(s): *various*
Sponsor: *Southern Comfort 1991*
Other: *press office; market research*
UK promotion: *radio; local newspapers; regional*
tourist board; other attractions; leaflets/
information packs; ETB/BTA

SUDLEY
(national museum)
historic house; museum; gallery

Established: *1944*
Address: *Mossley Hill Rd, Liverpool, L18 5BX*
Telephone: *(051) 207 0001*
Access: (road) *M62/A561* (rail) *Mossley Hill*
Season: *all year*
Hours: *Mon to Sat – 10am to 5pm; Sun – 12am*
to 5pm. Closed Christmas, New Year's Day and
Good Friday
Admission (1992): *free*
No. visitors (1992): *26 256*

Facilities
Interpretation: *videos; leaflets; information*
boards; slides; tour guides; guide books
Languages: *French; German*
Schools: *educational literature; audio/visual*
presentation; lecture/talk; must book prior to
visit
Disabled: *easy access; access to ground floor only*
Catering: *1 self-service cafeteria*
Franchisees: *Mon to Sat – 10am to 5pm; Sun –*
12am to 5pm. Closed Christmas, New Year's
Day and Good Friday
Retailing: *postcards/inexpensive souvenirs; gallery*
guide book
No. shops: *1*

Operations
Contacts: *R Foster (Director, NMGM); J Treuherz*
(Keeper of Art Galleries); A Archard (Head of
Personnel); C Hitchins (General Manager,
NMGM Enterprises); B Hope (Marketing
Manager)
No. employees: (high season) *12 full time*
Training: *F/T operations staff, F/T management,*
P/T operations staff, P/T management, casual
operations staff and casual management are
trained in-house and externally and on specific
courses and day-to-day on job using videos and
handbooks
Languages spoken: *French*

Marketing
Annual event(s): *on-going temporary exhibition*
and events programme
Sponsor(s): *Organised by NMGM Development*
Officer
Affiliations: *Museums Association*
Other: *press office; market research*
UK promotion: *television; national newspapers;*
radio; local newspapers; regional tourist board;
other attractions; leaflets/information packs;
ETB/BTA
Europe/USA promotion: *leaflets/brochures;*
British Tourist Authority

Environmental monitoring: *recycling; waste;*
hazardous materials; chemical usage; transport

SUFFOLK REGIMENT MUSEUM
(trust)
museum; military exhibits dating from 1685

Established: *1932*
Address: *The Keep, Gibraltar Barrack, Bury St*
Edmunds, Suffolk
Telephone: *(0284) 752394.* Fax: *(0284) 752026*
Access: (road) *A45* (rail) *Bury St Edmunds*
Parking capacity: (cars) *14*
Hours: *Weekdays – 10am to 12 noon and 2pm to*
4pm. Closed PH
Admission (1992): *free*
No. visitors (1992): *2000 (est.)*

Facilities
Interpretation: *tour guides*
Schools: *maximum no. 20; no special support*
Retailing: *postcards/inexpensive souvenirs*
No. shops: *1*

Operations
Contact: *Major A G B Cobbold (Hon Curator)*
No. employees: (high season) *1 full time*
Languages spoken: *French; German; Spanish;*
Japanese; Russian

Marketing
UK promotion: *regional tourist board*

Environmental monitoring: *recycling; energy*
consumption; hazardous materials

SULGRAVE MANOR
(charity)
historic house; garden

Established: *1921*
Address: *Manor Rd, Sulgrave, Banbury, Oxon,*
OX17 2SD
Telephone: *(0295) 760205*
Access: (road) *M40/M1/B4525*
(rail) *Banbury*
Parking capacity: (cars) *30* (coaches) *5*
Season: *all year*
Hours: *Mar and Oct to Dec – Thur to Tues –*
10.30am to 4pm; Apr to Sept – Thur to Tues –
10.30am to 5.30pm; Feb by appointment only
Admission (1992): *adults £3.00; children £1.50;*
OAP £3.00; student £1.50; group rates
No. visitors (1992): *20 000 (est.)*

Facilities
Interpretation: *videos; leaflets; tour guides; guide*
books
Languages: *Tours if booked*
Schools: *educational literature; audio/visual*
presentation; educational tour; lecture/talk
Catering: *1 picnic area*
Franchisees: *Mar and Oct to Dec – Thur to Tues –*
10.30am to 4pm
Retailing: *postcards/inexpensive souvenirs;*
confectionery and ice cream; craftwork; books;
reproductions of famous artefacts; souvenirs
No. shops: *1*

Operations
Contacts: *M Sirot-Smith (Resident Director); M*
Jeffery (Assistant Director)
No. employees: (high season) *2 full time; 7 part*
time (low season) *2 full time; 4 part time*

Marketing
Annual event(s): *various*
Sponsor(s): *EMA, EMMA, SNDC, NCC*
Other: *market research*
UK promotion: *radio; local newspapers; regional*
tourist board; other attractions; leaflets/
information packs; ETB/BTA
USA promotion: *leaflets/brochures; British*
Tourist Authority

Environmental monitoring: *emissions*

SUMMERLEE HERITAGE TRUST
(trust)
museum; gallery

Established: *1988*
Address: *West Canal St, Coatbridge, ML5 1QD*
Telephone: *(0236) 431261.* Fax: *(0236) 440429*
Access: (road) *M8/A89* (rail) *Coatbridge*
Parking capacity: (cars) *80* (coaches) *5*
Season: *all year*
Hours: *10am to 5pm daily except 25 and 26 Dec*
and 1 and 2 Jan
Admission (1992): *free*
No. visitors (1992): *138 848*

Facilities
Interpretation: *videos; leaflets; information*
boards; maps; tour guides; visitor services staff
Languages: *French; German; Italian; new*
information panels
Children: *play area; nappy changing*
Schools: *visitor services staff*
Disabled: *easy access; disabled toilets; helpers*
Catering: *1 picnic area*
Retailing: *postcards/inexpensive souvenirs;*
confectionery and ice cream; books;
reproductions of famous artefacts
No. shops: *1*

Operations
Contacts: *Mr S Kay (General Manager);*
Mr F Deeney (Personnel Officer);
Mr T Gallacher and Ms M Brown (Visitor
Services and Catering Services); Ms J Lambie
(Development Officer)

No. employees: (high season) 44 full time; 15 part
time (low season) 44 full time; 15 part time
Training: F/T operations staff, F/T management
and P/T operations staff are trained in-house
and externally and on specific courses and
day-to-day on job
Languages spoken: French; German

Marketing
Annual event(s): festivals, fairs and activities for
various interests
Other: market research
UK promotion: national newspapers; radio; local
newspapers; regional tourist board; other
attractions; leaflets/information packs

SUNDOWN KIDDIES ADVENTURELAND
(limited company)
theme park

Established: 1968
Address: Rampton, Retford, Notts, DN22 0HX
Telephone: (077) 248274
Access: (road) A57
Parking capacity: (cars) 700
Season: all year
Hours: 10am to 6pm (earlier in winter) daily
except Christmas Day and Boxing Day
Admission (1992): adults £2.75; children £2.75;
OAP £2.75; student £2.75; wheelchair visitors
free
No. visitors (1992): 250 000

Facilities
Interpretation: leaflets
Children: adventure playground; play area; nappy
changing
Schools: no special support
Disabled: disabled toilets; some play equipment
Catering: 3 picnic areas
Retailing: postcards/inexpensive souvenirs;
confectionery and ice cream; toys
No. shops: 4

Operations
No. employees: (high season) 36 full time (low
season) 7 full time; 5 part time
Languages spoken: French; Spanish

Marketing
Market research
UK promotion: regional tourist board; other
attractions; leaflets/information packs

Environmental monitoring: recycling

SUSSEX COMBINED SERVICES MUSEUM
(trust)
monument; museum

Established: 1976
Address: The Redoubt Fortress, Royal Parade,
Eastbourne, E Sussex, BN12 7AQ
Telephone: (0323) 410300. Fax: (0323) 638686
Access: (road) A22 (rail) Eastbourne
Hours: Easter to Nov – 9.30am to 5.30pm daily
Admission (1992): adults £1.60; children £1.00;
OAP £1.00; student £1.00; group rates
No. visitors (1992): 40 000 (est.)

Facilities
Interpretation: leaflets; information boards; maps
Schools: maximum no. 100; educational tour;
lecture/talk; musket firing demonstrations
Catering: 1 picnic area
Retailing: postcards/inexpensive souvenirs; books
No. shops: 1

Operations
Contact: M V Moss (Curator/Manager)
No. employees: (high season) 5 full time; 2 part
time (low season) 5 full time
Training: F/T operations staff and F/T
management are trained in-house and on
specific courses and day-to-day on job

Marketing
Annual event(s): 1812 concerts
Other: press office; market research

UK promotion: local newspapers; regional tourist
board; other attractions; leaflets/information
packs; ETB/BTA; guidebooks

SUTCLIFFE GALLERY
(local authority partnership)
gallery; photographic gallery

Established: 1956
Address: 1 Flowergate, Whitby, N Yorks, YO21
3BA
Telephone: (0947) 602239. Fax: (0947) 820287
Season: all year
Admission (1992): free

Facilities
Interpretation: leaflets; exhibitions
Schools: maximum no. 20; lecture/talk; leaflets
Retailing: postcards/inexpensive souvenirs; books;
framed photographs and prints
No. shops: 1

Operations
Contacts: Mr B Eglon Shaw (Senior Partner); Ms
S Boyes (Secretary); Mr M Shaw (Junior
Partner)
No. employees: (high season) 5 full time; 4 part
time
Training: F/T operations staff, F/T management,
P/T operations staff and P/T management are
trained in-house and day-to-day on job using
training courses

Marketing
Market research
UK promotion: local newspapers; regional tourist
board; leaflets/information packs
Australia promotion: distributor

SWAFFHAM MUSEUM
(local authority run)
museum

Established: 1987
Address: London St, Swaffham, Norfolk, PE37
7DQ
Telephone: (0760) 721230
Access: (road) A47/A1065
Hours: Apr to 31 Oct – 10am to 4pm
Admission (1992): adults £1.00; OAP £1.00
No. visitors (1992): 9000 (est.)

Facilities
Interpretation: leaflets
Schools: maximum no. 50; educational literature
Retailing: postcards/inexpensive souvenirs; books
No. shops: 1

Operations
Contacts: Miss G B Reith (Town Clerk); D C
Butters (Curator)
No. employees: (high season) 2 part time (low
season) 2 part time
Training: P/T operations staff and P/T
management are trained in-house and externally
and day-to-day on job
Languages spoken: French

Marketing
Annual event(s): historic vehicles spectacular
Sponsor: Friends of Swaffham Museum
Affiliations: Museums in Norfolk Group
UK promotion: radio; local newspapers; regional
tourist board; leaflets/information packs

Environmental monitoring: recycling

SWALEDALE FOLK MUSEUM
(privately owned)
museum

Established: 1974
Address: Reeth Green, Reeth, Nr Richmond,
N Yorks, DL11 6TX

Telephone: (0748) 84373
Access: (road) A6108/B6270
Hours: Easter to 31 Oct – 10.30am to 5.30pm
daily
Admission (1992): adults £0.75; children £0.40;
OAP £0.65; student £0.50; family ticket £2.00
No. visitors (1992): 9002

Facilities
Interpretation: information boards
Schools: maximum no. 50; personal help from
staff
Disabled: easy access; stairs may be difficult
Retailing: postcards/inexpensive souvenirs; books
No. shops: 1

Operations
Contact: Mrs D Law (Curator/Manager)
No. employees: (high season) 1 full time; 1 part
time (low season) 1 part time

Marketing
UK promotion: local newspapers; regional tourist
board; other attractions; leaflets/information
packs; ETB/BTA

SWISS GARDEN
(local authority run)
garden

Established: 1981
Address: Old Warden, Biggleswade, Beds. Postal
Address: Leisure Services Dept, Bedfordshire
County Council, County Hall, Bedford, MK42
9AP
Telephone: (0234) 228330. Fax: (0234) 228921
Access: (road) A1
Parking capacity: (cars) 200 (coaches) 10
Hours: Apr to Oct – Wed to Sat – 1.30pm to
6pm, Sun and BH – 11am to 6pm; Jan to Feb –
Sun and BH – 11am to 3pm; Mar – Sun – 11am
to 4pm
Admission (1992): adults £1.50; children £0.75;
OAP £0.75
No. visitors (1992): 27 505

Facilities
Interpretation: leaflets; information boards; tour
guides; guide books
Schools: maximum no. 50; educational tour;
lecture/talk; guided tours available
Disabled: easy access; disabled toilets; helpers;
guide dogs admitted
Catering: 1 picnic area
Retailing: postcards/inexpensive souvenirs; books
No. shops: 1

Operations
Contacts: S Wileman (Cultural and Community
Services Assistant); H McMahon (Marketing
and Publicity Officer)
No. employees: (high season) 2 full time; 5 part
time (low season) 2 full time; 3 part time
Training: F/T management and P/T operations
staff are trained in-house and externally and on
specific courses and day-to-day on job

Marketing
Affiliation: regional tourist board
Other: press office; market research
UK promotion: local newspapers; regional tourist
board; leaflets/information packs; ETB/BTA

SYON PARK
(limited company and (trust)
historic house; garden; butterfly house and garden
centre

Address: Brentford, Middx
Telephone: (081) 560 0881
Access: (road) M3/M4/A4 (rail) Kew Bridge
Parking capacity: (cars) 1000 (coaches) 100
Hours: gardens – 10am to 6pm daily except 25
and 26 Dec; house – Apr to Oct – 12 noon to
5pm
Admission (1992): adults £4.00; children £3.00;
OAP £3.00; student £3.00; school groups £1.00

Facilities

Interpretation: *leaflets; audio tapes; information boards; maps; tour guides; guide books*

Disabled: *easy access; disabled toilets; other audio facilities*

Catering: *1 picnic area*

Franchisees: *Gardens – 10am to 6pm daily except 25 and 26 Dec; house – Apr to Oct – 12 noon to 5pm*

Retailing: *postcards/inexpensive souvenirs; craftwork; Koi carp; garden centre; wholefood*

No. shops: *1*

Operations

Contact: *B Thornbull (Administrator)*

Marketing

Annual event(s): *craft fair*

Sponsor(s): *Decorex International*

Affiliations: *HHA*

UK promotion: *local newspapers; leaflets/ information packs; Thames and Chilterns Tourist Board*

Environmental monitoring: *recycling; waste; energy consumption; transport*

T

TABELY HOUSE COLLECTION
(trust)
historic house; museum; gallery; family chapel

Established: *1990*
Address: *Tabely House, Nr Knutsford, Ches,*
WA16 0HB
Telephone: *(0565) 750151.* Fax: *(0565) 653230*
Access: (road) *M6/A5033/A556* (rail) *Knutsford*
Parking capacity: (cars) *150* (coaches) *30*
Hours: *Apr to Oct – Thur to Sun and BH – 2pm*
to 5pm
Admission (1992): *adults £3.00; children £1.00;*
OAP £3.00; student £3.00; group discounts

Facilities
Interpretation: *information boards; tour guides;*
guide books; personnel
Languages: *French*
Schools: *maximum no. 36; educational tour;*
lecture/talk; slide show if required
Disabled: *easy access; disabled toilets; helpers;*
other audio facilities; guide book; information
sheets, feelers
Catering: *1 picnic area*
Retailing: *postcards/inexpensive souvenirs;*
craftwork
No. shops: *1*

Operations
Contacts: *P Startup (Administrator); B Folds*
(Assistant Administrator)

Marketing
Market research
UK promotion: *radio; local newspapers; regional*
tourist board; other attractions; leaflets/
information packs; NWTB, Cheshire County
Council, Vale Royal, Cheshire Peaks and Plains

Environmental monitoring: *water quality; no*
pesticides

TAIN AND DISTRICT MUSEUM
(trust)
museum

Established: *1966*
Address: *Castle Brae, Tain, Ross-shire*
Telephone: *(0862) 893054*
Access: (road) *A9* (rail) *Tain*
Parking capacity: (cars) *200* (coaches) *10*
Hours: *Easter to 30 Sept – Mon to Sat – 10am to*
4.30pm
Admission (1992): *adults £0.50; OAP £0.30*
No. visitors (1992): *5200*

Facilities
Interpretation: *videos; leaflets; audio tapes;*
information boards; slides; maps; tour guides;
guide books; various other methods
Languages: *French; German; Italian; Spanish*
Schools: *maximum no. 30; special arrangements*
Disabled: *easy access; disabled toilets; helpers*
Retailing: *postcards/inexpensive souvenirs; books;*
Clan Ross items
No. shops: *1*

Operations
Contacts: *Mrs M R I Mackenzie (Chairman of*
Trustees); Miss A M Franklin (Honorary
Secretary)
No. employees: (high season) *1 part time* (low
season) *1 part time*
Training: *P/T operations staff and casual*
operations staff are trained in-house and
externally and on specific courses and
day-to-day on job using videos and handbooks

Languages spoken: *French; German; Italian;*
Spanish

Marketing
Annual event(s): *street fair*
Affiliations: *SMC*
Other: *market research*
UK promotion: *local newspapers; regional tourist*
board; other attractions; leaflets/information
packs; Ross and Cromarty Tourist Guide
Australia/USA/N Zealand and Canada
promotion: *leaflets/brochures; Clan Ross*
Association abroad

TALES OF ROBIN HOOD, THE
(plc)
heritage centre; museum; interpretation centre

Established: *1988*
Address: *30–38 Maid Marian Way, Nottingham,*
NG1 6GF
Telephone: *(0602) 483284.* Fax: *(0602) 501536*
Access: (road) *M1/A52* (rail) *Nottingham*
Season: *all year*
Hours: *summer – 10am to 4.30pm daily; winter –*
10am to 3.30pm daily except 24, 25 and 26 Dec
Admission (1992): *adults £3.95; children £2.95;*
OAP £2.95; student £2.95; family ticket £10.95
No. visitors (1992): *200 000 (est.)*

Facilities
Interpretation: *videos; leaflets; information*
boards; tour guides; guide books; personnel
Languages: *Japanese; Dutch; French; German;*
Italian; Spanish; Urdu
Children: *play area; nappy changing*
Schools: *educational literature; audio/visual*
presentation; education officer and activities
Disabled: *easy access; disabled toilets; helpers;*
special signs; special car on the ride and access
to archery range
Catering: *1 picnic area*
Retailing: *postcards/inexpensive souvenirs;*
confectionery and ice cream; craftwork; books;
clothes; reproductions of famous artefacts
No. shops: *2*

Operations
Contacts: *Mr M Harris (Operations Manager); Ms*
J Hinch (Operations Manager); Mr M Pratt
(Retail Manager); Ms S Pearson (Marketing
Manager)
No. employees: (high season) *9 full time; 8 part*
time (low season) *9 full time; 4 part time*
Training: *F/T operations staff, F/T management,*
P/T operations staff, P/T management, casual
operations staff and casual management are
trained in-house and externally and on specific
courses and day-to-day on job

Marketing
Annual event(s): *events for children and interest*
days
Other: *market research*
UK promotion: *national newspapers; radio; local*
newspapers; regional tourist board; other
attractions; leaflets/information packs; ETB/
BTA; E Mids Tourist Board
Europe promotion: *leaflets/brochures; travel*
agents' brochures; British Tourist Authority

TALKIN TARN COUNTRY PARK
(local authority run)
park/reserve

Established: *1969*
Address: *Brampton, Cumbria, CA8 1HN*

Telephone: *(06977) 3129*
Access: (road) *M6/A69* (rail) *Carlisle/Brampton*
Parking capacity: (cars) *250* (coaches) *12*
Season: *all year*
Hours: *Easter to Nov – Mon to Sun – 9am to 6pm*
Admission (1992): *free*
No. visitors (1992): *N/A*

Facilities
Interpretation: *leaflets; information boards; maps;*
guide books
Schools: *maximum no. 40; educational literature;*
audio/visual presentation; lecture/talk
Disabled: *easy access*
Catering: *4 picnic areas*
Retailing: *postcards/inexpensive souvenirs;*
confectionery and ice cream; books
No. shops: *1*

Operations
Contacts: *D Hammond/A Jackson (Land Agents)*
No. employees: (high season) *2 full time; 4 part*
time (low season) *2 full time*
Training: *F/T operations staff are trained in-house*
and externally and on specific courses using
handbooks

Marketing
Annual event(s): *rowing/sailing regattas,*
mountain bike events
Other: *press office; market research*
UK promotion: *national newspapers; radio; local*
newspapers; regional tourist board; leaflets/
information packs; ETB/BTA; Cumbria Tourist
Board

Environmental monitoring: *energy consumption*

TALLBERG TAYLOR GALLERY
(limited company)
gallery

Established: *1991*
Address: *142a Greenwich High Rd, Greenwich,*
London, SE10 8NN
Telephone: *(081) 305 2113.* Fax: *(081) 293 1268*
Access: (road) *A102(M)/A102/A206*
(rail) Greenwich
Hours: *Feb to Nov – Tues to Fri – 10am to 6pm;*
Sat and Sun – 12 noon to 4pm
Admission (1992): *free*
No. visitors (1992): *2000 (est.)*

Facilities
Interpretation: *leaflets*
Schools: *maximum no. 50; no special support*
Disabled: *helpers*
Retailing: *books; limited edition prints; magazines*
No. shops: *1*

Operations
Contacts: *Ms L Kelly (Gallery Manager); Guitty*
Talberg (Director)
No. employees: (high season) *4 full time; 3 part*
time (low season) *4 full time; 3 part time*
Training: *F/T operations staff, F/T management,*
P/T operations staff and P/T management are
trained in-house and day-to-day on job using
Senr to Country Centres

Marketing
Press office
UK promotion: *local newspapers; regional tourist*
board; London Log; Visitor Card

Environmental monitoring: *recycling; waste;*
water quality

TALNOTRY COTTAGE BIRD GARDEN
(private ownership)
zoo/wildlife attraction

Established: *1981*
Address: *2 Crumlin Rd, Crumlin, Co. Antrim, BT29 4AD*
Telephone: *(08494) 22900*
Access: (road) *A52/A26* (rail) *Crumlin*
Season: *all year*
Hours: *Easter to Aug – Sun and BH – 2pm to 6pm. Other times by arrangement*
Admission (1992): *adults £1.70; children £0.80*
No. visitors (1992): *1500 (est.)*

Facilities
Interpretation: *information boards; tour guides*
Children: *nappy changing*
Schools: *maximum no. 40; educational tour; lecture/talk*
Disabled: *easy access; helpers*
Catering: *1 picnic area*
Retailing: *craftwork; oriflame skincare*
No. shops: *1*

Operations
Contact: *P Nevines (owner)*
No. employees: (high season) *2 full time; 1 part time* (low season) *2 full time*
Training: *F/T operations staff and F/T management are trained in-house and day-to-day on job using handbooks*
Languages spoken: *French; German*

Marketing
Affiliations: *World Pheasant Association, NI Ornamental Pheasant Society, Ulster Wildlife Trust, USPCA*
UK promotion: *local newspapers; regional tourist board; other attractions; leaflets/information packs; Antrim Borough Council*

Environmental monitoring: *recycling*

TALYLLYN RAILWAY
(statutory company)
steam railway

Established: *1866*
Address: *Wharf Station, Tywyn, Gwynedd, LL36 9EY*
Telephone: *(0654) 710472.* Fax: *(0654) 711755*
Access: (road) *A487/A493* (rail) *Tywyn*
Parking capacity: (cars) *40* (coaches) *4*
Hours: *Easter to Oct, and during the Christmas holidays, times available from the Talyllyn Railway*
Admission (1992): *on request*
No. visitors (1992): *61 919*

Facilities
Interpretation: *leaflets; information boards; guide books*
Languages: *Japanese; Dutch; French; German; Italian; Spanish; Swedish; Arabic*
Children: *nappy changing*
Schools: *maximum no. 50; educational literature; lecture/talk*
Disabled: *easy access; disabled toilets; helpers; leaflets; special coach for wheelchairs*
Catering: *3 picnic areas*
Retailing: *postcards/inexpensive souvenirs; confectionery and ice cream; craftwork; books; model railway items*
No. shops: *2*

Operations
Contacts: *Mr D Woodhouse MBE (General Manager); Ms M Wagland and Mr E Lund (Shop and Catering Managers)*
No. employees: (high season) *14 full time; 11 part time* (low season) *14 full time; 7 part time*
Training: *F/T operations staff, F/T management, P/T operations staff and casual operations staff are trained in-house and externally and on specific courses and day-to-day on job using handbooks*

Environmental monitoring: *recycling*

TAMAR VALLEY DONKEY PARK
(partnership)
theme park; park/reserve

Established: *1989*
Address: *At Ann's Chapel, Gunnislake, Cornwall, PL18 9HW*
Telephone: *(0822) 834072*
Access: (road) *A390* (rail) *Gunnislake*
Parking capacity: (cars) *75* (coaches) *4*
Hours: *Easter to end of Oct – 10am to 5.30pm daily; Sat and Sun in winter*
Admission (1992): *adults £2.00; children £1.50; OAP £1.50*
No. visitors (1992): *30 000 (est.)*

Facilities
Interpretation: *information boards; personnel*
Children: *adventure playground; play area; nappy changing*
Schools: *maximum no. 200; question and answer sheets*
Disabled: *easy access; disabled toilets; helpers; donkey cart for wheelchair*
Catering: *2 picnic areas*
Retailing: *postcards/inexpensive souvenirs; confectionery and ice cream; craftwork; clothes; donkey related; toys*
No. shops: *1*

Operations
Contacts: *Mr P Masters (Partner); Mr A Masters (Partner); Ms Y Masters (Partner)*
No. employees: (high season) *3 full time* (low season) *3 full time*
Training: *F/T operations staff and casual operations staff are trained in-house and day-to-day on job*

Marketing
Affiliations: *Donkey Breed Society, SE Cornwall Tourist Association*
Other: *market research*
UK promotion: *radio; local newspapers; regional tourist board; other attractions; leaflets/ information packs; SECTA; Tour Operators Guide, tourist handbook*

TAMWORTH CASTLE
(local authority run)
castle; museum

Established: *1899*
Address: *The Holloway, Tamworth, Staffs*
Telephone: *(0827) 63563.* Fax: *(0827) 52769*
Access: (road) *M42/A453/A5* (rail) *Tamworth*
Season: *all year*
Hours: *Mon to Sat – 10am to 5.30pm; Sun – 2pm to 5.30pm. Closed 25 and 31 Dec*
Admission (1992): *adults £2.75; children £1.00; OAP £1.50; student £1.50*
No. visitors (1992): *51 020*

Facilities
Interpretation: *leaflets; audio tapes; information boards; slides; tour guides; guide books; "living images"*
Children: *adventure playground*
Schools: *maximum no. 20; educational literature*
Retailing: *postcards/inexpensive souvenirs; confectionery and ice cream; craftwork; books; glassware, coasters, pens, etc.; toiletries, toys, maps, lace, etc.*
No. shops: *1*

Operations
Contacts: *E Ballard (Castle and Museum Curator); I Dougall (Training and Development Officer); J Reddaway (Tourism Officer)*
No. employees: (high season) *6 full time; 6 part time* (low season) *6 full time; 6 part time*
Training: *F/T operations staff, F/T management, P/T operations staff and casual operations staff are trained in-house and externally and on specific courses and day-to-day on job*

Marketing
Annual event(s): *Easter festivals, castle by candlelight, Tamworth flower club, Christmas*
Other: *press office; market research*

UK promotion: *national newspapers; radio; local newspapers; regional tourist board; other attractions; leaflets/information packs; HETB and EMTB publications*

Environmental monitoring: *recycling; waste; conservation and organic methods*

TANK MUSEUM
(registered charity)
museum

Established: *1947*
Address: *Bovington Camp, Wareham, Dorset, BH20 6JG*
Telephone: *(0929) 403329.* Fax: *(0929) 405360*
Access: (road) *M27/A35* (rail) *Wool*
Parking capacity: (cars) *800* (coaches) *40*
Season: *all year*
Hours: *10am to 5pm daily except 10 days over Christmas period*
Admission (1992): *adults £4.00; children £2.00; OAP £2.00; student £1.50; family ticket (2 + 2) £8.00*
No. visitors (1992): *175 812*

Facilities
Interpretation: *videos; leaflets; audio tapes; information boards; maps; tour guides; guide books*
Languages: *French; German*
Children: *adventure playground; nappy changing*
Schools: *maximum no. 80; educational literature; audio/visual presentation; lecture/talk; education officer*
Disabled: *easy access; disabled toilets; other audio facilities; special signs; parking*
Catering: *1 picnic area*
Franchisees: *10am to 5pm daily except 10 days over Christmas period*
Retailing: *postcards/inexpensive souvenirs; craftwork; books; clothes; reproductions of famous artefacts; military toys and models; fancy goods*
No. shops: *2*

Operations
Contacts: *Lt Col (Retd) G Forty (Director/ Curator); Mrs S Bardner (Aylesworth Fleming of Bournemouth)*
No. employees: (high season) *46 full time; 11 part time* (low season) *34 full time; 11 part time*
Training: *F/T operations staff and F/T management are trained in-house and externally and on specific courses and day-to-day on job using videos and handbooks*

Marketing
Annual event(s): *military days and classic car show*
Sponsor: *exchange and Mart*
Affiliation: *AIM*
Other: *PR company: Aylesworth Fleming, Bournemouth; press office; market research*
UK promotion: *national newspapers; radio; local newspapers; regional tourist board; other attractions; leaflets/information packs; ETB/ BTA*
Europe/Asia/Australia/USA/worldwide promotion: *leaflets/brochures; British Tourist Authority*

TANKERNESS HOUSE MUSEUM
(local authority run)
historic house; garden; museum

Established: *1968*
Address: *Broad St, Kirkwall, Orkney, KW15 1DH*
Telephone: *(0856) 873191*
Season: *all year*
Hours: *10.30am to 12.30pm and 1.30pm to 5pm daily*
Admission (1992): *adults £1.00; free for unemployed*
No. visitors (1992): *16 000 (est.)*

Facilities
Interpretation: *displays*
Schools: *maximum no. 25; tour on request*

Retailing: *postcards/inexpensive souvenirs; books*
No. shops: *1*

Operations
Contact: *B S Wilson (Museums Officer)*
No. employees: (high season) *5 full time; 2 part time* (low season) *5 full time; 1 part time*
Training: *F/T operations staff and F/T management are trained externally and on specific courses and day-to-day on job*
Languages spoken: *German*

Marketing
Annual event: *summer exhibition*
UK promotion: *radio; local newspapers; regional tourist board; leaflets/information packs*

Environmental monitoring: *energy consumption; transport*

TAPELEY PARK AND BRITISH JOUSTING CENTRE
(trust)
historic house; garden; jousting centre

Established: *1970*
Address: *Tapeley Park, Instow, Devon, EX39 4NT*
Telephone: *(0271) 860528*
Access: (road) *M5/A39*
Parking capacity: (cars) *100* (coaches) *4*
Hours: *Easter to Oct – Mon to Sun – 10am to 6pm, closed Sat. Jousting – Wed, Thur, Fri, Sun and BH Sat*
Admission (1992): *adults £3.50; children £2.00; OAP £2.80; these prices are for weekends, reduced prices for gardens and mid week*
No. visitors (1992): *10 000 (est.)*

Facilities
Interpretation: *leaflets; information boards; maps; tour guides; guide books; personnel*
Children: *play area*
Schools: *lecture/talk*
Disabled: *easy access; disabled toilets; special signs*
Catering: *1 picnic area*
Retailing: *postcards/inexpensive souvenirs; confectionery and ice cream; craftwork; dried flowers, jams*
No. shops: *1*

Operations
Contacts: *Ms K Christie; Ms L Cook; Mr H Christie*
No. employees: (high season) *2 full time; 5 part time* (low season) *2 full time; 2 part time*
Training: *F/T operations staff are trained in-house and day-to-day on job*

Marketing
Affiliation: *HHA*
Other: *market research*
UK promotion: *local newspapers; regional tourist board; other attractions; leaflets/information packs*

Environmental monitoring: *Humidity, temperature and UV*

TATTON
(local authority run)
theme park; historic house; park/reserve; garden; museum; zoo/wildlife attraction

Established: *1962*
Address: *Tatton Park, Knutsford, Ches, WA16 6QN*
Telephone: *(0565) 654822. Fax: (0565) 650179*
Access: (road) *M6/M56/A556* (rail) *Knutsford*
Parking capacity: (cars) *5000* (coaches) *100*
Season: *all year*
Hours: *Apr to Sept – Tues to Sun – 10.30am to 6pm; Oct to Mar – Tues to Sun – 11am to 5pm*
Admission (1992): *adults £2.30; children £1.60; group and family tickets*
No. visitors (1992): *723 000 (est.)*

Facilities
Interpretation: *videos; leaflets; information boards; maps; tour guides; guide books; personnel*
Languages: *Japanese; French; German*
Children: *adventure playground; nappy changing*
Schools: *maximum no. 2000; audio/visual presentation; educational tour; lecture/talk*
Disabled: *easy access; disabled toilets; Braille/sound posts; powered transport*
Catering: *2 picnic areas*
Franchisees: *Apr to Sept – Tues to Sun – 10.30am to 6pm Oct to Mar – Tues to Sun – 11am to 5pm*
Retailing: *postcards/inexpensive souvenirs; confectionery and ice cream; craftwork; books; garden shop, farm produce*
No. shops: *more than 4*

Operations
Contacts: *Mr Beaufoy (Director); L Dunn (Support Services Manager); D Hardman (Marketing Manager)*
No. employees: (high season) *48 full time; 12 part time* (low season) *48 full time; 12 part time*
Training: *F/T operations staff, F/T management, P/T operations staff, P/T management and casual operations staff are trained in-house and externally and on specific courses and day-to-day on job*

Marketing
Annual event(s): *various*
Sponsor(s): *various*
Affiliations: *NT*
Other: *PR company: Barrington Johnson Lorains, 623 Sunlight House, Quay St, Manchester; press office; market research*
UK promotion: *television; national newspapers; radio; local newspapers; regional tourist board; other attractions; leaflets/information packs; various; ETB/BTA*
Europe/Asia/USA promotion: *leaflets/brochures; British Tourist Authority*

Environmental monitoring: *recycling*

TEHIDY COUNTRY PARK
(local authority run)
park/reserve; country park

Established: *1983*
Address: *Countryside Services Office, Tehidy Country Park, Tehidy, Camborne, Cornwall, TR14 0HA*
Telephone: *(0209) 714494. Fax: (0872) 70340*
Access: (road) *M5/A30*
Parking capacity: (cars) *250* (coaches) *3*
Season: *all year*
Admission (1992): *free*
No. visitors (1992): *130 000 (est.)*

Facilities
Interpretation: *leaflets; information boards; maps; personnel; ranger service*
Schools: *maximum no. 50; no special support; educational literature; audio/visual presentation; educational tour; lecture/talk*
Disabled: *easy access; disabled toilets; Braille/sound posts; helpers*
Catering: *1 snack bar/food stall*
Franchisees: *all year*

Operations
Contacts: *J Kay (Project Officer); P Folland (Countryside Ranger)*
No. employees: (high season) *3 full time; 2 part time*
Training: *F/T operations staff, F/T management, P/T operations staff and casual operations staff are trained in-house and externally and on specific courses and day-to-day on job using handbooks*
Languages spoken: *French; German*

Marketing
Annual event(s): *various*
Other: *press office; market research*
UK promotion: *radio; local newspapers; regional tourist board; other attractions; leaflets/information packs*

Environmental monitoring: *recycling; waste; water quality; energy consumption*

TEIFI VALLEY RAILWAY
(limited company)
tourist railway and leisure park

Established: *1985*
Address: *Henllan Station, Henllan, Llandysul, Dyfed, SA44 5TD*
Telephone: *(0559) 371077*
Access: (road) *M4/A484* (rail) *Carmarthen*
Parking capacity: (cars) *60* (coaches) *5*
Hours: *Good Friday to Oct – Mon to Sun – 11am to 4pm (July and Aug – to 5pm)*
Admission (1992): *adults £3.00; children £1.50; OAP £2.70; dogs £0.50*
No. visitors (1992): *30 000 (est.)*

Facilities
Interpretation: *leaflets; information boards; guide books*
Children: *play area; nappy changing*
Schools: *maximum no. 70; lecture/talk; wildlife display*
Disabled: *easy access; disabled toilets; helpers*
Catering: *2 picnic areas*
Franchisees: *Good Friday to Oct – Mon to Sun – 11am to 4pm July and Aug – to 5pm*
Retailing: *postcards/inexpensive souvenirs; confectionery and ice cream; craftwork; books; clothes*
No. shops: *1*

Operations
Contact: *Raymond Sanderson (Commercial Director)*
No. employees: (high season) *4 full time; 6 part time* (low season) *4 full time; 2 part time*
Training: *F/T operations staff, F/T management, P/T operations staff and casual operations staff are trained in-house and on specific courses and day-to-day on job using handbooks*

Marketing
Annual event(s): *Easter Sunday, Victorian Day, Hallowe'en, Santa Specials*
Other: *market research*
UK promotion: *local newspapers; regional tourist board; other attractions; leaflets/information packs; Welsh Tourist Board*

Environmental monitoring: *recycling; waste; water quality; energy consumption; hazardous materials; chemical usage; transport; emissions*

TEIGNMOUTH MUSEUM
(trust)
museum

Established: *1978*
Address: *29 French St, Teignmouth, Devon, TQ14 9EG*
Telephone: *(0626) 777041*
Access: (road) *A38* (rail) *Teignmouth*
Hours: *May to Sept – Mon to Fri – 10am to 4.30pm (Thur – 7pm to 9pm); Sun – 2pm to 4.30pm*
Admission (1992): *adults £0.50; OAP £0.50; student £0.50*
No. visitors (1992): *2500*

Facilities
Interpretation: *tour guides*
Languages: *French*
Children: *nappy changing*
Schools: *maximum no. 30; educational literature; audio/visual presentation; educational tour; lecture/talk*
Disabled: *easy access; special signs; guide book*
Retailing: *postcards/inexpensive souvenirs; books*
No. shops: *1*

Operations
Contact: *G M W Ruddock (Curator)*
No. employees: (high season) *1 full time; 15 part time* (low season) *1 full time*

Training: *F/T operations staff, F/T management and P/T operations staff are trained in-house and day-to-day on job using handbooks and Rule books*
Languages spoken: *French; Welsh*

Marketing
Affiliations: *AIM*
UK promotion: *local newspapers; regional tourist board; leaflets/information packs; West of England; ETB/BTA*
Europe promotion: *leaflets/brochures; British Tourist Authority*

Environmental monitoring: *transport; emissions*

TENBY MUSEUM AND PICTURE GALLERY
(trust)
museum; gallery

Established: *1878*
Address: *Castle Hill, Tenby, Dyfed, SA70 7BP*
Telephone: *(0834) 842809*
Access: *(road) M4 (rail) Tenby*
Season: *all year*
Hours: *Easter to 31 Oct – 10am to 6pm daily; 1 Nov to Easter – 10am to 12 noon and 2pm to 4pm – Mon to Fri. Other times by arrangement*
Admission (1992): *adults £1.00; children £0.30; OAP £0.50*
No. visitors (1992): *41 240*

Facilities
Interpretation: *videos; leaflets; information boards; tour guides; guide books*
Children: *nappy changing*
Schools: *maximum no. 30; lecture/talk*
Disabled: *access may be difficult*
Retailing: *postcards/inexpensive souvenirs; books*
No. shops: *1*

Operations
Contact: *Mr D Bleines (Museum Assistant)*
No. employees: (high season) *1 full time; 5 part time* (low season) *1 full time; 1 part time*
Languages spoken: *French; German*

Environmental monitoring: *energy consumption; humidity, lighting, UV, etc.*

TEWKESBURY MUSEUM
(local authority run)
historic house; museum

Established: *1962*
Address: *64 Barton St, Tewkesbury, Glos, GL20 5PX*
Access: *(road) M5/M50/A38 (rail) Cheltenham*
Season: *all year*
Hours: *10am to 1pm and 1.30pm to 4pm daily*
Admission (1992): *adults £0.50; OAP £0.25; student £0.25*
No. visitors (1992): *3080 (est.)*

Marketing
UK promotion: *regional tourist board; museums and galleries*

THAMESIDE COMPLEX
(local authority run)
museum; theatre and library

Address: *Orsett Rd, Grays, Essex, RM17 5DX*
Telephone: *(0375) 382555*
Access: *(road) M25 (rail) Grays*
Season: *all year*
Hours: *9am to 8pm daily. Later closing when theatre is open*
Admission (1992): *N/A*
No. visitors (1992): *12 000 (est.)*

Facilities
Interpretation: *leaflets; information boards; signs*
Children: *nappy changing*
Schools: *maximum no. 300; educational literature*

Disabled: *easy access; disabled toilets*
Catering: *1 bar/public house*
Retailing: *confectionery and ice cream*
No. shops: *1*

Operations
Contacts: *Mark Allinson (Manager); Pat Jolliffe (Duty Officer); Linda Clampett (Duty Officer)*
Training: *F/T operations staff, F/T management, P/T operations staff and P/T management are trained in-house and externally and on specific courses and day-to-day on job*

Marketing
UK promotion: *radio, local newspapers; regional tourist board; leaflets/information packs*

THETFORD MUSEUM
(local authority run)
historic house; garden; museum

Established: *1924*
Address: *21–23 White Hart St, Thetford, Norfolk, IP24 1AA*
Telephone: *(0842) 752599*
Access: *(road) M11/A11 (rail) Thetford*
Hours: *Mon to Sat – 10am to 5pm daily; June to Sept – Sun – 2pm to 5pm*
Admission (1992): *free except in Aug – £0.30 to £0.60*
No. visitors (1992): *15 000 (est.)*

Facilities
Interpretation: *leaflets; information boards; signs*
Schools: *maximum no. 35; educational literature; handling sessions*
Retailing: *postcards/inexpensive souvenirs; books; reproductions of famous artefacts; maps, guides*
No. shops: *1*

Operations
Contacts: *Oliver Bone (Curator); Hilary Slater (0603) 223628 (Publications Officer); Doug Chinnery (0603) 223646 (Assistant Director)*
No. employees: (high season) *1 full time; 2 part time* (low season) *1 full time; 2 part time*
Training: *F/T management and P/T operations staff are trained in-house and externally and on specific courses and day-to-day on job using videos and handbooks*
Languages spoken: *French; Japanese*

Marketing
Annual event(s): *temporary exhibitions*
Affiliations: *Museums Association, Norfolk Museums Service*
Other: *market research*
UK promotion: *local newspapers; leaflets/information packs; ETB/BTA*

Environmental monitoring: *recycling*

THIRLESTANE CASTLE
(trust)
historic house; castle; museum

Established: *1982*
Address: *Lauder, Berwickshire, TD2 6RU*
Telephone: *(05782) 430. Fax: (05782) 761*
Access: *(road) A68/A697*
Parking capacity: *(cars) 60 (coaches) 6*
Hours: *Easter and May to end Sept – Wed ,Thur and Sun – 2pm to 5pm (plus July and Aug – Mon, Tues and Fri – 2pm to 5pm)*
Admission (1992): *adults £3.00; OAP £3.00; student £3.00; family ticket £8.00; groups £2.50 for 30 or more*
No. visitors (1992): *15 102*

Facilities
Interpretation: *information boards; tour guides; guide books*
Schools: *lecture/talk; with support of school*
Disabled: *disabled toilets*

Catering: *1 picnic area*
Retailing: *postcards/inexpensive souvenirs; confectionery and ice cream; books; toys and own label whisky*
No. shops: *1*

Operations
Contacts: *P Jarvis (Castle Administrator); Mrs F Jarvis (House Manager)*
No. employees: (high season) *3 full time; 12 part time* (low season) *3 full time; 3 part time*
Training: *F/T operations staff and casual operations staff are trained externally and on specific courses using handbooks*
Languages spoken: *French*

Marketing
Annual event: *Scottish Horse Trial Championship*
Sponsor: *Kimberly Clark*
Affiliations: *HHA, Museums Council, Border Heritage and Borders Museum Forum*
Other: *market research*
UK promotion: *national newspapers; radio; local newspapers; regional tourist board; other attractions; leaflets/information packs*

THREAKE GARDENS
(trust)
garden; school of horticulture

Established: *1959*
Address: *National Trust for Scotland, Castle Douglas, Dumfries and Galloway*
Telephone: *(0556) 2575*
Access: *(road) A75*
Parking capacity: *(cars) 80 (coaches) 3*
Season: *all year*
Hours: *Gardens – 9am to sunset daily. Visitor centre – 9am to 5.30pm – Apr to Oct. Restaurant – 10am to 5pm – Apr to Oct*
Admission (1992): *adults £2.80; children £1.40; OAP £1.40; student £1.40; party rate £2.20 (adults) and £1.10*
No. visitors (1992): *11 000*

Facilities
Interpretation: *leaflets; information boards; maps; guide books*
Children: *nappy changing*
Schools: *maximum no. 30; educational literature; lecture/talk*
Disabled: *easy access; disabled toilets; powered transport*
Catering: *1 picnic area*
Franchisees: *Gardens – 9am to sunset daily. Visitor centre – 9am to 5.30pm – Apr to Oct*
Retailing: *postcards/inexpensive souvenirs; confectionery and ice cream; craftwork; books; clothes*
No. shops: *1*

Operations
Contacts: *W R Hean (Administrator, Threave); Director (Head Office, Edinburgh); Merchandising (Head Office, Edinburgh); Bruce Mackie (Head Office, Edinburgh)*
No. employees: (high season) *13 full time; 12 part time* (low season) *13 full time*
Training: *casual operations staff are trained in-house and on specific courses*

Marketing
Affiliation: *NT*
Other: *press office*
UK promotion: *national newspapers; local newspapers; regional tourist board; leaflets/information packs*

THRIGBY HALL WILDLIFE GARDENS
(limited company)
zoo/wildlife attraction

Established: *1979*
Address: *Filby, Great Yarmouth, Norfolk, NR29 3DR*
Telephone: *(0493) 369477. Fax: (0493) 368256*
Access: *(road) A1064*
Parking capacity: *(cars) 400 (coaches) 20*
Season: *all year*

Hours: *summer – 10am to 6pm; winter – 10am to 4pm*
Admission (1992): *adults £3.40; children £2.00; OAP £2.90; student £2.00*
No. visitors (1992): *72 000 (est.)*

Facilities
Interpretation: *information boards; maps; guide books; signs*
Children: *adventure playground; nappy changing*
Schools: *maximum no. 500; audio/visual presentation*
Disabled: *easy access; disabled toilets; helpers*
Catering: *1 picnic area*
Retailing: *postcards/inexpensive souvenirs; craftwork; clothes; souvenirs*
No. shops: *1*

Operations
Contact: *Ken Simms (Director)*
No. employees: (high season) *5 full time; 10 part time* (low season) *5 full time; 1 part time*
Training: *F/T operations staff are trained in-house and day-to-day on job using videos*

Marketing
Affiliation: *British Zoo Federation*
Other: *PR company: Paula Babb PR, Tudor Lodge, Upton, Acle, Norfolk; market research*
UK promotion: *local newspapers; regional tourist board; other attractions; leaflets/ information packs; EATB Guide, Welcome to East Anglia*

THURSFORD COLLECTION
(limited company)
museum

Established: *1977*
Address: *Thursford, Fakenham, Norfolk, NR21 0AS*
Telephone: *(0328) 878477*
Access: (road) *A148*
Parking capacity: (cars) *1000* (coaches) *50*
Hours: *Apr, May, Sept and Oct – 1pm to 5pm daily; June July and Aug – 11am to 5pm daily*
Admission (1992): *adults £4.20; children £1.80; OAP £3.80; student £3.30; group rate £3.30*
No. visitors (1992): *170 000*

Facilities
Interpretation: *information boards; guide books; personnel; live musical shows and organ demonstrations*
Children: *adventure playground; play area; nappy changing*
Schools: *maximum no. 1500*
Disabled: *easy access; disabled toilets; guide book*
Catering: *1 picnic area*
Retailing: *postcards/inexpensive souvenirs; confectionery and ice cream; books; quality gifts*
No. shops: *4*

Operations
Contacts: *Ms G Rye (Administrator); Ms L Palmer (Personnel)*
No. employees: (high season) *10 full time; 40 part time* (low season) *10 full time; 10 part time*
Training: *F/T operations staff, F/T management, P/T operations staff and casual operations staff are trained in-house and externally and on specific courses and day-to-day on job using correspondence course*
Languages spoken: *French*

Marketing
Annual event(s): *Christmas shows*
Other: *market research*
UK promotion: *television; local newspapers; regional tourist board; other attractions; leaflets/information packs; ETB/BTA*
Europe promotion: *leaflets/brochures; British Tourist Authority*

Environmental monitoring: *recycling; waste; water quality; energy consumption; hazardous materials; chemical usage; transport; emissions*

THURSO HERITAGE MUSEUM
(trust)
heritage centre; gallery

Established: *1972*
Address: *Town Hall, Thurso, Highland*
Telephone: *(0847) 62692*
Hours: *June, July, Aug and part Sept*
Admission (1992): *adults £0.50; children £0.10; OAP £0.25; student £0.25*
No. visitors (1992): *2300*

Facilities
Interpretation: *leaflets; information boards; maps*
Schools: *maximum no. 30; lecture/talk*
Disabled: *easy access; disabled toilets*
Retailing: *postcards/inexpensive souvenirs; books*
No. shops: *1*

Operations
Contact: *Mrs E C Angus (Chairperson)*
No. employees: (high season) *7 part time*
Training: *P/T operations staff are trained in-house and day-to-day on job using videos*
Languages spoken: *French; Spanish*

Marketing
UK promotion: *local newspapers; regional tourist board; STB, Factfinder and Caithness Explorer*

Environmental monitoring: *waste; energy consumption; hazardous materials; chemical usage*

TIMESPAN HERITAGE CENTRE
(company limited by guarantee)
heritage centre; garden; museum

Established: *1987*
Address: *Dunrobin St, Helmsdale, Sutherland*
Telephone: *(04312) 327*
Access: (road) *A9* (rail) *Inverness – Wick*
Parking capacity: (cars) *50* (coaches) *6*
Hours: *Easter to Oct – Mon to Sat – 10am to 5pm, Sun – 2pm to 5pm (July and Aug – to 6pm)*
Admission (1992): *adults £2.40; children £1.50; OAP £1.90; student £1.90; family ticket £6.00*
No. visitors (1992): *17 000*

Facilities
Interpretation: *videos; leaflets; audio tapes; information boards; maps; guide books; life size sets and sound effects*
Languages: *French; German; Italian*
Schools: *educational literature*
Disabled: *easy access; disabled toilets; helpers*
Retailing: *postcards/inexpensive souvenirs; confectionery and ice cream; craftwork; books*
No. shops: *1*

Operations
Contact: *Mrs M Mackenzie (Project Co-ordinator)*
No. employees: (high season) *2 full time; 6 part time* (low season) *2 part time*
Training: *F/T operations staff, P/T operations staff and P/T management are trained in-house and on specific courses and day-to-day on job*

Marketing
Affiliation: *ASVA*
Other: *market research*
UK promotion: *local newspapers; regional tourist board; leaflets/information packs*

Environmental monitoring: *recycling; water quality*

TIMOTHY HACKWORTH VICTORIAN AND RAILWAY MUSEUM
(local authority run)
historic house; museum

Established: *1975*
Address: *Soho Cottages, Hackworth Close, Shildon, Co. Durham, DL4 2QX*
Telephone: *(0388) 777999*

Access: (road) *A6072* (rail) *Shildon*
Parking capacity: (cars) *50* (coaches) *20*
Hours: *Easter Fri to last Sun in Oct – Wed to Sun – 10am to 5pm*
Admission (1992): *adults £1.25; children £0.75; OAP £0.75; student £0.75; family ticket £3.50*
No. visitors (1992): *2500 (est.)*

Facilities
Interpretation: *videos; leaflets; slides; tour guides*
Children: *nappy changing*
Schools: *maximum no. 200; educational literature; lecture/talk; discounts available*
Disabled: *helpers*
Retailing: *postcards/inexpensive souvenirs; books*
No. shops: *1*

Operations
Contacts: *Mr A Pearce (Manager); Ms J Patterson (Promotions and Marketing Officer)*
No. employees: (high season) *1 full time; 1 part time* (low season) *1 full time; 1 part time*
Training: *F/T operations staff, F/T management, P/T operations staff and casual operations staff are trained externally and on specific courses*

Marketing
Annual event: *festival day*
Affiliations: *NEMS, NTB, Transport Trust, etc.*
Other: *market research*
UK promotion: *local newspapers; regional tourist board; other attractions; leaflets/information packs; ETB/BTA; NTB*

TINGWALL AGRICULTURAL MUSEUM
(personal collection)
museum; farmlife attraction

Established: *1975*
Address: *2 Veensgarth, Gott, Shetland*
Telephone: *(0595) 84344*
Hours: *June, July and Aug – 2pm to 5pm daily*
Admission (1992): *adults £1.00; children £0.50; OAP £0.50; student £0.50; groups £0.50 per head*
No. visitors (1992): *700 (est.)*

Facilities
Interpretation: *audio tapes; slides; tour guides*
Children: *play area*
Schools: *maximum no. 50; educational literature; audio/visual presentation; lecture/talk*
Catering: *1 picnic area*

Operations
Languages spoken: *French; Spanish*

Marketing
UK promotion: *radio; local newspapers; regional tourist board*

TITHE BARN MUSEUM AND ARTS CENTRE
(trust)
historic house; museum; exhibition centre

Established: *1976*
Address: *Church Hill, Swanage, Dorset*
Telephone: *(0929) 424566*
Access: (road) *M3/A31/A351* (rail) *Wareham*
Parking capacity: (cars) *300* (coaches) *50*
Hours: *Easter to mid Sept – Weekdays – 10.30am to 12.30pm; 2.30pm to 4.30pm and 7.30pm to 9.30pm; Sun – 2.30pm to 4.30pm. Groups at other times by arrangement*
Admission (1992): *adults £0.30; children £0.15; OAP £0.30; student £0.30; school groups £0.30 (adults) and £0.10 (children)*
No. visitors (1992): *5879*

Facilities
Interpretation: *information boards; maps; models, paintings, showcases*
Schools: *maximum no. 50; educational literature; lecture/talk*
Disabled: *easy access*
Retailing: *postcards/inexpensive souvenirs; craftwork; books; geological specimens*
No. shops: *1*

Operations
Contacts: *Mr D Hayson (Curator); Ms D
Billington (Purchasing); Mr C Harde (Publicity)*
No. employees: (high season) *30 part time* (low
season) *30 part time*
Training: *P/T operations staff are trained
in-house and day-to-day on job*
Languages spoken: *Norwegian*

Marketing
Market research
UK promotion: *local newspapers; leaflets/
information packs*

TIVERTON CASTLE
(privately owned)
castle

Established: *1971*
Address: *Tiverton, Devon, EX16 6RP*
Telephone: *(0884) 253200*
Access: (road) *M5/A361* (rail) *Tiverton Parkway*
Parking capacity: (cars) *30*
Hours: *Easter to last Sun in Sept – Sun to Thur –
2.30pm to 5.30pm*
Admission (1992): *adults £2.75; children £1.75;
OAP £2.75*

Facilities
Interpretation: *information boards; tour guides*
Schools: *maximum no. 60; lecture/talk; tours
tailored to needs*
Catering: *1 waiter/waitress served*
Retailing: *postcards/inexpensive souvenirs;
confectionery and ice cream; craftwork; books;
toy arms and armour*
No. shops: *1*

Operations
Contact: *Mrs A Gordon (owner)*
No. employees: (high season) *12 part time*
Training: *casual operations staff are trained
in-house and day-to-day on job*
Languages spoken: *French; German; by
arrangement*

Marketing
Affiliation: *HHA*
Other: *market research*
UK promotion: *regional tourist board; other
attractions; leaflets/information packs*

TIVERTON MUSEUM
(independent and charity)
museum

Established: *1960*
Address: *St Andrew St, Tiverton, Devon, EX16
6PH*
Telephone: *(0884) 256295*
Access: (road) *M5/A361* (rail) *Tiverton Parkway*
Parking capacity: (cars) *300* (coaches) *5*
Hours: *Feb to Christmas – Mon to Sat – 10.30am
to 4.30pm*
Admission (1992): *adults £1.00; OAP £1.00;
students and under 16s free*
No. visitors (1992): *20 000*

Facilities
Interpretation: *displays*
Schools: *maximum no. 50; no special support*
Retailing: *postcards/inexpensive souvenirs;
books*
No. shops: *1*

Operations
Contacts: *Dr M Nix (Curator); Mr T Hassall
(Shop Administrator)*
No. employees: (high season) *1 full time; 5 part
time* (low season) *1 full time; 5 part time*
Training: *F/T management are trained in-house
and externally and on specific courses and
day-to-day on job*

Marketing
Affiliations: *Area Museum Council SW, AIM,
MA*
Other: *market research*

UK promotion: *local newspapers; regional tourist
board; leaflets/information packs*

TOLPUDDLE MARTYRS MUSEUM
(trust)
museum

Established: *1981*
Address: *Tolpuddle, Dorchester, Dorset, DT2
7EH*
Telephone: *(0305) 848237*
Access: (road) *A35*
Season: *all year*
Hours: *1 Apr to 31 Oct – Tues to Sat – 10am to
5.30pm; Sun – 11am to 5.30pm; 1 Nov to 31
Mar – Tues to Sat – 10am to 4pm, Sun – 11am
to 4pm; open BH Mon. Closed Christmas week*
Admission (1992): *donations*
No. visitors (1992): *20 000 (est.)*

Facilities
Interpretation: *leaflets; information boards*
Schools: *maximum no. 50; no special support*
Disabled: *will be available*
Retailing: *postcards/inexpensive souvenirs; books;
1st day cover stamps*

Operations
Contact: *Mr R Pickering (Warden)*

Marketing
Annual event: *Tolpuddle rally*
Affiliation: *Dorset Museums Association*
UK promotion: *regional tourist board*

Environmental monitoring: *temperature; light;
humidity*

TOLSEY MUSEUM
(trust)
historic house; museum

Established: *1960*
Address: *126 High Street, Burford, Oxon, OX18
4QU*
Access: (road) *M40/A40/A424/A361*
Hours: *Mar to Oct – 2pm to 5pm daily*
Admission (1992): *adults £0.30; children £0.10;
OAP £0.20; student £0.20*
No. visitors (1992): *5503*

Facilities
Interpretation: *information boards*
Schools: *maximum no. 20; educational tour*
Retailing: *postcards/inexpensive souvenirs;
booklets*
No. shops: *1*

Operations
Contact: *C R Baines (Chairman)*

Marketing
UK promotion: *regional tourist board*

TOROSAY CASTLE AND GARDENS
(partnership)
historic house; garden

Established: *1975*
Address: *Craignure, Isle of Mull, Argyll, PA65
6AY*
Telephone: *(06802) 421.* Fax: *(06802) 470*
Access: (road) *A849 and ferry* (rail) *Oban*
Parking capacity: (cars) *20* (coaches) *3*
Season: *all year*
Hours: *house – late Apr to mid Oct – 10.30am to
5pm daily. Gardens – summer – 9am to 7pm,
winter – daylight hours*
Admission (1992): *adults £3.50; OAP £2.75;
concession rates for garden only and groups*
No. visitors (1992): *40 000*

Facilities
Interpretation: *guide books; extensive captions*

Languages: *Japanese; French; German; Italian;
Spanish*
Children: *play area*
Disabled: *easy access; disabled toilets; helpers*
Catering: *1 bar/public house*
Retailing: *postcards/inexpensive souvenirs;
confectionery and ice cream; craftwork; books;
clothes*
No. shops: *3*

Operations
Contact: *Mr C James (owner)*
No. employees: (high season) *14 full time* (low
season) *6 full time*

Marketing
Affiliations: *HHA, West Highlands and Islands of
Argyll Tourist Board*
UK promotion: *local newspapers; regional tourist
board; other attractions; leaflets/information
packs*

TORQUAY MUSEUM
(society)
museum

Established: *1894*
Address: *529 Babbacombe Rd, Torquay, Devon,
TQ1 1HG*
Telephone: *(0803) 293975*
Access: (road) *A380* (rail) *Torquay*
Season: *all year*
Hours: *Easter to Oct – Mon to Sat – 10am to
4.45pm; July and Aug – Sun – 2pm to 4.45pm*
Admission (1992): *adults £1.50; children £0.75;
OAP £0.75; student £0.75*
No. visitors (1992): *14 000*

Facilities
Interpretation: *leaflets; tour guides; guide books;
lectures*
Schools: *maximum no. 60; educational literature;
educational tour; lecture/talk; hands on,
schoolroom*
Retailing: *postcards/inexpensive souvenirs; books;
clothes; reproductions of famous artefacts;
models*
No. shops: *1*

Operations
Contacts: *A Insckar (Curator); B Hamment-
Arnold (Hon Programme Officer)*
No. employees: (high season) *3 full time; 6 part
time* (low season) *3 full time; 6 part time*
Training: *F/T operations staff, F/T management,
P/T operations staff and casual operations staff
are trained in-house and externally and on
specific courses and day-to-day on job using
videos*
Languages spoken: *French; German; Indonesian*

Marketing
Annual event(s): *special exhibitions*
Sponsor: *SW Museums Association*
Affiliations: *Private Museums Association, SW
Museums Association, SW Naturalists Union*
UK promotion: *radio; local newspapers; regional
tourist board; other attractions; leaflets/
information packs; Tourist Trade Manual;
ETB/BTA*
Europe/Asia/Australia/USA promotion: *British
Tourist Authority*

Environmental monitoring: *water quality; energy
consumption; chemical usage*

TORRE ABBEY
(local authority run)
historic house; monument; gallery

Established: *1930*
Address: *The Kings Drive, Torquay, Devon, TQ2
5JX*
Telephone: *(0803) 293593*
Access: (road) *M5/A380* (rail) *Torquay*
Season: *all year*
Hours: *Apr to Oct – 10am to 6pm daily; Nov to
Mar – Mon to Fri – by appointment*

Admission (1992): *adults £2.00; children £1.00; OAP £1.00; family £4.50*
No. visitors (1992): *30 000 (est.)*

Facilities
Interpretation: *information boards; tour guides; guide books*
Schools: *maximum no. 40; educational literature; educational tour; lecture/talk*
Catering: *1 snack bar/food stall*
Franchisees: *Apr to Oct – 10am to 6pm daily*

Operations
Contact: *L Retallick (Senior Curator)*
No. employees: (high season) *3 full time; 3 part time* (low season) *3 full time*
Languages spoken: *French; German; Italian; Spanish*

Marketing
Annual event: *flower festival*
UK promotion: *radio; local newspapers; regional tourist board; leaflets/information packs*

Environmental monitoring: *energy consumption*

TORRINGTON MUSEUM
(society)
museum

Established: *1974*
Address: *Town Hall, Torrington, Devon*
Telephone: *(0805) 24324*
Access: (road) *M3/A386* (rail) *Barnstaple*
Hours: *May to Sept – Mon to Fri – 10.15am to 12.45pm and 2.15pm to 4.45pm; Sat – 10.15am to 3pm*
Admission (1992): *free*
No. visitors (1992): *3000 (est.)*

Facilities
Interpretation: *information boards; volunteer staff*
Schools: *maximum no. 40; educational literature; lecture/talk; liaison with school*

Operations
Contacts: *E Trimm (Chairman); Mrs E Hallett (Secretary)*
No. employees: (high season) *30 part time*
Training: *P/T operations staff and P/T management are trained in-house and on specific courses and day-to-day on job*

Marketing
UK promotion: *town guide*

TOTNES (ELIZABETHAN) MUSEUM
(trust)
historic house; garden; museum; historical study centre

Established: *1962*
Address: *70 Fore Street, Totnes, Devon, TQ9 5RU*
Telephone: *(0803) 863821*
Access: (road) *M5/A38* (rail) *Totnes*
Hours: *Easter to Oct – Mon to Fri – 10.30am to 5pm (Sat in high season)*
Admission (1992): *adults £0.50; children £0.25; student £0.20*
No. visitors (1992): *10 000 (est.)*

Facilities
Interpretation: *leaflets; information boards; maps; tour guides; guide books*
Schools: *maximum no. 50; educational literature; educational tour; lecture/talk; teachers pack and worksheet*
Retailing: *postcards/inexpensive souvenirs; books*
No. shops: *1*

Operations
No. employees: (high season) *2 full time; 1 part time* (low season) *2 full time; 1 part time*
Training: *F/T management are trained in-house and externally and on specific courses and day-to-day on job*
Languages spoken: *French; German; by arrangement for groups*

Marketing
Affiliations: *MA, Devonshire Association, National Heritage, National Art Collections*
UK promotion: *local newspapers; regional tourist board; other attractions; leaflets/information packs; South Hams Museums Group*

TOTNES CASTLE
(English Heritage, local authority run)
castle

Established: *1980*
Address: *Castle St, Totnes, Devon, TQ9 5NE*
Telephone: *(0803) 864406*
Access: (road) *A38* (rail) *Totnes*
Season: *all year*
Hours: *1 Apr to 30 Sept – 10am to 6pm daily; Tues to Sun – 1 Oct to 31 Mar – 10am to 4pm*
Admission (1992): *adults £1.20; children £0.60; OAP £0.90; student £0.90; ub40s £0.90*
No. visitors (1992): *31 000*

Facilities
Interpretation: *leaflets; information boards; guide books*
Languages: *Japanese; French; German*
Schools: *maximum no. 400; audio/visual presentation; talk by arrangement*
Disabled: *not suitable*
Catering: *1 picnic area*
Retailing: *postcards/inexpensive souvenirs; books*
No. shops: *1*

Operations
Contact: *Mr A Henshaw (Group Custodian)*
No. employees: (high season) *1 full time; 1 part time* (low season) *1 full time; 1 part time*
Training: *F/T operations staff, F/T management, P/T operations staff and casual operations staff are trained on specific courses*

Marketing
Annual event(s): *themed events*
Sponsor(s): *various*
Other: *press office; market research*
UK promotion: *television; national newspapers; local newspapers; regional tourist board; other attractions; leaflets/information packs; ETB/BTA*

TOTNES GUILDHALL
(local authority run)
historic house; museum

Established: *1982*
Address: *High St, Totnes, Devon, TQ9 5QH*
Telephone: *(0803) 862147*
Access: (road) *M5/A38* (rail) *Totnes*
Hours: *Easter to Oct – Mon to Fri – 10am to 5pm; Sat and Sun – groups by arrangement*
Admission (1992): *adults £0.50; children £0.20*
No. visitors (1992): *10 000 (est.)*

Facilities
Interpretation: *leaflets; information boards; maps; tour guides; guide books*
Languages: *Dutch; French; German; Italian; Spanish*
Schools: *maximum no. 50; educational literature; lecture/talk*
Disabled: *helpers*
Retailing: *postcards/inexpensive souvenirs; confectionery and ice cream; craftwork; books; clothes; reproductions of famous artefacts*
No. shops: *1*

Operations
Contact: *P Langridge (Town Clerk)*
No. employees: (high season) *4 full time; 4 part time*
Training: *F/T operations staff, F/T management and P/T operations staff are trained in-house and on specific courses and day-to-day on job using videos and handbooks*

Marketing
Annual event: *mayor choosing ceremony*
Other: *press office; market research*

UK promotion: *local newspapers; regional tourist board; other attractions; leaflets/information packs; ETB/BTA*

Environmental monitoring: *recycling; waste; energy consumption; hazardous materials*

TOWER BRIDGE
(local authority run)
bridge and national landmark

Established: *1982*
Address: *London, SE1 2UP*
Telephone: *(071) 403 3761.* Fax: *(071) 357 7935*
Access: (road)
Parking capacity: (cars) *200* (coaches) *50*
Season: *all year*
Hours: *Apr to Oct – 10am to 6.30pm daily; Nov to Mar – 10am to 4.45pm daily*
Admission (1992): *adults £2.50; children £1.00; OAP £1.00*
No. visitors (1992): *467 244*

Facilities
Interpretation: *videos; information boards*
Languages: *Japanese; Dutch; French; German; Italian; Spanish*
Schools: *maximum no. 100*
Disabled: *easy access; disabled toilets*
Retailing: *postcards/inexpensive souvenirs; confectionery and ice cream; books; clothes; reproductions of famous artefacts*
No. shops: *1*

Operations
Contacts: *C Stevens (Bridge Master); Mr M Waters (Tourism Manager)*
No. employees: (high season) *24 full time* (low season) *23 full time*
Training: *F/T operations staff and F/T management are trained in-house and externally and on specific courses and day-to-day on job using handbooks*

Marketing
Affiliation: *MA*
Other: *market research*
UK promotion: *regional tourist board; leaflets/information packs; ETB/BTA*
Europe/Australia/USA promotion: *leaflets/brochures; British Tourist Authority*

TOWER WORLD
(plc)
indoor leisure attraction and historic monument

Established: *1894*
Address: *The Promenade, Blackpool, FY1 4BJ*
Telephone: *(0253) 22242.* Fax: *(0253) 25194*
Access: (road) *M55*
Season: *all year*
Hours: *10am to 11pm daily*
Admission (1992): *adults £5.95; children £4.95; OAP £3.95; student £3.95; under 5s free*

Facilities
Interpretation: *leaflets; maps; tour guides; guide books*
Children: *adventure playground; play area; nappy changing*
Schools: *educational literature; educational tour*
Disabled: *easy access; disabled toilets*
Catering: *3 bars/public houses*
Retailing: *postcards/inexpensive souvenirs; craftwork; clothes*
No. shops: *3*

Operations
Contacts: *S Brailey (Executive General Manager); M McKee (Assistant Manager); M Verren (Deputy Manager); C Titherington (Sales and Promotion Manager)*
No. employees: (high season) *260 full time; 40 part time* (low season) *50 full time*
Training: *F/T operations staff, F/T management, P/T operations staff, P/T management, casual operations staff and casual management are trained in-house and on specific courses*
Languages spoken: *French; German; Spanish*

Marketing
Annual event: *junior dance festival*
Sponsor: *Junior Dance Festival*
Other: *press office; market research*
UK promotion: *television; national newspapers; radio; local newspapers; regional tourist board; other attractions; leaflets/information packs; ETB/BTA*

Environmental monitoring: *energy consumption; hazardous materials*

TOWN DOCKS MUSEUM
(local authority run)
museum

Established: *1975*
Address: *Queen Victoria Square, Hull, HU1 3DX*
Telephone: *(0482) 593902.* Fax: *(0482) 595062*
Access: (road) *M62/A63* (rail) *Hull Paragon*
Season: *all year*
Hours: *Mon to Sat – 10am to 5pm; Sun – 1.30pm to 4.30pm. Closed Christmas Day, Boxing Day, New Year's Day and Good Friday*
Admission (1992): *free*
No. visitors (1992): *127 198*

Facilities
Interpretation: *information boards; guide books*
Languages: *Dutch*
Schools: *maximum no. 200; educational literature; audio/visual presentation; lecture/talk*
Disabled: *easy access; helpers; lift*
Retailing: *postcards/inexpensive souvenirs; craftwork; books; maritime items; greeting cards, etc*
No. shops: *1*

Operations
Contact: *Mr A Credland (Keeper of Maritime History)*
No. employees: (high season) *11 full time*
Training: *F/T operations staff and F/T management are trained in-house and externally and on specific courses and day-to-day on job using videos and handbooks*

Marketing
Press office; market research
UK promotion: *local newspapers; regional tourist board; other attractions*

TOWNELEY HALL ART GALLERY AND MUSEUM
(local authority run)
historic house; park/reserve; garden; museum; gallery; zoo/wildlife attraction

Established: *1903*
Address: *Towneley Park, Burnley, Lancs, BB11 3RQ*
Telephone: *(0282) 24213*
Access: (road) *M66/A646* (rail) *Burnley*
Parking capacity: (cars) *60* (coaches) *3*
Season: *all year*
Hours: *Mon to Fri – 10am to 5pm; Sun – 12am to 5pm*
No. visitors (1992): *122 151*

Facilities
Interpretation: *tour guides; guide books; labels and displays*
Languages: *French*
Children: *play area*
Schools: *maximum no. 60; educational tour; lecture/talk; activity sessions*
Disabled: *easy access; disabled toilets; helpers; other audio facilities; Braille labels*
Catering: *2 picnic areas*
Franchisees: *all year – Mon to Fri – 10am to 5pm, Sun – 12am to 5pm*
Retailing: *postcards/inexpensive souvenirs; books; reproductions of famous artefacts; pens, geological kits, pottery*
No. shops: *1*

Operations
Contact: *S Bourne (Curator)*

No. employees: (high season) *15 full time; 2 part time* (low season) *15 full time; 1 part time*
Training: *F/T operations staff, F/T management, P/T operations staff and P/T management are trained in-house and externally and on specific courses and day-to-day on job and visits to other sites using videos and handbooks*

Marketing
Annual event(s): *Victorian games day, vintage vehicle cavalcade, etc.*
Affiliations: *MA, NW Federation of Museums and Gardens, Lancashire Curators Group, NWAMS, etc.*
Other: *market research*
UK promotion: *national newspapers; local newspapers; regional tourist board; other attractions; leaflets/information packs; Lancashire's hill country publications*

Environmental monitoring: *energy consumption; hazardous materials*

TOWNER ART GALLERY AND LOCAL HISTORY MUSEUM
(local authority run)
museum; gallery

Established: *1923*
Address: *High St, Old Town, Eastbourne, E Sussex, BN20 8BB*
Telephone: *(0323) 411688.* Fax: *(0323) 648182*
Access: (road) *A22* (rail) *Eastbourne*
Season: *all year*
Hours: *Tues to Sat – 10am to 5pm; Sun and BH – 2pm to 5pm*
Admission (1992): *free*
No. visitors (1992): *51 000*

Facilities
Interpretation: *leaflets; information boards*
Schools: *maximum no. 35; educational literature; educational tour; lecture/talk*
Disabled: *easy access*
Retailing: *postcards/inexpensive souvenirs; books*
No. shops: *1*

Operations
Contact: *P Johnson (Curator)*
No. employees: (high season) *6 full time; 4 part time*
Training: *F/T operations staff, F/T management and P/T operations staff are trained in-house and externally and on specific courses using videos*
Languages spoken: *French*

Marketing
Press office; market research
UK promotion: *local newspapers; ETB/BTA; specialist visual arts magazines*

Environmental monitoring: *recycling; energy consumption; hazardous materials; chemical usage*

TOY AND TEDDY BEAR MUSEUM
(private)
museum

Established: *1989*
Address: *373 Clifton Drive North, St Anne's, Lancs, FY8 2PA*
Telephone: *(0253) 713705*
Access: (road) *M6/A585* (rail) *St Anne's*
Parking capacity: (cars) *6*
Season: *all year*
Hours: *Apr to Oct – Wed to Mon – 11am to 5pm; winter – Sun – 12 noon to 5pm. Other times by arrangement*
Admission (1992): *adults £1.50; children £1.00; OAP £1.00; student £1.00*
No. visitors (1992): *12 000*

Facilities
Interpretation: *leaflets; information boards*
Schools: *maximum no. 70; lecture/talk; fun quiz and worksheet*

Retailing: *postcards/inexpensive souvenirs; books; collectors bears and ceramics*
No. shops: *1*

Operations
Contact: *Irene Thompson (owner)*
No. employees: (high season) *2 part time*

Marketing
Market research
UK promotion: *national newspapers; regional tourist board; other attractions; leaflets/information packs; UK Teddy Bear Guide, Dolls House International, NWTB discovery map and group visits, Lan; ETB/BTA*
Europe promotion: *Teddy Bear Guide*

Environmental monitoring: *light and humidity levels*

TRAFFORD ECOLOGY PARK
(Trafford Park Development Corporation)
park/reserve; zoo/wildlife attraction

Established: *1990*
Address: *Mosley Rd North, Trafford Park, Manchester*
Telephone: *(061) 873 7182*
Access: (road) *M63/M602/A5081*
Parking capacity: (cars) *20* (coaches) *1*
Season: *all year*
Hours: *Mon to Fri – 9.30am to 4.30pm; Sun – 1pm to 4.30pm*
Admission (1992): *free*
No. visitors (1992): *7403*

Facilities
Interpretation: *leaflets; information boards; maps*
Schools: *maximum no. 40*
Disabled: *easy access; disabled toilets*
Catering: *4 picnic areas*

Operations
Contacts: *D Rodger (Project Officer); W Brooks (Executive Director); D Slight (Finance and Administration)*
No. employees: (high season) *1 full time* (low season) *1 full time*

Marketing
Market research
UK promotion: *national newspapers; radio; local newspapers; regional tourist board; other attractions; leaflets/information packs*

TRAQUAIR HOUSE
(privately owned)
historic house

Established: *1958*
Address: *Innerleithen, Peebleshire, EH44 6PW*
Telephone: *(0896) 830323.* Fax: *(0896) 830639*
Access: (road) *A703*
Hours: *Easter week and 1 May to 30 Sept – 1.30pm to 5.30pm daily; July and Aug – 10.30am to 5.30pm daily*
Admission (1992): *adults £3.50; children £1.50; OAP £3.00; groups £2.75; grounds only £1.50 (adults) and £1.00 (children)*
No. visitors (1992): *45 000*

Facilities
Interpretation: *leaflets; audio tapes; information boards; maps; tour guides; guide books*
Languages: *Japanese; Dutch; French; German; Italian; Spanish*
Children: *play area*
Schools: *educational literature*
Disabled: *easy access; disabled toilets*
Catering: *1 licensed restaurant*
Retailing: *postcards/inexpensive souvenirs; confectionery and ice cream; craftwork; books; clothes; reproductions of famous artefacts*
No. shops: *1*

Operations
Contacts: *Ms C Maxwell Stuart (owner/Administrator); Mrs F Maxwell Stuart (owner)*

No. employees: (high season) *3 full time; 28 part time (low season) 3 full time; 1 part time*
Languages spoken: *French; Spanish*

Marketing
Annual event(s): *sheep and wool day, Traquair fair*
Sponsor(s): *various from year to year*
Affiliations: *HHA, Scottish Tourist Board*
Other: *market research*
UK promotion: *local newspapers; regional tourist board; other attractions; leaflets/information packs*
Europe/USA promotion: *leaflets/brochures; British Tourist Authority*

TREBAH GARDEN
(trust)
garden

Established: *1987*
Address: *Mawnan Smith, Nr Falmouth, Cornwall, TR11 5JZ*
Telephone: *(0326) 250448.* Fax: *(0326) 250781*
Access: (road) *A39/A394* (rail) *Truro/Falmouth*
Parking capacity: (cars) *140* (coaches) *7*
Season: *all year*
Hours: *10.30am to 5pm daily*
Admission (1992): *adults £2.50; children £1.00; OAP £2.50; student £2.50; disabled £1.00; under 5s free*
No. visitors (1992): *52 200*

Facilities
Interpretation: *leaflets; information boards; maps; tour guides; guide books*
Languages: *Dutch; French; German*
Children: *adventure playground; play area*
Schools: *maximum no. 40; educational literature; lecture/talk; children's trails*
Disabled: *not suitable*
Catering: *3 picnic areas*
Retailing: *postcards/inexpensive souvenirs; confectionery and ice cream; craftwork; books; clothes; plants*
No. shops: *2*

Operations
Contacts: *J Hibbert (Manager); Ms J Sutcliff (Secretary); Mrs K Ainsley/Mrs A Black (Shop/Plant Sales)*
No. employees: (high season) *5 full time; 5 part time (low season) 5 full time; 1 part time*
Training: *F/T operations staff and P/T operations staff are trained in-house and externally and on specific courses and day-to-day on job*
Languages spoken: *French; Spanish*

Marketing
Annual event: *Trebah Icicle*
Affiliations: *HHA, Country Landowners Association, Horticultural Trades Association, CTB, WCTB*
Other: *market research*
UK promotion: *local newspapers; regional tourist board; other attractions; leaflets/information packs; Coach drivers Club; ETB/BTA; Cornwall Tourist Board, WC Tourist Board, Kerrier District Council*

TREFRIW WELLS SPA
(limited company)
museum; medicinal spa

Established: *1987*
Address: *Trefriw, Snowdonia National Park, Gwynedd, LL27 0JS*
Telephone: *(0492) 640057.* Fax: *(0492) 641590*
Access: (road) *M6/A55/B5106*
Season: *all year*
Hours: *Summer – Mon to Sun – 10am to 5.30pm; Nov to Easter – Mon to Sat – 10am to 5pm, Sun – 12 noon to 5pm*
Admission (1992): *adults £2.50; OAP £2.25; student £1.50; under 10s free*
No. visitors (1992): *20 000 (est.)*

Facilities
Interpretation: *leaflets; audio tapes; information boards; maps*

Disabled: *helpers; guided tour; terrain unsuitable*
Catering: *1 picnic area*
Retailing: *postcards/inexpensive souvenirs; confectionery and ice cream; craftwork; books; medicinal spa water, etc.*
No. shops: *1*

Operations
Contact: *Tony Rowlands (Managing Director)*
No. employees: (high season) *4 full time; 2 part time (low season) 2 full time; 1 part time*
Training: *F/T operations staff, F/T management and P/T operations staff are trained in-house and externally and on specific courses and day-to-day on job using handbooks*
Languages spoken: *French; German*

Marketing
Press office; market research
UK promotion: *regional tourist board; other attractions; leaflets/information packs*

Environmental monitoring: *recycling; water quality; chemical usage*

TREGWYNT MILL
(sole trader)
working woollen textile mill

Established: *1950*
Address: *Tregwynt Mill, Castle Morris, Haverfordwest, Dyfed, SA62 5UX*
Telephone: *(03485) 225644.* Fax: *(03485) 694*
Access: (road) *M4/A487* (rail) *Fishguard*
Parking capacity: (cars) *50* (coaches) *10*
Season: *all year*
Hours: *Mon to Fri – 9am to 5.30pm. Shop open on weekends*
Admission (1992): *free*
No. visitors (1992): *50 000 (est.)*

Facilities
Interpretation: *leaflets; information boards; maps; guide books*
Languages: *Welsh*
Children: *adventure playground; play area*
Schools: *maximum no. 40; educational literature*
Disabled: *easy access*
Catering: *1 picnic area*
Retailing: *postcards/inexpensive souvenirs; craftwork; books; clothes; woollens made at mill*
No. shops: *1*

Operations
Contacts: *Eifion Griffiths (Director); Kath Owen (Administrator); Amanda Griffiths (Director)*
No. employees: (high season) *17 full time; 3 part time (low season) 17 full time*
Training: *F/T operations staff and F/T management are trained in-house and on specific courses and day-to-day on job*

Marketing
Market research
UK promotion: *regional tourist board; leaflets/information packs; national magazines*
Europe promotion: *leaflets/brochures; consumer magazines*

Environmental monitoring: *recycling*

TRENOUTH FARM RARE BREEDS CENTRE
(partnership)
zoo/wildlife attraction; rare breeds farm

Established: *1987*
Address: *Trenouth, St Ervan, Wadebridge, Cornwall*
Telephone: *(0841) 540606*
Access: (road) *A39*
Parking capacity: (cars) *40*
Hours: *17 Apr to 30 Sept – 10am to 5pm daily*
Admission (1992): *adults £2.25; children £1.50; OAP £1.50*
No. visitors (1992): *10 000 (est.)*

Facilities
Interpretation: *leaflets; guide books*

Languages: *French; German*
Children: *play area*
Schools: *maximum no. 40; educational literature; audio/visual presentation; lecture/talk*
Disabled: *easy access*
Catering: *1 picnic area*
Retailing: *postcards/inexpensive souvenirs; craftwork; books; paintings, prints, stoneware*
No. shops: *1*

Operations
Contacts: *Mr and Mrs P O'Shea*
No. employees: (high season) *1 full time; 3 part time (low season) 1 part time*

Marketing
UK promotion: *leaflets/information packs*

Environmental monitoring: *water quality; energy consumption; hazardous materials*

TRINITY HOUSE NATIONAL LIGHTHOUSE CENTRE
(limited company registered charity)
museum

Established: *1990*
Address: *The Old Buoy Store, Wharf Rd, Penzance, Cornwall, TR18 4BN*
Telephone: *(0736) 60077*
Access: (road) *A30* (rail) *Penzance*
Hours: *Apr to end Oct – 11am to 5pm daily*
Admission (1992): *adults £2.00; children £1.00; OAP £1.00; student £1.00; family ticket (2 + 3) £5.00*
No. visitors (1992): *10 000 (est.)*

Facilities
Interpretation: *videos; leaflets; information boards; tour guides*
Schools: *maximum no. 50; audio/visual presentation; lecture/talk*
Disabled: *easy access*
Retailing: *postcards/inexpensive souvenirs; books; nautical related*
No. shops: *1·*

Operations
Contact: *Mr M Hooley (Manager)*
No. employees: (high season) *1 part time (low season) 1 part time*
Languages spoken: *French; German*

Marketing
Market research
UK promotion: *regional tourist board; leaflets/information packs*
Europe promotion: *leaflets/brochures*

Environmental monitoring: *conservation*

TROPICAL BIRD PARK
(limited company)
park/reserve, zoo/wildlife attraction

Established: *1972*
Address: *Old Park, St Lawrence, Ventnor, Isle of Wight, PO38 1XS*
Telephone: *(09838) 52583.* Fax: *(09838) 54920*
Parking capacity: (cars) *100* (coaches) *6*
Season: *all year*
Hours: *10am to 5pm daily except Christmas Day*
Admission (1992): *adults £2.20; children £1.50; OAP £1.75; student £1.75*
No. visitors (1992): *30 000 (est.)*

Facilities
Schools: *maximum no. 50; educational literature; lecture/talk*
Catering: *1 picnic area*
Retailing: *postcards/inexpensive souvenirs; confectionery and ice cream; books; clothes*
No. shops: *1*

Operations
Contacts: *Mr R Thornton (Director)*
No. employees: (high season) *4 full time; 3 part time (low season) 3 full time*

Training: *F/T operations staff, P/T operations staff and casual operations staff are trained in-house and day-to-day on job*

Marketing
Market research
UK promotion: *regional tourist board; leaflets/information packs; Southern Tourist Board*
Europe promotion: *leaflets/brochures*

TROPICAL WORLD
(local authority run)
park/reserve; garden; zoo/wildlife attraction; butterfly and insect house

Established: *1984*
Address: *Canal Gardens, Roundhay Park, Leeds, LS8 1DF*
Telephone: *(0532) 661850*
Access: (road) *M62/M1/A58* (rail) *Leeds*
Parking capacity: (cars) *250* (coaches) *50*
Season: *all year*
Hours: *summer – 10am to 9pm daily winter – 10am to dusk daily*
Admission (1992): *free*
No. visitors (1992): *1 250 000 (est.)*

Facilities
Interpretation: *leaflets; maps; guide books*
Children: *adventure playground*
Disabled: *easy access; disabled toilets; helpers by arrangement*
Catering: *2 bars/public houses*
Retailing: *postcards/inexpensive souvenirs; confectionery and ice cream; books*
No. shops: *1*

Operations
Contact: *Mr K Roberts (Manager)*
No. employees: (high season) *28 full time; 2 part time* (low season) *28 full time*
Training: *F/T operations staff and casual operations staff are trained in-house and day-to-day on job*

Marketing
Annual event(s): *pop concerts*
Other: *press office*
UK promotion: *regional tourist board; leaflets/information packs; ETB/BTA*

Environmental monitoring: *recycling; waste; energy consumption*

TROWBRIDGE MUSEUM
(local authority run)
museum

Established: *1990*
Address: *The Shires, Court St, Trowbridge, Wilts, BA14 8AT*
Telephone: *(0225) 751339.* Fax: *(0225) 777147*
Access: (road) *M4/A361* (rail) *Trowbridge*
Parking capacity: (cars) *1000*
Season: *all year*
Hours: *Tues to Fri – 12 noon to 4pm; Sat – 10am to 5pm*
Admission (1992): *free*
No. visitors (1992): *20 000*

Facilities
Interpretation: *videos; leaflets; information boards; maps; tour guides; guide books; personnel; exhibitions*
Languages: *French; German*
Schools: *maximum no. 60; educational literature; lecture/talk; schoolroom activities*
Disabled: *easy access; disabled toilets*
Retailing: *postcards/inexpensive souvenirs; craftwork; books; reproductions of famous artefacts; cloth woven at museum*
No. shops: *1*

Operations
Contact: *Ms L Wigley (Curator)*
No. employees: (high season) *1 full time; 2 part time* (low season) *1 full time; 2 part time*

Training: *F/T operations staff, F/T management, P/T operations staff and casual operations staff are trained externally and on specific courses*

Marketing
Annual event(s): *lectures, talks , exhibitions*
Sponsor(s): *various*
Affiliations: *MA, SWFMG, Wiltshire Museums Association*
Other: *market research*
UK promotion: *radio; local newspapers; regional tourist board; other attractions; leaflets/ information packs; leisure magazines; ETB/ BTA*

Environmental monitoring: *recycling; energy consumption; chemical usage; biological control*

TRURO CATHEDRAL
(Governed by Dean and Chapter)
church

Established: *1880*
Address: *Truro Cathedral Office, 21 Old Bridge St, Truro, Cornwall, TR1 2PE*
Telephone: *(0872) 76782.* Fax: *(0872) 77788*
Access: (road) *A30* (rail) *Truro*
Season: *all year*
Hours: *7.30am to 5.30pm daily. Closed Nov to Mar – Sun – 11am to 5pm*
Admission (1992): *free*
No. visitors (1992): *250 000 (est.)*

Facilities
Interpretation: *leaflets; information boards; tour guides; guide books*
Languages: *French; German*
Schools: *maximum no. 100; educational literature; lecture/talk*
Disabled: *easy access; Braille/sound posts*
Catering: *1 picnic area*
Retailing: *postcards/inexpensive souvenirs; books*
No. shops: *1*

Operations
Contact: *J Holifield (Bursar)*
No. employees: (high season) *20 full time; 10 part time* (low season) *20 full time; 10 part time*
Training: *F/T operations staff, F/T management, P/T operations staff, P/T management and casual operations staff are trained in-house and day-to-day on job*

Environmental monitoring: *temperature and humidity*

TUDOR HOUSE MUSEUM
(local authority run)
historic house; garden; museum

Established: *1912*
Address: *St Michael's Square, Bugle St, Southampton*
Telephone: *(0703) 332513*
Access: (road) *M27* (rail) *Southampton*
Season: *all year*
Hours: *Tues to Fri – 10am to 12 noon and 1pm to 5pm; Sat – 10am to 12 noon and 1pm to 4pm; Sun – 2pm to 5pm*
Admission (1992): *free, hire by arrangement*
No. visitors (1992): *40 000*

Facilities
Interpretation: *leaflets; audio tapes; information boards; tour guides*
Schools: *maximum no. 40; private visits and workshop*
Disabled: *easy access; disabled toilets*
Retailing: *postcards/inexpensive souvenirs; confectionery and ice cream; books; reproductions of famous artefacts*
No. shops: *1*

Operations
Contacts: *Mr S Hardy (Heritage Manager); Ms J Case (Leisure Personnel); Mrs H Spillett (Research Officer)*

No. employees: (high season) *6 full time* (low season) *6 full time*
Training: *F/T operations staff and F/T management are trained in-house and externally and on specific courses*
Languages spoken: *French; German*

Marketing
Press office; market research
UK promotion: *local newspapers; regional tourist board; leaflets/information packs; ETB/BTA*

TULLIEHOUSE MUSEUM AND ART GALLERY
(local authority run)
museum; gallery

Established: *1991*
Address: *Castle St, Carlisle, CA3*
Telephone: *(0228) 34781.* Fax: *(0228) 810249*
Access: (road) *M6* (rail) *Carlisle Citadel*
Season: *all year*
Hours: *10am to 5pm daily*
Admission (1992): *adults £3.10; children £1.60; OAP £1.60; student £1.60; Carlisle residents admitted free with Tullie card.*
No. visitors (1992): *240 000*

Facilities
Interpretation: *audio-visual displays, exhibits, set pieces*
Languages: *Japanese; German*
Children: *nappy changing*
Schools: *educational literature; audio/visual presentation; lecture/talk; education officer/ department.*
Disabled: *easy access; disabled toilets; helpers; other audio facilities*
Catering: *1 bar/public house*
Franchisees: *10am to 5pm daily*
Retailing: *postcards/inexpensive souvenirs; craftwork; books; clothes; reproductions of famous artefacts*
No. shops: *1*

Operations
Contacts: *Nick Winterbottom (Director, Tullie House); City Council Personnel Department (Carlisle); Mike Taylor (Commercial Marketing Manager)*
No. employees: (high season) *16 full time; 27 part time* (low season) *16 full time; 27 part time*
Training: *F/T operations staff, F/T management, P/T operations staff, P/T management, casual operations staff and casual management are trained in-house and on specific courses and day-to-day on job*

Marketing
Affiliations: *Museums Association*
Other: *market research*
UK promotion: *television; local newspapers; regional tourist board; other attractions; leaflets/information packs; ETB/BTA*
Europe promotion: *British Tourist Authority*

Environmental monitoring: *hazardous materials*

TUTANKHAMUN EXHIBITION
(privately owned)
museum

Established: *1987*
Address: *High West St, Dorchester, Dorset*
Telephone: *(0305) 269571.* Fax: *(0305) 268885*
Access: (road) *A35/A37*
Season: *all year*
Hours: *9.30am to 5.30pm daily except 24–26 Dec*
Admission (1992): *adults £2.95; children £1.95; OAP £2.50; student £2.50; family ticket (2 + 2) £8.95*
No. visitors (1992): *173 000 (est.)*

Facilities
Interpretation: *videos; audio tapes; information boards; guide books; reconstructions*
Schools: *maximum no. 100; lecture/talk*
Disabled: *easy access*

Retailing: *postcards/inexpensive souvenirs; craftwork; books; reproductions of famous artefacts; ancient Egyptian theme*
No. shops: *1*

Operations
Contacts: *Mr T Batty (General Manager); Ms J Ridley (Director); Ms T McDonald (Merchandising Manager);*
No. employees: (high season) *11 full time; 12 part time* (low season) *8 full time; 9 part time*
Training: *F/T operations staff, P/T operations staff and casual operations staff are trained in-house and day-to-day on job using videos and handbooks and role play*

Marketing
Annual event(s): *occasional special exhibitions*
Other: *press office; market research*
UK promotion: *national newspapers; radio; local newspapers; regional tourist board; other attractions; leaflets/information packs*
Europe/USA promotion: *British Tourist Authority*

Environmental monitoring: *recycling; energy consumption*

TWEEDHOPE SHEEP DOGS
(privately owned)
sheepdog visitor centre

Established: *1987*
Address: *Tweedhopefoot, Tweedsmuir, By Biggar, Lanarkshire, ML12 6QS*
Telephone: *(08997) 302*
Access: (road) *M74/A701*
Season: *all year*
Hours: *Weekdays – demonstrations at 11am, 2pm, and 3.30pm. Centre open – 11am to 4.30pm. Weekends and during Winter by appointment*
Admission (1992): *adults £2.00; children £1.00*
No. visitors (1992): *7000 (est.)*

Facilities
Interpretation: *leaflets; information boards; tour guides; guide books*
Schools: *maximum no. 200; educational literature; lecture/talk*
Catering: *1 snack bar/food stall*
Retailing: *postcards/inexpensive souvenirs; craftwork; books; clothes*
No. shops: *1*

Operations
Contact: *Ms V Billingham (owner)*
Languages spoken: *French*

Marketing
Annual event(s): *sheep dog trial*
UK promotion: *television; national newspapers; radio; local newspapers; regional tourist board; leaflets/information packs; ETB/BTA*
Europe/USA promotion: *leaflets/brochures; travel agents' brochures; British Tourist Authority*

TWYCROSS ZOO
(trust)
zoo/wildlife attraction

Established: *1963*
Address: *Atherstone, Warks, CV9 3PX*
Telephone: *(0827) 880250.* Fax: *(0827) 880700*
Access: (road) *M1/M42/A444*
Parking capacity: (cars) *4000* (coaches) *150*
Season: *all year*
Hours: *summer – 10am to 6pm; winter – 10am to 4pm*
Admission (1992): *adults £3.80; children £2.00; OAP £2.60; group rates*
No. visitors (1992): *400 000 (est.)*

Facilities
Interpretation: *leaflets; information boards; maps; guide books; signs*
Children: *adventure playground; play area; nappy changing*
Schools: *educational literature; lecture/talk*

Disabled: *easy access; disabled toilets*
Catering: *1 bar/public house*
Retailing: *postcards/inexpensive souvenirs; confectionery and ice cream; books; clothes*
No. shops: *More than 4*

Operations
Contacts: *M W Badham (Director); S N Evans (Director); V J Richards*
No. employees: (high season) *50 full time; 100 part time* (low season) *50 full time; 5 part time*
Training: *F/T operations staff are trained in-house and day-to-day on job*

Marketing
Press office
UK promotion: *national newspapers; local newspapers; regional tourist board; other attractions; leaflets/information packs; ETB/BTA; TICs, hotels, libraries, etc.*

TWYFORD PUMPING STATION
(limited company and trust)
monument; museum

Established: *1985*
Address: *Hazeley Rd, Twyford, Nr Winchester, Hants*
Telephone: *(0794) 522842*
Access: (road) *M3/A33/B3335* (rail) *Shawford*
Parking capacity: (cars) *40* (coaches) *2*
Hours: *11am to 4pm – 1st Sun in May and Oct; also by appointment*
Admission (1992): *adults £1.50; children £0.50; OAP £1.50; schools £0.40, higher education £0.75*
No. visitors (1992): *1500 (est.)*

Facilities
Interpretation: *leaflets; audio tapes; information boards; slides; maps; tour guides; guide books*
Schools: *maximum no. 50; educational literature; audio/visual presentation; lecture/talk; exploratory visit by staff*
Catering: *1 picnic area*
Retailing: *postcards/inexpensive souvenirs*
No. shops: *1*

Operations
Contacts: *Mr M Mapp (Administrator); Dr E Course (Trust Chairman); Mrs P Moore (Trust Secretary)*

Marketing
Annual event(s): *open days*
Other: *market research*
UK promotion: *radio; local newspapers; regional tourist board; other attractions; leaflets/information packs*

U

ULLAPOOL MUSEUM
(company limited by guarantee)
museum; former Telford Church and listed
building

Established: *1988*
Address: *7-8 West Argyle St, Ullapool, Ross and
Cromarty, IV26 2TY*
Telephone: *none*
Access: (road) *A835*
Parking capacity: (cars) *150* (coaches) *50*
Hours: *week before Easter until mid Oct –
weekdays only – 11am to 5pm; from June
onwards – also 7pm to 9pm*
Admission (1992): *adults £0.50; OAP £0.50;
student £0.50*
No. visitors (1992): *10 000 (est.)*

Facilities
Interpretation: *leaflets; information boards;
photographs*
Schools: *maximum no. 25; lecture/talk*
Retailing: *postcards/inexpensive souvenirs; books;
coins and tapestry*
No. shops: *1*

Operations
Contacts: *Mrs A Eaton (Treasurer); Mrs R
Mackenzie (Vice Chairman); Mr R Poor
(Secretary)*

Marketing
Affiliation: *AIM*
UK promotion: *leaflets/information packs*

Environmental monitoring: *chemical usage*

ULSTER FOLK AND TRANSPORT MUSEUM
(central government Dept of Education)
museum; open air museum

Established: *1964*
Address: *Cultra, Holywood, Belfast, BT18 0EU*
Telephone: *(0232) 428428.* Fax: *(0232) 428728*
Access: (road) *A2*
Parking capacity: (cars) *1000* (coaches) *20*
Season: *all year*
Hours: *Open all year except Christmas. Oct to
Mar – Mon to Fri – 9.30am to 4pm; Sat and
Sun – 12.30pm to 4.30pm*
Admission (1992): *adults £2.50; children £1.25;
OAP £1.25; student £1.25; family ticket £5.50
and groups 50% discount; disabled free*
No. visitors (1992): *150 000 (est.)*

Facilities
Interpretation: *leaflets; information boards;
maps; tour guides; guide books; guides on
request*
Languages: *Japanese; French; German; Italian*
Schools: *maximum no. 100; educational literature;
audio/visual presentation; lecture/talk; by
arrangement*
Disabled: *easy access; disabled toilets*
Catering: *2 picnic areas*
Franchisees: *Open all year except Christmas. Oct
to Mar – Mon to Fri – 9.30am to 4pm; Sat and
Sun – 12.30pm to 4.30pm*
Retailing: *postcards/inexpensive souvenirs;
craftwork; books; clothes*
No. shops: *2*

Operations
Contacts: *Dr A Gailey (Director); Mr D Blemings
(Personnel Officer); Mr S Scott (Administrator);
Mrs A Campbell (Marketing Officer)*
Languages spoken: *French; German; Spanish;
Dutch*

Marketing
Annual event(s): *various, craft days and
demonstrations*
Affiliation: *Heritage Island*
Other: *press office; market research*
UK promotion: *television; local newspapers;
regional tourist board; leaflets/information
packs; NI Holiday News and Coach Tours*

ULSTER HISTORY PARK, THE
(local authority run)
theme park; heritage centre

Established: *1990*
Address: *Cullion, Omagh, Co. Tyrone, BT79 7SU*
Telephone: *(06626) 48188*
Access: (road) *B48*
Parking capacity: (cars) *120* (coaches) *9*
Season: *all year*
Hours: *Apr to Sept – Mon to Fri – 11am to 6pm,
Sat – 11am to 7pm, Sun – 1pm to 7pm; Oct to
Mar – Mon to Fri – 11am to 5pm*
Admission (1992): *adults £1.50; children £1.00;
OAP £1.00; student £1.00*
No. visitors (1992): *25 000 (est.)*

Facilities
Interpretation: *leaflets; information boards; slides;
tour guides; guide books*
Schools: *maximum no. 250; educational literature;
audio/visual presentation; lecture/talk; craft
demonstrations*
Disabled: *easy access; disabled toilets*
Catering: *1 picnic area*
Retailing: *postcards/inexpensive souvenirs;
craftwork; books; reproductions of famous
artefacts*
No. shops: *1*

Operations
Contacts: *Anthony Candon (Manager); Mrs
Elizabeth Harkin (Education and promotions
Officer)*
No. employees: (high season) *5 full time; 19 part
time* (low season) *5 full time; 16 part time*
Training: *F/T operations staff, F/T management,
P/T operations staff and casual operations staff
are trained in-house and on specific courses*
Languages spoken: *French; German*

Marketing
Annual event(s): *Bealtine spring festival*
Other: *market research*
UK promotion: *radio; local newspapers; regional
tourist board; other attractions; leaflets/
information packs*
Europe/Republic of Ireland promotion: *NITB*

ULSTER MUSEUM
(NDPB)
museum; gallery

Established: *1929*
Address: *Botanic Gardens, Belfast, BT9 5AB*
Telephone: *(0232) 381251.* Fax: *(0232) 665510*
Access: (road) *M2* (rail) *Belfast*
Season: *all year*
Hours: *Mon to Fri – 10am to 5pm; Sat – 1pm to
5pm; Sun – 2pm to 5pm*
Admission (1992): *free*
No. visitors (1992): *290 000*

Facilities
Interpretation: *videos; leaflets; audio tapes;
information boards; slides; maps; guide books;
permanent and temporary exhibitions*
Children: *nappy changing*
Schools: *educational literature; lecture/talk;
gallery lessons, bus*
Disabled: *easy access; disabled toilets; other
audio facilities; leaflets; Stannah wheelchair
lifts*
Catering: *1 licensed restaurant*
Retailing: *postcards/inexpensive souvenirs;
craftwork; books; reproductions of famous
artefacts; educational toys and games;
stationery, etc.*
No. shops: *1*

Operations
Contacts: *M McKee (Keeper of Museum Services);
G Herron (Administration Officer); S Neill
(Marketing and Development Officer)*
Training: *F/T operations staff, F/T management,
P/T operations staff, P/T management, casual
operations staff and casual management are
trained in-house and externally and on specific
courses and day-to-day on job*

Marketing
Affiliations: *Museums Association, Contemporary
Art Society, Museums Store Association (USA)*
Other: *press office; market research*
UK promotion: *television; national newspapers;
radio; local newspapers; regional tourist board;
other attractions; leaflets/information packs; NI
TB information bulletins*
Europe/USA promotion: *Heritage Island (Dublin)*

UNIVERSITY BOTANIC GARDEN
(university dept)
garden

Established: *1975*
Address: *Riverside Drive, Dundee, DD2 1QH*
Telephone: *(0382) 66939*
Access: (road) *M90/A85* (rail) *Dundee*
Parking capacity: (cars) *16* (coaches) *2*
Season: *all year*
Hours: *Mar to Oct – Mon to Sat – 10am to
4.30pm, Sun – 11am to 4pm; Nov to Feb –
Mon to Sat – 10am to 3pm, Sun 11am to
3pm*
Admission (1992): *adults £1.00; children £0.50;
OAP £0.50; student £0.50; local students and
friends of garden free*
No. visitors (1992): *10 000 (est.)*

Facilities
Interpretation: *leaflets; maps; tour guides;
displays in visitor centre*
Schools: *educational literature; lecture/talk; staff
tutor*
Disabled: *easy access; disabled toilets; wheelchair
available*
Retailing: *postcards/inexpensive souvenirs; books;
plants and seeds*
No. shops: *1*

Operations
Contacts: *L Bisset (Curator); Mrs M More
(Secretary)*
No. employees: (high season) *4 full time* (low
season) *4 full time*
Languages spoken: *French; German; Italian;
Russian*

Marketing
UK promotion: *national newspapers; local
newspapers; other attractions; leaflets/
information packs; STB*

Environmental monitoring: *energy consumption;
hazardous materials; chemical usage*

UNIVERSITY GALLERY
(education institution)
gallery

Established: *1977*
Address: *University of Northumbria, Library
    Building, Sandyford Rd, Newcastle upon Tyne,
    NE1 8ST*
Telephone: *(091) 235 8424.* Fax: *(091) 235 8559*
Access: (rail) *Newcastle and Metro*
Season: *all year*
Hours: *Termtime – Mon to Thur – 10am to 5pm,
    Fri and Sat – 10am to 4pm. Vacations – Mon to
    Fri – 10am to 5pm*
Admission (1992): *free*
No. visitors (1992): *80 000 (est.)*

Facilities
Interpretation: *videos; leaflets; information
    boards; guide books*
Schools: *maximum no. 100; educational literature*
Disabled: *easy access; disabled toilets*
Retailing: *postcards/inexpensive souvenirs;
    craftwork; books; reproductions of famous
    artefacts; posters*
No. shops: *1*

Operations
Contact: *Ms M Wood (Director)*
No. employees: (high season) *2 full time* (low
    season) *2 full time*
Training: *F/T operations staff are trained in-house
    and day-to-day on job*

Marketing
Annual event(s): *exhibitions*
Sponsor(s): *Laing Construction plc*
Other: *press office; market research*
UK promotion: *television; national newspapers;
    radio; local newspapers; leaflets/information
    packs; ETB/BTA; listings in guides*

UNIVERSITY OF DURHAM BOTANIC
GARDEN
(university)
garden

Established: *1978*
Address: *Hollingside Lane, Durham, DH1 3TN*
Telephone: *(091) 374 2670*
Access: (road) *A1(M)/A167* (rail) *Durham*
Parking capacity: (cars) *42* (coaches) *1*
Season: *all year*
Hours: *Garden open all year (opening hours
    under review). All year – 9am to 4pm
    glasshouses only daily. Visitor centre – Apr
    to Oct – Mon to Fri – 10am to 5pm, Sat
    and Sun – 2pm to 4pm. Restricted winter
    opening*
Admission (1992): *under review*
No. visitors (1992): *35 000 (est.)*

Facilities
Interpretation: *leaflets*
Schools: *maximum no. 40; educational literature*
Disabled: *easy access; disabled toilets*
Catering: *1 picnic area*
Retailing: *postcards/inexpensive souvenirs;
    confectionery and ice cream; plants and seeds*
No. shops: *1*

Operations
Contacts: *Miss J Cobb (Horticultural Officer and
    Curator)*
No. employees: (high season) *7 part time* (low
    season) *2 part time*
Training: *P/T operations staff are trained
    in-house and on specific courses using practical
    experience*
Languages spoken: *French; Italian*

Marketing
Annual event(s): *Flower show and 2 bring and
    buy sales*
Other: *press office; market research*
UK promotion: *radio; local newspapers; regional
    tourist board; ETB/BTA; posters*

Environmental monitoring: *recycling*

UNIVERSITY OF HULL ART COLLECTION
(university)
gallery

Established: *1963*
Address: *University of Hull, Cottingham Rd,
    Hull, HU6 7RX*
Telephone: *(0482) 465035.* Fax: *(0482) 440541*
Access: (road) *M62/A63* (rail) *Hull Paragon*
Season: *all year*
Hours: *Mon to Fri – 2pm to 4pm (Wed – 12.30pm
    to 4pm) except PH*
Admission (1992): *free*
No. visitors (1992): *5000 (est.)*

Facilities
Interpretation: *leaflets; labels*
Schools: *no special support*
Disabled: *easy access; disabled toilets*
Catering: *3 bars/public houses*
Retailing: *postcards/inexpensive souvenirs; books*
No. shops: *1*

Operations
Contacts: *Mr J Bernasconi (Hon Curator)*
Languages spoken: *German*

Marketing
Annual event(s): *exhibitions*
Sponsor(s): *various*
Affiliations: *Yorks and Humbs Museum Council,
    University Museums Group*
Other: *PR company: Kingston PR, 23 Sorrell
    Drive, Hull*
UK promotion: *local newspapers; leaflets/
    information packs; ETB/BTA*
Europe/Asia/Australia/USA promotion: *British
    Tourist Authority*

Environmental monitoring: *university policy*

UNIVERSITY OF LIVERPOOL ART GALLERY
(local authority run)
museum; gallery

Established: *1977*
Address: *3 Abercromby Square, Liverpool, L69
    3BX*
Telephone: *(051) 794 2347.* Fax: *(051) 708 6502*
Hours: *1 Sept to 31 July – Mon, Tues and Thur –
    12 noon to 2pm, Wed and Fri – 12 noon to
    4pm. Other times by appointment*
Admission (1992): *free during usual opening
    times*
No. visitors (1992): *4000 (est.)*

Facilities
Interpretation: *leaflets; information boards; maps*
Schools: *maximum no. 40; educational literature;
    lecture/talk*
Retailing: *postcards/inexpensive souvenirs*

Operations
Contacts: *Ms J Carpenter (Curator, Art
    Collections)*
No. employees: (high season) *2 full time; 50 part
    time* (low season) *2 full time; 50 part time*
Languages spoken: *Italian*

Marketing
Affiliations: *MA*
Other: *market research*
UK promotion: *leaflets/information packs; Arts
    Review, Arts Around Merseyside and museums
    and galleries*

UPMINSTER TITHE BARN AGRICULTURAL
MUSEUM
(voluntary)
museum; folk museum

Established: *1978*
Address: *c/o Mr P Butler, 7 Mendoza Close,
    Hornchurch, Essex, RM11 2RP*
Telephone: *(0708) 447535*
Access: (road) *A127* (rail) *Upminster*
Parking capacity: (cars) *100* (coaches) *10*
Hours: *Apr to Oct – 1st weekend – 2pm to 6pm*
Admission (1992): *free*

No. visitors (1992): *2500 (est.)*

Facilities
Interpretation: *leaflets; information boards*
Schools: *no special support*
Catering: *1 picnic area*
Retailing: *postcards/inexpensive souvenirs;
    books*
No. shops: *1*

Operations
Languages spoken: *French; Italian; Spanish*

Marketing
UK promotion: *regional tourist board; leaflets/
    information packs; ETB/BTA*

V

VALENCE HOUSE MUSEUM
(local authority run)
historic house; park/reserve; garden; museum;
gallery

Established: *1938*
Address: *Becontree Avenue, Dagenham, Essex,
RM8 3HT*
Telephone: *(081) 592 4500.* Fax: *(081) 595 8307*
Access: (road) *A13* (rail) *Chadwell Heath*
Parking capacity: (cars) *50* (coaches) *10*
Season: *all year*
Hours: *Mon to Fri – 9.30am to 1pm and 2pm to
4.30pm*
Admission (1992): *free*
No. visitors (1992): *10 000 (est.)*

Facilities
Interpretation: *leaflets; information boards; slides;
maps; tour guides; personnel*
Languages: *German*
Children: *play area; nappy changing*
Schools: *maximum no. 30; educational literature;
lecture/talk; advisory teachers*
Disabled: *disabled toilets*
Catering: *1 picnic area*
Retailing: *postcards/inexpensive souvenirs; books;
fresh herbs; stationery*
No. shops: *1*

Operations
Contact: *Ms S Curtis (Curator)*
No. employees: (high season) *7 full time; 3 part
time*

Marketing
Annual event(s): *theatrical project, friends
concerts*
Sponsor(s): *Friends of Valence House*
Affiliations: *MA, AMSSEE, NECCG*
Other: *PR company: London Borough of Barking
and Dagenham PR Office; press office; market
research*
UK promotion: *radio; local newspapers; regional
tourist board; leaflets/information packs*
Europe/USA promotion: *leaflets/brochures*

VALLEY HERITAGE CENTRE AND MUSEUM,
THE
(local authority run)
heritage centre; museum

Established: *1989*
Address: *Valley Rd, Hednesford, Cannock, Staffs,
WS12 5QX*
Telephone: *(0543) 877666.* Fax: *(0543) 462317*
Access: (road) *M6/A460* (rail) *Hednesford*
Parking capacity: (cars) *60* (coaches) *10*
Season: *all year*
Hours: *Apr to Sept – daily; Oct to Mar – Mon to
Fri (closed mid Dec to mid Jan)*
No. visitors (1992): *14 000 (est.)*

Facilities
Interpretation: *exhibition*
Schools: *maximum no. 60; educational literature;
lecture/talk*
Disabled: *easy access; disabled toilets*
Catering: *1 picnic area*
Retailing: *postcards/inexpensive souvenirs;
confectionery and ice cream; books*
No. shops: *1*

Operations
Contacts: *A Whitehouse (Curator); J O'Brian
(Assistant Curator)*
No. employees: (high season) *2 full time; 6 part
time (low season) 2 full time; 4 part time*

Training: *F/T operations staff, F/T management,
P/T operations staff and casual operations staff
are trained in-house and on specific courses and
day-to-day on job using handbooks and craft
materials*
Languages spoken: *French; Irish*

Marketing
Annual event(s): *various*
Affiliations: *West Midlands Area Museum
Services*
UK promotion: *radio; local newspapers; regional
tourist board; other attractions; leaflets/
information packs*

VAUXHALL ST PETER'S HERITAGE CENTRE
(limited company)
heritage centre; church

Established: *1991*
Address: *310 Kennington Lane, London, SE11
5U7*
Telephone: *(071) 793 0263*
Access: (rail) *Vauxhall*
Hours: *Mon to Fri – 10am to 4pm*
Admission (1992): *free*
No. visitors (1992): *9000 (est.)*

Facilities
Interpretation: *leaflets; information boards; slides;
maps; guide books*
Schools: *maximum no. 100; educational literature;
lecture/talk*
Disabled: *easy access; disabled toilets*
Retailing: *postcards/inexpensive souvenirs; books;
maps*
No. shops: *1*

Operations
Contacts: *Ms Z Brooks (Manager)*
No. employees: (high season) *1 full time (low
season) 1 full time*
Training: *F/T management, P/T operations staff,
P/T management, casual operations staff and
casual management are trained in-house and
externally and on specific courses and
day-to-day on job*
Languages spoken: *German*

Marketing
Annual event(s): *open days*
Sponsor(s): *various*
Other: *market research*
UK promotion: *local newspapers; regional tourist
board; other attractions; leaflets/information
packs*

Environmental monitoring: *recycling*

VENTNOR BOTANIC GARDEN
(local authority run)
park/reserve

Established: *1973*
Address: *The Undercliffe Drive, Ventnor, Isle of
Wight*
Telephone: *(0983) 855397*
Access: (road) *A3055*
Parking capacity: (cars) *160* (coaches) *20*
Season: *all year*
Hours: *Botanic Garden open all year. Temperate
house – Good Friday to 31 Oct – 10am to 5pm
daily, 1 Nov to Maundy Thursday – Sun only –
11am to 4pm*
Admission (1992): *adults £0.50; children £0.20;
charges for temperate house*
No. visitors (1992): *180 000 (est.)*

Facilities
Interpretation: *leaflets; information boards; tour
guides; guide books*
Children: *play area*
Schools: *maximum no. 15; educational literature;
lecture/talk*
Disabled: *easy access; disabled toilets; special
signs; raised beds containing highly scented
plantings*
Catering: *1 licensed restaurant*
Franchisees: *Botanic Garden open all year.
Temperate house – Good Friday to 31 Oct –
10am to 5pm*
Retailing: *postcards/inexpensive souvenirs;
confectionery and ice cream; craftwork; books;
seeds and plants*
No. shops: *2*

Operations
Contacts: *Mr S Goodenough (Curator); Mrs J
Ringer*
No. employees: (high season) *6 full time; 5
part time (low season) 6 full time; 3 part
time*
Languages spoken: *German*

Marketing
Affiliations: *RHS and other related organisations*
Other: *market research*
UK promotion: *radio; local newspapers; regional
tourist board; other attractions; leaflets/
information packs*

Environmental monitoring: *environmental*

VICTORIA AND ALBERT MUSEUM
(Dept of National Heritage, trust)
museum

Established: *1852*
Address: *Cromwell Rd, London, SW7 2RL*
Telephone: *(071) 938 8500.* Fax: *(071) 938 8341*
Access: (rail) *South Kensington*
Season: *all year*
Hours: *Mon to Sat – 10am to 5.50pm; Sun –
2.30pm to 5.50pm*
Admission (1992): *adults £3.50; OAP £1.00; these
are suggested donations*
No. visitors (1992): *1 066 000 (est.)*

Facilities
Interpretation: *leaflets; audio tapes; information
boards; maps; tour guides; guide books*
Languages: *Japanese; Dutch; French; German;
Italian; Spanish*
Children: *nappy changing*
Schools: *educational literature; lecture/talk;
outreach programmes*
Disabled: *easy access; disabled toilets; Braille/
sound posts; helpers; other audio facilities;
leaflets; tours by arrangement*
Catering: *1 picnic area*
Franchisees: *Mon to Sat – 10am to 5.50pm;
Sun – 2.30pm to 5.50pm*
Retailing: *postcards/inexpensive souvenirs;
craftwork; books; reproductions of famous
artefacts; ceramics, etc.*
No. shops: *2*

Operations
Contacts: *Mr J Close (Assistant Director); Ms G
Henchley (Personnel); Mr M Cass (Director,
V&A Enterprises); Ms R Griffith-Jones
(Marketing/PR)*
Training: *F/T operations staff, P/T operations
staff and casual operations staff are trained
in-house and on specific courses and day-to-day
on job*
Languages spoken: *French; Latin*

Marketing
Press office; market research
UK promotion: *leaflets/information packs*
Europe/Asia/Australia/USA promotion:
   leaflets/brochures; British Tourist Authority

Environmental monitoring: *water quality; energy
   consumption; chemical usage*

VICTORIAN REED ORGAN MUSEUM
(privately owned)
museum

Established: *1985*
Address: *Victoria Hall, Victoria Rd, Saltaire,
   Shipley, W Yorks, BD18*
Telephone: *(0274) 585601*
Access: (road) *M606/A650* (rail) *Saltaire*
Hours: *Sun to Thur – 11am to 4pm except 2
   weeks at Christmas and New Year*
Admission (1992): *moderate charges*
No. visitors (1992): *N/A*

Facilities
Interpretation: *tour guides; personal guided tour*
Schools: *maximum no. 20; educational literature*
Retailing: *books; recordings*
No. shops: *none*

VIEWPOINT PHOTOGRAPHY GALLERY
(local authority run)
gallery

Established: *1987*
Address: *Old Fire Station, The Crescent, Salford,
   Lancs, M5 4NZ*
Telephone: *(061) 737 1040.* Fax: *(061) 745 7806*
Access: (road) *M602/A6* (rail) *Salford Crescent*
Parking capacity: (cars) *50*
Season: *all year*
Hours: *Tues to Fri – 10am to 5pm; Sun – 2pm to
   5pm*
Admission (1992): *N/A*
No. visitors (1992): *20 000 (est.)*

Facilities
Interpretation: *videos; leaflets; information
   boards; guide books*
Schools: *maximum no. 150; audio/visual
   presentation; lecture/talk*
Disabled: *easy access; disabled toilets; leaflets*
Retailing: *postcards/inexpensive souvenirs;
   books*
No. shops: *1*

Operations
No. employees: (high season) *3 full time; 1 part
   time*
Training: *F/T operations staff, F/T management
   and P/T operations staff are trained in-house
   and on specific courses*

Marketing
Press office; market research
UK promotion: *local newspapers; regional tourist
   board; leaflets/information packs; ETB/BTA*

VINTAGE RAILWAY CARRIAGE MUSEUM
(trust)
museum

Established: *1990*
Address: *Ingrow Railway Centre, Ingrow,
   Keighley, W Yorks, BD22 8NJ*
Telephone: *(0535) 646472*
Access: (road) *A629* (rail) *Keighley*
Parking capacity: (cars) *50* (coaches) *6*
Season: *all year*
Hours: *every weekend throughout the year. Easter
   week and BH except Christmas Day. July and
   Aug – 11.30am to 5pm daily*
Admission (1992): *adults £0.80; children £0.50;
   OAP £0.50; student £0.50*
No. visitors (1992): *12 000 (est.)*

Facilities
Interpretation: *videos; leaflets; audio tapes;
   information boards; guide books*
Schools: *maximum no. 50; lecture/talk*
Disabled: *helpers*
Retailing: *postcards/inexpensive souvenirs; books*
No. shops: *1*

Operations
Contact: *M Cope (Hon Secretary)*
Languages spoken: *French*

Marketing
Affiliation: *Association of Railway Preservation
   Societies*
UK promotion: *regional tourist board; leaflets/
   information packs; YHTB*

VINTAGE TOY TRAIN MUSEUM
(privately owned)
museum

Established: *1982*
Address: *Field's Department Store, Market Place,
   Sidmouth, Devon, EX10 8LU*
Telephone: *(0345) 515124*
Access: (road) *M5/A3052* (rail) *Honiton*
Hours: *Easter to end Oct – Mon to Sat – 10am to
   5pm except BH*
Admission (1992): *adults £1.00; children £0.50;
   OAP £0.50*
No. visitors (1992): *13 950*

Facilities
Interpretation: *leaflets*
Retailing: *books; old toys and trains*
No. shops: *1*

Operations
Contact: *J Salisbury (owner)*
No. employees: (high season) *1 full time* (low
   season) *1 full time*
Languages spoken: *French*

Marketing
Affiliation: *AIM*
UK promotion: *other attractions; leaflets/
   information packs; collectors magazines*

VOLKS ELECTRIC RAILWAY
(local authority run)
railway

Established: *1883*
Address: *Madeira Drive, Brighton*
Telephone: *(0273) 681061.* Fax: *(0273) 777409*
Access: (road) *M23/A259/A23/A27* (rail)
   Brighton
Hours: *Easter to Sept – 10am to 6pm daily*
Admission (1992): *adults £0.85; children £0.35*
No. visitors (1992): *130 000 (est.)*

Facilities
Interpretation: *information boards*
Disabled: *disabled toilets*
Retailing: *postcards/inexpensive souvenirs;
   confectionery and ice cream*
No. shops: *More than 4*

Operations
Contact: *C Holm (Resort Services Manager)*
No. employees: (high season) *8 full time; 2 part
   time* (low season) *4 full time*

Marketing
Affiliation: *Museums and Galleries' Commission*
Other: *press office*
UK promotion: *regional tourist board; leaflets/
   information packs*

W

WAKEFIELD ART GALLERY
(local authority run)
gallery

Established: *1936*
Address: *Wentworth Terrace, Wakefield, W Yorks, WF1 3QW*
Telephone: *(0924) 295796.* Fax: *(0924) 295632*
Access: (road) *M1/M62* (rail) *Wakefield Westgate*
Season: *all year*
Hours: *Mon to Sat – 10.30am to 5pm; Sun – 2.30pm to 5pm; open BH except Christmas and New Year*
Admission (1992): *free*
No. visitors (1992): *15 000 (est.)*

Facilities
Interpretation: *leaflets; information boards; displays and exhibitions*
Schools: *maximum no. 40; educational literature; audio/visual presentation; lecture/talk; projects and animators*
Disabled: *helpers*
Retailing: *postcards/inexpensive souvenirs; books; reproductions of famous artefacts; prints and posters*
No. shops: *1*

Operations
Contact: *Ms M Sanderson (Administrator)*
No. employees: (high season) *6 full time; 4 part time* (low season) *6 full time; 4 part time*
Training: *F/T operations staff, P/T operations staff and casual operations staff are trained in-house and externally and on specific courses using videos and hand books and seminars*

Marketing
Press office
UK promotion: *local newspapers; regional tourist board; leaflets/information packs; ETB/BTA*

Environmental monitoring: *recycling; water quality*

WAKEFIELD CATHEDRAL
(charity)
church

Established: *1100*
Address: *Northgate, Wakefield, W Yorks, WF1 1HG*
Telephone: *(0924) 373923.* Fax: *(0924) 383842*
Access: (road) *M1/M62* (rail) *Wakefield Westgate*
Season: *all year*
Hours: *Mon to Sat – 8am to 5pm except during services. Closed to visitors Sun and BH Mon*
Admission (1992): *free*
No. visitors (1992): *60 000 (est.)*

Facilities
Interpretation: *leaflets; information boards; tour guides; guide books*
Schools: *maximum no. 300; educational literature; lecture/talk; children's days by arrangement*
Disabled: *easy access; disabled toilets; helpers; special signs; induction loop; parking*
Retailing: *postcards/inexpensive souvenirs; books*
No. shops: *1*

Operations
Contacts: *Mr P Beckett (Administrator); Very Revd J Allen (Provost)*
No. employees: (high season) *10 full time* (low season) *10 full time*
Training: *F/T operations staff and F/T management are trained in-house and day-to-day on job*

Marketing
Market research

Environmental monitoring: *recycling; hazardous materials*

WAKEFIELD MUSEUM
(local authority run)
museum

Established: *1936*
Address: *Wood St, Wakefield, W Yorks, WF1 2SR*
Telephone: *(0924) 295350.* Fax: *(0924) 295632*
Access: (road) *M1/M62* (rail) *Wakefield Westgate*
Season: *all year*
Hours: *Mon to Sat – 10.30am to 5pm; Sun – 2.30pm to 5pm. Closed Christmas and New Year*
Admission (1992): *free*
No. visitors (1992): *30 000 (est.)*

Facilities
Interpretation: *leaflets; information boards; personnel; displays and exhibitions*
Languages: *French*
Schools: *maximum no. 40; education officer and activities*
Retailing: *postcards/inexpensive souvenirs; books; reproductions of famous artefacts; posters and prints*
No. shops: *1*

Operations
Contact: *Ms M Sanderson (Administrator)*
No. employees: (high season) *6 full time; 5 part time* (low season) *6 full time; 5 part time*
Training: *F/T operations staff, P/T operations staff, casual operations staff are trained in-house and externally and on specific courses and day-to-day on job*
Languages spoken: *French; Swahili*

Marketing
Press office
UK promotion: *local newspapers; regional tourist board; leaflets/information packs*

WALKER ART GALLERY
(national museum)
monument; gallery

Established: *1877*
Address: *William Brown St, Liverpool, L3 8EL*
Telephone: *(051) 207 0001.* Fax: *(051) 298 1816*
Access: (road) *M62/A59/A57/A580/A5038* (rail) *Liverpool Lime Street*
Parking capacity: (cars) *20* (coaches) *4*
Season: *all year*
Hours: *Mon to Sat – 10am to 5pm; Sun – 12am to 5pm. Closed Christmas, New Year's Day and Good Friday*
Admission (1992): *free*
No. visitors (1992): *209 505*

Facilities
Interpretation: *videos; leaflets; audio tapes; information boards; slides; tour guides; guide books*
Languages: *French; German*
Children: *nappy changing*
Schools: *educational literature; audio/visual presentation; lecture/talk; teacher courses available*
Disabled: *easy access; disabled toilets; other audio facilities*
Catering: *1 waiter/waitress served*

Franchisees: *Mon to Sat – 10am to 5pm; Sun – 12am to 5pm. Closed Christmas, New Year's Day and Good Friday*
Retailing: *postcards/inexpensive souvenirs; books; posters, greeting cards, etc.*
No. shops: *1*

Operations
Contacts: *R Foster (Director, NMGM); J Treuherz (Keeper of Art Galleries); A Archard (Head of Personnel); C Hitchins (General Manager, NMGM Enterprises); B Hope (Marketing Manager)*
No. employees: (high season) *70 full time; 4 part time*
Training: *F/T operations staff, F/T management, P/T operations staff, P/T management, casual operations staff and casual management are trained in-house and externally and on specific courses and day-to-day on job*

Marketing
Annual event(s): *ongoing temporary exhibition and events programme*
Sponsor(s): *contact NMGM's Development Officer*
Affiliations: *Museums Association*
Other: *press office; market research*
UK promotion: *television; national newspapers; radio; local newspapers; regional tourist board; other attractions; leaflets/information packs; ETB/BTA*
Europe/USA promotion: *leaflets/brochures; British Tourist Authority*

Environmental monitoring: *recycling; hazardous materials*

WALKLEY CLOGS
(limited company)
industrial/retail centre

Established: *1981*
Address: *Canal Wharf Sawmills, Hawksclough, Hebden Bridge, W Yorks*
Telephone: *(0422) 842061.* Fax: *(0422) 844372*
Access: (road) *M62/A646*
Parking capacity: (cars) *225* (coaches) *5*
Season: *all year*
Hours: *Mon to Fri – 10am to 5pm; Sat and Sun – 10am to 5.30pm*
Admission (1992): *free*
No. visitors (1992): *750 000 (est.)*

Facilities
Interpretation: *leaflets; information boards*
Children: *play area; nappy changing*
Schools: *educational literature*
Disabled: *easy access; disabled toilets*
Catering: *1 picnic area*
Franchisees: *Mon to Fri – 10am to 5pm; Sat and Sun – 10am to 5.30pm*
Retailing: *postcards/inexpensive souvenirs; confectionery and ice cream; craftwork; books; clothes; reproductions of famous artefacts; clogs; most except food and electrical*
No. shops: *more than 4*

Operations
Contacts: *Ms J Warman (Finance Director); Ms J Lord/Mr R Dower (Product Directors); Ms J Sheriden (PR)*
No. employees: (high season) *80 full time*
Languages spoken: *French; German; Spanish; Japanese; Russian*

Marketing
Annual event(s): *various*
Affiliation: *NW Tourist Board*
Other: *PR company: The Media Store, Halifax, W Yorks; press office; market research*

UK promotion: *radio; local newspapers; regional tourist board; other attractions; leaflets/ information packs*
Europe/USA promotion: *leaflets/brochures; travel agents' brochures*

Environmental monitoring: *recycling; energy consumption; hazardous materials*

WALTER ROTHSCHILD ZOOLOGICAL MUSEUM, THE
(national museum)
museum

Established: *1892*
Address: *Akeman St, Tring, Herts, HP23 6AP*
Telephone: *(0442) 824181.* Fax: *(0442) 890693*
Access: (road) *M1/M25/A41* (rail) *Tring*
Parking capacity: (cars) *35*
Season: *all year*
Hours: *Mon to Sat – 10am to 5pm; Sun – 2pm to 5pm*
Admission (1992): *adults £1.50; children £0.75; OAP £1.00; student £1.00; family ticket £3.50; under 5s free*
No. visitors (1992): *74 000 (est.)*

Facilities
Interpretation: *leaflets; guide books*
Schools: *audio/visual presentation*
Disabled: *disabled toilets*
Catering: *2 picnic areas*
Retailing: *postcards/inexpensive souvenirs; craftwork; books; pottery, minerals, gift items*
No. shops: *1*

Operations
Contacts: *I R Bishop (Curator); A Chapman (Administrator); S Ferri (Shop Manager)*
No. employees: (high season) *28 full time; 7 part time* (low season) *28 full time; 7 part time*
Training: *F/T operations staff, F/T management, P/T operations staff, P/T management and casual operations staff are trained in-house and externally and on specific courses and day-to-day on job*
Languages spoken: *French; German*

Marketing
Sponsor: *British Gas*
Other: *press office*
UK promotion: *radio; local newspapers; regional tourist board; other attractions; leaflets/ information packs; Where to Go in the Thames and Chilterns*

Environmental monitoring: *hazardous materials*

WALTZING WATERS LTD
(limited company)
aqua theatre

Established: *1990*
Address: *Balavil Brae, Newtonmore, Inverness-shire, PH20 1DR*
Telephone: *(0540) 673752*
Access: (road) *A9*
Parking capacity: (cars) *100* (coaches) *6*
Hours: *20 Feb to 5 Jan – 10am to 6pm and 7.45pm to 9.45pm daily*
Admission (1992): *adults £3.50; children £1.00; OAP £3.00; student £3.00*
No. visitors (1992): *120 000*

Facilities
Interpretation: *live on stage*
Children: *play area*
Schools: *maximum no. 180; audio/visual presentation; lecture/talk*
Disabled: *easy access; disabled toilets; helpers; leaflets*
Catering: *1 picnic area*
Retailing: *postcards/inexpensive souvenirs; confectionery and ice cream; craftwork; books; clothes; reproductions of famous artefacts; high quality craft*
No. shops: *1*

Operations
Contacts: *Mr A Donald (General Manager); Ms M Binnie (Reception Manager)*
No. employees: (high season) *8 full time; 8 part time* (low season) *6 full time; 2 part time*
Training: *F/T operations staff, F/T management and P/T operations staff are trained in-house and externally and on specific courses and day-to-day on job*

Marketing
Market research
UK promotion: *television; national newspapers; radio; local newspapers; regional tourist board; other attractions; leaflets/information packs; ETB/BTA; various*

WARRINGTON MUSEUM AND ART GALLERY
(local authority run)
museum; gallery

Established: *1857*
Address: *Bold St, Warrington, Ches*
Telephone: *(0925) 444400*
Access: (road) *M6/M62/M56/A49/A57* (rail) *Warrington Bank Quay*
Season: *all year*
Hours: *Mon to Fri – 10am to 5.30pm; Sat – 10am to 5pm*
Admission (1992): *free*
No. visitors (1992): *67 426*

Facilities
Interpretation: *videos; leaflets; information boards; exhibits and labels*
Children: *nappy changing*
Schools: *maximum no. 40; educational literature; audio/visual presentation; lecture/talk; worksheets, craft sessions*
Disabled: *disabled toilets; lift*
Retailing: *postcards/inexpensive souvenirs; books; reproductions of famous artefacts; fine art prints; geological specimens, local art*

Operations
Contact: *A Leigh (Curator)*
No. employees: (high season) *12 full time; 1 part time* (low season) *12 full time; 1 part time*
Training: *F/T operations staff and F/T management are trained externally and on specific courses using videos and handbooks*
Languages spoken: *French; German*

Marketing
Affiliation: *Area Council and Museums Association*
Other: *market research*
UK promotion: *television; national newspapers; radio; local newspapers; regional tourist board; other attractions; leaflets/information packs; museums and galleries*

Environmental monitoring: *waste; water quality; chemical usage*

WARWICK CASTLE
(limited company)
castle

Established: *1700*
Address: *Warwick, CV34 4QU*
Telephone: *(0926) 495421.* Fax: *(0926) 401692*
Access: (road) *M40/A429* (rail) *Warwick*
Parking capacity: (cars) *250* (coaches) *30*
Season: *all year*
Hours: *Mar to Oct – 10am to 5.30pm daily; Nov to Feb – 10am to 4.30pm daily*
Admission (1992): *adults £6.25; children £3.80; OAP £4.25; student £4.75; family tickets £17.50 and £19.50*
No. visitors (1992): *685 000 (est.)*

Facilities
Interpretation: *videos; leaflets; audio tapes; information boards; slides; maps; tour guides; guide books; personnel*
Languages: *French; German*
Children: *nappy changing*

Schools: *maximum no. 200; no special support*
Disabled: *disabled toilets*
Catering: *3 picnic areas*
Retailing: *postcards/inexpensive souvenirs; craftwork; books; clothes; reproductions of famous artefacts; mugs, bookmarks, wine, videos, etc.*
No. shops: *4*

Operations
Contacts: *P Watson (Visitor and Administrative Services Manager); E Rogers (Personnel and Training Manager); C Underhill (Souvenir/ Merchandise Manager); S Montgomery (Marketing Manager)*
No. employees: (high season) *104 full time; 156 part time* (low season) *62 full time; 134 part time*
Training: *F/T operations staff, F/T management, P/T operations staff and casual operations staff are trained in-house and externally and on specific courses and day-to-day on job*

Marketing
Annual event(s): *various*
Affiliations: *HETB, BITOA, CAVCA, Treasure Houses of England*
Other: *market research*
UK promotion: *television; national newspapers; local newspapers; regional tourist board; other attractions; leaflets/information packs; ETB/ BTA*
Europe/USA promotion: *leaflets/brochures; British Tourist Authority*

WAT TYLER COUNTRY PARK
(local authority run)
park/reserve; museum; marina

Established: *1984*
Address: *Wat Tyler Way, Pitsea, Basildon, Essex, SS16 4UW*
Telephone: *(0268) 550088*
Access: (road) *M25/A13* (rail) *Pitsea*
Parking capacity: (cars) *500*
Season: *all year*
Hours: *8am to dusk*
Admission (1992): *free*
No. visitors (1992): *150 000 (est.)*

Facilities
Interpretation: *leaflets; information boards; maps; tour guides; guide books*
Schools: *maximum no. 180; educational literature; lecture/talk; owl displays and games*
Disabled: *easy access; disabled toilets*
Catering: *2 picnic areas*
Franchisees: *8am to dusk*
Retailing: *craftwork*
No. shops: *More than 4*

Operations
Contacts: *Mr D Standen (Countryside Manager)*
No. employees: (high season) *8 full time; 2 part time* (low season) *8 full time; 2 part time*
Training: *F/T operations staff, F/T management and P/T operations staff are trained in-house and externally and on specific courses and day-to-day on job using videos and handbooks*
Languages spoken: *French; German; Italian; Spanish; Flemish*

Marketing
Annual event(s): *craft and heritage fairs*
Sponsor: *Mark Anthony's Living Heritage*
Affiliation: *AMSSEE*
Other: *market research*
UK promotion: *radio; local newspapers; regional tourist board; leaflets/information packs*

WATCHET MARKET HOUSE MUSEUM
(trust)
museum

Established: *1979*
Address: *Market St, Watchet, Somerset, TA23 0AN*
Telephone: *(0643) 707132*
Access: (road) *M5/A39/B3191* (rail) *Taunton*

Hours: *Easter weekend and mid May to 30 Sept –
10.30am to 12.30pm and 2.30pm to 4.30pm
(also July and Aug – 7pm to 9pm)*
Admission (1992): *adults £0.10; children £0.05;
OAP £0.10; student £0.10*
No. visitors (1992): *18 678*

Facilities
Interpretation: *videos; tour guides; tour guides for
groups*
Schools: *maximum no. 25; educational literature;
lecture/talk*
Disabled: *helpers*
Retailing: *postcards/inexpensive souvenirs; books*
No. shops: *1*

Operations
Contacts: *Mr W Norman (Curator); Mr M Brown
(Chairman); Mr M Sully (Secretary)*

Marketing
Affiliation: *SW Area Museum Council, SW
Federation of Museums and Galleries, Somerset
Archaeological and Natural History Society*
UK promotion: *local newspapers; regional tourist
board; other attractions; leaflets/information
packs; Exmoor Visitor*

Environmental monitoring: *water quality;
landscape based on SSSI*

**WATERFOWL SANCTUARY AND RESCUE
CENTRE, THE**
(private/family run)
park/reserve; zoo/wildlife attraction; sanctuary
and rescue centre

Established: *1989*
Address: *Wiggington Heath, Nr Hook Norton,
Banbury, Oxon, OX15 4LB*
Telephone: *(0608) 730252*
Access: (road) *M40/A361* (rail) *Banbury*
Parking capacity: (cars) *40* (coaches) *3*
Season: *all year*
Hours: *10.30am to 7.30pm daily*
Admission (1992): *adults £2.00; children £1.00;
group discounts*
No. visitors (1992): *17 000 (est.)*

Facilities
Interpretation: *leaflets; maps*
Children: *adventure playground; play area*
Schools: *maximum no. 150; educational literature;
hands on experience*
Disabled: *easy access; disabled toilets*
Catering: *1 picnic area*
Retailing: *postcards/inexpensive souvenirs;
confectionery and ice cream*

Operations
Contact: *M Warner (owner)*
No. employees: (high season) *2 part time* (low
season) *2 part time*

Marketing
UK promotion: *local newspapers; regional tourist
board; leaflets/information packs; Thames and
Chilterns; ETB/BTA; Southern Tourist Board*

Environmental monitoring: *energy consumption;
hazardous materials; chemical usage; transport*

WATERFRONT MUSEUM
(local authority run)
museum

Established: *1989*
Address: *4 High St, Poole, Dorset, BH15 1BW*
Telephone: *(0202) 683138. Fax: (0202) 660896*
Access: (road) *A35* (rail) *Poole*
Season: *all year*
Hours: *Mar to Oct – Mon to Sat – 1pm to 5pm,
Sun – 2pm to 5pm; Nov to Feb – Sat – 10am to
5pm, Sun 2pm to 5pm*
Admission (1992): *adults £2.95; children £1.50;
OAP £2.25; student £2.25; family ticket £7.25,
price includes Scalpen's Court Museum*
No. visitors (1992): *40 000*

Facilities
Interpretation: *videos; leaflets; information
boards; slides; maps; computers and hands on*
Languages: *French*
Schools: *maximum no. 60; 2 advisory teachers*
Disabled: *easy access; disabled toilets*
Catering: *1 snack bar/food stall*
Retailing: *postcards/inexpensive souvenirs; books;
clothes; reproductions of famous artefacts;
quality gifts*
No. shops: *1*

Operations
Contacts: *Mr G Smith (Curator); Mr C Fisher
(Visitor Services)*
No. employees: (high season) *25 full time; 10 part
time* (low season) *25 full time; 10 part time*
Training: *F/T operations staff, F/T management,
P/T operations staff, P/T management, casual
operations staff and casual management are
trained in-house and externally and on specific
courses and day-to-day on job*
Languages spoken: *French*

Marketing
Affiliations: *MA, Area Museum Council for SW*
Other: *market research*
UK promotion: *local newspapers; regional tourist
board; other attractions; leaflets/information
packs; Southern Tourist Board, Poole Tourism
Services, Bournemouth Tourism; ETB/BTA*

WATERMOUTH CASTLE
(privately owned)
theme park; castle; garden; museum

Established: *1989*
Address: *Nr Ilfracombe, Devonshire, EX34 9SL*
Telephone: *(0271) 863879. Fax: (0271) 865864*
Access: (road) *M5/A399* (rail) *Barnstaple*
Parking capacity: (cars) *400* (coaches) *6*
Hours: *Apr to Oct from 11am*
Admission (1992): *adults £4.50; children £3.50;
OAP £4.00*
No. visitors (1992): *150 000 (est.)*

Facilities
Interpretation: *leaflets; tour guides; guide books;
personnel*
Children: *adventure playground; play area; nappy
changing*
Schools: *maximum no. 200*
Disabled: *disabled toilets; leaflets; guide book;
alternative route*
Catering: *2 picnic areas*
Retailing: *postcards/inexpensive souvenirs;
confectionery and ice cream; craftwork; books;
clothes; reproductions of famous artefacts;
holiday souvenirs*
No. shops: *3*

Operations
Contacts: *R Haines (Partner); A Haines (Partner);
J Haines (Partner)*
No. employees: (high season) *20 full time; 40 part
time* (low season) *15 full time; 10 part time*
Training: *F/T operations staff, F/T management,
P/T operations staff, P/T management, casual
operations staff and casual management are
trained in-house and externally and on specific
courses and day-to-day on job using videos and
outside bodies and council*
Languages spoken: *French*

Marketing
Affiliation: *British Association of Leisure Parks
and Attractions*
Other: *market research*
UK promotion: *television; radio; local
newspapers; regional tourist board; other
attractions; leaflets/information packs; ETB/
BTA; local guides*

Environmental monitoring: *collections*

WEALD AND DOWNLAND OPEN AIR MUSEUM
(trust)
museum

Established: *1970*

Address: *Singleton, Chichester, W Sussex*
Telephone: *(024363) 348. Fax: (024363) 475*
Access: (road) *A286*
Parking capacity: (cars) *1000* (coaches) *20*
Season: *all year*
Hours: *Mar to Oct – 11am to 5.30pm daily; Nov
to Feb – Wed and Sun – 11am to 4pm; Dec and
Jan – 11am to 4pm daily*
Admission (1992): *adults £3.60; children £1.50;
OAP £3.00; student £1.50; family £9.50*
No. visitors (1992): *160 000*

Facilities
Interpretation: *audio tapes; information boards;
tour guides; guide books; personnel*
Languages: *Dutch; French; German*
Children: *nappy changing*
Schools: *educational literature; educational tour*
Disabled: *disabled toilets*
Catering: *1 picnic area*
Franchisees: *Mar to Oct – 11am to 5.30pm
daily*
Retailing: *postcards/inexpensive souvenirs;
craftwork; books*
No. shops: *1*

Operations
Contacts: *C Zeuner (Museum Director);
R Pailthorpe (Assistant Director)*
No. employees: (high season) *14 full time; 10
part time* (low season) *14 full time; 16 part
time*
Languages spoken: *German*

Marketing
Annual event(s): *various*
Sponsor(s): *various*
Affiliations: *AIM, SETB*
Other: *market research*
UK promotion: *local newspapers; regional tourist
board; leaflets/information packs*
Europe promotion: *British Tourist Authority*

Environmental monitoring: *recycling; waste;
water quality; energy consumption; hazardous
materials; chemical usage; transport; emissions*

WELCH REGIMENT MUSEUM, THE
(trust)
castle; park/reserve; museum; zoo/wildlife
attraction

Established: *1978*
Address: *Cardiff Castle, Cardiff, CF1 2RB*
Telephone: *(0222) 229367*
Access: (road) *M4*
Season: *all year*
Admission (1992): *adults £2.00; children £1.00;
OAP £1.00*
No. visitors (1992): *70 000*

Facilities
Interpretation: *audio tapes; information boards;
maps*
Languages: *French; German; Welsh*
Schools: *educational literature*
Catering: *1 picnic area*
Retailing: *postcards/inexpensive souvenirs; books;
regimental souvenirs*
No. shops: *1*

Operations
Contacts: *LT (RN) (Retd) Bryn Owen FMA
(Curator); Major (Retd) P L Cutler MBE
(Administrative Officer)*
No. employees: (high season) *2 full time; 10 part
time* (low season) *2 full time; 10 part time*
Training: *P/T operations staff are trained
in-house and day-to-day on job*

Marketing
Affiliation: *National Museum of Wales*
UK promotion: *local newspapers; regional tourist
board; leaflets/information packs*

Environmental monitoring: *waste; water quality;
hazardous materials; transport*

WELLESBOURNE AVIATION GROUP
(trust)
museum

Established: *1986*
Address: *c/o Mr A Barker (Hon Sec), 15 Mountbatten Avenue, Kenilworth, Warks, CV8 2PY*
Telephone: *(0926) 55031*
Access: *(road) M40/A429*
Parking capacity: *(cars) 10*
Hours: *Sun and BH except Christmas and New Year – 10am to 4pm*
Admission (1992): *adults £1.00; children £0.50; OAP £1.00; student £1.00*
No. visitors (1992): *3000 (est.)*

Facilities
Interpretation: *leaflets; information boards; maps; trust members*
Schools: *maximum no. 20; no special support; lecture/talk; talks by members*
Disabled: *easy access*
Retailing: *aircraft photos and models*

Marketing
UK promotion: *regional tourist board; leaflets/ information packs; ETB/BTA*

WELLS AND WALSINGHAM LIGHT RAILWAY
(private railway)
light railway

Established: *1982*
Address: *Wells-next-the-Sea, Norfolk, NR23 1QB*
Access: *(road) A149 (rail) King's Lynn/Norwich*
Parking capacity: *(cars) 30 (coaches) 1*
Hours: *Good Friday to end Sept – 7 days a week*
Admission (1992): *adults £3.50; children £2.50*
No. visitors (1992): *20 000 (est.)*

Facilities
Interpretation: *leaflets; information boards; maps; guide books*
Schools: *maximum no. 76; train must be prebooked*
Catering: *1 self-service cafeteria*
Retailing: *postcards/inexpensive souvenirs; confectionery and ice cream; books; badges*
No. shops: *1*

Operations
Contact: *Cmdr R Francis RN (Rtd)*
No. employees: *(high season) 1 full time (low season) 1 full time*
Training: *F/T operations staff are trained in-house and day-to-day on job*
Languages spoken: *French; German; Russian*

Marketing
Affiliation: *ARPS*
UK promotion: *regional tourist board; leaflets/ information packs*

WELLS CATHEDRAL
(cathedral)
church

Established: *1238*
Address: *West Cloister Offices, Wells, Somerset, BH5 2PA*
Telephone: *(0749) 674483*
Access: *(road) A39/A371*
Season: *all year*
Hours: *7.15am to 6pm or until dusk or 8.30pm in summer*
Admission (1992): *donations requested, £2.00 adults, others £1.00*
No. visitors (1992): *400 000 (est.)*

Facilities
Interpretation: *leaflets; information boards; guide books*
Languages: *French; German*
Children: *nappy changing*

Schools: *maximum no. 400; educational literature; lecture/talk*
Disabled: *easy access; disabled toilets; other audio facilities*
Catering: *1 picnic area*
Retailing: *postcards/inexpensive souvenirs; craftwork; books*
No. shops: *1*

Operations
Contact: *J Shillingford (Chapter Clerk)*
No. employees: *(high season) 35 full time; 50 part time (low season) 35 full time; 20 part time*
Training: *F/T operations staff and P/T operations staff are trained in-house and externally and on specific courses and day-to-day on job*

Marketing
Annual event(s): *concerts and special services*
Sponsor(s): *various*
Affiliations: *WC Tourist Board, Wells Tourist Board, various Church of England bodies*
UK promotion: *local newspapers; regional tourist board; leaflets/information packs; ETB/BTA; West Country and Wells*

Environmental monitoring: *water quality*

WELLS MUSEUM
(trust)
museum

Established: *1932*
Address: *8 Cathedral Green, Wells, Somerset*
Telephone: *(0749) 673477. Fax: (0749) 676013*
Access: *(road) M5 (rail) Bath/Bristol*
Hours: *Easter to Oct – Mon to Sat – 10am to 5.30pm, Sun – 11am to 5.30pm; Nov to Easter – Wed to Sun – 11am to 4pm*
Admission (1992): *adults £1.00; children £0.50; OAP £0.50; student £0.50; MA members and visitors in wheelchairs free*
No. visitors (1992): *20 000 (est.)*

Facilities
Interpretation: *information boards; displays*
Schools: *maximum no. 25; no special support; some worksheets on request*
Disabled: *access to wheelchairs on ground floor only*
Retailing: *postcards/inexpensive souvenirs; books*
No. shops: *1*

Operations
Contact: *H Gillian (Administrator)*
No. employees: *(high season) 3 part time (low season) 3 part time*
Training: *P/T operations staff and P/T management are trained in-house and day-to-day on job using firetraining*
Languages spoken: *French; German*

Marketing
Market research
UK promotion: *local newspapers; leaflets/ information packs*

Environmental monitoring: *chemical usage; stone and stained glass*

WELSH FOLK MUSEUM
(trust)
heritage centre; museum

Established: *1946*
Address: *St Fagans, Cardiff, CF5 6XB*
Telephone: *(0222) 569441. Fax: (0222) 578413*
Access: *(road) M4/A4232*
Parking capacity: *(cars) 300 (coaches) 40*
Season: *all year*
Hours: *Apr to Nov – 10am to 5pm daily; Nov to Apr – Mon to Sat – 10am to 5pm*
Admission (1992): *adults £3.50; children £1.75; OAP £2.60; student £2.60; ub40s £2.60; under 5s free*
No. visitors (1992): *296 000*

Facilities
Interpretation: *videos; leaflets; information boards; guide books*

Languages: *Japanese; French; German; Spanish*
Children: *play area*
Schools: *educational literature; lecture/talk*
Disabled: *easy access; disabled toilets; special signs*
Catering: *1 picnic area*
Franchisees: *Apr to Nov – 10am to 5pm daily*
Retailing: *postcards/inexpensive souvenirs; craftwork; books; clothes*
No. shops: *1*

Operations
Contacts: *Dr Eurwyn Williams (Curator); Gwylan Williams (Head of Personnel); Mark Humphries (Commercial Manager); Onllwyn Brace (Marketing Manager)*
Training: *F/T operations staff and F/T management are trained in-house and externally and on specific courses*

Marketing
Annual event(s): *May fair, harvest festival, Christmas tree*
Sponsor: *South Wales Electricity*
Other: *press office; market research*
UK promotion: *television; national newspapers; radio; local newspapers; regional tourist board; leaflets/information packs; Wales Tourist Board*
Europe/USA promotion: *leaflets/brochures; travel agents' brochures*

WELSH HIGHLAND RAILWAY
(limited company)
narrow gauge railway

Established: *1980*
Address: *Portmadog, Gwynedd, LL49 9DY*
Telephone: *(0766) 513402. Fax: (051) 608 2696*
Access: *(road) A487 (rail) Portmadog*
Parking capacity: *(cars) 50 (coaches) 3*
Hours: *Easter to Nov – 10am to 5.30pm daily*
Admission (1992): *adults £1.00; children £0.50; OAP £0.50; family ticket £2.50*
No. visitors (1992): *18 000*

Facilities
Interpretation: *leaflets; audio tapes; information boards; tour guides; guide books*
Schools: *maximum no. 50; educational literature; lecture/talk*
Disabled: *easy access; helpers*
Catering: *2 picnic areas*
Retailing: *postcards/inexpensive souvenirs; confectionery and ice cream; books; railway books/videos, models*
No. shops: *1*

Operations
Contacts: *Les Blackwell (Treasurer); David Allen (Commercial Director/Publicity Officer)*
Training: *P/T operations staff and casual operations staff are trained in-house and on specific courses and all staff/volunteers using videos and handbooks*
Languages spoken: *Welsh*

Marketing
Annual event(s): *Vale of Ffestiniog steam gala*
Affiliations: *Association of Railways Conservation Societies and Tourist Organisations, Great Little Trains*
Other: *press office; market research*
UK promotion: *local newspapers; other attractions; leaflets/information packs*

WELSH SLATE MUSEUM
(local authority run)
museum

Established: *1971*
Address: *Gilfach Ddu, Llanberis, Gwynedd*
Telephone: *(0286) 870630. Fax: (0286) 871331*
Access: *(road) A5/A55 (rail) Bangor*
Parking capacity: *(cars) 150 (coaches) 10*
Hours: *Easter to Sept – 9.30am to 5.30pm daily. Other times by arrangement*
Admission (1992): *adults £1.50; children £0.90; OAP £0.90; student £0.90*
No. visitors (1992): *31 952*

Facilities
Interpretation: *videos; information boards; tour guides; guide books*
Languages: *Welsh*
Schools: *maximum no. 100; educational literature; audio/visual presentation*
Catering: *1 picnic area*
Retailing: *postcards/inexpensive souvenirs; confectionery and ice cream; craftwork; books; reproductions of famous artefacts*
No. shops: *1*

Operations
Contacts: *Dr Dafydd Roberts (Keeper); Nia Williams (Administrative Officer); Dewi Ellis (Shop Manager); John Bevan (Head of Public Services)*
No. employees: (high season) *6 full time; 4 part time* (low season) *6 full time*
Training: *F/T operations staff, F/T management and P/T operations staff are trained in-house and on specific courses and day-to-day on job*

Marketing
Press office; market research
UK promotion: *local newspapers; regional tourist board; other attractions; leaflets/information packs; North Wales Tourism*

WELSHPOOL AND LLANFAIR LIGHT RAILWAY
(limited company)
steam railway

Established: *1963*
Address: *The Station, Llanfair Caereinion, Powys*
Telephone: *(0938) 810441*
Access: (road) *M54/A458* (rail) *Welshpool*
Parking capacity: (cars) *100* (coaches) *6*
Hours: *Easter to Oct – 10.45am to 5.15pm daily*
Admission (1992): *adults £5.80; children £2.90; OAP £5.00; student £5.00*
No. visitors (1992): *27 200 (est.)*

Facilities
Interpretation: *videos; information boards; guide books*
Languages: *Japanese; Dutch; French; German*
Children: *nappy changing*
Schools: *maximum no. 150; educational literature*
Disabled: *disabled toilets; 2 coaches can take wheelchairs*
Catering: *2 picnic areas*
Retailing: *postcards/inexpensive souvenirs; confectionery and ice cream; books*
No. shops: *1*

Operations
Contact: *A Careym (General Manager)*
No. employees: (high season) *2 full time; 2 part time* (low season) *2 full time*
Languages spoken: *Welsh*

Marketing
Annual event(s): *Friends of Thomas the Tank Engine and gala weekend*
Other: *press office; market research*
UK promotion: *national newspapers; local newspapers; regional tourist board; other attractions; leaflets/information packs*

Environmental monitoring: *energy consumption; transport*

WELWYN ROMAN BATHS
(local authority run)
monument

Established: *1972*
Address: *Welwyn Bypass, Old Welwyn, Herts, AL6 9HT*
Telephone: *(0707) 271362*
Access: (road) *A1(M)/A1000* (rail) *Welwyn North*
Parking capacity: (cars) *10* (coaches) *1*
Season: *all year*
Hours: *Tues, Fri, Sat, Sun and BH – 2pm to 5pm*
Admission (1992): *adults £0.80; OAP £0.80; residents free*
No. visitors (1992): *8000*

Facilities
Interpretation: *leaflets; information boards; personnel*
Languages: *French; German*
Schools: *maximum no. 45; educational literature; educational tour*
Catering: *1 picnic area*
Retailing: *postcards/inexpensive souvenirs*
No. shops: *1*

Operations
Contact: *Sue Kirby*
No. employees: (high season) *1 full time; 4 part time* (low season) *1 full time; 4 part time*
Training: *F/T management and P/T operations staff are trained in-house and on specific courses and day-to-day on job*
Languages spoken: *Welsh*

Marketing
Affiliations: *Museums Association, AMSSEE*
Other: *market research*
UK promotion: *local newspapers; regional tourist board; other attractions; leaflets/information packs; ETB/BTA*

WESLEY'S CHAPEL
(Methodist chapel)
historic house; museum; church

Established: *1778*
Address: *49 City Rd, London, EC1Y 1AU*
Telephone: *(071) 253 2262*
Access: (road) *A501* (rail) *Moorgate*
Season: *all year*
Hours: *Mon to Sat – 10am to 4pm; Sun – after 11am service*
Admission (1992): *adults £3.00; children £1.50; OAP £1.50; student £1.50; includes house and museum*
No. visitors (1992): *10 000 (est.)*

Facilities
Interpretation: *videos; leaflets; audio tapes; information boards; slides; tour guides; guide books*
Schools: *maximum no. 50; lecture/talk*
Disabled: *easy access; disabled toilets*
Catering: *2 picnic areas*
Retailing: *postcards/inexpensive souvenirs; books; reproductions of famous artefacts*
No. shops: *1*

Operations
Contacts: *Mr P Hulme (Minister); Ms A Taylor (Curator); Mr L Dyson (Shop Manager)*
No. employees: (high season) *2 part time* (low season) *2 part time*
Languages spoken: *French; German*

Marketing
Affiliations: *MA, Area Museums Council*
Other: *market research*
UK promotion: *local newspapers; other attractions; leaflets/information packs; ETB/BTA*

Environmental monitoring: *relative humidity and temperature*

WEST HIGHLAND MUSEUM
(trust)
museum

Established: *1922*
Address: *Cameron Square, Fort William, Inverness-shire, PH33 6AJ*
Telephone: *(0397) 702169*
Access: (rail) *Fort William*
Season: *all year*
Hours: *2pm to 5pm daily. Closed Sun except July and Aug*
Admission (1992): *adults £1.00; children £0.40; OAP £0.60; student £1.00*
No. visitors (1992): *30 000 (est.)*

Facilities
Interpretation: *information boards; maps; guide books*

Schools: *maximum no. 30; no special support*
Retailing: *postcards/inexpensive souvenirs; books*
No. shops: *1*

Operations
Contact: *Ms F C Marwick (Curator)*
No. employees: (high season) *1 full time; 6 part time* (low season) *1 full time; 4 part time*
Languages spoken: *German*

Marketing
UK promotion: *local newspapers; regional tourist board; leaflets/information packs*

WEST LANCASHIRE LIGHT RAILWAY
(society)
museum; railway

Established: *1977*
Address: *Station Rd, Hesketh Bank, Nr Preston, Lancs*
Telephone: *(0772) 815581.* Fax: *(0772) 627815*
Access: (road) *M6/A59/A565* (rail) *Rufford*
Parking capacity: (cars) *60* (coaches) *5*
Season: *all year*
Hours: *Easter to Oct – Sun, Mon, Fri and BH – 12 noon to 5.30pm*
Admission (1992): *adults £1.00; children £0.50; OAP £1.00; family £2.50*
No. visitors (1992): *9500 (est.)*

Facilities
Interpretation: *leaflets; guide books*
Schools: *maximum no. 50; educational tour; lecture/talk; by appointment only*
Catering: *1 picnic area*
Retailing: *postcards/inexpensive souvenirs; confectionery and ice cream; books; railway related goods*
No. shops: *1*

Operations
Contacts: *M Spall (Traffic Manager); S Highes (Retail Manager); J Simm (Publicity Manager)*
No. employees: (high season) *15 part time* (low season) *15 part time*

Marketing
Annual event(s): *enthusiasts' gala day, Santa specials*
Other: *market research*
UK promotion: *regional tourist board; other attractions; leaflets/information packs*

WEST PARK MUSEUM
(trust)
museum

Established: *1897*
Address: *Prestbury Rd, Macclesfield, Ches*
Telephone: *(0625) 619831/613210*
Access: (road) *M6/B5087* (rail) *Macclesfield*
Season: *all year*
Hours: *Tues to Sun – 2pm to 5pm except Christmas, New Year and Good Friday*
Admission (1992): *free*
No. visitors (1992): *16 000 (est.)*

Facilities
Interpretation: *leaflets; information boards; exhibits*
Schools: *maximum no. 35; educational literature*
Disabled: *easy access; single ground floor gallery*
Retailing: *postcards/inexpensive souvenirs; books*
No. shops: *1*

Operations
Contacts: *M Stevenson (Museum Director); C Wasche (Administrative Assistant); C Wasche/ A Beard (Shop Manageress)*
No. employees: (high season) *1 part time*
Training: *F/T operations staff, F/T management, P/T operations staff, P/T management, casual operations staff and casual management are trained in-house and externally and on specific courses and day-to-day on job*
Languages spoken: *German; Spanish*

Marketing
Press office; market research
UK promotion: *regional tourist board; other attractions; leaflets/information packs; Cheshire CC, Macclesfield BC, NWTB*

Environmental monitoring: *energy consumption; hazardous materials*

WEST SOMERSET RURAL LIFE MUSEUM
(trust)
museum

Established: *1984*
Address: *The Old School, Allerford, Minehead, Somerset, TA24 6HN*
Telephone: *(0643) 862529*
Access: (road) *A39*
Parking capacity: (cars) *30*
Hours: *Apr to Oct – Mon to Sat – 10.30am to 4.30pm*
Admission (1992): *adults £0.60; children £0.25; OAP £0.60; student £0.60*
No. visitors (1992): *8000*

Facilities
Interpretation: *information boards*
Schools: *maximum no. 36; educational tour; Victorian lessons*
Catering: *1 picnic area*
Retailing: *postcards/inexpensive souvenirs*
No. shops: *1*

Operations
No. employees: (high season) *2 part time*
Training: *P/T operations staff are trained on specific courses using videos*
Languages spoken: *French; German; Spanish*

Marketing
UK promotion: *local newspapers; leaflets/information packs*

WEST WYCOMBE CAVES
limited company)
underground caves

Established: *1950*
Address: *West Wycombe, High Wycombe, Bucks*
Telephone: *(0494) 524411. Fax: (0494) 471617*
Access: (road) *M40/A40* (rail) *High Wycombe*
Parking capacity: (cars) *200* (coaches) *10*
Season: *all year*
Hours: *May to Sept – 11am to 6pm; Oct to Apr – 2pm to 5pm*
Admission (1992): *adults £2.50; children £1.25; OAP £1.25*
No. visitors (1992): *70 000 (est.)*

Facilities
Interpretation: *leaflets; audio tapes; information boards; maps; guide books*
Schools: *maximum no. 50; audio/visual presentation*
Disabled: *leaflets*
Catering: *3 picnic areas*
Retailing: *postcards/inexpensive souvenirs; confectionery and ice cream; books*
No. shops: *1*

Operations
Contacts: *Mrs Bird (Manageress); Mr Dashwood (Director)*
No. employees: (high season) *2 full time; 2 part time* (low season) *1 full time; 1 part time*

Marketing
Annual event(s): *various*
Affiliations: *HHA*
Other: *market research*
UK promotion: *radio; local newspapers; leaflets/information packs; Coach Journal*

WESTMINSTER ABBEY
(charity)
church

Established: *1065*

Address: *London, SW1P 3PA*
Telephone: *(071) 222 5152. Fax: (071) 233 2072*
Access: (rail) *Westminster*
Season: *all year*
Hours: *8am to 6pm (limited on Sun)*
Admission (1992): *adults £3.00; children £1.00; OAP £1.50; student £1.50; ub40s £1.50; prices are for royal chapels; nave and cloisters are free*
No. visitors (1992): *3 000 000 (est.)*

Facilities
Interpretation: *leaflets; audio tapes; tour guides; guide books*
Languages: *Japanese; Dutch; French; German; Italian; Spanish; Russian*
Schools: *maximum no. 25; lecture/talk; by arrangement*
Disabled: *easy access*
Retailing: *postcards/inexpensive souvenirs; confectionery and ice cream; books; reproductions of famous artefacts; London souvenirs*
No. shops: *2*

Operations
Contacts: *Rear Admiral K Snow CB (Receiver General); Mr K Oakley (Assistant Receiver General); Dr A Waller (Bookshop Manager); Ms E St John-Smith (Press Secretary)*
Training: *F/T operations staff and P/T operations staff are trained in-house and day-to-day on job*

Marketing
Press office; market research
UK promotion: *national newspapers; local newspapers; leaflets/information packs*
USA/BTA promotion: *leaflets/brochures; British Tourist Authority*

Environmental monitoring: *waste*

WESTMINSTER CATHEDRAL
(charity)
church

Established: *1903*
Address: *(Postal), 42 Francis St, London, SW1P 1QW*
Telephone: *(071) 834 7452. Fax: (071) 834 4257*
Access: (rail) *Victoria*
Season: *all year*
Hours: *7am to 8pm daily; BH – 8am to 4.30pm*
Admission (1992): *free*
No. visitors (1992): *500 000 (est.)*

Facilities
Interpretation: *leaflets; guide books; chaplain may give a faith tour*
Schools: *maximum no. 30; lecture/talk*
Disabled: *easy access*
Retailing: *postcards/inexpensive souvenirs; craftwork; religious objects*
No. shops: *1*

Operations
Contacts: *Revd Mgr P O'Donoghue (Administrator); Mr M Volkes (Manager)*
No. employees: (high season) *50 full time* (low season) *50 full time*
Training: *F/T operations staff are trained in-house and day-to-day on job*
Languages spoken: *French; German; Italian; Spanish; Japanese; Welsh*

Marketing
Annual event(s): *Christmas celebration and others*
Sponsor(s): *various*
UK promotion: *national newspapers; local newspapers; ETB/BTA*

WETHERIGGS COUNTRY POTTERY
(sole proprietor)
heritage centre; garden; museum; working pottery

Established: *1855*
Address: *Clifton Dykes, Penrith, Cumbria, CA10 2PH*
Telephone: *(0768) 62946. Fax: (0768) 899472*
Access: (road) *M6/A66* (rail) *Penrith*

Parking capacity: (cars) *200* (coaches) *6*
Season: *all year*
Hours: *10am to 6pm daily*
Admission (1992): *adults £2.50; children £1.00; OAP £1.00; student £1.00*
No. visitors (1992): *50 000 (est.)*

Facilities
Interpretation: *videos; leaflets; information boards; maps; guide books*
Children: *adventure playground; play area; nappy changing*
Schools: *maximum no. 15; educational literature; audio/visual presentation; lecture/talk; pottery making*
Disabled: *easy access; helpers*
Catering: *1 picnic area*
Retailing: *postcards/inexpensive souvenirs; confectionery and ice cream; craftwork; books; clothes*
No. shops: *1*

Operations
Contacts: *Chris Merchant (Chief Executive); Shelly Daly (Administrator)*
No. employees: (high season) *9 full time; 6 part time* (low season) *7 full time; 1 part time*
Training: *F/T operations staff, F/T management, P/T operations staff and casual operations staff are trained in-house and externally and on specific courses and day-to-day on job*

Marketing
Annual event(s): *steam event*
Other: *market research*
UK promotion: *radio; local newspapers; regional tourist board; other attractions; leaflets/information packs; ETB/BTA*

WETLANDS WATERFOWL RESERVE
(private company)
zoo/wildlife attraction

Established: *1982*
Address: *Sutton Cum Lound, Retford, Notts*
Telephone: *(0777) 818099*
Access: (road) *A638*
Parking capacity: (cars) *150* (coaches) *20*
Season: *all year*
Hours: *summer – 10am to 5.30pm; winter – 10am to dusk*
Admission (1992): *adults £1.50; children £1.00; OAP £1.00; student £1.00; disabled half price*
No. visitors (1992): *20 000 (est.)*

Facilities
Interpretation: *leaflets; tour guides*
Children: *adventure playground; play area*
Schools: *educational literature; lecture/talk; by arrangement*
Disabled: *easy access*
Catering: *3 picnic areas*
Retailing: *postcards/inexpensive souvenirs; confectionery and ice cream; craftwork*
No. shops: *1*

Operations
Contacts: *Mr J Oxford (owner)*
No. employees: (high season) *2 full time; 1 part time* (low season) *2 full time*
Languages spoken: *French*

Marketing
UK promotion: *national newspapers; local newspapers; regional tourist board; leaflets/information packs*

WEYMOUTH SEA LIFE PARK
(limited company)
zoo/wildlife attraction

Established: *1982*
Address: *Lodmoor Country Park, Weymouth, Dorset, DT4 7SX*
Telephone: *(0305) 761070. Fax: (0305) 760165*
Access: (road) *A352/A353/A354* (rail) *Weymouth*

Season: *all year*
Hours: *10am to 6pm (later in summer) daily
except Christmas Day*
Admission (1992): *adults £4.35; children £2.95;
OAP £2.95; student £2.45; disabled £2.45*

Facilities
Interpretation: *videos; leaflets; audio tapes;
information boards; slides; tour guides; guide
books*
Languages: *French; German*
Children: *adventure playground; play area; nappy
changing*
Schools: *educational literature; audio/visual
presentation; lecture/talk; projects and touch
pools*
Disabled: *easy access*
Catering: *1 picnic area*
Retailing: *postcards/inexpensive souvenirs;
confectionery and ice cream; craftwork; books;
clothes*
No. shops: *2*

Operations
Contacts: *Mr N Biles (Manager); Ms N Warnock
(Shop Supervisor); Ms P Corp-Palmer
(Publicity/promotions Officer)*
Training: *F/T operations staff, F/T management,
P/T operations staff and casual operations staff
are trained in-house and on specific courses and
day-to-day on job*

Marketing
Affiliation: *Regional Tourist Board*
Other: *press office; market research*
UK promotion: *television; national newspapers;
radio; local newspapers; regional tourist board;
other attractions; leaflets/information packs;
ETB/BTA*

**WHEELWRIGHTS MUSEUM AND GYPSY
FOLKLORE COLLECTION**
(sole trader)
museum; visitor centre and working museum

Established: *1990*
Address: *Webbington, Loxton, Nr Axbridge,
Somerset, BS26 2HX*
Telephone: *(0934) 750841*
Access: (road) *M5/A38*
Parking capacity: (cars) *35* (coaches) *2*
Season: *all year*
Hours: *10am to 7pm daily*
Admission (1992): *adults £2.00; children £1.25;
OAP £1.50; student £1.50; disabled £1.50;
group rates*

Facilities
Interpretation: *leaflets; information boards; maps;
personnel*
Children: *play area*
Schools: *maximum no. 50; educational tour;
lecture/talk*
Disabled: *easy access; disabled toilets*
Catering: *1 picnic area*
Retailing: *postcards/inexpensive souvenirs;
confectionery and ice cream; craftwork; books;
models of gypsy caravans, etc.; crafts*
No. shops: *1*

Operations
Contact: *K Atkinson (Proprietor)*
No. employees: (high season) *2 full time; 2 part
time* (low season) *1 full time; 1 part time*

Marketing
Annual event: *arts and craft fair*
Affiliation: *AIM*
Other: *market research*
UK promotion: *radio; local newspapers; regional
tourist board; other attractions; leaflets/
information packs*

Environmental monitoring: *recycling; waste;
water quality; energy consumption; hazardous
materials; chemical usage; transport;
emissions*

WHINLATTER VISITOR CENTRE
(Forestry Commission)
forest centre

Established: *1977*
Address: *Braithwaite, Keswick, Cumbria*
Telephone: *(07687) 78469*
Access: (road) *B5292*
Parking capacity: (cars) *100* (coaches) *4*
Hours: *Feb to Christmas – 10am to 5.30pm daily*
Admission (1992): *admission free, car park
charge*
No. visitors (1992): *100 000 (est.)*

Facilities
Interpretation: *information boards; slides;
computers, working models, displays*
Children: *adventure playground; play area; nappy
changing*
Schools: *maximum no. 60; educational literature;
audio/visual presentation; lecture/talk, etc.*
Disabled: *disabled toilets*
Catering: *1 picnic area*
Franchisees: *Feb to Christmas – 10am to 5.30pm
daily*
Retailing: *postcards/inexpensive souvenirs;
craftwork; books; clothes; souvenirs*
No. shops: *1*

Operations
Contact: *Mr M Pearson (Head Ranger,
Recreation)*
No. employees: (high season) *2 full time; 3 part
time* (low season) *2 full time; 3 part time*
Training: *F/T operations staff, F/T management,
P/T operations staff, P/T management, casual
operations staff and casual management are
trained in-house and externally and on specific
courses and day-to-day on job*

Marketing
Market research
UK promotion: *local newspapers; regional tourist
board; other attractions; leaflets/information
packs*

Environmental monitoring: *no plastics in gift shop*

WHIPSNADE WILD ANIMAL PARK
(limited company)
zoo/wildlife attraction

Established: *1931*
Address: *Dunstable, Beds, LU6 2LF*
Telephone: *(0582) 872171.* Fax: *(0582) 872649*
Access: (road) *M1* (rail) *Luton*
Season: *all year*
Hours: *summer – 10am to 6pm daily; winter –
10am to dusk daily*
Admission (1992): *adults £6.95; children £4.95;
OAP £5.60; student £5.60; group rates*
No. visitors (1992): *500 000 (est.)*

Facilities
Interpretation: *videos; leaflets; information
boards; maps; guide books*
Children: *adventure playground; nappy changing*
Schools: *educational literature; audio/visual
presentation; educational tour; lecture/talk*
Disabled: *disabled toilets*
Catering: *1 bar/public house*
Retailing: *postcards/inexpensive souvenirs;
confectionery and ice cream; books; clothes*
No. shops: *3*

Operations
Contacts: *L Killorn (Operations Manager); C
Robinson (Marketing Manager)*
No. employees: (high season) *71 full time* (low
season) *71 full time*
Languages spoken: *French*

Marketing
Annual event(s): *Easter egg hunt, steam up
weekend, teddy bears' party, Christmas*
Other: *press office; market research*
UK promotion: *television; radio; local
newspapers; regional tourist board; leaflets/
information packs; ETB/BTA*

Environmental monitoring: *recycling; water
quality; energy consumption*

WHITBY ARCHIVES HERITAGE CENTRE
(trust)
heritage centre; museum; gallery; historic resource
and research facilities

Established: *1983*
Address: *17–18 Grape Lane, Whitby, N Yorks,
YO22 4BE*
Telephone: *(0947) 600170*
Access: (road) *A171/A174*
Season: *all year*
Hours: *10.30am to 4.30pm daily*
Admission (1992): *free*
No. visitors (1992): *30 000*

Facilities
Interpretation: *audio tapes; information boards;
maps; tour guides; guide books*
Schools: *maximum no. 50; educational literature;
lecture/talk; by arrangement*
Disabled: *not ground floor, access difficult*
Retailing: *postcards/inexpensive souvenirs;
craftwork; books; Whitby jet, photographs*
No. shops: *1*

Operations
Contact: *Mr C Waters (Director)*
No. employees: (high season) *6 full time; 20 part
time* (low season) *4 full time; 11 part time*
Training: *F/T operations staff, P/T operations
staff and casual operations staff are trained
in-house and on specific courses and day-to-day
on job*

Marketing
Annual event(s): *family history weekends and
exhibitions*
Affiliations: *Y&H Museums Council, AIM,
Captain Cook Assocation*
UK promotion: *local newspapers; regional tourist
board; other attractions; leaflets/information
packs; Yorks Out and About, A Guide to
Captain Cook Country*
Europe/Australia promotion: *family history
publications*

Environmental monitoring: *Conservation*

WHITE CASTLE
(local authority run) castle

Established: *1992*
Address: *Llantillio, Crossenvy, Nr Abergavenny,
Gwent*
Telephone: *(060085) 380*
Parking capacity: (cars) *10*
Hours: *Mar to Nov – 9.30am to 6.30pm daily*
Admission (1992): *adults £1.00; children £0.60;
OAP £0.60; student £0.60*
No. visitors (1992): *6000 (est.)*

Facilities
Interpretation: *leaflets; information boards; guide
books*
Schools: *educational literature*
Retailing: *postcards/inexpensive souvenirs*
No. shops: *1*

Operations
Contacts: *David Pitman (Site Operations
Co-ordinator); Angela Stewart (Personnel
Officer); Peter Gerring (Marketing Manager)*
No. employees: (high season) *1 full time; 1 part time*
Training: *F/T operations staff, F/T management,
P/T operations staff and casual operations staff
are trained externally and on specific courses*

Marketing
PR company: *Golley Slater PR, The Hayes,
Cardiff, S Glamorgan; press office; market
research*
UK promotion: *local newspapers; regional tourist
board; other attractions; leaflets/information
packs*
Europe/Asia/Australia/USA promotion:
leaflets/brochures; British Tourist Authority

WHITE CLIFFS EXPERIENCE, THE
(local authority run)
heritage centre; museum

Established: *1991*
Address: *Market Square, Dover, Kent, CT16 1PB*
Telephone: *(0304) 214566.* Fax: *(0304) 212057*
Access: (road) *M20/A2* (rail) *Dover Priory*
Season: *all year*
Hours: *Mar to Nov – 10am to 5pm daily; Nov to Mar – 10am to 3pm daily*
Admission (1992): *adults £4.00; children £2.50; OAP £3.50; student £4.00; school parties £2.00*
No. visitors (1992): *233 064*

Facilities
Interpretation: *videos; audio tapes; information boards; slides; maps; guide books; personnel*
Languages: *Dutch; French; German*
Children: *adventure playground; nappy changing*
Schools: *maximum no. 100; educational literature; lecture/talk; education officer available*
Disabled: *easy access; disabled toilets; helpers; other audio facilities; special signs*
Catering: *1 picnic area*
Retailing: *postcards/inexpensive souvenirs; confectionery and ice cream; books; clothes; reproductions of famous artefacts; gift items, cards, potpourri*
No. shops: *1*

Operations
Contacts: *P Pinnock (Centre Manager); S Wookey (Marketing Manager)*
No. employees: (high season) *13 full time; 39 part time* (low season) *13 full time; 30 part time*
Training: *F/T operations staff, F/T management, P/T operations staff, P/T management, casual operations staff and casual management are trained in-house and externally and on specific courses and day-to-day on job*

Marketing
Annual event(s): *various*
Other: *press office; market research*
UK promotion: *television; local newspapers; regional tourist board; other attractions; leaflets/information packs; AA, RADAR, coaching venues and excursions; ETB/BTA*
Europe/USA promotion: *leaflets/brochures; travel agents' brochures; British Tourist Authority*

Environmental monitoring: *energy consumption*

WHITE POST MODERN FARM CENTRE
(privately owned)
zoo/wildlife attraction; working farm park

Established: *1988*
Address: *Farnsfield, Nr Newark, Notts, NG22 8HL*
Telephone: *(0623) 882977.* Fax: *(0623) 883499*
Access: (road) *M1/A614*
Parking capacity: (cars) *2000* (coaches) *40*
Season: *all year*
Hours: *Mon to Fri – 10am to 5pm daily; Sat and Sun – 10am to 6pm daily*
Admission (1992): *adults £2.50; children £1.50; OAP £1.50; student £1.50; under 4s free*
No. visitors (1992): *190 318*

Facilities
Interpretation: *information boards; maps; tour guides; guide books*
Languages: *French; German*
Children: *adventure playground; play area; nappy changing; creche*
Schools: *maximum no. 900; educational literature; lecture/talk; teachers pack*
Disabled: *easy access; disabled toilets; helpers; special signs; wheelchairs free; also sign language*
Catering: *4 picnic areas*
Retailing: *postcards/inexpensive souvenirs; confectionery and ice cream; craftwork; books; clothes*
No. shops: *1*

Operations
Contacts: *Mr T Clark (owner); Mrs A Clark; Ms M Allen*

No. employees: (high season) *15 full time; 65 part time* (low season) *10 full time; 35 part time*
Training: *F/T operations staff; F/T management; P/T operations staff and casual operations staff are trained in-house and externally and on specific courses and day-to-day on job*

Marketing
Annual event(s): *craft/wildlife weekends, family fun days and barn dances*
Other: *market research*
UK promotion: *television; national newspapers; radio; local newspapers; regional tourist board; other attractions; leaflets/information packs; ETB/BTA*

WHITHORN DIG
(trust)
heritage centre

Established: *1988*
Address: *45 George St, Whithorn, Wigtownshire, DG8 8NS*
Telephone: *(09885) 508*
Access: (road) *A75*
Hours: *Easter until 31 Oct – 10.30am to 5pm daily*
Admission (1992): *adults £2.50; children £1.25; OAP £1.25; season ticket £5.00 and £2.50, family ticket £6.00; groups £2.25 and £1.15*
No. visitors (1992): *16 000 (est.)*

Facilities
Interpretation: *videos; leaflets; information boards; slides; maps; tour guides; guide books*
Languages: *French; German*
Children: *nappy changing*
Schools: *maximum no. 200; educational literature; audio/visual presentation; lecture/talk; by arrangement*
Disabled: *easy access; disabled toilets; leaflets; guide book; sign language*
Catering: *1 picnic area*
Retailing: *postcards/inexpensive souvenirs; craftwork; books; clothes; reproductions of famous artefacts*
No. shops: *1*

Operations
Contact: *Mrs C L Wilson (Project Manager)*
No. employees: (high season) *7 full time; 8 part time* (low season) *3 full time; 2 part time*
Training: *F/T operations staff, P/T operations staff and casual operations staff are trained in-house and day-to-day on job using videos and handbooks*
Languages spoken: *French; German*

Marketing
Annual event: *Whithorn lecture*
Sponsor: *Friends of the Whithorn Trust*
Affiliation: *Historic Scotland*
Other: *press office; market research*
UK promotion: *local newspapers; regional tourist board; leaflets/information packs*
Europe/USA promotion: *leaflets/brochures; British Tourist Authority*

Environmental monitoring: *recycling; water quality; hazardous materials; trees and nature trails*

WHITMORE HALL
historic house; garden

Established: *1984*
Address: *Whitmore, Newcastle under Lyme, Staffs, ST5 5HW*
Telephone: *(0782) 680 478.* Fax: *(0728) 680 906*
Access: (road) *M6/A53* (rail) *Stoke on Trent*
Parking capacity: (cars) *60* (coaches) *5*
Hours: *May to Aug – Tues and Wed*
Admission (1992): *adults £2.00; children £0.50*
No. visitors (1992): *500 (est.)*

Facilities
Interpretation: *tour guides*

Operations
Contact: *Mrs C Cavenagh–Mainwaring*

No. employees: (high season) *4 part time*
Languages spoken: *French; German*

Marketing
Affiliation: *HHA*
UK promotion: *regional tourist board; ETB/BTA; Heart of England Tourist Board*

Environmental monitoring: *hazardous materials*

WHITWORTH ART GALLERY, THE
(university owned)
gallery

Established: *1889*
Address: *University of Manchester, Oxford Rd, Manchester, M15 6ER*
Telephone: *(061) 273 4865.* Fax: *(061) 274 4543*
Access: (road) *M6/M62/M63* (rail) *Mandester Piccadilly*
Parking capacity: (cars) *35*
Season: *all year*
Hours: *Mon to Sat – 10am to 5pm (Thur – to 9pm)*
Admission (1992): *free*
No. visitors (1992): *123 100*

Facilities
Interpretation: *leaflets; information boards; maps; guide books*
Children: *nappy changing*
Schools: *maximum no. 20; educational literature; audio/visual presentation; lecture/talk; workshop*
Disabled: *easy access; disabled toilets; helpers; other audio facilities; wheelchair, outreach facilities*
Catering: *1 licensed restaurant*
Franchisees: *all year – Mon to Sat – 10am to 5pm (Thur – to 9pm)*
Retailing: *postcards/inexpensive souvenirs; craftwork; books; prints, stationery*
No. shops: *1*

Operations
Contacts: *A Smith (Director); P Hamilton (Gallery Services Officer)*
No. employees: (high season) *23 full time; 4 part time*
Training: *F/T operations staff, F/T management, P/T operations staff and P/T management are trained in-house and externally and on specific courses using videos and handbooks*
Languages spoken: *French*

Marketing
Annual event(s): *various*
Other: *press office; market research*
UK promotion: *local newspapers; art magazines*
Europe promotion: *art newspapers*

Environmental monitoring: *recycling; energy consumption; hazardous materials; chemical usage; emissions*

WILBERFORCE HOUSE
(local authority run)
historic house; museum

Established: *1906*
Address: *High St, Hull*
Telephone: *(0482) 593902.* Fax: *(0482) 595062*
Access: (road) *M62/A63* (rail) *Hull Paragon*
Parking capacity: (cars) *30*
Season: *all year*
Hours: *Mon to Sat – 10am to 5pm; Sun – 1.30pm to 4.30pm. Closed Christmas Day, Boxing Day, New Year's Day and Good Friday*
Admission (1992): *free*
No. visitors (1992): *49 894*

Facilities
Interpretation: *audio tapes; information boards; guide books; period rooms*
Languages: *Dutch*
Schools: *maximum no. 100; educational literature; audio/visual presentation; lecture/talk*
Catering: *1 picnic area*

Retailing: *postcards/inexpensive souvenirs; craftwork; books; slavery packs; English civil war related*
No. shops: *1*

Operations
Contact: *Ms J Tyler (Keeper of Social History)*
No. employees: *(high season) 10 full time*
Training: *F/T operations staff and F/T management are trained in-house and externally and on specific courses and day-to-day on job*

Marketing
Annual event(s): *various*
Sponsor(s): *various*
Other: *press office; market research*
UK promotion: *regional tourist board; other attractions; leaflets/information packs*

WILDFOWL AND WETLANDS CENTRE
(trust)
park/reserve; zoo/wildlife attraction

Established: *1975*
Address: *Washington, Tyne and Wear, NE38 8LE*
Telephone: *(091) 416 5454. Fax: (091) 416 5801*
Access: *(road) A19*
Parking capacity: *(cars) 100 (coaches) 20*
Season: *all year*
Hours: *summer – 9.30am to 5.30pm; winter – 9.30am to 4.30pm except Christmas Eve and Christmas Day*
Admission (1992): *adults £2.95; children £1.50; OAP £2.20; family ticket £7.50; group rates*
No. visitors (1992): *84 000*

Facilities
Interpretation: *leaflets; information boards; guide books; guides and slide shows by arrangement*
Children: *adventure playground; play area; nappy changing*
Schools: *educational literature; lecture/talk; schools membership scheme*
Disabled: *easy access; disabled toilets*
Catering: *1 picnic area*
Retailing: *postcards/inexpensive souvenirs; confectionery and ice cream; craftwork; books*
No. shops: *1*

Operations
Contacts: *Mr C Francis (Curator); Ms V Mordue (Shop Manager); Ms Y Irving (Marketing Officer)*
Training: *F/T operations staff, P/T operations staff and casual operations staff are trained in-house and externally and on specific courses and day-to-day on job using videos and handbooks*
Languages spoken: *French*

Marketing
Annual event(s): *various*
Other: *market research*
UK promotion: *national newspapers; local newspapers; regional tourist board; leaflets/information packs*

Environmental monitoring: *energy consumption; hazardous materials*

WILDFOWL AND WETLANDS TRUST MARTIN MERE, THE
(trust)
park/reserve; zoo/wildlife attraction

Established: *1975*
Address: *Burscough, Nr Ormskirk, Lancs, L40 0TA*
Telephone: *(0704) 895181. Fax: (0704) 892343*
Access: *(road) M6/M58/A59*
Season: *all year*
Hours: *Summer – 9.30am to 5.30pm daily; winter – 9.30am to 4.30pm daily except Christmas Eve and Christmas Day*
Admission (1992): *adults £3.50; children £1.75; OAP £2.50; student £2.50; family and group rates*
No. visitors (1992): *18 400*

Facilities
Interpretation: *leaflets; information boards; maps; tour guides; guide books*
Languages: *French; German*
Children: *play area; nappy changing*
Schools: *maximum no. 400; educational literature; audio/visual presentation; lecture/talk*
Disabled: *easy access; disabled toilets; Braille/ sound posts; other audio facilities; rest room*
Catering: *1 picnic area*
Retailing: *postcards/inexpensive souvenirs; confectionery and ice cream; craftwork; books; clothes; reproductions of famous artefacts; garden shop*
No. shops: *2*

Operations
Contacts: *P Wisniewski (Curator); L Seddon (Administrator); M Duthie (Shop Manager); E Beesley (Promotions Officer)*
No. employees: *(high season) 30 full time; 1 part time (low season) 30 full time; 1 part time*
Training: *F/T operations staff and F/T management are trained externally and on specific courses using handbooks*
Languages spoken: *French; German; Italian; Spanish*

Marketing
Press office; market research
UK promotion: *national newspapers; radio; local newspapers; regional tourist board; other attractions; leaflets/information packs; NWTB, Merseyside Tourist Board*

Environmental monitoring: *recycling; waste; hazardous materials*

WILDFOWL AND WETLANDS TRUST – WELNEY CENTRE
(trust)
park/reserve; zoo/wildlife attraction

Established: *1970*
Address: *Hundred Foot Bank, Welney, Nr Wisbech, Cambs, PE14 9TN*
Telephone: *(0353) 860711*
Access: *(road) A1101*
Parking capacity: *(cars) 80 (coaches) 3*
Season: *all year*
Hours: *10am to 5pm daily except Christmas Eve and Christmas Day*
Admission (1992): *adults £2.95; children £1.50; OAP £2.20; student £2.20*
No. visitors (1992): *32 500*

Facilities
Interpretation: *maps; guide books*
Schools: *maximum no. 60; educational literature*
Disabled: *disabled toilets; helpers*
Catering: *2 picnic areas*
Retailing: *postcards/inexpensive souvenirs; craftwork; books; clothes*
No. shops: *1*

Operations
Contacts: *Mr D Revett (Reserve Manager); Ms M Goodale (Shop Manager); Mr T Cox (Education Officer)*
No. employees: *(high season) 6 full time; 4 part time (low season) 6 full time; 2 part time*
Training: *F/T operations staff, F/T management, P/T operations staff and P/T management are trained in-house and externally and on specific courses and day-to-day on job using handbooks*

Marketing
Annual event(s): *various*
Other: *press office; market research*
UK promotion: *local newspapers; regional tourist board; leaflets/information packs*

WILLSBRIDGE MILL
(trust and charity) historic house; park/reserve; garden; mill houses and exhibitions

Established: *1986*
Address: *Avon Wildlife Trust, Willsbridge Mill, Willsbridge Hill, Bristol, BS15 6EX*

Telephone: *(0272) 326885*
Access: *(road) M4/A431/A4 (rail) Keynsham*
Parking capacity: *(cars) 50*
Season: *all year*
Hours: *nature reserve open all year; other facilities – Mar to end Oct*
Admission (1992): *adults £1.50; children £1.00; OAP £1.25; student £1.25; disabled and unwaged £1.25*
No. visitors (1992): *12 000*

Facilities
Interpretation: *leaflets; information boards; maps; tour guides; guide books; trails and routed signs*
Schools: *maximum no. 60; educational literature; hands on activities*
Disabled: *easy access; disabled toilets; helpers; special signs*
Catering: *2 picnic areas*
Retailing: *postcards/inexpensive souvenirs; craftwork; books; clothes*
No. shops: *1*

Operations
Contacts: *Mr C Townsend (Education Officer); Ms R Worsley (Promotions Officer)*
No. employees: *(high season) 2 full time; 2 part time (low season) 2 full time; 1 part time*
Training: *P/T operations staff are trained in-house and externally and on specific courses and day-to-day on job*

Marketing
Annual event(s): *many varied special interest days*
Sponsor(s): *NRA and Countryside Commission*
Affiliations: *Wansdyke Tourism Association*
Other: *press office; market research*
UK promotion: *television; radio; local newspapers; regional tourist board; other attractions; leaflets/information packs; Bath Tourist Office, Days Out Avon CC*

Environmental monitoring: *recycling; waste; energy consumption; chemical usage; transport; emissions*

WINCHESTER CATHEDRAL
(cathedral)
museum; gallery; church

Established: *1093*
Address: *5 The Close, Winchester, Hants, SO23 9LS*
Telephone: *(0962) 853137*
Access: *(road) M3/A34/A31 (rail) Winchester*
Season: *all year*
Hours: *7.15am to 6.30pm daily*
Admission (1992): *suggested donations*
No. visitors (1992): *400 000 (est.)*

Facilities
Interpretation: *leaflets; information boards; maps; tour guides; guide books*
Languages: *Japanese; French; German; Italian; Spanish*
Schools: *educational literature; audio/visual presentation; lecture/talk; workshops*
Disabled: *easy access; helpers; special signs; chair lift to east end*
Catering: *1 self-service cafeteria*
Retailing: *postcards/inexpensive souvenirs; craftwork; books; clothes; reproductions of famous artefacts; music, tapes, videos*
No. shops: *1*

Operations
Contacts: *Mr K Bamber (Receiver General)*
No. employees: *(high season) 20 full time; 38 part time*
Training: *F/T operations staff are trained in-house and on specific courses using handbooks*

Marketing
Annual event(s): *concerts, exhibitions and small theatre productions*
Sponsor(s): *various*
UK promotion: *local newspapers; regional tourist board; leaflets/information packs; ETB/BTA*
USA promotion: *leaflets/brochures; travel agents' brochures*

Environmental monitoring: *recycling; waste; water quality; energy consumption; chemical usage; transport; water conservation*

WINCHESTER HERITAGE CENTRE
(trust)
heritage centre

Established: *1984*
Address: *52–54 Upper Brook St, Winchester, Hants*
Telephone: *(0962) 851664*
Access: (road) *M3/A34/A33* (rail) *Winchester*
Hours: *Easter to end Oct – Tues to Sat – 10.30am to 12.30pm and 2pm to 4pm, Sun – 2pm to 4pm. Winter weekends – exhibition programme*
Admission (1992): *adults £1.00; children £0.50; OAP £0.50; student £0.50*
No. visitors (1992): *1500 (est.)*

Facilities
Interpretation: *videos; information boards*
Schools: *maximum no. 35; audio/visual presentation; lecture/talk; talk if required, quiz*
Retailing: *postcards/inexpensive souvenirs; books; Winchester video*
No. shops: *1*

Operations
Contacts: *Mr T Hunter (Centre Manager); Ms R Kinnaird–Smith; Ms G Buchanan (Marketing and Publicity Officer)*
Languages spoken: *French; German; Italian; Polish*

Marketing
Market research
UK promotion: *local newspapers; leaflets/ information packs*

WINDERMERE STEAMBOAT MUSEUM
(trust)
museum; transport heritage attraction

Established: *1977*
Address: *Rayrigg Rd, Windermere, Cumbria, LA23 1BN*
Telephone: *(05394) 45565.* Fax: *(05394) 45847*
Access: (road) *M6/A591/A592*
Parking capacity: (cars) *85* (coaches) *10*
Hours: *Easter to end Oct – Mon to Sun – 10am to 5pm*
Admission (1992): *adults £2.20; children £1.40; OAP £1.80; student £1.80; group discounts*
No. visitors (1992): *40 723*

Facilities
Interpretation: *information boards; tour guides; guide books; personnel; showcases, artefacts*
Children: *nappy changing*
Schools: *educational literature; lecture/talk*
Disabled: *easy access; disabled toilets; helpers*
Catering: *1 picnic area*
Retailing: *postcards/inexpensive souvenirs; confectionery and ice cream; craftwork; books; clothes; reproductions of famous artefacts; plants, model boats, plans; general nauticalia, jewellery*
No. shops: *1*

Operations
Contacts: *Catherine Allard (Manager); Ian Robinson (Marketing Consultant)*
No. employees: (high season) *3 full time; 40 part time* (low season) *3 full time; 40 part time*
Training: *F/T operations staff, F/T management, P/T operations staff and casual operations staff are trained in-house and day-to-day on job*

Marketing
Annual event(s): *model boat rally, classic motorboat rally, steamboat association rally*
Affiliations: *Museums Association, NW Museum and Art Gallery Service, Association of Independent Museums*
Other: *market research*
UK promotion: *local newspapers; regional tourist board; other attractions; leaflets/information packs; Coach Drivers Yearbook, group visits manuals; ETB/BTA*

WINDSOR SAFARI PARK
(limited company)
theme park; park/reserve; zoo/wildlife attraction

Established: *1970*
Address: *Winkfield Rd, Windsor, Berks, SL4 4AY*
Telephone: *(0753) 830886.* Fax: *(0753) 861045*
Access: (road) *M4/M3/B3022* (rail) *Windsor*
Parking capacity: (cars) *4000*
Season: *all year*
Hours: *Nov to Mar – 10am to 4/5pm daily; Apr to July and Sept to Oct – 10am to 5pm daily; June, July and Aug – 10am to 6/7pm daily*
Admission (1992): *adults £9.50; children £7.95; OAP £4.95; student £4.50; groups £5.95*
No. visitors (1992): *850 000 (est.)*

Facilities
Interpretation: *leaflets; maps; guide books*
Languages: *French*
Children: *adventure playground; play area; nappy changing*
Schools: *educational literature; audio/visual presentation; educational tour; lecture/talk*
Disabled: *easy access; disabled toilets; powered transport*
Catering: *1 bar/public house*
Franchisees *Nov to Mar – 10am to 4/5pm daily*
Retailing: *postcards/inexpensive souvenirs; confectionery and ice cream; craftwork; books; clothes; reproductions of famous artefacts; safari theme goods*
No. shops: *More than 4*

Operations
Contacts: *M Etches (General Manager); A Crissel (Personnel Manager); P Lowe/D Bradbury (Retail Manager/Catering Manager); J Gould (Marketing Manager)*
No. employees: (high season) *500 full time* (low season) *150 full time*
Training: *F/T operations staff, F/T management, P/T operations staff, P/T management, casual operations staff and casual management are trained in-house and on specific courses and day-to-day on job using videos*
Languages spoken: *French*

Marketing
Market research
UK promotion: *television; national newspapers; radio; local newspapers; regional tourist board; other attractions; leaflets/information packs; ETB/BTA*
Europe promotion: *British Tourist Authority*

WINE AND SPIRIT MUSEUM
(limited company)
museum

Established: *1982*
Address: *Palace Green, Berwick upon Tweed, Northumberland*
Telephone: *(0289) 305153*
Access: (road) *A1* (rail) *Berwick upon Tweed*
Parking capacity: (cars) *30* (coaches) *3*
Season: *all year*
Hours: *Apr to end Sept – Mon to Sat – 9.30am to 5pm; Oct to Mar – Mon to Fri – 9.30am to 5pm*
Admission (1992): *free*
No. visitors (1992): *50 000 (est.)*

Facilities
Schools: *maximum no. 50; lecture/talk*
Disabled: *easy access*
Catering: *1 picnic area*
Retailing: *postcards/inexpensive souvenirs; confectionery and ice cream; craftwork; mead and hand made pottery*
No. shops: *3*

Operations
Contact: *Mr R Tait (Director)*
No. employees: (high season) *6 full time; 3 part time* (low season) *5 full time; 2 part time*
Training: *F/T operations staff, P/T operations staff and casual operations staff are trained in-house and day-to-day on job using videos and handbooks*

Marketing
UK promotion: *local newspapers; regional tourist board; other attractions; leaflets/information packs; ETB/BTA*

Environmental monitoring: *recycling; chemical usage*

WISBECH AND FENLAND MUSEUM
(trust)
monument; museum; gallery

Established: *1847*
Address: *Museum Square, Wisbech, Cambs, PE13 1ES*
Telephone: *(0945) 583817*
Access: (road) *A47*
Hours: *Tues to Sat – 10am to 5pm (Oct to Mar – to 4pm)*
Admission (1992): *free*
No. visitors (1992): *19 090*

Facilities
Interpretation: *leaflets; information boards; guide books; displays*
Languages: *French*
Schools: *maximum no. 40; no special support; educational literature; lecture/talk*
Retailing: *postcards/inexpensive souvenirs; books; reproductions of famous artefacts*
No. shops: *1*

Operations
Contacts: *D Devenish (Curator); W Weston (Hon Treasurer of Friends)*
No. employees: (high season) *2 full time; 3 part time* (low season) *2 full time; 3 part time*

Marketing
Annual event: *lecture*
Affiliation: *MA*
UK promotion: *local newspapers; regional tourist board; other attractions; leaflets/information packs; ETB/BTA*

Environmental monitoring: *recycling; energy consumption; hazardous materials*

WOBURN ABBEY
(trust)
historic house

Established: *1955*
Address: *Woburn, Beds, MK43 0TP*
Telephone: *(0525) 290666.* Fax: *(0525) 290271*
Access: (road) *M1/A4012* (rail) *Bletchley/Flitwick*
Parking capacity: (cars) *4000* (coaches) *100*
Hours: *Jan to Mar – Sat, Sun and BH – 11am to 4pm; Mar to Oct – 11am to 5pm daily*
Admission (1992): *adults £5.50; children £2.00; OAP £4.00; student £4.00; handicapped £2.00*

Facilities
Interpretation: *leaflets; tour guides; guide books*
Languages: *French; German*
Schools: *maximum no. 120; educational literature; lecture/talk*
Disabled: *easy access; disabled toilets*
Catering: *1 picnic area*
Retailing: *postcards/inexpensive souvenirs; confectionery and ice cream; craftwork; books; clothes; reproductions of famous artefacts; books, pictures, gifts*
No. shops: *3*

Operations
Contact: *P A Gregory (Administrator)*
No. employees: (high season) *45 full time; 230 part time* (low season) *45 full time; 20 part time*
Training: *F/T operations staff, F/T management, P/T operations staff and casual operations staff are trained in-house and day-to-day on job*
Languages spoken: *French; Spanish; Chinese*

Marketing
Annual event(s): *various*
Affiliation: *HHA, Treasure Houses of England*

Other: *market research*
UK promotion: *local newspapers; regional tourist board; leaflets/information packs; Travel Guide, etc.; ETB/BTA*
Europe promotion: *leaflets/brochures; British Tourist Authority*

Environmental monitoring: *emissions*

WOLFERTON STATION MUSEUM
(sole trader)
historic house; museum

Established: *1977*
Address: *Wolferton, King's Lynn, Norfolk, PE31 6HA*
Telephone: *(0485) 540674*
Access: (road) *A149* (rail) *King's Lynn*
Parking capacity: (cars) *60* (coaches) *10*
Hours: *1 Apr or Easter whichever is earlier to 30 Sept*
Admission (1992): *adults £1.75; children £0.75; OAP £1.30; disabled £1.00*
No. visitors (1992): *18 000 (est.)*

Facilities
Interpretation: *tour guides; guide books; signs*
Children: *play area; nappy changing*
Schools: *maximum no. 60; educational literature*
Disabled: *easy access; helpers*
Catering: *1 picnic area*
Retailing: *postcards/inexpensive souvenirs; confectionery and ice cream; craftwork; books*
No. shops: *1*

Operations
Contacts: *R E Hedley-Walker (owner); M L P Hedley-Walker (owner)*
No. employees: (high season) *2 full time*
Training: *F/T operations staff are trained in-house and day-to-day on job*
Languages spoken: *French; German; Italian*

Marketing
UK promotion: *local newspapers; other attractions; leaflets/information packs*

Environmental monitoring: *energy consumption; chemical usage*

WOOD END MUSEUM OF NATURAL HISTORY
(local authority run)
historic house; museum

Established: *1951*
Address: *The Crescent, Scarborough, N Yorks, YO11 2PW*
Telephone: *(0723) 367326.* Fax: *(0723) 376941*
Season: *all year*
Hours: *Tues to Sat – 10am to 1pm and 2pm to 5pm. Spring BH to end of Sept – Sun – 2pm to 5pm. Open BH Mon*
Admission (1992): *free*
No. visitors (1992): *28 907*

Facilities
Interpretation: *displays*
Schools: *maximum no. 50; educational literature; by arrangement and visit*
Retailing: *postcards/inexpensive souvenirs; books; natural history related*
No. shops: *1*

Operations
Contact: *C Massey (Senior Museums Officer)*
No. employees: (high season) *4 full time* (low season) *4 full time*
Training: *F/T operations staff and F/T management are trained externally and on specific courses*

Marketing
Affiliation: *Yorks and Humbs Area Museums Council*
Other: *press office; market research*
UK promotion: *local newspapers; regional tourist board; leaflets/information packs; specialist museum journals*

Europe promotion: *leaflets/brochures; trade fairs*

WOOD GREEN ANIMAL SANCTUARY
(charity)
park/reserve; zoo/wildlife attraction; animal shelter open to the public

Established: *1986*
Address: *London Rd, Godmanchester, Cambs*
Telephone: *(0480) 830014.* Fax: *(0480) 830566*
Access: (road) *M11/A1198/A604* (rail) *Huntingdon*
Parking capacity: (cars) *2000*
Season: *all year*
Hours: *9am to 3pm daily*
Admission (1992): *free*
No. visitors (1992): *600 000 (est.)*

Facilities
Interpretation: *videos; leaflets; information boards; slides; maps; tour guides*
Children: *nappy changing*
Schools: *educational literature; audio/visual presentation; lecture/talk*
Disabled: *easy access; disabled toilets; helpers*
Catering: *1 bar/public house*
Retailing: *postcards/inexpensive souvenirs; confectionery and ice cream; craftwork; books; clothes; pet supplies*
No. shops: *3*

Operations
Contacts: *Mr G Fuller MBE (Chief Executive); Mr M Hawkins (Personnel Manager); Mr D Barnes (Retail Development Manager); Ms V Munnings (PR Officer)*
Training: *F/T operations staff, F/T management, P/T operations staff, P/T management, casual operations staff and casual management are trained in-house and externally and on specific courses and day-to-day on job*

Marketing
Annual event(s): *various*
Sponsor(s): *Pedigree Petfoods, Sherleys, etc.*
Affiliations: *World Society for the Protection of Animals*
Other: *press office; market research*
UK promotion: *national newspapers; radio; local newspapers; regional tourist board; other attractions; leaflets/information packs; ETB/BTA*
Europe promotion: *leaflets/brochures*

Environmental monitoring: *Local national history habitats*

WOODHAM CHURCH MUSEUM
(local authority run)
museum; gallery

Established: *1972*
Address: *Woodham Village, Ashington, Northumberland*
Telephone: *(0670) 817371*
Access: (road) *A819*
Parking capacity: (cars) *20*
Season: *all year*
Hours: *May to Aug – Wed to Sun and BH – 11am to 12.30pm and 1pm to 5pm; Sept to Apr – Wed to Sun and BH – 10am to 12.30pm and 1pm to 4pm*
Admission (1992): *free*
No. visitors (1992): *17 000 (est.)*

Facilities
Interpretation: *videos; leaflets; information boards*
Schools: *maximum no. 40; educational literature; lecture/talk; workshops*
Catering: *1 picnic area*
Retailing: *postcards/inexpensive souvenirs; craftwork; books; clothes*
No. shops: *1*

Operations
Contacts: *Ms P Wilkinson (Museum and Cultural Services Officer); Ms H Edward*
No. employees: (high season) *2 full time* (low season) *2 full time*

Training: *F/T operations staff are trained in-house and day-to-day on job using videos and handbooks*

Marketing
Annual event(s): *various*
UK promotion: *local newspapers; regional tourist board; other attractions; leaflets/information packs*

Environmental monitoring: *recycling; waste; water quality; energy consumption; hazardous materials; transport; emissions; wind generator and bottle banks*

WOODHORN COLLIERY MUSEUM
(local authority run)
museum; gallery

Established: *1989*
Address: *Woodhorn, Ashington, Northumberland*
Telephone: *(0670) 856968*
Access: (road) *A189*
Parking capacity: (cars) *40* (coaches) *10*
Season: *all year*
Hours: *May to Aug – Wed to Sun and BH – 11am to 5pm; Sept to Apr – Wed to Sun and BH – 10am to 4pm*
Admission (1992): *free*
No. visitors (1992): *25 000 (est.)*

Facilities
Interpretation: *videos; leaflets; audio tapes; information boards*
Languages: *German*
Schools: *maximum no. 40; educational literature*
Catering: *1 picnic area*
Retailing: *postcards/inexpensive souvenirs; books*
No. shops: *1*

Operations
Contacts: *Ms P Wilkinson (Museum and Cultural Services Officer); Ms D Bramley (Tourism Officer)*
No. employees: (high season) *4 full time; 3 part time* (low season) *4 full time; 3 part time*
Training: *F/T operations staff, F/T management, P/T operations staff, P/T management and casual operations staff and casual management are trained in-house and day-to-day on job*

Marketing
Annual event: *open day*
Sponsor: *British Alcan*
Other: *market research*
UK promotion: *local newspapers; regional tourist board; other attractions; leaflets/information packs; ETB/BTA; Holiday magazines*
Europe promotion: *leaflets/brochures; local tourist board*

WOODSIDE FARM AND WILD FOWL PARK
(limited company)
park/reserve; zoo/wildlife attraction

Established: *1987*
Address: *Farm Shop, Mancroft Rd, Aley Green, Nr Slip End, Luton, Beds, LU1 4DG*
Telephone: *(0582) 841044*
Access: (road) *M1/M25/A5/A6*
Parking capacity: (cars) *200* (coaches) *15*
Season: *all year*
Hours: *Mon to Sat – 8am to 5.30pm*
Admission (1992): *adults £1.40; children £1.10; OAP £1.10; student £1.10*
No. visitors (1992): *110 000 (est.)*

Facilities
Interpretation: *videos; leaflets; information boards; maps; tour guides*
Children: *adventure playground; play area; nappy changing*
Schools: *maximum no. 1000; educational literature; lecture/talk*
Disabled: *easy access; disabled toilets*
Catering: *5 picnic areas*
Retailing: *postcards/inexpensive souvenirs; confectionery and ice cream; craftwork; books*
No. shops: *4*

Operations
Contact: *P Jempson (owner)*
No. employees: *(high season) 10 full time; 13 part time (low season) 10 full time; 13 part time*

Marketing
Annual event(s): *various*
UK promotion: *local newspapers; regional tourist board; leaflets/information packs*

WOODSPRING MUSEUM
(local authority run)
museum

Established: *1974*
Address: *Burlington St, Weston super Mare, Avon, BS23 1PR*
Telephone: *(0934) 621028*
Access: (road) *M5/A370* (rail) *Weston super Mare*
Season: *all year*
Hours: *Tues to Sun – 10am to 5pm*
Admission (1992): *free*
No. visitors (1992): *70 000 (est.)*

Facilities
Interpretation: *static interpretative displays*
Schools: *maximum no. 60; no special support*
Disabled: *disabled toilets*
Catering: *1 snack bar/food stall*
Retailing: *postcards/inexpensive souvenirs; books*
No. shops: *1*

Operations
Contacts: *Mr P Berridge (Archaeology Officer); Mr S Davison (Museum Curator); Ms S Bingley (Shop)*
No. employees: *(high season) 5 full time; 9 part time*
Training: *F/T management, P/T operations staff, P/T management and casual operations staff are trained in-house and externally and on specific courses and day-to-day on job*

Marketing
Press office; market research
UK promotion: *local newspapers; other attractions; leaflets/information packs*

WOOLHOUSE MARITIME MUSEUM
(local authority run)
historic house; museum

Established: *1960*
Address: *Bugle St, Southampton*
Telephone: *(0703) 223941*
Access: (road) *M27* (rail) *Southampton*
Season: *all year*
Hours: *Tues to Fri – 10am to 1pm and 2pm to 5pm; Sat – 10am to 1pm and 2pm to 4pm; Sun – 2pm to 5pm*
Admission (1992): *free, hire by arrangement*
No. visitors (1992): *29 000*

Facilities
Interpretation: *videos; leaflets; information boards*
Schools: *maximum no. 40; school visits and workshops*
Retailing: *postcards/inexpensive souvenirs; books; maritime related and Titanic*
No. shops: *1*

Operations
Contacts: *Mr S Hardy (Southampton Heritage Manager); Mrs H Spillett (Research Officer)*
No. employees: *(high season) 2 full time (low season) 2 full time*
Training: *F/T operations staff are trained in-house and externally and on specific courses using videos and handbooks*

Marketing
Press office; market research
UK promotion: *local newspapers; regional tourist board*

Environmental monitoring: *internal environment*

WORDSWORTH GALLERY
(trust and sole trader)
museum; gallery

Established: *1992*
Address: *Gallows Hill, Brompton By Sawdon, Scarborough, N Yorks, YO13 9QF*
Telephone: *(0723) 863298.* Fax: *(0723) 862287*
Access: (road) *A64/A170* (rail) *Scarborough*
Parking capacity: (cars) *35* (coaches) *1*
Hours: *3 Mar to 24 Dec – Mon to Sat – 10am to 5pm, Sun – 11am to 5pm*
Admission (1992): *adults £1.00; children £0.50; OAP £1.00*
No. visitors (1992): *25 000 (est.)*

Facilities
Interpretation: *leaflets; information boards; maps; guide books; exhibitions and displays*
Children: *nappy changing*
Schools: *maximum no. 20; educational literature; lecture/talk*
Disabled: *disabled toilets*
Catering: *1 waiter/waitress served*
Retailing: *postcards/inexpensive souvenirs; books; original prints and paintings; gifts and antiques*
No. shops: *2*

Operations
Contact: *Mrs R Harrison (owner)*
No. employees: *(high season) 4 full time; 4 part time (low season) 4 full time; 3 part time*
Training: *F/T operations staff and P/T operations staff are trained in-house and day-to-day on job*

Marketing
Affiliations: *Yorks and Humbs Tourist Board*
Other: *market research*
UK promotion: *national newspapers; local newspapers; regional tourist board; other attractions; leaflets/information packs; ETB/BTA*
Europe/USA/Japan promotion: *leaflets/brochures; British Tourist Authority*

Environmental monitoring: *hazardous materials*

WORDSWORTH HOUSE
(trust)
historic house; garden

Established: *1984*
Address: *Main St, Cockermouth, Cumbria, CA13 9RX*
Telephone: *(0900) 824805*
Access: (road) *M6/A66* (rail) *Penrith/Carlisle*
Hours: *Apr to Nov – Mon to Fri – 11am to 5pm*
Admission (1992): *adults £2.40; children £1.20; free to NT members*
No. visitors (1992): *24 000*

Facilities
Interpretation: *videos; leaflets; information boards; guide books; introductory talk*
Languages: *Japanese; French; German*
Schools: *maximum no. 25; educational literature; lecture/talk*
Disabled: *Braille/sound posts*
Catering: *1 waiter/waitress served*
Retailing: *postcards/inexpensive souvenirs; craftwork; books; models of house, sheet poetry; Lake District goods*
No. shops: *1*

Operations
Contact: *David Crosbie (Regional Enterprises Manager)*
No. employees: *(high season) 2 full time; 11 part time (low season) 2 full time; 11 part time*
Training: *F/T operations staff, F/T management and P/T operations staff are trained in-house and externally and on specific courses and day-to-day on job*
Languages spoken: *French*

Marketing
Affiliations: *National Trusts for Scotland, Australia and New Zealand and Royal Oak Foundation*
Other: *press office; market research*
UK promotion: *television; national newspapers; radio; local newspapers; regional tourist board; other attractions; leaflets/information packs; ETB/BTA*

Environmental monitoring: *water quality; energy consumption; no smoking*

WORDSWORTH TRUST, THE
(trust)
historic house; garden; museum

Established: *1891*
Address: *Dove Cottage, Town End, Grasmere, Cumbria, LA22 9SH*
Telephone: *(05394) 35544/35547.* Fax: *(05394) 35748*
Access: (road) *M6/A591* (rail) *Oxenholme/ Windermere*
Parking capacity: (cars) *45* (coaches) *2*
Season: *all year*
Hours: *Feb to Jan – 9.30am to 5.30pm daily*
Admission (1992): *adults £3.70; children £1.85; OAP £3.70; student £3.70; family and group tickets*

Facilities
Interpretation: *videos; leaflets; audio tapes; information boards; maps; tour guides; guide books*
Languages: *Japanese; French*
Schools: *maximum no. 60; educational literature; audio/visual presentation; lecture/talk; guided walk in country*
Disabled: *easy access; disabled toilets*
Catering: *1 waiter/waitress served*
Retailing: *postcards/inexpensive souvenirs; craftwork; books; reproductions of famous artefacts; posters, catalogues*
No. shops: *1*

Operations
Contacts: *Dr R S Woof (Hon Secretary and Treasurer); Ms Anne Lambert (Personnel Officer); Mr Gavin Smith (Shop Manager); Mrs Sylvia Wordsworth (Marketing Officer/ Conference Manager)*
No. employees: *(high season) 30 full time; 1 part time*
Training: *F/T operations staff, F/T management, P/T operations staff, P/T management, casual operations staff and casual management are trained in-house and externally and on specific courses and day-to-day on job and induction for new staff*
Languages spoken: *French*

Marketing
Annual event(s): *winter school, book collectors conference, summer conference*
Affiliations: *Museums Association, North West Museums, Cumbria Tourist Board, North West Tourist Board*
Other: *press office; market research*
UK promotion: *regional tourist board; other attractions; leaflets/information packs; ETB/BTA*
USA/Japan Promotion: *leaflets/brochures; British Tourist Authority; England's North Country Coast*

Environmental monitoring: *recycling; waste; water quality; energy consumption; hazardous materials; chemical usage*

WORLD OF THE HONEY BEE
(privately owned)
zoo/wildlife attraction

Established: *1990*
Address: *Hebble End Works, Hebble End, Hebden Bridge, W Yorks, HX7 6HJ*
Telephone: *(0422) 845557.* Fax: *(0422) 845557*
Access: (road) *M62/A646* (rail) *Hebden Bridge*
Season: *all year*
Hours: *May to Sept – 10am to 5pm daily; Oct to May – 2pm to 5pm; winter weekends – 11am to 5pm*
Admission (1992): *adults £0.75; children £0.50*
No. visitors (1992): *10 000 (est.)*

Facilities
Interpretation: *videos; leaflets; information boards; tour guides; guide books*
Languages: *French; German*

Schools: *maximum no. 100; educational literature; audio/visual presentation; lecture/talk*
Disabled: *helpers*
Catering: *1 snack bar/food stall*
Retailing: *postcards/inexpensive souvenirs; craftwork; books; honey and bee products*
No. shops: *1*

Operations
Contact: *Mr P Kennedy (owner)*
No. employees: (high season) *1 full time; 1 part time* (low season) *1 part time*
Training: *F/T operations staff, F/T management, P/T operations staff and casual operations staff are trained in-house and externally and on specific courses and day-to-day on job using videos and handbooks*
Languages spoken: *Italian; Spanish; Arabic*

Marketing
Other: *market research*
UK promotion: *national newspapers; local newspapers; regional tourist board; other attractions; leaflets/information packs*
Europe promotion: *leaflets/brochures*

WORLD OF TOYS
(privately owned)
museum

Established: *1987*
Address: *The Purbeck Toy and Musical Box Museum, Arne House, Arne, Nr Wareham, Dorset*
Telephone: *(0929) 552018*
Access: (road) *A351*
Parking capacity: (cars) *30* (coaches) *1*
Hours: *1 Apr or Easter until end Sept – Apr to June – 1.30pm to 5pm, July and Aug – 11am to 5.30pm and Sept – 1.30pm to 5pm. Closed Sat and Mon (open BH)*
Admission (1992): *adults £1.65; OAP £0.85*
No. visitors (1992): *11 500 (est.)*

Facilities
Interpretation: *videos; leaflets*
Schools: *maximum no. 80; no special support; audio/visual presentation*
Disabled: *easy access; helpers*
Catering: *1 self-service cafeteria*
Retailing: *postcards/inexpensive souvenirs; confectionery and ice cream*
No. shops: *1*

Operations
Contacts: *Mr and Mrs B Eitches (owners)*
No. employees: (high season) *2 full time*

Marketing
Affiliations: *Dorset Museums Association, AIM*
UK promotion: *radio; regional tourist board; leaflets/information packs; ETB/BTA*

WORLDWIDE BUTTERFLIES LTD
(limited company)
historic house; zoo/wildlife attraction

Established: *1976*
Address: *Compton House, Nr Sherborne, Dorset, DT9 4QN*
Telephone: *(0935) 74608. Fax: (0935) 29937*
Access: (road) *A30* (rail) *Sherborne*
Hours: *Apr to Oct – 10am to 5pm daily*
No. visitors (1992): *75 000 (est.)*

Facilities
Interpretation: *videos; leaflets; audio tapes; information boards; guide books*
Children: *play area*
Schools: *lecture/talk; explore sheets*
Catering: *1 picnic area*
Retailing: *postcards/inexpensive souvenirs; confectionery and ice cream; craftwork; books*
No. shops: *1*

Operations
Contact: *R Goodden (Director)*
No. employees: (high season) *10 full time* (low season) *3 full time*

Training: *F/T operations staff and P/T operations staff are trained in-house and on specific courses and day-to-day on job*

Marketing
Market research
UK promotion: *national newspapers; local newspapers; other attractions; leaflets/information packs*

WORSBROUGH COUNTRY PARK
(local authority run)
park/reserve; zoo/wildlife attraction

Established: *1975*
Address: *Worsbrough, Barnsley, S Yorks, S70 5LJ*
Telephone: *(0226) 774565*
Access: (road) *M1/A61* (rail) *Barnsley*
Parking capacity: (cars) *80* (coaches) *10*
Season: *all year*
Hours: *open all year*
Admission (1992): *free*
No. visitors (1992): *150 000 (est.)*

Facilities
Interpretation: *leaflets; information boards; maps*
Schools: *maximum no. 30; educational literature*
Disabled: *easy access; disabled toilets*
Catering: *1 snack bar/food stall*
Franchisees: *open all year*

Operations
Contact: *Mr K Robertson (Senior Ranger)*
No. employees: (high season) *1 full time; 2 part time* (low season) *1 full time*
Training: *F/T operations staff and P/T operations staff are trained in-house and day-to-day on job*

Marketing
Annual event(s): *guided walks on specific subjects*
UK promotion: *leaflets/information packs*

Environmental monitoring: *recycling; waste; water quality*

WORTLEY TOP FORGE INDUSTRIAL MUSEUM
(trust)
monument; museum

Established: *1967*
Address: *Cote Lane, Thurgoland, Nr Sheffield, S Yorks*
Telephone: *(0742) 887576*
Access: (road) *M1/A616/A629*
Parking capacity: (cars) *100* (coaches) *10*
Season: *all year*
Hours: *Sun – 11am to 5pm*
Admission (1992): *adults £0.50; children £0.25; OAP £0.25*
No. visitors (1992): *2000 (est.)*

Facilities
Interpretation: *leaflets; tour guides; guide books*
Schools: *maximum no. 50; educational literature; audio/visual presentation; lecture/talk*
Disabled: *easy access; leaflets; guide book*
Catering: *1 picnic area*
Retailing: *postcards/inexpensive souvenirs*
No. shops: *1*

Operations
Contact: *K Hawley (Custodian)*

Marketing
Annual event(s): *Easter steam weekend*
UK promotion: *radio; local newspapers; regional tourist board; leaflets/information packs*

Environmental monitoring: *water quality; environmentally sensitive*

WREST PARK HOUSE AND GARDENS
(English Heritage)
historic house; monument; garden

Established: *1954*

Address: *Silsoe, Beds, MK45 4HS*
Telephone: *(0525) 860152*
Access: (road) *M1/A6* (rail) *Luton*
Parking capacity: (cars) *1000* (coaches) *100*
Hours: *Apr to Sept – Sat to Sun and BH – 10am to 6pm*
Admission (1992): *adults £1.50; children £0.75; OAP £1.10; student £1.10; ub40s and handicapped £1.10*
No. visitors (1992): *35 000 (est.)*

Facilities
Interpretation: *leaflets; information boards; maps; guide books; introduction talks*
Languages: *French; Spanish*
Schools: *maximum no. 50; lecture/talk*
Catering: *1 snack bar/food stall*
Retailing: *postcards/inexpensive souvenirs; books*
No. shops: *1*

Operations
Contact: *R Clarke (Head Custodian)*
No. employees: (high season) *4 full time*
Training: *F/T operations staff and F/T management are trained in-house and externally and on specific courses*

Marketing
Annual event(s): *crafts festival, homes and gardens festival*
UK promotion: *radio; local newspapers; regional tourist board; other attractions; leaflets/ information packs*

WYE VALLEY FARM PARK
(partnership)
farm park

Established: *1986*
Address: *Goodrich, Ross on Wye, Herefordshire, HR9 6JN*
Telephone: *(0600) 890296*
Access: (road) *M50/A40* (rail) *Gloucester*
Parking capacity: (cars) *200* (coaches) *20*
Hours: *Easter to Oct – Mon to Sun – 10am to 5pm*
Admission (1992): *adults £3.00; children £2.00*
No. visitors (1992): *22 000*

Facilities
Interpretation: *videos; information boards; maps*
Children: *play area; nappy changing*
Schools: *maximum no. 300; educational literature; lecture/talk*
Catering: *1 picnic area*
Retailing: *postcards/inexpensive souvenirs; confectionery and ice cream; books*
No. shops: *1*

Operations
Contacts: *R Vaughan (Partner); S Vaughan (Partner)*
No. employees: (high season) *2 full time; 1 part time* (low season) *2 full time*
Training: *F/T operations staff, P/T operations staff and casual operations staff are trained in-house and day-to-day on job using videos and handbooks*
Languages spoken: *French; Spanish*

Marketing
Annual event(s): *ploughing*
Affiliation: *Rare Breeds Survival Trust*
Other: *press office; market research*
UK promotion: *radio; local newspapers; regional tourist board; other attractions; leaflets/ information packs; HETB; Local Guides*

Environmental monitoring: *recycling; waste*

WYMONDHAM HERITAGE MUSEUM
(trust)
museum

Established: *1984*
Address: *14A Middleton St, Wymondham, Norfolk, NR18 0AD*
Access: (road) *A11* (rail) *Wymondham*
Hours: *Easter weekend to end Sept – 2pm to 4pm (Sat – from 10am)*

Admission (1992): *adults £0.50; children £0.10;
OAP £0.25; student £0.25*
No. visitors (1992): *1500 (est.)*

Facilities
Interpretation: *information boards; tour guides*
Schools: *maximum no. 20; no special support*
Retailing: *postcards/inexpensive souvenirs*

Marketing
Affiliations: *Museums in Norfolk Group (MINE),
CPRE, Norfolk Society, Civic Trust*
UK promotion: *local newspapers; regional tourist
board; other attractions; leaflets/information
packs*

Environmental monitoring: *good countryside
behaviour*

WYTHOP MILL
(private company)
museum

Established: *1979*
Address: *Embleton, Cockermouth, Cumbria,
CA13 9YP*
Telephone: *(07687) 76394*
Access: (road) *M6/A66* (rail) *Penrith/Carlisle*
Parking capacity: (cars) *8*
Hours: *Apr to Oct – Tues to Sun – 10.30am to
5.30pm; Nov to Dec – Fri to Sun – 10.30am to
4pm*
Admission (1992): *adults £1.50; children £0.70;
OAP £1.50; student £0.70*
No. visitors (1992): *7000 (est.)*

Facilities
Interpretation: *leaflets; information boards*
Schools: *maximum no. 20; educational literature*
Catering: *1 waiter/waitress served*

Operations
Contacts: *J Sealby (owner); C Sealby (Partner)*
No. employees: (high season) *3 full time; 3 part
time* (low season) *3 full time; 2 part time*
Training: *F/T operations staff are trained in-house
and day-to-day on job*

Marketing
Affiliation: *Cumbria Tourist Board*
Other: *market research*
UK promotion: *local newspapers; regional tourist
board; other attractions; leaflets/information
packs; ETB/BTA*

Y

YORK MINSTER
(Church of England)
church

Established: 627
Address: York
Telephone: (0904) 624426
Access: (road) A1/A64 (rail) York
Season: all year
Hours: summer – 7am to 8.30pm daily; winter –
7am to 6pm daily
Admission (1992): free
No. visitors (1992): 2 250 000 (est.)

Facilities
Interpretation: leaflets; information boards; tour
guides; guide books
Languages: Japanese; Dutch; French; German;
Italian; Spanish; Swedish; Hebrew
Schools: educational literature; audio/visual
presentation; lecture/talk; education centre
Disabled: easy access; disabled toilets; Braille/
sound posts; other audio facilities; leaflets
Catering: 1 self-service cafeteria
Franchisees: summer – 7am to 8.30pm daily;
winter – 7am to 6pm daily
Retailing: postcards/inexpensive souvenirs;
craftwork; books; reproductions of famous
artefacts
No. shops: 1

Operations
Contacts: Major Gen K Bach/Mrs P Hunter
(Chapter Clerk/visitors Office); Mr G Ward
(Shop Manager); Mrs D Lee (PA to Chapter
Clerk)
No. employees: (high season) 150 full time; 70 part
time (low season) 150 full time; 20 part time
Training: F/T operations staff and P/T operations
staff are trained in-house and on specific
courses and day-to-day on job

Marketing
Affiliations: ALVA, Yorks and Humbs Tourist
Board
Other: press office; market research
UK promotion: York leaflet; ETB/BTA

Environmental monitoring: no smoking

YORKSHIRE CAR COLLECTION
(plc)
museum

Established: 1992
Address: Orange St, Keighley, W Yorks, BD21 3EJ
Telephone: (0535) 690499
Access: (road) A650
Parking capacity: (cars) 16
Season: all year
Hours: Easter to end Oct – 10am to 5pm daily.
Weekends throughout the year
Admission (1992): adults £3.00; children £2.00;
OAP £2.00; student £2.00; unemployed £2.00
No. visitors (1992): 30 000 (est.)

Facilities
Interpretation: information boards; guide books
Schools: maximum no. 100; quiz
Disabled: easy access; disabled toilets
Retailing: postcards/inexpensive souvenirs;
confectionery and ice cream; books; clothes
No. shops: 1

Operations
Contacts: Mr G Tuley (Curator); Ms A Hooley
(Personnel Manager); Ms J Tuley (Supervisor);
Mr P Downey (PR)

No. employees: (high season) 5 full time; 10 part
time (low season) 5 full time; 4 part time
Training: F/T operations staff, P/T operations
staff and casual operations staff are trained
in-house and day-to-day on job using handbooks
Languages spoken: French; German

Marketing
PR company: Lynx PR, The Rookery, Rodley
Lane, Leeds; market research
UK promotion: radio; local newspapers; regional
tourist board; other attractions; leaflets/
information packs

YORKSHIRE CARRIAGE MUSEUM
(trust)
museum; old flat mill, then flour mill

Established: 1965
Address: Yore Mill, Aysgarth Falls, Leyburn, N
Yorks
Telephone: (0748) 823725
Parking capacity: (cars) 100 (coaches) 20
Hours: Good Friday to mid Oct – 11am to 5pm
daily
Admission (1992): adults £2.00; children £0.75;
OAP £1.50; student £0.75
No. visitors (1992): 8000 (est.)

Facilities
Schools: maximum no. 40; educational literature;
by arrangement
Disabled: steps make access difficult
Retailing: postcards/inexpensive souvenirs;
confectionery and ice cream; craftwork; clothes
No. shops: 1

Operations
Contact: Mr G Shaw (owner/Curator)
No. employees: (high season) 3 part time

Marketing
UK promotion: local newspapers; regional tourist
board; leaflets/information packs; AIM; ETB/
BTA

YORKSHIRE DALES FALCONRY AND
CONSERVATION CENTRE
(privately owned)
zoo/wildlife attraction; all weather attraction

Established: 1991
Address: Crows Nest, Nr Giggleswick, Settle, N
Yorks, LA2 8AS
Telephone: (0729) 822832
Access: (road) M6/A65 (rail) Settle
Season: all year
Hours: 10am to 5.30pm daily
Admission (1992): adults £3.95; OAP £2.50;
student £2.95; school groups £3.25 (adults)
£2.00 (children)
No. visitors (1992): 100 000 (est.)

Facilities
Interpretation: videos; leaflets; information
boards; slides; tour guides; falconers
Children: adventure playground; play area; nappy
changing; creche
Schools: maximum no. 140; educational literature;
audio/visual presentation; lecture/talk
Disabled: easy access; disabled toilets; helpers;
special signs; leaflets
Catering: 1 picnic area
Retailing: postcards/inexpensive souvenirs;
confectionery and ice cream; craftwork; books;
clothes; reproductions of famous artefacts
No. shops: 2

Operations
Contact: Mrs S O'Donnell (owner)
No. employees: (high season) 7 full time; 30
part time (low season) 7 full time; 10 part
time
Training: F/T operations staff, F/T management,
P/T operations staff and casual operations staff
are trained in-house and day-to-day on job

Marketing
Annual event(s): barbecues, Christmas functions
Other: market research
UK promotion: television; national newspapers;
radio; local newspapers; regional tourist board;
other attractions; leaflets/information packs;
ETB/BTA
Europe promotion: leaflets/brochures; British
Tourist Authority

YORKSHIRE MUSEUM
(local authority run registered charity)
museum

Established: 1830
Address: Museum Gardens, York, YO1 2DR
Telephone: (0904) 629745. Fax: (0904) 651221
Access: (road) M62/A1/A64/A59 (rail) York
Season: all year
Hours: Apr to Oct – 10am to 5pm daily; Nov to
Mar – Mon to Sat – 10am to 5pm, Sun – 1pm
to 5pm
Admission (1992): adults £3.00; children £1.75;
OAP £1.75; student £1.75; prices are for
dinosaurs exhibition, special rates for groups
No. visitors (1992): 200 000 (est.)

Facilities
Interpretation: leaflets; information boards; guide
books
Languages: French; German; Chinese
Children: nappy changing
Schools: maximum no. 50
Disabled: easy access; disabled toilets; helpers;
special signs
Catering: 1 picnic area
Franchisees: Apr to Oct – 10am to 5pm daily;
Nov to Mar – Mon to Sat – 10am to 5pm,
Sun – 1pm to 5pm
Retailing: postcards/inexpensive souvenirs;
confectionery and ice cream; craftwork; books;
reproductions of famous artefacts; models;
giftware
No. shops: 2

Operations
Contacts: Miss F Jones (Services Manager); Ms S
Lewis (Commercial/Marketing Officer)
No. employees: (high season) 19 full time; 16 part
time (low season) 19 full time; 11 part time
Training: F/T operations staff, F/T management,
P/T operations staff, P/T management, casual
operations staff and casual management are
trained in-house and externally and on specific
courses and day-to-day on job using videos and
handbooks

Marketing
Annual event(s): natural history exhibitions
Sponsor(s): many
Affiliations: MA
Other: press office; market research
UK promotion: national newspapers; radio; local
newspapers; regional tourist board; other
attractions; leaflets/information packs;
education, group tour, holiday and coach tour
magazines; ETB/BTA
Europe/Holland/Norway promotion: leaflets/
brochures; travel agents' brochures; British
Tourist Authority

Environmental monitoring: *conservation of birds*

YORKSHIRE WATER MUSEUM
(plc)
museum

Established: *1989*
Address: *Springhead Avenue, Willerby Rd, Hull,*
   HU5 5HZ
Telephone: *(0482) 652283*
Access: (road) *A164*
Parking capacity: (cars) *20* (coaches) *2*
Hours: *Jan to Nov – Tues to Sun and summer*
   BH – 2pm to 4pm
Admission (1992): *free*
No. visitors (1992): *6000 (est.)*

Facilities
Interpretation: *leaflets; audio tapes; information*
   boards; slides; maps; tour guides
Schools: *maximum no. 30; educational literature;*
   audio/visual presentation; lecture/talk
Disabled: *disabled toilets*
Retailing: *postcards/inexpensive souvenirs; books;*
   clothes; to support railway stock fund; to
   support water aid to 3rd world
No. shops: *1*

Operations
Contacts: *D Atkinson (Senior Keeper); E Gore–*
   Brown (Conservation and Recreation Officer)
No. employees: (high season) *2 part time* (low
   season) *2 part time*
Training: *P/T operations staff and P/T*
   management are trained in-house and
   day-to-day on job
Languages spoken: *French; German; Spanish*

Marketing
Market research
UK promotion: *local newspapers; regional tourist*
   board; other attractions; leaflets/information
   packs; ETB/BTA

Z

ZETLAND LIFEBOAT MUSEUM
(private committee)
museum

Established: *1981*
Address: *5 King St, Redcar, Cleveland*
Telephone: *(0642) 484402*
Access: (road) *A19/A174*
Hours: *May to Sept – 11am to 4pm daily. Also Easter and Boxing Day and other times by request*
Admission (1992): *free*
No. visitors (1992): *18 760*

Facilities
Interpretation: *leaflets; information boards; maps; tour guides; guide books*
Schools: *maximum no. 60; educational literature; lecture/talk*
Retailing: *postcards/inexpensive souvenirs; books; clothes*
No. shops: *1*

Operations
Contacts: *H Hurst (Curator); Ms V Robinson (Rota Secretary); Mr G Smith*
No. employees: (high season) *50 part time* (low season) *3 part time*
Training: *P/T operations staff and casual operations staff are trained in-house and day-to-day on job*

APPENDIX A
UK VISITOR ATTRACTIONS DATABASE

SUMMARY OF INFORMATION HELD PER ENTRY

Information is held on the following:

Name of attraction
RTB area
Address
Telephone no.
Fax no.
Telex no.
Type of attraction
Year opened
Road access
Rail access
Car/coach parking
Opening details
Admission charges
Size (number of visitors)
Interpretation and languages

Facilities for children
Facilities for school parties
Facilities for disabled
Catering facilities
Retail outlets and goods sold
Parent and associated companies
Contacts
Staff employed
Staff training details
Languages spoken by staff
Special events and sponsors
Affiliations
Promotion UK and overseas
Environmental policies

The following table on retailing is given as an illustrative example. Other cross-tabulations, mailing lists or groupings can be provided on request.

Percentage analysis of retailing

	Postcards and souvenirs	Confectionery/ice creams	Craftwork	Books	Clothes	Reproductions	Other related goods	Other unrelated goods
Theme park	91.18	82.35	76.47	73.53	70.59	20.59	0.00	0.00
Historic house	90.16	33.46	50.39	74.02	22.83	21.65	0.00	0.00
Castle	90.57	39.62	50.94	73.58	18.87	26.42	0.00	0.00
Monument	91.49	36.17	38.30	78.72	17.02	36.17	0.00	0.00
Heritage centre	94.44	47.78	57.78	93.33	40.00	28.89	1.11	0.00
Park/reserve	86.40	52.00	61.60	76.80	35.20	13.60	0.00	0.00
Garden	82.57	39.83	55.19	68.88	27.80	14.11	0.00	0.00
Museum	93.34	30.12	38.44	83.19	22.80	24.46	0.00	0.00
Gallery	90.48	16.33	47.62	85.03	17.69	29.93	0.00	0.00
Zoo, etc.	91.60	72.27	68.07	79.83	53.78	13.45	0.00	0.00
Church, etc.	87.78	12.22	37.78	74.44	10.00	33.33	0.00	0.00
Other	90.80	53.71	56.08	78.04	36.50	14.54	0.00	0.00

APPENDIX B
LISTING OF ATTRACTIONS BY NAME

Name	RTB Area
A Day at the Wells	South East
Abbeydale Industrial Hamlet	Yorkshire & Humberside
Abbot Hall	Cumbria
Abbotsbury Sub Tropical Gardens	Southern
Abbotsbury Swannery	Southern
Abbotsbury Tithe Barn Museum	Southern
Abbotsford	Scotland
Adlington Hall	North West
Aerospace Museum, The	Heart of England
Age Exchange Remininscence Centre	London
Albert Dock	North West
Aldeburgh Moot Hall Museum	East Anglia
Alfriston Heritage Centre & Blacksmith's	South East
Alice in Wonderland Visitor Centre, The	Wales
All Saints Church	North West
Allhallows Museum	West Country
Almond Valley Heritage Trust	Scotland
Almondell & Calderwood Country Park	Scotland
Almonry Museum	Heart of England
Alton Towers*	East Midlands
Amgueddfa'r Gogledd/Museum of the North	Wales
Ancient High House, The	Heart of England
Ancient House Museum	East Anglia
Anglesey Abbey	East Anglia
Anglesey Sea Zoo*	Wales
Animal World	North West
Anne of Cleves House Museum	South East
Appleby Castle Conservation Centre	Cumbria
Apuldram Roses	South East
Arbeia Roman Fort & Museum	Northumbria
Arbury Hall	Heart of England
Ardencraig Gardens	Scotland
Ardfearn Nursery Plant Centre	Scotland
Ardington Pottery	Thames & Chilterns
Argyll Forest Park	Scotland
Armagh County Museum	Northern Ireland
Armagh Planetarium	Northern Ireland
Arran & Argyll Transport Museum	Scotland
Arreton Manor	Southern
Art Gallery and Museum*	Scotland
Arundel Toy and Military Museum	South East
Ashmolean Museum	Thames & Chilterns
Association Gallery	London
Athelhampton House and Gardens	West Country
Atwell Wilson Motor Museum	West Country
Auchindrain Township Open Air Museum	Scotland
Auckland Castle	Northumbria
Automobilia Transport Museum	Yorkshire & Humberside
Avon Valley Country Park	West Country
Avon Valley Railway	West Country
Avoncroft Museum of Buildings	Heart of England
Ays Coughfee Hall Museum	East Midlands
Ayton Castle	Scotland
Baddesley Clinton	Heart of England
Baden Powell House Hostel	London
Badsell Farm Park	South East
Bagshaw Museum	Yorkshire & Humberside
Baird Institute Museum	Scotland
Ballance House, The	Northern Ireland
Balmoral Estates	Scotland
Bank of England Museum	London
Bankfield Museum	Yorkshire & Humberside
Bankside Gallery	London
Barleylands Farm Museum	East Anglia
Bartley Mill	South East
Barton Clay Pits*	Yorkshire & Humberside
Barton Manor Garden & Vineyards	Southern
Basildon Zoo	East Anglia
Bass Museum, Visitor Ctr & Shire Horse Stables	Heart of England
Bateman's (The National Trust)	South East
Batley Art Gallery	Yorkshire & Humberside
Battle Abbey and Battlefield of Hastings	South East
Battle of Britain Memorial Flight (Visits)	East Midlands
Bayle Museum	Yorkshire & Humberside
Beacon Country Park	North West
Beacraigs Country Park	Scotland
Bear Museum	Southern
Beatles Story, The	North West

Name	RTB Area
Beatrix Potter Gallery*	Cumbria
Beaulieu National Motor Museum, House & Abbey*	Southern
Beaumaris Gaol and Court	Wales
Beck Isle Museum of Rural Life	Yorkshire & Humberside
Bedford Museum	Thames & Chilterns
Beeston Hall	East Anglia
Bekonscot Model Village*	Thames & Chilterns
Bellfoundry Museum, The	East Midlands
Belvoir Castle	East Midlands
Bennetts Water Gardens	West Country
Bentley Wildfowl & Motor Museum	South East
Bersham Heritage Centre and Ironworks	Wales
Bessie Surtees House	Northumbria
Bethnal Green Museum of Childhood	London
Beverley Minster	Yorkshire & Humberside
Bexhill Museum of Costume & Social History	South East
Bexley Museum	South East
Bickleigh Castle	West Country
Bicton Park Gardens	West Country
Big Sheep, The	West Country
Bignor Roman Villa	South East
Bill Quay Community Farm*	Northumbria
Billingham Beck Valley Country Park	Northumbria
Binchester Roman Fort	Northumbria
Birdland	Heart of England
Birmingham Cathedral	Heart of England
Birmingham Railway Museum	Heart of England
Bishops' House	Yorkshire & Humberside
Black Country Museum	Heart of England
Blackburn Cathedral	North West
Blackburn Museum and Art Gallery	North West
Blackpool Pleasure Beach	North West
Blackshaw Farm Park	Scotland
Blair Castle*	Scotland
Blair Drummond Safari and Leisure Park	Scotland
Blaise Castle House Museum	West Country
Blenheim Palace*	Thames & Chilterns
Blickling Hall*	East Anglia
Blue Pool	Southern
Bluebell Railway, The	South East
Boat Museum, The	North West
Bod of Gremista	Scotland
Bodmin and Wenford Railway	West Country
Bodmin Town Museum	West Country
Bodnant Gardens	Wales
Bodrhyddan Hall	Wales
Bolling Hall	Yorkshire & Humberside
Bolton Abbey Estate*	Yorkshire & Humberside
Book Museum	West Country
Border History Museum	Northumbria
Botanic Centre	Northumbria
Boughton House	East Midlands
Boughton Monchelsea Place	South East
Bournemouth Heritage Transport Centre	Southern
Bowes Railway Centre	Northumbria
Bowhill House and Country Park	Scotland
Bowood House	West Country
Bradford Industrial Horses at Work Museum	Yorkshire & Humberside
Bradford on Avon Museum	West Country
Bramham Park	Yorkshire & Humberside
Branklyn Garden	Scotland
Breamore House & Museums	Southern
Brecon Beacons Mountain Centre	Wales
Bressingham Steam Museum and Gardens	Cumbria
Brighton Sea Life Centre	South East
Bristol Cathedral	West Country
Bristol Industrial Museum	West Country
Bristol Zoo Gardens*	West Country
British Engineerium Steam Museum	South East
British in India Museum	North West
Brixham Museum & History Society	West Country
Broadleas Gardens Charitable Trust	West Country
Broads Museum	East Anglia
Brodick Castle & Country Park & Goatfell	Scotland
Bromham Mill	Thames & Chilterns
Bromley Museum	London
Brooklands Museum	South East
Brookside Miniature Railway	North West
Broughton Castle	Thames & Chilterns
Browhouse Yard Museum*	East Midlands
Bruce Castle Museum	London
Bryn Bras Castle	Wales
Buckfast Butterflies & Dartmoor Otter Sanctuary	West Country
Bucklers Hard Village & Maritime Museum*	Southern
Buckleys Yesterdays World	South East
Bude Museum	West Country
Buffers	Yorkshire & Humberside
Buildings of Bath Museum, The	West Country
Bungay Castle	East Anglia
Bure Valley Railway	East Anglia

Name	RTB Area
Burnby Hall Gardens & Museum	Yorkshire & Humberside
Burns Cottage.and Museum	Scotland
Burns Monument and Gardens	Scotland
Burrell Collection*	Scotland
Burton Agnes Hall	Yorkshire & Humberside
Burton Constable Hall	Yorkshire & Humberside
Bute Museum	Scotland
Butterfly and Falconry Park, The	East Midlands
Butterfly World	North West
Butterfly World and Fountain World	Southern
Buxton Micrarium	East Midlands
Buxton Museum and Art Gallery	East Midlands
Cadbury World*	Heart of England
Cadhay	West Country
Calderglen Country Park	Scotland
Calke Abbey*	East Midlands
Cambo Country Park	Scotland
Camborne School of Mines Geological Museum	West Country
Cambrian Railway Soc. & Oswestry Cycle Museum	Heart of England
Cambridge and County Folk Museum	East Anglia
Camera Obscura	Scotland
Canongate Kirk	Scotland
Canterbury Cathedral	South East
Capel Manor	London
Capesthorne Hall	North West
Captain Cook Schoolroom Museum	Yorkshire & Humberside
Carew Castle and Tidal Mill	Wales
Carfax Tower	Thames & Chilterns
Carisbrooke Castle	Southern
Carlisle Cathedral	Cumbria
Carrick-A-Rede Rope Bridge*	Northern Ireland
Carrickferggus Castle*	Northern Ireland
Cartwright Hall	Yorkshire & Humberside
Castle Eden Walkway Country Park*	Northumbria
Castle Howard*	Yorkshire & Humberside
Cathedral Church of St Nicholas	Northumbria
Cawdor Castle	Scotland
Cecil Higgins Art Gallery and Museum	Thames & Chilterns
Cefn Coed Colliery Museum	Wales
Central Church of the Royal Air Force	London
Centre for Alternative Technology	Wales
Ceredigion Museum	Wales
Chambercombe Manor	West Country
Chard & District Museum	West Country
Charles Dickens Birthplace Museum	Southern
Charles Manning's Amusement Park*	East Anglia
Charles Rennie Mackintosh Society	Scotland
Chatelherault Country Park	Scotland
Chatsworth*	East Midlands
Chatterley Whitfield Mining Museum	Heart of England
Chavenage	Heart of England
Chelmsford and Essex, Essex Regiment Museums	East Anglia
Chelmsford Cathedral	East Anglia
Chelsea Physic Garden	London
Chesil Gallery	Southern
Chessington World of Adventures*	London
Chester Cathedral	North West
Chester Visitor Centre	North West
Chester Zoo*	North West
Chestnut Centre	East Midlands
Chettle House	Southern
Chicheley Hall	Thames & Chilterns
Child-Beale Wildlife Park*	Thames & Chilterns
Children's Farm, The	Heart of England
Chilham Castle	South East
Chillingham Castle	Northumbria
Chillingham Wild Cattle Association Ltd	Northumbria
Chiltern Open Air Museum	Thames & Chilterns
Chingle Hall	North West
Cholderton Rare Breeds Farm Park	West Country
Christ Church Cathedral*	Thames & Chilterns
Christchurch Priory	West Country
Christchurch Spitalfields	London
Christchurch Tricycle Museum	Southern
Church of St Cuthbert & Turner Mausoleum	Northumbria
Church of St Martin-Within-Ludgate	London
Church of the Holyrude Stirling	Scotland
Churchill Gardens Museum	Heart of England
Cider Museum and King Offa Distillery	Heart of England
Cilgwyn Candles Workshop and Mini Museum	Wales
Clan Macpherson Museum	Scotland
Clandon Park	South East
Clapton Court Gardens	West Country
Cluanie Deer Farm Park	Scotland
C M Booth Collection of Historic Vehicles, The	South East
Coach House Museum	Southern
Coats Observatory	Scotland
Cobham Manor Riding Centre & Country Pursuits	South East
Cockley Cley Iceni Village & Museums	East Anglia
Cockthorpe Hall Toy Museum	East Anglia

Name	RTB Area
Colchester Zoo*	East Anglia
Collection of the Worshipful Company of Clockmakers	London
Colliford Lake Park	West Country
Colne Valley Museum	Yorkshire & Humberside
Colne Valley Railway	East Anglia
Colour Museum	Yorkshire & Humberside
Combe Martin Wildlife & Dinosaur Park	West Country
Commonwealth Institute*	London
Compton Acres Gardens	Southern
Coniston Boating Centre	Cumbria
Conwy Castle	Wales
Conwy Visitor Centre*	Wales
Cooper Gallery	Yorkshire & Humberside
Corinium Museum	Heart of England
Cornish Seal Sanctuary	West Country
Cornwall Donkey & Pony Sanctuary	West Country
Corsham Court	West Country
Coton Manor Gardens	East Midlands
Cotswold Countryside Collection	Heart of England
Cotswold Motor Museum	Heart of England
Coughton Court	Heart of England
Council for the Port of Rural England	North West
County and Regimental Museum	North West
Courage Shire Horse Centre	Thames & Chilterns
Courtauld Institute Galleries*	London
Coventry Cathedral	Heart of England
Coventry Toy Museum, The	Heart of England
Crabble Corn Mill	South East
Cranmore Tower	West Country
Crombie Country Park	Scotland
Cromer Lifeboat Museum	East Anglia
Cromer Museum	East Anglia
Croxteth Hall and Country Park	North West
Cumberland Pencil Museum & Exhibition Centre	Cumbria
Cumbria Crystal Ltd*	Cumbria
Cuming Museum	London
Cyfarthfa Castle Museum, Art Gallery and Park	Wales
D H Lawrence Birthplace Museum	East Midlands
Dalemain Historic House	Cumbria
Dales Countryside Museum	Yorkshire & Humberside
Dalmeny House	Scotland
Damside Garden Herbs	Scotland
Dan-Yr-Ogof Showcaves	Wales
Darlington Museum	Northumbria
Darnaway Farm Visitor Centre	Scotland
Darnoch Cathedral	Scotland
Dartmouth Museum	West Country
Deal Castle	South East
Dean Castle & Country Park	Scotland
Denmans Garden	South East
Derby Cathedral	East Midlands
Derby Industrial Museum	East Midlands
Derby Museum and Art Gallery*	East Midlands
Derwent Walk Country Park	Northumbria
Devonshire Regiment Museum	West Country
Dewey Museum, The	West Country
Dewsbury Museum	Yorkshire & Humberside
Dick Institute	Scotland
Dickens House Museum	London
Dickens House Museum, Broadstairs	South East
Didcot Railway Centre*	Thames & Chilterns
Dinmore Manor and Gardens	Heart of England
Dinosaur Museum*	West Country
Dinosaur Safari	Southern
Dinton Pastures Country Park*	Thames & Chilterns
Dochfour Gardens	Scotland
Doddington Place Gardens	South East
Donkey Sanctuary, The	West Country
Dorset County Museum	Southern
Dorset Heavy Horse Centre	Southern
Dorset Military Museum	West Country
Down County Museum*	Northern Ireland
Drummond Castle Gardens	Scotland
Drusillas Park	South East
Duart Castle	Scotland
Duke of Cornwall's Light Infantry Museum	West Country
Dulwich Picture Gallery	London
Dunaverig Farm Life Centre	Scotland
Duncombe Park	Yorkshire & Humberside
Dunham Massey Hall and Park	North West
Dunrobin Castle	Scotland
Dunstable Downs Country Park	Thames & Chilterns
Durham Heritage Centre	Northumbria
Durham Light Infantry Museum & Art Gallery	Northumbria
Duxford Airfield*	East Anglia
Dyffryn House Conference Centre and Gardens	Wales
Dyson Perrins Museum	Heart of England
Earlshall Castle and Gardens	Scotland
Easdale Island Folk Museum	Scotland
East Anglian Railway Museum	East Anglia

Name	RTB Area
East Ham Nature Reserve	London
East Lambrook Manor Garden	West Country
East Lancashire Railway	North West
East Riddlesden Hall	Yorkshire & Humberside
Eden Camp Modern History Theme Museum*	Yorkshire & Humberside
Edinburgh Canal Centre	Scotland
Edinburgh Museum of Childhood	Scotland
Edinburgh Zoo*	Scotland
Edmondsham House & Garden	Southern
Elizabethan Exhibition Gallery	Yorkshire & Humberside
Elsham Hall Country & Wildlife Park	Yorkshire & Humberside
Elstow Moot Hall	Thames & Chilterns
Elvisly Yours Centre	London
Ely Cathedral*	East Anglia
Ely Museum	East Anglia
Embsay Steam Railway	Yorkshire & Humberside
Epping Forest District Museum	East Anglia
Erddig Hall	Wales
Erith Museum	London
Escot Aquatic Centre & Gardens	West Country
Eskdale Corn Mill	Cumbria
Ethnic Doll and Toy Museum	South East
Etruria Industrial Museum	Heart of England
Eureka! The Museum for Children	Yorkshire & Humberside
Exbury Gardens	Southern
Exeter Cathedral*	West Country
Exmoor Bird Gardens	West Country
Eyemouth Museum	Scotland
Fair Maid's House	Scotland
Falls of Clyde Nature Reserve	Scotland
Falmouth Maritime Museum	West Country
Family Heritage Museum	Northern Ireland
Famous Old Blacksmiths Shop Centre*	Scotland
Farmworld*	East Midlands
Fasque	Scotland
Felbrigg Hall	East Anglia
Felin Crewi Working Watermill	Wales
Felsted Vineyards	East Anglia
Fenny Lodge Gallery	Thames & Chilterns
Ferens Art Gallery	Yorkshire & Humberside
Ffestiniog Railway	Wales
Filey Museum	Yorkshire & Humberside
Fishbourne Roman Palace and Museum	South East
Fitzwilliam Museum*	East Anglia
Flambards Village Theme Park*	West Country
Fletcher Moss Botanical Garden	North West
Fleur De Lis Heritage Centre	South East
Flimwell Bird Park	South East
Floors Castle	Scotland
Florencecourt House	Northern Ireland
Ford Green Hall	Heart of England
Forge Mill Museum & Bordesley Abbey Vis. Ctr.	Heart of England
Formakin Estate	Scotland
Forncett Industrial Steam Museum	East Anglia
Foxfield Steam Railway	Heart of England
Freud Museum	London
Frewen College	South East
Frigate Unicorn	Scotland
Frome Museum	West Country
Frontierland Western Theme Park*	North West
Gainsborough's House	East Anglia
Gairloch Heritage Museum	Scotland
Galloway Forest Park	Scotland
Garden House, The	West Country
Gem Rock Museum	Scotland
Gibraltar Point National Nature Reserve*	East Midlands
Gladstone's Land	Scotland
Glanbarr Abbey Visitors Centre	Scotland
Glasgow Botanic Gardens	Scotland
Glasgow Vennel Museum	Scotland
Glasgow Zoo Park	Scotland
Glen Trool Visitor Centre	Scotland
Glengoulandie Deer Park	Scotland
Gloucester Cathedral*	Heart of England
Gods House Tower Museum	Southern
Golden Hill Fort	Southern
Goosedale Model Aviation Centre	East Midlands
Gorse Blossom Railway & Woodland Park	West Country
Gosford Forest Park	Northern Ireland
Gosford House	Scotland
Goss and Crested China Ltd	Southern
Graham Sutherland Gallery	Wales
Grampian Transport Museum	Scotland
Grantham Museum	East Midlands
Graves Art Gallery	Yorkshire & Humberside
Gray Art Gallery	Northumbria
Graythwaite Hall Gardens	Cumbria
Great Orme Tramway	Wales
Great Western Railway Museum	West Country
Greenwich Borough Museum	London

Name	RTB Area
Greyfriars, The	Heart of England
Greyfriars Kirk	Scotland
Grizedale Forest Park*	Cumbria
Groam House Museum Trust	Scotland
Grosvenor Museum	North West
Guildford Cathedral	South East
Guildhall Beverley	Yorkshire & Humberside
Guinness World of Records Exhibition*	London
Gullivers Kingdom	East Midlands
Gurkha Museum	Southern
Haggs Castle	Scotland
Halifax Piece Hall*	Yorkshire & Humberside
Hamerton Wildlife Centre	East Anglia
Hamilton District Museum	Scotland
Hammerwood Park	South East
Hampton Court Palace*	London
Hanbury Hall (National Trust)	Heart of England
Hancock Museum	Northumbria
Hardys Wessex Exhibition	West Country
Harlow Carr Botanical Gardens	Yorkshire & Humberside
Harris Museum and Art Gallery	North West
Harrold Odell Country Park*	Thames & Chilterns
Harrow Museum & Heritage Centre*	London
Hartlepool Maritime Museum	Northumbria
Harveys Wine Museum	West Country
Harwich Redoubt	East Anglia
Haseley Manor	Southern
Hastings Museum and Art Gallery	South East
Hastings Sea Life Centres*	South East
Hatch Court	West Country
Hatchlands Park	South East
Hatfield Forest	Thames & Chilterns
Hatfield House*	Thames & Chilterns
Havant Museum	Southern
Haverfordwest Castle Museum and Art Gallery	Wales
Heale Gardens and Plant Centre	West Country
Heaven Farm	South East
Hebden Crypt	Yorkshire & Humberside
Helmshore Textile Museums	North West
Herb Farm and Saxon Maze, The	Thames & Chilterns
Hereford Cathedral	Heart of England
Herefordshire Waterworks Museum	Heart of England
Heritage Farm Park	Northern Ireland
Heritage Motor Centre*	Heart of England
Heron Corn Mill and Museum of Papermaking	Cumbria
Hever Castle	South East
Hexham Abbey	Northumbria
High Beeches Gardens	South East
Highclere Castle	Thames & Chilterns
Hirsel, The	Scotland
Historic Dockyard Chatham, The	South East
HM Tower of London*	London
HMS Belfast*	London
HMS Victory	Southern
Hogarth's House	London
Holburne Museum & Crafts Study Centre	West Country
Holker Hall and Gardens	Cumbria
Holkham Hall	East Anglia
Hollingworth Lake Country Park	North West
Hornsea Freeport*	Yorkshire & Humberside
Hornsea Museum	Yorkshire & Humberside
Hoskins Brewery	East Midlands
Houghton Hall	East Anglia
Houghton Lodge Garden & Hydroponicum	Southern
Houghton Mill	East Anglia
Hove Museum and Art Gallery	South East
How We Lived Then Museum of Shops	South East
Howletts Zoo Park	South East
Huddersfield Art Gallery	Yorkshire & Humberside
Hughenden Manor	Thames & Chilterns
Hull and East Riding Museum	Yorkshire & Humberside
Hunterian Art Gallery	Scotland
Hutton-in-the-Forest	Cumbria
Iden Croft Herbs	South East
Iford Manor Gardens	West Country
Ilfracombe Museum	West Country
Incredibly Fantastic Old Toy Show	East Midlands
International Helicopter Museum, The	West Country
Inveraray Jail	Scotland
Inverewe Garden	Scotland
Ironbridge Gorge Museum*	Heart of England
Isle of Arran Heritage Museum	Scotland
Isle of Gigha	Scotland
Isle of Wight Rare Breeds & Waterfowl Park	Southern
Itchen Valley Country Park	Southern
Izaak Walton's Cottage	Heart of England
J.M. Barrie's Birthplace	Scotland
Jane Welsh Carlyle Museum	Scotland
Jenner Museum	Heart of England
Jervaulx Abbey	Yorkshire & Humberside

Name	RTB Area
John Moore Countryside Museum, The	Heart of England
John Wesley's Chapel	West Country
Jonah's Journey	Scotland
Jorvik Viking Centre*	Yorkshire & Humberside
Kailzie Gardens	Scotland
Keighley & Worth Valley Railway*	Yorkshire & Humberside
Kelburn Country Centre	Scotland
Kellie Castle	Scotland
Kelmscott Manor	Heart of England
Kenilworth Castle	Heart of England
Kennet Horse Boat Company	Thames & Chilterns
Kew Bridge Steam Museum	London
Kielder Forest and Castle	Northumbria
Kielder Water	Northumbria
King's Lynn Museums	East Anglia
Kingdom of the Sea	Cumbria
Kingdom of the Sea Gt Yarmouth*	East Anglia
Kingdom of the Sea Hunstanton*	East Anglia
Kings Own Scottish Borders Regimental Museum	Northumbria
Kingston Bagpuize House and Garden	Thames & Chilterns
Kingston Maurward Gardens and Farm	West Country
Kirk of St Nicholas	Scotland
Kirkcaldy Museum & Art Gallery	Scotland
Kirklees Light Railway	Yorkshire & Humberside
Knaresborough Castle & Courthouse Museum	Yorkshire & Humberside
Knole	South East
Knowsley Safari Park	North West
Lace Centre*, The	East Midlands
Lace Hall, The	East Midlands
Lackham Gardens & Agricultural Museum	West Country
Lady Lever Art Gallery	North West
Laidhay Croft Museum	Scotland
Lake District National Park Visitor Centre*	Cumbria
Land Farm Garden	Yorkshire & Humberside
Land's End*	West Country
Landmark Highland Heritage and Adventure Park	Scotland
Lanreath Folk Farm Museum	West Country
Largs Museum	Scotland
Larne Tourist Info. & Interpretation Centre	Northern Ireland
Lea Gardens	East Midlands
Lee Valley Park Farms	East Anglia
Leeds Castle	South East
Leeds City Museum	Yorkshire & Humberside
Leeds Industrial Museum	Yorkshire & Humberside
Legbourne Railway Museum	East Midlands
Leighton Buzzard Railway	Thames & Chilterns
Leighton House	London
Leith Hall	Scotland
Lennoxlove House	Scotland
Leonardslee Gardens	South East
Levens Hall and Topiary Gardens	Cumbria
Lewes Castle and Museums	South East
Lichfield Cathedral	Heart of England
Lightwater Valley Theme Park*	Yorkshire & Humberside
Lincoln Cathedral	East Midlands
Lincolnshire Light Railway & Heritage Centre	East Midlands
Lincolnshire Poultry Park, The	East Midlands
Liverpool Cathedral	North West
Liverpool Museum	North West
Llangollen Motor Museum	Wales
Llewellyn Alexander (Fire Paintings) Ltd	London
Lloyd George Museum and Highgate His Home, The	Wales
Local Interest Museum, The	North West
Lochore Meadows Country Park	Scotland
Lochwinnoch Community Museum	Scotland
Lochwinnoch Nature Centre	Scotland
Logan Botanic Garden	Scotland
London Butterfly House*	London
London Canal Museum	London
London Ecology Centre	London
London Toy and Model Museum	London
Longdale Craft Centre & Museum*	East Midlands
Longdown Dairy Farm	Southern
Longleat House and Safari Park	West Country
Longstone Heritage Centre	West Country
Look out*, The	Thames & Chilterns
Lost Gardens of Heligan, The	West Country
Lotherton Hall Bird Garden*	Yorkshire & Humberside
Lulworth Cove Heritage	Southern
Luton Museum and Art Gallery	Thames & Chilterns
Lyme Regis Experience	West Country
Lympne Castle	South East
Maes Astro Tourist Attraction	Wales
Mall Galleries	London
Malton Museum	Yorkshire & Humberside
Malvern Museum	Heart of England
Manchester Cathedral	North West
Manchester United Museum & Tour Centre	North West
Manderston	Scotland
Manningford Gardens & Nursery	West Country

Name	RTB Area
Mannington Gardens and Countryside	East Anglia
Manor Farm Country Park	Southern
Manor House Museum/Alfred East Art Gallery	East Midlands
Mapledurham House and Watermill*	Thames & Chilterns
Marazion Marine Aquarium	West Country
Marble Arch Caves*	Northern Ireland
Margam Park*	Wales
Margaret Waudby Oriental Garden	Yorkshire & Humberside
Margate Old Town Hall Local History Museum	South East
Maritime Museum	West Country
Maritime Museum Ramsgate	South East
Mark Hall Cycle Museum and Gardens	East Anglia
Marle Place Gardens and Nursery	South East
Marsh Farm Country Park*	East Anglia
Marwell Zoological park*	Southern
Marx Memorial Library	London
Maxwelton House	Scotland
McLean Museum and Art Gallery	Scotland
McLellan Galleries	Scotland
Mercer Art Gallery	Yorkshire & Humberside
Merchant's House (Little Museum)	Heart of England
Metroland*	Northumbria
Michelham Priory	South East
Midland Motor Museum	Heart of England
Mill Green Museum and Mill	Thames & Chilterns
Mill of Towie	Scotland
Milton's Cottage	Thames & Chilterns
Miniature Pony Centre	West Country
Minsmere RSPB Nature Reserve	East Anglia
Minster Church of St Cuthberga*	Southern
Minterne Gardens	West Country
Model Farm and Folk Museum	Wales
Model House Craft and Design Centre	Wales
Model Village	Heart of England
Monkey Sanctuary, The	West Country
Moors Valley Country Park	Southern
Morpeth Chantry Bagpipe Museum	Northumbria
Morwellham Quay	West Country
Mouldsworth Motor Museum	North West
Mount Edgcumbe House & Country Park	West Country
Mount Ephraim Gardens	South East
Mount Stewart House and Gardens*	Northern Ireland
Much Wenlock Museum	Heart of England
Mull & West Highland Narrow Gauge Railway	Scotland
Mullaghbawn Folk Museum	Northern Ireland
Mummies and Magic	Southern
Museum of Army Flying	Southern
Museum of Army Transport	Yorkshire & Humberside
Museum of British Road Transport	Heart of England
Museum of Childhood	Wales
Museum of Childhood, The	North West
Museum of Costume	West Country
Museum of East Anglian Life	East Anglia
Museum of English Naive Art	West Country
Museum of Fire	Scotland
Museum of Flight	Scotland
Museum of Installation	London
Museum of Kent Life	South East
Museum of Lead Mining	Scotland
Museum of London*	London
Museum of Mechanical Music	Yorkshire & Humberside
Museum of Staffordshire Regiment	Heart of England
Museum of the Cumbraes	Scotland
Museum of the Home	Wales
Museum of the Moving Image*	London
Museum of the Order of St John	London
Museum of Transport	North West
Museum of Transport*	Scotland
Musical Museum	London
Myddelton House Gardens	London
Myreton Motor Museum	Scotland
National Ambulance Museum	West Country
National Army Museum	London
National Cycle Museum	East Midlands
National Gallery*	London
National Horseracing Museum	East Anglia
National Maritime Museum	North West
National Maritime Museum Greenwich*	London
National Motorcycle Museum, The	Heart of England
National Museum of Labour History	North West
National Pinetum (Bedgebury), The	South East
National Postal Museum	London
National Railway Museum*	Yorkshire & Humberside
National Shire Horse Centre*	West Country
National Sound Archive (British Library)	London
Natural History Museum*	London
Natural World*	Southern
Naworth Castle	Cumbria
Neidpath Castle	Scotland
Nelson Museum and Local History Centre, The	Wales

Name	RTB Area
Ness Gardens	North West
New Forest Butterfly Farm	Southern
New Forest Museum and Visitor Centre	Southern
New Lanark Village	Scotland
New World Tapestry Centres	West Country
Newark Air Museum	East Midlands
Newark Museum	East Midlands
Newham Grange Leisure Farm	Northumbria
Newhaven Fort	South East
Newlyn Art Gallery	West Country
Newport Museum and Art Gallery	Wales
Newstead Abbey*	East Midlands
Nidderdale Museum	Yorkshire & Humberside
Norfolk Rural Life Museum and Union Farm	East Anglia
Normanby Hall Country Park	Yorkshire & Humberside
North Ayrshire Museum	Scotland
North Carr Lightship Anstruther Harbour	Scotland
North Cornwall Museum and Gallery	West Country
North Devon Maritime Museum	West Country
North Down Heritage Centre	Northern Ireland
North East Aircraft Museum	Northumbria
North Norfolk Railway*	East Anglia
North Woolwich Old Station Museum	London
Northbourne Court Gardens	South East
Northern Ireland Aquarium*, The	Northern Ireland
Norton Conyers	Yorkshire & Humberside
Norton Priory Museum and Gardens	North West
Norwich Castle Museum*	East Anglia
Norwich Cathedral*	East Anglia
Norwich Gallery	East Anglia
Nothe Fort	West Country
Number One the Royal Crescent	West Country
Nunnington Hall	Yorkshire & Humberside
Nunwell House & Gardens	Southern
Oakwell Hall Country Park	Yorkshire & Humberside
Oban Sea Life Centre	Scotland
Oceanarium	Wales
Offa's Dyke Association	Wales
Old Byre	Scotland
Old Crown Court and Cells	West Country
Old Dairy Farm Centre	East Midlands
Old Grammar School	Yorkshire & Humberside
Old Operating Theatre Museum	London
Old Rectory, The	Yorkshire & Humberside
Old Semeil Herb Garden	Scotland
Old Smithy Tourist Centre	Southern
Oldway Mansion	West Country
Once Brewed National Park Visitor Centre	Northumbria
Oriel Mostyn	Wales
Oriental Museum	Northumbria
Otter Trust, The	East Anglia
Our Little Farm	East Midlands
Oxburgh Hall	East Anglia
Oxfordshire County Museum	Thames & Chilterns
Oxford Story, The	Thames & Chilterns
Padstow Shipwreck Museum	West Country
Paignton & Dartmouth Steam Railway	West Country
Paignton Zoo*	West Country
Paisley Museum & Art Galleries	Scotland
Palace of Holyroodhouse*	Scotland
Palace Stables Heritage Centre, The	Northern Ireland
Pallant House	South East
Paradise Mill	North West
Paradise Wildlife Park	Thames & Chilterns
Parcevall Hall Gardens	Yorkshire & Humberside
Parham Elizabethan House & Gardens	South East
Parke Rare Breeds Farm	West Country
Parracombe Garden Railway	West Country
Parsonage Farm Rural Heritage Centre	South East
Passmore Edwards Museum	London
Paulton's Park	Southern
Paxton House	Scotland
Peatlands Park*	Northern Ireland
Peckforton Castle	North West
Pecorama	West Country
Pembroke Castle	Wales
Pencarrow	West Country
Pendle Heritage Centre	North West
Pennyarcadia	Yorkshire & Humberside
Penrhyn Castle	Wales
Pensthorpe Waterfowl Trust	East Anglia
People's Palace Museum*	Scotland
Percival David Foundation of Chinese Art	London
Peter Pan's Playground*	East Anglia
Peter Scott Gallery	North West
Peterborough Cathedral*	East Anglia
Petrie Museum of Egyptian Archaeology	London
Pettitt's Feathercraft & Animal Adventure Park	East Anglia
Pickford's House Museum	East Midlands
Pilkington Glass Museum	North West

Name	RTB Area
Plas Newydd (The National Trust)	Wales
Pleasure Beach*	East Anglia
Pleasurewood Hills American Theme Park*	East Anglia
Plymouth Dome*	West Country
Polesden Lacey	South East
Pollock's Toy Museum	London
Pollok House*	Scotland
Ponsonby Farm Park	Cumbria
Pontefract Castle	Yorkshire & Humberside
Pontefract Museum	Yorkshire & Humberside
Pontypool and Blaenavon Railway	Wales
Poole Pottery	Southern
Poole's Cavern	East Midlands
Port Lympne Zoo Park, Mansion & Gardens	South East
Port of Harwich Maritime Museum	East Anglia
Portland Castle	West Country
Portsmouth Cathedral	Southern
Portsmouth Sea Life Centre	Southern
Potters Museum of Curiosity	West Country
Powysland Museum & Montgomery Canal Centre	Wales
Preston Tower	Northumbria
Prideaux Place	West Country
Priest's Mill	Cumbria
Probus County Demonstration Garden	West Country
Provand's Lordship	Scotland
Pugney's Country Park	Yorkshire & Humberside
Pumphouse Educational Museum	London
Puppet Centre Trust	London
Puppet Theatre Museum, The	Heart of England
Quay Arts	Southern
Queen Elizabeth Country Park	Southern
Queen's Own Highlanders Regimental Museum	Scotland
Quex House & Gardens & Powell-Cotton Museum	South East
Radstock Midsomer Norton Museum	West Country
Ragged School Museum	London
Ragley Hall	Heart of England
Rare Farm Animals of Hollanden	South East
Ravenglass and Eskdale Railway*, The	Cumbria
Red House Museum Art Gallery & Gardens	Southern
Red Lodge	West Country
Regiments of Gloucestershire Museum	Heart of England
Rhondda Heritage Park	Wales
Rhyl Sea Life Centre	Wales
Riber Castle Wildlife Park*	East Midlands
Ripley's Believe it or Not	East Anglia
Ripon Cathedral*	Yorkshire & Humberside
Ripon Prison & Police Museum	Yorkshire & Humberside
Robert Owen Museum	Wales
Rochdale Art Gallery	North West
Rochester Castle	South East
Rock Circus*	London
Rock Garden and Cave	West Country
Rockingham Castle	East Midlands
Roman Baths Museum*	West Country
Roman Villa, Brading	Southern
Romany Folklore Museum & Workshop	Southern
Romney, Hythe & Dymchurch Railway	South East
Rother Valley Country Park*	Yorkshire & Humberside
Rotherfield Park	Southern
Rougemont House Museum	West Country
Royal Air Force Museum*	London
Royal Albert Memorial Museum	West Country
Royal Ancient & Monastic Church of St Paul	Northumbria
Royal Botanic Gardens Kew*	London
Royal Cornwall Museum	West Country
Royal Engineers Museum	South East
Royal Green Jackets Museum	Southern
Royal Horticultural Society Garden	West Country
Royal London Hospital Archives & Museum	London
Royal Marines Museum	Southern
Royal Museum of Scotland*	Scotland
Royal Navy Submarine Museum	Southern
Royal Observatory Visitor Centre	Scotland
Royal Pavilion, Art Gallery and Museum	South East
Royal Photographic Society	West Country
Royal Pump Room Museum	Yorkshire & Humberside
Royal Scottish Academy	Scotland
Royal Signals Museum	Southern
Royal Victoria Country Park	Southern
Royalty and Empire*	Thames & Chilterns
RSPB North Cliffs and West Light Platform	Northern Ireland
Rural Life Centre	South East
Ruskin Museum	Cumbria
Russell-Cotes Art Gallery & Museum	Southern
Rutherglen Museum	Scotland
Ruthin Craft Centre	Wales
Rydal Mount	Cumbria
Ryhope Engines Museum	Northumbria
Saffron Walden Museum	East Anglia
Salcombe Maritime & Local History Museum	West Country

Name	RTB Area
Salford Museum and Art Gallery	North West
Salisbury and South Wiltshire Museum	West Country
Salisbury Cathedral*	West Country
Sally Lunn's Refreshment House & Museum	West Country
Salt Museum, The	North West
Salvation Army International Heritage Centre	London
Sand	West Country
Sandtoft Transport Centre	Yorkshire & Humberside
Satroshere	Scotland
Savill Garden, The	Thames & Chilterns
Saxon Tower Church of St Michael	Thames & Chilterns
Scaplen's Court Museum	Southern
Scone Palace*	Scotland
Scotland Street School Museum	Scotland
Scottish Agricultural Museum	Scotland
Scottish Industrial Railway Centre	Scotland
Scottish Maritime Museum	Scotland
Scottish Mining Museum	Scotland
Scottish Whisky Heritage Centre*	Scotland
Scottish Wildlife Trust	Scotland
Scunthorpe Museum	Yorkshire & Humberside
Sea Life Centre	North West
Sea Life Centre*	Yorkshire & Humberside
Seaford Tropical Butterfly House/Gardens/Maze	Northern Ireland
Seaton Delaval Hall	Northumbria
Selby Abbey	Yorkshire & Humberside
Sellafield Visitors Centre	Cumbria
Sellet Hall Gardens	North West
Selly Manor Museum	Heart of England
Shaftesbury Abbey Museum & Ruins	Southern
Shakespeare Globe Museum	London
Shaldon Wildlife Trust	West Country
Shandy Hall	Yorkshire & Humberside
Sheffield Botanical Gardens	Yorkshire & Humberside
Sherborne Abbey	West Country
Sheriff Hutton Park	Yorkshire & Humberside
Sherlock Holmes Museum	London
Sherwood Forest Visitor Centre*	East Midlands
Shetland Croft House Museum	Scotland
Shetland Museum	Scotland
Shibden Hall	Yorkshire & Humberside
Shipwreck & Heritage Centre	West Country
Shirehall Museum	East Anglia
Shugborough	Heart of England
Shuttleworth Collection, The	Thames & Chilterns
Sidmouth Museum	West Country
Silk Museum, The	North West
Sion Hill Hall	Yorkshire & Humberside
Sir John Soane's Museum	London
Skipton Castle*	Yorkshire & Humberside
Skipton Holy Trinity Parish Church	Yorkshire & Humberside
Smugglers Adventure	South East
Smuggling Experience, The	Yorkshire & Humberside
Snibston Discovery Park	East Midlands
Snowdon Mountain Railway	Wales
Sobriety Waterways Adventure Centre & Museum	Yorkshire & Humberside
Somerset Rural Life Museum	West Country
Sooty's World	Yorkshire & Humberside
South London Art Gallery	London
South Shields Museum & Art Gallery	Northumbria
South Wales Borderers Museum, The	Wales
Southend Central Museum & Planetarium	East Anglia
Southport Railway Centre	North West
Southport Zoo and Conservation Trust	North West
Southwark Cathedral	London
Southwick Country Herb Centre	West Country
Speke Hall, The	North West
Spencer House	London
Speyside Heather/Garden Visitor Centre	Scotland
Spitbank Fort	Southern
Spitting Image Rubberworks*	London
Springburn Museum Trust	Scotland
Springhill	Northern Ireland
Spurn Lightship	Yorkshire & Humberside
SS Great Britain	West Country
SS Shieldhall	Southern
St Andrew's Cathedral (Episcopal)	Scotland
St Andrew's Cathedral Inverness	Scotland
St Andrews Botanic Garden	Scotland
St Andrews Preservation Trust Museum	Scotland
St Andrews Sea Life Centre	Scotland
St Ann's Church	North West
St Colume's Cathedral	Northern Ireland
St Edmundsbury Cathedral	East Anglia
St Fin Barre's Cathedral	Northern Ireland
St George's Cathedral	London
St George's Chapel*	Thames & Chilterns
St Giles' Cathedral	Scotland
St Ives Society of Artists	West Country
St Martin-in-the-Fields	London

Name	RTB Area
St Mary Redcliffe Church Bristol	West Country
St Mary's Episcopal Cathedral	Scotland
St Mary's Parish Church	North West
St Mary's Priory Old Malton	Yorkshire & Humberside
St Michael the Archangel Church	Yorkshire & Humberside
St Michael's Parish Church	Scotland
St Mungo's 13thc Church	Northumbria
St Nicholas Priory	West Country
St Olave's Church	London
St Paul's Cathedral	London
St Wilfrid's Church	Yorkshire & Humberside
Stags Holt Farm and Stud	East Anglia
Stained Glass Museum	East Anglia
Staintondale Shire Horse Farm	Yorkshire & Humberside
Stamford Museum	East Midlands
Stamford Shakespeare Company	East Midlands
Stanborough Park	Thames & Chilterns
Stanford Hall	East Midlands
Stanford Hall Motorcycle Museum	East Midlands
Stanstead Park	Southern
Stanway House	Heart of England
Star Cottage Garden	Southern
Steam Brewery Museum	East Midlands
Steamtown Railway Centre	North West
Stewartry Museum	Scotland
Stewarts Garden – Lands	Southern
Stockgrove Country Park	Thames & Chilterns
Stockport War Memorial and Art Gallery	North West
Stockwood Craft Museum & Gardens	Thames & Chilterns
Stott Park Bobbin Mill	Cumbria
Stourton House Garden	West Country
Stow Mill	East Anglia
Stowe Landscape Gardens	Thames & Chilterns
Strangers' Hall Museum	East Anglia
Stranraer Museum	Scotland
Stratford Butterfly Farm	Heart of England
Strawberry Hill	London
Streetlife – Hull Museum of Transport	Yorkshire & Humberside
Stromness Museum	Scotland
Strumpshaw Hall Steam Museum	East Anglia
Sudbury Hall & Museum of Childhood	East Midlands
Sudley	North West
Suffolk Regiment Museum	East Anglia
Sulgrave Manor	Thames & Chilterns
Summerlee Heritage Trust	Scotland
Sundown Kiddies Adventureland	East Midlands
Sussex Combined Services Museum	South East
Sutcliffe Gallery	Yorkshire & Humberside
Swaffham Museum	East Anglia
Swaledale Folk Museum	Yorkshire & Humberside
Swiss Garden	Thames & Chilterns
Syon Park	London
Tabely House Collection	North West
Tain and District Museum	Scotland
Tales of Robin Hood*, The	East Midlands
Talkin Tarn Country Park	Cumbria
Tallberg Taylor Gallery	London
Talnotry Cottage Bird Garden	Northern Ireland
Talyllyn Railway	Wales
Tamar Valley Donkey Park	West Country
Tamworth Castle	Heart of England
Tank Museum	Southern
Tankerness House Museum	Scotland
Tapeley Park & British Jousting Centre	West Country
Tatton	North West
Tehidy Country Park	West Country
Teifi Valley Railway	Wales
Teignmouth Museum	West Country
Tenby Museum & Picture Galery	Wales
Tewkesbury Museum	Heart of England
Thameside Complex	East Anglia
Thetford Museum	East Anglia
Thirlestane Castle	Northumbria
Threaye Gardens	Scotland
Thrigby Hall Wildlife Gardens	East Anglia
Thursford Collection*	East Anglia
Thurso Heritage Museum	Scotland
Timespan Heritage Centre	Scotland
Timothy Hackworth Victorian & Railway Museum	Northumbria
Tingwall Agricultural Museum	Scotland
Tithe Barn Museum & Arts Centre	Southern
Tiverton Castle	West Country
Tiverton Museum	West Country
Tolpuddle Martyrs Museum	West Country
Tolsey Museum	Thames & Chilterns
Torosay Castle & Gardens	Scotland
Torquay Museum	West Country
Torre Abbey	West Country
Torrington Museum	West Country
Totnes (Elizabethan) Museum	West Country

Name	RTB Area
Totnes Castle	West Country
Totnes Guildhall	West Country
Tower Bridge*	London
Tower World	North West
Town Docks Museum	Yorkshire & Humberside
Towneley Hall Art Gallery and Museum	North West
Towner Art Gallery & Local History Museum	South East
Toy and Teddy Bear Museum	North West
Trafford Ecology Park	North West
Traquair House	Scotland
Trebah Garden	West Country
Trefriw Wells SPA	Wales
Tregwynt Mill	Wales
Trenouth Farm Rare Breeds Centre	West Country
Trinity House National Lighthouse Centre	West Country
Tropical Bird Park	Southern
Tropical World*	Yorkshire & Humberside
Trowbridge Museum	West Country
Truro Cathedral*	West Country
Tudor House Museum	Southern
Tulliehouse Museum and Art Gallery	Cumbria
Tutankhamun Exhibition	West Country
Tweedhope Sheep Dogs	Scotland
Twycross Zoo*	East Midlands
Twyford Pumping Station	Southern
Ullapool Museum	Scotland
Ulster Folk and Transport Museum*	Northern Ireland
Ulster History Park, The	Northern Ireland
Ulster Museum*	Northern Ireland
University Botanic Garden	Scotland
University Gallery	Northumbria
University of Durham Botanic Garden	Northumbria
University of Hull Art Collection	Yorkshire & Humberside
University of Liverpool Art Gallery	North West
Upminster Tithe Barn Agricultural Museum	London
Valence House Museum	London
Valley Heritage Centre and Museum, The	Heart of England
Vauxhall St Peter's Heritage Centre	London
Ventnor Botanic Garden*	Southern
Victoria and Albert Museum	London
Victorian Reed Organ Museum	Yorkshire & Humberside
Viewpoint Photography Gallery	North West
Vintage Railway Carriage Museum	Yorkshire & Humberside
Vintage Toy Train Museum	West Country
Volks Electric Railway	South East
Wakefield Art Gallery	Yorkshire & Humberside
Wakefield Cathedral	Yorkshire & Humberside
Wakefield Museum	Yorkshire & Humberside
Walker Art Gallery	North West
Walkley Clogs	Yorkshire & Humberside
Walter Rothschild Zoological Museum, The	Thames & Chilterns
Waltzing Waters Ltd	Scotland
Warrington Museum and Art Gallery	North West
Warwick Castle*	Heart of England
Wat Tyler Country Park*	East Anglia
Watchet Market House Museum	West Country
Waterfowl Sanctuary and Rescue Centre, The	Thames & Chilterns
Waterfront Museum	Southern
Watermouth Castle	West Country
Weald and Downland Open Air Museum	South East
Welch Regiment Museum, The	Wales
Wellesbourne Aviation Group	Heart of England
Wells & Walsingham Light Railway	East Anglia
Wells Cathedral*	West Country
Wells Museum	West Country
Welsh Folk Museum*	Wales
Welsh Highland Railway	Wales
Welsh Slate Museum	Wales
Welshpool and Llanfair Light Railway	Wales
Welwyn Roman Baths	Thames & Chilterns
Wesley's Chapel	London
West Highland Museum	Scotland
West Lancashire Light Railway	North West
West Park Museum	North West
West Somerset Rural Life Museum	West Country
West Wycombe Caves	Thames & Chilterns
Westminster Abbey*	London
Westminster Cathedral*	London
Wetheriggs Country Pottery	Cumbria
Wetlands Waterfowl Reserve	East Midlands
Weymouth Sea Life Park	Southern
Wheelwrights Museum & Gypsy Folklore Collection	West Country
Whinlatter Visitor Centre*	Cumbria
Whipsnade Wild Animal Park*	Thames & Chilterns
Whitby Archives Heritage Centre	Yorkshire & Humberside
White Castle	Wales
White Cliffs Experience, The	South East
White Post Modern Farm Centre*	East Midlands
Whithorn Dig	Scotland
Whitmore Hall	Heart of England

Name	RTB Area
Whitworth Art Gallery, The	North West
Wilberforce House	Yorkshire & Humberside
Wildfowl & Wetlands Centre	Northumbria
Wildfowl & Wetlands Trust, Martin Mere, The	North West
Wildfowl & Wetlands Trust – Welney Centre	East Anglia
Willsbridge Mill	West Country
Winchester Cathedral	Southern
Winchester Heritage Centre	Southern
Windermere Steamboat Museum*	Cumbria
Windsor Safari Park*	Thames & Chilterns
Wine and Spirit Museum	Northumbria
Wisbech & Fenland Museum	East Anglia
Woburn Abbey	Thames & Chilterns
Wolferton Station Museum	East Anglia
Wood End Museum of Natural History	Yorkshire & Humberside
Wood Green Animal Sanctuary*	East Anglia
Woodham Church Museum	Northumbria
Woodhorn Colliery Museum	Northumbria
Woodside Farm & Wild Fowl Park	Thames & Chilterns
Woodspring Museum	West Country
Woolhouse Maritime Museum	Southern
Wordsworth Gallery	Yorkshire & Humberside
Wordsworth House	Cumbria
Wordsworth Trust, The	Cumbria
World of the Honey Bee	Yorkshire & Humberside
World of Toys	Southern
Worldwide Butterflies Ltd	West Country
Worsbrough Country Park*	Yorkshire & Humberside
Wortley Top Forge Industrial Museum	Yorkshire & Humberside
Wrest Park House and Gardens	Thames & Chilterns
Wye Valley Farm Park	Heart of England
Wymondham Heritage Museum	East Anglia
Wythop Mill	Cumbria
York Minster*	Yorkshire & Humberside
Yorkshire Car Collection	Yorkshire & Humberside
Yorkshire Carriage Museum	Yorkshire & Humberside
Yorkshire Dales Falconry & Conservation Centre	Yorkshire & Humberside
Yorkshire Museum	Yorkshire & Humberside
Yorkshire Water Museum	Yorkshire & Humberside
Zetland Lifeboat Museum	Northumbria

INDEX 1
LISTING OF ATTRACTIONS BY CATEGORY

Category	Name of attraction

CASTLE

Appleby Castle Conservation Centre
Auckland Castle
Ayton Castle
Balmoral Estates
Belvoir Castle
Bickleigh Castle
Blair Castle*
Brodick Castle & Country Park & Goatfell
Bungay Castle
Carew Castle and Tidal Mill
Carisbrooke Castle
Carrick-A-Rede Rope Bridge*
Carrickferggus Castle*
Chilham Castle
Chillingham Castle
Conwy Castle
Darnaway Farm Visitor Centre
Deal Castle
Dean Castle & Country Park
Duart Castle
Dunrobin Castle
Earlshall Castle and Gardens
Floors Castle
Gosford Forest Park
Haverfordwest Castle Museum and Art Gallery
Hever Castle
HM Tower of London*

Kellie Castle
Kenilworth Castle
Kielder Forest and Castle
Knaresborough Castle & Courthouse Museum
Leeds Castle
Lewes Castle and Museums
Lympne Castle
Margam Park*
Naworth Castle
Neidpath Castle
Norwich Castle Museum*
Peckforton Castle
Pembroke Castle
Penrhyn Castle
Pontefract Castle
Portland Castle
Rochester Castle
Skipton Castle*
Tamworth Castle
The Welch Regiment Museum
Thirlestane Castle
Tiverton Castle
Totnes Castle
Warwick Castle*
Watermouth Castle
White Castle

CHURCH, ETC.

All Saints Church
Auckland Castle
Beverley Minster
Birmingham Cathedral
Blackburn Cathedral
Bolton Abbey Estate*
Bristol Cathedral
Canongate Kirk
Canterbury Cathedral
Carlisle Cathedral
Carrick-A-Rede Rope Bridge*
Cathedral Church of St Nicholas
Central Church of the Royal Air Force
Charles Rennie Mackintosh Society
Chelmsford Cathedral
Chester Cathedral
Christ Church Cathederal*
Christchurch Priory
Christchurch Spitalfields
Church of St Cuthbert & Turner Mausoleum
Church of St Martin-within-Ludgate
Church of the Holyrude Stirling
Cockley Cley Iceni Village & Museums
Coventry Cathedral
Darnoch Cathedral
Derby Cathedral
Dinmore Manor and Gardens
Durham Heritage Centre
Ely Cathederal*
Exeter Cathederal*
Gloucester Cathederal*
Greyfriars Kirk
Guildford Cathedral
Hereford Cathedral
Hexham Abbey
HM Tower of London*
John Wesley's Chapel
Kirk of St Nicholas
Lichfield Cathedral
Lincoln Cathedral
Liverpool Cathedral
Manchester Cathedral
Manor Farm Country Park
Maxwelton House

Minster Church of St Cuthberga*
Museum of the Order of St John
Norwich Cathedral*
Peterborough Cathedral*
Portsmouth Cathedral
Ripon Cathedral*
Royal Ancient & Monastic Church of St Paul
Royal London Hospital Archives & Museum
Saint Andrew's Cathedral, Inverness
Salisbury Cathedral*
Saxon Tower Church of St Michael
Selby Abbey
Sherborne Abbey
Skipton Holy Trinity Parish Church
Southwark Cathedral
St Andrew's Cathedral (Episcopal)
St Ann's Church
St Columbs Cathedral
St Edmundsbury Cathedral
St Fin Barre's Cathedral
St George's Cathedral
St George's Chapel*
St Giles' Cathedral
St Martin-in-the-Fields
St Mary Redcliffe Church, Bristol
St Mary's Episcopal Cathedral
St Mary's Parish Church
St Mary's Priory, Old Malton
St Michael the Archangel Church
St Michaels Parish Church
St Mungo's 13th Century Church
St Olave's Church
St Paul's Cathedral
St Wilfrid's Church
Stanstead Park
Truro Cathedral*
Vauxhall St Peter's Heritage Centre
Wakefield Cathedral
Wells Cathedral*
Wesley's Chapel
Westminster Abbey*
Westminster Cathedral*
Winchester Cathedral
York Minster*

GALLERY

Abbeydale Industrial Hamlet
Abbot Hall

Albert Dock
Anglesey Abbey

Category	Name of attraction

Appleby Castle Conservation Centre
Art Gallery and Museum*
Ashmolean Museum
Association Gallery
Auckland Castle
Ays Coughfee Hall Museum
Bagshaw Museum
Bankfield Museum
Bankside Gallery
Batley Art Gallery
Beatrix Potter Gallery*
Bexley Museum
Blackburn Museum and Art Gallery
Blenheim Palace*
Bowhill House and Country Park
Bromham Mill
Burton Agnes Hall
Buxton Museum and Art Gallery
Calderglen Country Park
Camborne School of Mines Geological Museum
Cartwright Hall
Cecil Higgins Art Gallery and Museum
Chesil Gallery
Cilgwyn Candles Workshop and Mini Museum
Cooper Gallery
County and Regimental Museum
Courtauld Institute Galleries*
Cranmore Tower
Cyfarthfa Castle Museum, Art Gallery and Park
Dean Castle & Country Park
Derby Museum and Art Gallery*
Dewsbury Museum
Dick Institute
Durham Light Infantry Museum & Art Gallery
Fenny Lodge Gallery
Ferens Art Gallery
Fitzwilliam Museum*
Frome Museum
Gainsborough's House
Glasgow Vennel Museum
Gosford House
Graham Sutherland Gallery
Graves Art Gallery
Gray Art Gallery
Halifax Piece Hall*
Harris Museum and Art Gallery
Haverfordwest Castle Museum and Art Gallery
Heritage Motor Centre*
Hogarth's House
Holburne Museum and Crafts Study Centre
Houghton Mill
Hove Museum and Art Gallery
Huddersfield Art Gallery
Hunterian Art Gallery
Ironbridge Gorge Museum*
Kailzie Gardens
Kirkcaldy Museum & Art Gallery
Lady Lever Art Gallery
Land Farm Garden
Leighton House
Llewellyn Alexander (Fire Paintings) Ltd
Lochwinnoch Community Museum
London Ecology Centre
Longdale Craft Centre & Museum*
Mall Galleries
Manor House Museum/Alfred East Art Gallery
Margam Park*
McLean Museum and Art Gallery
McLellan Galleries
Mercer Art Gallery
Model House Craft and Design Centre

Moors Valley Country Park
Museum of the Cumbraes
National Gallery*
Newlyn Art Gallery
Newport Museum and Art Gallery
North Ayrshire Museum
North Cornwall Museum and Gallery
Norwich Castle Museum*
Norwich Cathedral
Norwich Gallery
Oriel Mostyn
Paisley Museum & Art Galleries
Pallant House
Paxton House
Penrhyn Castle
Peter Scott Gallery
Pilkington Glass Museum
Plas Newydd "The National Trust"
Puppet Centre Trust
Quay Arts
Red House Museum Art Gallery & Gardens
Rochdale Art Gallery
Royal Botanic Gardens, Kew*
Royal Cornwall Museum
Royal Pavilion, Art Gallery and Museum
Royal Photographic Society
Royal Scottish Academy
Russel-Cotes Art Gallery & Museum
Ruthin Craft Centre
Salford Museum and Art Gallery
Somerset Rural Life Museum
South London Art Gallery
South Shields Museum & Art Gallery
Springburn Museum Trust
St Edmundsbury Cathedral
St Ives Society of Artists
St Martin-in-the-Fields
Star Cottage Garden
Stockport War Memorial and Art Gallery
Stranraer Museum
Sudley
Summerlee Heritage Trust
Sutcliffe Gallery
Tabely House Collection
Tallberg Taylor Gallery
Tenby Museum and Picture Gallery
The Ancient High House
The Nelson Museum and Local History Centre
The Old Rectory
The Whitworth Art Gallery
Thurso Heritage Museum
Torre Abbey
Towneley Hall Art Gallery and Museum
Towner Art Gallery & Local History Museum
Tulliehouse Museum and Art Gallery
Ulster Museum*
University Gallery
University of Hull Art Collection
University of Liverpool Art Gallery
Valence House Museum
Viewpoint Photography Gallery
Wakefield Art Gallery
Walker Art Gallery
Warrington Museum and Art Gallery
Whitby Archives Heritage Centre
Winchester Cathedral
Wisbech & Fenland Museum
Woodham Church Museum
Woodhorn Colliery Museum
Wordsworth Gallery

GARDEN

Abbotsbury Sub Tropical Gardens
Alton Towers*
Anglesey Abbey
Apuldram Roses
Arbury Hall
Ardencraig Gardens
Ardfearn Nursery Plant Centre
Arreton Manor
Athelhampton House and Gardens
Ays Coughfee Hall Museum
Baddesley Clinton
Balmoral Estates
Barton Manor Gardens & Vineyards
Bateman's (The National Trust)
Beaulieu National Motor Museum, House & Abbey*
Beeston Hall
Bennetts Water Gardens

Bentley Wildfowl & Motor Museum
Bexley Museum
Bickleigh Castle
Bicton Park Gardens
Blenheim Palace*
Blickling Hall*
Bodnant Gardens
Bodrhyddan Hall
Bowhill House and Country Park
Bowood House
Bramham Park
Branklyn Garden
Bressingham Steam Museum and Gardens
Broadleas Gardens Charitable Trust Ltd
Brodick Castle & Country Park & Goatfell
Bromley Museum
Brookside Miniature Railway

Category	Name of attraction

Broughton Castle
Browhouse Yard Museum*
Bryn Bras Castle
Burnby Hall Gardens & Museum
Burns Cottage and Museum
Burns Monument and Gardens
Burton Agnes Hall
Butterfly World
Cadhay
Calderglen Country Park
Calke Abbey*
Capel Manor
Capesthorne Hall
Carrick-A-Rede Rope Bridge*
Cawdor Castle
Centre for Alternative Technology
Chambercombe Manor
Chatsworth*
Chelsea Physic Garden
Chester Zoo*
Chettle House
Chicheley Hall
Child-Beale Wildlife Park*
Chilham Castle
Chillingham Castle
Chiltern Open Air Museum
Cholderton Rare Breeds Farm Park
Churchill Gardens Museum
Clandon Park
Clapton Court Gardens
Compton Acres Gardens
Corsham Court
Coton Manor Gardens
Coughton Court
Croxteth Hall and Country Park
Damside Garden Herbs
Denmans Garden
Dinmore Manor and Gardens
Dochfour Gardens
Doddington Place Garden
Drummond Castle Gardens
Drusillas Park
Dulwich Picture Gallery
Duncombe Park
Dunham Massey Hall and Park
Dunrobin Castle
Dyffryn House Conference Centre and Gardens
Earlshall Castle and Gardens
East Lambrook Manor Garden
Edmondsham House & Garden
Elsham Hall Country & Wildlife Park
Erddig Hall
Escot Aquatic Centre & Gardens
Exbury Gardens
Felbrigg Hall
Fletcher Moss Botanical Garden
Florencecourt House
Formakin Estate
Frewen College
Glasgow Botanic Gardens
Gosford House
Graythwaite Hall Gardens
Harlow Carr Botanical Gardens
Haseley Manor
Hatch Court
Hatchlands Park
Hatfield House*
Heale Gardens and Plant Centre
Heritage Farm Park
Hever Castle
High Beeches Gardens
Hogarth's House
Holburne Museum & Crafts Study Centre
Holker Hall and Gardens
Houghton Lodge Garden & Hydroponicum
Hutton-in-the-Forest
Iden Croft Herbs
Iford Manor Gardens
Inverewe Garden
Isle of Gigha
Izaak Walton's Cottage
Jenner Museum
Kailzie Gardens
Kelburn Country Centre
Kellie Castle
Kingston Bagpuize House and Garden
Kingston Maurward Gardens and Farm
Lackham Gardens & Agricultural Museum
Land Farm Garden
Lea Gardens

Leeds Castle
Leonardslee Gardens
Levens Hall and Topiary Gardens
Logan Botanic Garden
London Butterfly House*
Longleat House and Safari Park
Manderston
Manningford Gardens & Nursery
Mannington Gardens and Countryside
Manor Farm Country Park
Margam Park*
Margaret Waudby Oriental Garden
Mark Hall Cycle Museum and Gardens
Marle Place Gardens and Nursery
Maxwelton House
Michelham Priory
Minterne Gardens
Mount Edgcumbe House & Country Park
Mount Ephraim Gardens
Mount Stewart House and Gardens*
Myddelton House Gardens
Neidpath Castle
Ness Gardens
Newstead Abbey*
Normanby Hall Country Park
Northbourne Court Gardens
Norton Conyers
Norton Priory Museum and Gardens
Norwich Cathedral
Nunnington Hall
Nunwell House & Gardens
Oakwell Hall Country Park
Old Semeil Herb Garden
Old Smithy Tourist Centre
Oldway Mansion
Oxburgh Hall
Pallant House
Parcevall Hall Gardens
Parham Elizabethan House & Gardens
Parracombe Garden Railway
Paxton House
Pecorama
Pencarrow
Plas Newydd "The National Trust"
Probus County Demonstration Garden
Quex House & Gardens & Powell-Cotton Museum
Red House Museum Art Gallery & Gardens
Rock Garden and Cave
Rockingham Castle
Rotherfield Park
Royal Botanic Gardens
Royal Botanic Gardens Kew*
Royal Horticultural Society Garden
Rural Life Centre
Russel-Cotes Art Gallery & Museum
Rydal Mount
Sand
Scone Palace*
Seaford Tropical Butterfly House/Gardens/Maze
Seaton Delaval Hall
Sellet Hall Gardens
Selly Manor Museum
Shaftesbury Abbey Museum & Ruins
Shandy Hall
Sheffield Botanical Gardens
Shibden Hall
Shugborough
Southwick Country Herb Centre
Speyside Heather/Garden Visitor Centre
Springhill
St Andrews Botanic Garden
Stanstead Park
Stanway House
Star Cottage Garden
Stewarts Garden – Lands
Stockwood Craft Museum & Gardens
Stourton House Garden
Stowe Landscape Gardens
Sudbury Hall & Museum of Childhood
Sulgrave Manor
Swiss Garden
Syon Park
Tankerness House Museum
Tapeley Park & British Jousting Centre
Tatton
The Garden House
The Greyfriars
The Herb Farm and Saxon Maze
The Hirsel
The John Moore Countryside Museum

Category	Name of attraction

The Lloyd George Museum and Highgate His Home
The Lost Gardens of Heligan
The Monkey Sanctuary
The National Pinetum (Bedgebury)
The National Trust, Speke Hall
The Old Rectory
The Savill Garden
The Wordsworth Trust
Thetford Museum
Threake Gardens
Timespan Heritage Centre
Torosay Castle & Gardens
Totnes (Elizabethan) Museum

Towneley Hall Art Gallery and Museum
Trebah Garden
Tropical World*
Tudor House Museum
University Botanic Garden
University of Durham Botanic Garden
Valence House Museum
Watermouth Castle
Wetheriggs Country Pottery
Whitmore Hall
Willsbridge Mill
Wordsworth House
Wrest Park House and Gardens

HERITAGE CENTRE

A Day at the Wells
Albert Dock
Alfriston Heritage Centre & Blacksmith's
Almond Valley Heritage Trust
Almonry Museum
Bartley Mill
Barton Clay Pits*
Battle of Britain Memorial Flight (Visits)
Beaulieu National Motor Museum, House & Abbey*
Bexley Museum
Blue Pool
Bolton Abbey Estate*
Bowes Railway Centre
Bromham Mill
Camera Obscura
Carrick-A-Rede Rope Bridge*
Coach House Museum
Conwy Visitor Centre*
Down County Museum*
Dunaverig Farm Life Centre
Durham Heritage Centre
Embsay Steam Railway
Family Heritage Museum
Felin Crewi Working Watermill
Ffestiniog Railway
Fleur De Lis Heritage Centre
Forge Mill Museum & Bordesley Abbey Vis. Ctr.
Goss and Crested China Ltd
Groam House Museum Trust
Heritage Farm Park
Isle of Arran Heritage Museum
Isle of Gigha
John Wesley's Chapel
Jonah's Journey
Land's End*
Leeds Industrial Museum
Lincolnshire Light Railway & Heritage Centre
London Canal Museum
Longstone Heritage Centre
Lulworth Cove Heritage
Margam Park*
Marx Memorial Library
Mill of Towie
Morwellham Quay
National Ambulance Museum

New Forest Museum and Visitor Centre
New Lanark Village
Newark Air Museum
Norwich Cathedral
Old Byre
Oldway Mansion
Parsonage Farm Rural Heritage Centre
Pendle Heritage Centre
Plymouth Dome*
Poole Pottery
Pumphouse Educational Museum
Quay Arts
Rhondda Heritage Park
Royal Victoria Country Park
Salvation Army International Heritage Centre
Scottish Maritime Museum
Scottish Whisky Heritage Centre*
Scottish Wildlife Trust
Shakespeare Globe Museum
Shipwreck & Heritage Centre
Smugglers Adventure
Snibston Discovery Park
Speyside Heather/Garden Visitor Centre
St George's Cathedral
Staintondale Shire Horse Farm
The Ancient High House
The Guildhall, Beverley
The Historic Dockyard, Chatham
The Lace Hall
The Look Out*
The Oxford Story
The Palace Stables Heritage Centre
The Shuttleworth Collection
The Tales of Robin Hood*
The Ulster History Park
The Valley Heritage Centre and Museum
The White Cliffs Experience
Thurso Heritage Museum
Timespan Heritage Centre
Vauxhall St Peter's Heritage Centre
Welsh Folk Museum*
Wetheriggs Country Pottery
Whitby Archives Heritage Centre
Whithorn Dig
Winchester Heritage Centre

HISTORIC HOUSE

Abbot Hall
Abbotsford
Adlington Hall
Alton Towers*
Anglesey Abbey
Anne of Cleves House Museum
Arbury Hall
Arreton Manor
Athelhampton House and Gardens
Auckland Castle
Ays Coughfec Hall Museum
Baddesley Clinton
Bagshaw Museum
Bateman's (The National Trust)
Beaulieu National Motor Museum, House & Abbey*
Beaumaris Gaol and Court
Beeston Hall
Bentley Wildfowl & Motor Museum
Bessie Surtees House
Bexley Museum
Bishops' House
Blair Castle*
Blenheim Palace*
Blickling Hall*
Bod of Gremista
Bodrhyddan Hall
Bolling Hall
Boughton House

Boughton Monchelsea Place
Bowhill House and Country Park
Bowood House
Bramham Park
Breamore House & Museums
Bromley Museum
Broughton Castle
Browhouse Yard Museum*
Bruce Castle Museum
Bryn Bras Castle
Burns Cottage and Museum
Burton Agnes Hall
Burton Constable Hall
Cadhay
Calke Abbey*
Capesthorne Hall
Captain Cook Schoolroom Museum
Carrick-A-Rede Rope Bridge*
Castle Howard*
Cawdor Castle
Cecil Higgins Art Gallery and Museum
Chambercombe Manor
Charles Dickens Birthplace Museum
Chatelherault Country Park
Chatsworth*
Chavenage
Chelmsford and Essex, Essex Regiment Museums
Chettle House

Category	Name of attraction

Chicheley Hall
Chilham Castle
Chiltern Open Air Museum
Chingle Hall
Clandon Park
Cockley Cley Iceni Village & Museums
Corsham Court
Cotswold Countryside Collection
Coughton Court
Courtauld Institute Galleries*
Cranmore Tower
Croxteth Hall and Country Park
Cyfarthfa Castle Museum, Art Gallery and Park
D H Lawrence Birthplace Museum
Dalemain Historic House
Dalmeny House
Darnaway Farm Visitor Centre
Dartmouth Museum
Dickens House Museum
Dickens House Museum, Broadstairs
Dinmore Manor and Gardens
Duncombe Park
Dunham Massey Hall and Park
Earlshall Castle and Gardens
East Riddlesden Hall
Edmondsham House & Garden
Elsham Hall Country & Wildlife Park
Erddig Hall
Fair Maid's House
Fasque
Felbrigg Hall
Floors Castle
Florencecourt House
Ford Green Hall
Formakin Estate
Freud Museum
Frewen College
Gainsborough's House
Gladstone's Land
Glanbarr Abbey Visitors Centre
Gosford House
Hamilton District Museum
Hammerwood Park
Hanbury Hall (National Trust)
Harrow Museum & Heritage Centre*
Haseley Manor
Hatch Court
Hatchlands Park
Hatfield House*
Heale Gardens and Plant Centre
Heritage Farm Park
Hever Castle
Highclere Castle
Hogarth's House
Holburne Museum & Crafts Study Centre
Holker Hall and Gardens
Holkham Hall
Hornsea Museum
Houghton Hall
Houghton Lodge Garden & Hydroponicum
Houghton Mill
Hughenden Manor
Hunterian Art Gallery
Hutton-in-the-Forest
Ironbridge Gorge Museum*
Isle of Gigha
Izaak Walton's Cottage
Jenner Museum
Kelburn Country Centre
Kellie Castle
Kelmscott Manor
Kingston Bagpuize House and Garden
Knole
Leeds Castle
Leighton House
Leith Hall
Lennoxlove House
Levens Hall and Topiary Gardens
Lewes Castle and Museums
Lincoln Cathedral
Longleat House and Safari Park
Manderston
Mannington Gardens and Countryside
Manor Farm Country Park
Mapledurham House and Watermill*
Margam Park*
Maxwelton House
Merchant's House (Little Museum)
Michelham Priory
Milton's Cottage

Mount Edgcumbe House & Country Park
Mount Stewart House and Gardens*
Mullaghbawn Folk Museum
Museum of the Order of St John
Newstead Abbey*
Normanby Hall Country Park
Northbourne Court Gardens
Norton Conyers
Norwich Cathedral
Number One the Royal Crescent
Nunnington Hall
Nunwell House & Gardens
Oakwell Hall Country Park
Oldway Mansion
Oxburgh Hall
Oxfordshire County Museum
Palace of Holyroodhouse*
Pallant House
Parham Elizabethan House & Gardens
Paxton House
Peckforton Castle
Pencarrow
Pendle Heritage Centre
Penrhyn Castle
Pickford's House Museum
Plas Newydd "The National Trust"
Polesden Lacey
Pollok House*
Powysland Museum & Montgomery Canal Centre
Prideaux Place
Provand's Lordship
Quex House & Gardens & Powell-Cotton Museum
Ragley Hall
Red Lodge
Rockingham Castle
Rotherfield Park
Rougemont House Museum
Royal Botanic Gardens Kew*
Royal Pavilion, Art Gallery and Museum
Russel-Cotes Art Gallery & Museum
Rydal Mount
Sally Lunn's Refreshment House & Museum
Sand
Scone Palace*
Seaton Delaval Hall
Selly Manor Museum
Shandy Hall
Sheriff Hutton Park
Shibden Hall
Shugborough
Sion Hill Hall
Sir John Soane's Museum
Sooty's World
Spencer House
Springhill
St George's Cathedral
St Nicholas Priory
Stanford Hall
Stanstead Park
Stanway House
Stowe Landscape Gardens
Strangers' Hall Museum
Strawberry Hill
Sudbury Hall & Museum of Childhood
Sudley
Sulgrave Manor
Syon Park
Tabely House Collection
Tankerness House Museum
Tepeley Park & British Jousting Centre
Tatton
Tewkesbury Museum
The Ancient High House
The Ballance House
The Coventry Toy Museum
The Greyfriars
The Guildhall Beverley
The John Moore Countryside Museum
The Lloyd George Museum and Highgate His Home
The National Trust, Speke Hall
The Old Rectory
The Wordsworth Trust
Thetford Museum
Thirlestane Castle
Timothy Hackworth Victorian & Railway Museum
Tithe Barn Museum & Arts Centre
Tolsey Museum
Torosay Castle & Gardens
Torre Abbey
Totnes (Elizabethan) Museum

Category	Name of attraction

Totnes Guildhall
Towneley Hall Art Gallery and Museum
Traquair House
Tudor House Museum
Valence House Museum
Wesley's Chapel
Whitmore Hall
Wilberforce House

Willsbridge Mill
Woburn Abbey
Wolferton Station Museum
Wood End Museum of Natural History
Woolhouse Maritime Museum
Wordsworth House
Worldwide Butterflies Ltd
Wrest Park House and Gardens

MONUMENT

Abbeydale Industrial Hamlet
Arbeia Roman Fort & Museum
Battle Abbey and Battlefield of Hastings
Beaulieu National Motor Museum, House & Abbey*
Binchester Roman Fort
Blenheim Palace*
Bowes Railway Centre
Burns Monument and Gardens
Carrick-A-Rede Rope Bridge*
Carrickferggus Castle*
County and Regimental Museum
Cranmore Tower
Dunstable Downs Country Park
Durham Heritage Centre
Golden Hill Fort
Halifax Piece Hall*
Harwich Redoubt
Ironbridge Gorge Museum*
Jervaulx Abbey
Kenilworth Castle
Lady Lever Art Gallery
Liverpool Museum
National Maritime Museum
New Lanark Village

Newhaven Fort
Norton Priory Museum and Gardens
Norwich Cathedral
Offa's Dyke Association
Port of Harwich Maritime Museum
Portland Castle
Rochester Castle
Roman Villa, Brading
Shaftesbury Abbey Museum & Ruins
Shakespeare Globe Museum
Shugborough
Somerset Rural Life Museum
Spitbank Fort
St Edmundsbury Cathedral
Stowe Landscape Gardens
Sussex Combined Services Museum
Torre Abbey
Twyford Pumping Station
Walker Art Gallery
Welwyn Roman Baths
Wisbech & Fenland Museum
Wortley Top Forge Industrial Museum
Wrest Park House and Gardens

MUSEUM

A Day at the Wells
Abbeydale Industrial Hamlet
Abbot Hall
Abbotsbury Tithe Barn Museum
Albert Dock
Aldeburgh Moot Hall Museum
Alfriston Heritage Centre & Blacksmith's
Allhallows Museum
Almond Valley Heritage Trust
Almonry Museum
Amgueddfa's Gogledd/Museum of the North
Ancient House Museum
Anne of Cleves House Museum
Arbeia Roman Fort & Museum
Armagh County Museum
Armagh Planetarium
Arran & Argyll Transport Museum
Arreton Manor
Art Gallery and Museum*
Arundel Toy and Military Museum
Ashmolean Museum
Atwell Wilson Motor Museum
Auchindrain Township Open Air Museum
Automobilia Transport Museum
Avoncroft Museum of Buildings
Ays Coughfee Hall Museum
Baden Powell House Hostel
Bagshaw Museum
Baird Institute Museum
Bank of England Museum
Bankfield Museum
Barleylands Farm Museum
Bartley Mill
Barton Clay Pits*
Bass Museum, Visitor Ctr & Shire Horse Stables
Battle Abbey and Battlefield of Hastings
Bayle Museum
Bear Museum
Beaulieu National Motor Museum, House & Abbey*
Beaumaris Gaol and Court
Beck Isle Museum of Rural Life
Bedford Museum
Bentley Wildfowl & Motor Museum
Bersham Heritage Centre and Ironworks
Bethnal Green Museum of Childhood
Bexhill Museum of Costume & Social History
Bexley Museum
Bickleigh Castle
Bicton Park Gardens
Bignor Roman Villa
Birmingham Railway Museum
Bishops' House
Black Country Museum
Blackburn Museum and Art Gallery

Blaise Castle House Museum
Blue Pool
Bod of Gremista
Bodmin Town Museum
Bolling Hall
Book Museum
Border History Museum
Bournemouth Heritage Transport Centre
Bowhill House and Country Park
Bradford Industrial Horses at Work Museum
Bradford on Avon Museum
Breamore House & Museums
Bressingham Steam Museum and Gardens
Bristol Industrial Museum
British Engineerium Steam Museum
British in India Museum
Brixham Museum & History Society
Broads Museum
Bromham Mill
Bromley Museum
Brooklands Museum
Brookside Miniature Railway
Browhouse Yard Museum*
Bruce Castle Museum
Bucklers Hard Village & Maritime Museum*
Buckleys Yesterdays World
Bude Museum
Burnby Hall Gardens & Museum
Burns Cottage and Museum
Burrell Collection*
Bute Museum
Buxton Museum and Art Gallery
Camborne School of Mines Geological Museum
Cambrian Railway Soc & Oswestry Cycle Museum
Cambridge and County Folk Museum
Captain Cook Schoolroom Museum
Carlisle Cathedral
Carrick-A-Rede Rope Bridge*
Castle Howard*
Cecil Higgins Art Gallery and Museum
Cefn Coed Colliery Museum
Ceredigion Museum
Chambercombe Manor
Chard & District Museum
Charles Dickens Birthplace Museum
Chatterley Whitfield Mining Museum
Chelmsford and Essex, Essex Regiment Museums
Chesil Gallery
Chester Visitor Centre
Chillingham Castle
Chiltern Open Air Museum
Christchurch Tricycle Museum
Churchill Gardens Museum
Cider Museum and King Offa Distillery

Category	Name of attraction

Cilgwyn Candles Workshop and Mini Museum
Clan Macpherson Museum
Clandon Park
Coach House Museum
Coats Observatory
Cockley Cley Iceni Village & Museums
Cockthorpe Hall Toy Museum
Collection of the Worshipful Co of Clockmakers
Colliford Lake Park
Colne Valley Museum
Colne Valley Railway
Colour Museum
Commonwealth Institute*
Corinium Museum
Corsham Court
Cotswold Countryside Collection
Cotswold Motor Museum
County and Regimental Museum
Courage Shire Horse Centre
Courtauld Institute Galleries*
Crabble Corn Mill
Cranmore Tower
Cromer Lifeboat Museum
Cromer Museum
Croxteth Hall and Country Park
Cumberland Pencil Museum & Exhibition Centre
Cuming Museum
Cyfarthfa Castle Museum, Art Gallery and Park
D H Lawrence Birthplace Museum
Dales Countryside Museum
Darlington Museum
Darnaway Farm Visitor Centre
Dartmouth Museum
Dean Castle & Country Park
Derby Industrial Museum
Derby Museum and Art Gallery*
Devonshire Regiment Museum
Dewsbury Museum
Dick Institute
Dickens House Museum
Dickens House Museum Broadstairs
Didcot Railway Centre*
Dinosaur Museum*
Dinosaur Safari
Dorset County Museum
Dorset Military Museum
Down County Museum*
Duke of Cornwall's Light Infantry Museum
Dulwich Picture Gallery
Dunaverig Farm Life Centre
Dunrobin Castle
Durham Heritage Centre
Durham Light Infantry Museum & Art Gallery
Duxford Airfield*
Dyson Perrins Museum
Easdale Island Folk Museum
East Anglian Railway Museum
Eden Camp Modern History Theme Museum*
Edinburgh Canal Centre
Edinburgh Museum of Childhood
Elstow Moot Hall
Ely Museum
Embsay Steam Railway
Epping Forest District Museum
Erith Museum
Ethnic Doll and Toy Museum
Etruria Industrial Museum
Eureka! The Museum for Children
Eyemouth Museum
Falmouth Maritime Museum
Family Heritage Museum
Famous Old Blacksmiths Shop Centre*
Ffestiniog Railway
Filey Museum
Fishbourne Roman Palace and Museum
Fitzwilliam Museum*
Flambards Village Theme Park*
Fleur De Lis Heritage Centre
Forge Mill Museum & Bordesley Abbey Vis Ctr
Forncett Industrial Steam Museum
Foxfield Steam Railway
Freud Museum
Frome Museum
Gairloch Heritage Museum
Gem Rock Museum
Glanbarr Abbey Visitors Centre
Glasgow Vennel Museum
Gods House Tower Museum
Golden Hill Fort
Goosedale Model Aviation Centre

Graham Sutherland Gallery
Grampian Transport Museum
Grantham Museum
Gray Art Gallery
Great Western Railway Museum
Greenwich Borough Museum
Groam House Museum Trust
Grosvenor Museum
Gurkha Museum
Haggs Castle
Halifax Piece Hall*
Hamilton District Museum
Hancock Museum
Harris Museum and Art Gallery
Harrow Museum & Heritage Centre*
Hartlepool Maritime Museum
Harveys Wine Museum
Harwich Redoubt
Hastings Museum and Art Gallery
Hatch Court
Havant Museum
Haverfordwest Castle Museum and Art Gallery
Heaven Farm
Helmshore Textile Museums
Hereford Cathedral
Herefordshire Waterworks Museum
Heritage Farm Park
Heritage Motor Centre*
Heron Corn Mill and Museum of Papermaking
HM Tower of London*
HMS Belfast*
Hogarth's House
Holburne Museum & Crafts Study Centre
Holker Hall and Gardens
Holkham Hall
Hornsea Freeport*
Hornsea Museum
Hoskins Brewery
Hove Museum and Art Gallery
How We Lived Then Museum of Shops
Hull and East Riding Museum
Ilfracombe Museum
Incredibly Fantastic Old Toy Show
Inveraray Jail
Ironbridge Gorge Museum*
Isle of Arran Heritage Museum
Izaak Walton's Cottage
J M Barrie's Birthplace
Jane Welsh Carlyle Museum
Jenner Museum
Jonah's Journey
Jorvik Viking Centre*
Kew Bridge Steam Museum
Kielder Water
King's Lynn Museums
Kings Own Scottish Borders Regimental Museum
Kirkcaldy Museum & Art Gallery
Knaresborough Castle & Courthouse Museum
Lackham Gardens & Agricultural Museum
Lady Lever Art Gallery
Laidhay Croft Museum
Lanreath Folk Farm Museum
Largs Museum
Leeds Castle
Leeds City Museum
Leeds Industrial Museum
Legbourne Railway Museum
Leighton Buzzard Railway
Leighton House
Lewes Castle and Museums
Lincolnshire Light Railway & Heritage Centre
Liverpool Museum
Llangollen Motor Museum
Local Interest Museum
Lochwinnoch Community Museum
London Canal Museum
London Toy and Model Museum
Longdale Craft Centre & Museum*
Luton Museum and Art Gallery
Maes Astro Tourist Attraction
Malton Museum
Malvern Museum
Manchester United Museum & Tour Centre
Manderston
Manor Farm Country Park
Manor House Museum/Alfred East Art Gallery
Margate Old Town Hall Local History Museum
Maritime Museum
Maritime Museum Ramsgate
Mark Hall Cycle Museum and Gardens

Category	Name of attraction

Maxwelton House
McLean Museum and Art Gallery
Michelham Priory
Midland Motor Museum
Mill Green Museum and Mill
Miltons Cottage
Model Farm and Folk Museum
Morpeth Chantry Bagpipe Museum
Morwellham Quay
Mouldsworth Motor Museum
Much Wenlock Museum
Mullaghbawn Folk Museum
Mummies and Magic
Museum of Army Flying
Museum of Army Transport
Museum of British Road Transport
Museum of Childhood
Museum of Costume
Museum of East Anglian Life
Museum of English Naive Art
Museum of Fire
Museum of Flight
Museum of Installation
Museum of Kent Life
Museum of Lead Mining
Museum of London*
Museum of Mechanical Music
Museum of Staffordshire Regiment
Museum of the Cumbraes
Museum of the Moving Image*
Museum of the Order of St John
Museum of Transport
Museum of Transport*
Musical Museum
Myreton Motor Museum
National Ambulance Museum
National Army Museum
National Cycle Museum
National Horseracing Museum
National Maritime Museum
National Maritime Museum Greenwich*
National Museum of Labour History
National Postal Museum
National Railway Museum*
National Shire Horse Centre*
National Sound Archive (British Library)
Natural History Museum
Neidpath Castle
New Forest Museum and Visitor Centre
New Lanark Village
Newark Air Museum
Newark Museum
Newham Grange Leisure Farm
Newhaven Fort
Newport Museum and Art Gallery
Newstead Abbey*
Nidderdale Museum
Norfolk Rural Life Museum and Union Farm
Normanby Hall Country Park
North Ayrshire Museum
North Cornwall Museum and Gallery
North Devon Maritime Museum
North Down Heritage Centre
North East Aircraft Museum
North Woolwich Old Station Museum
Norton Priory Museum and Gardens
Norwich Castle Museum*
Norwich Cathedral
Nothe Fort
Nunwell House & Gardens
Offa's Dyke Association
Old Operating Theatre Museum
Oriental Museum
Oxfordshire County Museum
Padstow Shipwreck Museum
Paisley Museum & Art Galleries
Paradise Mill
Parsonage Farm Rural Heritage Centre
Passmore Edwards Museum
Pennyarcadia
Penrhyn Castle
People's Palace Museum*
Percival David Foundation of Chinese Art
Petrie Museum of Egyptian Archaeology
Pickford's House Museum
Pilkington Glass Museum
Plas Newydd "The National Trust"
Pollock's Toy Museum
Pontefract Museum
Poole's Cavern

Port of Harwich Maritime Museum
Potters Museum of Curiosity
Powysland Museum & Montgomery Canal Centre
Pumphouse Educational Museum
Quay Arts
Queen's Own Highlanders Regimental Museum
Quex House & Gardens & Powell-Cotton Museum
Radstock Midsomer Norton Museum
Ragged School Museum
Red House Museum Art Gallery & Gardens
Red Lodge
Regiments of Gloucestershire Museum
Ripon Prison & Police Museum
Robert Owen Museum
Rock Circus*
Roman Baths Museum*
Roman Villa, Brading
Romany Folklore Museum & Workshop
Rougemont House Museum
Royal Air Force Museum*
Royal Albert Memorial Museum
Royal Cornwall Museum
Royal Engineers Museum
Royal Green Jackets Museum
Royal London Hospital Archives & Museum
Royal Marines Museum
Royal Museum of Scotland*
Royal Navy Submarine Museum
Royal Observatory Visitor Centre
Royal Pavilion, Art Gallery and Museum
Royal Photographic Society
Royal Pump Room Museum
Royal Signals Museum
Royal Victoria Country Park
Royalty and Empire*
Rural Life Centre
Ruskin Museum
Russel-Cotes Art Gallery & Museum
Rutherglen Museum
Ryhope Engines Museum
Saffron Walden Museum
Salcombe Maritime & Local History Museum
Salford Museum and Art Gallery
Salisbury and South Wiltshire Museum
Salvation Army International Heritage Centre
Sandtoft Transport Centre
Scaplen's Court Museum
Scotland Street School Museum
Scottish Agricultural Museum
Scottish Industrial Railway Centre
Scottish Maritime Museum
Scottish Mining Museum
Scunthorpe Museum
Selly Manor Museum
Shaftesbury Abbey Museum & Ruins
Shakespeare Globe Museum
Shandy Hall
Sherlock Holmes Museum
Shetland Croft House Museum
Shetland Museum
Shibden Hall
Shipwreck & Heritage Centre
Shirehall Museum
Shugborough
Sidmouth Museum
Sion Hill Hall
Sir John Soane's Museum
Smugglers Adventure
Snibston Discovery Park
Sobriety Waterways Adventure Centre & Museum
Somerset Rural Life Museum
Sooty's World
South Shields Museum & Art Gallery
Southend Central Museum & Planetarium
Southend Planetarium
Southport Railway Centre
Spitbank Fort
Spitting Image Rubberworks*
Springburn Museum Trust
Springhill
SS Great Britain
St Andrews Preservation Trust Museum
St Columbs Cathedral
St Nicholas Priory
Stags Holt Farm and Stud
Stained Glass Museum
Stamford Museum
Stanford Hall Motorcycle Museum
Steam Brewery Museum
Steamtown Railway Centre

Category	Name of attraction

Stewartry Museum
Stockwood Craft Museum & Gardens
Strangers' Hall Museum
Stranraer Museum
Streetlife – Hull Museum of Transport
Stromness Museum
Strumpshaw Hall Steam Museum
Sudbury Hall & Museum of Childhood
Sudley
Suffolk Regiment Museum
Summerlee Heritage Trust
Sussex Combined Services Museum
Swaffham Museum
Swaledale Folk Museum
Tabely House Collection
Tain and District Museum
Tamworth Castle
Tank Museum
Tankerness House Museum
Tatton
Teignmouth Museum
Tenby Museum & Picture Gallery
Tenby Museum and Picture Gallery
Tewkesbury Museum
Thameside Complex
The Aerospace Museum*
The Bellfoundry Museum
The Boat Museum
The Building of Bath Museum
The C M Booth Collection of Historic Vehicles
The Coventry Toy Museum
The Dewey Museum
The Hirsel
The International Helicopter Museum
The John Moore Countryside Museum
The Lace Centre*
The Lace Hall
The Lincolnshire Poultry Park
The Lloyd George Museum and Highgate His Home
The Local Interest Museum
The Lost Gardens of Heligan
The Museum of Childhood
The National Motorcycle Museum
The Nelson Museum and Local History Centre
The Old Rectory
The Puppet Theatre Museum
The Ravenglass and Eskdale Railway*
The Salt Museum
The Shuttleworth Collection
The Silk Museum
The Smuggling Experience
The South Wales Borderers Museum
The Tales of Robin Hood*
The Valley Heritage Centre and Museum
The Walter Rothschild Zoological Museum
The Welch Regiment Museum
The White Cliffs Experience
The Wordsworth Trust
Thetford Museum
Thirlestane Castle
Thursford Collection*
Timespan Heritage Centre
Timothy Hackworth Victorian & Railway Museum
Tingwall Agricultural Museum
Tithe Barn Museum & Arts Centre
Tiverton Museum
Tolpuddle Martyrs Museum

Tolsey Museum
Torquay Museum
Torrington Museum
Totnes (Elizabethan) Museum
Totnes Guildhall
Town Docks Museum
Towneley Hall Art Gallery and Museum
Towner Art Gallery & Local History Museum
Toy and Teddy Bear Museum
Trefriw Wells SPA
Trinity House National Lighthouse Centre
Trowbridge Museum
Tudor House Museum
Tulliehouse Museum and Art Gallery
Tutankhamun Exhibition
Twyford Pumping Station
Ullapool Museum
Ulster Folk and Transport Museum*
Ulster Museum*
University of Liverpool Art Gallery
Upminster Tithe Barn Agricultural Museum
Valence House Museum
Victoria and Albert Museum
Victorian Reed Organ Museum
Vintage Railway Carriage Museum
Vintage Toy Train Museum
Wakefield Museum
Warrington Museum and Art Gallery
Wat Tyler Country Park*
Watchet Market House Museum
Waterfront Museum
Watermouth Castle
Weald and Downland Open Air Museum
Wellesbourne Aviation Group
Wells Museum
Welsh Folk Museum*
Welsh Slate Museum
Wesley's Chapel
West Highland Museum
West Lancashire Light Railway
West Park Museum
West Somerset Rural Life Museum
Wetheriggs Country Pottery
Wheelwrights Museum & Gypsy Folklore Collect
Whitby Archives Heritage Centre
Wilberforce House
Winchester Cathedral
Windermere Steamboat Museum*
Wine and Spirit Museum
Wisbech & Fenland Museum
Wolferton Station Museum
Wood End Museum of Natural History
Woodham Church Museum
Woodhorn Colliery Museum
Woodspring Museum
Woolhouse Maritime Museum
Wordsworth Gallery
World of Toys
Wortley Top Forge Industrial Museum
Wymondham Heritage Museum
Wynthop Mill
Yorkshire Car Collection
Yorkshire Carriage Museum
Yorkshire Museum
Yorkshire Water Museum
Zetland Lifeboat Museum

PARK/RESERVE

Argyll Forest Park
Auckland Castle
Avon Valley Country Park
Badsell Farm Park
Barton Clay Pits*
Battle Abbey and Battlefield of Hastings
Beacon Country Park
Beacraigs Country Park
Beeston Hall
Bentley Wildfowl & Motor Museum
Bill Quay Community Farm*
Billingham Beck Valley Country Park
Blackshaw Farm Park Ltd
Blenheim Palace*
Blickling Hall*
Blue Pool
Boughton House
Bowhill House and Country Park
Brodick Castle & Country Park & Goatfell
Calderglen Country Park
Calke Abbey*

Cambo Country Park
Capel Manor
Carrick-A-Rede Rope Bridge*
Castle Eden Walkway Country Park*
Chatelherault Country Park
Chestnut Centre
Child-Beale Wildlife Park*
Colliford Lake Park
Crombie Country Park
Croxteth Hall and Country Park
Cyfarthfa Castle Museum, Art Gallery and Park
Dean Castle & Country Park
Derwent Walk Country Park
Dinton Pastures Country Park*
Drusillas Park
Dunham Massey Hall and Park
Dunstable Downs Country Park
Earlshall Castle and Gardens
East Ham Nature Reserve
Falls of Clyde Nature Reserve
Felbrigg Hall

Category	Name of attraction	

Florencecourt House
Forge Mill Museum & Bordesley Abbey Vis Ctr
Gibraltar Point National Nature Reserve*
Glengoulandie Deer Park
Gosford Forest Park
Harrold Odell Country Park*
Haseley Manor
Hatch Court
Hatfield Forest
Hatfield House*
Heritage Farm Park
Heritage Motor Centre*
Holker Hall and Gardens
Holkham Hall
Hollingworth Lake Country Park
Hughenden Manor
Isle of Gigha
Isle of Wight Rare Breeds & Waterfowl Park
Itchen Valley Country Park
Kielder Water
Knowsley Safari Park
Lackham Gardens & Agricultural Museum
Landmark Highland Heritage and Adventure Park
Lochore Meadows Country Park
Lochwinnoch Nature Centre
Longleat House and Safari Park
Mannington Gardens and Countryside
Manor Farm Country Park
Margam Park*
Minsmere RSPB Nature Reserve
Moors Valley Country Park
Mount Edgcumbe House & Country Park
National Shire Horse Centre*
New Lanark Village
Newstead Abbey*
Normanby Hall Country Park
Once Brewed National Park Visitor Centre
Our Little Farm
Paxton House
Peatlands Park*
Pensthorpe Waterfowl Trust
Poole's Cavern

Pugneys Country Park
Pumphouse Educational Museum
Ragley Hall
Rare Farm Animals of Hollanden
Rock Garden and Cave
Rother Valley Country Park*
Royal Victoria Country Park
RSPB North Cliffs and West Light Platform
Scottish Wildlife Trust
Sherwood Forest Visitor Centre*
Shugborough
Snibston Discovery Park
Southwick Country Herb Centre
Staintondale Shire Horse Farm
Stanborough Park
Stockgrove Country Park
Talkin Tarn Country Park
Tamar Valley Donkey Park
Tatton
Tehidy Country Park
The Hirsel
The Lincolnshire Poultry Park
The Lost Gardens of Heligan
The National Pinetum (Bedgebury)
The Waterfowl Sanctuary and Rescue Centre
The Welch Regiment Museum
The Wildfowl & Wetlands Trust Martin Mere
Towneley Hall Art Gallery and Museum
Trafford Ecology Park
Tropical Bird Park
Tropical World*
Valence House Museum
Ventnor Botanic Garden*
Wat Tyler Country Park*
Wildfowl & Wetlands Centre
Wildfowl & Wetlands Trust – Welney Centre
Willsbridge Mill
Windsor Safari Park*
Wood Green Animal Sanctuary*
Woodside Farm & Wild Fowl Park
Worsbrough Country Park*

THEME PARK

Alton Towers*
Avon Valley Country Park
Badsell Farm Park
Beaulieu National Motor Museum, House & Abbey*
Blackpool Pleasure Beach
Centre for Alternative Technology
Chessington World of Adventures*
Cluanie Deer Farm Park
Cranmore Tower
Farmworld*
Flambards Village Theme Park*
Frontierland Western Theme Park*
Gorse Blossom Railway & Woodland Park
Gullivers Kingdom
Hornsea Freeport*
Jonah's Journey
Kelburn Country Centre

Kirklees Light Railway
Lightwater Valley Theme Park*
Margam Park*
Metroland*
Museum of Mechanical Music
National Shire Horse Centre*
Paultons Park
Pecorama
Peter Pan's Playground*
Pleasurewood Hills American Theme Park*
Sundown Kiddies Adventureland
Tamar Valley Donkey Park
Tatton
The Big Sheep
The Ulster History Park
Watermouth Castle
Windsor Safari Park*

ZOO, ETC.

Abbotsbury Swannery
Almond Valley Heritage Trust
Anglesey Sea Zoo*
Animal World
Appleby Castle Conservation Centre
Ardencraig Gardens
Avon Valley Country Park
Badsell Farm Park
Barton Clay Pits*
Basildon Zoo
Bennetts Water Gardens
Birdland
Blair Drummond Safari & Leisure Park
Bolton Abbey Estate*
Brighton Sea Life Centre
Bristol Zoo Gardens*
Brodick Castle & Country Park & Goatfell
Buckfast Butterflies & Dartmoor Otter Sanct.
Buffers
Butterfly World
Butterfly World and Fountain World
Calderglen Country Park
Capel Manor
Chambercombe Manor
Chessington World of Adventures*
Chester Zoo*
Chestnut Centre

Child-Beale Wildlife Park*
Chillingham Wild Castle Association Ltd
Cluanie Deer Farm Park
Colchester Zoo*
Colliford Lake Park
Combe Martin Wildlife & Dinosaur Park
Cornish Seal Sanctuary
Cranmore Tower
Dean Castle & Country Park
Drusillas Park
Edinburgh Zoo*
Elsham Hall Country & Wildlife Park
Escot Aquatic Centre & Gardens
Exmoor Bird Gardens
Falls of Clyde Nature Reserve
Flimwell Bird Park
Formakin Estate
Glasgow Zoo Park
Glengoulandie Deer Park
Gosford Forest Park
Hamerton Wildlife Centre
Hastings Sea Life Centres*
Heaven Farm
Heritage Farm Park
Hornsea Freeport*
Howletts Zoo Park
Isle of Wight Rare Breeds & Waterfowl Park

Category	Name of attraction

Kingdom of the Sea, Hunstanton*
Knowsley Safari Park
Lackham Gardens & Agricultural Museum
Leeds Castle
Liverpool Museum
London Butterfly House*
Longdown Dairy Farm
Longleat House and Safari Park
Lotherton Hall Bird Garden*
Maes Astro Tourist Attraction
Manor Farm Country Park
Marazion Marine Aquarium
Marwell Zoological Park*
Miniature Pony Centre
National Shire House Centre*
Natural World*
New Forest Butterfly Farm
Oban Sea Life Centre
Oceanarium
Paignton Zoo*
Paradise Wildlife Park
Parke Rare Breeds Farm
Pensthorpe Waterfowl Trust
Pettitts Feathercraft & Animal Adventure Park
Port Lympne Zoo Park, Mansion & Gardens
Portsmouth Sea Life Centre
Pumphouse Educational Museum
Rhyl Sea Life Centre
RSPB North Cliffs and West Light Platform
Scottish Wildlife Trust
Sea Life Centre
Sea Life Centre*
Seaford Tropical Butterfly House/Gardens/Maze

Shaldon Wildlife Trust
Southport Zoo and Conservation Trust
St Andrews Sea Life Centre
Staintondale Shire Horse Farm
Stratford Butterfly Farm
Talnotry Cottage Bird Garden
Tatton
The Big Sheep
The Monkey Sanctuary
The Waterfowl Sanctuary and Rescue Centre
The Welch Regiment Museum
The Wildfowl & Wetlands Trust, Martin Mere
Thrigby Hall Wildlife Gardens
Towneley Hall Art Gallery and Museum
Trafford Ecology Park
Trenouth Farm Rare Breeds Centre
Tropical Bird Park
Tropical World*
Twycross Zoo*
Wetlands Waterfowl Reserve
Weymouth Sea Life Park
Whipsnade Wild Animal Park*
White Post Modern Farm Centre*
Wildfowl & Wetlands Centre
Wildfowl & Wetlands Trust – Welney Centre
Windsor Safari Park*
Wood Green Animal Sanctuary*
Woodside Farm & Wild Fowl Park
World of the Honey Bee
Worldwide Butterflies Ltd
Worsbrough Country Park*
Yorkshire Dales Falconry & Conservation Centre

INDEX 2
LISTING OF ATTRACTIONS BY RTB AREA

RTB Area	Name

CUMBRIA

Abbot Hall
Appleby Castle Conservation Centre
Beatrix Potter Gallery*
Bressingham Steam Museum and Gardens
Carlisle Cathedral
Coniston Boating Centre
Cumberland Pencil Museum & Exhibition Centre
Cumbria Crystal Ltd*
Dalemain Historic House
Eskdale Corn Mill
Graythwaite Hall Gardens
Grizedale Forest Park*
Heron Corn Mill and Museum of Papermaking
Holker Hall and Gardens
Hutton-in-the-Forest
Kingdom of the Sea
Lake District National Park Visitor Centre*

Levens Hall and Topiary Gardens
Naworth Castle
Ponsonby Farm Park
Priests Mill
Ruskin Museum
Rydal Mount
Sellafield Visitors Centre
Stott Park Bobbin Mill
Talkin Tarn Country Park
The Ravenglass and Eskdale Railway*
The Wordsworth Trust
Tulliehouse Museum and Art Gallery
Wetheriggs Country Pottery
Whinlatter Visitor Centre*
Windermere Steamboat Museum*
Wordsworth House
Wythop Mill

EAST ANGLIA

Aldeburgh Moot Hall Museum
Ancient House Museum
Anglesey Abbey
Barleylands Farm Museum
Basildon Zoo
Beeston Hall
Blickling Hall*
Broads Museum
Bungay Castle
Bure Valley Railway
Cambridge and County Folk Museum
Charles Manning's Amusement Park*
Chelmsford and Essex, Essex Regiment Museums
Chelmsford Cathedral
Cockley Cley Iceni Village & Museums
Cockthorpe Hall Toy Museum
Colchester Zoo*
Colne Valley Railway
Cromer Lifeboat Museum
Cromer Museum
Duxford Airfield*
East Anglian Railway Museum
Ely Cathedral*
Ely Museum
Epping Forest District Museum
Felbrigg Hall
Felsted Vineyards
Fitzwilliam Museum*
Forncett Industrial Steam Museum
Gainsborough's House
Hamerton Wildlife Centre
Harwich Redoubt
Holkham Hall
Houghton Hall
Houghton Mill
King's Lynn Museums
Kingdom of the Sea, Gt Yarmouth*
Kingdom of the Sea, Hunstanton*
Lee Valley Park Farms
Mannington Gardens and Countryside
Mark Hall Cycle Museum and Gardens

Marsh Farm Country Park*
Minsmere RSPB Nature Reserve
Museum of East Anglian Life
National Horseracing Museum
Norfolk Rural Life Museum and Union Farm
North Norfolk Railway*
Norwich Castle Museum*
Norwich Cathedral*
Norwich Gallery
Oxburgh Hall
Pensthorpe Waterfowl Trust
Peter Pan's Playground*
Peterborough Cathedral*
Pettitts Feathercraft & Animal Adventure Park
Pleasure Beach*
Pleasurewood Hills American Theme Park*
Port of Harwich Maritime Museum
Ripley's Believe It or Not
Saffron Walden Museum
Shirehall Museum
Southend Central Museum & Planetarium
St Edmundsbury Cathedral
Stags Holt Farm and Stud
Stained Glass Museum
Stow Mill
Strangers' Hall Museum
Strumpshaw Hall Steam Museum
Suffolk Regiment Museum
Swaffham Museum
Thameside Complex
The Otter Trust
Thetford Museum
Thrigby Hall Wildlife Gardens
Thursford Collection*
Wat Tyler Country Park*
Wells & Walsingham Light Railway
Wildfowl & Wetlands Trust – Welney Centre
Wisbech & Fenland Museum
Wolferton Station Museum
Wood Green Animal Sanctuary*
Wymondham Heritage Museum

EAST MIDLANDS

Alton Towers*
Ays Coughfee Hall Museum
Battle of Britain Memorial Flight (Visits)
Belvoir Castle
Boughton House
Browhouse Yard Museum*
Buxton Micrarium
Buxton Museum and Art Gallery
Calke Abbey*
Chatsworth*
Chestnut Centre
Coton Manor Gardens
D H Lawrence Birthplace Museum
Derby Cathedral
Derby Industrial Museum

Derby Museum and Art Gallery*
Farmworld*
Gibraltar Point National Nature Reserve*
Goosedale Model Aviation Centre
Grantham Museum
Gullivers Kingdom
Hoskins Brewery
Incredibly Fantastic Old Toy Show
Lea Gardens
Legbourne Railway Museum
Lincoln Cathedral
Lincolnshire Light Railway & Heritage Centre
Longdale Craft Centre & Museum*
Manor House Museum/Alfred East Art Gallery
National Cycle Museum

RTB Area	Name

Newark Air Museum
Newark Museum
Newstead Abbey*
Old Dairy Farm Centre
Our Little Farm
Pickford's House Museum
Poole's Cavern
Riber Castle Wildlife Park*
Rockingham Castle
Sherwood Forest Visitor Centre*
Snibston Discovery Park
Stamford Museum
Stamford Shakespeare Company
Stanford Hall

Stanford Hall Motorcycle Museum
Steam Brewery Museum
Sudbury Hall & Museum of Childhood
Sundown Kiddies Adventureland
The Bellfoundry Museum
The Butterfly and Falconry Park
The Lace Centre*
The Lace Hall
The Lincolnshire Poultry Park
The Tales of Robin Hood*
Twycross Zoo*
Wetlands Waterfowl Reserve
White Post Modern Farm Centre*

HEART OF ENGLAND

Almonry Museum
Arbury Hall
Avoncroft Museum of Buildings
Baddesley Clinton
Bass Museum, Visitor Ctr & Shire Horse Stables
Birdland
Birmingham Cathedral
Birmingham Railway Museum
Black Country Museum
Cadbury World*
Cambrian Railway Soc & Oswestry Cycle Museum
Chatterley Whitfield Mining Museum
Chavenage
Churchill Gardens Museum
Cider Museum and King Offa Distillery
Corinium Museum
Cotswold Countryside Collection
Cotswold Motor Museum
Coughton Court
Coventry Cathedral
Dinmore Manor and Gardens
Dyson Perrins Museum
Etruria Industrial Museum
Ford Green Hall
Forge Mill Museum & Bordesley Abbey Vis Ctr
Foxfield Steam Railway
Gloucester Cathedral*
Hanbury Hall (National Trust)
Hereford Cathedral
Herefordshire Waterworks Museum
Heritage Motor Centre*
Ironbridge Gorge Museum*
Izaak Walton's Cottage

Jenner Museum
Kelmscott Manor
Kenilworth Castle
Lichfield Cathedral
Malvern Museum
Merchant's House (Little Museum)
Midland Motor Museum
Model Village
Much Wenlock Museum
Museum of British Road Transport
Museum of Staffordshire Regiment
Ragley Hall
Regiments of Gloucestershire Museum
Selly Manor Museum
Shugborough
Stanway House
Stratford Butterfly Farm
Tamworth Castle
Tewkesbury Museum
The Aerospace Museum*
The Ancient High House
The Children's Farm
The Coventry Toy Museum
The Greyfriars
The John Moore Countryside Museum
The National Motorcycle Museum
The Puppet Theatre Museum
The Valley Heritage Centre and Museum
Warwick Castle*
Wellesbourne Aviation Group
Whitmore Hall
Wye Valley Farm Park

LONDON

Age Exchange Reminiscence Centre
Association Gallery
Baden Powell House Hostel
Bank of England Museum
Bankside Gallery
Bethnal Green Museum of Childhood
Bromley Museum
Bruce Castle Museum
Capel Manor
Central Church of the Royal Air Force
Chelsea Physic Garden
Chessington World of Adventures*
Christchurch Spitalfields
Church of St Martin-within-Ludgate
Collection of the Worshipful Co of Clockmakers
Commonwealth Institute*
Courtauld Institute Galleries*
Cuming Museum
Dickens House Museum
Dulwich Picture Gallery
East Ham Nature Reserve
Elvisly Yours Centre
Erith Museum
Freud Museum
Greenwich Borough Museum
Guinness World of Records Exhibition*
Hampton Court Palace*
Harrow Museum & Heritage Centre*
HM Tower of London*
HMS Belfast*
Hogarth's House
Kew Bridge Steam Museum
Leighton House
Llewellyn Alexander (Fire Paintings) Ltd
London Butterfly House*
London Canal Museum
London Ecology Centre
London Toy and Model Museum
Mall Galleries

Marx Memorial Library
Museum of Installation
Museum of London*
Museum of the Moving Image*
Museum of the Order of St John
Musical Museum
Myddelton House Gardens
National Army Museum
National Gallery*
National Maritime Museum Greenwich*
National Postal Museum
National Sound Archive (British Library)
Natural History Museum*
North Woolwich Old Station Museum
Old Operating Theatre Museum
Passmore Edwards Museum
Percival David Foundation of Chinese Art
Petrie Museum of Egyptian Archaeology
Pollock's Toy Museum
Pumphouse Educational Museum
Puppet Centre Trust
Ragged School Museum
Rock Circus*
Royal Air Force Museum*
Royal Botanic Gardens Kew*
Royal London Hospital Archives & Museum
Salvation Army International Heritage Centre
Shakespeare Globe Museum
Sherlock Holmes Museum
Sir John Soane's Museum
South London Art Gallery
Southwark Cathedral
Spencer House
Spitting Image Rubberworks*
St George's Cathedral
St Martin-in-the-Fields
St Olave's Church
St Paul's Cathedral
Strawberry Hill

RTB Area	Name

Syon Park
Tallberg Taylor Gallery
Tower Bridge*
Upminster Tithe Barn Agricultural Museum
Valence House Museum

Vauxhall St Peter's Heritage Centre
Victoria and Albert Museum
Wesley's Chapel
Westminster Abbey*
Westminster Cathedral*

NORTH WEST

Adlington Hall
Albert Dock
All Saints Church
Animal World
Beacon Country Park
Blackburn Cathedral
Blackburn Museum and Art Gallery
Blackpool Pleasure Beach
British in India Museum
Brookside Miniature Railway
Butterfly World
Capesthorne Hall
Chester Cathedral
Chester Visitor Centre
Chester Zoo*
Chingle Hall
Council for the Port of Rural England
County and Regimental Museum
Croxteth Hall and Country Park
Dunham Massey Hall and Park
East Lancashire Railway
Fletcher Moss Botanical Garden
Frontierland Western Theme Park*
Grosvenor Museum
Harris Museum and Art Gallery
Helmshore Textile Museums
Hollingworth Lake Country Park
Knowsley Safari Park
Lady Lever Art Gallery
Liverpool Cathedral
Liverpool Museum
Local Interest Museum
Manchester Cathedral
Manchester United Museum & Tour Centre
Mouldsworth Motor Museum
Museum of Transport
National Maritime Museum
National Museum of Labour History
Ness Gardens

Norton Priory Museum and Gardens
Paradise Mill
Peckforton Castle
Pendle Heritage Centre
Peter Scott Gallery
Pilkington Glass Museum
Rochdale Art Gallery
Salford Museum and Art Gallery
Sea Life Centre
Sellet Hall Gardens
Southport Railway Centre
Southport Zoo and Conservation Trust
St Ann's Church
St Mary's Parish Church
Steamtown Railway Centre
Stockport War Memorial and Art Gallery
Sudley
Tabely House Collection
Tatton
The Beatles Story
The Boat Museum
The Local Interest Museum
The Museum of Childhood
The National Trust, Speke Hall
The Salt Museum
The Silk Museum
The Whitworth Art Gallery
The Wildfowl & Wetlands Trust, Martin Mere
Tower World
Towneley Hall Art Gallery and Museum
Toy and Teddy Bear Museum
Trafford Ecology Park
University of Liverpool Art Gallery
Viewpoint Photography Gallery
Walker Art Gallery
Warrington Museum and Art Gallery
West Lancashire Light Railway
West Park Museum

NORTHERN IRELAND

Armagh County Museum
Armagh Planetarium
Carrick-A-Rede Rope Bridge*
Carrickferggus Castle*
Down County Museum*
Family Heritage Museum
Florencecourt House
Gosford Forest Park
Heritage Farm Park
Larne Tourist Info & Interpretation Centre
Marble Arch Caves*
Mount Stewart House and Gardens*
Mullaghbawn Folk Museum
North Down Heritage Centre

Peatlands Park*
RSPB North Cliffs and West Light Platform
Seaford Tropical Butterfly House/Gardens/Maze
Springhill
St Columbs Cathedral
St Fin Barre's Cathedral
Talnotry Cottage Bird Garden
The Ballance House
The Northern Ireland Aquarium*
The Palace Stables Heritage Centre
The Ulster History Park
Ulster Folk and Transport Museum*
Ulster Museum*

NORTHUMBRIA

Arbeia Roman Fort & Museum
Auckland Castle
Bessie Surtees House
Bill Quay Community Farm*
Billingham Beck Valley Country Park
Binchester Roman Fort
Border History Museum
Botanic Centre
Bowes Railway Centre
Castle Eden Walkway Country Park*
Cathedral Church of St Nicholas
Chillingham Castle
Chillingham Wild Cattle Association Ltd
Church of St Cuthbert & Turner Mausoleum
Darlington Museum
Derwent Walk Country Park
Durham Heritage Centre
Durham Light Infantry Museum & Art Gallery
Gray Art Gallery
Hancock Museum
Hartlepool Maritime Museum
Hexham Abbey
Kielder Forest and Castle

Kielder Water
Kings Own Scottish Borders Regimental Museum
Metroland*
Morpeth Chantry Bagpipe Museum
Newham Grange Leisure Farm
North East Aircraft Museum
Once Brewed National Park Visitor Centre
Oriental Museum
Preston Tower
Royal Ancient & Monastic Church of St Paul
Ryhope Engines Museum
Seaton Delaval Hall
South Shields Museum & Art Gallery
St Mungo's 13th Century Church
Thirlestane Castle
Timothy Hackworth Victorian & Railway Museum
University Gallery
University of Durham Botanic Garden
Wildfowl & Wetlands Centre
Wine and Spirit Museum
Woodham Church Museum
Woodhorn Colliery Museum
Zetland Lifeboat Museum

RTB Area	Name

SCOTLAND

Abbotsford
Almond Valley Heritage Trust
Almondell & Calderwood Country Park
Ardencraig Gardens
Ardfearn Nursery Plant Centre
Argyll Forest Park
Arran & Argyll Transport Museum
Art Gallery and Museum*
Auchindrain Township Open Air Museum
Ayton Castle
Baird Institute Museum
Balmoral Estates
Beacraigs Country Park
Blackshaw Farm Park Ltd
Blair Castle*
Blair Drummond Safari & Leisure Park
Bod of Gremista
Bowhill House and Country Park
Branklyn Garden
Brodick Castle & Country Park & Goatfell
Burns Cottage and Museum
Burns Monument and Gardens
Burrell Collection*
Bute Museum
Calderglen Country Park
Cambo Country Park
Camera Obscura
Canongate Kirk
Cawdor Castle
Charles Rennie Mackintosh Society
Chatelherault Country Park
Church of the Holyrude, Stirling
Clan Macpherson Museum
Cluanie Deer Farm Park
Coats Observatory
Crombie Country Park
Dalmeny House
Damside Garden Herbs
Darnaway Farm Visitor Centre
Darnoch Cathedral
Dean Castle & Country Park
Dick Institute
Dochfour Gardens
Drummond Castle Gardens
Duart Castle
Dunaverig Farm Life Centre
Dunrobin Castle
Earlshall Castle and Gardens
Easdale Island Folk Museum
Edinburgh Canal Centre
Edinburgh Museum of Childhood
Edinburgh Zoo*
Eyemouth Museum
Fair Maid's House
Falls of Clyde Nature Reserve
Famous Old Blacksmith's Shop Centre*
Fasque
Floors Castle
Formakin Estate
Frigate Unicorn
Gairloch Heritage Museum
Galloway Forest Park
Gem Rock Museum
Gladstone's Land
Glanbarr Abbey Visitors Centre
Glasgow Botanic Gardens
Glasgow Vennel Museum
Glasgow Zoo Park
Glen Trool Visitor Centre
Glengoulandie Deer Park
Gosford House
Grampian Transport Museum
Greyfriars Kirk
Groam House Museum Trust
Haggs Castle
Hamilton District Museum
Hunterian Art Gallery
Inveraray Jail
Inverewe Garden
Isle of Arran Heritage Museum
Isle of Gigha
J M Barrie's Birthplace
Jane Welsh Carlyle Museum
Jonah's Journey

Kailzie Gardens
Kelburn Country Centre
Kellie Castle
Kirk of St Nicholas
Kirkcaldy Museum & Art Gallery
Laidhay Croft Museum
Landmark Highland Heritage and Adventure Park
Largs Museum
Leith Hall
Lennoxlove House
Lochore Meadows Country Park
Lochwinnoch Community Museum
Lochwinnoch Nature Centre
Logan Botanic Garden
Manderston
Maxwelton House
McLean Museum and Art Gallery
McLellan Galleries
Mill of Towie
Mull & West Highland Narrow Gauge Railway
Museum of Fire
Museum of Flight
Museum of Lead Mining
Museum of the Cumbraes
Museum of Transport*
Myreton Motor Museum
Neidpath Castle
New Lanark Village
North Ayrshire Museum
North Carr Lightship Anstruther Harbour
Oban Sea Life Centre
Old Byre
Old Semeil Herb Garden
Paisley Museum & Art Galleries
Palace of Holyroodhouse*
Paxton House
People's Palace Museum*
Pollok House*
Provand's Lordship
Queen's Own Highlanders Regimental Museum
Royal Museum of Scotland*
Royal Observatory Visitor Centre
Royal Scottish Academy
Rutherglen Museum
Saint Andrew's Cathedral Inverness
Satroshere
Scone Palace*
Scotland Street School Museum
Scottish Agricultural Museum
Scottish Industrial Railway Centre
Scottish Maritime Museum
Scottish Mining Museum
Scottish Whisky Heritage Centre*
Scottish Wildlife Trust
Shetland Croft House Museum
Shetland Museum
Speyside Heather/Garden Visitor Centre
Springburn Museum Trust
St Andrew's Cathedral (Episcopal)
St Andrews Botanic Garden
St Andrews Preservation Trust Museum
St Andrews Sea Life Centre
St Giles' Cathedral
St Mary's Episcopal Cathedral
St Michaels Parish Church
Stewartry Museum
Stranraer Museum
Stromness Museum
Summerlee Heritage Trust
Tain and District Museum
Tankerness House Museum
The Hirsel
Threake Gardens
Thurso Heritage Museum
Timespan Heritage Centre
Tingwall Agricultural Museum
Torosay Castle & Gardens
Traquair House
Tweedhope Sheep Dogs
Ullapool Museum
University Botanic Garden
Waltzing Waters Ltd
West Highland Museum
Whithorn Dig

SOUTH EAST

A Day at the Wells
Alfriston Heritage Centre & Blacksmith's
Anne of Cleves House Museum

Apuldram Roses
Arundel Toy and Military Museum
Badsell Farm Park

RTB Area	Name

Bartley Mill
Bateman's (The National Trust)
Battle Abbey and Battlefield of Hastings
Bentley Wildfowl & Motor Museum
Bexhill Museum of Costume & Social History
Bexley Museum
Bignor Roman Villa
Boughton Monchelsea Place
Brighton Sea Life Centre
British Engineerium Steam Museum
Brooklands Museum
Buckleys Yesterdays World
Canterbury Cathedral
Chilham Castle
Clandon Park
Cobham Manor Riding Centre & Country Pursuits
Crabble Corn Mill
Deal Castle
Denmans Garden
Dickens House Museum Broadstairs
Doddington Place Gardens
Drusillas Park
Ethnic Doll and Toy Museum
Fishbourne Roman Palace and Museum
Fleur De Lis Heritage Centre
Flimwell Bird Park
Frewen College
Guildford Cathedral
Hammerwood Park
Hastings Museum and Art Gallery
Hastings Sea Life Centres*
Hatchlands Park
Heaven Farm
Hever Castle
High Beeches Gardens
Hove Museum and Art Gallery
How We Lived Then Museum of Shops

Howletts Zoo Park
Iden Croft Herbs
Knole
Leeds Castle
Leonardslee Gardens
Lewes Castle and Museums
Lympne Castle
Margate Old Town Hall Local History Museum
Maritime Museum, Ramsgate
Marle Place Gardens and Nursery
Michelham Priory
Mount Ephraim Gardens
Museum of Kent Life
Newhaven Fort
Northbourne Court Gardens
Pallant House
Parham Elizabethan House & Gardens
Parsonage Farm Rural Heritage Centre
Polesden Lacey
Port Lympne Zoo Park, Mansion & Gardens
Quex House & Gardens & Powell-Cotton Museum
Rare Farm Animals of Hollanden
Rochester Castle
Romney, Hythe & Dymchurch Railway
Royal Engineers Museum
Royal Pavilion, Art Gallery and Museum
Rural Life Centre
Smugglers Adventure
Sussex Combined Services Museum
The Bluebell Railway
The C M Booth Collection of Historic Vehicles
The Historic Dockyard Chatham
The National Pinetum (Bedgebury)
The White Cliffs Experience
Towner Art Gallery & Local History Museum
Volks Electric Railway
Weald and Downland Open Air Museum

SOUTHERN

Abbotsbury Sub Tropical Gardens
Abbotsbury Swannery
Abbotsbury Tithe Barn Museum
Arreton Manor
Barton Manor Gardens & Vineyards
Bear Museum
Blue Pool
Bournemouth Heritage Transport Centre
Breamore House & Museums
Bucklers Hard Village & Maritime Museum*
Butterfly World and Fountain World
Carisbrooke Castle
Charles Dickens Birthplace Museum
Chesil Gallery
Chettle House
Christchurch Tricycle Museum
Coach House Museum
Compton Acres Gardens
Dinosaur Safari
Dorset County Museum
Dorset Heavy Horse Centre
Edmondsham House & Garden
Exbury Gardens
Gods House Tower Museum
Golden Hill Fort
Goss and Crested China Ltd
Gurkha Museum
Haseley Manor
Havant Museum
HMS Victory
Houghton Lodge Garden & Hydroponicum
Isle of Wight Rare Breeds & Waterfowl Park
Itchen Valley Country Park
Longdown Dairy Farm
Lulworth Cove Heritage
Manor Farm Country Park
Marwell Zoological Park*
Minster Church of St Cuthberga*
Moors Valley Country Park
Mummies and Magic
Museum of Army Flying

Natural World*
New Forest Butterfly Farm
New Forest Museum and Visitor Centre
Nunwell House & Gardens
Old Smithy Tourist Centre
Paultons Park
Poole Pottery
Portsmouth Cathedral
Portsmouth Sea Life Centre
Quay Arts
Queen Elizabeth Country Park
Red House Museum Art Gallery & Gardens
Roman Villa, Brading
Romany Folklore Museum & Workshop
Rotherfield Park
Royal Green Jackets Museum
Royal Marines Museum
Royal Navy Submarine Museum
Royal Signals Museum
Royal Victoria Country Park
Russel-Cotes Art Gallery & Museum
Scaplen's Court Museum
Shaftesbury Abbey Museum & Ruins
Spitbank Fort
SS Shieldhall
Stanstead Park
Star Cottage Garden
Stewarts Garden – Lands
Tank Museum
Tithe Barn Museum & Arts Centre
Tropical Bird Park
Tudor House Museum
Twyford Pumping Station
Ventnor Botanic Garden*
Waterfront Museum
Weymouth Sea Life Park
Winchester Cathedral
Winchester Heritage Centre
Woolhouse Maritime Museum
World of Toys

THAMES & CHILTERNS

Ardington Pottery
Ashmolean Museum
Bedford Museum
Bekonscot Model Village*
Blenheim Palace*
Bromham Mill
Broughton Castle
Carfax Tower

Cecil Higgins Art Gallery and Museum
Chicheley Hall
Child-Beale Wildlife Park*
Chiltern Open Air Museum
Christ Church Cathedral*
Courage Shire Horse Centre
Didcot Railway Centre*
Dinton Pastures Country Park*

RTB Area	Name

Dunstable Downs Country Park
Elstow Moot Hall
Fenny Lodge Gallery
Harrold Odell Country Park*
Hatfield Forest
Hatfield House*
Highclere Castle
Hughenden Manor
Kennet Horse Boat Company
Kingston Bagpuize House and Garden
Leighton Buzzard Railway
Luton Museum and Art Gallery
Mapledurham House and Watermill*
Mill Green Museum and Mill
Milton's Cottage
Oxfordshire County Museum
Paradise Wildlife Park
Royalty and Empire*
Saxon Tower Church of St Michael
St Georges Chapel*
Stanborough Park

Stockgrove Country Park
Stockwood Craft Museum & Gardens
Stowe Landscape Gardens
Sulgrave Manor
Swiss Garden
The Herb Farm and Saxon Maze
The Look Out*
The Oxford Story
The Savill Garden
The Shuttleworth Collection
The Walter Rothschild Zoological Museum
The Waterfowl Sanctuary and Rescue Centre
Tolsey Museum
Welwyn Roman Baths
West Wycombe Caves
Whipsnade Wild Animal Park*
Windsor Safari Park*
Woburn Abbey
Woodside Farm & Wild Fowl Park
Wrest Park House and Gardens

WALES

Amgueddfa'r Gogledd/Museum of the North
Anglesey Sea Zoo*
Beaumaris Gaol and Court
Bersham Heritage Centre and Ironworks
Bodnant Gardens
Bodrhyddan Hall
Brecon Beacons Mountain Centre
Bryn Bras Castle
Carew Castle and Tidal Mill
Cefn Coed Colliery Museum
Centre for Alternative Technology
Ceredigion Museum
Cilgwyn Candles Workshop and Mini Museum
Conwy Castle
Conwy Visitor Centre*
Cyfarthfa Castle Museum, Art Gallery and Park
Dan-Yr-Ogof Showcaves
Dyffryn House Conference Centre and Gardens
Erddig Hall
Felin Crewi Working Watermill
Ffestiniog Railway
Graham Sutherland Gallery
Great Orme Tramway
Haverfordwest Castle Museum and Art Gallery
Llangollen Motor Museum
Maes Astro Tourist Attraction
Margam Park*
Model Farm and Folk Museum
Model House Craft and Design Centre
Museum of Childhood

Museum of the Home
Newport Museum and Art Gallery
Oceanarium
Offa's Dyke Association
Oriel Mostyn
Pembroke Castle
Penrhyn Castle
Plas Newydd "The National Trust"
Pontypool and Blaenavon Railway
Powysland Museum & Montgomery Canal Centre
Rhondda Heritage Park
Rhyl Sea Life Centre
Robert Owen Museum
Ruthin Craft Centre
Snowdon Mountain Railway
Talyllyn Railway
Teifi Valley Railway
Tenby Museum and Picture Gallery
The Alice in Wonderland Visitor Centre
The Lloyd George Museum and Highgate His Home
The Nelson Museum and Local History Centre
The South Wales Borderers Museum
The Welch Regiment Museum
Trefriw Wells Spa
Tregwynt Mill
Welsh Folk Museum*
Welsh Highland Railway
Welsh Slate Museum
Welshpool and Llanfair Light Railway
White Castle

WEST COUNTRY

Allhallows Museum
Athelhampton House and Gardens
Atwell Wilson Motor Museum
Avon Valley Country Park
Avon Valley Railway
Beaulieu National Motor Museum, House & Abbey*
Bennetts Water Gardens
Bickleigh Castle
Bicton Park Gardens
Blaise Castle House Museum
Bodmin and Wenford Railway
Bodmin Town Museum
Book Museum
Bowood House
Bradford on Avon Museum
Bristol Cathedral
Bristol Industrial Museum
Bristol Zoo Gardens*
Brixham Museum & History Society
Broadleas Gardens Charitable Trust Ltd
Buckfast Butterflies & Dartmoor Otter Sanct
Bude Museum
Cadhay
Camborne School of Mines Geological Museum
Chambercombe Manor
Chard & District Museum
Cholderton Rare Breeds Farm Park
Christchurch Priory
Clapton Court Gardens
Colliford Lake Park
Combe Martin Wildlife & Dinosaur Park
Cornish Seal Sanctuary
Cornwall Donkey & Pony Sanctuary
Corsham Court
Cranmore Tower

Dartmouth Museum
Devonshire Regiment Museum
Dinosaur Museum*
Dorset Military Museum
Duke of Cornwall's Light Infantry Museum
East Lambrook Manor Garden
Escot Aquatic Centre & Gardens
Exeter Cathedral*
Exmoor Bird Gardens
Falmouth Maritime Museum
Flambards Village Theme Park*
Frome Museum
Gorse Blossom Railway & Woodland Park
Great Western Railway Museum
Hardys Wessex Exhibition
Harveys Wine Museum
Hatch Court
Heale Gardens and Plant Centre
Holburne Museum & Crafts Study Centre
Iford Manor Gardens
Ilfracombe Museum
John Wesley's Chapel
Kingston Maurward Gardens and Farm
Lackham Gardens & Agricultural Museum
Land's End*
Lanreath Folk Farm Museum
Longleat House and Safari Park
Longstone Heritage Centre
Lyme Regis Experience
Manningford Gardens & Nursery
Marazion Marine Aquarium
Maritime Museum
Miniature Pony Centre
Minterne Gardens
Morwellham Quay

RTB Area	Name

Mount Edgcumbe House & Country Park
Museum of Costume
Museum of English Naive Art
National Ambulance Museum
National Shire Horse Centre*
New World Tapestry Centres
Newlyn Art Gallery
North Cornwall Museum and Gallery
North Devon Maritime Museum
Nothe Fort
Number One the Royal Crescent
Old Crown Court and Cells
Oldway Mansion
Padstow Shipwreck Museum
Paignton & Dartmouth Steam Railway
Paignton Zoo*
Parke Rare Breeds Farm
Parracombe Garden Railway
Pecorama
Pencarrow
Plymouth Dome*
Portland Castle
Potters Museum of Curiosity
Prideaux Place
Probus County Demonstration Garden
Radstock Midsomer Norton Museum
Red Lodge
Rock Garden and Cave
Roman Baths Museum*
Rougemont House Museum
Royal Albert Memorial Museum
Royal Cornwall Museum
Royal Horticultural Society Garden
Royal Photographic Society
Salcombe Maritime & Local History Museum
Salisbury and South Wiltshire Museum
Salisbury Cathedral*
Sally Lunn's Refreshment House & Museum
Sand
Shaldon Wildlife Trust
Sherborne Abbey
Shipwreck & Heritage Centre
Sidmouth Museum
Somerset Rural Life Museum

Southwick Country Herb Centre
SS Great Britain
St Ives Society of Artists
St Mary Redcliffe Church Bristol
St Nicholas Priory
Stourton House Garden
Tamar Valley Donkey Park
Tapeley Park & British Jousting Centre
Tehidy Country Park
Teignmouth Museum
The Big Sheep
The Building of Bath Museum
The Dewey Museum
The Donkey Sanctuary
The Garden House
The International Helicopter Museum
The Lost Gardens of Heligan
The Monkey Sanctuary
Tiverton Castle
Tiverton Museum
Tolpuddle Martyrs Museum
Torquay Museum
Torre Abbey
Torrington Museum
Totnes (Elizabethan) Museum
Totnes Castle
Totnes Guildhall
Trebah Garden
Trenouth Farm Rare Breeds Centre
Trinity House National Lighthouse Centre
Trowbridge Museum
Truro Cathedral*
Tutankhamun Exhibition
Vintage Toy Train Museum
Watchet Market House Museum
Watermouth Castle
Wells Cathedral*
Wells Museum
West Somerset Rural Life Museum
Wheelwrights Museum & Gypsy Folklore Collect
Willsbridge Mill
Woodspring Museum
Worldwide Butterflies Ltd

YORKSHIRE & HUMBERSIDE

Abbeydale Industrial Hamlet
Automobilia Transport Museum
Bagshaw Museum
Bankfield Museum
Barton Clay Pits*
Batley Art Gallery
Bayle Museum
Beck Isle Museum of Rural Life
Beverley Minster
Bishops' House
Bolling Hall
Bolton Abbey Estate*
Bradford Industrial Horses at Work Museum
Bramham Park
Buffers
Burnby Hall Gardens & Museum
Burton Agnes Hall
Burton Constable Hall
Captain Cook Schoolroom Museum
Cartwright Hall
Castle Howard*
Colne Valley Museum
Colour Museum
Cooper Gallery
Dales Countryside Museum
Dewsbury Museum
Duncombe Park
East Riddlesden Hall
Eden Camp Modern History Theme Museum*
Elizabethan Exhibition Gallery
Elsham Hall Country & Wildlife Park
Embsay Steam Railway
Eureka! The Museum for Children
Ferens Art Gallery
Filey Museum
Graves Art Gallery
Halifax Piece Hall*
Harlow Carr Botanical Gardens
Hebden Crypt
Hornsea Freeport*
Hornsea Museum
Huddersfield Art Gallery
Hull and East Riding Museum
Jervaulx Abbey

Jorvik Viking Centre*
Keighley & Worth Valley Railway*
Kirklees Light Railway
Knaresborough Castle & Courthouse Museum
Land Farm Garden
Leeds City Museum
Leeds Industrial Museum
Lightwater Valley Theme Park*
Lotherton Hall Bird Garden*
Malton Museum
Margaret Waudby Oriental Garden
Mercer Art Gallery
Museum of Army Transport
Museum of Mechanical Music
National Railway Museum*
Nidderdale Museum
Normanby Hall Country Park
Norton Conyers
Nunnington Hall
Oakwell Hall Country Park
Old Grammar School
Parcevall Hall Gardens
Pennyarcadia
Pontefract Castle
Pontefract Museum
Pugneys Country Park
Ripon Cathedral*
Ripon Prison & Police Museum
Rother Valley Country Park*
Royal Pump Room Museum
Sandtoft Transport Centre
Scunthorpe Museum
Sea Life Centre*
Selby Abbey
Shandy Hall
Sheffield Botanical Gardens
Sheriff Hutton Park
Shibden Hall
Sion Hill Hall
Skipton Castle*
Skipton Holy Trinity Parish Church
Sobriety Waterways Adventure Centre & Museum
Sooty's World
Spurn Lightship

RTB Area	Name

St Mary's Priory, Old Malton
St Michael the Archangel Church
St Wilfrid's Church
Staintondale Shire Horse Farm
Streetlife – Hull Museum of Transport
Sutcliffe Gallery
Swaledale Folk Museum
The Guildhall Beverley
The Old Rectory
The Smuggling Experience
Town Docks Museum
Tropical World*
University of Hull Art Collection
Victorian Reed Organ Museum
Vintage Railway Carriage Museum
Wakefield Art Gallery

Wakefield Cathedral
Wakefield Museum
Walkley Clogs
Whitby Archives Heritage Centre
Wilberforce House
Wood End Museum of Natural History
Wordsworth Gallery
World of the Honey Bee
Worsbrough Country Park*
Wortley Top Forge Industrial Museum
York Minster*
Yorkshire Car Collection
Yorkshire Carriage Museum
Yorkshire Dales Falconry & Conservation Centre
Yorkshire Museum
Yorkshire Water Museum

INDEX 3
INDEX OF CONTACTS

Contact Name	Contact Title	Attraction

BUSINESS OPERATIONS

Contact Name	Contact Title	Attraction
Mr J Abraham	General Manager	Sally Lunn's Refreshment House & Museum
Ann Abramson	Curator	Strumpshaw Hall Steam Museum
H H Ackers	Senior Landscape Manager	Animal World
H H Ackers	Senior Landscape Manager	Butterfly World
Jean Adams	Museum Curator	Easdale Island Folk Museum
Ms B Adams	Curator	Petrie Museum of Egyptian Archaeology
J Aidiniantz	Director	Sherlock Holmes Museum
Mr M Aldridge	Factor	Drummond Castle Gardens
Mr C J Allan	Deputy Director	Hunterian Art Gallery
Catherine Allard	Manager	Windermere Steamboat Museum*
Mr T Allen	Team Leader	Barton Clay Pits*
Mrs B Allen	Tourism Manager	Bolton Abbey Estate*
C Allender	Museum Manager	National Railway Museum*
Mark Allinson	Manager	Thameside Complex
Mr T McAllister	Chief Museum Assistant	Passmore Edwards Museum
Mr D Allsop	Country Park Warden	Poole's Cavern
Mr D Alston/Ms A Goodchild	Deputy Director of Arts	Graves Art Gallery
M Amey	Owner	Hardys Wessex Exhibition
Ellis T Amos	Chapter Clerk	Carlisle Cathedral
M Andrews	Museum Director	Museum of Army Flying
Miss D Andrews/Mrs R Brooks	Partners	Old Smithy Tourist Centre
Mrs E C Angus	Chairperson	Thurso Heritage Museum
M & K Ann	Managing Partners	Drusillas Park
H Armitage	Information Officer, City of Oxford	Carfax Tower
Mr R Armstrong	Centre Manager	Jorvik Viking Centre*
Mr J Arnold	Managing Director	New Lanark Village
P Arnott	Operations Manager	Shugborough
T Ash	Proprietor	Parke Rare Breeds Farm
Mr D Asquith	Administrator	Clandon Park
Mr D Asquith	Administrator	Hatchlands Park
D Atkinson	Senior Keeper	Yorkshire Water Museum
Dr R L Atkinson	Curator	Camborne School of Mines Geological Museum
K Atkinson	Proprietor	Wheelwrights Museum & Gypsy Folklore Collect.
Mrs E Atkinson	Secretary	Frome Museum
Mr D Attwood	Deputy Gen Manager Operations	Chessington World of Adventures*
R & H Atwell		Atwell Wilson Motor Museum
Lt Col E H L Aubrey-Fletcher	Administrator	Stanford Hall
Lt Col E H L Aubrey-Fletcher	Administrator	Stanford Hall Motorcycle Museum
Mr B Ayres	Custodian/Team Leader	Newstead Abbey*
Maj Gen K Bach/Mrs P Hunter	Chapter Clerk/Visitors Office	York Minster*
M W Badham	Director	Twycross Zoo*
Ms J Bagnall	Curator	Roman Villa, Brading
Mrs B Bailes	Gift Shop Manageress	Cathedral Church of St Nicholas
Mr B Bailles	Administrator	Chillingham Castle
C R Baines	Chairman	Tolsey Museum
Ms D Baker	Manager	Spitting Image Rubberworks*
E Ballard	Castle and Museum Curator	Tamworth Castle
Mr K Bamber	Receiver General	Winchester Cathedral
Ms J Banham	Curator	Leighton House
Ms R Bannister	Parish Administrator	Beverley Minster
M Barbour	Business Manager	Ragley Hall
Dr A Barclay	Ranger	Scottish Wildlife Trust
Mrs Patricia Bardon	Museum Administrator	Down County Museum*
E H Barfoot	Regional Visitor Services Manager	Rochester Castle
M Barker	Curator	Midland Motor Museum
Miss J Barnard	Owner	Blue Pool
M E Barton	Museum Director	Brooklands Museum
Mr C Barton	Warden	The Old Rectory
Mr T Batty	General Manager	Dinosaur Museum*
Mr T Batty	General Manager	Dinosaur Safari
Mr T Batty	General Manager	Mummies and Magic
Mr T Batty	General Manager	Tutankhamun Exhibition
Ms E Baxter and Ms V Ford	Duty Managers	The Lace Hall
Mr H Bayntun-Coward	Owner	Book Museum
Mr Beaufoy	Director	Tatton
P W Beavis	Church Admin	Saxon Tower Church of St Michael
Lieutenant Commander J Beck	Trustee Secretary & Curator	Falmouth Maritime Museum
Mr P Beckett	Administrator	Wakefield Cathedral
Mrs S Beeley, Mr L James	Curator, Secretary	National Cycle Museum
H Belsey	Curator	Gainsborough's House
Ms C Belton		Cornwall Donkey & Pony Sanctuary
J Bennett	Partner	Bennetts Water Gardens
Ms J Bennette	Gallery Manager	Newlyn Art Gallery
R J Benson	Hon Secretary	Herefordshire Waterworks Museum
C Beresford	Curator	Regiments of Gloucestershire Museum
Mr J Bernasconi	Hon Curator	University of Hull Art Collection
Mr P Berridge	Archaeology Officer	Woodspring Museum

Contact Name	Contact Title	Attraction
Miss M Beston	Administrator	Norton Conyers
P T Bidwell	Principal Keeper	Arbeia Roman Fort & Museum
Mr N Biles	Manager	Weymouth Sea Life Park
Ms V Billingham	Owner	Tweedhope Sheep Dogs
Mrs Bird	Manageress	West Wycombe Caves
I R Bishop	Curator	The Walter Rothschild Zoological Museum
J Bishop	Museum Assistant	Much Wenlock Museum
Miss S Bishop	Sales/Reception	Haseley Manor
Mr C Bishop	Exhibition Manager	Rock Circus*
L Bisset	Curator	University Botanic Garden
Ms B Derby/Mr S Black	Curators	Christchurch Tricycle Museum
Mr and Mrs K Blackburn	Owners	Buffers
Dr S Blackden	Resident Representative	Kellie Castle
Ms R Blackmore	Shop Manager	Newark Air Museum
Les Blackwell	Treasurer	Welsh Highland Railway
J Blades	Administrator	Hanbury Hall (National Trust)
Mr G Blades	Operations Director	Lightwater Valley Theme Park*
Mrs S L Blaylock	Personal Assistant	Dalemain Historic House
David Bleines	Museum Assistant	Tenby Museum and Picture Gallery
Valerie Boa	Curator	McLean Museum and Art Gallery
Board of Directors		Blackpool Pleasure Beach
J D Bond	Keeper of the Gardens	The Savill Garden
Oliver Bone	Curator	Thetford Museum
Mr C Booth	Proprietor	The C M Booth Collection of Historic Vehicles
Mr C Borthwick/Mr M Cousins	Office Man/Arts Admin	St Edmundsbury Cathedral
Ms A Boscawen & Ms S Bray		High Beeches Gardens
J Boston	Managing Director	Land's End*
Rev A Botwright		Skipton Holy Trinity Parish Church
Mr B Boulton		Rock Garden and Cave
Mr P Bourke		Chettle House
S Bourne	Curator	Towneley Hall Art Gallery and Museum
R Boutwood/M Lockyer	Admin Director/Animal Director	Port Lympne Zoo Park, Mansion & Gardens
Mrs Jean Bowe	Hon Curator	Eyemouth Museum
Mr I Bowes	Museum Manager	North East Aircraft Museum
Mr N Boxall		Bickleigh Castle
K Bradbury	Curator	Cider Museum and King Offa Distillery
Mrs U Bradley		Old Byre
S Brailey	Executive General Manager	Tower World
Dr M Brambell	Director	Chester Zoo*
Lys De Bray	Owner	Star Cottage Garden
Mr P Brears	Director	Leeds City Museum
Ms E Bredsdorff	Museum Curator	Powysland Museum & Montgomery Canal Centre
M Brewster	Curator	Museum of English Naive Art
Rebe Brick	Correspondence Secretary	Offa's Dyke Association
Mr J Bridges	Administrator	Sion Hill Hall
Mr and Mrs A Brierley	Owners	Our Little Farm
Bristol Museums & Art Gallery	Curator of Applied Art	Red Lodge
A Broadhurst & A Broadhurst Jr	Partners	Llangollen Motor Museum
Mr J I Brockie MBE	Park Manager	Chatelherault Country Park
H S Brodie	Proprietor	Old Dairy Farm Centre
Gordon H Brookes	Curator	Rydal Mount
Ms Z Brooks	Manager	Vauxhall St Peter's Heritage Centre
Heather Broughton	Project Director	Snibston Discovery Park
Katherine Brown	Curator	King's Lynn Museums
Mr and Mrs Brown	Managers	Steam Brewery Museum
Robert Brown	Owner	Museum of Childhood
P McMillan Browse	Principal Horticultural Officer	Probus County Demonstration Garden
S Bruce		Chingle Hall
Mr & Mrs J Brumer	Proprietor	Cobham Manor Riding Centre & Country Pursuits
T Bryan	Museum Keeper	Great Western Railway Museum
A Buckley	Owner/Curator	Buckleys Yesterdays World
L M Budreau-Ross	Curator	Grantham Museum
C Buggy	Countryside Officer	Dinton Pastures Country Park*
Dr S Bull	Curator	County and Regimental Museum
Colonel and Mrs Bullivant	Owners	Stourton House Garden
Mrs P Bullock	Assoc Chairman	Bexhill Museum of Costume & Social History
Mr I Burdon	Partner	Jervaulx Abbey
S Burge	Curator	Colour Museum
L Burgess	Sales and Admin Officer	Luton Museum and Art Gallery
L Burgess	Sales and Admin Officer	Stockwood Craft Museum & Gardens
Mr J Burgess	Manager	London Butterfly House*
Mrs E Burgess	Hon Secretary	Nidderdale Museum
I M Burgoyne	Curator	Pilkington Glass Museum
Paul Burke	Head Recreation Ranger	Grizedale Forest Park*
Mr D Burrows	Cathedral Administrator	Chester Cathedral
Lady Burton		Dochfour Gardens
Mr A Burton	Head of Museum	Bethnal Green Museum of Childhood
Mr and Mrs M Busk	Owners	Houghton Lodge Garden & Hydroponicum
B & J Butler	Proprietors	Kennet Horse Boat Company
J W Butler	Managing Director	Heaven Farm
Mrs A Butler	Representative	Gladstones's Land
M A Byrne	Managing Director	The Beatles Story
Mr P Bywalski	Managing Director	Barton Manor Gardens & Vineyards
Ian Cadogan	Park Director	Margam Park*
Mr F Savage Caldwell	Curator	Gray Art Gallery
Mr F Savage Caldwell	Curator	Hartlepool Maritime Museum
Ms E Cameron	Secretary/Curator	Laidhay Croft Museum
Ms H Cameron	Administrator	Duncombe Park
G M Candler	Site Co-ordinator	Carew Castle and Tidal Mill

Contact Name	Contact Title	Attraction
Anthony Candon	Manager	The Ulster History Park
R Cannidy	Major – Curator	Royal Green Jackets Museum
A Careym	General Manager	Welshpool and Llanfair Light Railway
R Carman	Hon Curator	Ely Museum
M Carmichael	Administrator	Castle Howard*
Mr P Carpenter	Property Admin Officer	Oldway Mansion
Ms J Carpenter	Curator Art Collections	University of Liverpool Art Gallery
Major J Carroll	Curator	Dorset Military Museum
Mr H Carroll	Head Boatman	Coniston Boating Centre
D S and I M Carrothers	Owners	Family Heritage Museum
V Carslaw	Acting Manager	Museum of Kent Life
Mary Carter	House & Theatre Manager	Bowhill House and Country Park
Mr B Carter	Administrator	Oxburgh Hall
Mrs Janet Carter	Director	Buxton Micrarium
Miss K Carver	Museum Officer	Epping Forest District Museum
P M Cater	Visitors Centre Manager	Sellafield Visitors Centre
M Cates	Director	Maritime Museum Ramsgate
Mrs E Cartwright-Hignett	Owner	Iford Manor Gardens
Mr M Cavanagh	Owner	Cotswold Motor Museum
Mrs C Cavenagh-Mainwaring		Whitmore Hall
Countess Cawdor	Director	Cawdor Castle
R Cawthorne	Curator	Dartmouth Museum
The Chairman	Museum Sub-committee	Wymondham Heritage Museum
Dr N Chalmers	Director	Natural History Museum*
Miss F Chalmers	Countryside Officer	Itchen Valley Country Park
Mr L Channer	Custodian	Hogarth's House
Lynda Checketts	Curator	Norwich Gallery
Mr R Chesters	Curator	Almond Valley Heritage Trust
Mr K Childs	Retail Manager	Poole Pottery
Mr D Chinery	Assistant Director	Strangers' Hall Museum
D Chinnery	Assistant Director	Norwich Castle Museum*
G Christer	Manager	Lochwinnoch Nature Centre
Ms K Christie		Tapeley Park & British Jousting Centre
Fiona Clark	Custodian	Beatrix Potter Gallery*
M Clark	Director of Zoological Gardens	Exmoor Bird Gardens
Mr T Clark	Proprietor	White Post Modern Farm Centre*
Ms S Clark	Director	Famous Old Blacksmiths Shop Centre*
R D Clark	Honorary Curator	Bradford on Avon Museum
Miss Coryn E Clarke	Owner/Manager	Priests Mill
R Clarke	Head Custodian	Wrest Park House and Gardens
Rev D Clarke	Rector	St Wilfrid's Church
Miss S M Cleaver	Administrator	Houghton Hall
Mr S Clews	Keeper of Local History	Roman Baths Museum*
Mr J Close	Assistant Director	Victoria and Albert Museum
Mrs M Clough	Countryside Information Assistant	Castle Eden Walkway Country Park*
J Cobar	Director & General Manager	Paignton & Dartmouth Steam Railway
Miss J Cobb	Horticultural Officer & Curator	University of Durham Botanic Garden
Major AGB Cobbold	Hon Curator	Suffolk Regiment Museum
D Coke	Curator	Pallant House
Mrs B Cole	Partner	Felsted Vineyards
Mr A Coles	Principal Keeper	Hancock Museum
Captain F Collins	Director	HMS Belfast*
Mr A Collins	Park Manager/District Ranger	Calderglen Country Park
Mr B Collins/Ms S Collins	Partners	Automobilia Transport Museum
Mr J Collins	Assistant Curator Transport	Mark Hall Cycle Museum and Gardens
Commanding Officer HMS Victory		HMS Victory
Committee		Upminster Tithe Barn Agricultural Museum
B & G Compton	Curators	Bignor Roman Villa
Mr R Compton	General Manager	Harveys Wine Museum
Mr A Condick	Manager	Kew Bridge Steam Museum
J Connolly	Admin	Sidmouth Museum
Mrs D Cook	Church Warden/Verger	Church of St Cuthbert & Turner Mausoleum
Mrs G Cook	Proprietor	Old Semeil Herb Gardens
P Cooke		Athelhampton House and Gardens
M Cope	Hon Secretary	Vintage Railway Carriage Museum
Christopher Corry-Thomas	Administrator	Florencecourt House
Lady Anne Cowdray	Curator	Broadleas Gardens Charitable Trust Ltd
W Cowlin	Manageress	The International Helicopter Museum
Rev J Cowling	Rector	St Olave's Church
Mr S Cox	Director-General	Commonwealth Institute*
Mr W Crawford	Manager	Cluanie Deer Farm Park
Mr A Credland	Keeper of Maritime History	Town Docks Museum
Major T H Baker Cresswell		Preston Tower
Ms D Cripps	Manager	London Ecology Centre
Mr P Crockford	Owner	Stags Holt Farm and Stud
Mr D Crompton	Head Warden	Moors Valley Country Park
David Crosbie	Regional Enterprises Manager	Wordsworth House
Mr K Cross	Business Manager/Director	Oceanarium
Mr & Mrs S Cruickshank	Joint Owners	Damside Garden Herbs
Mr P Cullard	Deputy Controller	Museum of the Moving Image*
Ms S Curtis	Curator	Valence House Museum
Alison Cutforth	Curator	Springburn Museum Trust
E Dale	Senior Warden	Hollingworth Lake Country Park
Mr R Dance	Administrator	Centre for Alternative Technology
Mr J Darbyshire	Head Ranger	Falls of Clyde Nature Reserve
C Davidson	Admin	The National Trust, Speke Hall
John Hatton Davidson	Hon Curator	Robert Owen Museum
Ms D Davies	Manager	Bank of England Museum
Ms E Davies	Director	Freud Museum
Su Davies	Museum, Gallery and TIC Manager	Manor House Museum/Alfred East Art Gallery

Contact Name	Contact Title	Attraction
Mr N Davis	Financial Director	Association Gallery
R J Davis	Proprietor	Padstow Shipwreck Museum
Susanna Davis	Museum and Tourist Info Officer	Ays Coughfee Hall Museum
L & M Dawes	Manager/Owner	Mount Ephraim Gardens
J Dawson	Hon Curator	Ruskin Museum
M Dean & J Howse	General Manager & Marketing Exec.	Didcot Railway Centre*
The Dean		Norwich Cathedral*
The Dean and Chapter		Lichfield Cathedral
T Deary	Arts Development Manager	Durham Light Infantry Museum & Art Gallery
Mr I Dempster	Development Manager	Mill of Towie
Mr and Mrs A Dennis	Proprietors	Miniature Pony Centre
A Denyer	Manager	Crabble Corn Mill
D Devenish	Curator	Wisbech & Fenland Museum
Dr D F Devereux	Curator	Stewartry Museum
Robert Dillon	Administrator	Erddig Hall
Mr G Doban	Deputy Director	Royal Navy Submarine Museum
Mr A Donald	General Manager	Waltzing Waters Ltd
E G Donaldson	Acting Curator	Glasgow Botanic Gardens
N Donaldson	Deputy Park Ranger	Lochore Meadows Country Park
Stephen Done	Curator	Cyfarthfa Castle Museum, Art Gallery and Park
Ms P Douglas	Director	Charles Rennie Mackintosh Society
Hon Caroline Douglas-Home	Estate Factor	The Hirsel
Dr S Dowbiggin	Principal	Capel Manor
F C Downer	Admin	Knole
Dr A I Doyle	Chairman/Secretary of Trust/Company	Durham Heritage Centre
Ms C Dudley	Director	Royal Cornwall Museum
P F D Duffie	Administrator	Blenheim Palace*
Mr P G Duffy	Forestry Officer	Gosford Forest Park
K Dunning	Museum Manager	Oxfordshire County Museum
Lt Col D P Earlam	Director of Visits	Canterbury Cathedral
The Baron of Earlshall	Owner	Earlshall Castle and Gardens
Ms P Eastwood	Administration Officer	Halifax Piece Hall*
Mr H Eaton	Administrator	Blickling Hall*
Mrs A Eaton	Treasurer	Ullapool Museum
D Eccles	Cathedral Secretary	Blackburn Cathedral
S Eddy	Head Keeper	Combe Martin Wildlife & Dinosaur Park
Ms J Edom	Centre Manager	New Forest Museum and Visitor Centre
Miss Tessa Edwards	Conservation Centre Manager	Appleby Castle Conservation Centre
Mr and Mrs B Eitches	Owners	World of Toys
Richard Ellam	Development Manager	Royal Observatory Visitor Centre
Graham F Ellis	Director	Mull & West Highland Narrow Gauge Railway
Mrs L Ellis	Secretary	Colne Valley Museum
Ms C Ellis	Keeper	Cuming Museum
J R Emary	Admin	Mapledurham House and Watermill*
G Emerson	Director	Morwellham Quay
M England	Curator	Bodmin Town Museum
Mr Len England	Managing Director	Cumbria Crystal Ltd*
M Etches	General Manager	Windsor Safari Park*
E Evans	Dean Verger	Christ Church Cathedral*
J Evans	Head Custodian	Carisbrooke Castle
Mr J Evans	Archivist	Royal London Hospital Archives & Museum
Mr D Eveleigh	Curator	Blaise Castle House Museum
I Everett	Fort Manager	Newhaven Fort
J Facey	Owner	Lanreath Folk Farm Museum
Major J Fairbank	Archivist/Director	Salvation Army International Heritage Centre
Dr D Farr CBE	Director	Courtauld Institute Galleries*
Mr H Fattorini	Administrator	Skipton Castle*
Mr J Fawdry	Director – Pollock's Toy Theatres Ltd	Pollock's Toy Museum
Mrs C Feakins	Administrator	Sheriff Hutton Park
Mr M Fearon	Honorary Curator	Filey Museum
Grp Captain T Ferguson OBE	Director	Cockley Cley Iceni Village & Museums
Douglas Ferreira	General Manager	The Ravenglass and Eskdale Railway*
W S Ferris	Centre Manager	A Day at the Wells
D J Field	Director	Buckfast Butterflies & Dartmoor Otter Sanct
Mr R Field	Honorary Curator	The Dewey Museum
I B Fisher	Director	Courage Shire Horse Centre
Mr G Fitzpatrick	Director	Boughton House
J W A Fleming	Cathedral Administrator	Guildford Cathedral
Dr A Flett	General Manager	Satroshere
Mr K Flude	Curator	Old Operating Theatre Museum
Dr M Fopp	Director	Royal Air Force Museum*
Mr J Ford	Manager	Plymouth Dome*
The Rev Canon D Ford	Visitors Canon	Ripon Cathedral*
Mr Patrick Forde	Owner	Seaford Tropical Butterfly House/Gardens/Maze
Mr T Forer	Manager	RHYL Sea Life Centre
Mr R Forrest	Custodian (Miller)	Houghton Mill
Lt Col (Rtd) G Forty	Director & Curator	Tank Museum
Ms C Foss	Curator/Chairman/Trustee	Aldeburgh Moot Hall Museum
Mr I Foster	Manager	Kingdom of the Sea Hunstanton*
D Fox	Administrator	Bateman's (The National Trust)
Mr R Fox	Director	Lyme Regis Experience
Dr A Foxon	Keeper of Archaeology	Hull and East Riding Museum
Cmdr R Francis RN (Rtd)		Wells & Walsingham Light Railway
Dr R Francis	Director	Forncett Industrial Steam Museum
J A Francis	Museum Manager	The Aerospace Museum*
Mr C Francis	Curator	Wildfowl & Wetlands Centre
J Franklin	Branch Manager	Ford Green Hall
Mrs J Franklin	Administrator	Nunnington Hall
Mr D Fraser	Museums and Arts officer	Derby Museum and Art Gallery*
Grant Fraser-Tytler	Proprietor	Cambo Country Park

Contact Name	Contact Title	Attraction
V Frearson	Manager	Flimwell Bird Park
Michael Freeman	Curator	Ceredigion Museum
H E Frost	Curator and Company Secretary	Dyson Perrins Museum
Mr G Brown FRSA	Director	Longdale Craft Centre & Museum*
A H Fryer	Custodian	Almonry Museum
Mr G Fuller MBE	Chief Executive	Wood Green Animal Sanctuary*
Danny Fullerton	General Manager	Landmark Highland Heritage and Adventure Park
Dr A Gailey	Director	Ulster Folk and Transport Museum*
Ms S Gair	Administrator	Dulwich Picture Gallery
Mr G Gallen	Visitor Centre Manager	Battle of Britain Memorial Flight (Visits)
P Garnham	Owner	Bartley Mill
H Garraway	Parish Assistant	Christchurch Spitalfields
Mrs Steve Le Gassick	Resident Representative	Leith Hall
M Gavagan/A Rawlings	Gallery Director/Gallery Asst	Peter Scott Gallery
C J George	Administrator	Broughton Castle
H Gillian	Administrator	Wells Museum
B Gillow	Curator	Greenwich Borough Museum
Mrs Karen Gilmour	Property Representative	J M Barrie's Birthplace
Earl of Glasgow	Owner/Manager	Kelburn Country Centre
Mr H Gledhill	General Manager	Guinness World of Records Exhibition*
Mr R R Gledson	Factor	Gosford House
Mr P Glen	Chairman	Beck Isle Museum of Rural Life
C Goddard	Head Custodian	Battle Abbey and Battlefield of Hastings
Mr S Goldie	Business Manager	Botanic Centre
C Gooch	Owner	Boughton Monchelsea Place
R Goodden	Director	Worldwide Butterflies Ltd
Mr S Goodenough	Curator	Ventnor Botanic Garden*
Mr S Goodhard	Keeper of Transport	Streetlife – Hull Museum of Transport
Ms J Goodridge	Museums Officer	Border History Museum
K Goodway	Marketing Manager	Avon Valley Railway
D Gordon	Custodian	Hughenden Manor
Mrs A Gordon	Owner	Tiverton Castle
A C Gottlieb	Director	Michelham Priory
Captain J Gowen RN	The Agent	Stanstead Park
H Graham	Curator	Cecil Higgins Art Gallery and Museum
Mr B Graham	Chief Museum Assistant	East Ham Nature Reserve
Rev D Graham	Parish Minister	Jonah's Journey
Ms C Graham-Brown	Chief Executive	St Martin-in-the-Fields
Mr D Grainger	Curator	Ayton Castle
Mr R Grange	Tourism Promotion Manager	The Guildhall Beverley
Very Rev Malcolm E Grant	Provost & Rector	Saint Andrew's Cathedral Inverness
J Gray		Sellet Hall Gardens
Mrs Yvonne Gray	Museum Supervisor	Cumberland Pencil Museum & Exhibition Centre
Mrs M Gray-Parry		Bryn Bras Castle
G R Greed	Director	Bristol Zoo Gardens*
Canon D Green		Ely Cathedral*
Mr E Green	Estate Agent	Abbotsbury Sub Tropical Gardens
Mr E Green	Estate Agent	Abbotsbury Swannery
Mr E Green	Estate Agent	Abbotsbury Tithe Barn Museum
Ms C Green	Marketing Director	Strawberry Hill
R J W Greenland	Director	Model Farm and Folk Museum
E Greenwood	Keeper of Museum	Liverpool Museum
P A Gregory	Administrator	Woburn Abbey
P Gresnam	Managing Director	Pennyarcadia
Mr M Gresswell	Curator	Dales Countryside Museum
W Gricks	Director	Hebden Crypt
Dr Ian Griffen	Director	Armagh Planetarium
Mr P Griffith	Director	Butterfly World and Fountain World
Eifion Griffiths	Director	Tregwynt Mill
Ms M Gryspeerdt	Keeper Rural Life	Somerset Rural Life Museum
Mr L Gunn	Custodian	John Wesley's Chapel
Mr S Guron	Manager	National Postal Museum
M Guy	Park Manager	Queen Elizabeth Country Park
R Guy-Jobson	Managing Director	Albert Dock
Ian Gwilim	Manager	Dan-Yr-Ogof Showcaves
Mr P Hadden	Operations Director	Pleasurewood Hills American Theme Park*
Mr B Haigh	Community Curator	Bagshaw Museum
Mr B Haigh	Community Curator	Dewsbury Museum
R Haines	Partner	Watermouth Castle
Mr J Hale	Managing Director	Flambards Village Theme Park*
Tim Haley	Brockhole Centre Manager	Lake District National Park Visitor Centre*
Miss Hall	Curator	Largs Museum
Mr R Hall	Senior Curator Art Galleries	Huddersfield Art Gallery
Mr T Hall	Director	National Ambulance Museum
Mrs S Hallett	Manageress	Lulworth Cove Heritage
C E M Halsall	Owner Operator	Brookside Miniature Railway
Ms R Hardiman	Keeper of Art	Charles Dickens Birthplace Museum
Mr S Hardy	Southampton Heritage Manager	Gods House Tower Museum
Mr S Hardy	Heritage Manager	Tudor House Museum
Mr S Hardy	Southampton Heritage Manager	Woolhouse Maritime Museum
W F Harper	Owner	Colliford Lake Park
Siobhan Harpur	Commercial Manager	National Museum of Labour History
Mr M Harris	Operations Manager	The Tales of Robin Hood*
Ms L Harris	Manageress	Chambercombe Manor
D Harrison	General Manager	Stamford Shakespeare Company
Mrs R Harrison	Owner	Wordsworth Gallery
Mrs S Harrison	Director	Museum of Mechanical Music
P D Harrop	District Forester	Argyll Forest Park
Mr P Hart	Managing Director	Bure Valley Railway
D Hartley	General Manager	Smugglers Adventure

Contact Name	Contact Title	Attraction
A R Harwood	Keeper of Social History	Cotswold Countryside Collection
Mr C Hawke	Senior Warden	Gibraltar Point National Nature Reserve*
K Hawley	Custodian	Wortley Top Forge Industrial Museum
Mr D Hayson	Curator	Tithe Barn Museum & Arts Centre
D S E Hayward	Director	The Puppet Theatre Museum
W R Hean	Administrator at Threave	Threake Gardens
Mr R Heap	Partner	Chestnut Centre
Mary Heathcote	Administrator	Oriel Mostyn
R E Hedley-Walker	Owner	Wolferton Station Museum
J D Hegarty	Admin	Capesthorne Hall
A Helme	Curator	The Nelson Museum and Local History Centre
V Hemingway	Administrator	The Greyfriars
Mrs D Henderson	Owner & Administrator	Arundel Toy and Military Museum
Mr A Henshaw	Group Custodian	Totnes Castle
E M Henslowe	Curator/Manager	Selly Manor Museum
Mr J and Mrs S Hernu	Joint Owners	Alfriston Heritage Centre & Blacksmith's
Mr S Hession	Chapter Clerk	Peterborough Cathedral*
F Hetherington	Agent	Seaton Delaval Hall
Mr J Heyes	Keeper Childhood Collections	Edinburgh Museum of Childhood
Mr A Heywood	Traffic & Commercial Manager	Ffestiniog Railway
J Hibbert	Manager	Trebah Garden
P Hickman	General Manager	Marwell Zoological Park*
Graham Hicks	Administrator	Felbrigg Hall
H Higman	Museum Admin	Cambrian Railway Soc & Oswestry Cycle Museum
Catherine Hill	Director	Rhondda Heritage Park
Mr D Hillman	Principal Outdoor Manager	Pugneys Country Park
D Hillyard	Chief Ranger	Dunstable Downs Country Park
D Hillyard	Chief Ranger	Harrold Odell Country Park*
D Hillyard	Chief Ranger	Stockgrove Country Park
R M Hobby	Administrator	Ashmolean Museum
Lt Col C G O Hogg	Regimental Secretary	Kings Own Scottish Borders Regimental Museum
S A Holden	Curator, Owner and TIC Manager	North Cornwall Museum and Gallery
J Holifeild	Bursar	Truro Cathedral*
Mr A Hollingsworth	Divisional Director	Alton Towers*
C Holm	Resort Services Manager	Volks Electric Railway
Mr J Homer	Curator	Dean Castle & Country Park
Ian Hook	Site Manager	Chelmsford and Essex, Essex Regiment Museums
Mr M Hooley	Manager	Trinity House National Lighthouse Centre
J Horsley	General Manager	Leighton Buzzard Railway
A Howard	Manager	Child-Beale Wildlife Park*
D R Howlett	Curator	Quex House & Gardens & Powell-Cotton Museum
Mr J G Hughes	Director	Model House Craft and Design Centre
Mr P Hulme	Minister	Wesley's Chapel
E Hulse	Owner	Breamore House & Museums
Mr D Humas	Manager	Colne Valley Railway
Mr J Hunter	Curator	Dick Institute
Mr T Hunter	Centre Manager	Winchester Heritage Centre
H Hurst	Curator	Zetland Lifeboat Museum
J Hutchinson	Director	Chatterley Whitfield Mining Museum
Mr and Mrs R Hutchinson	Joint Owners	Incredibly Fantastic Old Toy Show
Mr H R Hutchman	Administrator	Mount Stewart House and Gardens*
Mr P Ingram	Owner	Romany Folklore Museum & Workshop
Mr E Inman	Director	Duxford Airfield*
A Insckar	Curator	Torquay Museum
E E Jackson	Head of Croxteth Hall	Croxteth Hall and Country Park
G Jackson	Managing Director	Leeds Castle
Mr H Jackson	Owner	Rural Life Centre
Mr R Jackson	Administrator	Shakespeare Globe Museum
Mr N Jacques	Park Manager	Normanby Hall Country Park
Hon C James	Owner/General Manager	Northbourne Court Gardens
Mr C James	Owner	Torosay Castle & Gardens
Mr S Jaques	Managing Director	Eden Camp Modern History Theme Museum*
P Jarvis	Castle Administrator	Thirlestane Castle
Ms J Jawaskyi	Manager	Kingdom of the Sea Gt Yarmouth*
Ms V Jeffries	MD	Bournemouth Heritage Transport Centre
P Jempson	Owner	Woodside Farm & Wild Fowl Park
F Jenkins	Partner	Avon Valley Country Park
Mr T Jenkins	Proprietor	Staintondale Shire Horse Farm
Trevor S Jennings	Curator	The Bellfoundry Museum
C Jewitt	Acting Director	National Sound Archive (British Library)
Mrs Inger John	Proprietor	Cilgwyn Candles Workshop and Mini Museum
Canon P F Johnson	Canon Treasurer	Bristol Cathedral
Mr A Johnson	Manager	Camera Obscura
Mrs C Johnson	Administrator	Holker Hall and Gardens
P Johnson	Lay Administrator	Birmingham Cathedral
P Johnson	Curator	Towner Art Gallery & Local History Museum
Miss F Jones	Services Manager	Yorkshire Museum
Mr B Jones	Administrator	Portsmouth Cathedral
Mr J Jones	Managing Director	Pleasure Beach*
Mr M Jones	Director	Royal Museum of Scotland*
Mr P Jones	Owner	Manningford Gardens & Nursery
Mr S Jones	Director	Spencer House
L Jordan	Marketing Manager	Museum of Army Transport
R Jury	Administrator	Stowe Landscape Gardens
Ms L Karlsen	Principal Keeper	Ferens Art Gallery
J Kay	Project Officer	Tehidy Country Park
Mr S Kay	General Manager	Summerlee Heritage Trust
Mr T Kay	Director	Pettitts Feathercraft & Animal Adventure Park
Ms D Keasal	District Curator	Glasgow Vennel Museum

Contact Name	Contact Title	Attraction
Ms D Keasal	District Curator	Museum of the Cumbraes
Ms D Keasal	District Curator	North Ayrshire Museum
Mr P Kelly	Curator	Leeds Industrial Museum
Ms L Kelly	Gallery Manager	Tallberg Taylor Gallery
F H C Kendall	Curator	Bude Museum
Mr and Mrs Kennaway	Managing Directors	Escot Aquatic Centre & Gardens
Miss Helen Kennedy	Director	Dyffryn House Conference Centre and Gardens
Mr P Kennedy	Proprietor	World of the Honey Bee
P Kennedy	Administrator	Parham Elizabethan House & Gardens
Mrs M Kershaw	Curator	Knaresborough Castle & Courthouse Museum
Mrs M Kershaw	Curator	Mercer Art Gallery
Mrs M Kershaw	Curator	Royal Pump Room Museum
Mr R Pond/Mrs C Key	Chapter Clerk/Marketing Officer	Lincoln Cathedral
G Kichenside	Managing Director	Gorse Blossom Railway & Woodland Park
David Kidd	Proprietor	Cockthorpe Hall Toy Museum
L Killorn	Operations Manager	Whipsnade Wild Animal Park*
A King	Asst Curator	Bristol Industrial Museum
David King	Manager	Eskdale Corn Mill
Dr R J King	Curator	The John Moore Countryside Museum
Dr R King	Curator	Merchant's House (Little Museum)
S Kirby	Curator	Mill Green Museum and Mill
Sue Kirby		Welwyn Roman Baths
C Kitts	Manager	Stanborough Park
Ms J Knatt	Tourism Officer	Old Crown Court and Cells
Mr J Kneale	Owner	Shipwreck & Heritage Centre
Mr B Knight	Chairman	Chard & District Museum
Mary Konik	Senior Ranger	Almondell & Calderwood Country Park
Ms C Krzesinka	Senior Officer Arts & Exhibitions	Cartwright Hall
Mr J Lackenby	Reservoir Manager	Kielder Water
Miss J Laidlan	Co-ordinator	Greyfriars Kirk
R Lamb	Manager	Stratford Butterfly Farm
Ms E Lambie	Proprietor	Speyside Heather/Garden Visitor Centre
J Lamond	Curator	Gurkha Museum
Ms I Lang	Secretary/Curator	St Ives Society of Artists
Colonel the Lord Langford	Owner	Bodrhyddan Hall
P Langridge	Town Clerk	Totnes Guildhall
Ms K Latham/Mr H Rudge	Visitor Services/Farm Manager	Marsh Farm Country Park*
Mr J Lavin	Deputy Director, Operations	Royal Botanic Gardens Kew*
Mrs D Law	Curator/Manager	Swaledale Folk Museum
Mrs H P Law	Property Manager	Springhill
G Lawes	Chief Executive	Ironbridge Gorge Museum*
David Lea-Wilson	Partner	Anglesey Sea Zoo*
Mr R Leak/Mrs P Edwards	Partners	The Smuggling Experience
M Leber	Principal Officer – Museum & Heritage	Salford Museum and Art Gallery
Mr C Lee	Community Museums Officer	Lochwinnoch Community Museum
Mrs M Lee	Administrator	Hexham Abbey
S A Legge	Co-owner	Legbourne Railway Museum
A Leigh	Curator	Warrington Museum and Art Gallery
A Leonard	Centre Manager	The Oxford Story
John Leslie	Manager	Heritage Farm Park
The Very Rev B H Lewers	Provost	Derby Cathedral
Mrs J Lillystone	Museum Manager	D H Lawrence Birthplace Museum
M Lindop/S Matthews	Support Officer/Curatorial Officer	Grosvenor Museum
J Linley	Governor	Inveraray Jail
B Littlewood	Managing Director	Museum of British Road Transport
Mr J Livingstone	Recreation Officer	Galloway Forest Park
Mr J Livingstone	Recreation Officer	Glen Trool Visitor Centre
T Loasby	Manager	Kingston Maurward Gardens and Farm
Mr S Locke	Director	Red House Museum Art Gallery & Gardens
R Boutwood/M Lockyer	Admin Director/Animal Director	Howletts Zoo Park
Capt S Loder	Proprietor	Clapton Court Gardens
R R Loder	Manager	Leonardslee Gardens
Ms B J Logan	Curator	The Ballance House
C Longley	Verger	St Ann's Church
Mr D Lowsley-Williams	Owner	Chavenage
Mr Bernard Mitchell Luker	Curator	Arran & Argyll Transport Museum
G Lyndon Jones	Operations Manager	Peckforton Castle
Mr R Macalindin	Ships Manager	North Carr Lightship Anstruther Harbour
A Macalister 5th Laird of Glenbarr	Curator	Glenbarr Abbey Visitors Centre
J MacDonald	Curator	Auchindrain Township Open Air Museum
Mr A J MacDonald	Custodian	Neidpath Castle
Mr C MacDonald	Palace Director	Hampton Court Palace*
Paul S MacDonald	Administrator	Naworth Castle
Mr H Macgillivray	Curator	London Toy and Model Museum
Mr N MacGregor	Director	National Gallery*
Mrs M Mackenzie	Project Co-ordinator	Timespan Heritage Centre
Mrs M R I Mackenzie	Chairman of Trustees	Tain and District Museum
T F Mackenzie	Museum Curator	Hamilton District Museum
W J Mackinnon	Hostel Manager	Baden Powell House Hostel
Sir L Maclean	Owner	Duart Castle
Very Rev G Macmillan	Min of St Giles' Dean of Thistle	St Giles' Cathedral
Mr A Macpherson	Museum Curator	Clan Macpherson Museum
D Madden	General Manager	North Norfolk Railway*
Mr H Maddison	Railway Centre Assistant	Bowes Railway Centre
Mr S Maguire	Owner	Spitbank Fort
Ms S Major	Administrator	Prideaux Place
Sqn Ldr R J Major (Rtd)	Curator	Museum of Flight
J Makin (appt by Walsingham Coll)	Garden Administrator	Parcevall Hall Gardens
Richard Malliwell	Assistant Curator	Buxton Museum and Art Gallery
Mr R Mancey	Dir/General Manager	Paultons Park

Contact Name	Contact Title	Attraction
Rev J Manchester		St Mary's Priory, Old Malton
Mr C Manning	Partner	Charles Manning's Amusement Park*
S Mansfield	General Manager	Royalty and Empire*
John Manson	Curator	Burns Cottage and Museum
John Manson	Curator	Burns Monument and Gardens
Mr M Mapp	Administrator	Twyford Pumping Station
Ms C March	Development Director	Puppet Centre Trust
Mr H Margary	Director	Lympne Castle
Elizabeth Marshall	Hon Curator	Groam House Museum Trust
P Marshall	Manager	Steamtown Railway Centre
Miss Martin		Chilham Castle
Ms F C Marwick	Curator	West Highland Museum
C Massey	Senior Museums Officer	Wood End Museum of Natural History
Mr P Masters	Partner	Tamar Valley Donkey Park
Sandra E Matchett	Supervisor	The Palace Stables Heritage Centre
M Maxfield	Manager	Manchester United Museum & Tour Centre
Mrs P Maxwell-Scott OBE		Abbotsford
T G May	Curator	Miltons Cottage
Mrs H McAdam	Secretary	Glengoulandie Deer Park
G McBribe	Museum & Visitor Centre Admin	Bass Museum, Visitor Ctr & Shire Horse Stables
Col D G McCord	Curator	Hatfield House*
Mr P McCormack	Observatory Officer	Coats Observatory
Eva McDonald	Proprietor	Fair Maid's House
Mr M McDonald	Manager	Ripley's Believe It or Not
A McEvoy	Principal Museum Officer	The Local Interest Museum
Mr R McHugh	Keeper of Technology	Bradford Industrial Horses at Work Museum
M McKee	Keeper of Museum Services	Ulster Museum*
C McLaren-Throckmorton	Managing Partner	Coughton Court
Major R McLean	Curator	Museum of Staffordshire Regiment
Mr C McLean	Director	Scottish Mining Museum
W R McLeod	Administrator	Baddesley Clinton
B Mead	Manager	Forge Mill Museum & Bordesley Abbey Vis Ctr
D Mead	Bursar	Coventry Cathedral
Ms Dallas Mechan	Curator	Kirkcaldy Museum & Art Gallery
Mr W T Meikle	Admin Sec	Royal Scottish Academy
Mr G Melville	General Manager	Scottish Whisky Heritage Centre*
Mr and Mrs M Menist	Owners	Southwick Country Herb Centre
Mrs R Mercer	Director & General Manager	Dorset Heavy Horse Centre
Chris Merchant	Chief Executive	Wetheriggs Country Pottery
Paul Meredith	Head Custodian	Conwy Castle
Mr Robert Merrill	Manager	Cefn Coed Colliery Museum
P Middleton	Manager	Rother Valley Country Park*
J Milford	Museums & Heritage Manager	Newark Museum
E M J Miller	Director	Pendle Heritage Centre
M Miller	Operations Manager	The Bluebell Railway
Mr P Miller	Managing Director	Peter Pan's Playground*
Mrs Miller		Fenny Lodge Gallery
Mr R Milliam	Visits Officer	St Paul's Cathedral
M Millo	Head of Commercial Activities	National Army Museum
M Millward	Curator/Manager	Blackburn Museum and Art Gallery
Ms P Millward	Senior Officer	Bankfield Museum
Mr P Milner	Accountant/Administrator	Levens Hall and Topiary Gardens
Ms S Minter	Curator	Chelsea Physic Garden
Mr B Mitchell	Property Administrator	Branklyn Garden
Mr P Mitchell	Managing Director	Heritage Motor Centre*
Mr R J Mitchell	Hon Curator	St Andrews Botanic Garden
J Moir	Project Director	Chiltern Open Air Museum
Moltu	Director	Pumphouse Educational Museum
Mrs J Monkman	Hon Curator	Shandy Hall
Miss A Montgomery	Organising Secretary (Hon)	Bute Museum
J Moody	Landscape Manager	Newham Grange Leisure Farm
M Moore	Exec Director	Shaldon Wildlife Trust
Ms A Moore	Museum Curator	Morpeth Chantry Bagpipe Museum
T R W Moore	Land Agent	Longleat House and Safari Park
Mr T Mor	Designer & Owner	New World Tapestry Centres
Mr G Moray	Administrator	Anglesey Abbey
C Morgan	Curator	The National Pinetum (Bedgebury)
R Morgan	Proprietor	The Coventry Toy Museum
Mrs L Morison	Administrator	Dalmeny House
Mr P Morris	Principal	Lackham Gardens & Agricultural Museum
Mrs T J Morris	Museums Officer	Haverfordwest Castle Museum and Art Gallery
P Morris	Director	Model Village
R Morris	Partner	Maritime Museum
Major W D Morris-Barker	Administrator	Arbury Hall
M Morton	Hon Deputy Curator	Ripon Prison & Police Museum
M V Moss	Curator and Manager	Sussex Combined Services Museum
Mrs S E Moss	Officer in Charge	Graham Sutherland Gallery
Ms D Moss	Keeper of Decorative Arts	Pickford's House Museum
T Muir (The Lady)		Kingston Bagpuize House and Garden
R Mullins	Curator/Manageress	Potters Museum of Curiosity
Mr R Murphy	Chairman	Dinmore Manor and Gardens
A Murray	Curator	Nothe Fort
Mr P Murrow	Clerk of the Trust	Bungay Castle
M Mutch	Curator	Myreton Motor Museum
Mr P Nangle	Director of Leisure Facilities	Lee Valley Park Farms
Col G W Napier	Director	Royal Engineers Museum
P Neaves	Admin/Secretary	The Monkey Sanctuary
Mr H Nelson	Director	British in India Museum
Carole Netting	Craft Development Officer	Ruthin Craft Centre
M J Neve	Managing Director	Denmans Garden

Contact Name	Contact Title	Attraction
Ms A Nevill/Mr S Blake	Secretary/Finance	Royal Photographic Society
P Nevines	Proprietor	Talnotry Cottage Bird Garden
Ms B Newbury	Park Manager	Manor Farm Country Park
Ms T Newland BA MSc	Librarian	Marx Memorial Library
B Newman	Managing Director	Bekonscot Model Village*
Lt Col N J Newman	Chapter Clerk	St Georges Chapel*
The Rev B Newth		St Michael the Archangel Church
Mr M J Nield	Chief Technician/Mill Manager	Stott Park Bobbin Mill
Dr M Nix	Curator	Tiverton Museum
Brian H Nodes	Administrator	Blair Castle*
Mr W Norman	Curator	Watchet Market House Museum
David North	Director, Education and Conservation	Pensthorpe Waterfowl Trust
W Northam/R Maddicott	Museum/FME Ltd	Fitzwilliam Museum*
Mr D Northmore	Education Officer	Spurn Lightship
Mr H Noyes	Owner	Isle of Wight Rare Breeds & Waterfowl Park
Mr C Nunn		Broads Museum
A Nuttall	Manager	Etruria Industrial Museum
Mr B Nuttall	Administrator	Harlow Carr Botanical Gardens
Mrs S O'Donnell	Proprietor	Yorkshire Dales Falconry & Conservation Centre
Rev Mgr P O'Donoghue	Administrator	Westminster Cathedral*
R J P O'Grady	Director–Secretary	Glasgow Zoo Park
Mr and Mrs P O'Shea		Trenouth Farm Rare Breeds Centre
M Oarden	Group Custodian	Kenilworth Castle
Dr and Mrs R Odgers	Owners	Hatch Court
Mrs Oldfield	Owner	Doddington Place Gardens
Mr S Olding	Head of Museums Service	Russel-Cotes Art Gallery & Museum
N Oliveira/N Oxley/M Petry	Directors	Museum of Installation
Mr E Oliver		Chatsworth*
Ms J Orr	Manager	Museum of Lead Mining
Very Rev D C Orr	Dean	St Columbs Cathedral
Mr C Orr-Ewing	Managing Agent	Exbury Gardens
Bryn Owen FMA LT RN (Rtd)	Curator	The Welch Regiment Museum
Ms D Owen	Administrator	East Riddlesden Hall
L & B Owens	Joint Partners	Ardington Pottery
Mr J Oxford	Owner	Wetlands Waterfowl Reserve
Dr C Palmer	Curator	Havant Museum
The Lord Palmer		Manderston
Very Rev Canon J Pannett		St George's Cathedral
Mrs M Frewen Parsons	Curator	Frewen College
Patti Partridge	Partner	Felin Crewi Working Watermill
Mr B Pass	Farm Manager	Longdown Dairy Farm
Rev I Paterson	Minister	St Michaels Parish Church
Mr M Pawley	Countryside Officer	Crombie Country Park
P Peach	Curator	Corsham Court
Mr J Peacop	Director	Mouldsworth Motor Museum
Mr A Pearce	Manager	Timothy Hackworth Victorian & Railway Museum
S Pearsall	Operations Manager	Cadbury World*
Mr M Pearson	Head Ranger (Recreation)	Whinlatter Visitor Centre*
Mr O Pearson	Estate Secretary	Graythwaite Hall Gardens
Ms J Peatman	Keeper of Industrial Sites	Abbeydale Industrial Hamlet
S Penney	Curator	The Salt Museum
Mr B Perkins	Shop Manager	Dickens House Museum
R Peters/P Cooley	Golf Professional/W Lancs Council	Beacon Country Park
Mr & Mrs Petrie	Directors	Southport Zoo and Conservation Trust
Mr R De Peyer	Curator	Dorset County Museum
M Phillips	Administrator	Allhallows Museum
P J H Philpot	Director	Barleylands Farm Museum
B Pickering	Curator and Director	Ethnic Doll and Toy Museum
Mr R Pickering	Warden	Tolpuddle Martyrs Museum
Mr N Pine	Managing Director (Publications)	Goss and Crested China Ltd
Pinmegar Family		Hammerwood Park
P Pinnock	Centre Manager	The White Cliffs Experience
G Piper	Chairman, Priory Pilgrims & Tourism	Christchurch Priory
David Pitman	Site Operations Co-ordinator	White Castle
Mr Andrew Plane	Administrator	Hutton-in-the-Forest
Mr J Platt	Senior Keeper of Industry	Derby Industrial Museum
Ms P Plumb	Administrator	Ragged School Museum
Mr L Pole	Curator	Saffron Walden Museum
Ms L Poley	Administrator	Stanway House
H Poole	Admin	Lewes Castle and Museums
W Powlett	Lady	Cadhay
Mr J Prentice	Church Warden	Church of St Martin-within-Ludgate
C M Preston	Owner/Manager	Badsell Farm Park
Sir Ronald Preston	Owner	Beeston Hall
Canon R Price	The Rector	St Mary's Parish Church
Rev Canon D Price	Rector	Minster Church of St Cuthberga*
Rev Canon S V Prins	Rector	St Mungo's 13thc Church
S C Pritchard	Chairman	Pecorama
Mr C Probert	Recreation & Information Officer	Kielder Forest and Castle
Ms E Proudfoot	Chairman of Trust	St Andrews Preservation Trust Museum
M R Puddle	Head Gardener and General Manager	Bodnant Gardens
R A Pullin	Managing Director	Hever Castle
I B Ramsden	Secretary/Manager	Pembroke Castle
Mrs C Raper	Countryside Information Officer	Billingham Beck Valley Country Park
M A Ratcliffe	Managing Director	The Alice in Wonderland Visitor Centre
R G Rawlins	Farmer	The Childrens Farm
D Rawlinson	Custodian	Jenner Museum
Ms O Raymond	Administrator	Brodick Castle & Country Park & Goatfell
Ms P Redmonds	Managing Director	Sooty's World

Contact Name	Contact Title	Attraction
L J Reed	Secretary	Foxfield Steam Railway
The Regimental Secretary		Queen's Own Highlanders Regimental Museum
Billy Ried/Alistair Davison	Manager/Asst Manager	The Northern Ireland Aquarium*
Ms A Reid	Curator	Stranraer Museum
Miss G B Reith/D C Butters	Town Clerk/Curator	Swaffham Museum
Ms A Rennick	Manager/Director	Blair Drummond Safari & Leisure Park
L Retallick	Senior Curator	Torre Abbey
Mr D Revett	Reserve Manager	Wildfowl & Wetlands Trust – Welney Centre
Mrs S Reynolds	Supervisor	Stained Glass Museum
D Richards	Heritage Manager	Izaak Walton's Cottage
D Richards	Heritage Manager	The Ancient High House
Mr J Richards	Chairman	The Lace Centre*
W R Richards	Founding Trustee	The National Motorcycle Museum
J Ro		Chicheley Hall
Dereck Roberts	Transport Manager	Great Orme Tramway
Dr D Roberts	Keeper	Amgueddfa'r Gogledd/Museum of the North
Dr Dafydd Roberts	Keeper	Welsh Slate Museum
Lt Col D R Roberts	Asst Curator	Devonshire Regiment Museum
Mr K Roberts	Manager	Tropical World*
Mrs P Roberts	Organiser	Jane Welsh Carlyle Museum
B Robertson	Chief Executive	The Historic Dockyard Chatham
Hamish Robertson	Development Manager	Frigate Unicorn
Mr K Robertson	Senior Ranger	Worsbrough Country Park*
Rev C Robertson	Minister	Canongate Kirk
A R Robinson	Administrator	Scone Palace*
K G Robinson	Managing Director	Beaulieu National Motor Museum, House & Abbey*
D Rodger	Project Officer	Trafford Ecology Park
P Roper	Development Director	National Maritime Museum Greenwich*
Ms B Roscoe	Curator	Holburne Museum & Crafts Study Centre
D H Ross		Knowsley Safari Park
Ms P Rossetter	Administrative Director	Age Exchange Reminiscence Centre
M Rothwell	Park Manager	Frontierland Western Theme Park*
Mr C Rougier	Director, Rosemoor	Royal Horticultural Society Garden
Mrs M Rowe	Hon Treasurer	Radstock Midsomer Norton Museum
Tony Rowlands	Managing Director	Trefriw Wells SPA
G M W Ruddock	Curator	Teignmouth Museum
Mrs P Ruddock	Senior Keeper & Keeper of Costume	Museum of Costume
D J Rudkin	Director	Fishbourne Roman Palace and Museum
J Ruffle	Keeper	Oriental Museum
Mr R Rusack	Managing Director	Edinburgh Canal Centre
Mr D Russell	Administrator	Pencarrow
J Rutherford	Director and Head of Museums	Royal Pavilion, Art Gallery and Museum
Mr A Rutter	Secretary	Harwich Redoubt
Mr A Rutter	Secretary	Port of Harwich Maritime Museum
Mr M Ryder	Chairman	Musical Museum
Ms G Rye	Administrator	Thursford Collection*
Mr N Sadler	Curator/Director	London Canal Museum
J Salisbury	Owner & Sole Member of Staff	Vintage Toy Train Museum
Mrs C Salt	Administrator	Number One The Royal Crescent
Mrs W Salter	Sec to Exec Committee	Brixham Museum & History Society
S Sampson	Manager	Paradise Wildlife Park
Ms M Sanderson	Administrator	Pontefract Museum
Ms M Sanderson	Administrator	Elizabethan Exhibition Gallery
Ms M Sanderson	Administrator	Pontefract Castle
Ms M Sanderson	Administrator	Wakefield Art Gallery
Ms M Sanderson	Administrator	Wakefield Museum
Raymond Sanderson	Commercial Director	Teifi Valley Railway
P R Saunders	Curator	Salisbury and South Wiltshire Museum
R Saville	Curator	Coach House Museum
Ms D Sawday	Owner	Apuldram Roses
Mr J Sayers	Company Accountant/Secretary	Mall Galleries
Mrs J Schroeder	Owner	Arreton Manor
Mr K Scotland	Executive Director	Paxton House
Ms R Scott	Curator	Percival David Foundation of Chinese Art
R Scott	Proprietor	The Herb Farm and Saxon Maze
Sir James Scott	Owner	Rotherfield Park
Vaj Scowe	Director	Abbot Hall
J Sculley	Senior Visual Arts Officer	Stockport War Memorial and Art Gallery
C Scurrah	Manager	Brighton Sea Life Centre
J Sealby	Proprietor	Wythop Mill
K Searle	General Manager	Bodmin and Wenford Railway
Mr G Seimann	Managing Director	Conwy Visitor Centre*
Mr K Sellwood	Manager	Hornsea Freeport*
F Shahbahrami	Proprietor	Cranmore Tower
Dr E J Sharples	Business Admin	Ness Gardens
Mr B Eglon Shaw	Senior Partner	Sutcliffe Gallery
Mr G Shaw	Owner and Curator	Yorkshire Carriage Museum
Mr S Shaw	Director	Elvisly Yours Centre
J Shillingford	Chapter Clerk	Wells Cathedral*
M Sifford	Honorary Manager	Fleur De Lis Heritage Centre
Ken Simms	Director	Thrigby Hall Wildlife Gardens
Ms J Simpson	Museums Services Manager	Rougemont House Museum
Ms J Simpson	Museums Services Manager	Royal Albert Memorial Museum
Ms J Simpson	Museums Services Manager	St Nicholas Priory
M Sirot-Smith	Resident Director	Sulgrave Manor
Mrs J Slocombe	Curator	Ilfracombe Museum
Mrs G Small	Chairperson I of AMT	Isle of Arran Heritage Museum
Mr T Smit	Project Director	The Lost Gardens of Heligan
A Smith	Director	The Whitworth Art Gallery

Contact Name	Contact Title	Attraction
J Smith	Hon Secretary	Cromer Lifeboat Museum
J Smith	Curator	Fasque
Major R P Smith	Curator	The South Wales Borderers Museum
Mr G Smith	Manager	Portsmouth Sea Life Centre
Mr G Smith	Curator	Scaplen's Court Museum
Mr G Smith	Curator	Waterfront Museum
Mr J Smith	Curator and Manager	Stamford Museum
Mrs J Smith	Owner	Edmondsham House & Garden
Ms H Smith	Curator	Harrow Museum & Heritage Centre*
Ms J Smith	Hon Curator	Dickens House Museum Broadstairs
Rev D W Smith	Vicar	All Saints Church
J B Snell	Managing Director	Romney, Hythe & Dymchurch Railway
Rear Admiral K Snow CB	Receiver General	Westminster Abbey*
Ms M Somerville	Organiser	Chesil Gallery
M Spall	Traffic Manager	West Lancashire Light Railway
Mr and Mrs J Sparrow	Owners	Bear Museum
Ms J Speller	Assistant Curator, Art	Batley Art Gallery
Mr M Spender	Director	Bankside Gallery
Mr R Spinks	Secretary	Captain Cook Schoolroom Museum
Mr G Sprott	Curator	Scottish Agricultural Museum
Michael Stammers	Keeper	National Maritime Museum
M Stanbury	Chairman	East Anglian Railway Museum
Mr D Standen	Countryside Manager	Wat Tyler Country Park*
Mr K Stanfield	Warden	Peatlands Park*
David Stanley	Partner	Ponsonby Farm Park
P Startup	Admin	Tabely House Collection
David Steele	Castle Manager	Carrickferggus Castle*
H Poole/L Steene	Admin/Custodian	Anne of Cleves House Museum
Mr G Stenhouse	Manager	Oban Sea Life Centre
Roderick Stenhouse	Estate Administrator	Maxwelton House
Mr Stephens	Chairman	Natural World*
M Stephenson/R Haynes	Dep Gen Mgrs	Sea Life Centre
Mr T Stephenson FGA	Proprietor	Gem Rock Museum
C Stevens	Bridge Master	Tower Bridge*
Mr P Stevens	Executive Director	Paignton Zoo*
M Stevenson	Museum Director	Paradise Mill
M Stevenson	Museum Director	The Silk Museum
M Stevenson	Museum Director	West Park Museum
Mr M Stewart	Managing Director	Stewarts Garden-Lands
Mrs S Stewart	Director/Partner	Dunaverig Farm Life Centre
Rev James C Stewart	Minister	Kirk of St Nicholas
St John & J Stimson	Owners	Museum of the Home
N T Stobbs	Administrator	Heron Corn Mill and Museum of Papermaking
Lord Strathnaver & Mrs S Broad	Director & Administrator	Dunrobin Castle
Ms K Streets	Asst Keeper of Social History	Bishops' House
J Strickson/C Alford	Admin/Asst Admin	Dunham Massey Hall and Park
Ms C Maxwell Stuart	Owner/Adminstrator	Traquair House
Mr A Suddes	Curator	Darlington Museum
M Sulter	Art Gallery Services Officer	Rochdale Art Gallery
Mr Peter Sunderland	Assistant Director	Beacraigs Country Park
Y Surcouf	Owner	Basildon Zoo
B Sutherland	Manager	Bentley Wildfowl & Motor Museum
Mr A Sutherland	Partner	Ardfearn Nursery Plant Centre
Mr J Sutton	Partner	The Lincolnshire Poultry Park
Dr E D Svendsen	Administrator	The Donkey Sanctuary
A Swinney	Centre Manager	The Look Out*
Ms L Sword	Manager	St Andrews Sea Life Centre
DW & PR Sydenham	Proprietors	Cholderton Rare Breeds Farm Park
P Symes	General Manager	The Shuttleworth Collection
Ms M Szabo	PA to Managing Director	Llewellyn Alexander (Fire Paintings) Ltd
Mr C Tabiner	Manager	Farmworld*
Mr R Tait	Director	Wine and Spirit Museum
D Talbot	Chairman	Museum of Transport
Jim Taylor	Warden in Charge	Carrick-A-Rede Rope Bridge*
M Taylor	Manageress	Heale Gardens and Plant Centre
Mr B Taylor	Managing Director	Kirklees Light Railway
M G L Thomas	Director	Avoncroft Museum of Buildings
M Thomas	Managing Director	Cornish Seal Sanctuary
Mr K Thomas	General Manager	Sea Life Centre*
Ms G Thomas	Director	Eureka! The Museum for Children
Nest Thomas	Museums Development Officer	The Lloyd George Museum and Highgate His Home
T Thomas	Trustee	Birmingham Railway Museum
Canon T Thompson	Vice Provost	Chelmsford Cathedral
Irene Thompson	Owner	Toy and Teddy Bear Museum
Mervyn Thompson	Manager	Bressingham Steam Museum and Gardens
Mr V Thomson	Estates Ranger	Darnaway Farm Visitor Centre
Ms C Thomson	Head Curator	Bessie Surtees House
B Thornbull	Administrator	Syon Park
Mr P Thornton	Curator	Sir John Soane's Museum
Mr R Thornton	Director	Tropical Bird Park
Mr D Thorpe	Manager	South London Art Gallery
Dr P Thwaites	Deputy Director	Royal Signals Museum
Mr W Timmis	Curator	Lotherton Hall Bird Garden*
R & D Titterington	Owner/Manager	Iden Croft Herbs
Ms A Todhunter	Marketing Manager	New Forest Butterfly Farm
Mr J Tonner	Estate Manager	Formakin Estate
Mr C Townsend	Education Officer	Willsbridge Mill
R Trelt	Curator	Newport Museum and Art Gallery
J Treuherz	Keeper of Art Galleries	Lady Lever Art Gallery

Contact Name	Contact Title	Attraction
Mr J Wilks	Senior Curator	South Shields Museum & Art Gallery
Ann Williams	Curator	Bersham Heritage Centre and Ironworks
Dr Eurwyn Williams	Curator	Welsh Folk Museum*
Gareth Williams	Principal Archivist and Museum Officer	Beaumaris Gaol and Court
L Williams		Marle Place Gardens and Nursery
Mr D Williams	Horticultural Education Officer	Sheffield Botanical Gardens
Mr J Williams	Owner	Land Farm Garden
V Williams	Curator	Hastings Museum and Art Gallery
Ms P Willis	Curator	Museum of the Order of St John
I Willsher	Owner	Longstone Heritage Centre
Mr P Willsher	General Manager	Compton Acres Gardens
B S Wilson	Museums Officer	Tankerness House Museum
C Wilson	Museum Officer	Margate Old Town Hall Local History Museum
Captain J R Wilson	Administrator	Balmoral Estates
H Wilson	Cathedral Secretary	Liverpool Cathedral
I A Wilson	Manager	North Down Heritage Centre
M Wilson	Company Secretary	Burton Agnes Hall
Mr K Wilson	Director	Chester Visitor Centre
Mrs C L Wilson	Project Manager	Whithorn Dig
Nick Winterbottom	Director Tullie House	Tulliehouse Museum and Art Gallery
J Wisenfeld	Head Warden	Hatfield Forest
P Wisniewski	Curator	The Wildfowl & Wetlands Trust Martin Mere
Mrs D Wood	Tour Organiser	Hoskins Brewery
Ms M Wood	Director	University Gallery
Col M J Woodcock	Chapter Clerk	Exeter Cathedral*
L A Wooder	Proprietor	Parracombe Garden Railway
Mr D Woodhouse MBE	General Manager	Talyllyn Railway
Mr C Woodward	Curator/Director	The Building of Bath Museum
Dr R S Woof	Hon Secretary and Treasurer	The Wordsworth Trust
Mr S Woolf	General Manager	Metroland*
K Wootton	Guide	Adlington Hall
Peter Worth	Director	The Butterfly and Falconry Park
Mr D Wrench	Director	Burton Constable Hall
D Wright	General Manager	Bicton Park Gardens
Mr A Wright	Curator	Southend Central Museum & Planetarium
Bridget Yates	Curator	Norfolk Rural life Museum and Union Farm
A D Yule	Warden	Auckland Castle
C Zeuner	Museum Director	Weald and Downland Open Air Museum

MARKETING/ADVERTISING

Contact Name	Contact Title	Attraction
Mr M Abbott/Mr G Gilbey	PR/Marketing	Shakespeare Globe Museum
H H Ackers		Animal World
H H Ackers		Butterfly World
Jean Adams		Easdale Island Folk Museum
Marlene Adams	Deputy Manager	Cefn Coed Colliery Museum
G Albison	Publicity Officer	Manchester Cathedral
Mr C Aldred	Events Officer	Halifax Piece Hall*
Mrs M Alexander	Treasurer	Isle of Arran Heritage Museum
David Allen	Commercial Dir/Publicity Officer	Welsh Highland Railway
M Amey	Owner	Hardys Wessex Exhibition
C Anderson	Senior Museum Officer	Oxfordshire County Museum
Mr Tom Anderson	Publicity Convener	Kirk of St Nicholas
Ms B Andresen	Events Manager	Stanstead Park
Miss D Andrews/Mrs R Brooks	Partners	Old Smithy Tourist Centre
M & K Ann	Publicity and PR Managers	Drusillas Park
Canon M Arundel	Rector	St Ann's Church
T Ash	Proprietor	Parke Rare Breeds Farm
Mr J Ashton	Head of Admin and Marketing	Pleasure Beach*
Mr D Asquith	Admin	Clandon Park
Mr D Asquith	Administrator	Hatchlands Park
Dr R L Atkinson	Curator	Camborne School of Mines Geological Museum
P Atkinson	Curator	Wheelwrights Museum & Gypsy Folklore Collect
Mr S Aubrey	Security and Bookings	Blaise Castle House Museum
Ms L Austin/Ms J Greenhalf	Information Officers	Bank of England Museum
Mrs S E Bagot	Owner	Levens Hall and Topiary Gardens
Ms J Bailey		Red House Museum Art Gallery & Gardens
Mr B Bailles	Administrator	Chillingham Castle
Mrs C E Baines	Administrative Officer	Carlisle Cathedral
Ms D Baker		Spitting Image Rubberworks*
G Baldwin	Marketing Manager	Cadbury World*
Mr D Jenkins & Mr M Baldwin	Publicity & Marketing	Centre for Alternative Technology
A Bamford	Education & Publications	National Sound Archive (British Library)
M Barbour	Business Manager	Ragley Hall
Dr A Barclay	Ranger	Scottish Wildlife Trust
Mrs S Bardner	Aylesworth Fleming of Bournemouth	Tank Museum
Ms J Barrie (Shop only)	Administrative Assistant	Hunterian Art Gallery
Mr M Barry	Marketing	Royal Air Force Museum*
Mr C Barton	Warden	The Old Rectory
Mrs J Batchelor	Marketing	Natural History Museum*
Mr T Batty		Dinosaur Museum*
Mr T Batty		Dinosaur Safari
Mr T Batty		Mummies and Magic
Mr T Batty		Tutankhamun Exhibition
Ms E Baxter	Exhibition/Marketing Manager	The Lace Hall
Mr H Bayntun-Coward	Owner	Book Museum
Mr P Beale/Ms M McCullough	Marketing Assistants	Bromley Museum
Mr P Beckett		Wakefield Cathedral
Mrs S Beeley		National Cycle Museum
E Beesley	Promotions Officer	The Wildfowl & Wetlands Trust Martin Mere
Mrs A Bell	Development Officer	New Lanark Village

Contact Name	Contact Title	Attraction
I A Bennett		Bennetts Water Gardens
C Beresford	Curator	Regiments of Gloucestershire Museum
Mr J Bernasconi	Hon Curator	University of Hull Art Collection
Mr D Bett	Exhibitions Officer	Dick Institute
Mr J Bevan	Head of Public Services	Welsh Slate Museum
Mr J Bevan	Head of Public Services	Amgueddfa'r Gogledd/Museum of the North
C Billen	Marketing Officer (Central Office)	Brighton Sea Life Centre
Ms C Billen	Marketing Officer (Central Office)	Hastings Sea Life Centres*
Ms C Billen	Marketing Officer	Oban Sea Life Centre
Mr S Bird	Asst Director Museums	Roman Baths Museum*
Ms S Bird	Museums Curator	Museum of Costume
John Birmingham	Marketing Manager	Model House Craft and Design Centre
L Bisset		University Botanic Garden
Mr and Mrs K Blackburn	Owners	Buffers
Mrs M Blacker	Publicity Officer	Nidderdale Museum
J Blades	Administrator	Hanbury Hall (National Trust)
Mrs S L Blaylock	Personal Assistant	Dalemain Historic House
Valerie Boa	Curator	McLean Museum and Art Gallery
Mr C Booth	Proprietor	The C M Booth Collection of Historic Vehicles
Ms A Boscawen & Ms S Bray		High Beeches Gardens
Ms L Bossine	Assistant Manager	Kew Bridge Steam Museum
J Boston		Land's End*
Mr B Boulton & Mrs D Boulton		Rock Garden and Cave
S Bourne	Curator	Towneley Hall Art Gallery and Museum
Ms R Bowden	Marketing Manager	Jorvik Viking Centre*
Mr N Boxall		Bickleigh Castle
C Boycs	Development Manager	Museum of British Road Transport
Onllwyn Brace	Marketing Manager	Welsh Folk Museum*
Mrs U Bradley		Old Byre
Ms D Bramley	Tourism Officer	Woodhorn Colliery Museum
Mr P Brears		Leeds City Museum
Mr J Bridges		Sion Hill Hall
Mrs S Broad		Dunrobin Castle
A Broadhurst & A Broadhurst Jr	Partners	Llangollen Motor Museum
D Brown	Regional Public Affairs Manager	Baddesley Clinton
E Gore-Brown	Conservation & Recreation Officer	Yorkshire Water Museum
J J R Brown	Deputy Curator & Education Officer	Hamilton District Museum
Mr D Brown	Publicity Officer	Sandtoft Transport Centre
Mrs Joan Brown	Director	Museum of Childhood
P McMillan Browse	Principal Horticultural Officer	Probus County Demonstration Garden
Mr & Mrs J Brumer	Proprietors	Cobham Manor Riding Centre & Country Pursuits
M Brunier	Regional Development Officer	Rochester Castle
B Buchan	Publicity	Museum of Flight
Ms B Buchan	Press/Advertising Officer	Royal Museum of Scotland*
Ms B Buchan	PR Officer Nat Museum of Scotland	Scottish Agricultural Museum
J Buchanan	Custodian	Drummond Castle Gardens
Ms G Buchanan	Marketing and Publicity Officer	Winchester Heritage Centre
R Buckley	Promotions Manager	Buckleys Yesterdays World
Ms E Bunurrti	Sales and PR	Guinness World of Records Exhibition*
S Burge	Curator	Colour Museum
L Burgess		Stockwood Craft Museum & Gardens
I M Burgoyne	Curator	Pilkington Glass Museum
Ms S Burke	Press & Publicity Officer	Sea Life Centre*
Paul Burke	Head Recreation Ranger	Grizedale Forest Park*
Ms A Burr	Marketing Director	Colchester Zoo*
Mr D Burrows	Cathedral Administrator	Chester Cathedral
Mr Butcher	Proprietor	Combe Martin Wildlife & Dinosaur Park
B Butler	Proprietor	Kennet Horse Boat Company
Caroline Butler	Assistant Manager	Bressingham Steam Museum and Gardens
M A Byrne	Managing Director	The Beatles Story
Cadogan Management		Spencer House
Mr F Savage Caldwell	Curator	Gray Art Gallery
Mr F Savage Caldwell	Curator	Hartlepool Maritime Museum
Cambridge Office		Wrest Park House and Gardens
Ms E Cameron	Secretary/Curator	Laidhay Croft Museum
Ms H Cameron	Administrator	Duncombe Park
Mrs A Campbell	Marketing Officer	Ulster Folk and Transport Museum*
Mrs M Campbell		Bexhill Museum of Costume & Social History
G M Candler	Site Co-ordinator	Carew Castle and Tidal Mill
Major R Cannidy	Curator	Royal Green Jackets Museum
R Carman		Ely Museum
Mr P Carpenter	Property Admin Officer	Oldway Mansion
Ms J Carpenter	Curator Art Collections	University of Liverpool Art Gallery
T Carr	Promotions Consultant	Cider Museum and King Offa Distillery
Major J Carroll	Curator	Devonshire Regiment Museum
Major J Carroll	Curator	Dorset Military Museum
Mrs Janet Carter	Director	Buxton Micrarium
Miss K Carver		Epping Forest District Museum
Mr J Castledine	Marketing Officer	Abbeydale Industrial Hamlet
Mr M Cavanagh	Owner	Cotswold Motor Museum
Countess Cawdor	Director	Cawdor Castle
Miss F Chalmers	Countryside Officer	Itchen Valley Country Park
D Chamberlain	Admin	Maritime Museum, Ramsgate
Katharine Chant	Head of Museums Service	Chelmsford and Essex, Essex Regiment Museums
D Chapman	House Steward	Kelmscott Manor
Mrs M Chapman	Marketing Consultant	Dalmeny House
Mr D Charles	Publicity Manager	North East Aircraft Museum
R I H Charlton	Publications Officer	Ashmolean Museum
Mr K Childs	Retail Manager	Poole Pottery
Doug Chinnem	Assistant Director (Business)	Norfolk Rural Life Museum and Union Farm

Contact Name	Contact Title	Attraction
D Chinnery	Assistant Director	Norwich Castle Museum*
Mr H Christie		Tapeley Park & British Jousting Centre
Linda Clampett	Duty Officer	Thameside Complex
M Clark	Director of Zoological Gardens	Exmoor Bird Gardens
Mr T Clark		White Post Modern Farm Centre*
Gwen Clarke	Administrator	Frigate Unicorn
Miss Coryn E Clarke	Owner/Manager	Priests Mill
G Compton		Bignor Roman Villa
Ms V Connell	Marketing Manager	Metroland*
Mrs G Cook	Proprietor	Old Semeil Herb Garden
P Cooke		Athelhampton House and Gardens
Ms P Corp-Palmer	Publicity/Promotions Officer	Weymouth Sea Life Park
Mrs Joy Coupe		Bristol Cathedral
Mr T Cox	Education Officer	Wildfowl & Wetlands Trust – Welney Centre
Mr W Crawford		Cluanie Deer Farm Park
T Croft	Asst Manager	Bodmin and Wenford Railway
Mr K Cross	Business Manager/Director	Oceanarium
Mr K Crowe	Keeper: Human History	Southend Central Museum & Planetarium
Ian Cruickshank	Marketing Manager/Press Officer	Anglesey Sea Zoo*
Mr & Mrs S Cruickshank	Joint Owners	Damside Garden Herbs
Ms S Curtis	Curator	Valence House Museum
Alison Cutforth	Curator	Springburn Museum Trust
Major (Rtd) P L Cutler MBE	Administrative Officer	The Welch Regiment Museum
E Dale	Senior Warden	Hollingworth Lake Country Park
Mr Dashwood	Director	West Wycombe Caves
Mr D David	Marketing Officer	Newham Grange Leisure Farm
June Davies/Nichola Walby Roberts	Conference and Marketing Officers	Dyffryn House Conference Centre and Gardens
R Davies	Business & Publicity Manager	Museum of Army Flying
C Dee	Marketing Exec	The Oxford Story
Mr I Dempster	Development Manager	Mill of Towie
Mr and Mrs A Dennis	Proprietors	Miniature Pony Centre
A Denyer	Manager	Crabble Corn Mill
D Devenish		Wisbech & Fenland Museum
Ms A Devonshire	Deputy Curator	Museum of the Order of St John
Mr P Dickson	Reg Public Affairs Manager	Oxburgh Hall
Director & Board of Trustees		Whitby Archives Heritage Centre
Mr G Doban	Deputy Director	Royal Navy Submarine Museum
Mrs P Doherty	Marketing Co-ordinator	Edinburgh Canal Centre
Mr A Donald		Waltzing Waters Ltd
Ms V Donaldson	Marketing Manager	Scottish Mining Museum
N Donaldson		Lochore Meadows Country Park
Stephen Done	Curator	Cyfarthfa Castle Museum, Art Gallery and Park
J Douglas	Partner	Avon Valley Country Park
Ms P Douglas		Charles Rennie Mackintosh Society
Hon Caroline Douglas-Home	Estate Factor	The Hirsel
Mr A Downend	Principal Librarian	Hogarth's House
Mr P Downey	PR	Yorkshire Car Collection
Dr A I Doyle		Durham Heritage Centre
Dreweatt Neate	Agents	Roman Villa, Brading
Ms C Dudley	Director	Royal Cornwall Museum
S Duff	Marketing Officer	Howletts Zoo Park
S Duff	Marketing Officer	Port Lympne Zoo Park, Mansion & Gardens
P F D Duffie	Administrator	Blenheim Palace*
A Dunne	Heritage Assistant	Izaak Walton's Cottage
A Dunne	Heritage Assistant	The Ancient High House
D Eccles	Cathedral Secretary	Blackburn Cathedral
Ms J Edom		New Forest Museum and Visitor Centre
Ms H Edward		Woodham Church Museum
Mr and Mrs B Eitches	Owners	World of Toys
Richard Ellam		Royal Observatory Visitor Centre
Ms L Ellingham	PR Executive	Hornsea Freeport*
Graham Ellis		Mull & West Highland Narrow Gauge Railway
Ms E Elwood	Marketing Manager	Boughton House
J R Emary	Admin	Mapledurham House and Watermill*
G Emerson	Director	Morwellham Quay
Commander K England	Trustee	Falmouth Maritime Museum
English Heritage		Stott Park Bobbin Mill
Ms M Evans	Visitor Services	Saffron Walden Museum
S Falconer	PR Officer	Bekonscot Model Village*
Dorothy Fenton	Marketing Officer	National Museum of Labour History
Grp Captain T Ferguson OBE	Director	Cockley Cley Iceni Village & Museums
Douglas Ferreira	General Manager	The Ravenglass and Eskdale Railway*
S Ferri	Shop Manager	The Walter Rothschild Zoological Museum
Mr C Fisher	Visitor Services	Scaplen's Court Museum
Mr C Fisher	Visitor Services	Waterfront Museum
1st Lt HMS Victory		HMS Victory
J W A Fleming		Guildford Cathedral
Diane Forbes	Regional Park Affairs Manager	Carrick-A-Rede Rope Bridge*
Mrs D Forbes	Regional Marketing Manager	Florencecourt House
Ms Diane Forbes	Regional Public Affairs Manager	Mount Stewart House and Gardens*
Ms Diane Forbes	Public Affairs Manager	Springhill
Mr J Ford	Manager	Plymouth Dome*
S Forrester	Regional Public Affairs Manager	Hughenden Manor
K Foster	Head of PR	Ironbridge Gorge Museum*
Dr A Foxon	Keeper of Archaeology	Hull and East Riding Museum
Dr R Francis	Director	Forncett Industrial Steam Museum
J A Francis	Museum Manager	The Aerospace Museum*
Mr H Francis/Catherine Vance		Larne Tourist Info & Interpretation Centre
Miss A M Franklin	Honorary Secretary	Tain and District Museum
Mr D Fraser	Museums and Arts Officer	Derby Museum and Art Gallery*

Contact Name	Contact Title	Attraction
Ms L Fraser	Marketing Manager	Edinburgh Museum of Childhood
V Frearson	Manager	Flimwell Bird Park
Mrs A Frewen	Advertising Manager	Frewen College
H E Frost	Curator and Company Secretary	Dyson Perrins Museum
Mrs S Furnell	Shop Manager	St Edmundsbury Cathedral
Miss B Galvin		Steam Brewery Museum
A Garnham		Bartley Mill
C J George	Administrator	Broughton Castle
Peter Gerring	Marketing Manager	White Castle
H Gillian	Administrator	Wells Museum
Mr D Glover		Cathedral Church of St Nicholas
D Goddard	Director	Midland Motor Museum
R Goodden	Director	Worldwide Butterflies Ltd
Mr S Goodhard	Keeper of Transport	Streetlife – Hull Museum of Transport
K Goodway	Marketing Manager	Avon Valley Railway
P J Gordon	Town Clerk	Almonry Museum
A C Gottlieb	Director	Michelham Priory
J Gould	Marketing Manager	Windsor Safari Park*
H Graham	Curator	Cecil Higgins Art Gallery and Museum
Ms C Graham-Brown		St Martin-in-the-Fields
Mr J Grainger		Burnby Hall Gardens & Museum
Mr R Grange	Tourism Promotion Manager	The Guildhall, Beverley
J Gray		Sellet Hall Gardens
E Graybill	Owner/Director	Peckforton Castle
Ms A Green	PR	Freud Museum
Ms C Green	Marketing Director	Strawberry Hill
R J W Greenland		Model Farm and Folk Museum
J Gresnam		Pennyarcadia
Mr M Gresswell	Curator	Dales Countryside Museum
Ms C Griffith	Director	Butterfly World and Fountain World
Ms R Griffith-Jones	Marketing/PR	Victoria and Albert Museum
Eifion Griffiths	Director	Tregwynt Mill
Mr L Gunn		John Wesley's Chapel
M Guy		Queen Elizabeth Country Park
B Gwynne	Promotions Officer	Ford Green Hall
R Gwynne	Promotions Officer	Etruria Industrial Museum
Dr Douglas Gyte	Leisure and Economic Dev Officer	Ays Coughfee Hall Museum
Mr B Haigh	Community Curator	Bagshaw Museum
Mr B Haigh	Community Curator	Dewsbury Museum
J Haines	Partner	Watermouth Castle
Mr T Hall	Director	National Ambulance Museum
P Hamilton	Gallery Services Officer	The Whitworth Art Gallery
B Hamment-Arnold	Hon Programme Officer	Torquay Museum
Mr C Harde	Publicity	Tithe Barn Museum & Arts Centre
Mr D Harding	Cathedral Steward	Hereford Cathedral
D Hardman	Marketing Manager	Tatton
Mrs Elizabeth Harkin	Education & Promotions Officer	The Ulster History Park
Harlow Council Information Services		Mark Hall Cycle Museum and Gardens
Ms L Harnet	Publicity Manager	Bucklers Hard Village & Maritime Museum*
L Harnett	PR Manager	Beaulieu National Motor Museum, House & Abbey*
W F Harper	Owner	Colliford Lake Park
Ms L Harris	Manageress	Chambercombe Manor
D Harrison		Stamford Shakespeare Company
Mrs R Harrison	Owner	Wordsworth Gallery
Mrs S Harrison	Director	Museum of Mechanical Music
Mr P Hart		Bure Valley Railway
D Hartley/A Donnelly		Smugglers Adventure
Mrs A Harvey	PA to General Manager	Bodnant Gardens
Mr C Hawke	Senior Warden	Gibraltar Point National Nature Reserve*
Ms J Hawkes	Publicity & Promotions Executive	Harveys Wine Museum
M Hawksworth	Commercial Manager	Bass Museum, Visitor Ctr & Shire Horse Stables
Mr R Heap	Partner	Chestnut Centre
Mary Heathcote	Administrator	Oriel Mostyn
MLP Hedley-Walker	Owner	Wolferton Station Museum
Mr H Heeley	Publicity Director	Newark Air Museum
J D Hegarty		Capesthorne Hall
A Helme	Curator	The Nelson Museum and Local History Centre
Mr J Hemstock	Interpretation Officer	Derwent Walk Country Park
M Henderson	Marketing	Paignton & Dartmouth Steam Railway
Mrs M Henderson	Owner	Rydal Mount
Mr A Henshaw	Group Custodian	Totnes Castle
E M Henslowe	Curator/Manager	Selly Manor Museum
Mr S Hession		Peterborough Cathedral*
F Hetherington	Agent	Seaton Delaval Hall
June Hewitt	Retail/Factory Shop Manager	Cumbria Crystal Ltd*
J Hibbert	Manager	Trebah Garden
P Hickman		Marwell Zoological Park*
Ms J Hodgkins	Marketing	Royal Marines Museum
Ms S Hogben	Publicity and Exhibitions	HMS Belfast*
Ms D Holloway	Marketing Manager	Paignton Zoo*
C Holm	Resort Services Manager	Volks Electric Railway
Mrs D Holmes	Partner	The Lincolnshire Poultry Park
Mr M Hooley	Manager	Trinity House National Lighthouse Centre
Mrs B Hope	Marketing Manager	⎧ Lady Lever Art Gallery ⎪ Liverpool Museum ⎨ Sudley ⎪ Walker Art Gallery ⎩ National Maritime Museum
Ms S Howall	Assistant Director	Bankside Gallery

Contact Name	Contact Title	Attraction
A Howard	Manager	Child-Beale Wildlife Park*
Carys Howell	Regional Public Affairs Manager	Erddig Hall
Mr D Howell	Assistant Curator	The Dewey Museum
D R Howlett	Curator	Quex House & Gardens & Powell-Cotton Museum
J Howse	Marketing Manager	Didcot Railway Centre*
Mr N Hudson	Consultant	Rockingham Castle
S Hudson	Marketing Manager	The Historic Dockyard, Chatham
E Hulse		Breamore House & Museums
Mr D Humas	Manager	Colne Valley Railway
J Humphreys	PR	National Army Museum
J Hutchinson	Director	Chatterley Whitfield Mining Museum
Mr and Mrs R Hutchinson	Joint Owners	Incredibly Fantastic Old Toy Show
Mr B Ilett		National Postal Museum
Ms Y Irving	Marketing Officer	Wildfowl & Wetlands Centre
D Brever/H Jackson	Principal Marketing Manager	Royal Pavilion, Art Gallery and Museum
Mr N Jacques		Normanby Hall Country Park
Hon C James	Owner/General Manager	Northbourne Court Gardens
Mr C James	Owner	Torosay Castle & Gardens
Mr S Jaques		Eden Camp Modern History Theme Museum*
P Jarvis		Thirlestane Castle
M Jeffery	Asst Director	Sulgrave Manor
P Jempson	Owner	Woodside Farm & Wild Fowl Park
Mr T Jenkins		Staintondale Shire Horse Farm
Dr Brian John		Cilgwyn Candles Workshop and Mini Museum
Ms E St John-Smith	Press Secretary	Westminster Abbey*
Mr A Johnson		Camera Obscura
Mrs C Johnson	Administrator	Holker Hall and Gardens
Mr T Johnstone	Advertising	Beck Isle Museum of Rural Life
Mr R Joiner	Marketing	Royal Botanic Gardens Kew*
Ms L Karlsen	Principal Keeper	Ferens Art Gallery
Ernie Kary		Offa's Dyke Association
Mr T Kay		Pettitts Feathercraft & Animal Adventure Park
Ms J Kelly		Association Gallery
Ms L Kelly		Tallberg Taylor Gallery
Mr Kennaway		Escot Aquatic Centre & Gardens
P Kennedy	Administrator	Parham Elizabethan House & Gardens
Mrs M Kershaw	Curator	Knaresborough Castle & Courthouse Museum
Mrs M Kershaw	Curator	Mercer Art Gallery
Mrs M Kershaw	Curator	Royal Pump Room Museum
G Kichenside		Gorse Blossom Railway & Woodland Park
David Kidd	Proprietor	Cockthorpe Hall Toy Museum
Ms M Kidner	Marketing Executive	Kingdom of the Sea, Gt Yarmouth*
Ms M Kidner	Marketing Executive	Kingdom of the Sea, Hunstanton*
Ms M Kidner	Marketing Executive	Pleasurewood Hills American Theme Park*
Ms M Kidner	Marketing Executive	Ripley's Believe It or Not
Mr B Kilner		Colne Valley Museum
C Kilpatrick	Secretary/Treasurer	Burns Cottage and Museum
A King	Asst Curator	Bristol Industrial Museum
Dr R J King	Curator	The John Moore Countryside Museum
S Kirby	Curator	Mill Green Museum and Mill
Sue Kirby		Welwyn Roman Baths
A Kirkhope	Marketing Manager	Frontierland Western Theme Park*
Mrs I Kitt	Arts and Museum Officer	Sobriety Waterways Adventure Centre & Museum
C Kitts	Manager	Stanborough Park
Mr J Kneale		Shipwreck & Heritage Centre
Ms P Knowson	Sales and Marketing	Lightwater Valley Theme Park*
Mr J Lackenby	Reservoir Manager	Kielder Water
L Ladd		Bradford on Avon Museum
A G M Lamb	Cathedral Education Advisor	Birmingham Cathedral
Mr D A Lambie	Proprietor	Speyside Heather/Garden Visitor Centre
Ms J Lambie	Development Officer	Summerlee Heritage Trust
Mr J Paton/Mr D Lane	Managers	Carisbrooke Castle
P Langridge	Town Clerk	Totnes Guildhall
Ms K Latham		Marsh Farm Country Park*
Mrs D Law	Curator/Manager	Swaledale Folk Museum
Mr R Leak/Mrs P Edwards	Partners	The Smuggling Experience
Mrs D Lee	PA to Chapter Clerk	York Minster*
M Legge	Co-owner	Legbourne Railway Museum
A Leigh	Curator	Warrington Museum and Art Gallery
Leisure Services Marketing		Leeds Industrial Museum
Gerard Lennon	Community Education Officer	Down County Museum*
M Lennox	Deputy Custodian	Jenner Museum
James Leslie	Proprietor	Heritage Farm Park
Ms S Lewis	Commercial/Marketing Officer	Yorkshire Museum
Ms J Liddiard	Press & PR	National Gallery*
M Lindop	Support Service Officer	Grosvenor Museum
J Linley		Inveraray Jail
Mr J Livingstone	Recreation Officer	Galloway Forest Park
Mr J Livingstone	Recreation Officer	Glen Trool Visitor Centre
Mr R Loader	GC Manager	Stewarts Garden – Lands
M Lockhart	Regional Information Officer	Gladstone's Land
Mrs M Lockhart	Regional Information Officer	Kellie Castle
Ms Y Lockwood		Botanic Centre
Ms B J Logan	Curator,	The Ballance House
Ms H Long	Publicity and Promotions Officer	St Andrews Sea Life Centre
Mr A Lovett	Senior Officer	Coniston Boating Centre
R Lunghi		Rother Valley Country Park*
J P Lyons	Marketing Consultant	Abbot Hall
Ms J Macalister	Curator	Glenbarr Abbey Visitors Centre
J MacDonald	Curator	Auchindrain Township Open Air Museum

Contact Name	Contact Title	Attraction
Mrs H B MacDonald	Asst Custodian	Neidpath Castle
Paul S MacDonald	Administrator	Naworth Castle
Mrs M Mackenzie	Project Co-ordinator	Timespan Heritage Centre
Bruce Mackie	Head Office – Edinburgh	Threake Gardens
W J Mackinnon	Hostel Manager	Baden Powell House Hostel
Lady Maclean		Duart Castle
Ms S Macpherson	Secretary – Trustees	Clan Macpherson Museum
Ms C Mahon	Head of Visitor Services/Marketing	Duxford Airfield*
Ms S Major	Administrator	Prideaux Place
J Makin (appt by Walsingham Coll)	Garden Administrator	Parcevall Hall Gardens
C Mamion	Marketing & Promotions Officer	The Local Interest Museum
Mr C Manning	Partner	Charles Manning's Amusement Park*
C Mannion	Marketing and Promotions Officer	Local Interest Museum
Mr H Margary	Director	Lympne Castle
Miss Martin		Chilham Castle
T Martin	Marketing Officer	Battle Abbey and Battlefield of Hastings
Ms F C Marwick	Curator	West Highland Museum
C Massey	Senior Museums Officer	Wood End Museum of Natural History
Ms Y Masters	Partner	Tamar Valley Donkey Park
Sandra E Matchett	Supervisor	The Palace Stables Heritage Centre
Mrs S Matthews		Stained Glass Museum
M Maxfield	Manager	Manchester United Museum & Tour Centre
Mrs H McAdam	Secretary	Glengoulandie Deer Park
Ms L McAuley	District Council Marketing Officer	Glasgow Vennel Museum
Ms L McAuley	District Council Marketing Officer	Museum of the Cumbraes
Ms L McAuley	District Council Marketing Officer	North Ayrshire Museum
Mr D McConnell	Estates Manager	Darnaway Farm Visitor Centre
Col D G McCord	Curator	Hatfield House*
Miceal McCoy		Mullaghbawn Folk Museum
L McCracken	Asst Public Affairs Manager	Bateman's (The National Trust)
B McDavitt	Marketing and Promotions Manager	Great Western Railway Museum
Eva McDonald	Proprietor	Fair Maid's House
A McLaren	Partner	Coughton Court
H McMahon	Marketing and Publicity Officer	Bromham Mill
H McMahon	Marketing and Publicity Officer	Harrold Odell Country Park*
H McMahon	Marketing and Publicity Officer	Swiss Garden
Mrs C McWilliam	Publications Convener	Greyfriars Kirk
B Mead	Manager	Forge Mill Museum & Bordesley Abbey Vis Ctr
D Mead	Bursar	Coventry Cathedral
S Meads	Museums Officer, N Cornwall Council	Bodmin Town Museum
Mr W T Meikle	Admin Sec	Royal Scottish Academy
Mr and Mrs M Menist	Owners	Southwick Country Herb Centre
Chris Merchant	Chief Executive	Wetheriggs Country Pottery
J Milford	Museums & Heritage Manager	Newark Museum
E M J Miller	Director	Pendle Heritage Centre
M Miller	Marketing Trustee	East Anglian Railway Museum
M Miller		The Bluebell Railway
Miss Cathy Miller	Partner	Ponsonby Farm Park
Mrs Miller		Fenny Lodge Gallery
R Millett	Marketing Manager	North Norfolk Railway*
Mr R Milliam		St Paul's Cathedral
C S Mills	Sales/Publicity Director	Southport Railway Centre
Ms P Millward		Bankfield Museum
Christine Mineham	Shop Manager	Beatrix Potter Gallery*
Ms S Minter	Curator	Chelsea Physic Garden
M Moir	Project Director	Chiltern Open Air Museum
Lady Molesworth-St Aubyn	Wife of Owner	Pencarrow
S Montgomery	Marketing Manager	Warwick Castle*
M Moore		Shaldon Wildlife Trust
Ms A Moore	Museum Curator	Morpeth Chantry Bagpipe Museum
Mrs P Moore	Trust Secretary	Twyford Pumping Station
Mr T Mor		New World Tapestry Centres
Rita More & Doreen McIntyre	Shop Manageress & Co-ordinator	Blackshaw Farm Park Ltd
C Morgan	Curator	The National Pinetum (Bedgebury)
B Morley	Regional Public Affairs Manager	Durham Massey Hall and Park
Mrs S Morris	PR Promotions	Peter Pan's Playground*
P Morris	Director	Model Village
S Morris	Exhibitions Officer	Blackburn Museum and Art Gallery
Major W D Morris-Barker	Administrator	Arbury Hall
M Morton	Hon Deputy Curator	Ripon Prison & Police Museum
Mrs S E Moss	Officer in Charge	Graham Sutherland Gallery
Ms D Moss	Keeper of Decorative Arts	Pickford's House Museum
T Muir (The Lady)		Kingston Bagpuize House and Garden
Ms V Munnings	PR Officer	Wood Green Animal Sanctuary*
F Munro	Marketing Manageress	Liverpool Cathedral
Mr R Murphy	Chairman	Dinmore Manor and Gardens
V & A Museum		Bethnal Green Museum of Childhood
M Mutch	Curator	Myreton Motor Museum
Ms J Naismith	Publicity Officer	Holburne Museum & Crafts Study Centre
Ms B Nash	Administrator	The Building of Bath Museum
P Neaves	Admin/Secretary	The Monkey Sanctuary
S Neill	Marketing and Development Officer	Ulster Museum*
Mr H Nelson	Director	British in India Museum
M J Neve	Managing Director	Denmans Garden
Ms T Newland BA MSc	Librarian	Marx Memorial Library
Mr A Nicholson	Publicity Officer	Bowes Railway Centre
Dr M Nix		Tiverton Museum
J Goodson/N Nixon	Marketing Officer/Senior Curator	Much Wenlock Museum
Brian H Nodes	Administrator	Blair Castle*
David North		Pensthorpe Waterfowl Trust

Contact Name	Contact Title	Attraction
W Northam/R Maddicott	Museum/FME Ltd	Fitzwilliam Museum*
Mr H Noyes		Isle of Wight Rare Breeds & Waterfowl Park
Mr C Nunn		Broads Museum
J O'Brian	Asst Curator	The Valley Heritage Centre and Museum
Mr D O'Grady	Merchandising Officer	Bishops' House
Mr and Mrs P O'Shea		Trenouth Farm Rare Breeds Centre
Ms B Oakley	Publicity/Promotions	Portsmouth Sea Life Centre
Mr C Oglivie	Secretary	Keighley & Worth Valley Railway*
Mrs Oldfield	Owner	Doddington Place Gardens
N Oliveira/N Oxley/M Petry	Directors	Museum of Installation
Mr E Oliver		Chatsworth*
L Orams	Secretary	Hove Museum and Art Gallery
Mr C Orr-Ewing	Managing Agent	Exbury Gardens
J Oswin	Marketing Manager	Leeds Castle
Mr M Overton	Owner	Sally Lunn's Refreshment House & Museum
Ms D Owen	Administrator	East Riddlesden Hall
L & B Owens	Joint Partners	Ardington Pottery
Ms P Owens	Marketing	Museum of the Moving Image*
R Pailthorpe	Asst Director	Weald and Downland Open Air Museum
Dr C Palmer	Curator	Havant Museum
J Palmer	Marketing Manager	Bristol Zoo Gardens*
Mr D Parker		Dickens House Museum
Mr R Parsons	Dir of Fabric Fund	Lincoln Cathedral
Patti Partridge	Partner	Felin Crewi Working Watermill
Lucy Paton	Visitors Officer	Norwich Cathedral*
Mr G Patterson		Barton Manor Gardens & Vineyards
Ms I Patterson	Publicity & Special Events	Kelburn Country Centre
Ms J Patterson	Promotions & Marketing Officer	Timothy Hackworth Victorian & Railway Museum
Mr M Pawley	Countryside Officer	Crombie Country Park
Mr M Pearson	Information/Tourism Officer	Abbotsbury Sub Tropical Gardens
Mr M Pearson	Information/Tourism Officer	Abbotsbury Swannery
Mr M Pearson	Information/Tourism Officer	Abbotsbury Tithe Barn Museum
Mr M Pearson	Head Ranger (Recreation)	Whinlatter Visitor Centre*
Ms S Pearson	Marketing Manager	The Tales of Robin Hood*
S Penney	Curator	The Salt Museum
A Percival	Honorary Director	Fleur De Lis Heritage Centre
Neil Perry	Commercial Manager	Margam Park*
Mr M Peters	Marketing/PR Operations	Bournemouth Heritage Transport Centre
Mr & Mrs Petrie		Southport Zoo and Conservation Trust
Mr R De Peyer	Curator	Dorset County Museum
M Phillips		Allhallows Museum
Mr N Pine		Goss and Crested China Ltd
Pinmegar Family		Hammerwood Park
Ms V Pirie	Keeper of Interpretation	Russel-Cotes Art Gallery & Museum
Mr J Platt	Senior Keeper of Industry	Derby Industrial Museum
Ms P Plumb	Administrator	Ragged School Museum
H Poole	Admin	Lewes Castle and Museums
Mr R Poole	Marketing Director	The Lost Gardens of Heligan
Mr R Poor	Secretary	Ullapool Museum
Ms M Powell	Marketing Manager	Battle of Britain Memorial Flight (Visits)
C M Preston	Owner/Manager	Badsell Farm Park
Sir Ronald Preston		Beeston Hall
J Procter	Sales and Marketing Manager	Royalty and Empire*
C Prout	Sales and Publicity Officer	Hever Castle
Ms J Purcell	Manager	Longdale Craft Centre & Museum*
Ms J Pye	Visitors Manager	Ely Cathedral*
Dr Ian Griffen/Eamon Rafferty	Director/Secretary	Armagh Planetarium
Ms D Ralpus	Publicity Officer	Charles Dickens Birthplace Museum
R S Ramsdale	Administrator	Church of St Cuthbert & Turner Mausoleum
Ms R Randall	Press & Public Events Officer	Rougemont House Museum
Ms R Randall	Press & Public Events Officer	Royal Albert Memorial Museum
Ms R Randall	Press & Public Events Officer	St Nicholas Priory
Mrs C Raper	Countryside Information Officer	Castle Eden Walkway Country Park*
M Ratcliffe (Mrs)	Director	The Alice in Wonderland Visitor Centre
J M Rawlins		The Childrens Farm
Ms J Rayner		London Toy and Model Museum
J Reddaway	Tourism Officer	Tamworth Castle
Ms P Redmonds		Sooty's World
Ms H Redwood	Press	Rock Circus*
E Rees	Founder/Trustee	The International Helicopter Museum
J Regan	Development Officer	Harris Museum and Art Gallery
S Regan	Publicity Executive	Stratford Butterfly Farm
Billy Reid/Alistair Davison	Manager/Asst Manager	The Northern Ireland Aquarium*
Ms A Reid	Curator	Stranraer Museum
Miss G B Reith/D C Butters	Town Clerk/Curator	Swaffham Museum
Ms A Rennick		Blair Drummond Safari & Leisure Park
Mrs B Reynolds	Personnel Manager	Cumberland Pencil Museum & Exhibition Centre
C Rice	W Lancs District Council	Beacon Country Park
Mr J Richards		The Lace Centre*
V J Richards		Twycross Zoo*
M Ridgers	Tourism Site Manager	Pecorama
Mrs J Ringer		Ventnor Botanic Garden*
Mr K Roberts	Manager	Tropical World*
Mrs P Roberts	Organiser	Jane Welsh Carlyle Museum
Ms C Roberts	Community & Development	Pumphouse Educational Museum
Mr K Robertson	Senior Ranger	Worsbrough Country Park*
Revd C Robertson	Minister	Canongate Kirk
A R Robinson	Administrator	Scone Palace*
C Robinson	Marketing Manager	Whipsnade Wild Animal Park*

Contact Name	Contact Title	Attraction
Ian Robinson	Marketing Consultant	Windermere Steamboat Museum*
Mr N Robinson	Publicity	SS Shieldhall
H Roe	Publicity Officer	Coach House Museum
P Roper		National Maritime Museum Greenwich*
Ms P Rossetter	Administrative Director	Age Exchange Reminiscence Centre
Mrs M Rowe		Radstock Midsomer Norton Museum
Tony Rowlands	Managing Director	Trefriw Wells Spa
G M W Ruddock	Curator	Teignmouth Museum
D J Rudkin	Director	Fishbourne Roman Palace and Museum
Ms A Ruffell	Marketing	Paultons Park
J Ruffle		Oriental Museum
Ms J Rushton	Marketing	Capel Manor
Mr A Rutter	Secretary	Harwich Redoubt
Mr A Rutter	Secretary	Port of Harwich Maritime Museum
Ms G Rye		Thursford Collection*
Mr N Sadler	Curator/Director	London Canal Museum
Mrs C Salt	Administrator	Number One the Royal Crescent
S Sampson	Manager	Paradise Wildlife Park
Mr R Sandell	Marketing Officer	Newstead Abbey*
Ms M Sanderson	Administrator	Pontefract Museum
Ms M Sanderson	Administrator	Elizabethan Exhibition Gallery
Ms M Sanderson	Administrator	Pontefract Castle
Ms M Sanderson	Administrator	Wakefield Art Gallery
Ms M Sanderson	Administrator	Wakefield Museum
Raymond Sanderson	Commercial Director	Teifi Valley Railway
Mr R Sandwell	Marketing	Browhouse Yard Museum*
Mrs J Schroeder	Owner	Arreton Manor
National Trust for Scotland		J M Barrie's Birthplace
Mary Scourfield	Marketing Assistant	Rhondda Heritage Park
D M Scragg	Press/Publicity Officer	Foxfield Steam Railway
J Sculley		Stockport War Memorial and Art Gallery
Mr B Sedgley	Sales	Chessington World of Adventures*
Mr G Seimann	Managing Director	Conwy Visitor Centre*
Mr S Selvester	Marketing Assistant	Edinburgh Zoo*
Ms H Sewell	Marketing and Publicity	Commonwealth Institute*
Vicki Seymour	Exhibition Officer	Kirkcaldy Museum & Art Gallery
Dr E J Sharples		Ness Gardens
Mr M Shaw	Junior Partner	Sutcliffe Gallery
Mr S Shaw		Elvisly Yours Centre
Ms L Shead	Marketing	Hampton Court Palace*
Mr J Sheard	Agent	Bolton Abbey Estate*
Mrs G Shephard	Sales Supervisor	Ffestiniog Railway
Ms J Sheriden	PR	Walkley Clogs
Tony Shorthose	Marketing Director	Kingdom of the Sea
J Simm	Publicity Manager	West Lancashire Light Railway
Mr P Simmonds	Senior Museums Officer	Haverfordwest Castle Museum and Art Gallery
Ken Simms	Director	Thrigby Hall Wildlife Gardens
Mr M Simpson FBIPP	Director	Lyme Regis Experience
Mrs M Simpson	Bookshop Manager	Selby Abbey
Mrs M Sivyer	PR	HM Tower of London*
R Skinner	Marketing Manager	Royal Engineers Museum
Ms H Slater		Strangers' Hall Museum
D Smith	Marketing Manager	Romney, Hythe & Dymchurch Railway
J Smith	Curator	Fasque
Mrs H Smith		Harrow Museum & Heritage Centre*
Ms J Smith	Hon Curator	Dickens House Museum, Broadstairs
Ms R Smith	Marketing	Eureka! The Museum for Children
N Smith	Museum Curator	Barleylands Farm Museum
Mrs L Snowdon	P A	Earlshall Castle and Gardens
Ms C Somerset	Secretary	Aldeburgh Moot Hall Museum
Mr and Mrs J Sparrow	Owners	Bear Museum
Mr J Spicer	Sponsorship & Development	Dulwich Picture Gallery
J Spier	Marketing Manager	Shugborough
Mr R Spinks		Captain Cook Schoolroom Museum
Ms P Spooner	Marketing Consultant	Dorset Heavy Horse Centre
Ms P Spooner	Marketing	Lulworth Cove Heritage
Mr D Standen	Countryside Manager	Wat Tyler Country Park*
Mr K Stanfield	Warden	Peatlands Park*
David Steele	Castle Manager	Carrickferggus Castle*
L Steene	Custodian	Anne of Cleves House Museum
Mr Stephens	Chairman	Natural World*
Mr T Stephenson		Gem Rock Museum
Mr P Stewart	Director/Partner	Dunaverig Farm Life Centre
N T Stobbs	Administrator	Heron Corn Mill and Museum of Papermaking
Mr R Street		Christchurch Tricycle Museum
Mr C Stringer/Ms C Brooke	Publicity/Promotions	Lee Valley Park Farms
G Stroud	Marketing, PR Manager	Leighton Buzzard Railway
Ms C Maxwell Stuart		Traquair House
D M Sturdy	Marketing Officer	Sea Life Centre
Mr D Sturdy	Publicity/Promotions Officer	Rhyl Sea Life Centre
Mr M Sully	Secretary	Watchet Market House Museum
M Sulter	Art Gallery Services Officer	Rochdale Art Gallery
Mr Peter Sunderland	Assistant Director	Beacraigs Country Park
Y Surcouf	Owner	Basildon Zoo
B Sutherland/P Andrews	Manager/Secretary	Bentley Wildfowl & Motor Museum
Mr J Sutherland	Partner	Ardfearn Nursery Plant Centre
Rosemary Sutton	Marketing Officer	Great Orme Tramway
P Svendsen	Asst Admin	The Donkey Sanctuary
D W & P R Sydenham	Proprietors	Cholderton Rare Breeds Farm Park
Mr C Tabiner	Manager	Farmworld*

Contact Name	Contact Title	Attraction
Mr R Tait	Director	Wine and Spirit Museum
Mr W Tayleur	Head of Marketing	Museum of London*
M Taylor	Manageress	Heale Gardens and Plant Centre
Mike Taylor	Commercial Marketing Manager	Tulliehouse Museum and Art Gallery
Mr B Taylor	Managing Director	Kirklees Light Railway
M Thomas	Marketing Officer	A Day at the Wells
M Thomas		Cornish Seal Sanctuary
Nest Thomas	Museum Development Officer	Beaumaris Gaol and Court
Nest Thomas	Museums Development Officer	The Lloyd George Museum and Highgate His Home
T Thomas	Trustee	Birmingham Railway Museum
Ms A Thomson	Visitor Services Manager	St Giles' Cathedral
D Thornton	Head of Sales and Marketing	Blackpool Pleasure Beach
Mr R Thornton	Director	Tropical Bird Park
Mr D Thorpe	Manager	South London Art Gallery
Dr P Thwaites		Royal Signals Museum
C Titherington	Sales and Promo Manager	Tower World
R & D Titterington		Iden Croft Herbs
Ms A Todhunter	Marketing Manager	Longdown Dairy Farm
Ms A Todhunter	Marketing Manager	New Forest Butterfly Farm
Mr J Tonner	Estate Manager	Formakin Estate
Tourism Committee		Minster Church of St Cuthberga*
G Traynor	Press Officer	Pallant House
Ms J Traynor	Development Officer	Satroshere
D Tucker	Museum Curator	Lackham Gardens & Agricultural Museum
Mr J Round Turner		National Horseracing Museum
Mr J Turner/Mrs S Turner	Co Directors	Lincolnshire Light Railway & Heritage Centre
Mr R Turner		The Big Sheep
M Twelves	Principal Marketing Officer	Arbeia Roman Fort & Museum
M Twelves	Principal Marketing/Commercial	Hancock Museum
M Twelves	Principal Marketing Officer	South Shields Museum & Art Gallery
Ms J Tyler	Keeper of Social History	Old Grammar School
Ms J Tyler	Keeper of Social History	Wilberforce House
University		University of Durham Botanic Garden
Mr B Unwin	Assistant Curator	Logan Botanic Garden
Mr G and Mrs J Upton	Owners	How We Lived Then Museum of Shops
K Usher	Administrator	Calke Abbey*
Mr M Valizadeh	Proprietor	Maes Astro Tourist Attraction
Mr N Varney	Marketing Director	Alton Towers*
R Vaughan	Partner	Wye Valley Farm Park
C Vere	Marketing Manager	Chester Zoo*
G Vevers	Publicity Director	East Lancashire Railway
D Viner	Curator	Corinium Museum
D Viner	Curator of Museums	Cotswold Countryside Collection
Mr M Volpe	Marketing and Publicity	Leighton House
Mr D Walker		Chester Visitor Centre
Mr J Walker	Hon Secretary to the Trustees	Bayle Museum
Mr S Walker	Business & Marketing Manager	Embsay Steam Railway
Mr P Wall	Marketing Manager	Heritage Motor Centre*
C Walthe	Asst Land Agent	Corsham Court
K Ward	Admin Assistant	The Shuttleworth Collection
V Ward	Director	Goosedale Model Aviation Centre
Mr R Wardroper	Head of Public Affairs	National Railway Museum*
M Warhurst	Museum Director	Norton Priory Museum and Gardens
C Warren	Marketing Officer	The Look Out*
Mr M Waters	Tourism Manager	Tower Bridge*
A J Watts	Director	Potters Museum of Curiosity
G Watts	Publicity Officer	Nothe Fort
B Websdale	Sales Manager	Sidmouth Museum
Mr N Weiss/Mr J Griffin	Marketing/Marketing Director	Portland Castle
Ms R Westwood	Museums Officer	Shibden Hall
Mr P Wetherall	Dept of Arts & Libraries	Lochwinnoch Community Museum
Mr P Wetherall	Deputy Director, Arts & Libraries	Paisley Museum & Art Galleries
Ms P Wheatcroft	Curator	Bruce Castle Museum
Ms J Whittaker	Arts Marketing Officer	Cartwright Hall
Ms J Whittaker/Ms L Killick	Marketing Officers Arts & Museums	Bradford Industrial Horses at Work Museum
Mr D Wickes		Palace of Holyroodhouse*
Mrs P Wiggle	Senior Assistant	Malton Museum
D Wild		The Museum of Childhood
Mrs Wildgust		D H Lawrence Birthplace Museum
R Wilkes	Marketing Manager	Brooklands Museum
Ann Williams	Curator	Bersham Heritage Centre and Ironworks
J Williams	Museum Asst	Margate Old Town Hall Local History Museum
L Williams		Marle Place Gardens and Nursery
P Williams	Publicity Officer	Museum of Transport
Peter Williams	Assistant Manager	Brecon Beacons Mountain Centre
V Williams	Curator	Hastings Museum and Art Gallery
I Willsher	Owner	Longstone Heritage Centre
Mr P Willsher	General Manager	Compton Acres Gardens
B S Wilson	Museums Officer	Tankerness House Museum
B Wilson	Hon Curator	Stromness Museum
I A Wilson	Manager	North Down Heritage Centre
K Wilson	PR Officer	The National Motorcycle Museum
M Wilson	Company Secretary	Burton Agnes Hall
Mrs C L Wilson	Project Manager	Whithorn Dig
Ms S Wilson	Marketing Officer	Border History Museum
R Wilson	Publicity Officer	Salisbury and South Wiltshire Museum
Mr D Woodhouse MBE	General Manager	Talyllyn Railway
S Wookey	Marketing Manager	The White Cliffs Experience
Mrs Sylvia Wordsworth	Marketing Officer/Conference Mgr	The Wordsworth Trust

Contact Name	Contact Title	Attraction
Ms R Worsley	Promotions Officer	Willsbridge Mill
Peter Worth		The Butterfly and Falconry Park
Frances Wortley	Marketing Officer	Snibston Discovery Park
D Wright	General Manager	Bicton Park Gardens
R Young	Principal	Haseley Manor
A D Yule	Warden	Auckland Castle

PERSONNEL

Contact Name	Contact Title	Attraction
Ms J Achroyd	PA to MD	Hornsea Freeport*
Ms L Adamson	Personnel, Exeter City Council	Rougemont House Museum / Royal Albert Memorial Museum / St Nicholas Priory
Mr D Aitchison	Chairman	Eyemouth Museum
Mr C J Allan	Deputy Director	Hunterian Art Gallery
Catherine Allard	Manager	Windermere Steamboat Museum*
Mrs B Allen	Tourism Manager	Bolton Abbey Estate*
Very Rev J Allen	Provost	Wakefield Cathedral
C Allender	Museum Manager	National Railway Museum*
M Amey	Owner	Hardys Wessex Exhibition
Ellis T Amos	Chapter Clerk	Carlisle Cathedral
E Anderson	Senior Exhibitions Officer	Harris Museum and Art Gallery
Miss D Andrews/Mrs R Brooks	Partners	Old Smithy Tourist Centre
A Archard	Head of Personnel	Lady Lever Art Gallery / Liverpool Museum / Sudley / Walker Art Gallery / National Maritime Museum
D Armitage	Curator	Museum of Army Flying
T Ash	Proprietor	Parke Rare Breeds Farm
D Asquith	Admin	Clandon Park
Mr D Asquith	Administrator	Hatchlands Park
Mr D Asquith		Fishbourne Roman Palace and Museum
Dr R L Atkinson	Curator	Camborne School of Mines Geological Museum
P Atkinson		Wheelwrights Museum & Gypsy Folklore Collect
Ms S Attanson		Kingdom of the Sea, Gt Yarmouth*
Ms F Baigent	Personnel	Rock Circus*
Mr C Bailes	Curator	Royal Horticultural Society Garden
Mr B Bailles	Administrator	Chillingham Castle
Mr K Bamber	Receiver General	Winchester Cathedral
M Barbour	Business Manager	Ragley Hall
Dr A Barclay	Ranger	Scottish Wildlife Trust
Julie Bareham	Secretary/PA	Manderston
R Barnes	Personnel Manager	The Donkey Sanctuary
Mr C Barton	Warden	The Old Rectory
Mr D Bashford	Assistant	Roman Villa, Brading
Mr A Bates	Administration Director	Eureka! The Museum for Children
Mr H Bayntun-Coward	Owner	Book Museum
Lieutenant Commander J Beck	Trustee Secretary & Curator	Falmouth Maritime Museum
C Beresford	Curator	Regiments of Gloucestershire Museum
Mr J Bernasconi	Hon Curator	University of Hull Art Collection
Miss M Beston	Administrator	Norton Conyers
Mr N Biles	Manager	Weymouth Sea Life Park
Ms N Binnie	Reception Manager	Waltzing Wartes Ltd
Cath Birchall	Administrator	National Museum of Labour History
Mrs Bird	Manageress	West Wycombe Caves
Miss S Bishop	Sales/Reception	Haseley Manor
Mr and Mrs K Blackburn	Owners	Buffers
Dr S Blackden	Resident Representative	Kellie Castle
J Blades	Administrator	Hanbury Hall (National Trust)
Mr G Blades	Operations Director	Lightwater Valley Theme Park*
Mrs S L Blaylock	Personal Assistant	Dalemain Historic House
Mr D Blemings	Personnel Officer	Ulster Folk and Transport Museum*
C E Blott	Group Custodian	Rochester Castle
Valerie Boa	Curator	McLean Museum and Art Gallery
L Bond	PA to Owner	Peckforton Castle
Oliver Bone	Curator	Thetford Museum
Mr C Booth	Proprietor	The C M Booth Collection of Historic Vehicles
Mr C Borthwick/Mr M Cousins	Office Man/Arts Admin	St Edmundsbury Cathedral
Ms A Boscawen & Ms S Bray		High Beeches Gardens
S Bourne	Curator	Towneley Hall Art Gallery and Museum
Mr N Boxall		Bickleigh Castle
Mr W Boyd	Regional Personnel Manager	Florencecourt House
Mrs U Bradley		Old Byre
Mr P Brears	Director	Leeds City Museum
Mr M Bridger	Personnel	Hampton Court Palace*
Mrs B Bridges	Curator	Sion Hill Hall
A Broadhurst & A Broadhurst Jr	Partners	Llangollen Motor Museum
Gordon H Brookes	Curator	Rydal Mount
W Brooks	Executive Director	Trafford Ecology Park
Mrs Joan Brown	Director	Museum of Childhood
M Browne	Secretary	Iden Croft Herbs
P McMillan Browse	Principal Horticultural Officer	Probus County Demonstration Garden
H Bruford	Deputy Centre Manager	A Day at the Wells
Mr & Mrs J Brumer	Proprietor	Cobham Manor Riding Centre & Country Pursuits
R Buckley		Buckleys Yesterdays World
B Burford	Education Service/Assist Curator	Greenwich Borough Museum
S Burge	Curator	Colour Museum
Mr J Burgess	Manager	London Butterfly House*
I M Burgoyne	Curator	Pilkington Glass Museum

Contact Name	Contact Title	Attraction
Paul Burke	Head Recreation Ranger	Grizedale Forest Park*
D Burn		Chingle Hall
Mr D Burrows	Cathedral Administrator	Chester Cathedral
Mr & Mrs R Butcher	Proprietors	Combe Martin Wildlife & Dinosaur Park
M A Byrne	Managing Director	The Beatles Story
Mr D Byrne	Assistant Principal	Capel Manor
Ms A Cadd	Administration Officer	Museum of Lead Mining
Ian Cadogan	Park Director	Margam Park*
Miss Mary Cadwallader	Honorary Secretary	Offa's Dyke Association
Mr F Savage Caldwell	Curator	Gray Art Gallery
Mr F Savage Caldwell	Curator	Hartlepool Maritime Museum
Cambridge Office		Wrest Park House and Gardens
Mr D Cameron	Director of Admin	Gladstones's Land
Ms E Cameron	Secretary/Curator	Laidhay Croft Museum
Ms H Cameron	Administrator	Duncombe Park
G M Candler	Site Co-ordinator	Carew Castle and Tidal Mill
Anthony Candon	Manager	The Ulster History Park
Major R Cannidy	Curator	Royal Green Jackets Museum
Mr P Carpenter	Property Admin Officer	Oldway Mansion
Ms J Carpenter	Curator Art Collections	University of Liverpool Art Gallery
Major J Carroll	Curator	Dorset Military Museum
Mr B Carter	Administrator	Oxburgh Hall
Ms A Carter	Curator	Red House Museum Art Gallery & Gardens
Mr P Cartman	Admin & Personnel Officer	Hancock Museum
Mr P Cartman	Personnel Officer	South Shields Museum & Art Gallery
Ms J Case	Leisure Personnel	Tudor House Museum
Mr N Cavanagh	Owner	Cotswold Motor Museum
Countess Cawdor	Director	Cawdor Castle
Miss F Chalmers	Countryside Officer	Itchen Valley Country Park
D Chamberlain	Admin	Maritime Museum Ramsgate
Katharine Chant	Head of Museums Service	Chelmsford and Essex, Essex Regiment Museums
A Chapman	Administrator	The Walter Rothschild Zoological Museum
D Chapman	House Steward	Kelmscott Manor
The Chapter Clerk		Lincoln Cathedral
Mr K Childs	Retail Manager	Poole Pottery
City Council Personnel Department	Carlisle	Tulliehouse Museum and Art Gallery
Fiona Clark	Custodian	Beatrix Potter Gallery*
M Clark	Director of Zoological Gardens	Exmoor Bird Gardens
Mr T Clark	Proprietor	White Post Modern Farm Centre*
Gwen Clarke	Administrator	Frigate Unicorn
Miss Coryn E Clarke	Owner/Manager	Priests Mill
Ms S Clarke	Tourism Assistant	Old Crown Court and Cells
Mr G Clay	Head Guide	Newstead Abbey*
Ms P Cleaver	Director of Finances & Personnel	Lee Valley Park Farms
Mr G Clitheroe	Curator	Beck Isle Museum of Rural Life
J Cobar	Director & General Manager	Paignton & Dartmouth Steam Railway
J Coleman	Animal Supervisor	Animal World
C Coles	Personnel and Training	Drusillas Park
S Colley	Office Manager	The National Pinetum (Bedgebury)
B & G Compton	Curators	Bignor Roman Villa
Mr A Condick	Manager	Kew Bridge Steam Museum
Mrs G Cook	Proprietor	Old Semeil Herb Garden
P Cooke		Athelhampton House and Gardens
Ms L Coote/Mr A Lane	Finance/Curator	Royal Marines Museum
Mrs Joy Coupe	Administrator	Bristol Cathedral
Dr E Course	Trust Chairman	Twyford Pumping Station
Coventry City Council		Museum of British Road Transport
Mr R Craig	Secretary	Royal Air Force Museum*
Mr A Crawford	Director	Cluanie Deer Farm Park
A Crissel	Personnel Manager	Windsor Safari Park*
T Croft	Asst Manager	Bodmin and Wenford Railway
Mr K Cross	Business Manager/Director	Oceanarium
Mr H Croxford	Guiding Manager	Selby Abbey
Mr & Mrs S Cruickshank	Joint Owners	Damside Garden Herbs
M Culley	Planetarium Lecturer	Southend Planetarium
Ms S Curtis	Curator	Valence House Museum
Alison Cutforth	Curator	Springburn Museum Trust
Major (Rtd) P L Cutler MBE	Administrative Officer	The Welch Regiment Museum
E Dale	Senior Warden	Hollingworth Lake Country Park
Shelly Daly	Administrator	Wetheriggs Country Pottery
Major P Dare	Company Secretary	The Historic Dockyard, Chatham
C Davidson	Admin	The National Trust, Speke Hall
Ms D Davies	Manager	Bank of England Museum
Ms M Davies	Personnel	Portland Castle
P Davies	Chairman Museum Committee	Bodmin Town Museum
Mr N Davis	Financial Director	Association Gallery
Ms A Davis	Clerical Assistant	Somerset Rural Life Museum
Susanna Davis	Museum and Tourist Info Officer	Ays Coughfee Hall Museum
Mr S Davison	Museum Curator	Woodspring Museum
G Dawes	Park Curator	Avon Valley Country Park
The Dean		Norwich Cathedral*
Mr F Deeney	Personnel Officer	Summerlee Heritage Trust
Mr I Dempster	Development Manager	Mill of Towie
Mr and Mrs A Dennis	Proprietors	Miniature Pony Centre
Ms S Dent	Sales Administrator	Sooty's World
A Denyer	Manager	Crabble Corn Mill
Ms K Derbyshire	Personnel	HM Tower of London*
D Devenish	Curator	Wisbech & Fenland Museum
D Devlin	Personnel Manager	Leeds Castle
Director	Head Office – Edinburgh	Threake Gardens

Contact Name	Contact Title	Attraction
Director & Board of Trustees		Whitby Archives Heritage Centre
Mr G Doban	Deputy Director	Royal Navy Submarine Museum
Mrs L Dobson	Personnel Officer	Duxford Airfield*
N Donaldson	Deputy Park Ranger	Lochore Meadows Country Park
Stephen Done	Curator	Cyfarthfa Castle Museum, Art Gallery and Park
A Donnelly	Asst Manager	Smugglers Adventure
Ms J Dornan	House Manager	Boughton House
I Dougall	Training and Development Officer	Tamworth Castle
Ms C Douglas	Personnel Officer	Ely Cathedral*
Hon Caroline Douglas-Home	Estate Factor	The Hirsel
Mr A Downend	Principal Librarian	Hogarth's House
P F D Duffie	Administrator	Blenheim Palace*
L Dunn	Support Services Manager	Tatton
K Dunning	Museum Manager	Oxfordshire County Museum
G Ealam	Director	Land's End*
The Baron of Earlshall	Owner	Earlshall Castle and Gardens
Ms C Easton	Administration Officer	Russel-Cotes Art Gallery & Museum
D Eccles	Cathedral Secretary	Blackburn Cathedral
G Edgar, D Stephenson, T Ward	Reception/Shop, Restorer, Gen Asst	National Cycle Museum
Ms J Edom	Centre Manager	New Forest Museum and Visitor Centre
Mr and Mrs B Eitches	Owners	World of Toys
G Elkin	Deputy Director	Shugborough
J P Ellender	Admin Officer	Royal Engineers Museum
R Elliott	Verger	All Saints Church
J R Emary	Admin	Mapledurham House and Watermill*
Mr Len England	Managing Director	Cumbria Crystal Ltd*
Essex County Council		Marsh Farm Country Park*
S N Evans	Director	Twycross Zoo*
Ms F Fairburn	Museum Development Assistant	Border History Museum
Ms R Fairfax	Visitors' Officer	Portsmouth Cathedral
E Feeney	Deputy Manager	The Oxford Story
Grp Captain T Ferguson OBE	Director	Cockley Cley Iceni Village & Museums
Douglas Ferreira	General Manager	The Ravenglass and Eskdale Railway*
N Ferris	Attendant	Museum of Staffordshire Regiment
Mr R Field	Honorary Curator	The Dewey Museum
C Fitton	Personnel Manager	Blackpool Pleasure Beach
Ms S Fitzgerald		Pleasurewood Hills American Theme Park*
J W A Fleming	Cathedral Administrator	Guildford Cathedral
Mr C Flower	Personnel	Museum of the Moving Image*
B Folds	Asst Admin	Tabely House Collection
P Folland	Countryside Ranger	Tehidy Country Park
Mr J Ford	Manager	Plymouth Dome*
Mr T Forer	Manager	Rhyl Sea Life Centre
F Formby	Personnel and Retail Manager	Frontierland Western Theme Park*
Lt Col (Retd) G Forty	Director & Curator	Tank Museum
Ms L Foulkes	Personnel Manager	Alton Towers*
Dr A Foxon	Keeper of Archaeology	Hull and East Riding Museum
Dr R Francis	Director	Forncett Industrial Steam Museum
J A Francis	Museum Manager	The Aerospace Museum*
Mr H Francis/Catherine Vance		Larne Tourist Info & Interpretation Centre
Mrs A Francis	Area Admin Officer	Queen Elizabeth Country Park
Mr D Fraser	Museums and Arts Officer	Derby Museum and Art Gallery*
V Frearson	Manager	Flimwell Bird Park
H E Frost	Curator and Company Secretary	Dyson Perrins Museum
Danny Fullerton	General Manager	Landmark Highland Heritage and Adventure Park
Mrs A M Gaffron	Supervisor	Jonah's Journey
P Garnham	Owner	Bartley Mill
C J George	Administrator	Broughton Castle
Rev A George	Warden	John Wesley's Chapel
H Gillian	Administrator	Wells Museum
Mr H Gledhill		Guinness World of Records Exhibition*
Mr N Glossop	Head Gardener	Houghton Lodge Garden & Hydroponicum
Mr E Goodall	Floor Manager	Satroshere
M Goodchild	Office Manager	Paradise Wildlife Park
R Goodden	Director	Worldwide Butterflies Ltd
Mr S Goodenough	Curator	Ventnor Botanic Garden*
Mr S Goodhard	Keeper of Transport	Streetlife – Hull Museum of Transport
Mr K Goodrick	Park Supervisor	Metroland*
K Goodway	Marketing Manager	Avon Valley Railway
P J Gordon	Town Clerk	Almonry Museum
E Gore-Brown	Conservation & Recreation Officer	Yorkshire Water Museum
A C Gottlieb	Director	Michelham Priory
Mr P Gough	Owner	Spitbank Fort
Mr D Govler	Chapter Clerk	Cathedral Church of St Nicholas
Captain J Gowen RN	The Agent	Stanstead Park
H Graham	Curator	Cecil Higgins Art Gallery and Museum
Mr J Grainger	Administrator	Burnby Hall Gardens & Museum
Mr R Grange	Tourism Promotion Manager	The Guildhall Beverley
Gavin Grant	Assistant Curator	Kirkcaldy Museum & Art Gallery
J Grant	Warden	Kingston Maurward Gardens and Farm
J Gray		Sellet Hall Gardens
Ms C Green	Marketing Director	Strawberry Hill
R J W Greenland		Model Farm and Folk Museum
P Gresnam	Managing Director	Pennyarcadia
Mr M Gresswell	Curator	Dales Countryside Museum
Ms L Grew	Personnel	National Gallery*
Dr Ian Griffen	Director	Armagh Planetarium
Mr P Griffith	Director	Butterfly World and Fountain World
Mr D Griffiths	Manager	Elvisly Yours Centre
Ian Gwilim	Manager	Dan-Yr-Ogof Showcaves

Contact Name	Contact Title	Attraction
Mr B Haigh	Community Curator	Bagshaw Museum
Mr B Haigh	Community Curator	Dewsbury Museum
A Haines	Partner	Watermouth Castle
D Hall	Butterfly Supervisor	Butterfly World
Mr T Hall	Director	National Ambulance Museum
Ms J Hall	Retail Manager	Bure Valley Railway
Mrs E Hallett	Secretary	Torrington Museum
Mrs A Hamilton	Personnel Officer	New Lanark Village
D Hammond/A Jackson	Land Agents	Talkin Tarn Country Park
Ms C Hannant		Ripley's Believe It or Not
Mr D Hardingham	Art Gallery Assistant	Durham Light Infantry Museum & Art Gallery
Ms A Hargreaves	Restaurant	St Martin-in-the-Fields
W F Harper	Owner	Colliford Lake Park
J Harris	Secretary	Boughton Monchelsea Place
Ms L Harris	Manageress	Chambercombe Manor
Mrs R Harrison	Owner	Wordsworth Gallery
Mrs S Harrison	Director	Museum of Mechanical Music
Mr C Hawke	Senior Warden	Gibraltar Point National Nature Reserve*
Mr M Hawkins	Personnel Manager	Wood Green Animal Sanctuary*
Mrs J Hay	Personnel Manager	Bucklers Hard Village & Maritime Museum*
Mrs M Haywood	Membership Secretary	Colne Valley Museum
Mr R Heap	Partner	Chestnut Centre
Mary Heathcote	Administrator	Oriel Mostyn
R E Hedley-Walker	Owner	Wolferton Station Museum
J D Hegarty	Admin	Capesthorne Hall
A Helme	Curator	The Nelson Museum and Local History Centre
Ms G Henchley	Personnel	Victoria and Albert Museum
Mr A Henshaw	Group Custodian	Totnes Castle
E M Henslowe	Curator/Manager	Selly Manor Museum
G Herron	Administration Officer	Ulster Museum*
Mr S Hession	Chapter Clerk	Peterborough Cathedral*
F Hetherington	Agent	Seaton Delaval Hall
Graham Hicks	Administrator	Felbrigg Hall
H Higman	Museum Admin	Cambrian Railway Soc & Oswestry Cycle Museum
J Hilder	Front of House Manager	Royalty and Empire*
Catherine Hill	Director	Rhondda Heritage Park
Ms J Hinch	Operations Manager	The Tales of Robin Hood*
R M Hobby	Administrator	Ashmolean Museum
J Holifield	Bursar	Truro Cathedral*
C Holm	Resort Services Manager	Volks Electric Railway
Mrs D Holmes	Partner	The Lincolnshire Poultry Park
Mr M Hooley	Manager	Trinity House National Lighthouse Centre
Ms A Hooley	Personnel Manager	Yorkshire Car Collection
P Horrocks	Personnel and Training Officer	The Salt Museum
J Horsley	General Manager	Leighton Buzzard Railway
A Howard	Manager	Child-Beale Wildlife Park*
D R Howlett	Curator	Quex House & Gardens & Powell-Cotton Museum
J Howse	Marketing Executive	Didcot Railway Centre*
J Hoy	Personnel Manager	Beaulieu National Motor Museum, House & Abbey*
Ann Hoyles	Part Time Secretary	Stamford Shakespeare Company
E Hulse	Owner	Breamore House & Museums
Mr D Humas	Manager	Colne Valley Railway
Maj Gen K Bach/Mrs P Hunter	Chapter Clerk/Visitors Office	York Minster*
J Hutchinson	Director	Chatterley Whitfield Mining Museum
Mr and Mrs R Hutchinson	Joint Owners	Incredibly Fantastic Old Toy Show
Mr H R Hutchman	Administrator	Mount Stewart House and Gardens*
A Insckar	Curator	Torquay Museum
Mr N Jacques	Park Manager	Normanby Hall Country Park
D A James	Financial Administrator	Hever Castle
Hon C James	Owner/General Manager	Northbourne Court Gardens
Mr A James	Director	The Lace Hall
Mr C James	Owner	Torosay Castle & Gardens
W James	Personnel Officer Borough Council	North Down Heritage Centre
Mr D Janes	Deputy City Curator	Edinburgh Museum of Childhood
Ms R Janssen	Assistant Curator	Petrie Museum of Egyptian Archaeology
P Jarvis	Castle Administrator	Thirlestane Castle
Ms J Jawaskyi	General Manager	Kingdom of the Sea
M Jeffery	Assistant Director	Sulgrave Manor
P Jempson	Owner	Woodside Farm & Wild Fowl Park
C Johnson	Sales Manager	East Anglian Railway Museum
Mrs J Johnson & Mrs G Small	Secretaries	Isle of Arran Heritage Museum
P Johnson	Lay Administrator	Birmingham Cathedral
Pat Jolliffe	Duty Officer	Thameside Complex
Miss F Jones	Services Manager	Yorkshire Museum
Mr D Jones	Visitor Services Manager	Bessie Surtees House
Mr J Jones	Managing Director	Pleasure Beach*
Mr K Jones & Mr R Riley	Curator & Semi Retired Curator	Dunrobin Castle
Mr S Jones	Director	Spencer House
Mrs J M Jones	Honorary Curator	Durham Heritage Centre
Ms L Karlsen	Principal Keeper	Ferens Art Gallery
Ms D Keasal	District Curator	Glasgow Vennel Museum
Ms D Keasal	District Curator	Museum of the Cumbraes
Ms D Keasal	District Curator	North Ayrshire Museum
Mr and Mrs Kennaway	Managing Directors	Escot Aquatic Centre & Gardens
Mr P Kennedy	Chief Administrative Officer	Commonwealth Institute*
Ms M Kennedy	Hon Administrator	Hornsea Museum
P Kennedy	Administrator	Parham Elizabethan House & Gardens
Mr S Kerry	Principal Officer Visitor Services	Bradford Industrial Horses at Work Museum

Contact Name	Contact Title	Attraction
Mr S Kerry		Cartwright Hall
Mrs M Kershaw	Curator	Knaresborough Castle & Courthouse Museum
Mrs M Kershaw	Curator	Mercer Art Gallery
Mrs M Kershaw	Curator	Royal Pump Room Museum
G Kichenside	Managing Director	Gorse Blossom Railway & Woodland Park
David Kidd	Proprietor	Cockthorpe Hall Toy Museum
A King	Asst Curator	Bristol Industrial Museum
Dr R J King	Curator	The John Moore Countryside Museum
Mrs J King	Director & Manageress	The Lace Centre*
Ms B Kingwood		Kingdom of the Sea, Hunstanton*
S Kirby	Curator	Mill Green Museum and Mill
Sue Kirby		Welwyn Roman Baths
C Kitts	Manager	Stanborough Park
Ms R Kneale	Owner	Shipwreck & Heritage Centre
A Kydd	Dir Leisure and Rec, NEFDC	St Andrews Botanic Garden
Mr J Lackenby	Reservoir Manager	Kielder Water
R Lamb	Manager	Stratford Butterfly Farm
Ms Anne Lambert	Personnel Officer	The Wordsworth Trust
Mr D A Lambie	Proprietor	Speyside Heather/Garden Visitor Centre
Mr R Lambie	Administrator	Ripon Cathedral*
D Langham	Museum Secretary	National Army Museum
P Langridge	Town Clerk	Totnes Guildhall
Mrs D Law	Curator/Manager	Swaledale Folk Museum
C Lawrence-King	Deputy Director	Morwellham Quay
Alison Lea-Wilson	Partner	Anglesey Sea Zoo*
Mr R Leak/Mrs P Edwards	Partners	The Smuggling Experience
Ms A Ledgard	Education Officer	Puppet Centre Trust
M Legge	Co-owner	Legbourne Railway Museum
A Leigh	Curator	Warrington Museum and Art Gallery
Leisure Services Personnel		Leeds Industrial Museum
John Leslie	Manager	Heritage Farm Park
Mr M Lilley	Partner	Felsted Vineyards
J Linley	Governor	Inveraray Jail
Mr J Livingstone	Recreation Officer	Galloway Forest Park
Mr J Livingstone	Recreation Officer	Glen Trool Visitor Centre
Ms Y Lockwood	PR/Personnel Manager	Botanic Centre
M Loftus	Administrative Officer	National Sound Archive (British Library)
Ms M Long	Personnel	Royal Botanic Gardens Kew*
S Lord	Publicity Officer	Museum of Transport
Mr A Lovett	Senior Officer	Coniston Boating Centre
R Lunghi	Administrator	Rother Valley Country Park*
B Mabbs	Visitor Centre Manager (AV)	Coventry Cathedral
Ms J Macalister	Curator	Glenbarr Abbey Visitors Centre
J MacDonald	Curator	Auchindrain Township Open Air Museum
Mrs H B MacDonald	Asst Custodian	Neidpath Castle
Paul S MacDonald	Administrator	Naworth Castle
Mrs M Mackenzie	Project Co-Ordinator	Timespan Heritage Centre
Mrs M R I Mackenzie	Chairman of Trustees	Tain and District Museum
T F Mackenzie	Museum Curator	Hamilton District Museum
W J Mackinnon	Hostel Manager	Baden Powell House Hostel
Sir L Maclean	Owner	Duart Castle
Very Rev G Macmillan	Min of St Giles' Dean of Thistle	St Giles' Cathedral
D Madden	General Manager	North Norfolk Railway*
Ms J Maher	Resident Warden	Sir John Soane's Museum
Ms S Major	Administrator	Prideaux Place
J Makin (appt by Walsingham Coll)	Garden Administrator	Parcevall Hall Gardens
Mr J Mancey	Managing Director	Paultons Park
Mr C Manning	Partner	Charles Manning's Amusement Park*
Mrs E Manning	Clerical Officer	Southend Central Museum & Planetarium
Mr H Margary	Director	Lympne Castle
S Marriott	Personnel Manager	Baddesley Clinton
Prof R Marrs	Director	Ness Gardens
Ms F C Marwick	Curator	West Highland Museum
C Massey	Senior Museums Officer	Wood End Museum of Natural History
Mr A Masters	Partner	Tamar Valley Donkey Park
Sandra E Matchett	Supervisor	The Palace Stables Heritage Centre
Mrs P Mathieson	Hon Sec, Soc of Friends	Greyfriars Kirk
Mrs H Matthews	Administration	St Paul's Cathedral
M Maxfield	Manager	Manchester United Museum & Tour Centre
Mrs H McAdam	Secretary	Glengoulandie Deer Park
C McCarthy	Business Development Manager	British Engineerium Steam Museum
J McCrossen/G Lefeure	Personnel Officer/Head of Personnel	Battle Abbey and Battlefield of Hastings
Ms K McCusker	Assistant Manager	Spitting Image Rubberworks*
Eva McDonald	Proprietor	Fair Maid's House
Ms R McEwan	Personnel	Chessington World of Adventures*
D McFarlane	General Manager	Brookside Miniature Railway
Mrs Jill McIvor	Chairman, Ulser New Zealand Trust	The Ballance House
M McKee	Asst Manager	Tower World
A McLaren	Partner	Coughton Court
Mr C McLean	Director	Scottish Mining Museum
Mr B McWilliam	Assistant Director	Strangers' Hall Museum
B McWilliams	Principal Assistant Director	Norwich Castle Museum*
B Mead	Manager	Forge Mill Museum & Bordesley Abbey Vis Ctr
Mr W T Meikle	Admin Sec	Royal Scottish Academy
Mr G Melville	General Manager	Scottish Whisky Heritage Centre*
O Menhinick	Horticulture Dept Manager	Lackham Gardens & Agricultural Museum
Mr and Mrs M Menist	Owners	Southwick Country Herb Centre
S Mennell		National Maritime Museum Greenwich*
Mrs R Mercer	Director & General Manager	Dorset Heavy Horse Centre
Mr Robert Merrill	Manager	Cefn Coed Colliery Museum

Contact Name	Contact Title	Attraction
J Milford	Museums & Heritage Manager	Newark Museum
E M J Miller	Director	Pendle Heritage Centre
Miss Cathy Miller	Partner	Ponsonby Farm Park
Mr M Miller	Manager	Peter Pan's Playground*
Mrs Miller		Fenny Lodge Gallery
Ms P Millward	Senior Officer	Bankfield Museum
Ms B Milner	Assistant Curator	Holburne Museum & Crafts Study Centre
Ms S Minter	Curator	Chelsea Physic Garden
J & M Moir	Project Directors	Chiltern Open Air Museum
Mrs J Monkman	Hon Curator	Shandy Hall
J Moody	Landscape Manager	Newham Grange Leisure Farm
Ms A Moore	Museum Curator	Morpeth Chantry Bagpipe Museum
Mrs M More	Secretary	University Botanic Garden
R E Morgan	Hon Treasurer	Herefordshire Waterworks Museum
P Morris	Director	Model Village
Major W D Morris-Barker	Administrator	Arbury Hall
M Morton	Hon Deputy Curator	Ripon Prison & Police Museum
A C Moss	Administrator	Old Dairy Farm Centre
Mrs S E Moss	Officer in Charge	Graham Sutherland Gallery
Ms D Moss	Keeper of Decorative Arts	Pickford's House Museum
S Muir	Director	Shaldon Wildlife Trust
T Muir	The Lady	Kingston Bagpuize House and Garden
R Mullins	Curator/Manageress	Potters Museum of Curiosity
Mr R Murphy	Chairman	Dinmore Manor and Gardens
V & A Museum		Bethnal Green Museum of Childhood
M Mutch	Curator	Myreton Motor Museum
Ms B Nash	Administrator	The Building of Bath Museum
National Trust for Scotland		J M Barrie's Birthplace
Ms R Neave	Curator	St Andrews Preservation Trust Museum
P Neaves	Admin/Secretary	The Monkey Sanctuary
Mr J Nelson	Restoration of Buildings	The Lost Gardens of Heligan
M J Neve	Managing Director	Denmans Garden
Ms A Nevill/Mr S Blake	Secretary/Finance	Royal Photographic Society
Ms B Newbury	Park Manager	Manor Farm Country Park
Ms T Newland BA MSc	Librarian	Marx Memorial Library
Lt Col N J Newman	Chapter Clerk	St Georges Chapel*
Roger Nicholas	Operations Manager	Mull & West Highland Narrow Gauge Railway
J Nicholls	Personnel Officer	Ironbridge Gorge Museum*
Dr M Nix	Curator	Tiverton Museum
N Nixon		Much Wenlock Museum
Mr M Noble	P/A to above	Staintondale Shire Horse Farm
Brian H Nodes	Administrator	Blair Castle*
Mr P Norman	Railway Secretary	Bowes Railway Centre
Mr W Norman		Watchet Market House Museum
W Northam/R Maddicott	Museum/FME Ltd	Fitzwilliam Museum*
Mr and Mrs H Noyes	Joint Owners	Isle of Wight Rare Breeds & Waterfowl Park
Mr C Nunn		Broads Museum
A Nuttall	Manager	Etruria Industrial Museum
M O'Lone	Estate Agent	Hatfield House*
Mr and Mrs P O'Shea		Trenouth Farm Rare Breeds Centre
Mr K Oakley	Assistant Receiver General	Westminster Abbey*
Mrs Oldfield	Owner	Doddington Place Gardens
N Oliveira/N Oxley/M Petry	Directors	Museum of Installation
Mr Gerben Oppermans	Manager	Buxton Micrarium
Mrs P Orchard	Personnel	Natural History Museum*
Mr C Orr-Ewing	Managing Agent	Exbury Gardens
Kath Owen	Admin	Tregwynt Mill
Miss C Owen	Manageress	Goss and Crested China Ltd
Ms D Owen	Administrator	East Riddlesden Hall
L & B Owens	Joint Partners	Ardington Pottery
Dr C Palmer	Curator	Havant Museum
Ms L Palmer	Personnel	Thursford Collection*
Mr D Parker	Curator	Dickens House Museum
Patti Partridge	Partner	Felin Crewi Working Watermill
Mr B Pass	Farm Manager	Longdown Dairy Farm
Mr G Patterson	Marketing	Barton Manor Gardens & Vineyards
Ms S Pattpay	Assistant Manager	Camera Obscura
Mr M Pawley	Countryside Officer	Crombie Country Park
P Peach	Curator	Corsham Court
Mr A Pearce	Manager	Timothy Hackworth Victorian & Railway Museum
Mr M Pearson	Head Ranger (Recreation)	Whinlatter Visitor Centre*
Ms R Pearson	Deputy Manager	Sea Life Centre*
Ms J Peatman	Keeper of Industrial Sites	Abbeydale Industrial Hamlet
Mrs Pemberton	Bursar	Frewen College
Mr R Penhallwrick	Curator	Royal Cornwall Museum
Personnel Department	County Hall, Carmarthen	Haverfordwest Castle Museum and Art Gallery
Personnel Dept	Thamesdown B C	Great Western Railway Museum
K Petch/M Stephen	Secretaries	Manchester Cathedral
R Peters/P Cooley	Golf Professional/W Lancs Council	Beacon Country Park
Mr R De Peyer	Curator	Dorset County Museum
P J H Philpot	Director	Barleylands Farm Museum
Ms V Pickering	Director	Chester Visitor Centre
Ms M Pigott	Curator	Harveys Wine Museum
Pinmegar Family		Hammerwood Park
P Pinnock	Centre Manager	The White Cliffs Experience
Mrs M Pittman	Publicity Officer	Derby Cathedral
Mr J Platt	Senior Keeper of Industry	Derby Industrial Museum
Mr B Playle	Assistant Dir Museums	Browhouse Yard Museum*
Ms P Plumb	Administrator	Ragged School Museum

Contact Name	Contact Title	Attraction
Mr L Pole	Curator	Saffron Walden Museum
H Poole	Admin	Lewes Castle and Museums
Mr R Postill	Assistant Manager	Eden Camp Modern History Theme Museum*
J E Potter	Co Secretary	The Bluebell Railway
J Powell	Admin	Pallant House
P Powell	Centre Services Manager	Cadbury World*
Miss Moira Pratt	Personnel and Wages	Dyffryn House Conference Centre and Gardens
C M Preston	Owner/Manager	Badsell Farm Park
Lady Preston		Beeston Hall
Rev Canon D Price	Rector	Minster Church of St Cuthberga*
Assistant Priests		St George's Cathedral
Norman Proctor	Administrative Officer	Snibston Discovery Park
M R Puddle	Head Gardener and General Manager	Bodnant Gardens
Ms J Purcell	Manager	Longdale Craft Centre & Museum*
Commander C Le Quezenec	Deputy Director	HMS Belfast*
V Quick	Personnel Manager	Pecorama
M Ratcliffe (Mrs)	Director	The Alice in Wonderland Visitor Centre
J M Rawlins	Visits Co-ordinator	The Childrens Farm
D Rawlinson	Custodian	Jenner Museum
Ms J Rayner	Operations	London Toy and Model Museum
L J Reed	Secretary	Poxfield Steam Railway
Billy Ried/Alistair Davison	Manager/Asst Manager	The Northern Ireland Aquarium*
Ms A Reid	Curator	Stranraer Museum
Miss G B Reith/D C Butters	Town Clerk/Curator	Swaffham Museum
Mrs B Reynolds	Personnel Manager	Cumberland Pencil Museum & Exhibition Centre
Mrs S Reynolds	Supervisor	Stained Glass Museum
D Richards	Heritage Manager	Izaak Walton's Cottage
D Richards	Heritage Manager	The Ancient High House
W R Richards	Founding Trustee	The National Motorcycle Museum
Mr M Riddell	Chief Game Warden	Blair Drummond Safari & Leisure Park
Ms J Ridley	Director	Dinosaur Museum*
Ms J Ridley	Director	Dinosaur Safari
Ms J Ridley	Director	Mummies and Magic
Ms J Ridley	Director	Tutankhamun Exhibition
Mr D Robb	Gardener	Dochfour Gardens
Dereck Roberts	Transport Manager	Great Orme Tramway
J Roberts	Admin Manager	Romney, Hythe & Dymchurch Railway
Lt Col D R Roberts	Asst Curator	Devonshire Regiment Museum
Mr K Roberts	Manager	Tropical World*
Mrs P Roberts	Organiser	Jane Welsh Carlyle Museum
Ms A Roberts	Assistant Manager	Bill Quay Community Farm*
Mr K Robertson	Senior Ranger	Worsbrough Country Park*
Revd C Robertson	Minister	Canongate Kirk
A R Robinson	Administrator	Scone Palace*
Ms V Robinson	Rota Secretary	Zetland Lifeboat Museum
P Robinson	Curator	Southport Zoo and Conservation Trust
E Rogers	Personnel and Training Manager	Warwick Castle*
Ms P Rossetter	Administrative Director	Age Exchange Reminiscence Centre
Mrs M Rowe		Radstock Midsomer Norton Museum
Tony Rowlands	Managing Director	Trefriw Wells SPA
H Royden	Secretary	Southport Railway Centre
P Rudd	Personnel Officer	Chester Zoo*
G M W Ruddock	Curator	Teignmouth Museum
Mrs P Ruddock	Senior Keeper & Keeper of Costume	Museum of Costume
J Ruffle	Keeper	Oriental Museum
Mr G Rushton	General Manager	Ffestiniog Railway
L Russell	Restaurant Manager	Goosedale Model Aviation Centre
Mr D Russell	Administrator	Pencarrow
Mr A Rutter	Secretary	Harwich Redoubt
Mr A Rutter	Secretary	Port of Harwich Maritime Museum
Mr N Sadler	Curator/Director	London Canal Museum
Mrs C Salt	Administrator	Number One the Royal Crescent
Mrs W Salter	Curator	Brixham Museum & History Society
Ms M Sanderson	Administrator	Pontefract Museum
		Elizabethan Exhibition Gallery
		Pontefract Castle
		Wakefield Art Gallery
		Wakefield Museum
Raymond Sanderson	Commercial Director	Teifi Valley Railway
P R Saunders	Curator	Salisbury and South Wiltshire Museum
R Saville	Curator	Coach House Museum
Mrs J Schroeder	Owner	Arreton Manor
Lady Scott		Rotherfield Park
J Sculley	Senior Visual Arts Officer	Stockport War Memorial and Art Gallery
C Scurrah	Manager	Brighton Sea life Centre
L Seddon	Administrator	The Wildfowl & Wetlands Trust, Martin Mere
Susan Seright	Assistant to Curator	Groam House Museum Trust
Mr B Eglon Shaw	Senior Partner	Sutcliffe Gallery
S Sheather	Wages and Personnel Manager	Howletts Zoo Park
S Sheather	Wages and Personnel Manager	Port Lympne Zoo Park, Mansion & Gardens
Mr W Shepherd	Administrator	St Olave's Church
Ms V Sheppard	Curator	Pollock's Toy Museum
G Shindley	Personnel Officer	Local Interest Museum
M Sifford	Honorary Manager	Fleur De Lis Heritage Centre
Ken Simms	Director	Thrigby Hall Wildlife Gardens
Ms Leslie Simpson	Assistant Curator	Down County Museum*
Mr R Skorupa	Station Officer	Museum of Fire
A Smith	Director	The Whitworth Art Gallery
J Smith	Curator	Fasque
Mr G Smith	Manager	Portsmouth Sea Life Centre

Contact Name	Contact Title	Attraction
Mr N Smith	Personnel Officer	Roman Baths Museum*
Ms J Smith	Hon Curator	Dickens House Museum Broadstairs
Ms S Smith	Dep Head Personnel	Carisbrooke Castle
Mr G Snelling	Curator	National Horseracing Museum
Ms C Somerset	Secretary	Aldeburgh Moot Hall Museum
Mr and Mrs J Sparrow	Owners	Bear Museum
Ms J Speller	Assistant Curator, Art	Huddersfield Art Gallery
Mr M Spender		Bankside Gallery
Mr R Spinks	Secretary	Captain Cook Schoolroom Museum
Mr G Sprott	Curator	Scottish Agricultural Museum
Miss L Stafford	PA to Director	Marwell Zoological Park*
Mr D Standen	Countryside Manager	Wat Tyler Country Park*
Mr K Stanfield	Warden	Peatlands Park*
David Steele	Castle Manager	Carrickferggus Castle*
H Poole/L Steene	Admin/Custodian	Anne of Cleves House Museum
Mr G Stenhouse	Manager	Oban Sea Life Centre
Mrs J Stephens	Admin and Education Manager	Epping Forest District Museum
Stephens	Chairman	Natural World*
Mrs R Stephenson	Joint Proprietor	Gem Rock Museum
C Stevens	Bridge Master	Tower Bridge*
Mr P Stevens	Executive Director	Paignton Zoo*
Angela Stewart	Personnel Officer	White Castle
Mrs S Stewart	Director/Partner	Dunaverig Farm Life Centre
N T Stobbs	Administrator	Heron Corn Mill and Museum of Papermaking
Stoke on Trent City Council		Ford Green Hall
Mrs Stratford		Chilham Castle
J Strickson/C Alford	Admin/Asst Admin	Dunham Massey Hall and Park
Mrs J Strode	Harrow Arts Council	Harrow Museum & Heritage Centre*
Ms C Maxwell Stuart	Owner/Administrator	Traquair House
Ms S Stubbins		Centre for Alternative Technology
M Sulter	Art Gallery Services Officer	Rochdale Art Gallery
Dr A Sumner	Keeper	Dulwich Picture Gallery
Mr Peter Sunderland	Assistant Director	Beacraigs Country Park
Ms S Sunderland	Secretary	Automobilia Transport Museum
Y Surcouf	Owner	Basildon Zoo
H Sussex	Support Services Officer	The Look Out*
Ms J Sutcliff	Secretary	Trebah Garden
B Sutherland	Manager	Bentley Wildfowl & Motor Museum
Mr A Sutherland	Partner	Ardfearn Nursery Plant Centre
Ms E Sutherland	Administrator	Dean Castle & Country Park
Ms E Sutherland	Administration Officer	Dick Institute
Ms L Sword	Manager	St Andrews Sea Life Centre
D W & P R Sydenham	Proprietors	Cholderton Rare Breeds Farm Park
P Symes	General Manager	The Shuttleworth Collection
Mr C Tabiner	Manager	Farmworld*
Mr I Tait	Assistant Curator	Shetland Museum
Mr R Tait	Director	Wine and Spirit Museum
Guitty Talberg	Director	Tallberg Taylor Gallery
C Taylor	Regional Personnel Manager	Bateman's (The National Trust)
M Taylor	Manageress	Heale Gardens and Plant Centre
Mr B Taylor	Managing Director	Kirklees Light Railway
Ms A Taylor	Curator	Wesleys Chapel
Mr E Third	Seasonal Ranger	Falls of Clyde Nature Reserve
Canon H Thomas	Canon Treasurer	Liverpool Cathedral
Nest Thomas	Museums Development Officer	The Lloyd George Museum and Highgate His Home
T Thomas	Trustee	Birmingham Railway Museum
Mr V Thomson	Estates Ranger	Darnaway Farm Visitor Centre
Mr R Thorne	Admin Officer	Charles Dickens Birthplace Museum
Mrs J Thorne	Personnel Administration	Stewarts Garden – Lands
Mr R Thornton	Director	Tropical Bird Park
Mr D Thorpe	Manager	South London Art Gallery
Mrs P Tinning	Custodian	Stott Park Bobbin Mill
Aileen Todd	Administrator	Blackshaw Farm Park Ltd
Mr P Todd/Mr S Underhay	Supervisors	Halifax Piece Hall*
Ms A Todhunter	Marketing Manager	New Forest Butterfly Farm
Ms A Toms	Director	Quay Arts
M Tonkins	PA	Cornish Seal Sanctuary
Mr J Tonner	Estate Manager	Formakin Estate
Mr J Troup	Hon Secretary	Stromness Museum
Trustees of Ely Museum		Ely Museum
Mr F Turner	Operations Manager	Heritage Motor Centre*
Mr J Turner/Mrs S Turner	Co-Directors	Lincolnshire Light Railway & Heritage Centre
Peter Tye	Assistant Manager	Lea Gardens
Ms J Tyler	Keeper of Social History	Old Grammar School
Ms J Tyler	Keeper of Social History	Wilberforce House
Mr B Unwin	Assistant Curator	Logan Botanic Garden
Mr G and Mrs J Upton	Owners	How We Lived Then Museum of Shops
K Usher	Administrator	Calke Abbey*
Mr M Valizadeh	Proprietor	Maes Astro Tourist Attraction
S Vaughan	Partner	Wye Valley Farm Park
Mr A Vella	Keeper of Art	
Mr M Venn	Accountant	Abbotsbury Sub Tropical Gardens
Mr M Venn	Accountant	Abbotsbury Swannery
Mr M Venn	Accountant	Abbotsbury Tithe Barn Museum
D Viner	Curator	Corinium Museum
Mr M Volkes	Manager	Westminster Cathedral*
Mr J Walker	Hon Secretary to the Trustees	Bayle Museum
Mr S Walker	Business & Marketing Manager	Embsay Steam Railway
S Walker	Land Agent	Hughenden Manor

Contact Name	Contact Title	Attraction
A Wallman	Keeper of Art	Blackburn Museum and Art Gallery
M Warhurst	Museum Director	Norton Priory Museum and Gardens
Ms J Warman	Finance Director	Walkley Clogs
C Wasche	Administration Assistant	Paradise Mill
C Wasche	Administration Assistant	The Silk Museum
C Wasche	Administration Assistant	West Park Museum
A Watson	PA to Director	Brooklands Museum
Cdr L M M Saunders Watson	Owner	Rockingham Castle
E Webb	Custodian	Nothe Fort
Mr T Weston	Conservation Officer	Derwent Walk Country Park
Ms R Westwood	Museums Officer	Shibden Hall
Mr P Wetherall	Dept of Arts & Libraries	Lochwinnoch Community Museum
Mr P Wetherall	Deputy Director, Arts & Libraries	Paisley Museum & Art Galleries
Ms P Wheatcroft	Curator	Bruce Castle Museum
A Whitehouse	Curator	The Valley Heritage Centre and Museum
Mr D Wickes	Superintendent	Palace of Holyroodhouse*
Mr A Widdows	Warden	Chillingham Wild Cattle Association Ltd
Mrs P Wiggle	Senior Assistant	Malton Museum
T Wilcox	Curator	Hove Museum and Art Gallery
D Wild		The Museum of Childhood
Mr N Wild	Manager	Hastings Sea Life Centres*
Mrs J Wildgust	Leisure Development Officer	D H Lawrence Birthplace Museum
S Wileman	Cultural & Community Services Asst	Bromham Mill
S Wileman	Cultural & Community Services Asst	Elstow Moot Hall
S Wileman	Cultural & Community Services Asst	Swiss Garden
Ann Williams	Curator	Bersham Heritage Centre and Ironworks
Gwylan Williams	Head of Personnel	Welsh Folk Museum*
L Williams		Marle Place Gardens and Nursery
Ms N Williams	Administrative Officer	Amgueddfa'r Gogledd/Museum of the North
Nia Williams	Administrative Officer	Welsh Slate Museum
Peter Williams	Assistant Manager	Brecon Beacons Mountain Centre
V Williams	Curator	Hastings Museum and Art Gallery
I Willsher	Owner	Longstone Heritage Centre
Mr P Willsher	General Manager	Compton Acres Gardens
B S Wilson	Museums Officer	Tankerness House Museum
M Wilson	Company Secretary	Burton Agnes Hall
Mrs C L Wilson	Project Manager	Whithorn Dig
Mary Withall/Anna Davidson	Assistant Curators	Easdale Island Folk Museum
Col M J Woodcock	Chapter Clerk	Exeter Cathedral*
Mr D Woodhouse MBE	General Manager	Talyllyn Railway
Julie Worth	Director	The Butterfly and Falconry Park
D Wright	General Manager	Bicton Park Gardens
Miss Sheila O Wright	Convener of Wardens	Kirk of St Nicholas
Mrs Hazel Wright	Sexton	St Columbs Cathedral
Ms H Wright	Manager	Conwy Visitor Centre*
Ms H Wright	Co Secretary	Pettitts Feathercraft & Animal Adventure Park
Ms L Wright	Finance Officer	Museum of Army Transport
Bridget Yates	Curator	Norfolk Rural Life Museum and Union Farm
N Yates	Acting Director	Museum of Kent Life
Ms S Young	Personnel	Graves Art Gallery
A D Yule	Warden	Auckland Castle

PURCHASING

H H Ackers		Animal World
H H Ackers		Butterfly World
Jean Adams		Easdale Island Folk Museum
Marlene Adams	Deputy Manager	Cefn Coed Colliery Museum
Mrs K Ainsley/Mrs A Black	Shop/Plant Sales	Trebah Garden
Ms C Alderson	Retail Manager	National Railway Museum*
Mrs M Alexander	Treasurer	Isle of Arran Heritage Museum
Catherine Allard	Manager	Windermere Steamboat Museum*
B Allen	Treasurer	Foxfield Steam Railway
Mrs B Allen	Tourism Manager	Bolton Abbey Estate*
Mark Allinson	Manager	Thameside Complex
J Amey	Shop Supervisor	Museum of Kent Life
M Amey	Owner	Hardys Wessex Exhibition
Ellis T Amos	Chapter Clerk	Carlisle Cathedral
Ms C Anderson	Museum Assistant	Shetland Museum
Miss D Andrews/Mrs R Brooks	Partners	Old Smithy Tourist Centre
Ms R Andrews	Shop Supervisor	Rhyl Sea Life Centre
M & K Ann	Purchasing Managers	Drusillas Park
T Ash	Proprietor	Parke Rare Breeds Farm
Mrs V Ashman		Radstock Midsomer Norton Museum
Mr D Asquith	Administrator	Clandon Park
Mr D Asquith	Administrator	Hatchlands Park
Dr R L Atkinson	Curator	Camborne School of Mines Geological Museum
P Atkinson		Wheelwrights Museum & Gypsy Folklore Collect
Mrs S E Bagot	Owner	Levens Hall and Topiary Gardens
Mrs B Bailes		Cathedral Church of St Nicholas
Mr B Bailles	Administrator	Chillingham Castle
Ms N Balamash	Retail	Spitting Image Rubberworks*
M Barbour	Business Manager	Ragley Hall
Dr A Barclay	Ranger	Scottish Wildlife Trust
Mrs Patricia Bardon	Museum Administrator	Down County Museum*
Mr D Barnes	Retail Development Manager	Wood Green Animal Sanctuary*
Ms J Barrie (Shop only)	Administrative Assistant	Hunterian Art Gallery
Mr C Barton	Warden	The Old Rectory
Mr D Bashford	Assistant	Roman Villa, Brading
Mr H Bayntun-Coward	Owner	Book Museum
A Beard/C Wasche	Shop Managers	Paradise Mill

Contact Name	Contact Title	Attraction
Lieutenant Commander J Beck	Trustee Secretary & Curator	Falmouth Maritime Museum
Mr P Beckett		Wakefield Cathedral
Mrs S Beeley		National Cycle Museum
Miss M Bennett	Asst Curator	Rydal Mount
Mrs C Benson	Manager	Ripon Cathedral*
C Beresford	Curator	Regiments of Gloucestershire Museum
Miss H Bermingham	Regional Enterprises Manager	Florencecourt House
Ms Maire Bermingham	Regional Enterprises Manager	Mount Stewart House and Gardens*
Mr J Bernasconi	Hon Curator	University of Hull Art Collection
Miss M Beston	Administrator	Norton Conyers
P Biffen	Shop Manager	Fishbourne Roman Palace and Museum
Ms D Billington	Purchasing	Tithe Barn Museum & Arts Centre
Ms S Bingley	Shop	Woodspring Museum
Mrs Bird	Manageress	West Wycombe Caves
Miss S Bishop	Sales/Reception	Haseley Manor
Mrs J Bishop	Shop	Brixham Museum & History Society
L Bisset		University Botanic Garden
Mr and Mrs K Blackburn	Owners	Buffers
Dr S Blackden	Resident Representative	Kellie Castle
J Blades	Administrator	Hanbury Hall (National Trust)
Mrs S L Blaylock	Personal Assistant	Dalemain Historic House
Valerie Boa	Curator	McLean Museum and Art Gallery
Mr C Booth	Proprietor	The C M Booth Collection of Historic Vehicles
Ms A Boscawen & Ms S Bray		High Beeches Gardens
S Bossence	Clerk	North Down Heritage Centre
Ms D Boulton/Ms B Stirrat	Shop Manager/Restaurant Manager	St Giles' Cathedral
S Bourne	Curator	Towneley Hall Art Gallery and Museum
Ms S Boyes	Secretary	Sutcliffe Gallery
Mrs U Bradley		Old Byre
M Brennan	Gallery Asst	Stockport War Memorial and Art Gallery
C Bretherton	Buyer	Royalty and Empire*
Mrs B Bridges	Curator	Sion Hill Hall
Mrs S Broad		Dunrobin Castle
A Broadhurst & A Broadhurst Jr	Partners	Llangollen Motor Museum
Mr T Browbridge/Mr T Silver	Operation/Retail	Lightwater Valley Theme Park*
Mr M Brown	Chairman	Watchet Market House Museum
Mrs Joan Brown	Director	Museum of Childhood
P McMillan Browse	Principal Horticultural Officer	Probus County Demonstration Garden
H Bruford		A Day at the Wells
Mr & Mrs J Brumer	Proprietor	Cobham Manor Riding Centre & Country Pursuits
B & A Buckley	Owners	Buckleys Yesterdays World
S Burge	Curator	Colour Museum
L Burgess		Stockwood Craft Museum & Gardens
I M Burgoyne	Curator	Pilkington Glass Museum
Paul Burke	Head Recreation Ranger	Grizedale Forest Park*
Mr D Burrows	Cathedral Administrator	Chester Cathedral
Caroline Butler	Assistant Manager	Bressingham Steam Museum and Gardens
Mrs A Butler	Shop Supervisor	Satroshere
M A Byrne	Managing Director	The Beatles Story
Mr P Bywalski		Barton Manor Gardens & Vineyards
Mr J Caldon	General Manager	Pleasure Beach*
Mr F Savage Caldwell	Curator	Gray Art Gallery
Mr F Savage Caldwell	Curator	Hartlepool Maritime Museum
Cambridge Office		Wrest Park House and Gardens
Ms E Cameron	Secretary/Curator	Laidhay Croft Museum
Ms H Cameron	Administrator	Duncombe Park
G M Candler	Site Co-ordinator	Carew Castle and Tidal Mill
Anthony Candon	Manager	The Ulster History Park
Major R Cannidy	Curator	Royal Green Jackets Museum
R Carman	Hon Curator	Ely Museum
Mr P Carpenter	Property Admin Officer	Oldway Mansion
Ms J Carpenter	Curator, Art Collections	University of Liverpool Art Gallery
Steven Carrington	Retail Manager	Snibston Discovery Park
Major J Carroll	Curator	Devonshire Regiment Museum
Major J Carroll	Curator	Dorset Military Museum
Ms S Carter	Shop Manageress	Oxburgh Hall
Miss K Carver		Epping Forest District Museum
Mr M Cass	Director, V & A Enterprises	Victoria and Albert Museum
C Cattle	Retail Manageress	Bristol Zoo Gardens*
Mr M Cavanagh	Owner	Cotswold Motor Museum
Lady Cavendish	Owner	Holker Hall and Gardens
Countess Cawdor	Director	Cawdor Castle
E Centelleche	Catering Manager	Capesthorne Hall
Miss F Chalmers	Countryside Officer	Itchen Valley Country Park
D Chamberlain	Admin	Maritime Museum Ramsgate
Katharine Chant	Head of Museums Service	Chelmsford and Essex, Essex Regiment Museums
D Chapman	House Steward	Kelmscott Manor
Mr K Childs	Retail Manager	Poole Pottery
M Clark	Director of Zoological Gardens	Exmoor Bird Gardens
Mr T Clark/Mrs A Clark/Ms M Allen		White Post Modern Farm Centre*
Gwen Clarke	Administrator	Frigate Unicorn
Miss Coryn E Clarke	Owner/Manager	Priests Mill
J Cobar	Director & General Manager	Paignton & Dartmouth Steam Railway
Miss M Cochrane	Supervisor, Public Enterprises	Palace of Holyroodhouse*
Mr R Coe	Front of House	Rock Circus*
Ms H Cole	Shop Manager	Museum of Army Transport
P Coleman	Manageress, Bookshop	St Georges Chapel*
Ms J Collier	Services	Association Gallery
Judith Collins	Senior Administrator	Margam Park*

Contact Name	Contact Title	Attraction
B Compton		Bignor Roman Villa
Mr A Condick	Manager	Kew Bridge Steam Museum
Mrs G Cook	Proprietor	Old Semeil Herb Garden
Ms L Cook		Tapeley Park & British Jousting Centre
P Cooke		Athelhampton House and Gardens
Mr O Cooper	Retail Sales	Musical Museum
Ms L Coote		Royal Marines Museum
Mr R Copeman	Retail Director	Alton Towers*
A Core	Senior Admin Asst	Salford Museum and Art Gallery
Mrs Joy Coupe	Administrator	Bristol Cathedral
Mr John R Cowdy	Treasurer, Ulster New Zealand Trust	The Ballance House
Mrs P Cox	Stock Manager	Clapton Court Gardens
Mr R Craig		Royal Air Force Museum*
W Crane	Sales Manager	Allhallows Museum
Mr W Crawford		Cluanie Deer Farm Park
L Crennell	Admin Officer	Great Western Railway Museum
T Croft	Asst Manager	Bodmin and Wenford Railway
Mr K Cross	Business Manager/Director	Oceanarium
Mr & Mrs S Cruickshank	Joint Owners	Damside Garden Herbs
Ms S Curtis	Curator	Valence House Museum
Alison Cutforth	Curator	Springburn Museum Trust
Major (Rtd) P L Cutler MBE	Administrative Officer	The Welch Regiment Museum
P Dabbs	Museum Assistant	Cider Museum and King Offa Distillery
E Dale	Senior Warden	Hollingworth Lake Country Park
Ms D Dale & Mr B Boulton		Rock Garden and Cave
Shelly Daly	Administrator	Wetheriggs Country Pottery
M Dando	Assistant Governor	Inveraray Jail
Simon Daniel	Retail Manager	Dan-Yr-Ogof Showcaves
M Davidson	Administration Assistant	Lochore Meadows Country Park
Chris Davis	Shop Manager	Royal Observatory Visitor Centre
Ms C Davis	Curatorial Assistant	Museum of Lead Mining
M Dean	General Manager	Didcot Railway Centre*
Mr I Dempster	Development Manager	Mill of Towie
V Denney	Retail Manager (Shop)	Brooklands Museum
Mr and Mrs A Dennis	Proprietors	Miniature Pony Centre
Mrs H Denton	Bookstall & Gift Shop	Christchurch Priory
Departmental Managers		North Norfolk Railway*
Mr P Dibdon	Senior Supervisor	Southend Central Museum & Planetarium
S Dickson	Retail Manager	Smugglers Adventure
Director & Board of Trustees		Whitby Archives Heritage Centre
Ms A Ditum	Administrator	Puppet Centre Trust
Mr G Doban	Deputy Director	Royal Navy Submarine Museum
Mr A Donald		Waltzing Waters Ltd
Stephen Done	Curator	Cyfarthfa Castle Museum, Art Gallery and Park
I Dougall	Training and Development Officer	Tamworth Castle
Hon Caroline Douglas-Home	Estate Factor	The Hirsel
Mr A Downend	Principal Librarian	Hogarth's House
Dr A I Doyle		Durham Heritage Centre
Ms D Dudley		Bickleigh Castle
P F D Duffie	Administrator	Blenheim Palace*
S Dugal	Finance	Commonwealth Institute*
M Duthie	Shop Manager	The Wildfowl & Wetlands Trust, Martin Mere
Valerie Dyamond	Gift Shop Manageress	Manderston
Mrs K Dyer	Retail Services Manager	Museum of Costume
Mrs K Dyer	Shops Manageress	Roman Baths Museum*
Mrs E Dymott	Shop	Breamore House & Museums
Mr L Dyson	Shop Manager	Wesley's Chapel
G Ealam		Land's End*
The Baroness of Earlshall		Earlshall Castle and Gardens
Ms J Ebdon	Shop Supervisor	Portsmouth Sea Life Centre
D Eccles	Cathedral Secretary	Blackburn Cathedral
Ms H Edward		Woodham Church Museum
Mrs V Edwards	Shop Manager	Chatsworth*
Mr and Mrs B Eitches	Owners	World of Toys
D Ellis	Shop Manager	Amgueddfa'r Gogledd/Museum of the North
Dewi Ellis	Shop Manager	Welsh slate museum
Graham Ellis		Mull & West Highland Narrow Gauge Railway
J R Emary	Admin	Mapledurham House and Watermill*
A Emerson	Shops Director	Morwellham Quay
Mr Len England	Managing Director	Cumbria Crystal Ltd*
English Heritage	Buying Office, London	Rochester Castle
English Heritage		Stott Park Bobbin Mill
S N Evans	Director	Twycross Zoo*
S Evitt	Regional Enterprises Manager	Hughenden Manor
Ms F Fairburn		Border History Museum
Ms B Farr	Manager, A Zwemmer at Courtauld	Courtauld Institute Galleries*
R Farrell	Shop Buyer	Stratford Butterfly Farm
Ms V Faulkner	Commercial Officer	Hancock Museum
Ms V Faulkner	Commercial Officer	South Shields Museum & Art Gallery
E Feeney	Deputy Manager	The Oxford Story
Ms S Fellows	Trading	Carisbrooke Castle
Ms S Fellows	Head of Trading	Portland Castle
Grp Captain T Ferguson OBE	Director	Cockley Cley Iceni Village & Museums
Douglas Ferreira	General Manager	The Ravenglass and Eskdale Railway*
S Ferri	Shop Manager	The Walter Rothschild Zoological Museum
Mr R Field	Honorary Curator	The Dewey Museum
Mrs E Fielding		St Columbs Cathedral
Mr L Fishpool	Sales	Beck Isle Museum of Rural Life
Mr G Fitzpatrick		Boughton House
C Ford	Retail Manager	Shaldon Wildlife Trust

Contact Name	Contact Title	Attraction
M Ford	Visitor Centre Bookshop Manager	Coventry Cathedral
Mr J Ford	Manager	Plymouth Dome*
F Formby	Personnel and Retail Manager	Frontierland Western Theme Park*
Lt Col (Rtd) G Forty	Director & Curator	Tank Museum
Ms M Fox	Director	Lyme Regis Experience
Dr A Foxon	Keeper of Archaeology	Hull and East Riding Museum
Dr R Francis	Director	Forncett Industrial Steam Museum
J A Francis	Museum Manager	The Aerospace Museum*
Mrs A Francis		Queen Elizabeth Country Park
Miss A M Franklin	Honorary Secretary	Tain and District Museum
Mr D Fraser	Museums and Arts Officer	Derby Museum and Art Gallery*
V Frearson	Manager	Flimwell Bird Park
H E Frost	Curator and Company Secretary	Dyson Perrins Museum
Mrs S Furnell	Shop Manager	St Edmundsbury Cathedral
Ms L Gabriels	Shop Supervisor	Hastings Sea Life Centres*
Mr T Gallachir & Ms M Brown	Visitor Services & Catering Services	Summerlee Heritage Trust
Ms M Gallacher	Senior Receptionist	Dean Castle & Country Park
Ms M Gallacher	Senior Receptionist	Dick Institute
Miss B Galvin	Curator	Steam Brewery Museum
P Garnham	Owner	Bartley Mill
Ms A Gemmell	Shop Manager	Jorvik Viking Centre*
C J George	Administrator	Broughton Castle
P Gifford	Reception & Retail Services Mgr	Chatterley Whitfield Mining Museum
H Gillian	Administrator	Wells Museum
Ms J Gillies	Administrator	Scottish Mining Museum
Countess of Glasgow		Kelburn Country Centre
Ms M Goodale	Shop Manager	Wildfowl & Wetlands Trust – Welney Centre
R Goodden	Director	Worldwide Butterflies Ltd
Mr S Goodenough	Curator	Ventnor Botanic Garden*
Mr S Goodhard	Keeper of Transport	Streetlife – Hull Museum of Transport
J Goodson		Much Wenlock Museum
K Goodway	Marketing Manager	Avon Valley Railway
P J Gordon	Town Clerk	Almonry Museum
E Gore-Brown	Conservation & Recreation Officer	Yorkshire Water Museum
A C Gottlieb	Director	Michelham Priory
Mrs S Gower	Shop Manageress	Peterborough Cathedral*
H Graham	Curator	Cecil Higgins Art Gallery and Museum
Mr R Grange	Tourism Promotion Manager	The Guildhall, Beverley
A Grant	Warden	Kingston Maurward Gardens and Farm
Ms C Grant	Merchandising	Chessington World of Adventures*
J Gray		Sellet Hall Gardens
Mrs Yvonne Gray	Museum Supervisor	Cumberland Pencil Museum & Exhibition Centre
E Graybill	Owner/Director	Peckforton Castle
Mrs C Green		The South Wales Borderers Museum
Ms C Green	Marketing Director	Strawberry Hill
P M Greenland		Model Farm and Folk Museum
J Gresnam	Secretary	Pennyarcadia
Mr M Gresswell	Curator	Dales Countryside Museum
Ms C Griffith	Director	Butterfly World and Fountain World
Amanda Griffiths	Director	Tregwynt Mill
Mr L Gunn		John Wesley's Chapel
Dr Douglas Gyte	Leisure and Economic Dev Officer	Ays Coughfee Hall Museum
Mr B Haigh	Community Curator	Bagshaw Museum
Mr B Haigh	Community Curator	Dewsbury Museum
A Haines		Watermouth Castle
Mrs F Haitto	Shop Manager	Gurkha Museum
Mr M Hall	Museum Registrar	Bankfield Museum
Mr T Hall	Director	National Ambulance Museum
Ms J Hall		Bure Valley Railway
Mrs M Hanley	Buyer	Nidderdale Museum
G Hannam	Deputy Custodian	Jenner Museum
D Hanson	Shop Manager	Exeter Cathedral*
Ms L Hardcastle	Curator	Museum of the Moving Image*
Ms A Hargreaves		St Martin-in-the-fields
W F Harper	Owner	Colliford Lake Park
Ms L Harris	Manageress	Chambercombe Manor
M Harrison	Treasurer	Coach House Museum
Mrs R Harrison	Owner	Wordsworth Gallery
Mrs S Harrison	Director	Museum of Mechanical Music
Mr T Hassall	Shop Administrator	Tiverton Museum
Mr C Hawke	Senior Warden	Gibraltar Point National Nature Reserve*
Ms J Haynes	Secretary	National Horseracing Museum
Mr T Hayward	Maintenance	London Toy and Model Museum
Mr R Heap	Partner	Chestnut Centre
Mary Heathcote	Administrator	Oriel Mostyn
M L P Hedley-Walker	Owner	Wolferton Station Museum
A Helme	Curator	The Nelson Museum and Local History Centre
Mr A Henshaw	Group Custodian	Totnes Castle
E M Henslowe	Curator/Manager	Selly Manor Museum
F Hetherington	Agent	Seaton Delaval Hall
P Hickman		Marwell Zoological Park*
S Highes	Retail Manager	West Lancashire Light Railway
C Hitchins	General Manager (NMGM Enterprises)	Lady Lever Art Gallery Liverpool Museum Sudley Walker Art Gallery National Maritime Museum
J Hoare	Staff Sgt	Royal Engineers Museum
R M Hobby	Administrator	Ashmolean Museum
C Holm	Resort Services Manager	Volks Electric Railway

Contact Name	Contact Title	Attraction
Mrs D Holmes	Partner	The Lincolnshire Poultry Park
Mr M Hooley	Manager	Trinity House National Lighthouse Centre
D R Howlett	Curator	Quex House & Gardens & Powell-Cotton Museum
Mr D Hughes		Burnby Hall Gardens & Museum
Mr M Hull/Ms P Eastwood	Registrar/Administrator	Halifax Piece Hall*
Mr D Humas	Manager	Colne Valley Railway
Mark Humphries	Commercial Manager	Welsh Folk Museum*
Mr P Hunt	Treasurer	North East Aircraft Museum
Mr and Mrs R Hutchinson	Joint owners	Incredibly Fantastic Old Toy Show
Mr B Ilett	Administrator	National Postal Museum
A Insckar	Curator	Torquay Museum
Ms D Ireland	Merchandising	Royal Photographic Society
Mr R Jackson		Shakespeare Globe Museum
D A James	Financial Administrator	Hever Castle
Hon C James	Owner/General Manager	Northbourne Court Gardens
Mr C James	Owner	Torosay Castle & Gardens
Mr S Jaques		Eden Camp Modern History Theme Museum*
Mrs F Jarvis	House Manager	Thirlestane Castle
M Jeffery	Asst Director	Sulgrave Manor
P Jempson	Owner	Woodside Farm & Wild Fowl Park
Ms A Jenkins	Retail Proprietor	Staintondale Shire Horse Farm
P Jennings	General Manager, Trading Company	Ironbridge Gorge Museum*
Mr A Johnson		Camera Obscura
P Johnson	Lay Administrator	Birmingham Cathedral
A Jones	Retail Sales Manager	Chester Zoo*
K Jones	Manager	The National Motorcycle Museum
Mr S Jones	Director	Spencer House
Ms K Jones	Administration	Cartwright Hall
S Joyce	Visitor Services Admin	Bass Museum, Visitor CTR & Shire Horse Stables
Ms L Karlsen	Principal Keeper	Ferens Art Gallery
Mr T Kay		Pettitts Feathercraft & Animal Adventure Park
Ms D Keasal	District Curator	Glasgow Vennel Museum
Ms D Keasal	District Curator	Museum of the Cumbraes
Ms D Keasal	District Curator	North Ayrshire Museum
Ms L Kelly		Tallberg Taylor Gallery
Mrs P Kendal	Administration	Bradford Industrial Horses at Work Museum
Mrs Kennaway		Escot Aquatic Centre & Gardens
P Kennedy	Administrator	Parham Elizabethan House & Gardens
C Kent	Visitor Services Manager	Museum of East Anglian Life
Mrs M Kershaw	Curator	Knaresborough Castle & Courthouse Museum
Mrs M Kershaw	Curator	Mercer Art Gallery
Mrs M Kershaw	Curator	Royal Pump Room Museum
P Kichenside	Commercial Director	Gorse Blossom Railway & Woodland Park
David Kidd	Proprietor	Cockthorpe Hall Toy Museum
Mr B Kilner	Executive Committee Member	Colne Valley Museum
A King	Asst Curator	Bristol Industrial Museum
Dr R J King	Curator	The John Moore Countryside Museum
Mrs King		The Lace Centre*
Ms R Kinnaird-Smith		Winchester Heritage Centre
S Kirby	Curator	Mill Green Museum and Mill
Sue Kirby		Welwyn Roman Baths
C Kitts	Manager	Stanborough Park
Mr J Kneale		Shipwreck & Heritage Centre
D Knight	Shops Manager	Beaulieu National Motor Museum, House & Abbey*
Mr J Lackenby	Reservoir Manager	Kielder Water
L Ladd		Bradford on Avon Museum
Mr D A Lambie	Proprietor	Speyside Heather/Garden Visitor Centre
P Langridge	Town Clerk	Totnes Guildhall
Andrew Larter/Martin Wilson	Catering Manager/Retail Manager	Kingdom of the Sea
Mrs S Lasson	Retail and Buying	Natural History Museum*
Mrs D Law	Curator/Manager	Swaledale Folk Museum
Mr R Leak/Mrs P Edwards	Partners	The Smuggling Experience
M Legge	Co-owner	Legbourne Railway Museum
A Leigh	Curator	Warrington Museum and Art Gallery
Ms A Leigh/Ms J Warner	Gift Shop/Farm Secretary	Marsh Farm Country Park*
James Leslie	Proprietor	Heritage Farm Park
Ms S Lewis	Commercial/Marketing Officer	Yorkshire Museum
Philip Lewis	Miller	Felin Crewi Working Watermill
Mr J Livingstone	Recreation Officer	Galloway Forest Park
Mr J Livingstone	Recreation Officer	Glen Trool Visitor Centre
M Loftus		National Sound Archive (British Library)
Ms J Lord/Mr R Dower	Product Directors	Walkley Clogs
Mr A Lovett	Senior Officer	Coniston Boating Centre
Mrs L Lowe	Manageress	Abbotsbury Swannery
P Lowe/D Bradbury	Retail Manager/Catering Manager	Windsor Safari Park*
C Lumb	Admin Assistant (purchasing)	Local Interest Museum
Ms J Macalister	Curator	Glenbarr Abbey Visitors Centre
J MacDonald	Curator	Auchindrain Township Open Air Museum
Mrs H B MacDonald	Asst Custodian	Neidpath Castle
Ms C MacDonald	Shop Manager	Dulwich Picture Gallery
Paul S MacDonald	Administrator	Naworth Castle
Mrs M Mackenzie	Project Co-ordinator	Timespan Heritage Centre
Mrs R Mackenzie	Vice Chairman	Ullapool Museum
T F Mackenzie	Museum Curator	Hamilton District Museum
W J Mackinnon	Hostel Manager	Baden Powell House Hostel
Lady Maclean		Duart Castle
Ms S Major	Administrator	Prideaux Place
J Makin (appt by Walsingham Coll)	Garden Administrator	Parcevall Hall Gardens
J Malpas	TIC Assistant	Izaak Walton's Cottage

Contact Name	Contact Title	Attraction
J Malpas	TIC Assistant	The Ancient High House
Mr C Manning	Partner	Charles Manning's Amusement Park*
Mr H Margary	Director	Lympne Castle
Ms D Marriott	Shop Supervisor	New Forest Museum and Visitor Centre
Elizabeth Marshall		Groam House Museum Trust
Miss M Martin	Shop Manager	Hereford Cathedral
Ms F C Marwick	Curator	West Highland Museum
C Massey	Senior Museums Officer	Wood End Museum of Natural History
Mr A Masters	Partner	Tamar Valley Donkey Park
Sandra E Matchett	Supervisor	The Palace Stables Heritage Centre
W M Matins	Director	Pensthorpe Waterfowl Trust
M Maxfield	Manager	Manchester United Museum & Tour Centre
Mrs H McAdam	Secretary	Glengoulandie Deer Park
Mr T J McCormack	Project Officer	Chatelherault Country Park
Eva McDonald	Proprietor	Fair Maid's House
Ms T McDonald	Merchandising Manager	Dinosaur Museum*
Ms T McDonald	Merchandising Manager	Dinosaur Safari
Ms T McDonald	Merchandising Manager	Mummies and Magic
Ms T McDonald	Merchandising Manager	Tutankhamun Exhibition
A McEvoy		The Local Interest Museum
Mrs S McHale	Deputy Manager	Bank of England Museum
A McLaren	Partner	Coughton Court
H McMahon	Marketing and Publicity Officer	Stockgrove Country Park
		Dunstable Downs Country Park
		Harrold Odell Country Park*
Fiona McQuarrie	Secretary/Shop Manager	Kirkcaldy Museum & Art Gallery
Mr M McVay	Retail Trading	Hampton Court Palace*
B Mead	Manager	Forge Mill Museum & Bordesley Abbey Vis Ctr
Mr G Melville	General Manager	Scottish Whisky Heritage Centre*
Mrs M Melvin	Administration	Peter Pan's Playground*
A Menhinick	Gardens & Museum Reception	Lackham Gardens & Agricultural Museum
Mr and Mrs M Menist	Owners	Southwick Country Herb Centre
Mrs R Mercer	Director & General Manager	Dorset Heavy Horse Centre
Merchandising	Head Office – Edinburgh	Threake Gardens
P Middleton		Rother Valley Country Park*
J Milford	Museums & Heritage Manager	Newark Museum
E M J Miller	Director	Pendle Heritage Centre
Miss Cathy Miller	Partner	Ponsonby Farm Park
Mrs Miller		Fenny Lodge Gallery
Mr N Milner	Sales	Browhouse Yard Museum*
Mr N Milner	Teamleader Trading	Newstead Abbey*
Christine Mineham	Shop Manager	Beatrix Potter Gallery*
Ms S Minter	Curator	Chelsea Physic Garden
Kapila Mistry	Administrative Officer	National Museum of Labour History
Mr A Mitha	Curator Multi Cultural Services	Huddersfield Art Gallery
J Moody	Landscape Manager	Newham Grange Leisure Farm
Ms A Moore	Museum Curator	Morpeth Chantry Bagpipe Museum
Ms V Mordue	Shop Manager	Wildfowl & Wetlands Centre
Rita More & Doreen McIntyre	Shop Manageress & Co-ordinator	Blackshaw Farm Park Ltd
C Morgan	Curator	The National Pinetum (Bedgebury)
P Morris	Director	Model Village
Major W D Morris-Barker	Administrator	Arbury Hall
A Morritt	Shop Supervisor	Museum of British Road Transport
Caroline Mortimer	Administrative Officer	Rhondda Heritage Park
M Morton	Hon Deputy Curator	Ripon Prison & Police Museum
Mrs S E Moss	Officer in Charge	Graham Sutherland Gallery
Ms D Moss	Keeper of Decorative Arts	Pickford's House Museum
Mr J Muir	Shop Manager	HMS Belfast*
T Muir (The Lady)		Kingston Bagpuize House and Garden
R Mullins	Curator/Manageress	Potters Museum of Curiosity
F Munro	Marketing Manageress	Liverpool Cathedral
Mr R Murphy	Chairman	Dinmore Manor and Gardens
A Murray	Curator	Nothe Fort
M Mutch	Curator	Myreton Motor Museum
Ms J Naismith	Administrator	Holburne Museum & Crafts Study Centre
Ms B Nash	Administrator	The Building of Bath Museum
National Trust for Scotland		J M Barrie's Birthplace
Mrs F Navabpour	Custodian	Oriental Museum
P Neaves	Admin/Secretary	The Monkey Sanctuary
Mrs D Nelson	Director	British in India Museum
M J Neve	Managing Director	Denmans Garden
Ms T Newland BA MSc	Librarian	Marx Memorial Library
Mr E Newton	Shop Manager	St Paul's Cathedral
Brian H Nodes	Administrator	Blair Castle*
W Northam/R Maddicott	Museum/FME Ltd	Fitzwilliam Museum*
Mrs J Noyes		Isle of Wight Rare Breeds & Waterfowl Park
Mr C Nunn		Broads Museum
A Nuttall	Manager	Etruria Industrial Museum
J O'Brian	Asst Curator	The Valley Heritage Centre and Museum
Ms S O'Cleary		Freud Museum
Mr D O'Grady	Merchandising Officer	Abbeydale Industrial Hamlet
Mr and Mrs P O'Shea		Trenouth Farm Rare Breeds Centre
Mrs Oldfield	Owner	Doddington Place Gardens
N Oliveira/N Oxley/M Petry	Directors	Museum of Installation
Mrs C Oliver	Shop Manager	Minster Church of St Cuthberga*
Mrs Nicki Oppermans	Manager	Buxton Micrarium
Mr C Orr-Ewing	Managing Agent	Exbury Gardens
Ms D Owen	Administrator	East Riddlesden Hall
L & B Owens	Joint Partners	Ardington Pottery
Dr C Palmer	Curator	Havant Museum

Contact Name	Contact Title	Attraction
Mr M Pawley	Countryside Officer	Crombie Country Park
P Peach	Curator	Corsham Court
Mr A Pearce	Manager	Timothy Hackworth Victorian & Railway Museum
Mr M Pearson	Head Ranger (Recreation)	Whinlatter Visitor Centre*
S Penney	Curator	The Salt Museum
A Percival	Honorary Director	Fleur de Lis Heritage Centre
Mr B Perkins		Dickens House Museum
R Peters/P Cooley	Golf Professional/W Lancs Council	Beacon Country Park
Mr & Mrs Petrie		Southport Zoo and Conservation Trust
Mrs M Petty		Leeds City Museum
Ms M Petty	Purchasing and Stock Controller	Leeds Industrial Museum
Mr R De Peyer	Curator	Dorset County Museum
Ms H Phillips	Buyer	Royal Cornwall Museum
Major R Pickard	Curator	Royal Signals Museum
Mr D Walker & Ms V Pickering		Chester Visitor Centre
J Pine	Regional Enterprises Manager	Baddesley Clinton
Mrs L Pine	Director (Porcelain)	Goss and Crested China Ltd
Pinmegar Family		Hammerwood Park
Mr J Platt	Senior Keeper of Industry	Derby Industrial Museum
Ms P Plumb	Administrator	Ragged School Museum
Mr L Pole	Curator	Saffron Walden Museum
J Pollock	Merchandising	Museum of Transport
J Pomfret	Bookshop Manageress	Oxfordshire County Museum
Mr M Pratt	Retail Manager	The Tales of Robin Hood*
R Pratt	Shop Manager	Child-Beale Wildlife Park*
C M Preston	Owner/Manager	Badsell Farm Park
Lady Preston		Beeston Hall
M R Puddle	Head Gardener and General Manager	Bodnant Gardens
Ms J Purcell	Manager	Longdale Craft Centre & Museum*
L Purchase	Shop Manager	Pallant House
J Pyzer	Shop Manager	Corinium Museum
Eamon Rafferty	Secretary	Armagh Planetarium
M Ratcliffe (Mrs)	Director	The Alice in Wonderland Visitor Centre
P Rawlins	Shop Manager	The Childrens Farm
Mr S Ray	Retail and Admissions	Paultons Park
Ms S Read	Shop Manager	Bankside Gallery
N Read	Sales Manager	Leighton Buzzard Railway
Mr P Reader	Purchasing Manager	Museum of the Order of St John
Mr B Redmonds	Director	Sooty's World
J Reeve/T Fallon	Secretary/Shop Manager	Salisbury and South Wiltshire Museum
Ms P Reeve	Shop Supervisor	Oban Sea Life Centre
Billy Ried/Alistair Davison	Manager/Asst Manager	The Northern Ireland Aquarium*
Ms A Reid	Curator	Stranraer Museum
Miss G B Reith/D C Butters	Town Clerk/Curator	Swaffham Museum
Ms A Rennick/Mrs S Keary		Blair Drummond Safari & Leisure Park
Mrs E Renwick	Head of Central Buying	Gladstones's Land
Mrs S Reynolds	Supervisor	Stained Glass Museum
M Ridgers	Tourism Site Manager	Pecorama
J Bleach/J Rix	Senior Custodians	Lewis Castle and Museums
Dereck Roberts	Transport Manager	Great Orme Tramway
Mr K Roberts	Manager	Tropical World*
Mrs P Roberts	Organiser	Jane Welsh Carlyle Museum
Mr K Robertson	Senior Ranger	Worsbrough Country Park*
Rev C Robertson	Minister	Canongate Kirk
A R Robinson	Administrator	Scone Palace*
G Robinson	Head Verger	Manchester Cathedral
Ms G Robinson	Shop	SS Shieldhall
Ms E Roche	Shop Supervisor	St Andrews Sea Life Centre
M Lindop/S Rogers	Support Officer/Admin Officer	Grosvenor Museum
J Rolfe	Administration Manager	Model House Craft and Design Centre
B Roper	Director	Cornish Seal Sanctuary
Ms P Rossetter	Administrative Director	Age Exchange Reminiscence Centre
Ms M Rowland	Buyer	Eureka! The Museum for Children
Tony Rowlands	Managing Director	Trefriw Wells SPA
G M W Ruddock	Curator	Teignmouth Museum
Mrs Russell		Pencarrow
Mr A Rutter	Secretary	Harwich Redoubt
Mr A Rutter	Secretary	Port of Harwich Maritime Museum
Ms G Rye		Thursford Collection*
Mr N Sadler	Curator/Director	London Canal Museum
Mrs C Salt	Administrator	Number One the Royal Crescent
S Sampson	Manager	Paradise Wildlife Park
Mr K Sanders	Administrator	Manor Farm Country Park
Ms M Sanderson	Administrator	Pontefract Museum
Ms M Sanderson	Administrator	Elizabeth Exhibition Gallery
Ms M Sanderson	Administrator	Pontefract Castle
Ms M Sanderson	Administrator	Wakefield Art Gallery
Ms M Sanderson	Administrator	Wakefield Museum
Raymond Sanderson	Commercial Director	Teifi Valley Railway
Mrs J Scarrat	Administration Assistant	Abbot Hall
Mrs J Schroeder	Owner	Arreton Manor
Mr S Scott	Administrator	Ulster Folk and Transport Museum*
C Sealby	Partner	Wythop Mill
Mr G Seimann	Managing Director	Conwy Visitor Centre*
Mr K Sellwood/Mr T Pearce	Manager/Director	Hornsea Freeport*
Mr R Shah	Finance Manager	Heritage Motor Centre*
Mr S Shannon	Regimental Assistant	Durham Light Infantry Museum & Art Gallery
Dr E J Sharples		Ness Gardens
J Shaw	Shop Manageress	Lochwinnoch Nature Centre

Contact Name	Contact Title	Attraction
Mr S Shaw		Elvisly Yours Centre
Mrs G Shephard	Sales Supervisor	Ffestiniog Railway
Mr C Shillito	Retail	Royal Botanic Gardens Kew*
F Shipton/J Lawson	Giftshop/Bookshop Managers	Guildford Cathedral
Shop Manager RSA enterprises		Royal Scottish Academy
P Shreeve	Shop Manager	Chiltern Open Air Museum
Mr W Silver	MD Nat Gallery Publications	National Gallery*
Mr P Simmonds	Senior Museums Officer	Haverfordwest Castle Museum and Art Gallery
Ms J Pye/Mr J Simmons	Visitors/Shops	Ely Cathedral*
Ken Simms	Director	Thrigby Hall Wildlife Gardens
Ms J Simpson		Rougemont House Museum
Ms J Simpson		Royal Albert Memorial Museum
Ms J Simpson		St Nicholas Priory
J Slack	Senior Technician	Blackburn Museum and Art Gallery
Ms H Slater	Sales Manager	Norwich Castle Museum*
Ms H Slater	Sales Officer	Norfolk Rural Life Museum and Union Farm
Ms H Slater	Publications Officer	Thetford Museum
Ms H Slater	Publications Officer	Strangers' Hall Museum
D Slight	Finance and Admin	Trafford Ecology Park
Mr T Smit		The Lost Gardens of Heligan
A Smith	Director	The Whitworth Art Gallery
B Smith	Commercial Manager	Romney, Hythe & Dymchurch Railway
E Smith	Shop Manageress	Hatfield House*
J Smith	Curator	Fasque
Mr Gavin Smith	Shop Manager	The Wordsworth Trust
Mr G Smith		Zetland Lifeboat Museum
Mrs H Smith		Harrow Museum & Heritage Centre*
Ms J Smith	Hon Curator	Dickens House Museum Broadstairs
N Smith	Museum Curator	Barleylands Farm Museum
Ms C Somerset	Secretary	Aldeburgh Moot Hall Museum
Ms J Sparkes	Shop Manager	Somerset Rural Life Museum
Mr and Mrs J Sparrow	Owners	Bear Museum
Ms T Spencer	Sales Executive	Harveys Wine Museum
Mrs H Spillett	Research Officer	Gods House Tower Museum
Mrs H Spillett	Research Officer	Tudor House Museum
Mrs H Spillett	Research Officer	Woolhouse Maritime Museum
Mr I Sproates	Treasurer	Captain Cook Schoolroom Museum
Mr G Sprott	Curator	Scottish Agricultural Museum
Mr R Stamford	General Manager	Guinness World of Records Exhibition*
Mr D Standen	Countryside Manager	Wat Tyler Country Park*
Mr K Stanfield	Warden	Peatlands Park*
David Steele	Castle Manager	Carrickferggus Castle*
L Steene	Custodian	Anne of Cleves House Museum
Mr Stephens	Chairman	Natural World*
Mrs K Stephenson	Joint Buyer	Gem Rock Museum
C Stevens	Bridge Master	Tower Bridge*
Angela Stewart	Personnel Officer	White Castle
Miss I Stewart	Stock Controller	Greyfriars Kirk
Mr A Stewart	Retail/Catering Manager	Metroland*
Mr P Stewart	Director/Partner	Dunaverig Farm Life Centre
H Stewart-Laidlaw	Shop Supervisor	Brighton Sea Life Centre
N T Stobbs	Administrator	Heron Corn Mill and Museum of Papermaking
Mr P Stone	Trading Manager	Charles Dickens Birthplace Museum
Ms L Stotners	Sales Administration Assistant	Edinburgh Museum of Childhood
Mrs Stratford		Chilham Castle
Mrs G Strathie	Visitor Centre Supervisor	New Lanark Village
Mr R Street	Director & Owner	Christchurch Tricycle Museum
J Strickson/C Alford	Admin/Asst Admin	Dunham Massey Hall and Park
F Stringer/J Carauna	Gift Shop Manager/Catering Manager	Howletts Zoo Park
F Stringer/J Carauna	Gift Shop Manager/Catering Manager	Port Lympne Zoo Park, Mansion & Gardens
Mrs F Maxwell Stuart	Owner	Traquair House
M Sulter	Art Gallery Services Officer	Rochdale Art Gallery
Mr Peter Sunderland	Assistant Director	Beacraigs Country Park
Y Surcouf	Owner	Basildon Zoo
H Sussex	Support Services Officer	The Look Out*
C Sutherland/C Keep	Shop/Birds	Bentley Wildfowl & Motor Museum
Mr J Sutherland	Partner	Ardfearn Nursery Plant Centre
P Svendsen	Asst Admin	The Donkey Sanctuary
Ms L Swales/Ms D Remm	Retail/Catering	Sea Life Centre*
D W & P R Sydenham	Proprietors	Cholderton Rare Breeds Farm Park
Mr C Tabiner	Manager	Farmworld*
Mr R Tait	Director	Wine and Spirit Museum
J Taylor	Asst Manager	Crabble Corn Mill
M Taylor	Manageress	Heale Gardens and Plant Centre
Mr B Taylor	Managing Director	Kirklees Light Railway
Ms C Taylor	Assistant Curator	Red House Museum Art Gallery & Gardens
R Taylor	Regional Enterprises Manager	Bateman's (The National Trust)
Mrs K Thirsk	Accountant/Shop Manager	Museum of Army Flying
Nest Thomas	Museums Development Officer	The Lloyd George Museum and Highgate His Home
T Thomas	Trustee	Birmingham Railway Museum
Mr I Thompson	Shop & Gardens Manager	Botanic Centre
Rita Thompson	Shop Manageress	Norwich Cathedral*
Mr V Thomson	Estates Ranger	Darnaway Farm Visitor Centre
Mr R Thornton	Director	Tropical Bird Park
Mrs L Thornton	Administration Officer	Sobriety Waterways Adventure Centre & Museum
Mr D Thorpe	Manager	South London Art Gallery
Y Threlfall/D Westgate		Blackpool Pleasure Beach
Ms L Tilbury	Visitor Officer	Lincoln Cathedral
J Tilt	Retail Manager	Cadbury World*

Contact Name	Contact Title	Attraction
Ms A Todhunter	Marketing Manager	Longdown Dairy Farm
Ms A Todhunter	Marketing Manager	New Forest Butterfly Farm
Ms A Toms	Director	Quay Arts
Mr J Tonner	Estate Manager	Formakin Estate
A Townsend	Shop Manager	Ford Green Hall
Mrs A Tropeano	Director	Colchester Zoo*
Mr W Trussler		Bexhill Museum of Costume & Social History
Ms J Tuley	Supervisor	Yorkshire Car Collection
Mr J Turner/Mrs S Turner	Co Directors	Lincolnshire Light Railway & Heritage Centre
Jenny Tye		Lea Gardens
Ms J Tyler	Keeper of Social History	Old Grammar School
Ms J Tyler	Keeper of Social History	Wilberforce House
C Underhill	Souvenir/Merchandise Manager	Warwick Castle*
University		University of Durham Botanic Garden
Mr B Unwin	Assistant Curator	Logan Botanic Garden
Mr G and Mrs J Upton	Owners	How We Lived Then Museum of Shops
K Usher	Administrator	Calke Abbey*
Mr N Valizadeh	Proprietor	Maes Astro Tourist Attraction
Catherine Vance		Larne Tourist Info & Interpretation Centre
S Vaughan	Partner	Wye Valley Farm Park
M Verren	Deputy Manager	Tower World
B F Virgo	Shop Organiser	North Devon Maritime Museum
Ms M Wagland & Mr E Lund	Shop and Catering Managers	Talyllyn Railway
Mr J Walker	Hon Secretary to the Trustees	Bayle Museum
Mr S Walker	Business & Marketing Manager	Embsay Steam Railway
Dr A Waller	Bookshop Manager	Westminster Abbey*
Mr E Walters		Bucklers Hard Village & Maritime Museum*
Mr G Ward	Shop Manager	York Minster*
Ms G Warden	Manager	Pollock's Toys Museum
M Warhurst	Museum Director	Norton Priory Museum and Gardens
Ms N Warnock	Shop Supervisor	Weymouth Sea Life Park
A Beard/C Wasche	Shop Manageress	The Silk Museum
C Wasche/A Beard	Shop Manageress	West Park Museum
D W Watkins	Treasurer	Southport Railway Centre
E Watkiss/L McNally	Gift and Book Buyers	Battle Abbey and Battlefield of Hastings
Mrs G Saunders Watson		Rockingham Castle
D Watts	Shop Manager	Bodmin Town Museum
Ms E Webster	Clerk/Typist	Normanby Hall Country Park
Mr T Weston	Conservation Officer	Derwent Walk Country Park
W Weston	Hon Treasurer of Friends	Wisbech & Fenland Museum
Ms R Westwood	Museums Officer	Shibden Hall
Mr P Wetherall	Dept of Arts & Libraries	Lochwinnoch Community Museum
Mr P Wetherall	Deputy Director, Arts & Libraries	Paisley Museum & Art Galleries
Ms P Wheatcroft	Curator	Bruce Castle Museum
S White	Merchandising Manager & Marketing	Leeds Castle
A Wickens	Nursery Manager	Iden Croft Herbs
Mrs P Wiggle	Senior Assistant	Malton Museum
T Wilcox	Curator	Hove Museum and Art Gallery
D Wild		The Museum of Childhood
Mrs Wildgust		D H Lawrence Birthplace Museum
S Wileman	Cultural & Community Services Asst	Bromham Mill
S Wileman	Cultural & Community Services Asst	Elstow Moot Hall
S Wileman	Cultural & Community Services Asst	Swiss Garden
Ms P Wilkinson		Woodhorn Colliery Museum
Hilary Williams	Administrator	Bersham Heritage Centre and Ironworks
L Williams		Marle Place Gardens and Nursery
Miss J Williams	Manageress	Abbotsbury Sub Tropical Gardens
Peter Williams	Assistant Manager	Brecon Beacons Mountain Centre
V Williams	Curator	Hastings Museum and Art Gallery
Mr D Wills	GC Manager	Stewarts Garden – Lands
I Willsher	Owner	Longstone Heritage Centre
Mr P Willsher	General Manager	Compton Acres Gardens
B S Wilson	Museums Officer	Tankerness House Museum
B Wilson	Hon Curator	Stromness Museum
M Wilson	Company Secretary	Burton Agnes Hall
Mr M Wilson		Kingdom of the Sea GT Yarmouth*
Mr M Wilson		Kingdom of the Sea Hunstanton*
Mr M Wilson		Pleasurewood Hills American Theme Park
Mrs C L Wilson	Project Manager	Whithorn Dig
Ms M Wilson		Ripley's Believe It or Not
Ms S Wilson	Sales & Info Asst	Falls of Clyde Nature Reserve
A Wood	Office Manager	Shugborough
Julie Worth		The Butterfly and Falconry Park
T Wray	Secretary	Combe Martin Wildlife & Dinosaur Park
D Wright	General Manager	Bicton Park Gardens
Iris Wyper	Receptionist	Almondell & Calderwood Country Park
A D Yule	Warden	Auckland Castle

INDEX 4
INDEX OF PARENT/HOLDING COMPANIES, ETC.

Parent Company	Attraction
221b Ltd	Sherlock Holmes Museum
Abbey Lawn Trust	The John Moore Countryside Museum
Abbey Lawn Trust	Merchant's House (Little Museum)
Age Exchange Theatre Trust Ltd	Age Exchange Reminiscence Centre
Allhallows Museum Society	Allhallows Museum
Almond Valley Heritage Trust	Almond Valley Heritage Trust
Apuldram Roses	Apuldram Roses
Arbury Hall	Arbury Hall
Ardington Pottery	Ardington Pottery
Ards Borough Council	The Northern Ireland Aquarium*
Argyll & Bute District Council	Ardencraig Gardens
Armagh District Council	The Palace Stables Heritage Centre
Armagh Planetarium/Observatory	Armagh Planetarium
Arran & Argyll Transport	Arran & Argyll Transport Museum
Arrowcroft Group Plc	Albert Dock
Atholl Estates	Blair Castle*
Auchindrain Trust	Auchindrain Township Open Air Museum
Avon Wildlife Trust	Willsbridge Mill
Ayrshire Railway Preservation Group	Scottish Industrial Railway Centre
Bank of England	Bank of England Museum
Barnsley Metropolitan Borough Council	Worsbrough Country Park*
Barrington Leisure Ltd, Dept of	Butterfly World and Fountain World
Bartley Mill	Bartley Mill
Basildon District Council	Wat Tyler Country Park*
Bass Brewers	Bass Museum, Visitor Ctr & Shire Horse Stables
Bath City Council	Museum of Costume
Bath Preservation Trust	Number One the Royal Crescent
Bath Preservation Trust	The Building of Bath Museum
Bayle Museum Trustees	Bayle Museum
Beck Isle Trustees	Beck Isle Museum of Rural Life
Bedford County Council	Swiss Garden
Bedford County Council	Bromham Mill
Bedford County Council	Elstow Moot Hall
Beetham Trust	Heron Corn Mill and Museum of Papermaking
Bekonscot Ltd	Bekonscot Model Village*
Belvoir Estate	Belvoir Castle
Bennetts Water Lily Farm	Bennetts Water Gardens
Beverley Borough Council	The Guildhall, Beverley
Bexley London Borough	Bexley Museum
Bexley London Borough	Erith Museum
Bicton Park Trust Co	Bicton Park Gardens
Bitton Railway Co Ltd	Avon Valley Railway
Black Country Museum Trust Ltd	Black Country Museum
Blackpool Pleasure Beach	Frontierland Western Theme Park*
Blackpool Pleasure Beach Group of Companies	Blackpool Pleasure Beach
Blackshaw Farm Park Ltd	Blackshaw Farm Park Ltd
Bletchley Timbee	Fenny Lodge Gallery
Boat Museum Trust	The Boat Museum
Bodmin and Wenford Railway Plc	Bodmin and Wenford Railway
Bolton Metro Leisure Services	Butterfly World
Bolton Metro Leisure Services	Animal World
Borough of Newport Civic Centre	Newport Museum and Art Gallery
Borough of Redditch	Forge Mill Museum & Bordesley Abbey Vis Ctr
Bournemouth Borough Council	Russel-Cotes Art Gallery & Museum
Bournemouth Heritage Transport	Bournemouth Heritage Transport Centre
Bourville Village Trust	Selly Manor Museum
Bow Trust (Durham) Ltd	Durham Heritage Centre
Bracknell Forest Borough Council	The Look Out*
Bradford Metropolitan Council	Cartwright Hall
Bradford on Avon Museum Society	Bradford on Avon Museum
Breamore Estate Co Ltd	Breamore House & Museums
Brecon Beacons National Park	Brecon Beacons Mountain Centre
Brighton Borough Council	Volks Electric Railway
Brighton Borough Council	Royal Pavilion, Art Gallery and Museum
Bristol City Council	Blaise Castle House Museum
Bristol City Council	Bristol Industrial Museum
Bristol, Clifton & W. of England Zoological Soc	Bristol Zoo Gardens*
British Film Institute	Museum of the Moving Image*
British Library	National Sound Archive (British Library)
British Motor Industry Heritage Trust	Heritage Motor Centre*
British Nuclear Fuels Plc	Sellafield Visitors Centre
British Rotorcraft Museum	The International Helicopter Museum
Broadland Properties Ltd	Hever Castle
Brooklands Museum Trust Ltd	Brooklands Museum
Brookside Garden Centre Ltd	Brookside Miniature Railway
Broxtowe Borough Council	D H Lawrence Birthplace Museum
BTR Plc	Poole Pottery
Buccleuch Heritage Trust	Bowhill House and Country Park

Parent Company	Attraction
Bungay Castle Trust Ltd	Bungay Castle
Burnley Borough Council	Towneley Hall Art Gallery and Museum
Burton Agnes Hall Preservation Trust Ltd	Burton Agnes Hall
Burton Constable Foundation	Burton Constable Hall
Bute Museum Trust	Bute Museum
Buxton & District Civic Assoc	Poole's Cavern
C A Morris Ltd	Model Village
Cadbury Schweppes	Cadbury World*
Calder Valley Cruising	World of the Honey Bee
Calderdale MBC	Halifax Piece Hall*
Calderdale MBC Halifax	Shibden Hall
Cambrian Railways Society Ltd	Cambrian Railway Soc & Oswestry Cycle Museum
Cambridge and County Folk Museum Assoc	Cambridge and County Folk Museum
Cannock Chase Council	The Valley Heritage Centre and Museum
Carlisle Cathedral Buttery Co Ltd	Carlisle Cathedral
Carlisle City Council	Tulliehouse Museum and Art Gallery
Castle Hill Museum Partnership	Museum of the Home
Castle Howard Estate Ltd	Castle Howard*
Castle Morpeth Borough Council	Morpeth Chantry Bagpipe Museum
Cawdor Castle (Tourism) Ltd	Cawdor Castle
Ceredigion District Council	Ceredigion Museum
Channings Ltd	Model Farm and Folk Museum
Chatterley Whitfield Mining Museum	Chatterley Whitfield Mining Museum
Chelsea Physic Garden Company	Chelsea Physic Garden
Cheshire County Council	The Salt Museum
Cheshire County Council	Tatton
Chester City Council	Grosvenor Museum
Chester Visitor Centre Ltd	Chester Visitor Centre
Chillingham Wild Cattle Association	Chillingham Wild Cattle Association Ltd
Chiltern Open Air Museum Ltd	Chiltern Open Air Museum
Choice High Ltd	Walkley Clogs
Church Commissioners	Auckland Castle
Church of England	St Mary's Priory, Old Malton
Church of Scotland	Jonah's Journey
Church of Scotland	St Michael's Parish Church
Church of Scotland	Church of the Holyrude, Stirling
Cilgwyn Candles	Cilgwyn Candles Workshop and Mini Museum
City Museum and Art Gallery	Etruria Industrial Museum
City of Bradford Metropolitan District Council	Bolling Hall
City of Bristol Council	Red Lodge
City of Liverpool	Croxteth Hall and Country Park
City of Sheffield Recreation Department	Sheffield Botanical Gardens
Clan Macpherson Museum Trust	Clan Macpherson Museum
Cleveland County Council	Castle Eden Walkway Country Park*
Cleveland County Council	Billingham Beck Valley Country Park
Cleyfield Farms Ltd	Cockley Cley Iceni Village & Museum
Cliffhead Hotel	Shipwreck & Heritage Centre
Close Harmony Trading Co Ltd	Salisbury Cathedral*
Clwyd County Council	Bersham Heritage Centre and Ironworks
Clwyd County Council	Ruthin Craft Centre
Coke Estates Ltd	Holkham Hall
Colne Valley Railway Co Ltd	Colne Valley Railway
Cornwall County Planning Dept	Tehidy Country Park
Corporation of London	Tower Bridge*
Cotswold District Council	Corinium Museum
Cotswold District Council	Cotswold Countryside Collection
Council of the National Army Museum	National Army Museum
Coventry City Council	Museum of British Road Transport
CPRE	Council for the Port of Rural England
Crabble Corn Mill Trust Ltd	Crabble Corn Mill
Cranmore Tower Leisure	Cranmore Tower
Crawford Farm Enterprises Ltd	Cluanie Deer Farm Park
Cultural Heritage Resources	Old Operating Theatre Museum
Cumberland Pencil Co	Cumberland Pencil Museum & Exhibition Centre
Cumbrae Holdings	Cumbria Crystal Ltd*
Cumbria County Council	Talkin Tarn Country Park
Cumbria County Council	Eskdale Corn Mill
Cummock & Doon Valley District Council	Baird Institute Museum
Cunninghame District Council	Glasgow Vennel Museum
Cunninghame District Council	North Ayrshire Museum
Cunninghame District Council	Museum of the Cumbraes
CWS Agriculture	Farmworld*
D Stewart & Son Ltd	Stewarts Garden – Lands
Darlington Borough Council	Darlington Museum
Dart Valley Light Railway Plc	Paignton & Dartmouth Steam Railway
Dean & Chapter of Bristol	Bristol Cathedral
Dean & Chapter of Lincoln	Lincoln Cathedral
Dean & Chapter of Winchester	Winchester Cathedral
Dean & Chapter, St Paul's Cathedral	St Paul's Cathedral
Dean and Canons, The Cathedral Manchester	Manchester Cathedral
Dean and Chapter of Canterbury	Canterbury Cathedral
Dean and Chapter of Exeter	Exeter Cathedral*
Dean and Chapter of Hereford Cathedral	Hereford Cathedral
Dean and Chapter, Ripon Cathedral	Ripon Cathedral*
Dean and Chapter, Westminster Abbey	Westminster Abbey*
Denmans Ltd	Denmans Garden
Department of Agriculture (Northern Ireland)	Gosford Forest Park
Department of Environment (N. Ireland)	Carrickferggus Castle*
Department of National Heritage	Victoria and Albert Museum
Department of Welsh Office	White Castle

Parent Company	Attraction
Dept Tourism & Amenities	Wood End Museum of Natural History
Derby City Council	Derby Museum and Art Gallery*
Derby City Council	Derby Industrial Museum
Derby City Council	Pickford's House Museum
Dickens House & Dickens House Fund	Dickens House Museum
Dinmore Manor Estate	Dinmore Manor and Gardens
Diocese of Bradford	Skipton Holy Trinity Parish Church
Diocese of Bradford	St Michael the Archangel Church
Diocese of Salisbury	Sherbourne Abbey
Donkey Sanctuary, Cornwall	Cornwall Donkey & Pony Sanctuary
Douglas & Angus Estates	The Hirsel
Drummuir Castle Estate	Mill of Towie
Duart Castle Partnership	Duart Castle
Duke of Cornwall's Light Infantry Museum Trust	Duke of Cornwall's Light Infantry Museum
Dunaverig Farm Life Centre	Dunaverig Farm Life Centre
Duncombe Park Partnership	Duncombe Park
Durham County Council	Durham Light Infantry Museum & Art Gallery
Durham County Council	Binchester Roman Fort
Dyson Perrins Museum Trust	Dyson Perrins Museum
Earl of Carlisle (Owner)	Naworth Castle
East 15 Acting School	Sheriff Hutton Park
East Anglian Railway Museum	East Anglian Railway Museum
East Dorset District Council	Moors Valley Country Park
East Kent Maritime Trust	Maritime Museum, Ramsgate
East Kilbride District Council	Calderglen Country Park
East Lancashire Light Railway Co Ltd	East Lancashire Railway
Eastbourne Borough Council	Sussex Combined Services Museum
Eastleigh Borough Council	Itchen Valley Country Park
Edinburgh City Museums & Galleries	Edinburgh Museum of Childhood
Elvisly Yours Ltd	Elvisly Yours Centre
Ely Museum Trustees	Ely Museum
English Heritage	Stott Park Bobbin Mill
English Heritage	Kenilworth Castle
English Heritage	Wrest Park House and Gardens
English Heritage	Bessie Surtees House
English Heritage	Battle Abbey and Battlefield of Hastings
English Heritage	Rochester Castle
English Heritage	Deal Castle
English Heritage	Carisbrooke Castle
English Heritage	Portland Castle
English Heritage	Totnes Castle
Epping Forest District Council	Epping Forest District Museum
Essex County Council	Marsh Farm Country Park*
Evesham Town Council	Almonry Museum
Exbury Gardens Ltd	Exbury Gardens
Exeter City Council	Royal Albert Memorial Museum
Exeter City Council	St Nicholas Priory
Falstaff Antiques	The CM Booth Collection of Historic Vehicles
Farm Partnership, G Palmer and Sons	Parsonage Farm Rural Heritage Centre
Fasque Estates	Fasque
Faversham Society	Fleur De Lis Heritage Centre
Federation of British Artists	Mall Galleries
Ferguson International Holdings Plc	Appleby Castle Conservation Centre
Fermanagh District Council	Marble Arch Caves*
Ffestiniog Railway Company	Ffestiniog Railway
Fife Regional Council	Lochore Meadows Country Park
First Leisure Corporation Plc	Tower World
Five Star Management Ltd	Potters Museum of Curiosity
Forent Ltd	New Forest Museum and Visitor Centre
Forestry Commission	Grizedale Forest Park*
Forestry Commission	Whinlatter Visitor Centre*
Forestry Commission	Argyll Forest Park
Forestry Commission	Galloway Forest Park
Forestry Commission	Glen Trool Visitor Centre
Forestry Commission	Kielder Forest and Castle
Forestry Commission	The National Pinetum (Bedgebury)
Fortescue Garden Trust	The Garden House
Foxfield Light Railway Society Ltd	Foxfield Steam Railway
Frome Museum Trustees	Frome Museum
Fujita (UK) Ltd	London Toy and Model Museum
Funday Ltd	Metroland*
Funday Ltd	Spitting Image Rubberworks*
G&P Kichenside Ltd	Gorse Blossom Railway & Woodland Park
Gairloch & District Heritage Society	Gairloch Heritage Museum
Gascoyne Estates	Hatfield House*
Gateshead MBC	Derwent Walk Country Park
Gateshead MBC	Bill Quay Community Farm*
General Trustees of the Church of Scotland	Kirk of St Nicholas
Glasgow City Council	Glasgow Botanic Gardens
Glasgow City Council	People's Palace Museum*
Glasgow City Council	Pollok House*
Glasgow City Council	Provand's Lordship
Glasgow City Council	Rutherglen Museum
Glasgow City Council	Haggs Castle
Glasgow City Council	McLellan Galleries
Glasgow City Council	Art Gallery and Museum*
Glasgow City Council	Museum of Transport*
Goss & Crested China Ltd	Goss & Crested China Ltd
Grampian Transport Museum Trust	Grampian Transport Museum
Graybill Ltd	Peckforton Castle

Parent Company	Attraction
Greater Manchester PTE	Museum of Transport
Gretna Museum and Tourist Services Ltd	Famous Old Blacksmiths Shop Centre*
Greyfriars Tolbooth & Highland Kirk	Greyfriars Kirk
Gricks Ltd, 316a High St, North London E12 6SA	Hebden Crypt
Grimstone & Drummond Castle Trust Ltd	Drummond Castle Gardens
Grwp Aberconwy	Great Orme Tramway
Guinness Plc	Guinness World of Records Exhibition*
Guitty Talberg Illustration Agents	Tallberg Taylor Gallery
Gulf Resources Pacific Ltd	Land's End*
Gurkha Museum Trading Co Ltd	Gurkha Museum
Gwynedd County Council	Beaumaris Gaol and Court
Gwynedd County Council	The Lloyd George Museum and Highgate His Home
H Griffiths and Son	Tregwynt Mill
H W Mawer Trust	Sion Hill Hall
Hamilton District Council	Hamilton District Museum
Hamilton District Council	Chatelherault Country Park
Hampshire County Council	Queen Elizabeth Country Park
Hampshire County Council	Royal Victoria Country Park
Hampshire County Council	Manor Farm Country Park
Hampshire County Museum Service	Havant Museum
Hampshire County Museum Service	Red House Museum Art Gallery & Gardens
Harlow District Council	Mark Hall Cycle Museum and Gardens
Harrogate Borough Council	Royal Pump Room Museum
Harrogate Borough Council	Mercer Art Gallery
Harrogate Borough Council	Knaresborough Castle & Courthouse Museum
Harrow Arts Council	Harrow Museum & Heritage Centre*
Hartlepool Borough Council	Gray Art Gallery
Hartlepool Borough Council	Hartlepool Maritime Museum
Harveys of Bristol Ltd	Harveys Wine Museum
Harwich Society	Harwich Redoubt
Harwich Society	Port of Harwich Maritime Museum
Hastings Borough Council	Hastings Museum and Art Gallery
Hastings Heritage Ltd	Smugglers Adventure
Heaven Farm Leisure	Heaven Farm
Heligan Gardens Project Ltd	The Lost Gardens of Heligan
Helmsdale Heritage Society	Timespan Heritage Centre
Hendon Mill Co Ltd	British in India Museum
Hereford Cider Museum Trust	Cider Museum and King Offa Distillery
Hereford City Museum	Churchill Gardens Museum
Herefordshire Waterworks Museum	Herefordshire Waterworks Museum
Heritage Projects (Management) Ltd	The Oxford Story
Heritage Projects (Management) Ltd	The White Cliffs Experience
Heritage Projects (Management) Ltd	A Day at the Wells
Historic Royal Palaces Agency	HM Tower of London*
Historic Royal Palaces Agency	Hampton Court Palace*
Holder Estate Company Ltd	Holker Hall and Gardens
Holt Leisure Parks Ltd	Isle of Gigha
Hornchurch & District Historical Society	Upminster Tithe Barn Agricultural Museum
Hornsea Museum Trust	Hornsea Museum
Hoskins Brewery Plc	Hoskins Brewery
Houghton Lodge Farms	Houghton Lodge Garden & Hydroponicum
How We Lived Then	How We Lived Then Museum of Shops
Howe and Davis Ltd	Pecorama
Howletts & Port Lympne Est Ltd	Howletts Zoo Park
Howletts & Port Lympne Est Ltd	Port Lympne Zoo Park, Mansion & Gardens
Hull City Museums and Art Galleries	Hull and East Riding Museum
Hull City Museums and Art Galleries	Streetlife – Hull Museum of Transport
Hull City Museums and Art Galleries	Ferens Art Gallery
Hull City Museums and Art Galleries	Old Grammar School
Hull City Museums and Art Galleries	Spurn Lightship
Hull City Museums and Art Galleries	Town Docks Museum
Hull City Museums and Art Galleries	Wilberforce House
Ilchester Estate (Strangeways Enterprises)	Abbotsbury Tithe Barn Museum
Ilchester Estate (Strangeways Enterprises)	Abbotsbury Swannery
Ilchester Estate (Strangeways Enterprises)	Abbotsbury Sub Tropical Gardens
Imperial War Museum	Duxford Airfield*
Imperial War Museum	HMS Belfast*
In receivership	Windsor Safari Park*
Incredibly Fantastic Old Toy Show	Incredibly Fantastic Old Toy Show
International Shakespeare Globe Centre Ltd	Shakespeare Globe Museum
Inverclyde District Council	McLean Museum and Art Gallery
Ironbridge Gorge Museum Trust	Ironbridge Gorge Museum*
Isle of Arran Museum Trust and Association	Isle of Arran Heritage Museum
Jenner Appeal Trustees	Jenner Museum
K F Boulton & Son	Rock Garden and Cave
Keighley & Worth Valley Rly. Preservation Soc	Keighley & Worth Valley Railway*
Kew Bridge Engines Trust	Kew Bridge Steam Museum
Kirklees Cultural Services	Oakwell Hall Country Park
Kirklees Light Railway Co Ltd, The Railway Sta	Kirklees Light Railway
Kirklees Metropolitan Council	Dewsbury Museum
Kirklees Metropolitan Council	Bagshaw Museum
Kirklees Metropolitan Council	Huddersfield Art Gallery
Kirklees Metropolitan Council	Batley Art Gallery
Lackham College	Lackham Gardens & Agricultural Museum
Laidhay Preservation Trust	Laidhay Croft Museum
Lake District Art Gallery and Museum Trust	Abbot Hall
Lake District National Park Authority	Coniston Boating Centre
Lake District Special Planning Board	Lake District National Park Visitor Centre*
Lamp of Lothian Trust	Jane Welsh Carlyle Museum
Lancashire County Council	Helmshore Textile Museums

Parent Company	Attraction
Lancashire County Museum Service	County and Regimental Museum
Lancashire Heritage Trust	Pendle Heritage Centre
Lancaster University	Peter Scott Gallery
Landmark	Camera Obscura
Larne Borough Council	Larne Tourist Info & Interpretation Centre
Laurence Sterne Trust	Shandy Hall
Lea Rhododendron Gardens Ltd	Lea Gardens
Lee Valley Regional Park Authority	Lee Valley Park Farms
Leeds Castle Foundation	Leeds Castle
Leeds City Council	Leeds Industrial Museum
Leeds City Council	Tropical World*
Leeds City Council	Leeds City Museum
Leighton Buzzard Narrow Gauge Railway Society	Leighton Buzzard Railway
Leisure Enterprises Ltd	Lyme Regis Experience
Lemanis Ltd	Lympne Castle
Lennoxlove Trust	Lennoxlove House
Lewes District Council	Newhaven Fort
Lichfield Cathedral Trust	Lichfield Cathedral
Lightwater Valley Holdings	Lightwater Valley Theme Park*
Lincolnshire County Council	Battle of Britain Memorial Flight (Visits)
Lincolnshire County Council	Stamford Museum
Lincolnshire Trust for Nature Conservation	Gibraltar Point National Nature Reserve*
Lindisfarne Ltd	Wine and Spirit Museum
Living Landscape Trust	Boughton House
Local Authority Leisure Services	Hove Museum and Art Gallery
London Borough of Barking and Dagenham	Valence House Museum
London Borough of Bromley	Bromley Museum
London Borough of Enfield	Capel Manor
London Borough of Greenwich	Greenwich Borough Museum
London Borough of Haringey	Bruce Castle Museum
London Borough of Hounslow	Hogarth's House
London Borough of Southwark	Cuming Museum
London Diocese	St Olave's Church
Lord Wemyss Trust, Stanway	Stanway House
Lothian & Borders Fire Brigade	Museum of Fire
Luton Borough Council	Stockwood Craft Museum & Gardens
Luton Borough Council	Luton Museum and Art Gallery
LVRPA	Myddelton House Gardens
Madame Tussaud's Ltd	Rock Circus*
Malvern Museum Society Abbey	Malvern Museum
Marwell Preservation Trust Ltd	Marwell Zoological Park*
Marx Memorial Library	Marx Memorial Library
Merthyr Tydfil Borough Council	Cyfarthfa Castle Museum, Art Gallery and Park
Methodist Church	John Wesley's Chapel
Metropolitan Borough of Calderdale	Bankfield Museum
Mid Glamorgan County Council Planning Dept	Rhondda Heritage Park
Middlesbrough Borough Council	Newham Grange Leisure Farm
Milton Cottage Trust	Milton's Cottage
Ministry of Defence	Museum of Staffordshire Regiment
Model Aviation Museum Ltd	Goosedale Model Aviation Centre
Model House (Llantrisant) Ltd	Model House Craft and Design Centre
Monmouth Borough Council	The Nelson Museum and Local History Centre
Montagu Ventures Ltd	Bucklers Hard Village & Maritime Museum*
Montagu Ventures Ltd	Beaulieu National Motor Museum, House & Abbey*
Moray Estates Development Co	Darnaway Farm Visitor Centre
Morris and Co (Shrewsbury) Ltd	Midland Motor Museum
Morwellham and Tamar Valley Trust	Morwellham Quay
Mostyn Gallery Ltd	Oriel Mostyn
MUFC	Manchester United Museum & Tour Centre
Mull & West Highland Narrow Gauge Railway Co	Mull & West Highland Narrow Gauge Railway
Mullaghbawn Folk Museum	Mullaghbawn Folk Museum
Museum of Army Flying Ltd	Museum of Army Flying
Museum of Kent Life Trust	Museum of Kent Life
Musical Museum	Musical Museum
Naron Plc	Hastings Sea Life Centres*
National History Museum	The Walter Rothschild Zoological Museum
National Horseracing Museum	National Horseracing Museum
National Motorcycle Museum Trust	The National Motorcycle Museum
National Museum	National Maritime Museum Greenwich*
National Museum of Labour History Co Ltd	National Museum of Labour History
National Museum of Scotland	Museum of Flight
National Museum of Scotland	Scottish Agricultural Museum
National Museum of Wales	Welsh Slate Museum
National Museum of Wales	Welsh Folk Museum*
National Museum of Wales	Graham Sutherland Gallery
National Museum of Wales	Amgueddfa'r Gogledd/Museum of the North
National Museums and Galleries on Merseyside	National Maritime Museum
National Museums and Galleries on Merseyside	Liverpool Museum
National Museums and Galleries on Merseyside	Walker Art Gallery
National Museums and Galleries on Merseyside	Lady Lever Art Gallery
National Museums and Galleries on Merseyside	Sudley
National Trust	Springhill
National Trust	Penrhyn Castle
National Trust	Florencecourt House
National Trust	Mount Stewart House and Gardens*
National Trust	Wordsworth House
National Trust	Beatrix Potter Gallery*
National Trust	Shugborough
National Trust	Erddig Hall
National Trust	The Greyfriars

Parent Company	Attraction
National Trust	Baddesley Clinton
National Trust	Hatfield Forest
National Trust	Hughenden Manor
National Trust	Stowe Landscape Gardens
National Trust	Hatchlands Park
National Trust	Bateman's (The National Trust)
National Trust	Polesden Lacey
National Trust	Knole
National Trust	Clandon Park
National Trust	Hanbury Hall (National Trust)
National Trust	Anglesey Abbey
National Trust	Sudbury Hall & Museum of Childhood
National Trust	Calke Abbey*
National Trust	Houghton Mill
National Trust	Oxburgh Hall
National Trust	Blickling Hall*
National Trust	East Riddlesden Hall
National Trust	The National Trust, Speke Hall
National Trust	Dunham Massey Hall and Park
National Trust for Scotland	Gladstones's Land
National Trust for Scotland	Branklyn Garden
National Trust for Scotland	Kellie Castle
National Trust for Scotland	Threake Gardens
National Trust for Scotland	Inverewe Garden
National Trust for Scotland	J M Barrie's Birthplace
National Trust for Scotland	Leith Hall
National Trust for Scotland	Brodick Castle & Country Park & Goatfell
National Trust Queen Anne's Gate London	Nunnington Hall
New Lanark Conservation Trust	New Lanark Village
Newark Air Museum Ltd	Newark Air Museum
Newark and Sherwood District Council	Newark Museum
Newham Council	East Ham Nature Reserve
Newham Council	North Woolwich Old Station Museum
Newham Council	Passmore Edwards Museum
Newlyn Orion Galleries Ltd	Newlyn Art Gallery
Nidderdale Museum Society	Nidderdale Museum
Norfolk County Council	Shirehall Museum
Norfolk County Council	Cromer Museum
Norfolk Museums Service	Strangers' Hall Museum
Norfolk Museums Service	Norfolk Rural Life Museum and Union Farm
North Bedfordshire Borough Council	Bedford Museum
North Devon Museum Trust	North Devon Maritime Museum
North Down Borough Council	North Down Heritage Centre
North East Aircraft Museum	North East Aircraft Museum
North East Fife District Council	North Carr Lightship Anstruther Harbour
North of England Zoological Society	Chester Zoo*
North Yorkshire County Council	Dales Countryside Museum
North Yorkshire County Council	Yorkshire Museum
Northbourne Farming Partnership	Northbourne Court Gardens
Northern Horticultural Society	Harlow Carr Botanical Gardens
Northumberland Estates	Syon Park
Northumberland National Park Dept	Once Brewed National Park Visitor Centre
Northumbrian Water Ltd	Kielder Water
Norton Priory Museum Trust Ltd	Norton Priory Museum and Gardens
Nottingham City Council	Newstead Abbey*
Nottingham County Council	Browhouse Yard Museum*
Nottingham Lace Centre Ltd	The Lace Centre*
Offa's Dyke Association	Offa's Dyke Association
Omagh District Council	The Ulster History Park
Order of St John	Museum of the Order of St John
Orkney Islands Council	Tankerness House Museum
Orkney Natural History Society Museum Trust	Stromness Museum
Oxford City Council	Carfax Tower
Oxfordshire County Council	Oxfordshire County Museum
Paisley Museum and Art Gallery	Coats Observatory
Pallant House Gallery Trust	Pallant House
Parkside Leisure Ltd	Paradise Wildlife Park
Patsy B Marketing Ltd	Sooty's World
Paultons Park Ltd	Paultons Park
Paxton Trust	Paxton House
Pearson Group Plc	Alton Towers*
Pearson Plc	Warwick Castle*
Pembrokeshire Coast National Park	Carew Castle and Tidal Mill
Peter Black Holdings Plc	Hornsea Freeport*
Peterborough Cathedral	Peterborough Cathedral*
Pilkington Glass Plc	Pilkington Glass Museum
PJN & E G Prideaux-Brume	Prideaux Place
Pleasure and Leisure Corporation Plc	Pleasure Beach*
Pleasureworld	Ripley's Believe It or Not
Pleasureworld	Pleasurewood Hills American Theme Park*
Pleasureworld	Kingdom of the Sea Gt Yarmouth*
Pleasureworld	Kingdom of the Sea Hunstanton*
Pleasureworld Ltd	Kingdom of the Sea
Poole Borough Council	Waterfront Museum
Poole Borough Council	Scaplen's Court Museum
Portsmouth City Council	Charles Dickens Birthplace Museum
POW Camp	Eden Camp Modern History Theme Museum*
Powys County Council	Powysland Museum & Montgomery Canal Centre
Preston Borough Council	Harris Museum and Art Gallery
Provost and Chapter of the Cathedral	Cathedral Church of St Nicholas

Parent Company	Attraction
Pumphouse Educational Trust	Pumphouse Educational Museum
Puppet Centre Trust	Puppet Centre Trust
RSPB	Lochwinnoch Nature Centre
R/C Archdiocese of Southwark	St George's Cathedral
Rabbit Hole (Llandudno) Ltd	The Alice in Wonderland Visitor Centre
Ragged School Museum Trust	Ragged School Museum
Regimental HQ Queen's Own Highlanders	Queen's Own Highlanders Regimental Museum
Renfrew District Council	Paisley Museum & Art Galleries
Renfrew District Council	Lochwinnoch Community Museum
Ripon Museum Trust	Rippon Prison & Police Museum
Robert Owen (Memorial) Museum	Robert Owen Museum
Robin Hood Centre Plc	The Tales of Robin Hood*
Rochdale Metropolitan Borough Council	Hollingworth Lake Country Park
Rochdale Metropolitan Borough Council	Rochdale Art Gallery
Romney, Hythe and Dymchurch Railway Plc	Romney, Hythe & Dymchurch Railway
Rotherham Metropolitan Borough Council	Rother Valley Country Park*
Royal Air Force Museum	The Aerospace Museum*
Royal Borough of Kensington & Chelsea	Leighton House
Royal Botanic Garden Edinburgh	Logan Botanic Garden
Royal Green Jackets Museum Trust	Royal Green Jackets Museum
Royal Horticultural Society	Royal Horticultural Society Garden
Royal Household Royal Collection	Palace of Holyroodhouse*
Royal Institution of Cornwall	Royal Cornwall Museum
Royal London NHS Trust	Royal London Hospital Archives & Museum
Royal Mail National	National Postal Museum
Royal National Lifeboat Institution	Cromer Lifeboat Museum
Royal Observatory (Edinburgh) Trust	Royal Observatory Visitor Centre
Royal Scottish Academy	Royal Scottish Academy
Royal Signals Institution	Royal Signals Museum
Royal Zoological Society of Scotland	Edinburgh Zoo*
RSPB	RSPB North Cliffs and West Light Platform
RSPB	Minsmere RSPB Nature Reserve
SS Great Britain Project Ltd	SS Great Britain
Salford and Trafford Groundwork Trust	Trafford Ecology Park
Salford City Council	Viewpoint Photography Gallery
Salisbury and South Wiltshire Trust Ltd	Salisbury and South Wiltshire Museum
Salvation Army	Salvation Army International Heritage Centre
Samuel Smith	Steam Brewery Museum
Sandtoft Transport Society	Sandtoft Transport Centre
Satroshere Ltd	Satroshere
School of Oriental and African Studies	Percival David Foundation of Chinese Art
Science Museum	National Railway Museum*
Scottish Episcopal Church	St Andrew's Cathedral (Episcopal)
Scottish Episcopal Church	Saint Andrew's Cathedral, Inverness
Scottish Maritime Museum Trust	Scottish Maritime Museum
Scottish Wildlife Trust	Falls of Clyde Nature Reserve
Scottish Wildlife Trust	Scottish Wildlife Trust
Scout Association	Baden Powell House Hostel
Scunthorpe Borough Council	Normanby Hall Country Park
Scunthorpe Borough Council	Scunthorpe Museum
Sea Life Centres (Holdings)	Sea Life Centre
Sea Life Centres Ltd	Sea Life Centre*
Sedgefield District Council	Timothy Hackworth Victorian & Railway Museum
Shaftesbury Abbey & Museum Preservation Trust	Shaftesbury Abbey Museum & Ruins
Shaldon Wildlife Trust Ltd	Shaldon Wildlife Trust
Sheffield City Council	Graves Art Gallery
Sheffield City Museum	Abbeydale Industrial Hamlet
Shetland Islands Council	Shetland Museum
Shetland Islands Council	Shetland Croft House Museum
Shetland Islands Council	Bod of Gremista
Shropshire County Council	Much Wenlock Museum
Shuttleworth Remembrance Trust	The Shuttleworth Collection
Sid Vale Association	Sidmouth Museum
Sir Humphrey Wakefield & Partners	Chillingham Castle
Slimbridge	Wildfowl & Wetlands Centre
Society of Antiquaries of London	Kelmscott Manor
Society of Dyers and Colourists	Colour Museum
Solent Steam Packet Ltd	SS Shieldhall
Somerset County Museums Service	Somerset Rural Life Museum
South Wales Borderers Museum	The South Wales Borderers Museum
South Wight Borough Council	Ventnor Botanic Garden*
South Yorkshire Trades Historical Trust	Wortley Top Forge Industrial Museum
Southampton City Council	God's House Tower Museum
Southampton City Council	Woolhouse Maritime Museum
Southampton City Council	Tudor House Museum
Southend Museums Service	Southend Central Museum & Planetarium
Southwark Leisure	South London Art Gallery
Spencer House Ltd	Spencer House
Springburn Museum Trust	Springburn Museum Trust
St Andrew's Preservation Trust	St Andrew's Preservation Trust Museum
St David's Sea Life Centre	Oceanarium
St Martin-In-The-Fields	St Martin-In-The-Fields
St Mary's College	Strawberry Hill
St Mary's Parochial Church Council	St Mary's Parish Church
St Wilfrid's Church Parochial Church Council	St Wilfrid's Church
Stafford Borough Council	The Ancient High House
Stafford Borough Council	Izaak Walton's Cottage
Stanford Hall	Stanford Hall Motorcycle Museum
Stanstead Park Foundation	Stanstead Park
Steamport Southport Ltd	Southport Railway Centre

Parent Company	Attraction
Stewart's Burnby Hall Gardens & Museum Trust	Burnby Hall Gardens & Museum
Stewartry District Council	Stewartry Museum
Stockport Metropolitan Borough Council	Stockport War Memorial and Art Gallery
Stockvale Ltd	Peter Pan's Playground*
Stoke on Trent City Council	Ford Green Hall
Stratford Butterfly Farm	Stratford Butterfly Farm
Subsidiary of W M Muir (Bond 9)	Scottish Whisky Heritage Centre*
Suffolk Regiment Museum Trustees	Suffolk Regiment Museum
Sulgrave Manor Board	Sulgrave Manor
Summerlee Heritage Trust	Summerlee Heritage Trust
Sussex Archaeological Society	Michelham Priory
Sussex Archaeological Society	Anne of Cleves House Museum
Sussex Archaeological Society	Fishbourne Roman Palace and Museum
Sussex Archaeological Society	Lewes Castle and Museums
Sutherland Trust	Dunrobin Castle
Tain & District Museum Trust	Tain and District Museum
Talnotry Cottage Crafts	Talnotry Cottage Bird Garden
Talyllyn Railway Co	Talyllyn Railway
Tamworth Borough Council	Tamworth Castle
Tank Museum & Tank Museum Trading Co	Tank Museum
Tayside Regional Council	Crombie Country Park
Teifi Valley Railway Company Ltd	Teifi Valley Railway
Teignmouth Historical Society	Teignmouth Museum
Thamesdown Borough Council	Great Western Railway Museum
Thanet District Council	Margate Old Town Hall Local History Museum
The Dean and Canons of Windsor	St Georges Chapel*
Thomas Fattorini Ltd	Skipton Castle*
Throckmorton Estates	Coughton Court
Thursford Collection	Thursford Collection*
Thurso Heritage Society	Thurso Heritage Museum
Tithe Barn Trust	Tithe Barn Museum & Arts Centre
Torbay Borough Council	Torre Abbey
Torquay Natural History Society	Torquay Museum
Totnes Museum Trust	Totnes (Elizabethan) Museum
Totnes Town Council	Totnes Guildhall
Trades Union Congress	Tolpuddle Martyrs Museum
Trebah Garden Trust	Trebah Garden
Trefriw Wells Spa Ltd	Trefriw Wells Spa
Trust for the Viscount Stormont	Scone Palace*
Trustees for Watchet Town Council	Watchet Market House Museum
Trustees of Burns Monument	Burns Monument and Gardens
Trustees of Burns Monument	Burns Cottage and Museum
Trustees of Colne Valley Museum	Colne Valley Museum
Trustees of MEM Sandys 1956 Settlement	Graythwaite Hall Gardens
Tussaud Group London	Chessington World of Adventures*
Twyford Waterworks Trust	Twyford Pumping Station
Tyne & Wear Museums	Arbeia Roman Fort & Museum
Tyne & Wear Museums	South Shields Museum & Art Gallery
Tyne & Wear Museums	Hancock Museum
Tynedale Council	Border History Museum
Ullapool Museum Trust Ltd	Ullapool Museum
Ulster Museum	Armagh County Museum
Ulster New Zealand Trust	The Balance House
Unicorn Preservation Society	Frigate Unicorn
University of Bath	Holburne Museum & Crafts Study Centre
University of Dundee	University Botanic Garden
University of Durham	Oriental Museum
University of Durham	University of Durham Botanic Garden
University of Glasgow	Hunterian Art Gallery
University of Hull	University of Hull Art Collection
University of Liverpool	University of Liverpool Art Gallery
University of Liverpool	Ness Gardens
University of Northumbria	University Gallery
University of Oxford	Ashmolean Museum
Uttlesford District Council	Saffron Walden Museum
V & A Museum	Bethnal Green Museum of Childhood
Victoria University of Manchester	Tabely House Collection
Visitor Centres Ltd	Landmark Highland Heritage and Adventure Park
Visitor Centres Ltd	Inveraray Jail
W F Harper	Colliford Lake Park
Wakefield Metropolitan District Council	Pugneys Country Park
Wakefield Metropolitan District Council	Elizabethan Exhibition Gallery
Wakefield Metropolitan District Council	Pontefract Museum
Wakefield Metropolitan District Council	Wakefield Art Gallery
Wakefield Metropolitan District Council	Pontefract Castle
Wakefield Metropolitan District Council	Wakefield Museum
Walsingham College (Yorkshire Properties) Ltd	Parcevall Hall Garden
Wanlockhead Museum Trust	Museum of Lead Mining
Wansbeck District Council	Woodham Church Museum
Wansbeck District Council	Woodhorn Colliery Museum
Warminster History Society	The Dewey Museum
Warrington Borough Council	Warrington Museum and Art Gallery
Watermouth Castle Estates	Watermouth Castle
Weald and Downland Open Air Museum	Weald and Downland Open Air Museum
Welsh Highland Railway (1964) Ltd	Welsh Highland Railway
Welsh Historic Monuments	Conwy Castle
Welwyn Hatfield District Council	Mill Green Museum and Mill
Welwyn Hatfield District Council	Stanborough Park
Welwyn Hatfield District Council	Welwyn Roman Baths
Wemyss & March Estates Management	Gosford House

Parent Company	Attraction
Wemyss & March Estates Management	Neidpath Castle
West Dorset District Council	Old Crown Court and Cells
West Glamorgan County Council	Margam Park*
West Lancashire Light Railway Assoc	West Lancashire Light Railway
West Lothian District Council	Almondell & Calderwood Country Park
West Lothian District Council	Beacraigs Country Park
West Somerset Archaeological Society	West Somerset Rural Life Museum
West Wycombe Caves Ltd	West Wycombe Caves
Westminster Roman Catholic Cathedral	Westminster Cathedral*
Weymouth Civic Society	Nothe Fort
Whitby Pictorial Archives Trust	Whitby Archives Heritage Centre
Whithorn Board of Management	Whithorn Dig
Whitley Wildlife Conservation Trust	Paignton Zoo*
Wigtown District Council	Stranraer Museum
Wildfowl & Wetlands Trust	Wildfowl and Wetlands Trust – Welney Centre
Wimborne Minster Ltd	Minster Church of St Cuthberga*
Winchester Preservation Trust	Winchester Heritage Centre
Windermere Nautical Trust Ltd	Windermere Steamboat Museum*
Windsor Station Ltd	Royalty and Empire*
Wokingham District Council	Dinton Pastures Country Park*
Woodside Eggs Ltd	Woodside Farm & Wild Fowl Park
Woodspring District Council	Woodspring Museum
World Heritage	Mummies and Magic
World Heritage	Dinosaur Safari
World Heritage	Dinosaur Museum*
World Heritage	Tutankhamun Exhibition
World Methodist Council	The Old Rectory
Yorkshire Car & Exhibition Company Plc	Yorkshire Car Collection
Yorkshire Water Services Ltd	Yorkshire Water Museum
Zoo Operations Ltd	Whipsnade Wild Animal Park*
Zoological Society of Glasgow & W Scotland	Glasgow Zoo Park

INDEX 5
INDEX OF CATERING FRANCHISEES

Franchisee Name	Attraction
1066 Public House	Buckleys Yesterdays World
Amanda's Tearooms	Felin Crewi Working Watermill
Annie Fryer Catering	Chelsea Physic Garden
Apple Catering	Welsh Folk Museum*
Banquets of Oxford	Blenheim Palace*
Barton Manor Tea Rooms	Barton Manor Gardens & Vineyards
Beaufort Catering	Holburne Museum & Crafts Study Centre
Beacraigs Restaurant	Beacraigs Country Park
Black Mrs J	Laidhay Croft Museum
Blackforest Catering	Colne Valley Railway
Bluebird Cafe	Coniston Boating Centre
Bonners Cuisine	Museum of Kent Life
Cafe Catering Direct	Scotland Street School Museum
Cafe in the Park	Cyfarthfa Castle Museum, Art Gallery and Park
Calderdale Education Service	Shibden Hall
Carte Blanche Catering	Walker Art Gallery
Carte Blanche Catering	Sudley
Castle Catering Services	National Army Museum
Castle Garden Restaurant	North Down Heritage Centre
Caterbake, Kirkcaldy	Kirkcaldy Museum & Art Gallery
Caterbirds Restaurant	Threake Gardens
Caterleisure	Cartwright Hall
Charlotte's Pantry & Orangery Function Room	Margam Park*
Chats Cafe	Royal London Hospital Archives & Museum
Clandon Park Restaurant	Hatchlands Park
Classic Caterers	Carisbrooke Castle
Coach House Cafe	Queen Elizabeth Country Park
Coatesworth, Mrs H	Burton Agnes Hall
Coburg Caterers	Marsh Farm Country Park*
Coghlan Mrs A	Seaford Tropical Butterfly House/Gardens/Maze
Compass Caterers	Eureka! The Museum for Children
Cookhouse Cafeteria Emmitoza	Museum of Army Transport
Country Chefs	Museum of Army Flying
Cow and Plough	Farmworld*
Cozy Cafe	Dinton Pastures Country Park*
D'Averia Bros	Stanborough Park
De Blanks	Natural History Museum*
Direct Services, Caterclean Division	Hollingworth Lake Country Park
Ellis, Mrs P	Abbeydale Industrial Hamlet
Evans, Mrs S	Haseley Manor
Everett, W K	Newhaven Fort
Fraters Restaurant	Coventry Cathedral
Frearson Mrs V	Flimwell Bird Park
Gadson, Mrs	The Hirsel
Gallery Bistro	The Whitworth Art Gallery
Garden Room Restaurant	Harlow Carr Botanical Gardens
Gardner Merchant	Tulliehouse Museum and Art Gallery
Gardner Merchant	Salisbury Cathedral*
Gardner Merchant	Durham Light Infantry Museum & Art Gallery
Garwood Ms S	Stanway House
Grants House Cafe	Museum of Flight
Hudson Rowe Ltd	The Shuttleworth Collection
Hulme, Mr M	Brookeside Miniature Railway
ICL Catering	Rhondda Heritage Park
In Focus Restaurant	Royal Photographic Society
Johnson, Mr C	Marble Arch Caves*
Key Services	Snibston Discovery Park
Korntner F & M	Courtauld Institute Galleries*
Leisure and Pleasure Catering	Glasgow Zoo Park
Leiths Good Food Ltd	Hampton Court Palace*
Leiths Good Food Ltd	Leighton House
Lovejoy, Miss J	Burnby Hall Gardens & Museum
LPD Ltd	Badsell Farm Park
Mayfield Concessions	Royal Navy Submarine Museum
Mayfield Concessions	Marwell Zoological Park*
McShane, Ballintoy	Carrick-A-Rede Rope Bridge*
Michelham Country Foods	Michelham Priory
Milburns Ltd	Victoria and Albert Museum
Milburns Ltd	National Gallery*
Milburns Ltd	Museum of London*
Milburns Ltd	Roman Baths Museum*
Milburns Ltd	National Railway Museum*
Milburns Ltd	York Minster*
Monkey House Restaurant	Formakin Estate
NMGM Enterprises	National Maritime Museum
NMGM Enterprises	Liverpool Museum
Norfolk County Services	Norwich Castle Museum*
Orangery Restaurant	Mount Edgcumbe House & Country Park

Franchisee Name	Attraction
Party Plan	Commonwealth Institute*
Payne & Curtis	Syon Park
Peacock, Mrs J	Ironbridge Gorge Museum*
Peters, R	Beacon Country Park
Pizza Express	Southwark Cathedral
Poets Corner Catering Services	Kew Bridge Steam Museum
Probus	Probus County Demonstration Garden
Ranch Kitchen Restaurant	Blair Drummond Safari & Leisure Park
Read, Mrs	Breamore House & Museums
Restaurant, Clandon Park	Clandon Park
Ring & Brymer	HMS Belfast*
Ring & Brymer	Royal Air Force Museum*
Ring & Brymer	Beaulieu National Motor Museum, House & Abbey*
Rowe, Mr H	National Horseracing Museum
Scunthorpe Catering Services	Normanby Hall Country Park
Simmons Baker Ltd	Hatfield House*
Simmons Bakeries	Child-Beale Wildlife Park*
Society Catering Ltd	Tatton
Southern Group Caterers	Longleat House and Safari Park
Sovereign Catering Services	Shugborough
Stables Restaurant	The Palace Stables Heritage Centre
Stockdale K	Fishbourne Roman Palace and Museum
Taylor Catering	Pensthorpe Waterfowl Trust
Teifi Valley Railway Society	Teifi Valley Railway
The Catering Company	The Historic Dockyard Chatham
The Silks Buttrie	The Silk Museum
The Workhouse	Model House Craft and Design Centre
Torbay & Dartmouth Railway Soc Trading Co Ltd	Paignton & Dartmouth Steam Railway
Town & County Catering	Tank Museum
Town & Country Caterers	Royal Botanic Gardens Kew*
Walpole, R.	Sulgrave Manor
Watsons Confectioners	Walkley Clogs
Webb, Mr P M W	Guildford Cathedral
Whitnal L & C	Paradise Wildlife Park
Wise Catering Ltd	Royal Victoria Country Park
Wray, Mr M	Ventnor Botanic Garden*
Yorvale	Yorkshire Museum
Yours Naturally	London Ecology Centre
Yum Yum Catering	Windsor Safari Park*

INDEX 6
INDEX OF RETAIL FRANCHISEES

Franchisee Name	Attraction
A Zwemmer Ltd	Courtauld Institute Galleries*
Alexon	Hornsea Freeport*
Aquascutum	Hornsea Freeport*
Barton Manor Gifts	Barton Manor Gardens & Vineyards
Berketex	Hornsea Freeport*
Booklocker	The Historic Dockyard Chatham
Border Fine Arts Gallery	Famous Old Blacksmiths Shop Centre*
Chillingham Antiques	Chillingham Castle
Concourse Enterprises	The Whitworth Art Gallery
Cornwall Craft Assoc	Pencarrow
Crafts and Things	Graham Sutherland Gallery
Dash	Hornsea Freeport*
Dillons Books	Hornsea Freeport*
Duxford Displays Ltd	Duxford Airfield*
Essence	Hornsea Freeport*
Frearson, Mrs V	Flimwell Bird Park
Friends of Museum	Wisbech & Fenland Museum
Fudge Kitchen	Lightwater Valley Theme Park*
Gallaghan, Mrs T	Farmworld*
Genesis	Hornsea Freeport*
Greenwich Zero (Nauticalia)	National Maritime Museum Greenwich*
Harlow Carr Gift Shop and Plant Centre	Harlow Carr Botanical Gardens
Hernhill Craft Centre	Mount Ephraim Gardens
Independent Craft Workshops	Traquair House
JCJ Pottery	Drusillas Park
Knickerbox	Hornsea Freeport*
Knoll Craft	Rother Valley Country Park*
Laura Ashley	Hornsea Freeport*
London Brass Rubbing Centre	St Martin-in-the-Fields
Lowes Mower Shop	Stewarts Garden–Lands
Michelham Country Foods	Michelham Priory
National Trust	Stowe Landscape Gardens
National Trust	Shugborough
National Trust	Coughton Court
National Trust	Syon Park
NMGM Enterprises	National Maritime Museum
NMGM Enterprises	Liverpool Museum
NMGM Enterprises	Walker Art Gallery
NMGM Enterprises	Lady Lever Art Gallery
NMGM Enterprises	Sudley
Nugent, J	Museum of Flight
Paul's Newsagents	Royal London Hospital Archives & Museum
Rayne Shoes	Hornsea Freeport*
Southern Aquatics	Stewarts Garden–Lands
Torbay & Dartmouth Railway Soc Trading Co Ltd	Paignton & Dartmouth Steam Railway
V & A Enterprises	Bethnal Green Museum of Childhood
W H Smith	Royal London Hospital Archives & Museum
Wine Warehouse	Apuldram Roses
World of Difference	London Ecology Centre
Wrangler	Hornsea Freeport*
Wray, Mr M	Ventnor Botanic Garden*